A Companion to the Reformation World

BLACKWELL COMPANIONS TO EUROPEAN HISTORY

This series provides sophisticated and authoritative overviews of the scholarship that has shaped our current understanding of the past. Defined by theme, period and/or region, each volume comprises up to forty concise essays written by individual scholars within their area of specialization. The aim of each contribution is to synthesize the current state of scholarship from a variety of historical perspectives and to provide a statement on where the field is heading. The essays are written in a clear, provocative, and lively manner, designed for an international audience of scholars, students, and general readers.

Published

A Companion to Europe 1900–1945
Edited by Gordon Martel

A Companion to Nineteenth-Century Europe
Edited by Stefan Berger

In preparation

A Companion to Europe Since 1945
Edited by Klaus Larres

A Companion to Eighteenth-Century Europe
Edited by Peter H. Wilson

A Companion to the Worlds of the Renaissance
Edited by Guido Ruggiero

A Companion to the Reformation World
Edited by R. Po-chia Hsia

A Companion to the Medieval World
Edited by Carol Lansing and Edward D. English

BLACKWELL COMPANIONS TO BRITISH HISTORY

Published

A Companion to Roman Britain
Edited by Malcolm Todd

A Companion to Britain in the Later Middle Ages
Edited by S. H. Rigby

A Companion to Tudor Britain
Edited by Robert Tittler and Norman Jones

A Companion to Stuart Britain
Edited by Barry Coward

In preparation

A Companion to the Early Middle Ages: Britain and Ireland
Edited by Pauline Stafford

A Companion to Eighteenth-Century Britain
Edited by H. T. Dickinson

A Companion to Nineteenth-Century Britain
Edited by Chris Williams

A Companion to Early Twentieth-Century Britain
Edited by Chris Wrigley

A Companion to Contemporary Britain
Edited by Paul Addison and Harriet Jones

BLACKWELL COMPANIONS TO HISTORY

Published

A Companion to Western Historical Thought
Edited by Lloyd Kramer and Sarah Maza

A Companion to Gender History
Edited by Teresa A. Meade and Merry E. Wiesner-Hanks

BLACKWELL COMPANIONS TO AMERICAN HISTORY

Published:

A Companion to the American Revolution
Edited by Jack P. Greene and J. R. Pole

A Companion to 19th-Century America
Edited by William L. Barney

A Companion to the American South
Edited by John B. Boles

A Companion to American Indian History
Edited by Philip J. Deloria and Neal Salisbury

A Companion to American Women's History
Edited by Nancy A. Hewitt

A Companion to Post-1945 America
Edited by Jean-Christophe Agnew and Roy Rosenzweig

A Companion to the Vietnam War
Edited by Marilyn B. Young and Robert Buzzanco

A Companion to Colonial America
Edited by Daniel Vickers

A Companion to 20th-Century America
Edited by Stephen J. Whitfield

A Companion to the American West
Edited by William Deverell

on to American Foreign Relations
Edited by Robert D. Schulzinger

A Companion to the Civil War and Reconstruction
Edited by Lacy K. Ford

A Companion to American Technology
Edited by Carroll Pursell

A Companion to African-American History
Edited by Alton Hornsby

A Companion to American Immigration
Edited by Reed Ueda

BLACKWELL COMPANIONS TO WORLD HISTORY

Published

A Companion to the History of the Middle East
Edited by Youssef M. Choueiri

In preparation

A Companion to Latin American History
Edited by Thomas Holloway

A Companion to Japanese History
Edited by William M. Tsutsui

A Companion to Russian History
Edited by Abbott Gleason

A COMPANION TO THE REFORMATION WORLD

Edited by

R. Po-chia Hsia

Blackwell
Publishing

BLACKWELL PUBLISHING
350 Main Street, Malden, MA 02148-5020, USA
9600 Garsington Road, Oxford OX4 2DQ, UK
550 Swanston Street, Carlton, Victoria 3053, Australia

First published 2004
First published in paperback 2006 by Blackwell Publishing Ltd

1   2006

Library of Congress Cataloging-in-Publication Data

A companion to the reformation world / edited by R. Po-chia Hsia.
        p. cm. – (Blackwell companions to European history)
Includes bibliographical references and index.
    ISBN 0-631-22017-8 (alk. paper)
    1. Reformation.   I. Hsia, R. Po-chia, 1953–   II. Series.
BR309.C62 2003
270.6–dc21

                                                                2002156493

ISBN-13: 978-0-631-22017-6 (alk. paper)
ISBN-13: 978-1-4051-4962-4 (pbk. : alk. paper)
ISBN-10: 1-4051-4962-0 (pbk. : alk. paper)

A catalogue record for this title is available from the British Library.

Set in 10 on 12 pt Galliard
by SNP Best-set Typesetter Ltd., Hong Kong
Printed and bound in the United Kingdom
by TJ International Ltd, Padstow, Cornwall

The publisher's policy is to use permanent paper from mills that operate a sustainable forestry policy, and which has been manufactured from pulp processed using acid-free and elementary chlorine-free practices. Furthermore, the publisher ensures that the text paper and cover board used have met acceptable environmental accreditation standards.

For further information on
Blackwell Publishing, visit our website:
www.blackwellpublishing.com

Contents

List of Contributors

Dan Beaver is Associate Professor of History at the Pennsylvania State University. He is the author of *Parish Communities and Religious Conflict in the Vale of Gloucester, 1590–1690*, and is currently working on hunting and the cultural history of violence in early modern England.

Miriam Bodian is Associate Professor of History and Jewish Studies at Pennsylvania State University. Her work has dealt with early modern Sephardic Jewry and, more generally, the history of Jewish–Christian relations. Her publications include *Hebrews of the Portuguese Nation: Conversos and Community in Early Modern Amsterdam* (1997) and "In the Cross-Currents of the Reformation: Crypto-Jewish Martyrs of the Inquisition, 1570–1670," *Past and Present*, 176 (November, 2002).

Johannes Burkhardt is Professor of History at the University of Augsburg, Germany, and Director of the Fugger-Archiv. He has published on diplomatic, economic, and political history. Recent books include *Der Dreißigjährige Krieg* (1992) and *Das Reformationsjahrhundert: Deutsche Geschichte zwischen Medienrevolution und Institutionenbildung 1517–1617* (2002).

Euan Cameron is the Henry Luce III Professor of Reformation Church History at Union Theological Seminary in New York City, and is also a Professor in the Department of Religion at Columbia University.

He is the author of *The European Reformation* (1991). He has also written *Waldenses: Rejections of Holy Church in Medieval Europe* (2000) and both edited and contributed to *Early Modern Europe: An Oxford History* (1999; paperback edition 2001).

Olivier Christin is Professor of Modern History at the University of Lyon-2 and member of the Institut Universitaire de France. He has published several studies on art and the Reformation (*Une révolution symbolique: L'iconoclasme huguenot et la reconstruction catholique*, 1991; *Les Yeux pour le croire: Les Dix commandements en images (XVe–XVIIe siècles)*, 2003; and, with François Boespflug, *Johannes Molanus traité des saintes images*, 1996) and on the search for compromise and secular peace between denominations in sixteenth-century France and Germany (*La Paix de religion: L'autonomisation de la raison politique au XVIe siècle*, 1997).

After entering the Society of Jesus in London, **Michael Cooper** worked at Sophia University, Tokyo, where he edited the academic quarterly *Monumenta Nipponica* for 26 years. In 1999 he retired to Honolulu, where he continues research on Jesuit activity in sixteenth-century Japan. He obtained his doctorate at Oxford University with a thesis on João Rodrigues (d. 1633), a Portuguese Jesuit who worked in both

Japan and China. Among Cooper's published works are *They Came to Japan* (1965, 1995), *Rodrigues the Interpreter* (1974), and *João Rodrigues's Account of Sixteenth-Century Japan* (2001). He is at present writing a book on the Japanese mission to Europe in the 1580s.

Barbara B. Diefendorf is Professor of History at Boston University. She is the author of *Paris City Councillors in the Sixteenth Century: The Politics of Patrimony* (1983) and *Beneath the Cross: Catholics and Huguenots in Sixteenth-Century Paris* (1991). Her recently completed study of pious women and the Catholic Reformation in France will be published by Oxford.

Massimo Firpo is Professor of Modern History at the University of Turin. His most recent books concerning the religious crisis in sixteenth-century Italy are *Riforma protestante ed eresie nell'Italia del Cinquecento: Un profilo storico* (1993), *Gli affreschi di Pontormo a San Lorenzo: Eresia, politica e cultura nella Firenze di Cosimo I* (1997), *Dal sacco di Roma all'Inquisizione: Studi su Juan de Valdés e la Riforma italiana* (1998), *Artisti, gioiellieri, eretici: Il mondo di Lorenzo Lotto tra Riforma e Controriforma* (2001), and *Studi sulla vita religiosa nel Cinquecento italiano* (2003).

Hans-Jürgen Goertz is Professor of Social and Economic History at the University of Hamburg. He is the author of many studies on the radical Reformation in Germany. Recent books include *Thomas Müntzer: Apocalyptic Mystic and Visionary* (1993), *Antiklerikalismus und Reformation: Sozialgeschichtliche Untersuchungen* (1995), and *Anabaptists* (1996).

Bruce Gordon is Reader in Modern History and Deputy Director of the Reformation Studies Institute at the University of St. Andrews. He has recently published (with Peter Marshall) *The Place of the Dead: Death and Remembrance in Late Medieval and Early Modern Europe* (2000) and a translation of Hans Guggisberg, *Sebastian Castellio, Humanist and Defender of Religious Toleration in a Confessional Age* (2003). His most recent book is *The Swiss Reformation* (2002).

Brad S. Gregory is Associate Professor of History at Stanford University. His first book, *Salvation at Stake: Christian Martyrdom in Early Modern Europe*, was published in 1999 and received six book awards. He is also the editor of *The Forgotten Writings of the Mennonite Martyrs*, published in 2002.

Kaspar von Greyerz is Professor of History at the University of Basel. His books include *Late City Reformation in Germany: The Case of Colmar, 1522–1628* (1980), *England im Jahrhundert der Revolutionen 1603–1714* (1994), and *Religion und Kultur: Europa 1500–1800* (2000).

Christopher Haigh teaches history at the University of Oxford. His major publications include *The Reign of Elizabeth I* (1984), *The English Reformation Revised* (1987), *Elizabeth I* (1988, 2nd ed. 1998), and *English Reformations: Religion, Politics and Society under the Tudors* (1993). He is now writing on the official church and its parishioners in post-Reformation England.

R. Po-chia Hsia is Edwin Erle Sparks Professor of History at Pennsylvania State University. He has published several books on Reformation Germany and the history of anti-Semitism. Recent books include *The World of Catholic Renewal 1540–1770* (1998), translated into German and Italian. He is now working on the relations between Catholic Europe and China between the sixteenth and eighteenth centuries. He is an elected member of the Academia Sinica, Taiwan.

Benjamin J. Kaplan is Professor of Dutch History at University College London, and he holds an appointment in early modern religious history at the University of Amsterdam. His publications include *Calvinists and Libertines: Confession and Community in Utrecht, 1578–1620*, which received the Philip Schaff Prize and the Roland Bainton Prize in History and Theology. Kaplan's current book project, titled *Divided by Faith*, is a social history of religious toleration in early modern Europe.

Robert M. Kingdon is Professor Emeritus of History at the University of Wisconsin-Madison. He has been involved in a number of editions of documents of the Reformation period, most recently of the *Registres du Consistoire de Genève au temps de Calvin*, vols. 1 and 2 (1996, 2001), with T. A. Lambert, I. M. Watt, and M. W. McDonald. He has also written a number of books and articles on aspects of the history of the Calvinist Reformation, including *Myths about the St. Bartholomew's Day Massacres, 1572–1576* (1988) and *Adultery and Divorce in Calvin's Geneva* (1995).

Robert Kolb is Missions Professor of Systematic Theology, Concordia Seminary, Saint Louis, Missouri, and was associate editor and editor of *The Sixteenth Century Journal* (1973–94, 1994–7). He is the author of *Martin Luther as Prophet, Teacher, and Hero: Images of the Reformer, 1520–1620* (1999), *Luther's Heirs Define His Legacy: Studies on Lutheran Confessionalization* (1996), and co-editor, with Timothy J. Wengert, of *The Book of Concord: The Confessions of the Evangelical Lutheran Church* (2000).

Amy E. Leonard received her PhD in history from the University of California at Berkeley in 1999. She is Assistant Professor of History at Georgetown University, Washington, DC, and President of the Society for Early Modern Catholic Studies. She has just completed a manuscript on Dominican nuns in Strasbourg, titled "Nails in the Wall: Catholic Nuns in Reformation Strasbourg."

William Monter is Professor Emeritus of History at Northwestern. Among recent publications are "The Fate of the French and English Reformations, 1555–1563," *Bibliothèque d'Humanisme et Renaissance*, 64 (2002), 7–19; "The Roman Inquisition and Protestant Heresy Executions in 16th-Century Europe," in *Atti del Simposio internazionale sull'Inquisizione (29–31 ottobre 1998)*, ed. Agostino Borromeo (2003), pp. 535–44; and "Witch-Trials in Continental Europe, 1560–1660," in S. Clark and B. Ankarloo, eds., *The Athlone History of Witchcraft*, vol. 5 (2002), pp. 1–79.

John W. O'Malley is Professor of Church History, Weston Jesuit School of Theology, Cambridge, MA. He is a Fellow of the American Academy of Arts and Sciences and member of the American Philosophical Society; past president of the American Catholic Historical Association and of the Renaissance Society of America; author of *Praise and Blame in Renaissance Rome*, *The First Jesuits*, *Trent and All That*; and co-editor of *The Jesuits: Cultures, Sciences, and the Arts, 1540–1773*.

José Pedro Paiva studied for his PhD at the European University Institute (Florence) and is Professor Auxiliar at the Faculty of Arts of the University of Coimbra. His main research fields are popular culture and religious and ecclesiastical history during the modern age. His publications include *Bruxaria e superstição num país sem caça às bruxas: 1600–1774* (1997) and five chapters in the more recent religious history of Portugal, *História Religiosa de Portuga*, ed. Carlos Moreira Azevedo (2000), vol. 2. He also edited *Religious Ceremonials and Images: Power and Social Meaning (1400–1750)* (2002).

James R. Palmitessa is Associate Professor at Western Michigan State University. He is the author of *Material Culture and Daily Life in the New City of Prague in the Age of Rudolf II* (1997) and "The Prague Uprising of 1611: Property, Politics and Catholic Renewal in the Early Years of Habsburg Rule," *Central European History*, 31/4 (1998). He is working on a book on Prague on the eve of the Thirty Years' War.

Tom Scott is Reader in History at the University of Liverpool and received his LittD from the University of Cambridge (2002). Relevant publications include *Freiburg and the Breisgau: Town–Country Relations in the Age of Reformation and Peasants' War* (1986); *Thomas Muentzer: Theology and Revolution in the German Reformation* (1989); (ed. with Bob Scribner), *The German Peasants' War: A History in Documents* (1991); *Regional Identity and Economic Change: The Upper Rhine, 1450–1600* (1997); (ed.), *The Peasantries* *of Europe from the Fourteenth to the Eighteenth Centuries* (1998); and *Society and Economy in Germany, 1300–1600* (2002).

James A. Sharpe is a Professor at the University of York, England. His early researches were into the field of crime in early modern England, a subject on which he published extensively. More recently he has turned his attention to witchcraft, and has a number of publications on the subject, notably *Instruments of Darkness: Witchcraft in England 1550–1750* (1996). Current research interests include the history of violence in England and the legal system of the early modern Isle of Man.

Joke Spaans teaches the history of Christianity at the University of Amsterdam. She is the author and editor of the following books: *Een golf van beroering: De omstreden opwekking in de Republiek in het midden van de achttiende eeuw* (2001); *Armenzorg in Friesland, 1500–1800. Publieke zorg en particuliere liefdadigheid in zes Friese steden: Leeuwarden, Bolsward, Franeker, Sneek, Dokkum en Harlingen* (1998); and *Haarlem na de Reformatie: Stedelijke cultuur en kerkelijk leven 1577–1620* (1989).

Larissa Taylor is Associate Professor of History at Colby College. She is the author of *Soldiers of Christ: Preaching in Late Medieval and Reformation France* (1992; paperback edition 2003), winner of the John Nicholas Brown Prize of the Mediaeval Academy of America, as well as *Heresy and Orthodoxy in Sixteenth-Century Paris* (1999) and *Preachers and People in the Reformations and Early Modern Period* (2001). A specialist in late medieval preaching, her current research focuses on pilgrimage and sacred space.

Kevin Terraciano is an Associate Professor of Latin American History at the University of California, Los Angeles. His recent book, *The Mixtecs of Colonial Oaxaca*, was published in 2001. Other recent publications include "Crime and Culture in Colonial Mexico: The Case of the Mixtec Murder Note," *Ethnohistory*, 45/4 (1998) and "The Colonial Mixtec Community," *Hispanic American Historical Review*, 80/1 (2000). In 2001, he won the UCLA Distinguished Teaching Award.

István György Tóth is Professor of History at the Central European University, Budapest, and Head of the Early Modern History Department at the Institute of History of the Hungarian Academy. His main interests are the social and cultural history of early modern central Europe. Recent publications include *Literacy and Written Culture in Early Modern Central Europe* (1999), "Hungarian Cultural History in the Early Modern Age," in Laszlo Kosa, ed., *A Cultural History of Hungary* (1999), *Litterae missionariorum de Hungaria et Transylvania 1572–1717* (2002, Latin texts with English introduction). He is editor-in-chief of the *Millennium History of Hungary* (2001, in Hungarian; English edition in preparation).

Ines G. Županov is a Research Fellow at the Centre National de la Recherche Scientifique in Paris. She has taught early modern history at the University of California at Berkeley, at Jawaharlal Nehru University in New Delhi, and at the École des Hautes Études en Sciences Sociales in Paris. She is author of *Disputed Mission: Jesuit Experiments and Brahmanical Knowledge in Seventeenth-Century India* (1999). Her articles in English, French, Portuguese, Italian, and Croatian are published in edited books and journals (*Annales, Representations, Etnosistemi, Studies in History, Indian Economic and Social History Journal, Archives de sciences sociales des religions,* etc.).

Introduction: The Reformation and its Worlds

R. Po-chia Hsia

In commenting on the Book of Daniel in 1530, Luther reflected on the eschato-logical mood of the Reformation movement: "Everything has come to pass and is fulfilled: the Roman Empire is at the end, the Turk has arrived at the door, the splendor of popery has faded away, and the world is crackling in all places, as if it is going to break apart and crumble." The world that Luther lived in had indeed come to an end. Once, Latin Christendom, united in faith and allegiance to the Roman pontiff, had resisted many forces that threatened to break it apart: the struggles between popes and kings, the critique of medieval reformers and prophets, and the mixture of social, national, and anticlerical movements branded as heretical – Lollardy and the Hussite Revolution of the late Middle Ages. Now, challenged by new theologies, the Latin Church jostled for orthodoxy amidst a growing array of churches and sects, each claiming for itself the apostolic mantle of pristine evangelical Christianity.

Suspended as it were between heaven and earth, the world of the Reformation existed simultaneously in different temporal and spatial dimensions. Drawing their inspiration from the world of the Gospels, the reformers and their supporters called themselves evangelicals and clamored for a pure Christianity, purged of its human and papal encrustations. Critics of the Roman Church harked back to a golden ecclesiastical age, much as the humanists advocated returning to the Greco-Roman sources of moral philosophy and rhetorical elegance, for many of the latter were found among the defenders of the *causa Lutheri*. This imagined world of primitive Christianity was invoked in order to discredit the present world of corruption: there, the true shepherds of Christ, here wolves in clerical garment; then, apostolic poverty in imitation of Christ, now, the pomp of prelates mocking the *passio Christi*; a past world of the true Kingdom of God struck a poignant comparison with this present world in the clutches of the devil. Yet, "the world is crackling in all places," as Luther reminded us, for the corrupt world would yield to a new time, to the Second Coming of Christ, to a new world subsumed under heaven.

Convinced though he was of the imminence of the end-time, Luther refused to prophesy its precise advent. For the true church of the new world was like an unborn child, a representation and simile of the Church, as the baby in the womb is surrounded and wrapped with a thin skin, which in Greek is called a *chorion*. . . . The *chorion* does not break until the fruit is ripe and timely and is brought forth into the light of the world. And thus also is the Church wrapped up and enclosed by the Word and seeks no other teaching of God's will, except what is revealed and shown in the very same Word, with which it is at peace, and remains steadfast through the faith until such a time, that it will see in that other life God's light and countenance and hear God Himself preaching on the mysterious and now hidden things, which we have here in faith, but only there in beholding.

Not all waited patiently for the birth of the new world. In their midwifely zeal, radical reformers ruptured the *chorion*, only to bring forth premature matter and aborted children, as Luther would castigate the Anabaptists "and other enthusiasts and hordes of rebellious spirits."

Indeed, for the radicals of the Reformation, Luther had stopped dead in the tracks of reform. In the words of Thomas Müntzer, reformer turned prophet of the rebellious peasants and townsmen of Thuringia, Luther was "the spiritless, soft-living flesh at Wittenberg, who has most lamentably befouled pitiable Christianity in a perverted way by his theft of holy Scripture."[1] Once a follower of Luther, Müntzer became disenchanted with the Wittenberg reformer for his refusal to call on the princes to root out godless popery with the sword. Urging the princes to wield the surgeon's knife to rip through the womb of the corrupt body ecclesiastic in order to deliver the newborn evangelical church, Müntzer and the other radical reformers failed to understand Luther's reluctance to hasten a divine delivery. What separated the Reformation of the established Protestant churches and the radical movements was a fundamental disagreement over the timing of the new world of redemption. Eager as they might have been for the Second Coming, the Lutheran Church refused to give in to the eschatological temptation: the imminent end of the world signified not a reordering of society and congregation, as the radicals would have it, whether by violence or peace, but an infinite patience to await the will of God.

If expectations for the future – the end of time itself – created a chasm between the Protestant and radical reformations, it was memory of a past world that cemented the permanent schism between the Roman Catholic Church and the new evangelical churches. History itself was up for grabs. After the battle lines were drawn, the doctrinal fronts stabilized, both the Protestant and Catholic churches turned to create a new understanding of the past world of apostolic Christianity and the present world of confessional conflicts. The blood of martyrs ensured the wounds would not heal, that the world torn asunder would not come together again in desecration of their memory. For the Protestants, the blood of their martyrs flowed in a continuous stream from the persecutions of the pagan tyrants to the repression of papal tyrants. Hence, the *Acts and Monuments* of John Foxe or the *Actes Martyrs* of Jean Crespin represented the English and French Protestant martyrs of the sixteenth century completing a redemptive history that stretched back to the world of apostolic Christianity. This was one area in which the Protestants and the Anabaptists held the moral high ground for some time, as initially Catholics played the role of killers rather than martyrs. England, however, proved an exception: the executions of Thomas More and John Fisher gave the Catholic world, especially English Catholics, their martyrdoms and just cause. The bonfires of the Marian reign yielded to the quarterings under Elizabeth, as English Jesuit missionaries shed their blood to blot out the moral triumph of Protestant martyrdom during the Marian years.

Crucial to the Catholic world's recovery of redemptive history was not so much its present martyrs, but the discovery of a past world of Christian heroism and sacrifice centered in Rome. The wonder of corporeal perfection after the opening of St. Cecilia's tomb, the discovery of the full extent of the catacombs, and the cognizance of the bloody baptism of the apostolic church restored the full confidence of the Roman Catholic Church. Publications in the early seventeenth century described the sacred subterranean world of Rome, the horror of instruments of torture and martyrdom, and the stories of early Roman virgins and their families, whose exempla served both to inspire the elites of a resurgent Catholicism and to affirm the legitimacy of the Roman Church, built literally upon the soil soaked through by the blood of martyrs.[2] Parallel to this Tridentine discourse of martyrology, the Catholic renewal fashioned a new ecclesiastical history: Cesare Baronius's *Annales Ecclesiastici* was published in 12 volumes between 1564 and 1588, to refute the claims of Lutheran ecclesiastical history, exemplified by Matthias Flacius Illyricus's *Centuriae Magdeburgenses*, that represented the papacy as an aberration of the apostolic tradition. Contesting the Protestant assertion of martyrdom, the Tridentine Church affirmed its own continuous martyrological history, with new chapters written by Catholic missionaries who testified with their lives to the traditional faith in lands far from the doctrinal struggles of Latin Christianity.

As early as 1535, during the turmoil of the Anabaptist kingdom of Münster, the Carthusian monk Dionysius of Cologne linked the confessional struggles at home with the European voyages overseas:[3]

> When Greece was involved in various heresies, finally became schismatic, and hence was cast away by God, it fell into the hands of the Muslims. . . . Did, therefore, the faith or the church perish? To be sure, it has perished with those in the Orient, but meanwhile in the Occident it has increased and remained. Even if here in the Occident – on account of our sins – faith, obedience, and finally the holy sacrifice have been taken away from many cities and territories, they nevertheless remain healthy and unimpaired with others. . . . For God is able to arouse other sons of Abraham even in the most distant nations. . . . But why do we say God can do this, since we know that the same is just now happening in America, Cuba, New Spain, and in other regions, populations, and languages of Great Asia through the Spaniards. And what is happening in Ethiopia, Arabia, Persia, India, and on the surrounding southern isles through the Portuguese?

This was a remarkable statement. Tucked away in a Latin manuscript in the Carthusian monastery of Cologne, these lines by Dionysius foreshadowed already the close connections between the confessional struggles in central Europe – where the Protestant schism originated – and the restorative evangelizations in the wider non-European Catholic world. Even as the Holy Roman Empire was torn between the Lutheran, Calvinist, and Catholic churches and rocked by popular revolts, it survived the carnage of the Thirty Years' War and the witch-craze to furnish reinforcements for the Catholic overseas missions.

Among the Catholic centers that published the annual reports (*Litterae Annuae*) of the newly founded Jesuit missions was Dillingen, seat of the bishop of Augsburg and a Jesuit university. There, the mission reports to Japan from 1577 to 1581 were translated into German and published for the defense of the Catholic faith in the Holy Roman Empire. The dedication stated "that the Almighty good God, in the place of so many thousand souls in Upper and Lower Germany who were tempted by the Evil Enemy – through numerous unstable new teachings, particularly by the Lutheran, Calvinist, and Zwinglian heretical preachers . . . has elected another people from the other side of the world, who has hitherto known nothing of the holy faith." No wonder that Catholic Germany was ready for the missions. During the Jesuit Nicolas Trigault's fundraising tour in Europe (1615) for the China mission, all the leading Catholic princes in the Holy Roman Empire pledged financial support. After the trauma of war and economic recovery in the late seventeenth century, Jesuits from German-speaking provinces would join a steady stream of missionaries who went to Asia and the Americas to serve their God. The worlds of Protestant and Catholic Germanies would have very different geographical references.

The Reformation world is very different today than it was 20 years ago. In 1985 Lewis W. Spitz, late Professor of Reformation History at Stanford University, published his synthesis, *The Protestant Reformation 1517–1559*, the last volume in the series "The Rise of Modern Europe" begun in the 1950s under the editorship of William Langer, which covered the span of European history from 1250 to 1945. The frames 1517 and 1559 encapsulated the history of the Reformation, as it were, between Luther's *Ninety-Five Theses* and the Peace of Cateau-Cambrésis. This was a framework adopted earlier in another series across the Atlantic, the "History of Europe" under the editorship of J. H. Plumb, with Geoffrey Elton writing the volume in question (*Reformation Europe 1517–1559*, London, 1963). The history of confessional conflict and Catholicism were not neglected in these series; rather, they were relegated to separate treatments that dealt with the period 1560 to 1598/1610, emphasizing respectively the Catholic Reformation or the confessional struggle.

There was much to be said then for this periodization. Examination fields in early modern Europe in departments of history were often organized around a century; and an orderly match between chronology and theme made good pedagogic sense. The only trouble is that university curricula tend to lag behind developments in scholarship. In my review of *The Protestant Reformation 1517–1559* published in 1986, I had called for a unified analysis of both Protestant and Catholic Europe, taking in the full length of the sixteenth century, in order to compare the disciplinary effects of religion in the entire early modern period.[4] I was, of course, only reading the latest signs in historiographical trends. And since the mid-1980s, many studies indeed have been published that stretch the classic terminal dates beyond recognition. Under the late Heiko A. Oberman and his students, the focus of the Reformation was shifted backward in time to the scholastic debates of the late medieval university. Fewer scholars today would suggest that the Reformation was "born deep within a single individual but emerged to become a public matter and a powerful historical force," as Spitz had claimed. Instead, the battles between the *via antiqua* and *via moderna*, and the influence of German mysticism on Luther, were very much crucial to the development of Reformation theology. The late Middle Ages also presented an urgent interpretative problem: if the thesis of an increasingly more corrupt clergy and declining church has been rejected on the evidence of new scholarship, why was it then that dissident movements in late medieval England and Bohemia – the Lollard and the Hussite – failed to threaten the hegemony of the Roman Catholic Church? The contributions in Part I by Euan Cameron and Larissa Taylor suggest ways to understand the relationship between society and religion, and between official and heterodox religions in the late Middle Ages, without implying a point of origin for explaining the events of 1517 and after.

Grasping the larger structures of society and religion allows us to focus in on the particulars of the early Reformation, located in the German-speaking lands of central Europe. In this area of scholarship, the theoretical debates from the 1960s to the 1980s proved stimulating; the Marxist concept of an "early bourgeois revolution," the model of communal Reformation, and the theory of confessionalization have spurned various studies, but the utility of any one hegemonic theory is now quite exhausted in the agenda of research. An enduring legacy of these fruitful decades of scholarship is the recognition of the need for a better integration of the history of social movements and the history of theology. While focusing on the years between Luther and the Religious Peace of Augsburg, the four contributions in Part II on the Reformation in the Holy Roman Empire explore the various connections between ideas and structures, theology and society. Concerned above all with giving a balanced exposition of the extraordinarily diverse religious and social movements of protest in the first decades of the German Reformation, the authors have desisted from allegiance to hegemonic theories that had dominated the German-language scholarship in the field.

From the cradle of the Reformation in Germany, new religious movements spread to other European lands, as if the one Saxon heresy had begotten a multitude of monstrous offspring to plague Latin Christendom. For the faithful of the Roman Church, like the sixteenth-century French physician Antoine Valet, it was a divine warning:[5]

> A witness, a witness, will be for us Germany
> When she opposed Christ with fraudulent Lutheran perjury
> Stuffed with innumerable offspring monstrous
> Saxony suffered and felt divine wrath wondrous.

Saxony, however, did not suffer alone. Within a few short years of the *Ninety-Five Theses*, the first evangelical martyrs – two Augustinian friars – were burned at the stake in Brussels. In western Europe and Italy, Luther's Latin treatises made a significant impact among intellectuals, although the German and hence national dimension of his appeal necessarily limited the Wittenberg reformer's influence on larger society. However, in Scandinavia, with extensive ties to the Hanseatic cities, and in eastern Europe, thanks to the extensive German settlements – in urban trading centers along the Baltic and in Bohemia and in the compact villages of Transylvania – Luther's message and evangelical reform made rapid progress.

For western Europe 1534 represented a crucial year for the Reformation breakthrough. On the surface, it seemed as if the Protestant challenge had been successfully contained. The Anabaptists represented a nuisance in the Low Countries, but hardly the menace they were in neighboring Westphalia; harsh repressive measures kept the peace in the Habsburg lands even while the Anabaptists seized power in Münster in northwestern Germany. In France, the incipient evangelical communities seemed shattered by royal ordinance, faced with the determination of Francis I to crush all heresies after the Affair of the Placard. In the Iberian peninsula, the Protestant heresy remained a distant echo. Even in England, where Henry VIII was about to break with the papacy in pursuance of his marital and dynastic goals, the allegiance of a deeply traditional Catholic England seemed not to have been in danger. Yet, the flight of one French evangelical to escape the dragnet of Francis I's repression would help to change the confessional landscape of western Europe in the decades to come. The remarkable career of Jean Calvin and the equally dramatic history of the city of Geneva sent a second shockwave to rock the foundations of the Roman Catholic Church. Often called "the Second Reformation," the Calvinist movement roared into France and the Low Countries, unleashing a series of religious civil wars in the former and an uprising against Spain in the latter. In England, the regrouping of Protestantism after the Catholic interlude of Queen Mary assumed an increasingly Calvinist character, thereby slowly transforming the Anglican Church, with its heavy Catholic vestiges, into a national Protestant Church during the long reign of Elizabeth. In Italy, Calvinism seduced some influential intellectual and clerical elites, before it was crushed in the 1550s in the cities of northern and central Italy. Even in Lutheran Germany, the Calvinist Reformation won allegiance, thus igniting bitter intra-Protestant strife that lasted until the eve of the Thirty Years' War. But it was in eastern Europe that the Calvinist Reformation gained the most brilliant though impermanent success: of short duration as it turned out in Bohemia, before being crushed by Emperor Ferdinand II after 1619; of great fashion among the Polish nobility, before Jesuit devotion won back the elites of the nation in the mid-seventeenth century; and of endurance in Hungary-Transylvania, where Calvinism became the confession of the ruling dynasties of Transylvania into the late seventeenth century and the allegiance of Hungarian communities down to the present day. This complex development in eight countries of Europe is told in Part III, where readers can discern the parallel trends in eastern and western Europe.

Unscathed by the Protestant Reformation, the Iberian kingdoms of Spain and Portugal emerged to become bulwarks of the Catholic renewal. In these staunch Catholic lands, the history of religiosity evolved without any perceptible breaks; and the ready reception of the decrees of the Council of Trent signified not so much reform but an affirmation of Catholic allegiance. This Catholic energy was manifest above all in the founding of new religious orders, both male and female, positive energy one may say, but also in the impulse to control and repress, as exemplified by the institution of the Holy Office, the Inquisition. While this papal institution remained in clerical hands in Italy (with the exception of Venice), in the Iberian peninsula it functioned as a royal institution with judicial competence extending to the far corners of the Spanish and Portuguese dominions from Lima to Goa. These developments, scrutinized in the chapters of Part IV, also included the large-scale international confessional struggles of the early seventeenth century – the Thirty Years' War and the English Civil War. Together with the French religious civil wars and the Netherlands Uprising, the 90 years from 1560 to 1650 were indeed the age of religious violence.

Extending across the confines of the oceans, it seemed as if God had rewarded the Catholic faith of the Iberian nations with maritime conquests. The Reformation world, as the chapters in Part V remind us, was no longer confined to the quarrels between Lutherans, Zwinglians, Calvinists, Anabaptists, and Catholics. The titanic struggle between Christian confessions and the bloody martyrdom of religious dissenters played alongside an equally dramatic story that unfolded on the world historical stage. An earlier generation of historians and missiologists used the term "spiritual conquests" to describe above all the Catholic conversion of the Spanish Empire. Long discarded for its Eurocentric and restricted ecclesiological perspective, historians of religion are exploring new topics in the history of early modern global Christianity. The stories of Latin America, India, China, and Japan were different tales that constituted a single discourse: the encounter of Catholicism and non-European religions and cultures developed in different contexts of power relations. Whereas Christianization accompanied Hispanization or Lusitanization in the Americas, with its relatively dense network of colonial institutions and settlements, the Spanish and Portuguese religious dominions were much more tenuous in Asia. The south Asian case highlights the dependence on a single Portuguese stronghold – Goa – and the steady dilution of Portuguese colonial and cultural goals the further Christian conversions worked away from the enclave. Likewise, the Catholic missions in China and Japan developed into independent mission fields only loosely bound to the anchor of Portuguese Macao. That Catholicism suffered horrific martyrdom in Tokugawa Japan in the seventeenth century while suffering a slow decline in eighteenth-century Qing China are stories that edified and entertained generations of pious European readers.

And finally, after the long peregrinations of chronology and continents, we reach the further shores of Part VI, which provides an anchor for the tired passenger after the multiple crossings of the vast oceans of historical events. "Structures of the Reformation World" offers readers some central themes common to both Protestant and Catholic Europe in the course of the early modern centuries. Some common developments were bloody and violent: the campaigns to control popular uses of magic and repress witchcraft led to persecutions stretching from Calvinist Scotland under James VI to the Catholic bishoprics of Central Germany. Likewise, religious violence made martyrs out of all Christian confessions, thus highlighting the structural parallels of their bloodletting while maintaining different martyrological memories built out of doctrinal disagreements. Amidst the shouts of truth and clamors of religious arms, the Reformation world also experienced more reassuring moments of peace. From the start of the religious civil wars in France, communities of their own accord concluded local and regional peace treaties to escape the larger madness, mirroring at a lower level of society the larger religious peace treaties that settled abiding differences. The colloquies and religious peacemaking of the sixteenth and seventeenth centuries were a reminder of the lingering legacy of the leading Christian humanist Erasmus, for whom true Christian piety lay not in doctrinal precision and ceremonial observance, but in charity and peace.

In the ruins of this new Reformation world, the fragments of Old Christendom were used to build the new parishes of the contending confessional churches. Drawing tighter boundaries against one another, the churches also bound their faithful closer to ecclesiastical control through bookkeeping and moral discipline: the parish registers, visitations, synodal admonition, and sanctions by secular authorities complemented the picture of a new parish clergy, gaining in intellectual and moral rigor, and standing more aloof from the common folk. Discipline could only coerce so much religious conformity. Lest we think of the Reformation world as one in which the early modern states used the confessional churches to make disciplined and obedient subjects of all, we need to remember the sheer force of apathy, passivity, and inertia that thwarted the goals of social discipline. Together with a sense of practicality and tolerance, seemingly widespread in all confessional settings, a regime of peaceful religious coexistence provided an alternative to the religious conformity imposed by the state. In time, this was even extended to the Jews, who of course stood outside the arena of fierce Christian confessional competition and suffered relatively little, in comparison to their lot in the Christian Middle Ages, from renewed Christian religiosity, even in the tense initial years of the German Reformation.

The 29 contributions to this volume come from scholars working (or who have worked) in the United States, Britain, Germany, Switzerland, the Netherlands, Italy, Hungary, Portugal, France, India, and Japan. Several are retired senior scholars; others are still on the first path of their career. Together, they reflect a wide spectrum of national scholarship, as well as generational and gender perspectives. Their vastly different historical backgrounds and styles are amply reflected in the contents of the essays. Far from wanting to impose an intellectual or theoretical agenda of my own, I see the diversity of historical scholarship represented in this volume as one of its strengths. It mirrors the complexity and creativity of the Reformation world and its peoples, eschewing both the restrictions of ecclesiastical discipline and the limitations of hegemonic theories; and it provides detailed guides for readers in their own explorations of this world.

NOTES

1   The full title of Müntzer's 1524 anti-Luther treatise. For an English translation see Michael G. Baylor, ed., *The Radical Reformation* (Cambridge, 1991), pp. 74ff.
2   See the discussion by Simon Ditchfield, "An Early Christian School of Sanctity in Tridentine Rome," in Simon Ditchfield, ed., *Christianity and Community in the West: Essays for John Bossy* (Aldershot, 2001), pp. 183–205.
3   Cited and translated in Sigrun Haude, *In the Shadow of "Savage Wolves": Anabaptist Münster and the German Reformation During the 1530s* (Boston/Leiden, 2000), pp. 67–8.
4   Published in *Renaissance Quarterly*, 39/1 (1986), pp. 99–100.
5   "Testis erit nobis, testis Germania: quae cum se Christo opposuit perjuri fraude Lutheri, Saxonia innumera monstrorum prole referta. Condoluit, justas ac sensit numinis iras." Cited in Jean Céard, *La Nature et les prodiges: l'insolite au XVIe siècle en France* (Geneva, 1977), p. 272. My translation.

PART I

On the Eve of the Reformation

ONE

Dissent and Heresy

EUAN CAMERON

"There was hardly a period in the second millennium of ecclesiastical history which accepted with less resistance the Catholic Church's absolutist claims in matters of dogma" (Moeller, "Religious Life," p. 15). Moeller's verdict, however applicable to Germany, does not apply equally to the rest of Europe. Dissent there certainly was: however, it was generally localized, diverse, and uncoordinated. Few would now argue that the Reformation followed upon a crescendo of rising protest against the spiritual and dogmatic claims of the Catholic Church. Many of the strongest movements of medieval religious protest had died down considerably from their previous intensity; the Cathars, in western Europe at least, had died out (Lambert, *Cathars*, pp. 291–6; Cameron, *Waldenses*, pp. 172–3). One might even ask whether, in most of Europe, the remaining flickering embers of dissent represented the barest residual level of discontent and disobedience, which no system of religious harmonization or repression could be expected to stamp out entirely. Nevertheless, the perennial question of "medieval heresy and the Reformation" cannot be answered so simply. In various parts of Europe medieval dissent and early modern Protestantism overlapped, met, conversed, and mingled with each other. These encounters repay study and comparison.

Many, though not all, movements of religious dissent originated with an intellectual founder or "heresiarch," who possessed both the learning and the confidence to raise his voice in protest against the received pieties, and inspired the less articulate to follow in his footsteps. Any such potential leader from the theological elite would, however, normally expect to face the challenge of "heresy" long before breaking out, or being forced out, from the academic citadel. The accusation of "heresy" at times meant nothing more than a particularly aggressive ploy in the game of theological disputation. Few academic theologians, in the half-century or so before the Reformation crisis, were willing to air their disputes in public. Wessel Gansfort questioned some conventional wisdom in pastoral theology and on indulgences, but in a paradoxical and profoundly inaccessible scholasticism (Oberman, *Forerunners*, pp. 93–120; Cameron, *European Reformation*, p. 86). Johann Rucherat of Wesel challenged the persistently inflated claims made for indulgences, and was hauled back into line in 1479 (Ritter, "Romantic and Revolutionary Elements," p. 27; Oberman, *Harvest*, pp. 403ff.). Konrad Summenhart even dared argue that withholding tithes might not after all be a mortal sin: but did so discreetly and in Latin (Oberman, *Masters*, pp. 115–24). By the later fifteenth century, the theological elite seemed sure that academic explanations of theological points ought not to be aired in front of a lay public, let alone any disagreements over them. "In the affairs of the faith, skilled spiritual men are said to understand: the rest of the people only simply to believe," wrote Thomas Netter of Walden, with the damaging effects of the Lollard heresy at the forefront of his mind (Lambert, *Medieval Heresy*, p. 234; cf. Cameron, *European Reformation*, pp. 83, 450 n. 23).

In the late fourteenth and early fifteenth centuries, it had briefly seemed possible for the debates of philosophers and theologians to strike fire among a broader community. In Oxford and Prague, a revival of realist Aristotelianism brought renewed certainty that "universals" were real entities rather than semantic abstractions. If there were, as Hus had reportedly argued, a universal donkey, then there was also a universal church, whose attributes could be discussed and compared against those of the real, visible church (Betts, *Essays*, pp. 29–62, 86–106, 132–59, 176–235; Oberman, *Forerunners*, pp. 208–37; Lambert, *Medieval Heresy*, p. 232). In this scenario, *via antiqua* realism became the ideology of challenge and protest, *via moderna* terminism or "nominalism" the underpinning for fideism and acquiescence in the status quo. However, after ca. 1450, if not before, the distinctions within scholastic theology proved far too subtle for such subversive potentialities to be realized. A new form of neo-Thomism grew up, exemplified by Johannes Capreolus (ca. 1380–1444) and represented in Luther's era by such pillars of orthodoxy as Tommasso di Vio Caietanus and Jakob van Hochstraten. Neo-Thomists habitually argued that divine power inhered in the traditional rites of the church, whereas nominalists regarded the link between the divine plan and its earthly manifestations as a matter of convention or *pactum* (Oberman, *Harvest*, passim). While theological disagreement and dissent might in theory have spilled over into the squares and marketplaces, such disagreement was so confused by cross-currents, interconnections, and jargon that it remained, for practical purposes, confined to the academy.

So, across western Europe, and even to some extent within Bohemia, dissent tended to become intellectually proletarianized. This process makes the sources for popular heresy problematic. Late medieval heresy and dissent offer different facets, which are not always easy to relate to each other. Judicial records reveal the evidence of heresy needed to secure conviction, usually in the form of epigraphic statements admitted by the accused, which may be internally inconsistent and lack explanation of their underlying beliefs. Because interrogators looked for a "complete" confession, these statements can sometimes homogenize and exaggerate the nature of heretical dissent. The behavior and conduct of heretics, as important to the historian as their alleged beliefs, may have to be deduced from fragmentary references. On the other hand, literary remains also survive for popular Lollardy and popular Waldensianism. Sermons, pastoral tracts, catechetical materials bear witness to a stern moralistic piety, whose roots were as often from within the shared medieval culture as from within authentic dissent. Though reasoned argument and continuous discourse are present, it is not clear who owned such manuscripts on the eve of the Reformation, how they read them, and what they made of them.

The Geography and Taxonomy of Heresy in Europe

The oldest surviving heretical movement in Europe on the eve of the Reformation was that which churchmen called by the name "Waldensian." In the writings of medieval theologians, and of most historians since, this movement was traced back to the spontaneous movement of self-abnegation, voluntary poverty, and vernacular preaching initiated and led by Valdesius of Lyon in the 1170s. In its origins it was nothing more than an obstinate insistence that its members preach in public, whether the hierarchy approved or not. It became gradually transmuted, as organized inquisition took shape ca. 1230–50, into a variety of wide-ranging anticlerical and antisacerdotal protest movements, led by itinerant, celibate pastors or "brethren" and conserved amongst sedentary lay followers or "friends." Other dissenting strands, especially in Lombardy, surely cross-fertilized and reshaped the movement; but the relative silence of the sources makes any clear narrative impossible.

From ca. 1260–1300 onwards Waldensian dissent was persistently and continuously entrenched in specific areas. In some of its earliest milieux, in Quercy and the west-central Pyrenean regions of present-day France, it was wiped out by the middle of the fourteenth century. However, a successor movement rooted itself in the southwestern Alps and became immovably fixed on both sides of the mountain passes. The Waldenses of Piedmont-Savoy and the Dauphiné emerge into the light of the historical record shortly before 1300, their origins unclear. From their tenacious and successful defense of their mountain valleys, it is most likely that they were native peoples of the region, and that the idea of dissent was brought to them from outside. Although locally based inquisitors and bishops made the Waldenses their business from the 1330s at the latest, the difficult terrain and the fierce self-defense of these communities frustrated ecclesiastical justice over and over again. A coalition of ecclesiastical and secular officials finally obtained a crusade bull from Pope Innocent VIII and attacked the Waldensian lay followers of the Dauphiné with armed force over the winter of 1487–8. A total of 160 people were killed; perhaps ten times that number were dragged through the humiliation of ritual penance. Yet even this did not subdue them. They made full (and surprising) use of all legal means to seek redress: after a 20-year legal process they obtained from a special ad hoc royal-cum-papal tribunal at Paris the cancellation of the acts of the inquisition and the crusade made against them (Cameron, *Waldenses*, pp. 11–95, 151–200). Meanwhile it appears that their Piedmontese cousins were not even attacked.

The Alpine Waldenses established links with similar groups further north in France, around Valence, and sent out colonies of Franco-Provençal speakers into parts of Apulia inland west of Manfredonia, and part of Calabria just inland from the port of Paola. A particularly large and important wave of migrations established Waldensian communities in the Luberon, east of Avignon in Provence, in the fifteenth century. Another important early heartland of Waldensian protest was in central northern Italy, in Lombardy, and possibly some regions further south. However, these groups vanished into all but impenetrable obscurity well before the end of the Middle Ages (Cameron, *Waldenses*, pp. 200–6). In the Marche d'Ancona and Spoleto they may have met or interacted, in the second half of the fifteenth century, with the fugitive remnants of the Fraticelli "of the opinion." These were vehemently antisacerdotal, though hostile ecclesiastical reporting makes ascertaining their precise beliefs and practices very difficult (Douie, *Nature and Effect*, pp. 243–5; Cohn, *Europe's Inner Demons*, pp. 42–54).

It is fairly certain that the Lombard Waldenses promoted the spread of their heresy northwards into what is now Austria and eastern Germany in the early thirteenth century. Waldensian heretics were settled in many small communities along parts of the Danube valley no later than the 1260s and remained at least until ca. 1400; their evangelizers carried the message northwards into the German communities of southern and central Bohemia, and into the Brandenburg Mark along the River Oder. Despite many defections of their leaders in the 1360s and 1390s, and the attentions of some exceptionally dedicated, effective (and surprisingly merciful) inquisitors, a small remnant of dissenters were still receiving ministrations from heretic pastors of some sort in the second half of the fifteenth century. Meanwhile, in a somewhat different fashion, growths of Waldensian protest had appeared around 1400 in several southern German towns and cities, notably Mainz, Augsburg, and Strasbourg, also Bern and Freiburg im Uechtland (Fribourg) in the Swiss Confederation (Cameron, *Waldenses*, pp. 96–150 and refs.). Even this geographical diversity may underrepresent the Waldensian presence: reports compiled of some heretics in Hungary and Bosnia in the middle fifteenth century listed "errors" in many respects similar to those of classic Waldensianism, though some importations from late Hussite rhetoric ensure that these groups defy classification.

England remained untouched by Waldensianism properly so called. However, by the end of the Middle Ages the indigenous heretical movement, the Lollard heresy, had established itself as a vehicle for lay anticlerical and antisacerdotal protest, almost a parallel evolution to Waldensianism. Lollardy arose from an intellectual protest against prevailing theological trends. The Oxford arch-realist John Wyclif (d. 1384) united a firm belief in the reality of universals with a strict predestinarianism and a conviction that only those who were in a state of grace could validly bear dominion and exercise ministry in the church. Applied in the real world, these beliefs led some academic followers of Wyclif to inspire others to bypass the hierarchy through a ministry of traveling "poor preachers." These men, canonically ordained Catholic priests, took the vernacular Scriptures to laypeople and disseminated a morally earnest Gospel, which (if realized in practice) would radically have simplified the ritual and cultic life of late medieval Christianity. They produced a large vernacular literature of sermons and scriptural exegesis, some of it written in massive tomes more appropriate to settled ministry in a church pulpit than to clandestine teaching in private houses (Lambert, *Medieval Heresy*, pp. 225–69; Hudson, *Premature Reformation*, pp. 60–173; Hudson and Gradon, *English Wycliffite Sermons*; Aston, *Lollards and Reformers*). Sporadic ecclesiastical persecution, the failure of some ill-conceived efforts at political revolt in 1414 and 1431, and the progressive defection of their learned leadership caused Lollardy to dwindle into a movement based on informal gatherings in private houses for reading and discussion by the second quarter of the fifteenth century. Any real threat to the structural institutions of the English Church was by then long past.

After a "dip" in the quantity of documentary evidence for Lollard heresy in the middle fifteenth century, trial records reappear in large quantities from ca. 1480 to ca. 1520, and in many of the same areas as before, especially Kent, London, the Thames Valley and Chilterns, and around Coventry and Bristol. Despite such geographical and possibly personal continuity, the Lollardy found in England ca. 1500 was different from that seen during the heroic decades of the early 1400s. The traveling ministry of ordained priests ceased: no new ministers were ordained to replace those who died off in the 1440s. In its place less-well-educated lay evangelizers carried around contraband English books and maintained contact between the conventicles of (mostly) small-town artisans where Lollard beliefs persisted. Secondly, no new devotional, educational, or homiletic works can definitely be proved to have been written within this later period (Lambert, *Medieval Heresy*, pp. 269–83; Hudson, *Premature Reformation*, pp. 446–507; Thomson, *Later Lollards*). The sermons and Bible translations were still circulated; some Lollard tracts would even find their way into print in the sixteenth century. However, it is not known who owned the quite numerous still-surviving manuscripts nor what use they made of them. Paradoxically, for a movement grown from the work of an inaccessible academic, Lollardy's intellectual proletarianization does not seem to have led to inevitable atrophy. The clearer, cruder, antisacerdotal protests of the later period may even have been easier for lay hearers to comprehend.

The great Czech movement of dissent, the Hussite heresy, was beyond question the most formidable challenge to the ecclesiastical hierarchy in the later Middle Ages. Alone of the movements to be discussed in this chapter, it succeeded in supplanting the priesthood and the worship of the Catholic Church, over a large part of Bohemia. It alone included a recognizable functioning "priesthood," which offered something resembling a complete religious service to its adherents. However, here as elsewhere, an earlier heroic phase had been followed by decades of mutual acrimony, compromises, and schisms. The picture of Hussitism on the eve of the Reformation is therefore complex.

The Hussite movement had arisen out of a fortuitous confluence of three spiritual strands. From the late fourteenth century a succession of vigorous, accessible preachers at Prague had inveighed against sin, especially the sins committed by the most materialistic and corrupt of the clergy. Secondly, Czech academics had striven to restore the prestige of the Czech "nation" within the Charles University in Prague against the institutionalized preponderance of ethnic Germans. Thirdly, Wyclif's philosophical ultra-realism was imported both as an intellectual counterweight to German nominalism and as underpinning for a sharp denunciation of moral abuses in the church. As reforming preacher, philosophical realist, and Czech nationalist, the theologian Jan Hus combined all three strands. However, Jan Hus was not Wyclif, and Hussitism was not Lollardy. In his theological writings Hus did not teach a neo-Donatist rejection of the sacramental ministry of sinful priests as Wyclif did. Hus became a martyr, and an inspiration to a range of diverse religious movements, because his cause was entangled in the complex and shifting ecclesiastical politics at the end of the Great Schism. The king of Bohemia, Václav IV, first encouraged the Czech reformists at the university to secure its adherence to the Pisan papacy, then abandoned their cause when the fathers of the Council of Constance made their hostility to Hus clear. Hus was burned, by the cruelest of ironies, because he refused to recant errors which (he claimed) he never held in the first place and were not present in his writings: he was therefore, in canon law, an obstinate and unrepentant heretic (Lambert, *Medieval Heresy*, pp. 284–316; Fudge, *Magnificent Ride*, pp. 1–88; Kaminsky, *Hussite Revolution*, pp. 7–23, 97–140).

The Hussite movement was led, in spirit, by a "heresiarch" who was no longer there to direct its course, and who almost certainly would have disapproved of many of the forms which it took. At the risk of oversimplification, one can identify four strands to mid-fifteenth-century Hussitism. Most conservative and hieratic were elements within the Czech priestly and academic elite who insisted, on the inspiration of Hus's colleague Jakoubek of Stribro, on giving lay communicants the chalice of consecrated wine in the Eucharist: laypeople had traditionally been refused the chalice in western Catholic practice in the Middle Ages. These "Utraquists" (who gave communion *sub utraque specie*, in both kinds) rapidly formed a separate allegiance within the Czech clergy, supported by a regional nobility outraged by the slur on their nation caused by Hus's condemnation and burning. In most other respects, socially and liturgically, the Utraquists were conservatives. A second strand was represented by the radical urban protest which flared up among the lesser guildsmen and artisans of Prague at the preaching of the former Premonstratensian canon Jan Želivský: by force of pulpit oratory and popular insurrection he exerted decisive influence in Prague until a coup led to his overthrow and execution in 1422 (Lambert, *Medieval Heresy*, pp. 316–26; Kaminsky, *Hussite Revolution*, pp. 141–264, 434–94; Fudge, *Magnificent Ride*, pp. 90ff.).

The third strand, on which Želivský depended but which outlived him, was the radical, millenarian reformism of the so-called "Taborites." To the alarm of the university masters and the aristocracy, these fervent apocalyptic believers gathered together at five towns designated as gathering-places of the elect, and set up a new order, social as well as religious. Under Jan Žižka (d. 1424) they became an astonishingly effective fighting force: their victories undoubtedly saved the entire Hussite enterprise against repeated Catholic crusades during the 1420s. In their liturgical life they practiced the utmost simplicity, in contrast to the relative conservatism of the Utraquists (Lambert, *Medieval Heresy*, pp. 323–4, 328–32; Heymann, *Žižka*; Kaminsky, *Hussite Revolution*, pp. 310–433; Fudge, *Magnificent Ride*, pp. 95–107, 140–1). In their so-called "little bishop" Mikuláš of Pelhrimov they possessed a theologian who articulated their founding documents and gave them some continuity. Ultimately, the Utraquists came to find the church-in-arms of the Taborites an encumbrance as they negotiated with the fathers of the Council of Basel. A coalition of moderate Utraquists and their allies defeated the Taborites in battle at Lipany (May 30, 1434) and outflanked them in negotiation, shaping an agreement with the Council of Basel known as the *Compactata*. This document gave some quasi-legal status to the Utraquist Church within the Roman communion, though problems over the ordination of priests and the apostolic succession dogged it for decades. Taboritism persisted in its hilltop fortress of the Hradiště (renamed Tábor) until it surrendered to the Hussite King of Bohemia George of Podebrady in 1452. The Utraquists, meanwhile, consolidated their position in the Kutná Hora agreement of 1485, which was made permanent in 1512 (Lambert, *Medieval Heresy*, pp. 344–8, 356–8; Williams, *Radical Reformation*, pp. 317–20; Odlozilik, *Hussite King*; Heymann, *George of Bohemia*).

Although Taboritism was a spent force by the Reformation, it influenced the fourth strand of Hussite dissent, the politically pacifist but theologically radical "Unity of Brethren." Petr Chelčický (ca. 1380–ca. 1467), formerly called Peter of Zahorka, became disillusioned with the Taborites because of their dependence on violence and political force to spread the word. By a dialectical process rather like that seen later in Anabaptism, Chelčický turned away from the idea of political conquest in a religious cause to the opposite extreme: he advocated complete renunciation of political office and political structures, and rejected not only warfare but all use of the sword to kill, even in justice. Around 1458 Gregory Krajcí, nephew of the Hussite Archbishop-elect of Prague Jan Rokycana, founded a community at Kunvald to live by Chelčický's teachings. This grew into the "Unity of Brethren," which consisted after 1467 of a separate, self-sustaining priesthood and a lay fellowship to which it ministered. Its first ordinands received a form of ordination from a follower of the Hussite-Waldensian German missionary Friedrich Reiser, who had been executed in 1458 (Lambert, *Medieval Heresy*, pp. 352–6; Williams, *Radical Reformation*, pp. 320–32; Cameron, *Waldenses*, pp. 149–50). The Unity became the theological repository of Taborite ideas, shorn of their militant features. Though gradual attenuation of some of its doctrines regarding participation in secular society caused a schism in the 1490s, it survived into the sixteenth century and grew in influence. Its leading theologian on the eve of the Reformation, Lukas of Prague (ca. 1458–1528), wrote works of real stature in the radical Hussite tradition.

The Hussite Church was exclusively a Czech-speaking phenomenon based in parts of Bohemia and Moravia. However, Friedrich Reiser (d. 1458) received some form of ordination from Mikuláš of Pelhrimov in 1431 and led missionary expeditions into Germany in the 1430s and 1450s until his capture and execution. His followers espoused more of traditional clandestine popular heresy, and less of the church-building ambition of the Hussites. In northeastern Germany they approached the same villages as the Waldensian pastors of a century or so before. Though it would be rash to make any claims about either their survival or disappearance, they caused little serious concern to the church and were barely known to the reformers, if at all.

Living Heresy

To the inquisitor and ecclesiastical judge, dissent consisted essentially in a set of affirmations – or perhaps merely reluctant admissions – that the accused person had rejected some element of the church's agreed teachings. To the historian, it is just as vital to see how the heretics lived. Too much concentration on doctrinal statements can mask vital differences between the Reformation and its antecedents, and thus betray the essential quality of the reformers' achievements.

The remainder of this discussion will follow thematic lines rather than examining each heretical movement in turn. The purpose of this approach is simply to avoid repetition. Many of the popular dissenting movements of the late Middle Ages turned against the same traits of a hierarchical, wealthy, ritualized church and its worship: one might even argue that the very nature of such a church provoked such repeated reactions. The dissenters' behavior followed similar lines, because sheer necessity and the behavior of officialdom dictated that certain survival strategies be followed. Similarities in conduct and attitudes can be discerned between movements which we know to be historically quite unrelated, such as Waldensianism and Lollardy. Given that such similarities exist between unrelated movements, historians must be wary of assuming that any two heretic groups who exhibit similarity of "official" ecclesiastical nomenclature, and similarity of behavior, were in very truth sprung from a common source or inspired by a shared founder.

Before the Reformation, unless there was some alternative religious establishment set up (as in Bohemia), "heretics" normally attended the services of the Catholic Church in their parishes. In the primitive years of English Lollardy, it was possible in some regions to hear a Lollard priest preaching within the parish church itself. However, after ca. 1450 one could only attend a Catholic church service. Church attendance may have served chiefly to allay the suspicions of the majority. Some Lollards apparently claimed sickness to excuse those occasions when they did not attend. Occasional comments from witnesses, for instance that Lollards looked to heaven rather than at the host when it was elevated, confirm that they attended mass; others confessed to breaking fasts before attending services (Hudson, *Premature Reformation*, pp. 149–51; Thomson, *Later Lollards*, pp. 68–9, 264–5). The evidence from across continental Europe suggests the same for late Waldensianism. Waldenses attended services in their churches; sometimes they even made pilgrimages or required masses to be said for their relatives. Their behavior while in church, in respect of the use of holy water, or adoration of the host, might be in some respect abnormal: but they still turned up for regular worship. Likewise, such popular heretics, by the general consent of the sources, usually made their annual confession of sins and received communion at Easter. Masters and followers, wrote the late fourteenth-century inquisitor Peter Zwicker, received baptism and the Eucharist from the Catholic clergy (Cameron, *Reformation of the Heretics*, pp. 84–7, 92–5, 100–1; *Waldenses*, pp. 123, 132–7). Even in the early years of the Reformation, when to admit to participation in Catholic rites was a great embarrassment, a Waldensian pastor or *barbe* like Georges Morel could admit to Johannes Oecolampadius, with unconscious paradox, that the sacraments were given to the people not by the *barbes* but by the "members of Antichrist." The reformers would express grave misgivings at this self-contamination by participation in idolatrous worship (Cameron, *Waldenses*, pp. 213, 237–8; Vinay, *Confessioni di fede*, pp. 42–3, 52–4, 84).

However, minimal conformity to the rites and cults of the late Middle Ages was itself a statement of sorts. A close economic and legal survey of the Waldensian communities of the Luberon, in Provence, has shown that they, like others, endowed obit masses for their deceased relatives and bequeathed money for masses for themselves, but did so on a less flamboyant scale than their neighbors. They kept to ancient, more restrained post-mortem devotions, while their Catholic neighbors willingly paid up for the great inflation of those devotions popular at the time (Audisio, *Vaudois du Luberon*, pp. 202–24, 264–74). It would be fascinating to discover how far Waldensian followers absented themselves from patronal celebrations, Corpus Christi processions, or other manifestations of late medieval voluntary religion. In theory they disapproved of them all. All the movements studied in this chapter held that some, most, or all of the Catholic priesthood were contaminated by sin: above all by their abandonment of apostolic poverty, their acceptance of worldly authority, their simoniacal and materialistic practices. To receive the sacraments from such priests ought to have troubled consciences. Heretics might have tried to seek out those priests who were better or less sinful than most (as the Patarenes of Milan allegedly did in the late eleventh century). However, there is no sign that late medieval heretics appraised the priesthood in this way. Some priests made approving noises about a group of Waldenses, while another spoke of the same people with exasperation and enmity: but one cannot deduce how far such diverse sentiments responded to religiously motivated hostility shown by the heretics (Cameron, *Reformation of the Heretics*, p. 76).

Outside the universities, heresy was a communal activity: like-minded groups came together for mutual instruction, support, and discipline. Outside Bohemia, such behavior was necessarily somewhat clandestine. Heretical gatherings took place typically in private homes, in the evenings or at night. Waldenses in the Alpine valleys would sometimes meet further up the valleys; those who lived in the German towns of fourteenth-century Bohemia sometimes constructed hidden rooms or cellars where they could gather undetected (Cameron, *Reformation of the Heretics*, p. 89; *Waldenses*, p. 114). Many Lollards were literate in the vernacular (though not usually in Latin) and could therefore read to each other from their Biblical translations and books of sermons and tracts. Later Lollardy, it would appear, was a cooperative exercise (Hudson, *Premature Reformation*, pp. 180–200). Waldenses were, in contrast, generally less literate. They had, however, an itinerant, celibate elite of pastors or *barbes*, who could read the books that they carried with them, and also knew parts of Scripture by heart. These pastors preached to the assembled gatherings as well as advising individuals in private (Cameron, *Waldenses*, pp. 216–26).

Waldensian *barbes*, with their greater reputation for austerity and holiness than the Catholic priesthood, were expected to hear the confessions of their followers and assign penances to them. Whereas Lollards and Hussites appear to have regarded the paraphernalia of canonical absolution as a needless concentration of spiritual power into earthly hands, Waldenses had, from the middle thirteenth century onwards, seen auricular confession as a rite to imitate. Neither the sins confessed nor the penances assigned were distinctive or unusual; penitents were told to fast on simple food, to learn and repeat the standard prayers of the church (Cameron, *Reformation of the Heretics*, pp. 90–2; *Waldenses*, pp. 72, 83, 115, 128, 130, 158, 185, 187–8). Confession was the only sacrament that the Waldensian pastorate claimed to dispense: *barbes* neither baptized nor consecrated. Popular heretics were consistently reluctant to "usurp" the ritual acts of the priesthood in any other respect. When a handful of German Waldenses performed a form of Eucharist, others vehemently criticized them (Cameron, *Waldenses*, pp. 128–9 and nn. 162–3). In Lollardy, there were occasional rumors of individual laypeople consecrating a form of irregular Eucharist, but they were so rare as to arouse special comment (Hudson, *Premature Reformation*, p. 151). Mainstream Utraquist Hussites, who had ordained priests to dispense the sacraments, were very sensitive about ensuring apostolic succession and due ordination. As a result, great backlogs of ordinands built up when canonically ordained bishops were not available. Emergency measures, for instance the importation of an Italian bishop in 1482, relieved the pressure (Lambert, *Medieval Heresy*, pp. 356–7). Even the more radical Unity of Brethren sought legitimation of its priesthood from outside, through its links with Friedrich Reiser's spiritual heirs. From the perspective of the sixteenth century, the issue of whether medieval heretics "rebaptized" followers when they converted from Catholicism to dissent would become highly sensitive. In 1530 Martin Bucer warned the Provençal Waldenses in copious and unnecessary detail against the evils of rebaptizing (Vinay, *Confessioni di fede*, pp. 86–102). The only later medieval heretics who appear to have rebaptized those who joined them from the ranks of

Catholicism were some of the Unity of Brethren; and they gradually abandoned the practice in the early sixteenth century (Cameron, *Waldenses*, p. 239; Lambert, *Medieval Heresy*, p. 385).

Though rebaptism was a red herring, it raises the important issue of how dissenting groups perceived themselves as social entities. Most late medieval heretics evinced some unease at participation in the messy and bloody business of everyday politics and government. Both Lollards and Waldenses at various times objected to killing people in judicial execution or otherwise, an objection which (if taken consistently) would have precluded wielding the office of magistrate. Lollards also objected to the idea of "just war" and denounced crusading (Hudson, *Premature Reformation*, pp. 367–70; Cameron, *Waldenses*, pp. 34, 46, 52, 85, 103, 234). Similar objections were attributed to Nicholas of Dresden, the German radical who briefly associated himself with the Prague Hussites in the 1410s. Most pacifist of all the Hussites, of course, was Petr Chelčický. The Unity of Brethren, however, demonstrate how a radical rejection of killing could pose intractable problems. The first members of the Unity were expected by their founding fathers to renounce all attributes of worldly power entirely; yet as the movement grew toward the end of the fifteenth century, and attracted more well-born adherents, it proved necessary to attenuate the primitive founders' ideals. The "major Unity" from the 1490s onwards dispensed with these strict prohibitions, and their theologian Lukas of Prague justified their doing so (Lambert, *Medieval Heresy*, pp. 352, 355; Brock, *Political and Social Doctrines*). Of course, heretics from isolated rural communities, who had little prospect of wielding high justice, lost little by repudiating it. In reality Waldensian villages, whether in the northeast German Uckermark or the southwestern Alps, did supply members of their number to serve as magistrates. In the Alps (though not in Germany) they were also ready to use lethal force to defend themselves, as the sixteenth-century reformers would discover to their chagrin (Cameron, *Reformation of the Heretics*, pp. 17–20, 163, 193; *Waldenses*, pp. 141, 196, 276–8).

The swearing of oaths poses further problems of apparent inconsistency in the heretics' behavior. Christ told his followers "not to swear at all," although that prohibition had been attenuated and glossed in the church for many centuries (Matthew 5: 33–7). To refuse to swear an oath to tell the truth under interrogation, or to withhold an oath of fealty or allegiance, was to cast oneself into virtual outlawry among other Christians. Yet allegations were persistently made against Lollards and Waldenses, as well as against some radical Hussites, that they would not take even a legal oath. Many heretics, under interrogation, said that to ask for the swearing of an oath, or to swear one, was a sin. Sometimes, especially in early fourteenth-century French and German Waldensianism, followers stubbornly (and potentially suicidally) refused to swear when urged to do so before ecclesiastical judges (Limborch, *Liber Sententiarum*, pp. 289–91; Cameron, *Waldenses*, p. 116). However, even as early as the thirteenth century, Waldenses allegedly found ways to wriggle out of the prohibition, or to justify minimal cooperation with the judicial oath; a similarly equivocal or balanced approach is found among some Lollards (Cameron, *Waldenses*, pp. 105–7 and refs.; Hudson, *Premature Reformation*, pp. 371–4). By the late fifteenth century, the Waldenses of Provence, beyond question, swore oaths to make contracts and verify legal documents. Their Alpine cousins even took oaths from each other to preserve the secrecy of the movement (Audisio, *Vaudois du Luberon*, pp. 205–8;

Cameron, *Waldenses*, pp. 190–1). All heretics, Lollards and Waldenses alike, objected to the promiscuous and blasphemous affirmation of every possible statement by a casual oath: so, one might add, did many medieval moralistic writers (Cameron, *Waldenses*, pp. 225–6). Context is crucial here. Among ordinary late medieval layfolk, to keep one's speech ostentatiously pure and modest was to stand out from one's neighbors. To avoid blasphemy might not have been a theological "offense," but it must have been a clear and visible cultural marker.

Another potential social marker of late medieval heretics was their attitude to intermarriage with the rest of the Catholic population. Since most late medieval dissenters performed mandatory Catholic practices, intermarriage was not absolutely impracticable. Some German Waldenses married Catholic spouses fairly readily. However, if a group had secrets to hide, or a strong self-consciousness as a defensive and persecuted minority, endogamy could result. Alpine Waldenses usually avoided intermarriage with Catholics, and were accused of holding themselves aloof and superior. In their colonies, in Provence or southern Italy, language, customs, and group identity tended to make them marry even more exclusively with each other. Though no such reason existed for the Lollards of London, an ecclesiastical investigator in 1521 asked whether it was a Lollard practice to marry only amongst each other's families (Audisio, *Vaudois du Luberon*, pp. 110–14; Cameron, *Reformation of the Heretics*, pp. 105–6; *Waldenses*, pp. 131, 191, 201; Brigden, *London and the Reformation*, p. 87).

A debate has grown up in recent years over the role of women in popular dissenting movements. In the Middle Ages, clerical writers alleged, to show how utterly subversive and disorderly dissenting movements were, that they allowed not only laymen but also laywomen to lead their religious activities. In the early years of Waldensian protest, some women were reported as traveling around in the company of the preaching and supposedly celibate "brethren." From time to time occasional references are made to "female masters" of the sect, or to "sisters" with whom the traveling brethren stayed while in training. Given that the clergy would have seized on any signs of female participation with scornful glee, it is striking just how little evidence there is of it. Recent work on the Lollards and the Waldenses has argued, independently, that dissenters did not transcend the social values of their world. Women remained confined to secondary roles (McSheffrey, *Gender and Heresy*; Shahar, *Women in a Medieval Heretical Sect*; but cf. Biller, "Preaching of the Waldensian Sisters"). When dissent was practiced in private homes, women were intimately and indispensably involved as the hosts, protectors, concealers, and hearers of traveling heretical teachers. Women on trial were often as articulate and defiant in their heresy as their menfolk (see e.g. Cameron, *Waldenses*, pp. 137, nn. 230, 232). However, their role was fundamentally little different from that of Catholic laywomen.

These behavioral traits tended to accrue around religious dissenters at the end of the Middle Ages: minimal participation in the official cult; private exhortation and reading from vernacular Scriptures and works of piety; reservations, rarely taken to extremes, regarding participation in civic office, oath-swearing, and killing people in war or justice; plain, modest, controlled speech; and a tendency to become a people apart, more visibly devout and contained than was normal. A late fourteenth-century inquisitor lamented that the "heresiarchs" did not "preach to great sinners, to the litigious, fornicators, deceivers, thieves, . . . usurers, rapists, and other criminals; you only draw to yourselves those whom you have heard are peaceful, quiet, silent, composed, who but for you would remain sons of the kingdom" (cited in Cameron, *Waldenses*, p. 137). Heresy promoted a quiet, interiorized devotion, hostile to the crassness of the everyday, materialistic cult. Its vehemence was verbal; its rejections of the spiritual claims of the church largely theoretical.

Believing Badly

Jacobus Simancas summed up the problem: a heretic was "not one who lives badly, but one who believes badly" (Simancas, *De Catholicis Institutionibus*, p. 228). Many heretics actually lived rather well by contemporary ethical standards, but their beliefs doomed them to hostility and attack from the majority. Heresy, as a legal offense, consisted in affirmations of disbelief. These affirmations, as encapsulated in thousands of "repetitions" of heretics' beliefs read out at the conclusion of an inquisitorial trial, pose real problems as historical sources. They tell us only that the judges formed the impression that a heretic believed such-and-such, and therefore incorporated a given point into the trial record. How they formed that impression, and how truly such an impression was grounded in the facts, becomes a matter of historical judgment. Jan Hus's sentence contains the absurd claim that he believed himself to be a fourth person of the Trinity (Fudge, *Magnificent Ride*, p. 85 and n. 78). Admittedly an extreme example, it reflects the medieval ecclesiastics' typical conviction, that heretics "really" believed what the inquisitors and their manuals thought they believed, rather than whatever untidy equivocations or bewildered statements the accused themselves produced. Interrogating a heretic often meant extracting evidence of the interrogator's preconceptions.

One key problem was that heretical words were rarely, if ever, backed up by consistent actions on those words. It is not difficult to draw up some sort of schema of popular heresy, with due allowance for the nuances of individual interpretation and the differences between various groups. One must not assume, however, that those assigned such beliefs always behaved as though they held them. The starting point for any presentation of heretical beliefs must be their attitude to the Catholic Church. Late medieval heretics argued that the church was tainted by sin; the possession of great wealth and political power had corrupted it. They were not unique in saying such things: many reforming preachers and Doctors of Theology said much the same. However, most heretics went beyond mere anticlericalism to argue that a church so sinful, and priests so flawed, could not rightly bear spiritual dominion, preach the Gospel, absolve sinners, or administer the sacraments of grace. Spiritual power, as some Waldensian followers put it, depended on sanctity (Cameron, *Reformation of the Heretics*, pp. 79–80). In its crude form, such an argument constituted a revival of the Donatist heresy, which had long since been argued down in the works of Augustine. Wyclif, with his towering certainty that spiritual power belonged to the elect only, could go down this road. Jan Hus did not; and indeed in the St. Wenceslas's Synod held at Prague on September 28, 1418, leading followers of Hus explicitly disavowed this and other such radical beliefs (Lambert, *Medieval Heresy*, pp. 297, 322). However, the Hussites repeatedly played on the graphic contrasts between the apostolic church with its simplicity, poverty, and humility, and the modern church with its power, greed, pride, and pomp. Illustrations on church walls and in manuscripts showed Christ humbly washing the feet of the apostles while the pope grandly allowed rulers to kiss his feet (Fudge, *Magnificent Ride*, pp. 230–1, 235–49). Whether theological "Donatism" was taught or not, the effect was much the same: the pomp and grandeur of the modern church showed its anti-Christian nature.

Many other doctrines depended on the belief that the church on earth had received, as it were by divine delegation, the responsibility to mediate and transmit grace, and to give or withhold absolution. Most movements, though by no means all heretics, taught people to reject those beliefs. The doctrine of purgatory, in its developed late medieval form, derived from the argument that sins absolved on earth too late for earthly penance to be completed must be worked out through suffering in the hereafter. All manner of religious rituals practiced by the living on earth might work for the benefit of souls in purgatory, above all the memorial mass. Waldenses, many Lollards, and the Taborite wing of Hussitism all renounced belief in purgatory, though many individuals found it difficult to live by such statements (Cameron, *Waldenses*, pp. 46, 75–6, 85, 90–1, 103, 115, 135–6, 187–8, 230; Hudson, *Premature Reformation*, pp. 309–10, 323, 469). A Taborite text argued that the godly were purged of their sins in this life: by the word of God, works of faith and piety, almsgiving, suffering adversities, through abundance of charity, by forgiving offenses, and by turning sinners away from their way of life.

Pilgrimages, saints, their images and their relics, and the whole concept of a host of heavenly intercessors linked to the earthly church likewise aroused withering skepticism. Lollards drew poignant contrasts between the needy poor, the true images of God, who often lacked necessary alms, and the wealthy images to which pilgrimages were commonly made. Inert and senseless idols were covered with vast wealth while human beings went in want, and stories of false miracles were spread around to encourage yet more largesse from pilgrims (Hudson, *Selections*, pp. 83–8). Taborites, drawing heavily on Wyclif's *Trialogus*, argued that Christ was the sole mediator, and that it was foolish to address saints as though God "were like an earthly sovereign whose anger needs to be calmed by their intercessors." God alone was to be worshipped, said many Waldenses. Yet here as elsewhere, beliefs are hard to pin down, and practice often belied theory. Waldenses ought not to have learned the Ave Maria if they believed prayers to saints to be superfluous, yet many did. Why, indeed, did the entirely Waldensian village of Freissinières press the archbishop of Embrun to restore the "ornaments and jewels" of their parish church which had been removed in the aftermath of the 1487/8 crusade (Cameron, *Waldenses*, pp. 89–90, 128, 132–3, 187–8; *Reformation of the Heretics*, p. 100)?

Late medieval heretics were ambivalent about the sacraments of the church. Some doubts about the sacraments might arise simply from the suspicion that the priests were not good enough truly to administer them. Also, the elaborateness of the ritual, and the claim to provide infallible grace, might invite doubt and rejection. Some later Lollard confessions, and many treatises written against the Waldenses, reeled off a list of rejections of each of the sacraments in turn. God's grace, the argument ran, did not need to be routed through ceremonies performed by an earthly institution (see e.g. Tanner, *Heresy Trials in . . . Norwich*, pp. 94–5, 111, 159–60, 165, 176–7, 179, 185, 194, 196–9, 205). While Taborites retained the seven sacraments, they took a different approach: every sacrament as currently performed in the church was full of redundant and excessive ceremonial, and needed rigorous pruning and simplification to return it to the primitive ideal. The supreme sacrament, of course, was the Eucharist: it was performed many times daily and watched by the laity in the hope of specific spiritual benefits. Lollard beliefs about the Eucharist are somewhat complex; Wyclif's philosophical objections to transubstantiation were barely susceptible of transmission to lay readers. By the eve of the Reformation most Lollards rejected a transubstantiated presence in favor of a symbolic or representational one. Even the Taborites, sprung from the supremely Eucharistic Hussite movement, came to reject transubstantiation as it was generally taught. The consecrated host was "the body of Christ by resemblance, and by the cogitations and affections of those who receive it," as Mikuláš of Pelhrimov put it (Fudge, *Magnificent Ride*, pp. 142–3 and nn. 80–1). Some Waldenses also had reservations about the real presence. The Austrian Andreas Hesel thought that if the host were really Christ's body, it would long since have been entirely eaten up by the faithful (Döllinger, *Dokumente*, pp. 343–4). However, since doubts over the Eucharistic presence were not part of the standard repertoire of questions asked of suspected Waldenses, such statements were rare. Because Waldenses were baptized, confessed, took communion, and married like other Christians, doubts about the sacraments only found expression, at most, in casual statements or unostentatious withdrawal from voluntary aspects of the cult.

Apocalypticism and prophecy were so widely diffused throughout later medieval and early modern culture that it becomes difficult to say how far apocalypticism was a feature of heresy. Belief in a coming judgment can offer attractive compensation to a minority which suffers persecution in the here and now. The first Taborites really thought that the elect should gather together in places of refuge to await a new order in the world. The administration of the chalice to the laity became a symbol that the world was being renewed in readiness for the end-time (Lambert, *Medieval Heresy*, p. 324; Kaminsky, *Hussite Revolution*, pp. 336–60; Fudge, *Magnificent Ride*, pp. 143ff., 166). The problem with such expectations was the same as at any other period: the more concentrated and imminent the expectation, the sooner disappointment set in. More moderate beliefs, which incorporated the long run of world history into the time-frame of the Book of Revelation, proved more durable. Several Lollard tracts interpreted their own age as that in which Satan had been loosed from his thousand-year period in chains, and allowed to wreak destruction in the church (Revelation 20: 1–3; Hudson, *Selections*, pp. 93, 112, 126). The same chronology would be appropriated in the schemes of church history produced by John Foxe in the reformed tradition (Foxe, *Acts and Monuments*, vol. 1, pp. 4–5; Cameron, "Medieval Heretics as Protestant Martyrs," pp. 205–6). Millennial expectations, if not too specific, could last a long time: the early sixteenth-century Lollard evangelizer John Hacker taught his London followers about a future millennium in which all evil priests would be killed (Brigden, *London and the Reformation*, p. 106 and n. 125).

Dissenting Texts

The priestly hierarchy kept its distance from the common herd by conserving a literature and a system of law in Latin, the language of the educated. Dissenters, who sought to establish a pattern of religious life independent of the hierarchy, naturally enough sought access to the Scriptures and other religious literature in the vernacular. Valdesius at Lyon in the 1170s arranged to have certain key extracts from Scripture translated into the vernacular at the very inception of his movement, and thereafter learning of Scripture texts in translation became very common (Patschovksy, "Literacy of Waldensianism," pp. 113–23). Hussitism long retained Latinate scholars within the movement, though even conservative Utraquists wished the Scripture lessons in the mass to be read in Czech: like the lay chalice, the vernacular helped to dismantle the wall between priests and laity (Lambert, *Medieval Heresy*, p. 333). After Wyclif, Lollards produced a copious vernacular literature. The mere possession of religious books in English came to be regarded as a convenient means to identify a heretic at the end of the Middle Ages (Hudson, *Premature Reformation*, pp. 470–1, 486–7). Apart from language and ownership, there was often little else that was "heretical" about heretics' books. The key text was of course the Bible itself. Waldensian translations were in various languages, and most are lost. There survive five incomplete Bibles in an Alpine version of Franco-Provençal. Usually the New Testament is nearly complete, while only selected books of moral and homiletic value from the Old Testament are included (Cameron, *Waldenses*, p. 217 n. 29; Papini, *Valdo di Lione*, pp. 347–74). The Lollard Bible was, by contrast, a full translation which went through two distinct recensions. The early version was a verbatim rendering into cumbersome and scholarly English, only suitable for use by a priest who already knew some Latin; this was succeeded, in the late 1390s, by a much more flowing translation in idiomatic Middle English (Hudson, *Selections*, pp. 40–1, 46–9; Lambert, *Medieval Heresy*, p. 247; Deanesly, *Lollard Bible*).

In both Lollard and Waldensian milieux there was preserved a large literature of sermons, catechesis, and moral tracts. At the end of the Middle Ages a curious line of filiation linked the three movements discussed in this chapter. Wyclif's later writings were imported into Bohemia, and helped to shape the more radical ecclesiological criticism of the Taborites and the Unity of Brethren. By the 1520s, some of these works from the Taborites and the Unity were translated into Alpine Franco-Provençal. Though the exact means of transmission are unknown, the antisacerdotal legacy of Wyclif, Mikuláš of Pelhrimov, and Lukas of Prague became briefly available in the language of the Waldenses. However, it is not always clear that such works were prized for their dissenting content. Collections of manuscripts sometimes contained works of uncontroversial Catholic instruction mixed up with anticlerical criticism. Many heretical sermons, from whatever source, resorted to the same laborious and, to modern eyes, unsatisfactory allegorizing as their Catholic counterparts (Brenon, "Waldensian Books," pp. 150–8; Cameron, *Waldenses*, pp. 216–31). The sermon literature offers a useful corrective to the impression given by the trial records. The former dwells, overwhelmingly, on the moral obligations of the Christian. Christianity appears as a stern, demanding code of moral righteousness. Such sermons convey precisely the heaping-up of moral demands and obligations that Martin Luther would later look back on with such horror. To criticize the hollow ceremonial consolations of the priesthood was half the story. The other half was that heretics expected their followers to live by a strict moral law of purity and self-restraint (Cameron, *Waldenses*, p. 302; but cf. Lambert, *Medieval Heresy*, pp. 355–6).

Heresy and the Reformation

In the later sixteenth century, Protestant apologists would claim the late medieval dissenters as their forebears, as the hidden "true church" that existed while Satan was unbound and the visible church was given over to error. That identification was not made immediately. Indeed, at first it was Catholic critics, theologians like Johann Eck, who hoped to blacken and shame the reformers by associating them with disreputable and already outcast heretics (Cameron, "Medieval Heretics as Protestant Martyrs," pp. 187–8). It is tempting to assume that a preexistent body of dissent must have provided a useful seed-bed for the Reformation to take root. However, there is an issue of scale to consider here. The reformers aspired to reshape whole churches, not cells of followers in private houses. The Waldenses of the southwestern Alps, an exceptionally compact and numerous group of dissenters, comprised a few thousand. Abjurations of Lollards in England, at their peak, usually ran into dozens rather than hundreds in any given diocese (Hudson, *Premature Reformation*, pp. 450, 466). Heretics were always a minority. If a minority's heretical inclinations predisposed the majority against dissent, then the reformers' task could actually be made harder, not easier. Then again, if a compact, defiant heretical community were confronted, as the Waldenses were from the 1530s, with evangelists from a new creed, sprung from the clergy whom they despised, they might find that shared hostility to Catholicism was not quite enough to build an easy or immediate alliance.

In the event, most heretical communities were gradually overwhelmed by the greater seismic shifts in sixteenth-century church history. In Bohemia, where the Utraquist Church and the Unity of Brethren had a visible identity and public structures, there was frequent dialogue with the reformers, but no formal union until the adoption of the *Confessio Bohemica* of 1575; even then the separate communions retained their identities. The Unity of Brethren in particular grew in influence and confidence in the later sixteenth century. The Waldenses of the Alps, according to an old historical tradition, were thought to have taken a collective decision to adhere to reformed teachings in a meeting of the *barbes* in the autumn of 1532. Close study of both of the sources alleged to demonstrate that decision, and of the founding and early history of the Reformed churches of the Alps and Provence, has shown a different story. From the 1550s onwards the Church of Geneva was able to offer the Alpine churches a wholly new cadre of trained ministers, who would reshape the religious life of the Waldensian communities and give them, for the first time, settled Reformed churches worshipping in the reformed manner. Great efforts and disproportionately large numbers of ministers were expended in creating this enclave of rebellious Protestantism in a Savoy dominated by Catholicism (Cameron, *Waldenses*, pp. 232–84; cf. Audisio, *Vaudois du Luberon*, pp. 409–26). The Lollards experienced a long period of gradual integration into the untidy and confused world of the early English Reformation. Early reforming evangelizers behaved rather like Lollard colporteurs, and their objections to the Catholic Church often used similar rhetorical devices. Geographical studies suggest that some areas of previous Lollard strength were particularly welcoming to Protestantism at parish level (Hudson, *Premature Reformation*, pp. 473–507; Davis, *Heresy and Reformation*).

Ultimately, though, medieval popular heretics and reformers were engaged in different enterprises. Heretics largely shared the ethical standards of the Catholic

Church, including its belief that the ideal for a priest was to be chaste and pure, living as a poor, apostolic ascetic. They objected above all to the church's perceived gross failure to live up to those standards. Reformers would argue that the whole system of works righteousness built on those ethical values was radically misconceived. The Reformation presented a new theological message, from which an entire program of reform could be rolled out with relative consistency. Where that program established itself, not only the medieval church, but also the dissenting remnants who opposed it, would be swept away.

BIBLIOGRAPHY

Aston, M., *Lollards and Reformers: Images and Literacy in Late Medieval Religion*. London: Hambledon Press, 1984.

Audisio, G., *Les Vaudois du Luberon: Une minorité en Provence, 1460–1560*. Aix-en-Provence: Association d'études vaudoises et historiques du Luberon, 1984.

Betts, R. R., *Essays in Czech History*. London: Athlone Press, 1969.

Biller, P., "The Preaching of the Waldensian Sisters," in *La Prédication sur un mode dissident: Laïcs, femmes, hérétiques*, in *Heresis*, 30 (1999), pp. 137–68.

Brenon, A., "The Waldensian Books," in P. Biller and A. Hudson eds., *Heresy and Literacy, 1000–1530*. Cambridge: Cambridge University Press, 1994, pp. 137–59.

Brigden, S., *London and the Reformation*. Oxford: Clarendon Press, 1989.

Brock, P., *The Political and Social Doctrines of the Unity of the Czech Brethren in the Fifteenth and Early Sixteenth Centuries*. The Hague: Mouton, 1957.

Cameron, E., *The Reformation of the Heretics: The Waldenses of the Alps 1480–1580*. Oxford: Clarendon Press, 1984.

Cameron, E., *The European Reformation*. Oxford: Clarendon Press, 1991.

Cameron, E., "Medieval Heretics as Protestant Martyrs," in *Martyrs and Martyrologies: Papers Read at the 1992 Summer Meeting and the 1993 Winter Meeting of the Ecclesiastical History Society*, ed. D. Wood, Studies in Church History, vol. 30. Oxford: Blackwell, 1993, pp. 185–207.

Cameron, E., *Waldenses: Rejections of Holy Church in Medieval Europe*. Oxford: Blackwell, 2000.

Cohn, N., *Europe's Inner Demons: An Enquiry Inspired by the Great Witch-Hunt*. London: Chatto, Heinemann, 1975; rev. ed., Chicago: University of Chicago Press, 2000.

Davis, J. F., *Heresy and Reformation in the South-East of England, 1520–1559*, Royal Historical Society Studies in History, vol. 34. London: Royal Historical Society, 1983.

Deanesly, M., *The Lollard Bible and Other Medieval Biblical Versions*. Cambridge: Cambridge University Press, 1920.

Döllinger, J. Ignaz v., ed., *Dokumente vornehmlich zur Geschichte der Valdesier und Katharer (Beiträge zur Sektengeschichte des Mittelalters)*, vol. 2. Munich: C. H. Beck, 1890.

Douie, D. L., *The Nature and the Effect of the Heresy of the Fraticelli*. Manchester: Manchester University Press, 1932.

Foxe, J., *The Acts and Monuments of John Foxe*, ed. Josiah Pratt, 8 vols. London: The Religious Tract Society [1877].

Fudge, T. A., *The Magnificent Ride: The First Reformation in Hussite Bohemia*. Aldershot: Ashgate, 1998.

Heymann, F. G., *John Žižka and the Hussite Revolution*. Princeton, NJ: Princeton University Press, 1955.

Heymann, F. G., *George of Bohemia, King of Heretics*. Princeton, NJ: Princeton University Press, 1965.

Hudson, A., *The Premature Reformation: Wycliffite Texts and Lollard History*. Oxford: Clarendon Press, 1988.

Hudson, A., ed., *Selections from English Wycliffite Writings*. Cambridge: Cambridge University Press, 1978.

Hudson, A. and Gradon, P., eds., *English Wycliffite Sermons*, 5 vols. Oxford: Clarendon Press, 1983–96.

Kaminsky, H., *A History of the Hussite Revolution*. Berkeley: University of California Press, 1967.

Lambert, M., *Medieval Heresy: Popular Movements from the Gregorian Reform to the Reformation*, 2nd ed. Oxford: Blackwell, 1992.

Lambert, M., *The Cathars*. Oxford: Blackwell, 1998.

Limborch, Philippus van, *Historia Inquisitionis. Cui Subjungitur Liber sententiarum inquisitionis Tholosanae ab anno Christi MCCCVII ad annum MCCCXXIII*. Amsterdam, 1692 [the *Liber Sententiarum*, an edition of British Library, Add. MS 4697, is paginated separately after the *Historia Inquisitionis*.]

McSheffrey, S., *Gender and Heresy: Women and Men in Lollard Communities, 1420–1530*. Philadelphia: Pennsylvania University Press, 1995.

Moeller, B., "Religious Life in Germany on the Eve of the Reformation," in G. Strauss, ed., *Pre-Reformation Germany*. London: Macmillan, 1972, pp. 13–42.

Oberman, H. A., *The Harvest of Medieval Theology: Gabriel Biel and Late Medieval Nominalism*. Cambridge, Mass.: Harvard University Press, 1963.

Oberman, H. A., *Forerunners of the Reformation: The Shape of Medieval Thought Illustrated by Key Documents*, 2nd ed. Philadelphia: Fortress Press, 1981.

Oberman, H. A., *Masters of the Reformation: The Emergence of a New Intellectual Climate in Europe*, trans. D. Martin. Cambridge: Cambridge University Press, 1981.

Odlozilik, O., *The Hussite King: Bohemia in European Affairs, 1440–1471*. New Brunswick, NJ: Rutgers University Press, 1965.

Papini, C., *Valdo di Lione e i "poveri nello spirito": Il primo secolo del movimento valdese (1170–1270)*. Turin: Claudiana, 2001.

Patschovsky, A., "The Literacy of Waldensianism from Valdes to c.1400," in P. Biller and A. Hudson, eds., *Heresy and Literacy, 1000–1530*. Cambridge: Cambridge University Press, 1994, pp. 112–36.

Ritter, G., "Romantic and Revolutionary Elements in German Theology on the Eve of the Reformation," in S. E. Ozment, ed., *The Reformation in Medieval Perspective*. Chicago: Quadrangle Books, 1971, pp. 15–49.

Shahar, S., *Women in a Medieval Heretical Sect: Agnes and Huguette the Waldensians*, trans. Y. Lotan. Woodbridge: Boydell, 2001.

Simancas, Jacobus de, *De Catholicis Institutionibus Liber, ad praecavendas & extirpandas haereses admodum necessarius*. Rome: In aedibus Populi Romani, 1575.

Tanner, N. P., ed., *Heresy Trials in the Diocese of Norwich, 1428–31*, Camden 4th series, vol. 20. London: Offices of the Royal Historical Society, 1977.

Thomson, J. A. F., *The Later Lollards 1414–1520*. Oxford: Clarendon Press, 1965.

Vinay, V., *Le Confessioni di fede dei Valdesi riformati*. Turin: Claudiana, 1975.

Williams, G. H., *The Radical Reformation*, 3rd ed. Kirksville, Mo.: Sixteenth Century Essays and Studies, 15, 1992.

FURTHER READING

General histories of heresy are rare. Fortunately, the second edition of M. Lambert, *Medieval Heresy*, offers an exceptionally thorough and careful introduction. Gordon Leff, *Heresy in the*

Later Middle Ages: The Relation of Heterodoxy to Dissent, c.1250–c.1450 (Manchester: Manchester University Press, 1999; originally published as 2 vols., Manchester: Manchester University Press, 1967) is centered on theology rather than society. There are many important essays in P. Biller and A. Hudson, eds., *Heresy and Literacy, 1000–1530* (Cambridge: Cambridge University Press, 1994).

Introductions to Waldensianism include Gabriel Audisio, *The Waldensian Dissent: Persecution and Survival, c.1170–c.1570*, translated by Claire Davison (Cambridge: Cambridge University Press, 1999), and E. Cameron, *Waldenses*. P. Biller, *The Waldenses, 1170–1530: Between a Religious Order and a Church* (Aldershot: Ashgate, 2001) offers a collection of often controversial essays. Of the work published in other languages, C. Papini, *Valdo di Lione e i "poveri nello spirito"* and the older J. Gonnet and A. Molnar, *Les Vaudois au moyen âge* (Turin: Claudiana, 1974) both concentrate on the early period. Martin Schneider, *Europäisches Waldensertum im 13. und 14. Jahrhundert*, Arbeiten zur Kirchengeschichte, 51 (Berlin: De Gruyter, 1981) is particularly well grounded in the primary sources.

On Lollardy, the corpus of Anne Hudson, especially her *Premature Reformation*, is fundamental, though she always attributes the maximum degree of intellectual sophistication and historical impact possible to her subjects. Her essays are collected in A. Hudson, *Lollards and their Books* (London: Hambledon, 1985). A. Hudson and P. Gradon, eds., *English Wycliffite Sermons*, 5 vols., is an exemplary edition of one of the largest bodies of surviving heretical texts. J. A. F. Thomson, *The Later Lollards 1414–1520*, explores the inquisitorial records of the period, while M. Aston, *Lollards and Reformers*, gathers together some important essays.

The largest English-language discussion of Hussitism, Howard Kaminsky's *A History of the Hussite Revolution*, does not take the story beyond 1424. It is continued in F. M. Bartos, *The Hussite Revolution, 1424–1437* (Boulder, Colo.: East European Monographs and Columbia University Press, 1986). František Šmahel, *La Révolution hussite: Une anomalie historique* (Paris: Presses Universitaires de France, 1985) offers a short introduction in French. T. A. Fudge's *The Magnificent Ride* is particularly valuable on the cultural and visual aspects of Hussite literature. The best discussion in English of the theological underpinning of Hussite thought remains that in older works, especially the papers in R. R. Betts, *Essays in Czech History*. P. Brock, *The Political and Social Doctrines of the Czech Brethren*, is one of very few books in English to explore the later history of the Hussite movement, alongside Rudolf Řican, *The History of the Unity of Brethren: A Protestant Hussite Church in Bohemia and Moravia*, translated by C. Daniel Crews (Bethlehem, Pa.: Moravian Church in America, 1992).

Two

Society and Piety

LARISSA TAYLOR

The ruling Taleban expelled the BBC from Afghanistan . . . for transmitting criticism of the group's destruction of ancient statues, including two of the Buddhas in Bamian. . . . "The destruction of the two statues has been completed," [information minister Qudratullah Jamal] told the Afghan Islamic Press . . . "The work was completed last evening, and now there is no trace of the two statues there." . . . The Taleban, which has vowed to eliminate all Afghanistan's historic statues on the grounds they are heathen idols, were angered by a broadcast on Tuesday. (Reuters News Agency, March 15, 2001)

[O]n July 28, 1936, at Cerro de los Ángeles near Madrid, a monumental outdoor stone statue representing the Sacred Heart of Christ was sentenced to death by Spanish Republicans and "executed" by firing squad. This, of course, proved rather ineffective, so the monument was dynamited on July 31. It still stood, so dynamite experts were called in on August 1, but to no avail. On August 6, the Republicans tried to pull the statue down with a cable attached to a tractor, but the cable broke. Finally, on the next day, symbolically a Friday, the monument was leveled and broken into fragments with sledge-hammers. The bullet-pocked heart and the mutilated head are preserved as relics. (Nolan and Nolan, *Christian Pilgrimage*, p. 211)

On November 9, 1793, at the beginning of the Terror, St. Geneviève's reliquary was carried to the Hôtel des Monnaies and dismantled. . . . These bones were put on trial, were found guilty of collaboration with royal authorities, and were condemned to be publicly burned at the Place de Grève. . . . The *auto-da-fé* took place on December 3, and the saint's ashes were thrown into the Seine. . . . Revolutionary Paris purified itself of its patron saint. (Sluhovsky, *Patroness*, pp. 208–9)

Perhaps it is strange to begin a chapter on late medieval society and piety in a book on the Reformation with examples from the eighteenth to twenty-first centuries. Yet such examples from modern times could be multiplied endlessly, demonstrating what I believe are three timeless themes in the study of popular religiosity: (1) the fear of the sacred, however it is defined, by both secular and some religious authorities; (2) the continuing need for material aspects of holiness; and (3) the differences and continuities in practice over time. As Ruth Harris points out in her study of Lourdes, "[r]elegating the study of such religious phenomena to the Middle Ages and early-modern period is one of the ways historians have maintained a division between our 'modern,' 'rational' age and the 'irrational,' ecstatic world that preceded it" (Harris, *Lourdes*, p. 12). R. Swanson puts it succinctly: "[a]s for arguments based on 'rationality,' they presuppose that twentieth-century rationality is necessarily better than the pre-Reformation variety. Yet, from that pre-Reformation perspective, could there be anything less rational than the denial of God . . . ?" (Swanson, *Catholic England*, pp. 6–7). Edward Muir shows that however much we dismiss or even demolish, there is always a need to replace what has been lost: "[t]he rituals of modern mass culture have created a shifting and transient sense of the sacred, now invested in the political ideology of the moment, romantic love of nature, charismatic leaders, jingoistic nationalism, idealized domesticity, or endless cults, fads, ephemera. If societies demand rituals, then changing societies will produce changing rituals" (Muir, *Ritual*, p. 274). As historians have come to terms with their own biases, they have recognized the need to try to understand the medieval past on its own terms (Gregory, *Salvation*, pp. 11, 13, 15). The quotations that began this chapter demonstrate that we need only scratch the surface of modern life to see both likeness and difference. The images, statues, and rituals so dear to medieval people and beyond cannot be reduced to "art" (Wandel, *Voracious Idols*, pp. 26–7) – their meanings had little to do with art as we know it. As James Tracy has argued, "I agree with De Rosa and Van Kley (and I believe also Mack Holt) in the 'premise' that a historian who takes the moral personality of past actors seriously must presume an understanding of human consciousness in which any one recognizably distinct dimension of conscious experience – such as religious experience – is not necessarily reducible to others: '[t]he men and women of the past were people like ourselves, and we owe them the same consideration that we would like to receive from contemporaries and from future historians . . . they were complex creatures whose motives, like ours, were not one-dimensional'" (Tracy, "Believers," p. 412). The need for ritual expression and objects, acts of iconoclasm, and responses to such actions are deeply interconnected, and not simply part of a past to be studied. *Plus ça change, plus ça reste la même chose.*

A curious thing happens when scholars begin to look at non-traditional sources as they have done in recent decades – they begin to ask new and different questions. The not-so-surprising result is new answers and further questions. Fundamentally flawed questions produce expectable results. As most scholars have finally stopped speaking of "decay" as the characteristic feature of the late Middle Ages, a new picture has emerged. As Euan Cameron has pointed out, the question about "what caused" the Reformation exemplifies the old approach. It assumes that "people wanted the Reformation . . . [and] that the state of late medieval religion ought to make understanding the causes of the Reformation easier." He suggests that "in fact it makes it much harder. The Christianity of the later Middle Ages was a supple, flexible, varied entity, adapted to the needs, concerns and tastes . . . of the people who created it. . . . It threatened, but it also comforted; it disciplined, but it also entertained" (Cameron, *European Reformation*, p. 19).

The richness and complexity of late medieval society and culture is so great that this chapter cannot possibly explore it in depth: the religious cosmos; the cult of the saints; ritual and liturgy; Eucharistic devotion; pilgrimage; prayer; processions; life, death, and beyond; magic; the differences (or not) between popular and elite culture; religion and gender; the interactions of people and clergy; and attitudes to the "Other." The chapter will instead discuss the historiography that has begun to reshape our knowledge and understanding of the medieval past.

Generalizations about what constituted Christianity in a given time and place have done more to obscure our study of belief and practice than to advance it. Jean Delumeau has spoken of the "Christianization" of European society, contrasting it with a "folklorization" that preceded it. He cites the 1697 life of Fr. Maunoir: "One must not be surprised to see in the missions something akin to what the pagans experienced when the first Apostles preached to them, because in many places of lower Brittany the mysteries of Religion were so little known it was a question of establishing the faith (kerygma) rather than of teaching Christian doctrine (parenesis)" (Delumeau, *Catholicism*, p. 175). Swanson admits that "folklorization" may be an accurate characterization, but it "can only be identified with hindsight, and perhaps with a deliberate rejection of the rationale for the actions. Contemporaries simply lived their lives. . . . Yet to call this a relapse into paganism is to distort: it imposes the historian's definition of Christianity onto what Christianity actually was" (Swanson, *Religion and Devotion*, p. 187). Medieval people did understand and practice much of what the Catholic Church taught as orthodoxy. If the church had been successful in its efforts to triumph over "paganism" in the early centuries of Christianity by converting ancient shrines and feasts into churches and holy days, how can the people of late medieval Christian Europe be faulted for having learned their lessons too well? Can we even ask this question without implying a supposed cultural superiority? As William Christian says, "[n]o longer is nature invested with the kind of sensitivity to the sacred that made the dove come and land in the transept during the petitionary mass to Saint Sebastian . . . that led the dog in Albalate de Zorita to discover the buried cross, or the horse of the Knights of Saint John to shy before the image of Our Lady of Salceda. . . . Or is it that these things still happen, and nobody, no devout and curious monarch, wants to know?" (Christian, *Local Religion*, p. 208). This powerful insight should alert us to the danger of labels, a subject to which we shall return.

In an astute analysis of late medieval culture, Jean-Claude Schmitt emphasizes the complexity of late medieval religious culture and society. Insisting that the "accent should also be placed on internal variations instead of being satisfied with a reconciliatory, customary, and mellifluous image that poorly masks the ideological preconceptions of certain authors" (Schmitt, "Religion," p. 380), he highlights the problem of discussing the religion of the Middle Ages. It was "above all participation in rituals and even more generally participation in an entire social organization and in the sum of symbolic practices and relationships of meaning among men, between men and nature, and between men and the divine. All of this transcends to a large extent what we generally call 'religion,' and thus it would be necessary at least to speak about 'the religious'" (ibid., p. 384). Conceived in these terms, it is easier to comprehend the deeply religious culture of late medieval Europe while accepting its infinite variations. Schmitt's study of the "dog saint" Guinefort is particularly instructive. Depending on the reader, his book *The Holy Greyhound* tells a story related by the Dominican Étienne de Bourbon (d. 1261) that could be considered sad, silly, or unusually helpful in our understanding of late medieval religious culture.

After the husband, wife, and nurse had left the manor, a snake (*serpens maximus*) insinuated itself through a hole in the wall:

> the greyhound, which had remained behind, chased the serpent and, attacking it beneath the cradle, upset the cradle and bit the serpent all over, which defended itself, biting the dog equally severely. Finally, the dog killed it and threw it well away from the cradle. The cradle, the floor, the dog's mouth and head were all drenched in the serpent's blood. Although badly hurt by the serpent, the dog remained on guard beside the cradle. . . . [T]he knight, when he arrived, thought [the dog had devoured the child] and drew his sword and killed the dog. Then, when they went closer to the baby they found it safe and sound, sleeping peacefully. . . . Realising the true facts of the matter, and deeply regretting having unjustly killed so useful a dog they threw it into a well in front of the manor door, threw a great pile of stones on top of it, and planted trees beside it, in memory of the event. . . . But the peasants, hearing of the dog's conduct and of how it had been killed, although innocent, and for a deed for which it might have expected praise, visited the place, honoured the dog as a martyr, prayed to it when they were sick or in need of something. . . . Above all, though, it was women with sick or weak children who took them to this place. (Schmitt, *Holy Greyhound*, pp. 4–5)

While Schmitt examines comparative legends, and also traces the existence of human St. Guineforts, his conclusion tells us the most about medieval religiosity: "for the peasants, there was no contradiction between the notion of sanctity and the memory of a dog" (ibid., p. 177). The reasons for that will become apparent. Indeed, although Étienne de Bourbon thought he had eradicated the pilgrimage site, its draw continued into the nineteenth century.

Although attempts to make sainthood the sole province of the papacy were formalized in 1234, this never inhibited the veneration of "local" and even living saints. Saints succeeded or failed based on whether or not their cult "took" – whether the saint performed miracles and pilgrims continued to resort to the saint for help. "An incompetent saint was an embarrassment. . . . In most cases neither success nor failure were empirically unequivocal. What mattered was the willingness of those not present at the scene of the action to believe the reports of others" (Kleinberg, *Prophets*, pp. 159, 162). With the veneration of St. Guinefort, we glimpse the degree to which medieval people did understand the tenets of their faith, even if their reasoning in this case contained two incongruous elements. Guinefort exhibited all the traits of a martyred saint except that he was not human and presumably was not cognizant of Christian religious belief. A saint typically had to have two characteristics, although these were not essential in the case of martyrs: holiness of life and heroic virtue. We could presume a certain holiness of life in Guinefort from the manner in which the story began – the husband, wife, and nurse left the baby unattended; Guinefort alone stayed. Guinefort was a greyhound, not the most fearsome of dogs. In waging a battle that resulted in the death of *serpens maximus*, he exhibited a heroic level of virtue uncommon to his breed. Killed by his again negligent master who acted on impulse, Guinefort suffered for his heroism. Some time after his unceremonious disposal, the local people came to believe Guinefort performed miracles associated with the healing of children. The peasants understood most of what constituted sanctity. As Kleinberg points out, "[t]he medieval perception of sainthood was fluid; it was personal, concrete, and of an ad hoc nature" (ibid., p. 5). Even Étienne de Bourbon, the famed

Dominican author of the tale, while condemning the veneration as superstition, implies a judgment of his own when he offhandedly remarks: "by divine will, the manor was destroyed, and the estate, reduced to a desert, was abandoned by its inhabitants" (Schmitt, *Holy Greyhound*, p. 5).

Using anthropological methods, Christian has studied saints and apparitions in Spain from the Renaissance to the present. One of many cases he has found in the records is typical:

> The reason why this feast of Saint Ambrose was vowed was because of the worm that was eating the villas [towns? vines?]. And when the town vowed it – so they have heard from their ancestors – the worm stopped immediately. But one person from this town did not want to keep the day, and the worms got into his house, so that he vowed once again the day and observed it, and there was no more worm. (Christian, *Local Religion*, p. 42)

A contractual type of relationship, trial and error, observation, and performance record all figured into the cult of a given saint and his or her relationship with the community. Local, popular veneration has not only continued to our day; it was also not limited to the forms of Christianity that accept a theological role for the saints. In his study of late sixteenth-century southwestern France, Raymond Mentzer argues that

> [e]radicating the old ways, many of which the Reformers considered pagan or idolatrous, and instilling new forms of piety and belief was an arduous task. The mandatory cultural shifts proved impossible for some members of the community to accept.... [P]opular religion proved a paradox of human tenacity and vulnerability. Its broad appeal spoke to a richness of imagery and a traditional belief system based on memory and sociability. The Reformed church, despite its many adherents, distinctive attraction, and unique meaning, represented authority and change. The requisite transformations were not always welcome, even when they were deemed theologically correct. (Mentzer, "Persistence," pp. 232, 233)

On a journey in 1597, eerily reminiscent of the Guinefort story, three mountain women took an infant to be healed in the cemetery behind St. Peter's church in the Calvinist town of Ganges. As a result, two townswomen were summoned by the Consistory for having aided and abetted the "superstitions and idolatries" of the mountain women (ibid., p. 225). Mentzer cites numerous instances in which even self-professed Calvinists clung tenaciously to Catholic practices and rituals (ibid., pp. 223, 228, 229). Not surprisingly, he discovered that in the 1940s, a Protestant pastor in the region was still condemning the "credulity of simple folk" (ibid., p. 220). Even in Protestant lands, the practices and beliefs of the people of late medieval Europe have persisted well into modern times.

Peter Burke, speaking of Renaissance Italy, argues that "[t]he distinction between the sacred and profane was not drawn in quite the same place and it was not drawn as sharply as it would be in the later sixteenth century" (Burke, *Italian Renaissance*, p. 210). But was it drawn even then? Mentzer argues that "[p]eople understood the religion of their ancestors – those reassuring daily habits that they had learned from parents and grandparents. For ordinary believers, their faith described and shaped a familiar world, providing a sense of continuity and community, and helping to define the character of social relationships" (Mentzer, "Persistence," p. 233). Liturgical and extra-sacramental practices celebrated important stages of life, turning points such as marriage, birth, and death in the community, as well as the cycles of the seasons and harvests. Local traditions, sometimes frowned upon by the church, supplemented but did not replace prescribed worship. The timelessness of these activities attests to the vitality of local religious culture in the late Middle Ages. Many studies emphasize the corporate aspects of late medieval religious practice that promoted a sharing in which the pious and the communal were closely entwined. As Cameron points out, whether it was a procession, pilgrimage, the Stations of the Cross, Rogations, guild festivities, or plays, "all the most popular activities of late medieval religion were based on doing something, on participation, activity, movement, essentially on experiencing an event more than on learning or understanding a message" (Cameron, *European Reformation*, p. 16). The statement is true on some levels and not on others. If the doing appears primary, that hardly proves that understanding was lacking, even if it is not the same kind of understanding we might expect. For example, the "reading" of religious imagery was far better developed then than now, and served as a form of education that went hand in hand with sermons and worship (see e.g. Camille, *Gothic Art*, pp. 12–25). But the sacraments of the church "demonstrated and confirmed membership of the Christian body and adherence to Christian life; they also marked stages in spiritual development, and human relationships" (Swanson, *Religion and Devotion*, p. 31). Whether rural or urban, rituals were powerful bonds in medieval society. "Rituals . . . give both form and content to abstract attachments, fix them in time and space, and mobilize powerful emotions and feelings among the people who hold the rituals to be of special significance. . . . [T]hese rituals turned Paris into a sacred space and its people into a sanctified community" (Sluhovsky, *Patroness*, p. 4). Muir has posited this as one explanation for the persistence of ritual practice that we saw among some of Mentzer's French Calvinists: "Precisely because Catholic reformers still retained a vital role for ritual in religious life, they may have been more successful in sustaining lay piety than the Protestant churches which in some ways attempted the impossible – the broad propagation of an intellectualized religion in a society where only a small minority could read at all, let alone read something as difficult as scripture" (Muir, *Ritual*, p. 152). Robert Scribner has emphasized the shock value that must have accompanied "[t]he process of desacralising, deritualising and demystifying" daily life (Scribner, "Comparative Overview," p. 221).

What of the years immediately around 1500? It was an era whose piety Bernd Moeller characterized as one of "consistent churchliness" (Moeller, "Piety," p. 52). Despite the elements that collapse both time and space, geographical differences in the late medieval period cannot be minimized even if the basic beliefs that animated religious practice were much the same. The strongly "national" characters of the Reformations in different parts of Europe did not arise in a vacuum, but were part of preexisting patterns that structured pious behavior. Lionel Rothkrug points to the "profoundly regional character of different types of religious expression" (Rothkrug, "Popular Religion," p. 20), suggesting plausibly that the much later missionary efforts and spread of Christianity in Germany than in France resulted in fundamentally different choices in the focus of religious culture. He finds interest in relics stronger in places other than Germany, with shrines prominent in the latter

(Rothkrug, "Religious Practices," p. xii). Similarly, often going back to very early origins, desired qualities of saints differed according to place. The "delightful Englishness" of the South English Legendary used "national characteristics" to relate sainthood more convincingly to contemporary experience (Jankofsky, "National Characteristics," pp. 85, 87, 90). In France and elsewhere, having the physical remains of a saint (such as relics of Mary Magdalene at Vézelay and later La Sainte-Baume) strongly influenced attitudes and even building programs. Different traditions, customs, and cultures, incipient nationalist feelings especially in areas not under strong monarchical control, proximity to or distance from the papacy, and other conditions inevitably affected practices and beliefs. If Jacques Toussaert describes what could only be considered apathy in religious practice in Flanders (Toussaert, *Senti-ment*, pp. 494–502), both older and recent studies paint a different picture. Moeller shows that for most of western and central Europe "the intensity of piety actually increased greatly in these decades" with the growth of cults, new endowments for masses, processions, pilgrimages, and the rebuilding of the fabric of churches (Moeller, "Piety," pp. 52–3). Likewise, in his *Religions of the People in Sixteenth-Century Champagne*, A. N. Galpern describes an "Indian summer" of late medieval piety. In England, Eamon Duffy has argued that while there was some "privatizing" of devotion in the later Middle Ages,

> the overwhelming impression left by the sources for late medieval religion in England is that of a Christianity resolutely and enthusiastically oriented towards the public and the corporate, and of a continuing sense of the value of cooperation and mutuality in seeking salvation. At its most obvious this continuing and indeed growing commitment to corporate Christianity is witnessed by the extraordinary and lavish spate of investment by lay men and women in the fabric and furnishings of their parish churches. (Duffy, *Stripping of the Altars*, pp. 131–2)

His monumental study develops the full "character and range of late medieval English Catholicism, indicating something of the richness and complexity of the religious system by which men and women structured their experience of their world, and their hopes and aspirations within and beyond it" (ibid., p. 1).

While Italian religious culture was in many ways shaped by its nearness to the papal states and a much more highly developed and wealthy urban culture than elsewhere in Europe, recent studies demonstrate "not only the importance of religion in Renaissance culture: they have shown that it was far from being simply 'late medieval,' 'inertial,' or merely 'persistent'" (Peterson, "Out of the Margins," p. 856). This is evident even though, as David Peterson argues, Italians had probably suffered more from papal abuses than other Europeans in the fifteenth century (ibid., p. 855).

Another element in the varieties of religious behavior may lie in both the availability and type of preaching, as has been shown by Anne Thayer, who has traced the use of "rigorist," "moderate," and "absolutionist" model sermons in several regions of Europe (Thayer, "Penitence and Preaching," chap. 1). Her study suggests that the Protestant message was far less likely to be accepted in areas in which the models advocated an absolutionist or moderate approach to preaching and penance. Moreover, urban areas, which were both more likely to have access to regular preaching and were more commercially advanced, could in turn fund devotional art, pious

endowments, and preacherships, and thus would have differed in several respects in
their religious practices from those of their rural counterparts.

But if differences existed in the choices of saints, whether shrines or relics were
preferred objects of cults or pilgrimage, and specific local practices, there is a relative
consensus that has evolved over recent decades that popular and elite beliefs overlapped far more than was previously thought. Lee Palmer Wandel offers the best bibliographic study for the Reformation period (Wandel, *Voracious Idols*, pp. 1–6; see
also Rubin, *Corpus Christi*, p. 7; Cameron, *European Reformation*, pp. 9–14). For
the medieval period, Swanson has questioned whether we can even distinguish
between lay and clerical culture (Swanson, *Religion and Devotion*, p. 187). While differences existed, two examples will suffice to indicate the degree of overlap. "The
pattern of designating special days occurred at all levels of authority from the pope
in Rome to the most humble parish church" (Muir, *Ritual*, p. 76). A more telling
example is found in a 1497 letter written by Europe's leading humanist, Erasmus:
" 'Lately I fell into a quartan fever, but have recovered health and strength, not by
a physician's help (though I had recourse to one) but by the aid of Sainte Geneviève
alone, the famous virgin, whose bones, preserved by the canons regular, daily radiate
miracles and are revered; nothing is more worthy of her, or has done me more
good' " (quoted in Sluhovsky, *Patroness*, p. 26).

Local studies have substantially reshaped the contours of how we view late
medieval piety, helping to minimize the use of convenient labels such as decadence
and apathy that have been accepted since the sixteenth century. Piety to some became
more internalized at the end of the Middle Ages, but for most people this was
an addition to, rather than a replacement of, their external sacramental and extra-
liturgical behaviors and practices. Religious individualism, ranging from mysticism to
healing magic combined with prayers, coexisted with collective expressions of piety.
André Vauchez has demonstrated "the existence of major differences between the
actual religious practices of the laity and what was prescribed for them. . . . [O]ne of
the novel characteristics of the period . . . was the ability of laypeople to create
autonomous forms of piety which, while generally avoiding clashes with orthodoxy,
succeeded in reshaping the religious message disseminated by the clergy to meet their
feelings and specific needs. This is particularly obvious in the case of devotion to the
saints" (Vauchez, *Laity*, p. 265). Echoing Galpern, Vauchez speaks of an "Indian
summer" of female religiosity at the end of the Middle Ages (ibid., p. xx), a finding
that accords with many other studies that describe a feminization of sainthood in the
later Middle Ages (Herlihy, *Medieval Households*, p. 113). While offering important
insights, both Galpern and Vauchez have in their choice of terms unfortunately added
to the notion of "waning" or "autumn" popularized by Johan Huizinga at the beginning of the twentieth century. Such conceptualizations, in addition to (often inadvertently) reviving notions of decay, also imply a waiting for something to happen
(i.e., the Reformations).

As long as the late Middle Ages were depicted as a waning, ending, or period of
decadence, and as long as we framed questions in the form of "what caused the Reformation?" or "what were the problems in the late medieval church?" the answers were
predictable. If one changes the question, and asks why significant numbers of church
men and women refused to leave monasteries, why the laity of cities and villages
sometimes attacked and even killed those who either smashed images or attempted

to close monasteries, the answer is no longer obvious. Why, if people were apathetic, were preachers frequently banished, assaulted, or otherwise threatened for their words? Why, when they were exiled, did weeping throngs accompany them to the city gates (Taylor, "Dangerous Vocations")?

Framing new questions, using non-traditional sources, and studying material on a local level has shown us that while problems did exist in both clergy and people, the mere fact that those within the church had been calling for change and reform for well over a century before the Reformation should give us pause. As Cameron states accurately, "[t]he late medieval church was its own sternest critic" (Cameron, *European Reformation*, p. 49). At criticism, the church was probably too successful for its own good. My studies of preaching in late medieval France exemplify how often preachers lamented the evils of their day, saying that times had never been worse. Michel Menot (d. 1518) reiterated what was a commonplace then as now when he complained, "I have preached and I have labored, but I do not know how much I have accomplished: I ask God to bring forth the fruit. Either all scripture is wrong, or the city of Tours will not long endure in this state." Olivier Maillard (d. 1503) said virtually the same of Paris (Taylor, *Soldiers of Christ*, pp. 15–16). It is easy to accept such words at face value. But if one ponders these comments more closely, two interesting facts emerge. First are the obvious Scriptural topoi – for example, Tours and Paris are simply modern-day Ninevehs, Chorazins, and Bethsaidas. Secondly, there was an obvious willingness among popular preachers, whose influence was arguably far stronger than any work of literature in a time in which oral culture predominated, to criticize not only the people who attended their sermons but their fellow clerics, and to call for correction of abuses. The latter points to a church that could be called waxing rather than waning. Was the glass half-full or half-empty? Hervé Martin has spoken of a rising crescendo of preaching in the period from the Black Death to the Reformation, "with the rhythm accelerating after 1450. This period of strength in Christian pastoral work coincided with the renewal of society as a whole, with the growth of confraternities, as well as the construction of magnificent buildings (churches, chapels, oratories), the construction of which was financed by the parish and by generous donors" (Martin, *Métier*, p. 74). My research has shown that popular preaching in the decades before 1520 was for the most part (despite regional differences) not the stuff of eschatological nightmares described by Denis Crouzet in *Les Guerriers de Dieu*. Although by its nature the goal of popular preaching was to chastise rather than to flatter, the Savonarolas of the preaching world were not the norm. The aim, using the language of the people and a mnemonic structure, was teaching and moral regeneration. In France as elsewhere, "the preachers described a religion based on sin and atonement that offered the possibility of salvation to everyone willing to do what was in him [*facere quod in se est*]." Thus "[a] pessimistic anthropology was . . . balanced by an optimistic soteriology in which, thanks to God, everything was possible for the repentant sinner" (Taylor, *Soldiers of Christ*, pp. 84–6). The possibilities for salvation, which Thayer found most commonly advised as a teaching tool to preachers in Italy and Spain, may not have been the norm in the cities of the Holy Roman Empire and Switzerland, where Ozment describes a "psychologically burdensome" religion filled with demands for penitential action almost impossible for a human being to fulfill (Ozment, *Reformation in the Cities*, p. 50). There may be some merit in Ozment's view, but as Lawrence

Duggan has noted, "if severity had been the aim of the late medieval penitential system, it did not work that way" (Duggan, "Fear and Confession," p. 165). Not everyone was as consumed by angst as Martin Luther. My own findings corroborate this view, with preachers suggesting that people (then as now) took away from sermons as little or as much as they chose (Taylor, "God of Judgment, God of Love," pp. 264–6). For whatever reason, however, people came to sermons in huge numbers, often from great distances, to hear a famed preacher (Martin, *Les Ordres mendiants*, p. 319). In England, the passionate if quite extraordinary Margery Kempe noted in her *Booke* the great excitement people in King's Lynn felt at the anticipated preaching of a noted Franciscan. Responses to preaching are hard to gauge, often reliant on internal evidence, although occasionally the mass conversion of prostitutes, sacred bonfires, or violent action taken against the preacher suggest significant involvement by those in attendance (Taylor, *Soldiers of Christ*, chap. 2; "Dangerous Vocations").

It is impossible to discuss society and piety without a basic understanding of the relationship between people and clergy if we are to gauge religiosity. Bad news makes good headlines. Good news is seldom reported. If that is true in our own day, how much more so in times past? Even with the best and most nuanced teaching available, it is from the satires of Boccaccio or Erasmus that students form and retain their views of medieval religious culture. Efforts to balance the scales too often fail. That priests, monks, and nuns were sometimes apathetic, and that some engaged in criminal misconduct or sexual impropriety, cannot be denied. But until recently, this was the standard portrayal of the clergy in the late Middle Ages. Studies showing villagers quite content with their priest or the often substantial benefits accruing from the presence of a local monastery have begun to challenge the stereotypes propagated since the sixteenth century that all medieval clergymen and women were felons, sexual perverts, or greedy landlords. As long as Boccaccean stories or humanist critiques framed the portrayal, it was no surprise that a Protestant Reformation was needed! But as Swanson has shown, most complaints tended to be ad hominem attacks (Swanson, *Religion and Devotion*, p. 256). Indeed, parishioners studied in England for the most part "made few complaints about the learning, morals, or commitments of their clergy. . . . There were few neglectful parish priests, few grasping monastic appropriators, few greedy non-resident rectors, but added together these were more than a few occasions for dissatisfaction" (Haigh, *English Reformations*, pp. 48–9). Christopher Haigh's investigation suggests that for England in the late Middle Ages, "what parishioners expected of their clergy was, above all, the proper fulfilment of liturgical and pastoral responsibilities, and it was negligence in this respect that was most likely to be reported. . . . Though reformers might criticize, parishioners seemed satisfied. It is, perhaps, surprising just how well the parish clergy fulfilled their pastoral tasks" (ibid., p. 42).

In most non-urban environments, the priest was drawn from and was part of the village, which created natural social bonds. Haigh reiterates some of the findings of Moeller and Galpern, but interprets them in a new light:

> The recruitment of clergy had slumped in the late fourteenth century, but by the mid-fifteenth century it was booming, probably because of energetic lay endowment of masses, and the improved reputation of priests. . . . When there was denunciation of the worldliness of priests, it usually came from the clergy themselves. . . . There is very little

evidence that the conduct of the clergy was worse than it had been in earlier centuries, and a good deal to suggest that it was much better. [John] Colet's cry for reform was not provoked by a decline in the morals or commitment of priests; rather it stood in a long tradition of Christian protests against the contamination of God's priests by man's ambition. (Ibid., pp. 8–9)

Haigh reminds us (and we need reminding) that "the future had not yet happened" (ibid., p. 14). The cause-and-effect or Whiggish version of history "is seductively easy: it defines significant change, helps us to organize an explanation, and gives principles for selection of relevant evidence. . . . Since historians seek explanations for a Reformation cataclysm, they look for pre-Reformation troubles, and they pile up the troubles into evidence of mounting crisis. Calm, co-operation, and contentment are ignored, for they do not offer forces for the future" (ibid., p. 15). In like fashion, Jean-Claude Schmitt cautions us, asking, "Has there not been a great continuity from the ancient church to the modern university? And how can one not see that history, for those who today write it and make a profession of it, is like a mirror in which they hope to see a flattering reflection of what they think they are, but in which they discover instead a cruel image of what they really are?" (Schmitt, "Religion," p. 378). Haigh states simply that "one person's superstition may be another's spirituality" (Haigh, *English Reformations*, p. 15).

So why do stereotypes of both ordinary people and clergy in the Middle Ages continue to haunt the halls of academe and the popular imagination? Besides the obvious propaganda value after the Reformations, aided by a burgeoning spread of information through printed broadsheets and pamphlets, "historians have too often selected dramatic anecdotes from the court records, without placing them in their context" (ibid., p. 45). It is also easy to simply repeat what past texts have stated as truth.

It is not possible to cover the range of popular religious behaviors that have recently been studied by scholars. A prolific outpouring of work has been done on the piety of late medieval women, whose practices showed both similarities with and differences from those of men. Nor have I been able to look at specifics such as prayer, pilgrimage, attitudes to non-Christians, drama, etc., all of which have been the subject of numerous books. In a historiographic essay, I believe it is most important to challenge, despite the excellent result studies, that old but persistent view of the "decadent" Middle Ages, especially in a volume dedicated to the Reformation. Too many scholars and teachers still tread in the footsteps of Huizinga. In almost every sentence, his words indict the belief structures and religious culture of medieval men and women: "all that is meant to stimulate spiritual consciousness is reduced to appalling commonplace profanity"; "[p]iety had depleted itself in the image, the legend, the office. All its contents had been so completely expressed that mystic awe had evaporated"; "[e]ven the profound faith in the eucharist expands into childish beliefs"; "the naïve religious conscience of the multitude had no need of intellectual proofs in matters of faith. The mere presence of a visible image of things holy sufficed to establish their truth" (Huizinga, *Waning*, pp. 151, 176, 155, 165). Throughout most of history, it has been the great or the unusual who have attracted the attention of scholars, and of course it is important to study their thought. But we must not assume that every man was a Luther or Erasmus, or that every woman was a Catherine of Siena. It is not to denigrate the thought of great intellectuals or passionate religious leaders of the past that scholars of religious culture have studied belief and behavior in a more anthropological framework, but as part of an attempt to understand the ordinary person insofar as the sources allow.

In our modern wisdom, we reject positivism and yet employ it daily. Huizinga describes "the naïveté and childishness" in the religion of medieval people. Giving the benefit of the doubt to those statements, is there not something we are in danger of losing, something that they had, which the Gospels celebrate? Is the awe and innocence of a child not said by Jesus to be the fount of true wisdom? The persistence of belief over the centuries, even that which has been met with ridicule or dismissal, is witness to something we ought not to try to explain away but rather understand. One person's sacrality is another's foolishness. As Alphonse Dupront has asserted, "[b]ecause we are plunged by them into silence, plastic images of sacrality are inexhaustible. They allow a privileged access to inner voices. . . . Nowadays the mystery is primarily an intellectual or theological one. . . . Only through a proper sequence of historically rooted materials can we shed any light on what would either appear to be less and less experienced as a need, or represents a fear of treating objects as the repositories of the unfamiliar, or is an actual refusal to do so" (Dupront, "Religion and Religious Anthropology," p. 144). Instead of belittling the medieval man or woman for their connections to the sacred through pilgrimage, sainthood, or acts of ritual and devotion, perhaps we should look at our own fears of an understanding they possessed and we can only begin to imagine. Or maybe, as Christian suggests, we should simply look and ask.

While there were some dramatic examples of change in areas most affected by the Lutheran and Swiss Reformations, even those areas experienced significant difficulties in "reeducating" the populace (see e.g. Strauss, *Luther's House of Learning*). All evidence suggests that throughout Europe many of the same religious behaviors and beliefs of the Middle Ages – in the powers of saints and the Virgin Mary, in miracles, and in the religious meanings of pilgrimage – continued for centuries. They persist in our own day, and statistics support a dramatic revival in pilgrimage in the late twentieth century (Nolan and Nolan, *Christian Pilgrimage*, pp. 1–2). It is telling that a study for the year 2000 showed that for Europe as a whole, Roman Catholics constituted 39.2 percent of all who considered themselves Christian; Orthodox Christians, 21.7 percent; and all Protestants, Anglicans, and Independents combined, fewer than 20 percent (Barrett, Kurian, and Johnson, *World Christian Encyclopedia*, vol. 1, p. 14).

As Wandel says, "[i]n destroying, the acts of the [Reformation-era] iconoclasts have told us something about late medieval Christian culture that we might otherwise not know" (Wandel, *Voracious Idols*, p. 197). The Madrid statue in the opening epigraph should perhaps serve as a metaphor for the endurance of the sacral in the face of a rationalist society. This brings us back to the fundamental problem of how we ask questions. If both "medieval religious practices" and Roman Catholicism have persisted and in many cases spread since the Reformations, how can we possibly suggest that the Reformations of the sixteenth century were caused by abuses in the Catholic Church? To suggest this does a disservice not only to the beliefs and practices of medieval people, but also to positive theological messages put forward by Luther and the Swiss reformers.

BIBLIOGRAPHY

Barrett, D., Kurian, G., and Johnson, T., eds., *World Christian Encyclopedia: A Comparative Study of Churches and Religions in the Modern World.* Vol. 1: *The World by Countries: Religionists, Churches, Ministries.* Oxford: Oxford University Press, 2001.

Bossy, J., *Christianity in the West, 1400–1700.* Oxford: Oxford University Press, 1985.

Burke, P., *The Italian Renaissance: Culture and Society in Italy,* 2nd ed. Princeton, NJ: Princeton University Press, 1986.

Cameron, E., *The European Reformation.* Oxford: Clarendon Press, 1991.

Camille, M., *Gothic Art: Glorious Visions.* New York: Harry N. Abrams, 1996.

Christian, W. A., Jr., *Local Religion in Sixteenth-Century Spain.* Princeton, NJ: Princeton University Press, 1981.

Delumeau, J., *Catholicism Between Luther and Voltaire: A New View of the Counter-Reformation,* trans. Jeremy Moiser. London: Burns & Oates, 1977.

Duffy, E., *The Stripping of the Altars: Traditional Religion in England 1400–1580.* New Haven, Conn.: Yale University Press, 1992.

Duggan, L., "Fear and Confession on the Eve of the Reformation," *Archiv für Reformationsgeschichte,* 75 (1984).

Dupront, A., "Religion and Religious Anthropology," in J. Le Goff and P. Nora, eds., *Constructing the Past: Essays in Historical Methodology.* Cambridge: Cambridge University Press, 1985, pp. 123–50.

Galpern, A. N., *The Religions of the People in Sixteenth-Century Champagne.* Cambridge: Cambridge University Press, 1976.

Gregory, B. S., *Salvation at Stake: Christian Martyrdom in Early Modern Europe.* Cambridge, Mass.: Harvard University Press, 1999.

Haigh, C., *English Reformations: Religion, Politics, and Society under the Tudors.* Oxford: Oxford University Press, 1993.

Harris, R., *Lourdes: Body and Spirit in the Secular Age.* New York: Viking, 1999.

Herlihy, D., *Medieval Households.* Cambridge, Mass.: Harvard University Press, 1985.

Huizinga, J., *The Waning of the Middle Ages.* New York: Doubleday, repr. 1954.

Jankofsky, K., "National Characteristics in the Portrayal of English Saints in the South English Legendary," in R. Blumenfeld-Kosinski and T. Szells, eds., *Images of Sainthood in Medieval Europe.* Ithaca, NY: Cornell University Press, 1991, pp. 81–93.

Kleinberg, A., *Prophets in their Own Country: Living Saints and the Making of Sainthood in the Later Middle Ages.* Chicago: University of Chicago Press, 1992.

Martin, H., *Les Ordres mendiants en Bretagne, vers 1230–vers 1530: Pauvreté volontaire et prédication à la fin du moyen âge.* Rennes: Institut armoricain de recherches historiques, 1975.

Martin, H., *Le Métier du prédicateur à la fin du moyen âge, 1350–1520.* Paris: Cerf, 1988.

Mentzer, R. A., "The Persistence of Superstition and Idolatry among Rural French Calvinists," *Church History,* 65 (1996), pp. 220–33.

Moeller, B., "Piety in Germany around 1500," in Steven Ozment, ed., *The Reformation in Medieval Perspective.* Chicago: Triangle, 1971.

Muir, E., *Ritual in Early Modern Europe.* Cambridge: Cambridge University Press, 1997.

Nolan, M. L. and Nolan, S., *Christian Pilgrimage in Modern Western Europe.* Chapel Hill: University of North Carolina Press, 1989.

Ozment, S., *The Reformation in the Cities: The Appeal of Protestantism to Sixteenth-Century Germany and Switzerland.* New Haven, Conn.: Yale University Press, 1975.

Peterson, D., "Out of the Margins: Religion and the Church in Renaissance Italy," *Renaissance Quarterly,* 53 (2000), pp. 835–79.

Rothkrug, L., "Popular Religion and Holy Shrines: Their Influence on the Origins of the German Reformation and their Role in German Cultural Development," in J. Obelkevich, ed., *Religion and the People, 800–1700.* Chapel Hill: University of North Carolina Press, 1979, pp. 20–86.

Rothkrug, L., "Religious Practices and Collective Perceptions: Hidden Homologies in the Renaissance and Reformation," *Historical Reflections/Réflexions historiques,* 1980.

Rubin, M., *Corpus Christi: The Eucharist in Late Medieval Culture.* Cambridge: Cambridge University Press, 1991.

Schmitt, J.-C., *The Holy Greyhound: Guinefort, Healer of Children Since the Thirteenth Century,* trans. M. Thom. Cambridge: Cambridge University Press, 1983.

Schmitt, J.-C., "Religion, Folklore, and Society in the Medieval West," in L. K. Little and B. Rosenwein, eds., *Debating the Middle Ages: Issues and Readings.* Malden, Mass., and Oxford: Blackwell, 1998, pp. 376–87.

Scribner, R., "A Comparative Overview," in B. Scribner, R. Porter, and M. Teich, eds., *The Reformation in National Context.* Cambridge: Cambridge University Press, 1994, pp. 215–27.

Sluhovsky, M., *Patroness of Paris: Rituals of Devotion in Early Modern France.* Leiden: Brill, 1998.

Strauss, G., *Luther's House of Learning: Indoctrination of the Young in the German Reformation.* Baltimore: Johns Hopkins University Press, 1978.

Swanson, R. N., trans. and annot., *Catholic England: Faith, Religion and Observance Before the Reformation.* Manchester: Manchester University Press, 1993.

Swanson, R. N., *Religion and Devotion in Europe, c.1215–c.1515.* Cambridge: Cambridge University Press, 1995.

Taylor, L., *Soldiers of Christ: Preaching in Late Medieval and Reformation France.* New York: Oxford University Press, 1992.

Taylor, L., "God of Judgment, God of Love: Preaching in France, 1460–1560," *Historical Reflections/Réflexions historiques,* 26 (2000), pp. 264–8.

Taylor, L., "Dangerous Vocations: The Social History of Preaching in France in the Late Medieval Period and Reformations," in L. Taylor, ed., *Preachers and People in the Reformations and Early Modern Period.* Leiden: Brill, 2001, pp. 91–124.

Thayer, A., "Penitence and Preaching on the Eve of the Reformation: A Comparative Overview from Frequently Printed Model Sermon Collections, 1450–1520." Harvard University PhD dissertation, 1996.

Toussaert, J., *Le Sentiment religieux en Flandre à la fin du moyen âge.* Paris: Plon, 1963.

Tracy, J., "Believers, Non-Believers, and the Historian's Unspoken Assumptions," *Catholic Historical Review,* 86 (2000), pp. 403–19.

Vauchez, A., *The Laity in the Middle Ages: Religious Beliefs and Devotional Practices,* ed. D. E. Bornstein and trans. M. J. Schneider. Notre Dame and London: University of Notre Dame Press, 1993.

Wandel, L. P., *Voracious Idols and Violent Hands.* Cambridge: Cambridge University Press, 1995.

FURTHER READING

Bynum, C. W., *Holy Feast and Holy Fast: The Religious Significance of Good to Medieval Women.* Berkeley: University of California Press, 1987.

Bynum, C. W., *Fragmentation and Redemption: Essays on Gender and the Human Body in Medieval Religion.* New York: Zone Books, 1992.

Bynum, C. W. and Freedman, P., *Last Things: Death and the Apocalypse in the Middle Ages.* Philadelphia: University of Pennsylvania Press, 2000.

Christian, W. A., Jr., *Apparitions in Late Medieval and Renaissance Spain*. Princeton, NJ: Princeton University Press, 1981.

Crouzet, D., *Les Guerriers de Dieu: La Violence au temps des troubles de religion, vers 1525–vers 1610*. Paris: Champ Vallon, 1990.

Delaruelle, E., *La Piété populaire au moyen âge*. Turin: Bottega d'Erasmo, 1975.

Finucane, R. C., *Miracles and Pilgrims: Popular Beliefs in Medieval England*. New York: St. Martin's, 1977.

Goodich, M. E., *Violence and Miracle in the Fourteenth Century*. Chicago: University of Chicago Press, 1995.

Gordon, B. and Marshall, P., *The Place of the Dead: Death and Remembrance in Late Medieval and Early Modern Europe*. Cambridge: Cambridge University Press, 2000.

Gurevich, A., *Medieval Popular Culture: Problems of Belief and Perception*. Cambridge: Cambridge University Press, 1992.

Hsia, R. P., *The Myth of Ritual Murder: Jews and Magic in Reformation Germany*. New Haven, Conn.: Yale University Press, 1988.

Kieckhefer, R., *Unquiet Souls: Fourteenth-Century Saints and their Religious Milieu*. Chicago: University of Chicago Press, 1984.

Oberman, H. A., *Forerunners of the Reformation: The Shape of Medieval Thought Illustrated by Key Documents*, 2nd ed. Philadelphia: Fortress Press, 1981.

Reinburg, V., "Popular Prayers in Late Medieval and Reformation France." Boston College PhD dissertation, 1985.

Sumption, J., *Pilgrimage: An Image of Medieval Religion*. Totowa, NJ: Rowman & Littlefield, 1976.

Tentler, T., *Sin and Confession on the Eve of the Reformation*. Princeton, NJ: Princeton University Press, 1977.

Thomas, K., *Religion and the Decline of Magic*. New York: Charles Scribner's Sons, 1971.

Ward, B., *Miracles and the Medieval Mind*. Philadelphia: University of Pennsylvania Press, 1987.

Weinstein, D. and Bell, R., *Saints and Society: The Two Worlds of Western Christendom 1000–1700*. Chicago: University of Chicago Press, 1982.

Winston-Allen, A., *Stories of the Rose: The Making of the Rosary in the Middle Ages*. University Park: Pennsylvania State University Press, 1997.

PART II

The Reformation in the Holy Roman Empire

THREE

Martin Luther and the German Nation

ROBERT KOLB

At Martin Luther's funeral his colleague and pastor Johannes Bugenhagen described him as "a great teacher and prophet, a reformer sent by God to the church," a "holy apostle and prophet of Christ, the one who came to preach to us and be the evangelist for the German lands."[1] Although many of Luther's contemporaries vilified and demonized him, peasants, pastors, and princes of the time expressed views similar to Bugenhagen's. Whether friend or foe, his contemporaries found the Professor of Bible at the University of Wittenberg larger than life. Four hundred fifty years after his death, at the turn of the third Christian millennium, lists composed in western societies of those who had most decisively shaped the second millennium inevitably included Luther's name. Some 60 million Christians belong to churches called "Lutheran." Ripples from his life and thought continue to shape learned discourse, provoke scholarly dispute, and attract human interest into the twenty-first century. Yet recent research has called into question whether his thought and actions actually changed much in European life and culture. Such challenges continue to call forth new research into his theology and his career.

Luther Research

Luther studies are both eased and complicated by excellent editions of his writings, aids to their use, and secondary literature so extensive (Leppin; Hendrix, "American Luther Research"; "Martin Luther") that Luther is one of those about whom it is said "more has been written about him than anyone else besides Christ." Since 1956 pentennial meetings of the International Congress for Luther Research have gathered scholars to exchange views. The periodicals *Lutherjahrbuch* and *Archiv für Reformationsgeschichte Literaturbericht* provide annual bibliographies. The "Weimar edition" of Luther's works was produced as a model of scholarly editing; a significant amount of his oeuvre appears in English translation. Access to editions of his collected works is guided by Kurt Aland's *Hilfsbuch zum Lutherstudium*.

Julius Köstlin wrote the first critical biography of Luther (1875). The only work of comparable size is Martin Brecht's. Among dozens of others, particularly those by

Bernhard Lohse, Heiko Oberman, and Reinhard Schwarz command attention. Readers of English may begin with James Kittelson's, which has replaced Roland Bainton's introduction to his life.

Theodosius Harnack and Julius Köstlin inaugurated critical assessment of Luther's thought. Students today may begin with more compact studies by Gerhard Ebeling (*Luther*), Paul Althaus (*Theology of Martin Luther*), and Bernhard Lohse (*Martin Luther's Theology*). Following World War II Roman Catholic Luther scholarship blossomed, under the leadership of Joseph Lortz. European and North American Catholic theologians produced significant works on Luther (McSorley, Olivier, Pesch, Wicks); unfortunately, this trend has receded.

Two major twentieth-century discussions regarding Luther have also diminished. The first concerned the dating of his so-called "tower experience," better labeled his "evangelical breakthrough." The Holl School, followers of Karl Holl (Stayer), pursued this question; revision set in with work by Saarnivaara, Bizer, and Bayer (cf. Lohse, *Durchbruch*, 1958, 1988). This preoccupation with the "early Luther" and the moment of his "conversion" has given way to assessing his theological development in terms of an intellectual process in the midst of the broader context of social and political change. The call of Helmar Junghans (*Leben und Werk Martin Luthers*) and others for more attention to the "older Luther" is bearing fruit. The second focus was the interpretation of his significance and thought in Marxist terms. Since the collapse of Soviet-dominated regimes, especially in the German Democratic Republic, eradicated societal support for this approach, its contributions, particularly in interpreting of the social and political context of the Reformation, have been absorbed into the wider field of social-historical research.

Luther's Schooling

Born in the village of Eisleben in Mansfeld county, November 10, 1483, to a father (Hans) who had left the land to become a successful entrepreneur in copper-smelting and mother (Margarete Lindemann) from a merchant family in Eisenach, Luther was pushed toward a career in government by his parents, who hoped for his success following the study of law. After a normal course of schooling in Mansfeld, Magdeburg, and Eisenach, he matriculated at the University of Erfurt in 1501, completing bachelor and master's degrees in the arts in 1502 and 1505.

Soon after he began his legal training, in July 1505, his sensitive conscience, aroused by his terror in the face of God's wrath, death, and hell during a thunderstorm, drove him into Erfurt's Augustinian monastery. He conformed to the strictest monastic regulations to commend his soul to God, but his spiritual anxieties only deepened as his feelings of guilt and unworthiness mounted. Nonetheless, his monastic superiors encouraged his career, prescribing academic work at Erfurt and Wittenberg, arranging his ordination to the priesthood in early 1507. At the first mass he celebrated, the young priest almost collapsed in terror before the words of institution that brought Christ's body and blood to the altar. This struggle continued as he pursued further study and assumed administrative duties within the Augustinian order. He traveled to Rome (1510) to plead for strict reform in the order, proposals opposed by the head of its Saxon province, Johann von Staupitz. Staupitz nevertheless continued to promote Luther's career and give him pastoral counsel, combating the young monk's scrupulosity by emphasizing God's unconditional grace and election of believers as well as Christ's sacrifice for his sins (Steinmetz, Wriedt).

The Beginnings of Luther's Reformation

Staupitz laid instructional responsibilities at the infant university of Saxon Elector Frederick the Wise upon Luther as he completed his formal studies. On October 18, 1512, he received the degree Doctor of Bible, pledging to devote his life to searching Scripture and defending its truth at all costs. In accord with the medieval plan of learning and teaching, he had earlier lectured on Aristotle, the *Sentences* of Peter Lombard, and patristic texts, above all Jerome. In 1513 he assumed lectures on Biblical books, beginning with Psalms (1513–15), Romans (1515–16), Galatians (1516–17), Hebrews (1517–18), and then the Psalms again. To the end of his life he continued such lectures, the most important on Galatians (1531) and Genesis (1535–45). In the 1510s his departure from strict adherence to the "allegorical" method of medieval exegesis and his development of a literal-prophetic interpretation, coupled with the theological hermeneutic of the distinction of God's accusing law from his life-restoring Gospel, initiated a new era in Biblical exposition and theological method. Recent interest in the history of exegesis and hermeneutics has opened new fields of inquiry in the rich resources of Luther's sermons, commentaries, and other works (Ebeling, *Evangelische Evangelienauslegung*; Hagen).

While lecturing on Hebrews this young monk and professor at an obscure new university became a controversial figure of European prominence. Luther's spiritual struggles had sharpened his sensitivity to the crisis of pastoral care enveloping western Christendom by 1500. The medieval system of "Seelsorge," centered on the mass and penance, was not working well as societal change loosened the dependence upon the clergy of small but significant groups of merchants and artisans in towns. When Albrecht von Hohenzollern, brother of the elector of Brandenburg, employed the sale of indulgences for building St. Peter's basilica in Rome to pay fees required by his acquisition of his third high ecclesiastical office, the archbishopric of Mainz, Luther protested against attendant abuses which harmed laypeople's consciences. This protest, posted October 31, 1517, took the form of academic theses – proposals for public debate. They provoked a storm of discussion and propelled Luther into the role of reformer. Although the first of his *Ninety-Five Theses on Indulgences*, "the whole life of the Christian is a life of repentance," summarized a lifelong concern, the document's theological content was not of critical importance. Its significance lies in the fact that enterprising printers published it, without realizing that they were instituting a communications revolution. For this publication became the first modern media event, the first public relations happening, as Johannes Gutenberg's technology was placed at the service of Luther's thinking.

Luther lived in an oral culture; his message commanded popular attention above all because preachers – many former Wittenberg students – proclaimed it in villages and towns across Germany and lands beyond. Nonetheless, Mark Edwards correctly notes that "the printed word played a crucial role in the early Reformation, and when multiplied by the effects of preaching and conversation, can be said to be a major factor in spreading it as a relatively coherent message." The appeal for reform disseminated "with a rapidity that had been impossible before [the] invention [of the printing press, which] . . . allowed the central ideological leader, Martin Luther, to reach the 'opinion leaders' of the movement quickly, kept them all in touch with each other and with each other's experience and ideas, and allowed them to 'broadcast' their (relatively coordinated) program to a much larger and more geographically diverse audience than ever before had been possible" (Edwards, *Printing*, pp. 11, 37, 172, 7). By 1520 some 30 publications had appeared from Luther's pen, with estimated sales of 600,000 copies. Twenty percent of the pamphlets published in Germany between 1500 and 1530 bore his name. Edwards argues that the impact of these writings was limited, however, by selective publication of titles in specific areas. Further research will extend Edwards's own study of Strasbourg printing. Robert W. Scribner has laid groundwork for further investigation of the communication of Luther's thought to the German public with his assessment of how popular propaganda by and about Luther was constructed. Scribner examines visual images, such as Luther as monk, teacher, and man of the Bible, in addition to the oral and written/printed word, showing how Luther met and capitalized on the apocalyptic longings of the age.

These printed media appeared in the midst of a political and legal process launched by Roman Catholic officials in Germany and Rome soon after the *Ninety-Five Theses* were published. Pressure was put upon the German Augustinians to discipline the rebellious monk. Staupitz invited him to address the order's Reform Congregation in Heidelberg in April 1518. Instead of treating the ecclesiastical-political issues at hand, Luther advanced his "theology of the Cross." Contrasting it with medieval "theologies of glory," which glorified human reason and good works, he grounded theology upon Paul's "word of the Cross" (1 Corinthians 1: 18–2: 15). The term vanished from Luther's vocabulary; its principles remained lifelong presuppositions. His *Heidelberg Theses* distinguished the "hidden God" (*Deus absconditus*) (God beyond human ability to grasp or as he is shaped by human imagination) from "God revealed" (*Deus revelatus*) in Christ and Scripture. Access to God comes not through human paths to knowledge (signs or proofs and logic) but only through trust in his Word, which restores humanity by pronouncing the forgiveness of sins and new life. Forgiveness and new life rest upon God's act of atonement through Christ's death and resurrection. The Word brings upon sinners the judgment of God's law (his plan and standard for evaluating life) and gives them the Gospel (the good news of his mercy delivered through Christ). Finally, Luther's understanding of daily Christian living also followed Jesus's command to take up the cross to follow him, in a life of self-sacrificial love. Discussion of the theology of the Cross begun by von Loewenich continues in works by Ngien, Forde (*On Being a Theologian of the Cross*), Schwarzwäller (*Kreuz und Auferstehung*), and others. The centrality of Christ remained a pillar of Luther's thought throughout his life (see Lienhard and Siggins).

Luther's own order did not discipline him. Dominican curial theologians in Rome, led by the Master of the Sacred Palace Silvester Mazzolini Prierias, charged Luther with heresy and pressed for citing him to Rome for trial. Luther's prince, Elector Frederick the Wise of Saxony, intervened. At the imperial diet in Augsburg in autumn 1518 Luther was summoned before papal legate Thomas de Vio, Cardinal Cajetan, who refused to hear his argument for reform but simply demanded his recantation and submission to the pope. Luther fled Augsburg in fear that the popular association of his efforts with the Bohemian Jan Hus a century earlier would be realized in his being burned at the stake. Negotiations between papal diplomat Karl von Miltitz and Frederick over Luther's fate came to naught.

Johann Eck, professor in Ingolstadt, challenged Luther's Wittenberg colleague Andreas Bodenstein von Karlstadt to debate the Wittenberg reform program in Leipzig in June/July 1519. The topic was authority in the church. Drawing Luther into the debate, Eck led him to admit that he rejected the authority of popes and councils in favor of the sole authority of Scripture. Luther's view of the papacy developed between 1517 and 1522 from ambivalence to the conviction that the institution of papal power was the Antichrist (Hendrix, *Luther and the Papacy*).

Foundations of Luther's Thought

By 1519 the major components of Luther's theology were largely in place. A variety of factors formed his many-faceted thought. Investigating the ways in which late medieval monastic piety shaped Luther's thinking may offer new insights alongside those from study of influences from the popular mystical tradition, including Heinrich Tauler and the *Theologia Deutsch*, which Luther himself edited in 1516 (zur Mühlen). Among medieval authors Luther preferred Bernard of Clairvaux (Bell). Luther read patristic sources in florilegia and in new editions, above all Augustine, but ever more critically. His knowledge of scholastic theology was extensive. His own instructors had been trained in part by the Tübingen Ockhamist Gabriel Biel, whose writings Luther knew well. Both the positive and negative influences of the nominalists never left him (Oberman, *Harvest*; cf. Janz on Luther's relationship to Aquinas). Recent scholarship also emphasizes the influence upon him of Biblical humanists, including Johannes Reuchlin, Jacques Lefèvre d'Étaples, and Desiderius Erasmus (Spitz, Junghans, Grane), and especially Luther's Wittenberg colleague Philip Melanchthon, whose 500th birthday (1997) spawned significant investigations of his relationship with Luther and his own theological activity, advancing understanding of him as a thinker in his own right (Wengert, Frank, Loehr). Heinz Scheible's edition of Melanchthon's correspondence, begun with a comprehensive catalog, will aid further study immensely.

Guilt and terror in the face of the holy God's wrath against sin had long plagued Luther. He attributed his liberation from them to new insight into the Biblical definition of "righteousness." Through his spiritual struggles (*Anfechtungen*) and study of Scripture, with the aid of the linguistic studies of humanists, including Erasmus and Melanchthon, Luther came to understand several Biblical concepts in new ways. God's own righteousness – what makes God God, his essence – he redefined as divine mercy and love, as revealed in Christ's Cross and resurrection. Human righteousness he redefined by distinguishing what makes human beings truly human in relationship to God from that which constitutes the practice of humanity in relationship to others. God's love or favor alone determines human righteousness in his sight. Human performance of God's commands, in love and care for his world, is what defines righteousness among human beings.

From the nominalists Luther had absorbed the Old Testament conviction that God is almighty, absolutely sovereign, and thus completely responsible for everything in creation. At the same time they had taught that God had ordained a world in which human creatures were held totally responsible for their own obedience to

God's law. Biel synthesized these two concepts of responsibility by teaching that God gives grace, understood as that which enables obedience to God's law, to those who "out of purely natural powers" do their best (*facere quod in se est*). With that grace they have the ability to render performance worthy of salvation, supplemented by the grace of the forgiveness of sins bestowed through the church's sacramental system. Luther rejected this harmonization of God's grace and human works. Instead, within the framework of his distinction between two kinds of righteousness, he held total divine responsibility for everything in tension with total human responsibility for obedience to God. He distinguished between God's word of love or favor in Christ, which establishes the identity of his chosen people as children of God, from his word of command, which describes the performance expected from those who have been given the gift of being God's children, believers in Christ. Luther understood the relationship between Creator and chosen human children as the relationship of love and trust. Thus, he held that trust or faith in God, the response to the promise made in Christ, constitutes the essential humanity of the human creature.

Alongside this paradox of the two responsibilities Luther recognized the mystery of the continuation of evil and sinfulness in believers' lives. Because they are righteous and sinful at the same time (*simul justus et peccator*), they continue to repent, repeating the death to sin and resurrection to new life in Christ given them in their baptism. In baptism Luther found the foundation for his doctrine of justification, the restoration of the fullness of humanity to sinners (Trigg).

God bestows righteousness (*justitia*) through his act of justification, accomplished through his Word of Gospel, which comes in oral, written, and sacramental forms, labeled by Luther "the means of grace." From his nominalist training, Luther had learned that the word of almighty God determines reality. The Creator summoned all that exists into existence by speaking (Genesis 1), and Luther believed that God's promise of forgiveness of sins in the means of grace freed sinners from sin and restored them to the practice of righteousness.

Much twentieth-century discussion over Luther's evangelical breakthrough ignored Luther's understanding of the power of God's Word and therefore attempted to argue that Luther defined justification as "effective," that is, God's act that produces good works in believers because it changes them, rather than as "forensic," a "mere" pronouncement which did not effect change (Holl). Gerhard Forde correctly observes that this argument poses a false alternative. Luther believed that God's Word expresses his power and creates the fundamental reality of human existence through the forgiveness of sins, which restores human righteousness in God's sight: "the absolutely forensic character of justification renders it effective – justification actually kills and makes alive. It is, to be sure, 'not only' forensic, but that is the case only because the more forensic it is, the more effective it is!" (Forde, *Justification by Faith*, p. 36).

A more recent debate engages the argument of Tuoma Mannermaa that Luther's doctrine of justification centers upon the concept of "divinization" (*Vergottung*). Contrary to later sixteenth-century interpretation, according to Mannermaa and Simo Peura, Luther defined justification as a real ontic change in sinners, accomplished through union with Christ, which effects divinization. With such a view Mannermaa hoped to promote ecumenical rapprochement, especially with eastern Orthodoxy. Schwarzwäller ("Verantwortung des Glaubens") notes that fundamental to Luther's presuppositions is the Biblical writers' consistent separation of the Creator from the creation, broken only in the incarnation of the second person of the Trinity. There is no movement in the opposite direction, from human being into God, possible in Luther's reading of Scripture. Schwarzwäller questions the methodological and hermeneutical process involved in the "theosis" argument because of the lack of evidence in the sources that Luther's very occasional use of the language of *Vergottung* provides the "idea that structures Luther's thought." Schwarzwäller further subjects the argument to historical and logical criticism, also insisting that a confusion of metaphor and reality haunts the Mannermaa school's investigations. Finally, Schwarzwäller challenges the theological coherence of an interpretation of Luther based on Platonic paradigms he rejected (ibid., pp. 143–8; cf. Flogaus).

The Spread of Luther's Ideas

As Luther's theology developed, his public persona did, too. His ideas may not have always been clearly understood, but an aura of the apocalyptic prophet attracted many followers. Luther's writings encouraged further development of civic self-confidence in rising middle-class people in towns. Thus, his own and the tracts of others repeating and extending his ideas found a wide readership and hearership. In 1520/1521 he expressed his program for Reformation in five treatises. His *Open Letter to the Nobility of the German Nation* repeated the grievances (*gravimina*) of the German estates regarding a wide range of ecclesiastical and social practices, within his own theological critique of the church's abuse of power. The medieval doctrine of the sacraments, and the associated ascription of special status and power to the clergy, invited his assessment in *The Babylonian Captivity of the Church*. Luther defined the sacraments on the basis of his belief that God's Word, in sacramental form as well as oral and written forms, actually effects a change of the reality of the sinner's life, forgiving sin and effecting a "new creature in Christ." The Word in sacramental form rested, he believed, on Christ's explicit command and used external elements to convey remission of sins and new life. Therefore, he reduced the number of sacraments from seven to two or three (he wavered on whether absolution was a sacrament in itself or a continuation of baptism). He rejected reliance on Aristotelian physics to explain the presence of Christ's body and blood in the Lord's Supper (transubstantiation), insisting that his body and blood are truly present, in a mysterious way, because Christ said so. He rejected the medieval prohibition of lay reception of Christ's blood in the wine as tyranny over God and the laity. He rejected the concept of the mass as a repetition of Christ's sacrifice, arguing instead that it gives believers salvation.

The reformer expressed his doctrine of justification in *The Freedom of the Christian*, which taught that Christ has freed believers from their enemies, sin, death, Satan, condemnation by God's law, in order to bind them to their neighbors in love. *On Good Works* taught how trusting in Christ was to produce good works of love toward others. Luther regarded this everyday life of love as God's way of living, in contrast to monasticism, the object of his fierce critique in *On Monastic Vows*.

While Luther was formulating his program of reform, the legal processes set in motion by Prierias and Eck ground on, accomplishing their goal with his excommunication and condemnation as a heretic in January 1521. Luther's concept of reform of the church's teaching also offended the pious young German emperor, Charles V, who was concerned about its moral and institutional reform. Luther's Reformation threatened his plans for consolidating his power in Germany, just as it aided the desire of the princes and towns of the empire for more independence from the emperor. Charles summoned Luther before the imperial diet in Worms in May 1521, demanding his recantation. Luther probably did not actually utter the words placed in his mouth by later reports – "Here I stand; I cannot do other" – but he did confess his faith clearly. After the official close of the diet, Charles obtained a formal condemnation of Luther as an outlaw and pledged his government to eliminating Luther's publications and followers. Even princes faithful to Rome and Charles enforced this Edict of Worms with varying degrees of severity (Kohnle); it produced only a few martyrs. Nonetheless, it remained a significant factor in imperial politics until the Religious Peace of Augsburg gave Luther's followers legal (though inferior) standing in 1555.

The Indigenization of Luther's Reformation

Throughout the 1520s, at meetings of the imperial diet (Nuremberg 1522/23, 1524, Augsburg 1525/26, Speyer 1526, 1529), Charles maneuvered against the increasing number of Luther's princely and municipal supporters. In 1526 he seemed to allow them some freedom to pursue their own consciences in matters of reform; in 1529 he cracked down upon the Lutheran movement again, provoking a testimony of faith (*protestatio*) from the evangelical estates which won them the designation "Protestants." Charles rejected the explanation of reform presented at the Augsburg diet of 1530, formulated by Melanchthon, the *Augsburg Confession*, and had a commission of Roman Catholic theologians compose a *Confutation*, which elicited Melanchthon's *Apology of the Augsburg Confession* (1531) (Wenz, *Theologie der Bekenntnisschriften*, vol. 1, pp. 349–498). The emperor condemned Wittenberg reform again and demanded that its adherents return to the Roman obedience, without avail.

For the process of indigenizing reform had been advancing at court and in the German countryside during the 1520s. Elector Frederick hid Luther after his stand at Worms in his castle, the Wartburg. There the professor completed a translation of the New Testament into German. Not the first attempt to do so, his rendering nonetheless exhibited Luther's fine sense of language and exercised a wide influence, theologically and linguistically. At the same time he prepared the first section of a book of sermons, his postil, which served as a continuing education program for priests, many of whom had little idea how to preach. The postil provided both instruction in Luther's way of thinking and models for proclaiming his message. Further research is needed to assess how medieval priests were transformed into Lutheran pastors by such efforts (cf. Karant-Nunn's pioneering study). In subsequent years Luther and his associates produced a cornucopia of literature, including devotional tracts, occasional sermons, and hymns. Luther published a reformed Latin liturgy (1523) and his *German Mass* (1526).

Most importantly, he produced a children's handbook for daily living, his *Small Catechism*, in the form of a wall chart and a booklet, along with an instructor's manual, the *Large Catechism*, a recapitulation of his preaching on the medieval program of basic instruction, "the catechism" (Arand, Peters, Wenz). Luther took its core (Apostles Creed, Lord's Prayer, Decalog) and reordered its parts to frame Christian living under the law that diagnoses sin (Decalog), the Gospel that proclaims new life (Creed), and the exercise of faith (Lord's Prayer). The *Small Catechism* also treated the use of the sacraments (baptism, absolution, Lord's Supper), the devotional life of prayer and meditation, and the "table" of callings of the Christian life to serve the neighbor within the whole social structure. This "table" reflects Luther's adaptation of the medieval social structure of three "estates," oeconomia, politia, and ecclesia, to his understanding that God calls people to serve him by loving others. His ethics presupposed these situations and callings to responsibilities (offices) within them as the basis for living in obedience to God's commands (Wingren; Althaus, *Ethics of Martin Luther*).

This concept of the Christian's calling is an important element in what is often labeled Luther's "doctrine of two kingdoms." A conceptual framework or paradigm rather than a doctrine, Luther's distinction between the earthly realm and the heavenly realm reflected his rejection of the medieval equation of the sacred or religious with godliness and the profane or secular with a lower level of worth. He affirmed that God effects everything in the realm of faith, the realm which involves the relationship between God and human creatures, while human love acts in the earthly realm, in required obedience to God when sin does not interfere. Nineteenth-century German scholars put a version of this to use in supporting political aims (Brady), but early twentieth-century Scandinavian scholars began the study of Luther's intention, repudiating notions that Luther wanted to free the secular realm from moral obligations since the opposite was the case (Wingren). Debate continues about the proper interpretation of Luther's own understanding of the two realms and its significance of this distinction between earthly and heavenly realms within contemporary social questions (Cranz, Duchrow).

As Luther prepared literature and students at Wittenberg for introducing reform, the yeast of his thought and the general apocalyptic longing of the time led to critical ecclesiastical, social, and political developments of several kinds in 1524–9. In 1525 he married a former nun, Katharina von Bora. In addition to her vital role in his continued theological and ecclesiastical activities, his marriage exhibited his concept of the Christian calling dramatically. This relationship served as a model for the Protestant concept of married life.

The year also brought disjuncture, however. Luther's fears of public disorder, coupled with his eschatological convictions that Satan was using rebellious peasants to disrupt the spread of the Gospel, led him to fierce opposition to peasant revolts in 1524–6 (see chapter 4). Franz Lau's argument that the damage to Luther's reputation among the common people was exaggerated by Roman Catholic opponents then and modern scholars now requires further study.

In 1525 Luther's reply to the attack of Desiderius Erasmus on his views on the bondage of the human will in matters of faith also marked his break with his own generation of Biblical humanists. Luther thanked Erasmus for identifying a key issue in the gulf that he had long realized separated them; his emphasis on doctrinal reform did not match Erasmus's on moral and institutional reform. From Scripture, and reflecting his own experience, Luther asserted that the human will is active but its ability to choose to trust God is bound, turned away from him to false objects of trust. In *On Bound Choice* (1525) Luther replied to Erasmus's *Diatribe on Free Choice* (1524), describing his method of theology (emphasizing the assertion or confession of the Biblical message) and his convictions regarding what it means to be human. Schwarzwäller (*Shibboleth*) summarizes a century of debate over interpretations of the dispute; subsequent work should be surveyed in similar manner. Melanchthon supported Luther and felt the sting of the cantankerous Erasmus's disappointment (Wengert, *Human Freedom*). Many in the third generation of German humanists remained faithful to Luther and provided "the shock troops" of his Reformation.

Inevitably, Luther was challenged not only by the reform program of Erasmus's Biblical humanism but also by popular reform ideas that had arisen from time to time in the Middle Ages among groups that repeated a common pattern of Biblicistic revolt against ecclesiastical authority, insistence on strict moral performance rather than rote ritualism, antisacramentalism linked to anticlericalism, and millennialism. Reformation anticlericalism has commanded scholarly interest recently (Dykema and Oberman); further exploration of its role in Luther's life is warranted. Luther's colleague Karlstadt had captured his enthusiasm for reform but channeled into this traditional form for seeking improvement in church life. He abandoned his professorship, became a pastor in a village, shedding clerical garb, claiming a simplicity for himself in stark contrast to his former lifestyle. Luther particularly criticized his spiritualizing view of the Lord's Supper (Edwards, *Luther and the False Brethren*; Sider). Luther similarly rejected the theology and social practice of the Anabaptists.

Disputes over the Lord's Supper separated the Wittenberg reformers from colleagues, particularly in Switzerland, e.g., Johannes Oecolampadius and Huldrych Zwingli, whose Neoplatonic humanistic training made it impossible for him to grasp what for the nominalistically educated Luther was clear: that God could use selected elements of the created order to convey salvation. Zwingli argued that when Jesus said, "This is my body," he could not have meant that the bread became his body but that "is" meant "represents" or "symbolizes" because his Platonic presuppositions prevented him from believing that the material order could be put to such use in the spiritual realm. Luther's nominalistic presuppositions made such a use possible and the authority of Christ's words absolute. Furthermore, Zwingli argued that Christ's human nature had ascended to God's right hand in heaven and could not be present in bread and wine. Luther contended that in Hebrew thought "God's right hand" refers to Christ's human nature's assuming divine power as it shared with his divine nature its characteristics, all the while remaining essentially completely distinct from the divine nature within the union of the person of Christ.[2] The most important of Luther's replies to Zwingli was his *Confession Concerning Christ's Supper* (1528). In 1529 the two met, with colleagues, at Marburg in a colloquy arranged by Landgrave Philip of Hesse. They found widespread agreement but not on the Lord's Supper.

Philip actively introduced Luther's reform throughout his lands, as did Elector John of Saxony. His succession to the electorate after the death of his brother Frederick (1525) marked the onset of active support for Reformation in electoral Saxony. John instituted the equivalent of a medieval episcopal visitation of parishes in 1527–8. Led by Luther and Melanchthon and guided by *Visitation Articles* composed by Melanchthon with his colleague's assistance, this visitation shocked the Wittenberg theologians, who had hoped that their message would have transformed peasant life. That it had not done so shaped Luther's and Melanchthon's theologies by driving them both to a stronger use of the proclamation of the law of God to crush sin and accuse sinners (Wengert, *Law and Gospel*). Princes and town councils from Germany and beyond sought advice from the Wittenberg theologians on a wide range of matters, extending their influence on policy and practice in church and society. Bugenhagen often left Wittenberg to advise governments on the construction of constitutions for church, school, and social welfare (*Kirchenordnung*).

The Maturing of Luther's Reformation

At the imperial level the Wittenberg leaders continued to promote reform. Melanchthon's *Augsburg Confession* not only argued that Luther's theology repeated in a clear fashion what Scripture and the Catholic tradition had always taught; it also became a formal definition of Luther's alternative to the medieval way of conducting the church's teaching and life. After Pope Paul III called for a church council in 1536, Luther formulated a statement of the evangelical position for discussion at such a meeting, a statement designed to serve as his doctrinal last will and testament as well. In these *Schmalkaldic Articles* (1537) Luther briefly but clearly delineated the heart of his faith, trust in Christ for forgiveness and life, and differentiated it from Roman teaching on three key issues, the mass, monasticism, and the papacy; he further noted disagreement on other issues. The papally called council began its sessions in 1545 rather than 1537; nonetheless, the challenge of a council evoked Luther's detailed treatment of the doctrine of the church, above all in *On the Councils and the Church* (1539) and *Against Hans Wurst* (1542). For him the church was built upon its use of the Gospel, in preaching, in the sacraments, through the office of the ministry, in its liturgy and instruction. He believed that the church would always be in battle against Satan and thus always under the threat of persecution. He insisted that love for neighbor is always visible in the church's life. Luther expressed himself on a wide range of societal issues (Rieth), including commerce, but largely in quite traditional fashion. His polemic against the Jews reflected the most deplorable prejudices of his time (see Oberman, *Luther*, pp. 292–7; Edwards, *Luther's Last Battles*, pp. 115–42).

Parallel to Luther's theological efforts to further reform according to his teaching, evangelical princes and theologians were maneuvering to attain legal status for their confession against imperial opposition. Before 1530 some evangelical governments were shaping plans for armed resistance to the emperor on the basis of arguments from the German constitution and natural law (Wolgast). Luther rejected them sharply, but by 1531 hints of a justification for such resistance on the basis of imperial abandonment of God's calling to rule justly appeared in his *Warning to His Dear German People*: by 1539 this idea had matured in his writings (Edwards, *Luther's Last Battles*, pp. 20–67; cf. Wolgast). The princes formed a defensive league (1532); this Schmalkaldic League played a role not only within Germany but also in relationships with other powers, including France and England.

Luther's Legacy

Luther's death in 1546 coincided with the end of distractions which had kept Charles V from employing armed force against the German Lutherans. The further definition of Luther's contributions to church and society would have taken place under any circumstances, as part of the process scholars now label "confessionalization" (Schilling). In fact, this interpretation and further application of his ideas and actions took place in the shadow of the Schmalkaldic War, launched in 1546 by the Habsburg emperor against John Frederick of Saxony and Philip of Hesse. Isolating them from other Protestant princes, Charles defeated them in April 1547 and imposed a new religious policy upon evangelical German lands, his "Augsburg Interim," which was to bring them back to the Roman obedience under reformed medieval Catholic doctrine and practice. John Frederick's cousin (and Philip's son-in-law) Moritz of Saxony sided with the Habsburg brothers and was rewarded with the electorate of Saxony and territory, including Wittenberg. Melanchthon was drawn reluctantly into the construction of an alternative religious policy for Moritz's lands. In order to save Lutheran pulpits for Lutheran preachers, he agreed to certain compromises in "adiaphora," neutral ecclesiastical practices. Many of his and Luther's former students reacted against this compromise with deep and bitter feelings of betrayal, which were returned by equally bitter feelings of betrayal from Melanchthon and his associates, who believed that they were only trying in good faith to rescue the Lutheran churches from imperial suppression. Thus, the further indigenization and interpretation of Luther's legacy was conducted in a polemical atmosphere of mistrust among former friends. The disputes were solved to a large extent by the *Formula of Concord* of 1577, published with other defining documents of the Lutheran churches in 1580 in the *Book of Concord*, but resistance to this settlement in some evangelical churches continued (Dingel).

After his death some of his followers used Luther's writings as a secondary authority, the first instance for adjudicating doctrinal disputes, differences of Biblical interpretation, and other matters of church life, a kind of substitute for the authority of popes and councils. He was widely regarded as a teacher of the church, and particularly on certain issues his insights were reproduced (although with applications that reflected the input of other teachers and new factors in the intellectual and ecclesiastical environment of his successors). German evangelicals also regarded him as a hero of their people, in the battle against papal tyranny (Kolb).

Recent discussions of Luther's cultural significance have questioned whether he "succeeded" in conforming the world to his model. The debate opened by Gerald Strauss's *Luther's House of Learning* regarding the impact of Luther's Reformation and his theology continues. Criticisms of Strauss's findings that "if it was its [Luther's Reformation] central purpose to make people – all people – think, feel, and act as Christians, to imbue them with a Christian mind-set, motivational drive, and way of life, it failed" (ibid., p. 307) were lodged from several methodological perspectives (e.g., Kittelson, "Successes and Failures"; Hendrix, "Luther's Impact"). This debate, like the earlier over Luther's "evangelical breakthrough," too often reflects more of the modern scholar's presuppositions than the sixteenth-century situation. Further discussion about the relationship of the Reformation to, or between, Middle Ages and the modern age, and about the definition of Reformation and whether it was one movement or several, will also provoke reactions in the coming decade (Hamm, Moeller, and Wendebourg). Studies of the social setting and impact of Luther's person and message[3] are also needed. For Martin Luther continues to command the attention of people around the world at the beginning of the twenty-first century.

NOTES

1 *Eine christliche Predigt Vber der Leich vnd Begrabnus . . . Herrn D. Martini Lutheri . . .* (Wittenberg, 1546).
2 An expression of the ancient Christian doctrines of the personal or hypostatic union of Christ and the communication of the attributes of each of his natures with the other. The most detailed treatment remains Köhler; cf. Sasse. For further literature, see chapter 6.
3 For examples of several approaches, see Hsia, *German People and the Reformation*.

BIBLIOGRAPHY

Aland, K., *Hilfsbuch zum Lutherstudium*, 4th ed. Bielefeld: Luther-Verlag, 1996.
Althaus, P., *The Ethics of Martin Luther*, trans. Robert C. Schultz. Philadelphia: Fortress Press, 1972 (German, 1965).
Aulén, G., *Christus Victor*, trans. A. G. Hebert. London: SPCK, 1945 (Swedish, 1931).
Bagchi, D., *Luther's Earliest Opponents: Catholic Controversialists, 1518–1525.* Minneapolis: Fortress Press, 1991.
Bainton, R. H., *Here I Stand.* New York: Abingdon, 1950.
Bayer, O., *Promissio: Geschichte der reformatorischen Wende in Luthers Theologie.* Göttingen: Vandenhoeck & Ruprecht, 1971.
Die Bekenntnisschriften der evangelisch-lutherischen Kirche, 11th ed. Göttingen: Vandenhoeck & Ruprecht, 1992; trans. *The Book of Concord*, ed. Robert Kolb and Timothy J. Wengert. Minneapolis: Fortress Press, 2000.
Bell, T., *Divus Bernhardus: Bernhard von Clairvaux in Martin Luthers Schriften.* Mainz: Zabern, 1993.
Bizer, E., *Fides ex auditu: Eine Untersuchung über die Entdeckung der Gerechtigkeit Gottes durch Martin Luther.* Neukirchen: Erziehungsverein, 1958.
Brady, T. A., "Luther and the State: The Reformer's Teaching in its Social Setting," in James D. Tracy, ed., *Luther and the Modern State in Germany.* Kirksville, Mo.: Sixteenth Century Journal, 1986, pp. 31–44.
Cranz, F. E., *An Essay on the Development of Luther's Thought on Justice, Law and Society.* Cambridge, Mass.: Harvard University Press, 1959.
Dingel, I., *Concordia controversa: Die öffentlichen Diskussionen um das lutherische Konkordienwerk am Ende des 16. Jahrhunderts.* Gütersloh: Gütersloher Verlagshaus, 1996.
Duchrow, U., *Christenheit und Weltverantwortung: Traditionsgeschichte und systematische Struktur der Zweireichelehre.* Stuttgart: Klett, 1970.
Dykema, P. A. and Oberman, H. A., *Anticlericalism in Late Medieval and Early Modern Europe.* Leiden: Brill, 1993.
Ebeling, G., *Evangelische Evangelienauslegung, eine Unterschung zu Luthers Hermeneutik.* Munich: Lempp, 1942.
Edwards, M. U., Jr., *Luther and the False Brethren.* Stanford, Calif.: Stanford University Press, 1975.

Flogaus, R., *Theosis bei Palamas und Luther*. Göttingen: Vandenhoeck & Ruprecht, 1997.

Forde, G. O., *Justification by Faith: A Matter of Death and Life*. Philadelphia: Fortress Press, 1982.

Frank, G., ed., *Der Theologe Melanchthon*. Sigmaringen: Thorbecke, 2000.

Grane, L., *Martinus Noster: Luther in the German Reform Movement, 1518–1521*. Mainz: Zabern, 1994.

Hagen, K., *Luther's Approach to Scripture as Seen in his "Commentaries" on Galatians 1519–1538*. Tübingen: Mohr/Siebeck, 1993.

Hamm, B., Moeller, B., and Wendebourg, D., *Reformationstheorien: Ein kirchenhistoricher Disput über Einheit und Vielfalt der Reformation*. Göttingen: Vandenhoeck & Ruprecht, 1995.

Harnack, T., *Luthers Theologie*, 2 vols. Erlangen: Blaesing, 1862, 1886.

Hendrix, S., *Luther and the Papacy: Stages in a Reformation Conflict*. Philadelphia: Fortress Press, 1981.

Hendrix, S., "Luther's Impact on the Sixteenth Century," *Sixteenth Century Journal*, 16 (1985), pp. 3–14.

Hendrix, S., "American Luther Research in the Twentieth Century," *Lutheran Quarterly*, 15 (2001), pp. 1–23.

Hendrix, S., "Martin Luther und die Lutherischen Bekenntnisschriften in der englischsprachigen Forschung seit 1983," *Lutherjahrbuch*, 68 (2001), pp. 115–36.

Holl, K., "Die Rechtfertigungslehre in Luthers Vorlesung über den Römerbrief," in *Gesammelte Aufsätze zur Kirchengeschichte*. Vol. 1: *Luther*. Tübingen: Mohr/Siebeck, 1921, pp. 111–54.

Hsia, R. P., ed., *The German People and the Reformation*. Ithaca, NY: Cornell University Press, 1988.

Janz, D., *Luther on Thomas Aquinas*. Stuttgart: Steiner, 1989.

Junghans, H., ed., *Leben und Werk Martin Luthers von 1526 bis 1546*, 2 vols. Göttingen: Vandenhoeck & Ruprecht, 1983.

Junghans, H., *Der junge Luther und die Humanisten*. Göttingen: Vandenhoeck & Ruprecht, 1985.

Karant-Nunn, S., *Luther's Pastors: The Reformation in the Ernstine Countryside*. Philadelphia: American Philosophical Society, 1979.

Kittelson, J. M., "Successes and Failures in the German Reformation: The Report from Strasbourg," *Archiv für Reformationsgeschichte*, 73 (1982), pp. 153–75.

Köhler, W., *Zwingli und Luther: Ihr Streit über das Abendmahl nach seinen politischen und religiösen Beziehungen*, 2 vols. Leipzig: Heinsius, 1924, 1953.

Kohnle, A., *Reichstag und Reformation: Kaiserliche und ständische Religionspolitik von den Anfängen der Causa Lutheri bis zum Nürnberger Religionsfrieden*. Gütersloh: Gütersloher Verlagshaus, 2001.

Kolb, R., *Martin Luther as Prophet, Teacher, and Hero: Images of the Reformer, 1520–1620*. Grand Rapids, Mich.: Baker, 1999.

Köstlin, J., *The Life of Martin Luther*, trans. John G. Morris, 2 vols. Philadelphia: Lutheran Publication Society, 1883 (German, 1875).

Köstlin, J., *The Theology of Martin Luther*, trans. Charles E. Hay. Philadelphia: Lutheran Publication Society, 1897 (German, 1863).

Lau, F., "Der Bauernkrieg und das angebliche Ende der lutherischen Reformation als spontaner Volksbewegung," *Lutherjahrbuch*, 26 (1959), pp. 109–34.

Leppin, V., "Luther-Literatur seit 1983," *Theologische Rundschau*, 65 (2000), pp. 350–7, 431–54.

Lienhard, M., *Luther, Witness to Jesus Christ*, trans. Edwin H. Robertson. Minneapolis: Fortress Press, 1982 (French, 1973).

Loehr, J., ed., *Dona Melanchthoniana: Festgabe für Heinz Scheible*. Stuttgart-Bad Cannstatt: fromann-holzboog, 2001.

Loewenich, W. von, *Luther's Theology of the Cross*, trans. Herbert J. A. Bouman. Minneapolis: Augsburg, 1976 (German, 1929).

Lohse, B., ed., *Der Durchbruch der reformatorischen Erkenntnis bei Luther*. Darmstadt: Wissenschaftliche Buchgesellschaft, 1958.

Lohse, B., ed., *Der Durchbruch der reformatorischen Erkenntnis bei Luther: Neuere Untersuchungen*. Wiesbaden: Steiner, 1988.

Lohse, B., *Martin Luther*, trans. Robert C. Schultz. Philadelphia: Fortress Press, 1986 (German, 1980).

Lortz, J., *Die Reformation in Deutschland*. Freiburg a.B.: Herder, 1940.

Luther, M., *D. Martin Luthers Werke: Kritische Gesamtausgabe, Abteilung Werke*. Weimar: H. Böhlau, 1883–1993.

Luther, M., *Luther's Works*. St. Louis: Concordia/Philadelphia: Fortress Press, 1958–86.

Luther, M., *Sermons of Martin Luther*, ed. John Nicolaus Lenker, 8 vols. (1903–9). Grand Rapids, Mich.: Baker, 1993.

McSorley, H. J., *Luther: Right or Wrong? An Ecumenical-Theological Study of Luther's Major Work, The Bondage of the Will*. New York: Newman/Minneapolis: Augsburg, 1969.

Mannermaa, T., *Der im Glauben gegenwärtige Christus, Rechtfertigung und Vergottung. Zum ökumenischen Dialog*. Hanover: Lutherisches Verlagshaus, 1989.

Ngien, D., *The Suffering of God According to Martin Luther's "Theologia Crucis."* New York: Lang, 1995.

Oberman, H. A., *The Harvest of Medieval Theology: Gabriel Biel and Late Medieval Nominalism*. Cambridge, Mass.: Harvard University Press, 1963.

Olivier, D., *Luther's Faith*, trans. John Tonkin. St. Louis: Concordia, 1982 (French, 1978).

Pesch, O. H., *Theologie der Rechtfertigung bei Martin Luther und Thomas von Aquin*. Mainz: Grünewald, 1967.

Peters, A., *Kommentar zu Luthers Katechismen*, ed. Gottfried Seebaß, 5 vols. Göttingen: Vandenhoeck & Ruprecht, 1990–4.

Peura, S., *Mehr als Mensch? Die Vergöttlichung als Thema der Theologie Martin Luthers von 1513 bis 1519*. Mainz: Zabern, 1994.

Rieth, R., *"Habsucht" bei Martin Luther: Ökonomisches und Theologisches Denken*. Weimar: Böhlau, 1996.

Rublack, H.-C., ed., *Die lutherische Konfessionalisierung in Deutschland*. Gütersloh: Mohn, 1992.

Saarinen, R., *Gottes Wirken auf Uns*. Wiesbaden: Steiner, 1989.

Saarnivaara, U., *Luther Discovers the Gospel: New Light upon Luther's Way from Medieval Catholicism to Evangelical Faith*. St. Louis: Concordia, 1951.

Scheible, H., ed., *Melanchthons Briefwechsel*. Stuttgart-Bad Cannstatt: fromann-holzboog, 1977–95.

Schilling, H., "Confessional Europe," in Thomas A. Brady, Jr., Heiko A. Oberman, and James D. Tracy, eds., *Handbook of European History 1400–1600: Late Middle Ages, Renaissance and Reformation*. Leiden: Brill, 1995, vol. 2, pp. 641–70.

Schwarz, R., *Luther*. Göttingen: Vandenhoeck & Ruprecht, 1986.

Schwarzwäller, K., *Shibboleth: Die Interpretation von Luthers Schrift De servo arbitrio seit Theodosius Harnack*. Munich: Kaiser, 1969.

Schwarzwäller, K., "Verantwortung des Glaubens, Freiheit und Liebe nach der Dekalogauslegung Martin Luthers," in Dennis D. Bielfeldt and Klaus Schwarzwäller, eds., *Freiheit als Liebe bei/Freedom as Love in Martin Luther*. Frankfurt a.M.: Lang, 1995, pp. 133–58.

Schwarzwäller, K., *Kreuz und Auferstehung*. Göttingen: Vandenhoeck & Ruprecht, 2000.

Sider, R. J., *Andreas Bodenstein von Karlstadt: The Development of his Thought*. Leiden: Brill, 1974.

Spitz, L. W., *The Religious Renaissance of the German Humanists*. Cambridge, Mass.: Harvard University Press, 1963.

Stayer, J. M., *Martin Luther, German Saviour: German Evangelical Theological Factions and the Interpretation of Luther, 1917–1933*. Montreal and Kingston: McGill-Queens University Press, 2000.

Steinmetz, D. C., *Misericordia Dei: The Theology of Johannes von Staupitz in its Late Medieval Setting*. Leiden: Brill, 1968.

Strauss, G., *Luther's House of Learning: Indoctrination of the Young in the German Reformation*. Baltimore: Johns Hopkins University Press, 1978.

Wengert, T. J., *Law and Gospel: Philip Melanchthon's Debate with John Agricola of Eisleben over Poenitentia*. Grand Rapids, Mich.: Baker, 1997.

Wenz, G., *Theologie der Bekenntnisschriften der evangelisch-lutherischen Kirche*, 2 vols. Berlin: Aldine de Gruyter, 1996, 1998.

Whitford, D., *Tyranny and Resistance: The Magdeburg Confession and the Lutheran Tradition*. St. Louis: Concordia, 2001.

Wicks, J., *Man Yearning for Grace: Luther's Early Spiritual Teaching*. Washington, DC: Corpus, 1968.

Wolgast, E., *Die Wittenberger Theologie und die Politik der evangelischen Stände*. Gütersloh: Gütersloher Verlagshaus, 1977.

Wriedt, M., *Gnade und Erwählung: Eine Untersuchung zu Johann von Staupitz und Martin Luther*. Mainz: Zabern, 1991.

Zur Mühlen, K. H., *Nos extra nos: Luthers Theologie und zwischen Mystik und Scholastik*. Tübingen: Mohr/Siebeck, 1972.

FURTHER READING

Althaus, P., *The Theology of Martin Luther*, trans. Robert C. Schultz. Philadelphia: Fortress Press, 1966 (German, 1962).

Arand, C. P., *That I May Be His Own: An Overview of Luther's Catechisms*. St. Louis: Concordia, 2000.

Brecht, M., *Martin Luther*, trans. James L. Schaaf, 3 vols. Philadelphia: Fortress Press, 1985–93 (German, 1981–7).

Ebeling, G., *Luther: An Introduction to his Thought*, trans. R. A. Wilson. Philadelphia: Fortress Press, 1970 (German, 1964).

Edwards, M. U., Jr., *Luther's Last Battles: Politics and Polemics, 1531–1546*. Ithaca, NY: Cornell University Press, 1983.

Edwards, M. U., Jr., *Printing, Propaganda, and Martin Luther*. Berkeley: University of California Press, 1994.

Forde, G. O., *On Being a Theologian of the Cross: Reflections on Luther's Heidelberg Disputation, 1518*. Grand Rapids, Mich.: Eerdmans, 1997.

Kittelson, J. M., *Martin Luther: The Story of the Man and his Career*. Minneapolis: Fortress Press, 1986.

Lohse, B., *Martin Luther's Theology: Its Historical and Systematic Development*, trans. Roy A. Harrisville. Minneapolis: Fortress Press, 1999 (German, 1995).

Oberman, H. A., *Luther: Man Between God and the Devil*, trans. Eileen Walliser-Schwarzbart. New Haven, Conn.: Yale University Press, 1989 (German, 1982).

Sasse, H., *This is my Body: Luther's Contention for the Real Presence*. Minneapolis: Augsburg, 1959.

Scribner, R. W., *For the Sake of Simple Folk: Popular Propaganda for the German Reformation*. Cambridge: Cambridge University Press, 1981.

Siggins, I., *Martin Luther's Doctrine of Christ*. New Haven, Conn.: Yale University Press, 1970.

Trigg, J. D., *Baptism in the Theology of Martin Luther*. Leiden: Brill, 1994.

Wengert, T. J., *Human Freedom, Christian Righteousness: Philip Melanchthon's Exegetical Dispute with Erasmus of Rotterdam*. Oxford: Oxford University Press, 1998.

Wingren, G., *Luther on Vocation*, trans. Carl C. Rasmussen. Philadelphia: Muhlenberg, 1957.

Four

The Peasants' War

Tom Scott

I

In the summer of 1524 on the southern fringes of the Black Forest near the River Rhine and the border with the Swiss Confederation, according to contemporary accounts, the Peasants' War, which was to convulse the whole of southern and central Germany and the Austrian lands over the following two years, broke out. What grounds did contemporaries have for believing that localized unrest – a venerable tradition in the German southwest – would from mid-1524 onwards erupt into a war of liberation, transcending the particularity of feudal lordships to embrace overarching principles of Christian egalitarianism? Were the chroniclers simply writing with the benefit of hindsight? Might events in the southern Black Forest have taken a different turn? Are we even justified in speaking of a Peasants' War at all before the onset of armed rebellion – manifest in the formation of regional peasant bands – further to the east throughout the length and breadth of Upper Swabia in the spring of 1525?

These are nagging questions because the chroniclers themselves chose to pick out the seemingly trivial and adventitious. All agreed that the inception of rebellion occurred in the landgraviate of Stühlingen, a territory largely (though not exclusively) under the rule of the counts of Lupfen, at midsummer 1524, and several saw its trigger in the unconscionable insistence of the countess that the peasants during harvest-time should gather snail shells for her maidservants to wind yarn upon. This may be no more than a fairy tale, but the Stühlingers themselves subsequently set forth grievances of an equally bizarre nature: that they had been forced to gather roots, morels, juniper berries, and even barberries so that their lords could make barberry compôte. The sting, of course, lay in the very triviality of the task: how humiliating to have to perform such superfluous work to satisfy the self-indulgent whim of their overlords.

Yet the Stühlingers demanded to negotiate in the hope of redress; there was no initial recourse to arms. The judicial process dragged on (as it always does) through various fruitless meetings well into the autumn until the case was scheduled to be heard before the imperial court of chancery in April 1525, for which the Stühlingen subjects drew up a list of 62 articles in support of their demands. Amidst the welter of protests, negotiations, and accords which had stamped relations between lords and their subjects throughout so much of southern Germany during the preceding century – culminating in several instances in so-called treaties of lordship, in which both parties acted as signatories on an equal footing – what, if anything, made the revolt in the landgraviate of Stühlingen special? The short answer is that it threw up one of the most audacious, resolute, and militarily experienced commanders of the Peasants' War, Hans Müller, a serf from the abbey of St. Blasien's village of Bulgenbach, not far from Stühlingen, whose endeavors to raise the whole of the Black Forest and the Upper Rhine from the autumn of 1524 onwards (quite separately from the rebellion that engulfed Upper Swabia) were crowned by the capitulation of the Austrian stronghold of Freiburg im Breisgau in May 1525. The longer answer is that the Stühlingen revolt took place in a region of almost endemic military and polit-ical turmoil along the contested frontier with the Swiss. Into these already troubled waters there dropped the depth-charge of the communal Reforming doctrines ema-nating from Zwingli's headquarters in Zürich, or more especially from his radical acolytes in the countryside and neighboring territories.

For decades the example of the "free" or republican Swiss cantons had served as a source of constant irritation to the feudal lords of southern Germany. The attempt by Emperor Maximilian to bring them to heel had led in 1499 to a string of vicious campaigns along the border, cast in effect as a civil war between the "cow-Swiss" and the "sow-Swabians," which ended in ignominious defeat for the imperial troops at the battle of Dornach south of Basel. The commander-in-chief of Maximilian's army in the west had been Count Sigismund von Lupfen, and his lordship became the target of reprisals by the Swiss in the wake of their victory. After 1500 the loyalty of peasants north of the Rhine to their lords and to the Habsburgs as dynastic rulers of the Austrian lands, which lay scattered in the west along a belt stretching from Vorarlberg through Upper Swabia to the Upper Rhine and Alsace, came under strain from other quarters. The French crown quarried these borderlands for mercenaries to fight its campaigns in Italy (Hans Müller himself had seen service in French ranks), while Duke Ulrich, the ruler of Württemberg, the Swabian principality to the north-east of the Black Forest, used his fortress of Hohentwiel, perched on a volcanic outcrop dominating the western end of Lake Constance, as the base from which to regain control of his duchy after his expulsion in 1519. Ulrich's intrigues depended upon stirring up support amongst the local peasantry on both banks of the Rhine, for he had no other troops to call upon. For a time at the turn of 1524 it looked as though his campaign might succeed, for Hans Müller and his Black Foresters joined the early sorties northwards, but Ulrich's footsoldiers melted away as their pay was not forthcoming, and as news of the imperial victory over the French at Pavia in February 1525 (with many Swiss mercenaries falling on the field) filtered through.

By then, the Reforming doctrines emanating from Zürich had been thoroughly transvalued by local preachers and parishes in a broad swathe of countryside to the north of the city into a clarion for communal control of the church with openly antifeudal overtones. The issue over which Zwingli and his radical followers parted company was above all tithing, for many benefices had been incorporated not merely by powerful ecclesiastical corporations but by secular lords as well, including members of the Zürich magistracy, both singly and collectively. But tithing in many cases reflected a more general ideological desire for the Word of God to become the template of all human conduct and social relations. When the villagers of Hallau, a Schaffhausen village only a few miles from Stühlingen, declared in July 1524 that they would have no Lord but God alone, they proceeded to demand on that basis not only full congregational control of the appointment of pastors and their remuneration from tithes (which they had already voiced four years earlier), but also the abolition of all labor services and servile dues. That implicit rejection of feudal lordship had in fact already been explicitly addressed in the demands of the peasants of Zürich's village of Embrach in January 1524, who had roundly asserted that nowhere in the Holy Gospel or any other divine text was any passage to be found stating that one man should be the serf of another, or be subject to fines (such as merchets) arising from servile status.

In other words, at the very time when the Stühlingers rose up, their neighbors to the east and south had already embraced a general demand for liberation based on the Gospel. Hallau was to become a refuge for the Zürich radicals in 1525, while the preacher of Schaffhausen, Sebastian Hofmeister, was not backward in showing his support for the city's disaffected wine-growers and fishers, and in encouraging them to forge an alliance with the surrounding rural rebels.

To the west, however, the Stühlingers had an even more potent source of inspiration. The little community of Waldshut, one of the four so-called Forest Towns on the Upper Rhine under Austrian jurisdiction, had fallen under the spell of a charismatic evangelical preacher, Balthasar Hubmaier, who had arrived in the town as early as 1521, after a checkered career in Regensburg, where he had led calls in 1519 for the expulsion of Jews from the city and the destruction of their synagogue; the church erected on the site and dedicated to the Virgin became a popular place of pilgrimage. During his sojourn in Waldshut Hubmaier's own theological convictions underwent a radical transformation. By 1523 he had become an ardent follower of Zwingli, but by the end of that year it transpired that his sympathies lay more with the radical Congregationalists (such as Hofmeister), whose stance on tithing he fully shared. It was these contacts with the Zürich radicals which led Hubmaier ultimately to break with Zwingli and embrace Anabaptism, he himself being rebaptized at Easter 1525.

During the summer months of 1524 while negotiations were under way, detachments of rebellious Stühlingers twice marched to Waldshut in full array under their commander Hans Müller, on the second occasion, according to older accounts, in order to conclude an evangelical brotherhood with the citizenry. The fusion of secular protest and spiritual liberation – the hallmark of the Peasants' War as it swept through Germany – seems encapsulated in these actions. And that is certainly how the Austrian authorities, as upholders of the Catholic faith, saw it. At the beginning of June 1524 the Austrian military commander of the four Forest Towns warned that any failure to suppress the religious movement in Waldshut would soon lead to open revolt in the other Forest Towns and throughout the Black Forest as a whole. A month later, the Austrian roving ambassador, Veit Suter, outlined the danger posed by the evangelical adherents in Zürich, Schaffhausen, and Appenzell: in parts of Zürich's territory iconoclasm was in full swing, while the Reforming preacher of Konstanz, Jakob Windner, was denouncing from his pulpit all princes as tyrants. Within a few days Suter's fears had become a self-fulfilling prophecy, as peasants from the Thurgau and the Zürich countryside stormed the charterhouse at Ittingen near Frauenfeld, setting fire to the abbey (having taken care to drink its cellar dry first) and sacking it. The city fathers of Zürich understandably viewed these excesses with alarm, since they played straight into the hands of their Catholic opponents.

On closer inspection, the links between radical evangelism and social protest, as unrest fanned outwards from the southern Black Forest in the autumn and winter of 1524, are less compelling than the apprehensions of the authorities suggest. The Stühlingers' articles of grievance, it has often been noted, were concerned solely with infringements of their customary rights, for which they were seeking redress under the terms of feudal law. At no stage did they invoke radical Christian precepts to legitimate their demands, or seek to overthrow the feudal order and replace it with a Christian commonwealth. That verdict is broadly accurate, but requires further comment. The articles as they have been handed down are not the original griev-ances of June 1524, but rather the *pièces justificatives* of their suit before the imper-ial court of chancery, whose procedures would not have admitted claims grounded in divine law. At the end of their submission the peasants nevertheless came quite close to an overarching legitimating principle when they expressed the hope that their demands would be judged in the light of "godly, natural equity, reason, and under-standing." Moreover, although the bulk of their demands was quite specific in char-acter, Article 59 demanded the complete abolition of serfdom (even though no general justification was advanced).

Yet actions frequently speak louder than words. The Stühlingers' continuing tru-culence in the months after midsummer, and the repeated breakdown of negotia-tions in Schaffhausen, must surely indicate that something more than the rectifica-tion of local grievances was at stake. The truth is that the Stühlingers were split. When news of an agreement between Count Georg von Lupfen and 22 delegates from the landgraviate on September 10 reached the armed contingent under Hans Müller, fresh from its second march to Waldshut, there was uproar. Any acceptance of its terms, which involved swearing a renewed oath of fealty and surrendering their banner, was rejected out of hand by Müller's followers, so that the peasant negotia-tors abandoned any hope of compliance under the threat of coercion.

From his subsequent actions it is quite clear that Hans Müller was bent from the outset upon turning the Stühlingen uprising into a general war of liberation, in which the marches to Waldshut were a calculated act of defiance, designed to demonstrate the parlousness of the authorities' response and to strike a propaganda blow for his cause. At the beginning of October Müller began his campaign in earnest, embark-ing upon a sweeping march northwards to rally support from subjects of the abbey of St. Blasien in the Black Forest and peasants from the lordships of Fürstenberg and Schellenberg on its eastern fringes. In early December he led a second expeditionary force, with peasants from the landgraviate of Klettgau bordering Stühlingen to the southeast in tow, through the Black Forest, picking up recruits all the way, whose openly military intent was revealed when it laid siege to the abbey of St. Trudpert on the western slopes of the Black Forest overlooking the Upper Rhine, and plun-dered its inventory. By then peasants in the Baar to the east of the Black Forest, including subjects of the Austrian town of Villingen, as well as subjects of St. Blasien in the county of Hauenstein, were in open revolt. Müller's campaign had by and large been a resounding success – yet nowhere in these areas seized by rebellion was there any recourse to Biblical legitimation or slogans of divine justice. That was to change the following spring, but until then it seems that Müller's guiding star was the republican liberty of his unruly neighbors across the Rhine, the Swiss Confederates.

II

Although unrest and agitation continued in the Black Forest throughout the winter of 1524, by Shrovetide 1525 mass rebellion began to engulf Upper Swabia; from the outset these peasants claimed to be acting solely in accordance with the Word of God. There was no shortage of preachers in the towns and villages of Swabia to expound the Gospel according to Reforming understanding – Dr. Hans Zwick, the pastor of Riedlingen on the Upper Danube, in the thick of events, was named by the rebel leaders as one of their preferred choices to arbitrate on the justice of their cause – but religious inspiration took wing amongst the laity as well. The peasants in western Swabia south of Ulm, who rallied in the Baltringen band, approached a smith in the village of Sulmingen, Ulrich Schmid, to act as their leader and spokesman on account of his eloquence and wisdom. When confronted with representatives of the Swabian League, who had ridden out from its headquarters in Ulm, Schmid, a lay pastor in fact if not in name, rejected any appeal to the imperial court of chancery, and insisted instead that their grievances be heard under the divine law "that pronounces to each estate what it must do or not do." He was given three weeks – a remarkably indulgent gesture by the League, though it was obviously also buying time – to find doctors of law and Scripture who might act as arbiters. To that end, Schmid traveled eastwards to the imperial city of Memmingen, where he encountered the lay preacher Sebastian Lotzer, a journeyman furrier, who subsequently drew up the Twelve Articles of Upper Swabia, the main revolutionary program of the Peasants' War, with Biblical commentary provided by the city's Reforming preacher, Dr. Christoph Schappeler.

   Schmid's intentions had been essentially conciliatory: he had been more or less forced into the role of the Baltringers' leader and genuinely believed that the peasants' grievances could be addressed through negotiation. But the events in Memmingen forced him onwards. At his back he had a sizable force of western Swabians, and they were joined in the first days of March by two other bands (each composed of local detachments) from southeastern Swabia, the Allgäu, and from the sweep of countryside below (that is, north of) Lake Constance. The Allgäu and Lake Constance bands pressed for an alliance of the three armies, which was finally concluded in the Christian Union of Upper Swabia, though its regional bands continued to operate separately. Yet clear differences in objectives and militancy emerged at Memmingen. The Lake Constance band pressed for the rupture of negotiations and an immediate military campaign, according to Johannes Kessler of St. Gallen, whose account was fed by statements from Lotzer and Schappeler who fled thither after the peasants' defeat. But it was the Lake Constance band, under its allegedly moderate and temporizing leaders, which shied away from wider military undertakings and was willing to sign a peace treaty with the commander of the Swabian League five weeks later at Easter on the field at Weingarten. In fact, none of the constituent armies of the Christian Union of Upper Swabia took part in – or even sought to foment – any general uprising beyond their own region (though some Upper Allgäu peasants did cross the Lech onto Bavarian territory to plunder the abbey of Stein-gaden). Nor did the Swabian peasantry show themselves especially violent toward the seats of feudal power in castles and convents.

In that respect, it was left to two Franconian bands – the Odenwald-Neckar valley band in the west, the Taubertal band to the east – to undertake relentless and effec-tive sieges and destruction of nobles' castles – over two hundred were sacked in the space of ten days in the bishopric of Bamberg alone. The Mühlhausen-Thuringian army further north showed itself similarly implacable in destroying castles and con-vents in the archbishop of Mainz's exclave of the Eichsfeld in early May. The many small bands in Alsace, which never succeeded in forming a united army, were no less passionate in their attacks upon the numerous convents and ecclesiastical foundations strung out along the fertile foothills of the Vosges.

The one attempt to keep an army in the field for months and to march it in a con-certed plan of supraregional revolt was that of Hans Müller and his followers, who by the spring of 1525 had redesignated themselves the Christian Union of the Black Forest. From mid-April (spurning requests for support from their Christian brothers in Swabia), Müller and his men swept into the Hegau, then into the fringes of the Baar, across the Black Forest, and joined forces with the massed armies of the right bank of the Rhine – the Ortenauers, Kaiserstühlers, Breisgauers, Hachbergers, and Markgräflers – to force Freiburg im Breisgau to surrender. But even then, the longer-term military goal remained obscure. The fall of Freiburg was undoubtedly a feather in the peasants' cap, but short of putting its inhabitants to the sword, how were the rebels supposed to neutralize the town? No sooner had the civic fathers been obliged to swear allegiance to the Christian Union, which then moved off to take Breisach and Waldkirch, than they began urgent deliberations over pacification and reprisals. Meanwhile the Christian Union of the Black Forest had turned tail in response to an urgent summons from the Hegau peasants to rush back over the Forest to assist the fruitless beleaguerment of Radolfzell on Lake Constance.

The only other audacious campaign of general liberation, sweeping across terri-torial boundaries, was launched in the spring of 1526 from South Tirol by Michael Gaismair, first against the Habsburgs and their clients, the bishops of Brixen/Bressanone and Trent/Trento, and then rallying to the side of the Salzburg rebels, who, after having inflicted a significant defeat on a Styrian army at Schladming the pre-vious year, rose again, only to be routed by the Swabian League at Radstadt in July. Gaismair fled onto Venetian territory, whence over the next six years (until he was assas-sinated) he plotted further international offensives against the Habsburgs. Yet the beginnings of the Austrian revolt in Tirol were even more local and specific than elsewhere, and the negotiations that ensued over the summer months had led to a provisional agreement, until vitiated by political chicanery and religious obtuseness.

In February 1525 the miners in the North Tirolean Klondyke of Schwaz presented grievances over their working conditions, especially over the practices of the large oli-gopolistic merchant and finance companies from South German cities, the Fuggers to the fore, who held the Tirolean mining industry in a vice-like grasp. Resentment at the early capitalist trading firms struck an especially resonant chord in a part of the German-speaking lands which acted as a conduit for trade from the Mediterranean to northern Europe over the Alpine passes. When the Tirolean rebels assembled to present their demands at a diet in Meran/Merano at the end of May, as well as setting forth the familiar demands for the Gospel and communal-congregational control of the church, they rehearsed a litany of complaints over the commercialization of everyday life, the greed of merchants, the dubious practices of artisans, and usurious rates of interest, themes which Gaismair was subsequently to elaborate in his vision for a Christian commonwealth for Tirol.

When Archduke Ferdinand, in order to defuse the protest, brought forward his proposed territorial diet (in which the peasants were already represented) from July to June, he held out the prospect of a new territorial constitution that would go some way toward meeting the rebels' demands (it was indeed published the following spring, and remained in force until 1532). But for Gaismair this was a compromise too far, and he incited 18 districts in South Tirol to reject it. Matters might have remained thus inconclusive, had not Gaismair been arrested in Innsbruck in August, after complying with an invitation to continue discussions. His escape from custody, and his subsequent intrigues in eastern Switzerland over the winter, where he put out feelers to the Zürich Reformer Huldrych Zwingli, set the seal on a military showdown. A similar chain of events unfolded in Salzburg. After an initial uprising in May 1525, which threatened to spill over into the eastern Austrian heartlands, the archbishop, Cardinal Matthäus Lang, finally agreed to convene a territorial diet to consider the rebels' grievances. Had he shown better judgment by accommodating their desire to participate in the territorial government as a commons' Estate (an aspiration that they had temporarily achieved two generations earlier), the revolt might have been resolved without further recourse to arms. But Lang dragged his feet in calling the diet, and when it finally met in January 1526 showed half-hearted commitment to its proceedings. Out of frustration, the Salzburgers mounted a fresh rebellion, which, despite Gaismair's efforts to enlist support from Venice, Zürich, and France, was crushed. With that, the curtain was rung down on the Peasants' War as a military insurrection. In most areas the revolt had lasted no more than six weeks, from April through to mid-May 1525.

III

A rebellion that seized so many disparate areas of the German-speaking lands is unlikely to have been unleashed by a single cause – unless one clings to the venerable belief that the peasants and their allies took up arms solely to save the Gospel from dilution or defeat. The relationship of the Reformers' message to secular revolt remains controversial in the historical literature, but no one nowadays seriously questions that the etiology of the Peasants' War lay in the profound transformations that had taken place in the structure of rural economy and society in southern and central Germany in the century before 1525.

Several historians have chosen to interpret that transformation as a "crisis of feudalism," but this term arouses too many false associations. The Peasants' War was chronologically too remote from the period of the late medieval agrarian crisis up to the mid-fifteenth century – whose manifestations were a slump in population in the wake of epidemic disease, and a collapse in cereal prices – to be in any direct sense its consequence. On the contrary, the period from around 1470 onwards was marked by a steady recovery in population and in grain prices, and by the growing commercialization and diversification of the rural economy. Even the more tightly drawn bands of serfdom, which the rebels in 1525 were determined to cast off in the name of Christian liberty, can only partly be ascribed to a "feudal reaction" on the part of landlords (as occurred in England in the run-up to the Peasants' Revolt of 1381), and were rather a means of consolidating the political and jurisdictional authority of lords with diminutive or fragmented territories, on the one hand, or with subjects often scattered over a wide area and owing allegiance to more than one seigneur, on the other.

It has frequently been pointed out that the Peasants' War was largely confined to regions stamped by three distinguishing features: partible inheritance; dense urbanization (which encouraged strong market ties between town and country); and the spread of industrial crops and rural crafts amidst an already commercialized agriculture. These were the hallmarks of southwestern and central Germany. In those areas the recovery of population and the upturn in cereal prices proved a mixed blessing. The equal division of farms between all eligible heirs led to the parcelization of holdings, sometimes to a point where they could no longer sustain a peasant family. Siblings, it is true, might sell their share of the estate to enable farms to be recombined into viable units, but that entailed access to credit on the part of the inheriting tenant, and alternative employment and income for the remaining siblings. Upper Swabia, however, the very heartland of the uprising, is commonly supposed to have been an area of impartible inheritance, where farms were passed on intact, usually to the eldest son (primogeniture), with the non-inheriting siblings forced to seek employment elsewhere. The rise of a cottar class in the Swabian countryside and the prevalence of rural by-employment in the textile industry are often taken as a reflection of the social dislocation caused by impartibility. In fact, much of Upper Swabia, at least in the west, may still have been partible at the time of the Peasants' War, with impartibility only prevailing (often at the behest of landlords eager to attract tenants onto their farms) at the end of the sixteenth century. It is conceivable, therefore, that the war in Upper Swabia may have been occasioned partly in response to changes in inheritance practices then under way which stripped many villages of access to land.

The problem of partibility was alleviated (but not solved) in those areas given over to viticulture or horticulture, for both absorbed more labor and produced a greater return from smaller holdings than arable husbandry. But the opportunities afforded by the cultivation of primarily commercial, rather than subsistence, crops at the same time carried huge risks. It took only slight shifts in consumption patterns or changes in climate to tumble such agriculture into crisis. Indeed, overproduction (especially of poor-quality wine grown on unsuitable terrain) could be as much a hazard as harvest failure. The sustainability of such smallholdings depended greatly on access to the village common – water, forest, pasture, meadow – to supplement diet and income. That is why the demand to abolish the small tithe, which was levied on all garden produce, as well as sheep, goats, pigs, and chickens, was so often listed among the articles of grievance in 1525.

Exposure to the market affected peasants in other ways, too. While family farms were rarely alienated to non-kin, the smaller plots given over to market gardening were often treated as a commodity, to be bought and sold at will. That raises issues of rural debt and credit, which the sources all too rarely allow us to exploit before the late sixteenth century, but the dangers of injudicious involvement in the land market were certainly present. Yet the greatest impact on the structure of rural economy and society before the war was the spread of textile manufacturing to the countryside, controlled and organized as outwork by urban entrepreneurs and capitalists. The putting-out system, as it is known, had originally embraced weavers in the towns, who were forced into wage dependence from the status of masters in charge of their own workshops, but guild restrictions on production and pricing encouraged capitalists to transfer production to the unregulated countryside. Although deployed in linen production, outwork was prevalent in the rise of fustian manufacture – a linen and cotton blend – in the fifteenth century, since cotton was not grown in Upper Germany and had to be imported from the warmer climate of the Mediterranean by long-distance merchant companies. This rural by-employment undoubtedly provided a safety-valve in an age of population growth, but it left weavers at the mercy of capitalists as distributors, and exposed them to the fluctuation of markets and fashions about which they could have little knowledge. It also brought rural textile workers into direct competition with urban weavers, despite attempts by town councils and guilds to restrict the later and more skilled stages of production (with greater added value) to themselves. These tensions bore directly upon the willingness of townsfolk and countryfolk to make common cause in 1525.

Few of these tensions at grassroots level, perhaps understandably, surface in the rebels' main programs of demands: the pressing need was to stand shoulder to shoulder in the face of the lords' reprisals. Article 10 of the Twelve Articles does seek the restoration to common ownership of meadow and arable that had once belonged to the community, but whether its alienation was the result of lords' extending their sheep pastures by enclosure, or of landless men seizing the common to carve out smallholdings for themselves, is uncertain. Likewise, there is a fleeting mention of craftsmen in the countryside in the Federal Ordinance of the Upper Swabian peasants, the sister-manifesto to the Twelve Articles which regulated military discipline within the Christian Union and the conduct of negotiations with outsiders, namely, that they should return home to fight if required. Only from the events of the war itself is it possible to get a glimpse of the differing class interests and degree of radicalism within the villages which social and economic changes had wrought. The failure of the tenants of the abbey of Ottobeuren, close by Memmingen, to reach a settlement with the convent's officials in mid-April (the abbot himself had fled) allowed the initiative to pass from the possessing peasants to radicals bent on military action. These, it transpired, were the cottars and landless on the abbey's estates, whose voice had hitherto been drowned out, but who then set about storming and plundering the nobles' strongholds in the surrounding district.

It is self-evident that the Peasants' War was not unleashed by tensions within the village communes alone: the pressure of intensified lordship weighed heavily upon the peasants as well. The most obvious instance was the efforts of landlords and judicial seigneurs to consolidate their often diminutive and fragmented territories and manage them more efficiently. That could manifest itself both in attempts to exercise judicial powers more directly and harshly, thereby infringing traditional village rights of self-policing, and by seeking new sources of revenue, either by increasing feudal dues or by commercializing their estate management (which might include encroaching upon common land and communal usufructs).

Time and again, the peasants' articles of grievance complain of the lords' legal chicanery: jacking up court fines, imposing arbitrary arrest and imprisonment (often for trivial offenses), overturning court rulings that had found in favor of the peasants, curtailing rights of appeal, or interfering in civil suits over inheritance and property transactions. More broadly, the pursuit of territorialization provoked resentment among those peasants who had enjoyed preferential status, for instance, where they had been induced to clear and settle new land. One telling example comes from the county of Fürstenberg, where the counts were whittling away the rights of peasant colonists in the western districts up into the Black Forest, one of which had only been acquired in 1491. Their numerous grievances were submitted alongside those of the Stühlingers for imperial arbitration in mid-April 1525. By contrast, the Fürstenberg peasants on the old-settled lands further east along the Upper Danube drew up only one set of articles (though, significantly, from a commune also acquired very recently, in 1513). And it was largely from the western, not the eastern, Fürstenberg districts that Hans Müller and his Black Foresters drew their greatest following in the campaigns of incitement in the winter of 1524.

The principal means of achieving a consolidated territory with unitary jurisdiction, deployed by so many ecclesiastical lordships in Swabia, as well as by secular princes, including the counts of Fürstenberg, was serfdom. This was a different animal from the servile tenure found on the manors of the high Middle Ages throughout western Europe, with peasants tied to the soil. Rather, it was a reinforcement of judicial lordship by creating a uniform category of subjection, usually tied to residence under the lord's jurisdiction. Whether such servile status was oppressive, and what obligations might be attached to it, varied considerably. In some of the larger secular territories – Württemberg, the Rhineland Palatinate (as well as the much smaller margraviate of Baden) – it was a legal category without degrading connotations and with mostly nominal renders. But elsewhere it could be imposed brutally, forcing free peasants into servility as a means of extracting sizable dues, inheritance fines, and, not least, labor services. That was above all the case in the abbey of Kempten in the Allgäu in eastern Swabia, which at the time of the Peasants' War had been engaged in a bitter struggle with its peasants spanning more than a generation over its recourse to serfdom. Yet the rebels everywhere denounced serfdom as repugnant: the vision of Christian liberty contained in the Twelve Articles was enthusiastically taken up even in regions where serfdom had entirely disappeared!

IV

For it was in the Twelve Articles that demands for the easing of feudal burdens and the desire to make the Gospel the template of human society fused most potently. They embodied, in summary, four heads of demands: (1) communal control of pastors (who should preach the Gospel as the Reformers understood it) and their remuneration through tithing; (2) the abolition of serfdom and servile dues; (3) the restoration of communal usufructs; (4) the removal of legal and financial burdens upon individual tenants or peasant families. In their preamble the Articles refuted any charge of rebellious intent; it was not the Gospel, but rather attempts by its enemies to suppress it, which had caused the uprising. And in conclusion, the Articles insisted that, should any be found incompatible with the Word of God, they would be disclaimed. It is quite clear, however, that the Articles, if implemented, would have undermined the foundations of feudal lordship to the point of collapse. Their moderate language, in other words, concealed a revolutionary purpose.

Yet the rapid dissemination of the Twelve Articles of Upper Swabia throughout almost all areas of rebellion threatens to confer upon them a normative quality that they did not possess. Quite apart from the fact that the dislocations within rural society caused by the spread of a commercialized economy receive barely a mention, in some areas the Articles were modified to take account of local circumstances. That was true in Württemberg, where hostility was vented at the Austrian government of occupation rather than at the local feudal lords, and in Alsace, where the hatred of clerical lords, the attack on the use of ecclesiastical courts to hear temporal cases, and opposition to a host of tolls, excises, and taxes had a long pedigree. By contrast, in the archbishopric of Salzburg, where rural grievances closely paralleled those in Swabia, the Twelve Articles were not adopted at all. That raises the possibility that their invocation was sometimes contingent and tactical, rather than principled and ideological.

That applies particularly to the religious maxims contained in the Articles and embraced by the Christian Unions that fought under their banner. Were the slogans of divine justice and the Holy Gospel functional – not so much the cause of rebellion as the means of its rapid diffusion – or ideological – supplying both legitimation and program to the rebels? The peasants' understanding of divine justice was not clear-cut: some historians have suggested that they saw it in legal rather than theological terms; in other words, its foundations lay in natural godly justice (the order of Creation), rather than the Bible. Its deployment, it is argued, varied so widely that in the end it amounted to little more than the law which abetted the peasants and assailed their lords, a strangely voluntaristic attitude. Even if this view is overstated, it should warn us not to draw too sharp a distinction between the old (customary) law, tied to local circumstances, and the truly revolutionary divine justice implied in the Gospel.

Those who accord the Gospel its full weight in creating a general struggle of liberation spanning regions and classes insist that its ideological force was powerful enough effortlessly to override any tensions or differences of interest that existed within the countryside, or between the countryside and the towns. Yet even that solidarity was not always what it seemed. Of course, anticlerical resentment of the Catholic Church and its wealthy foundations forged a bond between the rural rebels and those towns where Reforming enthusiasm had already given fresh impetus to the venerable medieval tradition of "parson's storms" (*Pfaffenstürme*), violent attacks on the clergy. Perhaps the most striking instance is Erfurt in Thuringia, where in June 1521 the council had been the complicit beneficiary of such an attack, in which local students, journeymen, and peasants from the city's dependent territory had sacked 43 houses belonging to canons of collegiate chapters, as well as the archbishop of Mainz's consistory court. When the great rebellion engulfed Thuringia in the spring of 1525, the council was obliged to admit a huge peasant army on condition that it left the citizenry unharmed – the unspoken invitation being to harm the clergy instead. Thereupon a new bout of looting occurred, in which the archbishop's prison and archive were destroyed. A newly elected council had to submit all its decisions for scrutiny by two committees drawn from the urban guild opposition and the peasants, who in May 1525 together presented a list of 28 articles. Although known as the "peasant articles," in reality the grievances mirrored essentially inner-urban discontents – calls for greater financial transparency and an end to arbitrary taxation and illegal detention – and did not echo demands for the installation of an Eternal Council on theocratic principles, as had occurred under the religious revolutionary firebrand Thomas Müntzer in nearby Mühlhausen. Once the peasants had been defeated, the Erfurt council calmly proceeded to introduce Lutheran worship in the city, to reassert its authority over its territory, and to execute a handful of peasant ringleaders. Despite appearances, there was never any real danger that a "popular front" of peasants and burghers would tumble Erfurt into revolutionary upheaval.

In general, if councils were willing, either through conviction or expediency, to order clerical property to be inventoried, to confiscate church plate, to suspend clerical immunities, and to require the clergy to swear an oath of citizenship and pay civic taxes, then domestic unrest could be defused and the peasant rebels denied entry. That is what happened in Alsace, where imperial cities such as Wissembourg, Haguenau, Sélestat, and Colmar were all under threat, with fifth-columnists within their walls eager to ally with the peasant bands. Certainly, the peasants were able to win over hundreds of small towns that lived in symbiosis with their surrounding countryside, the so-called "peasant burgher towns." But the attitude of the larger craft towns was altogether lukewarm. Almost all who joined the peasant bands were coerced, or were preempting the threat of looting and destruction. Far from being principled alliances in the name of the Gospel, that is to say, communities of interest, most alliances were communities of action, that is, of mutual convenience or defensive necessity, with no active solidarity or ultimate common purpose. Even in Heilbronn, the north Swabian imperial city which opened its gates to the rebels and was to have been the venue of another "peasants' parliament" in May 1525, along the lines of the Memmingen assembly, the ideological clasp of Reforming doctrines, preached in the city by Johann Lachmann, was looser than it appears. One group of malcontents, around the wealthy wine-grower Hans Spet, sought to use the uprising as a springboard for ousting the council and installing Spet as mayor, while another faction, led by the baker Wolf Leip, did seek an active alliance with the rebels, whose precepts of Christian equality and brotherly love Leip undoubtedly adopted through his contacts with the militant leader of the Württemberg band, Jäcklin Rohrbach, rather than by following Lachmann, who upheld the Christian virtues of peace and obedience.

Furthermore, the principles of divine justice, exemplified in brotherly love and social egalitarianism, give us no sure indication of how the Christian commonwealth should be configured in the event of the peasants' victory. Leaving aside for the moment the radical religious program of Thomas Müntzer and Michael Gaismair's vision for Tirol, there is little trace of any widespread enthusiasm for a Christian socialist society, in which private property would disappear. Rather, the peasants were desperate to resist any encroachment upon their property rights and individual family livelihoods. Very few rebels (though some who subsequently embraced Anabaptism) renounced secular politics in favor of a community of saints. Instead, the peasants were seeking to recast the political order in their own interests by replacing hierarchical or feudal channels of authority by horizontal or republican ones. That goal was largely determined by existing patterns of lordship. Where territorial fragmentation was the rule, in Upper Swabia, on the Upper Rhine, and in Franconia, the rebels envisaged a corporative-confederal constitution (as the Federal Ordinance set out), whereby autonomous village and urban communes would voluntarily ally in Christian Unions while retaining their sovereign rights, in a clear parallel with the Swiss Confederation. But where unitary territories with a hierarchy of Estates existed, as in Württemberg, Salzburg, Tirol, and southern Baden, the peasants were prepared to recognize the political structures, provided that the constitution of Estates yielded to a commons' constitution, in which local communes would elect representatives to the diet, who in turn should nominate a commons' council to administer the government alongside the territorial ruler. In several of these territories the peasantry was in fact already represented: in Baden, Tirol, and obliquely in Württemberg. It was particularly in areas of territorial fragmentation, where the rebels had no natural focus for their demands, that negotiations with local lords quickly became pointless, so that the regional peasant bands came to demand a recasting of the political order on the basis of divine law.

Two contrasting blueprints for a Christian society reveal, in conclusion, how various the inspiration of divine justice and the Gospel might be. For Thomas Müntzer in central Germany, the rebellion was the sign that Christ's Second Coming was at hand; during the stations of his ministry he had founded leagues of the righteous and then, more narrowly, of the elect as conscious reconfigurations of the Old Testament covenant between God and his chosen people Israel. But although the leagues offered a disciplined and effective framework for supraregional action, Müntzer steadfastly refused to offer any detailed program for the leagues to adopt, believing that the imminent order of Christ's kingdom was not for man to determine. Indeed, after the defeat of the Thuringian rebels at Frankenhausen, Müntzer turned upon his followers in chagrin, accusing them of pursuing creaturely ends rather than God's purpose.

By contrast, Gaismair's plan for a peasant republic in Tirol was so full of detailed proposals that it has been the victim of conflicting assessments. There is no doubt that the Word of God was to form the legal framework of the republic, in which a university was to be established whose sole purpose was to teach Scripture. All ecclesiastical foundations were to be dissolved, their buildings converted into orphanages and hospitals, and their assets distributed as poor relief. But Gaismair went on to address the economic and commercial needs of Tirol, including the future of its extensive mining industry. Here he went much further than the simple rural arcadia, beloved of so many Reformers, with no social and economic divisions. Rather, he advocated increasing the agricultural output of Tirol by adopting the Italian system of mixed commercial agriculture (*coltura promiscua*). Manufacturing, on the other hand, was to be strictly regulated, with two markets under state control, while artisan production was to be centrally located and supervised by a state official. All foreign mining companies were to be expropriated, and the mines run as a state collective, with the price of ore determined by a state tariff, not market forces.

Gaismair's debt to Zwingli's religious republicanism is obvious; nevertheless, the Tirolean Constitution presents formidable problems of interpretation. Gaismair was not opposed to individual peasant proprietorship, or to the use of dependent wage laborers in the mines, and he said nothing to disturb the native Tirolean mining companies, with which his own family was involved. The thrust of his mining provisions was rather to shore up the position of the labor-employing petty-capitalist mining shareholders against the monopolistic merchant companies of the South German cities. More broadly, there are strongly mercantilist elements in Gaismair's plan, albeit inconsistently applied, all of which goes well beyond a simple Christian socialist society.

What Gaismair's Territorial Constitution shows is how far the Peasants' War could unleash creative energies in the pragmatic elaboration of a new society, indebted to Christian principles but willing to respond to the complexities of a society in Germany in the throes of profound economic and political change. That agenda survived the peasants' defeat.

FURTHER READING

Sources in translation for English-language readers include Tom Scott and Bob Scribner, eds., *The German Peasants' War: A History in Documents* (Atlantic Highlands, NJ: Humanities Press, 1991), and Peter Matheson, ed., *The Collected Works of Thomas Müntzer* (Edinburgh: T. & T. Clark, 1988). The principal modern interpretation of the war as a "revolution of the common man" is by Peter Blickle, *The Revolution of 1525: The German Peasants' War from a New Perspective*, translated from the 2nd edition (1981) and edited by Thomas A. Brady, Jr. and H. C. Erik Midelfort (Baltimore: Johns Hopkins University Press, 1982). Blickle's approach has not gone unchallenged. See Tom Scott, "The Peasants' War: A Historiographical Review," *Historical Journal*, 22 (1979), pp. 693–720, 953–74; Bob Scribner, "1525: Revolutionary Crisis?," in Monika Hagenmaier and Sabine Holtz, eds., *Krisenbewußtsein und Krisenbewältigung in der Frühen Neuzeit – Crisis in Early Modern Europe: Festschrift für Hans-Christoph Rublack* (Frankfurt a.M.: Peter Lang, 1992), pp. 25–45; and most recently Tom Scott, "The German Peasants' War and the 'Crisis of Feudalism': Reflections on a Neglected Theme," *Journal of Early Modern History*, 6 (2002), pp. 265–95. Further reflections on the reluctance of peasants and burghers to make common cause are contained in Tom Scott, *Freiburg and the Breisgau: Town–Country Relations in the Age of Reformation and Peasants' War* (Oxford: Clarendon Press, 1986).

For those who read German, a fundamental study on the social and economic background to the war is David Sabean, *Landbesitz und Gesellschaft am Vorabend des Bauernkriegs* (Stuttgart: Gustav Fischer, 1972); an English précis is contained in the collection of essays by Bob Scribner and Gerhard Benecke, eds., *The German Peasant War of 1525: New Viewpoints* (London: George Allen & Unwin, 1979). Sabean's anthropological approach is taken further by Govind Sreenivasan, "The Social Origins of the Peasants' War of 1525 in Upper Swabia," *Past and Present*, 171 (2001), pp. 30–65.

On the various aspects of religion in the war, see H. J. Cohn, "Anticlericalism in the German Peasants' War," *Past and Present*, 83 (1979), pp. 3–31; James M. Stayer, *The German Peasants' War and Anabaptist Community of Goods* (Montreal: McGill-Queen's University Press, 1991); and on Thomas Müntzer, Hans-Jürgen Goertz, *Thomas Müntzer: Apocalyptic, Mystic and Revolutionary*, translated by Jocelyn Jaquiery, edited by Peter Matheson (Edinburgh: T. & T. Clark, 1993); Tom Scott, *Thomas Müntzer: Theology and Revolution in the German Reformation* (Houndmills/London: Macmillan, 1989).

FIVE

Radical Religiosity in the German Reformation

Hans-Jürgen Goertz

The Concept and Phenomenon of Radical Religiosity

The concept of "radical religiosity" was introduced by George H. Williams in order to give a name to those figures, groups, and movements which, though they were part of the Reformation, hesitated to go the way of the confessional Reformation churches: Lutheran, Zwinglian, and Calvinist. They defined their own paths. They distanced themselves from the pressure of religious conformity imposed by spiritual and secular power elites, and, usually under dramatic and troubled circumstances, created ways of thinking and living of a quality that allowed Williams to speak of a "coherent, gripping and dramatic unity," thus of a confessional type *sui generis* (Williams, *Radical Reformation*, p. 1296).

Scholarship on "radical Reformation" has moved beyond Williams's typological conceptualization, and has come to be seen more as extreme religious revolt than as a belated confessional formation. This standpoint can be justified in three ways: First, the "radical Reformation" includes the entire spectrum of radical expressions and gestures of piety in the sixteenth century – violent disputes as well as irenic or pacifistic stances. Furthermore, one needs to ensure that the development of the radicalism of reform renewal is taken into account: the change from aggressive opposition to tempered, frequently even quietist nonconformity, from the inclusive and popular to the exclusionary, separatist free-church Reformation concept. Finally, one does not do justice to the concept of radicalism if it is considered only from a theological perspective. The theological concept of the *restitutio* of the original Christian communalism of material goods may have been a radical one and a bold resolution, but in practice frequently only a compromised version of the concept could be carried through.

This concept allows us to include the entire spectrum of those who broke with the Roman Church and shunned the hierarchical-Reformational pressure to conform. Among them we find those who were stigmatized by Luther as "enthusiasts," "heavenly prophets," "firebrands," and "murderous mobs," as well as irenic mystics like Hans Denck, pacifistic martyrs like Michael Sattler, innovative prophets of tolerance like Sebastian Franck, and faultlessly sedate spiritualists like Caspar von Schwenckfeld. This is the broad and thoroughly heterogeneous spectrum of radical religiosity that existed during the Reformation; a religiosity which is not to be historiographically captured in theological thought nor in dogmatic treatises, but rather in words and gestures, rituals, signs, and deeds, insofar as these effect, engage with, and attempt to vanquish the social reality that gives rise to them. The religiosity of the "radical Reformation," seen in this way, is the manifestation of a "utopian intention."

The radical tendencies that appeared in the so-called mainstream Reformation are not the subject of this enquiry – they belong in the early history of the Lutheran and reformed confessions. However, the authors of pamphlets like Heinrich von Kettenbach and Johann Rot-Locher, who publicized evangelical ideas in the context of strong anticlerical sentiments and language, should certainly be included; so too should the communal Reformation, in which the religiosity of the "masses" took on a social form.

Radical religiosity is a feature of Reformation movements that had not yet taken on a firm shape, that were still full of contradictions and illogic, were tentative and experimental, and therefore can hardly be defined in any conclusive way. Wolfhart Pannenberg described this type of piety in the context of which the doctrine of justification developed, as follows:

> The Reformation can be regarded in some ways as a new form of the striving for direct contact with God – a striving that always stood in a critical relation to the system of clerical mediation, if often only implicitly.

The framework of this type of piety, which Pannenberg sees as originating as early as the late Middle Ages, could give birth to Luther's doctrine of justification as much as to the spiritually inspired consciousness of the radicals. This commonality makes it difficult to describe radical religiosity as a singular, circumscribed spirituality, which can be differentiated from the Lutheran and reformed *praxis pietatis*, especially with reference to the period in which Luther's, Zwingli's, Bucher's, and Calvin's theological impulses initially mobilized Reformational impulses, but had not yet found any institutionalized grounding in states and territories. This presents us with an unavoidably confusing array of interconnected phenomena – and yet there are attitudes, words, and gestures that do allow us to distinguish the distinctive quality of the radical Reformational variant of piety.

Contrasts in the Social Spheres: Mobilization through the Experience of Radical Religiosity

Disagreements about the renewal of Christianity were the order of the day well before the Reformation. Having said that, the disagreements that took place in the wake of Luther's *Ninety-Five Theses* of 1517 were markedly more impassioned and embittered. They also involved significantly broader segments of the population. Faith or actions, there is no third choice: elect or damned, light or darkness, Christ or Belial, the Kingdom of Christ or that of the Antichrist – such dualisms confront anybody who casts even the most casual glance at the texts of the early Reformation. An uneducated member of the laity gave it its simplest expression, when he contributed to the Eucharistic debates of his day in 1527: "The last supper of Christ and the papestry are as different as black and white." This is how the decisive question of his day was described by Andreas Bodenstein of Karlstadt in a woodcut by Lukas Cranach the Elder.

Word and counter-word, image and counter-image, presented themselves as ways of comprehending the situation in which the long-smoldering debates of the late Middle Ages suddenly became entangled, came to a climax, and were dramatically enacted in spectacular ways. "This is the age of the Antichrist," wrote Thomas Müntzer to Nikolas Hausmann in 1521, giving expression to a general belief. It was believed that the apocalyptic chaos and tribulation had descended, and that they were taking the course that was prophesied in the Scriptures (Matthew 24). The Scriptures served to give meaning to the fears and sufferings of contemporary times, and to comfort the suffering. The world of the New Testament is moving inevitably toward destruction, but a new beginning is already within view.

The negative aspects of reality included, in the eyes of many contemporaries, above all the realm of power that the clergy had established for themselves over the course of the centuries: the usurpation and imitation of secular power, the fiscalization of church services, their imposition of their will upon the laity, the abuse of spiritual powers of sanction in legal rulings, their self-imposed immunity from vows of poverty and luxurious representation, the neglect of duties and decadent lifestyle, sexual excess, greed, and simony. Not alone in Reformation times, but also before, the clergy had been criticized for the fact that it had exercised power over the people rather than – following the example of Jesus – serving them. "Die Pfaffen sind Affen [the papists are apes]," went one widely circulated utterance, because they set all store in imitation of the powerful. Over and over again the "ape-like ways" of the religious was denounced. The priests wanted to be lords, and, as Karlstadt wrote, "to be more highly respected than laypeople" (*Von beiden Gestalten der heiligen Messe*). Although the laity were in part responsible for the desolate condition of Christianity, they had been led to it by the clergy, who should have known better. Müntzer expressed a similar opinion, when he complained about the fact that "all of Christendom prays to a silent God"; nevertheless, he did not neglect to mention that the "temple over the masses had been laid waste by the ignorant papists" (Müntzer, *Schriften*, p. 293). The power pretensions of the clerics lent common ground to criticism that was raised against them from discrete corners, and allowed a strong anticlericalism to take shape. Anticlericalism is the form of action in which the striving for direct contact with God took visible form, "in its critical relationship to the system of church mediation" (Pannenberg, *Spiritualität*, p. 8).

The forms taken by anticlericalism have been described in detail recently, so that these few details will suffice here. One thing above all is important: the anticlerical agitation in word, image, and act is the experiential background in the context of which the dualisms mentioned above become meaningful. These dualisms highlight the disputes with the clergy and play an important role in the quashing of the hope maintained in the early years of the Reformation that the clergy might be able to renew itself, and in the formation of the opinion that the religious hierarchy must be abolished, indeed, as Müntzer demanded, that the papists must be destroyed and "the laity must become our prelates and ministers." Radical religiosity is rooted in this deeply fissured anticlerical sphere.

Laymen Instead of Priests: Spiritual Authority, Receiving Salvation and the Pious Subject

Radical religiosity did not evade the problems of everyday life; rather, it took full consciousness of them, indeed it first took shape in the effort to overcome them. What was often seen as an "exodus from history" (Blickle, *Reformation*, p. 127) was fundamentally only a determined, indeed radical way of reacting to the problems that offered no other solution for some people than to break with established history, in order to be able to begin a new one. The background to the Anabaptist demand to separate oneself from the world was not a flight from negative reality, but rather the decisive intention to overcome the evil that ruled in the world and destroyed the relation of people to God and to one another.

The clergy had become a key problem; nobody obstructed the Reformation more than the religious: the pope, bishops, prelates, priests, monks, and nuns. This obstruction, where the problem became critical, had to be dealt with. Luther attacked the sacramental character of priestly ordination and criticized the hierarchical separation of the clergy from the laity. The walls that had been erected between the religious and the laity would have to fall. Crucially, Luther did not take issue with just any wall, but with the *first* one. This will also, therefore, have been the wall that obstructed the renewal of Christianity: that which was initiated by the religious. In the *Address to the German Nobility* Luther still expressed the hope that he might convince the priests to take his side; Müntzer expressed himself even more rigorously on the subject. He wanted to abolish the papists absolutely, and not just their institutionalized role (even if this was intended only in a hyperbolic sense), because they were, in his eyes, the truly guilty for the soulless condition of Christianity, and had been the enemies of the spirit of God since the death of the apostles and their followers. The clergy had claimed unique possession of access to the Spirit, in order to justify their monopoly on interpretation of the Holy Book and on the right to perform the office of the Eucharist, as described by Luther.

The aggressive attack on the clergy inevitably implied dealing with the problem of spiritual authority. Initially the authority of the pope and of the curial clergy was to be disposed of above all; soon, however, also the authority of the bishops, of the pastoral clergy, and of the religious orders. The exclusive monopoly of the clergy to authentically interpret the Scriptures was taken from them. Luther transferred the powers of interpretation to the Holy Book – which interprets itself. It alone can claim authority over the correct understanding of the Christian faith, thanks to the power of the divine spirit that is active in it, and that leads to truth. The *sola scriptura* points not only to the singularity of the source of revelation, but also simultaneously to the exclusive mediation of salvation. Salvation comes not from the spirit that is claimed by the clergy as a result of ordination, but rather from that which is at work in the Scriptures. The *sola scriptura* had found new resonance and had become the sign by which all those who had placed themselves on the side of the Reformation would be known. With amazement it was noted that even the peasants had begun to learn the alphabet and to read the Bible. That is not to say that the Holy Scriptures were read in the same way by all. Luther, Zwingli, and Melanchthon read them differently than Karlstadt and Müntzer, the spiritualists and Anabaptists differently than the peasant revolutionaries. The principle of interpretation followed by Luther was to interpret the text according to the measure of the message of justification, the offer of forgiveness. Karlstadt and Müntzer, on the other hand, were in the tradition of Augustine spiritualism, which had won increasing influence in the Middle Ages, and they differentiated between the letter (*signum*) and the spirit (*res*) of the text. The text, for example, was for Müntzer not the source but rather the revelation of Christ, which joined the divine to the mortal spirit. Spiritualists and Anabaptists also held this belief, although it could take on quite different characteristics in specific instances: in the most extreme form, an orthodox Biblicism in external matters as well as the subjective-enthusiastic calling of "heavenly voices," which one claimed to have heard and which one was prepared to follow. The Swiss Anabaptists were such Biblists, as well as the Hutterite Brothers and, in his own way, Menno Simons. The Appenzeller Prophets and the Uttenreuther Dreamers were enthusiasts; between them, maintaining a balance between spirit and letter, stood Pilgrim Marpeck. The two tendencies coalesced in Müntzer, who prescribed "practicing the holy books daily with singing, reading and preaching," as well as paying equal attention to the revelations of the divine spirit in dreams and visions (Müntzer, *Schriften*, p. 242) – an anticipation of the promise of eternal salvation being seen in the fact that the spirit of God poured out through all people (Joel 3).

This use of the Scriptures was radical, insofar as it claimed to proceed without help ("ohne Mittel"), that is, without the alphabet that was appropriate to mortals, and without the salvation-mediating priests or theologians. Luther had, however, repudiated this radical understanding of Scripture. He too believed, according to the *Magnificat* of 1521, that the Word of God would be revealed to people without mediation, indeed directly through the spirit of God; but not without the help of someone who was educated enough to interpret the Scriptures according to the hermeneutic rules – and not only educated, but also with a vocation for that activity. Along with this Luther warned against the arbitrariness that could become a feature of dealing with the Scriptures, if the borders between the subject and object of cognizance were not carefully observed. The defendants of spiritualistic Scriptural interpretation, as it might be called, saw it as the logical conclusion of Reformational cognizance of how to receive salvation directly from God, without recourse to any human mediation. This explains the unbridled passion with which they opposed Luther's criticism. Müntzer complained about the fact that the papists had not only stuffed the mouths of the laity, but also that of God, and that they prayed to a mute God. For him it was a question of the speaking God in the soul's abyss. Liberation from the clergy meant freedom of expression, in addition to taking personal responsibility for religious practice: reading the Scriptures oneself, actively offering oneself to the Holy Spirit and living one's life according to God's will. For Müntzer this meant exchanging the fear of mortal dominion for the fear of God, which would lead people back into the divine order from which they had strayed. For Karlstadt, it meant throwing off one's robes and starting a new life on the land, in the garb of a farmer, in order to work for the Reformation as part of the communal spirit. For the peasant revolutionaries, it meant shaping their social and economic relations to land and to territorial authorities according to the dictates of the Scriptures, for example by abolishing serfdom, and above all by autonomously arranging their own spiritual needs. For Anabaptists, it meant becoming disciples of Jesus, individually or collectively, often including the willingness to become a martyr. For spiritualists, it meant concentration on their inner lives, renouncing all exterior trappings and giving consideration only to the spiritual relation to God and to spiritual comrades. For Antitrinitarians, it meant opposing oneself to Trinitarian speculation and leading a life of simple morality. In this way there arose a piety which, although it took various forms, in general had the traits of a heightened individualism, specifically a subjectification or personalization of religious practice, and a consequential importance of the laity. As *homo religiosus* or *homo spiritualis*, the priest had refused this entire line of development; the religious ideal expressed by these concepts was now developed by pious members of the laity. Thus neither the dogmatic tracts nor the grand religious truths were the subject of theological exclusivity. The anti-intellectualism so typical of the radical Reformation also took root here: "the educated, who do not recognize eternity, are reversers of the Scriptures" (Krebs and Rott, *Quellen*, vol. 7, p. 139). The idiomatic catchword "Gelehrten den Verkehrten" (learned, perverted) had become widely used, as had the derogatory terms "Schriftgelehrten" (textually educated, i.e., educated from texts) and "Schriftstehlern" (Scripture stealers). Anticlerical sentiment was transferred from the priests to the educated, to the scholarly reformer. In the eyes of Karlstadt and Müntzer, the Wittenberg reformer had become the "new pope," who monopolized the interpretation of the Holy Scriptures as the Roman pope had once done. Thus throughout this spectrum a religiosity that was determined by anticlerically conceived contrasts was demonstrated: type (priest) and anti-type (laity). The former is repressed, marginalized, or eliminated, while the latter is built up.

This rhetorical structure, grounded in concrete experience, is the foundation for most of the opinions expressed by the radicals. This observation applies, for example, to differences in understanding justification. Luther's view was of a predominantly imputative character, that is, the believer was justified, but his status was not transformed to righteousness. He continued to languish in the status of a sinner. In contrast, Karlstadt, Müntzer, Anabaptists, and spiritualists refuted the Catholic doctrine of good works and posited a justification that was effective, that changed people internally, and that must be externally demonstrable. Menno Simons, for example, spoke of the "Rechtveerdigmakinge." Sebastian Franck expressed a similar idea in his talk of rebirth, and moved toward a mediation between the Lutheran *sola grata* and a partly "gruff morality." The belief that the righteous were without sin surfaced only rarely, but the belief that sin had lost its power was widespread, as well as the belief that, in the future, one should no longer concede it any power. This assumption reflects the by then already stereotypical claim of the radicals that faith could be identified by its fruits. The manner in which the status of priests in relation to the laity was changed in the sacrament of ordination had transformed the Christian, and distinguished him from the unbeliever, and above all from the clergy. This is the foundation for the intensely new notion of the individual's personal religiousness: a person who is told that the divine spirit transforms him internally, and of whom it is expected that he will contribute to it through acts of mortification, and that the transformation will be fully realized, becomes more intensively conscious of his own singularity than if he is told that his sinful self will henceforth be overlooked. This played a major role in the fact that women felt encouraged to take an active part in the Reformation process – above all in the Peasants' War and the Anabaptist movement. They participated in anticlerical agitation, they often took up arms, they became preachers and missionaries, they operated subversive communication networks, they hid and sheltered the persecuted, they supported their husbands, and they often left them when the spiritual harmony between them was disturbed. This certainly demonstrates a deeply rooted spiritual tendency toward egalitarianism, which also benefited women. This was not to have a prolonged effect, however. Patriarchal structures were stronger and swiftly shook these early moves toward the emancipation of women. On the other hand, the emergence of radical women was notable enough that the higher authorities indicated their concern, and sometimes even noted a particularly feminine affinity to mystic and apocalyptically motivated subversiveness: "[the spirit of Müntzer] always so formed in female persons that it effects more damage there than it does in men" (Fuchs, *Akten*, vol. 2, p. 478). The observation of individual religiosity is the foundation for strict morality, the following of Christ, or Christianity of action, in short, for the ethicization of faith. It is also the foundation for Anabaptist separatism: the separation from the world, that is, from evil, and from the opinions of all of those people who still live in sin – including even one's own spouse. The call to world-transformational activism is also ultimately rooted in this conception; this was observed by Müntzer and in Middle and Upper German Anabaptism, which was influenced by Hans Hut, as well as in Melchorite Anabaptism, and above all in the Anabaptist kingdom of Münster. Only the person who is inwardly purified and transformed is called to participate in the divine renewal of the world, indeed, to make himself available as an instrument of this process of renewal: ultimately with the sword (Müntzer, Hut), or without (Hoffman). The renewal of the individual and the renewal of the world were not precisely mutually implicated processes (one did not exactly "follow" the other). The idea that the renewal of the individual completes the renewal of the world is expressed nowhere more clearly than by Müntzer (p. 42), but this concept was ultimately the source of the pronounced consciousness of radicals of their mission on earth. The conception of justification based on change effected can also demonstrate a very different effect: it led, in the spiritualists and spiritually inclined Anabaptists, to Nicodemite, that is, nonconformist, secret behavior (e.g., the postponement of holy communion and baptism by Schwenckfeld and the moderation of apocalyptic expectations in Upper German Anabaptism and around David Joris), or even to an elitist practice of piety among spiritual comrades in complete isolation – unconcerned with worldly events, thus not toward the *vita activa* but toward the *vita contemplativa*.

Radical Reformation Concepts

When God becomes a closer presence, his omnipresence is assured. The borders between the sacred and the profane become permeable; furthermore, the barriers fall. God should no longer be worshipped in temples of stone but in the hearts of people. Repentance should no longer be limited to certain church services, but should rather, as Luther had already made clear, be conducted throughout one's life. The judgment of God on humankind would occur not only on the last day, but rather began with the apocalyptic winds that were already blowing. Where the laity had already acceded to positions of spiritual authority and responsibility, superseding the religious, such separation of sacred times and spaces was no longer tolerated.

The understanding of salvation

Thomas Müntzer followed the tradition of the medieval mystic, especially the suffering mysticism of Johannes Tauler and the *Theologia Deutsch*, and shared the concept of a process of purification that would have to involve suffering, in order to overcome internal sins and to create space for the workings of the divine spirit in the abyss of the soul. The soul became a place of divine presence. This demonstrates the essentially spiritualist feature of the understanding of salvation particularly clearly. Müntzer, although he rejected traditional work righteousness and very decisively the mediating role of the clergy in salvation, also staunchly criticized the fact that Luther concentrated solely on the "honey-sweet" and ignored the "bitter" Christ – who demanded suffering – and knew no better than the traditional papists "what God is in experience." The stress that Müntzer put on suffering in the salvation process was organized in a "Gospel of all creatures" by Hans Hut:

> Christ must suffer in all his limbs (. . .)
>   Nowhere is it understood, that this gospel is preached to creatures such as cats and dogs, cows and calves, leaf and grave, rather, as Paul said, the gospel that is preached to you is for all creatures. (Müller, *Glaubenszeugnisse*, vol. 1, p. 16)

From the instruction to preach the Gospel *to* all of creation (dative) (Mark 16: 15) was erroneously derived the concept of the Gospel *of* all creation (genitive). All of creation is destined to suffer, so also is man, as he can recognize suffering in every creature.

In a similar way, the Anabaptists found the seriousness of the belief lacking in the mainstream Reformation, the deep moral significance of the new understanding of salvation, in short, the "improvement of behavior." They were inspired by late medieval pious repentance and, like Menno Simons for example, were challenged to be reborn as "new men." Here also it is the spiritualist impulse that forms the core of the understanding of salvation. Beyond that, the active, conscious turning away of people from their lives as sinners toward a life in accord with God is significant. Müntzer formulated this caesura as the change from fear of creation to "fear of God," as the return from the fallen to the original "divine order." Menno Simons, who was most probably influenced by the *Devotio moderna*, saw it as the return to a life of obedience to God, and the Swiss Anabaptists as the decision to become disciples of Christ. Balthasar Hubmaier could even quite unguardedly write: "brothers, make your salvation."

It is, in all cases, a matter of the ethicization of faith. Practice becomes the visible preservation of salvation. This tendency was also noted among the peasant revolutionaries in Alsace. Franzisca Conrad opines that the soul's salvation was, for the revolutionaries, "less a gift from God than a goal that can be reached through one's own actions." Human participation in the process of salvation is also unmistakably stressed here. The pendulum can also swing the other way, as when Hans Denck takes up Origenes's heretical idea of the resurrection of all people after the last judgment and passes it on to Melchior Hoffman. Be that as it may: these examples, which point to a curious amalgam of Catholic and evangelical attitudes, fail to explain why divisions and disagreements, indeed even enmities, arose in the Reformation movement.

Beliefs regarding the sacraments: Communion and baptism

The radicals shared the mainstream Reformation critique of the sacraments. They refuted the idea of the mass as an offertory in the name of salvation, and reduced the septet of sacraments to communion and baptism. However, their attitudes to both sacraments put them at odds with Luther and Zwingli from the beginning.

Karlstadt took the spiritual understanding of the reception of salvation to its logical conclusion, and refuted every attempt to view the bread and wine as the real body and blood of Christ after consecration in the church service (the doctrine of transubstantiation), or to conclude a practical presence by privileging what was happening textually (consubstantiation, Luther). Karlstadt did not impute any salvational power to the Eucharistic celebration, in any shape or form. In the characteristic style of Augustinian spiritualism, the Eucharist was a spiritual eating and drinking of the body and blood of Christ, it was a symbolic celebration, the expression of mutual love. It was also crucial to Müntzer to eliminate every remnant element of Catholic belief from the Eucharist. The Eucharistic celebration now had only educational value. It should prepare the congregation to receive the spirit "in the abyss of the soul."

A symbolic understanding of the Eucharist had also been taught by Zwingli in Zürich. The Anabaptists followed him in this, although they placed more emphasis on the communal character of the meal, in which the community contemplated the death of Christ together. The Eucharist became the central element in the Anabaptist conception of the spiritual community. In this meal the unity of the body of Christ on earth was realized.

The Anabaptists also took part in the heated debates about the Eucharist that took place during the early years of the Reformation, and they brought to it a multitude of different and internally divisive arguments, from the incomprehension of simple Anabaptists, who could not fathom the baking of the Lord God in an oven, to the involved and complex arguments of Balthasar Hubmaier and Pilgrim Marpeck. The spiritualists made different decisions. Schwenckfeld, for example, contended that the Eucharist should be preserved as a service of celebration for a time, in order to avoid unnecessary conflict. God was present neither in the elements of creation nor in the external word, but alone in the "inner Word." Where the Eucharist was celebrated, this was the visible symbol of the unity of the body of Christ "and all become one bread and one body," precisely the visible expression of the "fraternal love" in this world. Hubmaier pointed to this aspect in particular, and spoke of the "public expression of Christian love."

The spiritualist understanding of salvation, which refutes every mediation of salvation from without, also had consequences for understandings of baptism. Both Karlstadt and Müntzer were of the opinion that baptism must stand in relation to the internally observable salvation in a fundamental way. Therefore they made the case that baptism should be delayed until the age of at least 6 or 7 years. The radical followers of Zwingli eventually decided, in 1525, to accept baptism as a declaration of faith. For all Swiss Anabaptists the baptism of faith was not only the entry into the community, a rite of initiation, but at the same time a public act in which the baptizee bound himself to remain a follower of Christ and declared himself willing to become a martyr. For Hans Hut and Upper German Anabaptism, baptism was a symbol of the connection that joined God to humankind. It is true of all of them that the new baptismal practice was not the particular characteristic that differentiated them from the members of other churches as such, but rather an integral part of the process of salvation and, as will presently be demonstrated, of their understanding of the community.

Community and community-building

Karlstadt and Müntzer, like Schwenckfeld and the early Anabaptists, wanted to renew the church in which they lived in a radical way. However, they did not want to create any autonomous, isolated churches. That happened to the Swiss Anabaptists only after the defeat of the peasant revolutionaries and their exclusion by Zwingli. Now the Anabaptists had a serious crisis on their hands, from which they felt they could only extract themselves by uniting on the issue of a strict separation from the world, as they did in the *Fraternal Union*. They retreated into their community, which was comprised only of those who, in Luther's formulation, "seriously wanted to be Christians" and who refused the directives of every secular authority. They refused to take the oath of allegiance, to do military service, and to assume positions of secular authority. They avoided secular courts in the settlement of internal disagreements. Ultimately, they avoided official church services, even when bailiffs of the secular authority tried to persuade them otherwise. They gathered for their own church services, read the Holy Book, interpreted it together, celebrated the Eucharist together, comforted one another in prayer and song – all in an unformalized liturgy. They helped and sheltered one another; the purity and coherence of the community was particularly strengthened by adherence to the so-called "rule of Christ."

In Swiss Anabaptism, the experience of divine immediacy, which was sought everywhere, led not to an *ecclesia invisibilis* but to a visible church – a visibility that did not consist in the ritual of the Catholic Church, nor in the ordinances of the Reformation churches, but rather in the depth and practice of the faith of the members of the community, who, despite their constrained situation, did not cease to strive for the best possible church form, a prototype for the togetherness of people now and in the kingdom that was promised to all.

Utopia: Motives and Goals of Radical Behavior – or Making Religious Rituals Quotidian

All of the movements, gatherings, groups, or figures that one includes in the radical Reformation were highly displeased with the condition of contemporary Christianity. This is expressed particularly clearly in a resolution of the Strasbourg city council: "That the Anabaptists, who are citizens, allow contrary words to be heard, which have injured other citizens. Now they are saying that things must be different, that something different must come of it" (Krebs and Rott, *Quellen*, vol. 8, p. 301). Apparently the council was concerned about the activities of Anabaptists in the city and about the unrest that might result from anti-authoritarian religiosity. Although the council had tolerated the migration of Anabaptists and passively observed their missionary activities, the situation could not be allowed to result in a divided population. Thus the radicalism of the Reformation outburst had reached its limits. Its effects could no longer be tolerated politically, even from a secular authority that had itself followed the path of Reformation.

Repentance and reversal, new human beings, and the Kingdom of God, were conceptions that implied participation in the process of change. This applied also to the Anabaptist gestures of refusal, above all to the refusal to swear oaths or to be conscripted. Each one was a symbol of protest and an indication of the hope for better times to come.

These were the grand signs. The smaller signs were less noticeable, but of equal effect, and they pointed to the fact that, for Anabaptists, *everything* had changed. Religious services took on a different character: the mass was abolished, the vestments had disappeared, golden chalices and silver monstrances were replaced by wooden beakers, from which the ecclesiastical wine was consumed. The loaf that was broken replaced the unleavened bread offering. The baptismal font was replaced, like the one in Waldshut, by a large milk tub. Baptisms took place most frequently in rivers and lakes. The community met for service in secret locations, in barns, forests, and caves. Instead of listening to a sermon, they read from and discussed the Scriptures. Thus those among the Anabaptists who took responsibility for dealing with the Scriptures came to be called "readers" by the Hutterites, "servants of the Word." The sermon in the usual sense was too thoroughly a form of expression of the priest, intellectual, or religious who had been appointed by the secular authority. Not only did Anabaptists themselves select their "shepherds," as they were called in Scheltheim's *Fraternal Union* (1527), but they selected them from among their own ranks, and even granted them the position indefinitely, as well as making it impossible to separate themselves from them, or to banish them, should they become difficult. Apart from this, the relations between readers, community leaders, and community members were not strictly ordered. It was acceptable for anybody who was capable to read from the Scriptures and to initiate conversations about them. Numerous Anabaptists roamed the land as emissaries, as the apostles once moved from place to place, and spread their insights among the people – they also visited their own kind, to comfort and encourage them. They were integrated into established groups or communities, and enlivened the missionary strength that emanated from this radical religiosity. Faith was a universal topic of conversation: in farmer's cottages, in the inns, at the kitchen hearth, in prisons. The quotidian not only became the sphere in which faith was perpetuated, it also provided the forms in which faith was expressed and took shape. The religious service, once a formalized ritualistic affair, was now reclaimed by the quotidian – and, during the Reformation, nowhere as consequentially as among Anabaptists. The seriousness of the intention to change everything became very tangibly evident. The belief that everything must change is not an incidental demand of radical followers of the Reformation, but rather – even if not always systematically developed – its essential concept or program.

Resistance against Secular Authority, and Martyrdom

It has now become abundantly clear that the radicals were not primarily interested in the abolition of the clerical hierarchy, but rather in the change of the hierarchical society as a whole, in many cases even its abolition. In spiritualistic or mystically inclined groups, who strove for the internalization of their religiosity and to some extent settled into an unnoticeable quietism, this aggressive intention to change society was less apparent or barely visible. Where spiritualistic-mystic tendencies were combined with apocalyptic imperatives to act, the aforementioned aggressiveness was manifested in spectacular ways. Interestingly, the pattern of anticlerical accusation and confrontation was carried over into relations with the secular power elites, who were considered culpable for the desolate condition of society, i.e., of Christianity as a whole. Thus critique of the clergy was transferred to critique of secular authorities. The example of Thomas Müntzer illustrates the fact that the princes were not criticized for conducting their secular business badly; they were attacked because they were not prepared to protect the God-fearing or the chosen, and to destroy the godless, i.e., the enemies of Christianity; and because they did not take care that their subjects, freed from the need to worry about the basic necessities for survival, were in a position to develop faith and to live in pure fear of God. The authorities who, in this respect, stood guilty before their subjects had themselves destroyed the legitimacy of their rule, and were themselves to blame, if the exercise of power once again fell to the common people. Thus Müntzer could court the Ernestine prince of Saxony, at the same time that he contested Knight Georg von Witzleben to hold any positions of secular authority. In terms of his attitude to secular authorities, Melchior Hoffman took a similar position; he had played a decisive leadership role in apocalyptic battles for the purification of Christianity in imperial cities like Strasbourg. Even in the moderate Anabaptism of Menno Simons, who had rooted out the principle of the overthrow of secular power espoused by the Anabaptists in Münster, and from the militant-apocalyptic Anabaptists in the Netherlands, there continued to exist a differentiated dislike of secular authorities. Balthasar Hubmaier lived in very different conditions, at first in Waldshut on Lake Constance and then in Moravian Nikolsburg, and he took it for granted that, as an Anabaptist, he should cooperate with the secular authorities, although not with the ruling house of the Habsburgs, but rather with subordinate authorities. The Swiss Anabaptists saw things differently after 1527. They had separated themselves from the militant revolutionaries during the Peasants' War, and had distanced themselves slightly also from their own roots in the peasant uprising, and had begun to see in secular authority an "order outside of the completeness of God." They followed their own pacifistic route and refused to take up secular offices of authority, as well as military or defense duties. They refused to take any oath of loyalty to the authority and made it their policy to deal with internal disagreements among themselves rather than in court. Thus the attitude of Anabaptists to secular authorities varied very widely. The spiritualists, like Schwenckfeld, had developed a trenchant position *vis-à-vis* secular authorities. In his early years as a reformer, he was one of those members of the nobility who had taken it upon themselves to introduce the Reformation in their own jurisdiction. Although Schwenckfeld was later obliged to give way to certain authorities (in Strasbourg and Ulm) which took offense at his nonconformist piety, on the other hand he did not seek out any conflict with the authorities and was even capable of making the necessary diplomatic compromises as the occasion demanded, as he in turn – as a member of the nobility – was treated with a certain diffidence. Sebastian Franck acted very differently. He was set on a collision course with the authorities, and was, for example, put in the stocks by the city council of Strasbourg after he attacked the emperor in his *Geschichtsbibel*. The authorities presented no fundamental problem to the Antitrinitarians and the Socinians. Their theological nonconformity did not pertain to secular authorities; although certainly many Antitrinitarians suffered persecution under secular authorities.

Radical protest and criticism in the spirit of utopianism were more than the spiritual and secular power elites were willing to tolerate. Accusations of heresy, blasphemy, and rebellion inevitably led, within the realm of the relevant authority, to persecution and strict punishment, in the worst case even to death by fire, water, strangulation, or the sword.

In the second *Reichstag* of Speyer in 1529 the Catholic and evangelical nobility agreed on the so called anti-Anabaptist mandate, which, although it intended the accused to be dealt with by a complex series of legal procedures, did condemn to death those who held fast to their baptism of faith – rebaptism in the eyes of its enemies. This mandate was basically an adaptation of a law from the sixth-century *Codex Iustitianeus*. It was followed fairly strictly in Catholic regions; in reformed regions it was applied less stringently: milder in Hessen, more strongly in Electoral Saxony and in parts of the Palatinate. The grounds for punishment were also revised in the Protestant regions – not heresy, but blasphemy and treason were cited. In this context, the practice of believers' baptism was forbidden by being declared a public offense. Persecution affected the Anabaptists above any other group, even before the anti-Anabaptist mandate was enacted. Felix Mantz was drowned in 1526; Michael Sattler was burned alive after a torturous trial in Rottenburg in 1527. Balthasar Hubmaier fell into the hands of the Habsburg authorities and was burned in Vienna in 1528; shortly afterwards his wife was drowned in the Danube. The Anabaptist apostles Leonard Schiemer and Hans Schaffer, who had been active in the Tirol, were also burned at the stake: both were former Roman Catholic clergy. Many women were also condemned to death. Reports about the martyrdom of many male and female Anabaptists were gathered in the so-called *Mirror of the Martyrs* of Tilman van Braght of 1660.

Spiritualists and independents like Andreas Bodenstein von Karlstadt, Sebastian Franck, or Gerhard Westerburg were sometimes banished, but they were able to escape the worst forms of punishment. Ludwig Hätzer, on the other hand, did not manage to let the bitter chalice pass him by. The most famous Antitrinitarian martyr was Michael Servetus, whose origins were in the lower Spanish nobility; he was burned in reformed Geneva in 1553, on the run from the Spanish Inquisition. It was above all his Antitrinitarian opinions that caused offense, but he was executed as an Anabaptist.

The consequence of radical piety was martyrdom. The circle around Konrad Grebel had already pointed to this in its famous letter to Thomas Müntzer of September 1524. The suffering was predicted and was understood as an integral part of the life of the faithful, not only among Swiss Anabaptists but also in a different way as a process that adumbrated the reception of salvation, in the Cross mysticism of Thomas Müntzer and Hans Denks, which survived among Upper German Anabaptists and in the circles of Pilgrim Marpeck. In this last context it led to a theologically reckless statement:

Fear, need, poverty, pain, hostility, persecution, imprisonment, weeping and misery: indeed suffering and the Cross itself is the path to blessedness, who does not want to follow it, he will not be blessed, no excuse will help. (*Aus dem Kunstbuch*, cited in Baumann, *Gewaltlosigkeit*, p. 184)

Talk of the suffering that leads to true tranquility arose above all among the Hutterites, but also in Schwenckfeld and Franck. Franck's statement on the subject is particularly poignant: "History is the suffering of people, that actually constitutes all theology" (Dejung, *Wahrheit*, p. 268).

Songs about martyrs, which came out of various regions of persecution, from Switzerland, Moravia, and the Netherlands, and which were sung at the gatherings of the persecuted, became widely known. These songs told of the suffering and death of countless brothers and sisters, of their steadfastness and the triumph of faith over the faithless world. They condemned the persecutors, judges, and executioners, but above all they condemned the popes: "How can you so claim / to teach others when you yourselves are dead blind / and disposed towards evil" (Lieseberg, *Märtyrerlied*, p. 218). Thus these songs became a means of communication that, even as the intensity of persecution receded, served to portray the piety of radicals in a positive light and to strengthen their internal coherence. The utopianism that was the kernel also of these songs of martyrdom was no flight from a bad and threatening world. They were the spark in the darkness of suffering, fear, and trembling, as Ernst Bloch once wrote about Thomas Müntzer, a spark that ignited the "zögernde Reich [hesitant kingdom]" (Bloch, *Münzer*, p. 67).

Constant Religious Flux

What has been described as the radical religiosity of the Reformation was, in reality, not as singular and coherent as it might appear here. Radicalism occurs spontaneously and develops a dynamic that destroys traditional orders and moves beyond the limits of spiritual and political agreement and balance. Radical religiosity is of an experimental and diffuse character, thus it can hardly be given a singular definition. The camp of the radicals was anything but an internally coherent unity as Williams contended; it offered, rather, a heterogeneous vision, not out of a lack of ability to articulate itself but as a matter of principle. This principle was the utopian intention. It could be of a stronger or weaker nature, but is characterized by the will to change not this and that, but everything. This will could express itself in a stubborn individualism – it could also be bound together with the communalism of "the common man" and be at work in the early "communal Reformation" (Blickle), it could be a driving force in revolutionary or even terrorist activities, as for example in the Anabaptist kingdom in Münster, the attack on the city hall of Amsterdam by nudist Anabaptists and prophets of doom in 1535, or the marauding gangs of Jan van Batenburg. It could be discharged as the revolutionary potential of apocalyptic images of fear and hope, which were derived from the Holy Scriptures and late medieval conceptualizations, in Müntzer both in the same breath. Only when the utopian intention is defined so broadly can it express the fundamental motif of the religiosity that was active in the radical Reformation. Radical religiosity and piety were characterized by the intensity of their existential concern, by stubborn individuality and practical engagement, which, in many cases, implied the readiness to bear the consequences of alternative attitudes and behaviors even to the point of martyrdom: a religiosity that was often sustained over long periods of time, because all Reformation movements were once, at their conception, radical, above all those that eventually became large confessional churches with confessions of faith, church ordinances, and affiliations with authority. They had to break with tradition, convention, and the law in order to realize religious change. Radical religiosity was constant religious flux.

BIBLIOGRAPHY

Baumann, C., *Gewaltlosigkeit im Täufertum*. Leiden: Brill, 1968.

Bloch, E., *Thomas Münzer als Theologe der Revolution*. Frankfurt a.M.: Suhrkamp, 1962.

Dejung, C., *Wahrheit und Häresie: Untersuchungen zur Geschichtsphilosophie bei Sebastian Franck*. Zürich: Samisdat, 1980.

Fast, H., ed., *Der linke Flügel der Reformation: Glaubenszeugnisse der Täufer, Spiritualisten, Schwärmer und Antitrinitarier*. Bremen: Carl Schünemann, 1962.

Fuchs, W. P., ed., *Akten zur Geschichte des Bauernkriegs in Mitteldeutschland*, vol. 2. Jena/Aalen: Scientia, 1942/1964.

George, T., "The Spirituality of the Radical Reformation," in Jill Raitt, ed., *Christian Spirituality: High Middle Ages and Reformation*. New York: Crossroad, 1987.

Goertz, H.-J., *Innere und äussere Ordnung in der Theologie Thomas Müntzers*. Leiden: Brill, 1967.

Goertz, H.-J., ed., *Umstrittenes Täufertum 1525–1975: Neue Forschungen*, 2nd ed. Göttingen: Vandenhoeck & Ruprecht, 1977.

Goertz, H.-J., ed., *Radikale Reformatoren: 21 biographische Skizzen von Thomas Müntzer bis Paracelsus*. Munich: Beck, 1978.

Goertz, H.-J., *Pfaffenhass und gross Geschrei: Reformatorische Bewegungen in Deutschland 1517 bis 1529*. Munich: Beck, 1987.

Goertz, H.-J., *Die Täufer: Geschichte und Deutung*, 2nd ed. Munich: Beck, 1988.

Goertz, H.-J., *Thomas Müntzer: Mystiker, Apokalyptiker, Revolutionär*. Munich: Beck, 1989.

Kobelt-Groch, M., *Aufsässige Töchter Gottes: Frauen im Bauernkrieg und in den Täuferbewegungen*. Frankfurt a.M.: Campus, 1993.

Krebs, M. and Rott, H. G., eds., *Quellen zur Geschichte der Täufer*, vols. 7–8. Gütersloh: G. Mohn, 1959, 1960.

Lieseberg, U., *Studien zum Märtyrerlied der Täufer im 16. Jahrhundert*. Frankfurt a.M.: Peter Lang, 1991.

Müller, L., ed., *Glaubenszeugnisse oberdeutscher Taufgesinnter*, vol. 1. Leipzig: M. Heinsius, 1938.

Pannenberg, W., *Christliche Spiritualität: Theologische Aspekte*. Göttingen: Vandenhoeck & Ruprecht, 1986.

Schraepler, H., *Die rechtliche Behandlung der Täufer in der deutschen Schweiz, Südwestdeutschland und Hessen, 1525–1618*. Tübingen: E. Fabian, 1957.

Seibt, F., *Utopica: Modelle totaler Sozialplanung*. Düsseldorf: L. Schwann, 1972.

Snyder, C. A. and Hecht, L. A. H., eds., *Profiles of Anabaptist Women: Sixteenth-Century Reforming Pioneers*. Waterloo, Ont.: Wilfrid Lauvier University Press, 1966.

Stayer, J. M., *Anabaptists and the Sword*, 2nd ed. Lawrence, Ks.: Coronado Press, 1976.

Stayer, J. M., *The German Peasants' War and Anabaptist Community of Goods*. Montreal: McGill-Queen's University Press, 1991.

FURTHER READING

Blickle, P., *Die Reformation im Reich*, 2nd ed. Munich: Beck, 1988.

Clasen, C.-P., *Anabaptism: A Social History, 1525–1618. Switzerland, Austria, Moravia, South and Central Germany*. Ithaca, NY: Cornell University Press, 1972.

Deppermann, K., *Melchior Hoffman: Soziale Unruhen und apokalyptische Visionen im Zeitalter der Reformation*. Göttingen: Vandenhoeck & Ruprecht, 1979.

Dipple, G. L., *Antifraternalism and Reformation. Anticlericalism in the German Reformation: Johann Eberlin von Günzburg and the Campaign against the Friars*. Aldershot: Scolar Press, 1996.

Goertz, H.-J., *Religiöse Bewegungen in der Frühen Neuzeit*. Munich: Beck, 1993.

Goertz, H.-J., *Antiklerikalismus und Reformation: Sozialgeschichtliche Untersuchungen*. Göttingen: Vandenhoeck & Ruprecht, 1995.

McLaughlin, R. E., *Caspar Schwenckfeld, Reluctant Radical: His Life to 1540*. New Haven, Conn.: Yale University Press, 1986.

Rempel, J. D., *The Lord's Supper in Anabaptism: A Study in the Christology of Balthasar Hubmaier, Pilgrim Marpeck, and Dirk Philips*. Scottdale, Pa.: Herald Press, 1993.

Williams, G. H., *The Radical Reformation*, 3rd ed. Kirksville, Mo.: Sixteenth Century Essays and Studies, 15, 1992.

Six

The Reformation in German-Speaking Switzerland

Kaspar von Greyerz

In 1500 the population of Switzerland (in its modern boundaries) amounted to slightly fewer than 800,000 and by 1600 to more than 1 million inhabitants. These figures are based on estimates. The population density was lowest in the Alpine zone. In the remainder of the country perhaps as many as 15 percent lived in towns. However, the significance of urbanization for early modern Switzerland should not be overestimated, for we are looking at cities of a comparatively small size. The most sizable among them in the sixteenth century were Basel (9,000–10,000 inhabitants) and Geneva (approx. 10,000), which in the heyday of Huguenot immigration around 1560 even reached as high a figure as 17,000. Bern had about 5,000 inhabitants, St. Gall 4,500 to 5,500, and Zürich's population ranged between 5,000 and 8,000 persons. The population estimates for sixteenth-century Solothurn, Fribourg, and Lucerne range between 2,000 and 4,500 inhabitants. Nonetheless, the significance of this urban network should not be overlooked.

Not surprisingly, the first impulse for the spread of the Reformation in the Swiss Confederation originated in the cities. Zürich took the lead, followed by Bern and, later, Basel and Schaffhausen. The role of these towns as territorial lords facilitated the propagation of the Reformation message in the countryside, as well as, chiefly due to Bern's "western design," its spilling over into the French-speaking part of Switzerland. In all three cities a coalition movement of artisans, evangelically minded priests, and individual councilors ensured its ultimate success, even when it was against the will of the acting urban regime, as in Bern and Basel. However, the Reformation message did not prove contagious in all cities of the Confederation. It ultimately failed in Lucerne, Fribourg, and Solothurn (Zünd, *Gescheiterte Stadt- und Landreformationen*).

The role of the countryside was far from uniform. While there are clear signs that villages surrounding Zürich adhered to the Reformation at an early stage, and while sources from other areas, notably in eastern Switzerland, point to similar rural developments, part of the Bernese peasantry was more reluctant to support ecclesiastical innovation wholeheartedly (Gordon, "Toleration," p. 137).

Zürich took the lead in the Swiss Reformation. Unwittingly, the city's role as trendsetter contributed at a relatively early date to a rallying of the forces of resistance against reform. This was notably the case in central Switzerland, where by 1524 the cantons of Lucerne, Uri, Schwyz, Unterwalden, and Zug, largely in opposition to Zürich's ecclesiastical policy, began to form the nucleus of the Catholic part of the Confederation. Within just a few years, this group was joined by Fribourg and Solothurn. In 1528 Zürich and the evangelical party within the Confederation gained the support of Bern, which was crucial in the further spread of the movement in Switzerland. In 1529 and especially in 1531, the confrontation between the two parties led to agreements, which created a stalemate stifling the further advancement of the Reformation and cementing the confessional factions and fronts for generations to come. The most important underlying principle of these agreements was that of confessional parity.

Major confessional conflict was thus averted in the interest of the political survival of the Confederation, a basic consensus that was to govern the individual policies of its members for generations to come. It was reconfirmed in the Villmergen treaties of 1656 and 1712, which ended renewed outbreaks of confessional war, and was maintained down to the creation of the modern Swiss federal state in 1848. The delicate balance between confessional and constitutional concerns that governed the policies of the 13 members of the Confederation from 1531 onwards is tellingly revealed in a statement addressed to the Reformed cantons by the Catholic members of the Confederation in 1585. In that statement, the initial emphasis on necessary unity in terms of religious belief is followed by the admission that "there is nobody we would rather share our house with than you" (Dommann, "Der barocke Staat," p. 46).

By about 1520, the turmoil of the Reformation reached Switzerland just as the late medieval process of territorial consolidation finally came to a halt. The last full members to join the complicated network of treaties that formed the backbone of the late mediaeval and early modern Confederation were Basel and Schaffhausen in 1501, and Appenzell in 1513. From then onwards there were 13 full members: Uri, Schwyz, Unterwalden (Obwalden/Nidwalden), Luzern, Zürich, Bern, Fribourg, Solothurn, Basel, Schaffhausen, and Appenzell (two half-cantons from 1596) – in the chronological order of their accession. The city cantons fully matched the rural members in terms of territorial expansion.

A second layer of the network of treaties in question comprised the so-called Associate Members (*Zugewandte Orte*), among them St. Gall, Mülhausen in the Upper Alsace, Biel and Rottweil in the Black Forest, as well as the county of Neuchâtel and the Benedictine abbey of St. Gall. In the course of the sixteenth century, Geneva and the bishop of Basel also joined their ranks, although, for largely confessional reasons, they were associated only with individual members of the Confederation. The Valais and the Grisons formed states of their own, which were, however, closely interconnected with the Confederation.

Associate members did not enjoy the same rights as the 13 full members of the Confederation. Generally, they took no part in the government and administration of the shared lordships (*Gemeine Herrschaften*), which were subject to the control of some or several of the full members. Mandated territories is an older, less precise connotation for this form of dominion. The area of Baden and its hinterland (the Freie Ämter), the Thurgau, the Rhine valley bordering on Appenzell and the Toggenburg region, as well as the area of Sargans, were shared lordships, and so were the several bailiwicks that made up the Ticino in the south (Head, "Shared Lordship"). An additional cluster of such territories was administered jointly by Bern and Fribourg in the west. The collectively governed shared lordships were to become the particular "zones of confessional irritation" (Stadler, "Eidgenossenschaft," p. 91). The agreements reached by the two confessional parties in 1529 and 1531 and their underlying principle of parity not only put a stop to the further spread of the Reformation, they also inhibited a possible further growth of the Confederation by way of additional association, which would have upset the prevailing confessional balance. It was only at the periphery of the Confederation that the advance of the Reformation did not come to a halt in 1531. This applies, of course, to French-speaking Switzerland, where the major successes of the Reformation were linked to Bern's occupation of the Pays de Vaud in 1536. In the remote Alpine world of the Valais, as well as in the bishopric of Basel, notably at Porrentruy, it made inroads into the educated section of the population, notably during the 1550s and 1560s, but failed to generate a broader movement. The ensuing decades witnessed the increasing hold of the Counter-Reformation on the hitherto Catholic regions of Switzerland, made evident by the establishment of Jesuit schools in Lucerne, Fribourg, and Porrentruy between 1574 and 1591. At the same time, the Capuchins founded monasteries at Altdorf, Stans, and Lucerne (1581–9). Although Catholic reform was noticeably slow in gaining a hold on the Valais, where its decisive progress had to wait until the following century, the "Indian summer" of the Protestant Reformation nonetheless remained a relatively short-lived episode, albeit with a vengeance at the level of constitutional politics, as we shall see below. Matters were different in the Grisons (Graubünden) owing to the thoroughgoing communalization of the Reformation of the 1520s, to which we have already referred. To this, too, we shall return in the following section.

The Course of the Reformation in German-Speaking Switzerland

In the cities, the century preceding the Reformation was marked by mounting secular pressure exerted on monastic and ecclesiastical privilege. The aim of this urban policy was the gradual integration of the church within the civic community. Similarly, the Swiss cantons managed to expand their control over the church in rural areas "to a considerable and probably even exceptional extent" (Peyer, *Verfassungsgeschichte*, p. 64). This undoubtedly was an important precondition of the Reformation.

The Swiss Reformation began in Zürich. Its earliest public advocate of some stature was Huldrych Zwingli (1484–1531), who had been a common priest at the city's Grossmünster church since December 1518. The simultaneous discovery of St. Augustine's theology, knowledge about Martin Luther's quest for reform, and experience of the plague of 1519, turned him into a reformer eager to combine ecclesiastical reform with social reform, as became apparent, for example, in his fierce opposition to the mercenary system so dear to many Swiss contemporaries. To the common people, especially those from the Alpine regions, the mercenary system was often an indispensable source of income, for the ruling class – chiefly of central Switzerland – one of considerable wealth, as Thomas More amongst other contemporaries knew well, when he castigated the venality of the Swiss in his *Utopia* of 1516.

The leading Zürich reformer differed from Luther in the way he linked inner and outer reform. The two churchmen were reared in differing theological traditions, the Wittenberg reformer in the *via media* (nominalism), Zwingli, like most other Upper German and Swiss reformers, in the *via antiqua* (realism). It is not surprising, therefore, that they should also differ in their theology of the Eucharist, a difference that was to become the symbol for all points of doctrinal contention separating Protestants of the Reformed (Zwinglian and, later, Calvinist) persuasion from those of Lutheran faith. While Luther insisted on Christ's physical presence in the Eucharist, Zwingli, in the wake of Cornelis Hoen, as well as Erasmus, interpreted the Lord's Supper as a communal remembrance of Christ's suffering.

Zwingli's marked advocacy of ecclesiastical and social reform soon won him not only a following in Zürich but also a number of influential opponents among the local clergy as well as amidst the city's councilors. In order to overcome this opposition, he appealed to the city council and was granted a disputation, which took place on January 29, 1523 under the auspices of the secular authorities. It brought Zwingli a decisive victory over his opponents and ensured the continuation of reform. At Easter 1525, this ended with the official introduction of the Reformation symbolized by the abolition of the mass and the official removal of images. Additional reforms of those years encompassed, *inter alia*, the abolition of pilgrimages and of saints' days, the reform of communal poor relief, as well as the city's refusal to renew a treaty with the king of France covering mercenary service. The first Zürich disputation of January 29, 1523 has rightly been claimed to have been a decisive event in the Protestant Reformation in that it laid the ground for the further creation of Reformed communal churches in Switzerland as well as abroad.

From 1523 the Reformation in Zürich was accompanied by considerable socioreligious turmoil in and outside the city, which erupted in acts of popular iconoclasm and, in 1524, merged with the beginnings of the Peasants' War. Together with a series of disputations held between September 1523 and June 1524, it led city authorities to order the removal of all images from the churches under their control. In accordance with Zwingli's stern opposition against all forms of what he considered idolatry, this ultimately brought about the destruction of all organs in 1527.

However, these measures did not suffice to temper the impatience of some of the more zealous sections of the rural population, who expected a combination of a thorough reform of the church and social reforms, such as the abolition of the tithe. The most radical among them joined the Anabaptists.

The polarization between the confessional parties dividing the Confederation increased considerably after the powerful city of Bern adhered to the Reformation in the spring of 1528, especially since Bern, Biel, Zürich, Constance, and Strasbourg concluded the Christliches Burgrecht, a mutual defense treaty. By 1529, a confessional war between the evangelical party, especially Zürich and Bern, and the Catholic cantons of central Switzerland became inevitable, not least in view of the increasing confessional conflict in the government of shared lordships, such as the Freie Ämter and the Thurgau, which were ruled jointly by Reformed and Catholic members of the Confederation. The first confrontation ended peacefully, however, as bloodshed was avoided at the last minute. The first Peace of Kappel of 1529, as we have seen, made the principle of confessional parity a basis for future reconciliation. So, too, did the second treaty of Kappel of 1531. This second treaty was far from beneficial to the growth of Swiss Protestantism. In fact, it was to stifle its further advance within the Confederation. It sealed the defeat of Protestantism at the hands of its Catholic opponents in two battles of October 1531, in the first of which Huldrych Zwingli and a considerable number of Zürich's political leaders perished.

The treaty of 1531 governed confessional matters within the Confederation until the mid-seventeenth century. It led to the dissolution of the Christliches Burgrecht as well as to the reinstatement of the abbot of St. Gall, who had been deprived of most of his possessions by the Reformation movement. It had a particularly pernicious effect on the hold of Protestantism in the shared lordships. It entailed a return to Catholicism in the Freie Ämter, in Gaster and Uznach, and notably in the towns of Rapperswil, Bremgarten, and Mellingen, as well as a partial reversion to the old faith in the Rheintal, and it curtailed any further progress of the Reformation in these jointly governed regions. For a while, the outcome of the battles of 1531 led to a serious crisis of Zürich's rule, especially in the territories subject to the city's control.

In Bern, the autonomy of the city authorities in ecclesiastical matters was far advanced on the eve of the Reformation. It is not surprising, therefore, that when a small but influential Reformation movement began to take shape in 1522, which occasioned the first open conflicts regarding the interpretation of the church's tradition, the city councilors evaded the bishop's jurisdiction and took matters into their own hands. They held a disputation between the Reforming priest Georg Brunner and his adversaries and decided that Brunner was to continue to preach since he did so according to the Scriptures. Ernst Walder has pointed out that this argument was completely in line with the council's late medieval ecclesiastical policy, that the council used the appeal to the authority of the Bible above all as a political justification for not involving the bishop. Did considerations of a religious nature play only a secondary role? It is difficult to gauge Walder's thesis on the basis of the available evidence. But it should be added that it is useful in pointing to the important aspects of continuity in line with other recent research on the political, cultural, and social aspects of the Reformation (Walder, "Reformation und moderner Staat," p. 502). On the other hand, it must be said that anticlericalism alone, although it may have marked urban ecclesiastical policy on the eve of the Reformation in more than one place, cannot have been the decisive factor that eventually tipped the local scales in favor of adopting the Reformation. Whatever their basic inclinations, the Bernese authorities stuck to their temporizing insistence on Scriptural preaching throughout the next five years. They did so in the face of a growing Reformation movement in town whose leading spokesmen were the painter, writer, and politician Nikolaus Manuel (1484–1530) and the preacher and reformer Berchtold Haller (1492–1536).

Ultimately it was pressure from the city's artisans which overcame the opposition of some influential councilors and prompted an official decision in favor of holding a disputation in the spring of 1527. This took place in January 1528 and led to the official introduction of the Reformation both within the city and within its extended territory. A consultation of the rural population (*Ämterbefragung*) was held on February 23, 1528 in the Bernese countryside, yielding a handsome majority in favor of the Reformation. In spite of this, the abolition of the old order for a while met with some fierce peasant resistance in the Bernese Oberland.

Next to the Reformation in Zürich, the movement's success in the powerful republic of Bern had the most decisive effect on the history of the Reformation in

Switzerland. Schaffhausen, where a Reformation movement formed around integration figures such as the physician Johannes Adelphi and the reformer Sebastian Hofmeister (1476–1533), is a good case in point. After the Peasant Revolt of 1524/25, which caused considerable unrest in this city, Schaffhausen did not follow Zürich's example. Instead, the council banned Sebastian Hofmeister, and there was a kind of stalemate until the orderly Reformation in Bern cleansed religious reform from the opprobrium of causing social unrest. On September 29, 1529 the Great and Small Council together finally opted in favor of abolishing Catholic worship in the presence of a delegation composed of emissaries from Zürich, Bern, Basel, St. Gall, and Mülhausen. A week later, it joined the Christliches Burgrecht.

In St. Gall, where the new order was introduced in the spring of 1527, the progress of the Reformation movement, headed by the learned Joachim Vadianus (1484–1551) and by Johannes Kessler (1502/03–1574), was accompanied by uncontrolled acts of iconoclasm, much as in contemporary Basel, following the council's decision on February 23, 1529 to secularize the church of the abbey. The council soon came to regret this rash decision taken against the recommendations received from Zürich. In 1532, in the wake of the Protestants' defeat at Kappel, the city authorities had to restore the abbot's secularized possessions at great cost, and the uniformly Protestant community henceforth had to tolerate the continued presence of the ancient Benedictine monastery in town.

The residence of the prince-bishop in former times, Basel managed in 1521 to cut the last constitutional ties linking its council elections to the participation of the bishop. In the same year, it acceded to the alliance with France along with other members of the Confederation – with the exception of Zürich. After a group of priests began to adhere to the Reformation, the council interfered for the first time in 1523 by silencing a vociferous group of conservatives at the university and by appointing the reformers Conrad Pellicanus (1478–1556) and Johannes Oecolampadius (1482–1531) as professors of theology. While the former soon moved on to Zürich, where he became a noted teacher of Hebrew, the latter was to become Basel's main reformer.

Following the example of Zürich, the Basel council in 1523 issued a mandate enjoining Scriptural preaching, soon to be imitated in Bern and Strasbourg. However, this marked a halfway position, and the authorities were in fact reluctant to take more decisive steps in favor of reform thereafter. The mandate of 1523, repeated and extended in the autumn of 1527 and at the end of February 1528, has been interpreted in the past as an expression of a policy of toleration. It is much more likely, however, that it was a sign of indecision in the face of deep divisions, which paralyzed the authorities as to whether or not age-old traditions were to be rejected (Guggisberg, "Tolerance," p. 147).

In 1525, when the peasantry of the Sundgau in the north end of Basel's own territory was in upheaval, an open socioreligious revolt in town by the unruly vintners, gardeners, and weavers in support of the peasants' rebellion could not be averted. After the turmoil subsided, even a temporary backlash occurred when influential councilors encouraged clerical defenders of Catholicism in their endeavors. But there was a clear change of heart in 1526, when the Catholic cantons of central Switzerland failed to participate in Basel's renewal of its treaty with the Confederation. This experience decisively strengthened the friends of reform. However, the final breakthrough of the Reformation, more and more impatiently awaited by the city's artisans, was slow in coming. It took increasing open unrest within the community, acts of spontaneous iconoclasm, and, finally, an open revolt against the oligarchic rule of the council on February 8 and 9, 1529, which forced the latter to exclude 12 conservative members, before the Reformation could triumph.

In the rural cantons of Appenzell and Glarus and in the Grisons of eastern Switzerland, the principle of communal decision played an important role. In Glarus matters remained in a delicate balance down to the spring of 1528, when individual cases of iconoclasm led to the convocation of a series of *Landsgemeinden* (regional meetings of all full citizens), in which a solution to the confessional problem was sought. It became clear that the evangelical party constituted a majority, but, at the same time, the deep divisions within the community on account of the Reformation became apparent. At the *Landsgemeinde* of May 2, 1529, a guarantee for domestic peace in confessional matters was ultimately found in the principle that each individual community should have the right to decide for or against the Reformation. Implicitly, this amounted to an official recognition of the Reformation, which survived the difficult years after 1531, even though it had not managed entirely to replace Catholicism. A similar decision was taken by the *Landsgemeinde* of Appenzell as early as April 1525. Here, too, the effect of the second Peace of Kappel of 1531 was to stop the further advance of Protestantism.

In the Grisons (Graubünden) a great many communities followed the example of the town of Chur, where the Reformation managed to establish itself in 1527. Chur was also the seat of a bishop who was the major feudal lord of the surrounding valleys. The spread of the Reformation combined in a major part of the Grisons with opposition against the secular power of the bishop and peasant resistance against the latter's feudal privileges, as demonstrated by the Ilanz Articles of 1524 and 1526. These document not only the secularization but also the communalization of episcopal rights, such as those of territorial rule, hunting and fishing, as well as appointing pastors, which the combined peasants' and Reformation movements successfully put into effect. Communalism was so strongly rooted here as a way of life that confessional coexistence within the same villages presented few problems before new confessional identities began to destroy this tradition of *de facto* toleration from the 1580s onwards (Head, "Catholics and Protestants").

Whereas confessionalization, Catholic as well as Reformed, proceeded in Graubünden without the assistance of a central state power, a small but influential Reformed community survived in the Valais into the early years of the seventeenth century without a proper church and despite mounting political pressure aiming at its suppression coming from all sides. It consisted largely of two groups of socially well-situated adherents based in the episcopal city of Sion and in the town of Leuk. Its suppression went hand in hand with an unprecedented assertion of republican rights by the estates representing the seven districts (*Sieben Zenden*) of the Upper Valais against the bishop's efforts to reclaim long-lost predominance as secular lord of the Valais. This reached its apogee in 1613 when the estates required the new bishop, as a condition of his election by the cathedral chapter of Sion, to agree to the principle that "the countrypeople of the Valais . . . are a free people [and have] a free democratic government" (Schnyder, *Reformation und Demokratie* p. 301).

If we turn very briefly to French-speaking Switzerland, it is only to highlight the fact that Bern's "western design" (i.e., mainly the city's politics *vis-à-vis* the duchy of Savoy) had important repercussions in this part of the country, which, short of the lower Valais and some smaller shared lordships, embraced the Reformation almost in its entirety from the 1530s onwards. In the county of Neuchâtel and the adjoining domain of Valangin (which together form the modern canton of Neuchâtel), the indefatigable preaching of Guillaume Farel (1489–1565) helped prepare the ground, so that a meeting of Neuchâtel's burghers on November 4, 1530 officially voted for the abolition of Catholic worship, albeit by a fairly narrow margin. In neighboring Valangin, the territorial lords saw themselves forced to introduce the Reformation when Bern conquered the Pays de Vaud and took it from the hands of the duke of Savoy in 1536. In Lausanne and the Vaud, milords of Bern lost no time in decreeing the abolition of Catholicism by mandates issued in October and December 1536 and in establishing an initially small group of Reformed preachers. Likewise they soon reformed the schools, founded the Academy of Lausanne, and reorganized poor relief.

It was thus only at the periphery of the Swiss Confederation, in the Grisons, in the Valais, and in the French-speaking western part of modern Switzerland, that Protestantism continued to expand after the pivotal year 1531. Considering the fact that the process of confessionalization slowly got under way in central Europe from the late 1520s onwards, it should be added that it was Reformed (rather than Lutheran) Protestantism that consolidated or established itself in Switzerland in those years. Confessional politics around the Augsburg diet of 1530 made it clear that the still very permeable northern border of Switzerland was to a large extent going to become a confessional frontier between the Reformed areas south of the border and the Lutheran ones to the north, especially after the introduction of the Reformation in the duchy of Württemberg in 1536 (see Brady, "Jacob Sturm").

On the Swiss side of this confessional borderline, the role of the exception to the rule fell to Basel. Between the 1550s and the 1580s its clerical leaders, notably the first minister (Antistes) Simon Sulzer (1508–85), pursued a Lutheranizing church policy, which was condoned by the political and social leadership of the city until changing political conditions forced the city's church to adhere more closely to the Reformed camp within the Confederation (Guggisberg, *Basel in the Sixteenth Century*, pp. 45–8). It was symptomatic of the change under way that that great stalwart of Zwinglianism, Thomas Erastus (1524–83), should spend the last months of his life in Basel.

At the prince-elector's court in Heidelberg, following the former's conversion to the Reformed faith, Erastus was an important model for the Zürich churchman Heinrich Bullinger (1504–75), who became leader of the Zürich ministers following Zwingli's death in 1531 and took a keen interest in developments at Heidelberg. In the struggle for influence among Calvinists and Zwinglians at the Heidelberg court during the 1560s and early 1570s, when it came to give the territorial church a more clearly defined structure, Erastus was the personification of the Zwinglian principles of unity between state and church – hence the modern notion of "Erastianism." In the end, he nonetheless lost out to the Genevan interest.

Heinrich Bullinger has been neglected by historiography to date, but he played an important part not only in the post-1531 consolidation of Protestantism in

German-speaking Switzerland but also, through his most extensive network of correspondents all over Europe, in the formation of Reformed Protestantism outside Switzerland, as the Palatine case well illustrates. In 1566, Palatine theologians and politicians in turn urged him to draft the "Confessio Helvetica Posterior," the first truly national confession of faith of Swiss Protestantism, joined by all local churches from Glarus to Geneva with the exception (for the reasons discussed above) of Basel.

The Impact of the Reformation on Social and Church Discipline

The Upper German Reformation (and that includes the Reformation in German-speaking Switzerland) differed from the Lutheran Reformation elsewhere in the Holy Roman Empire in the greater importance it attributed to the "sanctification" of the individual member of a church and of the parish community as a whole (Moeller, "Die Kirche"). The particular emphasis on church discipline (*Kirchenzucht*) and moral control (*Sittenzucht*), which characterized the Swiss Reformation from the outset, was adopted by the Reformation in French-speaking Switzerland and especially by that of Geneva. It was an area in which the interest of church and secular authorities coincided, although there were recurrent tensions regarding the autonomy of the church in this field between the early 1530s and the 1550s, notably in Basel, and later in Geneva, Bern, and the Vaud, and at mid-century again in Geneva. Despite such tensions, Swiss ministers everywhere became the mouthpiece of the secular government's drive for the reform of manners; countless were the mandates in question which the pastors regularly had to read from their pulpits. Although many men of the church would have liked to act independently in these matters, nowhere in Switzerland, not even in Geneva, did they manage to wrest control over and initiative for this reform of manners from the secular government. Zwingli firmly believed in the role of the Christian magistrate in this respect, whereas other reformers, such as Oecolampadius, wished to establish the right of ministers to excommunicate unruly members of the church but failed to get what they were striving for (Köhler, *Zürcher Ehegericht*, vol. 1, pp. 285–92).

There are three areas in which the new emphasis on communal discipline was particularly visible: poor relief, schooling, and the institutionalized control of public morality.

The reform of public welfare policy brought about the organization of communal support for the well-deserving, indigenous poor, who, following the drying up of traditional Catholic almsgiving on account of the Reformation, could no longer rely on spontaneous individual donations. Unlike traditional almsgiving, the new system categorically excluded the vagrant and, especially, the able-bodied beggar. In Zürich, from January 1525, it rested on the Mushafen, as well as the common chest, to provide daily food for the poor.

As far as education is concerned, the Reformation in the cities gave a new impetus to the reform of schooling. On occasion this brought about changes even before the final act of introducing the Reformation. In Schaffhausen, for example, the Latin school was reorganized two years before the introduction of the Reformation in 1527. In 1532, the city council also created a new German school for primary education. This was even more than was done by the government of Zürich, where reforms were restricted to a reorganization and strict supervision of the two Latin schools and the creation of a theological Hochschule. Zürich's German schools of that period, however, were privately run institutions. Owing to space limitations, the fact that from the 1530s onward catechism played a crucial role in primary education can be mentioned only in passing.

The most singular creation of the Swiss Reformation was the particular form of matrimonial court it engendered. This first materialized in Zürich in May 1525 and was subsequently imitated by all major Swiss cities, including Geneva. It was this institution in particular that allowed the Reformed alliance of church and state to establish a control of people's moral conduct, which on occasion did not stop short of invading domestic privacy. It also encouraged the spying out of less devout members of the community, as becomes apparent in the matrimonial court ordinance of Basel from 1533, which promised half of the five pound fine for a conviction for adultery to the city guard, who, through his spying, had brought the suspect person to court (Burckhardt, *Tagebuch des Johannes Gast*, p. 298, n. 70).

In Bern, the matrimonial court called *Chorgericht* was established in May 1528. It was constituted of six members, two representatives each from the Small and the Great Councils, and two preachers. The composition was different in other towns, but nowhere was this institution of moral surveillance manned by the clergy alone. From 1530, a *Chorgericht* was established in every parish of the Bernese countryside, and, only a few years later, this system was introduced into the Pays de Vaud as well. In Geneva, the consistory, which became one of the most important means of Calvin's reform, was founded upon the reformer's return to this city in 1540.

In Geneva, Bern, and Basel, the Reformation's quest for enhanced social discipline led to the prohibition of public prostitution. Where the prostitutes were not banished, as in Zürich, close control was institutionalized. At the same time, the ecclesiastical and secular authorities jointly intensified the battle against excessive drinking in inns and alehouses and at fairs. However, the drive for discipline reached far beyond this. The Reformation in Switzerland led to attempts at suppressing traditional expressions of popular culture, for example, in the clerical opposition against carnival, where people got "inebriated day and night, eat like gluttons, shout like wild beasts and sing inexpressibly base songs," as the contemporary chronicler noted in disgust (cited in Zehnder, *Volkskundliches*, p. 300). In Geneva and Lausanne, similar criticism led to the suppression of the abbeys of youth in 1538 and 1544, respectively. Almost everywhere, church ales likewise became the object of increasingly stringent moral control.

Later in the sixteenth century, this attack on specific manifestations of popular culture could lead in its most extreme form to persecution as witches or wise women and wizards, whose popularity is attested to by numerous contemporary sources. However, it must be added that such campaigns did not differ substantially from those going on simultaneously in Catholic areas, and that there were other forms of witch-hunting, too, as in Geneva, where from 1545 onwards alleged witches were repeatedly accused of having helped the spread of the plague.

These are only a few examples taken from the vast field in which the Reformed secular and ecclesiastical authorities jointly developed their efforts at disciplinary reform. The reduction of the number of saints' days, more radical than in Lutheran Germany, and the introduction of marriage and baptismal registers almost immediately after the final abolition of Catholic worship are additional cases in point. What was the reaction to all these measures? Were they wholeheartedly accepted?

The Appeal of the Reformation

In Switzerland, as well as in central Europe more generally, the Reformation message was conceived by a relatively small number of (largely clerical) reformers, retailed in town and countryside by a more numerous group of evangelically minded preachers, and, finally, received by the mass of common people. This complicated process could and did involve alterations and shifts in emphasis due, above all, to differences in the nature of the concerns of daily life, which gave shape to individual religious experience and thus strongly influenced the reception of sermons, pamphlets, and catechism. The initial confrontation between adherents and adversaries of the Reformation among the common people in and around Zürich typically did not concern central theological issues, which were more difficult to grasp for laypeople than other hotly debated items of the day, but concentrated on such problems as fasting, the veneration of saints and images, priestly marriage, and the like. Confusion and insecurity in this level of society must have been very widespread during the initial phase of the Reformation.

Although Peter Blickle's thesis on the central role of the communal corporation in bringing about the Reformation locally requires some modification in this respect, he is almost certainly correct (at least as far as German-speaking Switzerland is concerned) in suggesting that the Reformation became much more authoritarian and lost a good deal of its communal support after 1525. Following the suppression of the Peasants' Revolt, there was a noticeable loss of interest in the Reformation on the part of those common people who had linked social with religious reform, such as the Basel weavers and the peasants of the Zürich countryside, because the reformers, jointly with the secular authorities, had disavowed such a conception of reform. This disavowal resulted in a "divorce between doctrine and life" (Oberman, "Impact," p. 7).

On the political level this divorce was intensified in German-speaking Switzerland by the fact that the Reformation so strengthened the power of the urban authorities that the traditional *Ämteranfragen* (the consultation of the common people district by district on important issues), repeatedly used by the authorities of Bern and Zürich during the crisis of the early Reformation period, fell into disuse after 1531 – an unmistakable sign of the increasingly authoritarian hold of the cities on the countryside.

The year 1525 also marks the point at which the movement of Anabaptism, which in Switzerland was contained to the German-speaking part of the country, definitively veered from the course of the official Reformation. One of the several birthplaces of sixteenth-century believers' baptism was Zürich, where on January 21, 1525, in the house of Felix Mantz, Conrad Grebel baptized the former priest Georg Blaurock. At the same time, Anabaptism found many adherents in the villages surrounding Zürich. Many of these Brethren were involved in the Peasants' Revolt, which spread across northern and eastern Switzerland at the same time. Disillusionment with Zwingli's magisterial reform combined with deep disappointment about the increasingly authoritarian nature of the Reformation. The result was the growing seclusion of the Swiss Brethren, who separated from the established church and, with their strict rejection of oath-taking and warfare, initiated a decisive departure from their initial radicalism. Soon after 1525, the surprisingly widespread appeal of their movement led to its harsh and cruel suppression, especially by the city councils of Zürich and Bern.

Given the almost total lack of specific modern research, the longer-term impact of the Reformation in Switzerland is as yet very difficult to measure. It is certain, however, that it was more significant in the urban setting than in the countryside, where the spread of the Reformation was slowed down not only by the fact that many evangelical preachers were former priests, whose resonance was limited as far as bringing about the new order was concerned, but also by the strong attachment of the rural population to forms of traditional Catholic culture. Among several possible examples, the "Observations against the Heretics" of the Catholic city clerk of Lucerne, Renward Cysat (1545–1614), are a case in point. They contain interesting information regarding the unabating fascination of Protestants for exorcism and their secret veneration of saints' images and, despite their confessionalist nature, yield *ex negativo* many additional illustrations for the limits of the appeal of the Reformation for the common people.

Markus Schär, however, has drawn different conclusions for post-Reformation Zürich, which suggest that by the seventeenth century church control over individual people's lives was both thorough and substantial. Nevertheless, we should note the fact that his interpretation of the sources concerning cases of melancholy and suicide in Zürich has by no means remained undisputed (Schär, *Seelennöte*). Furthermore, we should not overlook the fact that Schär's observations concern only the urban environment, where the effect of the new discipline may have been felt and experienced more strongly.

To date we also lack a detailed study of the common people's Protestant culture. In trying to outline its contours, Richard Weiss has pointed to the fact that the Swiss Reformation strongly relativized the traditional role of "community and tradition" and that this involved a basic rejection of most traditional popular culture by the Swiss reformers (Weiss, "Grundzüge"). This resulted in a significant reduction in the number of annual feasts and the general asceticism which accompanied feasting as well as worship, to the extent, for example, that playing the organ was only reintroduced in Zürich's churches in the course of the nineteenth century. The religion of Swiss Protestants certainly was less a religion of ritual and much more a religion of the spoken and, above all, written word.

How successful was the Protestant reform of schooling? It has been suggested that it was unusually successful in the Zürich countryside, where between 30 and 40 percent of the adult population in the years 1650 to 1700 were able to read (Wartburg-Ambühl, *Alphabetisierung*, pp. 27ff. and 247ff.). These are surprising figures, for we know that in the mid-sixteenth century catechetical instruction in the same region suffered from the negligence of individual ministers and from the resistance it encountered among the rural population. Unfortunately, owing to the deficiency of comparable sources, we lack supplementary studies enabling us to verify these findings for other areas of Switzerland.

What was the impact of other Reformed disciplinary measures? It is almost certain that the attempt to reform church ales seems to have yielded very limited results.

This is mirrored by the almost countless mandates in this matter regularly reissued by the various authorities. In Basel, local youth in 1609 barricaded the door to the meeting place of the matrimonial court because it had suppressed the traditional nightly tricks of youth during the weeks preceding Christmas. However, we lack information as to whether this was an isolated act of resistance or rather part of a general reluctance of youth to conform to the standards these institutions sought to enforce. The reform of welfare inspired by the Reformation everywhere ran up against the great difficulties presented to the authorities by the dramatic increase in the number of the poor from the mid-sixteenth century onwards – an indirect result of the contemporary demographic growth.

Despite the fact that research in this area is continuously in progress, it is safe to claim that the appeal of the Reformation met its limits where it collided with alternative belief systems, such as the widespread attention paid to judicial astrology or the equally prominent reliance on traditional, Catholic expressions of popular culture. The latter manifested itself in the incorporation of exorcisms performed by Catholic priests, the use of sacramentals for magical purposes, and the participation in pilgrimages, to mention only a few examples (Greyerz, *Religion*, pp. 79–89).

In its early stages, the Reformation in German-speaking Switzerland had much in common with the Reformation in Upper Germany. However, there were some important differences, too, especially in respect of the control of Swiss cities over unusually large territories, which facilitated the spread of the Reformation, as well as regarding the central role of mercenary service.

The mercenary question was a central issue of the Swiss Reformation in the years prior to 1531. For Huldrych Zwingli and his close supporters, rejection of mercenary service was, like other social problems, inextricably linked to ecclesiastical reform. This linkage also helps to explain the serious obstacles the Reformation encountered in parts of the country. For the regions of central Switzerland, mercenary service was indispensable from an economic point of view. Next to the widespread fear that the Reformation would contribute to the destruction of all traditional authority, the mercenary issue was at the heart of the rejection of the Reformation by the political leadership of central Switzerland, Fribourg, and Solothurn (Zünd, *Gescheiterte Stadt- und Landreformationen*, pp. 90f.).

For a moment, between 1529 and 1531, the disruptions and tensions created by the Reformation threatened the very survival of the Swiss Confederation as a political entity, as they were to do once more during the 1630s. The danger was averted by subordinating, in the majority of Switzerland, the confessional question to the imperative of political unity. Thus, in comparison with the neighboring countries of Germany and France, a political solution to religious dissension, which inherently threatened the cohesion of the Confederation, was found at a very early stage.

BIBLIOGRAPHY

Brady, T. A., Jr., "Jacob Sturm of Strasbourg and the Lutherans at the Diet of Augsburg, 1530," *Church History*, 42 (June 1973), pp. 183–202.

Brügisser, T., "Frömmigkeitspraktiken der einfachen Leute in Katholizismus und Reformiertentum: Beobachtungen des Luzerner Stadtschreibers Renward Cysat (1545–1614)," *Zeitschrift für historische Forschung,* 17 (1990), pp. 1–26.

Burckhardt, P., ed., *Das Tagebuch des Johannes Gast* (*Basler Chroniken,* vol. 8). Basel: Schwabe, 1945.

Dommann, F., "Der barocke Staat in der Schweiz," in O. Eberle, ed., *Barock in der Schweiz.* Einsiedeln: Benziger, 1930.

Gordon, B., "Toleration in the Early Swiss Reformation: The Art and Politics of Niklaus Manuel of Berne," in O. P. Grell and R. Scribner, eds., *Tolerance and Intolerance in the European Reformation.* Cambridge: Cambridge University Press, 1996, pp. 128–44.

Greyerz, K. von, *Religion und Kultur: Europa, 1500–1800.* Göttingen: Vandenhoeck & Ruprecht, 2000.

Guggisberg, H. R., *Basel in the Sixteenth Century: Aspects of the City Republic before, during, and after the Reformation.* St. Louis, Mo.: Center for Reformation Research, 1982.

Guggisberg, H. R., "Tolerance and Intolerance in Sixteenth-Century Basle," in O. P. Grell and R. Scribner, eds., *Tolerance and Intolerance in the European Reformation.* Cambridge: Cambridge University Press, 1996, pp. 145–63.

Head, R. C., "Shared Lordship, Authority, and Administration: The Exercise of Dominion in the *Gemeine Herrschaften* of the Swiss Confederation, 1417–1600," *Central European History,* 30 (1997), pp. 489–512.

Head, R. C., "Catholics and Protestants in Graubünden: Confessional Discipline and Confessional Identities without an Early Modern State," *German History,* 17 (1999), pp. 321–45.

Köhler, W., *Zürcher Ehegericht und Genfer Konsistorium,* vol. 1 (*Quellen und Abhandlungen zur Schweizer Reformationsgeschichte,* vol. 7). Leipzig: Heinsius, 1932.

Moeller, B., "Die Kirche in den evangelischen freien Städten Oberdeutschlands im Zeitalter der Reformation," *Zeitschrift für Geschichte des Oberrheins,* 112 (1964), pp. 147–62.

Oberman, H. A., "The Impact of the Reformation: Problems and Perspectives," in E. I. Kouri and T. Scott, eds., *Politics and Society in Reformation Europe: Essays for Sir Geoffrey Elton on his Sixty-Fifth Birthday.* London: Macmillan, 1987, pp. 3–31.

Peyer, H. C., *Verfassungsgeschichte der alten Schweiz.* Zürich: Schulthess Polygraphischer Verlag, 1978.

Schär, M., *Seelennöte der Untertanen: Selbstmord, Melancholie und Religion im Alten Zürich, 1500–1800.* Zürich: Chronos, 1985.

Schnyder, C., *Reformation und Demokratie im Wallis (1524–1613)* (*Veröffentlichungen des Instituts für Europäische Geschichte,* Mainz, vol. 191), Mainz, 2002.

Stadler, P., "Eidgenossenschaft und Reformation," in H. Angermeier, ed., *Säkulare Aspekte der Reformationszeit* (*Schriften des Historischen Kollegs, Kolloquien,* vol. 5). Munich and Vienna: R. Oldenbourg, 1983, pp. 91–9.

Walder, E., "Reformation und moderner Staat," in *450 Jahre Berner Reformation* (*Archiv des Historischen Vereins des Kantons Bern,* vol. 64/65). Bern: Stämpfli, 1980, pp. 441–583.

Wartburg-Ambühl, M.-L. von, *Alphabetisierung und Lektüre: Untersuchung am Beispiel einer ländlichen Region im 17. und 18. Jahrhundert* (*Europäische Hochschulschriften,* series 1, vol. 459). Bern and Frankfurt a.M.: Peter Lang, 1981.

Weiss, R., "Grundzüge einer protestantischen Volkskultur," *Schweizerisches Archiv für Volkskunde,* 61 (1965), pp. 75–91.

Zehnder, L., *Volkskundliches in der älteren schweizerischen Chronistik* (*Schriften der Schweizerischen Gesellschaft für Volkskunde,* vol. 60). Basel: Krebs, 1976.

Zünd, A., *Gescheiterte Stadt- und Landreformationen des 16. und 17. Jahrhunderts in der Schweiz* (*Basler Beiträge zur Geschichtswissenschaft,* vol. 170). Basel: Helbing & Lichtenhahn, 1999.

FURTHER READING

A useful general introduction is provided by Rudolf Pfister, *Kirchengeschichte der Schweiz*, vol. 2: *Von der Reformation bis zum Villmerger Krieg* (Zürich: Zwingli, 1974) and by Gottfried W. Locher, *Die Zwinglische Reformation im Rahmen der europäischen Kirchengeschichte* (Göttingen and Zürich: Vandenhoeck & Ruprecht, 1979), which also covers the impact of Zwinglianism in the Holy Roman Empire. See also Hans Berner et al., "Schweiz," in Anton Schindling and Walter Ziegler, eds., *Die Territorien des Reichs im Zeitalter der Reformation und Konfessionalisierung: Land und Konfession 1500–1650*, vol. 5: *Der Südwesten* (Münster: Aschendorff, 1993), pp. 278–323. Peter Blickle, *Gemeindereformation: Die Menschen des 16. Jahrhunderts auf dem Weg zum Heil* (Munich: R. Oldenbourg, 1985; English translation by T. Dunlap, Atlantic Highlands, NJ: Humanities Press, 1992) highlights the role of communalism in the Swiss and South German Reformation. For the special case of the Graubünden, cf. Randolph C. Head, *Early Modern Democracy in the Grisons* (Cambridge: Cambridge University Press, 1995) and the article by the same author on "Catholics and Protestants" listed above. Peter Bierbrauer, *Freiheit und Gemeinde im Berner Oberland, 1300–1700* (*Archiv des Historischen Vereins des Kantons Bern*, vol. 74; Bern: Stämpfli, 1991) accounts for the different case of the Bernese Oberland, where the communes unanimously rejected the Reformation, which had to be imposed on them. To date there is no comprehensive social history of the Swiss Reformation. The *Geschichte der Schweiz und der Schweizer*, 3 vols. (Basel and Frankfurt a.M.: Helbing & Lichtenhahn, 1982–3), especially Martin Körner's contribution, offers some useful background information, but for additional information some of the recently published new cantonal histories should be consulted, e.g., *Geschichte des Kantons Zürich*, 3 vols. (Zürich: Wird, 1994–6); *Handbuch der Bündner Geschichte*, vol. 2 (Chur: Verein für Bündner Kulturforschung, 2000); Angelo Garovi, *Obwaldner Geschichte* (Sarnen: Staatsarchiv, 2000); *Nah dran, weit weg: Geschichte des Kantons Basel-Landschaft*, 6 vols. (Liestal: Verlag des Kantons Basel-Landschaft, 2001); Georg Kreis et al., eds., *Basel: Geschichte einer städtischen Gesellschaft* (Basel: Christoph Merian, 2001). Hans Conrad Peyer, *Verfassungsgeschichte der alten Schweiz* (see above) is indispensable in respect of the constitutional aspects. For Zürich, next to G. W. Locher's work, George Potter's *Zwingli* (Cambridge: Cambridge University Press, 1976) offers a valid treatment in English. The most authoritative work on Zwingli is still Ulrich Gäbler, *Huldrych Zwingli: Eine Einführung in sein Leben und sein Werk* (Munich: C. H. Beck, 1983). On Heinrich Bullinger and his times, cf. Hans Ulrich Bächtold, *Heinrich Bullinger vor dem Rat: Zur Gestaltung und Verwaltung des Zürcher Staatswesens in den Jahren 1531 bis 1575* (*Zürcher Beiträge zur Reformationsgeschichte*, vol. 12; Bern and Frankfurt a.M.: Peter Lang, 1982) and Pamela Biel, *Doorkeepers at the House of Righteousness: Heinrich Bullinger and the Zurich Clergy, 1535–1575* (New York: Peter Lang, 1991).

For Bern, an introduction is provided by Kurt Guggisberg, *Bernische Kirchengeschichte* (Bern: Paul Haupt, 1958). On Anabaptism and the radical Reformation see George Huntston Williams, *The Radical Reformation* (Philadelphia: Truman State University Press, 2000) and especially chapter 5 by Hans-Jürgen Goertz in this volume. For other important aspects of the Swiss Reformation see the works cited in the bibliography above, as well as Hans R. Guggisberg, "The Problem of 'Failure' in the Swiss Reformation: Some Preliminary Reflections," in E. I. Kouri and Tom Scott, eds., *Politics and Society in Reformation Europe: Essays for Sir Geoffrey Elton on his Sixty-Fifth Birthday* (London: Macmillan, 1987), pp. 188–209, who analyzes the "failed" urban reforms. This has since been expanded in A. Zünd, *Gescheiterte Stadt- und Landreformationen* (see above). Kurt Maeder, *Die Via Media in der Schweizerischen Reformation: Studien zum Problem der Kontinuität im Zeitalter der Glaubenskämpfe* (Zürich: Zwingli, 1970) investigates the links between humanism and the Reformation. A. Zimmerli-Witschi, *Frauen in der Reformationszeit* (Zürich: aku-Fotodruck, 1981) looks at the role of women, but there is as yet no comprehensive modern account of the history of women in sixteenth-century Switzerland. Susanna Burghartz, *Zeiten der Reinheit – Orte der Unzucht: Ehe und Sexualität während der frühen Neuzeit* (Paderborn: F. Schöningh, 1999) is indispensable on the Reformed conception of marriage and the Basel matrimonial court. Heinrich Richard Schmidt, *Dorf und Religion: Reformierte Sittenzucht in Berner Landgemeinden der frühen Neuzeit* (*Quellen und Forschungen zur Agrargeschichte*, vol. 41; Stuttgart: Gustav Fischer, 1995) offers an equally authoritative investigation of the control of morals in the Bernese countryside.

PART III

The European Reformation

SEVEN

Calvin and Geneva

ROBERT M. KINGDON

Before the Reformation the city of Geneva was the headquarters of a large ecclesiastical state ruled by a prince-bishop. It extended over a fairly large expanse of territory now covered by both the Swiss canton of Geneva and large parts of southwestern France. The largest secular power in the area was the duchy of Savoy, a state straddling the frontier now dividing France from Italy. The governments of Geneva and Savoy were closely linked. If the area had followed the historical course of most of Europe, the bishopric of Geneva would have been absorbed by Savoy. The last of the prince-bishops were aristocrats with close connections to the ruling house of Savoy, sometimes even members of that house. The bishop was assisted in his rule by a chapter of canons, most of them also Savoyard aristocrats. The duchy of Savoy provided Geneva with military protection. It also supervised the administration of most criminal justice in the city, through an officer it appointed who resided in the city in a special castle reserved for his use. The internal government of the city was handled by a hierarchy of councils elected from among middle-class men who lived in the city. They were led by officials called syndics, who represented the citizens in negotiations with the bishop. The councils were responsible for the control of business, morals, civil justice, and some criminal justice in cooperation with the duke's representative. The bishop controlled foreign policy, the minting of money, and some types of justice. The bishop's court, as in most parts of Europe, had jurisdiction over cases of certain kinds, most obviously all those involving marital problems. The bishop also supervised the church of the diocese. Teams representing him periodically visited all the rural parishes in the diocese. Within the city, seven parishes, each staffed by a group of secular priests, gave structure to religious life. There were also several religious houses located within the city. Altogether there were between two and three hundred clergymen and women living in Geneva. When one adds their dependents, mostly their servants, they totaled about 1,000 people, or 10 percent of a total population of around 10,000. These clergymen not only provided religious services to Geneva. They constituted its most important educated elite, and for that reason came to control education. They also constituted an economic elite, controlling a significant part of all the property in the city and its hinterland. They also controlled the administration of charity in the city.

The Reformation in Geneva began with a revolution against this episcopal regime. The bishop, most of the clergy, and the agents of Savoy were thrown out of the city and their property within it was confiscated. The city councils assumed sovereign powers, now controlling the government of the city and a few neighboring villages that had been the property of the bishop. The rest of the diocese remained under the control of the bishop in collaboration with the duchy of Savoy. This revolution was made possible by foreign support. The governments of some of the republics within the Swiss Confederation encouraged the Genevans in their revolt. The most important of them was the republic of Bern, one of the great military powers of the period. It sent troops to surround Geneva, to take control of some of the villages in its neighborhood, and to protect it against Savoyard counter-attack.

This political revolution was accompanied by a religious revolution. Bern had recently become Protestant, adopting the Zwinglian variety of Protestantism as first developed in Zürich. To help along those in Geneva inclined to revolt against the bishop, it sent into the city French-speaking Protestant missionaries, headed by an inflammatory preacher named Guillaume Farel. His impassioned sermons aroused the population and helped persuade them to drive out the Catholic clergy and to vote in 1536 henceforth "to live according to the Gospel," i.e., become Protestant. At the height of the uproar provoked by this agitation, a young French lawyer named Jean Calvin happened to come through Geneva on his way to Strasbourg, where he planned to settle. He had recently published a basic summary of Protestant doctrine called the *Institutes of the Christian Religion.* Farel persuaded the Genevans to hire Calvin as a public lecturer, to explain to them the meaning of the new form of religion they had just agreed to adopt.

Farel and Calvin then set about creating a new church for Geneva, with a radically new order of service, arrangements for education in the faith as now defined, and provisions for discipline of those who misbehaved. Some of their proposals seemed too radical to many native Genevans, who feared the creation of a new clerical tyranny to replace the old. Farel and Calvin and several of their supporters were thrown out of the city on short notice in 1538. Farel moved to nearby Neuchâtel and assumed direction of its newly Reformed church. Calvin moved to Strasbourg, then an imperial city in the Holy Roman Empire of the German nation, and became minister to a church of French refugees. He worked closely in Strasbourg with Martin Bucer, one of the seminal figures in the German Reformation, and learned a great deal from Bucer on how to organize a Reformed church.

Meanwhile, conditions in Geneva deteriorated. The remaining Protestant preachers were not capable of providing effective leadership. Leaders of the Roman Church in the area began putting pressure on Genevans to return to Catholicism. Preeminent among them was Cardinal Jacopo Sadoleto, one of the leaders in a Reforming faction within the hierarchy of the Roman Catholic Church, then resident in the French diocese of Carpentras, not far from Geneva. He sent a public letter to the people of Geneva urging them to return to the bosom of the Holy Mother Church. Geneva's leaders were frightened by this initiative. They had no wish to abandon their new-found political freedom by permitting return of a bishop. They persuaded Calvin to write a public letter in answer to Sadoleto. And they invited him back to Geneva to oversee the construction of the entire Reformed church establishment. After some hesitation and some hard negotiations, he accepted this invitation, returned, and spent the rest of his life in Geneva. There he created a significantly new form of Protestantism, then supervised an effort to export it to many other parts of Europe.

Calvin was invited back to Geneva because he possessed precisely the skills the Genevans needed at this juncture. He was not a clergyman trained in theology. In fact, he had never been ordained to the priesthood or received formal education in theology. As a young man he had, to be sure, received a church benefice in his native diocese of Noyon to finance his education in Paris, and later in Orléans and Bourges. But after a high-powered education in what was then called the humanities and what we would now call classical literature and philosophy, he had taken his advanced training in law. After receiving his university degrees in law, he had taken even more advanced training in the humanities, working with Guillaume Budé, a great specialist on the Greek versions of the Roman law who also held an appointment at the royal court. At some point still veiled in mystery, Calvin had become Protestant, resigned his benefice, and fled to Basel, during a period of a savage repression of French Protestantism sponsored by the royal government. It was in Basel, where he arrived in 1534, that Calvin had taught himself theology and had written his *Institutes.*

The combination of training in law and theology which Calvin had acquired was precisely what Geneva needed at this point. Among his earliest duties was the drafting of laws for the Genevan Republic. A first set of laws, the ecclesiastical ordinances, provided a kind of constitution for the Reformed Church of Geneva. A second set of laws, the ordinances on offices and officers, provided a kind of constitution for the Genevan state. Calvin got assistance in drafting these laws, but he was clearly the leading figure in drafting both sets. They did not take effect until they were ratified, with a few amendments, by the governing councils of the city. The ecclesiastical ordinances were ratified in 1541, only months after Calvin's return. The ordinances on offices and officers were ratified in 1543.

Both of these "constitutions" were built around the principle of collective government. Genevans wanted to wipe out all vestiges of the one-man rule by a bishop under which they had lived for centuries. In this they were parting company with most of the monarchies and feudal principalities of the period, as well as the Roman Catholic Church. They were joining the company of a number of other city-states of the period, primarily in Germany and Italy.

The constitution for the state codified institutions and practices that had grown up in the years since the establishment of the Reformation. At the base of its government was a General Council of all of the native-born citizens and *bourgeois.* It met at least once a year, in February, to elect members of all the other councils and standing committees. It also met on special occasions to ratify particularly important laws, for example the laws outlawing the Catholic mass and providing for Protestant preaching in 1536. At a next level was a Council of Two Hundred that met on occasion to participate in specified ways in the elections, to hear appeals in certain kinds of cases, and to handle other duties. At a next level was a Council of Sixty that met on occasion to handle certain other types of cases, often in the realm of foreign policy. At the top of the pyramid was a Narrow or Small Council of 25 citizens that met almost every day and provided most of the day-by-day government of the city. Members of these councils were technically elected every year, but were often continued in office year after year. From within the Small Council four syndics were elected annually for one year only. They held the chief executive powers in this government and represented it on ceremonial occasions. In addition there were also a number of standing committees elected every year that reported to the Small Council but included members of other councils as well. They supervised things like fortifications, a municipal grain supply, the administration of justice, and financial affairs.

The constitution for the church involved an even more radical break with the past. It created four orders of ministry for the Reformed Church. At the peak were pastors assigned to parishes within the city and in the villages still under city control. Their job was to preach the Word of God. They were not formally ordained, in the traditional Catholic way. They were simply nominated by the group of existing pastors, approved by the Small Council and members of the parishes to which they were to be assigned, and then put on the city payroll. They were not given independent income in the form of benefices, as were Catholic clergymen. They were rather paid salaries from the city treasury, usually supplemented with grain and wine rations, and often provided with free housing. At a second level were doctors. Their job was to teach the Word of God, primarily to those in training for the pastorate. In the beginning, doctors were often pastors as well. Calvin held both jobs and so did Theodore Beza, his eventual successor. Only after 1559, when Geneva established an Academy to train pastors and others, were independent scholars hired solely as doctors. Before then there were a number of men hired as schoolteachers. They do not seem to have been regarded as doctors, although the pastors often claimed a role in their appointment. Both doctors and teachers received financial support from the city treasury. At a third level were elders. These were laymen charged with maintaining discipline in the city. At a fourth level were deacons. These were laymen charged with administering charity to the poor of the city.

Each of these groups of ministers was organized into a collective. The pastors and doctors belonged to a Company of Pastors that met once a week to coordinate all religious activities within the city. There were no provisions in the ordinances for its governance, but in practice it came to be led by Calvin, who was often called its moderator. He presided over its weekly meetings and made petitions on its behalf to the Small Council, sometimes accompanied by some of his colleagues. Its decisions, however, were always advertised as collective decisions, never as decisions made by Calvin alone.

The elders, along with the pastors, belonged to a body called the consistory. It also met once a week to superintend the behavior of everyone in Geneva. It was in law one of the standing committees of the city government, although a committee of a special sort, since it included the pastors *ex officio*. It was always presided over by one of the syndics. Its lay members, the elders, were elected as commissioners to the consistory every year in the annual elections. They often continued in office for several years, but never for very long terms. Assigned to its support were a secretary and a summoner. Its reach was remarkably intrusive. Up to 7 percent of the entire adult population of the city was summoned before the consistory every year. In the beginning, many were summoned because they were not yet fully informed about the Reformation, still using Catholic practices, not as yet aware of the practices that Protestants wanted to substitute for them. Many were also summoned because of problems with marriages or related delinquencies in morals. In this the consistory was inheriting both the pre-Reformation bishop's court supervision of marriage and the pre-Reformation civic councils' supervision of morals. Many were also summoned because of quarrels, within families, among neighbors, among business associates. In this capacity, the consistory acted as a compulsory counseling service, designed to resolve these quarrels. In later years cases of surviving Catholic beliefs and practices tended to fade away, as the population became more fully aware of what was expected in the religious domain. But cases of marriage, morals, and quarrels became even more frequent, and the consistory remained a very intrusive institution.

The deacons were members of a body of procurators for the city's General Hospital, assisted by a hospitaller who actually directed that institution on a day-to-day basis. The General Hospital was not primarily an institution for caring for the sick. It was rather a kind of poor house. It supported a number of orphans, providing for their education until adolescence, then placing them as apprentices or domestic servants within city households. It also supported a few people incapable of caring for themselves, including cripples, the blind, and the very elderly. It also provided free rations of bread for households in the city temporarily too poor to support themselves. This institution and its officers had been created before Calvin's arrival in Geneva, to replace a number of small hospitals controlled by religious communities or confraternities that had provided charity before the Reformation. By calling its officers "deacons" Calvin was in effect sacralizing this institution, giving it a religious status, gaining more civic respect for its work. The board of procurators for the Hospital was also one of the standing committees of the city government, elected every year in the annual elections, presided over most years by one of the four syndics. The Small Council was supposed to consult with the pastors in advance of the yearly elections as it drew up the lists of nominees for the positions of both elder and deacon.

The main internal problem that developed within Geneva in the early years of the Reformation was over the powers of the consistory. The ordinances gave it only the power to scold the sinners called before it, and most of its cases did in fact end with a formal admonition or remonstrance, most often delivered by Calvin himself. Any more secular punishments, like fines, imprisonments, banishment, or the death penalty, were reserved to the secular government. The consistory could recommend to the Small Council investigation that could and did lead to punishments of these types. But it had no power to levy them itself. Before long, however, the members of the consistory demanded the right to excommunicate people called before it, to bar people who had made serious mistakes or who seemed unrepentant, from participation in the next quarterly communion service. This was a serious penalty in sixteenth-century society. Excommunication kept people from participating in a sacrament that was still thought to be a visible sign of invisible grace, evidence of God's willingness to extend to believers eternal salvation, a ritual that, furthermore, bound people together in a visible way into a community. Excommunication also kept people from participating in the sacrament of baptism, specifically made it impossible to serve as godparents, a privilege highly regarded in sixteenth-century society as tying families together in many important ways. Excommunication may have even constituted a measure of social disgrace, at least to the pious. In later years excommunication could even lead to banishment from the city entirely. Anybody who had been excommunicated was expected to reconcile himself or herself with the community as represented by the consistory within the next several months. A number of prominent people excommunicated by the consistory challenged its powers to issue this penalty without any supervision. Many of them were active in a political faction within the city that called themselves the "children of Geneva," led by a prominent local businessman and politician named Ami Perrin. They thought that at the very least excommunicates should have the right to appeal over the consistory's head to the Small Council to reverse a decision of excommunication or to readmit someone to communion who now thought herself or himself sufficiently penitent. Calvin and the other pastors flatly refused to recognize any such right of appeal. They insisted that the consistory alone had the right to levy and lift sentences of excommunication. They said they would not administer communion to anyone who had been excommunicated. They threatened to resign their positions and leave the city if they did not win their way on this issue. After a period of increasingly bitter local controversy, climaxing in a riot, the supporters of consistorial excommunication won decisively. Perrin and his most vocal supporters were driven out of the city or punished. A few of them were even put to death on charges of treason. From now on discipline, administered by an institution like the consistory, and enforced by excommunication, became an extremely important characteristic of Calvinism. It became the rule not only in Geneva, but also was introduced wherever possible and to whatever degree possible in every other community that decided to follow the lead of Calvinism.

The decisive victory of the followers of Calvin over the followers of Perrin on this issue had been made possible to an important degree by a flood of religious refugees into Geneva. In the first years after the Reformation, the population of Geneva had dropped, as the Catholic clergy and their supporters left the city, falling from about 10,000 to about 8,000. Once the Reformed regime created by Calvin was firmly established, however, the population began rising rapidly. That rise was brought about for the most part by a flood of religious refugees from France, driven by the increasing intolerance of the French royal government for all forms of religious deviation, attracted by the power of the religious message formulated by Calvin. They were joined by smaller numbers of refugees from other countries, notably from parts of Italy, also including refugees from Britain, the Netherlands, and yet other countries. The refugees from France were integrated into the Genevan Church. The refugees who spoke other languages were permitted to create their own churches. Particularly important ones were created for the Italians and the English. Among these refugees were people of social prominence, wealth, and advanced education. They came to dominate entire professions and to buy up much of the choicest property. Almost all of the pastors, for example, beginning with Jean Calvin himself, were refugees from France. Most of the printers who became particularly successful and visible members of the business community were refugees from France, including Robert Estienne, who had been official printer to the king of France. Many of the notaries and lawyers who helped give legal structure to the Genevan community were refugees from France, including Germain Colladon, who became the most important adviser to the Genevan government on how to draft and interpret laws. And there were refugees in other walks of life. Perhaps the most prominent refugee of all was the Marquis Galeazzo Caracciolo from Naples, from the ranks of the highest aristocracy in Italy, a great-nephew of Pope Paul IV. There were so many refugees that the city literally doubled in size, reaching about 20,000 in 1560, at the height of Calvin's career. A population of that size proved to be economically unsustainable, however, and in the following years the population declined, perhaps to about 15,000, as refugees either returned to their homes or moved on to other communities. In a very real sense the Calvinist Reformation was a Reformation of refugees.

The fact that there were so many refugees in Geneva, indeed, explains much about the city's history during the early Reformation. It helps to explain the mentality of the "children of Geneva." Many of them felt that they were being overwhelmed by foreign Frenchmen, introducing many customs new to them. They felt these foreigners were taking over their city. The fact that many of the foreigners were wealthier and more highly educated than most native Genevans made matters worse. Some of the foreigners were sensitive to this situation and tried to help out. It soon became clear, for example, that the General Hospital and the arrangements for charity could not handle substantial numbers of new people. So each group of foreigners agreed to handle those among them who needed public assistance. For the French that meant creating an institution called the *Bourse française*, a fund raised among the community of French refugees for the support of widows and other poor French refugees. The administrators of this fund were called deacons, and that word, in fact, was more frequently applied to them than to the native procurators of the General Hospital. The most prominent of these deacons was Jean Budé, son of the great scholar attached to the royal court who had provided Calvin with some of his education. Calvin himself, in fact, was quite active in the work of this institution, making generous gifts to it out of the salary he received from the city.

The foreign refugees, for their part, were ardent supporters of the Calvinist experiment in its entirety. That meant that they wanted to see the full establishment of a regime of discipline including consistorial excommunication. To help secure that, many of them sought voting rights within the city. The population of Geneva at that time was split into three categories. One category was of citizens. They had to be born within the city and the most important jobs in the city government, including membership in the Small Council, were reserved to them. A second category was of *bourgeois*, men of respectability who had taken oaths to support the community. Most of them were merchants and professional men, but some of them were artisans. Foreigners could be voted into this group free of charge in return for special services they were able to provide to the city. Many of the pastors became *bourgeois* in this way, although Calvin himself was not voted in until 1559. Or a man could obtain admission to this *bourgeoisie* by paying a substantial amount of money, adjusted individually to his background and resources. These sums were large enough to create a significant source of income to the city government. Once in the *bourgeoisie* a man was entitled to a vote in the Grand Council, could gain membership in the next higher councils in the hierarchy although not the Small Council, and might even win membership on some of the standing committees of the state government. Before the end of Calvin's career, for example, there were foreign-born *bourgeois* sitting as elders on the consistory. A third category of the population were inhabitants. They were mostly servants and day-laborers, although some of them were artisans. They possessed few political rights.

In the struggle over consistorial excommunication that led to the expulsion of the Perrinist "children of Geneva" and the triumph of the supporters of Calvin, these *bourgeois* of foreign origin played a crucial role. Their numbers increased dramatically in the years just before 1555, in effect packing the electorate, making possible the election of a number of new members to the Small Council, replacing Perrinist old-timers. While the triumph of Calvin's party would not have been possible without substantial native support, the margin making possible their victory over the Perrinists may well have been supplied by refugees.

It has even been argued that the theology that became characteristic of the Calvinist Reformation was a theology designed for refugees. That does not seem obvious when one considers how the Reformation began in France. It really started as a protest against Catholic Eucharistic theology. The earliest French Protestants objected with special vehemence to the mass and the theology of transubstantiation that lay behind it. They claimed that by insisting on the mass in its present form, Catholics were maintaining a form of idolatry. They were requiring people to worship manmade objects – the pieces of bread and cups of wine that Catholics believe are transubstantiated into the body and blood of Christ, rather than the only true God who can be worshipped in spirit alone. They railed against the "idolatry of the mass" and the Catholic practice of worshipping a "god of bread." A broadsheet making these claims had been posted in many parts of France in 1534. That broadsheet had provoked a firestorm of protest, leading to a vicious general crackdown on Protestants of every variety. It seems to have been this wave of persecution that persuaded Calvin to resign his benefice and leave France in that very year.

French Protestants still believed in a sacrament of communion. And they still believed that Christ is present in that sacrament. But they insisted that he could not be present in the elements of bread and wine served during the sacrament. They came to believe, with Calvin, that the souls of pious communicants are lifted up to heaven to commune with the body of Christ in triumph there, returning to their bodies on earth and the mundane life of this world after that moment of ecstasy. The lay leaders of Geneva were so suspicious of the mass that they did not want communion to be served frequently. On this point Calvin and the other pastors gave way. They agreed to celebrate it once every three months, or four times a year.

The abandonment of frequent communion led to a radical change in the form of worship in Calvin's Geneva. No longer was the primary form of worship a mass, a sacrament celebrated hundreds of time every week, with special attention on Sundays and feast days, which the pious came to observe. Now the primary form of worship was a sermon, an explanation of a passage from the Bible, the Word of God, interpreted by an expert, which the pious came to hear. Genevan sources of the period invariably call Catholic worship "the mass," and Protestant worship "the sermon." It took some time for many Genevans to get used to this change. In the beginning many, particularly elderly and often illiterate women, would come to church, shut their eyes, and repeat their prayers in a low voice, as they had been instructed to do as Catholic children. It must have come as a shock to many of them to be called before the consistory and to be told, in effect, to shut up and listen.

For a strand in Calvinist theology more relevant to the refugee mentality, one should turn to the doctrine of predestination. It is a theological doctrine with which Calvinism came to be closely associated. The belief that God alone deserves credit for the salvation of each individual who wins a place in heaven is an old one in the Christian churches of the west, dating back to St. Augustine at least. And it was shared in one form or another by all orthodox Christians of the sixteenth century, including both Catholics and Protestants. The corollary belief that God alone deserves responsibility for the damnation of each individual who descends to hell, however, was much less universal. Calvin insisted that God alone decides both who is to be saved and who is to be damned. This is called double predestination. He claimed that he found the doctrine in Scripture, explained and elaborated in Augustine, and that no person of piety could deny it. He also tended to believe that the number of those elected by God for salvation, the "saints," was fairly small, a minority of all humankind. These beliefs would seem to provide ideal support for a religious group that recognized that it was a minority, that it had to face persecution and exile, that it could never win over all of society, that its ultimate reward would be granted only after this temporal life, in heaven. It might thus be particularly appealing to a church of refugees.

Calvin's doctrine of double predestination was not without opposition, even in Geneva. In 1551 it was directly challenged by a man named Jerome Bolsec. Bolsec had been a Carmelite friar in Paris, had been converted to Protestantism and left the country, had somehow gained training in medicine and was supporting himself as physician to an emigrant French noble family living in the countryside near Geneva. He frequently came into the city and engaged in conversation with the local pastors and others interested in theology. At one point he attended a "congregation," a kind of adult Bible class, in which laymen were encouraged to express their ideas on theological topics. The topic for that date was a verse from the Bible that had been used to support arguments for predestination. Bolsec rose to attack the doctrine frontally, arguing that it encouraged a kind of fatalism, that it made the Christian God more of a tyrant like the pagans' Jupiter than a God of love. Bolsec's attacks provoked a perfect uproar. Calvin rose to refute them at length and with great erudition. Bolsec was immediately arrested, held in jail for a long time, cross-examined closely by a local court, calling in the Company of Pastors as expert witnesses, with opinions also elicited from Reformed theologians in other cities. In the end Bolsec was found guilty of misbelief and sedition. He was sentenced to perpetual banishment from Geneva. From then on, Calvin insisted with increasing vehemence on the doctrine of double predestination. He wrote entire treatises on it and inserted ever longer passages about it into his more general writings. It came in later years to be associated with Calvinism in a particularly close way.

Another celebrated theological dispute within these years was associated with the teachings of Michael Servetus. He was a Spaniard who had moved to Paris for his advanced education. His attacks on traditional Christian theology went even further than those of Bolsec. He rejected the doctrine of the Trinity, that God is composed of three beings, the Father, the Son, and the Holy Ghost. He had particular objections to the idea that the Son of God had existed from eternity, descending to this earth only for a brief lifetime as Jesus the Christ. In short, he rejected the co-eternity of the second person of the Trinity. He also rejected a number of other doctrines and practices that had become traditional in Christianity, like, for example, the baptism of infants. His views had been expressed in books that horrified Christians all over Europe. For a while he had kept in hiding, under an alias, supporting himself as a physician, and indeed made contributions to medical knowledge that still command respect. Finally his cover was blown, he was seized by Catholic authorities in France and put on trial for his life before a branch of the Inquisition. He escaped from a prison of the Inquisition, and imprudently made his way to Geneva in 1553. Calvin had known him when they were both students back in Paris. He had become increasingly upset by Servetus's ideas, especially after their publication. He demanded the arrest of Servetus. Like Bolsec, Servetus was examined by a local court, with the Company of Pastors again acting as expert witnesses, and theologians from other cities being consulted. This time opinions were even more unanimous than they were in the case of Bolsec, and the deviation from traditional belief seemed even more serious. Servetus was condemned to death by burning, the normal way of executing notorious heretics, and the penalty duly administered.

In both of these cases, most Genevans supported Calvin. There were a few who expressed some support of Bolsec, in part because they had found him a good physician. They were summoned before the consistory and chastised. But they were only a handful of people without prominence. There were almost none who expressed any support of Servetus. The city lieutenant in charge of his trial was a moderate member of the "children of Geneva." He presumably presided over the burning of Servetus. Calvin did not even attend. To provide a minister to accompany Servetus to the stake, urging him to recant so as to save his soul if not his body, Farel was drafted. He came down from Neuchâtel for this chore. The main opposition to the burning of Servetus came from outside Geneva, specifically from a man named Sebastian Castellio. He was a well-trained humanist who had served for a time as a teacher in the schools of Geneva after the Reformation. When he had been discouraged in his ambition to become a pastor there, he resigned, moved to Basel, and spent most of the rest of his life as an assistant to printers in that major publishing center. Castellio was one of the few people in sixteenth-century Europe who really believed in religious toleration. He was horrified that Servetus should have been burned solely because of his religious ideas. He wrote an eloquent defense of the principles of toleration in reaction to this event. His argument was savagely attacked in treatises drafted by Calvin and Beza. Little more came of this exchange. Clearly, most Europeans saw no point in toleration. They strongly believed that misbelievers deserved savage suppression. They disagreed on the precise identity of those who should be treated that harshly. Catholics thought most Protestants should be persecuted for heresy. Mainline Protestants thought most Catholics should be persecuted for idolatry. And both agreed that the wild fringe, consisting of people like Anabaptists and Servetus, deserved death.

After 1555, Calvin was in full control of almost everything that happened in Geneva. Unlike the earlier bishop, he had no formal powers of governing either state or church. But he was so widely respected that almost everyone was prepared to follow his suggestions. Now he and the other pastors were free to turn their attention to developments outside of Geneva. It seemed like a particularly propitious time for them to mount a missionary campaign in France. That is precisely what they did. A first missionary pastor was sent from Geneva to France in 1555, more and more were sent in following years, reaching a climax in 1561 and 1562. Most of these missionaries had initially been sent to Geneva for training in the Reformed faith by communities of French Protestants still worshipping in secrecy. Some of them had been Catholic priests and religious but more of them were educated laymen. Some of them took courses in the Genevan secondary schools before 1559, then in the Academy when it was founded in that year. Practically all of them attended the public lectures in Biblical exegesis which Calvin had begun delivering back in 1536 when he first arrived in Geneva, and which he continued throughout his career as Geneva's most prominent pastor. A number of these missionary candidates got practical experience, as preachers in village churches both within the Genevan state or in other parts of what is now French-speaking Switzerland. Others worked as chaplains or teachers in the city or as tutors in wealthy families. When the time came for them to return to France, each of them appeared before the Company of Pastors. Each seems to have been examined on his competence and orthodoxy. Then each was given some sort of certificate of approval by the Company and dispatched to a Protestant community that wanted his services. This was a highly dangerous enterprise, given the strict laws against heresy then being enforced in France. A few were in fact caught and burned. A good number of them, however, were successfully smuggled into France and began performing functions as the ministers of underground churches, serving "under the Cross."

It was not only events in Geneva but also events in France that made this missionary campaign possible. In 1559, King Henry II, who had been strongly opposed to Protestantism and had supported its suppression, had been wounded in a jousting accident that proved fatal. He was succeeded by his eldest son, still a boy, who became King Francis II, advised by the relatives of his new wife, of the fervently pro-Catholic Guise family. The role of the Guises in this government, however, was deeply resented by other powerful aristocrats, most prominently by relatives of the king of the Bourbon family. These opponents of the Guises, in searching for an ideological platform for mobilizing opposition to them, hit upon Protestantism. Then Francis II died prematurely, and his even younger brother became King Charles IX. He was so young that he had to have a regent who could rule in his name. That job was given to his mother, Catherine de' Medici, a member of the famous Florentine family of that name, and widow of Henry II. She tried to play a middle role between the Guises and the Bourbons, and to that end obtained legislation providing partial toleration of Protestantism. That created the opening through which missionaries trained in Geneva, and many other potential leaders in exile outside of the kingdom, could come. And come they did, particularly in 1561 and 1562, the very years of a measure of toleration. This experiment collapsed in religious warfare that began in 1562 and continued with interruptions until 1598. These wars ended with France officially Catholic but tolerating a small Protestant minority under very restricted conditions. Calvin did not live to see that happen. When he died, shortly after the first war of religion, he and his followers in Geneva still had some reason to believe that all of France might be won for the Reformed faith. That hope was only really squelched by the St. Bartholomew's massacres of 1572.

In addition to Calvin and his French compatriots, another group of refugees to Geneva during this period who achieved prominence were British. They arrived and organized their own church in 1555 and stayed until 1560. Their leader was John Knox. They had fled England because of the persecution launched by the government of "bloody" Mary Tudor, who, after her accession in 1553, worked strenuously to return England to Catholicism. They felt free to return to Britain on the accession in 1558 of Elizabeth I, whose position required her to become at least a cautious Protestant. Knox and several other of these refugees went to Scotland. They played an influential role in the revolt of the Lords of the Congregation against the Catholic government of Mary Stuart, then represented by her mother, Mary of Guise,

of the famous French Catholic family of strongly committed Catholics. They helped
create within Scotland a Reformed Kirk which became thoroughly Calvinist in its
theology, its liturgy, and its ecclesiology. Its creation of representative institutions
called "presbyteries" to organize groups of local churches has led to it being named
a Presbyterian church.

Other English refugees in Geneva returned to England. They brought with them
a Bible translated into English, first published in Geneva in 1560 and for that reason
called the "Geneva Bible." It was the most widely used Bible in all English-speaking
lands throughout the sixteenth century. It was eventually replaced by the Authorized
or King James Bible drafted in the early seventeenth century, but the Geneva Bible
continued in use even in later years among those strongly committed to Calvinism.
These refugees helped to persuade most English Protestants to adopt Calvinist theology, including a Calvinist view of communion and double predestination. They did
not persuade them all to adopt Calvinist liturgies or Calvinist ways of organizing
churches. The Protestant community in England split into two groups, an episco-
palian faction supported by the monarchy and led by the bishops of the Church of
England, and a puritan faction that wanted to go all the way in making England
Calvinist. This controversy helped to lead England into civil war in the seventeenth
century, with the eventual triumph of episcopalianism. But that, of course, happened
well after Calvin's death.

Men who came to be leaders of Reformed churches in yet other countries also
came through Geneva during the years of Calvin's dominance. They included the
Marnix van St. Aldegonde brothers, Jean and Philippe, Dutch noblemen of prominence and education. They spent a period in Geneva studying in the new Academy
from 1560 to 1561, shortly after its creation in 1559. They then returned to their
home provinces to assist the prince of Orange and others organize the Dutch revolt
against Spanish rule and establish a Calvinist church as the official church of the
northern provinces of the Netherlands. Jean died in the early stages of that revolt,
but Philippe lived on to become a leading adviser to the prince of Orange and an
important writer of Calvinist propaganda. These future leaders also included Kaspar
Olevianus, who was important in introducing a version of Calvinism into Germany.
He had first visited Geneva to make Calvin's acquaintance in 1558, and remained in
touch with Calvin and Beza through much of his life. In 1559, he returned to his
home town of Trier, headquarters of a Catholic electoral archdiocese, and tried to
use a position as teacher there to introduce a Reformed version of Protestantism into
that community. When that did not work, he moved to the Rhineland Palatinate and
gained considerable prominence as the chief theological adviser to its prince-elector.
He helped to make of the Palatinate a state that was, with occasional interruptions
of Lutheran rule, thoroughly Calvinist in its theology, its liturgy, and some of its
ecclesiology. And the Palatinate encouraged a number of other German principalities to turn to Calvinism, usually from some form of Lutheranism. In later years there
were among the visitors to Geneva men who became leaders of Czech and Polish
Reformed churches. Many of these developments blossomed only after Calvin died,
but the seeds for them had been sown during his ministry.

Geneva thus became, thanks to Calvin, an international center for a new form of
Protestantism, a form labeled "Reformed" as distinguished from the "evangelical"
or Lutheran form of Protestant Christianity. For the Reformed, Geneva became a

kind of Protestant Rome. It never had the resources or power base to exert really effective control over other Calvinist churches, and thus had less actual influence than Rome continued to exert over Catholics. But Geneva continued to be widely respected and honored throughout the Reformed world, not only in Europe but in such outposts of European countries as the English colonies in North America, and it continued to supply at least an element of intellectual leadership to the entire movement.

FURTHER READING

Bergier, J.-F. and Kingdon, R. M., eds., *The Register of the Company of Pastors of Geneva in the Time of Calvin*, trans. Philip E. Hughes. Grand Rapids, Mich.: Eerdmans, 1966.

Cottret, B., *Calvin: A Biography*. Grand Rapids, Mich.: Eerdmans, 2000.

Kingdon, R. M., *Geneva and the Coming of the Wars of Religion in France, 1555–1563*. Geneva: Droz, 1956.

Kingdon, R. M., "The Church in Calvin's Geneva," a section of four articles in *Church and Society in Reformation Europe*. London: Variorum Reprints, 1985.

Kingdon, R. M., "Popular Reactions to the Debate between Bolsec and Calvin," in Willem van't Spijker, ed., *Calvin: Erbe und Auftrag, festschrift für Wilhelm Neuser*. Kampen: Kok, 1991.

Lambert, T. A. and Watt, I. M., eds., *Registers of the Consistory of Geneva in the Time of Calvin*, vol. 1, trans. M. Wallace McDonald. Grand Rapids, Mich.: Eerdmans, 2000.

Monter, W., *Calvin's Geneva*. New York: Wiley, 1967.

Muller, R. A., *The Unaccommodated Calvin*. New York: Oxford University Press, 2000.

Naphy, W. G., *Calvin and the Consolidation of the Genevan Reformation*. Manchester: Manchester University Press, 1994.

Olson, J. E., *Calvin and Social Welfare: Deacons and the Bourse Française*. Selinsgrove: Susquehanna University Press, 1989.

Wendel, F., *Calvin: The Origins and Development of his Religious Thought*. New York: Harper & Row, 1963.

The theory that the Calvinist Reformation should be studied as a Reformation of refugees has been advanced by the late Heiko A. Oberman in a number of lectures and articles. It is to be developed in a full book to be published posthumously.

EIGHT

Reform in the Low Countries

JOKE SPAANS

In the sixteenth century the Low Countries sat at the crossroads of important trade routes. The estuary of the Rhine, Meuse, and Scheldt contained both the main ports of Antwerp and Amsterdam and a host of lesser sea and river ports. These handled traffic both on the overland route from the Mediterranean to the Atlantic, through Venice and Genoa, over the Alpine passes and via the Rhine valley on to England, and the sea route connecting the Baltic to the Mediterranean. Proximity to these arteries of wealth had created a favorable climate for the development of a heavily urbanized, highly literate society, in which international trade and manufacture for both export and a dense network of local and regional markets interlocked and flourished (Spufford, "Literacy").

Politically, this rich area was firmly in the hands of the House of Habsburg. Charles V had personally built the Low Countries around the Burgundian lands he inherited from his father. Conquests had made him ruler of the "seventeen Provinces" by 1543, and in 1548 he forged these possessions into a geographically well-defined unit, separate from the German Empire to which various parts had formerly belonged. In 1549 he made the Estates of all these provinces recognize their government as hereditary in the House of Habsburg. He capped this achievement with the installation of a state-of-the-art, modern set of federal councils: a supreme court at Mechelen, which was also court of appeal for the provincial law courts, the privy council, and the councils of state and finance to advise the ruler. These formed the central government of the whole area, but had to share the power of sovereignty with the provinces and their Estates, which fiercely defended their traditional privileges.

Welding together these heterogeneous lands – old possessions and new acquisitions, some densely populated, others only sparsely so, in which four languages were spoken and which represented a wide variety in government traditions, tangled jurisdictions, and divergent customs – was a task left to Philip II, who succeeded his father as overlord of the Low Countries in 1559. Within a decade of his rule, these rich and well-organized lands were in deep trouble. Philip ruled his lands from Spain and delegated executive power over the Low Countries to a regent, his half-sister Margaret, duchess of Parma. She was closely surrounded by advisers, many of foreign extraction, who were in the confidence of the king. At first a perceived preferment of foreign-born men to positions of power and influence, later a new, centrally decreed system of taxation introducing higher tariffs, led to strong opposition from the provinces to the central government. These problems meshed with, and were in time to be almost overshadowed by, a conflict over the religious policies of the Habsburg dynasty. The combination of political and religious discontent was at the root of the revolt that would divide the Low Countries into the Catholic Spanish Netherlands and the Reformed Dutch Republic (Parker, *Dutch Revolt*, pp. 19–67).

Evangelical Religion and Anabaptism

The easy accessibility of the area facilitated not only the trade in commodities but also the exchange of books, ideas, and rumors. Lutheran and Anabaptist religious views very rapidly found their way from the German Empire to audiences in the Low Countries and combined with local traditions critical of religious life and ecclesiastical organization into a diffuse mix of heresies that abhorred their rulers. In the 1520s they perceived widespread "Lutheranism." In actual fact the influence of the German Reformation may have been rather limited, but certainly a considerable change was afoot in both learned and popular views of what it took to be a good Christian.

Central to this change in religious sensibility was a growing interest in the Bible. Humanists, most influential among them Desiderius Erasmus, studied the Bible with a new interest in its literary form and as a guide to moral conduct. The development of the printing industry made the Biblical texts and "evangelical" literature available in the vernacular, and no doubt rumors about the "Luther affair" stimulated demand. The literate artisans in towns and cities bought both Bibles and devotional works that formerly were more the preserve of clerics and religious. In a still overwhelmingly oral culture the texts were divulged by word of mouth, in meetings in the houses of laymen where the best reader present read them to the others, and in open-air sermons, where often unnamed preachers expounded the message of the Gospel to willing audiences (Bredero, *Spaanse Brabander*, III.1349–61; Rooze-Stouthamer, *Zeeland*, p. 34; Spaans, *Haarlem*, p. 29).

It is unlikely that this popular interest in the Bible was willfully heretical. It did, however, strengthen criticism against the church, both among the learned and the unlearned. Priests lost faith in the way they had traditionally preached and ministered, and some of them shared their worries with parishioners who had access to Biblical texts and were interested in the new brand of evangelical devotion. Religious began to question their vows, and some of them left their communities, shed their habits, and started a new life as laypersons. Among the laity some degree of anti-clericalism had never been absent. The privileges of the clerical estate, often obtained by patronage rather than ability, and the cost of its maintenance evoked sentiments ranging from Erasmian irony to bitter resentment. Celibacy was formally required from priests and religious but not rigidly enforced – and concubinage was often socially accepted (Woltjer, *Friesland*, pp. 64–7, 124–6) – but the ambiguity made them the butt of ribald joking and reflected badly on their moral standing. The absence of formal training for the ministry lowered their professional, intellectual status in the esteem of their flocks, who either were literate themselves or saw other laypersons read and explain Scripture to them (Bijsterveld, *Pastoors*).

On the basis of this new understanding of the Scriptures, the focus of devotion shifted away from the sacraments, the saints and their images, pilgrimages, and other quests for indulgences to a more spiritualized and moralistic religion. Funding for traditional devotional practices plummeted in the 1520s (Verhoeven, *Devotie en negotie*, pp. 157–84; Mol, "Friezen"; Thijs, *Geuzenstad*, pp. 20–1). It may well be that at least part of it was deflected toward charity for the poor. All over Europe poor relief was reorganized, and in its new form, which was propagated as being both more efficient and more Christian, depended almost entirely on regular and frequent contributions from the population. One of the most ardent advocates of the reforms was Juan Louis Vives, secretary to the town council at Bruges (van Damme, *Armenzorg*, pp. 102–30). "Lutheranism" quickly became the umbrella term for all of these religious changes, and it is indeed not difficult to see the similarities between the new devotional preferences and Luther's message. Antwerp was, however, the only place in the Low Countries where a fully Lutheran community was formed (Estié, *Vluchtige bestaan*, pp. 7–15).

The emperor reviewed the heresy laws in the Low Countries and gave lay commissioners, provincial courts, and urban justices power of inquisition alongside, and often above, the regular episcopal courts to prevent the spread of the German Reformation, with which as German emperor he was intimately familiar, into these lands. Under the new laws reading, possessing, printing, and sale of forbidden books, attending conventicles to discuss the Bible or books by Protestant authors, breaking or defiling images, and disrespect to clergy and the sacraments were defined as heresy and *lèse-majesté*, and as such fell within the jurisdiction of secular courts (Goosens, *Inquisitions modernes*, vol. 1, pp. 47–62). A more active policing of religious orthodoxy resulted of course in a higher visibility of what was actually going on, but still the religious picture remains diffuse. The persecuting authorities found networks of people suspected of heretical opinions both locally, around readers and teachers of the Bible and the new doctrines, and supralocally, where such groups kept in contact through letters and visits. "Lutherans" were burned at the stake, were banned, or fled before they could be arrested. In many cases, however, accusations could not be made to stick. For most the change in devotion did not amount to separation from the church or a total negation of all it stood for, but rather reinforced preexisting criticism and anticlericalism (Decavele, *Dageraad*; Duke, *Reformation and Revolt*; Rooze-Stouthamer, *Zeeland*).

In the 1530s Anabaptism penetrated into the Low Countries from the northeast. Emissaries of Melchior Hoffman, then based at Emden, took up a wandering ministry in these lands. Anabaptism was from the start both much more radical and more organized than what had so far gone under the broad umbrella of "evangelicalism" or "Lutheranism." They practiced what they preached. Instead of the rather general criticism of the sacraments found in the adherents of the new evangelicalism, the Anabaptists from the beginning divided into several branches, following specific "prophets" and accepting only those doctrines they considered Biblical. Their abstention from the Easter celebration of the Eucharist and the baptism of newborns, in favor of their own version of the Lord's Supper and the baptism of believers, constituted open heresy. Those who were rebaptized formed tight, self-reliant cells, in which teaching was done by those most able, and support of the needy was modeled on the sharing of goods in the primitive Christian communities. A strict discipline kept them separate from the evils of the world and provided a shield of secrecy. Apart from this lay ministry of believers, the early Anabaptists had an ordained ministry of elders and missionary bishops, who supervised the local cells and were authorized to baptize new members. The Anabaptists may have recruited from earlier evangelical groups but had a radically different character from these (Augustijn, "Anabaptisme," pp. 16–23; Knottnerus, "Menno als tijdverschijnsel," pp. 105–12).

The Anabaptists were not only heretical, they were also considered a political danger. As the successor to a long line of popular evangelical movements, critical of the church and its entanglement in secular power and wealth, they believed the end of the world, the Second Coming of Christ, and the Last Judgment were imminent. In preparation for these events they kept themselves separate from society at large in order to remain unpolluted by worldly interests. They did not attend the services of the church, remained as much as possible in the company of co-religionists, and refused to swear oaths and bear arms – the usual prerequisites for civil citizenship. They made one decisive exception to their general abstention from armed violence. Anabaptists believed that they could expedite the Second Coming by preparing a New Jerusalem, a town held by the believers, from where Christ and his saints could rule the world. With this object in mind, in 1534 Anabaptists seized Münster in Westphalia through a political coup. They evicted all those who were not of their persuasion and reorganized the urban community according to their views of Paradise. They invited sympathizers from elsewhere to join them and help defend the city against the bishop of Münster, who intended to retake it by force. Thousands of Anabaptists started out from the Netherlands but were intercepted by the authorities on their way, in Spaarndam near Haarlem, and in the harbor of Kampen, where shiploads from North Holland landed after crossing the Zuyderzee. A number of them were executed for heresy, but the large mass were considered harmless souls misled by religious fervor and were released with a mere warning. Münster itself was recaptured and the Anabaptist leaders executed. In 1535 and 1536 several attempts were made to take other towns, most notably Amsterdam, but also Leiden, Deventer, and Hazerswoude, and in 1535 Anabaptists briefly occupied the convent of Bloemkamp near Bolsward. None of these actions was successful. Secular authorities were very alert and investigated closely into the trade in the kind of prophetic texts that justified the Anabaptist attempts, actively sought out cells in which this literature was read and new plans could be prepared, and brought suspects to trial. In the 1540s this policy slackened, as within Anabaptist groups eschatological expectations faded and a majority decided to bide the time until the Second Coming in patience, abstaining from all use of violence. An important architect of this new peaceful identity was Menno Simons, after whom Dutch Anabaptists are henceforth called Mennonites (Zijlstra, *Ware gemeente*, pp. 11–150, 170–96, 237–47).

Except for the period of the Anabaptist kingdom of Münster and the attempts to take other towns, local magistrates were not very keen on persecution of heresy, Anabaptist or otherwise. The anti-heresy policy emanating from Brussels was seen as one more example of central government infringing upon local jurisdictions. Resentment may not have been the only root of this lack of enthusiasm, interpreted as obstruction by the emperor. Local magistrates were reluctant to bring their own citizens to trial for harboring ideas that, although akin to those of Luther, might not quite represent an outright break from the traditional church, or that could be viewed as honest misconceptions. They seem to have adhered to an older definition of heresy as "willful and obstinate rejection of Christian doctrine and the authority of the church," rather than the new one focusing on transgression of the emperor's religious policies. The distinction between an interest in Biblical precepts or a spiritualized piety and heresy was, however, often a fine one. The ambiguity of the appeal to a Biblical Christianity can be demonstrated from the plays staged by the Chambers of Rhetoric. These plays usually addressed some actual discussion, and quite a few of them contain references to religious issues of the day. In some instances these were quite outspoken. The texts of the plays staged in Ghent in the course of a "rhetoricians' contest" in 1539 were subsequently placed on the Index. Obviously, the players and the magistrate of Ghent did not consider the subject matter or its interpretation as beyond the pale of orthodoxy, as a public display of heresy was unwise in the extreme. The royal inquisitioners in Brussels, however, thought otherwise (Decavele, *Dageraad*, pp. 193–203). Laxity or sympathy for heretic notions may have played a part, but this does not seem highly likely. There was an extensive gray zone between heresy and an acceptable appeal to the plain Gospel, however critical. The latter could be seen as a call for reforming the church from the inside. In fact, the desire for reform may have been widespread among magistrates and town councils (Spaans, *Haarlem*, pp. 31–2).

Calvinism

In the 1540s a new brand of religion entered the Low Countries. From France Calvinism spread into the southern provinces, at first gradually and diffuse in character, but then more systematically, especially in the French-speaking areas from 1560, under the guidance of Guy de Bres, who had earlier been active in London and Switzerland. Like Anabaptists, the Calvinists formed relatively autonomous cells, with a strong internal organization. They were ministered to by ordained preachers. A consistory made up of lay elders, mostly local notables, organized secret meetings, procured ministers and devotional books like the Bible and the Psalms – translated and set to music for communal singing – and maintained discipline, while deacons cared for the poor (Augustijn, "Opmars"). French Calvinism was not only a religion but also a political movement. Supported from Geneva, which trained and sent out ministers, the Calvinist congregations in France were used by the Huguenot faction to destabilize the crown that was in the power of the Catholic nobility. This policy would lead to intermittent civil war from 1562 to 1598, each period of warfare concluded by a peace settlement in which the rights and freedoms of both religions were formulated. Likewise, after 1559, in the Southern Netherlands the Calvinist consistories allied themselves with opposition against the centralizing policies of the Catholic King Philip II. His style of government, although building on the institutional structures his father had introduced, was strongly resented by the higher nobility. Noblemen from the Low Countries like William of Orange, Lamoral, count of Egmond, and Philip of Montmorency, count of Hornes, who claimed hereditary rights to high office, felt excluded from the real center of power, which was located in the small entourage of the regent. They rode the wave of Calvinism, which would propel Orange to fame as the successful leader of the revolt and founder of the Dutch Republic, and Egmond and Hornes to public execution (Cameron, *European Reformation*, pp. 372–81).

Calvinist provocations of the government in Brussels, in the form of public preaching and the singing of Psalms on the public streets (*chanteries*), preferably under a Catholic clergyman's windows, started early in the 1560s. The ministers who led these disturbances were theologically often ill informed and functioned more as military leaders than as pastors. They were in contact with the members of the noble faction who saw themselves excluded from the center of power, and who within years would openly present themselves as leaders of the Dutch Revolt. City magistrates did not suppress the sermons and *chanteries*, or prosecute participants with anything like the vigor the king and his regent ordered. This led to the impression that the cities and their magistrates were heavily infected with heresy. Magistrates themselves denied this, pointing to "foreign elements" as the inciters of religious unrest, and maintaining that most participants were there simply out of curiosity or had been unaware of the heretical character of the occasion. And although magistrates had a compelling interest in deflecting the attentions of central government, to protect their own autonomy, they may have had some point there: if the actions were mainly politically inspired, those in it for merely religious motives were unaware and innocent (Steen, *Chronicle of Conflict*, pp. 23–38).

In 1566 the league of discontented grandees, supported by a larger group of lesser nobles, felt strong enough to apply to the regent for a suspension of the heresy laws. In a moment of weakness, Margaret of Parma promised moderation. All over the south the Calvinist congregations grew in the summer of this Miracle Year 1566, and in the northern provinces, where so far very little Calvinist activity had been going on, new congregations emerged (Vis, *Arentsz.*, pp. 40–91). Existing groups changed character; more than before, members of local elites became involved. They reshaped the congregations into recruiting grounds and communications centers for the opposition. The open-air services they organized attracted large crowds. They grew into a show of strength for the opposition to royal policy, a fact underlined by the frequent presence of armed guards. The opposition did not, however, content itself with services in the open air, the so-called hedge-preaching: in August and September 1566, in a seemingly well-organized operation which started in Steenvoorde in the deep south of Flanders and swept from south to north through Antwerp into Gelderland, leading to many similar localized incidents as far north as Friesland and Groningen, little groups of iconoclasts, often with the help of local Calvinists or sympathizers, smashed the images in the churches in town after town.

By that time the king had been informed of the softening of his religious policy by his regent, and had predictably ordered immediate repression of all heretical innovations. In a subsequent accord, the regent tried to contain the damage by granting limited toleration, but limiting Protestant preaching to those places where they had been held before. Moderation, however, effectively ended in 1567 with the arrival of the duke of Alva, who was sent by the king with an army of Spanish *tercios* to restore order and punish those responsible for the "Troubles" of 1566 (Crew, *Calvinist Preaching*, pp. 1–38; Parker, *Dutch Revolt*, pp. 74–84).

Catholic Reformation, Conformity, and Exile

Repression was not, however, the only policy initiated by the king. The issues addressed by the Protestant Reformation – the need for higher standards of learning and morality in the clergy, the soft life lived in many monasteries, the demand among both the learned and the literate urban classes for a more spiritualized devotion, closer to the example of the early church – preoccupied many leading Catholics, including the papacy. From 1545 the Council of Trent, dedicated to the defense of Catholic doctrine against Protestantism and to church reform from within, had been in session. In the spirit of this Catholic Reform, in 1561 Philip II decreed a reorganization of the bishoprics in the Low Countries, which had been discussed from the reign of Charles V. Three archiepiscopal sees instead of one and 15 suffragan bishoprics instead of five would henceforth cover all of the territory of the Netherlands, where formerly the jurisdiction of ecclesiastical provinces had ignored state borders to the detriment of effective governance. The new bishoprics would initiate the Counter-Reformation program of regular synods and visitations, in order to improve pastoral care and combat heresy. As this reorganization infringed upon existing jurisdictions and privileges, it met with much resistance, notwithstanding a broader movement for reform (Rogier, *Katholicisme*, vol. 1, pp. 201–59; Post, *Kerkelijke verhoudingen*, pp. 114–16, 335–6, 452–5, 552).

The actual impact of both political and religious developments on the population at large is hard to calculate. By the 1560s the Low Countries contained one Lutheran congregation in Antwerp (Estié, *Vluchtige bestaan*). In the Dutch-speaking areas both north and south Mennonite groups were widely scattered, with denser concentrations in Frisia, North Holland, and Flanders. Organized Calvinist churches were found mainly in the south, both Flemish and Walloon. Despite humanist criticism of the traditional church and common age-old anticlericalism, the majority seem to have unprotestingly conformed to Catholicism. They may have harbored the wish for reform, but the conscious choice for a Protestant congregation, which meant a repudiation of traditional religion, was made only by the informed few. The emphasis here is on informed: hindsight and textbooks allow us to see the doctrinal and ecclesiological implications of the various blends of Christianity formed by such macro-developments of radical Reformation, magisterial Reformation, Counter-Reformation, and state formation, but for the average sixteenth-century layperson the finer theological distinctions were less obvious and perhaps quite irrelevant. Traditional religion was closely intertwined with family life and all levels of social organization, and a personal choice for a style of devotion that separated one from this familiar web of relations may have been inconceivable to most.

Those who did join Protestant congregations ran the risk of persecution, which at times could be fierce and deadly. Persecution drove heretics into exile. Most visible are the patterns of exile for the Calvinists. In the 1540s Calvinists from the southern Low Countries crossed the Channel into England and formed exile communities in several towns in the southeast, most of all in London. Several cities in the German Empire also harbored Dutch Protestant exile communities. These exile churches remained separate from the Protestant organization in the receiving countries, but operated with the tacit support of the authorities. They supported the secret congregations that remained on the continent, training and sending back ministers and printing and smuggling in books, just as Geneva did for French Calvinism. With the accession of the Catholic Queen Mary, the Dutch churches had to leave England. They relocated to Emden in East Frisia, which, also after the succession of the Protestant Queen Elizabeth, remained an important center of missionary Calvinism, supplying both the northern and the southern churches. Many of those involved in the

Troubles of 1566 in the northern provinces, either as iconoclasts or as members of the fledgling congregations, fled to Emden, and it was in synods held at Emden in 1568 and 1571 that a blueprint was devised for the organization of a Reformed Church once the revolt had been successful and these exiles could return (Pettegree, *Emden*).

Political Reformation

Armed insurrection would eventually determine the confessional configuration in the Low Countries. However widespread discontent and heresy had been in the preceding decades, it was the revolt against the harsh rule of Alva that would make the north officially Protestant and the south officially Catholic. In 1568 Orange, having fled to the safety of his German family possessions, orchestrated a four-pronged attack on Alva's forces, aided by the German Lutheran princes and his relations among the French Huguenot leaders, and by the exile consistories in England. This ambitious campaign failed, costing Orange both a fortune and the support of the French and Germans (Parker, *Dutch Revolt*, pp. 105–11). The first signal victory in the revolt was gained more or less by accident by the Sea Beggars, a loose association of pirate captains and crews privateering against the Spanish with letters of marque from Orange. Denied access to English ports by Elizabeth, they landed in the small port town of Den Briel, in the estuary of the Meuse River. As it happened, the town was practically defenseless, and on April 1, 1572 the Beggars took it "for the prince of Orange." Den Briel provided Orange and his Beggars a convenient bridgehead, from which in the early summer of that same year most of Holland was won. The fall of Den Briel would understandably come to be seen in later Protestant historiography as proof of God's guiding hand in the Reformation of the Netherlands.

One after the other, towns and cities declared their allegiance "to the prince," partly under the pressure of the Beggar troops before their gates, but also in no small measure aided by members of the local political elites sympathetic to the cause of the revolt. Although by no means all of these supporters were themselves Protestants, and the urban populations often preferred to remain loyal to the Catholic faith, in each town that joined the revolt, the Reformed Church was officially recognized. In 1572 and 1573, Catholics retained equal rights to public worship and access to public office under a religious peace arrangement dictated by the prince of Orange. From 1573 on, however, allegiance to the revolt meant also rejection of Catholicism, as among Catholics resistance to the Protestant political takeover was perceived to foment conspiracy with the royal forces. Catholics gradually came to be excluded from political office.

Royal armies proved unable to recapture the areas controlled by the Beggars. The war seriously hampered the economy of Flanders and Brabant, unpaid troops mutinied in Antwerp in 1574 and 1576, and in the latter year thoroughly sacked the city. A stalemate seemed to have been reached, and the 17 provinces wanted the war to end. In the 1576 Pacification of Ghent, the Estates General, overstepping the boundaries of their constitutional power, declared the war over and accepted the political and religious status quo. Holland and Zeeland would have the prince of Orange as their governor, and the Reformed Church would be their public church. The other provinces would remain royalist and Catholic, but the heresy laws were suspended. In the years that followed, religious peace settlements were tried out, but these experiments foundered on the growing polarization between north and south. In 1579 the Union of Arras and the Union of Utrecht effectively created two different federations of provinces. In the years 1580–5 in Antwerp, Ghent, Brussels, and Mechelen, "Calvinist republics" were proclaimed, in defiance of growing royalist and Catholic hegemony. At the same time, Groningen in the far north of the territory of the Union of Utrecht declared for the king and Catholicism, thereby creating a backlash of anti-Catholicism throughout the north. In each of these cities upwardly mobile guilds made a grab for political power against the traditional elite. In the south they were given ideological support by the militantly Calvinist ministers – a development not unlike the communal reform movements found in North German cities and, at the same time, heir to the politicized Calvinism of the consistories in France and the Netherlands in the 1550s and 1560s. The republics were overthrown by force of arms in 1585 (Marnef, "Brussel"; *Mechelen*; Israel, *Dutch Republic*, pp. 155–220; Woltjer, *Vrijheidsstrijd*).

The south reconciled itself with Spanish rule and was in 1599 entrusted by Philip II as a dowry to his daughter Isabella, who ruled it as an independent principality with her husband, Albert of Austria. The couple were given the title of archdukes. They were devoted to the cause of the Counter-Reformation and supported the reform of the Catholic Church in their lands. In 1581 the north renounced its allegiance to Philip II and became the Dutch Republic. All seven of the United Provinces introduced the Reformed Church as their public church.

New Religious Regimes

The military campaigns of Alexander Farnese, duke of Parma, consolidated the Southern Netherlands under Spanish rule. They culminated in the capture of Antwerp in 1585. The sea lanes to its harbor were controlled, however, by the Republic, stifling its commerce in favor of Amsterdam. Not only did the wealth generated by access to international trade routes shift to the north, leading it to its Golden Age, but so did large numbers of merchants and skilled artisans, many of them Calvinists, Lutherans, Jews, and Mennonites. They left the city and its industrial hinterland, partly because of the economic malaise that came in the wake of war, but also for religious reasons. The Spanish Netherlands was a Catholic country and its rulers demanded loyalty to the Catholic Church from its inhabitants. Protestants were purged from all public functions. The Catholic Church tried to reconcile Protestants, and this policy was moderately successful. Bishops could report large numbers of converts, although it is also clear that many merely outwardly conformed. Those who could not live with that had to leave, and many did (Marinus, "Verdwijnen van het protestantisme"; Thijs, *Geuzenstad*, pp. 31–59).

Calvinist, Lutheran, and Jewish merchant families from Antwerp were given four years in which to sell their real estate in the city and emigrate. Similar arrangements had been made for other cities in the south. Many went to Hamburg or Frankfurt at first, but eventually Amsterdam proved a magnet few could resist. Mennonite linen weavers and Calvinist wool weavers from Flanders and Brabant settled around Haarlem and Leiden, the main centers of these industries in Holland. Ministers and schoolmasters came from all over the south. Together with emissaries from the exile churches, they played an important role in building the public Reformed Church of the Republic and its French-speaking complement, the Walloon Reformed Church, as well as those Protestant churches that enjoyed a limited freedom in the north: the Evangelical Lutheran churches and the Mennonite communities.

For all churches the last decades of the sixteenth century were a period of building. Politics and war had demonstrated the need for, and determined the choice of, official churches for both the Spanish Netherlands and the Dutch Republic. Both the war and the uncertainties of the times had seriously diminished the wealth of the old church. Church buildings had been damaged, the lands and rents that provided their upkeep and the income of the clergy were diminished through violence and neglect, and title deeds had been lost. The priests needed for pastoral care had been harassed by Calvinists in the south; in the north Protestant ministers, officially in demand now for the first time, were equally scarce. Moreover, clergy now had to conform to the higher standards of learning, moral conduct, and pastoral ability set by both Protestant and Catholic Reformations. They had to teach their flocks a godly discipline that was stricter than traditional, medieval Catholicism had been.

In the south the appointment of able and active bishops to oversee and lead this construction work proved no easier in the 1580s than it had been in the 1560s. The organization of the new bishoprics, started by Philip II at the very beginning of his reign, was not yet completed, mainly due to problems of funding. The money needed for a well-appointed episcopal household, annex court, and office in most cases had to come from the incorporation of wealthy abbeys, who tried each and every possible legal strategy to retain their autonomy. Bishops were obliged under the decrees of the Council of Trent to hold regular diocesan synods and visitations of the churches under their jurisdiction. Synods and visitations had to instill in the diocesan clergy the spirit of the new Catholicism and to correct those who fell short – even parish priests who divided their attentions between farming and their priestly duties because of insufficient income from their benefice. Bishops had to see to it that the religious in cloisters lived according to their vows, and had to stimulate the work of active congregations in the care of the sick and the poor, and in elementary teaching. They were responsible for the recruitment and training of priests for their churches. They supported the Latin schools and stimulated promising pupils to continue their studies in their seminaries and eventually take the cloth. They had to ensure that the new teaching device, the catechism, was taught in schools. In their courts they disciplined all, both religious and lay, who in any way overstepped the rights and teachings of the church (Harline and Put, *Bishop's Tale*).

Where bishops and their secular clergy had a relatively hard time overcoming the after-effects of the revolt and changing into the more demanding Counter-Reformation gear, the regular clergy showed a remarkable resilience. Especially in Antwerp, but also more generally, the traditional orders quickly recovered. The contemplative, cloistered orders, which often demanded a sizable dowry from new members, appealed especially to the sons and daughters of the wealthy, and having a relative in such an order became a mark of social distinction. This in turn appears to have stimulated vocations to the less strict orders, and the active congregations. The monasteries attracted gifts from the faithful, which allowed them to rebuild, refurnish, and embellish their buildings with all the lushness of the then fashionable baroque style. Their chapels consequently became popular. Parishioners preferred them over the shabbier parish churches for their regular devotions and for receiving the sacraments. As in the latter donations from the faithful were expected, this bred resentment between the regular clergy and the seculars. At the same time, the "market forces" implied in this competition for patrons and income may have improved pastoral work, religious education, and discipline.

The help of regular clergy and the members of religious communities was also indispensable in inculcating the faithful with the new religious values and attendant practices. The Council of Trent advocated a focus on Christ and the Eucharist over the traditional cult of the saints. It prescribed a more frequent communion, and consequently frequent confession, for which the regular priests provided the necessary manpower. There was some measure of specialization in the different orders, which preached for the educated or for the masses, dedicated themselves to teaching or care of the sick and burying of the poor, but the most versatile order of all were the Jesuits. The religious orders promoted lay devotions, bringing people together in clubs and fraternities for a combination of pious exercises and conviviality. Many of these were socially exclusive, but others catered to the common people. Both regular and secular priests acted as father-confessors to loose groups of devout lay sisters, who combined a life of prayer and meditation with pious work, such as teaching children their catechism, caring for the sick and the poor, and engaging people in devout conversation. The arts, from the polemics for the intellectual few to the processions and religious theater for the population at large, were used to enhance the effect of this process of confessionalization. All this stimulated reverence for the church, new vocations, and pious donations, and gave society at large a distinctly Catholic stamp. Visitors from the north could not but be impressed by the splendor of the religious services which impacted all the senses, and by the many forms of popular devotion (Thijs, *Geuzenstad*, pp. 61–96, 161–85; Vroede, *"Kwezels"*).

In the north the Reformed Church had many of the same problems in building its new organization and finding able clergy. Here too adequate funding for the church was a problem. Secular government claimed a part of the income from the abolished Catholic monasteries, chapters, and chantries for the war effort, for the repair of war damage, and to pay for the new Protestant universities that would have to educate the elites of the Republic who had traditionally patronized Cologne and Louvain – both Catholic by now. The rest had to be used to pay the former monks and nuns a pension for life and for other pious purposes. In time these funds, together with those of the parishes, would guarantee the ministers of the public church an adequate salary, at least in the larger towns and cities. Rural parishes could be too poor to support a minister, and many had to share one. Even then, Protestant ministers were sometimes forced to work for additional income. Ministers were trained in the new universities. They formed supralocal governing bodies in the regional classes and provincial synods, which exercised many of the administrative and disciplinary functions handled by bishops in Catholic areas.

In the Dutch Republic the one minister in the village or the handful in larger towns had to do without the rivalry and support the secular clergy of the south experienced in the regulars. The ministers were expected to preach twice on Sundays and usually on one or more weekdays. Four times a year the Lord's Supper was celebrated, exclusively for those who had by a public profession of faith proven they had sufficient knowledge of and wholeheartedly subscribed to the doctrines of the church.

The Reformed version of the sacrament did not require prior confession by the faith-ful – a sermon of instruction and exhortation to self-examination of one's conscience was held some days in advance. Moreover, all full members of the church were visited personally by the minister and one of the elders, to inquire whether they were worthy of partaking. Those who were not were officially barred. Religious instruction for adults seems to have been given almost exclusively in the form of sermons. In the larger towns "comforters of the sick" visited the sick and dying in their houses. Parents were expected to teach the essentials to their children, while a more system-atic instruction was provided by schoolmasters, which consisted mainly of memo-rization of the catechism. The elders, a college of lay notables often partly made up of members of the magistrate, supervised the religious life of the congregation, and together with the minister handled cases of ecclesiastical discipline. The poor among the full members were supported by the deacons, who were often amalgamated in a wider board of welfare officers catering to all poor urban residents.

The requirement of some form of instruction, public profession of faith, and a godly lifestyle, under the permanent scrutiny of the consistory once one had attained full membership, demanded a measure of commitment that not all were prepared to make. The Reformed Church was, for a public church, rather exclusive, and it is esti-mated that by the end of the sixteenth century only 10 to 20 percent of the popu-lation could be counted as members. This is remarkable. It is an indication that all the humanism, evangelicalism, and anticlericalism of the preceding decades had not made many people into informed and convinced Protestants. It would take a process of confessionalization, of systematic inculcation of religious values, lasting deep into the seventeenth century to do that (Abels and Wouters, *Nieuw en ongezien*; Spaans, "Catholicism").

Reformed religious life was focused on the Bible and the truths contained therein. Religious culture was decidedly stark in comparison to the baroque splendor of the Counter-Reformation. The public church buildings were few, without the comple-ment of chapels that gave the Catholic faithful a choice of devotional styles and the possibility of social distinctiveness. Only in Utrecht was a shortlived experiment con-ducted with two rival congregations, offering two different modes of Reformed worship and community-building. One minister in one parish church conducted a relatively undemanding form of worship, without discipline and with access to the sacrament of the Lord's Supper for all who wished to partake. This so-called Liber-tine church was patronized by members of the city's social and political elite, but also by the poor, for whom the thresholds to membership were generally felt to be high, whereas the regular, more Calvinist congregation attracted the economically inde-pendent middle groups (Kaplan, *Calvinists and Libertines*). Within the Reformed Church at large social differentiation in religious behavior and display never played a part comparable to what Catholicism could offer. Sometimes it seems that being a member of the church was itself felt to be a mark of social distinction. Over time within the congregations finer distinctions would develop for the higher strata of Reformed society, in the form of seating arrangements and membership of conven-ticles promoting a more intimate knowledge of the faith and pious exercises.

The Reformed church interiors were plain and, although the arts flowered in the Republic, they depended on civic rather than ecclesiastical patronage. Even the splen-did and costly organs found in many churches were an expression of civic pride, used for concerts and not as an accompaniment to the singing of the Psalms in religious worship. Where in the Spanish Netherlands every possible allurement was deployed in order to integrate all subjects of a land that had been heavily infiltrated by evangelical, Anabaptist and Calvinist ideologies into a homogeneously Catholic culture, the Reformed Church of the Republic refused so much as to try. Even on the point of baptism and church marriage, in theory a service as the public church it could perform for all, the Reformed Church was ambiguous, often preferring to reserve these for members only.

The Problem of Diversity

Despite all the efforts to reconcile all subjects to the Catholic Church, small communities of Protestants and Jews remained in the Spanish Netherlands. They were condemned to obscurity, obliged to conform outwardly to the Catholic mainstream, attending services and even partaking of the sacraments. Their own forms of worship could only be practiced in secrecy. Dissidents living in border areas could and did cross over to places where they could join in the religious services of co-religionists, but such contacts were discouraged. In a city like Antwerp, which depended on the presence of foreign communities in the interest of trade, dissident communities were allowed some latitude, as long as they used it discreetly, without giving offense by attracting any attention to their existence, sometimes at the cost of special taxation. The official policy was that friendly persuasion and force of habit might eventually reconcile them to Catholicism, whereas active persecution would give the authorities in the Dutch Republic an excuse to harass their Catholic communities (Marinus, "Verdwijnen van het protestantisme").

The Dutch Republic was confessionally much more diverse. In the Union of Utrecht (1579), freedom of conscience was guaranteed for all the inhabitants of the United Provinces. This in itself did not imply freedom of worship: in fact, a succession of penal laws denied Catholics all forms of religious organization and communal worship, whereas Mennonites and Lutherans were never officially granted more freedom than they had had under Habsburg rule, except the freedom from persecution and inquisition into personally held beliefs. Jews were given specific privileges for worship and burial locally in the first decade of the seventeenth century. Freedom from persecution and inquisition and the exclusivity of the public Reformed Church did, however, create some space for religious minorities.

Catholics who were not prepared to live under an officially Protestant regime left the country for the south, or for the exile community in Cologne. Remnants of the indigenous Catholic hierarchy remained in place, however, and from these a new Catholic community was built under the direction of apostolic vicars. When hopes that the Northern Provinces could be regained for the Spanish king and Catholicism faded, the Republic was declared a mission field by Rome, denying ecclesiastical validity to the structures built in the meantime. This did not immediately affect the community as such. Programs were devised by the remaining clergy to train indigenous priests in seminaries in Cologne and Louvain. To this secular clergy were added regular priests, both Dutch and foreign born, leading here also to resentment on both sides over competition for positions and income. Monasteries had been abolished, but lay sisters, because they officially lacked the status of religious, operated in relative freedom as helpmates of the priests, catechists, and fundraisers (Monteiro, *Geestelijke maagden*). As long as Catholic organization, worship, and pastoral care kept out of public view, and, most important of all, as long as the clergy involved was not suspected of disloyalty to the Dutch Protestant authorities, Catholic devotion, inspired by the Counter-Reformation despite its subdued existence, was allowed to flourish. In the seventeenth century, in the territories to the south of the great rivers, which had for decades been part of the Spanish Netherlands, and the Achterhoek, which had long remained under Münster but were added by conquest to the Seven Provinces by the stadholders Maurice and Frederick Henry, Catholics were ruled by a small Reformed elite, but the overwhelming majority remained Catholic and in the exceptional case of Maastricht even enjoyed public status (Rogier, *Geschiedenis*; de Mooij, *Bergen*; Ubachs, *Twee heren*; Israel, *Dutch Republic*, pp. 387–8, 658–60).

More or less the same applied to the other religions. Lutheran communities were found in most of the larger towns. All except Woerden and Bodegraven, which had been given as a fief to one of Orange's German Lutheran allies, owed their existence to immigration from the south and subsequently grew on German labor migration. Their ministers were usually also Germans (Visser, *Lutheranen*). The Mennonite presence too was strengthened by exiles from Flanders and Brabant. Flemish, Frisian, and "Waterlander" Mennonites, the latter deriving their name from the marshy area north of Amsterdam, each formed their own communities, with a distinctive brand of piety. The "ethnic" character faded over time, but the names remained as labels for the larger denominations within the highly fragmented community. Often one town or village boasted more than one Mennonite congregation, and some of the smaller splinter groups were to be found in a limited area. They were led by lay preachers, recruited from their own midst (Zijlstra, *Ware gemeente*). Jews settled in towns which were prepared to allow them freedom of worship and often also a separate burial ground in exchange for the economic activities they generated. At the end of the sixteenth century these were mainly Sephardic Jews, denoting Iberian or, more generally, Mediterranean extraction; later in the seventeenth century they would be joined by Ashkenazi, or central European, communities. The largest Jewish presence was concentrated in Amsterdam. Especially the Sephardic Jews, born and raised as New Christians in Spain or Portugal, built a new religious identity, taught them initially by rabbis imported from the German Empire (Fuchs-Mansfeld, *Sefardim*; Bodian, *Hebrews*).

The nature of the religious settlement of the Dutch Republic, usually described as tolerant, was nevertheless a variety of the common European form of the confessional state. The magistrates supported the public church, both financially and morally, and guaranteed its monopoly on public worship. Political power and public office in general were reserved for members of the Reformed Church, or those who outwardly conformed to its precepts. Especially in the early Republic many exceptions to this rule can be found, as the Reformed Church locally often contained a minority of the population as a whole, and following it to the letter was not always possible or desirable, but a rule it remained. Members of dissident religious communities were excluded from positions of power and often socially at a disadvantage, and a distinctly hierarchical socioreligious differentiation would develop later on (Spaans, "Religious Policies").

BIBLIOGRAPHY

Abels, P. and Wouters, T., *Nieuw en ongezien: Kerk en samenleving in de classis Delft en Delfland 1572–1621*, 2 vols. Delft: Eburom, 1994.

Augustijn, C., "Anabaptisme in de Nederlanden," *Doopsgezinde Bijdragen*, 12–13 (1986–7), pp. 13–28.

Augustijn, C., "De opmars van de calvinistische beweging in de Nederlanden," *Theoretische Geschiedenis*, 20 (1993), pp. 424–38.

Bijsterveld, A. J. A., *Laverend tussen kerk en wereld: De pastoors in Noord-Brabant 1400–1570*. Amsterdam: VU Uitgeverij, 1993.

Bodian, M., *Hebrews of the Portuguese Nation: Conversos and Community in Early Modern Amsterdam*. Bloomington: Indiana University Press, 1997.

Bredero, G. A., *Spaanschen Brabander*, ed. C. F. P. Stutterheim. Culemborg: Tjeenk Willink/Noorduijn, 1974.

Cameron, E., *The European Reformation*. Oxford: Clarendon Press, 1991.

Crew, P. M., *Calvinist Preaching and Iconoclasm in the Netherlands 1544–1569*. Cambridge: Cambridge University Press, 1978.

Damme, D. van, *Armenzorg en de Staat*. Ghent: Author, 1990.

Decavele, J., *De dageraad van de Reformatie in Vlaanderen (1520–1565)*. Brussels: Koninklijke Academie voor Wetenschappen, Letteren en Schone Kunsten van België, 1975.

Duke, A., *Reformation and Revolt in the Low Countries*. London/Ronceverte: Hambledon Press, 1990.

Estié, P., *Het vluchtige bestaan van de eerste Nederlandse Lutherse gemeente, Antwerpen 1566–1567*. Amsterdam: Rodopi, 1986.

Fuchs-Mansfeld, R. G., *De Sefardim in Amsterdam tot 1795: Aspecten van een joodse minderheid in een Hollandse stad*. Hilversum: Verloren, 1989.

Goosens, A., *Les Inquisitions modernes dans les Pays-Bas Méridionaux (1520–1633)*, 2 vols. Brussels: Éditions de l'Université de Bruxelles, 1998.

Harline, C. and Put, E., *A Bishop's Tale*. New Haven, Conn.: Yale University Press, 2000.

Israel, J., *The Dutch Republic, Its Rise, Greatness and Fall 1477–1806*. Oxford: Oxford University Press, 1995.

Kaplan, B. J., *Calvinists and Libertines: Confession and Community in Utrecht, 1578–1620*. Oxford: Oxford University Press, 1995.

Knottnerus, O. S., "Menno als tijdverschijnsel," *Doopsgezinde Bijdragen*, n.s. 22 (1996), pp. 79–118.

Marinus, M. J., "Het verdwijnen van het protestantisme in de Zuidelijke Nederlanden," *De Zeventiende Eeuw*, 13 (1997), pp. 261–72.

Marnef, G., "Het protestantisme te Brussel, ca. 1567–1585," *Tijdschrift voor Brusselse geschiedenis*, 1 (1984), pp. 57–81.

Marnef, G., *Het calvinistisch bewind te Mechelen*. Kortrijk-Heule: UGA, 1987.

Mol, J. A., "Friezen en het hiernamaals: Zieleheilsbeschikkingen ten gunste van kerken, klosoters en armen in testamenten in Friesland tot 1580," in J. A. Mol, ed., *Zorgen voor zekerheid: Studies over Friese testamenten in de vijftiende en zestiende eeuw*. Leeuwarden: Fryske Akademy, 1994.

Monteiro, M., *Geestelijke maagden: Leven tussen klooster en wereld in Noord-Nederland gedurende de zeventiende eeuw*. Hilversum: Verloren, 1996.

Mooij, C. de, *Geloof kan Bergen verzetten: Reformatie en katholieke herleving te Bergen op Zoom 1577–1795*. Hilversum: Verloren, 1998.

Parker, G., *The Dutch Revolt*. Harmondsworth: Penguin, 1977.

Pettegree, A., *Emden and the Dutch Revolt: Exile and the Development of Reformed Protestantism*. Oxford: Clarendon Press, 1992.

Post, R. R., *Kerkelijke verhoudingen in Nederland voor de Reformatie*. Utrecht/Amersfoort: Het Spectrum, 1965.

Rogier, L. J., *Geschiedenis van het katholicisme in Noord-Nederland in de 16e en 17e eeuw*, 2 vols. Amsterdam: Urbi et Orbi, 1947.

Rooze-Stouthamer, C., *Hervorming in Zeeland*. Goes: De Koperen Tuin, 1996.

Spaans, J., *Haarlem na de Reformatie: Stedelijke cultuur en kerkelijk leven, 1577–1620*. The Hague: Stichting Hollandse Historische Reeks, 1989.

Spaans, J., "Catholicism and Resistance to the Reformation in the Northern Netherlands," in Philip Benedict, Guido Marnef, Henk van Nierop, and Marc Venard, eds., *Reformation, Revolt and Civil War in France and the Netherlands 1555–1585*. Amsterdam: Koninklijke Nederlandse Academie van Wetenschappen, 1999, pp. 149–63.

Spaans, J., "Religious Policies in the Seventeenth-Century Dutch Republic," in Ronnie Po-chia Hsia and Henk van Nierop, eds., *Calvinism and Religious Toleration in the Dutch Golden Age*. Cambridge: Cambridge University Press, 2002, pp. 72–86.

Spufford, M., "Literacy, Trade and Religion in the Commercial Centres of Europe," in Karel Davids and Jan Lucassen, eds., *A Miracle Mirrored: The Dutch Republic in International Perspective*. Cambridge: Cambridge University Press, 1995, pp. 229–83.

Steen, C. R., *A Chronicle of Conflict: Tournai, 1559–1567*. Utrecht: Hes Publishers, 1985.

Thijs, A. K. L., *Van Geuzenstad tot katholiek bolwerk: Antwerpen en de Contrareformatie*. Antwerp: Brepols, 1990.

Ubachs, P. J. H., *Twee heren, twee confessies: De verhouding van staat en kerk te Maastricht, 1632–1673*. Assen: Van Gorcum, 1975.

Verhoeven, G., *Devotie en negotie: Delft als bedevaartplaats in de late middeleeuwen*. Amsterdam: VU Uitgeverij, 1992.

Vis, G. N. M., *Jan Arentsz., de mandenmaker van Alkmaar, voorman van de Hollandse Reformatie*. Hilversum: Verloren, 1992.

Visser, C. Ch. G., *De lutheranen in Nederland tussen katholicisme en calvinisme, 1566 tot heden*. Dieren: De Bataafsche Leeuw, 1983.

Vroede, M. de, *"Kwezels" en "zusters": De geestelijke dochters in de Zuidelijke Nederlanden*. Brussels: Koninklijke Academie voor Wetenschappen, Letteren en Schone Kunsten van België, 1994.

Woltjer, J. J., *Friesland in Hervormingstijd*. Leiden: Universitaire Pers, 1962.

Woltjer, J. J., *Tussen vrijheidsstrijd en burgeroorlog: Over de Nederlandse Opstand 1555–1580*. Amsterdam: Balans, 1994.

Zijlstra, S., *Om de ware gemeente en de oude gronden: Geschiedenis van de dopersen in de Nederlanden 1531–1675*. Hilversum: Verloren, 2000.

FURTHER READING

The best place to start further research is the article "Niederlände" in the *Theologische Realenzyklopädie*, vol. 24 (1994), pp. 474–502. It is written by Cornelis Augustijn, who is easily the most sophisticated author on the early Dutch Reformation, and contains extensive bibliographical notes on primary sources and secondary literature. Post, *Kerkelijke verhoudingen*, is still authoritative for pre-Tridentine Catholicism, although Bijsterveld, *Pastoors*, nuances his opinion on parish priests. Decavele, *Dageraad*, presents a broad and insightful picture of the early Reformation in Flanders, as do several articles in Duke, *Reformation and Revolt*, (mainly) for Holland. Parker, *Dutch Revolt*, is good on political and military aspects of the revolt, Woltjer, *Vrijheidsstrijd*, on the ambiguous relation between religion and politics, and the importance of "middle groups" between Trent and Geneva. Israel, *Dutch Republic*, offers the longer chronological perspective, Cameron, *European Reformation*, the wider European context. There is a general tendency to overrate the impact of Protestant influence on the population at large, and to romanticize dissident groups. Thijs, *Geuzenstad*, and Harline and Put, *Bishop's Tale*, give lively impressions of Catholic renewal in the south. Reformation and beginning confessionalization in the north are best described in a number of books on city Reformation: Abels and Wouters, *Nieuw en ongezien*, on Delft, is a good example of this wider genre, and, moreover, also draws in the situation in the surrounding countryside. The history of the tolerated churches in the Republic has not yet been integrated into a broader religious history, a real and painful lacuna. Attempts toward such an integration can be found in de Mooij, *Bergen*, Spaans, *Haarlem* and "Religious Policies," and also in Israel, *Dutch Republic*. The references given in the text are for the most recent general histories of these churches.

NINE

The Reformation in England to 1603

CHRISTOPHER HAIGH

One thing seemed clear about England in 1529: it was not going to have a Reformation. King Henry VIII would not permit one: he had himself published a book against Martin Luther in 1521, the *Assertio Septem Sacramentorum* ("Defense of the Seven Sacraments"). The papal legate and lord chancellor, Cardinal Wolsey, was stifling any possibility of one: he had stage-managed bonfires of Luther's books in London in 1521 and 1526, to signal English rejection of the new heresy, and ordered bishops and magistrates to seek out heretics. England's leading theologians were arguing forcibly against one: in books and sermons, Bishop Fisher and others defended what Luther attacked and pointed out the shattering implications of the doctrine of justification by faith alone. The authorities of a powerful state and a powerful church stood firmly against Luther. England looked safe from Reformation.

Further, England did not need Reformation. It was once thought by historians that England in 1529 was ripe for Reformation and ready for Protestantism. This was not so. Sales of Catholic religious books were booming, and high levels of gifts and benefactions to religious causes suggested that laypeople were content with the religion on offer. Churches were crammed with votive altars and images of saints, and decorated with stained glass and paintings, funded voluntarily by parishioners. All the money given to religious guilds or bequeathed for prayers for souls created a huge demand for priests – and recruitment of young laymen to the priesthood reached unprecedented levels in the 1510s. Ordinations declined somewhat from about 1520, but that seems to have been because of high levels of royal taxation on poorly paid assistant clergy. Thomas More thought it would be better to have fewer, better priests – but there were so many because they were needed to say the services that people wanted, and they were generally well behaved and hard-working.

The Catholic Church in England was a going concern, and going well. Wolsey and his fellow-bishops encouraged a better-educated priesthood, and tightened discipline over both monks and parish clergy. The elaborate machinery of church courts and diocesan visitations kept the clergy in order and smoothed out frictions with the laity. Parishioners used the courts to settle their own disputes and to keep their neighbors in order. It would be hard to prove that tithes and church dues were paid enthusiastically, but they were paid: any arguments concerning such taxes and fees were usually about interpretation of local custom and were settled by compromise. Not every aspect of the church was perfect, and perhaps routine was more evident than fervor. But the church was part of the way things were: its role, the privileges of its clergy, and its beliefs were rarely questioned.

There were a few malcontents in 1529. There were Lollards, who criticized confession, images, pilgrimage, purgatory and transubstantiation, and passed around battered copies of the old Wycliffite translation of the Bible. Most Lollards were prosperous artisans in the smaller market towns of southern England, and in Amersham Lollard families were among the most respectable in the town – but there were few of them, their manuscripts were now a hundred years old, and they kept their opinions to themselves. Lollards were not going to make a Reformation. There were earnest reformers among the younger academics at Cambridge and Oxford, some influenced by Erasmus, some by Luther, and some by their own reading of the Bible. They wanted more emphasis on the saving power of Christ, and less on the mechanical processes of salvation by works. Most of them worked for a better religion rather than a different religion – and they were not going to make a Reformation either.

Among the orthodox, there may have been some who thought that churchmen had too much independence and too much authority. Christopher St. German wanted to shift the jurisdictional boundary between common law and canon law, and he got some support from lay lawyers who saw business they might have had going to church courts instead. Nobles close to the king may have resented the influence (and the arrogance) of Cardinal Wolsey, and perhaps they wanted to clip the power of the prelates if they could. And, for all his loyalty to the pope and the Catholic sacraments, Henry VIII could bridle at the pretensions of priests. When in 1515 the bishops insisted that their courts and not the king's should deal with errant clergy, Henry exploded: "the kings of England in time past have never had any superior but God alone. Wherefore know you well that we shall maintain the right of our crown and of our temporal jurisdiction as well in this point as in all others" (Guy, "Henry VIII," p. 497). But kings had been saying this sort of thing for centuries, and lawyers and nobles had griped when it suited them. In 1529 Christopher St. German, Thomas Howard, duke of Norfolk, and Henry Tudor were not about to start a Reformation.

But then the bulwarks fell. Cardinal Wolsey was overthrown in 1529, Bishop Fisher was executed in 1535, and by 1536 Henry VIII was making theological concessions to win a diplomatic alliance with the Lutheran princes of Germany. In 1539 England got an official English Bible; in 1549 it got an official English Prayer Book; in 1553 it got an official Protestant theology. England had a Reformation – against all the odds and probabilities. How did it happen? Well, first we have to understand what "it" was. "It" was not a swift German Reformation, deliberately imported, copied, and implemented – nor was "it" a Swiss Reformation. Germany and Switzerland provided some of the ideas, but not the motive or the motor or the model – much to the chagrin and discomfort of the Cambridge evangelicals who wanted a determined destruction of popish superstition and the erection of a godly church and commonwealth. Instead, England had decades of messy politics, religious change and reversals, faltering steps and occasional leaps, uncertainty and struggle, and blundering responses to threats and crises. In the end – and for our purposes the end was not until 1603 – "it" was a Reformation of sorts, but a Reformation by accidents and in installments. "It" was not what anyone intended, and not what many people liked.

When Henry VIII turned against Wolsey, and then against the clergy, and then against the pope, he did not mean to start a Reformation – he did not even mean to start a schism. For reasons partly political but mainly personal, Henry wanted to disown his wife, Catherine of Aragon, and marry Anne Boleyn; for reasons partly legal but mainly political, Pope Clement VII refused an annulment. But Henry was determined: he had persuaded himself that God disapproved of his relationship with Catherine, so it must be terminated. Cardinal Wolsey had tried legal argument and failed: he was brought down in a court coup in October 1529. Now Henry huffed and puffed and pleaded, and threatened the pope and the English Church. In 1530 his think-tank of divorce lawyers and theologians produced the "Collectanea satis copiosa" ("the sufficiently large collection"), documents, precedents, and spurious history designed to show that Henry did not need papal approval for an annulment: England was an independent jurisdiction, and its king had sovereign authority over church and state. This was indeed a blueprint for schism – but Henry did not follow it.

Henry used the "Collectanea" not to justify repudiation of papal authority, but to try to persuade the pope to allow the marriage case to be settled in England – and to help the pope give the right answer, in 1532 he threatened to block papal revenues from England. To ensure the English Church would then decide the suit as he wished, Henry flexed his muscles and squeezed his clergy as well: to protect their property, in 1531 they had to grant a tax of £118,000 and acknowledge that the king was "sole protector, supreme lord and head of the English Church and clergy" – though the bishops insisted this was only "as far as the law of God allows" (Guy, "Henry VIII," pp. 498–9). In 1532 the king's parliamentary manager, Thomas Cromwell, engineered a petition from the House of Commons about canon law and the church courts, and the clergy were forced to acknowledge that the king had authority over ecclesiastical law. To cap it all, in 1533 the Act of Appeals declared that there could be no appeal to Rome against decisions in England in temporal matters: testaments, tithes, and divorces. It had been an epic struggle: the bishops stood their ground, but were threatened and intimidated; the recalcitrant were punished, the king's councilors made concessions, MPs had to face the king himself; and finally everything was in place – if the pope would only agree, the English clergy would have to do as they were told and give Henry his annulment. No schism would be needed.

But the pope did not agree – and now the issue was urgent. Anne Boleyn was pregnant, and she and Henry were secretly married in January 1533. Catherine had to go. The new archbishop of Canterbury, Thomas Cranmer, declared the Aragon marriage invalid, and on June 1, 1533 crowned Anne queen of England. The pope responded by condemning the second marriage, and ordering Henry to return to his first wife or face excommunication. Now a schism was necessary. For excommunication would absolve Henry's subjects from obedience to him, and would surely lead to rebellion in England – perhaps to invasion from abroad as well. So the option of denying the pope's authority was attractive – especially as Henry was coming to believe the fake history of the "Collectanea" and to relish a new role as head of the English Church. In 1534 the Supremacy Act declared that Henry was indeed "the only supreme head on earth of the Church of England" – "any usage, custom, foreign laws, foreign authority, prescription or any other thing or things to the contrary hereof notwithstanding" (Elton, *Tudor Constitution*, pp. 364–5). England had broken from the Church of Rome: not yet from Rome's religion, but certainly from Rome's jurisdiction.

As things turned out, this was the beginning of England's Reformation – the Reformation that had seemed impossible only five years before. But only as things turned out, and they were a long time a-turning. There were some who hoped that the break with Rome would lead to Reformation, a Reformation like Germany's – and these included Archbishop Cranmer, who was a secret Lutheran, Thomas Cromwell, the king's secretary, and Queen Anne. There were others who thought that schism was good enough, with independence from Rome and royal control over the church – including perhaps the dukes of Norfolk and Suffolk and a few of the bishops, and certainly the king himself. But there were more, probably many, many more, who thought the breach with Rome was a temporary disruption, a tactic to get the king his annulment: it would not last, and it would not bring Reformation. The warden of New College, Oxford, warned his evangelical nephew to beware: "Remember that this world will not continue long. For (he said) although the king hath now conceived a little malice against the bishop of Rome because he would not agree to this marriage, yet I trust that the blessed king will wear harness [armor] on his own back to fight against such heretics as thou art" (Elton, *Policy and Police*, p. 353). Kings had fallen out with popes before, and it had always been mended. Perhaps things were not as bad as they looked.

But they got worse. Henry's schism had left England dangerously exposed, at risk from invasion by Emperor Charles V, Francis I of France, or both – and so in desperate need of improved defenses and foreign allies. To fund a program of naval building and repair, Henry turned to the wealth of the church: an annual income tax was imposed on the clergy in 1535, and in 1536 the smaller monasteries were suppressed and their lands seized. Henry had probably intended to leave the larger monasteries standing, but in 1538 he was short of cash again, to build a string of defensive fortresses on the south coast: the larger monasteries came down too. As for allies, who might join forces with a schismatic and cause trouble for Charles V? – the Lutheran princes of Germany. In negotiations in England and Germany, Henry had to make theological concessions to the Lutherans to entice them into an alliance. The Ten Articles of 1536 and the "Bishops' Book" of 1537 stated the new orthodoxies of the Church of England, incorporating compromises with the Lutherans on justification by faith and the nature of the sacraments. Henry VIII was not pleased: he refused to give the "Bishops' Book" his endorsement (hence its unofficial title), and sent Cranmer a list of 250 alterations he wanted made. He recognized diplomatic necessities, however, and allowed the book to be issued as an interim statement of what the English had to believe. But he was keeping his options open.

Henry had been pushed from schism into Reformation. The schism had led Henry to take advice from men who were reliably antipapal, evangelicals who wanted to go further than the king – Cranmer, Cromwell, Richard Foxe, and others. Their influence, and Lutheran demands, took Henry on toward Reformation. And Henry's own views were shifting. He had not set out to be supreme head of the church, but he found he rather liked it, caring for his subjects' souls as well as their bodies, purifying religion for the good of the realm. In royal injunctions for the church in 1536 and 1538, the king tackled "superstition" – veneration of images and relics was banned, pilgrimage was discouraged – and he ordered every parish church to have an English Bible. When the official "Great Bible" was published in 1539, its frontispiece showed Henry handing out Bibles to Cranmer and the bishops on his right and to Cromwell and the councilors on his left, who then passed "Verbum Dei" to the people – while Christ looked down approvingly from the clouds. That was how Henry had come to see himself, as God's agent bringing true religion.

Many of his people were less impressed. The common lawyers had been content to see Henry stripping the prelates of their power – until the king was forced to protect himself by seeking allies among heretics. Merchants were keen to see government funded by taxation on the clergy and confiscation of church property – until there was a risk of religious war, and disruption of the Flanders trades. From the time Henry's divorce project became public, there had been widespread, persistent criticism of the king, his ministers, and his policies: mutterings in the alehouse, sermons in the churches, local resistance to royal commissioners, and, in 1536, a great rebellion in the north. There, armies of 40,000 men mobilized in defense of the church and especially its monasteries, and Henry was able to deflect the protest only by agreeing to meet its demands and then reneging on promises given. Dissent was risky. Between 1532 and 1540, 883 people were investigated for treasonable opposition to the king: 329 were executed, including 69 simply for verbal criticism. It was not quite a reign of terror, but it was enough to make people careful of what they said and did. Magistrates watched priests, bishops watched magistrates, and they all had to report to Cromwell. But dissent continued.

By the autumn of 1538, Henry was in a dangerous position. There was growing evidence of public hostility to the royal injunctions – especially the introduction of English Bibles (seen as heretical) and parish registers (seen as a preparation for taxes on baptisms, marriages, and funerals). Henry was afraid of another rebellion, and back-tracked on religious change. He broke off negotiations with the German Lutherans, and signaled his orthodoxy by a new campaign against heretics – presiding himself over the trial of John Lambert, and then having him burned on November 22, 1538 with atrocious cruelty. It is a measure of Henry's fear of his own people (and his own distaste for key Lutheran ideas) that he pulled back from Reformation when the diplomatic situation was deteriorating: Charles V and Francis I formed an alliance against England, and Henry needed the Lutherans more than ever. But he refused to make the theological changes the German negotiators wanted, on the Eucharist, confession, clerical celibacy, and masses for the dead – exactly the issues which most bothered his subjects and made them hate heretics.

In 1539 Henry's new stance was given parliamentary backing in the Act of Six Articles, and in 1540 Bishop Stephen Gardiner led a Lenten sermon campaign against the evangelical doctrine of justification by faith alone. In July 1540 Thomas Cromwell was executed for treason – partly because he had pushed the king into a distasteful marriage alliance, but mainly because he had lost a struggle over the direction of religious policy. In 1541 Henry was even contemplating the possibility of a return to the Roman obedience, rather than risk international isolation. And in 1543 he tried to freeze England's faith solid by the Act for the Advancement of True Religion. The Act imposed a new formulary of faith to replace the "Bishops' Book" of 1537 –

incorporating many of Henry's own objections to the 1537 text, rejecting justification by faith alone, and emphasizing the mass, confession, obedience, and good
works. The Act also forbade Bible-reading by the lower ranks of society, on pain of
imprisonment, denying perhaps 90 percent of the population direct access to the
Scriptures. This looked like the end of Reformation in England.

In fact, it was not. By breaking away from Rome and setting the doctrine and
practice of the Church of England by royal instructions and parliamentary statutes,
Henry had made religion a political issue, always subject to political pressures and
calculations – and the 1543 Act could not take religion off the political agenda.
English religion would be whatever the king and Parliament could be persuaded it
was. Thomas Cranmer was still archbishop of Canterbury, and there were councilors
and courtiers who favored reformist change: military skills had gained Edward
Seymour and John Dudley royal favor, and Anthony Denny was close to the king.
In 1544 Henry endorsed a new English litany for use in churches, and in 1545 a
new English primer for use in schools: each one gave less attention to the saints than
traditional devotions had done. Also in 1545, a precautionary Chantries Act allowed
the king to seize endowments which funded masses for the dead – if he needed more
money for national defense. The future of prayers for souls depended upon the
demands of the defense budget – and the nature of English religion depended on
who had influence over the king of England.

By the middle of 1546, Henry VIII was 55 years old and in poor health. If he
had died in that summer, he would have left the young Edward VI in the care of a
Catholic-inclined regency council: a heresy hunt was in progress, the evangelicals
were on the defensive, and Bishop Gardiner and the duke of Norfolk seemed to be
in control. But when Henry actually died on January 28, 1547, things were very different. In a brilliant political coup in the autumn, evangelicals and their allies had
discredited Gardiner and convicted Norfolk of treason: in effect, evangelicals now
controlled the future. Edward VI would be their king, not the Catholics'. On Henry's
death, the regency council agreed that the new king's uncle should be duke of Somerset and protector of the realm: the duke bought support with a lavish distribution
of rewards, remodeled the council, and was voted regency powers. There would be
more Reformation – partly because of the sincere convictions of Somerset, Cranmer,
and others; partly to sideline Catholic politicians; and partly to provide theological
cover for the seizure of church property.

Although Somerset was afraid of both Charles V and popular discontent – as
Henry had been – Reformation proceeded briskly. The treason and heresy laws were
eased, censorship was relaxed, and the Act for the Advancement of True Religion
was repealed. In 1547 the chantries were suppressed and a book of model sermons
for the clergy took reformist ideas into the parishes. In 1548 the council ordered
images of saints to be removed from churches and destroyed, and part of the mass
was to be said in English not Latin. In 1549 Parliament substituted a half-Protestant
Book of Common Prayer in English for the old Latin rites, and the clergy were
allowed to marry. In 1550 the council demanded that altars should be taken down
and replaced by communion tables, and a new ordination service sought to change
the role and status of the clergy. In 1552 a second, more Protestant Book of Common
Prayer was introduced, and in 1553 a set of Articles defined the Protestant theology
of the Church of England. The Catholic service equipment made redundant by these

changes was collected up by royal commissioners – and precious chalices, candle-sticks, and such like were taken off to the mint.

Perhaps this was a determined reformist program implemented step-by-step by idealists; perhaps they knew where they were going, and how to get there safely. Perhaps it was less tidy (and less honorable) than that. The council stumbled rather than marched into the destruction of images and altars: in 1547–8 its hand was forced by visitation commissioners who (probably deliberately) misinterpreted new royal injunctions and caused contention in the parishes; and in 1550 it was bounced by bishops who encouraged radicals to pull down altars. In 1549 the flow of reforms was disrupted by rebellions and a coup – and Reformation continued by accident not design. There were revolts in Cornwall and Devon (and riots elsewhere) against the new English services, and agrarian protests in East Anglia and more widely: Somerset's rule was made to look both provocative and weak. There was a council coup against him in the autumn, and some of those involved meant to reverse religious policy – but the earl of Warwick deserted his conservative allies, brought more evangelicals onto the privy council, and picked up where Somerset had left off. By 1553 the Church of England had a Protestant liturgy, a Protestant theology, and a mainly Protestant episcopate. There had been a Reformation.

The driving forces had been political: the calculations, the ambitions, the self-interest, and the fortunes and misfortunes of princes and politicians had taken England from 1529 (when a Reformation seemed impossible) to 1553 (when it seemed to have happened) – despite the fact that very few wanted that Reformation and very many hated it. How had it been possible? – why had it not been stopped? There was rebellion in the north in 1536 and in the west in 1549; there was con-stant complaint everywhere, and frequent local struggles over the implementation of change – there was opposition, but only in 1538 had it scared a king into a policy shift (and then because Henry hadn't liked the policy anyway). In general, the Catholic English had obeyed their reformist rulers – and obedience was the key. Faced by a choice between what the state now demanded and the church had long taught, almost everyone obeyed the state: Thomas More argued that its claims were illegit-imate, but few others chose to test them. God had made Henry and Edward kings, and if they commanded wickedness that was God's business, not their subjects'. There was a habit of obedience, to the king and to the law – and Reformation came through the decrees of the king and the laws of Parliament. Reformation was grudgingly accepted.

This was partly because in England Reformation came in small doses, spread over 20 years and more, each dose just about bearable. The trimming of church jurisdic-tion, the breach with Rome, higher taxation of the clergy, the suppression of monas-teries, an English Bible, the attack on popular devotions, the dissolution of chantries, the pulling down of images and then of altars, the abolition of the mass – all were objectionable to traditionalists, but none caused national outrage. The early measures hit the clergy rather than the laity, and by the time parish religion was being altered the people had been habituated to change. The king rejected the pope, but God did not send floods or plagues or famine – the sky did not fall in. The king threw down abbeys, but the sky did not fall in; he committed sacrilege over and over again, but the sky did not fall in; and even when he stopped the mass, the sky did not fall in. The sun shone, the harvests came, and God did not seem so angry after all.

It was Reformation by installments, rather than by cataclysm – so it was not obvious that it was Reformation, that there was more to come. Groups and individuals took their stands on different issues: Archbishop Warham on clerical independence, Bishop Fisher and Thomas More on loyalty to the pope, the northern rebels of 1536 on the monasteries, Bishop Gardiner on the Eucharist, the western rebels of 1549 on traditional rites, Bishop Bonner on the doctrine of transubstantiation, Bishop Heath on ordination, Bishop Day on altars – Bishop Thirlby opposed all religious innovations by Edward's government, but put up with them. And it wasn't all bad. Perhaps the rejection of papal authority would give the English bishops more freedom, perhaps a drive against superstition would bring a better kind of Catholicism, perhaps the destruction of monasticism would free resources for schools and colleges. There were opportunities for gain, too – by the purchase of monastic and chantry lands, by buying redundant equipment at bargain prices. Michael Sherbrook, an Elizabethan clergyman, asked his father why he had joined in the ransacking of Roche abbey 30 years before: "What should I do, said he. Might I not as well as other men have some profit of the spoil of the abbey? For I did see all would away, and therefore I did as others did" (Dickens, *Tudor Treatises*, p. 125).

There were also enthusiasts for change, those for whom novelty brought liberation rather than despair. Evangelical tutors at the universities trained evangelical students – who then became evangelical preachers, supported and protected by Cranmer and the first evangelical bishops. Especially in 1535–8 and 1547–53, when government favored religious change, the preachers attacked idolatry and offered another way to God, by faith and the Bible – first Barnes, Bilney, and Latimer; later Bradford, Lever, and Rogers. In Edwardian London, there were great revivalist meetings at St. Paul's Cross, and the young in particular responded to the word preached. Some responded to the word read – both the English Bible, and the thousands of books published (often by immigrant printers) in a great campaign against the mass in 1547–9. Joan Waste, a blind Derby girl, was converted to Protestantism by Edwardian preachers and saved up to buy a New Testament: she got others to read it to her, and sometimes had to pay them. By 1553 there were Protestants throughout England, but mostly in a crescent from Norfolk round to Sussex, and in a spur from London through the Thames valley to Gloucestershire. But everywhere they were a minority – quite a large one in London, a tiny, tiny one in the north and the west.

So far, England had had its Reformation by chance – the chance that Henry VIII wanted an annulment, but the pope would not give it; the chance that for a time Charles V and Francis I planned to fight England rather than each other; the chance that Henry died in January 1547 rather than July 1546; the chance that when Somerset was overthrown Warwick deserted his conservative allies and looked to Protestants for support. And now Reformation was stopped by chance – the chance that Edward VI, educated as a Protestant, died at the age of 15, at the time when his regime's religious policy was at its most unpopular. In July 1553, the bishops were struggling to get parish clergy to subscribe to the Protestant Forty-Two Articles, and royal commissioners were struggling to get parishioners to surrender copes and candlesticks and chalices and pyxes and banners, and all the paraphernalia of the old liturgy. So when the privy council tried to put Henry VIII's Protestant great-niece on the throne, instead of his Catholic elder daughter Mary, it is not surprising that there was widespread popular support for Mary's claim. There was revolt in the provinces, the council buckled, Mary entered London in triumph, and the Reformation was over – it seemed.

But how was it to be undone? Mary may have thought that the Reformation legislation was ungodly and could be ignored; she was persuaded that it was parliamentary, and had to be repealed. There were a few hiccups over timing, and the order in which things should be done, but within two and a half years Mary had almost all she wanted – the mass, a celibate priesthood, the papal supremacy, the anti-heresy laws. What she did not get was the return of the property confiscated from the church by her father and brother: most of it had been sold, and the purchasers (and their political representatives) were not going to give it back. With that exception, it was a whirlwind Counter-Reformation and the parishes often moved even faster than the queen and Parliament. Altars were reerected and the mass celebrated again within weeks of Mary's accession, well ahead of the official restoration in December 1553. There were scuffles in some churches and the Protestants were outraged, but the Catholics were confident and they had their way.

At the parish level, Catholic worship was restored with eagerness and success: Reformation had been imposed from above, but Counter-Reformation was not. Congregations made huge investment in new equipment, repurchases, and repairs – high altar, vestments, service books, and cross in 1553; candlesticks, banners, and side-altars in 1554; rood and images in 1555–6; fabric and bell repairs thereafter. Often parishes ran ahead of official policy, putting up altars, images, and roods before they were ordered to do so. By 1556 almost all churches had been redecorated and supplied with the basic needs for Catholic services. Some parishes had wisely concealed prohibited equipment in Edward's reign, and were now able to bring it out of hiding, but for the others restoration was an expensive business. Michael Sherbrook (who was 20 at this time) noted later that "whereas the poor commons had taken from them their church goods in King Edward's time . . . , now in this queen's time they were compelled to buy new again, and thus God on the altar put the commons to no little charge by his going away and his coming again" (Dickens, *Tudor Treatises*, p. 141). A few parishes (especially in Essex and Kent) were reluctant to pay – but most raised large sums by church ales, bequests, and voluntary collections as well as by rates, and more was being spent on parish churches in Mary's reign than at any time since the 1520s.

For Catholics, it was a time of exuberance and renewal; for Protestants, a time of anguish and fear – especially after January 1555, when the heresy laws came into force again. Almost all the Protestants went to church and publicly conformed – much to the horror of their leaders who, like John Bradford, wrote tracts on *The Hurt of Hearing Mass*. Like Catholics before them, Protestants obeyed the law – though they tried to limit their compromises by little gestures of dissent. They faced some determined persecution, led by conservative gentry in Essex, Kent, and Suffolk, and in all more than 280 heretics were burned in less than four years. This was not what the government had intended: it had supposed that after a few salutary burnings Protestant loyalty would collapse. But Protestants would not keep quiet. Thomas Hudson of Aylsham in Norfolk drew attention to himself in 1558 by three days of psalm-singing, and villagers called the constable to have him arrested. Most heretics were reported by their neighbors, rather than weeded out by formal inquisition: Alice Benden was turned in by her husband, and John Fetty twice by his wife. There was trouble at some burnings, but usually the crowd watched the law take its course – and sometimes there was real hostility toward a heretic. When Christopher Wade was burned at Dartford in 1558, some threw faggots to silence him, and fruiterers brought cartloads of cherries to sell to those who came to watch him die.

The persecution did not crush Protestantism, but it did not discredit Catholicism either. Recruitment to the priesthood boomed, especially in 1557 and 1558, and giving to religious causes recovered well from the depths of Edward's reign. The Protestant leadership fragmented: lay leaders conformed to Catholic practice and retired from politics, or made their peace with Mary and entered her service; senior clergy were silenced or burned, or they went into exile where they were harmless. Protestant books were smuggled into England, but some advocated Mary's deposition or murder and probably did the cause more harm than good. The bulk of the Protestant leadership survived the persecution onslaught, but they were powerless: the Protestants were destined to be a small, sectarian minority, weaker than the Huguenots in France (because they had no protection from great magnates). And then Mary died, on November 17, 1558. It was another accident in the accidental Reformation.

As her father and her brother had done, Mary timed her death badly: it could hardly have come at a worse time for the future of Catholicism in England – during a war with France, and after harvest failures and an influenza epidemic. The only plausible Catholic candidate for the throne, Mary Stewart, was effectively disqualified: as wife of the French dauphin and Queen of Scots, she was an enemy. So Mary's half-sister Elizabeth, the daughter of Anne Boleyn, had a clear run at the crown and freedom of action. Elizabeth was a moderate Protestant, and had the will and the opportunity to reintroduce Reformation. The pro-French Pope Paul IV backed Mary's claim, and was unlikely to grant the dispensation necessary for Elizabeth's accession as a legitimate Catholic monarch – so it was safer to take the throne as a Protestant and ignore Rome. Spain was bound to support Elizabeth whatever she did, since Spain could not permit the French-backed Mary to succeed. At home, Elizabeth's closest allies and supporters were Protestants (or at least anti-Catholics), especially the displaced members of Edward VI's regime – and soon they dominated the new queen's council. Elizabeth would start where Edward had left off: she would have a Protestant Church. But it was not going to be easy.

In the Parliament of 1559, Elizabeth and her councilors tried to restore the royal supremacy and the Prayer Book of 1552, but they were initially blocked in the House of Lords by an alliance of Catholic bishops and conservative peers. In a second attempt, the council put forward separate supremacy and uniformity bills, and made concessions to appease critics. The Prayer Book was to be amended to allow a more Catholic understanding of the Eucharist, and the vestments, ornaments, and rituals of communion were to be more like those of the mass. With these alterations, the Prayer Book was approved – but by a margin of only three votes in the Lords, even after some opponents had been excluded. The supremacy bill also passed, and when the Catholic bishops refused the supremacy oath they were removed by the new supreme governor and replaced by Protestants. But the queen seems to have been shaken by her near-defeat, and made further gestures toward Catholic opinion by new injunctions in the summer of 1559 – in particular, the communion table was to stand where the altar had been, and wafers were to be used for communion (though the Prayer Book had prescribed ordinary bread). Thereafter Elizabeth tried to keep crosses in parish churches, to insist on Catholic vestments, and to forbid the marriage of priests – but in each case she had to back down when rebuffed by her new Protestant bishops. The queen had already lost a Catholic episcopate: she could not lose a Protestant one as well.

The Elizabethan Church of England was not planned: nobody would deliberately have invented such a monstrosity. It was too Protestant for the Catholics, and too Catholic for the Protestants. Nobody liked it, and certainly not the new Protestant bishops: Grindal of London explained in 1567: "You see me wear a cope or a surplice in [St.] Paul's. I had rather minister without these things, but for order's sake and obedience to the prince" (Nicholson, *Remains of Grindal*, p. 211). By any recognizably Protestant standard, the Elizabethan Church was inadequate – dismissed by a London minister in 1572 as "a certain kind of religion, framed out of man's own brain and fantasy, far worse than that of popery (if worse may be), patched and pieced out of theirs and ours together" (Collinson, *Godly People*, p. 336). It was not a true religion but a political compromise. Its official theology, confirmed by Convocation and the queen in 1563, was not too bad – but everything else was dreadful. It was still an episcopal church, with a clerical hierarchy, cathedrals, and diocesan courts. Its structures of patronage and finance were, if anything, even worse than before, with parish appointments in private hands and gross inequalities in clerical incomes. Worst of all, its services were popish: the ministers were meant to dress up like Catholic priests, and the communion service looked too much like a mass. Was this what the martyrs had died for, some were asking. The church was still contaminated by "dregs of popery," and all Protestants agreed it could not stay as it was.

All Protestants except the queen, that is – and, by another Reformation chance, she was to rule for 44 years and try to keep her church intact. For the first half of her reign, the Protestant Elizabeth had more trouble from her Protestant subjects than from the Catholics – and that was because she made so many concessions to Catholics that she kept most of them quiet, but only at the cost of a continuing battle with fellow-Protestants. Most of her bishops accepted a need for caution, waiting until the threat of Catholic rebellion subsided and the queen and council could be persuaded to adopt further reform – but they kept up the persuasion. Many preachers were so outraged by "popish abuses" that they campaigned against the Prayer Book and refused to follow its more objectionable rules: in 1572 they submitted an *Admonition to the Parliament*, detailing their demands. A tiny minority of ministers and laypeople concluded that a partly reformed church was still the Church of Antichrist, and they left it: by 1567 there were separatist groups meeting in London. For them, an official Reformation could not deliver a godly church.

Nor could it deliver a godly people. Elizabeth's Church was not Protestant enough, that was obvious. But it was also not evangelical enough: it had neither the manpower nor the organization to convert the people. The Protestants were in a missionary situation: they were a minority religion wishing to convert a hostile or indifferent majority. But theirs was not a missionary church. The east midlands diocese of Peterborough had 296 parishes: in 1561 it had 166 ministers, but only nine of them could preach; in 1576 it had 230 ministers, and only 40 of them could preach – after 17 years of official Protestantism, still only 40 preachers to convert 296 parishes. It was the same or worse elsewhere. By the 1570s the supply of preachers was increasing, and the printing presses were churning out catechisms – teaching aids for use with the children of a parish on Sunday afternoons. Prospects were improving and Protestant ideas were spreading, but not very fast. There had been a political Reformation, of sorts – but, outside London, not much of a popular Reformation. The growth of preaching was constrained by the teaching capacity of the universities, and the impact of preaching was restricted by the parochial organization of the church. As time passed there were more preachers, but each preacher formally served only one parish church; the other parishes were served by surviving Catholic priests who had conformed with more or less reluctance, or by untrained nominal Protestants who could not preach. It would be decades before every parish had a preacher and every parishioner had the chance of conversion – decades more to have a real Reformation. Meanwhile, popery survived, there was a danger of Catholic restoration, and souls were lost to the devil.

So some Protestant ministers tried to build a missionary church within the unhelpful structures of the Church of England. Many cooperated together in the organization of "exercises," a mix of in-service training for ministers and conversion campaign for laypeople: ministers and laity from miles around met together in a market town, inexperienced preachers practiced in front of the old hands, and a series of sermons offered Protestantism to the people. In some market towns, merchants or the borough council endowed a lectureship, a well-paid preaching post for the whole town: a lecturer would preach on market days and Sunday afternoons, and attract congregations from all the town's parishes and from neighboring areas. If there was no endowment for a new salaried lecture, then local preachers might take turns to give a market-day sermon – a system called "lectures by combination." And in some areas, especially in the midlands and East Anglia, clergy got together in team ministries, cooperating together, sharing duties, and reducing the significance of parish boundaries in a cooperative evangelical effort. These team ministries were called conferences or "classes," and they were copied from Calvinist organization in Switzerland, France, and the Netherlands. Some ministers saw them as a stage in the creation of a presbyterian Church of England and the abolition of bishops. But for most participants the aim was pastoral rather than political: the minute-book of the meetings at Dedham in Essex in the 1580s shows the ministers discussing how to make their people Protestants, not how to make the Church of England presbyterian.

There were just two problems with this missionary effort: it was distrusted by some in authority, and was only partly successful. The bishops generally supported the "exercises," and when their opinions were canvassed in 1576 three-quarters were in favor: some even forced ministers to attend. But Elizabeth was afraid that too much preaching would frighten the Catholics, and that revivalist Protestant meetings would be provocative: in 1577 she tried to close the "exercises" down, to the distress of her bishops. Most bishops supported lectureships, too – and privy councilors were enthusiastic founders. But lectureships also became suspect, especially as Protestant ministers who didn't like the Prayer Book were attracted to posts with only a preaching responsibility. And, of course, the "classes" looked subversive – and for a few ministers they deliberately were: the network was destroyed by a series of prosecutions from 1589, which for some confirmed that episcopacy was ungodly.

Bishops and ministers might create missionary structures, they might undertake evangelical campaigns – but they were, in the main, literally preaching to the converted. It was the converted who went to the "exercises," and it was the converted who went to town lectures. Perhaps a few others went along out of curiosity, but the congregations at lectures were drawn primarily from the godly – not Catholics who might be converted from popery, not mere conformists who might be given some fervor, nor the ignorant or indifferent who might learn how Christ saves, but the godly – those who already had Protestant faith and wanted some more. "Sermon-gadding" became a defining characteristic of the godly Protestants: they went to sermons whenever and wherever they could, taking note-pads with them and discussing the sermon afterwards. Not surprisingly, then, the lecturers preached to them, directing their words to the converted, to the insiders. And lectures became recognized gatherings of the godly, exclusive occasions for like-minded enthusiasts.

A few towns had godly councils, which tried to make people attend lectures and fined absentees – at Bury St. Edmunds, for example. But elsewhere, and nationally, there was no requirement to go to any service except to a parish church each Sunday and festival. So the vast majority of English men and women never went to a lecture: they heard sermons only if preached in their parish church. But parish sermons were uncommon. In Oxfordshire in 1589, only a quarter of parishes had frequent sermons; two-thirds only but one sermon every three months – and, as was said in 1585, "Four sermons in the year are as insufficient ordinarily to make us perfect men in Christ Jesus . . . as four strokes with an axe are unable to fell down a mighty oak" (*Parte of a Register*, p. 216). Intensive evangelical campaigns in some towns, especially if backed by energetic magistrates, could make effective local Reformations: across the country as a whole, that did not happen. The attempt to make a missionary church failed; the attempt to make a godly people failed. Had Reformation failed?

By 1603, England was a Protestant nation. The church's theology, in the Thirty-Nine Articles, was Protestant, and so were its working documents: catechisms, homilies, Foxe's *Acts and Monuments*, and piles of printed sermons. Its leadership was Protestant, and so was its ministry. The former Catholic priests were now dead, and half its clergy were university graduates who had learned their Calvin. Its services were usually Protestant – because godly zealots left out the bits they thought were not Protestant, and because others were persuaded that wearing a surplice and kneeling for communion could be Protestant. England's festival days were Protestant: the anniversary of the queen's accession, the defeat of the Spanish Armada, the failures of Catholic plots against Elizabeth's life, were marked by Protestant prayers, anti-Catholic rhetoric, bonfires and bells. In 1529 Protestantism had been a nasty foreign religion and Catholicism was English: in 1603 Catholicism was a nasty foreign religion and Protestantism was English.

But England was not a nation of Protestants. There was a Catholic minority, an underground sect served by English priests trained on the continent. This foreign link made Catholics suspect and liable to persecution; persecution led a few Catholics into plotting; plotting led to more persecution; and so on. Some Catholics were recusants, refusing to attend the services of the Church of England and paying fines if convicted; probably more were "church papists," evading prosecution by occasional conformity and gestures of obedience. The total number of those who regarded themselves as Catholics cannot have been much more than 5 percent, but they were a remnant who would not go away – and who loomed large in the fears of Protestants. The enthusiastic Protestants – the sermon-gadders, the Bible-readers, those who examined their consciences for the signs of election – were another minority, though a much larger one. Many of them hoped that the Reformation was not over, that the Church of England would become more Protestant, that the Catholics could be crushed, that the lukewarm might be converted – but their neighbors sneered at them as self-righteous hypocrites. And the rest, the lukewarm, the neighbors, the majority? They went to church; they learned the Prayer Book catechism; they paid their contributions to the parish: they had to. They probably thought that Christ had died for them too, and would help them to heaven if they prayed and tried to be good. They hated the pope, and hated the papists when there was a scare on; they called the godly "puritans," and hated them when Sunday games were stopped. England was now divided, and the divisions were sometimes bitter. It is too much to say that the Reformation had failed – but it is also too much to say it had succeeded.

BIBLIOGRAPHY

Collinson, P., *Godly People: Essays on English Protestantism and Puritanism*. London: Hambledon Press, 1983.

Dickens, A. G., ed., *Tudor Treatises*. Yorkshire Archaeological Society Record Series, vol. 123, 1959.

Elton, G. R., *Policy and Police: The Enforcement of the Reformation in the Age of Thomas Cromwell*. Cambridge: Cambridge University Press, 1972.

Elton, G. R., *The Tudor Constitution*, 2nd ed. Cambridge: Cambridge University Press, 1982.

Guy, J., "Henry VIII and the *Praemunire* Manoeuvres of 1530–1531," *English Historical Review*, 97 (1982), pp. 481–503.

Nicholson, W., ed., *The Remains of Edmund Grindal*. Cambridge: Parker Society, 1843.

A Parte of a Register, contayninge sundrie memorable matters, written by divers godly and learned men in our time. Middelburg, 1593.

FURTHER READING

The English Reformation has always been a highly controversial subject: current approaches and debates are surveyed by P. Collinson, "The English Reformation 1945–1995," in M. Bentley, ed., *Companion to Historiography* (London: Routledge, 1997); and C. Haigh, "The Recent Historiography of the English Reformation," in C. Haigh, *The English Reformation Revised* (Cambridge: Cambridge University Press, 1987). The classic synopses a generation ago were A. G. Dickens, *The English Reformation* (London: Batsford, 1964; 2nd ed., 1989); and G. R. Elton, *Reform and Reformation: England 1509–1558* (London: Edward Arnold, 1977), but later research undermined their stress on the decay of Catholicism and the rapid impact of Protestantism. J. J. Scarisbrick, *The Reformation and the English People* (Oxford: Blackwell, 1984); E. Duffy, *The Stripping of the Altars: Traditional Religion in England 1400–1580* (New Haven, Conn.: Yale University Press, 1992); and C. Haigh, *English Reformations: Religion, Politics, and Society under the Tudors* (Oxford: Oxford University Press, 1993) portrayed Reformation as difficult, unpopular, and slow – an interpretation which has been dubbed "revisionist."

The church before the Reformation is now best studied through T. Cooper, *The Last Generation of English Catholic Clergy* (Woodbridge: Boydell Press, 1999); and P. Marshall, *The*

Catholic Priesthood and the English Reformation (Oxford: Oxford University Press, 1994). The messy politics of the Reformation may be approached through J. Guy, *Tudor England* (Oxford: Oxford University Press, 1988); D. Starkey, *The Reign of Henry VIII: Personalities and Politics* (London: George Philip, 1985); D. MacCulloch, *Thomas Cranmer: A Life* (New Haven, Conn.: Yale University Press, 1996); and N. Jones, *Faith by Statute: Parliament and the Settlement of Religion 1559* (London: Royal Historical Society, 1982). In *Tudor Church Militant: Edward VI and the Protestant Reformation* (London: Allen Lane, 1999), MacCulloch argues that under Edward Reformation was more coherent, purposive, and successful than revisionist accounts allow. Most historians now agree that Protestantism worked only slowly, but that, late in Elizabeth's reign, it brought a major cultural shift: see P. Collinson, *The Birthpangs of Protestant England* (Basingstoke, Macmillan, 1988); and P. Marshall, ed., *The Impact of the English Reformation 1500–1640* (London: Edward Arnold, 1997).

TEN

The Religious Wars in France

BARBARA B. DIEFENDORF

In his epic "Les Tragiques," Huguenot poet Agrippa d'Aubigné memorably depicts France as a grieving mother whose warring sons – representing France's Catholic and Protestant factions – have made a battlefield of her fertile body. The strongest son, unwilling to share his mother's rich bounty with his twin, provokes the other to fight for his rightful inheritance, but the furious struggle destroys them both. Striking blindly at each other, they also demolish the mother, from whose once generous breasts only blood now flows (Book I, "Misères," ll. 97–130). A soldier as well as a poet, d'Aubigné was far from impartial in assessing blame for the civil and religious wars that wracked his homeland in the second half of the sixteenth century. French Catholics would have angrily denied provoking the quarrels. Indeed, ardent Catholics would have flatly rejected d'Aubigné's initial premise that members of the two faiths were twins, with an equal claim to a common mother's bounty. Regarding Protestantism rather as a monstrous birth, or a cancer on the social body, they vigorously denied its very right to exist. But wherever one placed the blame for the wars, one thing was not in dispute. The long decades of fratricidal war had devastated the mother land.

In order to understand just why the Protestant Reformation in France led to such prolonged and destructive civil war, we will need to look first at the rise of a militant Calvinist faith in the kingdom. Only then can we begin to understand the sequence of events that led to a cycle of warfare that was to prove very difficult to escape.

The Rise of Calvinism in France

The power and prestige of French kings was strongly rooted in Roman Catholic ritual and ceremonies. Anointed with special oils and receiving both bread and wine at the coronation communion, the monarchs enhanced their claim to rule by divine right by assuming sacerdotal powers. Both church and crown benefited from this close alliance; the kings promised in their coronation oath to protect the faith and drive out heretics. When Martin Luther's writings, which had spread quickly into France, were condemned as heretical by the theologians of the University of Paris in 1521, the king's courts criminalized religious dissent and began to prosecute suspected heretics. A great admirer of humanism, King Francis I was reluctant to identify evangelical scholars as heretics, but the more conservative members of his high court of Parlement took a harder line and attempted to stifle nonconformity. Their repressive campaign only drove the new ideas underground, where they continued to spread, particularly in university milieux but also among merchants and artisans whose trades brought them into contact with foreign dissenters. Forbidden books passed quietly from hand to hand; itinerant preachers delivered clandestine sermons and departed before they could be caught. Networks of family and friendship helped to spread the new teachings but also to preserve a secrecy that became all the more necessary as prosecution of accused heretics continued and even accelerated in the 1540s.

In order to prevent discovery, most men and women attracted to evangelical doctrines conformed outwardly, if minimally, to the Roman Catholic Church. In the 1540s, John Calvin, whose works were being clandestinely imported into France in increasingly large numbers, attacked the hypocrisy of outward conformity in several strongly worded tracts. Denouncing as "Nicodemites" those who consented to idolatry in order to protect their lives and property, he pronounced emigration the only viable option for men and women who recognized the errors of Catholic teachings. Calvin's attacks on Nicodemism spurred a thin stream of departures for Geneva, but many converts were unwilling or unable to pack up their lives and move. They read Protestant books smuggled into the kingdom, met secretly to discuss their readings and pray together, and looked forward to a day when they could worship regularly and receive the sacraments in a manner that conformed to their beliefs. Increasingly, they took for their ideal the ecclesiastical institutions and services that Calvin had introduced in Geneva.

The opportunity to form true churches occurred only in the mid-1550s, but once the movement began it spread rapidly. Delegates from 72 congregations attended the first national meeting, or synod, of the French Reformed churches in May 1559, just four years after the first churches were established in 1555. Scholars estimate that by 1562 more than a thousand congregations existed, with a membership totaling between 1.5 and 2 million people. Calvin's Geneva supplied ministers to some of these churches but was unable to meet more than a small part of the demand. Many congregations were forced to choose their initial pastor from among their own ranks or those of a neighboring church. When possible, they sent the chosen men to study, however briefly, in Geneva or with another French congregation. The Paris church, for example, receiving its first Genevan minister in 1556, almost immediately established an informal seminary where promising recruits could be trained. And yet the growth of the French congregations was so explosive that many churches were forced to press into immediate service converted priests or laymen who felt the call.

Ties between the French churches and Calvin's Geneva remained largely informal; the Genevan pastors did not want their city to become another Rome. They also feared invasion by the Catholic powers that surrounded them and did not dare too openly to encourage the spread of Protestantism in France. At the same time, most Genevan pastors were, like Calvin himself, French by nationality and remained vitally interested in the success of the Reformation in their homeland. They continued to offer guidance and advice. Winning over the elites who tended to dominate most local congregations, they insured the triumph of Calvinist orthodoxy in France. We know regrettably little about the exact process through which dissident opinion in the new churches was silenced, but it would appear that the immense moral authority of Calvin and the Genevan pastors and an appeal to strength through unity worked in favor of Calvinist hegemony. In 1557, Calvin himself drafted a confession of faith for the French churches. In 1559, he sent representatives to Paris to assist the French Reformed churches in revising this confession of faith and drafting a common ecclesiastical code, or "discipline." Grouped into regional colloquies and provinces, the churches adopted a hierarchical structure that, while leaving each congregation a good measure of independence, facilitated communication and mutual aid at the same time that it imposed standards of governance on the churches as a whole.

It proved easier, however, to impose structural unity on the French Reformed churches than to unify the ambitions of their members, who, as their numbers grew, were eager to practice their faith publicly, unhindered by fear of arrest or harassment by the Catholic populace. The growing demand to emerge from their shadowy, illegal status put the French Reformed churches on a collision course with both the crown and the majority Catholic population. By 1560, many congregations were becoming increasingly public in their worship. Calvinists gathered to sing psalms in city streets and listen to sermons in fields outside city gates. In some towns, preaching took place more daringly in market squares or, still more defiantly, in front of the cathedral. Wanting a sheltered space for regular services, Calvinist congregations began to demand that Catholic church buildings be reassigned to their use. Already in 1558, Calvinists appropriated a church in the Béarnais town of Nérac. Emboldened by the knowledge that Nérac's sovereigns, Jeanne d'Albret and Antoine de Bourbon, the queen and king of Navarre, were lax in the persecution of heresy, Protestants in the southern town took a step that fellow-believers in other cities took only in 1560 or 1561 (Benedict, "Dynamics of Protestant Militancy," p. 41).

Any public demonstration of faith by Calvinist sympathizers attracted the hostility of Catholic believers, whose attacks on Calvinist worshipers prompted the latter to arm to defend themselves. This only raised the level of mutual defiance still farther. The situation was further aggravated by the presence within many Reformed congregations of activists who demonstrated their opposition to Catholic errors by mocking Catholic processions, defacing saints' statues and shrines, and engaging in other acts that Catholics could only regard as blasphemy. The Reformed Church leadership kept a careful distance from such provocations. Recognizing, with Calvin, the need for French Protestants to present themselves as loyal subjects of the crown, church leaders regularly denied taking part in seditious acts and cast the blame instead on the excessive zeal of individual believers. Recent research has, however, shown that Protestant leaders engaged in a policy of deliberate ambiguity and concealed their more revolutionary aims so as to protect themselves and their churches from legal repression. Contrary to what a long – and largely Protestant – historiography has argued, the Protestant struggle in France was not simply about freedom of worship and belief. The very act of organizing churches was a violation of the laws, and the records show Reformed Church consistories approving the takeover of Catholic churches, providing it was accomplished peacefully, organizing the paramilitary forces that provided their defense, and engaging in other clearly illegal acts (Benedict, "Dynamics of Protestant Militancy").

The speed with which the Reformed churches expanded between 1555 and 1562 gave the movement a confidence born of its own dynamism. Protestant propaganda from the years 1560 and 1561 reflects this optimism in biting attacks on Catholic clerics, doctrine, and ceremonies, but also in demands for the restoration of a pure and evangelical church, a reformed polity, and a morally upright society. The radical renewal articulated in this propaganda finds clear echoes in demands for reform presented by delegates with Protestant inclinations to meetings of the provincial Estates and also the Estates General held in 1560 and 1561. If this vision was subsequently swept away by the force of the Catholic opposition it inspired, its revolutionary character should not be underestimated, nor should the threat that it posed to traditional structures of power, wealth, and prestige.

Monarchical Authority and the Outbreak of War

The turning point toward war is commonly dated to the accidental death of King Henry II as a result of an injury suffered while jousting in the tournament that celebrated the wedding of his daughter, Elisabeth de Valois, to King Philip II of Spain in June 1559. Having just ended long decades of foreign war with the peace of Cateau-Cambrésis, Henry was preparing to turn his attention to internal problems, chief among them the spread of heresy. His unanticipated death left France in the hands of a callow adolescent, King Francis II, dominated by his wife's uncles, Francis, duke of Guise, and Charles, cardinal of Lorraine. Under the influence of the ardently Catholic Guises, religious persecution intensified. Their ascendency, however, was brief. Even before King Francis II's own premature death in December 1560, his mother, Catherine de' Medici, emerged from the sidelines to advance a more moderate policy regarding religious dissent. In March 1560, the Edict of Amboise offered a general pardon to dissenters, heretical preachers excepted, providing they returned to the Catholic Church. Several months later, the Edict of Romorantin returned prosecution of heresy to church courts. Neither edict intended a complete reversal of policy. Royal courts still prosecuted dissenters for sedition – an elastic term that could include disseminating heretical literature, publicly uttering anti-Catholic sentiments, or failing to show proper respect for Catholic processions or shrines – but for the first time belief itself, if privately held, was decriminalized.

On Francis II's death, Catherine had herself declared regent for her 10-year-old son Charles IX and further attempted to ease religious tensions by policies of moderation. Believing that the Guises had acquired too much power during Francis II's brief reign, she tried to compensate by favoring other aristocratic clans. Appointing Antoine de Bourbon, king of Navarre and first prince of the blood, as lieutenant general for the kingdom, she also freed Antoine's younger brother Louis de Bourbon, prince of Condé, from the prison where he was charged with conspiring with other Protestant nobles to seize Francis II at Amboise in order to liberate him from Guise domination (March 1560). At the same time, Catherine further moderated laws against religious dissenters. In April 1561, a royal edict forbade injuring anyone on account of their religion. Like previous edicts, this one threatened punishment for seditious conduct. It went farther than the Edict of Amboise, however, in explicitly ordering toleration of dissident beliefs and even practices, so long as they took place in private. Catherine further sparked hopes of a peaceful religious settlement by announcing that Catholic and Protestant theologians would meet for a colloquy at Poissy in September 1561.

However well intentioned, Catherine de' Medici misjudged the willingness of theologians on either side of the religious debate to compromise. She also misjudged the Calvinists' will to profit from the slightest measure of toleration in order to assemble more openly. Despite the continued prohibition against public assemblies, French Calvinists (or Huguenots, as they came to be called by 1561) gathered in ever larger numbers. They seized more churches and engaged in ever more brazen acts of iconoclasm and calculated blasphemy, particularly in southern towns, where their numbers were strongest. The Catholic populace responded by increasing its own retaliatory acts of religious violence. Egged on by radical preachers who inflamed religious passions by describing the new faith as a gangrene corrupting the social body and threatening to bring down the wrath of God, Catholic crowds invaded known sites of Calvinist worship, attacked participants in Reformed Church services, and set fire to buildings and furniture. They disinterred the corpses of Protestants buried in church cemeteries as a desecration of hallowed ground. Just as Huguenots acted out their disdain for Catholic teachings by breaking religious images, mocking the consecrated Host, and other deliberate provocations, so Catholics defended their faith by conscious acts of public disobedience. In towns where they clashed head on, blood was spilled and cries for vengeance grew louder. Despite the escalation of civil disorder, a new edict in January 1562 permitted assemblies of the new faith so long as they took place outside town walls. Hoping to promote peace, Catherine instead prompted an escalation of civil disorder.

Disorder dissolved into war when, on March 1, 1562, troops commanded by the duke of Guise invaded a barn where Protestants were worshiping in the town of Vassy in Champagne. The ensuing clash left as many as 50 unarmed worshipers dead and another 150 injured. Greeted as a hero when he entered Paris two weeks later, Guise ignored the Huguenots' demand for an apology. In reaction, Louis, prince of Condé, who had taken the title of Protector of the French Reformed churches and assumed leadership of the Protestant faction, left Paris and prepared for war. Caught between the opposing parties, Catherine de' Medici solicited Condé's protection for the royal family, but he placed his hope in his army instead. On April 2, his troops seized the town of Orléans and made it their headquarters. Armed uprisings in a great many other towns from Normandy and the Loire Valley to Languedoc and Dauphiné placed them in Huguenot hands as well. Catherine, meanwhile, reluctantly accepted the protection offered by the Catholic leadership, a triumvirate consisting of Francis, duke of Guise, Antoine de Bourbon (who had abandoned any Protestant leanings), and Marshal de Saint-André. She nevertheless continued to try to negotiate peace.

Although the Huguenots remained a small minority of the population, they used the scattered nature of their strength to advantage in war, avoiding set battles whenever possible and forcing their enemies to resort instead to time-consuming and costly sieges to smoke them out of the cities they held. Only in December 1562, after a hard-won siege at Rouen, which cost Antoine de Bourbon his life, was the Catholic army finally able to engage the Huguenots in the field. The battle of Dreux took the life of the second triumvir, Marshal de Saint-André, and resulted in the capture of Condé. It also convinced the Huguenots that they lacked the force to win in the field. When the Catholic army, flushed with victory, went on to lay siege to Orléans, the Huguenots were ready to negotiate more seriously. The assassination of the duke of Guise, the remaining triumvir, in the Catholic camp outside Orléans (February 1563) brought the Catholics to agree to peace.

Because neither side had been decisively defeated, the peace negotiated at Amboise (March 1563) was a compromise settlement that allowed the Protestants freedom of conscience but permitted them to worship only in limited social and geographical settings. In this respect it resembled both the earlier edicts by which Catherine de' Medici had allowed dissenters a limited sphere of religious toleration and later religious settlements. The Edict of Amboise limited Protestant worship to the suburbs of one town in each judicial district, or bailiwick, except in the case of cities the Huguenots held at the end of the war, where they were allowed to continue holding services as long as they returned Catholic churches to their previous owners. The edict gave more generous privileges of worship to Protestant nobles, who were permitted to hold services for their households and, on lands where they held the rights of high justice, their subjects.

The compromise nature of the peace also, however, meant that each side was less than satisfied. Protestants wanted more churches and more religious freedom. Catholics, still equating the new faith with heresy, continued to oppose any right to worship. The high courts of Parlement showed their opposition by delaying registration of the edict and, after registration, only laxly enforcing it. Popular hostilities remained acute. In some areas Catholic nobles and commoners joined militant confraternities and leagues sworn to oppose the peace. Huguenots who had fled Catholic cities on account of the wars often did not dare to return for more than a year after the peace was signed. On the whole, however, Protestants were no more willing to abide by the edict than were their enemies. They reopened churches forbidden by the edict and worshiped as boldly as they dared. Royal governors and the commissioners chosen to assist them in administering the peace encountered enormous difficulties. Nor was tranquility restored at court. Despite the death of all three triumvirs, factional quarrels persisted among the magnate families closest to the crown. Tensions were particularly acute between the Guise and Montmorency clans. Blaming Protestant leader Gaspard de Coligny for the assassination of his brother, the duke of Guise, the cardinal of Lorraine also feuded with Coligny's Montmorency cousins, who, although Catholic, supported the queen's policy of moderation. Recent research suggests that the cardinal of Lorraine's influence at court may not have been as dominant in the interwar years as has traditionally been supposed (Carroll, *Noble Power*, pp. 126–7). As yet, however, no one has come up with a better explanation for the actions that led into the second civil war than the Huguenots' fear of an ultra-Catholic conspiracy to reverse the religious settlement.

Signs that Catholics were rearming fed rumors that the king intended to revoke the Edict of Amboise. Matters came to a head in the summer of 1567 when Huguenot leaders, fearing that the armies the duke of Alva was marching up France's eastern frontier in order to put a stop to heresy in the Spanish Netherlands were actually intended to be used against them, decided to seize the initiative. In a move that in many respects resembled the failed Conspiracy of Amboise, they plotted to seize the king so as to separate him from his Catholic advisers. As with the earlier conspiracy, they failed to keep their intentions a secret. The attempt to capture young Charles IX while he was hunting outside of Paris miscarried. He fled to the safety of his fiercely Catholic capital, and a second religious war broke out (September 1567). This time there was no question which side the royal family would take.

As with the first war, the Huguenots seized a number of towns. Their attempt to blockade Paris so as to starve the city into submission led in November 1567 to an indecisive battle at St.-Denis. Badly outnumbered and unable to defeat the Catholic army on the field, the Huguenots retreated to the east, where they awaited the arrival of German reinforcements. Slow to mobilize because of the enormous expense and time required to bring troops in from the border provinces where they were normally stationed, the royal army looked much stronger on paper than it did in the field. The Huguenots remained a sufficiently powerful threat that the king prudently chose to negotiate. The peace reached at Longjumeau in March 1568 reestablished the compromise settlement of Amboise but also, reflecting past difficulties, incorporated new provisions intended to make it easier to maintain the peace. Explicitly amnestying participants in the war, the edict forbade recriminatory acts, promised the return of lands, offices, and titles taken during the war, and also agreed that the crown would pay the cost of the foreign mercenaries hired to fight for the Huguenots.

The latter provision was a necessary one. Reduced to living off the land, unpaid mercenaries tended to wreak havoc on civilian populations. It nevertheless prompted enormous opposition from Catholic citizens, who resented being taxed to pay off the armies that had made war against them. Catholic resistance to the Peace of Longjumeau kept the country in a state of open hostility. Despite explicit prohibitions, Catholic leagues sprang up again. Charles IX's attempt to coopt the movement toward Catholic militance by placing himself at its head had the effect of further alarming the Huguenot leadership. Fearing an attempt on their lives, Condé and Coligny sought refuge in the Protestant town of La Rochelle in August 1568. A third war of religion began, with each side adopting a more radical stance.

By the Ordinance of St.-Maur (September 1568), Charles IX placed all responsibility for the quarrels onto the Huguenots, accused them of attempting to overturn royal sovereignty, and entirely revoked their rights to worship. For their part, the Protestants justified taking up arms in strident tones and began to articulate the theories of legitimate resistance that came to full fruition several years later. Personal enmities became more strident as well. When Condé was taken prisoner in the battle of Dreux, the duke of Guise, upholding ancient traditions of noble honor, treated him courteously and shared his meals and even his bed with his captive. Injured in the battle of Jarnac (March 1569), Condé again surrendered to a Catholic nobleman. This time he was ignobly dispatched with a shot in the head and his corpse, flung over a donkey, paraded derisively into the Catholic camp (Jouanna, *La France du XVIᵉ siècle*, p. 455).

As in the previous wars, the Huguenots proved resilient and despite suffering serious losses on the battlefield rallied to negotiate from a position of strength. The Peace of St.-Germain (August 1570) restored the rights to worship promised in early edicts and also granted an additional place of worship in every province or "government." Most important, recognizing that angers stirred up in the quarrels were slow to abate, the king promised the Protestants four fortified cities to used as places of refuge for two years, at which time they were to be surrendered back to the crown. The Huguenots insisted on the insertion of a similar clause in subsequent settlements. Despite explicit provisions intended to insure civil order, the Peace of St.-Germain was no more successful in putting an end to religious hatreds and violence than earlier settlements had been. Indeed, mutual recriminations only grew more bitter with time.

The Destructive Power of Civil War

The armies that fought the wars left a trail of destruction, only part of which was a direct consequence of the clash of arms. Their pay most frequently in arrears, soldiers descended on the countryside like hordes of locusts, robbing and pillaging to fill their bellies and supply their needs. In addition, Huguenot armies deliberately targeted churches and monasteries. They stole anything worth selling, destroyed statues and paintings to express their hatred for Catholic "idols," burned church buildings, and on occasion even massacred monks and nuns. Their outrages sparked retaliatory violence on the part of Catholic armies in Protestant-dominated regions.

And yet the wars had a broader and more profound impact on the civilian population than can be imagined from charting the movement of armies across the countryside. The Huguenots' tactic of seizing widely scattered towns meant that war became endemic even in the absence of princely armies. Few regions were spared the distress that resulted from clashes between neighboring towns of opposing faiths as they competed to defend the hinterland from which they drew provisions and the trade networks on which their economy depended. Improvised tactics of terror and surprise played a greater role here than cavalry, infantry, or artillery. It was far less costly and time-consuming to take a city by surprise, with the assistance of secret confederates within, than to lay siege to it in classic style. But the tactic worked both ways; a city taken from within could be lost in the same way. To protect against this fate, partisans often drove out their enemies. Even if not ordered to leave, members of the opposing faith usually departed in fear of their lives. Events that occurred in Nîmes at the outset of the second war demonstrate the wisdom of speedy departure. Seizing power from the Catholic officials installed by the king, Nîmois Huguenots slaughtered as many as a hundred men, including both Catholic notables and ecclesiastics serving the town's cathedral.

Refugee populations gathered in neighboring towns and pressed for revenge. Local warlords, lacking troops for formal retaliation, instead mounted terrorist campaigns in the countryside. They blew up bridges, seized stores of grain, pillaged farms, and held hostages for ransom in order to undermine enemy morale and finance their own war-making.

The financial exactions of the warlords but also the special taxes levied by cities to pay for their defense multiplied the burden of the wars. Royal taxes also mounted precipitously. The cost of moving the heavy cavalry companies normally stationed near the kingdom's frontiers to where they might be needed for battle, raising additional troops both internally and abroad, and transporting the heavy munitions required for siege warfare all placed enormous strain on the royal treasury. The problem was further exacerbated by the refusal of areas under Huguenot control to contribute their share of taxes, as well as the need to forgive the tax debt of towns devastated by combat. The financial burdens of war increasingly alienated French Catholics from the crown. As they saw it, they were paying more and more money and seeing no results. Each time that peace was made, the Protestants appeared to be in the same or a better position than before. The special taxes levied to pay off the mercenaries that Huguenot leaders had engaged were particularly infuriating to French Catholics, who protested loudly but with little effect.

Sermons, pamphlets, and public demonstrations condemned the Peace of St.-Germain. Some of these protests were violent. In Rouen, a crowd intent on rescuing five men arrested for attacking Huguenots returning from worship nearly massacred the men's jailers in their determination to set them free (Benedict, *Rouen during the Wars of Religion*, p. 121). In Paris, crowds attacked city officials ordered by the king to remove a monument to the religious hatreds known as the Cross of the Gastines. Here too the crowd freed prisoners arrested for participating in the riots. They also demonstrated their hatred by sacking and burning several houses belonging to Protestant families. The fact that residents of these same houses were among the first victims of the St. Bartholomew's massacres in August 1572 reminds us how intensely personal these religious hatreds could be (Diefendorf, *Beneath the Cross*, pp. 84–6).

The St. Bartholomew's Massacres and their Consequences

The most notorious event of the Wars of Religion is the slaughter of perhaps 10,000 Protestants in Paris and the provinces in the summer and fall of 1572. The killing that began in Paris on August 24, St. Bartholomew's Day, was touched off by a failed attempt two days earlier to assassinate Admiral Coligny as he returned to his lodgings from the Louvre. With other prominent Huguenots, Coligny was in Paris to celebrate the wedding of the Protestant prince Henry de Bourbon, king of Navarre, with the king's sister, Marguerite de Valois. Historians have speculated endlessly as to who was responsible for the assassination attempt. Traditional interpretations blamed Catherine de' Medici, jealous of Coligny's growing influence over Charles IX and fearful that the Huguenot leader was swaying the young king to mount a dangerous military intervention in support of the Protestant revolt in the Spanish Netherlands. This view has largely been discredited. It appears far less likely that Catherine so radically departed from her consistent policy of moderation than that another of Coligny's enemies should have seized the occasion to eliminate him from the scene, just as Condé was killed after the battle of Jarnac.

But the consequences of the act are far more important than the laying of blame. The Huguenots responded by demanding retribution and threatening a return to civil war. Although their anger was directed primarily against the Guises, whom they believed responsible for the attack, the rumor spread rapidly that they intended to seize the royal family in the Louvre. Responding to the perceived threat to the crown, Catherine de' Medici and the king's advisers are believed to have convinced him in a late night meeting on August 23 to eliminate the Huguenot leadership with a pre-emptive strike, so as to prevent them from carrying out their threats and organizing a return to war. Royal guards dispatched in the night to execute the king's orders touched off a popular massacre that spread far beyond the original target of the coup. Already in a state of near insurrection on account of the rumors of a Huguenot coup, the Catholic populace of Paris was quick to interpret the king's order, intended to encompass only the Huguenot leaders, as a blanket permission to slaughter any and all members of the Reformed faith. City officials were unable to regain order for nearly a week, by which time 2,000–3,000 Protestants of all ages and social classes lay dead. The ritualized nature of many of these killings – the mutilation of corpses, disembowelment of pregnant women, and so forth – can be seen as evidence of the extent to which the popular massacres were motivated by a desire to cleanse the city of the pollution that heresy represented for ardent Catholics (Diefendorf, *Beneath the Cross*, pp. 99–106).

Between the end of August and the middle of September, the massacres spread to at least eight major provincial cities and took another 6,000 or 7,000 lives. In Orléans alone, more than a thousand people were killed. A second wave of killings hit Bordeaux, Toulouse, and several smaller southern towns in early October. As in Paris, the perpetrators of the provincial massacres appear to have believed that the king had authorized the killing of Huguenots, although the evidence suggests that this was not the case. Letters from Charles IX explicitly ordered provincial governors to keep the peace. The cities where the worst massacres took place were ones that had experienced very high levels of religious conflict during the previous decade. Orléans, Lyon, Meaux, Bourges, and Rouen, for example, were all towns that the Huguenots had seized in 1562 but lost in subsequent struggles. The Huguenot populations of these towns, although systematically excluded from power, still represented a threatening minority, and religious hatreds still ran very deep. In several other towns, virulently anti-Protestant officials initiated "quasi-judicial" massacres in which Protestant citizens were rounded up and summarily executed. These killings displayed little of the ritualized violence or pillaging that characterized the popular massacres (Benedict, "Saint Bartholomew's Massacres in the Provinces," pp. 220–5).

In addition to the underlying level of popular animosities, the initial reaction of Catholic elites was very important in determining whether a town remained calm or exploded into violence upon hearing of the events in Paris. Catholic leaders in Limoges, for example, maintained the peace when they first got word of the events in Paris by placing the city on alert and arming all of the citizenry, including the small number of Protestant residents. The fact that their enemies were armed effectively discouraged hotheaded Catholics from taking matters into their own hands. On the other hand, the strategy was only workable in a city whose strong civic ethic (and small Protestant minority) had allowed citizens of contrary faiths to retain relatively harmonious relations through the earlier wars (Cassan, *Temps des Guerres de Religion*, p. 242). In a city where the situation was inherently more volatile, arming the citizenry might have been more likely to touch off a bloodbath than to guarantee the peace.

The St. Bartholomew's massacres provoked an erosion of Reformed Church membership that far exceeded the loss of lives. Geneva received a new wave of French immigrants. A far larger number of French Protestants simply returned to the Catholic Church. Some converted as a result of direct force, and some as a result of fear. Still others abandoned the Reformed Church because they could no longer confidently believe in the truth of its teachings or their own identity as God's chosen children. Although they admired and celebrated martyrs to the faith, the scale of the massacre was too great. They could not believe that God would allow the slaughter of his own.

Meanwhile, surviving Protestant leaders fled to La Rochelle, the most secure of the armed cities they held by the Peace of St.-Germain. Besieged by royal armies, they fought and lost a brief war. The punitive Edict of Boulogne (July 1573) permitted Reformed worship only in three towns and limited attendance at services held in noble households. Determined to reverse this unsatisfactory settlement, the Huguenots began almost immediately to plan a new offensive. They also sought to gain international support by publicizing the horrors of St. Bartholomew's Day and elaborating upon the theories of legitimate resistance to tyrannical rule advanced only tentatively in earlier writings. The Huguenots had created institutional structures that allowed them to raise arms, men, and money all across Languedoc as early as 1562. Now they took further steps to solidify the institutions that allowed them to speak with a common voice. In 1574, they forged an alliance with the moderate Catholic governor of Languedoc, Henry de Montmorency-Damville, who shared their conviction that extensive political and economic reforms were needed to repair the damage done by the wars and insure a lasting peace. Nicknamed the "Malcontents" because of their dissatisfaction with state policies, the moderate Catholics who allied with the Huguenots were pragmatically willing to accept religious coexistence as a price of peace. The break from Catholic unity was to be a key characteristic of the later religious wars.

French Catholics Divide: Ultra-Catholics and "Politiques"

The death of Charles IX in May 1574 brought his brother Henry, duke of Anjou and the recently elected king of Poland, to the throne. Anjou, serving as lieutenant general of the kingdom during the third and fourth civil wars, was credited with the Catholic victories of Jarnac and Moncontour and directed the siege of La Rochelle. Believing that he would lead them to glorious triumph over the Huguenots, Catholic militants eagerly awaited his return from Poland. He quickly disappointed them, delaying his return to sample the pleasures of Italy and then only reluctantly prosecuting the war. The latter delays were caused by the empty state of the treasury as much as a lack of will on Henry's part. The debts remaining from earlier wars were enormous; new tax levies were urgently required. None of this endeared the new king to his subjects, who protested and even flatly refused the demand for higher taxes. The situation worsened when Henry III's younger brother, Francis, duke of Alençon, held virtually a prisoner at court because of his moderate Catholic sympathies, escaped in 1575 and joined the Malcontents. Alençon's defection was particularly troubling because, until or unless Henry III produced a son, he was heir to the throne. In joining the Malcontents, he gave their cause a legitimacy it would not otherwise have had, as was evident by the number of Catholic noblemen who joined it in his wake. The arrival of an army of 30,000 from the Palatinate to bolster the Huguenot-Malcontent cause further convinced Henry III to negotiate a settlement.

The weak position from which the crown negotiated meant that the Edict of Beaulieu (May 1576) gave the Huguenots the most generous terms yet in a religious war. They were allowed to worship and even build churches in any place except Paris and its immediate surroundings. They were also given eight fortified towns, twice the number granted in the Peace of St.-Germain. The edict created special chambers of Parlement to hear lawsuits when plaintiffs feared that religious differences would otherwise deprive them of a fair trial. It included a formal expression of regret, if not quite apology, for the events of St. Bartholomew's Day and restored both

Malcontent and Huguenot leaders to the high honors and offices they had held before the war. The duke of Alençon was further rewarded by the now vacant title of duke of Anjou and the grant in appanage of lands and revenues associated with the title. As a final but important concession to the Malcontent platform of political reform, Henry III agreed to convoke the Estates General at Blois within six months.

Not surprisingly, the ultra-Catholics who had looked to Henry III to end the kingdom's religious divisions once and for all were as disappointed and angry with the Peace of Beaulieu as the Huguenots were pleased. Catholic leagues sprang up yet again, and this time the organizers aimed for national union. Historians have traditionally assumed that the Guises were the instigators of the movement, which took its hardiest start in Picardy with the League of Péronne. Recent scholarship has suggested, rather, that the initiative came from among the Picard nobility, who were angry that the Edict of Beaulieu made the Huguenot Henry, prince of Condé (son of the prince assassinated at Jarnac), governor of their province. Many early supporters of the League were nevertheless clients of the Guises, who favored the same hardline policies, even if political wisdom required them to proceed cautiously (Carroll, *Noble Power*, pp. 161–3; Constant, *Les Guise*, p. 81). Although the texts published by the movement declared fidelity to the crown, Henry III rightly perceived a threat to his power in the leaguers' plan to organize militarily for the defense of the faith. Attempting to co-opt the League by placing himself at its head, Henry hoped to use the organization to help raise troops and money to reverse the humiliating peace that had been forced on him in the previous war.

When the Estates General opened at Blois in December 1576, the religious question had an important place on the agenda. Although it had been the Huguenots and Malcontents who originally pushed for the meeting, they took their distance when they realized that elections had favored the return of ardent Catholics eager to use the meeting to reverse the peace. Meeting separately, as tradition dictated, each Estate debated proposals to abolish religious toleration. The clergy and nobility demanded a return to Catholic unity even if it meant a return to war. The Third Estate divided, with some representatives advocating war and others unwilling to countenance any threat to peace. In the end, they voted to forbid Protestant worship and banish Reformed Church ministers. Neither they nor members of the other Estates were willing, however, to vote the financial subsidies necessary to carry out a new war (Greengrass, "Day in the Life of the Third Estate"). Nor, in the end, were the representatives hardy enough to enact proposed governmental reforms that would have tempered royal authority by giving more power to the Estates. However much they wanted reform, they hesitated to further weaken monarchical authority in the face of a renewed Protestant threat.

Although few Protestants attended the Estates, they watched closely from a distance and returned to arms even before Henry III formally announced his decision to suppress freedom of worship. The failure of the Estates to vote subsidies needed for the war meant that actual fighting was limited. The Huguenots' position was nevertheless weakened by the defection of Francis, duke of Anjou, won over by the generous settlement he received in the Peace of Beaulieu and given titular command of the royal armies, and, two months into the war, of Henry de Montmorency-Damville. The peace reached at Bergerac in September 1577 rolled back the Protestants' freedom of worship and reduced the proportion of Protestant judges appointed to the special courts designated to try cases involving plaintiffs of different religions. Both sides were unhappy with these conditions, but fatigue and financial exhaustion allowed the uneasy peace to last, with a brief interruption in 1580, until 1585.

This was the longest cessation of hostilities since the wars began, though it can scarcely be considered a time of recovery. Rather, it was a time of widespread disorder. Grain shortages, escalating prices, marauding bands of unpaid troops, and the unrealistic demands of the king's tax assessors combined to provoke rural rebellion and social distress. Although perhaps the most intelligent and surely the most cultivated and devout of the later Valois kings, Henry III came to be despised by his subjects, whose deepening misery was fertile ground for ultra-Catholic and Protestant propagandists, who denounced the king as a sybarite more devoted to his own pleasures than his subjects' well-being. Henry's failure to produce a son also worked against him, feeding rumors of impotence, homosexual inclinations, and sexual disease. When Francis, duke of Anjou, became ill with tuberculosis and died in June 1584, a succession crisis pushed the troubled kingdom back into war.

The Wars of the League

By long tradition, the French throne passed through the male line by order of primogeniture. Barring the increasingly unlikely birth of a son to Henry III, the house of Valois would expire with Henry's death. The throne would pass to the house of Bourbon, descendants of a younger son of King Louis IX, and within this house to Henry of Bourbon, king of Navarre. But Navarre was a Protestant; indeed, he was by 1581 the Huguenots' protector and most powerful military leader. The prospect of a Protestant king was of course unacceptable to ardent Catholics, who insisted that the king's Catholic religion was as much a fundamental law of the kingdom as the rule prescribing descent through the line of the eldest son. Even before Anjou's death, ultra-Catholics had tried to pressure Henry III to declare Navarre ineligible to succeed to the throne. The king refused and, on Anjou's death, sent a favorite courtier to Navarre to try to convince him to convert to the Catholic faith. Navarre refused. This solution to the dilemma of the succession was in any event unacceptable to most devout Catholics, who believed that a conversion made under such circumstances could not be sincere or valid.

If the king would not resolve the succession crisis, the Guises determined that they would. They began to organize a new Catholic league, the Holy Union, and signed an alliance with Philip II to gain financial backing for yet another war. By the secret Treaty of Joinville (December 31, 1584), the Guises and Spain pledged mutual support for war against Protestants in France and the Netherlands and, declaring heretics ineligible to reign, named Cardinal Charles de Bourbon, Henry of Navarre's aged uncle, as heir to the throne. While the Guises raised an army and rallied aristocrats to join the Holy Union, urban leagues formed in a number of French cities, Paris foremost among them.

Although they made common cause with the aristocrats in their desire to purge the kingdom of heresy, the urban leagues had different priorities from the aristocratic Holy Union. Often depicted as single-minded in their defense of the Catholic Church, the Guises acted more to defend the family's position and honor than has often been recognized. Excluded from favor at court through much of the second half of the sixteenth century, they sought to compensate by strengthening their influence in the provinces and saw the Holy Union as a way to accomplish this goal (Carroll, *Noble Power*). The initial core of the league's army, formed by the Guises' own aristocratic clients, was soon joined by clients of the deceased Anjou and other disgruntled aristocrats. They too were motivated by a complex blend of self-interest and religious conviction. Historians generally agree that defense of the faith was a more central motive for organizers of the urban leagues, although here too political strategies played a part. Many cities, when they first allied with the Holy Union, looked to the league's aristocratic protectors to help defend municipal liberties that were being encroached upon by the crown. When these protectors proved as insensitive to civic traditions and determined to exert their control as the king had been, the alliance between aristocratic leaguers and city-dwellers was bound to fracture. This conflict of interest, however, only became apparent with time. What was evident in 1585 was not the internal weakness of the Catholic league but rather the growing numbers of troops that were rallying under its banners.

In July 1585, Henry III bowed to necessity and signed the Treaty of Nemours with the league's leaders. Even if the king emerged, as in 1576, as titular head of the Holy Union, the Treaty of Nemours was a humiliating capitulation. Promising to lead a war for the extermination of heresy, Henry III revoked previous edicts and ordered Calvinists to return to the Catholic faith. Calvinist ministers were to leave the country within six months; others were allowed to choose between abjuration and exile. The Huguenots again prepared for war. Thus began an awkward three-sided struggle. Although formally allied with the league, Henry III was secretly determined to cripple its power, along with that of the Huguenots. To this end, he sent the league's army east to battle the powerful German army arriving to aid the Huguenots, while the royal army marched south to challenge what was expected to be a weaker Huguenot force. The strategy failed. Guise ably defeated the German reiters, further burnishing his reputation as a military leader. At the same time, the royal army lost to Henry of Navarre at Coutras (October 1587). Henry III's nominal allies began to seem more of a threat than his declared enemies.

Fearing the duke of Guise's growing popularity, Henry III forbade him to come to Paris, where the Holy Union was already too strong. When the king learned that Guise planned to come anyway, he brought in troops to maintain order. The move had just the opposite effect. Like citizens of every other early modern town, Parisians had always resisted the stationing of troops inside their walls. Barricades went up in the streets, and a popular revolt broke out (May 1588). Unable to regain calm, Henry III fled his capital just three days after Guise's triumphant entry. Three months later, Henry III capitulated yet again to the power of the Guises and signed the Edict of Union (July 1588). Reconfirming his alliance with the Holy Union and determination to extirpate heresy, Henry III amnestied participants in the Day of the Barricades, made the duke of Guise lieutenant general of his armies, and rewarded the duke's allies with offices and other favors. He also agreed to call another meeting of the Estates General at Blois to resolve the continuing financial crisis and discuss projects of internal reform. Sometime during this meeting, which opened in October 1588, Henry III rashly decided to put an end to his problems by ordering the assassination of Henry of Guise. Summoning the duke to a private meeting early on the morning of December 23, Henry III had him cut down by his private guard. Arrested with other Guise allies, the duke's brother, Louis, cardinal of Guise, went to his death the following day.

But if Henry III thought that, in ridding himself of the Guises, his problems would disappear, he was badly mistaken. Guise kinsmen took over leadership of the Holy Union, while news of the deaths sent leaguer cities into open and violent revolt. In Paris, ultra-Catholic preachers denounced the king as a tyrant, as the league's radical leaders, known as the Seize, raised troops to make war against him. Frightening into silence those opponents who had dared to remain in the city, the Seize used their new authority to imprison and extort money from anyone who did not appear sufficiently supportive of their cause. Their revolt soon took on a religious dimension as well. A wave of penitential and apocalyptic piety swept over the city. For several months, the rituals of daily life gave way to an endless round of religious services, sermons, and processions to invoke God's aid and implore his mercy. Mourning for the "martyred" duke and cardinal of Guise took on overtones of a popular religious cult. Similar events took place in other leaguer cities. Henry III saw no alternative to forming an alliance with Henry of Navarre in order to put down the league's revolt. The allies planned to besiege Paris to regain control of the capital, but before this could happen, a Jacobin monk named Jacques Clement, begging an interview with the king, plunged a knife into his belly and killed him (August 1, 1589). One of Henry's last actions was formally to recognize Navarre as his heir.

Laying claim to the throne as Henry IV, Navarre fought on to defeat the Catholic league, which had grown still larger on Henry III's death with the defection of royalist cities and nobles who refused to accept a Protestant king. By August 1589, six of the eight major cities with courts of Parlement – Paris, Rouen, Toulouse, Dijon, Grenoble, and Aix – were in leaguer hands. Only Rennes and Bordeaux remained faithful to the crown. Many of France's other largest cities – including Lyon and Marseille – had gone over to the Holy Union as well. And yet, as a recent study of the league has shown, Henry IV was not in as unfavorable a position as most classic texts presume. If he did not hold France's largest cities, he nevertheless had a strong network of middle-sized and strategically important towns. In terms of the proportion of aristocrats who remained either neutral or faithful to the crown, his position was stronger still (Constant, *La Ligue*, pp. 313–16 and 325–31). The league was, moreover, beset by internal contradictions that would gradually undermine its force from within. But if all of the advantages were not on the side of the league, the task that lay before Henry IV in 1589 was nevertheless an enormous one.

Henry IV's leadership on the field of battle played an important role in his eventual triumph, but his strategy off the battlefield was important as well. Royalist propagandists combated the apocalyptic rhetoric of the league by depicting Henry IV's victories at Arcques (September 1589) and Ivry (March 1590) as signs of a divinely ordained mission to rescue France from its misery and restore it to a golden age of reason, honor, and peace (Crouzet, *Guerriers de Dieu*, vol. 2, pp. 577–81). The notion that Henry IV had been consecrated on the field of battle, if not in the traditional ceremonies at Reims, may not have converted ardent leaguers to his cause, but it was a clever beginning to the necessary task of convincing the French people that Henry IV was indeed their legitimate king. The truly important step was nevertheless Henry's conversion to the Roman Catholic religion. Henry's announcement in May 1593 that he would take instruction in the Catholic faith seriously undermined support for the league, which at that very moment was convening a meeting of the Estates General with the express purpose of naming a Catholic king. In July, Henry formally abjured Calvinism at St.-Denis. In February 1594, he was solemnly consecrated and crowned at Chartres cathedral. Reims was still in leaguer hands. The following month, supporters within Paris quietly opened the gates and allowed Henry IV to enter. What little resistance initially formed quickly melted away as Henry made his way to the cathedral of Notre-Dame, where he attended mass and a service of thanksgiving.

Contrary to popular legend, it was not Henry IV who said "Paris is worth a mass." His leaguer enemies coined the phrase as a way of accusing Henry of hypocrisy (Wolfe, *Conversion of Henri IV*, p. 1). Henry's conversion was nevertheless a politically calculated move. He might have undertaken it sooner, but he knew that a quick abjuration of Calvinism would appear too blatantly self-serving. He had to wait until enough of his Catholic subjects, exhausted by the prolonged quarrels, were ready to accept his conversion as sincere. When, in late 1592, a growing "Third Party" began to call on Henry to convert, he knew it was time to listen, although he still had to act cautiously so as to keep the Huguenots in the alliance. After all, Henry's coronation oath, like that of his predecessors, required him to expel all heretics so designated by the church, and ultra-Catholics wanted him to live up to the oath as proof of the sincerity of his conversion. The Huguenots had good reason to worry about what Henry's return to the Catholic Church would mean for them.

Paris was not the first leaguer city to rally to Henry IV. That honor goes to Meaux, which opened its gates in January 1594. Lyon followed in February, but it was only after Paris's move into the royalist camp that the rush was on to abandon the Catholic league. Henry's announced policy of appeasement brought many cities and governments over voluntarily; others he took by war. One by one, league leaders surrendered or were bought off with generous settlements. Peace seemed near when the duke of Mayenne, a younger brother of the duke of Guise and the head of the Holy Union after his death, surrendered in late 1595. Spain, however, prepared to assist the league's last holdouts by sending an army into northern France. The timing could not have been worse. The Huguenots were growing increasingly restive, worried that Henry was not doing enough to protect their rights in the peace treaties he signed with various league supporters. Henry had to promise them a new and more favorable peace – not just the return to the 1577 edicts that he had accorded them in 1591 – in order to gain their support for the war against Spain. Even so, key Huguenot nobles withdrew before the crucial siege of Amiens (September 1597), leaving it to royalist and ex-leaguer troops to aid Henry in driving out the Spanish army. Henry defeated the league's last warlord, the duke of Mercoeur, in January 1598. In April, he made peace with the Huguenots, who by their continued defiant posture secured important concessions in the settlement. In May, he made peace with Spain at Vervins.

The Edict of Nantes and After

Like earlier settlements, the Edict of Nantes was a compromise peace less than satisfactory to either side. The edict consisted of four separate documents. The first set out 92 "general articles." As with previous edicts, these articles forbade all reference to past quarrels. They promised freedom of conscience, specified where Reformed Church worship might take place, and outlined rules for adjudicating complaints. A second document, containing 56 "secret articles," modified the general articles in accordance with promises Henry had made to particular individuals or towns at the time of their surrender. In addition, two special warrants issued under the king's private seal promised the Huguenots an annual subsidy to pay the salaries of their ministers and allowed them to hold nearly 200 fortified towns, about half of which were to be garrisoned at the crown's expense, for a period of eight years. These were set out as the king's personal promises rather than as acts of state so that they did not need to be registered by the courts, which would almost certainly have refused to approve them. Even so, it took ten months to convince the Parlement of Paris to register the general and secret articles. The Parlement of Rouen resisted full registration for another ten years.

Henry IV's policy of appeasement gave a secure enough base for the kingdom to begin at last to rebuild. The last 12 years of Henry IV's reign witnessed an important economic and political recovery. If relations remained strained with the Huguenot nobility, French Calvinists nevertheless gained a necessary respite. However imperfect, the toleration accorded by the Edict of Nantes allowed the Huguenot communities time to nurture those traditions and values that insured the church's survival through later persecutions. What little research has been done on religious coexistence under the edict suggests, moreover, that a certain amount of social integration eventually took place as well. Within their local communities, people did learn to live together on a day-to-day basis. On the other hand, the Edict of Nantes was far from putting an end to religious dissension.

In the first place, neither Henry IV nor his contemporaries envisioned the religious divisions as permanent. Despite its designation as "perpetual and irrevocable," the edict was intended merely to allow the two faiths to live together peacefully until they could be reunited in one church. When it was no longer needed, another "perpetual and irrevocable" edict might replace it. What this meant in practice is that members of each faith still aimed to convert the members of the other to their own unique truth. Having failed to accomplish this through war, they would instead employ theological debate, preaching, and propaganda. With the seventeenth century's Catholic revival, members of new religious orders began fervent missions in the French countryside. They did not secure many outright conversions but did succeed in fostering a new and more ardent Catholicism, thereby furthering religious divisions rather than concord.

In the end, however, it was not the people's inability to live together but rather royal policy that put an end to the toleration granted in the Edict of Nantes. Henry IV, recognizing the need to reassure the Huguenots, renewed the special warrants when they expired, even if he cut the level of payments, already in arrears. Henry's careful attempts to achieve stability were, however, undermined after his assassination in 1610. His widow, Marie de' Medici, who became regent for Louis XIII after Henry's death, showered her favors on a few chosen courtiers, thereby destabilizing the aristocracy and pushing them into revolt. A devout Catholic, she also destabilized the religious balance by alienating the Huguenots and favoring the ultra-Catholic faction at court. Louis XIII was schooled in his mother's devout politics and convinced by his minister Richelieu that the Huguenots' military power was a threat to his sovereignty. He made war against the Huguenots to reestablish the Catholic Church in Béarn, which had become exclusively Calvinist under his grandmother, Jeanne of Navarre. He then went on to destroy the Huguenots' military power, leaving them vulnerable to the persecutions later begun by his son and heir, Louis XIV, whose callous campaigns of forcible conversion did what time and persuasion had failed to do. Those Calvinists who resisted conversion were forced to flee or go underground. In 1685, declaring France entirely reunited in the Catholic Church, Louis XIV revoked the Edict of Nantes.

BIBLIOGRAPHY

Barnavi, E., *Le Parti de Dieu: Étude sociale et politique des chefs de la Ligue parisienne, 1585–1594.* Louvain: Nauwelaerts, 1980.

Benedict, P., "The Saint Bartholomew's Massacres in the Provinces," *Historical Journal,* 21/2 (1978), pp. 205–25.

Benedict, P., *Rouen during the Wars of Religion.* Cambridge: Cambridge University Press, 1981.

Benedict, P. et al., eds., *Reformation, Revolt and Civil War in France and the Netherlands, 1555–1585.* Amsterdam: Royal Netherlands Academy of Arts and Sciences, 1999.

Carroll, S., *Noble Power during the French Wars of Religion: The Guise Affinity and the Catholic Cause in Normandy.* Cambridge: Cambridge University Press, 1998.

Cassan, M., *Le Temps des Guerres de Religion: Le cas du Limousin (vers 1530–vers 1630).* Paris: Publisud, 1996.

Christin, O., *Une révolution symbolique: L'iconoclasme huguenot et la reconstruction catholique.* Paris: Éditions de Minuit, 1991.

Constant, J.-M., *Les Guise.* Paris: Hachette, 1994.

Constant, J.-M., *La Ligue.* Paris: Fayard, 1996.

Crouzet, D., *Les Guerriers de Dieu: La violence au temps des troubles de religion (vers 1525–vers 1610),* 2 vols. Seyssel: Champ Vallon, 1990.

Davis, N. Z., *Society and Culture in Early Modern France: Eight Essays.* Stanford, Calif.: Stanford University Press, 1975.

Descimon, R., *Qui étaient les Seize? Mythes et réalités de la Ligue parisienne (1585–1594).* Paris: Fédération des Sociétés historiques et archéologiques de Paris et de l'Île-de-France, 1983.

Diefendorf, B. B., *Beneath the Cross: Catholics and Huguenots in Sixteenth-Century Paris.* Oxford and New York: Oxford University Press, 1991.

Gal, S., *Grenoble au temps de la Ligue: Étude politique, sociale et religieuse d'une cité en crise (vers 1562–vers 1598).* Grenoble: Presses Universitaires de Grenoble, 2000.

Garrisson, J., *Les Protestants au XVIᵉ siècle.* Paris: Fayard, 1988.

Goodbar, R. L., ed., *The Edict of Nantes: Five Essays and a New Translation.* Bloomington, Minn.: The National Huguenot Society, 1998.

Greengrass, M., "A Day in the Life of the Third Estate: Blois, 26th December 1576," in Adrianna E. Bakos, ed., *Politics, Ideology and the Law in Early Modern Europe.* Rochester, NY: University of Rochester Press, 1994, pp. 73–90.

Greengrass, M., *France in the Age of Henri IV,* 2nd ed. London and New York: Longman, 1995.

Harding, R. R., "The Mobilization of Confraternities Against the Reformation in France," *Sixteenth Century Journal,* 11/2 (1980), pp. 85–107.

Holt, M. P., *The French Wars of Religion, 1562–1629.* Cambridge and New York: Cambridge University Press, 1995.

Jouanna, A., *Le Devoir de révolte: La noblesse française et la gestation de l'État moderne, 1559–1661*. Paris: Fayard, 1989.

Jouanna, A., *La France du XVIᵉ siècle (1483–1598)*. Paris: Presses Universitaires de France, 1996.

Kingdon, R. M., *Geneva and the Coming of the Wars of Religion in France, 1555–1563*. Geneva: Droz, 1956.

Kingdon, R. M., *Geneva and the Consolidation of the French Protestant Movement, 1564–1572*. Geneva: Droz, 1957.

Konnert, M., *Civic Agendas and Religious Passion: Châlons-sur-Marne during the French Wars of Religion, 1560–1594*. Kirksville, Mo.: Sixteenth Century Essays and Studies, 1997.

Mariéjol, J.-H., *La Réforme, la Ligue, l'Édit de Nantes (1559–1598)*. Paris: Tallandier, 1983 (originally published 1904).

Monter, W., *Judging the French Reformation: Heresy Trials by Sixteenth-Century Parlements*. Cambridge, Mass.: Harvard University Press, 1999.

Roberts, P., *A City in Conflict: Troyes during the French Wars of Religion*. Cambridge: Cambridge University Press, 1996.

Salmon, J. H. M., *Society in Crisis: France in the Sixteenth Century*. New York: St. Martin's, 1975.

Stegmann, A., *Édits des Guerres de Religion*. Paris: J. Vrin, 1979.

Wolfe, M., *The Conversion of Henri IV: Politics, Power, and Religious Belief in Early Modern France*. Cambridge, Mass.: Harvard University Press, 1993.

Wood, J. B., *The King's Army: Warfare, Soldiers, and Society during the Wars of Religion in France, 1562–1576*. Cambridge: Cambridge University Press, 1996.

FURTHER READING

The best recent English language survey is Mack Holt's *The French Wars of Religion*, although J. H. M. Salmon, *Society in Crisis: France in the Sixteenth Century*, is still useful. On the spread of Protestantism, see Robert Kingdon, *Geneva and the Coming of the Wars of Religion in France*, but also, more recently, William Monter, *Judging the French Reformation*, and Philip Benedict, "The Dynamics of Protestant Militancy," pp. 35–50, in his *Reformation, Revolt and Civil War in France and the Netherlands*. The latter volume also has useful articles by Jean-Marie Constant on the Huguenot nobility, Denis Crouzet on Protestant political theory, Olivier Christin on royal policy, and Marc Venard on Catholic resistance. James Wood, *The King's Army*, is fundamental on the problems of raising, funding, and mobilizing armies. The seminal study of religious violence in the wars is Natalie Davis, "The Rites of Violence," in her *Society and Culture in Early Modern France*. Barbara Diefendorf's *Beneath the Cross* covers the events in Paris through St. Bartholomew's Day. On individual cities, see especially Philip Benedict's *Rouen during the Wars of Religion*, but also Penny Roberts's *A City in Conflict* on Troyes and Mark Konnert's *Civic Agendas and Religious Passion* on Châlons-sur-Marne. Catholic militance is addressed in Robert Harding, "The Mobilization of Confraternities"; see also Philip Benedict, "The Saint Bartholomew's Massacres in the Provinces." Political factionalism has received less attention than religious passions lately. Stuart Carroll's *Noble Power*, on the Guise affinity, aims to redress the balance. Little is available on the Wars of the League in English, but see Michael Wolfe, *The Conversion of Henri IV*, and Mark Greengrass, *France in the Age of Henri IV*, on the later stages of the wars and their settlement. Richard Goodbar has published a new translation of the Edict of Nantes, along with several useful interpretative essays.

ELEVEN

The Italian Reformation

MASSIMO FIRPO

I

The circulation of the Protestant doctrines in sixteenth-century Italy was widespread and precocious, above all in the towns of the northern part of the country. Not surprisingly, the first to know about and appreciate the German and Swiss reformers' new message of Christian freedom were ecclesiastics, beginning with Luther's Augustinian confrères, among whom were many friars who were "ill-disciplined as to the matters concerning the Catholic faith," such as Agostino Mainardi, Andrea Ghetti, Giuliano Brigantino, Ambrogio Cavalli, and Giulio Della Rovere. However, exponents of other orders, too, did not take long to side with them: the Franciscans Girolamo Galateo, Bartolomeo Fonzio, Baldo Lupatino, Giovanni Buzio, Bartolomeo della Pergola, Paolo Ricci (alias Camillo Renato), the Capuchins Bernardino Ochino and Girolamo da Molfetta, the Carmelite Giambattista Pallavicino, the Lateran regular canons Pietro Martire Vermigli, Celso Martinengo and Ippolito Chizzola, the Dominicans Bernardo Bartoli and Angelo da Messina (alias Ludovico Manna), the Cassinese Benedictines Francesco Negri, Benedetto Fontanini, Luciano Degli Ottoni, Giorgio Siculo, and Antonio da Bozzolo. Sooner or later, all would fall into the hands of the Inquisition, and eventually some would take the path of exile to become a minister or professor in the Swiss lands. Only clerics and scholars, such as Celio Secondo Curione, Francesco Porto, Aonio Paleario, and Ludovico Castelvetro, were able to understand the Latin of those texts, which, nevertheless, were not long in becoming available on the market disguised in translations under engaging titles, allusive pseudonyms, and false attributions. For instance, a booklet containing Lutheran writings had several editions, two of which were anonymous and three published under the name of Erasmus; furthermore, the version from the Dutch of the *Summario della santa Scrittura* enjoyed great success. The use of the vernacular in many texts that were differently characterized by a heterodox inspiration was not only the propaganda method used by pro-Reformation groups, it also reflected a large social demand, a widespread religious ferment, and a profound unrest due to the crisis that ecclesiastical institutions experienced.

On this side of the Alps in fact, pro-Reformation leanings were rooted in a particular historical experience, first of all in the old settlement of the papacy, with its various connections with aristocrats and patricians of the peninsula, with its political and financial presence, and with its mighty system of allocation of ecclesiastical offices. A widespread anticlerical attitude gives evidence of this, as is made clear by the famous words of Machiavelli according to whom Italians owed "to the church and priests the fact that they had become irreligious and wicked." While the ongoing wars between Habsburgs and Valois with their tragic repercussions of famine, pestilence, and fiscal oppression plunged the small states of the peninsula into an irreversible crisis, new prophetic tensions fueled many religious phenomena: Savonarola's subversive preaching in Florence, the Venetian reprints of Gioacchino da Fiore's writings, the great success of leaflets giving accounts of disturbing astrological combinations or of monstrous births, the penitential and apocalyptic messages of itinerant friars covered in sackcloth. The hermit Brandano da Petroio from Siena, for instance, went through the streets of Rome and openly insulted Pope Clement VII as a "sodomite and bastard," while Francesco Guicciardini hoped for "a world that would be free from the tyranny of these wicked priests" and confessed that only his "particular" interest had prevented him from loving Luther as himself: certainly not because of religious aspirations, which were far from his intellectual sensitivity, but rather because of his desire "to see this host of scoundrels reduced to due terms, namely to remain either without vices or without authority."

The favor that the Lutheran protest encountered in many parts of Italy also originated from the difficulties that had been caused by the assimilation of the peninsula into the Habsburg sphere of influence, by the fading of the city-states' freedom and of the republican tradition in the framework of the new regional states, by the collapse of princely and aristocratic families' ancient privileges, and by the growing role of the papacy in the frantic events of Italian politics and its nepotistic ambitions. The Medici popes' prominent Florentine interests help to explain the delay and lack of attention in Rome's response to the transalpine heresies; the late response facilitated their penetration in the peninsula, especially along the flourishing trade routes with the German world or in the sees of prestigious universities, such as Padua or Bologna, that were attended by foreign students. The measures against the clandestine importation of heterodox books in the 1520s bear witness to their widespread circulation more than to their repression. Only in 1542 was the Holy Office of the Inquisition founded and only at the end of 1546 was the long-awaited council able to meet in Trent, almost 30 years after the publication of the Wittenberg Theses. Yet, as early as in 1519, a bookseller from Pavia solicited Luther's works; in the following year a Venetian diarist recorded a notice, however contradictory, concerning the redoubtable "monster of Germany" but also "very erudite man who follows Saint Paul."

The identity crisis of the church, its loss of religious credibility, and the pastoral absenteeism of the clergy stressed even further the bewilderment of believers, who crowded under pulpits, learned to find their bearings among the preachers' doctrinal subtleties, and looked for answers to their doubts by reading the Bible. It is in light of this institutional crisis, of the widespread individual and collective malaise and doctrinal uncertainties, that we can understand the unprecedented investigation of theological discussions by the lower classes, to whom the success of the vernacular offered a tool of emancipation from the monopoly of the clerics. In Bologna, for instance, in the 1540s "a sect and congregation of many persons, women, men, friars, nuns and persons of any sort" met regularly and recognized a merchant as their leader. During those years there were innumerable worried reports on the dangerous spread of the religious debate "over squares, shops, taverns and even over the washhouses of women," where humble, common people, artisans, tailors, weavers, and fish merchants, dared to discuss faith and works, free will and predestination, sacraments "and other tangled questions and high dogmas of the faith." In 1542, in Lucca, one of the accusations made against Curione on the eve of his escape to Switzerland was "having translated into vernacular some of Luther's works, in order to give that food to the simple women of our town."

Hence, the success encountered by the complete editions of the Biblical translation by Florentine exile Antonio Brucioli is understandable. This translation was published in Venice in 1532 and the pages of the Apocalypse contained antipapal illustrations copied from Holbein's illustrations for the Basel print of 1523 of the New Testament of Luther. A year later, again in Venice, an illiterate carpenter was arrested; he was reputed to have learned by heart the entire Scripture in order to teach the new doctrines to the heterodox community that he led. For this reason, the nuncio Aleandro asked for and obtained from Rome a papal brief forbidding anyone from reading the Bible without authorization. Reluctantly, Catholic controversialists also had to recognize this new social frontier and cope with the need to confute the Lutheran heresies in the vernacular, by addressing the illiterate as well and by finding a language that was suitable for the "simple people." Hence, although only of short duration, the lively religious experimentation of those decades offered unforeseen spaces of freedom, whereas the acceptance of the new doctrines seemed to some to shatter ancient cultural and social barriers that were destined to stiffen during the post-Tridentine age.

II

In this essay, it is impossible to reconstruct town by town the early circulation of the Protestant heresies, their origins, their ability to take root and become more stable in organized groups, their embryonic forms of ecclesiastical life, and the definition of their doctrinal profile. In Piedmont the existing Waldensian communities embraced the Swiss Reformation in 1532, whereas new adherents would gradually end up swelling the ranks of immigrants. Among the Piedmontese were Celio Secondo Curione, the well-known Genevan printer Jean Girard, Giorgio Biandrata, and Gian Paolo Alciati. Many heretical communities gathered in Lombardy, in Milan, Como, Pavia, and in Cremona, where a real dissident church was founded. A similar situation occurred in Genoa and in Mantua, where for a few years Cardinal Ercole Gonzaga nurtured a curiosity for the new doctrines. In Ferrara, too, Duchess Renata of France welcomed Clement Marot and for a while Calvin himself in her court, where the Holy Supper was celebrated according to the Genevan custom. She also offered help to heterodox friars and exiles who were persecuted because of their faith, to the point that the duke had to have her arrested. A similar situation occurred in Modena, where patricians, intellectuals, and ecclesiastics created a heretical movement that was so strong and deep-seated that it prompted the episcopal vicar to depict the town as being as "contaminated by the infection of several heresies as Prague" and a German prince to evoke it as the "only city to be blessed in Italy." A similar situation occurred in Bologna, where in 1547, while the council was meeting, a bishop denounced the "countless number" of heretics that populated the city as well as the territories of the papal state in Emilia and Romagna. A similar situation occurred in Florence, where, after the early leanings of Savonarola's followers in favor of the Reformation had faded, it was the circles close to the Medici court of Cosimo that appropriated tendencies open to the new doctrines. A similar situation also occurred in Pisa, in Siena, and above all in Lucca, where in the middle of the century a large part of the dominant urban elite more or less openly sympathized with the Reformation. A similar situation occurred in Rome itself, where the general of the Capuchins Bernardino Ochino and that of the Augustinians Girolamo Seripando successfully preached the doctrine of justification by faith alone: "And everybody thronged there because they liked this doctrine." Finally, a similar situation occurred in the Spanish domains of southern Italy, not only in Naples but also in Apulia, Terra di Lavoro, Calabria, and Sicily; not even the isolated and closed island of Sardinia was exempt from heretical contaminations. In Trent, in October 1546, one bishop gave vent to his feelings of alarm and maintained that "by now all Italy has been infected and made secretly Lutheran."

However, as Ochino himself wrote on the day following his clamorous escape to Geneva in 1542, the real "door" to the Lutheran and Calvinist doctrines in Italy was Venice. The principal typographic center of Europe (numerous printers were suspected of being sympathetic to the Reformation), it was a fervent crossroads of trade between the Mediterranean and the German world and a welcoming refuge for intellectuals and political exiles. Here, some issues of the Reformation seemed for a while to follow the tracks of an ancient tradition separating jurisdiction between church and state, a tradition that was strengthened by the harsh conflicts with papal Rome. In March 1530, after an imperial request to expel all heretics from Venetian domains, the Signoria answered firmly "that our state and domain is free and therefore we cannot drive them away." Conspicuous pro-Reformation groups gradually formed in the mainland as well: in Padua (where in 1531 it was said that "it seemed that all who could read were Lutherans"), in Bergamo (where in the 1540s Bishop Vittore Soranzo himself did not conceal his favor for the Reformation), and similarly in Verona, Vicenza, Brescia, Rovigo, and in the towns in Friuli and Istria. There is evidence that attempts were made to spread the new doctrines even in the countryside: in 1550 some artisans from Bergamo were denounced for going on holy days to the villages of the countryside, where they climbed trees and "preached the Lutheran sect to peasants and the whole population."

Despite the diversity of the local aggregations that has gradually been defined by recent studies, the pro-Reformation groups and movements that were widespread in Italy in the central decades of the sixteenth century shared some common characteristics. First, they had in common forms of propaganda and conversion, through the preaching of famous itinerant preachers who drew huge crowds, many of whom soon shrewdly apprehended the undercurrents of the different religious messages, and through the clandestine circulation of pro-Reformation literature, first in Latin, then in translation, and finally also successful booklets that had been written and printed in Italy. Secondly, it is worth noting the social diversity of the followers of the new doctrines; they included humble workers and powerful aristocrats, clerics and laypeople, men and women, artisans and notaries, poor illiterates and intellectuals, who gathered in many cases in real communities of "brothers," endowed with permanent forms of clandestine organization, cult, and mutual solidarity. With their predominantly secular orientation, these groups shaped themselves as embryonic crypto-reformed communities: instruments for a collective and individual resumption of religious life, of a new relationship with God and his Word, of the daily gestures of the sacred, finally extracted from the arbitrary will of a church engaged in mystification and of a corrupt clergy. Therefore, the denunciation of the Roman Antichrist and the celebration of the Holy Supper confirmed the awareness of an ecclesiastical alterity that was also mirrored in forms of reciprocal solidarity able to shatter rigid social barriers.

Although bishops and inquisitors did not hesitate to classify as "Lutheran" every form of religious dissent, it is necessary to take into account the multifarious diversities of individual paths and to avoid imposing inflexible doctrinal constraints on different religious experiences, fluid religious identities, and communities that were often forced to the difficult compromises of Nicodemism. In fact, the absence of strong ecclesiastical structures and of connections with political power prevented religious dissenters from defining a precise doctrinal orientation and made possible many forms of religious eclecticism that were able to draw their inspiration from Luther as much as from Erasmus, from Calvin as much as from Valdés, in the framework of persistent hopes for a religious pacification destined to last until the conclusion of the Council of Trent and even beyond. First of all, at the core of this heritage was the controversy against the superstitious forms of traditional devotions, the rejection of the mendicant pharisaic piety, the principle of justification by faith, the denial of purgatory, intercession of saints and the veneration of images, papal authority, mass, auricular confession, indulgences, etc.; the Eucharistic question, which in those years divided the evangelical churches from the Reformed ones, remained somewhat marginal. The heretical groups began to define themselves on the basis of a more precise doctrinal profile only later, starting from the end of the 1540s, with the promulgation of early council decrees and with the fading of hope of the Reformation's success on the Italian side of the Alps.

In fact, since their early appearance in the peninsula, the Protestant doctrines seemed to many to consist of the rejection of a fruitless piety made up of processions, indulgences, blessed water, relics, and fasting and marked by those futile and repetitive rituals against which Erasmus had hurled his polemical arrows. For this reason, despite the fact that Erasmianism and Lutheranism would soon deeply diverge, in Italy they could appear essentially consistent and in agreement. The absence of an institutional Reformation in Italy condemned heretical groups to living underground and long protected a sort of embryonic doctrinal identity, largely focused against the papal church and its superstitious cults, and completely centered on the will to resume the genuine evangelical and Pauline matrix of the Christian's freedom. For instance, in 1539 in Modena, a Franciscan friar was denounced on suspicion of belonging to the "Lutheran sect" and of preaching from the pulpit "Erasmus's sect," namely, focusing in his homilies on that doctrine of justification by faith which represented the most authentic core of Reformation for inquisitors as well as for dissenters.

The trusting abandon to God's infinite mercy, to the sacrifice of the Cross, and to predestination as certainty of grace sometimes turned into the firm belief that "we are all saved [. . .] because the Lord Jesus Christ with his blood has given Paradise to all of us," as some heterodox inhabitants of Piran maintained. This explains why the upholders of the Catholic tradition precociously denounced the risks of disorder, lawlessness, and political and social turmoil that seemed implicit in the assertion that "believing is enough to save us," in the desire expressed to send everyone "to Paradise shod and dressed [. . .] by saying that the Lord has paid for us with his blood," with no more awe, no more works, no more priests, no more obedience. This was a message to which the establishment would not fail to pay attention, after the peasant revolt in Germany, the spreading of Anabaptism, the French civil wars, and the rebellion of Flanders seemed to reveal how easy it was to distort *in libertatem carnis* the evangelical freedom announced by the Reformation and to pass from revolt against the church to revolt against the state and its social and political balance. This helps us to clarify the specific originality of the Italian Reformation: it was, therefore, not only an unsuccessful expansion of the German or Swiss reforms, it also expressed a series of autonomous characteristics and creative elements, even though there is no doubt that from the 1550s – with the strengthening of a repression that was made increasingly effective by the consolidation of the Roman Inquisition – the heretical groups ended up loosening their expansive ability and leaning toward doctrinal choices that were mostly in agreement with Calvinism. After all, it was the Swiss cantons on the Italian borders, Geneva, Zürich, Basel, and Grisons, that hosted an increasing flow of emigrants *religionis causa*, who found here social structures, political traditions, and economic activities that did not much differ from those of their native land, where the profession of their faith had become impossible.

III

The circulation and duration of the pro-Reformation groups in Italy would remain inexplicable if we did not take into account the protection and complicity of aristocrats, patricians, and high prelates. The court of Renata of France in Ferrara has already been mentioned, but analogous leanings toward German and Swiss heresies were also present in the courts of the duchess of Savoy, Marguerite de Valois, and the duchess of Urbino, Eleonora Gonzaga. If between the 1540s and 1550s the patrician ruling class in Lucca was largely oriented toward heterodoxy (as is proved by the dense emigration of the Balbani, Diodati, Turrettini, and Micheli who settled in Geneva), the situation was similar in Modena in the 1540s, where religious dissent attracted many followers among the members of eminent households, such as the Rangoni, Grillenzoni, Valentini, and Sadoleto, before spreading widely among merchants and artisans during the following decade. A similar situation occurred in Venice, above all among the members of the minor patrician families, where the escape to Geneva of the doge's brother Andrea Da Ponte caused a sensation. Analogous observations could be extended to other Italian cities, such as Vicenza or Brescia, Imola or Bologna. Since the 1550s and 1560s, but with reference to events of the previous decade, the trials for heresy reached the point of involving persons close to the Mantuan court, starting with Endimio Calandra, former secretary to Cardinal Gonzaga, and to the Florentine court, where close collaborators of Duke Cosimo, such as Bartolomeo

Panciatichi, Pietro Gelido, Gian Battista Ricasoli, patricians of ancient stock, such as Pietro Carnesecchi (former secretary of Clement VII), and intellectuals of the Medici establishment, such as Benedetto Varchi or Cosimo Bartoli, did not conceal their various degrees of inclination toward the new doctrines. The same observations can be made for some representatives of great aristocratic families such as the duchess of Camerino, Caterina Cibo, Ascanio and Vittoria Colonna (the famous poetess), Giulia Gonzaga, Isabella Brisegna, Camillo Orsini, and Alessandro and Giulio Trissino, all of them suspected of heresy. The same can be said of some powerful Neapolitan and Sicilian barons, such as the marquis of Oria, Giovanni Bernardino Bonifacio, or the marquis of Vico, Galeazzo Caracciolo, who claimed the right to be not only prince but also "pope" in his fiefs (both were exiles in Switzerland). A similar religious orientation was shared by other prominent figures who were proud of their eminent lineages, namely, Brancaccio, Sanseverino, Galeota, d'Avalos, Villamarina, Delli Monti, Alois, and Spadafora. From this point of view, there is no doubt that the religious crisis of those decades was linked to the unrest of the traditional elites, whose power and autonomy suffered under the consolidation of new absolutist models, new political hegemonies, and a new balance of power.

The involvement in the new doctrines of many ecclesiastics sensitive to the need for a deep revival of the church and the religious life was even more significant, especially in light of the authoritative theological and institutional legitimacy that would develop from it. Even before the Theses of Wittenberg, a great Venetian patrician like Gasparo Contarini, destined to become cardinal and to devote himself vigorously to the reformation of the church and reconciliation with the Protestants, entrusted his hopes of salvation only to faith in the blood shed by Christ on the Cross. Analogous aspirations did not take long to surface over the course of the collective theological reflection devised among the collaborators of the bishop of Verona, Gian Matteo Giberti, the powerful datary of Clement VII, who was accountable for the anti-Habsburg politics that tragically led to the sack of Rome. After 1527, he decided to withdraw to his diocese, where his attempt to promote a serious reform from below and from the periphery would offer an enduring model in the post-Tridentine period. In his entourage there circulated doctrines, persons, and books that would later be considered unorthodox by the church. "Many years ago, religious questions in Italy were little regulated because the office of the Holy Inquisition had not yet been established or it was not yet well founded and strong," wrote Cardinal Giovanni Morone in 1557; he remembered how before the council everyone dared to talk "in every corner [. . .] of ecclesiastical dogmas and everyone acted as a theologian and books were composed and sold everywhere without consideration."

When he wrote these words, Morone had just been locked up in Castel Sant'Angelo, where over the course of a long trial he would have to account to the Inquisition for attitudes he had held in the past, when his irenic stance – inspired by Contarini and shaped during his long appointment as nuncio in Germany (almost without interruption from 1536 to 1542) – had undergone an evolution that developed finally into the doctrine of justification by faith. This choice was destined also to have repercussions in the government of his dioceses of Modena, where he had sent friars to preach who would later be tried for heresy; he had also encouraged the circulation of books that would be relegated to the Index, and had offered protection to suspect individuals. Morone acted in a similar fashion during his short period of assignment with the Bologna Legation, where he actually expressed the conviction that "it was good to tolerate these Lutherans since God, who could annihilate them with a nod, tolerated them."

Morone's behavior did not represent an isolated example in the 1540s, as is proven by the bishop of Capodistria, Pier Paolo Vergerio, the bishop of Bergamo, Vittore Soranzo, the patriarch of Aquileia, Giovanni Grimani, the bishop of Cyprus, Andrea Centani, the bishop of Messina, Giovan Francesco Verdura, the bishop of Chioggia, Iacopo Nacchianti, the archbishop of Otranto, Pietro Antonio Di Capua, the bishop of Cava dei Tirreni, Giovanni Tommaso Sanfelice, the bishop of Catania, Nicola Maria Caracciolo, and the bishop of Policastro, Antonio Francesco Missanelli. At different moments, all of these individuals became targets of suspicion and accusation, and were placed on trial. In the 1560s a Protestant dissenter from Caserta revealed to the inquisitors the names of at least 11 bishops and archbishops of the kingdom of Naples who had in the past embraced the doctrine according to which "man is justified only by faith because works are useless." Besides Cardinal Gonzaga, who has already been mentioned, other members of the Sacred College appreciated and sometimes contributed to the spread of ideas and books that would soon be condemned. Among them were Cristoforo Madruzzo (bishop and prince of Trent), the learned Federico Fregoso, the Benedictine Gregorio Cortese, the Dominicans Tommaso Badia and Pietro Bertano, the famous scholar Pietro Bembo, and the influential Reginald Pole, member of the English royal family and several times in line for papal election. Before the death of Contarini in August 1542, he himself became the target of malevolent suspicions that came out into the open during the 1550s when the intransigent inquisitor Gian Pietro Carafa, by then Pope Paul IV, would devote himself, in Carnesecchi's words, to "filling the prisons with cardinals and bishops."

However, it would be misleading to link these tendencies, then largely present in Italian society, only to conscious pro-Reformation choices. In fact, many continued to cherish increasingly faint and illusory hopes for possible reconciliation of the religious splits that racked European Christianity; they continued to hope not only until the failed religious colloquy with Protestants in Regensburg (1541), or until the establishment of the Roman Holy Office and the flight over the Alps of famous preachers such as Ochino and Vermigli (1542), but also until the approval of the first council decrees (1547), until the conclave in 1549 and beyond, until the death of Pope Julius III (1555), and until the conclusion of the Tridentine Council (1563). They hoped for a reconciliation that was based on an incisive reform of the church, starting with the profiteering and corruption that reigned in the Datary or in the apostolic Penitentiary, veritable "workshops of wickedness" according to Cardinal Gonzaga; they also hoped for a pacification based on some concessions to Protestant claims, such as priests' marriage and the chalice for the laity, but also on acceptance of the Lutheran theology of justification by faith alone. Soon, other crucial issues clustered round this doctrine; they can be summarized in the general question of its "consequences," as it was said, namely, its sacramental and ecclesiological "inferences," which concerned above all the approval or rejection of the mass, purgatory, confession, good works, alms, the cult of saints, the veneration of images, and the authority of the pope. These issues concerned the problem of ecclesiastical identity and affiliation, the choice to stand consciously on the Reformation side and to appropriate its doctrines as well as the struggle to overthrow the Roman Antichrist. It was a difficult and distressing choice, of course, that would entail risks, suffering, distressing duplicities, and sometimes courageous decisions which, until the end of the 1540s and beyond, many hoped to delay while waiting for council decrees and hoping for a religious pacification.

IV

As has been mentioned, there is no doubt that influential figures and prelates played a significant role in legitimizing such expectations and hopes by seeming to offer institutional compatibility and social rootedness to those religious tendencies. Yet, it would be difficult to understand such behavior without taking into account the original characteristics that religious dissent gradually took on during the 1540s as a result of the influence of Juan de Valdés, the Spanish dissenter who sought refuge in Rome in order to escape the proceedings that had been initiated against him by the Spanish Inquisition in 1529, following the publication of his *Diálogo de doctrina cristiana*. In fact, with Valdés the repercussions of the Spanish *alumbradismo* were far from negligible in Italy. *Alumbradismo* refers to that core of doctrines and religious attitudes that had been devised before Luther's protest in a world of *conversos, beatas,* common people, intellectuals, and even among a few great aristocrats. At its heart was above all the firm belief that knowledge of the "secretos de Dios" was based not so much on the authority of the Scriptures and of the church as on the inner revelation of the spirit, on the light that it instilled in everyone's conscience allowing genuine understanding of God's Word. It proposed a radical spiritualism intolerant of the theological and institutional norms, hostile to the teaching of the "letrados," and driven by profound inner certainties assuaged by the "peace of conscience." Theoretically, this resulted in the Christian's absolute freedom, in his abandonment to God's love, in the centrality of faith as the sole guarantor of salvation and the consequent contempt for the useless "little acts of devotion," namely, the obligations of rites, alms, masses, prayers, vows, and traditional precepts, in the rejection of confession and communion by the "perfectos," in the denial of papal authority and faith in universal salvation for all people. Soon, the Spanish inquisitors perceived several analogies between these doctrines and the new German heresies (from which they were completely independent), and promoted accusations and condemnations that contributed to increasing the *alumbrados'* Nicodemic cautions; but then, their spiritualism had induced them to theorize multiple levels of theological awareness, to practice forms of esoteric initiation and pedagogic gradualness, to avoid imprudent controversies and external expression of their dissent. Therefore, they created small communities "de doctrina secreta," as Melchor Cano would write, denouncing the way in which men and women of limited culture arrogated to themselves the right to read and explain the Gospel, to rely on the inner light of the spirit and on the pacifying freedom of conscience they felt in themselves by rejecting the church's authority and refraining from works and ceremonies.

The repercussions of this complex religious experience are clearly visible in the *Diálogo* of Juan de Valdés (also a descendant of a family of *conversos*), who was familiar with the Spanish *alumbradismo* milieu and synthesized its essential elements with Erasmian and Lutheran ideas. Even his brother Alfonso, Charles V's Latin secretary and a friend and correspondent of Erasmus, knew the German reformers' works and made no secret of his religious preference in the dialogues written after the sack of Rome in defense of Charles V's actions, in which he attributed that terrible tragedy to God's judgment and thereby blamed the corruption of papal Rome for the debacle. It was exactly this eclectic synthesis that Valdés elaborated and handed down during the years he spent in Italy, especially during his last stay in Naples between 1535 and 1541 (the year of his death). The many works he wrote in those years bear the unmistakable sign of a creative and original reflection, one that was free from a systematic character but endowed at the same time with great religious significance and the ability to involve his followers in a privileged spiritual experience. In fact, the Valdesian message in Naples encountered remarkable success, attracting not only intellectuals and ecclesiastics such as Ochino and Vermigli but also some members of important aristocratic families, such as his favorite disciple Giulia Gonzaga.

What Valdesianism offered, above all, was the chance to avoid the clash between opposing doctrines contending for the same arena, and also to avoid the splits that originated within the same church, the same town, the same family, and sometimes the same conscience. In fact, Valdesianism envisioned a way that unreservedly resumed the core of a recovered Christian identity implied in the evangelical announcement of justification by faith, but at the same time eluded in programmatic fashion the need to draw the necessary ecclesiological conclusions. According to his *alumbrados* masters and in Valdés's own opinion as well, taking knowledge of the truth from the theological norm and from the authority of the Scriptures and giving it to the illumination of the spirit alone meant, first of all, acknowledging the inalienable rights of the individual conscience. It meant recognizing the different levels of religious consciousness in everyone, the firm belief that the "Christian revival" was a process based not on abstract theological science but on concrete personal experience, destined therefore to develop over time and to have different results from person to person. It meant respecting this process without ever refraining from reciprocal charity, "in a way in which no man among those who have faith, even though limited by their humanity, would be regarded as alien from the Christian Church." Herein lies the need to refrain from every arrogance and human prudence and to respect those weak in faith, to try patiently to instruct them and to lead them step by step toward a new doctrinal awareness. Herein lie the Nicodemic cautions that had been theorized and practiced by Valdés and his followers, not only to avoid inquisitorial severity but also as a pedagogic means of propaganda and proselytism.

Hence, the profound spiritualism inspiring Valdesian reflection ended up entrusting the ecclesiastical institution only with the task of regulating external behavior and liturgical rites, leaving the individual the freedom of investing them with diverse theological meanings. It is not surprising, therefore, that many among the most sensitive consciences saw in Valdesianism a way to embrace the doctrine of justification by faith without necessarily entailing the doctrinal "consequences" that would have ensued from a break with the official church. According to Valdés's followers – as one of them, the above-mentioned Pietro Carnesecchi, maintained – whereas it was true that Luther "had said well on many subjects and had interpreted well many passages of the Scriptures," they deemed unacceptable the fact that he "had separated from the Catholic Church, because this separation can originate only from mere haughtiness." For this reason, when judging his heresy, it was necessary to draw a distinction between the two elements that composed it, namely, the "diversity of opinions" and the "refusal to obey," the former acceptable, the latter not, that had driven him to reject the authority of the council and to rebel against the apostolic see. For this reason, Valdés's followers did not completely accept "Luther's doctrine since it was *extra ecclesiam* and therefore *extra caritatem*," and they reserved the right to distinguish "gold from filth," in other words, the right to accept justification by faith alone and possibly to draw further doctrinal "inferences" on purgatory and confession, but to reject every possible consequence concerning the struggle against the papacy and the break with the Church of Rome.

It is evident that Valdesian spiritualism had an aristocratic connotation as well as an intrinsic political fragility in the years when the Catholic and Reformed orthodoxies were gradually defining their confessional profiles along the unyielding ridges of polemical controversies. Yet, in some measure, it was its very contradictions, its ability to distinguish between and operate on different levels, that guaranteed that refined religious message a remarkable success throughout Italy in the 1540s, against the background of the first and decisive council sessions. In this chapter, it is not possible to reconstruct the forms of Valdesian propaganda and the clustering of a complex group around the Spanish exile, in which intellectuals and clerics from every part of Italy gradually sided with the first Neapolitan disciples. Among them it is worth mentioning at least Ochino and Vermigli, both exiles in Switzerland in 1542, together with Vittore Soranzo, Pietro Carnesecchi, and Marcantonio Flaminio. In the case of Flaminio, who was a former collaborator of Giberti in Verona, the religious shift marked by the support of Valdesianism was evident in the stance he adopted in the course of an important epistolary debate between 1538 and 1540 on the crucial themes of redeeming grace and predestination, first with Contarini and then with Seripando.

The great success of such doctrines would be incomprehensible without considering that after Valdés's death the cautious action of proselytism by his disciples successfully involved personalities of great political authority such as Cardinal Pole and, shortly afterwards (and through him), Cardinal Morone, both of whom would be sent as papal legates to Trent in order to preside over the doomed inaugural council meeting. The entire group of Valdés's disciples, beginning with Flaminio, came together at the house of the English cardinal and gave birth to the group of so-called "spirituals" or *Ecclesia Viterbiensis*, named after the place where Pole had resided as papal legate to the patrimony of St. Peter, where he was able to involve Vittoria Colonna as well in Valdesianism. Pole and his friends did not confine themselves to intensive study; rather, they devoted themselves to the translation of Valdés's writings and to their circulation in a milieu open to the aspirations for revival, in a circumspect action of propaganda. Sometimes these works were addressed to preachers who would spread the doctrines from the pulpit, as happened in the diocese of Modena and Bergamo, which had been entrusted to the government of Morone and Soranzo.

The most famous outcome of such endeavors, which aimed to put forward Valdesianism as a response to the disastrous religious crisis of those decades, was the draft of the short treatise *Del beneficio di Cristo* ("The benefit of Christ's death"), published by an anonymous author in Venice in 1543 and destined for great success beyond Italy, as sixteenth-century French, English, and Croatian translations prove. Vergerio maintained that 40,000 copies of it were printed in Venice between 1543 and 1549; in almost all inquisitorial trials of the 1540s and 1550s it was recalled in the dissidents' usual readings. Although the book quoted copiously from Calvin's *Institutes of the Christian Religion*, it did not mention controversial themes such as the mass, purgatory, and the sacraments; in addition, it refrained from the antipapal controversy that was recalled in those years in dozens of books and pamphlets published in Switzerland and destined to evangelize Italy, such as Negri's *Tragedia del libero arbitrio*, Curione's *Pasquino in estasi*, and Ochino's *Prediche* and *Sermones*. Formulated positively as it was and revolving around the liberating announcement of salvation and grace, its intense religious message insisted with extraordinary effectiveness only on the "general forgiveness of the whole human generation" that was announced on the Cross, on its potential for making every soul "holy, innocent, fair, and divine," for healing the free will, defeating "sin, death, devil and hell," and even presenting the doctrine of the "most sweet" predestination as a message of universal salvation. Valdesian inspiration is evident, as suggested by the fact that a first draft of the text by the Benedictine Benedetto Fontanini from Mantua was elaborated, rewritten, and prepared for print by Flaminio at Cardinal Pole's house in Viterbo in 1542, on the eve of the first meeting in Trent and the decisive choices that the council was called to make.

For its capacity precisely to recover genuine aspirations and reformed doctrines and to reformulate them from a Valdesian viewpoint, *Il Beneficio di Cristo* stresses with great clarity the peculiarity of the so-called Italian Reformation; it suggests an explanatory cipher to it, and reveals some contradictions that are evident merely in the fact that it was the Tridentine assembly, even before the Index, which in 1546 condemned the very booklet that had been drafted and promulgated by one of the chairs of the same council. A year later, the English cardinal's bitter withdrawal from Trent on the eve of the approval of the council decree on justification (which he did not want to subscribe) theatrically underscored the failure of the attempt by the spirituals to use *Il Beneficio di Cristo* to direct the council fathers toward a viable reconciliation and to restore to the church the obedience of the dissenters who were swarming in Italian cities.

V

Certainly, these hopes were illusory and yet widespread during those years of crisis and disorientation, when the Catholic orthodoxy still held a margin of uncertainty, as is suggested by the great success of *Beneficio di Cristo* not only in the diversified world of Reform sympathizers, but also among some members of the College of Cardinals who read it as an edifying text. After all, the Habsburg court explicitly gave its steady support to the spirituals, whose religious leanings seemed to promote a hoped-for reformation of the church (it was said of Morone, for instance, that "he always talked of this reformation endlessly") and to indicate at the same time a possible path for the pacification of the empire. A conspicuous sign of these significant political collusions can be detected in the middle of the 1540s, with the initiation of the Tridentine sessions, when a prince such as Cosimo I de' Medici, who was very close to Charles V, entrusted Iacopo da Pontormo with the task of representing in the frescos of the choir of San Lorenzo (the ancient Florentine basilica that was consecrated to the Medici family's historical memory) the religious message that Valdés had left in the essential Christian pedagogy of his catechism *Qual maniera si devrebbe tenere a informare insino dalla fanciullezza i figliuoli de' christiani delle cose della religione*, published posthumously in Venice.

However, toward the end of the 1540s, above all following the council decrees on the sources of revelation, original sin, and justification, the margins of doctrinal uncertainty were drastically reduced. More and more clearly, the summit of the church came under the control of the Inquisition, the personal creation of the Theatine Cardinal Gian Pietro Carafa, the future Paul IV, who was completely devoted to the task of eradicating the weed of heresy from Italy. In fact, the unity of the aims of the new cardinals appointed by Paul III for prompting the reform of the church in view of the summoning of the council lasted only for a short time. The *Consilium de emendanda Ecclesia* they proposed to the pope in 1536 was signed by Contarini, Fregoso, and Pole, who later did not conceal their sympathies for some religious and doctrinal issues of the Reformation, as well as by Carafa, who in 1532 had already sent to Rome a memoir in which he urged a decisive battle against heterodoxy to be waged with the weapons of severe repression, on the basis of the principle that "heretics had to be treated as heretics." Although the forces of the so-called Catholic Reformation had been held together by a common will of revival and by opposition to the firm resistance of the Curia, they did not take long to diverge. More and more sharply, they split up into those who (like Contarini and then, more radically, the spirituals) thought that the Catholic Reformation should not be confined to a battle against the multiple abuses that infested the body of the church but should also incorporate essential elements of the Reformed doctrine and promote a reconciliation of the religious break, and those who (like Carafa), on the contrary, thought that the reformation of the church should aim at its institutional strengthening for a more energetic struggle against heresy on both sides of the Alps. Therefore, the summit of the Curia was marked in those years by a deep religious split that soon became open political confrontation, given that the so-called "intransigents" quickly identified the advocates of each different tendency, beginning with the spirituals who gathered around Pole and Morone, as the main enemies to be defeated.

Within this framework, the Roman Holy Office was instituted in July 1542 in order to check the spread of heresies all over Italy, and particularly – as it was said – in Naples, Lucca, and Modena, where Morone was involved with an attempt to reabsorb the heretical movement without resorting to the Inquisition, employing instead the weapons of mildness and mediation (it is not a coincidence that he had asked for and obtained the collaboration of Contarini). On the contrary, the new Roman tribunal intended to forsake this strategy once and for all, and to assert repression. In those days, the summons of Ochino and Vermigli to Rome (which both eluded by escaping) represented the most evident sign of a shift that left dangerously unprotected the Valdesian illusions and irenic strategies of the spirituals, who suddenly became targets of their opponents. In fact, thanks to the Inquisition, the latter were supplied with an extremely effective operating tool that would soon become the real ideological and political core of the Counter-Reformation Church. The religious history of those years was profoundly marked by it; those stances that were irreconcilable with curial claims came under suspicion and were sometimes the target of legal inquiries. Papal conclaves were deeply affected as well, during which the intransigents did not hesitate to formulate defamatory charges of heresy against the spirituals in

order to exclude those candidatures closest to success, such as Pole's in 1549 and
Morone's in 1550.

Eventually, the Holy Office celebrated its triumph when, between 1555 and 1559,
Carafa himself was elected Pope Paul IV; the tribunal had been further strengthened
at the beginning of the 1550s during the papacy of Julius III, whose authority the
Inquisition was able to challenge repeatedly. Trials were then initiated against Pole
and Morone: the former was deprived of the legation in England (where he died in
November 1558), and the latter was locked up in Castel Sant'Angelo, while other
inquiries were instigated against Carnesecchi, Soranzo, Di Capua, and many other
disciples of Valdés, all prominent figures in the religious life of the 1530s and 1540s.
By means of a series of dossiers that had been gathered in previous years, sometimes
in spite of the explicit prohibition of Julius III, the Inquisition was able to disrupt
that movement, in which – rightly or wrongly – it singled out the main responsibility for the atmosphere of tolerance and collusion in which heresy had been able to
take root and thrive. Although Paul IV's death in August 1559 prevented the Holy
Office from serving the predictable sentence on Morone, the group of spirituals was
subdued once and for all by these events. The new pope, Pius IV, tried to rid himself
of the onerous heritage of Carafa's pontificate, which had led to a new and irre-
sponsible war against Charles V and Philip II, who were accused of heresy and
dethroned. Quickly released, Morone (and many others with him) was absolved and
even dispatched as papal legate to the Council of Trent, where his incomparable
diplomatic talent allowed him to bring matters to a conclusion.

The troubled fortunes of Morone, papal legate in Trent in 1542, arrested and
indicted for heresy in 1557, absolved in 1560, and again sent to chair the council in
1563, but later again accused by Pius V, clearly indicate the rough paths, the breaks,
contradictions, and, finally, the outcomes of the sixteenth-century religious crisis at
the very summit of the church. The winner turned out to be the Inquisition, which,
after having conquered the summit of ecclesiastical hierarchy, met with no further
obstacles in its struggle for the repression of heresy. Increasingly isolated, increasingly deprived of political and social protections, the surviving heterodox groups
could do nothing other than retreat and maintain a migratory flow – dwindling to a
trickle in the 1570s – toward the Reformed lands, or to take refuge in Nicodemite
practices, which were harshly condemned by the orthodoxy in Geneva when their
subversive spiritualist premises became clear. The trials of the local Inquisitions, on
the increase after the 1550s, revealed the persistent firmness but also the substantial
exhaustion of the thrust propelling the heretical communities that were deeply rooted
in the peninsula and predominantly leaning toward Calvinism, while the great hopes
triggered by the Reformation were gradually fading away. It was especially under the
papacy of Pius V, who followed and continued Paul IV's work, that the Inquisition
was eventually able to defeat heresy by means of an effective alternation of mildness
and severity to the point of reabsorbing almost the entirety of religious dissent, whose
traces remained for decades and sometimes for centuries in the increasingly faded
penitential clothes worn by heretics in *autos-da-fě* hung in the vaults of cathedrals.
It succeeded easily thanks to the unhesitating collaboration by political authorities,
in states like Venice, Florence, Ferrara, or Mantua, which had once offered more or
less open spaces of toleration. By the 1580s the Reformed presence could be considered substantially uprooted.

VI

Any account, however succinct, of the Italian heretical movement would be incomplete without mentioning the Anabaptist radicalism that manifested itself in the first half of the century, especially in the Venetian mainland, but with significant ramifications all over the plain of the Po and in Tuscany. Linked as it was to the offshoots from Trent of the Peasants' War and to the propaganda coming from Switzerland, Italian Anabaptism spread in a world of small artisans, among whom it gained stable organizational forms, as is demonstrated by the fact that in 1550 a real council was summoned in Venice to tackle a few sensitive doctrinal issues that split the community, in particular that of the dogma of the Trinity, resulting in the denial of Christ's divinity. The Antitrinitarian outcome of the Venetian synod (a practically unique case in the history of European Anabaptism of those years) underscored once more the specificity of heterodoxy on the Italian side of the Alps in the sixteenth century. Furthermore, it is significant that a decisive role in this evolution was played by personalities linked to the tradition of Spanish *conversos* and epigones of Neapolitan Valdesianism. A detailed denunciation to the Inquisition in 1551 led to severe repression of the movement, which in future would find its only chance of survival in exile among the Moravian Hutterites, where groups from Veneto continued to offer their persistent testimony of an egalitarian and communitarian Christianity.

Antitrinitarian criticism was resumed, instead, with other levels of theological maturity by a group of Italian exiles in Switzerland, such as Lelio Sozzini, Giorgio Biandrata, and Gian Paolo Alciati, who found in it the cause for a controversy against the dogmatic and institutional tightening of the Calvinist Reformation, a process dramatically represented by the burning of Michael Servetus in Geneva in 1553 and of Valentino Gentile in Bern in 1566. Antitrinitarian doctrines would be linked more and more closely with the struggle in defense of religious freedom and toleration, along the lines that had been drawn in Basel by Sebastian Castellio and by the group of Italian exiles around him, while the new exegetic premises of Antitrinitarianism formulated by Lelio and then by his nephew Fausto Sozzini would open the long and fruitful history of Socinianism. In fact, the definitive break with Swiss Reformed orthodoxy at the end of the 1550s would also lead to the emigration of Antitrinitarians to eastern Europe. Yet, aside from these outcomes of extreme radicalism, which were to leave deep traces in the history of Europe in the following century, the role of hundreds and hundreds of individuals and families, for whom support for the new religious ideas meant leaving the peninsula, cannot be neglected. It also meant the transfer to the new countries that hosted them – from England to Lithuania, from Switzerland to Transylvania, from Flanders to Poland – of some fragments of the great intellectual and moral heritage of Italian humanistic culture, which, while it faded away in its homeland, could in this manner convey on the other side of the Alps something of the spirit of freedom that had animated it.

BIBLIOGRAPHY

Adorni-Braccesi, S., *"Una città infetta": La repubblica di Lucca nella crisi religiosa del Cinquecento*. Florence: Olschki, 1994.

Ambrosini, F., *Storie di patrizi e di eresia nella Venezia del '500* Milan: Angeli, 1999.

Caponetto, S., *La Riforma protestante nell'Italia del Cinquecento*. Turin: Claudiana, 1992. Published in English as *The Protestant Reformation in Sixteenth-Century Italy*. Kirksville, Mo.: Truman State University Press, 1998.

Firpo, M., *Tra alumbrados e "spirituali": Studi su Juan de Valdés e il valdesianesimo nella crisi religiosa del '500 italiano*. Florence: Olschki, 1990.

Firpo, M., *Inquisizione romana e Controriforma: Studi sul cardinal Giovanni Morone e il suo processo d'eresia*. Bologna: Il Mulino, 1992.

Firpo, M., *Riforma protestante ed eresie nell'Italia del Cinquecento*. Rome/Bari: Laterza, 1993.

Firpo, M., *Gli affreschi di Pontormo a San Lorenzo: Eresia, politica e cultura nella Firenze di Cosimo I*. Turin: Einaudi, 1997.

Firpo, M., *Dal sacco di Roma all'Inquisizione: Studi su Juan de Valdés e la Riforma italiana*. Alessandria: Edizioni dell'Orso, 1998.

Martin, J., *Venice's Hidden Enemies: Italian Heretics in a Renaissance City*. Berkeley/Los Angeles/London: University of California Press, 1993.

Perrone, L., ed., *Lutero in Italia*. Casale Monferrato: Marietti, 1983.

Peyronel Rambaldi, S., *Dai Paesi Bassi all'Italia. "Il Sommario della sacra Scrittura": Un libro proibito nella società italiana del Cinquecento*. Florence: Olschki, 1997.

Prosperi, A., *L'eresia del Libro Grande: Storia di Giorgio Siculo e della sua setta*. Milan: Feltrinelli, 2000.

Seidel Menchi, S., *Erasmo in Italia 1520–1580*. Turin: Bollati Boringhieri, 1987.

Tedeschi, J. (in association with J. M. Lattis), *The Italian Reformation of the Sixteenth Century and the Diffusion of Renaissance Culture: A Bibliography of the Secondary Literature (ca. 1750–1996)*. Modena: Franco Cosimo Panini, 1999.

FURTHER READING

As orientation to the sources and the vast historiography on this topic, the reader will need to refer to the monumental bibliography *The Italian Reformation of the Sixteenth Century and the Diffusion of Renaissance Culture: A Bibliography of the Secondary Literature (ca. 1750–1996)*, compiled by John Tedeschi in association with James M. Lattis. Among the works with the most updated synthesis see Silvana Seidel Menchi, *Erasmo in Italia 1520–1580*; Salvatore Caponetto, *La Riforma protestante nell'Italia del Cinquecento*; and Massimo Firpo, *Riforma protestante ed eresie nell'Italia del Cinquecento*.

TWELVE

The Reformation in Bohemia and Poland

JAMES R. PALMITESSA

In 1555 and 1558, the Jesuit Peter Canisius traveled to Bohemia and Poland, respectively, in the hope of finding local support for the establishment of Jesuit colleges in these lands. Canisius probably would not have felt that he was going to an exotic destination but to *another* part of Europe, a region that possessed traditions and customs similar to those in his native Low Countries. In this his experience was quite different from that of his fellow Jesuits Michele Ruggiero and Matteo Ricci, who approximately 25 years later began missionary work in China, or of many of us today, whose perspective, despite the ease and trendiness of travel these days to central Europe, is still shaped by the polarized world of the late twentieth century. Yet the story of the Reformation in Bohemia and Poland is not a mere variation of the German-Lutheran, Zürich-Zwinglian, or French- or Dutch-Calvinist story, but represents its own distinctive narrative of reform of religion and society. It cannot be denied that movements coming out of other areas of Europe influenced reforms in Bohemia and Poland. It would be a mistake, however, to overlook the fact that these two central European lands also were major contributors to the European Reformation as centers of theological innovation, social and political revolution, refuge, toleration, and repression.

It should be noted at the outset that not all scholars interested in religion in Bohemia and Poland place their work within the "Reformation" paradigm. Religion and religious reform are studied by scholars coming out of different academic traditions and disciplines: "late medieval" and "early modern," confessional and non-confessional historians, art historians, theologians and philosophers. Over a century before Luther's Reformation, Bohemia experienced a religious reform movement that erupted in the early fifteenth century into a social and political revolution ("the Hussite Revolution") that influenced developments in Poland and other countries. Although the idea that the Hussite Revolution influenced subsequent developments is widely accepted, many questions about the specifics of the impact have remained unexplored, and discussions about the relationship between "late medieval" and "early modern" developments have been embraced only hesitantly in some circles. One frame of reference for late medieval historians of Bohemia is "heretical" movements such as the Cathars and Waldensians; other medievalists have explored the Hussite legacy in confessional politics in the late fifteenth and early sixteenth centuries (Seibt and Eberhard, *Europa 1500*; Eberhard, "Konflikt und Integration"). Theologians have embraced the idea of a long "Bohemian Reformation" which extends from the beginning of the Hussite reform movement in the late fourteenth century to the life and work of the philosopher and educational reformer Jan Amos Komenský (Johannes Amos Comenius, 1592–1670), who was a member of the Bohemian Brethren, in the early seventeenth century. Amedeo Molnár distinguished between "the First Reformation," which he used to refer to the Hussite movement (which he discussed together with Waldensianism), and "the Second Reformation," referring to Lutheranism, both of which he considered part of a larger "world [i.e. European] Reformation" (Molnár, "Husovo místo v evropské reformaci"). In Poland, the Reformation had traditionally been viewed as a mere "episode," but in recent years has been reevaluated and is now recognized as a small, though vital, chapter in the history of Polish Christianity (Kłoczowski, *History of Polish Christianity*, pp. 84–117). By the middle of the seventeenth century, Catholic reform and Counter-Reformation were ultimately successful in making Catholicism the dominant force in both countries. In Bohemia, which underwent a forced transformation, Catholic Reform and Counter-Reformation have been viewed as extremely problematic (Mikulec, "Pobělohorská rekatolizace"); whereas in Poland where Catholic reform took place in "peaceful" fashion, the topic is unproblematic to the point of being taken for granted (Kłoczowski, *History of Polish Christianity*, pp. 109–16).

Aside from these historiographical reservations, religious developments in Bohemia and Poland fit in quite well with recent discussions of the diversity of the Reformation experience. In Bohemia and Poland, as in other European lands, "the Reformation" embraced a number of reforms or reformations: of church, popular religion, society, politics, art and culture, which were intimately connected to one another.

One convenient way of approaching the Reformation in Bohemia and Poland has been to simply divide the discussion into two national parts. Such an approach has much to commend it, since the starting point and source of much of modern scholarship on religion and society in Bohemia and Poland is the work of late nineteenth- and early twentieth-century historians who framed their research in national categories. That holds even for German *Ostforschung* scholarship from the early twentieth century, which was rooted in its own problematic national framework. Some Anglo-American scholars who began publishing in the 1960s and 1970s adopted a comparative approach focusing on "central Europe" (Evans, *Making of the Habsburg Monarchy*; Evans, *Rudolf II and His World*; Williams, *Radical Reformation*; Białostocki, *Art of the Renaissance*; Kaufmann, *Court, Cloister and City*); or at the very least engaged in dialogue with colleagues working in other European societies (Howard Kaminsky, the author of a major critical work on the Hussite Revolution, also co-translated a seminal work on late medieval landownership by the Austrian scholar Otto Brunner). At the same time, German scholars, who sought to redefine their discipline along less ideological and nationalist lines after World War II, focused on *Ostmitteleuropa*, a concept which has gained reception in some circles. Although the national framework remains an important focus of research on religion and other topics in the Czech Republic and Poland, one can identify since 1989 a quiet trend in the scholarship coming from these countries that has increasingly found it useful to look at points of comparison and encounter, not only between each other and Hungary (see chapter 13 in this volume), but also, in the case of Czech scholarship, with the German lands, England, and Italy (Lášek, *Jan Hus*; Bůžek et al., *Věk urozených*; Hojda, "Zastavení nad novým soupisem italik"; Graciotti, *Italia et Boemia*); and in the case of Polish scholarship, with Lithuania, Belarus, the Ukraine, and France (Kłoczowski et al., *Christianity in East Central Europe*; Kłoczowski et al., *Frontières*). This trend has been joined by new generations of German *Ostmitteleuropa* and Anglo-American scholars, in collaboration and dialogue with scholars of the German and European Reformation (Bahlcke and Strohmeyer, *Konfessionalisierung*; David and Holeton, *Bohemian Reformation*).

This chapter seeks to highlight these points of comparison and encounter, and trends in the recent secondary literature. For the sake of convenience, it will adopt a thematic and chronological approach, introducing Bohemia and Poland in the fourteenth and fifteenth centuries; the Hussite reform movement and Revolution; the Lutheran, Calvinist, "radical" and Catholic Reformations; and aspects of confessional society, 1550–1650.

Bohemia and Poland in the Fourteenth and Fifteenth Centuries: A Late Medieval Crisis?

Strictly speaking, Bohemia was one of a number of territories that together with Moravia, Silesia, and Lusatia made up the Bohemian crown lands (*země české koruny*). Since the twelfth century when the Holy Roman Empire recognized the elevation of the duchy of Bohemia to a kingdom, Bohemia (henceforth used to refer to the Bohemian crown lands) was loosely associated with the empire. The connection was strengthened in 1346 when the Bohemian king became a member of the imperial electoral college, and in 1526 when Ferdinand I became the first Habsburg elected to the Bohemian throne. Poland, one of the oldest states in Europe, also had a close relationship to the empire, but it enjoyed considerably more autonomy than Bohemia. In the late fourteenth and fifteenth centuries, Poland was composed of the Kingdom of Poland proper, made up of Great Poland and Little Poland; Lithuania, which had joined Poland in 1386 in a dynastic union; as well as Eastern Pomerania (also known as Royal Prussia), and other parts of the lower Vistula region acquired in 1466 as a result of Poland's earlier victory over the Order of the Teutonic Knights. In 1569, Poland and Lithuania came together even closer with the union of their diets, forming the Polish-Lithuanian Commonwealth (*Rzeczpospolita Polska* – henceforth referred to as "the Commonwealth").

Around 1420 Bohemia had a population of between 2 and 3 million and a population density of 36 to 42 people per square kilometer. Bohemia was bilingual, with Czech and German speakers who were distributed not only within the land as a whole but also within cities. Around 1370, before the dynastic union of Poland and Lithuania, the Polish kingdom had 2 million inhabitants with a population density of 8.6 persons per square kilometer. Around 1500 Poland-Lithuania had a combined population of around 7.5 million, with an average population density of around 6 people per square kilometer. The Polish-Lithuanian Commonwealth was multilingual with speakers of Polish, Lithuanian, German, Ruthenian, Latvian, Estonian, Prussian, and Serbo-Lusatian. Both Bohemia and Poland had sizable Jewish populations, and within the borders of the Polish Commonwealth also lived Muslim Tartars. The archbishopric of Prague, which embraced most of the Bohemian kingdom, had suffragan dioceses in Prague, Olomouc, and Litomyšl. The archdiocese of Gniezno had eight dioceses within Poland proper – in Gniezno, Cracow, Wrocław, Poznań, Lebus, Włocławek, Płock, and Chełmża – and another ten in other areas of the Commonwealth. Also within the Commonwealth were ten orthodox dioceses that were part of the province of Kiev, and Christian monophysite Armenians within the Catholic-Ormian province of Lviv.

Some important changes in church and religious life were already under way in the late fourteenth century. Both countries witnessed a rise in the number of ecclesiastical institutions and clergy. In the mid-fourteenth century, Charles IV, king of Bohemia and newly elected Holy Roman Emperor, invited reform preachers and new religious orders to Prague, successfully lobbied the pope for Prague's elevation from a bishopric to an archbishopric, and in 1348 established a university in the city, the first to be founded in central Europe, which later became a center of the religious reform movement. The foundation of the University of Cracow in 1364, the second university in central Europe, likewise developed into an important center for training priests and scholars of canon law. Between 1300 and 1500, the number of parishes in Poland doubled from ca. 3,000 to 6,000. Although Bohemia was only half as large in area as Poland, it had twice the number of parishes as Great Poland alone (4,700 parishes in ca. 1400). At the end of the fifteenth century, in Bohemia there was one clergy member for 100–150 individuals; in Poland (100 years later) the ratio was 1:400–500.

Many Czech historians have viewed the growth in the clergy and ecclesiastical institutions as being closely connected to changes in economy and society, which together made up what has been described as a "late medieval crisis." They have pointed to the fact that while the church owned a third of the usable land in Bohemia, the patronage of ecclesiastical institutions was largely in the hands of the nobility. This contributed not only to a great social differentiation among the clergy, many of whom were poor and dependent on the nobility, but also to tensions within the nobility and society in general. Polish historians have been keenly interested in developments in Bohemia because of many similarities with Poland, but have come to the general conclusion that no crisis existed in Poland (Bylina, "Krisen – Reformen – Entwicklungen"). Some Polish historians see the period before the Reformation as a golden age of Christianity, which was marked by a great encounter between learned and lay cultures. Jerzy Kłoczowski has described a slow but increasing voluntary "Christianization" of the Polish population during the thirteenth and fourteenth centuries, which can be seen in the spread of the cult of the Madonna, the use of Christian names, and the fusion of the old pagan Slavonic with the Christian calendar.

The Hussite Reform Movement and Revolution:
Causa ad disputandum

The beginnings of a religious reform movement in Bohemia date back to the late fourteenth century to individuals such as Jan Milíč of Kroměříž (d. 1374) and Matěj of Janov (ca. 1350–ca. 1393), who called for frequent preaching of the Gospel and frequent lay communion. Although influenced by the ideas of the Englishman John Wyclif (ca. 1330–84), contemporary scholarship no longer views the Bohemian reform movement as a mere offshoot of Wycliffism, but as a native movement that was characterized by a strong, eschatological tendency. Among the greatest innovations of the early Bohemian reformers were ideas and practices relating to the Eucharist; these included a rich variety of written works – ranging from Eucharistic theology to practical guides – and the actual implementation of frequent communion that brought together people of different backgrounds into a new religious-social community. David Holeton has noted that "nowhere else during this period was there a similar constellation of academics . . . producing theological works supporting frequent communion for the laity" and "nowhere else in this period is there any account of community of any sort" (Holeton, "Bohemian Eucharistic Movement," pp. 32, 29). In addition to Eucharistic innovations, early Bohemian reformers also engaged in fundamental debates about the use and display of religious images, which represented an important chapter in the history of iconoclastic thought and practice in Europe.

At the beginning of the fifteenth century, the center of the reform movement moved to the University of Prague and to the Bethlehem Chapel, which had recently been founded as a new place of worship focused on vernacular preaching. In 1402 Master Jan Hus (ca. 1372–1415) became the rector of the chapel. Continuing in the tradition of earlier Bohemian reformers and informed by Wycliffite teachings, Hus developed a theology stressing the primacy of "the Law of God." Along with other fellow Prague theologians, Hus also worked out a special understanding of predestination, infant communion, a rejection of indulgences, and other ideas that brought international attention (Kafka, "Bohemia," pp. 132–3). In 1414 the practice of the lay chalice was first introduced: the communion by the laity of both the bread and the wine, or as it became known in Bohemia, "in both kinds" (*sub utraque specie*). Although the lay chalice had not been a central issue for earlier Bohemian reformers (in contrast to frequent communion, which was a major concern), it had become a defining feature of the Bohemian Reformation at the beginning of the fifteenth century.

A century before the indulgence controversy in Saxony turned Luther's struggle into an imperial cause, Jan Hus got into trouble by protesting a papal ban against Wycliffite and other "heretical" teachings. Hus was forced to flee Prague and later explain his actions before the Council of Constance, which executed him as a heretic in 1415. Hus's execution gave support to a growing radical wing of the reform movement. On July 30, 1419, the Bohemian reform movement turned into a revolution when a procession led by Jan Želivský, "the preacher of the poor," ended up at the New City Hall in Prague where city officials were thrown from the windows. Almost immediately following the "defenestration," churches and monasteries in Prague were attacked and religious orders were forced to flee the city. Soon thereafter violence moved to the castle and then to other areas in the kingdom. Nobles, cities, and villages were forced to take sides between imperial and revolutionary forces. Joining the revolutionary forces were new "radical" groups – such as the Taborites in southern Bohemia – who had formulated a social-egalitarian theology and ideology based on a theory of just war, a rejection of legal decisions, and a criticism of private property. In 1420, the various revolutionary groups came together under the common banner of the Prague Articles, which called for free preaching, the lay chalice, divestment of church wealth, and purgation of public sins. However, in the years that followed, struggles developed between the radical and moderate wings of the Revolution that ended in the defeat of the radicals in the 1430s.

In the course of the Revolution the king died and the archbishop went over to the Hussite cause, leaving Bohemia without a secular or religious head, which was an unprecedented situation in Europe at this time. The clerical estate was abolished and replaced by the estate of the royal cities. Most of Bohemia, with the exception of some areas in the north and northwest, which had remained Catholic, came under the rule of a conservative Hussite elite of city councils and princes. Ecclesiastical properties, which had come into secular hands during the Revolution, were turned over to local communal organizations (called *záduší*) for administration. The Prague archdiocese was left in the hands of an administrator from the metropolitan church, St. Vitus, who had to deal with the absence of an archbishop, the loss of the clergy, and the lack of religious orders.

A number of fundamental questions have perplexed scholars about the Hussite Revolution. Why did it break out in Bohemia? Why at that particular time? Historians of the Czech nationalist school of history founded in the nineteenth century saw the Revolution as a watershed event, a high point in the history of the Czech people for the religious freedom and self-sovereignty it introduced. Some late twentieth-century scholars, such as František Graus, proposed that the outbreak of the movement and the Revolution in Bohemia could be explained by the late medieval crisis, which was more developed in Bohemia than in other countries (Graus, "Das Spätmittelalter als Krisenzeit"). Other scholars went in different directions, such as Howard Kaminsky, who focused on the collection and critical analysis of sources, and John Klassen, who studied the role of the nobility (Kaminsky, *Hussite Revolution*; Klassen, *Nobility*). One major area of debate has focused around the national question. German and Polish scholars have noted that there were German-speaking Hussites in Bohemia, neighboring Franconia, and even in areas of the empire not so close to the Bohemian border, and Polish-speaking Hussites in Great Poland and Cuyavia. In a 1965 study, Ferdinand Seibt sharply criticized the notion that Hussitism was a specific Czech phenomenon, arguing that nineteenth-century Czech nationalism obscured the medieval concept of *natio*, which had a territorial, not a national or linguistic, meaning (Seibt, *Hussitica*, pp. 92–7). František Šmahel has argued that one can identify distinctive features of Bohemian society that testify to the national dimension of Hussitism, but that this can be understood within the medieval European context (Šmahel, *Idea národa*, pp. 1–21, 250–63).

The British historian Anne Hudson's description of Lollardy as a "Premature Reformation" has stirred some discussion in central European circles about the relationship of Hussitism and other late medieval religious movements to later reform movements within and outside of Bohemia (Šmahel, *Häresie und vorzeitige Reformation*). Howard Kaminsky has pointed out that various distortions, omissions, and uncertainties exist in the paradigms "heresy" and "reformation," which obscure the complexities of the Hussite movement (Kaminsky, "Problematics"). František Šmahel suggests a practical approach, asking questions about the movement's *concrete* "successes" and areas of influence (Šmahel, "Zur Einführung," in *Häresie und vorzeitige Reformation*, pp. 9–11).

Religious belief and practice are two areas greatly impacted by the Hussite movement and Revolution. In recent work on Hussite popular religion, Thomas Fudge has argued that the figure of Jan Hus, the chalice, the Law of God, and the warrior Jan Žižka, which became popular motifs in pamphlets, songs, preaching, and images, served not only as rallying symbols for the Revolution but also gave identity to a Reformed tradition that continued into the late fifteenth century (Fudge, *Magnificent Ride*). Although the Hussite movement did not lead to a formal break *per se* with the Roman Church, it did set the context for the development of separate Reformed traditions. At the Council of Basel in 1436, the Roman Church entered into an agreement – called the *Compactata* – with the moderate wing of the Hussites (i.e., Utraquists), in the hope of someday reintegrating them back into the Roman fold. In agreeing to the *Compactata*, the Utraquists accepted the principle of apostolic succession, but *de facto* developed in time their own church structure and organization. In the 1460s, the Unity of Brethren (*Unitas Fratrum* or *Jednota bratrská*), which had formed a decade earlier out of the radical wing of the Hussites, broke with Rome and the Utraquists when they instituted their own separate priesthood.

The Hussite Revolution's call for social betterment and justice remained important ideals, especially among the Bohemian Brethren. The Brethren drew many of their earliest supporters from those laypeople who felt betrayed by the Revolution. A forerunner of the Brethren, Petr Chelčický (ca. 1380–ca. 1467), criticized contemporary inequalities and social distinctions, which he believed to be the antithesis of a Christian social order. He taught that the state must be totally rejected and Christ's Law of Love be put in its place. Later Brethren adopted this in their rejection of holding public office and taking oaths. In contrast, Jan Rokycana (ca. 1395–1471), archbishop-elect of the Utraquists, taught that civil government and the existing social order could be the instrument of God's will if rightly administered, and that public service was justified if officials were to act justly and not oppress the poor.

In the political realm, Robert Kalivoda has underscored the importance of appreciating and understanding the continuing, dynamic influence of Hussitism *after* the Revolution (Kalivoda, "Husitství a jeho vyústění," p. 3). According to Kalivoda, the defeat and elimination of the radical wing from the political picture meant not the defeat of the Revolution but a shift into a transforming, stabilizing constitutional process that was founded on consensus and coexistence. This can be seen in the Peace of Kutná Hora of 1485, which legally established a state of biconfessional parity, permitting only Catholics and Utraquists to freely exercise their religion and participate in public life. Although the Peace of Kutná Hora was envisioned as a provisional measure (like the *Compactata*), it remained in effect until 1609. Ferdinand Seibt and Winfried Eberhard have proposed that confession was a central factor in the continuing conflict between the Bohemian estates over competing ideas and concepts of rule, which led to a process of "integration through conflict" (Seibt and Eberhard, *Europa 1500*); Eberhard has followed the path of that process from the late fifteenth into the mid-sixteenth centuries in two studies (Eberhard, *Konfessionsbildung und Stände; Monarchie und Widerstand*).

In a new study of Polish Hussitism Paweł Kras looks at the attraction of the movement in Poland within the context of the exchange of beliefs and practices across the Bohemian–Polish border in late Middle Ages (Kras, *Husyci*). Beyond its spiritual appeal, Hussitism had an important impact on Polish foreign policy. While Polish conciliarists and bishops condemned the Hussites, Polish kings viewed them as a natural ally against the Order of the Teutonic Knights. In 1433, the Hussites even launched an expedition against the Teutonic Knights. At the end of the fifteenth century, Polish King Casimir the Jagiellonian (Kazimierz Jagiellończyk, 1447–92) defied the papal policy of isolating Bohemia and, drawing on the image of Poland as bulwark or *antemurale* of Christendom, which could defend Europe against the Turks, successfully lobbied to have his son, Wladysław, installed as king of Bohemia in 1471 (and in Hungary in 1490). The ascent of a Jagiellonian king to the Bohemian throne also assisted in paving the way for a religious conciliation of Bohemia with the rest of Western Christendom. The Jagiellonian age, a brief period of central European rapprochement, has become a focus of new interest in the last few years with a multi-volume synthesis by Josef Macek and an international, interdisciplinary research project conducted in Leipzig under the direction of Robert Suchale.

The Lutheran Reformation: New Directions in Bohemia; A Chapter in the History of Polish Christianity; Refuge in Moravia and Poland

The evangelical message entered Bohemia and Poland within a year after the posting of Martin Luther's *Ninety-Five Theses*. Its earliest and strongest reception was in German-speaking areas. In the 1520s the movement was responsible for popular uprisings in Gdańsk (Danzig) and other Baltic cities, and it was introduced into Ducal Prussia by Albrecht of Hohenzollern, the Grand Master of the Order of the Teutonic Knights, who secularized church properties and established the first state Lutheran Church in Europe. In 1525 Albrecht broke bonds with the Catholic Holy Roman Emperor and offered Ducal Prussia to the king of Poland as a fief.

In Bohemia the Lutheran Reformation was at first ardently adopted by Catholic nobles in the north and northwest. One of the most prominent was the count of Schlick, who expanded his power in the economically prosperous Elbogen region east of Eger (Cheb) where he founded the city of St. Joachimsthal. In a short period of time it became one of the fastest-growing cities in Europe, achieving renown for its Latin school and as a major Lutheran center. Other important Lutheran centers in Bohemia were the regions of Tetschen, Bensen, Kamnitz, and the city of Kaaden. In Moravia Lord Leonard Liechtenstein converted to Lutheranism and introduced it on his estates in Mikulov (Nicolsburg).

Not one single factor but a combination of factors – linguistic affinity, social, political, and economic features – help explain the attraction of Lutheranism in a particular area. Eastern Pomerania had lost its connection to other German-speaking communities and the empire a few decades earlier, as sovereignty changed from the Teutonic Order to the Polish Kingdom: becoming Lutheran was a way to mark off a boundary from their Polish-speaking neighbors. In northern Bohemia, economic factors seem to have played an important role, as many of the nobles originated from neighboring Saxony or at least had family and landholdings there. Petr Hlaváček is investigating religious reform in the city of Kaaden (Hlaváček, "Beginnings of the Bohemian Reformation in the Northwest," in David and Holeton, *Bohemian Reformation and Religious Practice*, vol. 4, pp. 43–6); and John Klassen, the author of a number of studies on the nobility in fifteenth-century Bohemia, is currently study-ing civic wills of Prague burghers in the early sixteenth century. Forthcoming studies by these scholars promise new insight into religious mentality.

In Bohemia Lutheranism reached beyond the German-speaking areas of the west and northwest into Czech-speaking areas, which brought about a close encounter between Lutheranism and the native Hussite reform traditions. As early as 1517, Thomas Müntzer preached in the Bethlehem Chapel in Prague, which had been the pulpit of Jan Hus. In 1519 in his Leipzig disputation with Johann Eck, Luther defended Hus's teaching as Christian and evangelical. Some Czechs present at the disputation brought his remarks back to two leading Utraquist clergymen in Prague, Jan Poduška and Václav Rozdalovský, who began a correspondence with Luther. In one of his letters Luther expressed optimism for cooperation between the evangeli-cal movement in the German lands and the Bohemian reform movement. Earlier Czech historiography saw Lutheranism as bringing about a fundamental division within Utraquism, which ultimately resulted in its absorption into Lutheranism. Recent scholarship has taken a more differentiated look at the encounter and its impact. Winfried Eberhard has pointed to an important division that took place within Utraquism in the decade before its encounter with Lutheranism that arose out of social and economic as well as religious changes. Furthermore, it has been noted that even those Utraquists who were early allies of Luther were not interested in simply adopting Lutheranism, but saw Luther as a companion who could help in finally breaking through with reform. And while there was much common ground between some Utraquists and Luther – such as in the importance of the Holy Scrip-ture, the reduction of sacraments to baptism and communion, and the rejection of the mass as sacrifice – there were also fundamental differences between the two groups. As early as 1524, Utraquists began to lean toward more radical views, such as the rejection of Christ's real presence in the Eucharist and the belief in salvation through faith alone. Thus, rather than being absorbed into the Lutheran movement, the arrival of Lutheranism was one of a number of ongoing factors that shaped the Utraquist movement. Zdeněk David has argued that Utraquism remained a contin-uing vital religious force throughout the sixteenth and early seventeenth centuries, which served as a sort of *via media* as Anglicanism did under Elizabeth I (David, "Bohuslav Bílevský," p. 73). Many Czech historians still view late sixteenth-century Utraquism as a listless, moribund movement.

Politics was another factor that played an important role in the reception of Lutheranism (and later other confessions) and, in turn, was also shaped by religion. In Bohemia, Lutheranism's encounter with Utraquism coincided with the ascent to the throne of Ferdinand I (1503–64), the first Habsburg Catholic king. During the early years of his reign, Ferdinand sought to uphold the religious status quo, as set forth in the Basel *Compactata* and the Peace of Kutná Hora. Although Lutheranism was officially illegal, the situation of unordained priests and affinity between some Utraquists and Lutherans allowed Lutheran preachers to be active in many Bohemian parishes. In Poland, strong bans imposed against it by the Polish King Sigismund I Jagiellonian, and the power of the clergy, which was a strong force in the Polish diet, helped to limit the spread of Lutheranism in the Commonwealth and to preclude it from becoming a political force. At the same time, Lutheranism's impact in Poland was not negligible either. (By the end of the sixteenth century, 32 of the 142 Lutheran

communities in Great Poland were Polish-speaking.) Janusz Tazbir has argued that
the success of Protestantism in Poland ultimately is to be viewed in qualitative rather
than quantitative terms (Tazbir, *Reformacja w Polsce*).

In the 1520s and 1530s, "radical" religious groups – such as the Anabaptists,
Mennonites, Spiritualists, and others – fleeing persecution in other areas of central
Europe by Catholic, Lutheran, Zwinglian, and other authorities found refuge in
Moravia, the area around the mouth of the Vistula River, and Royal and Ducal
Prussia. Their communities, formed on the basis of their own religious and social
ideals, became beacons for further refugees. In 1526, the Anabaptist Balthasar Hubmaier, fleeing Zürich, arrived in Mikulov at the request of Lord Leonard of Liechtenstein, where he transformed the German-speaking Lutheran parish into an
Anabaptist congregation. The new community attracted Anabaptist refugees from
South Austria, Tirol, and other regions. In 1527 the German Anabaptist Hans Hut
arrived in Mikulov from Passau. His arrival polarized the Anabaptist community,
which had been already divided over a number of issues. The main disagreement
related to "the use of the sword," the appropriateness of paying taxes for military
services in defense of Christendom, an issue that became the center of many "radical
reform" groups. In 1528, unhappy with the pacifistic program and the divisiveness
on his estates, Lord Liechtenstein asked the community to leave his territory, and
they moved on to Austerlitz (Slavkov), where they attracted additional refugees from
the Tirol and other areas. In 1529, the Austrian Anabaptist Johann Hutter came to
Moravia in an attempt to reconcile the Austerlitz community with other Anabaptist
groups in the area, creating the beginning of the Hutterite community which lasted
a long time in Moravia despite royal bans.

The political climate in Bohemia changed in 1546 when the royal cities rebelled
against the king's order to supply troops to fight in the Schmalkaldic War. The
defeat of the rebellion prompted a change of policy, moving religion from the background to the forefront of policy. In addition to punishing the royal cities through
fines, a revocation of their privileges, and installing royal offices in the courts and
city councils, King Ferdinand admonished the Utraquist and Catholic administrators
for allowing parishes to be run by people other than ordained priests and preachers
and issued a strong mandate against the Brethren, prompting an exodus out of
Bohemia.

The "Calvinist and "Radical" Reformations in Poland: Refuge and New Directions

Many of the Brethren fleeing Bohemia in the wake of the Schmalkaldic War sought
refuge in the Polish Commonwealth and Ducal Prussia. They joined the Anabaptists
and other "radical" reform groups who arrived two decades earlier, and the
Calvinists who had first entered Poland in the early 1540s soon after Geneva was
founded as a Calvinist republic. Many of the Brethren finally settled in Little Poland
on estates of noble families, such as the Ostoróg, Leszczyński, Górka, and Lipski,
where they were admired for their hard work and simple, pious lifestyle.

The Calvinists found strongest support among the Polish nobility. In the 1550s
the nobleman Nicholas Oleśnicki founded a Calvinist academy in Pinczów, and in
1554 the first Calvinist synod in Poland was held. By the end of the sixteenth century,

the Commonwealth had three independent Calvinist provinces, containing a total of approximately 500 parishes.

As with Lutheranism, not one but a number of factors explain Calvinism's attraction. Young Calvin's emphasis on the invisibility of the true church and the absolute autonomy of individual parishes appealed to nobles by creating a situation favorable to noble domination. Another attractive doctrine was Calvin's belief in the right to oppose royal authority persecuting the true faith, which was to be undertaken not by individuals but their lawful representatives (Tazbir, *State Without Stakes*, pp. 55–6). R. J. W. Evans has drawn attention to the importance of foreign contacts and intellectual alliances (Evans, "Calvinism in East Central Europe," pp. 173–5). Jean Calvin was personally interested in the fate of religious reform in Poland. In 1538 he dedicated his commentary on the mass to the heir to the Polish throne, Sigismund II Augustus, and later on corresponded with many of the Polish Reformed communities. Polish communities also had contacts with Calvinist printing centers in the Rhineland. And Polish students and their teachers attended Heidelberg, Leiden, Geneva, and other Calvinist universities. The spread of Calvinism in Poland and Poland's attraction as a place of refuge was also assisted by a change in monarch in the mid-sixteenth century. The new Polish king, Sigismund II Augustus (1548–72), though remaining strongly attached to the church and traditional forms of piety, was receptive to Erasmian ideas of reconciliation and sought practical compromise.

In 1551 the Italian Lelio Sozzino (Laelius Socinus, 1525–62) made a short visit to Poland. Sozzino was one of the most creative thinkers in Antitrinitarianism, a movement that was opposed to the dogma of the Holy Trinity, which became popular throughout Europe in the early sixteenth century. After the execution of Michael Servetus in Geneva, many Antitrinitarians, forced to leave Italy and the Swiss lands, found refuge and reception for their ideas in the Calvinist and "radical" communities of the Commonwealth. While Antitrinitarian ideas had been condemned earlier in Poland, the changed political climate of the mid-sixteenth century, and the presence of the Calvinists and "radical" groups, created an atmosphere that not only was receptive to Antitrinitarianism, but that contributed to a lively exchange of beliefs between different groups. The Antitrinitarians came to form a major group within the Polish Reformed community, known as the Polish Brethren (*Bracia polsci*) or the Minor (sometimes called Arian) Church, in contrast to the Major (Calvinist) Church.

An important moment in the history of the Polish Reformed community came in 1556 with the return to Poland of Jan Łaski (Johannes a Lasco, 1499–1560). A nephew of the archibishop of Gniezno, Łaski had converted to Calvinism and worked over ten years for the Reformed cause in England, Flanders, Friesland, and Denmark. On his return to Poland Łaski sought to unite the Evangelical and Protestant religions in Poland into one national church. But after his death the two Reformed parties went their separate ways. In 1569, the Polish Brethren founded their own community at Raków based on ideas of social egalitarianism. It became a vibrant community with schools and printing houses, and a theological seminary run by Fausto Sozzino (Faustus Socinus, 1539–1604), the nephew of Lelio, who had moved to Poland in 1580. By 1620 the community at Raków reached its height. The "radical Reformation" has been a lively area of Polish religious scholarship, and continues to be so.

The Beginnings of Catholic Reform

Some important efforts at reform of the church in Bohemia and Poland can be said to have taken place in the late fourteenth and late fifteenth centuries under Arnošt of Pardubice, archbishop of Prague (1305–64), and Jan Łaski, archbishop of Gniezno (1455–1531), the uncle of Jan Łaski (the Calvinist), respectively. But whatever might have come from these efforts is unclear, as they were eclipsed by the Hussite Revolution and reform movements of the sixteenth century. The beginning of a systematic Catholic reform movement dates back only to the establishment of Jesuit colleges in Bohemia and Poland in the 1550s, and the renewal of the Prague archbishopric in 1561, which had been vacant 140 years since the last archbishop converted to the Hussite cause. Both these moves involved various levels of cooperation between the papacy and its representatives, the Bohemian and Polish monarchies, the estates of these two lands, and local authorities.

The leading role in Catholic renewal was played by Archbishop Antonín Brus z Mohelnice (1518–80) and Cardinal Stanisław Hozjusz (Stanislas Hosius, 1504 or 1505–79). Both men had extraordinary careers. Before becoming archbishop, Brus served as preacher to the imperial troops at the Turkish front in Moravia, bishop of Vienna, and grand master of one of Bohemia's most influential religious orders (Order of the Knights of the Cross with the Red Star). He also served as one of two imperial representatives to the Council of Trent in 1561–2. Before becoming archbishop of Gniezno, Hosius was bishop of Warmia (Ermeland) and in 1569 was named cardinal. Hosius served as one of five presidents of the last assembly of the Council of Trent.

Both men were catalysts in the establishment of the first Jesuit colleges in their lands. In 1555, six years before being named archbishop, Brus hosted and assisted the provincial governor of the Jesuits in the German lands, Peter Canisius, who had traveled to Prague to study local conditions and create a plan for the establishment of a Jesuit college. A year later the first six Jesuits arrived in Prague and settled at the former Dominican monastery of St. Clement, which they began slowly to rebuild and expand into a grand complex. When Canisius traveled to Poland two years later, in 1558, he had problems finding local support. This was due in part because of the opposition of the University of Cracow, which was reluctant to see the establishment of Jesuit colleges. However, in 1563, the Jesuits found local support in Hosius, who was granted permission to settle the first Jesuits in his diocese. They came in 1564 and a year later the first college was founded in Braniewo. Jesuit colleges attracted students and others to their schools and brotherhoods, and reached out to the larger public through performances and theater presentations in squares. By the early seventeenth century Jesuits came to hold important positions of power. The Jesuit Piotr Skarga (1536–1612) served as the court chaplain of Polish King Sigismund III; William Larmormaini (1570–1648) was official confessor of the Bohemian king and Holy Roman Emperor, Ferdinand II.

In addition to the Jesuits, the papal nuncios were another major force of Catholic renewal. This was especially the case in Bohemia after the move of the imperial court to Prague in 1583, when the nuncios established permanent residence in the city. They were surely among the most vocal protagonists of renewal to the Bohemian and Polish kings. In a seminal 1969 study on the beginnings of Catholic renewal in Bohemia, František Kafka and Anna Skýbová noted the tension that existed between

King Ferdinand and various Catholic forces, and the difference between the potential of the beginnings of Catholic renewal, reminding us that their later success was neither inevitable nor linear (Kafka and Skýbová, *Husitský epilog*).

The founding of the Jesuits and the renewal of the Prague archbishopric are usually viewed in Bohemian history within the context of "recatholicization," the return of Bohemia to Roman Catholicism. In a piece first published in an underground (*Samizdat*) press in 1980, Josef Hanzal pointed out that "recatholicization" was important not just as a "filling" to a 200-year history but because it radically influenced the character, culture, thought, and feeling of the Bohemian nation. It was a long-term process with its own distinct history and phases (Hanzal, "Rekatholizace v Čechách"; Eberhard, "Entwicklungsphasen"). In Poland too, Jerzy Kłoczowski has noted that the inner dynamics and vitality of the movement have not yet been studied or presented in a satisfactory way (Kłoczowski, *History of Polish Christianity*, pp. 108–16).

Confessional Society, ca. 1550–1600: Art, Culture, and Religion; Tolerance or Peaceful Coexistence?

Religious reform coincided with the spread of the Renaissance style of literature and art in Bohemia and Poland. Humanism found an early reception in some Bohemian and Polish circles in the late fourteenth and early fifteenth centuries. Charles IV exchanged letters with Petrarch and the University of Cracow had links with Hungarian scholars who in turn were in contact with Italian humanists. Italian-style art and architecture were first introduced in central Europe at the court of Hungarian King Matthias Corvinus. Sigismund, son of Polish King Kazimierz IV, became acquainted with this art during a three-year stay in Buda at the court of his elder brother, Vladislav, who succeeded Corvinus as king in 1490 (since 1471 Vladislav was also king of Bohemia). After ascending to the Polish throne in 1506, Sigismund introduced Renaissance art in Poland. The first project was the commissioning of the tomb of his brother, Jan Olbracht. He went on to decorate his father's tomb in Renaissance style and initiated a rebuilding of the royal castle on Wawel Hill in Cracow that would continue for a quarter-century. Renaissance-style architecture also found other patrons among humanistically minded leaders, such as Jan Łaski, archbishop of Gniezno, who commissioned the first Renaissance chapel in Poland at his metropolitan church. Renaissance architecture first entered Bohemia through the efforts of Vladislav. Vladislav commissioned the renovation of the upper portion of the old palace of Charles IV into a larger hall to be used for tournaments, and the new addition to the castle. Between 1556 and 1563, King Ferdinand I commissioned the construction of the Belvedere villa near the Prague castle. At the same time, Renaissance architecture became fashionable with the Bohemian nobility, and stylistic elements began to appear in burgher homes as well. After moving the imperial court from Vienna to Prague in 1583, Bohemian King and Holy Roman Emperor Rudolf II assembled an international array of artists, artisans, and builders, which turned Prague into a major European center of late Renaissance culture.

Many earlier art historians viewed the Reformation as having a negative effect on art, but a more differentiated picture has emerged in the last few years which studies of Bohemian and Polish art have helped to shape. On the one hand, theological justification for commissioning works of religious art was clearly diminished by reform. On the other hand, however, religious art continued to flourish, though in quantitatively fewer terms and geared toward Protestant ideas and uses. Henryk Samsonowicz has argued that church art ca. 1520–1650 in Silesia – a region that retained a Lutheran majority despite becoming part of the Habsburg Empire in 1526 – contained a subtle though identifiable Protestant pictorial program, without representing a major break with tradition. In Bohemia Ferdinand I commissioned work on the organ loft of the cathedral church of St. Vitus. Further renovation of the cathedral continued under the patronage of Rudolf II. Rudolf also commissioned the All Souls Chapel, located near the castle, and the nearby Church of Sts. Sebastian and Rochus. In Bohemia and Poland, the Renaissance style became popular on tombs and burial stones of the nobility and burghers.

In literature, the sixteenth century was a golden age for Poland. Latin and vernacular writers, such as Jan Dantyszek (1495–1548), Mikołaj Rej (1505–69), and Jan Kochanowski (1530–84), produced works that were known all over Europe. Bohemia experienced a flowering of literary choirs or brotherhoods, societies of intellectuals who sang in Czech, German, or Latin, which were associated with mostly Protestant parishes. Religious and moral literature made up to two-thirds of all book collections of residents of large Bohemian and Polish cities, and up to a third in Lower Silesia. The most common religious book was the Bible, followed by sermon collections. Of the latter genre, the most common in Czech-speaking areas of Bohemia was the collection of sermons by Cyrill Spangenberg, which was the most common book published in Bohemia before 1620. In German-speaking areas and the city of Olomouc, Martin Luther's sermons were the most popular. Book collections of individuals, including members of the clergy, contained works representing a wide variety of confessions. Renaissance literature not only was a reflection of religious developments but could also influence them. According to R. J. W. Evans, Bohemians, Poles, and other central Europeans "were led to new religious experiences by humanist curiosity rather than by existing confessional commitment" (Evans, "Calvinism in East Central Europe," p. 173).

Another feature of confessional society in Bohemia and Poland is the state of confessional relations. Poland in the sixteenth century has long been recognized as one of the most religiously tolerant states in Europe. The reasons given for this include Poland's tradition of religious plurality before the Reformation and the strong position of the Polish nobility, who could choose their religious beliefs and destiny even against the wishes of the king. According to Janusz Tazbir, religious tolerance in the sixteenth century did not mean religious equality but the recognition of religious faiths other than the dominant one and the granting of a more or less limited freedom of worship on a class basis according to public interest and state policy (Tazbir, *State Without Stakes*, pp. 9–15, 21–2). The recognition of other faiths can be seen in the continuing attempt of Polish Protestantism to reach some kind of religious union. The first attempt was at the synod of Koźminek in 1555, when the Bohemian Brethren and the Calvinists entered into an agreement based on the articles of faith of the Brethren but with separate rites. The agreement did not last. The Consensus of Sandomierz in 1570, by which the Lutherans, Calvinists, and Bohemian Brethren acknowledged each other's distinctive character but agreed to hold general synods and consider the possibility of a common catechism in the future, was one of the most outstanding examples of tolerance in Europe. The Act of Warsaw Confederation from 1573 represents the political expression of toleration, which effectively gave nobles religious freedom, guaranteeing Protestants equal access to all political offices.

Josef Válka has described religious relations in sixteenth-century Bohemia as being in a state of peaceful coexistence rather than tolerance (Válka, "Tolerance či koexistence?"). Bohemia had its own tradition of dealing with religious pluralism arising out of the post-Hussite settlement and which, like Poland, was shaped by practical necessity rather than enlightened tolerance. There also were a number of moments of religious rapprochement between Lutherans, Utraquists, and the Brethren, but there does not appear to have ever been a serious program for religious unity. The struggle for a Bohemian Confession in 1575, which was influenced by the Sandomierz Consensus, represented an important step toward the political expression of religious tolerance. The Majesty of 1609, granted by Rudolf II out of political expedience, established religious freedom for all confessions for the first time. In the polarized climate of the seventeenth century, Jan Amos Komenský served as a voice for understanding and reconciliation among different confessions and nations of Europe.

The status of the Bohemian nobility and its relationship to the crown is an area of major difference from the Polish situation. The Polish nobility kept far-reaching privileges and were the major force shaping religious and political life in the sixteenth century. In Bohemia, the period after 1547 was characterized by a concerted effort of centralization and Catholic reform by Habsburg King Ferdinand I. R. J. W. Evans has proposed that Catholic reform was a tool of Habsburg state-building (Evans, *Making of the Habsburg Monarchy*). This brought about a movement of growing opposition by the estates along confessional lines, which is the subject of an important study by Jaroslav Pánek (Pánek, *Stavovská oposice*). Research into the Bohemian nobility, which has become a major focus of early modern scholarship in the Czech Republic, has shed light on some important aspects of religion and politics (Pánek, *Poslední Rožemberkové*; Bůžek et al., *Věk urozených*; Rejchrtová, *Václav Budovec z Budova*; see also Evans and Thomas, *Crown, Church and Estates*; and Klassen, *Warring Maidens*).

Confessional-Political Polarization and War, 1600–1650: Toward a Reassessment of "the Flood" and "the Dark Age"

The 1590s witnessed the beginning of a polarization in confessional politics in Bohemia, characterized by a tension between two groups of high estate leaders, one Catholic group supporting the king and the second Protestant group forming the opposition. This situation had implications that went beyond Bohemia and central Europe. In 1618, a revolt by the Protestant estates brought a change in royal government, as Frederick of the Palatinate, one of the major Calvinist territories in the Holy Roman Empire, was chosen by the Protestant estates as Bohemian king and, with international support, as emperor. In 1619 Calvinists associated with the court undertook an iconoclastic cleansing of Prague Cathedral in what were perhaps the last major Calvinist iconoclastic acts in Europe. A year later, an imperial Catholic army defeated Protestant forces at the battle of White Mountain. In the wake of the battle, Protestant estate leaders was executed and the property of Protestant nobles and burghers was confiscated, which unleashed an exile of Protestants from Bohemia into Saxony and other countries. Just as the Hussite Revolution was viewed in nationalist historiography as a high point, the battle of White Mountain was viewed as a low point because it resulted in the subordination of Bohemia and its integration into the Habsburg realm, bringing about what Alois Jirásek described in a historical novel of the early twentieth century as "the Darkness" (*Temno*). Since the 1970s the impact of the White Mountain is now viewed in a more differentiated light; and in the last ten years, Catholic piety and Baroque culture have become major topics of research, which is leading to a critical reassessment of the age from within Czech historiography (Hojda, *Kultura baroka*; Vlnas, *Jan Nepomucký*; Royt, *Obraz a kult*; Hausenblasová and Šroněk, *Gloria & Miseria*; Mikulec, "Pobělohorská rekatolizace"). This trend reached a new height at a scholarly conference held in December 1999 at the Vatican, which was organized in conjunction with the recent, unsuccessful, attempt by the conference of Czech bishops to seek from Pope John Paul II the rehabilitation of Jan Hus (Pánek and Polívka, *Jan Hus ve Vatikánu*).

Poland entered the conflict in 1624 when Sweden abandoned the coalition of Protestant states and went on a lone campaign against the Commonwealth, taking parts of the Baltic and attacking Ducal Prussia. In 1655, Sweden invaded Poland on two fronts, which precipitated attacks from other powers in the east and a civil war, and initiated one of the most destructive periods in Polish history, described in a nineteenth-century novel by Henryk Sienkiewicz as "the Flood" (*Potop*). Later ages looked back at the period as a time of heroic deeds, such as the legendary defense of the monastery of Jasna Góra at Częstochowa, which contained the icon dedicated to the Immaculate Virgin Mary. By the end of the seventeenth century, the Polish Commonwealth, like Bohemia, had also entered a new age, as a strong Catholic state and fully engaged participant in the European arena, which it would remain until its partitioning in the late eighteenth century.

BIBLIOGRAPHY

Bahlcke, J. and Strohmeyer, A., eds., *Konfessionalisierung in Ostmitteleuropa: Wirkungen des religiösen Wandels im 16. und 17. Jahrhundert in Staat, Gesellschaft und Kultur*. Forschungen zur Geschichte und Kultur des östlichen Mitteleuropa, 7. Wiesbaden: Steiner, 1999.

Białostocki, J., *The Art of the Renaissance in Eastern Europe: Hungary, Bohemia, Poland*. Ithaca, NY: Cornell University Press, 1976.

Bireley, R. L., *Religion and Politics in the Age of the Counterreformation: Emperor Ferdinand II, William Lamormaini, S.J., and the Formation of Imperial Policy*. Chapel Hill: University of North Carolina Press, 1981.

Bogucka, M., "Die Wirkungen der Reformation in Danzig," *Zeitschrift für Ostforschung*, 42 (1993), pp. 195–206.

Bredekamp, H., *Kunst als Medium sozialer Konflikte: Bilderkämpfe von der Spätantike bis zur Hussitenrevolution*. Frankfurt a.M.: Suhrkampf, 1975.

Brock, P., *The Political and Social Doctrines of the Unity of the Czech Brethren in the Fifteenth and Early Sixteenth Centuries*. The Hague: Mouton, 1957.

Burleigh, M., *Germany Turns Eastwards: A Study of Ostforschung in the Third Reich*. Cambridge: Cambridge University Press, 1988.

Bůžek, V., Hrdlička, J., Král, P., and Vybíral, Z., eds., *Věk urozených: Šlechta v českých zemích na prahu novověku*. Prague: Litomyšl: Paseka, 2002.

Bylina, S., "Krisen – Reformen – Entwicklungen," in F. Seibt and W. Eberhard, eds., *Europa 1400. Die Krise des Spätmittelalters*. Stuttgart: Klett-Cotta, 1984, pp. 82–302.

Bylina, S., "The Church and Folk Culture in Late Medieval Poland," *Acta Poloniae Historica*, 68 (1993), pp. 27–42.

David, Z. V., "Bohuslav Bílevský and the Religious *via media*: Czech Utraquism in the Sixteenth Century," in David R. Holeton, ed., *The Bohemian Reformation and Religious Practice*, vol. 1. Prague: Academy of Sciences of the Czech Republic Main Library, 1996, pp. 73–90.

David, Z. V., "The Strange Fate of Czech Utraquism: The Second Century, 1517–1621," *Journal of Ecclesiastical History*, 47/4 (1995), pp. 641–68.

David, Z. V., "A Brief Honeymoon in 1564–1566: The Utraquist Consistory and the Archbishop of Prague," *Bohemia*, 39 (1998), pp. 265–84.

David, Z. and Holeton, D. R., eds., *The Bohemian Reformation and Religious Practice*. Vol. 2: *Papers from the XVIII World Congress of the Czechoslovak Academy of Arts and Sciences, Brno, 1996*. Prague: Česká akademie věd, 1998.

Dmitrieva, M. and Lambrecht, K., eds., *Krakau, Prag und Wien: Funktionen von Metropolen im frühmodernen Staat*. Stuttgart: Franz Steiner, 2000.

Eberhard, W., *Konfessionsbildung und Stände in Böhmen 1478–1530*. Veröffentlichungen des Collegium Carolinum, vol. 38. Munich: R. Oldenbourg, 1981.

Eberhard, W., *Monarchie und Widerstand: Zur ständischen Oppositionsbildung im Herrschaftssystem Ferdinands I. in Böhmen*. Veröffentlichungen des Collegium Carolinum, vol. 54. Munich: R. Oldenbourg, 1985.

Eberhard, W., "Entwicklungsphasen und Probleme der Gegenreformation und katholischen Erneuerung in Böhmen," *Römische Quartalschrift für christliche Altertumskunde und Kirchengeschichte*, 84 (1989), pp. 235–57.

Eberhard, W., "Die deutsche Reformation in Böhmen 1520–1620," in Hans Rothe, ed., *Deutsche in den Böhmischen Ländern*. Cologne: Böhlau, 1992.

Eberhard, W., "Konflikt und Integration: Die Dynamik in den Ergebnissen der Hussitenrevolution," *Studia Comeniana et Historica*, 22/48 (1992), pp. 31–55.

Evans, R. J. W., *Rudolf II and His World: A Study in Intellectual History, 1576–1612*. Oxford: Clarendon Press, 1973.

Evans, R. J. W., *The Wechsel Presses: Humanism and Calvinism in Central Europe 1572–1627*. Oxford: Oxford University Press, 1975.

Evans, R. J. W., *The Making of the Habsburg Monarchy, 1550–1700*. Oxford: Clarendon Press, 1979.

Evans, R. J. W., "Calvinism in East Central Europe: Hungary and Her Neighbours, 1500–1700," in Menna Prestwich, ed., *International Calvinism 1541–1715*. Oxford: Clarendon Press, 1986, pp. 167–96.

Evans, R. J. W. and Thomas, T. V., eds., *Crown, Church and Estates: Central European Politics in the Sixteenth and Seventeenth Centuries*. New York: St. Martin's Press, 1991.

Fedorowicz, J. K., Bogucka, M., and Samsonowicz, H., eds., *A Republic of Nobles: Studies in Polish History to 1864*. Cambridge: Cambridge University Press, 1982.

Fučíková, E., ed., *Rudolf II and Prague: The Imperial Court and Residential City as the Cultural and Spiritual Home of Central Europe*. Prague, London, Milan: Prague Castle Administration, Thames & Hudson, Skira, 1997.

Fudge, T. A., *The Magnificent Ride: The First Reformation in Hussite Bohemia*. Aldershot: Ashgate, 1998.

Graciotti, S., *Italia e Boemia nella cornice del Rinascimento europeo*. Florence: L. S. Olschki, 1999.

Graus, F., "Das Spätmittelalter als Krisenzeit: Eine Literaturbericht als Zwischenbilanz," *Mediaevalia Bohemica*, 1 (1969), Supplement.

Hanzal, J., "Rekatolizace v Čechách: jeji historický smysl a význam," *Sborník historický*, 37 (1990), pp. 37–91.

Harasimowicz, J., *Treści i funkcje ideowe sztuki śląskiej reformacji, 1520–1650*. Wrocław, 1986.

Harasimowicz, J., "Die Glaubenskonflikte und die kirchliche Kunst der Konfessional-isierungszeit in Schlesien," *Berichte und Beiträge des Geisteswissenschaftliches Zentrums Osmitteleuropas* (1997), pp. 149–69.

Hausenblasová, J. and Šroněk, M., *Gloria & Miseria 1618–1648: Prague during the Thirty Years' War*. Prague, 1998.

Hlaváček, P., "Beginnings of the Bohemian Reformation in the Northwest: The Waldensians and the Reformers in the Deanery of Kadaň at the Turn of the Fourteenth Century," in Z. V. David and D. R. Holeton, eds., *The Bohemian Reformation and Religious Practice*, vol. 4. Prague: Main Library of the Academy of Sciences of the Czech Republic, 2002, pp. 43–56.

Hojda, Z., "Zastavení nad novým soupisem italik od Jaroslavy Kašparové a nad literaturou k českoitalským vztahům vůbec," *Folio Historica Bohemica*, 15 (1991), pp. 481–95.

Hojda, Z., ed., *Kultura baroka v Čechách a na Moravě*. Prague: Historický ústav Československé akademie věd, 1992.

Holeton, D. R., "The Bohemian Eucharistic Movement in its European Context," in David R. Holeton, ed., *The Bohemian Reformation and Religious Practice*, vol. 1. Prague: Academy of Sciences of the Czech Republic Main Library, 1996, pp. 23–48.

Kafka, F., "Bohemia," in B. Scribner, R. Porter, and M. Teich, eds., *The Reformation in National Context*. Cambridge: Cambridge University Press, 1994, pp. 131–54.

Kafka, F. and Skýbová, A., *Husitský epilog na koncilu tridenském a koncepce habsburské reka-tolizace Čech: Počátky obnoveného pražského arcibiskupství*. Prague: Univerzita Karlova, 1969.

Kalivoda, R., "Husitství a jeho vyústění v době předbělohorské a pobělohorské," *Studia Comeniana et Historica*, 25/13 (1993), pp. 3–44.

Kaminsky, H., "The Prague Insurrection of 30 July 1419," *Medievalia et Humanistica*, 17 (1966), pp. 106–26.

Kaminsky, H., *A History of the Hussite Revolution*. Berkeley: University of California Press, 1967.

Kaminsky, H., "The Problematics of 'Heresy' and 'The Reformation,'" in František Šmahel, ed., *Häresie und vorzeitige Reformation in Spätmittelalter*. Munich: R. Oldenbourg, 1998, pp. 1–22.

Kaufmann, T. D., *Court, Cloister, and City: The Art and Culture of Central Europe 1450–1800*. Chicago: University of Chicago Press, 1995.

Klassen, J. K., *The Nobility and the Making of the Hussite Revolution*. New York: Columbia University Press, 1978.

Klassen, J. K., *Warring Maidens, Captive Wives and Hussite Queens*. New York: Columbia University Press, 1999.

Kłoczowski, J., *A History of Polish Christianity*. Cambridge: Cambridge University Press, 2000. Revised and extended English translation of *Dzieje Chrześcijaństwa Polskiego*, 2 vols. Paris: Éditions du Dialogue, 1987, 1991.

Kłoczowski, J., Kras, P., and Polak, W., eds., *Christianity in East Central Europe: Late Middle Ages/La Chrétienté en Europe du Centre-Est: Le Bas Moyen Age*. Proceedings of the Commission internationale d'histoire ecclésiastique comparée. Lublin: Instytut Evropy Środkowo Wschodniej, 1999.

Kłoczowski, J., Plisiecki, P., and Łaszkiewicz, H., eds., *Frontières et l'espace national en Europe du Centre-Est. Exemples de quatre pays: Biélorussie, Lituanie, Pologne et Ukraine/The Borders and National Space in East-Central Europe. The Example of the Following Four Countries: Belarus, Lithuania, Poland and Ukraine*. Lublin: Instytut Europy Środkowo Wschodniej, 2002.

Kramář, V., *Zpustošení Chrámu svatého Víta v roce 1619*, ed. Michal Šroněk. Prague: Artefactum, 1998.

Kras, P., *Husyci w pifętnastowicznej Polsce*. Lublin: Towarzystwo Naukowe KUL, 1998.

Krmíčková, H., *K počátkám kalicha v Čechách: Studie a texty*. Brno, 1997.

Lášek, J. B., ed., *Jan Hus mezi Epochami, Národy a Konfesemi*. Sborník z mezinárodního sympozia, konaného 22.–26. září 1993 v Bayreuth, SRN. Prague: Česká křest'anská akademie, Husitská teologická fakulta Univerzity Karlovy, 1995.

Lortz, J., *Kardinal Stanislaus Hosius: Beiträge zur Erkenntnis der Persönlichkeit und des Werkes*. Münster, 1931.

Macek, J., *Jagellonský věk v českých zemích*. Prague: Academia, 1992–9.

Michalski, S., *The Reformation and the Visual Arts: The Protestant Image Question in Western and Eastern Europe*. London and New York: Routledge, 1993. Revised English translation of *Protestanti a Sztuka*. Warsaw, 1989.

Mikulec, J., "Pobělohorská rekatolizace: téma stále problematické," *Český časopis historický*, 96 (1998), pp. 824–30.

Mikulec, J., *Barokní náboženská bratrsva v Čechách*. Prague: Knižnice dějin a současnosti, 2000.

Molnár, A., "Husovo místo v evropské reformaci," *Československý časopis historický*, 14 (1966), pp. 1–14.

Palmitessa, J. R., *Material Culture and Daily Life in the New City of Prague in the Age of Rudolf II*. Krems: Medium Aevum Quotidianum, 1997.

Pánek, J., *Stavovská opozice a její zápas s Habsburky 1547–77. K politické krizi feudální třídy v přdbělohorském období*. Prague: Československá akademie věd, 1982.

Pánek, J., *Poslední Rožemberkové: velmoci české renescance*. Prague: Panorama, 1989.

Pánek, J. and Polívka, M., eds., *Jan Hus ve Vatikánu*. Prague: Historický ústav, 2000.

Pešek, J., "Knihovny pražských předbělohorských farářů," *Documenta Pragensia*, 9/2 (1991), pp. 417–38.

Pešek, J., *Měšt'anská vzdělanost a kultura v předbělohorských Čechách 1547–1620 (Všední dny kulturního života)*. Prague: Univerzita Karlova, 1993.

Polišenský, J., ed., *War and Society in Europe 1618–1648*. Cambridge: Cambridge University Press, 1978.

Polišenský, J., *Komenský, muž labyrintů a naděje*. Prague: Academia, 1996.

Popp, D. and Suckale, R., eds., *Die Jagiellonen: Kunst und Kultur einer europäischen Dynasti an der Wende zur Neuzeit*. Nuremberg: Germanisches Nationalmuseum, 2002.

Rejchrtová, N., *Václav Budovec z Budova*. Prague: Melantrich, 1984.

Royt, J., *Obraz a kult v Čechách 17. a 18. století*. Prague: Karolinum, 1999.

Schramm, G., *Der polnische Adel und die Reformation 1548–1607*. Wiesbaden: F. Steiner, 1965.

Seibt, F., *Hussitica: Zur Struktur einer Revolution*. Cologne and Graz: Böhlau, 1965.

Seibt, F. and Eberhard, W., eds., *Europa 1400. Die Krise des Spätmittelalters*. Stuttgart: Klett-Cotta, 1984.

Seibt, F. and Eberhard, W., eds., *Europa 1500. Integrationsprozesse im Widerstreit: Staaten, Regionen, Personenverbände, Christenheit*. Stuttgart: Klett-Cotta, 1987.

Šmahel, F., *Husitská revoluce*, 4 vols. Prague: Univerzita Karlova, 1993.

Šmahel, F., ed., *Häresie und vorzeitige Reformation in Spätmittelalter*. Munich: R. Oldenbourg, 1998.

Šmahel, F., ed., *Geist, Gesellschaft, Kirche im 13.–16. Jahrhundert*. Colloquia medievalia Pragensia, 1. Prague: Centrum medievistických studií, 1999.

Šmahel, F., *Idea národa v husitských Čechách*. Prague: Argo, 2000.

Tazbir, J., *A State Without Stakes: Polish Religious Toleration in the Sixteenth and Seventeenth Centuries*. New York: Kościuszko Foundation, Twayne Publishers, 1973.

Tazbir, J., *Reformacja w Polsce*. Warsaw: Książka i Wiedza, 1993.

Válka, J., "Tolerance či koexistence? (K povaze soužití různých náboženských vyznání v českých zemích v 15. až 17. století)," *Studia Comeniana et Historica*, 18/35 (1988), supplement.

Válka, J., "Komenský a nadkonfesijní křest'anství," *Studia Comeniana et Historica*, 24/51 (1994), pp. 124–9.

Vlnas, V., *Jan Nepomucký: Česká legenda*. Prague: Mladá fronta, 1993.

Williams, G. H., *The Radical Reformation*, 3rd ed. Kirksville, Mo.: Sixteenth Century Essays and Studies, 15, 1992.

FURTHER READING

The most up-to-date bibliography on the Hussite reform movement and Revolution is František Šmahel's *Husitská revoluce*, 4 vols. (A German translation is forthcoming in the *Monumenta Germaniae Historica* series.) For recent work on the Bohemian Reformation see contributions in the theological journal *Communio Viatorum*; papers from the biennial Prague symposium *Bohemian Reformation and Religious Practice* (vols. 1–4); *Berichte und Beiträge* of the Geisteswissenschaftliches Zentrum Ostmitteleuropas (GWZO) in Leipzig; and Jan Blahoslav Lášek, *Jan Hus mezi Epochami, Národy a Konfesemi*. On Moravia see Josef Válka, *Dějiny Moravy, II. Morava reforace, renesance a baroka* (Brno, 1996). Festschriften are an important forum for new scholarship: N. Rejchrtová, ed., *Směřování. Pohled do badatelské a literární dílny Amedea Molnára* (Prague: Kalich, 1983); Jaroslav Pánek et al., eds., *Husitství – Reformace – Renesance, Sborník k 60. narozeninám Františka Šmahela* (Prague: Historický Ústav Akademie věd České republiky, 1994); I. Hlaváček et al., eds., *Facta probant Homines. Sborník příspěvků k životnímu jubileu prof. dr. Zděnky Hledíkové* (Prague: Scriptorium, 1998). On international Comenius scholarship and intellectual/cultural history see the journals *Acta Comeniana* and *Studia Comeniana et Historica*. See also Howard Louthan and Randall Zachman, eds., *From Conciliarism to Confessional Church 1400–1618* (forthcoming).

For recent work on the Polish Reformation see H. Łaszkiewicz, *Churches and Confessions in East Central Europe* (Lublin: Instytut Europy Środkowo Wschodniej, 1999) and contributions in the journal *Odrodznie i Reformacja w Polsce*. For recent work on Calvinism and "radical" reform groups in Poland see Halina Kowalska, *Działalność reformatorska Jana Łaskiego w Polsce w latach 1556–1560* (Wrocław: Zaklad Narodowy im. Ossolinskich, 1969), Jolanta Dworzaczkowa, *Bracia czescy w Wielkopolsce w XVI–XVII wieku* (Warsaw: Wydaw. Naukowe Semper, 1997), Henryk Gmiterek, *Bracia Czescy a Kalwini w Rzeczpospolitej, połowa XVI–połowa XVII wieku* (Lublin: Wydaw. UMCS, 1987); Lech Szczucki, ed., *Socinianism and its Role in the Culture of the Sixteenth to Eighteenth Centuries* (Warsaw: PWN, 1983); Wacław Urban, *Der Antitrinitarismus in den böhmischen Ländern und in der Slowakei im 16. und 17. Jahrhundert* (Baden-Baden: Koerner, 1986). New biographies of Polish Protestants can be found in J. Szturc, *Ewangelicy w Polsce. Słownik biograficzny XVI–XX wieku* (Bielska-Biała: Augustana, 1998).

THIRTEEN

Old and New Faith in Hungary, Turkish Hungary, and Transylvania

ISTVÁN GYÖRGY TÓTH

The territory of the Hungarian Kingdom (including Croatia and Transylvania) has a special place in the history of Reformation and Counter-Reformation Europe because of the extraordinary richness of its denominations. While the Lutheran Reformation enjoyed complete victory in the Scandinavian countries and the Catholics defeated the Protestants' attacks in Spain and Italy, in early modern Hungary a surprisingly large number of denominations coexisted.

The Hungarian Reformation diverges in a number of ways from that of western Europe. However, if we compare it with the Polish Reformation rather than with the English or French, the difference is not nearly so marked. Distinctive to the Hungarian Reformation was that several Protestant denominations developed their own church organization and could thus become independently recognized. One reason for this was that in a politically dismembered Hungary many nationalities lived together: the Germans chose to follow Luther, the Hungarians preferred Calvin's doctrines, and the Romanians were Orthodox. Furthermore, in the Kingdom of Hungary the dominant political force, the Habsburg dynasty, was Catholic. It did not want to support one Protestant denomination against the others, which could have led to the victory of one Protestant church over the others. On the other hand, in the sixteenth century the weak and unsteady power of the Transylvanian principality was unable to give specific help to any particular denomination in gaining ascendancy. In addition, in all but seven years of the sixteenth century all the princes from the Szapolyai and Báthory dynasties had been Catholic; in other words, they adhered to the then minority denomination. What had contributed further to the country's multi-denominational nature was that the Catholic Habsburgs, ruling northwestern Hungary, always needed to be considerate of Protestant Transylvanian interests, and the converse also applied. During the seventeenth century, the Hungarian Protestants relied on the prince of Transylvania for protection of their churches, while the Transylvanian Catholics depended on the Habsburg king of Hungary's support.

Already in the Middle Ages, the Hungarian Kingdom (apart from Catholics) was comprised of Serbians, Greeks, and Romanians of Orthodox religion; to the south lived Bogomil and to the north Hussite heretics, in hiding to avoid persecution. Many towns also had thriving Jewish communities. However, even though we are unable to compile accurate data, by far the most dominant religion round 1500 was Roman Catholicism. In the sixteenth century, this situation was to change drastically. In Hungary, the territory of which was divided between the Habsburg Empire, the Ottoman Empire, and the semi-independent principality of Transylvania, the "papists" became a small minority. Following the Turkish occupation of the middle of the country, the great migration of the southern Slavs into the southern regions of Hungary caused a growth in the number of Orthodox adherents. With the Turkish occupation came many followers of Islam, but what brought the greatest changes of all to Hungary was the Reformation. By the end of the sixteenth century, at least three-quarters of the Hungarian population were adherents of Protestantism in one form or another.

In contrast to the majority of other European countries, after the Reformation Hungary truly became a multidenominational country. Despite the spread of Protestantism, Roman Catholicism survived and the proportion of the Orthodox population increased. Neither could the Catholics do away with the Protestant churches, nor did the Protestant denominations become exclusive, and Orthodoxy remained a powerful church too.

The First Steps of Reformation

After 1517 Luther's doctrines spread rapidly in Hungary within a couple of years. This comes as no surprise, as German was spoken in the royal cities in Hungary and among the Saxons in Transylvania just as it was spoken in Leipzig or Augsburg. In the following centuries it was precisely the Habsburg rulers who hindered the spread of Protestantism in Hungary, often by using military force. But in the 1520s it was in the court of Mary of Habsburg, the highly erudite wife of King Louis II (1516–1526) from the dynasty of the Jagellons, where with Erasmian humanists were to be found the first priests who sympathized with the Lutheran doctrine (e.g., Johann Henckel, Conrad Cordatus, and Johann Kresling). After the battle of Mohács in 1526, where the young Louis II died, it was Luther himself who prepared a book of condolence for the king's widow, who was sympathetic to his beliefs. Luther's doctrine spread in the royal capital Buda, in the German-speaking Erasmian circles of the Habsburg queen – no wonder the anti-Habsburg, anti-German Hungarian noblemen's faction became an enemy of the new faith. In 1524 the diet of Pest passed an anti-Lutheran law, according to which the followers of Luther were to be burned, "Lutherani comburantur" (this law was not put into practice) – the wrath of the noblemen at the diet was directed less toward the enemies of the Roman pope than toward the hated Germans in the court of the Habsburg queen.

In the mostly German-speaking royal and mining towns and cities the citizens avidly read the German pamphlets distributed by Luther's partisans. A century earlier, Hussites (active in Hungary too) could rely only on the spoken word or hand-copied works; now printing became Luther's greatest asset. For an era which was as yet unfamiliar with the newspaper, these one- or double-sided illustrated publications became a window on the world, not only for the literate minority but also for the illiterate, to whom they would be read aloud. Whether about belief or organization, the ideas behind the Reformation interested everyone. It was noted on spreading Luther's ideas in the western Hungarian town of Sopron that when citizens gathered in the tavern, "the one that can, will read, the rest – perhaps ten, twenty or however many, will listen." It was no different in Transylvania: concerning the realm of religion, "many arguments could be heard among the common people, whether in villages or towns, while eating or drinking, day or night," wrote the chronicler Ferenc Nagy Szabó. The teaching of Luther spread rapidly in Hungary, although, due to lack of sources, it is impossible to establish a concrete chronology.

Similarly to Luther, who was originally an Augustinian monk, many early reformers in sixteenth-century Hungary were from the mendicant orders who, through the reform movements of the Roman Church's religious orders demanding radical changes in church and society, came to support such new church reforms. Most of them were Observant Franciscans. This branch of the Franciscan order was founded by John Capestrano, who died and was buried in Hungary. It was extremely active and highly critical of the church and society at the end of the Middle Ages in Hungary. Among the first wave of successful reformers were several ex-Franciscans who had turned Protestant pastors: Mátyás Dévai Biró (ca. 1500–ca. 1545) and the priest and poet Mihály Sztárai, author of Hungarian dramas, as well as István Benczédi Székely, author of the first Hungarian world history, published in Cracow in 1559. Another group of early reformers in Hungary came from the Wittenberg University, such as Imre Ozorai and Imre Farkas, who were both students for the (Catholic) priesthood at the university but who there became adherents of Luther's doctrines. In other towns Catholic parish priests themselves turned to Protestantism, such as Gál Huszár in Magyaróvár, who not only became a Protestant priest but founded a very active printing house in the service of the new faith.

The Gradual Emergence of Different Protestant Churches

A twenty-first century reader of Catholic, Evangelical, and Reformed Church histories gains the false impression that in mid-sixteenth-century Hungary these churches fought with each other; however detailed, such works miss the essential point as they are projecting later realities back to an age when Protestant churches were not yet stabilized. In Hungary, unlike most other parts of Europe, for quite a long time the different denominations did not branch off. That the church of the Middle Ages was in need of general reform was quite clear to all. What did not become apparent for some time was the irrevocable breach between those who saw it being resolved by internal reform of the Roman Church, and those who saw it being attained through breaking with the pope.

In the first half of the sixteenth century, most people had not yet noticed that the Catholic Church of the Middle Ages in Hungary had finally and irrevocably split into several denominations. The followers of the old as well as the new church, each in their own way, hoped for a reformation that would encompass all Christians better than it had thus far. The aspiration that Luther's followers would return to the common church was only shattered after the closure of the Council of Trent (1563) proclaiming Catholic doctrines as dogma, and after the death in 1560 of Luther's highly esteemed successor Philip Melanchthon, who had endeavored to come to some agreement. The archbishop of Esztergom and primate of Hungary, Pal Varday (1483–1549), expressed the hope of many Hungarians when he wrote to the papal nuncio that a general reform would heal all wounds of the church and "then even a hundred Luthers cannot prevail over us!" One of the envoys of the Hungarian bishops to the Council of Trent, the bishop of Knin, Andreas Dudith (1533–89), was a highly active participant of this council – later, however, he married a lady in the court of the Polish king and continued his life as a Protestant scholar and humanist polyhistor.

The Protestants themselves split into different branches and churches even later; the complete separation between Lutherans and Calvinists in Upper Hungary was not achieved before 1610. For quite some time, the schism in the church did not seem irrevocable as the views did not seem to be irreconcilable. In the middle of the sixteenth century, everything in Hungary seemed transient: the most ardent supporters of Reformation among the magnates still clung to their well-tried rituals, "according to the Roman rite." These magnates, the pillars of Reformation in Hungary, requested burial for themselves according to the Roman rite and among their Catholic antecedents, whose remains rested within churches that they themselves had altered into Protestant churches. As a Protestant burial rite had not as yet been formed, they felt that the Roman rite was more in keeping with their status. This long transitional period is well characterized by a letter of the chief steward of Tamás Nádasdy, palatine of Hungary and great patron of Lutheran Reformation. The steward wrote in 1551 to his landlord with great enthusiasm that they celebrated the religious ceremony in question, not in the old papist way or with abuses but only with "evangelical songs and hymns" – however, the event was the procession of Corpus Christi, a thoroughly "papist" holiday and ceremony in itself!

Even though the Catholic Church did not permit the marriage of priests or the two types of communion, many parish priests who considered themselves to be genuine followers of Rome did both. At the 1561 synod presided over by Miklós Oláh (1493–1568), archbishop of Esztergom, of the 119 priests attending, 62 were married and 44 administered communion in both forms. Archbishop Oláh (earlier secretary to Queen Mary of Habsburg and a prolific humanist writer of Erasmite ideas himself) wrote to the Council of Trent saying that most priests in Hungary were married, and families of higher social status considered it a blessing if their daughter were married to a priest.

Consequently, it is difficult to ascertain which priests were Catholic and which considered themselves to be of the new faith midway through the sixteenth century. Many selected for themselves which aspects they accepted or rejected from the teachings of the church. At the same time, the villagers considered Protestant pastors as parish priests (*plebanus*) and referred to them as such. This is one reason for the difficulty in assessing at this time which village priests were followers of Luther and which priests, although married and administering both types of communion, would consider themselves faithful to the pope, even if they might choose to be selective regarding the church's teachings.

In the latter half of the sixteenth century, the Lutheran and Calvinist Protestant churches organized themselves, and subsequently the radical elements, such as the Antitrinitarians in Transylvania, broke away from these establishments. With the exception of the Transylvanian Saxons, where Lutheranism became the official and unique religion of their self-governing region, the new churches did not organize themselves into exclusive congregations. A characteristic peculiar to early modern

Hungary is that in one area could be found a Lutheran, Calvinist, and Catholic bishop simultaneously, because these denominations and churches were not regionally separated, a completely normal fact in the twenty-first century, but rather rare in the sixteenth.

First to begin was the Lutheran Church organization. Lénárt Stoeckel, a graduate of Wittenberg University and director of the Bártfa (Bardejov) city school, compiled the tenets of faith in 1549 for the Lutherans in the environs of Kassa (Kosice). This document was accepted by the alliance of five free cities and therefore had the name *Confessio Pentapolitana*. These tenets were more conservative than their German Lutheran counterparts and accepted more from the Catholic teachings. In subsequent years, an independent Lutheran Church became established in Upper Hungary (present-day Slovakia) on the estates of the magnates supporting the Reformation.

The Reformation was short-lived in Croatia, at this point a part of the Hungarian Kingdom. In the mid-sixteenth century, the great aristocratic families in Croatia turned to the Reformation: the Zrinyi, Frangepán, and Erdödy families supported the spread of Protestant ideas, had Protestant priests in their courts, and supported Calvinist missionaries in the region on the Ottoman border. However, Croatia was especially exposed to the Turkish danger and depended heavily on military and financial help from the inner Austrian provinces, where under the archdukes Charles and his son, later Emperor Ferdinand, the Counter-Reformation had already begun. The banus (governor of Croatia) was from 1567 to 1575 the bishop of Zagreb, György Draskovich, an active participant of the Council of Trent and vehement supporter of Catholic renewal. From 1567, according to the edict of the *sabor*, the Croatian diet, in Croatia only Catholics could obtain land possessions or hold offices. The Croatian aristocratic families returned to Catholicism, the two greatest of which, the Erdödy and Zrinyi, being the last to do so – both Tamás Erdödy and György Zrinyi junior returned to the old faith in order to be nominated by the emperor as banus of Croatia. While György Zrinyi senior expelled Catholic priests from his domains after 1623, his son did the same with Calvinist pastors, and the Catholic bishops acting as tutors to the latter's orphaned sons, Miklós and Péter Zrinyi, finished the work of Croatian Counter-Reformation. From the mid-seventeenth century, Croatia (with Slavonia and Dalmatia belonging to it) was a bastion of Counter-Reformation with a homogeneous Catholic population, apart from small, semi-clandestine Protestant communities.

After the great success of Lutheran teachings in Hungary, from the middle of the sixteenth century the Swiss-based Helvetic faith, Calvinism, spread there rapidly as well. A factor in its gaining ground among the Hungarian population was that many ethnic Hungarians regarded the Lutheran Reformation as "too Germanic." Among those first to proclaim Calvinist teachings in Hungary was Márton Kálmáncsehi Santa (ca. 1500–57). After his university studies in Cracow, he became a canon at Gyulafehérvár (Alba Iulia) in Transylvania. His great adversary Péter Bornemissza (1535–84), the Lutheran bishop and famous writer, wrote of Kálmáncsehi as "at the outset being a Catholic priest with great pretensions." Kálmáncsehi turned to the Reformation relatively late, in the 1540s. He immediately familiarized himself with the teachings of Calvin and Zwingli (i.e., he had no Lutheran phase in his life), and it is largely attributable to him that the 1552 synod of Beregszász (Berehovo, now in Ukraine) accepted the Helvetic teachings for the first time in Hungary.

In the following decades, the center for Hungarian Calvinism became Debrecen in eastern Hungary, a city belonging to the Transylvanian principality and also lying on the border of three countries: Habsburg Hungary, Transylvania, and Turkish Hungary. Its landlords, the powerful magnate dynasty of Török, were fervent adherents of Protestantism. Influenced by Péter Melius Juhász, later bishop of Debrecen, the priests of this region who sympathized with Calvin joined forces with the border castle soldiers and nobility of the town of Eger, outlining their teachings and professing their faith at the synod of Eger and Debrecen in 1562. This was followed by the 1567 synod of Debrecen accepting the Second Helvetic Confession of faith. With this fact, after many hesitations and doctrinal uncertainty, the young Hungarian Reformed Church joined the mainstream tendency of European Calvinism. Péter Melius Juhász well understood that the Calvinist doctrine would fall on particularly receptive ears among the inhabitants of the market towns. His collection of sermons of 1561 was dedicated to the merchants of Hungary, who, as he wrote, in their travels could share with others "the knowledge given to us from the Lord's mercy."

The real pillars of the Reformation, as in the case of the Catholic revival a century later, were those with the real power in the country – the aristocracy. This is evident from the first steps taken in the formation of Hungary's Reformed Church when (even before the above-mentioned Eger and Debrecen synod) the 1552 synod of Beregszász (Berehovo) first accepted the teachings of Calvinism. This scarcely populated and underdeveloped northeastern region of Hungary, devoid of great cities and inhabited by Orthodox Ruthenians, had never been at the forefront in adopting modern western European ideas. At first sight, it may seem peculiar to find Calvinism emerging here of all places. However, Péter Petrovics, one of Hungary's most influential magnates and a fervent supporter of the Reformation, had in the previous year been pressed to leave the southern region of Temesvár (Timisoara) and had settled in this northern county. Thus it was in this area that he used his influence to support the Calvinist doctrines. If he had stayed in his original power base, where earlier with his help the Lutherans had already organized their first Hungarian superintendencies, then it is most probable that the Hungarian Calvinist Reformation would have begun with a Temesvar synod.

The life of Mátyas Dévai Biró, often called "Hungary's Luther" by contemporaries, best illustrates the importance of the magnates' courts in the spread of Reformation. An Observant Franciscan much influenced during the course of his Wittenberg university studies, he became a follower of the new faith and subsequently visited one by one in different regions of Hungary the courts of those magnates drawn to the Reformation: the aristocrats Tamás Nádasdy, Ferenc Batthyány, Péter Perényi, Gáspár Drágffy, and so on. As a result of his influence, the priests throughout these regions joined the Reformation. In the new churches, the resident priest at the court of the magnate or patron would be chosen as bishop (a similar situation to seventeenth-century Transylvania, where the Calvinist bishop was also the prince's priest at court). It seemed entirely natural for the magnate to assume that the worthiest residence for this most illustrious spiritual leader was nowhere else but his court.

A distinctive feature of the Hungarian Reformation was that its development was for the most part bloodless. In the sixteenth century, in the age of bloody European wars of religion, only in exceptional cases can anyone be found in Hungary who had been killed for religious reasons. While the two rival kings of Hungary, Ferdinand of Habsburg (1526–64) and John of Szapolyai (1526–40), who embroiled in civil war, were both fervent Catholics (as was Szapolyai's widow, Queen Isabella of Jagellon), Protestantism could wage and win its battles virtually unhindered.

There are several interconnected reasons for the quick and bloodless triumph achieved by the Reformation in sixteenth-century Hungary. The most important factor in the rapid success of the Hungarian Reformation was the weakness of royal power. Because of the civil war and the life-and-death struggle with the Turks, the Catholics Ferdinand of Habsburg and John of Szapolyai simply could not allow questions of religion to cause further alienation among their supporters. At the same time, neither royal power could muster the strength to build up a formidable opposition to the Protestant cause. They also hoped that the papacy would head the Crusade that would expel the Turks. By the sixteenth century this was an already outdated viewpoint: the Christian princes spent more time warring against each other than with the pagans; furthermore, they would frequently seek direct alliance with the Turks. Even so, it was the pope who organized the Holy Leagues of 1571 and 1684 that triumphed over the Ottomans.

Throughout the sixteenth and seventeenth centuries, the papacy saw its task as the expulsion of the Turks from Hungary. A year after the fall of Buda in 1541, the future Pope Pius IV (then only a high-ranking official) was to be found in Hungary with the papal relief forces. In the fight against the Turks, the Holy See was to give repeated further assistance of both finance and troops. It agreed that the greater part of the church income from Hungary could be utilized for these purposes, as could the levy due upon the appointment of a bishop. Throughout the Long or Fifteen-Year War against the Turks (1593–1606), this assistance was of the utmost importance. Pope Clement VIII's nephew, Prince Aldobrandini, commanded 10,000 men for Hungary and this counted for a third of the Christian forces that were involved in the unsuccessful siege of Kanizsa (1601). During this period, the monthly fiscal assistance sent to Hungary from the pope was larger than the annual tax of the Transylvanian principality to the sultan. However far the pope's influence remained from the time of the twelfth- and thirteenth-century Crusades, it was Pius V's Holy League which defeated the Ottoman fleet at Lepanto. Pope Clement VIII achieved partial success in establishing the Christian coalition during the Fifteen-Year War, and finally the Holy League put together by Pope Innocent XI freed Hungary from the Turks at the end of the seventeenth century. Any Hungarian ruler with an ounce of sanity would have recognized the rashness of breaking with the pope.

The rapid victory of the new faith was further helped by the fact that in the middle of the sixteenth century Protestantism's intellectual superiority was evident. There was practically no single important scholar who supported the old religion. The only Catholic adversary of the spread of Reformation was the Franciscan prior of Várad, Gergely Szegedi. It was to his anti-Protestant writings that Mátyás Dévai Biró wrote his answer in 1537 (*Disputatio*). This situation slowly changed by the end of the sixteenth century with the emergence of the Archbishop of Esztergom Miklós Oláh's protégé, Bishop Miklós Telegdi (1535–86), who as vicar general directed the archdiocese of Esztergom. He was a recognized scholar and formidable opponent of Protestants in matters of religious argument. In 1562, he translated Peter Canisius's catechism. A reflection of this work's popularity is shown by the fact that it was retranslated at the end of the century by another Jesuit writer, Gergely Vásárhelyi (1562–1623). In his own works, Telegdi argued with Protestant writers, primarily with the Lutheran bishop and drama-writer Péter Bornemissza. In 1577, Telegdi purchased the printing equipment of the Viennese Jesuits and took it to Nagyszombat (Trnava) to be used in the service of promoting the Catholic faith.

If the sixteenth century saw the flourishing of Protestant literature, from the beginning of the seventeenth century Hungarian printing presses poured forth pro-Catholic works and discourses of a European standard, too. To hold their ground in this war of words, the Protestants needed help from abroad. Finding no one who could effectively counter the "Guide to Divine Truth" written in Hungarian by the archbishop of Esztergom, the Jesuit Péter Pázmány (1570–1637), its translation into Latin was funded by a Lutheran magnate, Palatine György Thurzó. The Latin translation of this Hungarian work was then sent to the University of Wittenberg, so that there a scholar could be found who would be able to mount a substantial counter-argument. However, in the middle of the sixteenth century, no writer or scholar of the old faith could endanger the intellectual superiority of Protestants in Hungary.

The Catholic Church in Hungary quickly collapsed without putting up great resistance. This is a further reason why no bloody wars of religion broke out between Catholics and Protestants – Catholics were for a long time simply too weak. The battle of Mohács fought between King Louis II and Sultan Suleiman had decapitated the Hungarian Catholic Church. Never had so many dioceses been emptied in one day as on August 29, 1526, the day of the battle. With the archbishops of Esztergom and Kalocsa, Lászlo Szalkai and Pál Tomori, half of all Hungarian bishops, six prelates lay dead on the battlefield.

By the middle of the sixteenth century there was still a severe shortage of Hungarian bishops, and of those who were in office few were concerned with the needs of their congregation. They served their kings as chancellors or diplomats, far from their flock. As a consequence of the double kingship, the popes (in contention with the Habsburg dynasty) supported neither one king nor the other; the popes did not accept the royal nominations to bishoprics and therefore the rare reconciliations between the Habsburg and Szapolyai kings were followed by the consecration of many bishops at once. Following the Peace of Várad (Oradea) in 1538 between Ferdinand Habsburg and John Szapolyai, Pope Paul III consecrated five bishops at once; there was an urgent need for this maneuver since at this time in all of Hungary there remained only three consecrated bishops. After 1554, the pope had to consecrate ten bishops simultaneously. However, by 1572, yet again there were only four living bishops in Hungary, of whom two were incapable even of attending the Hungarian coronation of Emperor Rudolf II on account of their age and infirmity.

Ferdinand I was in no hurry to appoint bishops, as the income from these unfilled positions could be rechanneled by him toward the upkeep of his border castles. This was the case for the income from the diocese of Eger in northern Hungary, one of the richest in the country, which was diverted for the upkeep of the strategic Eger border castle. The title of archbishop of Esztergom, after the death of the famous diplomat and humanist historian Antal Verancsics (1504–73), lay vacant for 23 years. Thus the Habsburgs did not have to reckon with the archbishop's power in Hungarian politics and could use the enormous income he usually commanded for their own purposes.

Secularization and Church Finances

In sixteenth-century Hungary, the Reformation gained not only a spiritual but a financial victory over the old church. The Catholic Church was on the verge of financial collapse by the end of the sixteenth century. Aristocratic supporters of the Reformation handled the estates of the bishops as though they were their own family estates, and the thought did not even occur to them that the stock from these should be handed over to Protestant bishops. The developing Protestant church organizations, after a great deal of uncertainty during a period of transition, adopted many aspects of the Catholic diocesan structures. The priests who headed their church districts were called bishops; Catholics raised objections against the use of the word "bishop" (*episcopus*), but to no avail. Despite the similarity in name, there was a great deal of difference between Catholic, Lutheran, and Reformed bishops. Catholic bishops, in accordance with their rank, belonged to the aristocracy and had a seat in the upper house in the diet, and as prelates were the owners of large estates, even though they were temporarily impoverished as a result of being relieved of their estates by the Turks or secular magnates. On the other hand, Protestant bishops could not take part in the diet; they had no estates and therefore their social standing and financial situation were no better than that of other clergy, their only source of income being tithes, congregational gifts, and the patronage of Protestant magnates. At most they might have been held in higher esteem than other Protestant priests.

In England or in the Lutheran provinces of the Holy Roman Empire, the shift of estates from ecclesiastic to secular hands was one of the great social changes brought about by the Reformation. One factor that encouraged magnates to become supporters of the new faith was the prospect of acquiring estates held by the church, and the release of these estates totally redefined status as regards wealth. In Hungary, as elsewhere, the secularization of church estates was a lop-sided achievement. The magnates, and to a lesser extent the rest of the nobility, carved out huge portions of the church estates for themselves, without their having undergone complete liquidation, as was the case in England.

The estates of the bishops were completely secularized only in Transylvania – ironically, under the ardent Catholic Queen Isabella of Jagellon and her governor György Martinuzzi, the Pauline monk, bishop, archbishop, and finally cardinal, who was, however, simultaneously Transylvania's treasurer and in constant need of money. In the Kingdom of Hungary the bishops' estates were drastically reduced, but they did not disappear completely. The followers of both old and new religions pounced on the estates of the weakened Catholic Church. Meanwhile, even King Ferdinand, an ardent upholder of the old faith, diverted revenue from bishops' estates and cloisters for the upkeep of his border castles. However, bishoprics, as a structure, survived the century of Reformation. Official procedures for their cessation were not even initiated by Protestants, since the aristocracy had to be mindful not only of the Catholic Habsburg dynasty, but also of the papacy. One explanation for the rapid triumph of the Catholic Restoration at the beginning of the seventeenth century, which arose seemingly out of nowhere, is the fact that the Catholic Church did not have to be rebuilt; only the existing framework needed to be filled in.

When Péter Pázmány, archbishop of Esztergom from 1615 to 1637, set about reviving the Catholic Church at the start of the seventeenth century, he considered one of his most important tasks the reacquisition of misappropriated estates and invested untold energy in pursuing any number of missing stock. He was well aware that material considerations were as important for the restoration of the Catholic Church and for the establishment of seminaries and the training of new priests as was the upkeep of gymnasiums, printing presses, churches, and the stipends of adequate numbers of Catholic priests, all of which required huge sums.

The free-for-all secularization affected not only the bishops' estates but also the cloister stock and the Catholic Church's most important source of income – the tithe. As with the misappropriation of estates, here also both Protestant and Catholic magnates displayed equal rapacity.

In comparison with western Europe, Hungary had always had fewer cloisters and monks; the numbers of nuns' convents in particular lagged behind. Other factors besides the Reformation that contributed to the decline in monastic life were a general crisis in monastic life and in the monks' lifestyle, where even prior to Luther a need for reform was apparent; the destruction meted out by the Turks; and, last but not least, the greed of the magnates which neither the weakened state power nor the ruptured Catholic Church could arrest. The old monastic houses with their estates were taken over by magnates regardless of their religious beliefs, since the associated income was a great temptation. Important Benedictine abbeys such as Tihany, Zalavár, and Szentmártonhegy (known also as Pannonhalma, where St. Gregory of Tours was believed to have been born) became border castles, while other abbeys were occupied by the Turks, who with few exceptions razed them to the ground. Most monastic orders completely disappeared from Hungary by the end of the sixteenth and the beginning of the seventeenth centuries. The extremely popular Observant Franciscan order survived best. Even so, while a century earlier Observant Franciscans were to be found in 70 monasteries, by 1605 only four of their cloisters functioned in the Kingdom of Hungary. At the same time, however, during the Turkish occupation the Observant Franciscan monasteries of Szeged and Gyöngyös in Ottoman territory and the monastery of Csiksomlyó in Transylvania were the last bastions of Catholicism, and their influence extended to whole regions.

The Catholic Church's third most important source of income was the tithe. This was normally paid in kind by the serf and the lesser nobility. In the sixteenth century the Hungarian treasury and magnates took control of this income, and on terms exceedingly favorable to themselves collected the amounts outstanding and handed over only a small portion to the bishops. In any event, the weakened bishoprics, despite their large estates, would probably not have been able to collect the tithes without the help of some show of force. In the seventeenth century, most Hungarian aristocrats converted to Catholicism and became fervent supporters of the Roman faith, although they still tried to keep the monasteries' lands and the bishops' tithes.

Transylvania: A Unique Case of Religious Freedom

In the newly emerging principality of Transylvania, a state that had never existed before, the spread of the Reformation differed in many respects from its occurrence in Hungary. Although the development to some extent is comparable to that in Poland, Transylvania's place on the map of European Reformation is exceptional because of the great number of denominations and churches that could freely function there. It is not due to some unusual level of tolerance that we find no fewer than four accepted state religions (Catholic, Reformed, Lutheran, and Unitarian), not to mention the Greek Orthodox religion of the Romanians. It is due rather to the weakness of the newly emerging state that one dominant religion could never be imposed upon the whole population.

Among the Transylvanian Saxons, as with the citizens of the Hungarian German-speaking cities, the spread of the Reformation occurred simultaneously with the spread of Luther's teachings throughout Germany. The most important Saxon city – Brassó (Brasov, Kronstadt) – was won over to the Wittenberg reformer's doctrines by János Honterus (1498–1549), a Brassó schoolmaster who had studied at Wittenberg, Cracow, and Basel universities. His successor, Valentinus Wagner (1510–57), was also a former student of the Wittenberg University and a direct pupil of Melanchthon.

After the Saxons of Transylvania had decided en masse to adopt Luther's religion, and over centuries had held on to it with great tenacity, they no longer took part in the Transylvanian Reformation's further turbulent developments. From the outset, Luther's doctrine was successful in many other non-Saxonian parts of Transylvania too, especially around the predominantly German-speaking Kolozsvár (Klausenburg, Cluj), where Kaspar Helth (ca. 1500–74) preached in the spirit of Luther; himself a Saxon by origin, he later Hungarianized his name to Gáspár Heltai and became an important Hungarian writer and printer. For a while after, the Hungarian Lutherans and the Saxon Lutherans had separate bishops. However, around 1550, the Calvinist Reformation gained ground, with Debrecen becoming its center, and gradually drew more followers from among the Transylvanians.

Decades later, followers of the Reformation's radical elements found refuge in Transylvania. The Mantuan Francesco Stancaro was forced to leave the by now mainly Protestant University at Vienna. He found employment as personal physician to the great castle lord Péter Petrovics, Calvinism's most successful patron in eastern Hungary. But he also preached in Transylvania against the Holy Trinity and Christ's divine nature. The Debrecen clergyman Tamás Arany, influenced by Stancaro, broadcast these Antitrinitarian doctrines, thereby becoming embroiled in a heated debate with the Calvinist bishop Péter Melius Juhász, an event from which Arany emerged the loser. Although strictly raised as a Catholic by the Pauline monk György Martinuzzi, Prince John Sigismund Szapolyai (1540–71), the only child of King John Szapolyai and Isabella of Jagellon and an extremely cultivated and open-minded young man, was a follower of Calvin by 1562. However, his Italian court physician Giorgio Biandrata and his court chaplain Ferenc Dávid (ca. 1510–79) both became adherents of the Antitrinitarian doctrine. In a life full of vicissitudes, Ferenc Dávid had been the bishop of three different churches, Lutheran, Calvinist, and Unitarian, before ending his days in the prison of the castle of Déva.

The Antitrinitarians broke into factions, the radicals being persecuted while the "moderate" wing became an organized church in Transylvania – a unique fact in sixteenth-century Europe – which was accepted and acknowledged by the state power; even the young prince, John Sigismund Szapolyai, adhered to this Antitrinitarian Church in the last years of his short life.

An even more radical wing of the Antitrinitarians, the Nonadorationists or Sabbatarians, rejected the New Testament and followed only the Old, to such an extent that the holy day was held to be Saturday or Sabbath. The chancellor of Prince Gabriel Bethlen (1613–29), Simon Péchy, was himself a Sabbatarian. However, Prince George Rákóczi I (1630–48), an orthodox Calvinist, forcibly did away with this branch of the Reformation in 1638 at the diet of Des. Simon Péchy was imprisoned, along with many other followers, and thereafter the Sabbatarians could only worship clandestinely, thus developing an interesting handwritten book culture.

In multinational Transylvania, no one denomination had the strength to declare itself the one true church. It was not only one "legendary" Torda (Turda) diet of 1568, as earlier Hungarian historiography thought, that proclaimed tolerance regarding the four religions but rather a continuous process from 1548 to 1571, during the reign of Prince John Sigismund, when several consecutive diets held at Torda helped lay the groundwork for an increasingly wider acceptance of Protestant denominations. First Lutherans, then Calvinists, and finally Antitrinitarians were accepted as a church. As yet, the tolerance declared at these diets did not apply to Catholics. Only in the reign of the next prince, the Catholic Stephan Báthory (1571–86; Polish king from 1576), was tolerance extended to the Catholic Church, i.e. to the church of the ruling prince. The Orthodox denomination of Romanians was not an accepted religion but was tolerated, however, with rights that extended, in the seventeenth century, further than those of Catholics, since unlike them it was allowed to have bishops and seminaries.

Reformation and Catholicism in the Land of the Sultan

The Reformation also drew believers from places where "Christendom's natural enemies," believers in the Prophet Mohammed, ruled – an almost unique case in the world history of Reformation. The Turks did not impede the spread of Reformation in the territory they occupied in the middle of the medieval Hungarian Kingdom, around the old capital Buda. The first generation of reformers had already achieved great success in the Turkish-occupied villages: the one-time Franciscan Mihály Sztárai was – if his reports are to be believed – the founder of Protestant congregations in 120 villages in Ottoman territory. In the first decades of the Reformation, European Protestants nursed a variety of illusions about the Turks; they considered the Ottomans to have been sent by God to punish the papists, and that under Turkish rule Protestants would be able freely to spread the Gospels. In 1557, the Calvinist priest and printer Gál Huszár wrote enthusiastically to Bullinger that in Hungary the Turks "are so much inclined to the servants of the Gospel that they never disturb them. Indeed, sometimes even Turkish soldiers are present at the church services, stay up to the sermon to the Christian faithful, and leave only when the Lord's supper begins." The enthusiasm of these years, however, soon disappeared: even if these illusions remained in far-off German universities, Hungarian reformers working in Turkish-occupied villages quickly realized that Turkish tolerance toward them was relative, and above all completely incidental, depending on the goodwill of one bey or another.

The Turks did not have a decisive and consistent policy toward the Christian churches operating within the territories they occupied. In the first decades after the Turkish occupation, they had some interest in the new disputes on Protestantism and the Christian faith; at this time, even Turkish beys participated in religious disputes, such as the beys of Pécs or Szeged. Sometimes the Turkish beys and pashas decided the outcome of a religious dispute: in 1574 in the village of Nagyharsány, in southern Hungary, the Turkish authorities ordered the Antitrinitarian preacher to be hanged after a religious dispute held in their presence – not only was he declared the loser against the Calvinist priest, but he had made derogatory remarks concerning the Koran, the holy book of Islam. In 1575, it was the governor of the whole of Turkish Hungary himself, the pasha of Buda Mustafa Sokollu (nephew of the grand vizir), who decided the outcome of a religious dispute, this time against the Calvinist priest, who had to pay a hefty fine. Later, however, this attention and sympathy vanished, and from the end of the sixteenth century the Turkish authorities looked with disinterest on these "sectarian squabbles." The pashas and the beys observed with obvious satisfaction when quarreling Christians looked to their new rulers for justice. Conflicts arising between Protestants and Catholics were often resolved by a Turkish judge or kadi, who frequently decided on matters of religion, or on whether a place of worship should be divided by a wall to allow access to Catholics as well as Protestants. Even rival Jesuit and Franciscan missionaries would seek justice through the Turkish legal process.

Islam considered Christian and Jewish teachings to have become stuck halfway along the true path. Those congregations "in need of succor" were under the protection and leadership of Islam in exchange for the payment of a poll tax. Christians (Orthodox, Protestant, Catholic, and Armenian alike) were able to retain their places of worship where they had already existed prior to the Turkish occupation, and if necessary they could also undertake repairs. However, new churches, or churches larger than those already in existence, could not be built. Outward expression of the Christian faith was forbidden; consequently, processions and bell-ringing fell into disuse.

The Ottoman Empire, based on an aggressive Islamic ideology, displayed an apparent religious tolerance which in many ways was far in advance of its Christian European counterparts. An adherent of the Reformation could enjoy greater freedom in religious practice in a Turkish vilayet than in Italy, while a Catholic was less at risk hearing mass in Belgrade than in London. Unlike heretic movements inside Islam, the Turks regarded the Christian faith as posing no threat to them; only the conversion of Muslims to Christianity was punishable by burning. Ottoman officials continually harassed the non-Muslim population. This had little to do with attempts to restrict religious practices and more to do with extorting surcharges over and above the poll tax. The beys frequently captured Protestant and Catholic priests alike and held them to ransom, proclaiming that Catholic priests were the spies of the pope who were preparing the way for insurrection against the sultan and therefore were to be impaled. Missionaries working in the captive territories frequently turned to the Holy See requesting it to contact the French ambassador in Istanbul, as Catholicism's patron within the Ottoman Empire, to help resolve specific cases. However, the fate of Christians was in the hands of individual beys and pashas and not centrally decided in Istanbul. Therefore, the situation among Catholics and Protestants of neighboring market towns was markedly different; where an activity was permitted in one, that same activity might be strictly forbidden in another, and vice versa. It depended on who the local Turkish commander was and to what extent he had been bribed. The local Turkish pashas and beys decided on matters of religion in the occupied territories, as did the Hungarian aristocrats in Habsburg Hungary – they were the real decision makers within the Kingdom of Hungary.

As the Turkish authorities did not persecute them, the Antitrinitarians (who were not accepted as a church in the Hungarian territory ruled by the Habsburgs) thrived in the Ottoman part of Hungary, especially in the southern region of Baranya around the city of Pécs, where there were several Antitrinitarian communities; indeed, a large number of the inhabitants of this town belonged to the Antitrinitarian Church. When at the end of the seventeenth century the Habsburgs took this region from the Turks, the Antitrinitarians' peaceful existence came to an end.

Among the denominations in the Hungarian province of the Turkish Empire, Catholics received the least understanding from the Ottoman ruling elite. The Orthodox priesthood had a much more trusting relationship with Turkish official-dom than did Latin churches. Cooperation between the Turks and the Byzantine Orthodox Church had centuries-old roots. A contributing factor was that ethnic Turks were in a minority in the ruling elite; most beys and pashas in Hungary spoke a southern Slavic mother tongue and could thus easily "come to some understand-ing" with the Serb-speaking Orthodox priesthood. The Orthodox Church, through the auspices of the patriarch of Constantinople, depended directly upon the good graces of the Turks; since the city's occupation, it had enjoyed special privileges within the Ottoman Empire. However, Orthodox bishops and archbishops had to donate a handsome annual sum in order to maintain this status, and to find this money, taxes from the Catholic and Protestant congregations were indispensable. Consequently, considering themselves to be the spiritual leaders of all Christians within the Turkish-occupied territories, Greek Orthodox bishops regularly levied taxes upon the Catholics and Protestants. When they resisted, the Orthodox Church would bring accusations against them and as a result the Turks would repeatedly arrest the "Latin" priests.

Among the Latin Christian denominations, the Turks had more trust in Protestants than in Catholics. The greater degree of tolerance they exercised toward Protestants had a religious as well as political basis. The austere church interiors of the Calvinists, devoid of altars, statues, and holy pictures, stood closer to the prerequisites of Islam than the richly decorated Catholic churches. The Turks sup-ported the Antitrinitarians largely because the monotheistic interpretation of their faith judiciously presented by their pastors was considered similar to that of Islam, whilst the Catholic belief in the Trinity was presented by these Antitrinitarian pastors as polytheistic. However, when some Antitrinitarian pastors preached about the similarity of their teachings to those of the Muslim faith, arguing for a merger of the two into one universal religion, Turkish beys quickly withdrew their sympathy for Antitrinitarians.

It was in the interest of the Turkish authorities to maintain religious division among their "infidel" subjects, and thus prevent unity among them leading to rebel-lion, but at the same time to keep the local population quietly in place and to prevent their migration to Christian territories; for this, toleration of the Christian churches was an excellent means. Thus Turkish beys invited Protestant pastors to come over from Habsburg Hungary to the Turkish part, or the local Turkish bey gave a church to Protestants living without one, as happened in 1566 in the Turkish-occupied market town of Gyöngyös. In other places, on the order of the beys, Protestants and

Catholics shared the use of the church and the two priests had to divide the tithe income between them, as ordered by Turkish authorities in the towns of Kecskemét, Pécs, Buda, and Pest.

For the Turkish pashas, the finer points of religious argument were far outweighed by political concerns, in which they favored the Protestants. The papacy, as a state power, was considered to be the Ottoman Empire's most important enemy, the driving force behind the Holy Leagues, while the Catholic bishops whose dioceses were on Turkish territory were appointed by the emperor and resided within the Habsburg Empire, and therefore were considered as the emperor's men.

Catholic bishoprics did not cease to exist under Turkish occupation. The Habsburg emperors as Hungarian kings continued to choose Hungarian bishops for those dioceses that were within the Ottoman sphere of interest. Already in the sixteenth century, and yet again in the seventeenth, the Holy See reminded the bishops of these dioceses to fill their posts or to renounce them. The Hungarian bishops were unwilling to meet these demands. It is also true to say that the Turks would not have allowed them to enter the area over which they were meant to preside. Therefore, the bishops chosen by the Habsburg king for dioceses in Turkish-controlled territories would frequently have remained unconsecrated by the pope. This did not seem to affect their enjoyment of their income and their voting rights in the diet, which were equivalent to those living in Habsburg Hungary. However, where the faithful were concerned, they could not fulfill important functions such as confirmation, ordination of priests, consecration of churches, and the blessing of holy oils. These "exiled" bishops endeavored to maintain contact with their flock through vicars who lived in the Turkish territories. In the sixteenth and seventeenth centuries, they also exercised the right to collect the tithe from their congregations in the Ottoman territories.

Clashes between the Hungarian Catholic bishops in exile and missionaries sent to Ottoman Hungary by the Holy Congregation for the Propagation of Faith were unavoidable. According to the bishops residing in Habsburg territory, Turkish Hungary was not missionary territory. The country had its own bishops and parishes and it was thought unnecessary for Rome to send missionaries here; it would have been more useful had Rome sent money for the Hungarian priests if it wanted to offer genuine help. In letters sent to Rome, in arguments couched in canon law, the main debate of the sixteenth and seventeenth centuries concerned Hungary's destiny. What had to be decided was whether Hungary was a province lost to Christendom for the foreseeable future, as had been the case with the Balkans, where the Serbian, Bosnian, and Bulgarian states had faded into Christendom's distant memory, or whether Hungary was merely temporarily occupied and could once more become, within a reasonable period, part of Christian Europe.

Rome took the former view, while the Hungarian bishops took the latter. Catholics in Turkish-occupied territory were claimed by two states and by two church hierarchies. Both Vienna and Istanbul regarded the area around Buda as their own, whose subjects' affairs in matters of religion they could decide upon. However, as with many other questions of church history in Hungary in the sixteenth and seventeenth centuries, this argument was decided not by canon law but by the canons; Christian forces at the end of the seventeenth century reoccupied Turkish territory and the "exiled" Catholic Church was reinstated once more. Political reunification at the end of the seventeenth century led to the reunification of Hungary, which in the sixteenth century had been divided into three parts, in matters of church and religion as well.

FURTHER READING

Andor, E. and Tóth, I. G., eds., *Frontiers of Faith: Religious Exchange and the Constitution of Religious Identities 1400–1750*. Budapest: Central European University/European Science Foundation, 2001.

Evans, R. J. W., *The Making of the Habsburg Monarchy, 1550–1700*. Oxford: Clarendon Press, 1979.

Evans, R. J. W. and Thomas, T. V., eds., *Crown, Church and Estates: Central European Politics in the Sixteenth and Seventeenth Centuries*. New York: St. Martin's Press, 1991.

Köpeczi, B., ed., *History of Transylvania*. Budapest: Akademiai, 1994.

Korade, M., Aleksic, M., and Matos, J., *Jesuits and Croatian Culture*. Zagreb: Croatian Writers' Association, 1992.

Kosa, L., *A Cultural History of Hungary*, vols. 1–2. Budapest: Osiris-Corvina, 2000.

Mannová, E., ed., *A Concise History of Slovakia*. Bratislava: Historical Institute, 2000.

Murdock, G., *Calvinism on the Frontier 1600–1660: International Calvinism and the Reformed Church in Hungary and Transylvania*. Oxford: Oxford University Press, 2000.

Péter, K., "Hungary," in Bob Scribner, Roy Porter, and Mikulas Teich, eds., *The Reformation in National Context*. Cambridge: Cambridge University Press, 1994.

Péter, K., "Tolerance and Intolerance in Sixteenth-Century Hungary," in O. P. Grell and R. Scribner, eds., *Tolerance and Intolerance in the European Reformation*. Cambridge: Cambridge University Press, 1996.

Tóth, I. G., ed., *Relationes missionariorum de Hungaria et Transilvania*. Rome/Budapest: Accademia d'Ungheria a Roma, 1994.

Tóth, I. G., ed., *Litterae missionariorum de Hungaria et Transilvania*. Rome/Budapest: Accademia d'Ungheria a Roma, 2002.

Tóth, I. G., ed., *Millennium History of Hungary*. Budapest: Osiris-Corvina, 2003.

PART IV

Catholic Renewal and Confessional Struggles

FOURTEEN

The Society of Jesus

JOHN O'MALLEY

The Society of Jesus, a religious order of men within the Catholic Church, officially came into being on September 27, 1540, with the bull of Pope Paul III, *Regimini militantis ecclesiae*. The bull approved the "plan of life" (*formula vivendi*) drawn up by ten young priests, mostly Iberians, who had met as students some years earlier at the University of Paris. Ignatius of Loyola, a Basque nobleman and unofficial leader of the group, there inspired the others through the book of *Spiritual Exercises* he had already almost completed while still a layman. The group included Francis Xavier (1506–65), who would later become the great missionary to India and Japan, and Diego Laínez, who would be an important theologian at the Council of Trent and succeed Ignatius as superior general of the order. The group determined to travel to Palestine to work for the conversion of the Muslims, but when they could not secure passage they decided to stay together and form a new order.

Within a few years of the founding, the members began to be known as Jesuits, a name that has stuck with them ever since. The Latin *Jesuita* appeared in fifteenth-century texts and originally meant a good Christian, a follower of Jesus, but later also began to connote a religious hypocrite. The Jesuits made the best of the situation, gradually accepted the term as a shorthand for the official name of the organization, and understood it of course in its positive sense. Ignatius was especially insistent on the inclusion of Jesus in the official name, even though it provoked persistent criticisms within the church for sounding arrogant, as if all Christians were not members of the society of Jesus.

The Jesuits were only one of a number of new religious orders of men and women founded in the early modern period, but by reason of their size, the influence of their schools and other ministries, their missionary activity, and their ventures into almost every aspect of culture they are the best known and the most controversial. Until recently the historiography of the order fell into two rather distinct camps, reflected in the ambiguity of the word *Jesuita* itself: the first depicted the Jesuits as exemplary followers of Jesus, as saints and savants, the second as the religious hypocrites *Jesuita* sometimes implied; almost all European languages have the equivalent of "jesuitical" to mean crafty and devious.

This latter historiography derived in large part from Protestant polemic but also from the Jesuits' many enemies within Catholicism itself, who ultimately achieved the worldwide suppression of the order by Pope Clement XIV in 1773. The primary Catholic font for this dark interpretation was the *Monita secreta* published anonymously in Cracow in 1614. It ran through 22 editions in seven languages by the end of the century, and, though often exposed as a crude forgery, continued to be reprinted and cited well into the twentieth century. Supposedly a collection of secret instructions from the head of the order, it firmly established the myth of the Jesuits as devils in a soutane, whose fundamental objective was to control the world through the systematic compiling of compromising secrets about friends, enemies – and each other.

Serious historians of course never bought either extreme, and in the past few years especially in France and North America they have turned to the Jesuits in record numbers to explore with less prejudice almost every aspect of the Jesuits' manifold activities. They have successfully challenged interpretations of the order that had long been taken for granted by friend and foe alike. They have shown, for instance, that the order was not founded to oppose the Reformation or even to "reform the Catholic Church" but had a much broader, primarily pastoral scope. They have shown that, despite the military imagery in the papal bull of 1540, the order was not grounded on a military model but on the more traditional model of a brotherhood or confraternity of "reformed priests." They have shown that the Jesuits' famous "Fourth Vow" was not an oath of Counter-Reformation loyalty to the pope but a vow of mobility expressive of their desire to be missionaries in imitation of the evangelizing St. Paul. By showing how much the order changed even within the first several decades of its life, they have subverted the common assumption that all was clear to the founders from the beginning, and they have especially demonstrated how profoundly the Jesuits' decision to undertake the running of schools changed their scope. They have broken the Eurocentric focus of most writings on the Jesuits by some fascinating studies of the various patterns of Jesuit encounters with "the Other" in Latin America, New France, the Philippines, India, Japan, and China.

The order grew rapidly. By the time Loyola died in 1556 it numbered about 1,000 members, already divided into 12 administrative units called provinces. The distribution of members among the provinces was, however, very uneven. In the earliest years the largest and most prosperous province was the Portuguese, due in part to the support of King John III, but soon Spain and then Italy began to catch up and even overtake it. Within about a decade there were only slightly over a dozen Jesuits in Paris, but 25 in Brazil and 30 in India. The single greatest concentration of members was in Rome, where for several decades some 10 to 15 percent of all Jesuits lived.

By 1565 the order numbered about 3,500 and 13,000 by 1615, and it continued to grow. In the middle of the eighteenth century there were some 3,000 Jesuits in France operating, besides their other institutions, 89 "colleges" (secondary schools) and 32 seminaries. In Italy at about the same time they ran, besides the prestigious Roman College, 132 other colleges and 22 seminaries. Their institutions were typically located in the center of large cities, but, as the very numbers indicate, many more were situated in towns of quite modest size, where their buildings were often among the most imposing in the environs.

How can we account for the growth of the Jesuits especially in their early years, when in comparison with other orders founded at about the same time they expanded incomparably faster and on a more international basis? Many factors helped them in this regard, not least of which were the great gifts of leadership possessed by Loyola and the fact that he lived long enough to give guidance and coherence through the first decade and a half. He also had a special talent for choosing men to assist him whose aptitudes complemented his own. Outstanding in this regard would be his secretary, Juan Alfonso de Polanco, and his plenipotentiary agent-in-the field, Jerónimo Nadal. Ignatius also bequeathed to the order his *Exercises*, which moved the members to a deeply interiorized sense of purpose and religious devotion. No other group had a book like it.

The Jesuit *Constitutions* were drawn up principally by Ignatius and Polanco beginning in 1547. This understudied document is strikingly different from correlative documents of other orders, which are simply collections of ordinances. The *Consitutions*, under the influence of the humanist tradition, broke new ground in the rationalized structure of their organization, in the psychological undergirding of their development from part to part, in their attention to motivation and general principles, in having an implicit but detectable theological grounding, in conveying a sense of overall direction, and, perhaps most important, in their insistence in particular and in general on flexible implementation even of their own prescriptions. Cluttered and overly detailed though they are, they served the Jesuits well and helped save them from the internal schisms so many other orders suffered.

Moreover, the group was not only international in its composition from the beginning but also determined to move "anywhere in the world where there was hope of God's greater glory and the good of souls." The other new orders were made up almost exclusively of one nationality and lacked the venturesome zeal for travel with which the Jesuits were imbued. The order had not yet been approved by Paul III when Xavier was already on his way to India. Xavier's letters back to Europe describing his missionary activity helped the Jesuits recruit new members, as would the letters of other Jesuit missionaries for the next two centuries. The Jesuits had, in other words, a modern sense of propaganda.

Moreover, in their original "plan of life" they articulated briefly yet more lucidly than any order up to that time their full commitment to a life of ministry. Symbolic of that commitment was their insistence that they not be bound to celebrate the canonical hours in common, so that they might be free at every hour of the day for preaching, teaching catechism, hearing confession, guiding persons through the *Exercises*, tending the sick, and performing other works of mercy. They mentioned these ministries specifically by name. Experience would soon lead them to expand the list.

Last but not least, the original members were all university-trained, which not only lent the group considerable prestige but set a pattern of cultural and intellectual excellence that attracted many young men. It was the academic training of the original members that enabled them to understand how the running of schools could be a new and important ministry, with the result that the Jesuits became the first teaching order in the Catholic Church. This ministry, unique to the Jesuits for some decades, made them special, palpably different from any of the other orders, and hence attractive to potential recruits.

When in 1539 the members drew up their "plan of life" for approval by Paul III, they envisaged themselves fundamentally as itinerant preachers modeled on Jesus's disciples and on St. Paul. They interpreted preaching in a broad sense to include formal sermons in church but also street preaching; it included lecturing on books of the Bible for the benefit of both clergy and laity, an early experiment in what we today call adult education; it included lessons in the catechism to children and adults, and even informal conversation with individuals or small groups. In these endeavors the early Jesuits built upon traditions established by the Franciscans, Dominicans, and other religious orders in the Middle Ages, but they often took them a step further. In their teaching of catechism, for instance, they exported almost around the world the Spanish tradition of setting the text to simple tunes so that questions and answers could be sung responsorially.

The Jesuits' pursuit of ministries like these was special because of the influence upon them of the *Spiritual Exercises*. One of the world's most famous books, it is one of the least read and understood. It was in fact never meant to be read in the conventional way because it was to be used as a handbook designed to help somebody guide another through a program of reflections and meditations that would lead to a deeper sense of purpose in life and to a deeper commitment to the ideals of Jesus. It is amazingly flexible in how it might be used and in just how a person or group might follow its suggestions. The book in effect created for the Jesuits the new ministry of the "retreat," days or weeks spent apart in prayer, but it also imbued their other ministries with certain emphases, like the fostering of greater inwardness that paradoxically issued in a commitment to greater service in the world.

Like the Dominicans and others, the Jesuits saw preaching closely connected with the reception of the sacraments of penance ("confession") and the Eucharist. One of the purposes of preaching was to motivate listeners to receive these two sacraments, and the Jesuits, unlike many Catholic clergy, advocated "frequent" reception, viz., every week. This was a break with the medieval tradition that Christians were not worthy to receive so often. Their advocacy of frequent reception brought the Jesuits under suspicion in some circles in the sixteenth century and was one of the factors leading in the next century to their bitter conflicts with the Jansenists in France that brought Pascal's wrath upon their head. The Jesuits also had by then adopted a form of moral reasoning called "probabilism" that struck the austere Pascal as lax and unprincipled. If the *Monita secreta* has acted through the centuries as primal source for anti-Jesuit myths, the viciously clever satire of Pascal's *Provincial Letters* dealt the order a heavy blow that made its suppression easier a hundred years later.

The Jesuits who founded the order saw compassion for the poor and oppressed as the most genuine expression of Christian sentiment, and they tried to practice and urge others to practice the so-called spiritual and corporal works of mercy such as feeding the hungry, clothing the naked, visiting prisoners, and instructing the ignorant. In such endeavors they called upon confraternities, those voluntary associations for pious purposes that flourished in the late Middle Ages, to carry on these ministries and give them a solid financial and organizational basis. They eventually developed their own form of such confraternities known as Marian Congregations or Sodalities of Our Lady.

In Venice the founding members saw the work of Gerolamo Miani (or Emiliani), who seems to have been the first person to establish refuges for homeless boys and girls, as distinct from abandoned infants, and thus create the first real orphanages. As early as 1541 Ignatius helped found in Rome a confraternity to carry on the work of two new orphanages, one for boys and one for girls. Others followed quickly in other cities. More impressive perhaps were their early efforts to establish what we would call halfway houses for courtesans and prostitutes who wanted to move to a better life. The latter often plied their trade in miserable conditions and out of sheer desperation. Ignatius founded the "House of St. Martha" in Rome in 1543 and promptly organized a confraternity to administer and financially support it. Such houses allowed the women some months of seclusion where they could break with their past and then provided them with dowries so that they could either marry or enter a convent. All through their history the Jesuits founded or inspired others to found works of social assistance along the same patterns as the orphanages and women's asylums. The administration and finances of these institutions were almost invariably in the hands of laymen and laywomen organized into confraternities for the purpose, which assured stability. The orphanage for boys founded by Ignatius in Rome, for instance, is still in existence in its original location, near the Pantheon in the very heart of the city.

The ministries and activities mentioned so far, for all that the Jesuits might have modified them, were pursued by members of other orders and some of them even by various lay groups. No other organization, however, undertook formal schooling in the organized and systematic way the Jesuits did, as a result of a decision taken in 1547 to open a school in Messina, Sicily, that turned out to be a great success. With that decision the Jesuits entered a dramatically new phase that entailed almost a new self-definition as they modified their understanding of themselves as primarily missionaries and itinerant preachers to combine it with being resident schoolmasters. Until that time they had, despite the advanced academic degrees many of them possessed, avoided permanent teaching assignments and even eschewed teaching their own younger members, but with the success of Messina and other schools like it designed in accordance with the principles of Renaissance humanism they recognized such institutions by 1560 as their primary ministry.

The decision also meant for the Jesuits a new relationship with culture, for they now had to learn many basically secular subjects so as to become skilled professionals in teaching them. This development largely explains why and how the Society began to earn its reputation for learning. Other orders had teachers and erudite members, but in the Jesuits learning based to a large extent on subjects outside the traditional clerical curriculum became systematic in ways and to a degree different from the others. The Jesuits interpreted the humanistic program to entail theater in which the students played the parts, which in turn often entailed singing and dancing, at least in the intervals between the acts. This was but one reason why the Jesuits were drawn into a notably close relationship with the arts. Like so many of their Catholic contemporaries, they also used the visual arts for instruction and evangelization, and to that end established in Japan in 1583, for instance, an "academy" to produce devotional art that would satisfy Japanese aesthetic tastes.

The Roman College, opened in 1551, soon developed into a university, though at first a very modest one indeed. It grew in prestige and complexity, as Jesuit faculty were recruited for it from around the Society, so that within several decades its reputation far exceeded that of its rival, the University of Rome. This situation persisted at least through the seventeenth century. Other Jesuit institutions developed in the same way, as for example the school founded by them in 1585 in Macau off the coast of Imperial China.

Most of the schools the Jesuits ran, however, were what we would call secondary, though of a particularly advanced and rigorous kind. They, as well as other schools founded on the humanist ideals, were the forerunners and models for what developed into the Latin Schools, *lycées*, and *Gymnasia* of later times. In them the Jesuits simply appropriated the goals and basic curriculum established by Italian humanists in the fifteenth century that by the time the Jesuits were founded were already widely diffused in Europe and utilized by Protestants and Catholics alike.

Why did the Jesuit schools, then, achieve so rapidly such success and begin to be considered superior to many of the others? Three special qualities must be singled out in this regard. First, the Jesuits did not charge any tuition and were open to any students who could pass the courses and would obey the rules. Second, they brought to these schools an organization and discipline that many of them had learned in Paris, the so-called "Parisian style," that were unknown in most other places. Most of the elements of the Parisian style proved so useful that we can hardly imagine schools without them: for instance, students were divided into classes, so that they progressed from one class to a higher one, from simpler skills to more complex; students were drilled in the subject matter and prompted to become active learners by doing homework, composing and delivering speeches, memorizing and reciting poetry. Students not only read great dramas, they took the parts of the characters in plays produced for the purpose.

The third feature was the development of a real faculty. Until the middle of the sixteenth century, many "schools" had but one teacher, sometimes assisted by one or two of the older students. This had begun to change before the Jesuits arrived on the scene, but even with the first school in Messina the Jesuits enlisted a faculty of five, which in actual fact almost immediately became a faculty of ten. Within a few years Ignatius insisted that no school should be opened without a Jesuit presence of at least 12 Jesuits, half of whom would be practically full-time in the school. This meant a much larger number of students could be accommodated. In 1556 enrollment ranged from a mere 60 in Venice to 800 in Billom, France. That same year there were 120 in Bologna, 280 in Palermo, and 300 in Cordoba. Soon the faculties in many schools became even larger, with a consequent increase in the number of students enrolled.

Why did the Jesuits take this dramatic turn? How did formal schooling fit with their scope? Contrary to what is often said, they did not undertake them primarily, at least in most parts of the world, to counteract the Reformation. Rather, they adopted the view of the humanists that "good literature" inspired noble sentiments and thus helped form upright character in the young men who studied them. The great public figures of the past who dedicated themselves to the public weal would inspire others to do the same, whether that be in the offices of church or state. Moreover, the development of powers of persuasion, of eloquence, would provide the skills to enable these public servants to sway others to similar dedication and to make the right choices in matters of the common good. This was the ancient ideal elaborated by classical authors like Cicero and Quintilian but now proposed in a Christian context.

The Jesuits hoped to accomplish many things through their schools. They were frank in seeing them as places where they might attract young men to join the Society. They saw them as providing them with an insertion into the life of a town or city quite different from what a church provided. They saw them as providing a base for their many other ministries, especially since each school had a church, sometimes a very large church, attached to it. In certain parts of the world, the Jesuits, by taking the long view, saw the schools as acting as a bulwark against Protestantism: the best way to combat Protestantism was through an educated and articulate laity. But most fundamental in the decision was the faith that the schools would produce Christian leaders for the benefit of all concerned.

If the Jesuits became enthusiastic promoters of humanistic education in their "colleges," they were just as dedicated to the scholastic philosophy and theology taught in the medieval and early modern universities. All Jesuits were required after their humanistic training to go on to philosophy and theology, "the higher disciplines," and in many of the colleges they went beyond the usual humanistic curriculum by offering to their students courses in "philosophy," which usually meant logic, ethics, and "natural philosophy," the rough equivalent of what we today consider the physical sciences. Indeed, although full programs of philosophy in Jesuit universities made ample room for metaphysics and similar disciplines, they gave even more attention to the three just mentioned. This explains how so many of the Jesuit schools boasted astronomical observatories and why the Jesuits wrote so many books on mathematics and the sciences. It is thus all the more ironic that a Jesuit, Roberto Bellarmino, played the important role he did in the papal condemnations of Galileo in the early seventeenth century, for many of his fellow Jesuits were convinced Galileo was correct and, even after the condemnation, tried to find ways to teach a heliocentric astronomy.

The training in theology the original group received at Paris virtually assured that scholastic theology would play a major role in the theological education they provided for their own members and for others, even though they were critical of it for being too cerebral. During the lifetime of Ignatius they adopted Thomas Aquinas as their official master in theology, a decision that helped promote the revival of interest in Thomas characteristic of Catholicism in the late sixteenth and seventeenth centuries.

The Dominicans had much earlier accorded Thomas the same similar position in their order, but they differed from the Jesuits in many points of interpretation, which exacerbated the rivalry between the two groups that began to take on serious form around the turn of the century with disputes about grace. The Dominicans accused the Jesuits of being Pelagians, that is, of attributing too much to human effort in the process of salvation and not enough to grace, whereas the Jesuits accused the Dominicans of being Calvinists in holding just the opposite emphasis.

This was the famous *De auxiliis* controversy that in 1607 evoked from Pope Paul V a decree stating that neither side could be justly accused of holding the heretical positions they attributed to each other. The issue still simmered beneath the surface, and, as mentioned, erupted again in the Jesuits' controversy with the Jansenists. In Louvain as early as 1570, both Leonard Lessius and Bellarmino had found themselves at odds with the teaching of Michel de Bay, the forerunner of Jansenism. The Jesuits in general held a more optimistic view of human potential than did many of their Catholic or Protestant contemporaries.

By the latter decades of the sixteenth century, the Jesuits had eclipsed the other orders in producing leading Catholic theologians – men like Bellarmino, Francisco de Toledo, Luis de Molina, and Francisco Suárez. Jesuits also published important works in other areas of learning, like José de Acosta's *Historia natural y moral de las Indias* (1590) based on his reflections on his experience in Peru, and Juan de Mariana's *Historia general de España* (1601) and his controversial *De rege et regis institutione* (1599), in which he allowed regicide under certain conditions. Suárez, who taught in Rome at the Roman College as well as in universities in Spain and Portugal, published many works on philosophical and theological topics, none more important than his *Disputationes metaphysicae* (1597), which exercised considerable influence even on contemporary Protestant philosophers because of its new method of not following the sequence of Aristotle's thought so as to develop an independent systematic treatment adapted to the needs of thinkers in his own day.

Ignatius several times early in his life had to appear before various inquisitions to answer charges that his *Exercises* or some of his other activities were unorthodox, and in Alcalá in 1527 he actually spent time in jail. While he was a student in Paris, the city and the university suffered considerable agitation over the infiltration of "Lutheranism," but he and his companions seem to have been relatively detached from it. They were intent on traveling to the Holy Land to live where Jesus lived and to work for the conversion of the Muslims. Although they certainly had no sympathy for "the Lutherans," they also had no intention of traveling to Wittenberg.

Nonetheless, as early as 1540 one of them, Pierre Favre, was invited to travel to Germany as part of a diplomatic entourage to the religious colloquies being held at Worms and Regensburg. He was the first Jesuit to see first-hand what the religious situation was like, and he conveyed to his brethren back in Italy how appalling he found the condition of the Catholic Church. He did not speak German, however, and was otherwise ill equipped to deal effectively with the situation. His most lasting achievement was in 1543 winning to the Society a young Dutch student of theology, Peter Canisius, who would turn out to be the single most important Catholic figure in the empire in the second half of the sixteenth century.

Bit by bit in the first decade Jesuit leadership in Rome became more concerned with the Reformation and in particular with Germany, and in 1550 they officially added "defense of the faith" to the stated purposes of the order. In Spain, Portugal, and Italy they supported the many ecclesiastical tribunals dealing with persons accused of heresy, although they in principle preferred to use directly pastoral remedies whenever possible. In 1549 Canisius, after a sojourn of a few years in Italy, returned to the empire, where he would remain until his death in 1597, active almost until the end. In 1555 Nadal made his first trip there and, horrified at what he found, sounded the alarm. From that time forward countering the Reformation would in many parts of Europe become an essential constituent of Jesuit self-definition. In his many travels around Europe after Ignatius died in 1556, Nadal loved to contrast him with Luther and to portray him as the David dealing mortal blows to the Goliath. He thus originated a diptych that later became standard for historians of every persuasion.

In the 1550s and 1560s their most concerted efforts to deal with the impact of Protestantism took place in German-speaking lands, where they were warmly supported by rulers like Emperor Ferdinand I (r. 1558–64) and Duke Albert V of Bavaria (r. 1550–79). In 1551–2 the Jesuits opened a college in Vienna, and in 1555 they settled with Albert for one in Ingolstadt, by which time there were about 50 Jesuits in the empire, led by Canisius. These schools accepted boys who were Lutherans or Hussites and made some concessions to them regarding the religious program – a truly unusual feature for the age. Just a year after the opening of the Roman College, Ignatius, prompted and assisted by Cardinal Giovanni Morone, opened in Rome the German College, whose purpose was to provide training as diocesan priests for young men from Germany and other areas of northern Europe "infected with heresy" such as Bohemia, Poland, and Hungary. In 1555 at the Roman College the Jesuits initiated a course in a new branch of theology – "controversialist theology" – that, as the name implies, taught students how to respond to Protestant teachings and refute them.

By 1600 the number of Jesuit schools in the empire had grown to 40. The enrollments were often large, between 700 and 1,000 students, and the physical size of these establishments grew accordingly. Besides teaching in their own institutions, Jesuits soon came to hold positions in theological faculties of universities like Cologne, Trier, and Mainz. By the later decades of the sixteenth century, the German College began finally to bear fruit, and from the alumni came a number of especially well-trained pastors and theologians. The Jesuits were the single most important agent for the consolidation and restoration of Catholicism in Austria, Bavaria, and the Rhineland.

By the outbreak of the Thirty Years' War the Jesuits held powerful positions in society at large and in the Wittelsbach and Habsburg courts. Wilhelm Lamormaini, confessor to Emperor Ferdinand II, used his position to promote a hard line against concessions to Protestants and thus exacerbated the situation. Jesuits in similar situations in other parts of Europe were consistently admonished by their superiors, including the superior general, not to meddle in politics. Most of them did their best to comply, though the line between religion and politics was often thin. Nonetheless, the image of Jesuits manipulating policy behind the scenes provided good ammunition for their enemies.

In the 1570s and 1580s the Jesuit Antonio Possevino led a bold, important, but ultimately unsuccessful venture in high-level conversion in Sweden and Russia. The Jesuits entered the Polish-Lithuanian Commonwealth in 1564 at a critical moment in the religious struggle there. Within ten years they were operating five schools and were able to establish a province, in which many of the most effective Jesuits came from Protestant families. Piotr Skarga's *Lives of the Saints from the Old and New Testaments* (1579) and Jakób Wujek z Wagrowca's translation of the Bible (1593–9) were powerful instruments for the Catholic cause that became classics of Polish literature. Many factors account for Poland's being won for Catholicism, but the Jesuits' importance can hardly be underestimated.

In 1580 Robert Parsons and Edmund Campion entered England. The latter was hanged, drawn, and quartered within a year. Under Elizabeth ten other Jesuits were executed, including the poet Robert Southwell. The English mission became embroiled in tactical and political disputes with other Catholics. Parsons contributed perhaps most effectively to the Catholic cause by founding at the end of the century the college of St.-Omer in Flanders for the sons of recusants. In 1623 the English province was established with 213 members.

Eleven years later, in 1634, three English Jesuits accompanied Leonard Calvert in the founding of the colony of Maryland as a haven in the New World for persecuted Catholics. They were the first Catholic priests to establish a permanent Catholic presence along the eastern seaboard of the English colonies. Waves of anti-Catholic animus battered Maryland periodically until the American Revolution, but the Jesuits stayed on. In 1789 one of them, John Carroll, founder of Georgetown College, became the first Catholic bishop in the new United States. In England, meanwhile, the Jesuits became especially anathema to the Protestant population after being effectively but falsely accused of involvement in the Titus Oates Plot to overthrow King Charles II, and they were also resented even by other Catholic clergy.

The Jesuit strategy in dealing with Protestantism took many forms. In it the schools proved in the long run to be the most effective. The Jesuits, like most of their Catholic counterparts, did not at first grasp the full potential of the printing press in this regard, but once they did so, apologetic and polemical works began to flow from their pens. A few Jesuits from even the first generation had a fairly precise and wide-ranging knowledge of Protestant authors, but they read them with polemical intent. As they attempted to refute the Protestants, they perforce gave a new emphasis to certain Catholic teachings that contributed to the imbalance in confessional statements of faith typical of the era.

The founding Jesuits were graduates of the University of Paris and held their alma mater in the highest esteem. They were especially shocked when in 1554 the Faculty of Theology declared their Society "a danger to the faith, a disturber of the peace of the church, destructive of monastic life, and destined to cause havoc rather than edification." They weathered this potentially mortal blow, but it presaged the resistance their efforts met in many sectors of French society through the rest of the sixteenth century. In 1603 King Henry IV lifted the exile from Paris imposed upon them in 1594, and a new era opened in which the Society was able to carry on its usual activities, including establishing the great network of schools mentioned earlier.

The seventeenth century is the *grand siècle* for France, and the Jesuits shared in some of its splendor. The schools developed into some of the most prestigious in the whole Society and numbered among their graduates Descartes, Molière, and, much later, Voltaire. Almost unique to France was the almost simultaneous creation of networks of schools for girls undertaken by various *compagnies* of women, many of which were encouraged or at least inspired by the Jesuits. But in France the Jesuits were particularly often embroiled in controversy with other Catholics, partly because of their close ties with the papacy, which offended Gallic sentiments, partly because of the increasing assertiveness of Jansenism, partly out of jealousy over the Jesuits' cultural prominence and the favor they seemed to enjoy with Louis XIV and Louis XV. François de la Chaize was confessor to the former for 34 years.

In 1632 French Jesuits arrived at the colonial city of Quebec, and three years later they opened a college. A few years later they welcomed an Ursuline nun, Marie de l'Incarnation, who at their invitation had come to join their mission among the Hurons. Shortly thereafter Marie founded at Quebec the first school for the education of women in North America. The efforts the Jesuits made to convert the Hurons suffered from every conceivable obstacle, including the incommensurability of the two cultures and the consequent mutual incomprehension, even when the two parties thought they understood each other.

Nonetheless, the Jesuits, along later with other missionaries, established among the French settlers a solidly Catholic society in the environs of Quebec and other settlements. Legendary about the Jesuits was the depth of their penetration into the interior of North America through the Great Lakes to beyond Lake Superior. In 1673 Jacques Marquette, companion to Louis Jolliet and others, sailed down the Mississippi in a journey of nearly 1,700 miles. The Jesuits in great detail reported their activities back to their superiors in France to produce the so-called *Relations*, the most extensive account available of life in the wilderness and of the habits of the Amerindians.

The Jesuit institutions in New France seem almost threadbare compared with those in Brazil, Peru, and New Spain. With the encouragement of King John III, six Portuguese Jesuits under the leadership of the talented and energetic nobleman Manuel da Nóbrega landed in Brazil in 1549, where they immediately set to work with the European colonists and then with the natives. Their activities soon fell into two parts. Along the seacoast they founded schools of various kinds, some of which soon flourished. As early as 1572, for instance, the college at Bahía introduced philosophy into its curriculum, and in 1575 conferred its first masters degree. Among the natives of the forests the objective of the Jesuits was to settle them in fixed communities, *aldeias*, where they hoped they could be weaned from cannibalism, strong drink, and superstitions.

In Spain King Philip II was ambivalent about the Jesuits, in contrast to the enthusiasm with which John III of Portugal received them, but bit by bit he became more comfortable at least with certain individuals among them. Besides their many schools, perhaps the most important aspect of the Jesuits' activities in Spain in the sixteenth century was the part they played in the great revival of scholastic philosophy and theology that had begun early in the century under the impetus at Salamanca of the great Dominican Francisco de Vitoria. The Jesuits were thus latecomers in an enterprise long under way, but they as a group and through individuals like Suárez and Molina helped the enterprise achieve respect outside Iberia and even in Protestant centers of learning.

Philip's ambivalence toward the Jesuits explains why the Spanish Jesuits did not arrive in the New World until 1566, 17 years behind their Portuguese brethren. Within six years they entered three major areas – Florida, Mexico, and Peru. The mission to Florida failed, but the others flourished. Typical of the Jesuit approach to the native peoples here and elsewhere was the work of Alonso Barzana, who beginning in Peru in 1569 produced a grammar, a lexicon, and a prayerbook in five Indian dialects. Diego de Torres Rubio meanwhile wrote the basic works for the study of Peruvian dialects. This attentiveness to what they saw and heard achieved a kind of culmination in Acosta's *Historia natural* (1590). Once again, however, the more enduring influence exercised by the Jesuits was through their schools, especially the college of San Pablo, founded in Lima in 1568, the first Jesuit school in Spanish America. San Pablo acted as a channel for intellectual exchange between Europe and Peru, as a center for Jesuit administration in the viceroyalty, and as a kind of research laboratory in medicine.

In Spanish America the most famous, distinctive, and controversial institution established by the Jesuits was the "Paraguayan Reductions." Helped by earlier Franciscan experiments along the same lines, the Jesuits established these settlements especially for the Guaraní because they felt they could not evangelize them in a truly effective way until they somehow got them to a more orderly way of life, and also because they could thus protect them against the predations of Spanish and Portuguese slave-traders. Whatever the merits or demerits of the Reductions, they almost from the beginning earned the Jesuits involved the distrust of many Spanish and Portuguese authorities because they sided with the Indians on contested issues. The breaking point came when the Jesuits resolutely defended the Indians against the incredible hardships visited upon them by the Boundary Treaty of 1750 between Spain and Portugal. Enemies of the Society especially in Portugal conducted a campaign of discredit that in 1759 helped lead to the royal edict expelling the Jesuits from Portugal, the first step in the general suppression of the order that followed two decades later.

The Jesuit missions in India, China, and Japan are treated in detail in other chapters of this volume (see chapters 21, 22, and 23). For the larger history of the Society, the only point that needs to be underscored here is the controversy within Catholicism over how radically the Jesuits in China had accommodated to Chinese ways, and especially over how tolerant they showed themselves toward certain Confucian rites, like the worship of ancestors and the veneration of Confucius. On the official level, the controversy over "Chinese Rites" was definitively settled by the papal bull *Ex illa die* (1715) condemning the Jesuit approach and forbidding its continuance. The Jesuits' enemies, who saw them as subversives within the fold, kept the issue alive as providing another reason why the Society should be disbanded.

By the eighteenth century, therefore, the Jesuits had managed to arouse the envy, distrust, and antagonism of powerful forces within Catholic Europe, especially in the courts of the Bourbon monarchs and in the Roman Curia. Given the preeminence of their institutions, it was easy to blame them for many ills and to sow suspicion about them, though in most parts of the world they remained much esteemed and even beloved by the population who knew them best. Their own missteps, their tendency particularly with the Jansenists to overplay their hand, and sometimes a naive complacency about their secure status contributed to the catastrophe that in 1773 befell them. Without warning, many of them were literally cast into the streets, packed into awaiting vessels with little more than the clothes on their backs, and sent into the open sea, destination undetermined.

The grand sweep of the story that ended in 1773 can create the false impression that the only problems the Jesuits faced came from outside the order. The older historiography that saw them as soldiers under marching orders contributed to this impression and masked the internal tensions the order had to face. Serious crises occurred early on. The most dangerous took place after the death of Loyola over the approval by the order of the *Constitutions* he had written and over the election of his successor. Two of the original band, now aided and abetted by Pope Paul IV, who had never fully trusted Ignatius and what he was about, threatened to throw the proceedings into disarray. Underneath the personal resentments lay disagreement over the degree of authority Ignatius had assumed as general and over the degree of regulation the Society, now a complex institution, needed to function. Because the pope lost interest in the affair, the proceedings eventually took a smooth course, but the incident early highlighted the inevitable tensions in a social body that on one level spoke to its members in the language of brotherhood, but on another had to operate as an institution with a mission, or many missions, to accomplish.

The most dramatic crisis in leadership occurred under Claudio Aquaviva, elected superior general in 1581. During his long term of office, membership in the Society almost tripled to 13,000, and the number of schools rose from 144 to 372. He was an extraordinarily talented Italian aristocrat, who, probably correctly, saw that further standardization of procedures had to be imposed on this rapidly growing and sprawling institution. In 1599, for instance, he achieved success with the publication of the definitive edition of a *Ratio Studiorum*, "Plan of Studies," for the schools of the order.

This document had been in the making almost from the opening of the first school but reached a culmination with an experimental and fully fledged "plan" in circulation since 1586, revised in 1591. The commission appointed to finalize the project consulted widely with Jesuits in the field and, with Aquaviva insisting on closure, produced a document that, for all the limitations obvious today, excited for many generations admiration and emulation even among Protestant educators. In its practical effects within the Society, the *Ratio* brought with it the advantage of articulating standards and the disadvantage of discouraging further experimentation. It was under the *Ratio*, in any case, that the Jesuit schools achieved in the seventeenth century their greatest renown.

The very achievements of the order's central authority suggest the issue that burned beneath the surface among a small but powerful percentage of the membership, especially in Spain. Those Jesuits, encouraged by Philip II's resentment of any foreign interference in ecclesiastical affairs, wanted to change the *Constitutions* by denying the general the power to appoint superiors and to vest that power in local chapters of the order. By their propaganda in Spain, this group aroused the suspicions of the Inquisition concerning the state of the Society and by a series of "memorials" sent to Rome stirred up uneasiness about the order in the minds of two successive popes, Sixtus V and Clement VIII.

The "memorialists," as they came to be known, convinced Pope Clement VIII that the unrest among the Spanish Jesuits was due to the worldliness of superiors and the vast powers invested in the general, and that the remedy was a general congregation of the Society to deal with the issues. The memorialists intended the congregation in effect to impeach the general and to change the *Constitutions* more to their own liking. In this they felt they had the support of their king. As it turned out, the Jesuits elected to the congregation backed the general almost unanimously, so that the memorialists utterly failed to achieve their goals but not without causing tense moments within the Society and badly strained relations between the Society and the Holy See. The crisis passed, but it serves as a reminder that there were serious disagreements in the order over serious issues, although this internal history has not received much attention from historians.

In recent years historians have, on the contrary, shown a new and intense interest in the Jesuits' relationship to the arts and to the production and dissemination of scientific knowledge. It is now widely recognized that, because of the schools, the order began to have a cultural as well as religious mission. The Jesuits' patronage of great artists like Bernini and Rubens has long been recognized, but the pervasiveness of the arts in all their activities around the world is now being assiduously studied. Special about their contribution to the sciences was the worldwide communication of scientific information from periphery to center and then back to periphery.

FURTHER READING

Alden, D., *The Making of an Enterprise: The Society of Jesus in Portugal, its Empire, and Beyond, 1540–1750.* Stanford, Calif.: Stanford University Press, 1996.

Bailey, G. A., *Art on the Jesuit Missions in Asia and Latin America, 1542–1773.* Toronto: University of Toronto Press, 2000.

Bangert, W. V., *A History of the Society of Jesus.* St. Louis, Mo.: Institute of Jesuit Sources, 1972.

Bireley, R. L., *Religion and Politics in the Age of the Counterreformation: Emperor Ferdinand II, William Lamormaini, S.J., and the Formation of Imperial Policy.* Chapel Hill: University of North Carolina Press, 1981.

Brodrick, J., *Saint Peter Canisius.* London: Sheed & Ward, 1935.

Burgaleta, C. M., *José de Acosta, S.J. (1540–1600): His Life and Thought.* Chicago: Loyola University Press, 1999.

Cohen, T. M., *The Fire of Tongues: António Vieira and the Missionary Church in Brazil and Portugal.* Stanford, Calif.: Stanford University Press, 1998.

Cordara, G. C., *On the Suppression of the Society of Jesus: A Contemporary Account*, trans. John P. Murphy. Chicago: Loyola University Press, 1999.

Gagliano, J. A. and Ronan, C. E., eds., *Jesuit Encounters in the New World: Jesuit Chroniclers, Geographers, Educators, and Missionaries in the Americas, 1549–1767.* Rome: Institutum Historicum Societatis Iesu, 1997.

Godman, P., *The Saint as Censor: Robert Bellarmine Between Inquisition and Index.* Leiden: Brill, 2000.

Lacouture, J., *Jesuits: A Multibiography*, trans. Jeremy Leggatt. Washington, DC: Counterpoint, 1995.

Lucas, T. M., *Landmarking: City, Church, and Jesuit Urban Strategy*, Chicago: Loyola University Press, 1997.

McCoog, T. M., *The Society of Jesus in Ireland, Scotland, and England 1541–1588: "Our Way of Proceeding?"* Leiden: Brill, 1996.

Martin, A. L., *The Jesuit Mind: The Mentality of an Elite in Early Modern France.* Ithaca, NY: Cornell University Press, 1988.

Martin, L., *The Intellectual Conquest of Peru: The Jesuit College of San Pablo, 1568–1767.* New York: Fordham University Press, 1968.

O'Malley, J. W., *The First Jesuits.* Cambridge, Mass.: Harvard University Press, 1993.

O'Malley, J. W. et al., eds., *The Jesuits: Cultures, Sciences, and the Arts, 1540–1773.* Toronto: University of Toronto Press, 1999.

Scaglione, A., *The Liberal Arts and the Jesuit College System.* Amsterdam and Philadelphia: Benjamins, 1986.

The Society of Jesus, Catalogue 1226. London: Bernard Quaritch, 1996.

Wittkower, R. and Jaffe, I. B., eds., *Baroque Art: The Jesuit Contribution.* New York: Fordham University Press, 1972.

FIFTEEN

Female Religious Orders

AMY E. LEONARD

The early modern period witnessed a variety of female religious activity in both Protestant and Catholic lands. From Teresa of Avila's mysticism and reform, to the founding of new active orders such as the Ursulines and the Visitation, to the many evangelical converts preaching the Word of God, women of the early modern period donned the mantle of a new spiritual fervor, both forming and being formed by the Reformations. This chapter focuses on one category of this spirituality, female religious orders – broadly defined to include both active and contemplative orders, as well as the individual experiences of nuns and other women religious – primarily during the sixteenth and early seventeenth centuries. Summarizing the recent research, we can see that although this was a period of a flowering of female spirituality, it was also a time of increasing panic about women's freedom and activities outside of the cloister or marriage. It is thus fair to categorize the female religious of the Reformation era as under attack, either by enclosure-minded clerics in Catholic areas, or by reformers bent on monastic dissolution in Protestant ones. How serious this attack was, and how the orders and religious women within them reacted to this seeming onslaught, will be addressed below.

This study splits geographically between Catholic, Counter-Reformation areas and Protestant ones. For Catholic regions – primarily Italy, Spain (including the Catholic Low Countries), and France – three issues are paramount: the debate over the active versus contemplative life for women; the remarkable rise of new orders; and the impact of the Council of Trent (1545–63), in particular the decree from the final session in 1563 stipulating monastic enclosure for all religious women. I will not address specifically the more informal groups of religious women (sometimes called semi-religious), known variously as *beatas, dévotes, pinzochere,* among others. Within Protestant lands, the focus will be on the forces behind the dissolution of the monasteries, its effects on the displaced religious, and, lastly, the often quite successful resistance efforts of the female religious. Finally, I will offer some suggestions of common themes between the experience of religious women in both Catholic and Protestant territories, including changing notions of utility and the convent's role in society, as well as the supposed empowering aspects of religion for women. The breadth of this topic, which covers different geographical regions, chronologies, and confessional traditions, does not lend itself to any easy generalizations, but I will attempt to draw some overarching conclusions.

Female Religious and the Catholic Counter-Reformation

While Kathryn Norberg could rightly assert in 1988 that "the women of Counter-Reformation Europe have not been the subject of a sustained analysis" as compared to those of the Protestant Reformation (Norberg, "Counter-Reformation and Women," p. 133), now one can rightly say that the topic of Catholic women is "indisputably a growth-industry" (Harline, "Actives and Contemplatives," p. 541). From a time when historians assumed nothing much changed for women in Catholic areas, we now know there was significantly more diversity, rebellion, and compromise within these territories than previously recognized. Although women in religious orders in Spain or Italy did not have to deal with the immediate and dramatic upheavals of monastic dissolution, they nonetheless had their own battles to wage and complicated waters to navigate. These complications centered on two linked debates about the female religious. First, how active should or could they be? And second, what role did the Council of Trent's decree of mandatory enclosure play for them?

The Counter-Reformation was typified on the one hand by an "innovative current of thought" brought on by changing times, which increasingly pushed for a more active spirituality. This trend was countered by a "restraining current" within the church hierarchy, confirmed at the Council of Trent, which, while it looked to reform the church, also wanted to control and enclose all female participation (Wright, "Visitation of Holy Mary," pp. 218–19). Thus, while the Catholic Reformation inspired women spiritually, it also tried to restrain them. These currents, following the traditional timeline for studying women religious and the Counter-Reformation, began with a period of religious enthusiasm in the fifteenth century, inspired by the monastic observance reform and other late medieval religious movements. This fervor led to an explosion of new orders. Following the consolidation and reaffirmation of Catholicism, however, there was a backlash against the new female orders and active religious women, which forced them into enclosed convents and shut down their public religious expression. This trajectory, although disputed and subsequently modified, still dominates the field and provides the model here, with certain qualifications. (For an excellent critique of this view see Harline, "Actives and Contemplatives.")

We must first distinguish between contemplative and active orders. Contemplative nuns, such as the Benedictines, Cistercians, Dominicans, or Poor Clares (which began as an uncloistered order but after the death of Clare of Assisi in 1253 became enclosed), were characterized by solemn (meaning permanent and public) vows of chastity, obedience, and poverty. These nuns devoted their days to prayer, contemplation, and the divine office. Once the nun took her final vows, she was theoretically "dead to the world" and enclosed forever behind the high walls of the convent. Active orders, such as Mary Ward's English Ladies, or the Daughters of Charity, and, initially, the Ursulines, usually took simple vows, did not necessarily live together in a community, and emphasized an active apostolate, through teaching, nursing, or other acts of charity.

This neat categorization was in reality more complex, with much confusion, diversity, and overlap between the two types of orders. One of the recent trends of the historiography has been to pull away from setting active and contemplative lives in such opposition, and instead traces a more nuanced relationship between the two (Harline, "Actives and Contemplatives"; Wright, "Visitation of Holy Mary"; Conrad, *Zwischen Kloster und Welt*). There is also criticism of the tendency to compare, often unfavorably, the contemplative, "passive" orders locked away from the world in lives of prayer with the active, more "useful" orders, which lost their autonomy and were forced into enclosure at the expense of their dynamism and creativity. As we shall see, contemplative nuns were anything but passive, and enclosure was never as complete as the theory made it, even after Trent. Furthermore, women of the active orders often emphasized prayer as a central part of their devotion; thus we must be careful about any generalizations.

The unclear borders between active and contemplative orders aside, women from both were unmistakable participants in what has been called the Counter-Reformation spirit (Evennett, *Spirit of the Counter-Reformation*). This spirituality has been described as particularly active (in Evennett's words, an "active, virile, exacting religious outlook"; p. 42), with a militant church rising in triumph from the ashes of corruption and near-death. The spirit of the times called for action, with the changing social and economic world, not to mention the challenge of the Protestant Reformation, giving rise to new forms of piety. This renewed Catholic spirituality led to the foundation of 30 new religious orders and congregations, many with female branches and nine devoted to women. All of the new male orders, excepting the Discalced Carmelites (founded by Teresa of Avila and the only order founded by a woman that includes men), "stressed active ministry to an unprecedented degree" (Donnelly, "New Religious Orders," pp. 283–5). Belying the "virile" characterization above, this burst of energy most definitely included women who, often trying to follow the ideal of Loyola's Society of Jesus (which famously resisted all attempts to create an order of "Jesuitesses"), strove to make their mark through teaching, helping the poor, or tending to the sick. These women can be seen as continuing the active spirit of medieval communities like the beguines or the tertiaries. Women searching for an active outlet in religion had always been a part of Christianity, so it is no surprise that with the upsurge of spirituality and activity that accompanied the Catholic Reformation, women were drawn into the mix.

This explosion of reforming activity also had an effect on the older, established orders. There was a growing number of women entering convents starting in the fifteenth and continuing through the seventeenth centuries (Rapley, *Dévotes*, p. 19; Evangelisti, "Wives, Widows, and Brides of Christ," p. 243). This increase is often linked to the rising cost of marriage dowries, particularly in Italy. Certain historians contend that many, if not most of these women were forced into the convent, for either financial reasons or because of male civic honor, having no true calling for the regular life (Klapisch-Zuber, "The Griselda Complex"; Sperling, *Convents and the Body Politic*). The outpouring of spirituality that led so many to enter an active apostolate, however, certainly motivated women to voluntarily enter the cloistered life as well. Barbara Diefendorf shows in France that there were also many women eager for the convent; so eager, in fact, they would defy their own families to enter one (Diefendorf, "Give Us Back Our Children").

Among the contemplative nuns of the Counter-Reformation, Teresa of Avila (d. 1582) is the best known and looms large among religious women, in both contemporary sources and historiography. Recent work on Teresa has battled the traditional view of her as the prototypical Catholic Reformation saint, showing instead the innovations within her reform. Whereas some writers have contended that Teresa was the living manifestation of Counter-Reformation spirituality, others have noted how hagiographers focused on aspects of her piety that meshed with the church's Reformation, and ignored her more radical actions (Zarri, "From Prophecy to Discipline," p. 110; Bilinkoff, *Avila of St. Teresa*, pp. 200–2). At a time of tightening control over active female religious, mystics, and "unorthodox" reformers, Teresa was all three. She lived an active, worldly life, even as she obediently preached a cloistered, contemplative one. She defended herself before the Inquisition, and wrote numerous mystical tracts, ostensibly for her nuns' eyes only, but with much broader appeal and circulation. She also founded a new branch of an order, established 15 female convents, helped form two male ones, and was a tireless activist for both Catholic reform and a woman's role in religion (Ahlgren, *Teresa of Avila*; Weber, *Teresa of Avila*).

Teresa exemplifies the dangers of using too narrow a definition of an "active" vocation. In the first place, Teresa would have disputed any characterization of her form of meditation and prayer that did not include action. Her quest for the perfect union with God was rigorously pursued, both mentally and physically, and required wholehearted dedication (Bilinkoff, "Teresa of Jesus and Carmelite Reform," p. 174). Secondly, in practical terms, Teresa was as much a part of the world as not, as she traveled around Spain, interacting with the clergy and laity to promote her cause. Teresa herself expressed frustration at the pull of the secular realm on her time and energy and waged a constant battle between her own spiritual desires and what society needed from her. "On the one hand, God was calling me," she writes, "[o]n the other, I was following the world" (cited in Bilinkoff, "Teresa of Jesus and Carmelite Reform," p. 168). Only after many years was Teresa able to wean herself away from what the world saw as her obligations and focus on her own reforms.

Despite Teresa's ultimate validation by the church (she was canonized in 1622), she was not immune to the clergy's overt suspicion of assertive women. A papal legate described the troublesome Teresa as a "restless wanderer, disobedient, and stubborn *femina* who, under the title of devotion, invented bad doctrines, moving outside the cloister against the rules of the Council of Trent and her prelates; teaching as a master against Saint Paul's orders that women should not teach" (cited in Costa, "Spanish Women in the Reformation," p. 99). Teresa had to be very careful to defer to the church hierarchy's authority and control, in particular through her male spiritual advisers.

This reaction to Teresa was part of a growing criticism by the organized church of women's religious activities, even those by cloistered nuns. Although grateful for the reforming enthusiasm of its female members, the church was increasingly worried about controlling the new rush of piety. The climax of this search for control came at the final session of the Council of Trent. The reform of the monasteries or religious life had not been Trent's top priority, but finally in 1563, before the participants went home, the council addressed the issue of monastic abuses and regulation. Since the celibate and monastic life had come under particular attack by the Protestants, it was an area the clergy knew must be reformed. The significant resolution for religious women came when the council decided to reaffirm the medieval prescription of female enclosure (*clausura*), first officially promulgated in 1298 with Boniface VIII's decree *Periculoso* (Tanner, *Decrees of the Ecumenical Councils*, vol. 2, pp. 777–8).

Enclosure meant the physical separation of the nun from the secular community. Not only was she symbolically dead to the world, but this death was reinforced by the architectural boundaries of tall walls, locked doors, and metal grilles. Enclosure was both active, meaning no professed nun could leave the cloister, and passive, that is, no one else could enter the cloister without specific reason or dispensation. Even the nuns' spiritual advisers had to hear confession through a shuttered window. Women religious were further restricted in 1566 when Pius V, in the bull *Circa pastoralis*, decreed that all female religious communities not practicing enclosure had to be suppressed, including tertiary, beguine, and other active orders. From the point of view of the organized church, therefore, the most important aspect of female religious life became its strict enclosure. This emphasis on the cloister seemed to place Trent and its handling of female religious out of step with the new reforming times. Just when the church and society were emphasizing a more active spirituality, women were *de jure* excluded from this form of piety.

There were practical benefits from enclosure, such as safeguarding nuns from disease or attacks, or reassuring elite families that their daughters were entering a secure house. The primary motivation, however, was as a means of protecting and controlling women's sexuality. Chastity became intimately linked with the female religious life, and the only way to ensure and protect nuns' virginity was through strict enclosure. The Catholic Church had already been under attack for the supposed rampant sexual debauchery in convents; the only way to avoid even the hint of sexual impropriety was to lock away the women as far as possible from public sight. This control of female sexuality was not limited to Catholics, but rather characterized early modern society. Women needed to be contained, either within marriage (or only marriage for Protestants) or behind the cloister walls (*aut maritus aut murus*); there was no in between (Strasser, "Bones of Contention," p. 276; Conrad, *Zwischen Kloster und Welt*, pp. 249–53).

In theory, then, strict enclosure cut the nun off from the public, lay world. One immediate effect of this was often impoverishment, as nuns could no longer beg for alms, participate in craftwork or other economic activities, or visit members of the community to raise donations for their house. With enclosure, the convents were forced to rely almost exclusively on dowries for financial solvency, making many orders and convents which had been socially diverse progressively more aristocratic (Blaisdell, "Angela Merici and the Ursulines," p. 110). Although enclosed convents would often have some lower-class entrants (mostly as lay nuns who took simple vows and were excluded from many religious duties of the house), the choir nuns were usually drawn from the wealthy elite.

But the Tridentine decrees were not always successfully enforced. Historians have challenged two popular misconceptions about enclosure: first, that it was ever completely implemented, either passively or actively; and second, that enclosure was a negative development against which most active religious women rebelled. Enclosure in practice was always more flexible than church decrees allowed, from *Periculoso*'s first expression through the Counter-Reformation, and Trent's implementation varied from country to country. The convent walls were certainly not impenetrable, and there was a wide variety of responses to attempts to make them so. Some convents eagerly welcomed enclosure, even agitated for it. Enclosure offered women more financial security (once dowries were levied and assured), and enclosed women enjoyed more respect in a society that still saw the cloistered nun as the ideal. Other nuns tacitly accepted enclosure, but their connection to the secular world continued, often with the approval and help of both the clergy and the nuns' families. Local necessity often dictated the extent to which enclosure was enforced or not, with nuns breaking cloister because of illness or financial hardship, to interact with their family and the community, to fund-raise, or just for spiritual outreach. Even nuns locked behind the cloister walls still corresponded with the world outside through letters, singing, plays, painting, and prayers. We must broaden our understanding of nuns' interaction with the lay world to include both spiritual and artistic expressions of community. In Milan, nuns used music to participate in the public sphere, as their "disembodied voices became perhaps the most direct means of contact for the citizenry at large with that hidden world within" (Monson, "Disembodied Voices," p. 191), while Franciscan nuns in Bavaria established a public persona for their convent as a spiritual locus of relic devotion (Strasser, "Bones of Contention," p. 256).

Many women actively opposed enclosure and fought to maintain their active mission. In Germany, religious women had to deal with a double assault, first from the Protestant reform looking to dissolve their houses, and later from the Catholic Reformation, which sought to enclose them. Many religious women vigorously resisted both (see below for Protestant examples). Convents in Catholic Bavaria felt repressive measures were being imposed upon them from the outside by that "other Reformation," comparing the Counter-Reformation unfavorably to the earlier, more acceptable Franciscan observance reform (Strasser, "Bones of Contention," p. 259). The beguines in Münster fought against their spiritual advisers the Franciscan friars when the friars tried to take over their house and turn it into an enclosed Poor Clares convent. Although eventually the beguines had to accede to many of the friars' demands, their opposition to enclosure was clear (Hsia, *Society and Religion in Münster*, pp. 142–7).

The biggest impact of Trent and enclosure was felt by the active orders, both old and new. Concentrating on the Ursulines, Mary Ward's English Ladies, and the Daughters of Charity shows the variety of experience. The Company of St. Ursula was founded in 1535 by Angela Merici (d. 1540), who wanted to establish a community of virgins, both lower and upper class, devoted to prayer, teaching, and charity. The Ursulines had connections to earlier lay movements, like the beguines and tertiaries, and were particularly associated with the Oratory of Divine Love, but Merici also envisioned them as a militant order of action, a precursor to the Jesuits, addressing the social needs of the day. The Company, given episcopal approval in 1535, was immediately popular with communities established in every major Italian city by 1600, and spreading into France and Germany. By this point, however, the Ursulines had undergone a profound transformation. After Merici's death, and with the support of the reforming bishop of Milan, Carlo Borromeo (d. 1584), the Company evolved from a lay community into a more formal order. The change was most dramatic outside of Italy. As Ursulines spread throughout Europe, what had been a loose and socially diverse affiliation of like-minded women, both virgins and widows, and many still living at home with their families, became structured as a religious community with solemn vows, enclosure, and an increased emphasis on virginity (Conrad, *Zwischen Kloster und Welt*, pp. 52–63). Families worried about their uncloistered daughters' safety, and society wondered about mixing together women from different classes. Gradually the Ursulines, particularly outside of Italy, became more like traditional orders, as the women took on a distinctive habit, began taking public vows, and moved into communal living. The Ursulines remained popular, however, and far from fighting enclosure many women within the order welcomed the changes. The order in France, for example, was divided over the issue of enclosure, with many in the younger generation supporting it, while the older women felt it would interfere with their active mission of charity (Lierheimer, "Redefining Convent Space," p. 214).

A more dramatic example of the conflict between active women's communities and the church hierarchy can be seen with Mary Ward's Institute of Mary (The English Ladies). Ward (d. 1645), an English Catholic who emigrated to the Low Countries in 1606, was inspired by the Jesuits to establish her own order in 1609, devoted to teaching and missionary activity (Rowlands, "Recusant Women"). She structured the order around a modified version of the Jesuit rule, including sworn obedience to a superior and the pope, simple vows, no enclosure, and no clear religious habit. As Ward's order, popularly known as Jesuitesses, spread, she went on to establish houses throughout Europe, including ones in Vienna, Munich, and Rome. Although the papacy in 1616 had given the community its approval, Ward's refusal to accept enclosure and her continued devotion to an active apostolate, coupled with the growing unpopularity of the Jesuits, garnered her many enemies. Her Ladies were derisively described as "noxious weeds" and labeled the "galloping girls" who did not know their place (Rapley, *Dévotes*, pp. 30–3). In 1630 Ward was condemned as a heretic and the following year her order was suppressed. The houses she established were enclosed and banned from honoring Ward as their founder. Only in 1909 was this prohibition lifted, at which point the order contained 200 houses, 6,000 members, and 70,000 female students (Warnicke, *Women of the English Renaissance*, p. 176).

One female association managed to stay true to its foundation as an active, unenclosed congregation, precisely because it avoided ever calling itself an order: the Daughters of Charity. Formally founded in 1633 but growing out of a confraternity established in France in 1617 by Vincent de Paul (d. 1660) and Louise de Marillac (d. 1660), the Daughters of Charity was another community devoted to nursing, education, and charity. Through an innovative alliance of elite women (the Ladies of Charity) and their lower-class associates (the Daughters of Charity), de Paul was able to create an active community with both the financial backing to survive (provided by the Ladies) and the pool of manual laborers to do charitable work often seen as beneath the wealthy women. Despite the Council of Trent's provision against unenclosed religious women, the Daughters of Charity survived outside the cloister. Four factors account for their survival: the alliance of the elite Ladies with lower-class Daughters; the community's close ties to the French royal family; its founders' successful soliciting of support from the church; and finally, the decision to describe themselves self-consciously as a confraternity rather than an order, to avoid enclosure (Dinan, "Confraternities as a Venue for Female Activism").

Female Religious and the Protestant Reformation

Moving now to Protestant areas we see many of the same tendencies to control and restrict women's active religious participation, with one key difference: where Catholic reformers sought to reform and eradicate abuses and corruption within the religious orders, Protestants sought to abolish the whole system. Attacks centered on the vocation itself, rather than just abuses within it. Martin Luther (d. 1546) and the Protestants denied the spiritual superiority of celibacy and challenged the efficacy of the monastic life, demanding that those women and men who had not truly been called to the celibate state should leave their convents and rejoin the world. Protestants took the Biblical maxim "be fruitful and multiply" and used it, within the realm of marriage, as the cornerstone of the new Christian community. It is important not to overemphasize the split between Protestants and Catholics over celibacy and marriage, since Catholics also praised women as wives and mothers and showed growing ambivalence about women's celibacy (see in particular Harrington, *Reordering Marriage*). However, a Catholic could still preach in the seventeenth century that "virginity [is] the Sun, chastity the dawn, and marriage the night," something antithetical to the new Protestant theology (cited in Rapley, *Dévotes*, p. 17).

Because of the Protestant focus on marriage and the attack on the monastic life, the female religious was "the first to confront the Protestant Reformation" (Wiesner, "Nuns, Wives, and Mothers," p. 9). Historians divide over the effects of this confrontation and the Protestant program of monastic dissolution. Some maintain that Luther and the other reformers liberated women from the corrupt and misogynist medieval institution of the cloister. Many girls were forced to enter convents when they were too young to have any kind of religious vocation, leading to the corruption within. Further, the medieval emphasis on celibacy and the perils of female sexuality had portrayed women as dangerous Eves, best to be avoided. Protestantism rejected that characterization and raised women and the family to a level above chastity and the convent (Ozment, *When Fathers Ruled*, pp. 9–25; Douglass, "Women and the Continental Reformation"). Other historians countered, however, that the closing of the convents limited women's options and denied them one of the only sanctioned careers available. "Thus although the Protestant reformers did champion a woman's role as wife and mother by closing the convents and forbidding female lay confraternities, they cut off women's opportunities for expressing their spirituality in an all-female context" (Wiesner, "Nuns, Wives, and Mothers," p. 26).

Just as with enclosure, the theory and reality of dissolution were very different. In areas that converted to Protestantism, religious women had several options: to accept the Reformation and give up the conventual life; to emigrate to a Catholic area; to leave the convent but continue to live communally outside the walls; or to resist and stay in their houses, either as Catholic or newly Protestant nuns. While many nuns did convert and leave the convent of their own free will (a fact Protestant propagandists were quick to point out), many others fought back, and in significantly greater numbers than their male counterparts (McNamara, *Sisters in Arms*, pp. 419–51). Examples exist from everywhere in Protestant Europe of nuns opposing the Reformation and/or dissolution. In Geneva, Jeanne de Jussie, the chronicler of the Poor Clares, deplored the "Lutheran heresy" that forced the nuns' exile to

Annecy in 1530 (Jussie, *Petite chronique*). Some nuns in Amsterdam refused to leave their convent and continued to celebrate the mass into the 1590s (Marshall, "Protestant, Catholic, and Jewish Women," p. 128). When the royal foundation of Syon Abbey in England was forcibly dissolved, the sisters remained together in small bands, many relocating to Flanders, waiting for the day when they could return to their abbey. They were reinstated briefly during Mary's reign in 1557, but forced to leave again with Elizabeth. They finally returned permanently in 1861, having successfully kept their community alive during the long banishment (Hutchison, "Syon Abbey"). In Germany the most famous example of resistance came from Caritas Pirckheimer who, using humanist rhetoric and theological arguments, battled the Protestant city council in Nuremberg until her death, refusing to leave her convent (Pfanner, *"Denkwürdigkeiten"*).

Although resistance took many forms, the formal pattern of dissolution was similar in all Protestant areas. The Reformation arrives (either by popular demand or as an act of state, usually preceded by pronounced anticlericalism); nuns, monks, and friars are told to leave their convents, sometimes by force; pensions are offered to the ex-religious to ease their transition back into lay life; finally, the empty houses, their goods, and their lands, are sold off to the benefit of the state and the wealthy. How thoroughly dissolution progressed, however, the fate of the former religious, and the interaction between lay and monastic institutions varied. Focusing primarily on England and Germany, one can see the very different effects of dissolution.

One finds the most dramatic example of dissolution in England. Motivated more by financial than theological concerns, Henry VIII saw the monasteries as rich pickings. The first Act of Suppression in 1536 stated that all monastic institutions with an annual income of less than £200 should be closed. The religious within could leave the cloistered life and accept yearly pensions, or they could merge with bigger houses. Although there were some extremely wealthy female houses, such as Syon Abbey or Dartford, 85 percent of female convents fell below this standard. In 1539 the final Act of Suppression closed all monastic houses, Waltham Abbey being the last to close in 1540 (Cooke, "English Nuns and the Dissolution").

Although there were substantially more men than women living in monastic houses (8,780 to 1,900), the effect of dissolution on women was disproportionately more devastating. First, the pensions offered were not equally distributed but rather based on the wealth of the house and the rank of the nun within the convent. Because the female houses were poorer, the ex-nuns on average had much lower pensions than the former monks or friars. For example, only 6 percent of the former male religious received pensions of £2 or less (essentially living in poverty), while 60 percent of the women did (Cooke, "English Nuns and the Dissolution," p. 296). This situation was peculiar to England, as we shall see below. The second reason for dissolution's harsher impact on nuns was that women had fewer options outside the cloister than men, who could more easily find other work or join the Protestant clergy. In the cruelest twist, Henry VIII decreed in the Act of Six Articles (1539) that former religious were banned from marrying, betraying his own ambivalence toward rejecting the celibate life. So what became the most common welfare system for ex-religious elsewhere – providing dowries for their marriage – was effectively barred in England. Unable to work or marry, many of the women ended up destitute. Although this Act was repealed by Edward VI in 1549, relief was short-lived.

When Mary came to the throne in 1553, the religious who had married were forced to separate.

The reaction of the English nuns to dissolution was mixed. Certainly some joined the new Anglican Church, but others worked to preserve their former religious lives as much as possible. Many nuns chose exile to the continent, in particular France and the Low Countries. The nuns could then continue their cloistered lives, often actively working for the restoration of Catholicism in their mother country (Walker, "Prayer, Patronage, and Political Conspiracy"). Mary Ward, as discussed above, provides an example of double resistance: first, to the Anglican religion of her native country when she emigrated to Flanders, and later as the founder of an active order of women at odds with the Counter-Reformation church.

In (primarily Lutheran) Germany, we find a different story for the convents. Because of the particularized nature of the Holy Roman Empire, there was much confusion during the Reformation and the nuns had more room to maneuver. The demand to close the convents could come from a newly Protestant city council, a territorial prince, the evangelical clergy, or from the nuns' families themselves. One dramatic example of familial pressure took place in Nuremberg, where a contingent of mothers appeared on the steps of Caritas Pirckheimer's Poor Clare house demanding that she turn over their daughters, even though this was clearly against their daughters' wishes. When the women finally resorted to forcibly removing their children, one mother (according to Abbess Pirckheimer) became so incensed by her daughter's tears and loud wailing that she punched her in the mouth (Pfanner, *"Denkwürdigkeiten,"* pp. 83). In Augsburg the convents were a focal point of hostility because of their wealth and powerful women (Roper, *Holy Household*, pp. 210–11). Yet families and local communities could also be instrumental in supporting the houses and pressuring civic authorities to allow the nuns to stay. The people of Strasbourg staunchly protected their convents and continued to attend mass there, give donations, and, most importantly, send their daughters to the nuns to be educated and to profess (Leonard, " 'Nails in the Wall,' " pp. 168–214).

Women (and men) in Germany were offered pensions if they chose to leave their houses, but unlike in England, all nuns from the same convent usually received equal amounts (although lay sisters received less than choir, and different convents could negotiate for higher settlements), and the sum was usually enough to live on comfortably. Many religious, however, refused to accept the pensions or to leave their convents. This resistance took different forms. Some nuns, while refusing to leave the cloister, converted voluntarily to Protestantism, establishing the somewhat incongruous image of a Lutheran convent. Others were more forcibly converted, and yet they too remained in their celibate, all-female environment. This happened especially within the noble abbeys (*Damenstifte*) where the women came from the highest social strata and had the connections to support their actions. This refusal of Protestant nuns to leave the convent shows that the communal life was often more important to the nuns than confessional religious ties (Wiesner, "Ideology Meets the Empire"). Many nuns, however, refused to leave or convert, and battled on (often successfully) against the Protestant churches and political authorities. German nuns resisted the repeated and increasingly adamant efforts of authorities to get the nuns to leave, to stop accepting novices, performing Catholic rituals (such as dry masses or the divine office), smuggling in priests to perform mass, and essentially making a mockery of the clergy's attempts to institute a uniform evangelical reform (Leonard, "'Nails in the Wall'"; Roper, *Holy Household*).

Historians have long recognized that many convents survived in the Holy Roman Empire, but only recently have they begun to explain how or why. Various factors played a role both in why the nuns resisted the Reformation and how they were successful. Fifteenth-century observance movements, the nuns' status and gender, their Catholic religiosity, familial connections, and social necessity all interacted to produce an environment conducive to the convents' survival. Nuns succeeded through tenacity, intelligence, support from family and influential friends, their strong sense of community and religious identity, not to mention the fact that civic authorities were loath to drag the women out of their convents kicking and screaming, especially if this would bring down the wrath of either the nuns' influential families or the Holy Roman Emperor.

Two of the key factors in the nuns' successful resistance were class and gender. Although class clearly played an important role in the convents' survival (almost all of the nuns were elite), gender was perhaps more decisive. Survival rates of monastic institutions were intimately linked to gender. In Strasbourg, the Dominican and Franciscan friars quickly left the city, but three Dominican convents refused to dissolve (Leonard, "'Nails in the Wall'"). In Augsburg, four female convents survived to witness the city's reintroduction of Catholicism, while none of the male houses remained (Roper, *Holy Household*, p. 235). Half of the convents in Magdeburg and Halberstadt were still there in 1648, whereas the male houses had a 20 percent survival rate (Wiesner, "Ideology Meets the Empire," p. 186). The role of gender was often more significant for the outside authorities than for the nuns themselves. Whereas the nuns would never define themselves solely by their gender, often preferring to focus on their religious affiliation, the fact that they were women was critical to how others viewed them and how leniently they were often treated.

In the face of such resistance, some authorities chose to modify the Protestant theology. Although in theory reformers wanted the dissolution of all convents, the reality was more difficult, with the reformers themselves showing a certain ambivalence toward complete closure. Even Luther realized the social upheaval closing the convents would cause. What would happen to the nuns, especially those who were too old to marry? While reformers did their best to dower and marry off the ex-nuns (the leading reformers themselves helping out, with Luther, Martin Bucer [d. 1551], and Matthew Zell [d. 1548] all marrying former nuns), there were still scores of women from each convent who would be left homeless. Returning these women to their families was not always feasible. In Strasbourg, for example, many families actively agitated to "liberate" their daughters from the convents. Once these former nuns were brought home, however, they proved to have such a difficult time reintegrating into society that many parents persuaded the city council to put their unhappy daughters back in the cloister (Leonard, "'Nails in the Wall,'" p. 171).

Governing authorities in Germany that had trouble closing their convents thus decided to make the best of the situation: if they could not close them, they would at least bring the houses under their complete authority. In many cities of the empire, financial administration of the convents had already been assumed by the councils during the Middle Ages, and this regulation was merely extended with the Reformation. Magistrates often assigned lay administrators to oversee all aspects of the houses, hired bursars to inspect financial transactions, forced the nuns to give up their habits and wear lay clothing, took over the election of officers, and subjected the nuns to frequent evangelical preaching in the hopes that they would convert and leave the cloister. Instead of forcing the nuns out, they decided to close the houses off, ban the acceptance of novices, and let the nuns die out naturally. As they took control, Protestants employed some of the same techniques the Catholic Reformation would use later in the century, especially enforcing full enclosure. Protestant authorities were as concerned about women's virginity as Catholic ones, and used, often word for word, the old Catholic ordinances outlining a strict cloister (Leonard, "Nails in the Wall"; Strasser, "Brides of Christ," pp. 236–7). Displaying a joint emphasis on surveillance and subordination, so long as the women were enclosed and under lay control, they could stay in their convents.

The Utility of the Convent

A fundamental question for Protestants regarding the female convents centered on their perceived usefulness. Initially, Protestant theology condemned the convents, since intermediary prayers, singing, or religious contemplation were useless in helping either the individual or society gain salvation; faith alone was all that was necessary. But once the social upheavals of dissolution became apparent, many areas redefined the cloister to fit in with a new Protestant definition of utility: that which would benefit one's neighbor practically, not spiritually. This shift in the utility of the cloister represents a fundamental change in mentality from Catholic theology, where the work of the nuns helped achieve salvation for the entire community, not just themselves. Religiously, the ideal portrayed the nun as praying for the souls of the entire community, participating in a system of transferable merit and penance. Now for Protestants their prayers were seen as a selfish act which brought no help for society as a whole. The efficacy of one's works was verified by how they benefited one's neighbors, but that benefit must be obvious to the naked eye; it was not expressed through spiritual succor but rather temporal. Within this utilitarian definition of Christian behavior, prayers and observances no longer sufficed; one must engage in reciprocal actions that served everyone.

The nuns themselves understood this new concept and structured their arguments accordingly. When the Protestant city council at Strasbourg attacked its female convents and the nuns within, accusing them of no longer benefiting the common good, one prioress responded that there were many ways in which they helped society. They taught manners and decorum to girls, protected the young daughters of the city in the safe haven of the convent until marriageable age, and provided a home for orphans and the old and unwanted women of the city. After careful deliberation, the magistrates decided to let the nuns stay in their convents, adding that it was an appropriate vocation for women to spend time in prayer. Significantly, it was the council that raised the spiritual utility of the convents, not the nuns. The prioress astutely downplayed their religious side – since it would only remind the council of the nuns' continued adherence to Catholicism – by emphasizing their practical, civic contributions to the community.

This increasing emphasis on utility was not limited to Protestants but appeared in Catholicism as well, as shown in the new active ethos of the Counter-Reformation spirit discussed above. Although early modern Catholic society still viewed convents as both spiritually and practically useful, more emphasis was being placed on the social, political, and economic roles these houses played within society. Convents were also schools, orphanages, hospices, halfway houses for repentant sinners, retirement homes, asylums, and centers of learning and artistic expression. The emphasis on utility does not negate the real power of the cloistered life and the important role a nun's prayers still played for the community at large. Despite enclosure, or maybe even emphasized by it, nuns were linked to the community through their piety, prayers for the living and the dead, and the belief that a convent of nuns improved the spiritual quality of all society. Even in Protestant lands, there is evidence that many continued to believe nuns played an important role spiritually for the community. We cannot ignore, however, the ambivalence authorities expressed about these enclosed institutions and what exactly their role in society should be.

One reason for this ambivalence about the convent was its appearance as an ambiguous space. At a time of a growing separation between the public and private spheres, with the public world of politics and culture increasingly seen as male, and the domestic sphere of the house and family as female, convents presented a serious problem because they were both and neither. Nuns had no clear status. They were not truly women, because they denied their biology, lived without the protection of men – at least, a father, husband, or brother – and did not confine themselves to the domestic sphere. Where did they belong? Protestants, and more and more Catholics, focused on women within the family and household, and the female convent did not fit that characterization (nor, one should note, did the male monastery). What was the cloister, a private or public space? And who held dominion, the nuns, the order, the bishop, or the lay community? After Trent, the papacy wanted the convents to be completely private, accountable to the bishop, even cutting the nuns off from their families. Many local ecclesiastics, however, realized it was not that simple. To the nuns' families, and the external population, these convents were an extension of their own households and kinship networks; the community did not want public access shut off.

For both Protestants and Catholics the way to handle this ambiguous – and possibly threatening – female space was to bring these houses under complete male control. Control and obedience, to either lay or religious authorities, became the hallmark of female religious life in the sixteenth and seventeenth centuries. For active orders, it meant negotiating around enclosure; for the mystics, the suspicious eye of the Inquisition; for the contemplative nun, renewed surveillance and a stricter chain of command ending in the bishop; and for the nuns in Protestant lands, it meant closure or the complete submission to the political authority, at least theoretically. The ecclesiastical and political authorities, in surprisingly similar ways, took over the convents, revamped their finances, got rid of old superiors, hired their own preachers and confessors for the nuns, and carried out periodic spot checks and interrogations of the women. The voice of the nun was to be redirected and modulated through male representatives: father confessor, bishop, or convent administrator. Religious women's very thoughts had to be vetted through their guardians and spiritual advisers. This search for control was not unusual to the sixteenth century, but rather was a standard reaction to reform and upheaval. In times of crisis throughout history, the common response was to tighten the bonds of authority to bring about stability and order, often in gendered terms.

The role of gender in this story has already been mentioned. On the one hand, society's definition of a woman's role, its view of female sexuality, and the real fear of single women in both Protestant and Catholic countries led to an increasing restriction of women's movements through the attack on active orders and strict enclosure. On the other hand, women, because of their supposed weaknesses and constrained existence, could use these same gender stereotypes to play on society's assumptions and manipulate authorities to get what they wanted. In Catholic countries, women accused of demonic visions might not be punished as severely as men, since they were weaker creatures who were easily misled. Nuns in Germany could protest that they did not mean to ignore the new evangelical doctrine, but they were such ignorant creatures they did not understand the council's decrees. Gender was a fluid variable that could work both positively and negatively for women.

Finally, one should not downplay the empowering aspects of religion for women during this time. The Catholic Reformation sparked an increased participation in religious activity by women, both lay and religious, cloistered or not. Just as religious movements of the Middle Ages often appealed dramatically to women, so too the early Reformation years were noteworthy for the number of female adherents, within both the Protestant and Catholic movements. The active orders gave women from all classes acceptable public vocations, ones that continued in more secular forms (nursing and teaching) long after the religious reforms ended (Rapley, *Dévotes*; Conrad, *Zwischen Kloster und Welt*). Teresa of Avila was able to establish "feminine powerhouses" where women enjoyed authority and respect (Pérez-Romero, "Get Thee to a Nunnery,'" p. 296). The convent offered women an escape from marriage and a notably feminine space in which to practice their piety. Be it through an education, or as a professional musician, the cloister afforded women the opportunity for intellectual and artistic self-expression. Even enclosure can be seen as liberating, as it gave women spiritual independence and created a female space and community (Lierheimer, "Redefining Convent Space," p. 215). This empowerment argument should be carefully drawn, however. Did nuns themselves feel they had more independence and power in the convent? Were they discouraged by the restricted opportunities for women available outside? Religious women were usually silent on any gender motivations for their actions. We should also not overstate the idea of the convent as a space of autonomy, creativity, freedom, and female expression. Craig Harline and Judith Brown have both shown the less-than-spiritual nature of cloistered nuns, as the cloistered realm could also be a world of intrigue, gossip, backbiting, and competition (Harline, *Burdens of Sister Margaret*; Brown, *Immodest Acts*).

I have focused in this essay on similarities between female religious orders throughout Europe, and although I certainly do not mean to downplay the very real differences that existed geographically, religiously, and chronologically on all the issues raised here, I also would argue for an increased look across confessional lines. Traditionally, by the very nature of the topic, most of the work done on nuns focused on Catholic countries, the Catholic Reformation, and Trent. Only recently have historians of the Protestant Reformation begun their own analysis of these women, led in large part by Merry Wiesner's 1992 essay "Ideology Meets the Empire," which showed that, contrary to popular belief, monastic dissolution was not as widespread or completely successful as previously thought. But now the topic could be enriched by viewing the subject more cross-confessionally and opening a dialogue between the two "Reformations." What were the effects of the Council of Trent on nuns remaining in Protestant areas? How would they find out about the decrees? And what were the benefits and detriments of trying to follow them? For religious women in Catholic areas, how much of the changes affecting their life come from religious reformation and how much from forces beyond Catholicism and Protestantism? Often the experience of these women was more similar than different, from the desire to control their activities to debates over their role in early modern society, indicating something common to these societies that transcended religious confession. A few historians are crossing this religious divide (for example, Gabriella Zarri and Ulrike Strasser) to ask what changed in the religious landscape for both Catholics and Protestants, and why and how that had such profound effects on everyone, in particular religious women.

BIBLIOGRAPHY

Ahlgren, G. T. W., *Teresa of Avila and the Politics of Sanctity*. Ithaca, NY: Cornell University Press, 1996.

Bilinkoff, J., *The Avila of St. Theresa*. Cornell, NY: Cornell University Press, 1989.

Bilinkoff, J., "Teresa of Jesus and Carmelite Reform," in R. L. DeMolen and J. C. Olin, eds., *Religious Orders of the Catholic Reformation: In Honor of John C. Olin on his Seventy-Fifth Birthday*. New York: Fordham University Press, 1994, pp. 165–86.

Blaisdell, C. J., "Angela Merici and the Ursulines," in R. L. DeMolen and J. C. Olin, eds., *Religious Orders of the Catholic Reformation: In Honor of John C. Olin on his Seventy-Fifth Birthday*. New York: Fordham University Press, 1994, pp. 99–136.

Brown, J. C., *Immodest Acts: The Life of a Lesbian Nun in Renaissance Italy*. New York: Oxford University Press, 1986.

Conrad, A., *Zwischen Kloster und Welt: Ursulinen und Jesuitinnen in der katholischen Reformbewegung des 16./17. Jahrhunderts*. Mainz: Philipp von Zabern, 1991.

Cooke, K., "The English Nuns and the Dissolution," in B. F. Harvey, J. Blair, and B. Golding, eds., *The Cloister and the World: Essays in Medieval History in Honour of Barbara Harvey*. Oxford and New York: Clarendon Press, 1996, pp. 287–301.

Costa, M. O., "Spanish Women in the Reformation," in S. Marshall, ed., *Women in Reformation and Counter-Reformation Europe: Public and Private Worlds*. Bloomington: Indiana University Press, 1989, pp. 89–119.

Diefendorf, B. B., "Give Us Back Our Children: Patriarchal Authority and Parental Consent to Religious Vocations in Early Counter-Reformation France," *Journal of Modern History*, 68 (1996), pp. 265–307.

Dinan, S. E., "Confraternities as a Venue for Female Activism during the Catholic Reformation," in J. P. Donnelly and M. W. Maher, eds., *Confraternities and Catholic Reform in Italy, France, and Spain*. Kirksville, Mo.: Truman State University Press, 1999, pp. 191–214.

Donnelly, J. P., "The New Religious Orders, 1517–1648," in T. A. Brady, Jr., H. A. Oberman, and J. D. Tracy, eds., *Handbook of European History, 1400–1600: Late Middle Ages, Renaissance, and Reformation*. Grand Rapids, Mich.: Eerdmans, 1995, pp. 283–307.

Douglass, J. D., "Women and the Continental Reformation," in R. R. Ruether, ed., *Religion and Sexism*. New York: Simon & Schuster, 1974, pp. 292–318.

Evangelisti, S., "Wives, Widows, and the Brides of Christ: Marriage and the Convent in the Historiography of Early Modern Italy," *Historical Journal*, 43 (2000), pp. 233–47.

Evennett, H. O., *The Spirit of the Counter-Reformation*. Notre Dame and London: University of Notre Dame Press, 1968.

Harline, C., *The Burdens of Sister Margaret*. New York: Doubleday, 1994.

Harline, C., "Actives and Contemplatives: The Female Religious of the Low Countries Before and After Trent," *Catholic Historical Review*, 89 (1995), pp. 541–67.

Harrington, J. F., *Reordering Marriage and Society in Reformation Germany*. Cambridge: Cambridge University Press, 1995.

Hsia, R. P.-C., *Society and Religion in Münster, 1535–1618*. New Haven, Conn.: Yale University Press, 1984.

Hutchison, A. M., "Syon Abbey: Dissolution, No Decline," *Birgittiana*, 2 (1996), pp. 245–59.

Jussie, J. de, *Petite chronique*, ed. H. Feld. Mainz: Philipp von Zabern, 1996.

Klapisch-Zuber, C., "The Griselda Complex: Dowry and Marriage Gifts in the Quattrocento," in *Women, Family, and Ritual in Renaissance Italy*. Chicago: University of Chicago Press, 1985, pp. 213–46.

Leonard, A. E., " 'Nails in the Wall': Dominican Nuns in Reformation Strasbourg," PhD dissertation, University of California at Berkeley, 1999.

Lierheimer, L., "Redefining Convent Space: Ideals of Female Community among Seventeenth-Century Ursuline Nuns," *Proceedings of the Western Society for French History*, 24 (1997), pp. 211–20.

McNamara, J. A. K., *Sisters in Arms: Catholic Nuns through Two Millennia*. Cambridge, Mass.: Harvard University Press, 1996.

Marshall, S., "Protestant, Catholic, and Jewish Women in the Early Modern Netherlands," in S. Marshall, ed., *Women in Reformation and Counter-Reformation Europe: Public and Private Worlds*. Bloomington: Indiana University Press, 1989, pp. 120–39.

Monson, C. A., "Disembodied Voices: Music in the Nunneries of Bologna in the Midst of the Counter-Reformation," in C. A. Monson, ed., *The Crannied Wall: Women, Religion, and the Arts in Early Modern Europe*. Ann Arbor: University of Michigan Press, 1992, pp. 191–210.

Norberg, K., "The Counter-Reformation and Women Religious and Lay," in J. O'Malley, ed., *Catholicism in Early Modern History: A Guide to Research*. St. Louis, Mo.: Center for Reformation Research, 1988, pp. 133–46.

Ozment, S., *When Fathers Ruled: Family Life in Reformation Europe*. Cambridge, Mass.: Harvard University Press, 1983.

Pérez-Romero, A., " 'Get Thee to a Nunnery': Women's Empowerment in Golden Age Spain," *Bulletin of Hispanic Studies*, 75 (1998), pp. 293–316.

Pfanner, J., ed., *Die "Denkwürdigkeiten" der Abtissin Caritas Pirckheimer (aus den Jahren 1524–1528)*. Landshut: Solanus, 1962.

Rapley, E., *The Dévotes: Women and Church in Seventeenth-Century France*. Montreal and Buffalo: McGill-Queen's University Press, 1990.

Roper, L., *The Holy Household: Women and Morals in Reformation Augsburg*. Oxford: Clarendon Press, 1989.

Rowlands, M. B., "Recusant Women, 1560–1640," in M. Prior, ed., *Women in English Society, 1500–1800*. London, 1985, pp. 149–80.

Sperling, J., *Convents and the Body Politic in Late Renaissance Venice*. Chicago: University of Chicago Press, 1999.

Strasser, U., "Brides of Christ, Daughters of Men: Nuremberg Poor Clares in Defense of their Identity (1524–1529)," *Magistra*, 1 (1995), pp. 193–248.

Strasser, U., "Bones of Contention: Cloistered Nuns, Decorated Relics, and the Contest Over Women's Place in the Public Sphere of Counter-Reformation Munich," *Archiv für Reformationsgeschichte*, 90 (1999), pp. 255–88.

Tanner, N. P., ed., *Decrees of the Ecumenical Councils*. London and Washington, DC: Sheed & Ward and Georgetown University Press, 1990.

Walker, C., "Prayer, Patronage, and Political Conspiracy: English Nuns and the Restoration," *Historical Journal*, 43 (2000), pp. 1–23.

Warnicke, R., *Women of the English Renaissance and Reformation*. Westport, Conn.: Greenwood Press, 1983.

Weber, A., *Teresa of Avila and the Rhetoric of Femininity*. Princeton, NJ: Princeton University Press, 1990.

Wiesner, M. E., "Nuns, Wives, and Mothers: Women and the Reformation in Germany," in S. Marshall, ed., *Women in Reformation and Counter-Reformation Europe: Public and Private Worlds*. Bloomington: Indiana University Press, 1989, pp. 8–28.

Wiesner, M. E., "Ideology Meets the Empire: Reformed Convents and the Reformation," in A. C. Fix and S. C. Karant-Nunn, eds., *Germania Illustrata: Essays of Early Modern Germany Presented to Gerald Strauss*. Kirksville, Mo.: Sixteenth Century Journal, 1992, pp. 181–96.

Wright, W. M., "The Visitation of Holy Mary: The First Years (1610–1618)," in R. L. DeMolen and J. C. Olin, eds., *Religious Orders of the Catholic Reformation: In Honor of John C. Olin on his Seventy-Fifth Birthday*. New York: Fordham University Press, 1994, pp. 217–50.

Zarri, G., "From Prophecy to Discipline, 1450 to 1650," in L. Scaraffia and G. Zarri, eds., *Women and Faith: Catholic Religious Life in Italy from Late Antiquity to the Present*. Cambridge, Mass.: Harvard University Press, 1999, pp. 85–112.

FURTHER READING

For general works and bibliographic essays, see J. McNamara's impressive *Sisters in Arms*, S. Evangelisti, "Wives, Widows, and the Brides of Christ," and R. P.-C. Hsia, *The World of Catholic Renewal 1540–1770* (Cambridge: Cambridge University Press, 1998), chaps. 2 and 9. Although now over 30 years old, R. P. Liebowitz's "Virgins in the Service of Christ: The Dispute Over an Active Apostolate for Women During the Counter-Reformation," in R. Ruether and E. McLaughlin, eds., *Women of Spirit: Female Leadership in the Jewish and Christian Traditions* (New York: Simon & Schuster, 1979), pp. 131–52, still provides a good entry into this subject. Much of Gabriella Zarri's important work has now been translated into English, including "Gender, Religious Institutions and Social Discipline: The Reform of the Regulars," in J. C. Brown and R. C. Davis, eds., *Gender and Society in Renaissance Italy* (London and New York: Routledge, 1998) and "From Prophecy to Discipline, 1450 to 1650." M. E. Wiesner looks at both Protestant and Catholic territories in *Women and Gender in Early Modern Europe*, 2nd ed. (Cambridge: Cambridge University Press, 2000), chap. 6, and addresses nuns specifically in the introduction to *Convents Confront the Reformation: Catholic and Protestant Nuns in Germany*, trans. and ed. J. Skocir and M. Wiesner-Hanks (Milwaukee: Marquette University Press, 1996), a translated collection of German nuns' letters.

On enclosure see E. M. Makowski, *Canon Law and Cloistered Women: Periculoso and its Commentators, 1298–1545* (Washington, DC: Catholic University of America Press, 1997) for a compelling reading of theological debates for the period preceding Trent, and Jutta Sperling's chapter on enclosure in *Convents and the Body Politic in Late Renaissance Venice*. P. R. Baernstein, *A Convent Tale: A Century of Sisterhood in Spanish Milan* (New York: Routledge, 2002), E. A. Lehfeldt, "Discipline, Vocation and Patronage: Spanish Religious Women in a Tridentine Microclimate," *Sixteenth Century Journal*, 30 (1999), pp. 1009–30, and U. Strasser, "Bones of Contention," study the varying degrees to which enclosure was followed.

A fast-growing field of study within the topic of female religious orders focuses on the arts, particularly within Italy. See R. L. Kendrick, *Celestial Sirens: Nuns and their Music in Early*

Modern Milan (Oxford: Clarendon Press, 1996), E. A. Matter and J. Coakley, eds., *Creative Women in Medieval and Early Modern Italy: A Religious and Artistic Renaissance* (Philadelphia: University of Pennsylvania Press, 1994), and C. Monson, ed., *The Crannied Wall*.

On the debate between active and contemplative orders, and the role of women within them, one should start with C. Harline, "Actives and Contemplatives," for a clear overview of the issues. Both E. Rapley, *Dévotes*, and A. Conrad, *Zwischen Kloster und Welt*, address women's active participation in religious movements of the early modern period, and Conrad is particularly useful for her geographical breadth. For a very useful summary of the new orders of the Catholic Reformation and their founders, see R. L. DeMolen and J. C. Olin, eds., *Religious Orders of the Catholic Reformation*, especially J. Bilinkoff's contribution, "Teresa of Jesus and Carmelite Reform," which has a thorough bibliography at the end. On the unique case of the Daughters of Charity, see S. E. Dinan, "Confraternities as a Venue for Female Activism," and Dinan, "Spheres of Female Religious Expression in Early Modern France," in S. E. Dinan and D. Meyers, eds., *Women and Religion in New and Old Worlds* (New York: Routledge, 2001).

Work on female religious orders in Protestant countries still tends to focus on dissolution rather than resistance or survival, with more work done on England. A great overview of the classic literature for England can be found in K. Cooke, "English Nuns and the Dissolution." Two works that do look beyond dissolution include B. Hill, "A Refuge from Men: The Idea of a Protestant Nunnery," *Past and Present*, 117 (1987), pp. 107–30, which shows how convents could still be useful as schools, and A. M. Hutchison, "Syon Abbey," outlining the trials of the Brigittine nuns.

Within Germany, the field is still relatively young. M. E. Wiesner's "Ideology Meets the Empire" provides essential reading on the theme of resistance and survival of nuns during the Reformation in central Germany, and the articles of M. Jung, in *Nonnen, Prophetinnen, Kirchenmütter: Kirchen- und frömmigkeitsgeschichtliche Studien zu Frauen der Reformationszeit* (Leipzig: Evangelische Verlagsanstalt, 2002), give a good overview. There is also much work on Caritas Pirckheimer, the best-known opponent of the Protestant Reformation, although we badly need a translation of the Nuremberg Poor Clare house memoir, the *Denkwürdigkeiten*. See further P. D. Barker, "Caritas Pirckheimer: A Female Humanist Confronts the Renaissance," *Sixteenth Century Journal*, 26 (1995), pp. 259–72, G. Krabbel, *Caritas Pirckheimer: Ein Lebensbild aus der Zeit der Reformation* (Münster: Aschendorff, 1982), and U. Strasser, "Brides of Christ, Daughters of Men." For examples of the Reformation and religious women in other cities of the empire, see A. E. Leonard, "'Nails in the Wall,'" D. J. Grieser, "A Tale of Two Convents: Nuns and Anabaptists in Münster, 1533–1535," *Sixteenth Century Journal*, 26 (1995), pp. 31–47, and L. Roper, *The Holy Household*. Ulrike Strasser is one of the few historians looking at both the Protestant and Catholic Reformations in Germany, and her forthcoming book, *State of Virginity: Gender, Politics and Religion in Early Modern Germany* (Ann Arbor: University of Michigan Press, 2003), will fill a great need.

Sixteen

The Inquisition

William Monter

In 1970, studying the Spanish, Roman, or Portuguese Inquisitions seemed the epitome of futility. It appeared to be a battlefield of antiquated polemics; a more complete dialogue of the deaf would be difficult to imagine. On one side stood a few besieged clerics, principally in the Vatican, assisted by collaborators from the reactionary and repressive regimes of Salazar's Portugal or Franco's Spain, holding positions which everyone else considered hopelessly outdated. On the other side stood noisy critics from liberal democracies, whose vehement condemnations of an antique nemesis were nearly always accompanied by complete ignorance of the original source materials, with the possible exception of Henry Charles Lea's four-volume anticlerical history of the Spanish Inquisition, which had been researched in the nineteenth century and published before World War I. Because the Vatican had always carefully guarded the archives of the Roman Inquisition against potentially hostile investigators, very little could be learned about its operations; apart from a few well-known cases, above all the records of Galileo's trial and condemnation in 1633, almost nothing was available in print. In 1965, a tiny oasis of modern scholarship appeared with Henry Kamen's pithy revisionist synthesis of the Spanish Inquisition. This noteworthy attempt, based on a reworking of available printed sources, subsequently translated into nearly a dozen different languages and revised twice (in 1985 and 1997), had the merit of introducing the oldest and largest of the modern Catholic Inquisitions to a contemporary audience without demonizing it.

Meanwhile, around 1970 a few pioneers were quietly laying the groundwork for reopening the scholarly study of these venerable symbols of doctrinal intolerance and bloody repression. With the wisdom of hindsight, we can identify John Tedeschi's article on "The Dispersed Archives of the Roman Inquisition," published in Italian in 1973, as truly pathbreaking.[1] It told potential historians of the Roman Inquisition what records were available, surveying all its known original documents preserved outside the Vatican (Dublin held the most important collection). Even more importantly, however, Tedeschi explained how much they would never be able to use, because nearly all of the original trials of the Roman Holy Office had been destroyed – first by a Roman mob celebrating the death of an unpopular pope in 1559, then in 1815 by Vatican officials unable to pay the cost of returning thousands of trials to Rome after Napoleon had carted them off to Paris. Even if the Vatican opened its secret inquisitorial archive to outsiders, Tedeschi predicted, they would find relatively few hidden riches. A quarter-century later, this sobering appraisal proved to be basically correct after the Roman Inquisition archives were suddenly opened. In the meantime, it has served as a cautionary reminder to potential investigators that any scholarly work on the Roman Inquisition must proceed on a base of original information which is both widely scattered and highly incomplete when compared to the volume of source material available from the central archives of the Spanish or Portuguese Inquisitions.

While Tedeschi, an Italian-born American, was outlining the single greatest problem facing potential historians of the Roman Inquisition, his Danish friend Gustav Henningsen was starting to explore the diametrically opposite problem facing contemporary historians of the Spanish Inquisition: a superabundance of information about its original trials. Despite assurances from his Spanish colleagues that most of the documentation left by Spain's Holy Office had been destroyed during the Napoleonic Wars, Henningsen found that, although most of the original records from its 20 branches had indeed perished, the central archive of the Spanish Inquisition had been preserved essentially intact within a special section of Spain's national historical archives. This discovery has finally permitted the present generation of Spanish Inquisition scholars to move beyond the remarkable achievement of Lea, who compiled an amazingly accurate synthesis without ever visiting Spain. As Henningsen has pointed out ("Database," p. 50), "the series of correspondence – in both directions – between the central body, *la Suprema*, and all the branch tribunals makes it possible to write the history of the Holy Office in the entire Spanish empire in spite of the almost systematic destruction of the tribunal's [branch] archives."

Trained as a folklorist and interested primarily in the problem of how the Spanish Inquisition treated witchcraft, Henningsen decided to plunge into this sea of documentation by concentrating on the central registers of case summaries, known as *relaciones de causas*, usually sent annually by each branch tribunal after the mid-sixteenth century. In the autumn of 1971, Henningsen began developing a method of analyzing and exploiting this huge "data bank" of the Spanish Inquisition. Subsidized by funding from Denmark, he hired a young Spanish historian, Jaime Contreras; after two years, they had inventoried about 25,000 cases. In 1975, a young French historian, Jean-Pierre Dedieu, preparing a doctoral thesis on the tribunal of Toledo, adopted their method and contributed over 4,000 *relaciones* to their project. By the end of 1977, this embryonic multinational collaboration had created about 42,000 handwritten cards, which they began sorting out in order to produce a preliminary statistical profile of the global activities of the Spanish Inquisition across the century and a half after 1550. Publications of their results began with Henningsen's pathbreaking article in 1977 ("Banco de datos"), followed by Dedieu's in 1978 ("Causes de foi").

By the mid-1970s, while the Salazar regime finally collapsed in Portugal and Franco finally died in Spain, historians from places as distant as Chicago and Copenhagen had quietly laid the groundwork for fundamental reassessments of the major modern Inquisitions. Because of the enormous discrepancy in the nature of the available source materials, the "Roman road" followed by historians of Italy would necessarily differ greatly from the "Spanish road" mapped out by Henningsen and Contreras, nearly as much as St. Peter's differs from Santiago de Compostela. To oversimplify, one could argue that studies on the Roman Inquisition during the past quarter-century have been most remarkable for their analytical depth, while historians of the Spanish Inquisition have often featured either chronological or geographical breadth. Let us begin by assessing recent developments in each of the three great modern Inquisitions, starting with the oldest, created by papal fiat in 1478 for Spain's "Catholic monarchs," Ferdinand and Isabella.

The "Boom Cycle" of the Spanish Inquisition

Not everything novel and significant which has been published about the Spanish Inquisition since the early 1970s has been connected to the Henningsen and Contreras rediscovery of its *relaciones de causas*. Two important projects which began publication well before the various commemorations of the 500th anniversary of the Spanish Inquisition in 1978 were completely independent, both of this project and of each other. One was undertaken by a young scholar in Spain, the other by a senior expert in Israel. Both, begun in the early 1970s and completed after 1980, were based on extensive research in the early archives of Spain's Holy Office, the period preceding the system of *relaciones*. Haim Beinart, continuing a Jewish tradition of investigating the early persecution of Sephardic "New Christians" by Spain's Holy Office, produced a critical edition of its first trials from Ciudad Real, providing our most minutely detailed introduction to its earliest operations in the heart of Castile. Meanwhile, Ricardo García Cárcel explored the considerable materials available in Valencia to produce our first well-documented portrait of the early workings of an Inquisition tribunal in Ferdinand's hereditary lands. His first volume (*Orígines de la Inquisición española*) ended in 1530, a period when "Judaizers" comprised nearly all of the Holy Office's victims; its sequel (*Herejía y sociedad*) continued this tribunal's history during a very different phase, ending with the expulsion of Valencia's Moriscos.

Despite the spate of publications in 1992 commemorating the 500th anniversary of the expulsions of Spanish Jews, relatively little important work about the early workings of the Spanish Inquisition – its bloodiest period, and a time when "Judaizers" virtually monopolized its attention – has appeared since 1980. Even less has appeared about the last century of the Spanish Inquisition, which was abolished three separate times beginning in 1808. During recent decades, research has instead concentrated on its quite different history across the intermediate century and a half when the system of *relaciones de causas* enables scholars to observe its operations from Madrid to Lima with unparalleled breadth and depth. This reorientation was already evident at the two very different international congresses held in 1978 to mark the 500th anniversary of its creation. The Spanish meeting proudly hailed the new approaches and new horizons of inquisitorial research in a post-Franco, "transitional" Spain, while a smaller but more international Danish meeting featured the provisional results of the *relaciones de causas* project. The proceedings from the Spanish congress (Pérez Villaneuva, *Inquisición Española*) appeared long before those from the Copenhagen congress (Henningsen and Tedeschi, *Inquisition in Early Modern Europe*).

The delicate balance between Spaniards and foreigners in Inquisition research, clearly revealed in 1978, soon led to frustrating consequences. On the one hand, the first concrete use of the almost complete Henningsen-Contreras data came in a preliminary but dazzling reinterpretation of Spain's Holy Office published in France (Bennassar, *Inquisition espagnole*), featuring several essays by their French collaborator J. P. Dedieu. Recalling the late 1970s as a period "borne by great enthusiasm," Henningsen ("Database," p. 54) recounted an abortive attempt to create a major international program on the Inquisitions of Spain, Italy, and Portugal under the aegis of the multinationally funded European Science Foundation (ESF). At a preliminary 1980 meeting in the Paris offices of a high-ranking Portuguese ESF official, the proposal was vetoed by the invited Spanish representative, whose recently created Center for Inquisitorial Studies was busily planning a new general history of the Spanish Inquisition in Europe and America written entirely by Spaniards (its first volume, 1,500 pages long, appeared in 1984). One consequence of this decision is that scholars still lack an online version of the Spanish *relaciones de causas* project, let alone any parallel projects from Portugal or Italy.

Nevertheless, Henningsen's recollection of "great enthusiasm" for studying the Spanish Inquisition around 1980 seems fully justified. While Spain established itself as a European parliamentary democracy and prepared to join the European Community, scholarly optimism spawned numerous Inquisition congresses both inside and outside Spain. A cluster of important new publications began in 1980 with Henningsen's investigation of the Spanish Holy Office's relatively enlightened attitudes about witchcraft, particularly evident in the Basque lands. In 1982, Contreras, his young Spanish collaborator, published a pathbreaking doctoral thesis on the remote northwestern tribunal of Santiago de Compostela, founded after the system of *relaciones de causas* was operative. Other Spaniards soon contributed an innovative study of early inquisitorial censorship (Pinto Crespo, *Inquisición y control ideologico*) and an examination of its workings in the Basque lands (Reguera, *Inquisición española*). French contributions, often published in Spain, filled the later 1980s, including the first investigation of the Inquisition's prosecution of homosexuals (Carrasco, *Inquisición y repression sexual*), innovative studies of Spain's Morisco minority (Vincent, *Minorias y marginados*), and an exemplary monograph on the tribunal of Toledo, providing our best available portrait of any individual tribunal (Dedieu, *Administration de la foi*). While Europeans provided useful studies of Spain's American tribunals (Alberro, *Inquisición y sociedad*; Castañeda and Hernández, *Inquisición de Lima*), Americans finally joined this "Spanish renaissance" with two English-language monographs on the Holy Office in the crown of Aragon (Haliczer, *Inquisition and Society*; Monter, *Frontiers of Heresy*), and a case study of the Inquisition's role in controlling popular prophecy and Castilian political opposition under Philip II (Kagan, *Lucrezia's Dreams*).

Significant Spanish contributions continued, including a study of inquisitorial censorship of scientific works (Pardo Tomás, *Ciencia y censura*). In the Canary Islands, Fajardo (*Hechicería y brujería*) used a unique source – more than 6,000 original denunciations made to the Inquisition between 1499 and 1714 – to study illicit magic and witchcraft (the basic charge in almost half of them), providing an interesting counterpart to Henningsen's earlier work. Meanwhile, Contreras (*Sotos contra Riquelmes*) exploited inquisitorial sources to reinterpret its last major persecution of

Castilian "Judaizers," which cost at least 165 lives in Murcia and Lorca between 1550 and 1570, as an unusually savage battle for local political power between rival factions, thereby dramatically and persuasively illustrating Kamen's argument that the Spanish Inquisition must be understood in the context of Spanish society while simultaneously providing our most important recent investigation of the Inquisition's original target, the *judeoconversos*. However, despite a few noteworthy exceptions (Haliczer, *Sex in the Confessional*; Nalle, *Mad for God*), this remarkable multinational renaissance of Spanish Inquisition scholarship seems to have slowed somewhat in the years since the second thick volume of the all-Spanish general history of the Spanish and American Holy Office appeared in 1993.

The Roman Inquisition

Aside from the fact that its records seem relatively sparse and widely scattered, as Tedeschi pointed out long ago, there are several reasons why no comparable surge of recent international scholarship has studied the modern Roman Inquisition. If Italian ecclesiastical historians have generally investigated less sinister aspects of the Catholic Reformation, foreign experts have usually preferred the Venetian or Florentine twilight of the Italian Renaissance to the subsequent, largely forgotten, centuries. Moreover, the Vatican's permanent Holy Office, founded in 1542, has remained a mysterious institution: supposedly it had been discontinued (or at least, it had been renamed in the mid-1960s), but no death certificate has ever been issued. Above all, its central archive has remained closed to outsiders until very recently.

Perhaps this relative scarcity of available evidence has been a blessing in disguise. Unlike scholars working on the Iberian Inquisitions, Roman Inquisition experts rarely worry about issues of breadth versus depth; in Italy, the case study virtually monopolizes scholarship. The proof for this proposition is in the pudding: while the boom cycle of Spanish Inquisition scholarship has encouraged general reinterpretations – Kamen, for example, has updated his 1965 overview twice,[2] and the Spaniards themselves have produced a truly massive synthesis – no general interpretation of the Roman Inquisition has appeared recently. Italian and foreign experts have held their own preparatory congresses (Rome 1981, Trieste 1988, Vatican City 1998) and published most of the results (contributions to the first congress appeared between 1983 and 1986 in the *Annuario dell'Istituto Storico Italiano per l'Età Moderna e Contemporanea*; Del Col and Paolin, *Inquisizione romano*; proceedings from the Vatican conference will appear soon). However, none of this work has yet produced either an individual or a collective attempt at synthesis; the apparent exception (Canosa, *Storia dell'Inquisizione in Italia*) does not claim to be a history of the Roman Inquisition but consists instead of numerous regional monographs.

Given the constraints under which Roman Inquisition specialists have labored, they can boast some remarkable recent achievements. If the in-depth case study is necessarily their forte, they have sometimes manipulated it with extraordinary brio. Two very different but equally outstanding examples come immediately to mind: Carlo Ginzburg's brief but dense examination of the mental universe of a Friulian miller condemned to death by the Roman Inquisition in 1599 (*Cheese and Worms*) and Massimo Firpo's multi-volume critical edition of the trial of Cardinal Morone (Firpo and Marcatto, *Processo inquisitoriale*). In the mid-1970s, while the "Spanish renaissance" gained momentum, Ginzburg produced the best example of "victim-based" inquisitorial history (a problem to which we shall return) while simultane-ously creating the prototype for the current fashion of microhistory. Shortly thereafter, Firpo began the reverse process of collecting all available evidence about one major early inquisitorial trial, pregnant with consequences for the sixteenth-century Catholic Reformation; after publishing five volumes, he and his collaborator Dario Marcatto finally obtained access to archival information from the institution which had conducted the original trial. Morone is not the only celebrity to benefit from recent scholarship; the Vatican has sponsored a critical edition of Galileo's fateful 1633 trial (Pagano, *Documenti del processo*), subsequently complemented by newly discovered information about his earliest brush with the Roman Inquisition in Venice (Poppi, *Cremonini e Galilei*). The once-obscure Menocchio, today a different kind of celebrity, has also received a critical edition of his two inquisitorial trials (Del Col, *Domenico Scandella*).

Many useful local monographs have been drawn from two dozen (mostly ecclesi-astical) Italian archives, scattered from Calabria to the Friuli, which are known to preserve sizable bodies of evidence about the Roman Inquisition. Regional studies of good quality abound, with clusters most evident in the Venetian Republic and Naples, but some of the richest work originating in such unexpected places as Capua (Scaramella, *"Con la Croce al core"*). Because the Roman Inquisition has had no readily accessible central archive, these various case studies, microhistories, and local accounts have seldom been able to incorporate a central Roman perspective – although few European institutions of this period were better centralized than the papacy. Unlike recent work on the Spanish Inquisition, only a handful of non-Italian Europeans have helped investigate the Roman Inquisition; as with Spain's Holy Office, North American scholarship, like John Martin's study of "Lutherans" pursued by the Venetian Holy Office (Martin, *Venice's Hidden Enemies*), is visible without being truly prominent. This situation is mildly ironic in a world where English has become the hegemonic scholarly language and Italian a relatively periph-eral one even in Europe, and where a majority of the world's Catholics now live in the Americas.

One important and closely related area, finally opened to outside investigators in 1998, holds enormous promise for international scholarship on European intellec-tual history. The virtually complete archives of the Vatican's Congregation of the Index are housed in the old *palazzo* of the Roman Holy Office, alongside those from the Congregation of the Inquisition: one created censorship policy, the other imple-mented it.[3] Papal censorship, a cornerstone of Tridentine Catholicism, exercised an influence far beyond the Italian peninsula, because Rome's censors had more com-plete information and more international resonance than their Iberian or Transalpine counterparts. Recent assessments of Italian inquisitorial enforcement of censorship began with Paul Grendler's optimistic investigation of its weaknesses at Venice (*Roman Inquisition*); however, subsequent studies of Italian censorship of Erasmus (Seidel Menchi, *Erasmo in Italia*), and especially Gigliola Fragnita's recent survey of early papal censorship of vernacular Bibles (Fragnita, *Bibbia al rogo*), have generally claimed that it was relatively thorough and effective. With the complete archives of the Roman Index to browse in, it seems safe to predict that Italian-based scholarship on censorship will increase exponentially in coming decades, becoming the next "growth sector" of Inquisition-related studies. Indeed, it has already begun (see Godman, *Saint as Censor*).

Portugal's Holy Office

By any standards one cares to employ, recent study of the third great Inquisition of early modern Europe has lagged far behind the other two. Its archival riches, largely complete and centralized in Portugal's national repository, closely resemble those of Spain. Its recent history closely resembles Spain's; after emerging from antiquated dictatorships, both nations joined the European Community at the same moment. However, its first international inquisitorial congress, co-sponsored by Portugal and Brazil, was not held until 14 years after Spain's and a decade after Italy's. Although its most controversial revisionist study (Saraiva, *Inquisição e critãos novos*) predated the 1974 revolution, and a sketch of its long-term quantitative history (Veiga Torres, "Uma longua Guerra social") appeared shortly after Henningsen described the Spanish "data bank," the first significant monograph drawn from Portuguese inquisitorial sources (Bethencourt, *Imagináro da magia*) appeared long after its Spanish or Italian counterparts. It seems more than coincidental that this study, like Ginzburg's original encounters with inquisitorial archives in northeastern Italy or Henningsen's in northern Spain, was driven by curiosity about the history of witchcraft. Indeed, this dynamic still seems to be operating with respect to the first monograph using inquisitorial trials discovered in the Roman Inquisition's recently opened central archive (Di Simplicio, *Inquisizione Stregoneria Medicina*).

Despite – or perhaps because of – its archival riches, the Portuguese Inquisition has generated much less recent scholarship than its Spanish or Roman counterparts. Its best-known expert, Francisco Bethencourt, admits that Portugal lacks a detailed modern synthesis of its Inquisition. While Portuguese projects have been announced and begun long ago to create inventories and research tools suitable for contemporary international scholarship, nothing concrete has yet appeared. Although a few noteworthy monographs exist (Paiva, *Bruxaria e superstição*), Portugal lags as far behind Italy in the riches of inquisitorial-based microhistory and local studies as it does behind Spain in the exploitation of quantitative data or the production of monographs on individual tribunals, and it lags behind both in attracting foreign scholars. The exception confirms the rule. Only in one specialized area, that of producing a critical edition of a famous account by an ex-prisoner of its Holy Office (Amiel, *Relation de l'Inquisition de Goa*), can Portugal claim scholarly priority over Italy or Spain – and both editor and the seventeenth-century prisoner are French.

Cross-Comparisons

Understandably, very few scholars have attempted archivally based investigations of problems affecting all three major Inquisitions. In fact, only two such enterprises have been undertaken before the Roman archives were officially opened in 1998. One (Bennassar and Bennassar, *Chrétiens d'Allah*) examined more than 1,000 inquisitorial trials of "renegades," baptized Christians (including many Greek Orthodox and Protestants, whose baptisms Rome accepted as valid) who had more or less voluntarily converted to Islam throughout the Mediterranean basin during the sixteenth and seventeenth centuries, subsequently returning to Christian territory and therefore to arrest and judgment as apostates by inquisitors from all three systems. The other (Bethencourt, *Inquisition à l'époque moderne*), a more comprehensive institutional comparison of all three systems, deploying almost every type of evidence except the original trials, is truly a product of the European Community, done in French by a Portuguese citizen as a thesis for an Italian-based university. It not only provides our best available current synthesis of how all three Inquisitions actually functioned in early modern Europe, but also includes our best available introduction to the workings of Portugal's Holy Office.

This comparative institutional synthesis, fortified by careful attention to long-term patterns of trials (summarized rapidly as the best-known aspect of his subject), therefore provides a springboard for the following generalizations. The order of presentation in Bethencourt's title – Spain, Portugal, Italy – not only reflects their respective dates of creation (1478, 1536, 1542), but also describes our relative level of information about their primary common activity, the detection and punishment of heretics. Given their fragmentary, discontinuous, and sometimes inaccessible sources, scholars of the Roman Inquisition, unlike experts on Spain or Portugal, have been understandably reluctant to create statistical series about its operations, thereby making comparisons of its trials with those of its older Iberian counterparts difficult; a pioneering attempt by John Tedeschi and myself (in Henningsen and Tedeschi, *Inquisition in Early Modern Europe*), revised by Tedeschi for the 1997 Italian version of his collected essays, remains controversial and isolated.

Nevertheless, several relatively non-controversial generalizations can be made among all three. In the first place, it seems clear that both in their organization and their primary purpose, the Spanish and Portuguese Inquisitions resembled each other far more closely than either of them resembled the Roman Inquisition. Both Iberian institutions were essentially state-run bureaucracies – in fact, royal councils – staffed mainly by men trained in canon law, operating under papal charter but normally completely independent of Roman influence. Both had been created in order to combat "Judaizers," the persistence of specifically Jewish beliefs and practices among a population of "New Christians" whose ancestors had accepted baptism for a variety of motives. (Indeed, many Portuguese "New Christians" had fled Spain in 1492 and were forcibly baptized in Lisbon a few years later.) Portugal differed from Spain because it had no significant minority of baptized Muslims, another type of "New Christian" who became a second major target of the Spanish Inquisition by the mid-sixteenth century.

Meanwhile, the Italian peninsula, including Rome, continued to permit Jewish worship; the handful of "Judaizers" among its "New Christian" population (Pullan, *Inquisition of Venice*) were at most a peripheral problem, while baptized Muslims posed no problem at all. The Roman Inquisition had instead been created to deal with the growth of Protestantism, or "Lutheranism," among Italy's "Old Christian" population; this problem affected Spain only very briefly around 1560, and Portugal scarcely at all. Even in the Italian peninsula, however, "Lutheranism" never posed a significant political threat, and most experts agree that Italy's Protestant movement was moribund by 1570. It is therefore not surprising that, with its most dangerous problem eliminated relatively quickly, the Roman Inquisition seems far less bloodthirsty than either of its Iberian cousins, who continued to execute "Judaizers" for heresy well into the eighteenth century.

Although Portugal's Inquisition continued to prosecute large numbers of "Judaizers" throughout its existence, both the Spanish and Roman Holy Office spent most of their energy after the Council of Trent in prosecuting lesser forms of heresy among ordinary "Old Christians." While all three Inquisitions investigated cases of heretical blasphemy, the Italian tribunals seem to have devoted proportionately more time than their Iberian cousins to investigating cases of "superstition" and illicit magical practices; under Philip II, the Castilians concentrated instead on correcting common misconceptions about the sinfulness of fornication. It is also noteworthy that both Iberian Inquisitions, hybrid tribunals dealing with "mixed" crimes that were both ecclesiastical and secular, prosecuted numerous cases of bigamy and homosexual "sodomy."

The Roman Inquisition resists generalizations – less because of the long-maintained secrecy and serious incompleteness of its central archives than because of the political fragmentation of early modern Italy, so unlike the unified Spanish and Portuguese monarchies. The pope was both the unchallenged head of Catholicism and the political ruler of part of Italy – but only a part. Although the Roman Inquisition contained almost twice as many tribunals as its two Iberian counterparts combined, its authority was far less than theirs outside the Papal States. Italian experts agree that (omitting the islands of Sicily and Sardinia, which belonged to the Spanish Inquisition) its authority was weakest at Venice and in the lands of the Venetian Republic. They are uncertain how to classify its standing in the remainder of Italy, although they know that it occupied a significantly different status in the southern Kingdom of Naples than it did anywhere in north-central Italy, where its exact situation varied somewhat in each polity. At a minimum, therefore, one must split the Roman Inquisition into four zones of influence, the last of which is both intermediate and miscellaneous. The key difference is that it was heterogeneous, whereas its Iberian cousins seem relatively homogeneous; even in the Crown of Aragon, local privileges or *fueros* interfered with its operations only sporadically and tangentially.

Compared with its older Iberian cousins, the Roman Inquisition seems institutionally underdeveloped. As Bethencourt noted (*Inquisition à l'époque moderne*, p. 94), the Holy Office of Italy, unlike its Iberian predecessors, never developed an autonomous system of emblems. Italian inquisitors, unlike those of Spain or Portugal, never visited their territories; compared to Iberian inquisitors, they were installed with minimal pomp, had smaller budgets, and supervised smaller staffs. Their repressive activities were less public: the closest approximation to an Iberian-style *auto-da-fé* in Italy occurred at Rome, under a Spanish pope, long before the Roman Inquisition was founded (ibid., p. 308). Italian inquisitors were always Dominican or Franciscan monks who could scarcely imagine promotion to their organization's governing board or Congregation, composed entirely of cardinals; Iberian inquisitors, mostly clerics trained in canon law, had a good chance of promotion to the governing boards of their respective national Holy Offices and of serving their respective royal governments in different capacities. In all three systems, a successful inquisitor in a significant location had some chance (about one in five) of becoming a bishop (ibid., pp. 119, 130–1, 139–41).

Italian scholars (Prosperi, *Tribunali della coscienza*; Brambilla, *Alle origini del Sant'Uffizio*) have recently insisted that, although the Roman Inquisition punished relatively few heretics in public spectacles, it was every bit as effective as its Iberian cousins in stifling religious dissent. They suggest that Tridentine Italy's peculiarly dense horizontal network of incrimination, making private confession and sacramental absolution dependent upon denunciation of religious nonconformity and therefore making all parish priests into agents of the Holy Office, bypassed any need for dramatic public executions in coercing ordinary Christians into thoroughgoing conformity. In this view, Italy's private style of punishment made denunciation – and the ultimate achievement of religious orthodoxy – easier than in the Iberian peninsula.

"Victim-Based" and "Internalist" Approaches

An enduring scholarly tension exists between authors primarily concerned with the major Inquisitions as loci of persecution, preoccupied by the beliefs and fate of the prisoners, and a minority of scholars with the reverse set of priorities, interested primarily in their institutional history and internal operations. The first and larger groups, whose roots go back to the sixteenth century, are outsiders, both metaphorically and literally. Collectively, they have created and maintained what modern scholarship has labeled the "black legend" of the Inquisition. But, as Bethencourt pointed out, the inquisitors themselves simultaneously built a sort of "white legend" celebrating their successful struggle to suppress heresy in southern Europe. This insider's vantage point, depicting the various Holy Offices as valiant defenders of besieged fortresses, has been reshaped by some recent scholars interested in them primarily as successful examples of early modern bureaucracies. It is relatively rare even today to find Inquisition experts who can engage emphatically with both historiographical traditions.

The "victim-based" school is united only in what it opposes. The major modern Inquisitions arrested thousands of people from very different religious traditions, as well as thousands of otherwise orthodox Catholics charged with such offenses as bigamy, superstition, or even sodomy. Scholarship emanating from each group of inquisitorial victims has been remarkably different. Representatives of the three major heresies attacked by the Holy Office – Jews, Muslims, Protestants – have responded to their respective persecutions in radically different ways. Moreover, there has been no ecumenicism in "victim-based" inquisitorial scholarship, because each major religious group cherishes and investigates its own martyrs exclusively. Of course, most other groups of inquisitorial prisoners outside the major heresies (for example those accused of bigamy, blasphemy, or bestiality) have yet to be defended posthumously, with the possible exception of accused witches and homosexuals.

"New Christians" of Jewish ancestry were originally the only target of the Spanish Inquisition, and remained the only important targets of the Portuguese Holy Office for two and a half centuries. However, Jews were long unable to attack the Iberian Inquisitions publicly; because the Ottoman Empire, where they enjoyed their greatest liberty, abhorred the printing press, the first printed account from a former prisoner accused of "Judaism" appeared (in English, and anonymously) only in 1713. Meanwhile, Sephardic "New Christians" composed many memoranda to the papacy against the injustices inflicted on them by both Iberian Inquisitions and even found a few Catholic defenders among seventeenth-century Portuguese Jesuits. Modern European Jewish scholarship has compensated for this long clandestinity with numerous publications on the early Spanish Inquisition. However, this topic remains highly polemical, long after Spanish Catholics of the post-Franco era have abandoned all public vestiges of anti-Semitism, because of a specifically Jewish and Zionist issue: were the Sephardic victims of the early Spanish Inquisition authentically Jewish? The dilemma for Jewish scholarship is precisely the reliability of the masses of information left behind by Torquemada's Holy Office; in order to place these *judeoconverso* martyrs within the long "lachrymose tradition" of Jewish history, one must accept all the information provided by the Spanish Inquisition as unvarnished truth, ignoring evidence both from assimilated Spanish *judeoconversos*, who considered their unfortunate kinsmen to be observant Christians, and from North African Sephardic rabbis, who shunned them as apostates.[4]

Muslim scholars, heirs of the second great religious tradition which the Spanish Inquisition attempted to eradicate, have traditionally shown little interest in exploring its records. Although a few Spaniards have enriched our knowledge of this subject, most recent experts who have investigated Holy Office policy toward Islam have been French; one in particular, the Bennassars' examination of Christian "renegades" to Islam across the northern half of Braudel's "Mediterranean world," examines its appeal to sixteenth-century Christians, Orthodox and Protestants as well as Catholics. Muslims have therefore left their history as victims of the Inquisitions to outsiders, who generally ignore Islamic archives. Protestantism, the third major heresy attacked by the three modern Inquisitions, struck back from the very beginning of persecution with effective use of printed rebuttals, including detailed accounts of its secretive procedures by former prisoners. Protestant scholarship, from Henry Charles Lea onwards, has been in the forefront of foreign investigations into inquisitorial history and remains visible even today.

Outside these major religious traditions, few other groups have investigated inquisitorial treatment of their historical ancestors. Current American feminist scholarship, for example, has encountered the Holy Office only quite recently and relatively tangentially. Although these clerical institutions displayed considerable condescension toward women who appeared before them and would therefore seem promising targets for feminists, most of the thousands of Jewish and Muslim "New Christian" women whom they punished were perpetuating private religious rituals in domestic contexts rather than exercising public agency, so feminist scholars have showed little interest in studying them. When confronted with the more individualistic and basically female offense of witchcraft, these Inquisitions usually behaved with unexpected gentleness. However, one vector of Holy Office activity has been privileged by feminist scholarship. Following Anne Schutte's case study of a woman prosecuted by the Roman Inquisition for "fictitious sanctity," largely based on her claims about having supernatural visions (Schutte, *Autobiography*), a recent collection of women's conflicts with the Inquisitions in Spain and its American colonies has similarly stressed "women's bid for authority on the basis of visions and other extraordinary gifts" as its principal theme (Giles, *Women in the Inquisition*, p. 11).

Rather than rebutting them, Catholic authorities have traditionally replied to critics of inquisitorial oppression and injustice as seldom and as discreetly as possible. If the first and only Vatican refutation of a prominent critic was published (anony-mously) in 1659, the Portuguese Inquisition, confident of domestic popular support, maintained an unbroken silence despite a chorus of foreign criticism of its "barbaric" operations, including the first printed criticism by a French Catholic ex-prisoner and a world-famous lampoon in Voltaire's *Candide*. Despite their relative public silence, these institutions carefully left behind a huge internal paper trail emphasizing their necessity and infallibility. Catholic apologists in Franco's Spain and Salazar's Portugal occasionally used these materials to defend their national Inquisitions; more recently, such secret archives have been used to reinterpret the Roman Holy Office's treatment of Galileo (Redondi, *Galileo Heretic*) by arguing that he was basically charged with extremely serious theological errors.

One branch of current inquisitorial scholarship exploits this large collection of internal documents in a different direction, studying these institutions primarily as early European bureaucracies whose records happen to be relatively well pre-served over a long time period. The most innovative studies of individual tribunals (Contreras, *Santo Oficio*; Dedieu, *Administration de la foi*) follow this agenda; they track the careers of inquisitors, explain their financial history, and try to locate their similarities and differences with other parts of Spanish royal administration. What they have done on a monographic level, Bethencourt (*Inquisition à l'époque moderne*) has attempted on a macro- and comparative level, blending investigations of Portuguese and Roman materials with better-known Spanish information in order to sketch an institutional portrait of all three across their long existence. And with the recent opening of the central archives of the Roman Inquisition, we can expect a modest surge in "internalist" scholarship about this special branch of papal adminis-tration in the near future.

What Have We Learned?

After examining the range of accomplishments by recent inquisitorial scholarship, one may attempt a provisional summary of our current state of information about them. I would argue that recent scholarship has moved beyond ancient polemics about two different yet related areas: the severity of inquisitorial repression, and the success of these Holy Offices in stifling religious dissent in southern Europe.

First, the Iberian and Roman Inquisitions executed relatively small numbers of people. Torquemada's new tribunal, establishing itself through a rigorous campaign which provoked extreme terror among Spain's Sephardic "New Christians," executed far more "Judaizers" during its first 50 years (1480–1530) than it did in the next three centuries. In all, about 2,000 people probably perished in the flames of early Spanish *autos-da-fé*, accompanied by an equal number of burned effigies of people condemned *in absentia*. After 1550, when the *relaciones de causas* enable us to see its record with unparalleled clarity, the Spanish Inquisition executed another thou-sand people, mostly Moriscos, foreign Protestants, or homosexuals. Its record was bloodier than that of the smaller Portuguese Inquisition, whose nearly complete records show over 1,000 "New Christians" executed at its *autos-da-fé* across two and a half centuries. However, unlike its Spanish counterpart, the Portuguese Holy Office rarely executed people for other offenses. And although we know far less about the overall condemnation of the Roman Inquisition, we know that it put far fewer people to death than either Iberian system – probably fewer than 150 people throughout its long existence, including a tiny handful of "Judaizers."[5]

These figures, large as they are, shrink to microscopic dimensions for any twentieth-century scholar aware of the Nazi Holocaust. More European Jews probably died in a single day in late 1944 than across the long history of the Iberian Inquisitions. Other comparisons reinforce this impression. However noisily they anathematized "Lutherans," they executed far fewer Protestants than did secular government in Reformation Europe. All three inquisitorial systems combined put far fewer people to death in three centuries, for whatever reasons, than the 40,000 people who were executed for witchcraft by secular authorities across Europe between 1580 and 1650. There is blood on the inquisitors' hands, which seems obscene for a Christian "Holy Office" aware of the sixth commandment, but there is much less of it than the "black legend" has supposed.

Second, inquisitorial repression usually achieved its primary purpose. Even its most adamant critics acknowledge that the Iberian and Roman Inquisitions played a major role in stifling religious dissent across southern Europe. For instance, indigenous Protestantism was snuffed out quickly in Spain and choked down a bit more slowly but no less effectively in the Italian peninsula. Although the subject remains extremely controversial among Jews, it does not seem outrageous to suggest that Spain's Holy Office succeeded in its original purpose of assimilating many thousand descendants of baptized Sephardim into Spanish Catholic society within two generations of the official prohibition of Jewish worship and the accompanying expulsion of unbaptized Jews in 1492.

There is only one notable exception to the generally successful Holy Office attacks on stubborn non-Catholics: Spain's baptized Muslim minority, whom the royal government finally felt compelled to expel in 1609 because its Inquisition was unable to make them learn and practice Tridentine Christianity. But even if they failed here, recent scholarship (for example, Nalle, *God in La Mancha*) also suggests that these Inquisitions played a positive role in implementing those same Tridentine reforms among ordinary Spanish or Italian Catholics. This question has not yet been examined with equal care for Latin America, where the Iberian Inquisitions – which punished European colonists and people of mixed blood rather than native converts – probably helped sustain a monolithic and orthodox Catholicism which presently supplies the core of Rome's adherents.

What Should We Expect Next?

After sifting through a basically impressive list of achievements by the past generation of inquisitorial experts, let us abandon the historian's instinctive looking backwards in order to predict a few developments (all of them will probably be disseminated in computer-assisted English and sold on small disks) that might occur in this field during the next generation of research. In this panorama, newcomers will explore each of the major Inquisitions, either opening new issues (especially at Rome) or reopening older ones with fresh variants of "victim-based" scholarship.

Rome. As a generation of international scholars, already accustomed to the Internet, becomes familiar with the rich archives of the Roman Index, we will see several intellectually committed investigations of post-Tridentine Catholic censorship, trying to identify its guiding principles and assessing its long-term effects both inside and beyond the zone policed by its sister Congregation, the Roman Holy Office. Latin American scholars should be prominent participants.

Lisbon. In Israel, Beinart's scholarly heirs will abandon their traditional concentration on the early Spanish Inquisition after discovering the remarkable riches of the Portuguese Inquisition, which they will exploit in order to examine the problem of Sephardic adaptations to Christian society across three centuries, probably in scholarly (and implicitly political) polemics with Netanyahu's more conservative Orthodox successors.

Madrid. Meanwhile, throughout the European Community, university-trained children of Muslim immigrants will begin to explore the records of the Spanish Inquisition in order to recover the only historical precedent to their own dilemmas of assimilation in an officially laicized, yet profoundly Christian, society.

Of course, none of this may happen. But, thinking back to 1970, who would have predicted the many important developments in this field by the current generation of scholars?

NOTES

1   First published in the *Rivista di storia e letteratura religiosa*, 9 (1973), pp. 298–312, Tedeschi's essay appeared in English 13 years later (Henningsen and Tedeschi, *Inquisition in Early Modern Europe*); it is most easily accessible in his collected essays (Tedeschi, *Pursuit of Heresy*).
2   Scholarship was evolving so rapidly in the mid-1980s that the Spanish edition of Kamen's 1985 synthesis, published a few months after the English version, contains a richer set of footnotes. No such problem affected his next revision, in 1997.
3   Although trials by the Roman Inquisition for possessing prohibited books are not very numerous, forming fewer than 5 percent of its total cases, they outnumber those from the Iberian Inquisitions.
4   The father of an Israeli prime minister, although saying nothing persuasive about the Inquisition's actual origins in his mammoth recent account (Netanyahu, *Origins of the Inquisition*), consistently diabolizes fifteenth-century Spanish Christian society and complements his previous revisionism about Spain's Marranos. Systematically rejecting all evidence left by the early Spanish Inquisition as hypocritical, he denies that the victims of the Spanish Inquisition can be considered as authentic practicing Jews and exactly reverses the traditional "lachrymose" perspective of such scholars as Beinart.
5   Rushing in where local experts fear to tread, I proposed this figure in 1998 to the Vatican experts preparing the papal apologia for the errors of the Inquisition during the 2000 Jubilee.

BIBLIOGRAPHY

Alberro, S., *Inquisición y sociedad en Mexico (1571–1700)*. Mexico: Fondo de Cultura Económica, 1988.
Amiel, C. and Lima, A., eds., *L'Inquisition de Goa: La relation de Charles Dellon (1687)*. Paris: Chandeigne, 1997.

"The Roman Inquisition and Protestant Heresy Executions in 16th-Century Europe," in *Atti del Simposio internazionale sull'Inquisizione (29–31 ottobre 1998)*, ed. Agostino Borromeo (Vatican City: Biblioteca Apostolica Vaticana, Studi e testi, 2003), pp. 535–44.

Beinart, H., ed., *Records of the Trials of the Spanish Inquisition in Ciudad Real*, 4 vols. Jerusalem: Israel National Academy of Sciences and Humanities, 1974–85.

Bennassar, B., *L'Inquisition espagnole, Xve–XIXe siècles*. Paris: Hachette, 1979.

Bennassar, B. and Bennassar, L., *Les Chrétiens d'Allah*. Paris: Perrin, 1989.

Bethencourt, F., *O imagináro da magia*. Lisbon: Centro de estudos de História e cultura portuguesa, 1987.

Brambilla, E., *Alle origini del Sant'Uffizio, Penitenza, confessione e giustizia spirituale dal medioevo al XVI secolo*. Bologna: Il Mulino, 2000.

Canosa, R., *Storia dell'Inquisizione in Italia, della metà del Cinquecento alla fine del Settecento*, 5 vols. Rome: Sapere 2000, 1986–90.

Carrasco, R., *Inquisición y repression sexual en Valencia*. Barcelona: Laertes, 1986.

Castañeda Delgado, P., and Hernández Aparicio, P., *La Inquisición de Lima (1570–1635)*. Madrid: Deimos, 1989.

Contreras, J., *El Santo Oficio de la Inquisición de Galicia (poder, sociedad y cultura)*. Madrid: Akal, 1982.

Contreras, J., *Pouvoir et Inquisition en Espagne au XVIe siècle*. Paris: Aubier, 1997 (French version of *Sotos contra Riquelmes*. Madrid, 1992).

Dedieu, J.-P., "Les causes de foi de l'Inquisition de Tolède (1483–1820)," *Mélanges de la Casa de Velázquez*, 14 (1978), pp. 143–71.

Dedieu, J.-P., *L'Administration de la foi: L'Inquisition de Tolède, XVI–XVIIe siècles*. Madrid: Casa de Velázquez, 1989.

Del Col, A. and Paolin, G., eds., *L'Inquisizione romano in Italia nell'età moderna*. Rome: Ufficio centrale per I beni archivistici, 1991.

Di Simplicio, O., *Inquisizione Stregoneria Medicina: Siena e il suo stato 1580–1721*. Siena: Il Leccio, 2000.

Fajardo Spinola, F., *Hechicería y brujería en Canarias en la Edad Moderna*. Las Palmas: Cabildo Insular de Gran Canaria, 1992.

Firpo, M. and Marcatto, D., eds., *Il processo inquisitoriale del Cardinal Giovanni Morone*, 6 vols. Rome: Istituto Storico Italiano per l'Età moderna e contemporanea, 1981–95.

Fragnita, G., *La Bibbia al rogo: La censura ecclesiastica e I volgarizzamenti della Scrittura (1471–1605)*. Bologna: Il Mulino, 1997.

García Cárcel, R., *Orígines de la Inquisición española: El tribunal de Valencia (1478–1530)*. Barcelona: Península, 1976.

García Cárcel, R., *Herejía y sociedad: La Inquisición en Valencia 1530–1609*. Barcelona: Península, 1980.

Giles, M., ed., *Women in the Inquisition: Spain and the New World*. Baltimore: Johns Hopkins University Press, 1999.

Godman, P., *The Saint as Censor: Robert Bellarmine Between Inquisition and Index*. Leiden: Brill, 2000.

Grendler, P., *The Roman Inquisition and the Venetian Press, 1540–1605*. Princeton, NJ: Princeton University Press, 1977.

Haliczer, S., *Inquisition and Society in the Kingdom of Valencia, 1478–1834*. Berkeley: University of California Press, 1990.

Haliczer, S., *Sex in the Confessional*. Berkeley: University of California Press, 1996.

Henningsen, G., "El 'banco de datos' del Santo Oficio: las relaciones de causas de la Inquisición española (1550–1700)," *Boletín de la Real Academia de la Historia*, 174 (1977), pp. 547–70.

Henningsen, G., *The Witches' Advocate: Basque Witchcraft and the Spanish Inquisition*. Reno: University of Nevada Press, 1980.

Henningsen, G., "The Database of the Spanish Inquisition: The *relaciones de causas* Project Revisited," in H. Mohnhaupt and D. Simon, eds., *Vorträge zur Justizforschung: Geschichte und Theorie*, 2 vols. Frankfurt a.M., 1993, vol. 2, pp. 43–85.

Kagan, R., *Lucrezia's Dreams*. Baltimore: Johns Hopkins University Press, 1990.

Martin, J., *Venice's Hidden Enemies: Italian Heretics in a Renaissance City*. Berkeley/Los Angeles/London: University of California Press, 1993.

Monter, W., *Frontiers of Heresy: The Spanish Inquisition from the Basque Lands to Sicily*. Cambridge: Cambridge University Press, 2003.

Nalle, S. T., *Mad for God: Bartolomé Sánchez, the Secret Messiah of Cardenete*. Charlottesville: University of Virginia Press, 2001.

Netanyahu, B., *Origins of the Inquisition in 15th-Century Spain*, 2nd ed. New York: Random House, 2000.

Pagano, S., ed., *I documenti del processo di Galileo Galilei*. Vatican City: Biblioteca Apostolica Vaticana, 1984.

Paiva, J. P., *Bruxaria e superstição num pais sem caça às bruxas, 1600–1774*. Lisbon: Editorial Notícias, 1997.

Pardo Tomás, J., *Ciencia y censura: La Inquisición española y los libros científicos en los siglos XVI y XVII*. Madrid: CSIC, 1991.

Pérez Villanueva, J., ed., *La Inquisición Española: Nueva visión, nuevos horizontes*. Madrid: Siglo XXI, 1980.

Pinto Crespo, V., *Inquisición y control ideologico en la España del siglo XVI*. Madrid: Taurus, 1983.

Poppi, A., *Cremonini e Galilei inquisiti a Padova nel 1604: Nuovi documenti d'archivio*. Padua: Antenore, 1992.

Prosperi, A., *Tribunali della coscienza: Inquisitri, confessori, missionari*. Turin, 1996.

Pullan, B., *The Inquisition of Venice and the Jews of Europe*. Totowa, NJ: Barnes & Noble, 1987.

Redondi, P., *Galileo Heretic*. Princeton, NJ: Princeton University Press, 1987 (Italian ed., 1983).

Reguera, I., *La Inquisición española en el Pais Vasco (El tribunal de Calahorra, 1513–1570)*. San Sebastian: Txertoa, 1985.

Saraiva, A. J., *Inquisição e critãos novos*. Porto: Inova, 1969.

Scaramella, P., *"Con la Croce al core": Inquisizione ed eresia in Terra di Lavoro (1551–1564)*. Naples, 1995.

Schutte, A. J., ed. and trans., *Autobiography of an Aspiring Saint*. Chicago: Chicago University Press, 1996.

Seidel Menchi, S., *Erasmo in Italia 1520–1580*. Turin: Bollati Boringhieri, 1987.

Tedeschi, J. A., *The Pursuit of Heresy*. Binghamton, NY: SUNY Press, 1991.

Veiga Torres, J., "Uma longua Guerra social: os ritmos da repressão inquisitorial em Portugal," *Revista de História Económico e Social*, 1 (1978), pp. 55–68.

Vincent, B., *Minorias y marginados en la España del siglo XVI*. Granada, 1987.

FURTHER READING

Bethencourt, F., *L'Inquisition à l'époque moderne: Espagne, Portugal, Italie XVe–XIXe siècles*. Paris: Fayard, 1995.

Del Col, A., *Domenico Scandella Known as Menocchio: His Trials before the Inquisition*

(1583–1599), trans. J. and A. Tedeschi. Binghamton, NY: SUNY Press, 1996 (original ed. Pordonene, 1990).

Ginzburg, C., *The Cheese and the Worms*, trans. J. and A. Tedeschi. Baltimore: Johns Hopkins University Press, 1980 (original ed. Turin, 1975).

Henningsen, G., and Tedeschi, J., eds., *The Inquisition in Early Modern Europe: Studies in Sources and Methods.* De Kalb: Northern Illinois University Press, 1986.

Kamen, H., *The Spanish Inquisition: A Historical Revision.* New Haven, Conn.: Yale University Press, 1997.

Nalle, S. T., *God in La Mancha: Religious Reform and the People of Cuenca, 1500–1650.* Baltimore: Johns Hopkins University Press, 1992.

Seventeen

The Thirty Years' War

Johannes Burkhardt

The Thirty Years' War has always occupied a special place in historical memory. Its almost mythical quality has been fostered by legendary war heroes such as Wallenstein and Gustavus Adolphus, by violence and misery on an unimaginable scale, and by an outpouring of written accounts by chroniclers, diarists, historians, and literary figures, whose treatments of the war include such outstanding works of world literature as Grimmelshausen's *Simplicissimus*, Friedrich Schiller's trilogy *Wallenstein*, Bertold Brecht's *Mutter Courage*, and Günther Grass's *Treffen von Telgte*, to name only a few among more than 500 texts of narrative literature alone (Hans Medick, Introduction to Krusenstjern and Medick, *Alltag*, p. 31). But the real basis for the creation of this myth has been the incomprehensible duration of a war that would not end for 30 years. On the other hand, the war was only one of many then under way in Europe and was itself comprised of numerous wars with varying adversaries, regional theaters, and several peace agreements in between. A thesis by Sigfrid Henry Steinberg, which has generated much confusion, has even contested the very existence of a "Thirty Years' War," declaring it a "figment of retrospective imagination."[1] This, however, has turned out to be an unacceptable misinterpretation, as Konrad Repgen's extensive research has proven beyond any doubt: even contemporaries perceived the war as a single event, counting the number of years as they mounted, and, following the peace treaty, referred to it as the "Thirty Years' War."[2] The term is contemporary and captures an authentic experience of the war. Thus, the war was indeed a "war of wars" in more than one sense: a war composed of many wars, and one that stood out from all other wars for its extraordinary length. This cumulative and distinctive meaning can be integrated into a typological one: the succession of wars in Europe became so dense that it was perceived at its height as a single war. This "prototype" of early modern "densification of war" (Burkhardt) facilitates the study of the epochal origins of war *per se*.

This was a European war, fought primarily on German battlefields. German history books traditionally break it down into a series of four "sub-wars," each named for a different opponent of the Habsburg Empire (and of the allied Spanish Habsburgs): the Bohemian-Palatinate War (1618–23) encompassed the uprising of the Bohemian estates against their Austrian ruler and future emperor, Ferdinand II, which had started with the Defenestration of Prague; their defeat under the newly elected Bohemian King Frederick, the elector of the Palatinate, in the battle of White Mountain (1620); and finally, the capture of Heidelberg and the Palatinate by the combined forces of the Spaniards and the Catholic League under Duke Maximilian I, who was subsequently elevated to the status of elector. In the Danish–Dutch (or the Lower Saxon) War (1625–9), the Dutch resumed their war of independence against Spain and, in alliance with France and England, erected a second front in northern Germany with the help of the Danish king. As the duke of Holstein and district captain of Lower Saxony, he intervened in favor of the Protestant princes but was defeated by the emperor's new general, Wallenstein, and withdrew from the war after the Peace of Lübeck (1629). The expansion of imperial power to the Baltic Sea and the promulgation of the confessionally explosive Edict of Restitution (1629) triggered the Swedish War (1630–5): Gustavus Adolphus led an unprecedented victory march through the whole of Germany, beginning and ending at Leipzig. The victory at Breitenfeld (1631) was followed by his death in the battle of Lützen (1632). In the battle of Nördlingen (1634), the Swedes lost their hold on all of southern Germany, and the German imperial princes rallied anew behind the emperor in the Peace of Prague (1635). France, under the leadership of Cardinal Richelieu, now openly entered into the war and thwarted a victory of the united forces of the Habsburgs and the empire in what became known as the Swedish–French War (1635–48). After attempts to expel the Swedes from northern Germany in the battle of Wittstock (1636) had failed, Spanish and imperial armies and contingents of German princes fought in ever-changing constellations with the Swedes and the French, until finally a peace compromise was reached.

All this reveals very little. The number of individual wars could be multiplied arbitrarily and differing versions circulate in the historiography. Thus, although the above-outlined narrative provides an initial chronological overview, it cannot by itself explain the war's magnitude, even if the respective domestic causes of each "sub-war" were taken into account as well. The causes go deeper and can only be understood in the overall context of European history and the era's broad constellations of conflict. The debate takes place on two levels, which today receive special attention in advanced German historical research. Each of these levels poses virtually intractable problems when viewed on its own, let alone when both are taken together. The first level is the classic level of war of religion (I), whose militancy has become increasingly apparent after a recent discovery and new access to sources; the second one is an entirely redefined political level, that of a European war of state-building, or rather a German constitutional war (II). I will first explain these two levels of conflict that constitute the war, and then address the much discussed interrelation of military developments and the recent historiographical attention to the wartime experiences of the populace in this seemingly unending war (III), in order to show how the Peace of Westphalia ultimately managed to solve both the religious and political conflicts (IV).

I

The war of religion has to be viewed in the context of the structural intolerance associated with the early modern "confessional formation" or "confessionalization."

These terms refer to the institutionalization of major religious groups at the outset of the modern age, a parallel process of standardizing religion, which was achieved by very similar means. Each side, however, regarded its own approach – the Lutheran "Primacy of Doctrine," the Catholic "Primacy of Organization," and the Reformed "Primacy of Practice" – as the only correct path toward the whole Christian truth. This was not a clash of different religions but rather a battle about the correct interpretation of one and the same religion. Therefore, the initial desire was not merely to distinguish between different confessions but to reverse the formation of the competing confessions. Each regarded itself as the sole heir to the old religion, denying the other groups their religious right to exist. These mutually exclusive claims to authenticity associated with the competing confessional formations resulted in a militancy that led to the use of violence and ultimately to a series of European wars of religion. Yet, even religious wars must eventually come to an end, and this was only possible in the long term if the question of religious truth were suspended and each confession recognized politically as well as legally. Such a precedent was set by the Religious Peace of Augsburg, which incorporated two confessions into the imperial constitution – albeit with gaps and jointly accepted "adjournments": thus, it remained unclear whether the territorial sovereign who determined the confession for his region (*cuius regio, eius religio*) would also rule over cloister and church lands; the reservation of the prince-bishoprics (*reservatum ecclesiasticum*) did not always find acceptance; and the biconfessional solution left no room for the third major confession, the Reformed Church. But in spite of all conflicts, this territorial peace agreement spared two generations the wave of religious wars that swept through half of western Europe. In terms of religious conflict management, the Holy Roman Empire's organization was so advanced compared to the rest of Europe that historians today doubt that it was indeed simply accumulated legal conflict over confessional matters which, propelled forward by a supposedly inner logic or even a certain degree of automatism, led to an irresoluble crisis and, ultimately, to the Thirty Years' War. So what did? To begin with, on the religious level itself, a series of exogenous and other causes that led to the breakdown of the existing confessional compromise in Germany has to be taken into account.

There are, on the one hand, the militant impulses from a confessionally turbulent Europe whose Calvinist and Catholic parties called into question the biconfessional system that already existed at its core. The "Calvinist internationalization," originally centered in the Netherlands, was broadening into a "Protestant internationalism" and found in the Elector Frederick of the Palatinate an envoy of the empire who led the Protestant Union, founded in 1608 and comprised of Lutheran and Reformed estates. When the Calvinist-inspired Bohemians elected Frederick their king in 1619, they added a confessional and political dimension of European-wide proportions to the initially rather marginal conflict over two churches and demanded anti-Catholic confessional solidarity. Although it came too late for them, it was this solidarity that would keep the whole war going. Conversely, the movement of Catholic internationalism had its center of operation in Rome. This stronghold of the Counter-Reformation promoted "the restoration of the Catholic religion in Germany" by means of the newly founded Congregation for the Propagation of the Faith, its permanent nunciatures in Vienna, Graz, and Cologne, and, ultimately, even war subsidies.[3] Pope Gregory XV in particular perceived the war explicitly as one of religion and supported the Catholic party with a rhetoric reminiscent of the "Holy War," along with considerable financial resources. For the worldwide Jesuit Order, confessionally mixed Germany soon became the main battleground, for it is here that its members attained their highest level of influence as instructors and advisers to the Catholic princes at the very time the war was beginning. Both Emperor Ferdinand II and the leader of the Catholic League, which was subsidized by the pope, had studied at a Jesuit university and maintained a special devotion for the Virgin Mary and the principles of the Counter-Reformation even in their roles as battle patrons. In contrast to both his predecessors and successors, Ferdinand II placed his engagement in confessional politics above his role as mediator in the empire that his imperial position implied. At the zenith of his political power and amid a wave of lawsuits before the imperial court, his Edict of Restitution endorsed the Catholic interpretation of the Religious Peace of Augsburg, leading to a "return" of cloisters and bishoprics to no longer existent owners and thus to the artificial construct of a "Catholic Church." According to an analysis by Bireley, Ferdinand II at times viewed the war not merely as one of religion but rather as an obligatory "Holy War" in the service of God against the Protestants (Bireley, *Religion and Politics*, pp. 127–31; "Thirty Years' War") – a perspective of the conflict common in contemporary Europe but utterly foreign to the imperial tradition.

Aside from such external influence, there was also a domestic intensification of the conflict by the media. The Thirty Years' War was, like no other, a war of leaflets, in which the single-page prints that had emerged at the time of the early Reformation, with their expressive combinations of pictures and text, reached their quantitative peak. While the more comprehensive pamphlets were henceforth reserved for political abstracts, the visual medium of leaflets, which presented the major actors and spectacles of war to a curious public in at times glorifying and at times satirical ways, particularly liked to base its interpretations upon the genre's catchy polemics from the time of the Reformation, elaborating on their confessional meanings and applying them to recent events.[4] Protestant leaflets offered satirical treatments of the pope or depicted Jesuits swarming out like locusts, sitting on cannon, or appearing as apocalyptic monsters. In the finest tradition of baroque art and symbolism, they presented endless variations of Gustavus Adolphus as a Protestant hero and God-sent savior, long awaited and hailed, then cheered on during what was perceived as his confessional victory march, and finally mourned by Protestant Germany with rallying calls. Conversely, Catholic leaflets mocked both the short rein of the Bohemian "Winter King" and his retreat – even portraying Luther, Zwingli, and Calvin posthumously as Bohemian exiles – or roused public opinion against the Protestant Congress of Leipzig. Such confessional antagonism also dominated sensational reports about the looting, burning, and overall destruction of Magdeburg, which was ascribed to the League commander Tilly, and subsequently recounted in poems, songs, and polemics. Hence the title of a leaflet, "Clerical Affray," depicting the pope, Luther, and Calvin wrestling with each other, which in the year 1617 seemed like a prophetic commentary on the media's reading of the war.[5] The power of these images has created a one-sided portrayal of the Thirty Years' War as a war of religion that persists to this very day. Yet these handbills – which were after all widely printed and sold – must have somehow struck a nerve among the population and emotionalized public opinion. The publicity and propaganda of religious warfare undoubtedly intensified and prolonged the war.

All this is assumed to have been the result of an almost incredible coincidence, which upon closer inspection does not appear to be a coincidence at all. For the Thirty Years' War began almost exactly 100 years after Martin Luther had posted his Theses in 1517, which was celebrated as a grand Reformation jubilee for the first time in late October of 1617. The jubilee lasted several days and took place in all Lutheran and most Reformed territories around Germany, where its outpouring of sermons and publications generated great publicity. Leading the way, the elector of Saxony celebrated this holiday to reinforce Lutheran identity and to mark the success of confessionalization in his principality. Although the Protestants did not intend it that way, to the Catholic camp the jubilee seemed like a terrible provocation. After all, the right to declare a "jubilee" had belonged to the pope since 1300, and its central feature was the acquisition of indulgences. Now, however, the Protestants were announcing a "pseudo-jubilee," as it was immediately dubbed,[6] not celebrating the year of Christ's birth but rather a symbolic act of Luther's who was attacking, of all things, the very idea of indulgences! Thus, Pope Gregory XV promptly ordered a counter-jubilee dedicated to the abolition of "heresies," and nothing could have been more likely to trigger a militant reenactment of the entire history of the Reformation and confessionalization than such competing jubilees. Thus, the Defenestration of Prague in the spring of 1618 was preceded only months earlier by an ideological and confessional mobilization which the media continued straight into the war. Even contemporary chroniclers in Ulm and Augsburg noticed this correlation of events and viewed the Protestant jubilee and Catholic counter-initiative as the "beginning" of the war.[7] A recent empirical reexamination of this thesis, based on sources from confessionally mixed border regions, has confirmed that the jubilee indeed had a polarizing effect, and that the Thirty Years' War was therefore perceived as a religious war, particularly in its early phase (Kohlmann, "'Von unsern Widersachern,'" pp. 149–60, esp. pp. 124, 211). Even more astonishing, however, is the exact repetition of events at the next important jubilee, the secular jubilee of the *Confessio Augustana*. This was the official Protestant confession of faith, which was first adopted at the imperial diet of Augsburg in 1530 and remains of fundamental importance to this day. For after the Edict of Restitution had placed the Protestants on the defensive in 1629, and it looked as though the emperor and the Catholic party had won the war, the fighting almost came to a standstill. At this point Gustavus Adolphus landed at the Baltic shore in what appeared to be a carefully staged move, just in time for the confessional jubilee of 1630. Protestant propaganda celebrated him as a "savior," but his intervention also brought Germany 20 more years of war. The Protestant electors, who had neither appealed to the Swedish king for help nor, for the most part, welcomed his presence, now found themselves under public pressure, generated by a new confessional pamphlet offensive, to join his ranks. Jubilees have long encouraged bellicosity, and are being studied today in the context of other wars as well. But in this case, the dual reference to the history of the Reformation was an additional factor that encouraged the confessional interpretation and militancy of the war.

Thus an exogenous confessional activism and a media war organized around the two jubilees contributed to the confessional mobilization of 1618 and the remobilization of 1630, and revived a war of religion which had been regarded as almost over. The term "guerra di religione" was used in papal diplomacy even at the time, whereas it was only obliquely referred to in the empire (Burkhardt, "Religionskrieg," pp. 681–2). However, such an interpretation has its complications and limits. From the very beginning, there were three, not two, competing confessions, which allowed for various possible alliances but essentially forced the Lutherans – who stood at the moderate center of the factions and were loyal to the empire – to choose between the extreme Calvinist and Roman camps. The Protestant Union, founded to protect the Protestant-Lutheran and Reformed-Calvinist estates against Catholic encroachments, fell apart right at the outset of the war. In order to prevent the escalation of events into a religious war, the Protestant elector of Saxony, who had remained outside the Union, explicitly declared the Bohemian uprising a purely political affair, and implemented a conciliatory policy of alliances and neutrality which kept shifting depending on the circumstances. Thus, he cooperated first with the Catholic emperor, then with Lutheran Sweden, then again with the emperor, and at times with neither or with both. Even the purported savior of Protestant Germany Gustavus Adolphus never mentioned the politically charged issue of religion in the war manifesto that legitimized his intervention. For some years the Catholic League of Maximilian of Bavaria, which had been reorganized only in 1619 and included a number of ecclesiastical estates, was a politically successful ad hoc alliance, although it was never formally institutionalized and lost its meaning long before its official demise in 1635. On the Catholic side, the pope and Richelieu occasionally led a kind of "religious war of the second variety," that is, a competition for the leadership of the Catholic camp. Tolerated for a long time by the francophile Pope Urban VIII, the French went as far as to enter into covert and finally open cooperation with the Protestants. Thus, there was never really a confrontation of confessionally homogeneous camps. By the time France officially entered the war on the confessionally "wrong" side of Sweden, it was obvious that there were also distinctly political motives behind the conflict. After all, even wars of religion were not waged by religions or confessions, but rather by the era's political warlords, who – although they saw their own actions as being motivated and legitimized by religious principles – would increasingly choose politics over religion if the two did not converge. It is, however, a common modern misinterpretation of the Thirty Years' War to simply argue that, between religious ideals and pragmatic political interests, the latter held the upper hand. In reality, politics consisted of ideas and ideals as well; and these, more than anything else, were the driving force behind the conflict.

II

On the political level, the Thirty Years' War was a "war of state-building." This term refers to the second important process of institutionalization in the modern age (Reinhard, *Geschichte der Staatsgewalt*), which not only transcended the process of confessional formation but ultimately rang in the end of the Reformation era. The Thirty Years' War was a war of state-building in so far as it concerned not only religious but also state matters. However, it was not yet a war between states, but rather literally a war of state-building – and precisely therefore caused a special degree of bellicosity. For at this pubescent stage of the state, the war presented a confrontation not between fully developed states but between different political allegiances and concepts. The need for an additional degree of organization, which we regard as essential to the existence of a state, already emerged on the historical agenda of modern Europe. Yet, as late as the age of Reformation, neither the overall constellation of European states nor even their approximate sizes or number had been decided upon. Thus, the Thirty Years' War can be truly regarded as the decisive test to determine the appropriate number and dimensions. The two possible constructs that emerged at the time competed and clashed continuously over the course of the war.

The first possible construct was a state for everyone, encompassing all of Europe. After all, the political unity of Europe, based on such concepts as Christianitas, Empire, or Monarchy, whose original meanings represented the universalist tradition, remained the political ideal of the time. According to the long tradition of hierarchical order, Europe was perceived as a pyramid, and while its highest position was often contested, it was widely accepted that there had to be one and that it had to be filled. In contrast, a mere plurality of territorial authorities was still considered to represent anarchy. As heirs to the imperial title and rulers over half of Europe, the Habsburgs tried to take advantage of their position to build a single European state. This was what Charles V envisioned under the programmatic term *"monarchia universalis"* (Bosbach, *Monarchia universalis*; Lutz, "Karl V."). Propagandist maps of Europe used analogies of the body in order to illustrate the ensuing division of labor, portraying Spain as the head of Europe and the Bohemian imperial residence as its heart. During the Thirty Years' War, the two lines of the Habsburgs – the central European imperial line and the now hegemonic Spanish-Atlantic line – reorganized their house union in the Oñate Treaty, entering the war as close allies. Just as any other wartime coalition, this one of course had its frictions. What is extraordinary, however, is not the emergence of occasional frictions, but rather the fact that – in contrast to the family feuds so common among European nobility – this union endured for more than 30 years of war, and that the emperor would ultimately abandon it only under enormous pressure. The stability of this union was based on the Habsburgs' conclusion that universalism only had a chance when pursued as a common cause. Their dynastic universalism operated in close agreement against Bohemia and the Netherlands – two territories at the edges of the Habsburg Empire which threatened to defect from the union – and against the French competitors. No wonder that there was much talk about Spanish *"superioridad,"* about the emperor as an absolute ruler, and, above all, again about the Habsburg *"monarchia universalis,"* albeit this time as a highly contested matter. With the Habsburg dynasty at the top of Europe, the war was indeed another attempt to resurrect this concept.

On the other hand, there were also early indications of the development of a pluralistic state system in Europe. Diametrically opposed to the universalist path was the formation of a pluralist state system from the bottom up, an idea promoted primarily by the estates. As representatives of a region they often supported the process of state-building. However, in the case of Switzerland, the Netherlands, and Bohemia, which were at conflict with the distant Habsburg universal rulers, the estates became independent and seceded. The Bohemian estates had long been administering their own finances, army, and church in a quasi-state manner when they staged a symbolically laden defenestration of the representatives of the empire from Prague Castle, formally established their sovereignty, and created a directorate. Just as the Swiss had founded the Confoederatio Helvetica, the estates of Bohemia, Moravia, Silesia, and Upper and Lower Lausitz founded a federal state, the Confoederatio Bohemica, controlling an impressively large population of 4 million. Similarly, the Dutch, who went through a series of various secessions and unions in their effort to break away from the Spanish Habsburgs, founded an individual state based on estates: "De Staten generael vande gheunierrde Nederlanden." In both cases, the estates initially invoked their right to object, then became the bearer of sovereignty and set up a semimonarchic public office – filled by the house of Orange in the Netherlands and by the "Winter King" Frederick of the Palatinate, who reigned for only one season, in Bohemia – in order to increase recognition for the single state and its chances for success in Europe. But the secession from the Habsburg universal dynasty was not possible without war. In each case the price to be paid for the building of a state was a war for its recognition. These wars of state-building, however, led to different outcomes. The Bohemian uprising that had triggered the Thirty Years' War was crushed as soon as 1620 in the lost battle of the White Mountain; many of the failed state founders were executed, and the futile experiment went down in history as a "revolt" or "rebellion." The Dutch, however, whose successful 80-year war of state-building, dating back to the sixteenth century, has been recorded as a "battle for freedom" or "war of independence," continued their war against the Habsburgs in 1621, the very year that ended a truce between the two. Strengthened by their European and worldwide economic power, the Netherlands became a center of the anti-Habsburg camp. Twice in a row, an experiment in state-building, undertaken by the estates, led to a conflict between the mutually exclusive concepts of a universal Europe and a pluralistic Europe, which could be solved not by compromise but only through force.

The universalism of the Habsburgs was challenged not only by such secessionist activities but also by competing designs of universalism. The classic historiographical tradition is overly inclined to present the rival powers France and Sweden as the defenders of the sovereign individual state. The Thirty Years' War, however, only makes sense upon realization that the invading powers originally had a much broader, universal objective. The very continuity of French politics leaves no doubt that Richelieu had such universal intentions. Accordingly, the cardinal's private memoranda closely resemble those of the Spanish premier, each demanding universal acknowledgment of their monarchs as "head" or "mightiest ruler" of Christendom, Europe, or even the entire world. In the case of Sweden, this ideology of universal rule was even more pronounced. Neither a defensive national security policy, as has been implied by older Swedish research, nor the Swedish interests in the Baltics alone can explain what Gustavus Adolphus was doing at the Rhine and Danube. His crusades, in the style of a new leader of the "barbarian conquests" (*Völkerwanderungsherrscher*), did, however, fit well into the Swedish cult of the Goths, which is nowadays increasingly acknowledged for its political relevance.[8] For under Gustavus Adolphus, who not only assumed the title *Rex Gothorum* but also internalized that role and called for a resumption of the Gothic conquests in his speeches, the concept of a Greater Gothic Empire (*störgöticism*) virtually became national ideology. This descendence from the Gothic heirs of the Roman Empire, together with other mythical and apocalyptic constructs, explains the Swedish bid for universal imperial power, which has always been seen as likely by a number of historians. Whereas the French universalism was based on the resources of a nation that already numbered 20 million, it is difficult to imagine, however, that Sweden, barely developed and home to fewer than 1 million inhabitants, was capable of formulating such sweeping objectives.

Taking into consideration this very Gothic ideology of identity, Erik Ringmar has therefore interpreted the Swedish intervention simply as a nationalist performance, meant to introduce Sweden as an actor on the European stage (Ringmar, *Identity, Interest and Action*). This is a dubious assumption which places Sweden too early on the side of those powers who favored a system of individual states and were in need of recognition. In terms of European universalism, "*störgoticism*" seems to have been capable of more than that. Only this triple claim to universalism, a maximum goal neither of the powers could attain, sufficiently explains the duration of the war.

Both the European conflict between the pluralistic and universal concepts of state-building and that among competing universalist powers were not only predominantly carried out on German battlegrounds, they also called into question the constitutional compromise that had already been reached there. The choice between the opposing concepts of state-building that had emerged in the sixteenth century posed a special challenge to German history. Facing this extraordinary constructive challenge, German history discovered a third way of statehood organization as early as the sixteenth century: the integration of universal and individual elements into a single system. Thus, on the lower territorial level, a kind of pluralistic state-building took place, including even highly organized political units such as regions and cities. But at the same time, Europe had already succeeded in incorporating the integrative universalism of the Habsburgs into the political system in the reduced form of a constitutional electoral emperorship as well as in establishing supraterritorial institutions such as the imperial diet and the imperial courts as a result of the sixteenth-century reform of the empire. But this complex early modern constitutional synthesis fell apart under the pressure generated by the European conflicts that were spreading into the empire, so that once again the choice seemed to be one between universalism and individual states. Thus, in the successful early stage of the war, in which General Wallenstein extended the immediate political power of the emperor to the Baltic Sea, Ferdinand II once again tried to rule by himself or in alliance with a small selection of princes. The 1629 Edict of Restitution, which brought changes to the political system as well, referred solely to absolute imperial power, and the 1635 Peace of Prague between the emperor and the estates even conceived of an imperial army as the only relevant military organization. This alternative, which envisioned a central state and is referred to as "imperial absolutism" in older historical studies, would have turned Germany into a dependence of the Habsburg universalism – which both wartime emperors placed above the constitutional duties of their office – rather than into a unified state. Conversely, an ecumenical counter-initiative of the princes brought about the first fall of the overly powerful Wallenstein in 1630; in fact, this opposition against the Habsburgs at times even displayed secessionist tendencies. For individual territories such as Hesse-Kassel and Electoral Brandenburg, and in the end even Electoral Saxony and Bavaria, fought their way through the war by forming alliances, neutrality agreements, and special peace treaties with all other war powers. The alliances between the German territorial states and Sweden often either disregarded clauses referring to the allegiance to emperor and empire or declared them invalid, which undermined the cohesion of the empire and could have led to the formation of individual states in Europe, just as in the case of the Netherlands, which had been previously part of the empire. Thus, the problems associated with the divergent confessional as well as political concepts, which clashed in Europe as antagonistic alternatives, were exported into the empire, where they were already thought to have been overcome. Here, they destabilized the political system in such a way that it was impossible to predict how this war could ever be led to a conclusion and many parties began to truly settle into it.

III

How can any single society fight a war for 30 years? What *economic* and *military* resources were needed for this effort, and what did this mean for the *population* at large? Economic objectives and material interests have turned out to be inadequate explanations for this war, for such classifications create more problems than they are able to solve by confusing ends and means and misjudging the governing priorities of the Reformation age. Thus, while the Spanish finance minister acknowledged that Spain stood on the brink of financial ruin, he held that its political reputation was at stake and that the war had to be continued (quoted in Elliot, "Foreign Policy," p. 193). Yet, it is valid to argue that Europe must have had abundant resources and great riches to be able to afford such a war without being destroyed by it. Miroslav Hroch and Heiner Haan have rightly pointed out the grim irony that central Europe's advanced socioeconomic development and long-lasting peacetime prosperity served as ideal material preconditions for the war (Haan, "Prosperität"; Hroch, "Wirtschaftliche und gesellschaftliche Voraussetzungen"), whereas the struggle for the last resources – no matter whether the economic situation reversed before or after the onset of the war – had nothing to do with the coming of war. In order to win access to these resources, however, the fledgling states had to be quite inventive. The resources of the early territorial and financial state were limited, but in Denmark and Sweden crown property and port tariffs were utilized to finance the war, and in regions with powerful or willing estates, like the Netherlands or Bavaria, taxes could yield considerable amounts of money despite low rates. An alternative route was foreign financing, either through "subsidies," which were transferred to the war regions from Rome and Spain or from the Netherlands and France, or through so-called "contributions" and other forms of coerced payments, which were collected by the army itself in the areas it occupied. Another significant source of money was the procurement of third-party funds, which made it possible to fight a war on credit: colonels and generals served as war entrepreneurs by paying their regiments advances and by taking over the task of recruiting and financing mercenaries. If the official warlord could not pay the soldiers even at a later point, they would be more than compensated by confiscated land and material. The last and greatest war entrepreneur was Albrecht of Wallenstein, who perfected the credit system with support from wealthy financiers, and managed to collect enough money via "contributions" to fully cover his expenses. Additional forms of war financing included drastic price reductions through the manipulation of coinage – although such practices were quickly abandoned once the ever-watchful press discovered them ("*Kipper- und Wipperzeit*")[9] – and a constant influx of conscripted farmers from Sweden, who were willing to work for as little as a third of a regular soldier's pay.

Not to be confused with the *causes* of the war, these economic *means* were an early indication of new forms of military organization and were utilized to facilitate the deployment of ever-larger armies. As late as the sixteenth century, 10,000 was still considered a respectable size for any army; during the Thirty Years' War, however, each of the powers maintained armed forces of 100,000 or more. The Swedes landed at the Baltic shore with a small military formation of 15,000; by the end of the war, however, they had 140,000 soldiers in Germany, while Spain as the strongest military power had command over up to 300,000 mercenaries throughout Europe. Therefore, the Thirty Years' War has been long regarded in the international historical debate as the main reference point for the thesis of a "military revolution" between 1560 and 1660, not only in terms of numbers but also the development of the entire notion of war.[10] Of fundamental importance was the "Orange army reform" in the Netherlands – based on the Roman *disciplina militaris*, rediscovered by the political philosopher Justus Lipsius and further developed by the counts of Nassau-Orange – which introduced drills, military exercises, and a new language of orders to achieve the artificially coordinated identical movements of soldiers which have since become a hallmark of the military and which added a whole new dimension to the power of firearms.[11] The explosive mix of antique military practices and modern gunpowder was adopted and refined by Gustavus Adolphus, the most famous student of the Dutch military system. This offensive "Swedish formation" contributed to victory in the battle of Breitenfeld and was soon imitated by other armies.

A true military innovation of this war was the "standing army" – a concept that would dominate military strategy throughout the subsequent era – or, to put it more pointedly, "the still-standing army." There already existed a tradition of part-time militias and defense units organized by the various estates which were developing into a standing military organization and were deployed, for example, by Württemberg and Saxony during the Thirty Years' War. Above all, the war was fought by freely available mercenaries of arbitrary national origin, who were called *Landsknechte*, *Kriegsknechte*, or *Kriegsvolk*, lived on wages and war spoils, and increasingly professionalized the field of soldiering. Originally only deployed for one season or campaign, their circumstances improved steadily over the course of this lengthy war. This 30-year long improvement of the mercenary system, which increasingly became a source of regular employment and turned out to be a lesser evil than the squads of soldiers who were out of work during certain phases of the war, was an important step toward the creation of a peacetime standing army. At the same time, the practice of half-private war entrepreneurs and sub-entrepreneurs, as a rule generals or colonels, to organize and deploy these mercenary armies in the name of a political warlord reached its zenith. For the state sovereign who needed these armies but had difficulties controlling them, this practice came to present both a great challenge and an important turning point, as can be seen in the spectacular case of Wallenstein. More interesting than Wallenstein's hypothetical conspiracy is what scholars today view as the "conspiracy against Wallenstein." After all, the "rebel of the empire" (Kampmann, *Reichsrebellion*) was removed from office, ostracized, and killed, and his mercenary army was confiscated and put under state control, which seems to have been the whole point. In a similar vein, Richelieu put the army of the mercenary leader Bernhard von Weimar under the control of the French crown immediately after his death. Brandenburg discharged its expensive army when it decided to become a neutral power, before the Great Elector acknowledged this move as a security blunder and corrected it by founding the Prussian standing army before the war was over. In the end, it was difficult to get rid of at least some of the troops; thus, in order to discharge the Swedish mercenaries, Germany's opponents had to take on the payment of their overdue wages. Thus, the real essence of the "military revolution" was the 30-year military presence itself. Over the course of the war, Europe experienced a stabilization of mercenary armies, which provoked state sovereigns to take control of them, and saw early organizational indications for the development of standing armies.

What effects did a war, during which, according to an estimate by Geoffrey Parker, a total of 1 million people were under arms, have on the population at large? The population loss was tremendous, and the number of German citizens decreased from about 16 or 17 million to 10 or 11 million, thus being reduced by at least a third. Although there were "safe areas" in the southeast and northwest, such as in Hamburg, where the population remained more or less stable and the economy could prosper, there was also – as Günther Franz calls it – an "axis of destruction," spanning from Pomerania and Mecklenburg on the Baltic Sea to the Thuringian and Saxon lands in central Germany to the Palatinate and Swabia in the southwest, which lost more than half of their population.[12] Ever since Steinberg's study, these figures have often been regarded as exaggerated. Although Günther Franz compiled them in 1940 from regional studies without using any proper statistical method, and he is furthermore discredited as a representative of the Nazi regime's scientific establishment, he is nevertheless – and unfortunately – right.[13] In fact, modern demographic case studies have resulted in even higher mortality rates and have further expanded Franz's axis.[14] Accordingly, any doubts as to the significance of the extremely rich sources such as descriptions of violence, diary entries, damage lists, and death registers are certainly out of place. Admittedly, even terror has its own rhetoric. But it makes little difference whether human beings were really eaten or whether such incidents were simply imagined – the reports express the same degree of hunger people at the time must have experienced; and if individuals were reported as beaten to death, raped, or hanged by their genitals, this was certainly not a fabrication. But the most significant causes for the demographic catastrophe were rather indirect, such as the unholy trinity of violence, hunger, and epidemics. It was the wartime violence that generated this deadly matrix, for when already scarce resources were requisitioned for the war, a food crisis broke out and made the weakened population susceptible to infections. Roaming armies and the poor hygienic conditions of a general population hiding in close quarters behind safe city walls contributed to the spread of diseases. Famines in turn intensified the propensity to violence among civilian and military groups competing for the last food reserves. The "*soldateska*" too was a victim – after all, only every tenth Swedish soldier returned to his homeland, and, on average, a soldier survived only three years of war. Three out of four died not in battle, however, but from exhaustion, hunger, or disease. Thus contemporary chroniclers perceived a long range of threats that placed an entire culture in jeopardy: war, epidemics, and hunger, wrote one of them, reduced the population to such a low level that future generations would have difficulties imagining it – if there were to be future generations at all.

How did the people deal with all this? On the one hand, the populace perceived the war as an unprecedented negative event, which shattered their traditional everyday lives, in fact their entire static world and understanding of history in a lasting manner, as becomes evident from numerous elegies and the myth of the Thirty Years' War which records this intensive war experience. On the other hand, the widespread

religious interpretation of the war as God's punishment for the great sins of mankind
helped to explain and cope with the events. It is remarkable, for example, how many
sermons and rituals around the issue of repentance took place in the Protestant southwest. Their deep-seated religiosity helped people find comfort in their grief and cope
with the terrors of the war. Correspondingly, a research program on the experience
of the war differentiates between the two contrasting functions of religion: as
"legitimization" for the war on the one hand, and as "consolation" for the bereaved
and suffering on the other (Schindling, "Erfolgsgeschichte und Konfessionalisierung," p. 21). Thus, today's research gives special attention to the incredible vitality
and survival strategies within communities which managed to prevent a total breakdown of society (for more details see Burkhardt, "'Ist noch ein Ort?'"; "Schlußkommentar"). In contrast to popular assumptions that all social ties fell apart and
solidarity ceased to exist, the social units of house, family, and community remained
surprisingly stable and flexible: families of mercenaries who traveled along with the
army or all-female Swedish households preserved these well-established social structures throughout the war, even under the harshest conditions. Official residences of
the territorial landlords as well as abbeys and cities opened their gates to offer refuge
to subjects and neighbors fleeing from the war and for the storage of supplies necessary for survival – the abbot of Andechs abbey stored the state supply of grain in
the chapel and let the local cattle graze in the cloisters. Social relations and forms of
cooperation developed even between the military and the civilian population. The
most famous cooperation was the *salva guardia*: the population would pay a fee for
a document that would guarantee them protection by the soldiers, who in turn would
gain an additional source of livelihood. And even the contested issue of religious confessions was at times overcome when the different groups who had previously not
known each other came together as a community. In fact, the longer the war went
on, the more the population became dependent on interconfessional communication
and cooperation, such as a joint system of early warnings in case of an approaching
army, or the practice of granting refuge which increasingly ignored confessional differences and allowed for a peaceful coexistence of the various confessional groups,
essentially in anticipation of what would become the political and legal norm after
the war. Thus, even in the midst of catastrophe, the perseverance of traditional
regional community structures and new modes of cooperation even with the military
and among the different confessional groups opened up possibilities that would finally
point the way out of this seemingly never-ending war.

IV

The Peace of Westphalia, which finally brought this 30-year catastrophe to an end,
can be counted among the greatest political achievements in European and German
history. For four years, up to 82 legates negotiated in the neutralized cities of Münster
and Osnabrück, even as the parties continued to fight bitter battles in order to achieve
victory – or at least to prevent the opponent from winning the war, an objective eventually achieved by the empire's defensive political strategy. The successful peace treaty
had many architects, but if we want to look beyond the mythical "war heroes" and
focus on a "face of peace," then the imperial adviser and plenipotentiary Count
Maximilian of Trauttmansdorff would be the rightful candidate. An intelligent man

with high personal integrity, Maximilian used his skills to salvage even the most hopeless negotiations. Neutrality agreements and special peace treaties that were initiated by the individual estates, such as the one between the Saxon elector and Sweden at Kötzschenbroda, created *faits accomplis* or served as precedents. After the long learning process of 30 years of warfare, all parties had to realize that they could achieve neither their maximum political nor religious goals and that they had to accept a peace compromise. But the peace treaties that were finally concluded on September 24, 1648 offered creative solutions, which ushered in a new age and lasted for about 150 years. This grand peace framework produced three conceptual outcomes which finally succeeded in resolving the seemingly inextricable tangle of conflicts and had a lasting impact: the creation of a European system of states, the completion of the imperial constitution, and the elimination of religious warfare in Germany.

The system of states that emerged from the Peace of Westphalia was the answer to the contested political questions that lay at the core of the state-building process. No longer could any of the powers claim the universal legacy of Europe, occupy a clearly superior or dominant position, or even organize Europe into a single state. All of them had concluded that the plurality of states did not necessarily represent "anarchy" or some flawed political concept that had to be done away with, but rather the future political order. The Westphalian Peace Congress succeeded in ending the war of state-building by changing international law and introducing this new model of coexistence of equal states of moderate proportions as the legitimate organization of Europe. In elaborate parallel formulations of the peace treaties, the contracting partners or, rather, opponents, who were the former competitors for universal rule, now scaled back their demands and recognized each other as equal sovereigns once and for all. This resolution was accomplished between the emperor and the French king in Münster (*Instrumentum Pacis Monasteriense, IPM*) and between the emperor and the Swedish crown in Osnabrück (*Instrumentum Pacis Osnabrugense, IPO*). There were no winners in this war. The position of the emperor was made equal to those of the other crowns – a new relationship the visual media liked to depict by using the symbol of a cloverleaf or other triangular images. At the same time the Habsburg universal union was dissolved, for Spain had to continue its fight against France for 11 more years before it could constitute itself in the Peace of the Pyrenees as just another European power. But the other side did not win either. France and Sweden were required to return almost all of their conquests in the empire and to evacuate their garrisons. France contented itself with some territories in the region of Alsace-Lorraine and legal titles full of qualifying clauses over ten Alsatian imperial cities, which only later were used for an expansive revision of French borders. Sweden's control over German lands was reduced to several coastal regions at the river mouths of the Oder, Elbe, and Weser (including Western Pomerania and the bishopric of Bremen), which were in fact never really ceded but were administered by Sweden for the duration of one generation. At the other end of the spectrum, the individual states that had succeeded in their formation from the bottom up were now recognized and theoretically treated as equals. The best example is the Netherlands, which had pulled itself out from under Habsburg and imperial domination and which concluded its own peace treaty with Spain, thereby asserting its sovereign position within Europe. Switzerland shared similar results as the Netherlands, if not as clearly and perfectly. Despite its incompleteness and numerous revisions, the Peace

Congress of 1648 established a new model of political order based on the coexistence of equal powers, which was upheld by the development of international law.

The restoration of peace in the empire – where the war had at times threatened to trigger constitutional conflicts that could have caused its disintegration – followed a different, federal, principle of state-building, which according to the most recent studies was even more modern than the European system of multiple states. The emperor and the imperial cities, which had insisted on participating in peace negotiations, codified the political system, thus developing a state on two interlocking constitutional levels. On the lower level, the individual territorial states, who had fought their way through the war in a rather independent manner, demanded that the peace treaty explicitly confirm their supreme territorial rule. But they declined the French offer to become "sovereign" states, and what was often interpreted as their new right to form political alliances was nothing more than the continuation of the traditional right of the imperial estates to form unions, as long as they were not directed against the emperor and did not compromise their duties to the empire. Local self-administration of the territorial states would take place under the overarching authority of a unified state. Some institutions on this level had tried to resume their duties even in the midst of war, and were now finally incorporated into the constitution and further developed. Most important of all was the imperial diet (*Reichstag*), where the representatives of the estates would meet for consultations and which – according to the specifications of the peace treaty – was granted decision-making powers in matters of war and peace and of the constitution. In 1663 the "permanent imperial diet" became one of the first major standing Parliaments of estates in Europe, which would be in permanent session for the next 140 years. This federal constitutional level of a "dual imperial system" (Burkhardt) or "complementary imperial state" (Georg Schmidt), which was quite efficient for the next hundred years, was further represented by the imperial courts (*Reichshofrat* and *Reichskammergericht*), the regional self-government and defense organization of the ten imperial districts (*Reichskreise*), the imperial postal service (*Reichspost*), which had been expanded during the war to respond to the pressing need for adequate information and communication, and the newly established office of the emperor, which settled the question of the nature of the emperorship for all times (*Amtskaisertum*). Thus, the peace treaty, which was ratified by all European powers and formally adopted as imperial basic law by the next imperial diet in 1654, and above all article VIII of *IPO*, which contained a kind of constitutional balance of powers, came to be the earliest written constitution in German history.

Yet, the greatest achievement of the peace compromise was the end of the religious war. Those who believe that the problem of religious conflict somehow resolved itself in the chaos of war should take a look at the Peace of Osnabrück: almost half of all of the provisions touch upon the relationship between the different confessions. However, all religious problems which had plagued the empire since the Reformation could be solved with the help of two ingenious yet simple political and legal principles: the "normative date" (*Normaljahr*) and parity. The normative date was actually a legal rule to resolve how contested church property – including material furnishings, the actual church and cloister buildings, and their sources of income – would be redistributed among the confessions. The Protestant imperial estates demanded the restoration of prewar conditions, which of course favored their own side, while the Catholic camp would have preferred to leave matters as they had been under the Edict of Restitution of 1629. They finally agreed to accept a proposal by the elector of Saxony, who, as always, was propagating a compromise. Thus, the date was to be January 1, 1624. This normative date undermined the *jus reformandi* of the princes, for subjects, too, could invoke this right, even in regions that had been previously confessionally mixed, but also in future instances when territorial princes personally changed their confessions. In the absence of any other specific agreements, a person was henceforth to be Catholic or Protestant based on whether the particular place where he or she resided had been Catholic or Protestant in 1624, unless the person chose to make use of an additional provision in the peace treaty permitting the right of emigration. This solution did not exactly correspond to modern claims for self-determination, but this freezing of the status quo and the legal codification of the entire German confessional map did subdue otherwise irresoluble conflicts. The principle of parity meant that in the future two religious parties were recognized as legally equal. Organized as *Corpus Evangelicorum* and *Corpus Catholicorum* in the imperial diet, these two parties were to be equally powerful members of the imperial regime (and also, as a special case, the imperial city of Augsburg) and were not allowed in any event to overrule one another in the decision-making process. Instead, in all questions concerning confessional matters, they had to negotiate a common solution point by point. Calvinists were integrated into the *Corpus Evangelicorum* and were thereby officially recognized. This system did not lead to the end of religious conflicts in multi-confessional Germany, but such conflicts were henceforth settled within the court system or through political negotiations rather than with weapons. It is one of the greatest achievements of the Peace of Westphalia that it finally managed to integrate the various confessions into the political and legal order – even if they would continue to be caught in their structural intolerance for a long time to come. Thus, in the very cradle of the Reformation, the peace treaty brought an end to the era of religious wars for all time.

NOTES

1   Sigfrid Henry Steinberg, *The "Thirty Years' War" and the Conflict for European Hegemony 1600–1660* (London, 1966; reprinted 1971, 1975, 1977, 1981), p. 1. See the German translation, Steinberg, *Der Dreißigjährige Krieg und der Kampf um die Vorherrschaft in Europa 1600–1660* (Göttingen, 1967). Although this book triggered an interesting historical debate, it has been outdated by newer German research, for example in regard to the fundamental defensive encirclement fiction of France ("a defensive, often desperate struggle against her encirclement by the house of Habsburg," p. 5).

2   Konrad Repgen, "Über die Geschichtsschreibung" and "Seit wann gibt es den Begriff 'Dreißigjähriger Krieg?'" in Heinz Dollinger, ed., *Weltpolitik, Europagedanke, Regionalismus: Festschrift für Heinz Gollwitzer zum 65.* (Münster, 1982), pp. 59–70; Repgen, "Noch einmal zum Begriff 'Dreißigjähriger Krieg,'" *Zeitschrift für Historische Forschung*, 9 (1982), pp. 347–52.

3   "Istruzione für Giovanni Stefano Ferreri," January 20, 1604, in Klaus Jaitner, ed., *Die Hauptinstruktionen Clemens' VIII. für die Nuntien und Legaten an den europäischen Fürstenhöfen 1592–1605*, 2 vols. (Tübingen, 1984), vol. 2, p. 709; Georg Lutz, "Roma e il mondo germanico nel periodo della guerra di Trent' anni," in Gianvittorio Signorotto

and Maria Antonietta Visceglia, eds., *La corte di Roma tra Cinque e Seicento "teatro" della politicia europea* (Rome, 1998), pp. 425–60.

4 The Museum des Dreißigjährigen Krieges in Wittstock/Brandenburg shows an annotated slide collection of such leaflets by my student Jutta Schumann and myself; most of the illustrations discussed appear in Wolfgang Harms, *Deutsche illustrierte Flugblätter des 16. und 17. Jahrhunderts*, annotated ed., 4 vols. (Tübingen/Munich, 1980–9), vol. 2, nos. 148–97, 294–305.

5 Harms, *Illustrierte Flugblätter*, vol. 2, no. 124.

6 Petrus Roestius, *Pseudoiubilaeum, Das ist: Falscher Jubel so anno 1617 den 1. Tag Novembr. ⟨. . .⟩ von den Lutheranern angestelt und gehalten worden* (Molshemium [Molsheim], 1620).

7 Hans Heberle, "Zeytregister," in Gerd Zillhardt, ed., *Der Dreißigjährige Krieg in zeitgenössischer Darstellung* (Ulm, 1975), p. 93. See also Anton Ernstberger, "Drei Nürnberger Reformationsjubiläen," *Luther-Jahrbuch*, 31 (1964), pp. 9–28, p. 17.

8 Swedish research has been largely neglected in the field. See Sverker Arnoldsson, *Krigspropagandan i Sverige före trettioDriga kriget* (Göteborg, 1941); Kurt Johannesson, "Gustav II Adolf som retoriker," in Königl. Leibrüstkammer, ed., *Gustav II Adolf: 350 Jår efter Lützen* (Stockholm, 1982), pp. 11–30; Sverker Oredsson, *Gustav Adolf*.

9 Ulrich Rosseaux, *Die Kipper und Wipper als publizistisches Ereignis (1620–1625): Eine Studie zu den Strukturen öffentlicher Kommunikation im Zeitalter des Dreißigjährigen Krieges* (Berlin, 2001).

10 Clifford J. Rogers, ed., *The Military Revolution Debate: Readings on the Military Transformation of Early Modern Europe* (San Francisco/Oxford, 1995).

11 Wolfgang Reinhard, "Humanismus und Militarismus: Antike-Rezeption und Kriegshandwerk in der oranischen Heeresreform," in Franz Josef Worstbrock, ed., *Krieg und Frieden im Horizont des Renaissancehumanismus* (Wernheim, 1986), pp. 185–204. For background information see Justus Lipsius, *Politicorum sive civilis doctrinae Libri sex, ex instituto Matthiae Berneggeri* (Lichae, 1603), introduced and with a commentary by Wolfgang E. J. Weber, in *Klassiker der Politik (17. Jahrhundert)*, reprint project of the Thyssen Foundation (Hildesheim, 1998); Werner Hahlweg, *Die Heeresreform der Oranier und die Antike* (Berlin, 1941; 2nd expanded ed., Osnabrück, 1987); Gerhard Oestrich, *Neostoicism and the Early Modern State* (Cambridge, 1982).

12 Günther Franz, *Der Dreißigjährige Krieg und das deutsche Volk: Untersuchungen zur Bevölkerungs- und Agrargeschichte* (Jena, 1940; Stuttgart/New York, 1979).

13 A different opinion is formulated by Wolfgang Behringer, "Von Krieg zu Krieg: Neue Perspektiven auf das Buch von Günther Franz, 'Der Dreißigjährige Krieg und das deutsche Volk' (1940)," in Krusenstjern and Medick, *Alltag*, pp. 543–91; John Theibault, "The Demography of the Thirty Years' War Re-visited: Günter Franz and his Critics," *German History*, 15 (1997), pp. 1–21.

14 Werner Lengger, "Leben und Sterben in Schwaben: Studien zur Bevölkerungsentwicklung und Migration zwischen Lech und Iller, Ries und Alpen im 17. Jahrhundert," dissertation, University of Augsburg, 1996 (microfiche) talks about a mortality rate of 60–65 percent (according to the newest method of calculating communicants), in contrast to Franz's 30–50 percent. See also Erich Landsteiner and Andreas Weigl, " 'Sonsten finden wir die Sachen sehr übel aufm Landt beschaffen': Krieg und lokale Gesellschaft in Niederösterreich (1618–1621)," in Krusenstjern and Medick, *Alltag*, pp. 229–71.

BIBLIOGRAPHY

Asch, R. G., "Warfare in the Age of the Thirty Years' War 1598–1648," in Jeremy Black, ed., *European Warfare 1453–1815*. Basingstoke: Macmillan, 1999, pp. 45–68, 250–6.

Bireley, R., *Religion and Politics in the Age of the Counterreformation: Emperor Ferdinand II,*

William Lamormaini, S.J., and the Formation of Imperial Policy. Chapel Hill: University of North Carolina Press, 1981.

Bireley, R., "The Thirty Years' War as Germany's Religious War," in K. Repgen, ed., *Krieg und Politik 1618–1648.* Munich: R. Oldenbourg, 1988, pp. 85–106.

Bosbach, F., *Monarchia universalis: Ein politischer Leitbegriff der Frühen Neuzeit.* Göttingen: Vandenhoeck & Ruprecht, 1988.

Burkhardt, J., "Der Dreißigjährige Krieg als frühmoderner Staatsbildungskrieg," in *Geschichte in Wissenschaft und Unterricht,* 45. Seelze: Erhard Friedrich, 1994, pp. 487–99.

Burkhardt, J., "Die Friedlosigkeit in der Frühen Neuzeit: Grundlegung einer Theorie der Bellizität Europas," in *Zeitschrift für Historische Forschung,* 24. Berlin: Duncker & Humblot, 1997, pp. 509–74.

Burkhardt, J., "Die entgipfelte Pyramide: Kriegsgrund und Friedenskompromiß der europäischen Universalmächte," in Klaus Bußmann and Heinz Schilling, eds., *1648: Krieg und Frieden in Europa,* 3 vols. Vol. 2: *Politik, Religion, Recht und Gesellschaft.* Münster and Osnabrück: Verlagsgesellschaft 350 Jahre Westfälischer Friede, 1998, pp. 51–60.

Burkhardt, J., "'Ist noch ein Ort, dahin der Krieg nicht kommen sey?' Katastrophenerfahrungen und Überlebensstrategien (misprinted: Kriegsstrategien) auf dem deutschen Kriegsschauplatz," in Horst Lademacher and Simon Groenveld, eds., *Krieg und Kultur: Die Rezeption von Krieg und Frieden in der Niederländischen Republik und im Deutschen Reich 1568–1648.* Münster: Waxmann, 1998, pp. 3–19.

Burkhardt, J., "Schlußkommentar und Ausblick," in B. von Krusenstjern and H. Medick, eds., *Zwischen Alltag und Katastrophe: Der Dreißigjährige Krieg aus der Nähe.* Göttingen: Vandenhoeck & Ruprecht, 1998, pp. 595–600.

Dickmann, F., *Der Westfälische Frieden.* Münster: Aschendorff, 1972.

Duchhardt, H., ed., *Der Westfälische Friede: Diplomatie – politische Zäsur – kulturelles Umfeld – Rezeptionsgeschichte.* Munich: R. Oldenbourg, 1998.

Elliot, J. H., "Foreign Policy and Domestic Crisis: Spain 1598–1659," in K. Repgen, ed., *Krieg und Politik 1618–1648.* Munich: R. Oldenbourg, 1988, pp. 185–202.

Englund, P., *Ofredsår: Om den svenska stormaktiden och en man i dess mitt.* Stockholm: Atlantis, 1993. German translation: *Die Verwüstung Deutschlands: Eine Geschichte des Dreißigjährigen Krieges,* trans. Wolfgang Butt. Stuttgart: Klett-Cotta, 1998.

Haan, H., "Prosperität und Dreißigjähriger Krieg," *Geschichte und Gesellschaft,* 7 (1991), pp. 91–118.

Hroch, M., "Wirtschaftliche und gesellschaftliche Voraussetzungen des Dreißigjährigen Krieges: Einige Überlegungen zu einem offenen Problem," in K. Repgen, ed., *Krieg und Politik 1618–1648.* Munich: R. Oldenbourg, 1988, pp. 133–50.

Kaiser, M., "Die Söldner und die Bevölkerung: Überlegungen zu Konstituierung und Überwindung eines lebensweltlichen Antagonismus," in Stefan Kroll and Kersten Krüger, eds., *Militär und ländliche Gesellschaft in der frühen Neuzeit.* Münster: Lit, 2000, pp. 79–120.

Kampmann, C., *Reichsrebellion und kaiserliche Acht: Politische Strafjustiz im Dreißigjährigen Krieg und den Verfahren gegen Wallenstein 1634.* Münster: Aschendorff, 1992.

Kohlmann, C., "'Von unsern Widersachern den Bapisten vil erlitten und ussgestanden': Kriegs- und Krisenerfahrungen von lutherischen Pfarrern und Gläubigen im Amt Hornberg des Herzogtums Württemberg während des Dreißigjährigen Krieges und nach dem Westfälischen Frieden," in M. Asche and A. Schindling, eds., *Das Strafgericht Gottes: Kriegserfahrungen und Religion im Heiligen Römischen Reich Deutscher Nation im Zeitalter des Dreißigjährigen Krieges.* Münster: Aschendorff, 2001, pp. 123–211.

Lademacher, H., and Groenveld, S., eds., *Krieg und Kultur: Die Rezeption von Krieg und Frieden in der niederländischen Republik und im Deutschen Reich 1568–1648.* Munich: Waxmann, 1998.

Langer, H., *1648, der Westfälische Frieden: Pax Europae und Neuordnung des Reiches.* Berlin: Brandenburgisches Verlagshaus, 1994.

Lutz, H., "Karl V.: Biographische Probleme," in Günter Vogler, ed., *Europäische Herrscher: Ihre Rolle bei der Gestaltung von Politik und Gesellschaft vom 16. bis zum 18. Jahrhundert*. Weimar: Böhlau, 1988, pp. 31–57.

Oredsson, S., *Gustav Adolf, Sverige och Trettioåriga kriget: Historieskrivning och kult*. Lund: Lund University Press, 1992. German translation: *Geschichtsschreibung und Kult: Gustav Adolf, Schweden und der Dreißigjährige Krieg*, trans. Klaus R. Böhme. Berlin: Duncker & Humblot, 1994.

Oschmann, A., *Der Nürnberger Exekutionstag 1649–1650: Das Ende des Dreißigjährigen Krieges in Deutschland*. Münster: Aschendorff, 1991.

Parker, G., *The Thirty Years' War*. London: Routledge & Kegan Paul, 1984.

Reese, A. and Uffelmann, U., eds., *Pax sit Christiana: Die westfälischen Friedensverhandlungen als europäisches Ereignis*. Düsseldorf: Schwann-Bagel, 1988.

Reinhard, W., *Ausgewählte Abhandlungen*. Berlin: Duncker & Humblot, 1997.

Reinhard, W., *Geschichte der Staatsgewalt: Eine vergleichende Verfassungsgeschichte Europas von den Anfängen bis zur Gegenwart*. Munich: R. Oldenbourg, 1999.

Repgen, K., *Die römische Kurie und der Westfälische Friede: Idee und Wirklichkeit des Papsttums im 16. und 17. Jahrhundert*, 2 vols. Tübingen: Niemeyer, 1962, 1965.

Ringmar, E., *Identity, Interest and Action: A Cultural Explanation of Sweden's Intervention in the Thirty Years' War*. Cambridge: Cambridge University Press, 1996.

Rudolph, H. U., *Der Dreißigjährige Krieg: Perspektiven und Strukturen*. Darmstadt: Wissenschaftliche Buchgesellschaft, 1977.

Schindling, A., "Erfolgsgeschichte und Konfessionalisierung," in M. Asche and A. Schindling, eds., *Das Strafgericht Gottes: Kriegserfahrungen und Religion im Heiligen Römischen Reich Deutscher Nation im Zeitalter des Dreißigjährigen Krieges*. Münster: Aschendorff, 2001, pp. 11–51.

Schmidt, G., *Der Dreißigjährige Krieg*, 2nd rev. ed. Munich: C. H. Beck, 1996.

Schormann, G., *Der Dreißigjährige Krieg*, 2nd ed. Göttingen: Vandenhoeck & Ruprecht, 1993.

Vogler, G., *Europäische Herrscher: Ihre Rolle bei der Gestaltung von Politik und Gesellschaft vom 16. bis zum 18. Jahrhundert*. Weimar: Böhlau, 1988.

FURTHER READING

Asch, R. G., *The Thirty Years' War: The Holy Roman Empire and Europe 1618–1648*. Basingstoke: Macmillan, 1997.

Asche, M. and Schindling, A., eds., *Das Strafgericht Gottes: Kriegserfahrungen und Religion im Heiligen Römischen Reich Deutscher Nation im Zeitalter des Dreißigjährigen Krieges*. Münster: Aschendorff, 2001.

Burkhardt, J., *Der Dreißigjährige Krieg*. Frankfurt a.M.: Suhrkamp, 1992; new ed., 1996; rev. ed., Darmstadt: Wissenschaftlichen Buchgesellschaft, 1997.

Burkhardt, J., *Das Reformationsjahrhundert: Deutsche Geschichte zwischen Medienrevolution und Institutionenbildung 1517–1617*. Stuttgart: Kohlhammer, 2002.

Kaiser, M., *Politik und Kriegführung: Maximilian von Bayern und die Katholische Liga im Dreißigjährigen Krieg*. Münster: Aschendorff, 1999.

Krusenstjern, B. von and Medick, H., eds., *Zwischen Alltag und Katastrophe: Der Dreißigjährige Krieg aus der Nähe*. Göttingen: Vandenhoeck & Ruprecht, 1998.

Repgen, K., ed., *Krieg und Politik 1618–1648*. Munich: R. Oldenbourg, 1988.

Repgen, K., *Dreißigjähriger Krieg und Westfälischer Friede: Studien und Quellen*. Paderborn: Schöningh, 1998.

Eighteen

Spain and Portugal

José Pedro Paiva

It makes perfect sense to study Spain and Portugal in conjunction. The manifold similarities and mutual influences of the various peninsular kingdoms at the time of the Catholic Renovation, or Reformation (a term preferable to Counter-Reformation in this geographical context, given the limited dimension of Protestantism in the Iberian peninsula), were vast. Assuming the concept of "confessionalization," as derived from German historiography in the work of Wolfang Reinhard and Heinz Schilling, it could be argued that Spain and Portugal constituted two magnificent examples of "confessional Tridentine Catholic states" (Schilling, "Confessionalisation," p. 26). Through the concept of "confessionalization," I intend to demonstrate that, in the sequence of events that led to the breakdown of the Christian medieval unity initiated by Protestantism, all the European territories tended toward greater internal homogenization through their political adhesion to a certain form of religious confession (not only at the level of institutions, doctrines, and relations between powers, but also at the level of individual and collective social and religious behavior). In the Iberian peninsula, the declared and felt attachment to Catholicism, vehemently reaffirmed after the Council of Trent, greatly contributed to the construction of a self-identity whose configuration consolidated lines of force deeply rooted in the period.

Religion constituted a strong determining factor in the formation of the various kingdoms which, since the seventeenth century, were defining their limits through the struggle to reinstate a Christianity apparently threatened by Muslim presence. From early on, the genesis of the monarchies' power was understood as a manifestation of divine will, as exemplified by the famous miracle of Ourique, in which Christ is said to have appeared before the founder of Portugal to guide him to victory in the decisive battle he was about to wage (Buescu, "Mito," pp. 49–69). Subsequently, discoveries and other maritime expansion, in which the peninsular kingdoms became involved from the beginning of the fifteenth century, and which turned the sea into an essential element of their self-identifications, were conceived of and utilized by the crowns as a Catholic crusade, especially by those with closer ties to the seat of the Catholic world.

In these decisive processes, the monarchs were portrayed as paladins in the defense of the religion, a portrayal that was insistently reaffirmed from the sixteenth century, when Protestantism began to splinter medieval Christian unity. From that point on, the kings of Portugal, along with those of Castile and Aragon, were to institute themselves as the defenders of the purity of the faith in accordance with the codes of Roman orthodoxy. In order to do so, they called for the establishment in their respective territories of an Inquisition, over which they would exercise some power and which would serve both as a standard bearer for the maintenance of doctrinal integrity in the territories and as an instrument of affirmation of a strong power that was becoming more centralized and modern. Pictorial expressions of this positioning emerge – one of the most celebrated is Titian's *Religion rescued by Spain* – that helped spread not only political propaganda but also, it must be admitted, word of the benevolence of some monarchs. John III (r. 1521–57) of Portugal, for example, was known as "the merciful," principally for establishing the Tribunal of the Holy Office (1536) and for intensifying his own religious practices, particularly at the end of his life. Philip II (r. 1556–98), nephew and son-in-law of John III, before his death at the Escorial palace, itself a vivid emblem of the faith and power of the king, ordered 30,000 mass services for his soul and that his body be adorned with 7,422 relics (Antonio, "Coleccionismo"). The benevolence of the monarch was fed by the example of the great Spanish spiritual figures, such as Luis de Leon, Luis de Granada, and Juan de Avila (González García, "Sombra de Dios," p. 185). It also assumed fundamental importance for the propagation and defense of the Catholic faith, for which Philip deployed an unequal military power, the most significant expression of which was the victory over the Turks at Lepanto in 1571 (Borromeo, "Felipe II," p. 186). Misunderstandings between the Iberian monarchs and the papacy – in 1556 the duke of Alva went so far as to invade the Papal States – which were aggravated in the first half of the seventeenth century and which resulted in complaints by the pontiff regarding the weak manner in which Tridentine reforms were being applied in Spain (Tellechea Idígoras, "Clemente VIII," pp. 210–11), do not invalidate this interpretation. The "Catholic kings" in Spain and Manuel I (r. 1495–1521) in Portugal began some initiatives that went along with the tendencies assumed by the various modern European states, who wanted to increase their control over the churches in their territories (Prodi, "Concilio di Trento," pp. 12–13). The conquest of the right to ecclesiastical patronage for the overseas empires, the financing of maritime enterprises through the establishment of the Bull of the Crusade, the takeover of control of the military orders by the kings, and the reformation of religious orders were some of the common and essential facets of the policies followed. This is why the quarrels that erupted were not fundamentally of a doctrinal nature but rather were motivated by the sudden assignment of charges in the national churches, the limitation of ecclesiastical jurisdiction, particularly concerning the competency of the papal nuncio, the economic exploitation of church finances by the crown, and by the creation of obstacles to the acquisition of new property by religious institutions (Paiva, "A Igreja," pp. 146–54; Carpintero Aguado, "Iglesia," pp. 547–51).

The power that the church and its clerics assumed over centuries in the Iberian kingdoms is unquestionable. That power, which manifested itself in different forms, derived from the importance of religion in the lives of the respective populations, who were circumscribed, as it were, from birth to death, by the performance of the sacraments, devotional acts, and numerous religious celebrations. In politics, and through the overlapping relations between the church and the state, the presence of clerics in several key administrative posts is exemplary. These positions would be attained not only through the "private" influence exercised by the regal confessors – a post that, beginning in the second half of the sixteenth century, was filled mostly by Dominicans and Jesuits (Domínguez Ortiz, "Regalismo," pp. 92–4; Marques, "Jesuítas") – but also by the preachers and other clerics of the royal chapel, some of whom enjoyed close proximity to the king's counsel, of which the Jesuit António Vieira was an exponent during the reign of John IV (r. 1640–56). It is logical to believe that many of the top titular heads of various councils of the central adminis-tration, as well as some governors, viceroys, and ambassadors, were clerics. In Portugal, the process by which, from the reign of John III to the second decade of the seventeenth century, the most visible and highest positions in the government were occupied by clerics has justly been described as a "clericalization of govern-ments" (Magalhães, "O rei," p. 72). This profound entanglement of competencies, to which was associated the desire to "sacralize" the monarchy, would have consti-tuted an obstacle to the creation of a modern state, in its Weberian sense as a cen-tralized and secular configuration of governance (Fernández Albaladejo, "Iglesia").

In economic life, the strength of the church was responsible for the accumulation of abundant riches in the hands of the clergy. At the end of the eighteenth century, the revenues of the church would be equivalent to government revenues (Domínguez Ortiz, "Aspectos sociales," p. 71): current calculations suggest that the church held a third of the national income (Godinho, *Estrutura*, pp. 88–9). This is a significant aspect, given our understanding that, in the mid-eighteenth century, the clergy (regular and secular) of Castile constituted close to 1.58 percent of the population and held 14.7 percent of the land and 24 percent of the agricultural income (Rey Castelao, "Fundamentos económicos," p. 392).

In the social structure, the large percentage of clerics is noticeable. Domínguez Ortiz informs us that, by the time of Philip II's death, there were 33,000 secular clergy and 90,000 monks and nuns, a figure that corresponds to 1.2 percent of the total population, a percentage which grew in the seventeenth century (Domínguez Ortiz, *Antiguo Regimen*, p. 168). In Portugal, taking as an example the case of the office of the archbishop of Evora, a steady or constant increase can be noted. From 1527 to 1532, there were 626 presbyters, corresponding to one priest for every 223 laypeople. At the end of the sixteenth century there were 1,008 mass-officiating clerics for 163,165 people (1:162 inhabitants), and in 1681 they totaled 1,500 (Paiva, "Portuguese Secular Clergy," p. 158). To these numbers we still have to add the population of regular clergy. It was, essentially, a clericalization of society. There was practically no place, no matter how small, that did not have a local cleric, even as some small parishes had problems maintaining a resident priest. In the cities, the distribution of the clergy was greater than in the country; in some places, at particu-lar moments, the rates of clerical emplacement are impressive. In the seventeenth century, in Chinchon in the archdiocese of Toledo, there came to be one clergyman for every 24 inhabitants (Sanchez González, "Clero rural," p. 430).

In the cultural and pedagogical sphere, clerical influence was unsurpassed. Some of the preeminent heavyweights of Catholic spirituality belonged to the religious elite, such as Luis de Granada, Ignatius of Loyola, Francis Xavier, Bartolomeu dos Mártires, Teresa of Avila, and John of the Cross, as well as some distinguished university professors such as Francisco Vitoria, Martin Azpilcueta Navarro, Luis de Leon, Luis de Molina, Francisco Suarez, and Pedro da Fonseca. In teaching, the religious orders and particularly the Jesuits, directors of numerous colleges, were outstanding; the vigilance exercised by bishops in their dioceses over those who taught the alphabet was also central for the church in the diffusion of knowledge.

In both rural and urban settings, the omnipresent silhouette of churches, convents, church plazas, bells, crosses, and the different habits of the different religions would transform the physical space of daily life into an essential instrument of insertion or emplacement into the divine and the ecclesiastical. The spread of information and orders throughout the territory and among its peoples, even late into the eighteenth century, was only possible through the structures set up by the ecclesiastical order. The effective control of space (the territory) greatly accelerated the capacity to send messages through the tight grid of parishes, which acted like cells of their own administration. The support of the kings of Castile and Portugal for the decisions of the Council of Trent was crucial in accentuating tendencies that would make the two peninsular kingdoms standard bearers of a triumphant Catholicism.

The necessity of applying conciliar measures was intensified by some flourishes of Protestantism, which tended to be more intense in Spain than in Portugal, and which contributed to the fierce climate of religious monism and intransigence in relation to other religions that dominated the seventeenth-century peninsula. Protestantism maintained a shadowy presence. The majority of cases pursued by the Spanish and Portuguese Inquisitions are reported to be foreign (English, French, and German). As Christine Wagner demonstrates (Wagner, "Luteranos," p. 497), the Protestantism persecuted by the Toledo Inquisition was mostly French and Calvinist. A similar situation occurred in Portugal, where it was not until March 11, 1571 that a Portuguese person received a death sentence (Tavares, "Em torno," p. 210). Despite this, the fear of contamination increased, around the mid-sixteenth century, in proportion to the growth in adherence to Lutheran doctrines externally, the increasing identification between Lutheranism and Erasmians (here the Valladolid assembly of 1527 may serve as a harbinger), and the deeper aversion and belligerence toward all forms of dissidence and free thought. The famous discovery in 1557–8 of "Protestant circles" in Seville and Valladolid gave rise to a great confrontation and intensified the fear that not even Spain was safe from Protestantism. The arrest on August 22, 1559 of the archbishop of Toledo, Bartolomé Carranza de Miranda, the most important figure of the Spanish church, who was accused of Lutheranism by the Inquisition, was an unprecedented scandal and served as justification for the tightening of vigilance (Tellechea Idígoras, *Arzobispo Carranza*).

It is this tightening of vigilance that explains many future persecutions. Among them were those waged against Luis de Leon, beginning in 1571, for his translation of the *Song of Songs*, as well as against other professors in the University of Valladolid and even against a theologian who had been at Trent, Miguel de Medina. In Portugal, Valentim da Luz was burned in an *auto-da-fé* in Lisbon in 1562 because of his Erasmian tendencies, which were believed to be a manifestation of his adhesion to Lutheran thought (Dias, *Erasmismo*). Professors from the Colégio das Artes, which between 1547 and 1552 had been an important instrument of the infiltration of

Christian humanism in Portugal, were visited by the Holy Office (Brandão, *Inquisição*). These examples bear witness to the repression unleashed against humanist and evangelical currents which, in the first half of the sixteenth century, had gained so much acceptance and diffusion in the Portuguese and Castilian royal courts and support the turn that was already under way in the direction of a climate of Catholic orthodoxy. The time had passed in which, as humanist João de Barros noted, it was possible in Lisbon to speak freely about Lutheran doctrines (Barros, *Ropica Pnefma*). The banishment of any external ideology was the result. In 1559, Philip II barred Spaniards from going abroad to study, except those who chose to go to Rome, Bologna, or Coimbra. A simple quantitative analysis of the production of religious literature in Portugal, in which 75 percent of published authors were Portuguese, 17 percent Spanish, and 5 percent Italian, confirms this interpretation (Sousa, "Algumas hipóteses," p. 122).

Spanish and Portuguese participation in the Council of Trent was scant. In the third and last phase, which had the most delegates, there were a mere 14 Spaniards and three Portuguese; the Italian delegation consisted of 85 clerics. The discreet Portuguese presence, especially in the first two phases of the council, was due to the agitated state of relations between John III and the Holy See on account of the conditions of the nascent Portuguese Inquisition and also because of problems arising from the pope's nomination of the bishop of Viseu, Miguel da Silva, to cardinal, a promotion that went against the king's will. On the other hand, the necessity for the council was not internally very convincing, given the relative insignificance of Protestantism in Portugal. One of the initial obstacles faced by the Spanish delegation was how to reconcile the interests of Charles V and of Francis I of France, even when Charles V was more interested in using the council to maintain the Germanic unity of the empire. Despite these conditions, the committees present were made up of distinguished figures who shaped many of the decisions that were ultimately approved, especially in the third phase of the council, which paid close attention to measures aimed at reforming episcopal and clerical conduct. From the Portuguese side, the work of the theologians Francisco Foreiro and Diogo Paiva de Andrade, but above all that of Bartolomeu dos Mártires, deserves special mention (Castro, "Os portugueses em Trento"). On the Spanish side, the bishop of Almeria, Antonio Carrionero, and the archbishop of Granada, Pedro Guerrero, were equally crucial (Lopez Martin, "Don Antonio Carrionero," p. 11).

It has been proposed that the spirit that animated Tridentine reform may have its origin in the actions of the various pre-reformist Spanish bishops, by which it is said that the Catholic reform was more internally than externally driven. This thesis is debatable, but in fact in Spain and Portugal, and most noticeably beginning in the last quarter of the fifteenth century, several bishops had already begun to renovate the life of their respective dioceses. The process was by no means universal, did not have the same chronology everywhere, and, since it was not impeded at all by the Roman central power, assumed a very different character than that of the systematization that occurred after the council. In the kingdom of Aragon, this process was begun later than in Castile (Miguel García, "El arzobispo reformador," p. 78). In the meantime, many loose measures were applied whose spirit would only later be explicitly stated in the Tridentine decrees. These interventions were not always effective. Nevertheless, there were bishops who completed their residence, instituted regular diocesan visits, edited constitutions, printed missals so as to regulate the liturgy, organized catechisms through which to teach the doctrine to the faithful, established schools for training the clergy, and maintained vigilance over their residence, attire, and behavior; suspicions, however, tended to fall more on the clergy than on the faithful. This is one of the aspects that distinguished these pre-reform efforts from the renewal started at Trent.

In the period immediately after, starting in December 1563, the decrees approved by the Council of Trent were well received by the Iberian monarchies. In June of 1564, Pius IV published the bull *Benedictus Deus*, which affirmed the decisions made at Trent. About a month later, a royal cell dated July 12, 1564 declared the Tridentine decrees be treated as law in Castile; Aragon followed suit on July 31. These norms contained no explicit references to clauses that might clash with the general law or with the prerogatives of the crown, but in practice royal power was extremely vigilant in this regard (Fernández Terricabras, *Felipe II*, pp. 112–15). In order to facilitate acceptance, the Franciscan bishop of Cuenca Bartolomé Fresneda, whose support the pope had been seeking since 1563 through the nuncio in Spain, was enlisted. In Portugal, a judicial writ in September 1564 adopted consular legislation as general law. The same ordinance ordered royal officials to help bishops arrest people, carry out decrees, and maintain guard over secular prisoners. It could be said that, despite huge support, which in the Spanish case might have been linked to a strategy by Philip II to gain control over the process (Fernández Terricabras, *Felipe II*, pp. 379–80), the level of acceptance was different in both cases. These differences had subsequent consequences in the fulfillment of some reforms, particularly for pastoral visits (Carvalho, "Jurisdição episcopal," pp. 138–49). In Portugal, acceptance of Trent knew no limitations whatsoever; it was no coincidence that, at the time, the acting regent was Henrique, cardinal, inquisitor general, and archbishop of Evora, since his nephew King Sebastian was still a minor. These converging conditions contributed to the situation that ensued.

The principles of reform approved in Trent fueled a gigantic change in the life of the church. The paths that reform took, however, were not unexpected. Many of the measures had already been proposed and, in some cases, had previously been applied. Four interconnecting planes of action can be identified:

1   Reinforcement of hierarchies and, in particular, of the authority of the bishops.
2   Diffusion and homogenization of the content of dogma, doctrine, and liturgy as approved by Trent and as reinforced by the repression of heterodoxies.
3   Moral and disciplinary reform of the secular and regular clergy.
4   Circumscription and deepening of believers' religiosity and a more attentive vigilance over their moral and religious conduct.

This program was firmly supported by the monarchs; the diligence of the kings was decisive in the first stage. The precedent established by Philip II's actions was paradigmatic in this respect. He accepted the Tridentine decrees, encouraged the practical implementation of Trent decisions, thus stimulating the convocation of provincial councils, oversaw the residency of bishops, reformed religious orders, supported the creation of seminaries, and so on. Philip II was the great supporter of the reform in Spain (Fernández Collado, "Felipe II," p. 447).

The concretization of this project was not immediate. There are some who believe that the most intense period occurred in the years following the council, when everything was still new, and began to decline at the beginning of the 1590s (Tellechea Idígoras, *Reforma tridentina*, p. lv). In fact, measures were taken that were almost all productive of a normative, or even structural, encasement indispensable for the application of subsequent actions. Provincial councils were convened as well as synods that established new diocesan constitutions; pastoral visits were started again with a renewed intensity and framework; ecclesiastical tribunals were reactivated to combat improper behavior by clergy and laypeople. This last aspect, for example, emerges clearly when the actions of the episcopal tribunal of the diocese of Coria in the period from 1500 to 1700 are examined. There a sudden rise in the number of cases can be detected after 1565 and a pronounced fall beginning in 1595, followed by a long seventeenth century marked by great irregularity in the actions of the tribunal (Perez Muñoz, *Pecar*, p. 22).

I believe, however, that this view is somewhat reductive. Undoubtedly, Catholic reform maintained a vigorous impulse in the decades following the council, but it only instituted itself definitively after a dynamic process that lasted the following two centuries. This time was necessary given the extent of the changes proposed by the program. Bishops were entrusted with the means for making the program bear fruit. Consequently, the application of reform fundamentally depended on their actions, which means that in the approximately 50 dioceses of the peninsula, not everything was run the same way, not to mention the variety of situations that obtained in the overseas dioceses, from the Orient to America.

The reinforcement of authority and of episcopal jurisdiction was an essential tool for the application of consular norms. Prelates were given new competencies and means, thus concentrating in them the functioning of the religious life of the dioceses, putting limitations on the multiple privileges that existed at the heart of the church. The bishops, who now enjoyed extensive jurisdiction over people and institutions which, until then, they had hardly controlled and who now acquired more effective means of correction and greater freedom to act, seemed like papal delegates in their own territory (Carvalho, *Visitas pastorais*, pp. 34–41). This process of episcopal reinforcement was responsible for the explosion of numerous conflicts with the chapters of the Holy See, the collegiate churches, military orders, and religious congregations. In many dioceses serious quarrels erupted, frequently in response to the application of Tridentine determinations, as was the case with the creation of seminaries or the carrying out of pastoral visits. These quarrels became more frequent in the period immediately after Trent and tended to decrease as time passed and episcopal authority became consolidated, often following the solemnization of covenants or concordats among the parties involved. In some cases the violence was severe and required the intervention of pontifical authority. In 1588 the bishop of Lérida wrote to the pope to inform him that he could not live in the cathedral, or implement any Tridentine decisions, because of the obstacles created for him by the chapters. In the same year, the Barcelona chapter was opposed to many of the measures that the prelate wanted to implement. Throughout the seventeenth century many Catalan bishops complained to the pope of the insubordination of the chapters (Kamen, *Phoenix and the Flame*, p. 115). In Portugal in 1612, in the office of the archbishop of Evora, a dispute that was common elsewhere over the contribution owed by the chapters for the functioning of the seminary turned into open conflict between the chapters and Archbishop José de Melo (Baptista, "Formação do clero," p. 61). For the most part, these problems did not have a religious dimension; they were mainly provoked by such things as attempts to reaffirm the jurisdictional power of the prelates, the diminution of rights that negatively impacted economic revenues, questions of social representation in public acts, or the purveyance of offices that would clash with the administration of clienteles.

Renewal passed to the reform of the prelates, who began to be chosen more carefully by the monarchs, with intellectual and moral qualities being taken into account. Studies conducted by Barrio Gonzalo demonstrate that, at the time of their appointment, the majority of prelates were older than 40, were literate in canon law or theology, and were previous officeholders either in the church or in the state, which "guaranteed" that they would fulfill their offices properly (Barrio Gonzalo, *Obispos de Castilla y Léon*, pp. 58–83). These tendencies have been observed with the Portuguese bishops of the same period (Paiva, "Os mentores," pp. 228–33). Over time, they became more attuned to the model of the Tridentine bishop. The famous examples of Pedro Guerrero of Granada or Bartolomeu dos Mártires of Braga are not the only ones that could be cited. Many figures who were lesser known in the period shone in subsequent periods, such as Luís da Silva, bishop of Lamego (1677–85), Guarda (1685–91), and Evora (1691–1703). Besides being a resident in the diocese, he officiated regularly at mass and during the sacraments, personally visited the bishop, taught the doctrine to the faithful, convened synods and printed diocesan constitutions, created mechanisms to improve the training of the secular clergy, welcomed new religious congregations, and spent the major part of his episcopal revenues on the needy, all of which earned him the title of "father of the poor."

The diffusion and homogenization of the content of dogma, doctrine, and the new discipline for the clergy and the faithful formed another essential axis of action. The Council of Trent stipulated that provincial councils be held every three years and diocesan synods annually. In this way, immediately after the council, there was an increase in the convocation of these meetings as well as in the compilation of new diocesan constitutions, where adjustment in accordance with the Tridentine dispositions was declared, even as the agreed frequency of celebrations was never upheld. These actions were nevertheless important instruments for the consummation of episcopal power, something that was marked in the ceremonial of its celebrations, as was demonstrated in relation to the synods (Paiva, "Public ceremonies," pp. 418–22).

The first provincial council was celebrated in Toledo in September 1565 and was marked by the active intervention of King Philip. It was no coincidence that Archbishop Carranza de Miranda, titular head of the metropolis, was at the time under arrest by the Inquisition. The king's diplomatic intervention was useful for overcoming the obstacles created above all by the chapters. Through the bishop of Cuenca and Francisco de Toledo, viceroy of Peru, the interference of the king was significant and the "agenda" of the sessions was marked by his directives: to obey all that was decreed in Trent; to establish the general doctrine without "descending" into details; to discuss patrimonial and jurisdictional matters; to bring up reform of the secular clergy and of public morality; to avoid overly polemical issues; and to try to balance the interests of the crown and those of Rome in order to avoid not only any submissions but also quarrels with the Holy See (Fernández Collado, "Felipe II," pp. 457–61). Similar interventions occurred in the first provincial councils of Braga (in September 1566) and Lisbon (in December of the same year). This last, which was convened by the regent, archbishop and cardinal Henrique, was attended by King Sebastian and the widowed queen, Catarina of Austria. Their presence was a significant sign of support by the monarchy for the burgeoning reform.

After the meeting of provincial councils, the bishops promoted the meeting of diocesan synods. In Spain, from 1565 until the end of the sixteenth century, 80 were convened (Reder Gadow, "Felipe II," p. 397) and 18 in Portugal; all of the dioceses had at least one during this period. These meetings would constitute an indispensable method for implementing the reforms, since it was from them that ecclesiastical legislation adapted to the new orientation emanated. This accounts for the vigilance of the regal power, which demanded the presence of a representative whose function it was to impede the adoption of clauses that would harm royal jurisdiction. This attitude provoked the reaction of some prelates, who did not accept such interference and who even refused to convene synods under such circumstances, as was the case with the archbishop of Lisbon, Miguel de Castro (1586–1625). In Portugal, all 13 continental dioceses adjusted their constitutions and edited printed versions: Miranda and Evora in 1565, Lisbon in 1569, Porto in 1585, Coimbra in 1591, Leiria in 1601, Guarda in 1621, Portalegre in 1632, Elvas in 1635, Algarve in 1674, Lamego in 1683, and, finally, Braga in 1697. The chronology of the editing of these texts is another indicator of how the reform movement was delayed and sustained a substantially different pace from diocese to diocese.

The diffusion of doctrine and the uniformization of the liturgy were even promoted through the abundant editions of religious books (devotionals, catechisms, confession manuals, syllabi of moral theology, hagiographies, devotional biographies, etc.). Many laypeople became used to handling them, while others were instructed by pastors, confessors, or spiritual guides who used the books for teaching. Some bishops decreed that parish priests should possess a personal library of such works. This decree was "verified" through pastoral visits. To a certain extent, this avalanche of religious texts was part of a larger Tridentine strategy, which consisted in flooding the market with texts that were religious and/or apologetic of Rome's actions. It was a "battle of words" against the dissidents, and the church had in the pulpits another fundamental instrument. The sacred oratory, preached everywhere from the pulpits of the royal chapel to the poorest church, on such different occasions as an *auto-da-fé*, the commemoration of the birth of a prince or during a mission, was an essential piece of the strategy.

Beyond books and preaching, art and the theater were also used to transmit the new message. Kings, bishops, chapters, religious congregations, brotherhoods, and almshouses, known as *Misericórdias* (which had relevant functions in the Portuguese world), sponsored various artistic programs. There was, moreover, an urgent preoccupation with finding a doctrinal language that would convincingly express Tridentine ideology, since art, particularly painting, was meant to have an exemplary function that would move the faithful by provoking in them feelings of devotion. In this context the role of images assumes profound relevance, since they allowed the illiterate to comprehend certain messages; they facilitated learning and served as a complement to the texts. Through the "intimate contemplative experience of the image" an "ideal of devotion strongly supported by the imagination" evolved which greatly shaped the piety of Iberians (González García, "Sombra de Dios," p. 192). Religious theater, which was spread by seventeenth-century Jesuits, was a means to disseminate Biblical scenes and episodes from the saints' lives, which were very popular. The tradition that was established influenced the theatrical production of such great dramatists of the golden age in Spain as Lope de Vega and Calderon de la Barca (Hornedo, "Teatro").

Equally decisive was the publication of texts elaborated by the papacy, such as the missal, breviary, ritual or ceremonial of the bishops, and the catechism. This last book can be used as an example. Originally promulgated by Pius V, it had its first edition in Rome in 1566 and appeared in Spain in 1577, printed in Medina del Campo. Soon efforts were made, with some "stimulation" from the papacy, to produce other versions in the various national languages. In Portugal, on the order of the archbishop of Lisbon, Miguel de Castro, it was translated in 1690. In Spain in 1567, the pope himself had charged the inquisitor general, Diego Espinosa, with translating the text. Despite this, the first Castilian version did not appear until 1777, in Pamplona, even though in 1596 there had been a Basque edition (Moreno Gallego, "Dominicos y letras," p. 350). There were some Spanish theologians who raised objections to certain interpretations in the Roman catechism, in particular its pronouncements on the doctrine of baptism. These objections, coupled with the fact that Archbishop Carranza de Miranda had shortly before written a catechism resembling the Roman one, prompted the Council of the Inquisition to raise obstacles against a Vulgate edition (Rodríguez, *El Catecismo romano*, pp. 38–58). Translations of theological texts or of the Bible were justified. It was argued that the unpreparedness of lay men and women could lead to free and incorrect interpretations that would have disastrous effects on the preservation of orthodoxy. On the other hand, keeping the texts in Latin turned clerics into privileged mediators of the divine word, helping to combat the Lutheran doctrine of universal priesthood. This situation contrasted with what had occurred in the Hispanic pre-reform period, during which regular contact between the faithful (as individuals) and the Biblical text had augmented. Nevertheless, as the seventeenth century advanced, direct contact between the people and the Holy Scriptures was increasingly discouraged. Priests were regularly asked to read the Gospel to the faithful, a request that was not always fulfilled or, if it was, was often performed with inadequate preparation in the Scriptures (Vázquez, "Controversias doctrinales," pp. 420–1). At the same time, in universities such as those at Coimbra and Salamanca, more attention was being given to Biblical studies and to theology (moral theology and Mariology occupying privileged places). The period after Trent until the middle of the 1600s was considered the golden century of Catholic exegesis, and Spain as well as Portugal possessed some of its most dignified representatives (Rodrigues, *A cátedra*).

The reform of the clergy was another essential pillar of the Catholic reform. The "clericalization" of the church was a Tridentine response to the Lutheran notion of universal priesthood, and it was justified by the knowledge that the urgent instruction of the faithful would be more achievable through a better-prepared clergy. It is true that 150 years after Trent many prelates were still be found, some already invigorated by Catholic enlightenment, who lamented the ignorance of the rural clergy, as was the case with the bishops of Coria and Badajoz in 1713 (Kamen,

Phoenix and the Flame, p. 341), or those of Lamego in the first half of the eighteenth century (Paiva, "Os mentores," pp. 223–4). But there is no doubt that reform of this body bore immense fruit. Humility, honesty, decorum, lucidity in language, use of attire, residency, zeal in the administration of the catechism, confession, and the sacraments to parishioners, and the rejection of secular and mundane behaviors (games and bull-runs, the handling of weapons, frequenting taverns, servile work) were all facets that slowly took root, contributing to the creation of a new image of the clergy, something that had important consequences for the church's actions. The cultural level of the clergy improved as well, as is demonstrated by studies of clerics who had university degrees before and after Trent in the dioceses of Coimbra (Fonseca, "Origem social," p. 36), Cuenca (Nalle, *God in La Mancha*, pp. 92–4), or Toledo, where in the seventeenth century half the priests already had the title of licentiate (Sanchez González, "Clero rural," p. 433).

The heterogeneity of the clerical body was staggering considering its diversity in terms of class, social background, and cultural formation. There was a wide difference between an archbishop of Toledo (who had an annual rent that varied between 200 and 300 ducados) and one from Evora (40 to 60 ducados per annum), and between the richest dioceses in Spain and Portugal, which were habitually occupied by the university-educated descendants of the highest nobility, and the multitude of priests who governed small parishes, many of them virtually illiterate and with rents that hardly allowed them to feed themselves. This does not even take account of the large number of unemployed clergy who survived by "lending" their services at masses and sundry religious events; in many churches, they constituted almost half of the clerical corpus, as was the case in Cuenca (Nalle, *God in La Mancha*, p. 73).

The improvements that were experienced resulted from greater care taken in granting admission to and administering the holy orders, facilitated by pastoral visitations and more vigilant policies on the part of bishops. Another decisive aspect was the institutionalization of a system of licenses, granted by bishops to enable clerics to officiate at mass, confess, or preach within the limits of each diocese.

Diocesan constitutions came to regulate the exams that were to be administered to candidates for orders in a much more rigorous manner. These demanded, besides knowledge of Latin grammar, the ability to sing, an adequate knowledge of basic Christian doctrines and sometimes even of theology (the sacraments, mysteries of the faith, matters of conscience), not to mention the need for candidates to have good moral conduct and a patrimony. These requirements were reproduced almost everywhere, as occurred in the constitutions in Valladolid in 1606 (Barrio Gonzalo, "Clero diocesano," p. 123).

The creation of seminaries and the institution by prelates of courses on matters of conscience and on the Holy Scriptures constituted another method of action. The first had been a Tridentine obligation, for which archbishop of Granada Pedro Guerrero had struggled; it was also not easy to implement. One of the initial difficulties was how to finance them. On the other hand, the existence of universities and Jesuit colleges was often invoked to justify the non-establishment of seminaries. Despite this, many were founded, particularly in the sixteenth century. In Spain, after Burgos and Granada, which was created in 1565, a further 18 were founded up to the end of the century, and eight more during the seventeenth (Martin Hernandez, *Seminarios españoles*). In Portugal, the first appeared in Lisbon in 1566 and in Braga in 1572; three more were built up to the end of the century, with a similar number in the following century (Paiva, "Os mentores," p. 215). In other words, this process was concluded only up to the second half of the eighteenth century. It should be noted that not every future priest went through the seminary. In fact, the number of priests who did was still relatively small, and the clergy continued to be trained through traditional channels. The available data suggest that frequenting the seminary conferred some advantages. A written report of the state of the clergy requested by the prelate of Cordoba in 1683 concluded that of the 400 clerics evaluated, only four of those who went to seminary had committed grievances (Ruiz de Adana, *Clero en el siglo XVII*, p. 138).

The result of all these efforts was that, with regional differences and in relation to the same clerical statutes, central problems such as residency and the non-increase in benefits were significantly improved. By the end of the seventeenth century, these two matters were practically resolved in dioceses such as Seville (Candau Chacon, *Clero rural*, pp. 315–17, 400) and Coimbra (Paiva, "Portuguese Secular Clergy," p. 165), to give just two examples. The same can be said in relation to the administration of the sacraments by the parish priests. Through the written accounts of pastoral visits to the clergy of Seville in the eighteenth century, we know that, among 337 clerics, almost all enforced the administration of the Eucharist (Martin Rego, "Eucaristia," p. 217). Naturally, there are many lacunae. From the point of view of social and moral behavior, maintaining the same regional and statute variability, the most common faults were nonconformity to celibacy and the excessive consumption of wine. From the point of view of sacerdotal leadership, failure to teach the doctrine was the most serious problem. But the most important thing to notice is that in the second half of the seventeenth century, only a small portion of the clergy had been found guilty of improprieties. In Toledo, they numbered only 10 percent of the total group (Sanchez González, "Clero rural," p. 435).

At the level of the regular clergy we find new orders, who were protagonists of Catholic reform and essential vehicles of the new values. They played a vital role not only in overseas evangelization, where the Franciscans in Spanish America and the Jesuits in the East and in Brazil distinguished themselves, but also in internal mission programs, particularly in teaching and lending assistance. One of these was the Company of Jesus, whose founder members included the Portuguese Simão Rodrigues. We should also not forget the great following that the Carmelites enjoyed, thanks in large part to the fame of St. Teresa of Avila and St. John of the Cross. Equally remarkable was the reform of some of the existing orders, part of a movement that had deep roots in the Iberian peninsula. In this domain, people originating in Spain unleashed many of the reforms made in Portugal (Fernandes, "Da reforma," p. 19).

The attraction for a religiosity reformed by the challenges of evangelizing a New World, the search for economic security, and the nobility's habit of placing second daughters in convents provoked such an explosive growth of new foundations – experienced, in Spain's case, more strongly in the south than in the north – that the monarchs were forced to attempt to slow down religious vocations. The golden period of this movement was the end of the sixteenth and first half of the seventeenth centuries; in the cities, the growth was more visible than in the country. In Valladolid and Medina del Campo there were 76 institutions for monks or nuns, of which 74 percent were founded in this period (Barrio Gonzalo, "Clero regular," p. 191). The Sisters of St. Clare alone, during the sixteenth century, were able to create 83 new foundations (Martínez de Vega, "Santa Ana," p. 336), and, in the subsequent century, close to 75 percent of religiously employed women were from this order. In Portugal, the implementation of new congregations occurred at a steady pace: Discalced Carmelites in 1581, Cartuxos in 1587, Franciscan Conceptionists in 1629, French Capuchins in 1647, Theatines in 1650, Discalced Augustinians in 1663, Oratorians in 1668, and Apostolic Missionaries in 1679.

The heterogeneity of the orders was great, something that had wide repercussions for some of the controversies that arose among them. Some of these controversies, embracing disputes over power by the monarchy or the aristocracy, involved almost all the orders, while others, provoked by differing doctrinal interpretations such as those that occurred in the 1620s over the Immaculate Conception, pitted Dominicans against Jesuits and Franciscans. There were even a few disputes over the different pedagogical conceptions and/or methodology for teaching Latin and natural philosophy; these constituted one of the great cultural polemics between the Oratorians and the Jesuits beginning in the 1600s.

Reform of the conduct and religiosity of the population was also an essential area of Catholic renewal after Trent. Some contend that the religious practice of the pious was scarcely affected by the Catholic reform (Christian, *Local Religion*, p. 147), and that the latter continued to ignore the rudiments of dogma and even the most simple prayers, a problem which, it is claimed, was further complicated in the peninsula by the presence of numerous communities of Jewish and Muslim converts. Recent studies have shown that, despite the difficulties that arose and the failure of some enterprises, there was a profound change in behavior. Suffice it to say that what happened to the Cuenca inquisitors in 1556, who were shocked by a priest accused of blasphemy who did not confess and knew none of the church's prayers (Nalle, *God in La Mancha*, p. 104), would hardly be repeated a century later. An analysis of inquisitorial procedures in the second half of the seventeenth century confirms that the majority of believers were already capable of reproducing the ten commandments and that they knew the principal prayers: the Creed, the Rosary, and the Lord's Prayer. Registers of those who confessed and the extensive furnishing of churches with confessionals prove that almost all complied annually with confession and communion. Portuguese episcopal visits demonstrate that few failed to observe the dominical precept, with higher rates of disobedience among men in certain parts of Catalonia (Kamen, *Phoenix and the Flame*, pp. 118–20). In the case of the diocese of Coimbra, the rates are made up by those who were accused of conduct not befitting the Christian ethic and who repented after being punished by the visitors (Paiva, "Administração diocesana," pp. 102–3). Finally, parochial registers are the best proof that the overwhelming majority of the population regularly performed baptism, marriage, and extreme unction and that the church made efforts to control this (Gouveia, "Sacramentalização," pp. 531–2). Granting that knowledge of the liturgy may have been superficial and that the sacraments may frequently have been received with little real conviction, absolute depravity, or near paganism, had been eradicated. It should be admitted that in some more distant regions action was taken too late, as Allyson Poska has pointed out in an excellent study of the Ourense diocese in Galicia, where a vision and practice of religion shaped by local structures predominated, proving that there were some pockets where the Tridentine spirit did not reign (Poska, *Regulating the People*).

Many forms of popular piety propagated by the church in this crusade were represented as the defense against attack by the Protestant Reformation (Egido, *Claves de la Reforma*, p. 97). In this way, to highlight the merits of its work, Catholicism stimulated the practices of penitence and pilgrimage, as long as they were properly circumscribed by the clergy. To reaffirm the doctrine of purgatory and the value of suffering, the church promoted indulgences, special masses for the dead, and the installation of a coffer for the souls that became a feature of almost every church. To make up for the costs of these interventions, it insisted on the cult of the Virgin Mary and of an immense court of saints (in Spain alone, 20 new saints were canonized in the seventeenth century), who were presented as models of conduct and protectors against calamity, and who overflowed temples and oratories deprived of relics and images, all of which contributed to a scenic spectacle characteristic of the landscape of modern Catholic temples. The cult of the Eucharist was stimulated through the creation of coffers, with solemn processions for Corpus Christi, lausperenes, Eucharistic thrones, and the 40-hour cult, one of the few completely new forms of devotion brought by the Catholic reform (Marques, "Rituais," pp. 564–5). In contrast, the Biblical text, the essential fountain of the reformed piety, was kept out of the "dangerous" hands of lay men and women.

In turn, this contributed to the creation of a "sensorial," "exterior" piety which has been characterized by many as baroque – magnificently displayed not only in processions put together for the most varied purposes, but also in the golden altars, filled with angels and seraphim, that began to embellish churches – and as a stimulus for some devotional sentiments particularly pleasing for the senses. In this category we can classify the Cross and the Passion, both of which invoke and represent Christ's pain; they were envisioned as tools for arousing reflection on the consequences of sin and the need for repentance, a constant trace of the affective spirituality of the post-Tridentine period, which found strong expression in the Lenten processions in Spain and in the celebrations of the Way of the Cross. Even devotion to the Child Jesus was accompanied by an explosion of iconographic representations (the Child of the Passion, the recumbent Child, the Child in his Majesty, the Child as Lord of the Universe), whether in painting or in sculpture, a magnificent collection of which can be found at the Museo de las Descalzas Reales in Madrid. Through these multiple outlets, and in contradistinction to the interiorization of devotion as proposed by Erasmian Neoplatonic idealism and to the humanist hostility for the image and for the ritualistic and formal aspects of religion, the Catholic reform enlarged, so to speak, the emotional and sensual aspects of common piety during religious manifestations, sometimes meeting them halfway in its taste for the marvelous, the excessive, and the surprising. The practical effect was the breathtaking and splendid spectacle of religious ceremonies and other solemnities (Bouza Alvarez, *Religiosidad*, p. 475).

But the reformation also owed much to the individual action of certain laymen and circles of devoted laypeople. Among these groups of beatified female and third orders gained prominence, who, stimulated by the devout, would practice both mental prayer and austere bodily mortification. Some cases provided the origin to the phenomena of faked sanctity, revelations, ecstasies, and visions that made up one facet of Iberian religiosity, thus necessitating the religious and clerical pressure that was exerted over laypeople and the vigilance of the Inquisition and bishops.

In parallel with more collective and exterior forms of piety, in some restricted circles there evolved a religion with a more spiritualist bent, where there was room for private prayer and even a certain religious individualism. The latter was strongly stimulated by the spread of individual confession, a vehicle that propelled the frequent exercise of introspection indicative of the intimate reform of the individual. The valorization of conscious self-examination by the penitent as preparatory to the act of confession, conjoined with the diffusion of a moralizing literature, signifies that, in fact, the church wanted to correct as much as to reform, including the correction of behaviors, tastes, and even gestures (Fernandes, "Da reforma," p. 35). Among these corrections can be counted the practice of bowing one's head before the Cross and images, of adoring the Holy Sacrament with humility, of kneeling during the reading of the Gospel, of maintaining silence during rituals, and of genuflecting when passing before a priest.

The battle against superstitions and ignorance that had characterized the religiosity of believers, which can now be classified as a systematic effort to reshape the faithful, was waged through patient and lasting campaigns so as to avoid ruptures and dissension – even if it meant using coercive methods, ranging from pastoral visits to inquisitorial persecution, to punish the more recalcitrant (García Carcél, "La iglesia triunfante," p. 86; Paiva, *Bruxaria*, pp. 352–4). The means used in this complex process of indoctrination and transformation of the ethic of conduct were extremely varied and were responsible for the eradication and change of the multiple facets of urban and rural culture. Altogether, even if the hierarchy might not have fully thought through these efforts, there was a strong disciplinary effect on society, something that has been recently theorized as relevant for the construction of the modern state (Prodi, *Disciplina*, p. 9). Among these means, mention should be made of pastoral visits, missions, the confession, the Inquisition, and the brotherhoods which, beyond the diffusion of certain cults, performed functions aimed at circumscribing the religious and moral life of parishioners. The first-mentioned had much greater regularity and efficacy over the conduct of the laity in Portugal than in Spain, which coincided with the means of correction at the bishops' disposal. Missions, which were systematically carried out by the Jesuits, Franciscans, and, later, Oratorians and Lazarists, were fundamental elements in the diffusion of cults and devotions, in the teaching of the doctrine, in the imposition of the habit of confession, and in the disciplining of behavior (Palomo del Barrio, *Fazer*, pp. 357–67). Confession, which facilitated the purification of the clergy's preparation as well as that of the faithful, brought the two together, sometimes too closely, leading to abuses that the Inquisition finally persecuted as "solicitation." The Inquisition, whose actions were intensified in the seventeenth century, saw to it that the language and religious beliefs of the population did not slip into heterodoxy, if not heresy. Bishop, missionary, confessor, and inquisitor never allowed believers to rest.

BIBLIOGRAPHY

Antonio, T. de, "Coleccionismo, devoción, y contrarreforma," in *Felipe II. Un monarca y su epoca: Un principe del Renacimiento*. Madrid: Sociedad Estatal para la Conmemoración de los centenarios de Felipe II y Carlos V, 1998, pp. 135–57.

Baptista, J. C., "A formação do clero na diocese de Évora," *A Cidade de Évora*, 61–2 (1978–9), pp. 5–90.

Barrio Gonzalo, M., "El clero diocesano: Beneficios y beneficiados," in *Historia de la diocesis de Valladolid*. Valladolid: Arzobispado de Valladolid; Diputación Provincial de Valladolid, 1996, pp. 23–149.

Barrio Gonzalo, M., "El clero regular: Monasterios y conventos," in *Historia de la diocesis de Valladolid*. Valladolid: Arzobispado de Valladolid; Diputación Provincial de Valladolid, 1996, pp. 191–214.

Barrio Gonzalo, M., *Los obispos de Castilla y Léon durante el Antiguo Régimen (1556–1834): Estudio socioeconómico*. Zamora, Junta de Castilla y León: Consejeria de Educación y Cultura, 2000.

Barros, J. de, *Ropica Pnefma*. Lisbon: Germão Galharde, 1532.

Borromeo, A., "Felipe II y el absolutismo confesional," in *Felipe II. Un monarca y su epoca: La monarquia Hispanica*. Madrid: Sociedad Estatal para la Conmemoración de los centenarios de Felipe II y Carlos V, 1998, pp. 185–95.

Bouza Alvarez, J. L., *Religiosidad contrarreformista y cultura simbolica del barroco*. Madrid: Consejo Superior de Investigaciones Cientificas, 1990.

Brandão, M., *A Inquisição e os professores do Colégio das Artes*, 2 vols. Coimbra: Universidade de Coimbra, 1948–69.

Buescu, A. I., "O mito das origens da nacionalidade: O milagre de Ourique," in Francisco Bethencourt and Diogo Ramada Curto, eds., *A memória da Nação*. Lisbon: Livraria Sá da Costa, 1991, pp. 49–69.

Candau Chacon, M. L., *El clero rural de Sevilla en el siglo XVIII*. Seville: Caja Rural de Sevilla, 1994.

Carpintero Aguado, L., "Iglesia y corte castellana en el siglo XVI: Contribucion y tributos," *Hispania Sacra*, 41 (1989), pp. 547–67.

Carvalho, J. R. de, *As visitas pastorais e a sociedade de Antigo Regime: Notas para o estudo de um mecanismo de normalização social*. Coimbra: Faculdade de Letras da Universidade de Coimbra, 1985.

Carvalho, J. R. de, "A jurisdição episcopal sobre leigos em matéria de pecados públicos: As visitas pastorais e o comportamento moral das populações portuguesas de Antigo Regime," *Revista Portuguesa de História*, 24 (1988), pp. 121–63.

Castro, J. de, "Os portugueses em Trento," *Lumen*, 25 (1961), pp. 739–76.

Christian, W. A., Jr., *Local Religion in Sixteenth-Century Spain*. Princeton, NJ: Princeton University Press, 1981.

Dias, J. S. S., *O erasmismo e a Inquisição em Portugal: O processo de Fr. Valentim da Luz*. Coimbra: Faculdade de Letras Universidade de Coimbra, 1975.

Domínguez Ortiz, A., "Aspectos sociales de la vida eclesiastica en los siglos XVII y XVIII," in Ricardo García-Villoslada, ed., *Historia de la Iglesia en España*. Madrid: Biblioteca de Autores Cristianos, 1979, vol. 4, pp. 5–72.

Domínguez Ortiz, A., "Regalismo y relaciones Iglesia–Estado en el siglo XVII," in Ricardo García-Villoslada, ed., *Historia de la Iglesia en España*. Madrid: Biblioteca de Autores Cristianos, 1979, vol. 4, pp. 73–121.

Domínguez Ortiz, A., *El Antiguo Regimen: Los reys catolicos y los Austrias*. Madrid: Alianza editorial, 1988.

Egido, T., *Las claves de la Reforma y la Contrarreforma 1517–1648*. Barcelona: Editorial Planeta, 1991.

Fernandes, M. de L. C., "Da reforma da Igreja à reforma dos cristãos," in Carlos Moreira Azevedo, ed., *História Religiosa de Portugal*. Lisbon: Círculo de Leitores, 2000, vol. 2, pp. 15–38.

Fernández Albaladejo, P., "Iglesia y configuración del poder en la monarquia católica (siglos

XV–XVII): Algunas consideraciones," in *État et Église dans la génèse de l'État Moderne: Actes du colloque organisé par le Centre National de la Recherche Scientifique et la Casa de Velázquez*. Madrid: Casa de Velázquez, 1986, pp. 209–16.

Fernández Collado, A., "Felipe II y su mentalidad reformadora en el concilio provincial toledano de 1565," *Hispania Sacra*, 50/101 (1998), pp. 447–66.

Fernández Terricabras, I., *Felipe II y el clero secular: La aplicacion del Concilio de Trento*. Madrid: Sociedad Estatal para la Conmemoración de los Centenarios de Felipe II y Carlos V, 2000.

Fonseca, F. T. da, "Origem social do clero conimbricense no século XVI (1581–1585)," *Actas do simpósio internacional comemorativo do IV Centenário da morte de Juão de Ruão*. Coimbra: Epartur, 1982, pp. 27–56.

García Carcél, R., "La iglesia triunfante," in *Arte y saber: La cultura en tiempos de Felipe III y Felipe IV*. Madrid: Ministerio de Educación y Cultura, 1999, pp. 77–87.

Godinho, V. M., *Estrutura da antiga sociedade portuguesa*. Lisbon: Arcádia, 1977.

González García, J. L., "La sombra de Dios: Imitatio Christi y contrición en la piedad privada de Felipe II," in *Felipe II. Un monarca y su epoca: Un príncipe del Renacimiento*. Madrid: Sociedad Estatal para la Conmemoración de los centenarios de Felipe II y Carlos V, 1998, pp. 185–201.

Gouveia, A. C., "A sacramentalização dos ritos de passagem," in Carlos Moreira Azevedo, ed., *História Religiosa de Portugal*. Lisbon: Círculo de Leitores, 2000, vol. 2, pp. 529–57.

Hornedo, R. M., "Teatro e Iglesia en los siglos XVII y XVIII," in Ricardo García-Villoslada, ed., *Historia de la Iglesia en España*. Madrid: Biblioteca de Autores Cristianos, 1979, vol. 4, pp. 309–58.

Kamen, H., *The Phoenix and the Flame: Catalonia and the Counter-Reformation*. New Haven, Conn.: Yale University Press, 1993.

Lopez Martin, J., "Don Antonio Carrionero, obispo de Almeria, Padre conciliar en Trento," *Anthologica Annua*, 30–1 (1983–4), pp. 11–44.

Magalhães, J. R., "O rei," in José Mattoso, ed., *História de Portugal*. Lisbon: Círculo de Leitores, 1993, vol. 3, pp. 61–73.

Marques, J., *A arquidiocese de Braga no século XV*. Lisbon: Imprensa Nacional Casa da Moeda, 1988, pp. 1122–72.

Marques, J., "Os jesuítas, confessores da corte portuguesa na época barroca (1550–1700)," *Revista da Faculdade de Letras – História*, 12 (1995), pp. 231–70.

Marques, J., "Rituais e manifestações de culto," in Carlos Moreira Azevedo, ed., *História Religiosa de Portugal*. Lisbon: Círculo de Leitores, 2000, vol. 2, pp. 517–601.

Martin Hernandez, F., *Los seminarios españoles: Historia y pedagogia*. Salamanca: Ediciones Sígueme, 1964.

Martin Rego, M., "La eucaristia en la archidiócesis hispalense a través de los libros de visitas pastorales. Siglo XVIII," *Isidorianum*, 3 (1993), pp. 203–30.

Martínez de Vega, M. E., "Santa Ana de Valencia de Alcantara: Un convento clariano bajo la jurisdiccion de la orden de Alcantara," in Enrique Martinez Ruiz and Vicente Suarez Grimon, eds., *Iglesia y Sociedad en el Antiguo Regimen*. Madrid: Associación Española de Historia Moderna, 1994, vol. 1, pp. 335–48.

Miguel García, I., "El arzobispo reformador," in *Don Hernando de Aragón: Arzobispo de Zaragoza y Virrey de Aragón*. Saragossa: Caja de Ahorros de la Immaculada de Aragón, 1998, pp. 75–131.

Moreno Gallego, V., "Dominicos y letras en la España ortosecular del XVII," in Enrique Martinez Ruiz and Vicente Suarez Grimon, eds., *Iglesia y Sociedad en el Antiguo Regimen*. Madrid: Associación Española de Historia Moderna, 1994, vol. 1, pp. 349–65.

Nalle, S. T., *God in La Mancha: Religious Reform and the People of Cuenca, 1500–1650*. Baltimore: Johns Hopkins University Press, 1992.

Paiva, J. P., "A administração diocesana e a presença da Igreja: O caso da diocese de Coimbra nos séculos XVII e XVIII," *Lusitania Sacra*, 3 (1991), pp. 71–110.

Paiva, J. P., *Bruxaria e superstição num país sem caça às bruxas, 1600–1774*. Lisbon: Editorial Notícias, 1997.

Paiva, J. P., "A Igreja e o poder," in Carlos Moreira Azevedo, ed., *História Religiosa de Portugal*. Lisbon: Círculo de Leitores, 2000, vol. 2, pp. 135–85.

Paiva, J. P., "Os mentores," in Carlos Moreira Azevedo, ed., *História Religiosa de Portugal*. Lisbon: Círculo de Leitores, 2000, vol. 2, pp. 201–37.

Paiva, J. P., "The Portuguese Secular Clergy in the Sixteenth and Seventeenth Centuries," in Eszter Andor and István György Tóth, eds., *Frontiers of Faith*. Budapest: Central European University and European Science Foundation, 2001, pp. 157–66.

Paiva, J. P., "Public ceremonies ruled by the ecclesiastical-clerical sphere: A language of political assertion (16th–18th centuries)," in J. P. Paiva, ed., *Religious Ceremonials and Images: Power and Social Meaning (1400–1750)*. Coimbra: Centro de História da Sociedade e da Cultura; European Science Foundation; Palimage Editores, 2002, pp. 415–25.

Palomo del Barrio, F., *Fazer dos campos escolas excelentes: Los jesuitas de Évora, la misión de interior y el disciplinamiento social en la época confesional (1551–1630)*. Florence: Instituto Universitario Europeo, 2000.

Paradas Pena, M. S., "Pere García, obispo de Barcelona (1490–1505), y la reforma," in Enrique Martinez Ruiz and Vicente Suarez Grimon, eds., *Iglesia y Sociedad en el Antiguo Regimen*. Madrid: Associación Española de Historia Moderna, 1994, vol. 1, pp. 65–80.

Perez Muñoz, I., *Pecar, delinquir y castigar: El tribunal eclesiastico de Coria en los siglos XVI y XVII*. Salamanca: Institucion Cultural "El brocense", Diputation Provincial de Caceres, 1992.

Poska, A. M., *Regulating the People: The Catholic Reformation in Seventeenth-Century Spain*. Leiden: Brill, 1998.

Prodi, P., ed., *Disciplina dell'anima, disciplina del corpo e disciplina della società tra medioevo ed etá moderna*. Bologna: Il Mulino, 1994.

Prodi, P., "Il concilio di Trento di fronte alla politica e al diritto moderno," in Paolo Prodi and Wolfang Reinhard, eds., *Il concilio di Trento e il moderno*. Bologna: Il Mulino, 1996, pp. 7–26.

Reder Gadow, M., "Felipe II, Trento y la diocesis de Málaga," *Hispania Sacra*, 52/105 (2000), pp. 389–401.

Rey Castelao, O., "Los fundamentos económicos de la Iglesia en la España del periodo Moderno: Quiebras y conflictos de mantenimiento," in Enrique Martinez Ruiz and Vicente Suarez Grimon, eds., *Iglesia y Sociedad en el Antiguo Regimen*. Madrid: Associación Española de Historia Moderna, 1994, vol. 1, pp. 391–408.

Rodrigues, M. A., *A cátedra de Sagrada Escritura na Universidade de Coimbra (1537–1640)*. Coimbra: Faculdade de Letras da Universidade de Coimbra, 1974.

Rodríguez, P., *El Catecismo romano ante Felipe II y la Inquisición española*. Madrid: Rialp, 1998.

Ruiz de Adana, J. C., *El clero en el siglo XVII: Estudio de una visita secreta a la ciudad de Córdoba*. Cordoba: Imprenta San Pablo, 1976.

Sanchez González, A., "El clero rural en el arzobispado de Toledo en el Seiscientos," *Hispania Sacra*, 46/94 (1994), pp. 427–47.

Schilling, H., "Confessionalisation and the Rise of Religious and Cultural Frontiers in Early Modern Europe," in Eszter Andor and István György Tóth, eds., *Frontiers of Faith*. Budapest: Central European University and European Science Foundation, 2001, pp. 21–36.

Silva, A. M. P., *O cardeal infante D. Henrique arcebispo de Évora: Um prelado no limiar da viragem tridentina*. Porto: Faculdade de Letras da Universidade do Porto, 1989.

Sousa, I. C. de, "Algumas hipóteses de investigação quantitativa acerca da Bibliografia Cronológica da Literatura de Espiritualidade em Portugal (1501–1700)," in *Congresso internacional Bartolomeu Dias e a sua época*. Porto: Tipografia Barbosa Xavier, 1989, vol. 5, pp. 115–38.

Tavares, P. V. B., "Em torno da história do Luteranismo ibérico do séc. XVI: Breves reflexões sobre alguns pressupostos, equívocos e encruzilhadas," *Humanística e Teologia*, 15 (1994), pp. 205–23.

Tellechea Idígoras, J. I., *El arzobispo Carranza y su tiempo*. Madrid: Ediciones Guadarrama, 1968.

Tellechea Idígoras, J. I., *La reforma tridentina en San Sebastian: El libro de "Mandatos de visita" de la parroquia de San Vicente (1540–1670)*. San Sebastian, 1970.

Tellechea Idígoras, J. I., "Clemente VIII y el episcopado español en las postrimerías del reinado de Felipe II (1596–1597)," *Anthologica Annua*, 44 (1997), pp. 204–53.

Vázquez, I., "Las controversias doctrinales postridentinas hasta finales del siglo XVII," in Ricardo García-Villoslada, ed., *Historia de la Iglesia en España*. Madrid: Biblioteca de Autores Cristianos, 1979, vol. 4, pp. 419–74.

Wagner, C., "Los Luteranos ante la Inquisicion de Toledo en el siglo XVI," *Hispania Sacra*, 46/94 (1994), pp. 474–505.

FURTHER READING

The historiography concerning the Catholic Reformation in Portugal is scarce. There are two reference studies, one more classical and institution-centered – Fortunato de Almeida, *História da Igreja em Portugal* (Coimbra, 1910) – and the other more up-to-date and open to new perspectives in the social history of religion – Carlos A. Moreira Azevedo ed., *História Religiosa de Portugal*, vol. 2 (Lisbon, 2001). Some good contributions are to be found in the *Dicionário de História Religiosa de Portugal* (4 vols., Lisbon, 2001). Concerning case studies on dioceses or specific aspects of the Catholic Reformation, there are very few references. On the Trent reception in Portugal see the excellent study by Joaquim Ramos de Carvalho, "A jurisdição episcopal sobre leigos em matéria de pecados públicos"; on the impact of Trent in local religion see Maria Fernanda Enes, *Reforma Tridentina e religião vivida: Os Açores na Época Moderna* (Ponta Delgada, 1991); for internal missions see Federico Palomo del Barrio, *Fazer dos campos escolas excelentes*. A well-documented study on pre-Reformation and the specific action undertaken by a bishop is contained in José Marques, *A arquidiocese de Braga no século XV*; for pastoral visitations in Braga, with abundant information but lacking coherence and a solid argument, see Franquelim Neiva Soares, *A arquidiocese de Braga no século XVII: Sociedade e mentalidades pelas visitações pastorais (1550–1700)* (Braga, 1997).

For Spain the panorama is rather different. Still the best general reference is Ricardo García-Villoslada, ed., *Historia de la Iglesia en España* (Madrid, 1979–80). More recently, for a collection of up-to-date contributions in very different areas (secular and regular clergy, brotherhoods, rural missions, church rents, etc.) see Enrique Martinez Ruiz and Vicente Suarez Grimon, eds., *Iglesia y Sociedad en el Antiguo Regimen* (Madrid, 1994). Substantial and well-documented studies on specific dioceses can be found in Sara Nalle, *God in La Mancha*; Henry Kamen, *Phoenix and the Flame*; and, with a more apologetic approach, *Historia de la diocesis de Valladolid* (Valladolid, 1996). Sharing a similar perspective, but insisting on the failure of the Catholic renewal in reformulating local popular religion, see Allyson Poska, *Regulating the People*. On the role played by Philip II in the application of Trent and relations between the state and the church see Ignasi Fernández Terricabras, *Felipe II y el clero secular* and Pablo Fernández Albaladejo's contribution in José Ignacio Fortea Perez, ed., *Imagines de la diversidad: El mundo urbano en la corona de Castilla (s. XVI–XVIII)* (Santander, 1997).

On secular clergy in a specific diocese see Maria Luisa Candau Chacon, *El clero rural de Sevilla en el siglo XVIII*, and for a general social study of the episcopate see Maximiliano Barrio Gonzalo, *Los obispos de Castilla y Léon durante el Antiguo Régimen (1556–1834)*. On the role played by images in private devotion see the brilliant article by Juan Luis González García, "La sombra de Dios." For a study focused on popular religion and confraternities see Tomás Antonio Montecón Movellán, *Contrarreforma y religiosidad popular en Cantabria: Las cofradias religiosas* (Santander, 1990).

NINETEEN

Parish Communities, Civil War, and Religious Conflict in England

DAN BEAVER

I

Since the seventeenth century the shifting cartographies of civil war during the 1640s have affected the entire landscape of early modern English historiography. As maps of the causes of war have come to stress the terrain of the late 1630s and early 1640s, broken by intense short-term conflicts, the contours of the early Stuart Church have softened into a more subtle landscape of fine shades. Under James, a diverse but effective episcopal leadership "attempted to construct a unified church based on a small number of key doctrines, in which advancement was open to a wide range of protestant opinion and from which only a minority of extreme puritans and papists were to be excluded" (Fincham, *Early Stuart Church*, pp. 24, 71–91). By the 1620s, Protestant emphasis on the qualities of clerical officeholders over the sacred powers of ceremonial office itself had produced in most dioceses a university-educated class of beneficed clergy. The evidence of an increasingly literate society and common exposure to the Protestant ceremonies prescribed in the Book of Common Prayer have been taken to suggest broad lay acceptance of this style of Protestantism during the early seventeenth century. Historians have reduced those styles of Protestant nonconformity loosely described as Puritanism from a formed opposition to the status of a subculture, an underground of private assemblies especially important in London. The English national church contained significant lay and clerical conflicts, but recent maps have indicated a subtle dynamism rather than sharp precipices in the church during the early seventeenth century. The blasted terrain of war and revolution now rises rapidly from Laudian efforts to enforce ceremonial uniformity during the 1630s. A series of contingent events and the cumulative effect of significant but small-scale grievances, crises, and panics now comprise the prelude to the crisis of the early 1640s. Yet small events may have large consequences, and the English civil wars exemplify

I thank Mike Braddick for his comments on this chapter and for many discussions of the English civil wars. John Walter suggested sources and offered valuable insights during an early phase in the work. Of course, any errors that remain are mine alone.

the revolutionary potential of such short-term crises, particularly in the profound religious changes of the 1640s and 1650s. Much important work remains to be done on the nature of these changes in the microhistorical context of the local parish.

This chapter does not presume to identify the causes of the English civil war. It seeks more narrowly to explore the impact of the war on parish communities and to explain some aspects of the violence committed in the course of the war. Even in this narrow sense, however, the English "wars of religion" began more than a year before the formal outbreak of hostilities. Parishes sustained damage of a cultural order long before shots were fired or pickaxes raised against religious objects. The politics of religion and the order of parish communities shifted profoundly in 1641. After the many local "root and branch" petition campaigns early in the year, the start on May 27 of the parliamentary debate on a "root and branch" bill against episcopacy, and the withdrawal of penal jurisdiction from the church in the statute against the high commission court, the system of church courts used to enforce conventional standards of ceremony and behavior in local parishes lost much of its authority and effective power. This suspension of ecclesiastical jurisdiction had a decisive impact on parish communities because, even during the 1630s, diocesan courts served important cultural ends quite apart from the enforcement of the Laudian ceremonial regime. Much of the recent work on church courts has stressed their reinforcement of communal discipline, especially on sexual and matrimonial matters, under the difficult social and economic circumstances of the late sixteenth and early seventeenth centuries. Just as importantly, these courts participated in the cultural process whereby parish communities formed. Among their distinctive qualities as communities, parishes were dependent on diocesan institutions in matters of authority and symbolism. Parishes by definition participated culturally in the diocesan system, were neither isolated nor self-contained.

The rituals of penance sanctioned by the church courts had expressed in a powerful visual form the moral boundaries of parish communities. Penitents had stood in their parish church on the Sabbath, their status marked by special clothes, props, and forms of demeanor. Most had worn a white sheet, held a white rod, and stood or knelt before the assembled parish to confess their sin and to implore divine mercy and forgiveness. These rites had aspired to transform the corrupting force of sin into the sanctifying force of love, in the form of absolution or charity. Moreover, the performances had been important religious events, as the spiritual health of parish communities had depended on the identification and correction of sin. Most penitents had been previously identified in the "public voice" or everyday talk of their neighbors as offenders against the public morality of the parish. The confession of sin and request for pardon in the parish church returned the penitent to the source of accusation, and the rituals of penance served as the means by which the soul and reputation of suspected neighbors were seen to be healed. The prosecution and visible punishment of the "moral offenders" previously identified by the collective conscience or "public voice" of the parish had played an important creative role in social order and community. This punishment, in the form of penance, had made the communal order visible in religious dramas, organized around the detection and destruction of sin.

As this process of symbolizing communal boundaries was suspended in 1641 and 1642, a flood of publications increasingly revealed the devilish plots of religion's many enemies. After the news of the Irish rebellion reached Parliament on November 1, pamphlet after lurid pamphlet cried further revelations of bloody-handed popish conspiracy. Such scares had a long history and built on the fervid Protestant commemorations of deliverance from the "Gunpowder Plot" in 1605, but the rumors of Catholic atrocities against Protestants in Ireland transformed the scare into a panic. A few illustrations can hardly convey the scale of publication or fear. On November 12, John Davis, "a plain country fellow and not able so fully to express himself," appeared before the Parliament to relate "a damnable plot at Ragland castle" in Monmouthshire, the seat of Henry Somerset, earl of Worcester, and a prominent Catholic (*A Great Discovery of a Damnable Plot at Ragland Castle* [1641], A2r–v). Davis shared his remarkable experiences as a guide for the perplexed "gentlemen" conspirators, unable to find their way to Ragland castle from Ross. After providing this service to a suspiciously striking gentleman, marked by his rich clothes, a montero or Spanish hunting cap, and curious ritual ablutions in a delicate container of Venice glass, Davis received from an obliging groom a grand tour of the military preparations at the castle, including 72 light horses "prepared for war" and a report of 40 more in an underground vault, as well as the "furniture" for 120 to 140 horses and "great store of match and powder and other ammunition" for 2,000 men in the same arsenal beneath the castle. This trusting groom tried to recruit Davis to the cause, boasting that the earl of Worcester had 700 men under arms and repeating the earl's promise "that any man who would be entertained should have sixteen pence a day, good pay from him, in case they would be true to him." In conclusion, the printed account of this plot posed the question of the hour: "whether we have not as just cause to fear the papists in England as they had in Ireland or Wales?" (*Damnable Plot*, A2v–A3r, A3r–v, A4r–v).

This dark vision of Spanish caps and subterranean arsenals did not confine the conspiracy to marginal provincial hamlets. On November 15 and 16, Thomas Beale, a tailor of Whitecross Street, revealed to Parliament "the treacherous practices of the papists now resident" in London (*Discovery of a Horrible and Bloody Treason and Conspiracy* [1641], A2r; *England's Deliverance* [1641], A1r). On a late-night walk through Moorfields, north of the city, Beale overheard "certain fellows talking and whispering together about their intended plot" to "murder diverse persons eminent in the house of parliament" on November 18, including "many protestant lords," John Pym, "and many other gentlemen" (*Discovery of a Treason*, A2v–A3r). Yet this murderous assault on Protestant leaders was only a part of their scheme. Beale heard the confederates "whisper" their grand design of forces from "the three next shires to Ragland castle," under the earl of Worcester's command, seizing the strongholds in Cheshire and Lancashire; "in that hurly burly and combustion, the plot was so laid . . . that by papists, at the same instant, the city of London should have been surprised and all the protestants' throats cut" (*Discovery of a Treason*, A3r). The provincial and metropolitan plots were strands of a single popish conspiracy.

This grand popish design may have posed the most obvious dangers to Protestant parishes but was not the only enemy in the field. One pamphlet invoked "arians, anabaptists, brownists, donatists, erticheans, familists, marcionists, montanists, nicolaitans, pelagians, papists, puritans, nonatians, and all other sorts of heresies and sects" as common enemies of religion. "Under the colors of a feigned piety," these "factions" fought each other "in a disunion and diversity among themselves" and shared only "a general, malignant, inveterate hatred" against "the government, the governors, and the true church" (*Religion's Enemies* [1641], A3–4). Richard Baxter later blamed "separatists, anabaptists, and the younger and unexperienced sort of religious people" in London for their campaign "to speak too vehemently and intemperately against the bishops and the church and ceremonies, and to jeer and deride at the common prayer and all that was against their minds" (Keeble, *Autobiography of Richard Baxter*, p. 29). At least in the short term, the dissolution of diocesan courts could only further the designs of religion's enemies by suspending the primary force for order in local churches. In 1641 and 1642, pamphlets on both sides of the conflict between crown and Parliament feared chaos. *Religion's Enemies*, published in 1641, lamented the profanation of religion, "now become the common discourse and table talk in every tavern and alehouse." Although the Book of Common Prayer had been established by authority of crown and Parliament and had served the ceremonial needs of parish churches for 90 years,

> one would have it to be cast out now, holding it a false worship; another is angry at the vestments and habits of the ministry; one will not kneel, another will not stand, one will sit down, one will not bow, another will not be uncovered, one holds all good manners to be popery, another that all decency is superstitious, another that rails are Romish (which is false, for the papists have no rails in their churches, nor anything so convenient). One foolishly assumes and presumes to save himself, and some of his neighbors too, by his good works; another will be saved by a bare and lazy faith that will do no work at all, and thus religion is puffed and blown to and fro with every wind of doctrine. (*Religion's Enemies*, 6)

Parish communities lost their boundaries and bulwarks in this "blind" confusion of the sacred. As the pamphlet concluded, "It shall be my hearty prayer that, as there is but one shepherd, God in his gracious goodness and mercy would make us all one sheepfold." After its denunciation of the London plot, another pamphlet asked its readers to "pray for the establishment of religion" (*England's Deliverance*, 4). A cultural crisis, evident in the dissolution of courts and confusion of symbolic boundaries, joined to fears of powerful religious enemies, may help to explain some of the patterns of violence during the civil war.

II

Of course, English parishes had never been "all one sheepfold," and the crisis of the early 1640s occurred in parish communities that, in many cases, had been divided since the reformations of the sixteenth century. The most recent conflicts had resulted from the efforts of the Laudian bishops during the 1630s to introduce a more uniform ceremonial discipline and strictly to enforce the ceremonial injunctions of the Book of Common Prayer. After his promotion as archbishop of Canterbury in 1633, William Laud used his metropolitan visitation to enforce the priority of the visible church in its sacraments and festivals; his commissioners moved communion tables to the site of traditional altars, surrounded by protective rails, repaired and "beautified" the church fabric, and in many places prohibited the customary use of churchyards for pasture. These innovations provoked reactions both as attacks on customary local practices and as assertions of a "beauty of holiness" that contradicted a strict "godly" emphasis on Scripture and sermons over ceremony and sacred objects in matters of salvation and church order. Laudian visitations divided many parishes and elicited passive and active forms of resistance in both the northern and southern provinces of the church. Despite their seriousness, these conflicts were adjudicated in the familiar arenas of the diocesan courts, as local factions attempted to use networks of influence and the politics of the courts themselves to resist the Laudian innovations in their parish churches. Unlike the crisis of the early 1640s, the conflicts of the 1630s, in most places, produced grievances for a Parliament rather than violence.

The suspension of ecclesiastical jurisdiction in 1641 dissolved the familiar sites of dispute, and power to adjudicate conflicts over the sacred dropped into the streets of local parishes. In the absence of a settled procedure to identify and prosecute religion's enemies, local factions resorted increasingly to violence. This pattern had surfaced first in northern England, in the aftermath of the war against the Scots, as the godly faction in Newcastle supported the iconoclasm of the Scots soldiers in their churches. After the withdrawal of the Scots army from the town in August 1641, violence erupted in the church when Yeldard Alvey, Laudian vicar of St. Nicholas, first attempted to conduct services in his accustomed style after his return from exile. As John Fenwick, a supporter of the Scots, described the scene,

> my wife, being less used to have her food so dressed, growing stomach sick, set some other weak stomachs on working, who fell upon the vicar's new dressing, the surplice and service book, which set the malignant, superstitious people in such a fire, as men and women fell upon my wife like wild beasts, tore her clothes, and gave her at least an hundred blows, and had slaine her if the mayor had not stepped out of his pew to rescue her; he and his officers both well beaten for their pains, such was the people's madness after their idols. (Howell, *Newcastle upon Tyne and the Puritan Revolution*, pp. 122–3, 142)

In 1641, the Parliament itself divided on the issues of iconoclasm and ceremonies in the church, creating an uncertainty in the law. Among many acts of popular iconoclasm in London, Nehemiah Wallington recorded of his own church, Leonard's Eastcheap, in October 1641, "the idol in the wall was cut down, and the superstitious pictures in the glass was broken in pieces, and the superstitious things and prayers for the dead in brass picked up and broken, and the pictures of the virgin Mary on the branches of candlesticks was broken" (Manning, *English People and the English Revolution*, pp. 46–7, 48). As the recent work of John Walter has revealed, this violence expressed a popular political consciousness and sometimes assumed strikingly conventional forms. In Suffolk and Essex, attacks focused on clerics suspected of popery in their support of Laudian innovations during the 1630s. Robert Warren, rector of Long Melford in Suffolk, had been nominated to his benefice by Elizabeth Strange, countess of Rivers, a powerful Catholic aristocrat, and had become an ally of the Laudian bishop Matthew Wren of Norwich in his attacks on the godly communities of Ipswich and Sudbury in 1636. In August 1642, Warren was "huffed and shuffed" by a large crowd – consisting in part of weavers from Sudbury – interrupted "in the midst of divine service, called a false prophet, and compelled to come out of the pulpit whilst in the midst of his sermon, and, returning home, one . . . beat a frying pan before him in derision, saying this is your saint's bell" (Walter, *Under-*

standing Popular Violence, pp. 191–7). This use of conventional forms of rough music or charivari expressed a popular desire to restore a traditional Protestantism, cleansed of popish influences. The crowd that attacked Warren formed only a small part of a much broader pattern of disturbances over northern Essex and southern Suffolk between August and December 1642, including attacks on the estates of such prominent Catholics as the countess of Rivers herself. Shortly before the battle of Edgehill in October, Ralph Josselin, godly vicar of Earls Colne in Essex, observed, "our poor people in tumults arose and plundered diverse houses, papists and others, and threatened to go farther, which I endeavored to suppress by public and private means" (Macfarlane, *Diary of Ralph Josselin*, p. 13).

After the outbreak of war, this unofficial violence continued from both sides. Both sides used stereotypes to promote their campaigns as part of a larger war against religion's enemies: royalists became "papists" determined to enslave and plunder the people; parliamentarians were "known to despise the common prayer book and to favor brownists, anabaptists, and other disturbers of all order and government" (Underdown, *Revel, Riot, and Rebellion*, pp. 164–5; Beaver, *Parish Communities*, pp. 165–80, 202–3). Although violent exchanges between neighbors over religious matters were hardly new, the presence of soldiers tended to magnify issues of principle and symbolism, to remove conflict from its local context and to escalate violence. In August 1642, Edwyn Sandys marched his regiment of Londoners into Kent, anticipating a local royalist coup. On their arrival in Canterbury,

> the soldiers entering the church and choir, giant-like began a fight with god himself, overthrew the communion table, tore the velvet cloth from before it, defaced the goodly screen . . . violated the monuments of the dead, spoiled the organs, brake down the ancient rails and seats, with the brazen eagle that did support the bible . . . mangled all our service books and books of common prayer, bestrewing the whole pavement with the leaves . . . and not content therewith, finding another statue of christ in the frontispiece of the southgate, they discharged against it forty shot at the least, triumphing much when they did hit it in the head or face. (Everitt, *Kent and the Great Rebellion*, pp. 111–16)

In July and August, the royalists harassed godly clerics in Warwickshire. Armed royalists entered his church and "violently assaulted" James Nalton, minister of Rugby, in an unsuccessful effort to make him use his pulpit on the king's behalf (Hughes, *Politics, Society, and Civil War in Warwickshire*, p. 144). In Tewkesbury, supporters of Parliament probably destroyed the abbey's "great window" early in the war because of its images; on the other side, Henry Bard, royalist governor of Worcester, later warned the villagers of Twyning, just north of the town, to pay their arrears to his garrison or to expect "an *unsanctified* party of horse amongst you, from whom, if you hide yourselves, they shall fire your houses without mercy [and] hang up your bodies wherever they find them" (Beaver, *Parish Communities*, pp. 214, 257). Among the grievous anxieties of civil war was the fear of a double death in the flesh and in memory, as attacks on churches often included the destruction of funeral monuments perceived as popish in design or rhetoric. In 1646, Edward Hunter alias Perry of Marholm, Northamptonshire, used his funeral monument to address "the courteous soldier: no crucifix you see, no frightful brand of superstition's here; pray let me stand" (Aston, *England's Iconoclasts*, p. 65). Spontaneous violence in the name of religion, even when supported in principle, was disquieting and difficult to interpret with confidence as divine will rather than divine wrath. "If this be not punished to the full," asked Nehemiah Wallington in 1646 after recording news of parliamentarian atrocities in Rutland, "can England ever look for a blessing or that god should ever end her troubles?" (Seaver, *Wallington's World*, p. 169). A few examples cannot do justice to the cultural damage sustained by parish communities during this war over the nature and meaning of community itself.

After 1643, the fear of violent disorders informed the grim circularity of parliamentarian iconoclasm. Many on both sides viewed a settlement, a restoration of common boundaries in the sacred, as the only means to forestall the violence of "profane liberty," yet a settlement required, for a significant proportion of the godly, the destruction of popish remnants in parish churches. As John Morrill has described the beliefs of William Dowsing, most notorious of parliamentarian iconoclasts, "God would build a New Jerusalem, if only the godly would clear the site" (Morrill, "William Dowsing," in Cooper, *Journal of William Dowsing*, p. 10). Only after the "trash and rubbish" of popery had been removed from parish churches could Nehemiah Wallington claim to receive divine ordinances "in a more sweet, pure, and powerful manner than ever our fathers knew" (Seaver, *Wallington's World*, p. 171). In April 1643, Sir Robert Harley and his parliamentary committee for "monuments of superstition and idolatry" in London finished the destruction of Cheapside cross and the windows in Westminster abbey, then entered Whitehall palace in pursuit of "superstitious pictures," pulling down the altar in Henry VII's chapel (Aston, *England's Iconoclasts*, p. 76). In late 1643 and 1644, Dowsing used commissions from Edward Montagu, earl of Manchester, commander of the eastern association for Parliament, to conduct a series of "visitations" in Cambridgeshire, Norfolk, and Suffolk, using "a network of relatives among the godly" and such shadowy figures as Clement Gilley of Troston, scourge of southern Norfolk churches, to smash windows, deface funeral monuments, and break altar rails in over 250 parishes. Richard Culmer, a vocal critic of Laudian innovations suspended from his ministry during the 1630s, received a parliamentary commission in December 1643 to cleanse Canterbury cathedral, climbing a 60-step ladder himself to destroy the "great idolatrous window" in the dean's chapel, despite an angry crowd "who cried out again for their great Diana" (Aston, *England's Iconoclasts*, pp. 85–6). The response to this violence often reflected the absence of any settled symbolism and ceremonies for the making of parish communities, and a rejection of iconoclasm as a basis for such a settlement. In Covehithe, Suffolk, Dowsing found "many inscriptions of Jesus, in capital letters, on the roof of the church, and cherubims with crosses on their breasts; and a cross in the chancel. All which, with diverse pictures that we could not reach in the windows, neither would they help us to raise the ladders." Southwest of Covehithe, in Ufford, several important villagers, officers of the parish known for their Protestant views of ministry, refused to turn over keys to the church. Samuel Canham and William Brown, a former churchwarden, warned that Dowsing had "sent men to rifle" and "pull down the church" (Cooper, *Journal of William Dowsing*, pp. 294, 305–7).

This official iconoclasm in parish churches had its counterpart in judicial violence against "that grand enemy of the power of godliness" (Macfarlane, *Diary of Ralph Josselin*, p. 31). Laud's trial and execution in January 1645, occurring at the same time as Parliament's suppression of the Book of Common Prayer and imposition of the directory of worship, reiterated the dreary process of violent purification as a prelude to godly settlement in the church. Laud stood accused of high treason, "to wit his traiterous endeavors to alter and subvert god's true religion by law established," and of setting up "popish superstition and idolatry by insensible degrees," as part of a grand scheme "to reconcile the Church of England to the Church of Rome" (Prynne, *Canterbury's Doom* [1646], frontispiece). After a lackluster trial in the Lords between March and October 1644, an unprecedented ordinance of attainder carried the conviction of Laud's guilt from its source in the Commons to the Lords. The sacrificial element in Laud's execution – the parliamentary desire to avoid crowd violence and to make the execution of one "delinquent" stand for many – lay beneath the surface of William Strode's words of warning to the Lords in late November 1644 to hasten their action on the ordinance. "The eyes of the country and City being upon this business," Strode intoned, "the expedition of it will prevent the demanding of justice by multitudes" (Gardiner, *Civil War*, vol. 2, p. 102). William Prynne made the point explicit in his prayer for deliverance from "such an hypocritical, false archiepiscopal generation of vipers, whose heads and hopes of succession we trust your honors have forever cut off in the decapitation of this archbishop of Canterbury, the very worst of his traitorous predecessors, their crimes being all concentred in him" (Prynne, *Canterbury's Doom*, 8v). Laud's death on the scaffold and the suppression of the Book of Common Prayer were intimately related to the new settlement in the church. At the moment of its inception, this godly order had taken the lifeblood of an anti-Christian enemy and destroyed an instrument of his evil design. After Laud's execution, the Parliament began a campaign to incorporate parish communities in this Presbyterian system of assemblies; a new godly hierarchy would enforce a uniform local conformity to the ceremonies prescribed by the directory of worship. The connections among these events were not lost on contemporaries. As Peter Heylyn observed, "the same day, 4 January, in which [the Lords] passed this bloody ordinance [of Laud's attainder], they passed another [ordinance] for establishing their new directory [of worship], which in effect was nothing but a total abolition of the common prayer book, and thereby showed the world how little hopes they had of settling their new form of worship, if the foundation of it were not laid in blood" (Heylyn, *Brief Relation*, p. 11; Laud, *History of the Troubles and Trial of William Laud* [1695], p. 447). Although Heylyn's royalism defined his view of events, Prynne's rhetoric revealed a remarkably similar awareness of the enemy's blood as a prerequisite of godly settlement and the restoration of order.

This violent expression of the desire for a settlement became even more pronounced in the witchcraft accusations and prosecutions linked to the "investigations" of Matthew Hopkins and John Stearne in 1645. Accusations and judicial violence against witches expressed a concern to restore the cultural boundaries of parish communities. These witchfinders consulted local clerics and neighbors to identify and cleanse parishes of witches, a conventional evil usually imagined as an elderly woman, impoverished, angry, and full of malice over her misfortunes. In 1645, the roughly 250 accusations in villages and towns across the counties of Essex, Norfolk, Suffolk, and, to a lesser extent, Bedford, Cambridge, Huntingdon, and Northampton generally remained faithful to this stereotype, indicting poor women for sinking ships, blasting the corn, and murdering adults, children, and cattle. These accusations had as their context cultural problems of authority and security, both large and small. In 1643 and 1644, parishes in Cambridgeshire and Suffolk had experienced William Dowsing's iconoclastic violence. In 1644, many Essex and Suffolk parishes had assisted parliamentarian committees to investigate and remove their parish priests for offenses ranging from Laudian innovations to drunkenness and sexual license. Parishes disturbed in their clerical leadership, assaulted in the sacred precincts of the church itself, or generally open to the rumors of such events elsewhere, easily experienced vulnerability to the familiar evil of witches. Yet accidents of mortality, such as the death of Thomas Witham, rector of Manningtree in Essex, the site of the first accusations in March 1645, could produce similar failures of leadership. As parishes seemed increasingly open and defenseless against the active minions of the devil, Hopkins and Stearne received invitations from villages and towns to examine local suspects and to offer opinions on their guilt. Parliamentarian committees purified parish churches and offices in order to sanctify the war effort and to secure control of the pulpit, but this strategy may have intensified a perceived vulnerability to religious enemies that had been discernible as early as 1641. Moreover, a few suspected witches attributed their own malign activities to fortunes and misfortunes of war. Two witches attacked parish officers in Essex and in the Isle of Ely for attempting to press their sons into military service, while Margery Sparham of Suffolk sent two imps "after her husband being a soldier to protect him" (Sharpe, *Instruments of Darkness*, pp. 128–47). Both parish communities and executed witches were unforeseen and unrecognized casualties of war.

III

The crisis and civil war of the 1640s suspended or destroyed many symbols and processes essential to the making of traditional parish communities. Although Parliament and civil officers attempted to maintain continuity in the exercise of discipline and then to impose a new Presbyterian settlement in 1645, many parishes dissolved in factional conflicts and in practice had to find their own informal settlements in the late 1640s and 1650s. These settlements brought an uneasy peace to the multiple Protestant communities, the splinters of godliness, created by the war and the bitter controversies over the nature of the peace. Among the most important long-term consequences of the civil war and revolution was this transformation of religious community from the customary parish, in which shared space suggested a common salvation, to spiritual networks understood in terms of shared beliefs and sympathy of conscience. Yet the destruction of the traditional church as a cultural system paradoxically fostered in many parishes new traditions of loyalty to the Book of Common Prayer and other customary symbols of religious identity. Ann Hughes has suggested, in her work on Warwickshire, how "the selfconfident, demanding, and intrusive puritanism" of the revolutionary church "crystallized and intensified a diffuse body of attitudes and behavior" which comprised an early form of Anglicanism (Hughes, *Warwickshire*, p. 322). In a survey of 150 eastern and western parishes, John Morrill uncovered a pattern of loyalty to the Book of Common Prayer over the new parliamentary directory after 1645; continuity in the custom of communion on the major festivals of Christmas, Easter, and Whitsunday; and a preference for the customary "open" communion over the "closed" or "railed" communion prescribed by Parliament to exclude the ungodly (Morrill, *English Revolution*, pp. 163–8). Yet the newly assertive loyalty to selected "traditions" of the national church remained a local response to the dissolution of the diocesan system. If some parishes escaped sectarian conflict in practice, it was impossible to remain unaffected by news of the profound divisions in many other places. In this sense, the informal parish settlements negotiated after the war represent fragile, often combustible, new forms of community made from elements of the traditional system and elements of the radical Protestant spiritualism intensified during the 1640s. This patchwork of local settlements became the basis of what was in practice an open church, the revolutionary church of the 1650s.

In the absence of the diocesan system, the disciplinary discourse of print became important in the making and sustaining of communities. Although print had always possessed this power to foster communities among dispersed populations, the circumstances of the late 1640s magnified its significance. Those involved in the great disputes over the nature of the formal settlement after the war "made the printed book function as a kind of ministerial magistrate," attempting to define and enforce through their texts the terms, symbols, and boundaries of new "reformed" communities. Protestant factionalism became the most serious problem of the peace, its dangers seeming greater to some than the earlier crisis of popery. As Thomas Edwards lamented in 1646, "our evils are not removed and cured but only changed" from the "popish innovations, superstitions, and prelatical tyranny" of the early 1640s to the current "damnable heresies, horrid blasphemies, libertinism, and fearful anarchy." Edwards viewed "this last extremity" as "far more high, violent, and dangerous in many respects" than the former, as "the worst of the prelates, in the midst of many popish tenets and innovations, held many sound doctrines and commendable practices," and even "the papists hold many articles of faith and truths of god, have some order among them, encourage learning, have fixed principles of truth, practices of devotion, and good works." By way of contrast, "the sects and sectaries in our days deny all principles of religion, are enemies to all holy duties, order, learning, overthrowing all, being vertiginous spirits, whirligig spirits." These enemies denied the divinity of Scripture and the Trinity, alleged the final death of the soul as well as the body, included Turks and pagans in the divine forgiveness secured by Christ's sacrifice, and, not least among their monstrous blasphemies, advocated a general toleration for Protestants, a "liberty of conscience and liberty of prophesying," as the only certain article of faith. This way lay madness, "dressing up a cat like a child to be baptized," "mechanics and women taking upon them to preach and baptize," "frogs out of the bottomless pit covering our land, coming into our houses, bedchambers, beds, churches . . . like Africa bringing forth monsters every day." "We are gone beyond Amsterdam," a supporter assured Edwards in 1645, "and are in our highway to Munster." Edwards and the many local correspondents whose fearful, angry letters were included in his book defended the Presbyterian settlement embodied in the new directory of worship as a godly bulwark against the "devilish" chaos of individual license and atheism. In his dedication to the Parliament, Edwards demanded a strict enforcement of church discipline as the only way to fight the sectarian threat. "You have made a reformation," Edwards intoned, "but with the reformation, have we not a deformation, and worse things come in upon us than ever we had before?" (Edwards, *Gangraena* [1646], vol. 1, A3r–A4r, 15, 17–18, 22, 24, 58; vol. 2, 12–13, 29, 58).

Despite its symbolic power, print could only acquire magisterial authority in the aftermath of a settlement. As consensus remained elusive, the printed discourse of the mid-1640s reflected the variety of communities fostered by war. Such polemical writers as Edwards merely intensified the conflict among Protestants and offered their opponents opportunities to use print for their own purposes. Edwards himself observed how Independents and sectarians gave "great and glorious names, swelling titles, to their books," using print and other techniques "to boast their party to be more and greater than they are, as if parliament, armies, city of London, country, all the godly, wise, judicious men were theirs or would be theirs" (Edwards, *Gangraena*, vol. 1, 55, 58). Among the many radical Protestant responses to Edwards, a series of pamphlets by William Walwyn in 1646 defined a distinctive form of fellowship in terms of "liberty of conscience" antithetical to the traditional parish, as "very many judicious persons" had become, "through a blessed opportunity, freedom of discourse, and clearer search of scripture than heretofore, fully satisfied in their understandings that to compel or restrain any peaceable person in matters of faith and the worship of god is as real a sin, and as odious in the sight of god, as murder, theft, or adultery." Simple, powerful images communicated the contrast between this fellowship of "liberties" and "this kind of tyranny, in the bishops and prelatical clergy" and the similar despotism of "master Edwards his work of bowing all to his rule" (Walwyn, *An Antidote against Master Edwards Old and New Poison* [1646], 2). Walwyn used, as effectively as Edwards, imagery which shoved his enemy beyond the bounds of human society. Edwards

> raged like an Irish, ravenous, hungry wolf, deprived of his prey by generous and true English mastifs, that watch both night and day to save the harmless and beneficial sheep, the Independents and separatists, who from the beginning of these our troubles have continually, without repining, contributed their fleece for clothing and their limbs and lives for nourishment and strength, to preserve not only their own liberties but the just liberties of this nation. (Walwyn, *Antidote*, 3)

The use of print served the purposes of all factions in the marshaling of dispersed support and the magnification of its importance, represented here by the claim on behalf of gathered churches and sects "that the numbers of them are daily increased and that their faithfulness to the parliament and commonwealth has caused them to grow in favor with all the people" (Walwyn, *Antidote*, 3–4). The traditional image of the godly "sheepfold" was recycled in this context to convey a new form of community based on liberty of conscience and protected by parliamentarian soldiers. This brief analysis is not intended to oversimplify the complex situation after 1645 as a confrontation of sides, but rather to suggest an approach to texts that reveals the uses of print in the building and sustaining of communities in the absence of a formal settlement.

Many parishes in the late 1640s contained multiple networks of families defined in terms of community. The more populous urban parishes, especially in London, might conceal a gathered church, and elements of smaller sects, in addition to the faction able to decide the ceremonies used in the parish church. In rural parishes, these networks often comprised small sects sustained by the broader radical discourse in print or sometimes by links to larger groups in nearby towns. If we are to apply the term "settlement" to English conditions in the late 1640s, it must be explored through a patchwork of informal local settlements. In Kidderminster, Worcestershire, an intensive pastoral discipline enabled Richard Baxter to build an inclusive godly community. Baxter and his assistant led separate meetings for youths and adults to discuss Baxter's weekly sermons, as well as biweekly catechism sessions for 14 families. An extraordinary pastoral effort in the cause of Baxter's "mere catholicism" or aloofness from all parties resulted in

> freedom from those sects and heresies which many other places were infected with. We had no private church, though we had private meetings; we had not pastor against pastor, nor church against church, nor sect against sect. But we were all of one mind, and mouth, and way. Not a separatist, anabaptist, antinomian in the town. (Keeble, *Autobiography of Richard Baxter*, pp. 80, 84)

Yet the distance traveled from traditional parish discipline, even in Kidderminster, was reflected in Baxter's difficulties with such routine disciplinary problems as "a common notorious drunkard." Although successfully excluded from communion, "when he was drunk he would stand at the market place and, like a quaker, cry out against the town and take upon him to prophesy god's judgments against them, and would rage at my door and rail and curse," eventually attacking Baxter in the churchyard (ibid., pp. 77–8, 80–2). On the other end of the spectrum, Ralph Josselin, vicar of Earls Colne in Essex, "began a little to be troubled with some in the matter of separation" as early as summer 1642, as the godly began to separate from their ungodly neighbors. Josselin could not resolve the resulting problem of "mixed communion" in the parish and, although troubled by "our confusions and disorders and want of communion," suspended the ceremony during the 1640s. In 1651, Josselin administered communion to his godly neighbors for the first time in nine years, the group being determined "to admit none but such as in charity we reckon to be disciples," yet conflict over such ordinances of the church as baptism continued, and "diverse christians" still refused to help or participate in the ceremony. By the mid-1650s, Quakers had "set up a paper on the church door" in Earls Colne, and Josselin had to weather a series of confrontations in the parish church, including charges of worldly vanity for his "cuffs" and verbal abuse sometimes bordering on assault. In 1656, Josselin thankfully recalled being "in the lane, set upon by one called a quaker; the lord was with my heart, that I was not dismayed" (Macfarlane, *Diary of Ralph Josselin*, pp. 12, 77, 96, 234–7, 350, 377, 379, 380, 384, 450). During the late 1640s and 1650s, local peace depended all too often on the delicate diplomatic transactions of precisely these kinds of confrontations.

In London, Parliament ordered the enforcement of the ordinance for the election of elders in June 1646, but parishes in the city already comprised a spectrum of distinct if interrelated communities. A series of weekly lectures near Coleman Street, established by women in 1645, attracted "a world of people" and promoted "confusion and disorder" (Porter, *London and the Civil War*, p. 14). Nehemiah Wallington, elected an elder of his parish under the new Presbyterian regime, lamented the discord among the godly that blasted the early promise of the covenant. Although Wallington hoped to contain and resolve conflicts in the new system, many of his neighbors "were going about settling a church by themselves" under the protection of the army (Seaver, *Wallington's World*, p. 171). Many English parishes experienced a similar diversity in the late 1640s, resulting in forms of community that reflected local negotiations. In Coventry, the Presbyterians John Bryan and Obadiah Grew, ministers of Trinity and St. Michael's, and Samuel Basnet, the pastor of a local Independent church appointed as lecturer by the corporation in 1653, maintained a common front against sectarianism and limited the local effectiveness of Anabaptism and Quakerism. In Tewkesbury, violent conflict between the Independent John Wells, minister of the parish, and the Presbyterian lecturer George Hopkins produced a petition to the council of state in 1656, an assault on Hopkins in 1658, and perhaps the opportunity for Baptists and Quakers to establish a presence in the town and its hinterland.

Among the distinctive features of the communities made in the late 1640s and 1650s was the complex subcultural interrelationship of parishes and sects. After such missionary campaigns as Samuel Oates's tour across the east midlands in 1647 and 1648, and the tireless efforts of George Fox and other Quakers in the rural north in 1652, thousands of Baptists and Quakers defined their communities in opposition to the dominant symbolism of parishes. Most Protestants feared this dissolution of the parish into multiple communities. Justices of the peace in Rutland accused Oates of "filling the county with diverse sects and schisms, withdrawing them from their own ministers into mutinous assemblies, and perverting whole families, working divisions even between nearest relatives" (McGregor and Reay, *Radical Religion*, p. 32). In the early 1650s, Nehemiah Wallington viewed the "liberty of conscience" that had supported Baptists, Ranters, Quakers, and Fifth Monarchists as a "national sin" (Seaver, *Wallington's World*, p. 171). Yet the failure to establish a national settlement fostered a creative interrelationship of parish and sect in fashioning new communities. The dominant factions of Presbyterians and Independents used the war against "diverse sects and schisms" to build parishes in the new order, just as Baptists evoked "sacrifices of the wicked" in parish churches and "the hardening of the people in their idolizing of the temple," just as Quakers expressed their contempt for "priests of Baal," "the fist of wickedness and bloody hands," and the "steeple house," to create the symbolic repertoire of subcultures and their own new fellowships of inter-related families (Beaver, *Parish Communities*, pp. 234–6, 273; Davies, *Quakers*, p. 77). These subcultures expressed the efforts of sectarian groups to create a break, an open space, in the conventional order of religion through representations of distinction from this conventional order in symbol, behavior, and ritual. Yet the creation of identity through the rejection of "idolatry" in the national church formed a subcultural dependence on the symbols of the parish and held the sect in a dialogic relationship to the dominant order. These new sectarian groups never demonstrated their dependence on traditional religious culture, nor their part in a new configuration of communities, more powerfully than in their various acts of rejection and separation.

In conclusion, it has become evident that the experience of community in English parishes was fundamentally transformed during the 1640s. Although many elements of traditional parish communities survived the crises of civil war and revolution, their new significance and the loyalty discovered during the 1640s to the customary calendar and ceremonies of the church, even to the church fabric itself, suggest the impact of war and its disorders on the local experience of familiar symbols and rites. The broad process of change followed an unexpected pattern, as the crisis over popery in the early 1640s helped to precipitate a war among Protestants; and a crisis over schism ultimately splintered the movement for further reformation in the aftermath of the parliamentarian victory. Although the despised popish device of episcopacy had ceased its nefarious influence in 1641, the dissolution of the church hierarchy effectively dissolved the cultural boundaries of local parishes. Several important forms of violence during the war, especially the official and unoffical iconoclasm and the judicial murder of 1645, reflect either responses to the absence of boundaries or efforts of reconstruction. After the failure of the Presbyterian settlement in the mid-1640s, new forms of community emerged from myriad negotiations among diverse Protestant factions. These factions derived unprecedented disciplinary power and support from the dynamic print culture of the 1640s. A new configuration of communities in many local parishes involved fellowships of sympathetic families defined in terms of church and sect, the symbiotic concerns of uniformity and persecution helping to build communities in the absence of the territorial solidarity of the traditional parish. In 1650, the republic abandoned all pretense of uniformity, as the Parliament repealed the laws that had compelled attendance in parish churches and left only a blasphemy law to mark the boundaries of Protestant community, and the formal toleration of 1653 confirmed this approach to the problem of Protestant diversity. Yet the general significance of the changes must be stated in relative rather than absolute terms, as an acute intensification of a process under way since the early Reformation. The result of the crisis during the 1640s was a form of Protestant community *more* divided and discursively defined, *more* open to interventions of civil authority in religious matters, and *more* sensitive to shifts in the currents of national debates.

IV

Since the seventeenth century, the restoration of the Stuart monarchy in 1660 has played an important symbolic role in grand historical narratives. If such narratives were considered in their morphology, as familiar folk narratives, the restoration would represent the magical sleep, the supreme moment of collective forgetfulness. A rhetoric of oblivion has been used repeatedly since 1660 to describe and interpret the return of monarchy. As Dryden observed, "the hateful names of parties" vanished from the political landscape in 1660, and "factious souls [were] wearied into peace" (Dryden, "Astraea Redux," ll. 312–13). Clarendon believed the painful religious contortions of the 1650s had prepared the "natural inclinations and integrity" of "hearts and affections" for the restoration of monarchy and obedience to royal authority (*Life of Edward Earl of Clarendon*, vol. 1, pp. 320–1, 327–8). This attitude has been transformed in modern historical narratives into a form of collective weariness. Charles returned to a country in need of a rest, exhausted by the failures of religious radicalism and constitutional innovation. The exhaustion of the creative spirit in 1660 and the essential popularity of restoration dominated the progressive narratives of David Ogg and Godfrey Davies during the 1950s and have continued to influence the varied revisionist accounts of John Kenyon and others.

Critical assaults on progressive interpretations of the civil wars and revolution have cast doubt on this interpretation of the restoration as a social, political, and religious boundary, an interlude of forgetfulness between the emotional upheavals of the 1640s and the rational politics of the late seventeenth century. The loss of an historiographic convention has effectively reunified the seventeenth century around the evident persistence of familiar conflicts in the localities after 1660 and deficiencies of power, policy, and authority in royal government itself. Recent discussions of Charles II, the Cavalier Parliament, and various local communities have found in each context important continuities between the bitter divisions of the civil war and the patterns of policy and conflict in the later seventeenth century. Yet this emphasis on continuity and conflict makes the process of restoration itself difficult to understand. If conflicts were unresolved, who wanted the restoration of the monarchy? To the extent that erstwhile republicans supported the process, how did these former enemies refashion identities to become allies and local leaders of the restoration?

Much recent work on the restoration has attempted to interrelate local understandings of events and a broader print discourse, generally supportive of the restored regime. This work has often focused on corporations, the complex civil communities formed by royal charters, because of their rich archives as well as their political importance in the reconstruction of the royal state. Moreover, corporations evoke the crucial problems of culture and identity in the restoration because, through their charters, they constituted intersections of a kind between local forms of community and governance and the symbolism and authority of the government in London. Historians have generally focused on a narrowly defined relationship between the corporations and the restored monarchy. The local councils have been approached as the primary sources of power and identity in their communities, and the restoration has been understood as a royalist invasion of corporate offices, an invasion less successful in some corporations than others but independent of place in its motivations and designs. This approach has defined power and politics in civil terms. If religious issues have been raised, the issues have concerned the ability of specific groups to defy the penal laws and retain power in the corporation. The restoration of parishes and their distinctive forms of power and identity have received less attention, despite the significance of the parish in the ceremonial culture of corporations in the seventeenth century. Many corporate councils required members to participate in processions to parish churches on the Sabbath and maintained separate seats in local churches to symbolize the authority and dignity of the corporation in the ceremonial hierarchy of the parish. Before historians can ask the right questions about the process of restoration, this complex relationship between forms of religious community and civic community must be recovered.

To understand the appeal of Charles's return for heterogeneous groups is to perceive the general fear of religious extremism in the late 1650s. As we have seen, the process of religious separation during the 1640s and early 1650s had formed communities of significant spiritual and discursive power as alternatives to the discipline of the customary parish. Baptists renounced local custom and hierarchy in the formal rules of their communities yet continued to profess their obedience to the authority of the state. Such radical groups as Quakers and Fifth Monarchists departed from Baptists in their exclusive reliance on the authority of personal revelation and experience of the Holy Spirit. This emphasis on personal experience over other forms of public authority, including Scripture, made Quakerism appear antisocial and dangerous both to supporters of the Book of Common Prayer and to Presbyterians and Independents. The vision of many Independents and other supporters of the protectorate had called for the reconstitution of parishes as more exclusive religious communities dominated by spiritual elites. These godly elites included persons of different social status but preserved a hierarchy in the relationship between the elect and the corrupt remnant of the parish. Quakerism destroyed this hierarchy by emphasizing universal access to the authority of the spirit. To Independents, the open church that harbored Quakerism began to symbolize the dissolution of social order.

The general fear of Quakers as antisocial spiritual levelers has dominated recent discussions of the religious motives for restoration (Reay, "Quakers"; "Authorities"). The intensity of this common fear sometimes resulted in violence. In June 1660, Quakers were assaulted in the village of Tirley in Gloucestershire. William Sparrow, a Quaker from Ross, had traveled to visit his friends and co-religionists in Tirley. Several villagers subsequently arrested Sparrow and assaulted one of his friends in an attack described by one participant as a civil action. Richard Broadwell, another Quaker, went to the house of one of the villagers on the following day to request Sparrow's release but was lured into a room and accosted by Edward Perry, servant of a local gentleman. Perry drew his sword and threatened to kill Broadwell unless he agreed to drink the king's health. In the confrontation that followed, Perry was physically restrained by his companions, as Broadwell fled from the house (Beaver, *Parish Communities*, p. 254). The enmity between Quakers and other Protestants surfaced in a second scuffle, this time between George Fox and some Independents in Tewkesbury. In 1655, Fox held a night meeting in the town and recorded its incidents in his journal. John Wells, the Independent minister of the parish, attended the meeting "with a great deal of rabble and rude people" and "boasted he would see whether he or [Fox] should have the victory." Fox began to preach and

> turned the people to the divine light, which Christ the heavenly and spiritual man had enlightened them withal; that with that light they might see their sins; and how that they were in death and darkness and without God in the world; and with the same light they might see Christ from whence it came, their savior and redeemer, who had shed his blood for them and died for them; who was their way to God, their truth and life. (Penney, *Journal of George Fox*, vol. 1, p. 197)

This approach to religious experience clearly disregarded election in favor of the "light of Christ" as a universal guide to salvation. In his exaltation of personal religious authority, Fox seemed to deny the principles of hierarchy and subordination in human society. The inevitable diffusion of religious authority in personal experience was repugnant to Independents, and Wells "began to rage against the light and denied it and so went away." His supporters remained behind and carried a "mischief in their hearts" but were restrained, according to Fox, by the power of the Lord.

Although the power of this concern over religious radicalism is not controversial, much remains unclear about the microhistories of restoration in the parishes. If the fascination of the restoration process lies in its mingling of general and highly specific or local influences, the diversity of local settlements lies very much in shadow. There is remarkably little work on the first wave of episcopal visitations, for example, surely key moments and sites for the making of the first restoration settlements in local parishes. A brief sketch may suggest the benefits of such an approach. A fear of sectarian movements, and Quakerism in particular, formed the context of the first episcopal visitation in Tewkesbury and its neighborhood in northern Gloucestershire. This visitation lasted from December 19, 1661 to September 9, 1662 as convocation revised the Book of Common Prayer, promoted a restrictive Act of Uniformity, and created a conservative religious settlement for the national church. At this time, the traditional process of visitation, with its presentment of local offenses, reasserted the ceremonial authority and moral jurisdiction of the territorial church. Just as the local commissioners appointed under the terms of the Corporation Act in 1662 created protective boundaries around restored borough councils, so the presentments made by churchwardens in the course of this visitation formed part of an effort to reconstruct the ceremonial boundaries of parish churches, although in practice the Act of Uniformity was less strictly enforced than the Corporation Act. Between October 1662 and March 1665 the consistory court focused almost exclusively on religious offenses and handled 70 presentments for 70 violations of the ceremonial code in the restored church. Despite the narrowness of the formal settlement in the church, however, churchwardens did not prosecute Presbyterians and Independents in the vale of Gloucester. On the contrary, the visitation was an unmistakable assault on Baptists and Quakers. Separatism was the principle of exclusion in the restored parish, and Independents in Tewkesbury were reluctant to separate from a church which had borne their stamp during the 1650s.

This first visitation and its prosecutions thus formed a campaign against Baptists and Quakers, the most visible local separatist communities. Both diocesan and parish officers used the campaign to mark the boundaries of the established church by prosecution of the most conspicuous offenders, but the rank-and-file separatists were not systematically prosecuted. This method was reflected in the prosecution of villagers known to hold private religious meetings or conventicles in their homes. In 1663, Edwin Millington of Tewkesbury was presented for "keeping a conventicle of Anabaptists" in his house. The Quakers prosecuted were sufficiently prominent to hold the Stoke Orchard monthly meeting in their Tewkesbury homes. This assault on separatist leaders and meeting sites was the primary objective of the visitation. Prosecutions occasionally touched the local rank and file for various offenses against the restored parish, including absence from church and more serious transgressions of the ritual cycle, such as keeping infants from baptism. The Baptist community centered on Tewkesbury had at least 17 of its 135 members presented in court, almost 13 percent of its membership. The number of prosecutions remained small and evenly distributed between movements. Of the 70 presentments made between 1662 and 1665 for violations of the ceremonial code, 35 offenders can be identified positively as either Baptists or Quakers. The small number of known separatists prosecuted suggests that this visitation was an attempt to establish boundaries rather than uniformity. The arrival of the bishop and the preparation of presentments was part of the process of marking the boundaries of the restored church and inducing neighbors beyond the boundaries to cross over.

This pressure on the leadership and margins of separatist communities in the restoration of the parish created and subsequently reinforced the distinction between the church and dissent. The importance of this boundary for local Presbyterians and Independents as well as the more shadowy community of Prayer Book Protestants helps to explain the diverse local support for the restoration. Protestantism had splintered during the 1640s and 1650s, and a pervasive fear of spiritual levelers induced even Independents to favor the building of formidable boundaries to protect the authority of Scripture and the societies of the godly from the destructive power of radical mysticism. This cooperation among Presbyterians, Independents, and Cavaliers in the "royalist restoration" saved the elect from the spiritually and socially subversive force of Quakerism. Yet this fragile alignment of diverse groups produced not the static relationships frequently implied by the concept of *the* restoration but a form of belonging characterized as much by unresolved conflicts as by the shared desire to preserve social and religious hierarchy.

The creation of boundaries between church and sect did not imply local consensus on the form of religious ritual to be practiced in the restored parish. Presbyterians, Independents, and Prayer Book Protestants agreed on the necessity of boundaries to protect formal hierarchy in parishes, but the precise relationship between prescribed forms of prayer and the authority of conscience in this restored hierarchy remained unclear. The parochial restoration thus failed to resolve longstanding conflicts over authority and ceremony in the church. Many nonconformists returned to the parish church in the early 1660s but refused to accept the restoration settlement as the last word on local religious practice. The first episcopal visitation distinguished Presbyterians, Independents, and Prayer Book Protestants as the restored parish and constructed boundaries to protect this form of belonging from sectarian neighbors. The restoration process thus represented neither a return to homogeneous parish communities nor a decisive break from the experience of the 1640s and 1650s but rather a redistribution of power among local factions expressed as an assault on sectaries and officers of the protectorate. The fundamental questions of ritual and authority had been rephrased but not resolved.

What is meant by restoration process? A process is defined by indeterminacy, the absence of closure or finality. This simple concept, applied to the return of monarchy in 1660, has already begun to shape a new historical perspective on the restoration. Just as the progressive landmarks of the English reformation have dissolved in contingency, the restoration has ceased to stand as a monolithic event, defined once and for all in royal decrees and parliamentary statutes. These local views and experiences of restoration in the corporation and parish of Tewkesbury only make sense in the context of earlier conflicts and alliances during the 1640s and 1650s and reveal a complex local politics of belonging in both corporation and parish, a politics of inclusion and exclusion. Nor did the restoration process resolve the related problems of authority, loyalty, and belonging or local identity. The experience of defeat was not the experience of destruction, and visions of the restored polity removed from power in the early 1660s survived to emerge in later conflicts and debates. The moment of restoration therefore should not be assumed as the norm for relations among factions.

BIBLIOGRAPHY

Aston, M., *England's Iconoclasts*. Oxford: Oxford University Press, 1988.
Beaver, D. C., *Parish Communities and Religious Conflict in the Vale of Gloucester, 1590–1690*. Cambridge, Mass.: Harvard University Press, 1998.
Bell, C., *Ritual Theory, Ritual Practice*. Oxford: Oxford University Press, 1992.
Capp, B. S., *The Fifth Monarchy Men: A Study in Seventeenth-Century English Millenarianism*. London: Faber, 1972.

Cohen, A. P., *The Symbolic Construction of Community*. London: Routledge, 1985.

Collinson, P., *The Religion of Protestants: The Church in English Society 1559–1625*. Oxford: Clarendon Press, 1982.

Cooper, T., ed., *The Journal of William Dowsing*. Woodbridge: Boydell Press, 2001.

Cust, R. and Hughes, A., eds., *Conflict in Early Stuart England: Studies in Religion and Politics 1603–1642*. London: Longman, 1989.

Davies, A., *The Quakers in English Society, 1655–1725*. Oxford: Oxford University Press, 2000.

Davies, G., *The Restoration of Charles II, 1658–1660*. San Marino, Calif.: Huntington Library, 1955.

Durston, C. and Eales, J., eds., *The Culture of English Puritanism, 1560–1700*. Basingstoke: Macmillan, 1996.

Everitt, A., *The Community of Kent and the Great Rebellion, 1640–1660*. Leicester: Leicester University Press, 1966.

Fincham, K., ed., *The Early Stuart Church, 1603–1642*. Basingstoke: Macmillan, 1993.

Gardiner, S. R., *History of the Great Civil War, 1642–1649*, 4 vols. Adlestrop: Windrush Press, 1987, 1991 (originally published 1893).

Green, I. M., *The Reestablishment of the Church of England*. Oxford: Oxford University Press, 1978.

Haigh, C., *English Reformations: Religion, Politics, and Society under the Tudors*. Oxford: Oxford University Press, 1993.

Halliday, P., *Dismembering the Body Politic*. Cambridge: Cambridge University Press, 1998.

Harris, T., Seaward, P., and Goldie, M., eds., *The Politics of Religion in Restoration England*. Oxford: Blackwell, 1990.

Hebdige, D., *Subculture: The Meaning of Style*. London: Methuen, 1979.

Heylyn, P., *Brief Relation of the Death and Sufferings of the Archbishop of Canterbury* (1645).

Howell, R., Jr., *Newcastle upon Tyne and the Puritan Revolution: A Study of the Civil War*. Oxford: Oxford University Press, 1967.

Hughes, A., *Politics, Society, and Civil War in Warwickshire, 1620–1660*. Cambridge: Cambridge University Press, 1987.

Hughes, A., *The Causes of the English Civil War*, 2nd ed. Basingstoke: Macmillan, 1998.

Hutton, R., *The Restoration*. Oxford: Oxford University Press, 1985.

Hutton, R., *Charles II*. Oxford: Oxford University Press, 1989.

Hyde, Edward, Earl of Clarendon, *The Life of Edward Earl of Clarendon*, 3 vols. (1827).

Ingram, M., *Church Courts, Sex, and Marriage in England, 1570–1640*. Cambridge: Cambridge University Press, 1987.

Jones, C., Newitt, M., and Roberts, S., eds., *Politics and People in Revolutionary England: Essays in Honour of Ivan Roots*. Oxford: Blackwell, 1986.

Jones, J. R., ed., *The Restored Monarchy, 1660–1688*. Totowa, NJ: Rowman & Littlefield, 1979.

Keeble, N. H., ed., *The Autobiography of Richard Baxter*, Rev. ed. Totowa, NJ: Rowman & Littlefield, 1974.

Kenyon, J. P., *Stuart England*, 2nd ed. Harmondsworth: Penguin, 1985.

Lake, P., *The Boxmaker's Revenge*. Stanford, Calif.: Stanford University Press, 2001.

Macfarlane, A., ed., *Diary of Ralph Josselin, 1616–1683*. Cambridge: Cambridge University Press, 1976.

McGregor, J. F. and Reay, B., eds., *Radical Religion in the English Revolution*. Oxford: Oxford University Press, 1986.

Maltby, J., *Prayer Book and People in Elizabethan and Early Stuart England*. Cambridge: Cambridge University Press, 1998.

Manning, B., *The English People and the English Revolution 1640–1649*, 2nd ed. London: Bookmarks, 1991.

Morrill, J., *The Nature of the English Revolution*. London: Longman, 1993.

O'Day, R., *The English Clergy: The Emergence and Consolidation of a Profession, 1558–1642*. Leicester: Leicester University Press, 1979.

Ogg, D., *England in the Reign of Charles II*, 2nd ed. Oxford: Clarendon Press, 1956.

Penney, N., ed., *The Journal of George Fox*, 2 vols. Cambridge: Cambridge University Press, 1911.

Porter, S., ed., *London and the Civil War*. London: Macmillan, 1996.

Reay, B., "The Authorities and Early Restoration Quakerism," *Journal of Ecclesiastical History*, 34 (1983), pp. 69–84.

Reay, B., "The Quakers, 1659, and the Restoration of the Monarchy," *History*, 63 (1978), pp. 193–213.

Richardson, R. C., ed., *Town and Countryside in the English Revolution*. Manchester: Manchester University Press, 1992.

Seaver, P. S., *Wallington's World: A Puritan Artisan in Seventeenth-Century London*. Stanford, Calif.: Stanford University Press, 1985.

Seaward, P., *The Cavalier Parliament and the Reconstruction of the Old Regime*. Cambridge: Cambridge University Press, 1989.

Sharpe, J., *Instruments of Darkness: Witchcraft in England 1550–1750*. London: Hamish Hamilton, 1996.

Sharpe, K., *The Personal Rule of Charles I*. New Haven, Conn.: Yale University Press, 1992.

Smith, N., *Literature and Revolution in England, 1640–1660*. New Haven, Conn.: Yale University Press, 1994.

Spurr, J., *The Restoration Church of England, 1646–1689*. New Haven, Conn.: Yale University Press, 1991.

Tyacke, N., *Anti-Calvinists: The Rise of English Arminianism, c.1590–1640*. Oxford: Clarendon Press, 1987.

Underdown, D., *Revel, Riot, and Rebellion: Popular Politics and Culture in England 1603–1660*. Oxford: Oxford University Press, 1987.

Underdown, D., *Fire from Heaven: Life in an English Town in the Seventeenth Century*. London: Fontana, 1993.

Walter, J., *Understanding Popular Violence in the English Revolution: The Colchester Plunderers*. Cambridge: Cambridge University Press, 1999.

Watts, M., *The Dissenters*. Oxford: Clarendon Press, 1978.

Withington, P., "Views from the Bridge," *Past and Present*, 170 (2001), pp. 121–4.

FURTHER READING

Any of the sources and secondary works included in the bibliography may serve as an introduction to the religious crises and changes of the 1640s. Overviews of the civil wars and revolution currently do not do justice to the intricacies of change in local parishes. This experience of war is best approached through such excellent local studies as Mark Stoyle, *Loyalty and Locality: Popular Allegiance in Devon during the English Civil War* (Exeter: Exeter University Press, 1994), on Devonshire parishes, Underdown, *Fire from Heaven*, on Dorchester, and Walter, *Understanding Popular Violence*, on the Stour valley, and through the many useful articles in the journals *Midland History*, *Northern History*, and *Southern History*, such as Mark Stoyle, "Whole Streets Converted to Ashes: Property Destruction in Exeter during the English Civil War," *Southern History*, 16 (1994), pp. 62–81. A major obstacle to writing the broader narrative of change in English parishes is the absence of systematic work on the local implications of the dissolution of diocesan authority in 1641 and 1642 and a similar paucity of detailed work on the first restoration visitations in late 1661 and 1662. Apart from impressionistic observations, very little is currently known about these key moments in the history of the cultural process whereby parish communities were created.

After an introduction through secondary works, consulting the wealth of primary evidence is the best way to understand the hopes and fears sparked by the violence of civil war and religious change during the 1640s. Bruno Ryves in his *Mercurius Rusticus* (1643) articulated a royalist view of parliamentarian atrocities committed in the name of godliness. John Corbet described from a parliamentarian perspective the resistance of Gloucester's besieged godly minority in *Historical Relation of the Military Government of Gloucester* (1645); and Brilliana Harley conveyed the many terrors of rural siege in letters to her husband and others, collected in *Letters of Lady Brilliana Harley* (Camden Society, 1854, vol. 58). A magnificent array of documents and commentary on the practice of godly iconoclasm under the parliamentarian regime in East Anglia has been collected in Trevor Cooper's beautifully produced edition of William Dowsing's journal. This text reveals in unique detail the use of violence against the fabric of local churches as a means to build new godly communities. Thomas Edwards's *Gangraena* (1646) conveyed common fears of sectarian disorder following the first civil war. Edwards's febrile rhetoric and intellectual horror reflected a common view of religious radicalism as a form of personal, social, and spiritual pollution. Taken together, the myriad perspectives expressed in these sources suggest the cultural dynamism essential to the process of religious change in the revolution.

Part V

Christian Europe and the World

Twenty

Religion and the Church in Early Latin America

Kevin Terraciano

In his *True History of the Conquest of New Spain*, Bernal Díaz del Castillo recounted how Hernando Cortés had mocked Moteuczoma for his "false gods." The Mexican ruler replied:

> I understand what you have said to my ambassadors about the three gods and the cross, and what you preached in the various towns through which you passed. We have given you no answer, since we have worshiped our own gods here from the beginning and know them to be good. No doubt yours are good also, but do not trouble to tell us any more about them at present. (Díaz del Castillo, *Conquest of New Spain*, p. 222)

Later, Cortés continued to scorn him, remarking with a laugh, "Lord Montezuma, I cannot imagine how a prince as great and wise as your Majesty can have failed to realize that these idols of yours are not gods but evil things." Moteuczoma responded, speaking to the translator, a native woman known as Malinche:

> Lady Malinche, if I had known that you were going to utter these insults I would not have shown you my gods. We hold them to be very good. They give us health and rain and crops and all the victories we desire. So we are bound to worship them and make offerings to them, and I beg you to say nothing more against them. (Ibid., p. 237)

This tense dialogue, whether fact or fiction, represents the collision of cultures and religious systems in Mexico. After the fall of Tenochtitlan in 1521, Moteuczoma's gods could provide neither health nor victory. The victors forced the vanquished to worship "the one god from Castile," as one Mixtec called him when he testified before the Holy Office of the Inquisition (Terraciano, *Mixtecs of Colonial Oaxaca*, p. 278). At the same time, the conquest and colonization of the Americas forced Spaniards to confront a series of theological, moral, and legal issues. Pope Alexander VI asserted in 1493 that Ferdinand and Isabella and their successors could claim dominion over the newly discovered islands and mainland. Although the bull prohibited Spaniards from inflicting hardships on native peoples, this provision was often overlooked or proved impossible to enforce in the conquest period. Members of the church played a key role in subsequent debates on the forced conversion and exploitation of indigenous peoples, arguing both for and against imperial ambitions.

This chapter provides a broad overview of research in three related areas of colonial Latin American history. The first part examines several sixteenth-century ecclesiastical writings on the Americas, focusing on debates over the forced conversion of indigenous peoples. The second section summarizes how the church operated in Spanish America and Brazil. The third part considers native and African responses to Christianity, the successes and limitations of the church, and the development of local forms of Christianity. In keeping with the literature on this topic, I will focus on the two most populous areas of the Americas, Mexico (Mesoamerica) and Peru (the Andes), especially in the sixteenth century.

Conquest and Conversion

Iberian intellectuals discussed the Castilian right to possess and colonize the Indies soon after Cristobal Colón's first voyage. In 1503, a group of civil lawyers and theologians concluded that the papal bulls of donation, which granted Castile "full, free, ample, and absolute authority and jurisdiction" over the Indies, guaranteed their right to conquer and enslave Indians in return for converting them to Christianity (Hanke, *Aristotle and the American Indians*, pp. 25–6; Brading, *First America*, p. 79). The assumption that God had chosen the Spaniards to instruct Indians and to do so by force, if necessary, was exemplified in the language of a notorious document called the *Requerimiento* (requirement), a speech that *conquistadores* were supposed to read (in Spanish or Latin) when they encountered a group of peoples in the Americas. Juan López de Palacios Rubios, a judge, university professor, and royal adviser, developed the text of the speech, which was approved by King Ferdinand in the first decade of the sixteenth century. The requirement was a legal ultimatum for native peoples to submit to the superiority of Christianity and the political authority of Spain or be warred upon. An excerpt from the speech captures the crusading spirit that Spaniards brought to the Americas:

> I beg and require of you as best as I can that you recognize the church as lord and superior of the universal world, and the Pope in its name, and His Majesty in his place, as superior and lord and king . . . and consent to what the religious fathers declare and preach . . . and His Majesty and I in his name will receive you and will leave your women and children free, without servitude, so that with them and with yourselves you can freely do what you wish . . . and we will not compel you to turn Christians. But if you do not do it, with the help of God, I will enter forcefully against you, and I will make war everywhere and however I can, and I will subject you to the yoke and obedience of the church and His Majesty, and I will take your wives and children, and I will make them slaves, and I will take your goods, and I will do to you all the evil and damages that a lord may do to subjects who do not obey or receive him. And I solemnly declare that the death and damages received from such will be your fault and not that of His Majesty, nor mine, nor of the gentlemen who came with me. (Seed, *Ceremonies of Possession*, p. 69)

Friars quickly followed in the footsteps of the conquerors. Twelve members of the Franciscan order arrived in New Spain in 1524. One of the 12, fray Toribio de

Benavente, who adopted the name Motolinia (a Nahuatl-language word meaning "the afflicted one"), embodied the euphoric optimism and energy of the "spiritual conquest." In his *Historia de los indios de la Nueva España* (1541), one of the earliest ecclesiastical chronicles on the Americas, he boasted that the Franciscans had baptized and civilized millions of people and had eradicated countless idolatries. He admired the fully sedentary Mesoamerican and Andean societies that resembled the Europeans in many ways, but condemned many of their practices and customs as evil. He denounced the mistreatment of native peoples but approved the use of force in converting unwilling infidels; the conquest was a bad means to a good end. Like many churchmen, Motolinia saw the conversion of the Indians as an opportunity to create a pure brand of Christianity, free from Jewish, Islamic, and Protestant interference.

In contrast to Motolinia's optimism, some religious objected to the ideological basis of Castile's power in the Indies and the treatment of native peoples, and questioned whether the papal bulls of donation entitled Castile to jurisdiction over the Indies. The Dominican fray Antonio de Montesinos was among the first to question the legality of the conquests when in 1511 he accused Spaniards of abusing and killing Indians on the island of Española. The crown's advisers responded to these doubts and criticisms by attributing their right to rule and possess the Indies, and to use indigenous labor for mining and other enterprises, to the supposed simplicity of native peoples. The Indians were "barbarians" who were incapable of creating their own civil societies, and thereby had forfeited their rights to property, according to the precepts of Roman law. Indians could be warred upon if they did not acknowledge the authority of the crown and Christianity. This explanation contradicted the widely accepted scholastic premise that men who lived in civil societies had the same natural rights as those who lived in the state of nature. John Major, a Scottish Dominican, was among the first to suggest that the Indian may represent a category called the "natural slave," a mentally inferior being who was destined to serve superior masters. Aristotle articulated a theory of natural slavery in books one and three of the *Politics* to justify the enslavement of non-Greeks. As natural slaves, Indians were incapable of possession or free will and were bound to serve the Spaniards (Pagden, *Fall of Natural Man*; Hanke, *Spanish Struggle*).

Francisco de Vitoria, a Dominican leader of the Thomist revival at the University of Salamanca, rejected the idea that Indians were slaves by nature and challenged the intellectual foundation of Spain's empire in the Americas. In *Relectio de Indis* (1557), Vitoria referred to the concept of *dominium* in Aquinas's *Summa Theologiae*, that is, the right to possess property according to civil and natural law. He argued that Indians possessed natural reason and complex societies based on civil customs. Vitoria could not reconcile the conquerors' reports of sophisticated societies with arguments that Indians were incapable of ruling themselves, nor did he believe that unnatural and sinful behavior, such as cannibalism and human sacrifice, justified the act of conquest. But he acknowledged the political inexpediency of Spain's withdrawal from the Indies, and he affirmed Spain's right to rule based on its Christian responsibility to tutor and civilize indigenous people. On the other hand, he argued that the crown had no more right to wage war on its subjects in the Indies than it did on citizens of Seville. His attempt to justify the empire without vilifying the Indian as a natural slave continued to serve the royal cause but rejected many traditional arguments for conquest and empire. The emperor Charles V responded by prohibiting public discussion on the matter and confiscating all papers on the subject. Still, the "Salamanca School" continued to debate the application of natural law to the Indies.

Vitoria's opposition to the theory of natural slavery caught the attention of Juan Ginés de Sepúlveda, a distinguished scholar who had completed a translation of Aristotle's *Politics* into Latin. In the early 1540s, Sepúlveda wrote a manuscript called *Democrates Secundus* that attempted to legitimate "just war" in the Indies by applying Aristotle's theory of natural slavery to the Indians. The author considered the Indians barbarous and inhuman peoples who did not deserve *dominium*. In *Tratado sobre las justas causas de la guerra contra los indios* (written in 1548), he cited Biblical examples of wars waged for holy purposes and argued that natural law dictated a hierarchy of "perfect" masters and "imperfect" slaves. He likened the difference between Indians and Europeans to that between adults and children, men and women, or even men and monkeys. Though Sepúlveda had never set foot in the Americas, he characterized the Indians as brutish pigs and pagan cannibals who possessed neither individual property nor any discernible culture. He acknowledged that Spaniards had committed wrongs and cruelties in the Indies, but he believed that the end justified the means (Sepúlveda, *Tratado*, pp. 99–105).

If Montesinos and Vitoria opened the door to criticisms of Spanish right and might in the Indies, and Sepúlveda sought to shut that door, fray Bartolomé de las Casas broke the door down in his prolonged attack on the imperial perspective. He had witnessed many atrocities as an ordained priest on the islands of Española and Cuba. Jolted by the protests of Montesinos and a passage in Ecclesiasticus, Las Casas divested himself of his own lucrative Cuban encomienda and dedicated his life to advocating on behalf of the Indians; he later entered the Dominican order in 1522. In *Apologia*, one of his many writings on Native Americans, he concluded that Indians were only barbarians in the sense that they were non-Europeans who lacked certain arts and cultural forms, which they were capable of learning and acquiring. He even drafted plans for and attempted to implement utopian native Christian settlements. One of Las Casas's most controversial arguments, raised earlier by Vitoria, concerned the rights of Christian subjects: if Indians had been Christianized by the millions, as ecclesiastical writers had claimed, should they not be free to rule themselves? At what point would Christian Indians be fully tolerated and acknowledged as free? Las Casas's idea of a just or legitimate government meant complete restitution to the indigenous. Whereas most of his contemporaries argued that the Indians did not deserve to be tolerated, or that they needed to attain a status worthy of toleration, Las Casas argued for full toleration as a precondition of conversion but he did not suggest that Indians be left alone entirely. He reserved an active, paternal role for friars in his utopian vision, and he suggested that African slaves might perform the labor that Europeans required. Later, he opposed African slavery as well (Hanke, *Aristotle and the American Indians*, p. 9).

The Dominican-led campaign against violent conquest and forced conversion culminated in a debate between Las Casas and Sepúlveda, held in Valladolid in 1550–1. Las Casas and Sepúlveda presented their views before a group of jurists and scholars appointed by the king, including representatives of the Salamanca School and the Councils of Castile and the Indies, who possessed no formal, legal power beyond their role as advisers. The two never met in the same room together. Rather, each read arguments before the appointed council. In the end, little came of the symbolic event, and both sides claimed victory. The council of advisers generated no records of their thoughts on the event and rendered no final judgment; their role as advisers did not entitle them to issue individual or collective statements to anyone besides the king and the Council of the Indies. Apparently, the king said and did nothing about the debate.

Whereas Las Casas used his position and connections to publish freely on these matters, Sepúlveda's writings were never published in Spain during the author's lifetime. The Council of the Indies, influential members of the Universities of Salamanca and Alcalá, the Dominican order, and Las Casas blocked the publication of *Democrates Secundus*. The Council of the Indies also decreed that Sepúlveda's one book on the subject, a summary of his ideas in Latin, published in Rome during the first year of the debate, should be banned from the Indies. Meanwhile, one year after the debate, Las Casas wrote a scathing work known as *A Short Account of the Destruction of the Indies*. This treatise attacked the contradictions of Christian rule in the Americas from the perspective of an eyewitness. He argued that "from the very outset, the Spanish have taken no more trouble to preach the Christian faith to these peoples than if they had been dealing with dogs or other animals," and he accused Spaniards of obstructing the work of friars "because they felt that the spread of the Gospel would in some way stand between them and the gold and wealth they craved" (Las Casas, *Short Account*, p. 126). He called Cortés and Pizarro and the other conquerors greedy tyrants who should have been beheaded rather than rewarded. In response to Sepúlveda's "just war" arguments, Las Casas countered that the natives could rightfully proclaim just war on the Spaniards (ibid., p. 23).

Las Casas antagonized many people by directly challenging and contradicting previous histories that praised Spanish and Christian accomplishments in the Indies. He dodged an attempted assassination in 1545 before he returned to Spain in 1547, where he lobbied on behalf of indigenous rights until his death in 1566. Motolinia accused Las Casas of being a false prophet and a hypocrite who had damaged Spain's international reputation, especially after the publication of *A Short Account* in multiple European languages. Whereas Las Casas condemned the conquest, Motolinia saw it as a divine, millennial event. Motolinia criticized Las Casas for being too busy agitating in Spain to take any serious interest in his own bishopric of Chiapas. Las Casas aimed his criticisms at greedy subjects of the crown who had ignored royal laws and Christian principles. By raising problems and proposing changes without implicating the king in any wrongdoing, typical of official correspondence to the crown, he did not directly threaten the royal agenda. On the contrary, Las Casas's defense of native peoples strengthened royal authority because it urged the crown to expand its prerogative at the expense of encomenderos, who stood to lose their perpetual grants of native tribute and labor. Las Casas's campaign contributed to the "New Laws" of 1542, which restricted the rights of encomenderos and eventually abolished the institution. Thus, the crown consolidated and extended its control in the Indies by allowing various constituencies and factions to compete against one another (Brading, *First America*, pp. 68, 72).

The justification of conquest and possession by way of condemning native cultures, a familiar theme of earlier writings, was no longer as prevalent in late sixteenth-century Spanish writings, when the storm of debate around the conquest had subsided. The writings of the Jesuit José de Acosta represent a significant shift in the Spanish discourse on native peoples, though he was clearly influenced by Las Casas and Vitoria. Acosta's *Historia natural y moral de las Indias* (1590) surpassed previous writings on native cultures in its sophistication, clarity, and innovation. Acosta sought to change Europeans' contempt and lowly opinion of the Indians by understanding native cultures on their own terms. He advocated the retention of native forms of organization and customs if they did not contradict Christian practices. Acosta dismissed the concept of natural slavery and emphasized the authority of empirical knowledge and experience over ancient texts in describing natural phenomena and human cultures. He opposed the idea that Christians could justly wage war upon non-Christians, even if they had refused to accept the faith. Like Las Casas and Vitoria (and Sepúlveda), however, he could not escape the analogy of the Indian as a promising child (Pagden, *Fall of Natural Man*, pp. 160–80).

Despite the humanitarian and progressive arguments of religious writers such as Las Casas and Acosta, many churchmen continued to hold indigenous people in low esteem. In New Spain, the first Mexican provincial council of 1555 forbade the ordination of Indians to the priesthood and prohibited them from touching the sacred vessels, contrary to earlier hopes that they were capable of becoming priests. Mestizos and blacks were also forbidden to be ordained. By the time of the third council in 1585, most members had concluded that the Indians failed to meet Christian expectations, and lamented the evolution of separate indigenous and Spanish churches in Mexico. This low image of the Indian among churchmen in New Spain conformed in many ways to the ideology of the Catholic Reformation, which reserved a sober, low opinion for human nature in general (Poole, "Declining Image," pp. 13–17). Whether optimistic or pessimistic about the future of the church in the Americas, most religious thought that the Indians were childlike and all believed that they needed permanent guidance in the faith. However, they could not agree on the best means of conversion.

In the last quarter of the sixteenth century, skepticism toward the outcome of the spiritual conquest, a nostalgic sense that the promise of the early period had not been realized, criticisms of the humanist project of learning indigenous languages, the continuing decline of the native population, and the waning power of the religious orders in Mexico all weighed heavily on Christians who reflected on the spiritual conquest's successes and failures. In his *Historia eclesiástica indiana* (1596), fray Gerónimo de Mendieta lamented the end of a golden era. The experience of Franciscans at the College of Santa Cruz Tlatelolco in Mexico, where indigenous nobles were groomed for priesthood, had taught the friars that "for the most part, the Indians are not fit to command or govern, but rather to be commanded and governed" (Brading, *First America*, pp. 113–15). Mendieta's pessimism was shared by a fellow Franciscan, fray Bernardino de Sahagún, who spent much of his life learning the Nahuatl language, teaching Nahua aides to write in the Roman alphabet, and overseeing the writing of a lengthy encyclopedia of Nahua culture and history. In 1575, Sahagún was ordered to send a Spanish version of the Nahuatl-language *Historia general de las cosas de Nueva España* to Spain. The author-compiler justified his work by comparing it to a doctor's examination of a sick patient, whose cure depended on a proper diagnosis of the disease. Sahagún intended to penetrate the Nahua mind and soul by studying their language and culture. Sahagún also responded to criticisms of these types of ethnographic projects, which recorded and kept alive the memory of ancient customs. In 1577, after Philip's decree to abort writings on native culture and history, all 12 books of the *Historia general* were confiscated and sent to Spain. In his prologue to the Spanish edition of the work, Sahagún revealed his doubts about the entire mission. No Indian had been admitted to the priesthood, he claimed, because none was able to guard the requirements of celibacy; the natural environment caused them to be "indolent and inclined to sensual vices." The Indians had been destroyed by the conquest, he concluded (Sahagún, *Historia general*, vol. 1, pp. 27–32; Ricard, *Spiritual Conquest*, pp. 230, 294).

Let us turn from ecclesiastical writings and questions of ideology to matters of practice by considering how the institution of the church operated in Spanish America and Brazil.

The Church

Like the encomienda, parishes were based on native communities in the sedentary areas of the Americas. A percent of the labor and tribute was directed toward building the church and maintaining the priest – a provision that often placed friars and encomenderos in direct competition for native labor, especially as the indigenous population declined rapidly in the second half of the sixteenth century. Churches were built in the middle of settlements, from the same stones and on the same sites as the preconquest temples. In the sedentary areas, people possessed the technical and organizational skills to build magnificent churches in the colonial period. Local native authorities were expected to oversee church construction and attendance. The religious investigated every potential enterprise to sustain their activities, from producing silk and sugar to selling African slaves. The orders (the Franciscans, Dominicans, and Augustinians, among others) were very competitive with one another, jostling for the best areas with the densest native populations.

In the early postconquest period, members of the orders set out to find and destroy temples, images, and the native priesthood. They confiscated and burned *codices* (pictographic writings on deerskin or fig-bark paper) and created new sacred texts in the form of native-language *doctrinas* or catechisms. They sought to learn as much as possible about native beliefs and customs in order to identify and extirpate idolatries. The religious underwent extensive native language-training programs so that they could communicate with people, preach to large audiences in the patio of their churches, and hear confession. They worked with male nobles and their sons in schools to develop native-language dictionaries and grammars, teaching them how to write their own languages with the Roman alphabet. There were so few priests that they could not have done it any other way. The orders also introduced edifying plays, established primary and technical schools, and founded hospitals for the sick. In the early period, the Spanish presence in the native countryside was often limited to ecclesiastical establishments.

Eventually, Spaniards who were born in the Americas, called *criollos*, joined ecclesiastical organizations as ordained clerics. Whereas membership in the orders represented a measure of prestige and high learning, joining the secular clergy had certain financial benefits that appealed to local, prominent families. Namely, in the regular orders, the money that a family donated to subsidize a son's entry into the order was no longer controlled by the family; in comparison, the funds used to set up a secular cleric could remain under family control through the foundation of a chaplaincy. Normally, a yearly income from one of the family's properties would be paid to the son as chaplain, under the direction of the family patron. The secular priest could also acquire and own property, which he would return to the rest of the family by bequest. Secular priests usually received the assignment of new parishes that were created after the sixteenth century, whereas the orders retained the parishes that they already controlled or acquired new parishes in peripheral areas, on the frontiers or edges of the colony. Within the mendicant orders, Spanish-born members, called *peninsulares*, maintained their numbers, and members born on both sides of the Atlantic competed for many of the same positions. In comparison, *criollos* became a majority of the secular clergy.

Bishoprics were based on major Spanish settlements, nearly all established before the 1570s. By the mid-seventeenth century the cathedrals of the viceregal capitals and other prominent cities were stone basilicas that reflected the prosperity of those regions' economies. In urban areas, convents of nuns grew in size and number until they rivaled the monasteries, drawing membership almost exclusively from prominent local families who paid a substantial dowry toward the support of their daughters and the establishment. Hospitals were often associated with both monasteries and convents. All monastic institutions received donations, which allowed them to acquire rural estates and urban rental properties as sources of income. The more peripheral the area, the larger a proportion of total Spanish landholding these estates represented. The premise that the church held most of the land in Latin America is due in part to the prominence of chaplaincies; most haciendas did have ecclesiastical encumbrances, but the properties and their incomes remained in the possession of laymen and often remained under family control (Lockhart and Schwartz, *Early Latin America*, pp. 154–6).

The church in Brazil reflected the economic conditions, size, and complexity of the population. It was slow to develop in comparison to Spanish America, and it never enjoyed the wealth and institutional strength that it had in Mexico and Peru. By 1700 Brazil had only one archiepiscopal see, at Salvador, with two suffragan bishoprics at Rio de Janeiro and Pernambuco, in comparison with the five archbishoprics and more than 25 bishoprics in the Spanish Indies. The regular orders in Brazil remained strong even after the initial conquest phase; in Spanish America, the regular orders remained dominant in the peripheral areas, which were in many ways comparable to Brazil (Lockhart and Schwartz, *Early Latin America*, p. 239).

The Jesuits came to the Spanish Indies in force after the 1570s. Whereas the mendicant orders were created in the late Middle Ages, Jesuit organization was the product of a later time. Instead of embracing the monastic tradition of the cloister, they reflected the secular, international interests of early modern Europe. The Jesuits immediately established their headquarters in the viceregal capitals, in Lima and Mexico City, and other large cities. They rivaled the Dominicans as an order of intellectuals and educators and specialized in the secondary education of the colonial elite. The donations they attracted went to their *colegios*, their churches, and their rural and urban properties. Jesuits normally invested in the most capital-intensive, lucrative areas of the economy and ran their properties directly, unlike the other orders whose holdings were usually leased out or run by lay managers. Once established in the most populous areas, Jesuit operations expanded to more per-ipheral regions, among semi-sedentary or non-sedentary indigenous populations. Whereas the Jesuits were latecomers in Spanish America, they were involved in Brazil almost from the beginning and tended to dominate the ecclesiastical and intellectual affairs of the Portuguese colony (Lockhart and Schwartz, *Early Latin America*, pp. 156–7).

In the peripheral areas of Latin America, Europeans could not rely on encomien-das and parishes, as they had done in the areas of sedentary native populations, or the centers of early Latin America. The encomienda could not function where there were no permanent settlements, no widely recognized indigenous rulers, and no tribute or labor mechanisms. Parishes could not be based on already existing communities or use their mechanisms to run the church, as was common in the sedentary areas. Thus, Iberians adopted the mission as a method of conversion and pacification. The mission differed from the parish church in that it was located in a relatively arbitrarily chosen location, where indigenous people were forced or enticed from a large surrounding area to live in the mission compound. Mission establish-ments represented an adaptation of the center's rural monasteries to the periphery. In the center, a cloister stood alongside the church, facing onto a large open atrium. The cloister enclosed the entire community, church, convent, storehouses, shops and workshops, and native residences. Its walls defended it against attack. The enclosure in some missions was large enough for grazing livestock. Mission settlements were supervised directly by Spanish priests. The Spaniards tried to make the native peoples of the frontiers more like those of the sedentary areas, by creating walled-in settle-ments and forcing them to plant and harvest crops and perform Spanish-style enter-prises. In New Spain, Spaniards relocated Nahuas from Tlaxcala, a major altepetl in central Mexico that helped the Spaniards invade and conquer Mexico Tenochtitlan, to act as intermediaries in mining towns and in distant New Mexico. Missions and forts (*presidios*) were Spanish adaptations to the frontier. The soldiers in these forts were plebeian Spaniards and mestizos who supplemented their meager salaries by capturing Indians and selling them as slaves.

In Northern Mexico, there were four areas of mission activity: New Mexico begin-ning in the late sixteenth century; the Gulf of California in the seventeenth and eigh-teenth centuries; Texas in the early and mid-eighteenth century; and Alta California in the late eighteenth century. As in central Mexico, the Franciscans were at first the most active order; by 1600 they had 25 establishments in the north. The Jesuits began to develop a northern mission program during the seventeenth century in Sonora, Arizona, and the coastal regions along the Gulf of California. In Brazil, Jesuits established *aldeas* or mission settlements that attempted to replicate indige-nous villages but resembled European communities in their plan and organization. Paraguay was another site of mission activity; over 100,000 natives were housed in as many as 30 Jesuit missions by the seventeenth century. Conflict between the Jesuits and Spanish and Portuguese settlers revolved around the right to control native Guaraní labor in the region. Although the Jesuits held the high moral ground in this controversy, they nonetheless relied on native labor to create profitable economic enterprises and supplied mining areas with the same types of goods that the Paraguayan Spaniards produced. Competition for scarce native labor was common-place on the fringes and frontiers of Latin America.

The Holy Office of the Inquisition was not established in the Indies until the early 1570s, with the founding of two tribunals in Mexico City and Lima. In Spanish America, the episcopal or apostolic Inquisition, under the direction of bishops and then archbishops, had jurisdiction over native idolatries. The Inquisition was concerned especially with cracking down on crypto-Jews, Protestants, foreigners, blasphemers, sorcerers, bigamists, and other social deviants. The Holy Office used the "purity of blood" code as an exclusionary, political device of extortion and control, often against "New Christians" and ethnic others. As a court with its own sovereign jurisdiction, the Inquisition was one of several independent agencies that vied for power under the crown and played an active role in local politics.

Responses to Christianity

Native and African responses to the introduction of Christianity ranged between the two extremes of full acceptance and outright resistance. Charles Gibson concluded that the Nahuas of central Mexico were drawn to the most overt forms of Christianity after the conquest; they did not understand many basic concepts, they never entirely abandoned their polytheistic beliefs, and they managed to maintain many elements of local religious systems, often in "syncretic compromise" with Christian doctrine (Gibson, *Aztecs*, pp. 101, 134–5). In his balanced assessment of continuity and change, Gibson rejected the notion advanced by George Kubler and Robert Ricard that Christianity replaced native beliefs and practices (Kubler, *Mexican Architecture*; Ricard, *Spiritual Conquest*). But even Ricard, who tended to reproduce the friars' own views of their accomplishments because he relied on their writings for sources, recognized the limitations of the so-called spiritual conquest and used Inquisition records from the early postconquest period to document outright resistance to Christianity. Ricard distinguished between "indifference and ignorance" and organized hostility; backsliding after baptism was due more to weakness and confusion than systematic resistance. Mexican neophytes unconsciously "mingled Christian elements with the practices and beliefs of their old religion" (Ricard, *Spiritual Conquest*, pp. 267–73). Serge Gruzinski also used inquisitorial records to consider how the shock of the Spanish conquest transformed indigenous cultures and mentalities (Gruzinski, *Man-Gods in the Mexican Highlands*). In his broader work on the conquest of Mexico, he examined changing systems of writing and representation, social memory, and the practice of idolatry to explore the cultural strategies that native peoples employed under Spanish rule. Native beliefs and practices imparted new meaning to Christian introductions, and elements of the two ritual systems coexisted in many places (Gruzinski, *Conquest of Mexico*, p. 152). Gruzinski concluded that the Europeanization of native cultures, or the "Christianization of the *imaginaire*," was devastating, but it was never complete or perfect.

Nancy Farriss cited the idolatry trials of the 1560s in Yucatan as evidence of the crisis and conflict that preceded the "creative synthesis" of future generations, and the "gap between the Maya's public acceptance of Christianity and their private activities" (Farriss, *Maya Society*, pp. 291, 318). Christian and Maya beliefs and practices were expressed at different corporate and household levels. Louise Burkhart highlighted the ideological gap between Christian moral precepts and Nahua ideology by examining Nahuatl-language church texts produced by the friars (Burkhart, *Slippery*

Earth, pp. 10, 184–93). For Farriss and Burkhart, the native–Christian synthesis represented cultural survival and creation more than substitution and loss. S. L. Cline and James Lockhart have used Nahuatl-language writings from the second half of the sixteenth century and beyond to examine Nahua-Christian piety and the local church in Nahua communities of central Mexico (Cline, *Colonial Culhuacan*; Lockhart, *Nahuas After the Conquest*). Recent work on the Mixtecs documents a spectrum of local responses to Christianity in Oaxaca, and considers how Mixtecs imagined and reinterpreted many Christian concepts in the light of specific local beliefs and practices (Terraciano, *Mixtecs of Colonial Oaxaca*).

For Peru, Sabine MacCormack studied Andean and Inca religion in the sixteenth and seventeenth centuries as "the focal point of a dialogue between Andeans and invaders" in which people on both sides acted within the constraints imposed by their religious traditions and by their perceptions and experiences. She distinguished between Inca religion in and around the region of Cuzco and the variety of regional, non-Inca cults and practices of the Andes, which were more resilient and continuous. MacCormack compares the Andes around 1600 to the late antique Mediterranean, where it was unclear how much of the pagan past could be accommodated by Christianity (MacCormack, *Religion in the Andes*, pp. 11–13). Kenneth Mills followed MacCormack's work by using the records of Spanish extirpators in the mid-colonial period to illustrate the uneven and unpredictable nature of Andean religious change more than a century after the conquest (Mills, *Idolatry and its Enemies*).

Despite the many obvious differences between Christian and native religions, and the many obstacles to conversion that these differences presented, some Christian practices and concepts were not entirely unfamiliar or incomprehensible to Mesoamericans or Andeans because they resembled native equivalents to some degree. In general, European introductions that converged with indigenous practices or precedents, or that were considered useful by native peoples, were more likely to take root among native populations. For example, in preconquest Mesoamerica, a large temple served as the ceremonial center of a community and a symbol of its identity and autonomy. The church building and the temple shared a similar function; Christians constructed churches on the ruins of temples, an ancient Mediterranean practice, often using the same stones. Mesoamericans built large churches in the sixteenth century and often referred to them in the same terms as the old temples; the Nahuas called the church *teocalli* or "sacred house," and the Mixtecs referred to the new structure in identical terms, as a *huahi ñuhu*. The church building became an important ritual center of the community in Mesoamerica, as it is in many places today.

In Mexico the temple complex influenced the monastery churches that were built in the largest native communities. The church itself looked very European, but the arrangement had many preconquest features. Most Mesoamerican religious practices occurred outdoors, on platform temples or in other sacred sites. Similarly, the monastery church faced onto a large enclosed *atrio* or patio and featured an open chapel that faced the patio, where mass was said to crowds standing in the open. Open-chapel churches represent an American innovation in church architecture (McAndrew, *Open-Air Churches*). A platform crowned with a cross usually stood in the center of the patio, resembling the sacrificial platform that adorned the center of temple compounds. Convents were built on high ground or were raised above the surrounding village ground. A native hierarchy of officials included stewards, sacristans, singers, and others who worked in the new churches. These men were associated with the nobility of a community, the same group of elites that had organized activities around the old temple and palace complex. They were not allowed to act as intercessors, however, and did not become priests.

Catholicism's collective practices, including public worship, processions, *cofradías*, and public feasts, must have appealed to many indigenous communities. No introduction was more successful than the Christian cult of saints; the patron saint of the local church became a symbolic head of the community, resembling a patron deity in many ways. Feasts on saints' days and Christian celebrations often featured dances and other native practices, including ritual drinking. A major general feast was the combined celebration of All Saints' Day and All Souls' Day in November, called "Todos Santos." Writing in the 1580s, fray Diego Durán suspected that Nahuas continued a preconquest tradition in a Christian guise when he observed a "feast of the little dead" and a "feast of the adults," complete with offerings of food and candied fruits, that corresponded with the Christian celebrations (Dúran, *Book of the Gods*, p. 442). Today, this holiday is known as "Día de los Muertos." Hugo Nutini has analyzed the indigenous roots of the Todos Santos complex and its continued celebration in Tlaxcala (Nutini, *Todos Santos*, pp. 86–9).

Like Native Americans, Africans adapted certain Christian customs to their own Bantu, Yoruban, Dahomey, or other West African practices. Africans also incorporated native traditions and influences, such as the use of tobacco in ritual and medicine and, in Brazil, the belief in *caboclo* spirit protectors. The Afro-Brazilian devotion of Candomblé combined African and Christian elements. In Candomblé, *orishas* or spirits embody particular sacred forces: for example, the orisha *Iemanja* is associated with the sea, *oxossi* with the forest and plants, *xango* with thunder and storms, and *ogum* with iron and war. Just as orishas were identified with specific natural forces, Christian saints possessed specialized powers to help people with particular needs and ailments. Many orishas were linked with Catholic saints for their particular associations: Ogum and St. George were identified with war, whereas Xango and St. Jerome were associated with thunder. Black saints such as Efigenia were adopted. In their Catholic confraternities (*cofradías*), Africans maintained many practices within a Christian context and forged ethnic ties with other peoples of African descent, including mulattos. In Brazil, the confraternity of "Our Lady of the Rosary" was especially popular among Congolese slaves; the Lady's day of celebration fell on the first Sunday of October, accompanied by the election of a king and queen and African song and dance, led by *batuqués* or brotherhood dance groups (Conrad, *Children of God's Fire*, pp. 185–92).

Despite the many possibilities for convergence and familiarity, even if indigenous people or Africans wanted to accept the new system they were bound to misunderstand it or reinterpret many new introductions in the light of deeply rooted cultural beliefs or ideologies. Many fundamental Christian principles simply had no corresponding cultural equivalent. Terminology for Christian concepts such as sin, heaven, hell, and the devil had no ready counterparts and were understood in many different ways by native peoples. Furthermore, if some people were willing to acknowledge the new deity or deities of a conqueror, because it was customary to do so, then their acceptance of the Christian God did not entail a rejection of all other deities, nor did their continuation of traditional practices and beliefs signify a rejection of Christianity. The native habit of practicing Christian acts without totally abandoning non-Christian rituals tended to exasperate priests. Another reason for the incomplete conversion of native peoples was the fact that friars and priests were always a tiny minority, especially in rural parishes, remote areas, and peripheral regions. Despite the writings of friars who exaggerated their own accomplishments, they could not teach more than the most basic tenets of the faith to those who were willing to learn. And if priests succeeded in dictating the most outward forms of worship, at the corporate level, they could not eradicate many beliefs and cultural practices in the home, the field, the mountain, or the forest. Thus, countless local forms of Christianity, reshaped by indigenous beliefs and practices, emerged in the early colonial past and continue to evolve in the present, sometimes alongside non-Christian practices.

In both Mexico and Peru, ecclesiastics drew upon the collected knowledge of predecessors to identify and extirpate fundamental characteristics of native religions. By the seventeenth century, beliefs and practices that were once associated with elaborate ceremonies had been reduced to clandestine practices in remote areas or humble rituals that retained only vestiges of the former ceremonies. As MacCormack observed, on the surface, Andean religion resembled the ancient residual paganism of European country people in the medieval or early modern period (MacCormack, *Religion in the Andes*, p. 405). But if public displays were Christian, native deities and ancestors proved extraordinarily resilient. The imperial religious institutions of the Incas were gone, but the Spaniards could not destroy the sacred topography or older Andean deities, *huacas* such as Pachacamac and Titicapa. Many indigenous sacred practices, called idolatries by Europeans, were so deeply rooted in daily cultural behavior that extirpators could not easily distinguish between what they thought were silly superstitions, which they ascribed to native ignorance, and diabolical practices that were attributed to the devil. Indeed, healers, midwives, and other bearers of specific knowledge drew upon a rich oral tradition that cannot be separated neatly from traditional sacred beliefs. In Mesoamerica, many of these specialists continued to use the ancient Mesoamerican calendar. Attentive and zealous priests such as Hernando Ruiz de Alarcón encountered a world of mundane, mainly household practices in the Nahua countryside that were not associated with the worship of Mexican deities such as Huitzilopochtli, and were not organized by a native priesthood, but were nonetheless non-Christian. These ancient, pervasive beliefs in *nahualli* spirits and lifecycle rituals were beyond the grasp of priests, regardless of their tenacity as extirpators (Ruiz de Alarcón, *Treatise on the Heathen Superstitions*).

Despite the persistence of some native practices in altered but still recognizable forms, countless local versions of Christianity had taken root throughout much of Latin America by the second half of the colonial period. In Mexico, the centerpiece of local and regional Christianity was the cult of the Virgin of Guadalupe, which spread especially after the second half of the seventeenth century. A shrine was dedicated to the Virgin of Guadalupe, established at some time during the sixteenth century at Tepeyacac, near Mexico City, on a site where there had been a temple of the preconquest goddess Tonantzin ("Our Mother" in Nahuatl). The Guadalupe devotion in Mexico and the image of the Virgin itself is based entirely on the Virgin of Guadalupe in Spain. Even the story of the Virgin's apparition in Mexico is modeled on the Spanish one; the main difference is that the Virgin appears to a humble native commoner, Juan Diego, rather than to a shepherd as in the original Spanish version. While local Spaniards had made their mark on the Guadalupe devotion, the Nahuas contributed a site already associated with a female deity, as well as the hero of the apparition account, Juan Diego, to whom the Virgin appeared. The Nahuas also rein-terpreted the Virgin by calling her "our precious mother" (*totlaçonantzin*), much like a preconquest divinity, and not just "our lady" or "the mother of God" as the Spaniards called her. Most importantly, many Nahuas were devoted to a saint that also appealed to Spaniards and mestizos. The shrine enjoyed a reputation only in and around Mexico City, both among native peoples and local Spaniards, until the middle of the seventeenth century, when the cult spread throughout central Mexico among both Spanish-speaking and Nahuatl-speaking people. Chapels were erected and images of the Virgin proliferated in churches and homes. By the end of the colonial period, the devotion had spread beyond the Nahuas to other native groups outside of central Mexico (Sousa, Poole, and Lockhart, *Story of Guadalupe*; Poole, *Our Lady of Guadalupe*).

In general, forms of local native Christianity were shaped by the nature and extent of the European presence. Where Spaniards were present in the region in force, as in central Mexico, Christianity and indigenous religious traditions tended to con-verge or coexist. In more remote areas, two separate and parallel cults emerged. In contrast to sedentary native peoples who came into close contact with Europeans, and who had much in common with them, peoples on the frontiers saw nothing familiar in European customs or Christianity. They were more hostile to Spanish introductions than the peoples of the sedentary areas and they tended to resist Christianity. Contact often involved conflict. The mission threatened to reorganize their whole way of life and made them more susceptible to deadly diseases such as smallpox and measles. The Pueblo and Apache revolt of 1680 that destroyed Spanish settlements and churches in Nuevo Mexico is one of the most famous cases of violent resistance on the frontier.

Remote, peripheral areas were also subject to violent, millenarian movements that called for a rejection of foreigners and a return to indigenous patterns. In the highland areas of Peru, a major rebellion known as Taqui Onqoy or "dance of disease" spread from La Paz to Lima in the 1560s. Leaders of the movement rejected Christianity's claim to the truth, anticipated a return of the Incas who had fled in exile to Vilcabamba, called for a restoration of the ancient *huacas*, and predicted the end of Spanish rule. Spaniards fought the revolt for several years, destroyed the Inca state in exile, and then executed Tupac Amaru, the last claimant of the Inca dynastic line, in 1572. Some millenarian movements employed Christian symbols or figures against the Spaniards. For example, in 1712, several communities among the Tzeltal, Tzotzil, and Chol Maya of highland Chiapas gathered in the village of Cancuc and rebelled in defense of a Maya cult of the Virgin Mary that local church author-ities had tried to suppress. A Maya army sacked churches and Spanish estates, ordained their own priests, and began to organize a regional government. Cancuc succumbed to colonial authorities after several months of violent warfare that ruined their crops and villages (Gosner, *Soldiers of the Virgin*). Racially charged, religious conflict revisited the area in the mid-nineteenth century, during the "Caste War" of Chiapas. At the same time, a similar conflict ravaged the Maya of Yucatan (Bricker, *Indian Christ*).

This brief discussion of religion in early Latin America can be summarized best by William Taylor's assessment of local native religions in late colonial Mexico as "great persistences within great changes" (Taylor, *Magistrates of the Sacred*, pp. 52–62). Gibson remarked nearly four decades ago that "our fullest evidence for preconquest survivals derives from modern Indian practices rather than from colonial records" (Gibson, *Aztecs*, p. 134). I would qualify "preconquest survivals" by suggesting that nothing remains unchanged, and add that non-Christian practices are not sought out and persecuted as vigorously as they were during much of the colonial period. Present-day practices and beliefs represent the ongoing impact of colonial introductions on local customs. Today, Roman Catholicism is the predominant religion in Latin America, but the church now competes with many Christian evangelical groups, some with ties to churches in North America. Indeed, Christianity continues to exert a profound influence on Latin America's religious traditions.

BIBLIOGRAPHY

Acosta, J. de, *Historia natural y moral de las Indias* [1590]. Valencia: Artes Gráficas Soler, 1977.
Bastide, R., *The African Religions of Brazil*. Baltimore: Johns Hopkins University Press, 1978.
Block, D., *Mission Culture on the Upper Amazon: Native Tradition, Jesuit Enterprise, and Secular Policy in Moxos, 1660–1880*. Lincoln: University of Nebraska Press, 1994.
Boxer, C., *The Church Militant and Iberian Expansion, 1440–1770*. Baltimore: Johns Hopkins University Press, 1978.
Bricker, V., *The Indian Christ, The Indian King: The Historical Substrate of Maya Myth and Ritual*. Austin: University of Texas Press, 1981.
Burgoa, fray F. de, *Palestra historial* [1670]. Mexico: Editorial Porrua, 1989.
Burkhart, L., *Holy Wednesday: A Nahua Drama from Early Colonial Mexico*. Philadelphia: University of Pennsylvania Press, 1996.
Cervantes, F., *The Devil in the New World: The Impact of Diabolism in New Spain*. New Haven, Conn.: Yale University Press, 1994.
Christian, W. A., Jr., *Local Religion in Sixteenth-Century Spain*. Princeton, NJ: Princeton University Press, 1981.
Cline, S. L., *Colonial Culhuacan, 1580–1600: A Social History of an Aztec Town*. Albuquerque: University of New Mexico Press, 1986.
Conrad, R. E., *Children of God's Fire: A Documentary History of Black Slavery in Brazil*. University Park: Pennsylvania State University Press, 1994.
Cuevas, M., *Historia de la iglesia en México*, 5 vols. Mexico: Editorial Patria, 1946–7.
Dávila Padilla, A., *Historia de la fundacion y discurso de la provincia de Santiago de México, de la orden de predicadores* [1596]. Mexico: Editorial Academia Literaria, 1955.
Díaz del Castillo, B., *The Conquest of New Spain*, trans. J. M. Cohen. London: Penguin, 1963.
Dúran, D. de, *Book of the Gods and Rites and the Ancient Calendar*, trans. and ed. F. Horcasitas and D. Heyden. Norman: University of Oklahoma Press, 1971.
Dúran, D. de, *The History of the Indies of New Spain*, trans. D. Heyden. Norman: University of Oklahoma Press, 1994.
Farriss, N. M., *Crown and Clergy in Colonial Mexico, 1759–1821*. London: Athlone Press, 1968.
García, G., *Origen de los indios del Nuevo Mundo* [1607]. Mexico: Fondo de Cultura Económica, 1981.

García Icazbalceta, J., *Bibliografía mexicana del siglo XVI: Catálogo razonado de libros impresos en México de 1539 a 1600*. Mexico: Fondo de Cultura Económica, 1954.

Garcilaso de la Vega el Inca, *Comentarios reales de los Incas* [1619], 2 vols. Mexico: Fondo de Cultura Económica, 1991.

Garcilaso de la Vega el Inca, *Royal Commentaries of the Incas and General History of Peru*, 2 vols. trans. H. V. Livermore. Austin: University of Texas Press, 1966.

Gibson, C., *The Aztecs Under Spanish Rule: A History of the Indians of the Valley of Mexico, 1519–1810*. Stanford, Calif.: Stanford University Press, 1964.

Gosner, K., *Soldiers of the Virgin: The Moral Economy of a Colonial Maya Rebellion*. Tucson: University of Arizona Press, 1992.

Greenleaf, R. E., ed., *The Roman Catholic Church in Colonial Latin America*. New York: Knopf, 1971.

Gruzinski, S., *Man-Gods in the Mexican Highlands: Indian Power and Colonial Society, 1520–1800*. Stanford, Calif.: Stanford University Press, 1989.

Hanke, L., *The Spanish Struggle for Justice in the Conquest of America*. New York: American Historical Association, 1949.

Hanke, L., *Aristotle and the American Indians: A Study in Race Prejudice in the Modern World*. Chicago: Henry Regnery, 1959.

Hanke, L., *All Mankind is One: A Study of the Disputation between Bartolomé de Las Casas and Juan Ginés de Sepúlveda in 1550 on the Intellectual and Religious Capacity of the American Indians*. De Kalb: Northern Illinois University Press, 1974.

Hu-De Hart, E., *Missionaries, Miners, and Indians: Spanish Contact with the Yaqui Nation of Northwestern New Spain, 1533–1820*. Tucson: University of Arizona Press, 1981.

Huertas Vallejos, L., *La religion en una sociedad rural andina, siglo XVII*. Ayacucho: Universidad Nacional de San Cristóbal de Huamanga, 1981.

Kamen, H., *Spain, 1469–1714: A Society of Conflict*. London: Longman, 1983.

Konrad, H. W., *A Jesuit Hacienda in Colonial Mexico: Santa Lucía, 1576–1767*. Stanford, Calif.: Stanford University Press, 1980.

Kubler, G., *Mexican Architecture in the Sixteenth Century*, 2 vols. New Haven, Conn.: Yale University Press, 1948.

Langer, E. and Jackson, R. H., eds., *The New Latin American Mission History*. Lincoln: University of Nebraska Press, 1995.

Las Casas, fray B. de, *Historia de las Indias*, 3 vols., ed. A. Millares Carlo. Mexico: Fondo de Cultura Económica, 1951.

Las Casas, fray B. de, *In Defense of the Indians*, trans. and ed. S. Poole. De Kalb: Northern Illinois University Press, 1974.

Las Casas, fray B. de, *A Short Account of the Destruction of the Indies* [1552]. London: Penguin, 1992.

Leite, S., *História da Companhia de Jesus no Brasil*, 10 vols. Lisbon: Livraria Portugalia, 1938–50.

Liebman, S., *The Jews in New Spain*. Coral Gables: University of Miami Press, 1970.

McAndrew, J., *The Open-Air Churches of Sixteenth-Century Mexico*. Cambridge, Mass.: Harvard University Press, 1965.

Megged, A., *Exporting the Catholic Reformation: Local Religion in Early-Colonial Mexico*. Leiden: Brill, 1996.

Mendieta, fray G. de, *Historia eclesiástica Indiana* [1596]. Mexico: Editorial Porrua, 1971.

Monaghan, J., *The Covenants of Earth and Rain: Exchange, Sacrifice, and Revelation in Mixtec Sociality*. Norman: University of Oklahoma Press, 1995.

Mörner, M., *The Political and Economic Activities of the Jesuits in the La Plata Region: The Hapsburg Era*. Stockholm: Victor Pettersons Bokindustri Aktiebolag, 1953.

Mörner, M. ed., *The Expulsion of the Jesuits from Latin America*. New York: Knopf, 1965.

Motolinia, fray T. de Benavente, *Historia de los indios de la Nueva España* [1541]. Madrid: Historia 16, 1985.

Muriel de la Torre, J., *Conventos de monjas en la Nueva España*. Mexico: Editorial Santiago, 1946.

Murphy, J. M., *Santería: An African Religion in America*. Boston: Beacon Press, 1988.

Nutini, H. G., *Todos Santos in Rural Tlaxcala: A Syncretic, Expressive, and Symbolic Analysis of the Cult of the Dead*. Princeton, NJ: Princeton University Press, 1988.

Pagden, A., *European Encounters with the New World: From Renaissance to Romanticism*. New Haven, Conn.: Yale University Press, 1993.

Palmer, C. A., *Slaves of the White God: Blacks in Mexico, 1570–1650*. Cambridge, Mass.: Harvard University Press, 1976.

Perry, M. E. and Cruz, A. J., eds., *Cultural Encounters: The Impact of the Inquisition in Spain and the New World*. Berkeley and Los Angeles: University of California Press, 1991.

Phelan, J. L., *The Millennial Kingdom of the Franciscans in the New World: A Study of the Writings of Gerónimo de Mendieta*. Berkeley and Los Angeles: University of California Press, 1956.

Poole, S., *Pedro Moya de Contreras: Catholic Reform and Royal Power in New Spain, 1571–1591*. Berkeley and Los Angeles: University of California Press, 1987.

Poole, S., "The Declining Image of the Indian among Churchmen in Sixteenth-Century New Spain," in S. E. Ramírez, ed., *Indian–Religious Relations in Colonial Spanish America*. Syracuse, NY: Maxwell School of Citizenship and Public Affairs, Syracuse University, 1989.

Powell, P. W., *Soldiers, Indians, and Silver: The Northward Advance of New Spain, 1550–1600*. Berkeley and Los Angeles: University of California Press, 1952.

Ramírez, S. E., *The World Upside Down: Cross-Cultural Contact and Conflict in Sixteenth-Century Peru*. Stanford, Calif.: Stanford University Press, 1996.

Restall, M. B., *The Maya World: Yucatec Culture and Society, 1550–1850*. Stanford, Calif.: Stanford University Press, 1997.

Ruiz de Alarcón, H., *Treatise on the Heathen Superstitions That Today Live Among the Indians Native to This New Spain, 1629*, trans. and ed. J. R. Andrews and R. Hassig. Norman: University of Oklahoma Press, 1984.

Russell-Wood, A. J. R., *Fidalgos and Philanthropists: The Santa Casa de Misericórdia of Bahia, 1550–1755*. Berkeley and Los Angeles: University of California Press, 1968.

Sahagún, fray B. de, *The Florentine Codex: General History of the Things of New Spain*, trans. A. J. O. Anderson and C. E. Dibble, 13 parts. Salt Lake City and Santa Fe: University of Utah Press and School of American Research, 1950–82.

Sahagún, fray B. de, *Historia general de las cosas de Nueva España*, 4 vols. Mexico: Editorial Porrua, 1996.

Salomon, F. and Urioste, G., eds. and trans., *Huarochirí Manuscript: A Testament of Ancient and Colonial Andean Religion*. Austin: University of Texas Press, 1991.

Sandstrom, A., *Corn is Our Blood: Culture and Ethnic Identity in a Contemporary Aztec Indian Village*. Norman: University of Oklahoma Press, 1991.

Schroeder, S., *Chimalpahin and the Kingdoms of Chalco*. Tucson: University of Arizona Press, 1991.

Schwaller, J. F., *The Church and Clergy in Sixteenth-Century Mexico*. Albuquerque: University of New Mexico Press, 1987.

Seed, P., *Ceremonies of Possession in Europe's Conquest of the New World, 1492–1640*. Cambridge: Cambridge University Press, 1995.

Sepúlveda, J. G. de, *Tratado sobre las justas causas de la guerra contra los indios* [1548]. Mexico: Fondo de Cultura Económica, 1941.

Spalding, K., *Huarochirí: An Andean Society under Inca and Spanish Rule*. Stanford, Calif.: Stanford University Press, 1984.

Spicer, E. H., *Cycles of Conquest: The Impact of Spain, Mexico, and the United States on the Indians of the Southwest, 1533–1960*. Tucson: University of Arizona Press, 1962.

Stern, S. J., *Peru's Indian Peoples and the Challenge of the Spanish Conquest: Huamanga to 1640*. Madison: University of Wisconsin Press, 1982.

Taylor, W. B. and Pease, F., eds., *Violence, Resistance, and Survival in the Americas: Native Americans and the Legacy of Conquest*. Washington, DC: Smithsonian Institution Press, 1994.

Vargas Ugarte, R., *Historia de la iglesia en el Peru*. Lima: Impresa Santa María, 1953.

Watanabe, J., *Maya Saints and Souls in a Changing World*. Austin: University of Texas Press, 1992.

Weber, D., *The Spanish Frontier in North America*. New Haven, Conn.: Yale University Press, 1992.

Wiznitzer, A., *Jews of Colonial Brazil*. New York: Columbia University Press, 1960.

FURTHER READING

Brading, D., *The First America: The Spanish Monarchy, Creole Patriots, and the Liberal State, 1492–1867*. Cambridge: Cambridge University Press, 1991.

Burkhart, L., *The Slippery Earth: Nahua-Christian Moral Dialogue in Sixteenth-Century Mexico*. Tucson: University of Arizona Press, 1989.

Farriss, N. M., *Maya Society Under Colonial Rule: The Collective Enterprise of Survival*. Princeton, NJ: Princeton University Press, 1984.

Greenleaf, R. E., *The Mexican Inquisition of the Sixteenth Century*. Albuquerque: University of New Mexico Press, 1969.

Gruzinski, S., *The Conquest of Mexico: The Incorporation of Indian Societies into the Western World, 16th–18th Centuries*. Cambridge: Polity Press, 1993.

Lockhart, J., *The Nahuas After the Conquest: A Social and Cultural History of the Indians of Central Mexico, Sixteenth through Eighteenth Centuries*. Stanford, Calif.: Stanford University Press, 1992.

Lockhart, J. and Schwartz, S., *Early Latin America: A History of Colonial Spanish America and Brazil*. Cambridge: Cambridge University Press, 1983.

MacCormack, S., *Religion in the Andes: Vision and Imagination in Early Colonial Peru*. Stanford, Calif.: Stanford University Press, 1991.

Mills, K., *Idolatry and its Enemies: Colonial Andean Religion and Extirpation, 1640–1750*. Princeton, NJ: Princeton University Press, 1997.

Pagden, A., *The Fall of Natural Man: The American Indian and the Origins of Comparative Ethnology*. Cambridge: Cambridge University Press, 1982.

Poole, S., *Our Lady of Guadalupe: The Origin and Sources of a Mexican National Symbol, 1531–1797*. Tucson: University of Arizona Press, 1995.

Ricard, R., *The Spiritual Conquest of Mexico: An Essay on the Apostolate and the Evangelizing Methods of the Mendicant Orders in New Spain, 1523–72*, trans. Lesley Byrd Simpson. Berkeley and Los Angeles: University of California Press, 1966.

Sousa, L., Poole, S., and Lockhart, J., eds. and trans., *The Story of Guadalupe: Luis Laso de Vega's Huei tlamahuiçoltica of 1649*. Stanford and Los Angeles: Stanford University Press and UCLA Latin American Center, 1998.

Taylor, W. B., *Magistrates of the Sacred: Priests and Parishioners in Eighteenth-Century Mexico*. Stanford, Calif.: Stanford University Press, 1996.

Terraciano, K., *The Mixtecs of Colonial Oaxaca: Ñudzahui History, Sixteenth through Eighteenth Centuries*. Stanford, Calif.: Stanford University Press, 2001.

TWENTY-ONE

Compromise: India

INES G. ŽUPANOV

Sebastião Gonçalves, a prolific Jesuit historian who resided in Goa in the first decade of the seventeenth century, musing over the Christianization of Asia under the Portuguese royal *padroado* (patronage), wove together three crucial historiographical strands for understanding Catholic expansion in India from the sixteenth to the late eighteenth centuries: Portuguese early regal messianism; a close relation between "temporal" and "spiritual" colonial intentions; and the central importance of the Society of Jesus in matters of missionary proselytism and conversion (Subrahmanyam, "Du Tage au Gange").

> Let me not forget to mention what happened at the time King Dom Manuel sent Vasco da Gama to discover India in the year of one thousand four hundred and ninety-seven, in the same year the Blessed Father Francis Xavier was born in Navarra. For it was understood that God had predestined him to bring the Gospel and to sow the Faith in those vast regions, as soon as the Portuguese armada had opened the way and taken possession; and to that purpose he created him, and he moved the heart of the King of Portugal to begin an adventure which many Portuguese considered to be uncertain and those who are ignorant of navigation considered to be insane. The good King intended it [i.e., the adventure] to disseminate the faith of Christ our Lord, as it was revealed to King Dom Afonso. (*Gonçalves*, part 1, vol. 1, p. 46)

Gonçalves's historical imagination fabricates, discursively and chronologically (by replacing, for example, the date of Francis Xavier's birth in 1506 with 1497), the story of cultural, social, religious, and economic encounters between the Portuguese and the inhabitants of the Indian subcontinent as a triumph of Christianity. Along similar lines, late seventeenth- and early eighteenth-century apologetic Catholic and missionary historians, such as Francisco de Sousa, Paulo da Trinidade, and Fernão de Queyroz, among the most important, continued the earlier tradition of depicting the progress of Christianity as a teleological and providential goal and as the result of the Portuguese presence in India and Asia in general. By digging beneath the fertile soil of such historical generalizations and outright epistemological projects, mostly peddled by the Jesuit missionary intelligentsia, a more complex set of scenarios is unearthed in the immense expanse of Indian cultural and religious encounters. One of the decisive factors throughout this period was Portuguese and Spanish (from 1580 to 1640) royal policy toward missionary activity, with alternating zeal or disinterest, which was often translated in terms of generous or nominal economic support (Gruzinski, "Mondes mêlés"). Putting into practice the royal desires and ordinances depended on the local government in Goa, or in other Portuguese enclaves, which had the means to speed up or delay decisions indefinitely. The tension between the center and periphery was also reflected in the workings of, on the one hand, the ecclesiastical institutions under direct royal temporal jurisdiction and, on the other hand, the spiritual, but indirect and often weak, jurisdiction of the papacy. Open or surreptitious rivalries between religious orders, between missionaries and diocesan priests, between European and non-European priests, between Portuguese missionaries and Italian missionaries, and so on, complicated the situation. The list of possible and effective divisions is not only long but also unstable, as the alliances were forged and unmade with remarkable speed and defied all predictability. The colonial chessboard on which various actors strove to pose and position themselves – from "official" Portuguese expatriates (*reinões*) to freelance merchants and outlaws (*casados, chatins, degredados*) whose lifestyle and progeny were rapidly indigenized, and to "New Christians" in search of a safe haven from intolerant metropolitan policies, as well as "Old" St. Thomas Christians encountered in Malabar – was further enlarged by mushrooming convert communities. With the establishment of the Congregation of the Propagation of Faith in 1622 by the papacy and the gradual erosion of the Portuguese royal *padroado* on Indian territory, new missionary enterprises came into being and new actors came to play important roles, such as Discalced Carmelites and French missionaries from the Société des Missions Étrangères (Launay, *Histoire des Missions*). The formation of an Indian clergy received a decisive fillip as well. With the Dutch, English, and French intruding politically, economically, and militarily in the region, with more or less defined "spiritual" goals, the Christianization of India haltingly separated into different directions. The "liberalization" of the Indian Christian market and the diversification of the supply of religious specialists multiplied in many ways the areas of friction between European actors and provided a space of creative (spiritual, economic, and cultural) freedom for the Indian Christian communities.

Early Portuguese Expansion Overseas: Messianism, Papal Bulls, and Patronage

Weakness or authoritarianism, or both, are evoked as explanations for regal messianism in early modern Europe. In the early sixteenth century, the Portuguese king Dom Manuel was not alone in dreaming of the Fifth Empire (*quinto império*), conceived as both a colonial empire and a Christian utopia, a new beginning under the banner of the dynasty of Avis. Portuguese maritime "discoveries" and progressive expansion along the West African coast were conceived already in the middle of the fifteenth century by Gomes Eanes de Zurara, Henry the Navigator's apologetic chronicler, as yet another utopian project. Besides gold and slave hunting, it was nothing less than a way to reach Prester John, the long-lost mythical Christian king of the East, inhabiting vaguely in European minds the country called Ethiopia, and to enroll him for the final annihilation of Islam and the reconquest of Jerusalem. What Zurara, on the other hand, was not even able to imagine was the fact that at the very moment of his writing, Islam, or rather, Arab and Persian traders, had already brought into being, and without the important work of proselytism, a whole "federation" of Muslim states and communities in Africa and Asia. All along the East African coast, the first Portuguese expeditions, that of Vasco da Gama in 1498 and of his successor Pedro Álvares Cabral in 1500, discovered to their surprise and dismay that the major commercial centers such as Sofala, Mozambique, Kilwa, Mombasa, Malindi, and Mogadiscio were administered by Muslim governors. Moreover, even in India in spite of da Gama's initial mistaken discovery of the lost Christians of the legend, maritime commerce in Calicut, Cochin, Cannanore, Quilon/Kollam, and many other places was solidly in the hands of Islamicized communities, indigenous and foreign. The crusading zeal of the Portuguese against infidels was thus nurtured in the Indian Ocean in combination with the mercantile desire of the state to capture and monopolize the spice trade with Europe.

The early Portuguese activities in the Indian Ocean, therefore, followed the behavior pattern already rehearsed during their violent capture and foundation of *presídios* in Morocco. Thus, in an act of vengeance after the conquest of Goa (1510), Afonso de Albuquerque ordered the massacre of all Muslims – except women, whom he planned to baptize and marry off to Portuguese settlers. Christianity was understood by these early military commanders more as an invigorating and unifying martial ideology than as a system of ethical rules and commandments. The confusion of religious and political goals was neither new nor a passing affair and although the distinction between them became paradoxically both less obvious and more refined, in the decades and centuries to come, the basic contradictions remained intact.

Besides the inherited spirit of the *reconquista*, Dom Manuel nurtured a brand of personal messianism. Had providence wanted to fulfill Dom Manuel's dreams, the Christianization of Asia, one might suppose, would have worked itself out naturally with the help of Prester John's Christians, which is at least partly the reason why proselyte missionary activity before John III's reign never gained impetus. Another important reason lies in the fact that the papacy and the church in general showed little initiative, except rhetorically, in such activity. From the 1440s, Eugene IV and his successors issued various bulls regulating the religious side of the future travels of discovery and conquests by Henry the Navigator (Witte, "Bulles pontificales"). As accorded by the papacy, Portuguese territorial and political sovereignty over the overseas conquests also implied patronage of the missions and churches within its geographical boundaries. With the power to appoint archbishops and bishops, and to distribute ecclesiastical benefices at his own will, Dom Manuel, and later John III, tried – without fully succeeding – to centralize and control all aspects of Portugal's overseas expansion. Royal privileges and prerogatives implicit in the *padroado* system were many, such as siphoning off church revenues and tithes, or creating a network of dependents from among the appointed benefice holders; but there were also certain important and costly obligations concerning the creation of missions, new bishoprics, convents, and sanctuaries. However, the overseas ecclesiastical institutions of the Portuguese, reinforced by direct state intervention, should not be equated, in spite of circumstantial convergence, with missionary activity. In fact, they were often at odds, especially from the second part of the sixteenth century when the transnational Society of Jesus "invented," captured, and monopolized the missionary field in Asia (O'Malley, *First Jesuits*).

Goa: The Center of Missionary Activity in Asia

All Portuguese expeditions in the Indian Ocean were accompanied by one or more official chaplains: members of religious orders or secular priests. On board ships, they acted as spiritual counselors and nurses and were also the first to plant crosses and to bless *padrões* (memorial stones) on the "virgin" land of discovery. The next step in religious implantation was the foundation of churches and chapels, usually built literally on or of the debris of mosques and Hindu temples. In the years to come, especially by the end of the sixteenth and in the seventeenth centuries, larger and more sumptuous religious edifices were erected, and official papal recognition followed through grants of ecclesiastical benefices.

Thus, the chapel of St. Catherine in Goa, initially a mud and palm-leaf construction built by Albuquerque shortly after the conquest in 1510, was replaced in the following decades by a larger stone building and became in 1534 the cathedral of the first Asian diocese, which consisted of a vast territory from the Cape of Good Hope to China. Before March 1539, when the first bishop of Goa, Juan de Albuquerque, a Franciscan Recollect (or Capucho), inaugurated the diocese, small parties of his co-religionists and some diocesan priests were already beginning the work of conversion, very closely following the commercial and political routes and networks of the Portuguese (Meersman, *Ancient Franciscan Provinces*).

The contemporary Portuguese dilemma concerning the overseas empire, contrasting free trade and royal monopoly and dirigisme, found an echo or simple parallelism among religious specialists (Subrahmanyam, *Portuguese Empire*). In addition, the overlapping jurisdictions of the royal *padroado* and of the papacy steadily grew, and the question of the center of ecclesiastical authority was therefore always open and disputable. Moreover, in spite of a call for the creation of a new Christian Goa, a kind of utopian dream starting with Afonso de Albuquerque's marriage arrangements for the Portuguese settlers (*casados*) and the Christianization of their native spouses, the proselytizing effort was mitigated by practical constraints, such as the fact that Hindu and Muslim merchants brought business into the city and facilitated diplomatic and commercial ties with the Deccan hinterland. Nevertheless, conversion on the Ilhas, the five islands of the original conquest of Goa, and on the later additions of Bardez and Salcete after 1543, accelerated, especially among lower and poorer agricultural classes, stimulated by well-orchestrated public rituals, such as solemn mass and baptism celebrations (D'Costa, *Christianization of the Goa Island*). It was through "charitable" institutions, such as the confraternity of Misericórdia, that the new Christian communities, including that of the Portuguese settlers with their local spouses and slaves, came under firmer ecclesiastical control. The exercise of Christian charity facilitated communal integration, particularly in far-removed territories where family, class, or regional ties were often tenuous because of the vagaries of commercial and military enterprises (Sá, *Quando o rico se faz pobre*). It was not before 1541 that the confraternity of the Holy Faith was established for the non-European Christians including a seminary for the education of the indigenous clergy. The finances for this enterprise were raised by taxing the non-Christians and appropriating revenues formerly associated with Hindu places of worship, which were on the way to being massively destroyed throughout the islands of Goa (Wicki, *Documenta Indica*, vol. 1, pp. 756–70).

The intensification of missionary efforts after 1542 consisted mostly in the branching out and refinement of former trends which had been set in motion shortly before the Jesuit arrival and which followed the moods of both metropolitan and local politics. Even if Francis Xavier did write to John III demanding that the Inquisition be established, the first "New Christian" (a Christian of Jewish origin) had been burned in Goa in 1539. The hardening of heart against the inhabitants of Jewish descent, provoked partly by local circumstances – the presence of, and rivalry with, Jewish merchants along the Malabar Coast and in Ormuz – was also part and parcel of a new Joanine policy in the second part of the sixteenth century when Spanish influence began to play a considerable role in Portuguese religious enterprise. During the regency under the dowager Queen Catarina and Infante-Cardinal Henrique, from 1557 until Sebastian's direct rule sometime before 1570, the royal house of Portugal endeavored to modify and efface its "spice merchant" image and began to emulate the Habsburg ideals of agrarian-based aristocracy, always ready to sacrifice commercial profits for the display of noble, pious actions and belated chivalry.

In Asia, moving within and along the frontiers of the expanding social, political, and economic world of the Portuguese, the missionaries, Jesuits in particular, were perfect *Doppelgänger* of the other prominent social group: the merchants. They were, in short, spiritual entrepreneurs who endeavored to open new markets and, as a general rule, the farther from the center the more open they were to structures, modes, and forms of belief and sociability of the peoples with whom they came in contact. Inversely, the closer to the center, Goa in the case of the Indian missionary field, religious orders endeavored to monopolize all activities regarding ecclesiastical and "spiritual" enterprises and thus inaugurated long and complicated rivalries between European colonial actors, both lay and religious. The conversion methods of the various missionary orders, on the other hand, remained the same: a combination of incentives (solemn baptism, acquisition of property and titles) and threats to use symbolic and "real" violence (eviction from the land, prohibition to use and display local marks of prestige such as the *palanquin*, etc.) (Thekkedath, *History of Christianity in India*).

Estheticization of Religious Propaganda, Inquisition, and the Indigenization

Religious feasts and processions in Goa and throughout the Asian strongholds of the Portuguese were social performances of great symbolic and ideological display geared toward strengthening communal solidarity, while at the same time opening a "reflexive" space and encouraging the integration of new social actors. It was often following such ostentatious events that individuals or groups, Christian and non-Christian, rushed to religious institutions and asked for spiritual instruction, confession, or baptism. After 1575, the magnificent adult baptism scenes, mostly organized by the Jesuits, were no longer in fashion because almost all of the village communities on the Goan islands were Christian. Nevertheless, Jesuits still noted about 500 conversions a year until the end of the century and an even larger number for the first part of the seventeenth century (Guerreiro, *Relação annual*, vol. 1, p. 4). The Goan religious calendar hardly became less impressive with the decline of solemn baptism, for numerous festivities continued to entertain, amuse, edify, and in some cases terrify the population. Various processions and acts of public devotion during the Holy Week presented the most stunning spectacles in which penitents performed flagellation and other mortifications (Rego, *História das Missões*, vol. 1, pp. 495–6).

The growing number of Christians and the simultaneous resistance to conversion posed a new problem: were these conversions sincere or only a shield for secret "pagan" practices? The ecclesiastical hierarchy, already casting a menacing shadow over the families of *cristãos novos* settled in Cochin and Goa, proved to be lastingly doubtful of Hindu converts, defining them as second-class Christians and often refusing to ordain even *mestiços* (born to Portuguese fathers) (Tavim, "From Setúbal to the Sublime Porte"). The third provincial council of Goa (1585) had decreed, moreover, that the adult converts could receive ordination only 15 years after baptism and were to be at least 30 years of age. The fifth provincial council (1606) added a local "caste" flavor to these highly selective restrictions: only Brahmans and other "noble" castes were to be admitted to the priesthood (Rivara, *Archivo Portuguez Oriental*, fasc. 4). Indigenous diocesan priests employed in Goan parishes rarely acquired ecclesiastical benefices, those being reserved for the Portuguese. Nevertheless, these "parish jobs" were much coveted and, in the seventeenth century, Indian diocesan priests resented the presence of religious orders, who still retained in their hands nearly two-thirds of the parishes (Melo, *Recruitment*). The religious orders were generally more sympathetic to their new converts, but very few natives or *mestiços* were permitted to join any religious order before the second half of the eighteenth century (Boxer, *Church Militant*, pp. 12–14). The same status was also reserved for Portuguese of Jewish ancestry. After 1622, the newly established Congregation for the Propagation of Faith (often abbreviated as Propaganda Fide) in Rome worked actively to undermine the Portuguese *padroado*, considered as ineffective, by stimulating the formation of the local clergy and even conferring higher ecclesiastical benefices on Goan priests (Metzler, *Sacrae Congregationis*). The seventeenth-century case of Mattheus de Castro, a Goan Brahman, is often taken as an example, although his mandate as a bishop continued to be marred by opposition from the Goan ecclesiastical hierarchy (Ghesquière, *Mathieu de Castro*). It was not until the last decades of the seventeenth century that the Goan diocesan priests, headed by Joseph Vaz, pulled their ranks together and founded their own congregation – Oratório do Santa Cruz dos Milagres – which was finally approved in 1686 by the pope and the king of Portugal under the rules of the Oratory of St. Phillip Neri – and all this in spite of the opposition of the Goan archbishop (Nunes, *Documentação*). A year later, Goan Oratorians started their own Catholic mission in Sri Lanka (Flores, *"Um Curto História de Ceylan"*).

Not all archbishops of Goa were adamantly against indigenous clergy. A famous Augustinian archbishop, Dom Aleixo de Menezes (1595–1609), appointed Indian priests to various parishes in Goa, Kanara, and the Bassein region. His ordinations *en masse* of St. Thomas Christians during the synod of Udayamperur (Diamper) is another sign of his policy of "indigenization" of ecclesiastical offices stimulated by similar Jesuit success stories in Japan. There was no consistent policy, however, concerning the recruitment of indigenous clergy and the prelate who replaced Menezes, Christóvão de Sá e Lisboa (1616–22), swore on the missal never to ordain any indigenous priest. What he was tacitly denouncing was also the incessant papal efforts to circumvent the Portuguese *padroado* by encouraging missions outside the direct control of the Estado da Índia in the midst of "heathen" and "infidel" kingdoms (Rubiés, "Jesuit Discovery of Hinduism"). The jurisdictional muddle arising from this struggle marked the whole of the seventeenth and eighteenth centuries, until the marquis of Pombal made sure that the Goan clergy officially achieved equality *vis-à-vis* their European counterparts. Another target of Pombal's reforms was the Inquisition, which he simply abolished (1774), although after his own fall from power it was briefly resuscitated until 1820.

Often associated with the second, "Spanish," phase of John III's reign, the Santo Ofício, the Inquisition, found its way to Goa only in 1560 during the regency of the dowager Queen Catarina and thrived for almost two and a half centuries, notwithstanding waves of opposition from the secular governments and even from the clergy and archbishops. Conceived as a royal weapon of centralization against the particular interests of just about everybody else in the kingdom, the implantation of the Inquisition in Goa – its jurisdiction often overlapping with that of the secular authorities – provoked endless disputes. This institution eventually grew to become a state within a state with elaborate bureaucracies and clients (Baião, *Inquisição de Goa*). In spite of its busy working schedule in Goa, financed by the local government, in setting up trials – from 1562 to 1774 there were 16,202 registered court cases – and organizing awe-inspiring *autos-da-fé*, only about 200 people were actually burned at the stake. More important was the extent to which the tribunal confiscated the property and riches of the local New Christian families in order to feed its own machine (Amiel, "Archives de l'Inquisition portugaise").

Missionary Frontiers Beyond Goa: The St. Thomas Christians and the Parava Converts

From the middle of the sixteenth century, the Portuguese factory-settlements that dotted the west and east coasts of India, Southeast Asia, and, later on, Japan and China endeavored to organize their own religious life in imitation of the Goan Catholic effervescence. Most of them had rather limited and short-lived success due to political, economic, and social conditions, while a few managed to survive long into the modern period. Around the time when Goa was elevated to the rank of archbishopric (1558), two dioceses were created – Cochin and Melaka – followed by Macao (1576), Funai in Japan (1588), Angamale on the Malabar Coast (1594; it became an archbishopric in 1608), and Mylapore (1600). In addition to being in charge of the diocesan priests, under the jurisdiction of the bishops, the Portuguese *padroado* was also obliged to provide for the upkeep of the missionaries belonging to different monastic orders. Franciscans, Dominicans, Jesuits, and Augustinians established their missions, colleges, monasteries, and other institutions before the end of the sixteenth century. A second wave of missionary orders directly financed by and responsible to the Propaganda Fide – Discalced Carmelites, Capuchins, Italian Oratorians, and Theatines – arrived in the seventeenth century. Although in theory they were sent to "help out" the *padroado* and were to be employed in the fields still not covered by the missionary staff, newcomers were often seen as intruders and treated as such by the Portuguese ecclesiastical and colonial administration.

The "discovery" of St. Thomas or Syrian Christians on the Malabar Coast was considered to be providential by Pedro Álvares Cabral and his successors engaged in Asian pepper empire-building. Due to its corporate control of commercial enterprises, its tradition of martial prowess, and its "noble" or "purity-conscious" lifestyle, this Christian group (estimated to have numbered between 80,000 and 200,000 in the course of the century) held a privileged position in the social and political fabric of sixteenth-century Kerala, and thus opened the way for the Portuguese traders to profit from local market opportunities. At the same time, St. Thomas or Syrian Christians accepted Portuguese patronage in expectation of an enhancement of their own economic and symbolic prestige. However, the centralizing nature of the political and colonial intentions of the Estado da Índia was soon in conflict with the existing, segmentary, power relations in Kerala, which had previously left to St. Thomas Christians a high degree of autonomy. It was through religious patronage that the Portuguese endeavored to gain control of this Indian community, which claimed as its founder one of Christ's disciples, St. Thomas, and had maintained ecclesiastical connections, from at least the fourth century, with the independent West Asian churches. These ancient religious ties came to be branded by the Portuguese ecclesiastical hierarchy as illegitimate since the doctrine of the Syrian patriarchs was known to be based on Nestorian teaching and was, therefore, "heretic." Furthermore, according to the regulation of the *padroado*, the appointment of the bishops was the prerogative of the Portuguese king and the pope, and thus all "foreign" ecclesiastical officials sent by the West Asian patriarchs were potentially seen as transgressors.

During the first half of the sixteenth century, Portuguese relations with St. Thomas Christians appear to have been relatively harmonious, primarily due to the lack of European missionaries (Mundadan, *History of Christianity*). However, in the long run, the Portuguese endeavored to curtail their religious, liturgical, social, and political "liberties." Throughout the second part of the sixteenth century, the Jesuits came to dominate the missionary scene along the southernmost Malabar and Fishery Coasts (today called the Gulf of Mannar), and some of them "specialized" in this particular field. Briefly, the European ecclesiastical pressure on the St. Thomas Christians increased from the 1550s onwards and various provincial councils of Goa, the third in particular (1585), issued strong decrees concerning the matter. Under such external weight, the community of St. Thomas Christians began breaking up into factions of those who were *pro* or *contra* "Latinization." An additional historical contingency that facilitated the splintering of this Christian community, which traditionally possessed an endemically unstable religious leadership, was the split (1551) within the Chaldean Church itself, with one patriarch acknowledging the union with Rome and the other denying it.

This highly conflictual situation came to a sudden resolution, at least temporarily, through a high-handed gesture of a zealous Goan archbishop, Dom Aleixo de Menezes. Imbued with religious idealism, this noble Portuguese prelate stormed the sacred territory of the Syrian Christians and imposed a complete Latinization of liturgy and customs at the synod of Udayamperur (Diamper) in 1599. The moment of "union" was short-lived and the religious leadership under the Jesuit bishops continued to be unstable, while other religious orders tried to break this and other Jesuit monopolies by encouraging opposing factions among the St. Thomas Christians. To make the situation more complicated, from 1622 the Propaganda Fide – with the barely dissembled intention to replace the Portuguese *padroado* – began to send Italian Discalced Carmelites as vicars apostolic among the Syrian Christians. The end result was a schism within the community in 1653. Two-thirds of the Christians returned to the Roman fold in 1662, mostly through Carmelite efforts, while the other "rebel" faction elected and consecrated its own bishop, Mar Thoma I (Brown, *Indian Christians of St. Thomas*, pp. 92–109). Except for the St. Thomas Christians, all other newly converted Christians in South India belonged to ritually low-status groups very often engaged in "polluting" activities such as manual labor and fishing. There were, of course, token Brahmans and some other high-caste lineages (such as the Nayars) who for exceptional reasons accepted European religious patronage, but they remained very few throughout the period.

The "romantic" plot of the evangelization of the Parava fishing villages and communities was one of the favorite Jesuit master narratives of conversion because it was an essential part of the biography of St. Francis Xavier, the first Jesuit missionary in Asia. In the early seventeenth century, in his history of the Jesuit missions in India, Sebastião Gonçalves referred to Xavier as *negoceador das almas*, a soul merchant, who came in search of the "precious stones which are souls of the infidels" in order to transform them through "the holy baptism into carbuncles, diamonds, safires, emerals and pearls" (Gonçalves, *História*, vol. 1, p. 133). Thus a commercial aspect of the Jesuit proselytizing was underlined in his text by a figurative equation of "infidel souls" and "precious stones." There is, undoubtedly, some truth in his statement, since Paravas can *de facto* be likened to pearls, in a metonymical sense. They were one of the pearl-fishing coastal groups in the Gulf of Mannar or, as the Portuguese would evocatively name it, the Fishery Coast (*Costa da Pescaria*). This particular skill was the currency with which they attracted Portuguese patronage and protection. The conversion of Paravas to Catholicism, at least in its early phase in the sixteenth century, came as a result of a conjunction of political, economic, and cultural factors threatening to undermine Parava corporate economic interests. It seems that the Portuguese presence along the South Indian coast and their naval skirmishes in the 1520s with the Mappilas and Maraikkayars, Muslim trading groups that controlled the pearl-fishery revenues and the bulk of other seaborne trade from the Coromandel Coast, disrupted the political and economic power relations in the region (Subrahmanyam, *Portuguese Empire*, p. 92). In addition, the Portuguese determination to edge out the Muslims from the local trade networks, by diplomacy or arms, enabled the Paravas to negotiate a more favorable niche in the regional division of pearl-trade profits. Converting to Christianity in the early sixteenth century was for the Paravas a way of symbolically and ritually cementing the new political alliance.

The "pearl" politics in the Gulf of Mannar was complicated by the shifting alliances between various local groups, and the Portuguese were ultimately able to exploit these divisions, although not without setbacks. According to the Christian foundation story, with a typical overture plot for communal conflict, the tension between Parava and Muslim divers from Palayakayal rose in 1532 when a woman was insulted by a Muslim and her husband mutilated. However, from insult to conversion, four years had passed and, incidentally, the initiative for this political move – to convert to the religion of the Portuguese – came from an "outsider," a "Malabar" horse merchant from Calicut (Roche, *Fishermen of the Coromandel*, p. 54). According to Sebastião Gonçalves, in 1536 a delegation of 85 Parava leaders officially presented their request to be baptized to the Portuguese captain in Cochin. The mass baptism took place as soon as a few clerics had been sent to the Fishery Coast and 20,000 Paravas were baptized in some 30 villages (Gonçalves, *História*, vol. 1, p. 138).

However, when Francis Xavier arrived in the area in 1542, himself a missionary novice, he commenced an intensive Catholic indoctrination and secured the field for Jesuit monopoly until the early seventeenth century. The Estado da Índia's weak presence, the rivalry with local political predators, and the sustained "spiritual" control of the Jesuits, combined with the preexisting social and family structure of the Paravas, produced in the long run, notwithstanding inevitable internal factional struggles, a coherent and tightly knit community, an endogamous caste with strong leadership and uniform religious and domestic customs (Bayly, *Saints, Goddesses and Kings*, pp. 321–79).

What the emerging Parava elite realized soon enough was that Catholicism could be used as a way of transforming their system of kinship into a political structure resembling a South Indian "little kingdom." For this particular task they needed a powerful god/father-figure, capable of bestowing a permanent sense of legitimation on the "noble" lineages headed by the *jati talaivan* (the caste headman) and his progeny. The confluence of Jesuit proselytism, with Francis Xavier elevated to the role of the Parava tutelary deity, and sociopolitical interests of the Parava elite, partly created by the Jesuits, succeeded in the next few decades in reformulating the Paravas' corporate identity, internal social relations, and cultural meanings. While Xavier, besides cutting the figure of a father, also brought a gift of "miracles," Henrique Henriques, a Jesuit missionary who came to the Fishery Coast in 1549 and stayed on until his death in 1600, gave the gift of "Tamil Christian" speech and captured it in writing. Not only did he write the first Tamil grammar and dictionary for the missionaries' use, he also, helped by some learned interpreters, wrote and published pious books for the edification of the Tamil Christians. The Tamil written and printed word became a conduit through which the Christian message poured into folk songs and was promptly appropriated by the indigenous religious and esthetic imagination, facilitating the growth of the particular politico-ecclesiastical order of the Paravas. The reorientation of communal life in and around churches, the growing popularity of Christian pilgrimage sites, lavish Christian festivals such as the Corpus Christi and the Assumption became the hallmarks of Parava life. When in 1582 Jesuits installed the statue of the Virgin Mary in the church in Tuticorin, the Paravas finally acquired their "mother." Henceforth, she was to nurture the Paravas' sense of corporate identity and enhance the role of the Parava elite, in particular that of the *jati talaivan*, who became a chief protector and donor of the church. When the office of the *jati talaivan* became hereditary, his lineage assumed the role of Parava "royalty." By the eighteenth century, the Parava community functioned as a South Indian "little kingdom." The Jesuits were gone and the Portuguese were replaced by the Dutch and later the British, but the structure of authority and solidarity remained firmly bound to Parava "Catholic" rituals, ceremonies, and beliefs.

Jesuit Social and Religious Experiments: The Madurai and the Mughal Missions

In the 1590s, a Jesuit mission for the small Christian Parava trading community which had migrated inland was established in Madurai, the capital of the Nayaka's kingdom in the heart of Tamil country. With the arrival, in 1606, of Roberto Nobili (1577–1656), a young Italian aristocrat educated in Rome, the famous Indian "accommodationist" experiment of the Jesuits came into existence, fashioned along the lines traced by Alessandro Valignano for the Japanese and by Matteo Ricci for the Chinese missions. The "new" Madurai mission established by Nobili was separated from the "old" church and residence in which an ex-soldier, Gonçalo Fernandes (1541–1619), continued to minister to the Parava Christians. At a safe distance from Goa, the "accommodationist" missions that existed in Tamilnadu until the middle of the eighteenth century happened to be by and large opposed to Portuguese colonial and ecclesiastical aspirations. For non-Portuguese Jesuit missionaries one thing was clear by the end of the sixteenth century – Christianization did not equal Portugalization (Županov, *Disputed Mission*).

Denounced as a convert to "Brahmanism" by Gonçalo Fernandes, Nobili had spent half a century refuting the accusations and defending the theory of *accommodatio* in his various letters and treatises. As a rule, the Jesuit adaptationist missions were elitist, if not aristocratic, projects. One of the reasons for this was that the missionaries recruited for these missions, which were often considered to be dangerous, were themselves of noble birth. Faced with a situation in which Christianity was perceived by the local non-Christian population as a "dirty," *Parangui* (i.e., foreign, Portuguese, etc.), low-caste religious practice, Nobili reinvented and customized Christianity to fit in with Tamil ideas of personal holiness and social authority. He disassociated Christianity from the Portuguese and linked it with Brahmanical normative precepts. His first move was to sever all ties with the "old" Madurai church – not permitting Paravas to attend his mass, not communicating publicly with Fernandes – while at the same time eating, dressing, and behaving like a Brahman hermit. He maintained that if one were to inculcate Christianity to the most learned (Brahmans) and the most noble (kings), they themselves would then spearhead the religious transformation in a trickle-down movement of cultural change.

His next move was anthropological. Helped by his Brahman teachers and interpreters, he acquired mastery over Tamil, Sanskrit, and Telugu and studied "religious" texts written in those languages. After acquiring indigenous "theological" knowledge, he endeavored to graft Christianity onto the local material through a series of allegories and metaphors and by playing on their mutual resemblances. In Nobili's view, Tamil society and culture, headed by the learned Brahmans, was comparable to the classical pre-Christian civilization with Jewish and Roman literati at its helm. He agreed with José de Acosta's precept that the strategy of conversion appropriate for this kind of "advanced" culture was persuasion and logical argument. Coercion was to be employed for those illiterate, stateless "barbarians" who were on the lower level of development. The missionaries in the Madurai mission were, in any case, unable to use coercion, as their co-religionists did in such territories as Salsette, south of Goa. According to the typical accommodationist principle, a successful conversion would be to celebrate Christian mass in the structure that from outside looked like a temple, or to call oneself a Christian while preserving the dress code and social customs of a Hindu. In a series of Latin treatises, Nobili concluded that, if in the early Christian centuries many "pagan" customs were allowed into both liturgical practice and Christian civilization, there was no reason to disallow certain Brahmanical customs, especially since they appeared to be indispensable for the conversion.

It was the distinction between religious and social customs and rites, still wrapped in adiaphoristic garb (i.e., the theory of "things indifferent"), that enabled Nobili to prove his point. If all social customs were "indifferent," as the argument goes, then, in the case of conversion to Christianity, they need not be modified. Thus Nobili argued that ritual baths, the use of the sandal paste and marking the body with sacred ashes, the custom of wearing the sacred thread, and similar "external" signs were purely social and were to be permitted to his Brahman converts. His arguments were, in fact, very persuasive to his contemporaries, especially the learned theologians in Europe and in Rome. In 1622, he won his case after a decade of disputes both with other Jesuits in India and with the Goan ecclesiastical clique. However, unwittingly, by inflating the social he almost effaced the religious. It was only taking one step further, as the Enlightenment *philosophes* certainly did in the next century, to perceive Christianity itself as just another set of customary rules, rituals, and beliefs, neither better nor worse than Hinduism, Islam, or any other religion. Nobili's approach, therefore, forged the instruments for opening the Pandora's box of both religious and cultural relativism which became the hallmark of modernity.

In his missionary field in Madurai, Nobili played a role of spiritual preceptor, guru, and miracle worker, of a Brahman *sannyasi* (i.e., renouncer, ascetic), a hybrid role based on both local and European ideas of holiness and religious competence. It is clear from his early missionary reports that most of his converts belonged to small groups of (1) disgruntled young Brahmans or other high-caste men facing financial and spiritual problems, (2) dethroned or contesting *palaiyakkarars* or military chiefs, and (3) more generally, various men and women facing social, psychological, and biological lifecycle crises. These were all unstable conversion groups and in spite of their "promise" to influence their relatives and kinsmen, backsliding and opposition from their families were a constant menace. Nevertheless, through his *sannyasi* missionary model, Nobili tried to position himself in a threshold space between the social and the divine, which he rightly identified as the central place for acquiring and establishing his own local "political" network. The problem was that in the fluid, segmentary political situation of early modern South India, leadership and "holiness" were up for grabs by numerous exalted spiritual gurus such as Nobili, inspired by a syncretic melange of Islam, popular Hinduism, and Christianity. The ability to gather followers, directly connected with the ability to raise funds, perform miracles, and distribute honors, produced patronage networks in which the leader himself, or rarely herself, becomes dispensable. A rival leader, often a disciple, might dethrone him with relative ease (Bayly, *Saints, Goddesses and Kings*).

By the 1630s, however, attempts to convert only Brahmans and other "high castes" were virtually given up, primarily for economic reasons. Henceforth, Nobili and his companions focused on those groups, mostly low-caste, that showed an eagerness to improve their ritual status through conversion and adherence to a spiritual leader. A new missionary model was devised for this purpose – the *pandarasami*, an adapted imitation of a local non-Brahman ritual specialist. The same climate of religious pluralism that facilitated the establishment of the Jesuit missions worked to undermine their global conversion project. In other words, Christianity became a personalized religion depending directly on the religious preceptor or guru in question, such as Nobili, João de Britto, Francis Xavier, and so on. According to the individual missionary's charisma, the network of followers either expanded or contracted. Upon the death of such a divine figure, his disciples often splintered away and established their own devotional, *bhakti*, sects, often independent from Jesuit missions.

When the Jesuits were expelled from India by the end of the eighteenth century, the Parava Catholic community continued to thrive, as did other scattered groups of Christians in the interior of Tamil country and on the Coromandel Coast that were attached to their "indigenized" Catholic worship, to their corporate ceremonies and rituals, to their churches, pilgrimage sites, and their leaders. But the project as conceived by Nobili of global, hierarchical Christianization, encompassing all social layers, from the Brahmans at the top to the Paraiyars at the bottom, failed to materialize.

At the root of missionary success or failure to make conversions was their ability to find local and rooted symbolic expressions for the new religious sensibility and sociability. Those rituals and ceremonies that fostered community, kinship, and the hierarchical organization of "honors" (*mariyatai*) served as vehicles for the implantation of Christianity. In a Durkheimian sense, only those communities of believers that found the way to worship themselves in Christian ritual adhered enthusiastically to a new religion.

Another equally elitist, but less accommodationist, mission was that at the Mughal court initiated in 1580. It continued with interruptions from 1580 until the suppression of the Society of Jesus at the end of the eighteenth century. The Portuguese Estado da Índia and the Mughal state in the hinterland came into closer contact through the latter's conquest of Gujarat; their complicated relationship, erupting at times into hostilities and violence (in 1613–15 and in 1632), did not preclude mutual curiosity and "cultural exchange," even if the results were not always satisfactory for both sides.

The Jesuit mission at the Mughal court solicited by Akbar (r. 1556–1605) raised the hopes of a Christian "triumph" over Islam, only to be thwarted in the end. The costly, and from the Jesuit point of view frustrating, project gave rise in the course of time to an immense correspondence and literary production in European and Persian languages, as well as a series of paintings by Mughal painters inspired directly or indirectly by Christian art. Ultimately, Jesuit writing and publications and Mughal paintings remained the only tangible results of the whole endeavor, since the mission never succeeded in producing a convert community.

What the Jesuits who were sent on the first mission – Rodolfo Acquaviva, António de Monserrate, and Francisco Henriques – did not know was that Akbar's dissatisfaction with the orthodox Sunni *ulema*, combined with his political efforts at centralization and his personal type of religious millenarians, had already brought to his court representatives of the major religious currents of the subcontinent: Brahmans, Jains, Shia Muslims, Persian Sufis, and Zoroastrians. His experiments with a "divine monotheism" (*tauhid ilahi*) or a "divine religion" (*din-i ilahi*) that would function as an umbrella for all the diverse, and often irreconcilable, religious experiences in his empire, and thus provide an ideological underpinning for the Mughal reign, led him to rather complicated syncretism. The result was a new Sunni orthodox reaction which worked at the same time to destabilize and delegitimize Akbar's divine and political pretensions.

When the Jesuits joined his "hall of adoration" – constructed near the mosque of Fatehpur Sikri – in order to debate the fine points of universal theology with other religious specialists, their task was quite difficult because of their ignorance of Persian and because as latecomers they were completely unaware of the rules and the goals of Akbar's religious pondering. From the early enthusiastic letters full of anticipation of Akbar's imminent conversion, it had become clear to the Jesuits by 1583 that he was too elusive, and too often on drugs, as they remarked, to "honestly change his heart."

The second Jesuit mission (1591–3) to the court of Akbar, this time in Lahore and headed by Duarte Leitão, was equally unsuccessful in producing the desired effect. It was the third and the most ambitious Jesuit mission, at least in the beginning, carefully studied and prepared in Goa, that persisted in spite of insurmountable difficulties. Linguistic expertise was once again brought to the forefront of the missionary effort. Thus, Jéronimo Xavier, grand-nephew of the "Apostle of the Indies," spent 20 years in the mission and even learned Persian and "Hindustani," while waiting, as he said, "for the fish to bite." In the meantime, he composed texts and treatises in Spanish, such as *Fuente da Vida*, a theologico-philosophical dialogue, written in Lahore in the 1590s, and then gradually translated them into Persian (Camps, *Jerome Xavier*). Just as Nobili thought that Sanskrit could become a new language of the mass and Ricci felt the same for Mandarin, Jéronimo Xavier extolled Persian as a refined language perfectly suitable to express Christian doctrine. As the hopes of converting either Akbar or Jahangir waned, and as Islam appeared, as always, completely impenetrable to Christian teaching, new strategies had to be devised. A contemporary Jesuit chronicle defines Muslims as being as "hard as diamonds to work upon" (Maclagan, *Jesuits and the Great Mogul*, p. 284).

One of the solutions, mentioned in Jesuit letters from the first decade of the seventeenth century, was to widen the mission field in order to include the non-Muslim population, particularly women, who expressed themselves in local vernacular languages, in particular in what they identified as "the vulgar speech." This interest grew steadily and by the middle of the seventeenth century some Jesuit missionaries, such as Antonio Ceschi and Heinrich Roth, developed an interest in Hinduism and its "sacred" language, Sanskrit. The transliteration of the Ave Maria and Paternoster into Sanskrit can still be seen in Athanasius Kircher's *China monumentis*, published in Amsterdam in 1667 (Kircher, *China monumentis*, p. 163).

An additional strategy employed in their "popular" mission field consisted in sumptuous celebrations of liturgical festivities with sermons in two or three languages (Portuguese, Persian, local vernacular), processions, and theater performances. Musical instruments – an organ was imported from Goa for the church in Agra – illuminations, fireworks, and flagellations were all geared to visually impress non-Christians. Jesuit sensorial and particularly visual approaches to proselytism and conversion reached an apogee with post-Tridentine religious painting, sculpture, and architecture. It was a happy coincidence, from the missionary point of view, that Akbar and Jahangir, known for their unorthodox Muslim practices, delighted in and patronized the visual arts. In the course of time, Mughal painters themselves started producing copies of the European imports and adopted certain western techniques and themes in their own works. At times of anti-Christian feelings, or when a Mughal sovereign wished to conciliate Muslim opinion, it was often the images that suffered the most. Thus the paintings from the Portuguese Hughli enclave, captured by Shah Jahan in 1632, were "insulted," hung on trees or cast into the Jamuna River. By that time, the Catholic visual influence of the Portuguese was losing ground, confronted with the new type of imagery that had been introduced by the British (Bailey, *Art on the Jesuit Missions*).

Conclusion

A brief survey of the main themes, events, and general trends in the encounter between Catholicism and other religious traditions in India from the sixteenth to eighteenth centuries is necessarily incomplete, not only because of the lack of reliable data and because of the shifts and displacements in historians' perspectives and epistemological grids, but also because it continues to be a neglected field of serious research and study. Without historical compendia, such as those written by Jesuit missionaries themselves, among many others, which were based on first-hand experience and "archival" work, many of the documents concerning the period would have been lost for us due to shipwrecks, earthquakes, and unwitting or deliberate destruction. At the same time, however, their own selection of what was important or insignificant, their personal judgments and hints, colored the opinions of historians who followed in their steps.

Hence, from the seventeenth century onwards, much of the traditional historiography on the spread of Catholicism in India followed two exclusive lines of interpretation, with barely disguised confessional, political, or national prejudices: either as a heroic drama of Christian victory over the forces of "heathenism" against all odds, or as a satire on the "dissembling" and the greed and bigotry of Catholic missionaries and clergy. While Protestant historians, in particular, reveled in vilifying "Catholic perfidy," from John Lockman to J. W. Kaye and J. N. Farquhar, various religious orders also continued their mutual rivalries on the pages of their historical texts, from Domingo Navarette to Tessier de Quéralay and others. Recent historiography of the Catholic venture in India in the early modern period privileges "anthropological" approaches. Historians generally profess interest in "local," "indigenous" histories and forms of knowledge, as well as in "subaltern voices" and resistance to overt and hidden modes of political, social, or religious domination. Nevertheless, the personal, confessional, and national agendas of the historians do reemerge in a new, complicated way as moral or partisan political views.

In spite of the different interpretations, however, the period of Catholic expansion in India under the Portuguese *padroado* falls roughly into three phases, with a certain degree of shifting and overlapping of calendars for different mission territories. The first phase, from 1500 until 1530, was characterized by a weak missionary presence but strong regal messianism; the second, ending with the sixteenth century, was a period of intense Christianization when post-Tridentine culture spread from Goa to all other mission territories; and the third phase consisted of the consolidation of the "conquered" territories, spiritual and/or political, and the slow and difficult progress, if any, of missionary activities beyond the Estado da Índia. The third phase dragged on into the eighteenth century when new actors, both Catholic and Protestant, engaged in a series of disputes.

The legacy of the first two centuries of Catholic expansion and proselytism in India is manifold. In terms of social geography, indigenous Christian communities sprang up in different parts of India. Some of them have preserved and nurtured their Catholic identity until today. In general, the religious interaction produced various types of syncretism affecting both Catholic and Hindu religious practices. And finally, not least importantly, Catholic missions often served as cultural and social laboratories for testing and experimenting with ideas, theories, and methods that were later to be appropriated and refined by the Enlightenment.

BIBLIOGRAPHY

Albuquerque, L. de, *Martim Afonso de Sousa*. Lisbon: Biblioteca da Expansão Portuguesa, 1989.

Albuquerque, V. A. C. B. de, "Congregação do Oratório de S. Felippe Nery em Goa," *O Oriente Portuguez*, 2 (1905).

Almeida, A. F. de, "Da demanda do Preste João à missão jesuíta da Etiópia: A cristandade da Abissínia e os portugueses nos séculos XVI e XVII," *Lusitania Sacra*, 11, 2nd ser. (1999), pp. 247–94.

Alves, J. M. Dos Santos, *Portugal e a missionação no século XVI: O Oriente e o Brasil*. Lisbon: Imprensa Nacional-Casa da Moeda (Portuguese and English version), 1997.

Amiel, C., "Les archives de l'Inquisition portugaise: Regards et réflexions," *Arquivos do Centro cultural português*, 14 (1979).

Amiel, C. and Lima, A., eds., *L'Inquisition de Goa: La relation de Charles Dellon (1687)*. Paris: Chandeigne, 1997.

Baião, A., *A Inquisição de Goa, tentativa de história da sua origem, estabelecimento, evolução e extinção*, 2 vols. Lisbon and Coimbra: Academia das Ciências, 1930–45.

Bailey, G. A., *Art on the Jesuit Missions in Asia and Latin America, 1542–1773*. Toronto: University of Toronto Press, 2000.

Bayly, S., *Saints, Goddesses and Kings: Muslims and Christians in South Indian Society, 1700–1900*. Cambridge: Cambridge University Press, 1992 (Indian ed.).

Besse, L, S.J., *La Mission du Maduré: Historiques de ses Pangous*, 2 vols. Trichinopoly, 1914.

Borges, C. J., *The Economics of the Goa Jesuits, 1542–1759: An Explanation of their Rise and Fall*. New Delhi: Oxford University Press, 1994.

Borges, C. J., "The Portuguese Jesuits in Asia: Their Economic and Political Networking within Asia and with Europe," in *A Companhia de Jesus e a Missionação no Oriente*. Lisbon: Brotéria & Fundação Oriente, 2000, pp. 203–24.

Boxer, C. R., *The Great Ship from Amacon: Annals of Macao and the Old Japan Trade, 1555–1640*. Lisbon: CEHU, 1959.

Boxer, C. R., *Race Relations in the Portuguese Colonial Empire*. Oxford: Oxford University Press, 1963.

Boxer, C. R., *Fidalgos in the Far East, 1550–1770*. The Hague: Martinus Nijhoff, 1948 (rpt. 1968, Hong Kong).

Boxer, C. R., *The Portuguese Seaborne Empire, 1425–1825*. London and New York: Weidenfeld & Nicolson, 1969.

Boxer, C. R., *The Church Militant and Iberian Expansion, 1440–1770*. Baltimore: Johns Hopkins University Press, 1978.

Boxer, C. R., *Portuguese India in the Mid-Seventeenth Century*. New Delhi: Oxford University Press, 1980.

Boyd, R. H. S., *India and the Latin Captivity of the Church: The Cultural Context of the Gospel*. Cambridge: Cambridge University Press, 1974.

Brou, A., "Notes sur les origines du clergé indigène au pays Tamoul," *Revue d'histoire des missions*, 7/2 (June 1930), pp. 188–210.

Brown, L., *The Indian Christians of St. Thomas*. Cambridge: Cambridge University Press, 1982 (1st ed., 1956).

Camps, A., O.F.M., *Jerome Xavier, S.J., and the Muslims of the Mogul Empire: Controversial Works and Missionary Activity*, Schöneck-Beckenried: Neue Zeitschrift für Missionwissenschaft (Nouvelle Revue de Science Missionaire), 1957.

Coates, T. J., *Degredados e Órfãs: Colonização dirigida pela coroa no império português, 1550–1755*. Lisbon: CNCDP, 1998.

Correia-Afonso, J., S.J., *Jesuit Letters and Indian History*. Bombay: St. Xavier's College, 1955.

Correia-Afonso, J., S.J., "More about Akbar and the Jesuits," *Indica*, 14 (1977).

Correia-Afonso, J., S.J., *Indo-Portuguese History: Sources and Problems*. Bombay: Oxford University Press, 1981.

Costa, J. P. O. e, "Em torno da criação do Bispado do Japão," in A. T. de Matos and L. F. F. R. Thomaz, eds., *As relações entre a India Portuguesa, a Asia do Sueste e o Extremo Oriente*. Macao and Lisbon: CNCDP, 1993.

Costa, J. P. O. e, "Os Portugueses e a cristandade siro-malabar (1498–1530)," *Studia*, 52 (1994).

Costa, J. P. O. e, "A crise financeira da missão jesuítica do Japão no início do século XVIII," in *A Companhia de Jesus e a Missionação no Oriente*. Lisbon: Brotéria & Fundação Oriente, 2000, pp. 235–46.

Coutinho, F., *Le Régime paroissial des diocèses de rite latin de l'Inde des origines (XIVe siècle) à nos jours*. Louvain/Paris: Publications Universitaires de Louvain/Béatrice-Nauwelaerts, 1958.

Couto, D. do, *O Soldado Prático*, ed. M. Rodrigues Lapa. Lisbon: Livraria Sá da Costa Editora, 1937.

Cruz, M. A. L., "Exiles and Renegades in Early Sixteenth-Century Portuguese India," *Indian Economic and Social History Review*, 23/3 (1986).

Cunha, A. C. da, *A Inquisição no Estado da Índia: Origens (1539–1560)*. Arquivos Nacionais/Torre do Tombo, 1995.

Curto, D. R., "Cultura escrita e práticas de identidade," in F. Bethencourt and K. Chaudhuri, eds., *História da Expansão Portuguesa*. Navarre: Círculo de Leitores, 1998, vol. 2., pp. 458–531.

Das, K., *Mughal Painting during Jahangir's Time*. Calcutta: The Asiatic Society, 1978.

D'Costa, A., *Christianization of the Goa Island, 1510–1567*. Bombay: St. Xavier's College, 1965.

Debergh, M., "Premiers jalons de l'évangélisation de l'Asie," in J.-M. Mayeur, Ch. and L. Pietri, A. Vauchez, and M. Venard, eds., *Histoire du Christianisme: Le temps des confessions (1530–1620)*. Paris: Desclée, 1992.

Dharampal, G., *La Religion des Malabars, Tessier de Quéralay et la contribution des missionnaires européens à la naissance de l'indianisme*. Immensee: Nouvelle Revue de Science Missionnaire, 1982.

Farquhar, J. N., *Modern Religious Movements in India*. London: Munshiram Manoharlal, 1929.

Ferroli, D., S.J., *The Jesuits in Malabar*, 2 vols. Bangalore: Bangalore Press, 1939–51.

Flores, J. M., *"Um Curto História de Ceylan": Five Hundred Years of Relations between Portugal and Sri Lanka*. Lisbon: Fundação Oriente, 2001.

García-Gallo, A., "Las Bullas de Alejandro VI y el ordenamiento jurídico de la expansión portuguesa y castellana en Africa e Indias," in *Los orígines españoles de las instituciones americanas: Estudios de derecho indiano*. Madrid: R. Academia de Jurisprudencia y Legislación, Conmemoración del V Centenario del descubrimiento de América, 1987.

Ghesquière, T., *Mathieu de Castro, premier vicaire apostolique aux Indes*. Louvain: Apostolat monastique et missionnaire, 1937.

Gonçalves, S., S.J., *Primeira Parte da Historia dos Religiosos da Companhia de Jesus e do que fizeram com a divina graça na conversão dos infieis a nossa sancta fee catholica nos reynos e provincias da India Oriental*, ed. José Wicki, S.J. Coimbra: Atlântida, Coimbra, 1957–62.

Gracias, F. da Silva, *Health and Hygiene in Colonial Goa (1510–1961)*. New Delhi: Oxford University Press, 1994.

Gracias, F. da Silva, *Beyond the Self: Santa Casa da Misericórdia de Goa*. Panaji, Goa: Surya Publications, 2000.

Gruzinski, S., "Les mondes mêlés de la monarchie catholique et autres 'connected histories,'" *Annales*, 56/1 (Jan.–Feb. 2001), pp. 85–117.

Guerreiro, F., S.J., *Relação Annual das Coisas que Fizeram os Padres da Companhia de Jesus nas suas Missões nos anos de 1600 a 1609*, 3 vols. Coimbra: Imprensa da Universidade, 1929–42.

Kamat, P., *Farar Far (Crossfire): Local Resistance to Colonial Hegemony in Goa, 1510–1912*. Panaji, Goa: Institute Menezes Braganza, 1999.

Kaye, J. W., *Christianity in India: An Historical Narrative*. London, 1859.

King, R., *Orientalism and Religion: Postcolonial Theory, India and "The Mystic East."* New Delhi: Oxford University Press, 1999.

Kircher, A., *China monumentis*. Amsterdam: J. Janssonium & E. Weyerstraet, 1667.

Launay, A., *Histoire des Missions de l'Inde: Pondichéry, Maïssour, Coïmbatour*, 4 vols. Paris, 1898.

Lopes, M. de Jesus dos Mártires, *Goa Setecentista: Tradição e Modernidade*. Lisbon: Universidade Católica Portuguesa, 1996.

Lopes, M. de Jesus dos Mártires, "A Inquisição de Goa na primeira metade do século XVIII: Uma visita pelo seu interior," *Mare Liberum*, 15 (1998).

Lopes, M. de Jesus dos Mártires, "Negócios e convivências dos jesuítas de Goa no século XVIII: Contributo para a sua história," in *A Companhia de Jesus e a Missionação no Oriente*. Lisbon: Brotéria & Fundação Oriente, 2000, pp. 235–58.

Loureiro, R. M., "O descrobrimento da civilização indiana nas caratas dos jesuítas (século XVI)," in *Encontro sobre Portugal e a Índia*. Lisbon: Fundação Oriente/Livros Horizonte, 2000, pp. 107–25.

Loureiro, R. M. and Gruzinski, S., eds., *Passar as fronteiras: II Colóquio International sobre Mediadores Culturais, séculos XV a XVIII*. Lagos: Centro de Estudos Gil Eanes, 1999.

Maclagan, E., *The Jesuits and the Great Mogul*. New York: Octagon Books/Farrar, Straus & Giroux, 1972 (1st ed., 1932).

Martins, J. F. F., *História de Misericórdia de Goa*, 3 vols. Nova Goa: Imprensa Nacional, 1910–14.

Meersman, A., *The Ancient Franciscan Provinces in India 1500–1835*. Bangalore: Christian Literature Society Press, 1971.

Melo, C. M. de, S.J., *The Recruitment and Formation of the Native Clergy in India*. Lisbon: Agência Geral do Ultramar, Divisão de Publicações et Biblioteca, 1955.

Metzler, J., O.M.I., *Sacrae Congregationis de Propaganda Fide Memoria Rerum: 350 Years in the Service of the Missions*, vol. 1, part 1 (1522–1700). Rome/Freiburg/Vienna: Herder, 1972.

Mitter, P., *Much Maligned Monsters: A History of European Reactions to Indian Art*. Chicago: Chicago University Press, 1992 (1st ed., 1977).

Mosse, D., "The Politics of Religious Synthesis: Roman Catholicism and Hindu Village Society in Tamil Nadu, India," in C. Stewardt and R. Shaw, eds., *Syncretism/Antisyncretism: The Politics of Religious Synthesis.* London: Routledge, 1994.

Mundadan, M., C.M.I., *History of Christianity in India.* Vol. 1: *From the Beginning up to the Middle of the Sixteenth Century (up to 1542).* Bangalore: Church History Association of India, 1989.

Nayagam, X. S. T., "The First Books Printed in Tamil," *Tamil Culture*, 4 (1956).

Neil, S., *A History of Christianity in India.* Cambridge: Cambridge University Press, 1985.

Newman, R. S., *Of Umbrellas, Goddesses and Dreams: Essays on Goan Culture and Society.* Mapusa: Other India Press, 2001.

Nunes, M. da Costa, *Documentação para a História da Congregação do Oratório da Santa Cruz dos Milagres do Clero Natural do Goa.* Lisbon: Instituto de Investigação Científica Tropical, 1966.

Oddie, G. A., *Hindu and Christian in South-East India.* London: Curzon/Riverdale, 1991.

O'Malley, J. W., *The First Jesuits.* Cambridge, Mass.: Harvard University Press, 1993.

Pearson, M. N., *The Portuguese in India.* Cambridge: Cambridge University Press, 1987.

Priolkar, A. K., *The Goa Inquisition*, 2nd ed. New Delhi: Voice of India, 1991.

Ramos, J. M., "The Invention of a Mission: The Brief Establishment of a Portuguese Catholic Minority in Renaissance Ethiopia," in E. J. Mucha, ed., *Dominant Culture as Foreign Culture: Dominant Group(s) in the Eyes of the Minorities.* New York: East European Monographs and Columbia University Press, 1999.

Ramos, J. M., "Machiavellian Empowerment and Disempowerment: The Violent Struggle for Power in XVIIth Century Ethiopia," in Angela Cheater, ed., *The Anthropology of Power: Empowerment and Disempowerment in Changing Structures.* London: Routledge, 1999, pp. 191–205.

Rego, A. da Silva, *História das Missões do Padroado Português do Oriente: Índia (1500–1542).* Lisbon: Agência Geral do Ultramar, 1949.

Rego, A. da Silva, "A primeira missão religiosa ao Grão Mogol," *Temas Sociomissionológicos e Históricos*, Lisbon, 1962.

Rivara, J. H. da Cunha, *Archivo Portueuz-Oriental*, 6 fasc. in 10 vols., 1st ed. Nova Goa: Imprensa Nacional, 1857–75; New Delhi/Madras, 1992.

Roche, P. A., *Fishermen of the Coromandel.* Manohar, New Delhi: Oxford University Press, 1984.

Rubiés, J.-P., *Travel and Ethnology in the Renaissance: South India through European Eyes, 1250–1625.* Cambridge: Cambridge University Press, 2000.

Rubiés, J.-P., "The Jesuit Discovery of Hinduism: Antonio Rubino's Account of the History and Religion of Vijayanagara (1608)," *Archiv für Religonsgeschichte*, 3 (2001), pp. 210–56.

Sá, I. dos Gimarães, *Quando o rico se faz pobre: Misericórdias, caridade e poder no império português, 1500–1800.* Lisbon: CNCDP, 1997.

Santos, C. M., *"Goa é a chave da toda a Índia": Perfil político da capital do Etado da Índia (1505–1570).* Lisbon: CNCDP, 1999.

Schurhammer, G., S.J., *The Malabar Church and Rome during the Early Portuguese Period and Before.* Trichinopoly, 1934.

Schurhammer, G., S.J., *Francis Xavier: His Life and Times*, trans. M. J. Costelloe, S.J., 4 vols. Rome: Jesuit Historical Institute, 1973–82.

Schurhammer, G., S.J., and Cottrell, G. W., S.J., "The First Printing in Indic Characters," *Orientalia*, Lisbon, 1963.

Schütte, J. F., S.J., *Valignano's Mission Principles for Japan*, trans. John J. Coyne, S.J., 2 vols. St. Louis: Institute of Jesuit Sources, 1980–5.

Silva, C. R. de, "The Portuguese and Pearl Fishing off South India and Sri Lanka," *South Asia*, 1/1 (March 1978).

Sousa, T. R. de, *The Medieval Goa: A Socio-Economic History*. New Delhi: Oxford University Press, 1979.

Subrahmanyam, S., *The Portuguese Empire in Asia, 1500–1700: A Political and Economic History*. London: Longman, 1993.

Subrahmanyam, S., *The Career and Legend of Vasco da Gama*. Cambridge: Cambridge University Press, 1997.

Subrahmanyam, S., "Connected Histories: Notes Towards a Reconfiguration of Early Modern Eurasia," *Modern Asian Studies*, 31/3 (1997), pp. 735–62.

Subrahmanyam, S., ed., *Sinners and Saints: The Successors of Vasco da Gama*. New Delhi: Oxford University Press, 1998.

Subrahmanyam, S., "Du Tage au Gange au XVIe siècle: Une conjoncture millénariste à l'échelle eurasiatique," *Annales, Histoire, Sciences Sociales*, 56 (Jan.–Feb. 2001), pp. 51–84.

Tavim, J. A. R. da Silva, "From Setúbal to the Sublime Porte: The Wandering of Jácome de Olivares, New Christian and Merchant of Cochin (1540–1571)," in S. Subrahmanyam, ed., *Sinners and Saints: The Successors of Vasco da Gama*. New Delhi: Oxford University Press, 1998.

Thekkedath, J., S.D.B., *History of Christianity in India*. Vol. 2: *From the Middle of the Sixteenth Century to the End of the Seventeenth Century (1542–1700)*. Bangalore: Church History Association of India, 1982.

Thomaz, L. F. F. R., "Le Portugal et l'Afrique au XVe siècle: Les débuts de l'expansion," *Arquivos do Centro Cultural Português*, 26 (1989).

Thomaz, L. F. F. R., "L'idée impériale manueline," in J. Aubin, ed., *La Découverte, le Portugal et l'Europe*. Paris: Fondation Calouste Gulbenkian/Centre Culturel Portugais, 1990.

Thomaz, L. F. F. R., "Factions, Interests and Messianism: The Politics of Portuguese Expansion in the East, 1500–1521," *Indian Economic and Social History Review*, 28/1 (1991).

Thomaz, L. F. F. R., *De Ceuta a Timor*. Lisbon: Difel, 1994.

Thomaz, L. F. F. R., "A crise de 1565–1575 na história do estado da Índia," *Mare Liberum*, 9 (1995).

Vaz, Can. F. X., "Primeiros clerigos indios," *O Oriente Portuguez*, 6 (1909).

Visvanathan, S., *The Christians of Kerala*. Madras: Oxford University Press, 1993.

Wicki, J., S.J., "Der einheimische Klerus in Indien," in J. Beckmann, ed., *Der einheimische Klerus in Geschichte und Gegenwart*. Schöneck-Beckenried: Neue Zeitschrift für Missionswissenschaft (Nouvelle Revue de Science Missionaire), 1950.

Wicki, J., S.J., *Missionskirche im Orient*. Immensee: Neue Zeitschrift für Missionwissenschaft (Nouvelle Revue de Science Missionaire), 1976.

Wicki, J., S.J., and Gomes, J., S.J., eds., *Documenta Indica*, 18 vols. Rome: Institutum Historicum Societatis Iesu, 1948–88.

Wilfred, F., S.J., "Christianity in Hindu Polytheistic Structural Mould: Converts in Southern Tamilnadu Respond to an Alien Religion During the 'Vasco da Gama Epoch,'" *Archives de sciences sociales des religions*, 103 (1998).

Witte, C. M. de, "Les bulles pontificales et l'expansion portugaise au XVe siècle," *Revue d'histoire ecclésiastique*, 48 (1953); 49 (1954); 51 (1956); 53 (1958).

Xavier, Â. B., "Assistir diferenciadamente: Ordem social e mundo da caridade em Goa nos séculos XVI e XVII," *Vértice*, 2nd ser. (Mar.–Apr. 1997), pp. 11–20.

Xavier, Â. B., "Amores e desamores pelos pobres: Imagens, afectos e atitudes (sécs. XVI e XVII)," *Lusitania Sacra*, 11, 2nd ser. (1999).

Xavier, Â. B., "'Correo logo a fama do milagre': Narrativas missionárias, motivações e devoções num oriente imaginado," *Centro de Historia da Cultura*, Terramar, Lisbon, 1999, pp. 207–18.

Xavier, Â. B., "The Martyrs of Cuncolim (Goa, 16th century): Portuguese Domination and the Resistance/Adaptation of Local Communities," paper presented at the Annual

Conference of the Society for Spanish and Portuguese Historical Studies, New York, April 27–30, 2000.

Xavier, Â. B., "Between Conversion and Political Death: The Case of Carambolim in 16th-Century Goa," paper presented at the International Conference on Religion and Violence, New York University/Max-Planck Institut/Universiteit van Amsterdam, Amsterdam, May 25–7, 2000.

Xavier, Â. B., "Uneasiness in the Village: Alliances, Conflicts and Conformity between Jesuits and Local Populations (Goa, 16th century)," paper presented at the workshop Jesuits as Intermediaries in the Early Modern World, October 11–13, 2001.

Županov, I. G., "Aristocratic Analogies and Demotic Descriptions in the Seventeenth-Century Madurai Mission," *Representations*, 41 (1991).

Županov, I. G., "Prosélytisme et pluralisme religieux: Deux expériences missionnaires en Inde aux XVIe et XVIIe siècles," *Archives de sciences sociales des religions*, 87 (Jul.–Sept. 1994).

Županov, I. G., "Le repli du religieux: Les missionnaires jésuites du XVIIe siècle entre la théologie chrétienne et une éthique païenne," *Annales*, 6 (1996).

Županov, I. G., "The Prophetic and the Miraculous in Portuguese Asia: A Hagiographical View of Colonial Culture," in S. Subrahmanyam, ed., *Sinners and Saints: The Successors of Vasco da Gama*. New Delhi: Oxford University Press, 1998.

Županov, I. G., *Disputed Mission: Jesuit Experiments and Brahmanical Knowledge in Seventeenth-Century India*. New Delhi: Oxford University Press, 2000.

Županov, I. G., "Lust, Marriage and Free Will: Jesuit Critique of Paganism in South India (Seventeenth Century)," *Studies in History*, 12/2, n.s. (2000).

FURTHER READING

Two Jesuit historians, Georg Schurhammer and Josef Wicki, have published indispensable articles and books and have edited primary sources on the Christianization of India. Schurhammer's *Francis Xavier: His Life and Times* is an unsurpassed biography of the Jesuit saint and the early Jesuit missions in Asia. A generally reliable survey of the Franciscan presence in India can be found in works by equally prolific Franciscan historian Achilles Meersman. His *Ancient Franciscan Provinces in India* is particularly useful.

Until recently all scholarship regarding missionary presence in India during the early modern period was the exclusive turf of partisan religious historians. Among the useful traditional "Catholic" narratives are Léon Besse, *La Mission du Maduré*, and Adrien Launay, *Histoire des Missions de l'Inde*. Works by the Jesuits John Correia-Afonso, *Jesuit Letters and Indian History*, and Anthony D'Costa, *Christianization of the Goa Island*, are pioneer studies in the social and cultural history of Christianization.

Two volumes published by the Church History Association of India in the series History of Christianity in India are the most authoritative contemporary reference works: A. Mathias Mundadan, C.M.I., *From the Beginning up to the Middle of the Sixteenth Century (up to 1542)*, and Joseph Thekkedath, S.D.B., *From the Middle of the Sixteenth Century to the End of the Seventeenth Century (1542–1700)*. Numerous descriptive articles of varying interest are published in two Portuguese journals, *Lusitania Sacra* and *Studia*. A high degree of scholarship is consistently found in texts by Luís Filipe F. R. Thomaz and João Paulo Oliveira e Costa (see Bibliography).

The most recent studies, endeavoring to combine the perspectives of anthropological and cultural history, as well as choosing to address questions such as caste, hegemony, and colonialism in a more global way, are written mostly, but not exclusively, by lay historians. Susan Bayly's *Saints, Goddesses and Kings* is a rich and stimulating book for the later period. A chapter on Mughal painting and Jesuit missionary propaganda in Gauvin Bailey's *Art on the Jesuit Mis-*

sions in Asia and Latin America is a welcome contribution to the long-neglected field of "esthetic accommodation." These and similar questions are also addressed in my book, *Disputed Mission*. For an excellent article on questions of indigenization and inculturation see Felix Wilfred, "Christianity in Hindu Polytheistic Structural Mould." Equally stimulating and in the process of being written and published are works by Ângela Barreto Xavier, Joan-Pau Rubiés, João Manuel Ramos (on Ethiopian historical nexus and its connection with the Goa Catholic institutions), and Rui Loureiro (see Bibliography).

TWENTY-TWO

Promise: China

R. PO-CHIA HSIA

In 1585 the printer Johann Mayer in Dillingen published a work in German, entitled *Historical Report of the Conversion of the Great Land and Island of Japan.* Consisting of translations from the Latin letters received by German Jesuits from missionaries of their own Society in Japan, this work provided a first glimpse of the Catholic missions in faraway Japan from 1577 to 1581. Dedicated to Bishop Marquardt of Augsburg (whose episcopal seat was in nearby Dillingen), the printer wanted to show "that the Almighty good God, in the place of so many thousand souls in Upper and Lower Germany who were tempted by the Evil Enemy . . . through numerous unstable new teachings, particularly by the Lutheran, Calvinist, and Zwinglian heretical preachers . . . has elected another people from the other side of the world, who has hitherto known nothing of the holy faith."

As it turned out, the Japanese did not become the new chosen people, as savage persecutions by the Tokugawa regime in the early seventeenth century crushed the flourishing Catholic mission (see chapter 23). But the publication of this book in 1585 pointed to a conjunction of events. As one of the strongest proponents of the Catholic Counter-Reformation, Bishop Marquardt had just provoked the Protestants in Augsburg into a fierce confrontation over the introduction of the new Gregorian calendar (1582), rejected by Protestants due to its papal origins. Also in those very years, two Italian Jesuits, Michele Ruggiero and Matteo Ricci, obtained permission to establish a residence in southern China (1583), thus inaugurating a Catholic mission that would bring a more enduring success than in Japan. The force behind the China mission, Ricci, had been a student at the Roman College of the Society of Jesus under Christopher Clavius, the Jesuit mathematician responsible for the new Gregorian calendar. In time, Ricci himself and his Jesuit successors would play an equally significant role in calendar reform in seventeenth-century China.

Although the Catholic princes in the Holy Roman Empire became supporters of the Jesuit China mission, Catholicism in sixteenth-century China owed its origins to the Iberian maritime expansion. Under the patronage of the Portuguese and Spanish crowns, sanctioned by Pope Alexander VI in 1493, Catholic missionaries accompanied Iberian sailors and merchants to the Americas, Africa, and Asia. China fell under the sphere of influence of the Portuguese crown; and after the establishment of the small Portuguese enclave of Macao in 1557, several abortive attempts were made to introduce missionaries to China proper, before the successful venture of Ruggiero and Ricci in 1583.

Chronology

1 Foundations, 1583–1630s

The major events in the history of Christianity in China are well known. As told in *The Christian Expedition to China* (1615), based on Ricci's memoirs and revised by the Belgian Jesuit Nicolas Trigault during a fundraising trip back to Europe, the story of the Catholic mission, at least during the first 20 years, represented to a large extent the personal triumph of one man, Ricci. Viewed initially by the Chinese as teachers of a new Buddhist sect from India, Ricci and a handful of Jesuits persisted in presenting a distinct message: Christianity, or the Teachings of Heaven, as Catholicism came to be called in the late Ming dynasty (1368–1644), was the only true universal religion; its monotheism, its moral rigor, and its intellectual foundations agreed essentially with the teachings of the ancient Chinese sages, as recorded in the canon of the Confucian tradition. Christian conversion in China, in other words, was undertaken very differently from the practice in the Americas. Faced with an ancient and self-confident civilization, and without colonial conquests, natural reason and moral philosophy became the rhetoric of persuasion. Ricci succeeded brilliantly after investing more than a decade in mastering written classical Chinese and learning the Confucian canon. By 1595, the Jesuits cast off Buddhist robes and assumed a new persona as "western literati"; dressed in the style of Chinese scholars, Ricci and his companions cultivated officials and literati, exchanged western gifts (clocks and maps) for patronage, and attracted enormous curiosity by the novelty and brilliance of their intellectual and social performance, exemplified by learned discourse, expertise in mathematics, and printed works in Chinese.

While no more than a dozen Jesuits worked in China during his lifetime, Ricci's personal reputation and elite network achieved enormous gains for the Catholic mission. With converts numbering probably no more than a few hundred before 1600, Ricci's patrons secured for him imperial permission to reside in the capital Beijing. In 1603 Ricci published *Tianzhu shiyi* ("True Meaning of the Lord of Heaven"), combining Aristotelian logic, Christian doctrines, and Confucian rhetoric to create a template of Sino-Catholic persuasion that would be crucial for the future history of the Catholic mission. When Ricci died in 1610, the Wanli emperor bestowed an official funeral and cemetery. Ricci's work was continued by the cooperation between the major Chinese converts – leading officials and renowned literati – and a handful of new Jesuit arrivals. Between 1610 and the 1630s, when the Jesuits (European missionaries and Chinese and Macaist brothers) ranged from 10 to 20, the number of converts shot up from ca. 2,500 in 1610 to some 40,000 in 1636 (Standaert, *Handbook*, p. 382).

The success of the Jesuit mission was not uninterrupted. Sporadic, local, and early opposition to Christianity crystallized in the 1616–17 campaign instigated by Shen Que, the vice-minister of the Nanjing Ministry of Rites. Shen accused the Jesuits in

Beijing – Diego de Pantoja (1571–1618) and Sabatino De Ursis (1575–1620) – of subverting the Confucian state order by their projected calendar reform, and similarly accused Alfonso Vagnone (1568–1640) and Alvaro de Semedo (1586–1658) in Nanjing, the southern capital, of creating a heterodox sect. Even though the leading Christian officials Xu Guangqi (Paul) and Yang Tingyun (Michele) composed apologies defending the orthodoxy and usefulness of Christianity, other officials supported Shen and an imperial edict of February 3, 1617 expelled the four Jesuits to Macao. Protected by Yang in his hometown of Hangzhou, the other missionaries rode out the storm, and renewed their success in the following decades.

2   Crisis, 1630s–1660s

The second period of Christianity lasted from the 1630s to the 1660s. This was a time of tumultuous changes. Famine and uprisings toppled the Ming dynasty; and China was invaded by the Manchus, who established a new dynasty, the Qing. For most of these decades, warfare and insecurity hampered the work of conversion, but the Christian Church survived remarkably well the years of conquest and internal warfare. The number of Christians remained stable between 60,000 and 80,000; and the Jesuit astronomers in Beijing, under the leadership of Johann Adam Schall von Bell, were taken into service by the new conquest dynasty. China was no longer an exclusive mission domain for the Jesuits, who operated under Portuguese crown patronage. In the 1630s, Spanish friars (two Dominicans and one Franciscan) arrived in the southeastern coastal province of Fujian from Manila, where the orders had worked among the large Chinese (Fujian) immigrant community.

The arrival of Spanish friars initiated a long dispute over the methods of conversion in China. Formed by their experience in the Americas (the friars traveled from Spain to the New World before arriving in the Philippines), the Spanish mendicants held a more rigid view of Christianity: conversion entailed renouncing indigenous customs and beliefs, labeled as superstitious, and the new Christian identity often implied Hispanicization. This alternative model of conversion worked well for the friars, for their work in the New World and in the Philippines was backed up by the secular arm of the Spanish colonial empire. In Fujian, the friars were disturbed by the Jesuit method of conversion, specifically the accommodation of Christianity to Chinese practices in ancestral and Confucian rituals. They also criticized the Jesuit use of Chinese terms to denote the Christian God, fearing a confusion of "superstitious" and true beliefs. Controversy over proper terminology had previously divided the Jesuits; Niccolò Longobardo (1565–1655), Ricci's successor, had opposed Ricci's accommodationist method. But the Jesuits resolved their division internally at the 1627 conference at Jiading, where the majority of Jesuit missionaries supported Ricci's methods against Longobardo's minority view. True to Jesuit obedience, the fathers would maintain an almost solid front against later criticisms. This issue first reached Rome when the Dominican friar Juan Baptista Morales, the first of his order to work in China, presented a list of objections to Rome. It resulted in a first judgment against Chinese rites issued in 1645 by the Congregation for the Propagation of Faith (Propaganda Fide). Jesuit counter-lobbying led to the dispatch of Martino Martini to Rome, who secured a favorable decree by Pope Alexander VII, affirming the civil character of Chinese rites and hence their approbation.

3   Ascent, 1664–1707

Differences over conversion strategies, in fact, reflected the national rivalry between the Portuguese and Spanish crowns, as well as competition between religious orders. During the third period of early modern Chinese Christianity, from 1664 to 1707, disagreements over Chinese rites intensified in a more complex missionary picture, with new religious orders entering the mission field and with papal intervention in the Portuguese patronage. The initial years of this period were marked by a political struggle against the Jesuit astronomers. In 1664, the Chinese official Yang Guangxian brought charges against Adam Schall, head of the Astronomical Bureau, of having selected an inauspicious date for the burial of an infant son of the Shunzhi emperor's favorite consort, thus resulting in the premature death of the consort and the emperor (1660/1661). Yang also condemned Christianity as a heterodox sect that undermined Confucian orthodoxy and social order. Deprived of Shunzhi's protection, in 1665 Schall and his Chinese colleagues at the Astronomical Bureau were arrested and condemned to death. The court executed the Chinese astronomers, five of whom were Christians, but pardoned Schall when Beijing was struck by a strong earthquake, which was interpreted as a sign of the wrath of the Christian God. The persecutions shook the foundations of the Christian mission. Except for four court Jesuits, all missionaries were rounded up and confined to prison and then house arrest in Canton (1665–71). Christianity was proscribed and churches were closed throughout the country. The Catholic mission only recovered from this grave crisis when Yang, who succeeded as director of the Astronomical Bureau, proved unequal to his task. The young emperor Kangxi allowed the Belgian Jesuit Ferdinand Verbiest to challenge Yang to an astronomical prediction. With western science triumphant, Kangxi restored the Jesuits to good graces. Condemned to death in 1669 for his intrigue, Yang's sentence was commuted to internal exile. Although Kangxi freed the missionaries from confinement in Canton and allowed churches to reopen, the edict forbidding Christianity was not formally rescinded. Christianity in early modern China would reach its zenith under the reign of Kangxi, but it flourished only under the benevolence of the emperor. An imperial edict of 1692 gave the mission a great boost. In response to Jesuit petitions against a local persecution, Kangxi issued an edict disassociating Christianity from seditious heterodox sects, specifying that in reward for the service of Jesuits in diplomatic missions with Russia, Christian worship was allowed for subjects of the emperor. Repeated favors bestowed by Kangxi on individual Jesuits vastly increased the prestige of Christianity. Between the Calendar Case of 1664/5 and the 1692 Edict, the number of Christians roughly doubled to 200,000.

The end of persecutions coincided with a new missionary enthusiasm in Europe. Having recovered from the Thirty Years' War, a confident Catholic Europe sent new generations of missionaries to China in answer to Verbiest's appeal. With fewer than 30 missionaries during the Calendar Persecution in 1665, the number rose to almost 40 by 1679, and jumped rapidly during the following two decades to reach a maximum of around 140 Europeans in 1701. In addition to Jesuits under Portuguese patronage, whose number included members from many nationalities, a fresh contingent of French Jesuits arrived in China in 1687. As agents of Louis XIV's diplomatic, scientific, and religious mission, the French Jesuits refused to submit to

Portuguese authority and eventually won approval from the general in Rome to establish a separate and independent mission. The mendicants also received reinforcements. Fujian became the dominant missionary field of the Dominicans; Franciscans
concentrated their effort in Shangdong and Guangdong provinces on the coast, and
Shaanxi in the interior; and the first Augustinians arrived in 1680. Swelling the ranks
of godly servants were missionaries sent by the Propaganda Fide in Rome. Aiming
to pry China away from the monopoly of Portuguese patronage, the papacy dispatched Italian mendicants as vicars apostolic to China. A new religious order, the
Missions Étrangères de Paris (MEP), created under Propaganda sponsorship, would
play a significant role after 1684.

Ecclesiastical administration was also restructured during this period. Under
Jesuit predominance, the China mission was originally subject to the province of
Japan, before the vice-province of China was created as a separate unit. Given
the small clerical presence in China during the first decades, the mission operated
rather autonomously from the ecclesiastical structure of Portuguese Asia, centered in
the archdiocese of Goa and in the diocese of Macao. In 1657 Pope Alexander VII
created apostolic vicariates for China and Southeast Asia, to operate outside of the
jurisdiction of the diocese of Macao. The first vicars apostolic entered China only
in the 1680s. By the next decade, the China mission was administratively divided
between the dioceses of Beijing, Nanjing, and Macao, in addition to the apostolic
vicariates.

Initial conflict over jurisdiction and hierarchy gradually subsided, but the complex
missionary presence ignited the dormant but persistent controversy over Chinese
rites. In general, the Dominicans and the MEP strongly opposed Jesuit methods, a
hostility linked to the Jesuit–Dominican rivalry in Europe and the strongly Jansenist
anti-Jesuitism of the MEP. The Franciscans and Augustinians wavered between the
two positions, trying to find a balance between the two.

The crucial initiative to ban Chinese rites came from Charles Maigrot, a member
of the MEP and vicar apostolic in Fujian. In 1693 he submitted to Rome a series of
articles on Chinese rites deemed superstitious. In 1697 Innocent XII ordered the
Holy Office to investigate thoroughly the longstanding controversy, a laborious
process interrupted by the death of the pope in 1700. Meanwhile, vigorous lobby-
ing went on from both sides; the Jesuits even secured a statement from Emperor
Kangxi to the effect that rites honoring ancestors and Confucius were essentially civil
and not religious ceremonies. Disagreement over conversion strategy in China rapidly
became a public matter in Catholic Europe and took on the character of an anti-
Jesuit campaign. In 1700 the theological faculty at the Sorbonne condemned a list
of proposals in a book on China written by the French Jesuit missionary Louis Le
Comte. By 1704, the Holy Office reached a decision on Maigrot's mandate. Referring to the 1645 and 1656 papal decisions, Clement XI's decree concurred with many
of Maigrot's propositions: the Chinese terms *tian* (heaven) and *shangdi* (Lord on
High) were forbidden; church tablets bearing the words *jing tian* (respect heaven)
were to be removed; Christians could not participate in sacrifices to Confucius or to
ancestors; ancestral tablets were allowed only if they bore the names of the deceased
and no other words. Clement appointed Charles Thomas Maillard de Tournon as
papal legate to China, instructing him to publish the papal decree at an appropriate
time.

Tournon arrived in Beijing in December 1705. Despite an initially favorable audience with Emperor Kangxi, Tournon incurred imperial anger when he openly sided with Maigrot, whom Kangxi held in contempt for his limited knowledge of classical Chinese. Expelled from the court in 1706, Tournon publicized Clement's decree in 1707, to great consternation among the Jesuits and Chinese converts. The condemnation of rituals honoring ancestors and Confucius profoundly alienated the Chinese elites and provoked strong opposition in many Christian communities. The injunction to remove tablets with the words *jing tian* from churches exposed Christianity to political repressions, for the words were bestowed by Kiangxi himself on the Jesuit church in Beijing. The emperor perceived Tournon's mission to be undue papal interference to his rule and required all missionaries to swear allegiance to the methods of Ricci and to remain forever in China. Those refusing the oath were denied a residence permit and ordered to leave.

4   Decline, 1707–1800

The fourth period of Christianity dated from 1707 to the end of the eighteenth century. Three main developments were characteristic. First, the Chinese rites prohibition led to a definitive rupture between Beijing and Rome, leading to the official ban on Christianity in 1724. Second, the strength and nature of Chinese Christianity changed substantially in the face of persecutions, launched usually by hostile provincial and local officials, who could invoke the imperial ban. The persecutions of 1746–52 and 1784–5 shocked public opinion in Europe owing to the martyrdom of European missionaries. Finally, Christianity in China came to be viewed increasingly as incompatible with Chinese traditions, while the Catholic Church became Sinicized, with European missionaries playing a diminishing role.

Years of ambiguity followed Tournon's debacle. The legate himself, elevated to cardinal, died in 1710 in Macao under house arrest. Christian communities followed different ritual practices, depending on their clerical leadership. Strict prohibition of Chinese rites was only achieved in those communities (in Fujian) where the Dominicans and MEP exercised clerical control; many Jesuits and Franciscans continued to adhere to a modified form of Chinese rites, attempting to follow in Ricci's footsteps while obeying papal injunction. Kangxi himself avoided an open break with Christianity and continued to employ Jesuits and missionaries of other orders in imperial service. Definitive rupture was postponed until 1720/1. In 1715 Clement XI issued an apostolic constitution *Ex illa die*, which affirmed the decree of Tournon and forbade disobedience under any subterfuge. In strong language, the constitution prescribed excommunication for all recalcitrant clergy, and specifically admonished the Society of Jesus to obedience. The promulgation of this document in Beijing aroused anew the wrath of Kangxi. While submitting to papal authority, many missionaries feared the destruction of Christianity and appealed for revisions. To clarify papal intentions, Clement XI appointed Carlo Mezzabarba as new papal legate in 1719. In the course of many audiences with Kangxi in the winter of 1720/1, Mezzabarba's legation proved equally disastrous. Irked by inter-order rivalry, Kangxi dismissed Mezzabarba's mission as a replay of that of Tournon and Maigrot. Intolerant of ecclesiastical intervention in China, contemptuous of the presumption of Europeans to judge Chinese culture, the emperor rejected *Ex illa die*: "After reviewing this proclamation, one can only speak of western ignoranti, and not of Chinese principles. More-over, no European understands Chinese texts, and their arguments are often ludi-crous. Now I see that this proclamation by the envoy is merely similar to the teachings of Buddhist monks, Daoist priests, and heterodox sectarians. Nothing can be more ridiculous and nonsensical than this. Hereafter, westerners do not need to preach their teachings in China. It ought to be forbidden to prevent troubles" (Chen Yuan, *Kangxi*, p. 96).

Kangxi's wish to proscribe Christianity was enacted only in 1724 by his successor, the Yongzhen emperor, who was troubled by the conversion of some imperial clans-men, sons of Sunu, a major supporter of Yongzhen's rivals to the throne. Zealous local officials closed down churches, but on the whole Christianity suffered little repression under Yongzhen's reign (1724–35), the only exceptions being the exile of Sunu's sons, who became celebrated in Jesuit letters to Europe, and the strangu-lation of the Portuguese Jesuit João Mourão (1681–1726), adviser to two rival impe-rial princes executed by Yongzhen. Clearly, the emperor's motivation was political; Christianity as such mattered little, it was a religion "without harm or benefit." Nevertheless, the loss of imperial favor dealt a severe blow to Chinese Christianity. From a high of 200,000 in 1701, the number of converts dropped almost in half to an estimated figure of 120,000 in 1740. It would grow only slightly over the eigh-teenth century, when China's population more than doubled from 160 to 350 million. Far more significant was the changing social profile of conversion: with a few exceptions, elite conversions dried up. The French Jesuit Antoine Gaubil, who arrived in China in 1722, stated the deplorable fact: "We only baptize poor people. The literati and the well-placed who had wanted to become Christians abandoned us the moment we published the decrees by order of the Supreme Pontiff, even with the permissions [exceptions to Chinese rites granted by Mezzabarba in China but later repudiated by Rome] given by Messieur Patriarch Mezzabarba" (Gaubil, *Correspondance*, p. 128). Many observations in the letters and annual reports of the Jesuits attested to this new social profile of Chinese Christianity: a handful of offi-cials, few elites, literati limited to local gentry of lower and middling sorts, large majority of artisanal and peasant membership, and a geographical shift from urban centers (Beijing being an exception) to rural areas.

The third and fourth developments – the disenchantment of Europe and the Sinicization of the Christian Church – responded to the same logic: the official proscription of Christianity and recurrent waves of persecution. After 1724, the only European missionaries tolerated in the Qing Empire were courtiers in the service of the Yongzhen and Qianlong emperors (r. 1735–95); their presence assured tacit tol-eration for a small but flourishing Catholic community in the imperial capital. In the provinces, foreign missionaries were forbidden to reside. When discovered, officials imprisoned or exiled them to Macao. In 1746, however, zealous local and provincial officials in Fujian arrested five Spanish Dominican missionaries. Despite the Grand Council's instruction to expel the Europeans to Macao, the provincial governor, citing the law of prohibition, executed the five in 1747 and 1748. Also in 1748, betrayed by an apostate angry over clerical intervention in a property dispute, two Jesuits in Suzhou were arrested and executed. These first European martyrdoms in China shocked public opinion in Europe. After the 1740s European taste for Chinese modes began to turn sour: the *chinoiserie* craze in decorative arts and architecture subsided in a rising discourse of oriental despotism, a rhetoric strengthened by the anti-Christian persecutions in the Qing Empire.

The danger for European missionaries necessitated the employment of Chinese priests. Although a handful of Chinese scholars had joined the Society of Jesus during the early years of Catholic mission, their inferior theological education prevented them from advancing to the priesthood. The first Chinese Jesuit priest was ordained in Portugal in 1664: Zheng Weixin (1633–73, alias Manuel de Siqueira) left Macao in 1645 and was trained in Rome, Bologna, and Coimbra. A small number of Chinese Jesuits followed his footsteps to France and Italy and began to play an important role in the mission field after the 1720s. Unlike the Jesuits, the Dominicans strongly advocated the training of an indigenous clergy from the beginning; one of their own, Luo Wenzao (1617–91, alias Gregory Lopez), ordained in Manila, became the first Chinese bishop in 1685. Paradoxically, those religious orders least accommodating to Chinese culture – the Dominicans and the MEP – strongly supported the training of an indigenous clergy, with the latter setting up a seminary in Siam for the education of Chinese priests. After 1732, an ex-China missionary, Matteo Ripa, established the Collegio Cinesi (Holy Family College) in Naples under the auspices of the Propaganda Fide. While there were only four Chinese clerics against 86 Europeans in 1724, their numbers rose to 26 out of a total of 109 in 1739 and 44 out of 101 in 1765 (Standaert, *Handbook*, p. 308). By the end of the century, native clergy constituted the core of the Chinese Christian Church.

Sources and Historiography

Our brief chronological survey of the history of Christianity in China reveals the salient features of a historiography which, with notable exceptions, is based primarily on sources in western languages. Until the late 1980s, the story of Christianity in China had been told in two distinct modes: classic missiological studies, focusing on the work of religious orders, individual missionaries, liturgies, religious works, and persecutions; and Sinological studies that framed the Catholic mission in the perspective of Chinese culture and history.

The first group of studies characterized the work of church historians, many of them missionaries in China before 1949, some with good Sinological training. Analyzing the history of Christianity from within, as it were, this tradition of scholarship is responsible for the major collections of published sources, examples being the ongoing publication of sources on the Franciscan mission in China, the *Sinica Franciscana* (9 volumes in 14 books covering the sixteenth century to 1698, published between 1933 and 1997) and Pasquale D'Elia's impressive edition of Matteo Ricci's original diaries. Ricci himself is the subject of many monographs, of which the biography by Henri Bernard, S.J. (1937) is still outstanding. Individual and group biographies of missionaries constituted a large output of scholarship. There are studies of particular groups of Jesuits by time period and nationalities: Dunne's work on Jesuits of the late Ming and Duteil's study of French Jesuits. There are detailed biographies of individual Jesuits: on Pereira, Bouvet, Stumpf, Schall, Verbiest, Thomas, and Laimbeckhoven, among others. For the Dominicans we find studies on Domingo Navarrete, the fierce critic of Jesuit accommodation, Gregory Lopez, and the martyrs of 1747/8. Franciscan historiography has produced many shorter studies of the

Italian, Spanish, and German friars in China, including the one Mexican missionary, Pedro de la Piñuela, who composed influential works in Chinese. Other religious orders also produced studies of missionaries of their orders, even though the sheer volume of Jesuit historiography has dominated the field.

Another focus of this approach is on liturgy. Understandably, much of the scholarship has centered on the Chinese rites controversy, both because of its importance for the history of the Chinese Christian Church and on account of the enormous volume of extant sources. Jesuit historiography has been particularly active in this field: the work of Francis A. Rouleau and George Minamiki represents pioneering studies that are by no means exhaustive; and the Ricci Institute at the University of San Francisco houses a large collection of materials devoted to this topic.

Related to the rites controversy, the diplomatic relations between Rome and Beijing have been the subject of studies by Antonio S. Rosso in English and Luo Kuang in Chinese, but the key figure of Tournon has yet to receive a critical full-length treatment. On the interesting subject of Catholic liturgy and sacraments in the early modern Chinese context, some preliminary work has been done on the 1615 papal concession of a Chinese-language liturgy (never practiced and later withdrawn), but we know very little of the actual sacramental practices, especially among the rural Christian communities.

The subject of Christian martyrdom is the focus of several fine monographs: González's source edition and study of the Dominican martyrs of 1747/8, Willeke's study of the 1784–5 persecutions under Qianlong, and Zhang Ze's survey of persecutions of Christianity under the Qing between 1724 and 1842 (when proscription was rescinded after China's defeat in the Opium War). The first two of these studies rely on European and missionary sources, while Zhang's book is drawn primarily from Chinese-language Qing government records and Chinese Catholic sources.

As a couple of Chinese studies cited above reflect, the internalist or church-historical approach is by no means limited to western works. Although far fewer in volume, a distinct Chinese Catholic historiography has made substantial contributions. The major themes are echoed in this tradition as well: Fang Hao's three-volume biography of leading Chinese Catholics (1973), Luo Kuang's study of papal–Qing diplomacy, and Zhang's study of persecutions. A longstanding tradition of local church history, biographies of Chinese Catholics, editions of Chinese Catholic sources, and a general reliance on both Catholic and state sources in Chinese give these works a distinct flavor. Interrupted after 1949, this tradition within church history has focused more recently on translations from western works, both from documents and studies.

The second approach to this scholarship before the late 1980s was undertaken by Sinologists. Naturally, there existed points of overlap between the missiological/ecclesiastical history mode and Sinological studies, since many missionaries were Sinologists and the field owed its origins to the Catholic mission (especially the Jesuits). Not surprisingly, a lay scholar of literature such as René Etiemble, author of books on the Chinese rites controversy and Chinese cultural impact on Europe, held the Jesuits in high esteem. This evaluation was shared by historians of China who represented the Jesuits as cultural pioneers and heroes, an eminent example being Jonathan Spence's interpretation of Ricci. Still, other Sinologists took exception to the Jesuit contribution. Jacques Gernet's 1982 classic, *Chine et Christianisme* (English translation 1985), argued for fundamental differences between Chinese, or more precisely Confucian, philosophy and Christianity, and faulted the Jesuits for intellectual dissimulation. Less critical than Gernet perhaps, the Dutch Sinologist Erik Zürcher compared Catholic conversion to the spread of Buddhism in early medieval China, and came away with a negative assessment of the long-term impact of the Jesuits. Still another approach in Sinology before the 1980s concentrated on the reception of China in early modern Europe, as exemplified by the research of David Mungello.

In Chinese-language historiography of the late Ming and early Qing, the interest in Christianity has been very limited outside of Chinese Catholic circles. For one, the question of foreign missionaries was bound up with the study of western colonialism and imperialism after 1842; and much effort in China and Taiwan went into the analysis of *jiao-an*, the hundreds of cases concerning litigational disputes and conflicts between Christians and Chinese between 1842 and 1900. However, Chinese historians are viewing the precolonial period in a more favorable light; they praise early Jesuits as bearers of western science and technology to China, a topic that continues to hold the interest of Chinese historians.

With both the missiological and Sinological approaches still active, a new energy has animated the historiography of early modern Chinese Christianity after the late 1980s. Three features are characteristic. First, a new generation of scholars in Europe and China is posing new questions and offering fresh perspectives. Instead of privileging the view of the missionaries and relying on western sources, new studies focus on the experience of the Chinese converts. Instead of asking how Matteo Ricci persuaded and converted the Chinese literati, these historians analyze the presence of the Jesuits through the lenses of Chinese society. A groundbreaking work was the 1988 study of Yang Tingyun (one of the Three Pillars of the early Chinese Church, in the words of Ricci) by Nicolas Standaert, a Jesuit and Sinologist, who analyzed the range of Yang's intellectual and spiritual experiences and followed Yang's conversion from Buddhism to Christianity. Another scholar is the Chinese historian Lin Jinshui, who tried to reconstruct the literati networks around Ricci and Giuglio Aleni, an Italian Jesuit hailed as a western sage and worthy successor to Ricci. Still another example is Mungello's book on the Chinese Christians of Hangzhou, focusing on Zhang Xingyao (1633–1715), one of the few Chinese literati active in publishing Christian works at the end of the seventeenth century. Besides correcting the Eurocentric and sacerdotalist view of traditional scholarship, these recent studies help us to understand the effectiveness of the early Jesuit mission. The translation and publication of scientific works, the preparation and printing of Chinese-language religious works, and the persona of Jesuits as western sages all resulted from collaboration. These were not so much the achievements of "a generation of giants" as the products of a novel and creative interaction between two intellectual elites in a specific historical setting of cultural curiosity and consciousness of crisis.

Interest in the Chinese collaborators goes beyond the small circle of literati converts, for the Jesuits enjoyed a much broader network of friends, wellwishers, and acquaintances, exalted officials and famous literati who discussed metaphysics and moral ethics, wrote prefaces to Jesuit books, and opened social and political doors without actually accepting the religious message of Christianity. The actual research into the Chinese dimension of Christianity, at least at the elite level, has been made possible by several key publications of Chinese-language Catholic works.

Altogether, European missionaries and Chinese converts composed more than 600 works in Chinese up to the mid-eighteenth century. The majority of these books were printed before 1700; some three-quarters were authored by European missionaries, with the Jesuits in a predominant position. In addition to some 120 texts on the sciences and geography of the West, the rest comprised compositions or translations on spiritual, moral, and liturgical subjects. Whereas scientific and philosophical texts tended to dominate in the first 50 years of Chinese Catholic printing, books for religious use (catechisms, prayer books, devotional treatises, handbooks on sacraments, etc.) made up the majority of titles by the end of the seventeenth century. Although all religious orders published Christian works in Chinese, the Jesuits were the only ones engaged in the production of scientific texts.

Until the late 1990s, the only collection of Chinese-language Catholic sources easily accessible was at the Bibliothèque de France (Division of Oriental Manuscripts). Thanks to recent publications, two further collections have been made accessible to research. Rome holds a significant deposit of Chinese Catholic works, primarily at the Historical Archives of the Society of Jesus and at the Vatican Library. A 2001 descriptive catalogue by Albert Chan, S.J., describes the Chinese works in the Jesuit collection, of which 500 date from the late Ming and early Qing. In 2002, Nicolas Standaert and Ad Dudink published 100 selected documents from this collection in 12 volumes. Also of note is the 1996 published collection of selected works from the former Jesuit Library at Zikawei (Shanghai), which represented the most important collection of its kind in pre-1949 China. A small portion of the library and some of the most valuable books were shipped out of China before the communist takeover and eventually found their way to Taiwan. The 1996 collection assembled 24 works from the late Ming to the mid-Qing; the entirety of this collection is accessible today on CD-Rom at the Institute of History and Philology at the Academia Sinica.

Using hitherto neglected or inaccessible Chinese sources has given a new burst of energy to research in the field. The writings by Standaert and Dudink mentioned above continue, albeit in an invigorated way, the Sinological and missiological traditions. A novel element, however, consists in the interests of Chinese scholars from a non-Christian tradition, such as Han Qi, Huang Yilong, Zhu Pingyi, and Li Tiangang who, since the 1990s, have published works on the scientific and cultural significance of the Catholic mission and on the Chinese rites controversy.

Without doubt, the intense interest in this corpus of Chinese Catholic works will yield yet more insights into the history of Christianity. Nevertheless, these printed and manuscript books provide few answers to the actual religious practices on the ground, especially in the lower social milieux. Compared to Dominican and Franciscan sources, the vast quantity of Jesuit documentation is still relatively underexplored. For example, the well-known collection *Lettres édifiantes et curieuses* published by the French Jesuits in the eighteenth century contains a wealth of information, but very few annual reports (*Litterae Annuae*), which give more precise information and often telling episodes, are actually published and analyzed. There is still a vast amount of information to be mined from the Historical Archives of the Society of Jesus in Rome; and copies from the collection of Jesuit documents of the Portuguese viceprovince in China, deposited at the Bibliotheca Ajuda in Lisbon, have formed the basis for the recent work of Liam Brockey, whose analysis shows the richness of the Ajuda collection. In the remaining pages of this chapter, I would like to outline some of the more interesting current topics of research and indicate areas that need more attention.

Themes

Missionaries

Even though this is the most thoroughly researched topic in the field, we still do not know the exact number of missionaries working in China during the entire period under consideration. We do know, however, the magnitude of missionaries working in selected years, with the peak years being 1700–6 (the numbers were 122, 153, and 148, respectively). Among the religious orders, information on the Jesuits is most detailed. Dehergne gives a figure of 563 Jesuits who left Europe for China between 1583 and 1723. Some worked in India, Southeast Asia, or Japan primarily; others died en route. Excluding these Jesuits, Pascale Girard comes up with a revised figure of 288 Jesuits actually in the China mission for the same period. A breakdown of the main nationalities shows the following order of predominance: Portuguese (129), French (58), Italian (56), Spanish (16), Belgians (15), German and Austrian (13) (Girard, *Religiosos Ocidentais*, pp. 172–3).

Until the dissolution of the Society of Jesus in 1772, its missionaries dominated the China mission. Except for the earliest period (1583–1630), when they represented an exclusive clerical presence in China, the Jesuits comprised between 50 and 80 percent of all missionaries. The Franciscans and Dominicans occupy second and third place in the numerical ranking, followed by roughly equal numbers of Augustinians, Missions Étrangères priests, and Propaganda Fide missionaries. Of all the non-European mission fields, China represented the region with the most diverse representation of religious orders and nationalities, and where the indigenous clergy played a significant role in the eighteenth century.

National rivalries played a crucial role in the conflict between Dominicans and Jesuits, and between the Portuguese vice-province and the French Jesuit mission. There is likewise scholarship on the European dimension of the Chinese rites controversy, located principally in the Jansenist hostility toward the Society in France. Less work has been done on the different formation and outlook of European missionaries in the seventeenth and eighteenth centuries – with the notable exception of Brockey's work on the Portuguese Jesuits – which had an important bearing on the perception of Chinese culture.

Converts

Except for the *Litterae Annuae* from the eighteenth century with precise figures of Christians, the number of converts can only be estimated in a general order. Standaert has evaluated the different figures and charted an approximate picture of steady growth from 1583 to 1690, with a golden period between 1690 and 1710 (ca. 200,000), followed by a substantial decline to ca. 120,000 by 1740 and slow and sporadic recovery thereafter.

As for the social profile of Chinese Christianity, again the general picture is clear enough. Catholicism reached the highest social level during 1600 to 1650: the conversion of officials and literati in the late Ming was followed by success among eunuchs, court noblewomen, and one Southern Ming emperor in the period of Manchu conquest. This ephemeral success nourished the Jesuit hope for a Chinese Constantine and redirected their effort during the early Qing dynasty toward the imperial throne. Apart from a couple of conversions among imperial Manchu clansmen in the eighteenth century, this imperial strategy remained unsuccessful, as we have seen. The persona of the missionaries, especially that of the Jesuits, was transformed in the course of the seventeenth century from western sage and European Christian-Confucian into servant of the imperial household under the Manchu. While giving the Jesuits some political patronage, this restricted their role in China and provoked more criticisms in Europe.

By the late seventeenth century, the Confucian literati class as a whole had become indifferent or hostile toward Christianity. The climate of crisis and spiritual vacuum among the intellectual elites in the late Ming was replaced by one of self-confidence and orthodoxy. Under the Qing emperors, the Chinese Confucian elites in the mandarinate and the gentry often opposed foreign missionaries, who enjoyed better relations with the Manchu nobility. Converts among the literati and gentry elites were limited to those with lower examination degrees. While several of them published works defending the Christian-Confucian synthesis, none exerted more than a local influence.

From the beginning commoners constituted the numerical majority of converts. Until the arrival of the mendicants, this concerned mostly the urban lower classes, as the Jesuits concentrated their work in the cities. During the seventeenth century, the Catholic mission penetrated deeper into the interior provinces and branched out to smaller towns and villages. Documents seldom mentioned the specific profession of commoners, but by the eighteenth century, especially after the Chinese rites controversy, missionary sources occasionally named the presence of boatmen, charcoal workers, and peasants in their writings. There seemed to have been a distinct social profile between the older established Christian centers in Jiangnan and Fujian on the coast, regions with dense urban networks, often retaining a gentry leadership, and the newer, interior communities with a predominantly lower-class profile.

There remains much work to be done. A key question that has yet to be answered is the role of kinship networks in the spread and maintenance of Christianity, especially in periods of persecution and clerical absence. Also, the role of women in Chinese Christianity deserves more attention. Adjusting to the sexual regime of early modern Chinese society, the missionaries established separate churches and held separate masses for the sexes, in order to avoid scandal. The only female testimony is a laudatory portrait of Candida Hu, the granddaughter of Paul Xu Guangqi, written by the Belgian Jesuit Philippe Couplet and translated into several European languages. Her biography describes the indispensable role of women leaders in the life of a household Catholicism centered on prayers, religious rituals, and works of charity. Unlike Buddhist monasticism, early modern Christianity did not create a niche for pious women outside of the patriarchal household. In one specific area, however, the Christian mission challenged the social status quo: in its insistence of monogamy and condemnation of concubinage, European Christianity confronted an elite morality that prized filial piety (and the responsibility to produce male heirs) above marital-sexual propriety. This would prove an enduring obstacle to the conversion of the elites during the Ming and Qing dynasties.

Christianity and Chinese Religions

Ricci classified the Chinese into three sects, using the meaning of *sectarii*, or followers of a teaching: the followers of Buddha, Dao, and the sect of the literati. His rudimentary "religious sociology" was augmented later by the encounter with Islam and Judaism in China. Subsequent missionaries (almost all Jesuits, as the other religious orders showed little or no interest in indigenous religions) followed Ricci's schemata, thereby giving perhaps an undue cultic emphasis to Confucianism. As I have mentioned above, Ricci and his literati collaborators created a Christian-Confucian synthesis: the ancient Chinese worshipped a monotheistic God, whose presence left traces in the ancient classics; over time, especially with the corrupting influence of idolatrous Buddhism and materialist neo-Confucianism, this knowledge of the true God was lost, but the Jesuit mission restored the knowledge of the true God and the correct interpretation of the ancient classics. This conversion strategy underlay the collective effort to introduce Confucianism to Europe in several pivotal translations of Confucian canonical books in the late seventeenth century. However, under attack for their cultural accommodation and faced with declining literati interest, the Jesuits, while not exactly repudiating this conversion strategy, generally abandoned it during the eighteenth century with the exceptions of the Figurists, several French Jesuits who pursued a Quixotic (and condemned) intellectual effort to find hidden prophecies in the *Yijing* (Book of Changes) and in ancient Chinese characters.

The Christian attitude toward Judaism and Islam was unambivalent. The latter represented an enemy, albeit not dangerous, on account of its low social esteem in China, and elicited few comments. Judaism, on the other hand, fascinated several generations of Jesuits. Ricci himself encountered and converted several Chinese Jews in Beijing; over the course of the seventeenth and early eighteenth centuries, the Jesuits paid at least two visits to the Jewish community at Kaifeng. There was even a plan to collect and ship all Jewish antiquities to Europe under the sponsorship of an imperial prince, a plan that came to naught.

Christianity's relationship with the two officially recognized indigenous cults – Daoism and Buddhism – changed over time from combat and competition to indifference. In the initial years of the mission, the Jesuits struggled to create a distinct identity and clarify mistaken attributes: they repudiated Daoist alchemy, explained the differences between Buddhist and Christian fasting, and insisted on the complete incompatibility between the true Christian and the false Buddhist beliefs, often to the incomprehension of their Chinese interlocutors. Daoism represented a less prominent competitor for Christian missionaries, who generally dismissed its magical and esoteric orientations. Buddhism, however, was a different matter. As the most popular religion in China since the ninth century, Buddhism enjoyed not only a distinguished tradition but a large canon of texts. In the mid-sixteenth century, Buddhism experienced an impressive revival, winning substantial imperial patronage, gentry sponsorship of monastic renewal, and attracting men of high intellectual caliber into the Buddhist priesthood. Some of these leading Buddhist monks met and debated with

Ricci; some exchanged polemical writings with him. The hostility between Buddhism and Christianity was provoked entirely by the early Jesuit missionaries, especially by Ricci, in the effort to establish a distinct Christian identity in the minds of the literati. Works of polemics were published between 1600 and 1640, with laymen of both beliefs joining in the fray. Fascinating from the perspective of intellectual encounter, this Christian–Buddhist polemic never approximated the bitterness of Protestant–Catholic polemic in Europe and died away after 1640. By the end of the seventeenth century, even if Chinese converts still criticized the false teachings of Buddha, the European missionaries became indifferent to a cult that seemed socially inferior and politically ineffectual in the Qing empire.

A far more perplexing question was the relationship with popular Chinese religions. Syncretistic and highly amorphous, folk beliefs in China assumed a political liability in the sixteenth century with the creation of millenarian sects based on Buddhist doctrines of karma and reincarnation and Daoist esoteric rituals. Dismissed under the categorical label of White Lotus Sect by the Confucian state, popular religious cults shared certain common characteristics: they were created and transmitted by charismatic cult leaders, frequently by family or kinship succession; they produced and transmitted religious texts, the so-called precious scrolls (*baojuan*) that often contained millenarian prophecies; they attracted adherents almost exclusively from the lower classes, many of whom were mobile in their work (migrant farmers, charcoal burners, boatmen, soldiers); they operated outside of the framework of Confucian orthodoxy and represented a potential challenge to the political and social order built on Confucian loyalties; female deities and women sometimes played the central roles in these cults.

Concurrent with the consolidation of Christianity in the early seventeenth century, the first of many sectarian uprisings broke out in northern China. Defending Christianity as distinct from these heterodox popular sects, Yang Tingyun and Xu Guangqi argued for the elite status of Christianity and its message of loyalty to the state and social order. Although repeated by subsequent generations of converts and missionaries, this defense never completely absolved Christianity of the suspicion of sedition because of its foreign origins. As converts came increasingly only from the lower strata of society, there were examples of infiltration of Christian communities by popular heterodox sectarians, who appropriated Christian rituals and doctrines for their own purposes. Some research into this question has been undertaken, but a more systematic investigation of the sources is necessary before we can come up with answers that would illuminate the nature of Christian conversion among the commoners, and the complex relationship between ritual and magic in folk beliefs.

Europe and China

One last area of research takes us back to the larger picture: the Christian mission in China formed part of the history of the early modern world. As Johann Mayer's work at the beginning of this chapter well testifies, the Catholic mission outside of Europe was part of the contest between Tridentine Catholicism and Protestantism for the mantle of true Christian apostleship. Besides the Iberian monarchies and their support of world Catholicism, the French monarchy, the Holy Roman Empire, and the German Catholic princes, especially the Wittelsbach dynasty, gave substantial financial backing to the China mission in the seventeenth and eighteenth centuries. And as late as 1757, the Jesuit mission still fueled the Protestant–Catholic polemic in the Holy Roman Empire, as Florian Bahr excoriated the Protestant Church historian Johann Lorenz Mossheim for his depiction of the Jesuit mission in China.

Embedded in the maritime empires of Portugal, Spain, and France, the history of Christianity constituted simultaneously the history of the early modern world. Ships from half a dozen European nations carried missionaries, envoys, converts, books, money, and scientific equipment across the oceans. Bills of exchange conveyed donations from Catholic Europe halfway around the world; and Jesuit letters portrayed heroic martyrs and cruel pagans to the imagination of European readers. Unlike the tender implant of Christianity in Mongol China during the thirteenth century, the Jesuit mission inaugurated a new era in the history of Chinese Christianity and in Sino-western relations.

BIBLIOGRAPHY

Bernard, H., *Le P. Matthieu Ricci et la société chinoise de son temps (1552–1610)*, 2 vols. Tientsin: Hautes Études, 1937.

Bontinck, F., *La Lutte autour de la liturgie chinoise aux XVIIe et XVIIIe siècles*. Louvain: Nauwelaerts, 1962.

Brockey, L. M., "Harvest of the Vine: The Jesuit Missionary Enterprise in China, 1575–1710," PhD dissertation, Brown University, 2002.

Chan, A., *Chinese Books and Documents in the Jesuit Archives in Rome: A Descriptive Catalogue*. Armonk, NY and London: M. E. Sharpe, 2002.

Chen Yuan, ed., *Kangxi yu Luoma shijie guanxi wenshu yingyin ben* (1932). Reprinted in *Zhongguo shixue congshu xubian*, 23. Taipei: Xuesheng shuju, 1973.

Criveller, G., *Preaching Christ in Late Ming China: The Jesuits' Presentation of Christ from Matteo Ricci to Giulio Aleni*. Taipei: Ricci Institute, 1997.

Cummins, J. S., *A Question of Rites: Friar Domingo Navarrete and the Jesuits in China*. Aldershot: Scolar Press, 1993.

Dehergne, J., "Les Chrétientés de Chine de la période Ming, 1581–1650," *Monumenta Serica*, 16 (1957), pp. 1–136.

Dehergne, J., *Répertoire des Jésuites de Chine de 1552 à 1800*. Rome and Paris: Institutum Historicum Societatis Iesu/Letouzey & Ané, 1973.

Dunne, G. H., *Generations of Giants: The Story of the Jesuits in China in the Last Decades of the Ming Dynasty*. South Bend, Ind.: University of Notre Dame Press, 1962.

Duteil, J.-P., *Le Mandat du Ciel: Le rôle des Jésuites en Chine*. Paris: Éditions Arguments, 1994.

Etiemble, R., *Les Jésuites en Chine: La Querelle des Rites 1552–1773*. Paris: Julliard-Gallimard, 1966.

Etiemble, R., *L'Europe chinoise*, 2 vols. Paris: Gallimard, 1988, 1989.

Fang Hao, *Zhongguo tianzhujiao shi renwu zhuan*, 3 vols. Hong Kong/Taizhong: Gongjiao zhenli hui/Guangqi, 1973.

Gaubil, A., *Correspondance de Pékin 1722–1759*, ed. Renée Simon. Geneva: Droz, 1970.

Gernet, J., *China and the Christian Impact*. Cambridge: Cambridge University Press, 1985.

Girard, P., *Os Religiosos Ocidentais na China na Época moderna*. Macao: Fundação Macáu, 1999.

González, J. M., *Historia de las Misiones Dominicanas de China*. Vol. 1: *1632–1700*; vol. 2: *1700–1800*. Madrid: Juan Bravo, 1962, 1964.

Han Qi, *Zhongguo kexue jishu de xichuan jiqi yingxiang.* Shijiazhuang: Hebei Remin chuban-she, 1999.

Hsia, R. Po-chia, "Mission und Konfessionalisierung in Übersee: Die Chinamission und das Heilige Römische Reich," in Wolfgang Reinhard and Heinz Schilling, eds., *Katholische Konfessionalisierung.* Münster: Aschendorff, 1995, pp. 114–19.

Huang Yilong, "Ming Qing tianzhujiao zai Shanxi Jiangzhou de fazhan ji qi fantan," *Zhongyang yanjiuyuan jindaishi yanjiusuo jikan*, 26 (1996), pp. 3–39.

King, G., "Couplet's Biography of Madame Candida Xu (1607–1680)", *Sino-Western Cultural Relations Journal*, 18 (1996), pp. 41–56.

Lancashire, D., "Anti-Christian Polemics in 17th-Century China," *Church History*, 38 (1969), pp. 218–41.

Lin Jinshui, "Ai Rulüe yu Fujian shidafu jiaoyou biao," *Zhongwai guanxishi luncong*, 5 (1996), pp. 182–202.

Lin Jinshui, *Li Madou yu Zhongguo.* Beijing: Zhongguo she hui ke xue chubanshe, 1996.

Li Tiangang, *Zhongguo liyi zhi zheng: Lishi, wenxian he yiyi.* Shanghai: Guji chubanshe, 1998.

Luo Kuang, *Jiao Ting yu Zhongguo shi jie shi.* Taipei: Zhuanji wenxue chubanshe, 1962.

Minamiki, G., *The Chinese Rites Controversy from its Beginning to Modern Times.* Chicago: Chicago University Press, 1985.

Mungello, D. E., *Curious Land: Jesuit Accommodation and the Origins of Sinology.* Stuttgart: F. Steiner, 1985.

Mungello, D. E., ed., *The Chinese Rites Controversy: Its History and Meaning.* Nettetal: Steyler, 1994.

Mungello, D. E., *The Forgotton Christians of Hangzhou.* Honolulu: University of Hawaii Press, 1994.

Noll, R. R. and Sure, D. F., eds., *100 Roman Documents Concerning the Chinese Rites Controversy (1645–1941).* San Francisco: Ricci Institute, 1992.

Peterson, W. J., "Learning from Heaven: The Introduction of Christianity and Other Western Ideas into Late Ming China," in D. Twitchett and F. W. Mote, eds., *The Cambridge History of China: The Ming Dynasty 1368–1644*, part 2. Cambridge: Cambridge University Press, 1998, pp. 789–839.

Ronan, C. E. and Oh, B. B. C., eds., *East Meets West: The Jesuits in China, 1582–1773.* Chicago: Loyola University Press, 1982.

Ross, A. C., *A Vision Betrayed: The Jesuits in Japan and China, 1542–1742.* Maryknoll, NY: Orbis Books, 1994.

Rosso, A. S., *Apostolic Legations to China: 18th Century.* South Pasadena: P. D. and I. Perkins, 1948.

Rouleau, F. A., "Chinese Rites Controversy," in *New Catholic Encyclopedia*, Washington, DC: Catholic University of America Press, 1967, vol. 3, pp. 611–17.

Rule, P. A., *K'ung-tzu or Confucius? The Jesuit Interpretation of Confucianism.* Sydney: Allen & Unwin, 1986.

Spence, J. D., *The Memory Palace of Matteo Ricci.* London and Boston: Faber, 1985.

Standaert, N., *Yang Tingyun, Confucian and Christian in Late Ming China: His Life and Thought.* Leiden: Brill, 1988.

Standaert, N., "New Trends in the Historiography of Christianity in China," *Catholic Historical Review*, 83/4 (1997), pp. 573–613.

Standaert, N., ed., *Handbook of Christianity in China.* Vol. 1: *635–1800.* Leiden: Brill, 2001.

Standaert, N. and Dudink, A., eds., *Chinese Christian Texts from the Roman Archives of the Society of Jesus*, 12 vols. Taipei: Ricci Institute, 2002.

Standaert, N., Dudink, A., Huang Yilong, and Zhu Pingyi, eds., *Chinese Christian Texts from the Zikawei Library*, 5 vols. Taipei: Fujen University, Faculty of Theology, 1996.

Uhalley, S. and Xiaoxin Wu, eds., *China and Christianity: Burdened Past, Hopeful Future.* Armonk, NY: M. E. Sharpe, 2001.

Wang Xiaochao, *Christianity and Imperial Culture: Chinese Christian Apologetics in the Seventeenth Century and their Latin Patristic Equivalent.* Leiden: Brill, 1998.

Willeke, B. H., *Imperial Government and Catholic Missions in China during the Years 1784–1785.* New York: Bonaventura, 1948.

Zhang Ze, *Qingdai jinjiao qi de Tianzhujiao.* Taipei: Guangqi chubanshe, 1992.

Zhu Pingyi, "Shenti, linghun yu tianzhu: Ming mo Qing chu xixue zhong de renti shengli zhishi," *Xinshixue*, 7 (1996), pp. 47–98.

Zürcher, E., "Bouddhisme et christianisme," in *Bouddhisme, christianisme et société chinoise (Conférences, essais et leçons du Collège de France)*, Paris: Julliard, 1990.

Zürcher, E., "Confucian and Christian Religiosity in Late Ming China," *Catholic Historical Review*, 83/4 (1997), pp. 614–53.

FURTHER READING

The best place to start is volume 1 of the *Handbook of Christianity in China*, edited by Nicolas Standaert, which brings together contributions by 20 authors covering a wide range of subjects. There is a good presentation of sources, historiography, and current state of knowledge. Absolute beginners may wish to read Andrew C. Ross, *A Vision Betrayed*, a succinct and well-balanced account by a church historian outside of the field. Jonathan Spence's *The Memory Palace of Matteo Ricci* is a good read and scholarly introduction to the life of the China mission pioneer. A large amount of published sources is available. For documents translated into English, see Matteo Ricci, *The True Meaning of the Lord of Heaven (T'ien-chu Shih-I)*, translated by Douglas Lancashire and Peter Hu Kuo-chen (1985), and the website of the Ricci Institute, University of San Francisco (www.usfca.edu/ricci/), with resource links to bibliographical and biographical databases connected with the history of Christianity in China.

TWENTY-THREE

A Mission Interrupted: Japan

MICHAEL COOPER

The history of Christianity in Japan during the sixteenth and seventeenth centuries offers an instructive case study of missiology. At that time, missionaries laboring in undeveloped societies in Asia and Latin America were often closely associated with Iberian colonialism and the two enterprises, religious and military, generally worked in tandem. Both Japan and then China greatly differed from the territories previously evangelized, for these two nations were too powerful, developed, and remote to allow the possibility of armed intervention, and thus missionaries had no colonial support to fall back on in time of need. A new approach was therefore called for, although it is probable that few Europeans in Japan were fully aware of this need and the urgency of its implementation.

The case of Japan shows a break from traditional missionary methods employed in India, Africa, and Latin America, yet at the same time falling short of the high degree of cultural and social adaptation later achieved in China. It represented, so to speak, the halfway mark in the development of missiological thought and practice, retaining some traditional elements but also incorporating new and untried ideas; it was a mixture of the old and new, the tried and untried. The missionary history of Japan, therefore, marks a turning point, the beginning of a new approach toward spreading among Asians a religious message that had been nurtured and developed in Europe and was now to be preached to sophisticated people unfamiliar with western values and thought. The fact that this enterprise came to a violent end after less than a century of endeavor was due more to political and social factors in Japan than to an intrinsic failure of missionary policy. Circumstances in China and Japan differed considerably, and even had the Jesuits in Japan acted in the same way as their confrères later did in China, the prevailing political reality would still have brought their best efforts to eventual failure. It may perhaps be argued that the insular Japanese were not ready or willing to embrace such a fundamentally alien way of thought, which some saw as inherently incompatible with deep-seated values and traditions.

The Beginning

The first recorded arrival of Europeans in Japan occurred by chance when in 1543 a storm blew a Chinese junk on to the small island of Tanegashima, located south of Kyushu, one of the main islands of Japan. At that time Portugal and Spain were the leading European maritime powers in Asia, and merchants and sailors of both nations were to be found throughout the region. On board this vessel were three Portuguese traders, credited with being the first Europeans to set foot on Japanese soil. News of their fortuitous discovery of Marco Polo's legendary island of Zipangu spread rapidly in trading circles in Asia. Within a few years Portuguese merchant vessels were calling in at Japan, thus inaugurating the era of European–Japanese relations that was to last for a century.

Japan at that time was in an unstable state of intermittent warfare waged by rival territorial barons, or daimyo, who strove to increase their holdings by violence and treachery. In earlier ages the emperor, residing in the capital at Kyoto, ruled the country through regional governors, but his authority had long since been relegated to the realms of religion and court ceremonial. For centuries a military commander, or shogun, had administered the country, nominally in the emperor's name, but eventually his authority had also diminished and his rule did not extend beyond the metropolitan region. During its prolonged era of civil wars, Japan was torn by military conflict. Describing this period, a Jesuit missionary wrote in 1565 with pardonable exaggeration, "There are sixty-six kingdoms [in Japan], but not even four of them enjoy peace" (*Cartas*, vol. 1, f. 193).

For Iberians, accustomed to strong monarchical rule, this was indeed a strange state of affairs, and at first glance the political and social instability might hardly seem to have been conducive for successful Portuguese trade. But the volatile situation had some advantages, for in the absence of central authority, no one had the power to forbid the entrance of foreigners nationwide (as was to happen later in China). If a local ruler proved inhospitable to European visitors, then they could, and did, transfer their custom to another area where they might receive a more congenial reception. In addition, constant warfare created a demand for wealth to finance armies and buy weapons, and commerce with the Portuguese proved to be highly profitable for both Europeans and Japanese alike. Territorial rulers therefore made efforts to attract foreign traders to their domains and generally accorded them a tolerant welcome. An illustration of the local benefits to be obtained by their arrival may be seen in Hirado in 1550. When a Portuguese ship docked in that remote part of Kyushu, wealthy merchants from Kyoto, Hakata, Sakai, and other large cities converged on the port to examine and purchase its cargo (Schurhammer, *Francis Xavier*, p. 137).

Traditionally the Chinese have always coveted silver more than gold, and this the Japanese could provide in abundance. On their part, the Japanese were eager to obtain superior Chinese raw silk. Ideally the two countries could exchange these two commodities directly, but the pillaging of Chinese coastal communities by pirate crews consisting of Japanese and other nationalities had prompted the mainland government to break off relations with Japan and forbid trade between the two countries. This prohibition was highly advantageous for the Portuguese, who utilizing their large merchant vessels acted profitably as middlemen by exchanging Chinese silk for Japanese silver.

Catholic missionaries first arrived in Japan in August 1549 when Francis Xavier (1506–52) and two Jesuit companions sailed into the port of Kagoshima and started evangelization. (Protestant missionary activity did not begin in the country until the nineteenth century.) Yajirō, a fugitive samurai, had met Xavier in Malacca in 1547 and had assured the priest that his countrymen would readily accept Christianity if only missionaries would teach them the faith. Encouraged by this optimistic claim, Xavier, a founder member of the Society of Jesus, or the Jesuit religious order, had left his work in India to convert the fabled island of Zipangu.

As the unstable conditions in Japan aided the Iberian merchants, so to some extent it also helped the first missionaries. Eager to attract lucrative Portuguese trade, which with some justification they associated with the newly arrived Jesuits, some Kyushu barons welcomed Xavier and his companions, and granted them permission to preach in their territories. Xavier faced formidable obstacles, for he had to rely on the poorly educated Yajirō as interpreter and translator, and within a short time the priest made an ill-informed decision that had an indirect effect for years to come. He was told that the Buddhist deity Dainichi was three-in-one, and so when compiling a cate-chism of Christian doctrine, translated with questionable accuracy into Japanese, Xavier proclaimed that the Christian God was none other than Dainichi and was to be called by that name. This was a grievous error, for whatever else Dainichi may be, he most certainly has nothing in common with the Christian deity. In his audience with the daimyo in Yamaguchi, Xavier explained that he had come from India to preach the religion of Dainichi, thus inadvertently giving the impression that he belonged to an Indian sect of Buddhism. As a result the missionaries were granted the use of a temple to promulgate "the law of the Buddha" (Schurhammer, *Francis Xavier*, p. 220).

Within a matter of months Xavier realized his error and no longer exhorted his listeners to worship Dainichi, for which he substituted the adapted Latin term *Deusu*. His mistake may have been short-lived, yet its effect persisted throughout the history of the Japanese mission. For later missionaries, despite their commendable efforts of adaptation in other areas, played it safe by employing Latin and Portuguese words, suitably adapted to Japanese pronunciation, to express Christian terms. In addition to *Deusu*, for example, "angel" and "sacrament" were rendered *angeru* and *sakura-mento*. This cautious policy may well have avoided preconceived notions embodied in Buddhist terms, but it inevitably introduced a foreign note into their teaching. Here we may contrast this policy with that of their colleagues who later worked in China, where they strove to express their teaching in wholly Chinese terms.

Despite the problems facing the first three missionaries, their work met with some success, partly perhaps owing to Xavier's patent zeal and charisma, although, unable to speak Japanese, he appears to have had little understanding of the political reali-ties of Japan. Thus in midwinter 1550 he set out on an arduous journey to the capital with a twofold purpose in mind – to meet the emperor and obtain permission to preach throughout the entire country, and to visit the "university" near Kyoto, in reality the Buddhist monastic complex on Mt. Hiei, to engage in religious discus-sion. As regards Xavier's first objective, any educated Japanese could have informed him of its futility for the powerless emperor resided obscurely in his palace, seldom seen except by court nobles. Even in the unlikely event of his granting an audience to the impoverished foreigner and allowing his petition, it would have been to no avail as the imperial writ did not extend beyond the confines of the ruined capital. Before setting out for Kyoto, Xavier had in fact been advised by the Yamaguchi daimyo, well versed in political matters, not to make the journey.

It took the Jesuit only two weeks in Kyoto to realize the futility of his journey, and he returned to Yamaguchi, perhaps a little wiser concerning the political realities then obtaining in Japan. In November 1551, after a stay of less than two and a half years, he left to deal with mission problems in India. During the voyage, Xavier decided that, instead of returning to Japan in the following year as intended, he would travel to China, for, he reasoned, if that great nation were converted to the faith, the Japanese would hopefully follow suit. On December 3, 1552, while awaiting passage to the mainland, Xavier died of exhaustion on Sancian (Schurhammer, *Francis Xavier*, pp. 640–3, 662–4), a small island used by Portuguese merchants to smuggle their goods into nearby Canton. He was 46 years old.

In due course Jesuit reinforcements, mostly Portuguese and Spaniards, arrived in Japan to continue and expand the apostolate. The mission always suffered from a shortage of manpower, and during its entire history there were never more than 50 Jesuit priests working in the country at any one time. Despite this lack of personnel, their labors achieved remarkable success, and by the end of the century the number of Christians, mostly in Kyushu, had increased to about 300,000. This expansion may be attributed to several factors in the mission's favor. The country was embroiled in military and civil strife, and the dangers threatening people's daily lives not unnaturally led their thoughts to religion. In addition, while Buddhism was in a state of decline in Japan, the zeal of the missionaries, most of them volunteers who had braved the perils and hardships of the two-year journey from Lisbon to Nagasaki, was much in evidence. With rare exceptions they never returned to Europe, but dedicated their lives to the conversion of Japan. Further, in that age the maxim *Extra ecclesiam nulla salus* ("No salvation outside the church") was interpreted literally, and inspired priests and brothers to toil unceasingly to bring people to salvation and save them from damnation.

"Top-Down" Policy

Another factor played a significant role in producing the large number of conversions in Kyushu. In addition to the Latin maxim quoted above, there was another European saying that was equally valid in Japan at that time – *Cuius regio, eius religio* ("whose territory, his religion"). This concept, although expressed in Latin, was not at all new to Japanese tradition, for local barons exercised power of life and death over their subjects, and throughout history there were not a few instances of people being obliged to change from one Buddhist sect to another at the behest of their rulers. The missionaries succeeded in bringing into the Christian fold a number of Kyushu daimyo, and although due caution should be taken in interpreting the reasons for their agreeing to receive baptism, conversions in some cases may well have been at least partially inspired by mixed motives. In this matter we may cite the example of the daimyo of Arima, who was received into the church in 1580. Events leading up to his much-postponed baptism are extremely complicated, but it is obvious that political factors were involved. Following his baptism, the Jesuits arranged for a Portuguese ship, a source of considerable income, to call at Arima. When the fief came under attack later in the same year, the missionaries had food distributed to besieged fortresses, and powder and lead, obtained from the ship, were supplied to the garrisons (Schütte, *Valignano's Mission Principles*, vol. 1, pp. 322–3). This is not to adopt a totally cynical view and suggest all the Christian rulers received baptism solely to encourage the lucrative Portuguese trade, for several daimyo, such as Ōtomo Yoshishige, Takayama Ukon, and Konishi Yukinaga, suffered hardship rather than renounce their faith. Nor should it be supposed that the Jesuits devoted themselves exclusively to the conversion of daimyo, for most of them worked in rural areas far removed from circles of political power.

A result of the top-down policy of attracting local rulers in Kyushu to the church was the mass conversion of people owing allegiance to some of the Christian daimyo who brought pressure to bear on them to follow their example and accept baptism. Daimyo could, and did, embrace or at least favor Christianity and then tell their subjects to follow suit. This happened, for example, in Ōmura in late 1574 under the orders of the local baron, and in 1576 in Arima (Schütte, *Valignano's Mission Principles*, vol. 1, pp. 322–5). Even more, in their misplaced zeal (whether religious or commercial) converted daimyo occasionally burned down Buddhist temples and expelled the monks from their domains. This happened in Arima, where more than 40 temples and shrines, "some of great beauty and renowned throughout Japan," according to a missionary, were demolished (Schütte, *Valignano's Mission Principles*, vol. 1, p. 324). Destruction in these instances was carried out on the orders of local rulers, and one missionary report of the time advocates that the buildings should be transformed into Christian churches instead of being razed (Valignano, *Sumario*, p. 166). But there is nothing in the records to suggest that the missionaries in fact protested against these wanton acts of demolition. In at least one recorded case in 1574, a priest actually suggested the use of arson to a Christian as a Lenten penance, with the result that "a large and lovely temple" was destroyed by fire soon after (Fróis, *Historia*, vol. 2, pp. 430–1). In light of modern standards of religious toleration it is impossible to justify these acts of violence, but such deplorable incidents were not uncommon at the time and possibly caused little surprise to local Japanese. The sixteenth century in Japan witnessed far worse atrocities against Buddhist establishments. In 1571, for instance, Oda Nobunaga had his troops destroy the hundreds of temples in the monastic complex on Mt. Hiei. In the two days of fire and carnage, thousands of monks and laity were slaughtered.

The missionaries' top-down policy was based on the desire to bring into the church large numbers of converts who hopefully would later be instructed more deeply in the Christian faith. In 1574 in Ōmura, for example, "more than forty thousand" people received baptism "in a few days" (Fróis, *Historia*, vol. 2, p. 427). In cases of such incredible numbers it is not difficult to agree with a modern Jesuit authority on early Christian history in Japan when he writes, "there could be no question of giving them all a thorough instruction in the faith" (Schütte, *Valignano's Mission Principles*, vol. 1, pp. 229–30). In view of Japan's social system in which rulers enjoyed absolute power over their subjects, the policy was attractive and possessed a certain logic. At the same time it involved obvious dangers, for this approach depended so much on the goodwill and cooperation of daimyo in an unsettled and unstable era.

The missionaries were certainly aware that people receiving baptism at the order of their liege lord would later require further instruction to strengthen and deepen their faith. In not a few instances, however, subsequent persecution did not allow this follow-up to take place. But the steadfastness shown by many Christians in times of persecution amply illustrates that, for whatever reason they had accepted baptism, their faith ran deep. Nevertheless, despite the encouraging numbers of people entering the church, Japanese embracing Christianity under pressure from their local lords could, and sometimes did, fall away with equal ease when their ruler experienced a change of heart. A case in point occurred in late 1576. After the death of the Christian daimyo of Arima, his successor threatened Christians with violence unless they apostatized, and according to Jesuit reports, most in fact did renounce their faith. But then, owing to external pressure, the new daimyo ended the persecution, and many of the Christians who had fallen away now returned to the faith (Schütte, *Valignano's Mission Principles*, vol. 1, p. 238).

The sudden downfall of rulers occurs so often in Japanese history that the term *gekokujō* specifically refers to the phenomenon of subjects overthrowing rulers. This perhaps should have given the Jesuits pause, for friendly daimyo could be abruptly replaced by hostile successors. Even without such a dramatic change in power, dependence on the favor of national and local rulers presented the disquieting possibility that they could with equal ease turn against Christianity, and in fact this happened on various occasions.

Alessandro Valignano

Many accounts of the early mission in Japan dwell on the role of Xavier, rightly maintaining that he was the founder of the enterprise. But Xavier stayed in the country for less than three years, and on his departure in 1551 left behind his two companions without any clear-cut plan of future work and organization. Although countless books have been devoted to him and his apostolate, only in recent years has scholarly attention been drawn (notably in the works of Schütte, Moran, and Ross) to the contribution of the mission's second founder, Valignano, whose policies made a deep impact on the evangelization of Japan, and who introduced a new approach to missionary work in Asia.

The Italian Jesuit Alessandro Valignano (1539–1606) was born of a distinguished family in Chieti in the Abruzzi region, then under Spanish domination. After receiving a doctorate in civil law at the University of Padua, he entered the Society of Jesus in 1566 and studied theology in Rome. Superiors recognized his administrative talent and after only seven years from entering the order, Valignano, then aged 34, was appointed visitor, or inspector, of the Jesuit missions in Asia (Schütte, *Valignano's Mission Principles*, vol. 1, pp. 30–43). In this capacity he visited Japan three times, spending a total of ten years in that country. His influence on the development of mission policy would be hard to exaggerate. Although Japan was outside the ambit of Iberian colonization and thus required fresh ideas for better spreading the Christian message, old ways of thought persisted among many of the missionaries, and it was Valignano more than anyone else who introduced a new approach.

Japan was obviously far different from many of the regions in Asia and Latin America where Christianity had already been introduced. The Japanese possessed a highly developed social system and a sophisticated culture that Europeans had seldom encountered elsewhere. Xavier himself had written that the Japanese he had met "are the best we have yet discovered" (Schurhammer, *Francis Xavier*, p. 82). The Jesuit chronicler Luis Fróis (1532–97) spent more than 30 years in Japan, and his voluminous writings amply testify to his admiration of the Japanese and their culture. The Italian Organtino Gnecchi-Soldi (d. 1609) enthused, "You should not think that these people are barbarians, because, apart from the Faith, however prudent we may believe we are, we are great barbarians compared with them" (Cooper, *Southern Barbarians*, p. 137). In the first of his two grammars of the Japanese language, the missionary João Rodrigues (ca. 1561–1633) quotes with approval classical poetry from imperial anthologies compiled four or five hundred years earlier, and in his treatise on Japanese life and culture, he devotes four chapters to a perceptive study of the practice and ethos of the tea ceremony (Rodrigues, *This Island*, pp. 250–96). Clearly, Japan was in a different league when compared with most other mission countries and thus called for a different approach from the policy generally employed elsewhere.

Although the far-sighted Valignano realized this need, there were other missionaries in Japan who were unwilling to shed their European mindsets, and saw little or no need for cultural adaptation. Much of this attitude could be found in the outlook of Francisco Cabral (1533–1609), the Portuguese mission superior from 1570 to 1581. After taking part in military action against the Turks, Cabral had entered the Society of Jesus in Goa in 1554 and thus had long experience of missionary life in India before being sent to Japan. He was undoubtedly a talented and energetic superior, but saw no need for missionaries to study the Japanese language, and made little or no effort to encourage adaptation to local customs and etiquette. He regarded Japanese members of the Jesuit order as inferiors, and treated them with severity and harshness, using (in Valignano's words) "a rod of iron, with blows and rough words" (Schütte, *Valignano's Mission Principles*, vol. 1, pp. 251–60). Cabral further believed the Japanese unfit to proceed to the priesthood, and in this opinion he was not alone. Somewhat surprisingly, João Rodrigues wrote in 1598 that not one of the Japanese recruits "has great zeal for souls or much disposition for Sacred Orders" (Cooper, *Rodrigues*, p. 173) – a puzzling criticism as in the previous year he had witnessed in Nagasaki the martyrdom of young Bro. Paul Miki (1564–97), who had fervently preached the faith en route to his execution and then from his cross.

The Euro-ethnocentric attitude of looking down on the Japanese was alien to the thought of Valignano, who stressed the urgent need for acculturation and adaptation if missionaries were to achieve lasting success. He was under no illusion about the difficulty of achieving this goal, for he appreciated the deep-seated differences between Japanese and Europeans. To illustrate this problem, he wrote with some exasperation, "They have rites and ceremonies so different from those of all other nations that it seems that they deliberately try to be unlike any other people. . . . It may truly be said that Japan is a world the reverse of Europe" (Cooper, *They Came to Japan*, front matter). Despite the obstacles to his program of acculturation, he believed that there really was no alternative if eventual success was to be obtained. He was not alone in this opinion. The Italian Gnecchi-Soldi shared his views on the need for adaptation, while the pioneering work later done by the Italians Roberto de Nobili (in India) and Matteo Ricci (in China) may also be mentioned in this context (see chapters 21 and 22).

This difference in viewpoints between Italians and Portuguese may perhaps not be entirely fortuitous. The former came from a country which had no imperialist pre-

tensions and was in fact partially under foreign rule, while the latter had been born
and educated in a country which was then at the peak of its colonial power. To avoid
conflict in distant parts of the globe, European treaties and papal bulls had arbitrarily
divided the Asian world into Spanish and Portuguese regions of commercial (and possibly military) interest, and the Portuguese maintained that Japan fell within their
zone. Although they could never overcome Japan by force of arms (as they had done
elsewhere in Asia), the notion that the country somehow belonged to the Portuguese
sphere of interest persisted. There were even some hotheads who advocated using
Spanish troops from the Philippines to invade Japan and place it under Christian rule.
Valignano treated such harebrained suggestions with scorn. Even though Japan was
politically divided at the time, he declared that any Iberian invasion would be unable
to capture even four spans of Japanese territory, and that the devout Christian general
Konishi Yukinaga would turn his sword against any missionaries who ventured to aid
and abet the invaders (Yuuki, *Twenty-Six Martyrs*, p. 23).

Valignano realized that the work of evangelization in Japan would inevitably be
impaired in the long run by outdated European views and policies. If no change were
made, the sophisticated Japanese would resent the foreigners' condescending attitude and would regard them with disdain. In fact they had already dubbed Europeans as *nanbanjin*, or "Southern Barbarians," although this unflattering sobriquet,
derived from Chinese thought, should not be interpreted too literally. Nevertheless
the term possessed a certain justification when Japanese politeness in social dealings,
eating habits, and personal cleanliness were compared with, or rather contrasted to,
those of Europeans.

Not without opposition, Valignano revamped mission policy during his three stays
in Japan. He insisted that Jesuits should study the language and that a dictionary and
grammar should be compiled for this purpose. Further, missionaries should not
expect converts to conform to European ways; instead, the Jesuits should adapt themselves as much as possible to local traditions and way of life. Valignano's treatise on
Japanese customs and etiquette, *Advertimentos e Avisos* (1581) spells out in detail
how the European Jesuits should treat their Japanese brethren and the laity. He insists
that they should adapt themselves to Japanese life, detailing the etiquette to be
observed when receiving visitors in Jesuit residences and on other occasions. The
Japanese attach much importance to social standing, and to make clear the different
grades among missionaries (such as regional superior, local superior, priest, and
brother) Valignano borrowed titles used to denote ranking in the Zen sect (Schütte,
Valignano's Mission Principles, vol. 2, pp. 159–62). That a Catholic missionary in
the late sixteenth century should appropriate Buddhist terms in this way illustrates
the length to which Valignano was prepared to go to achieve his ideal of adaptation.
His policy appears to have achieved some success, for in 1596 a visiting Spanish
layman reported about the missionaries, "They so imitate the Japanese that they wear
their clothes, speak their language, eat like them on the floor without cloths, tables,
or napkins. Nor do they use their hands but eat with a small stick, observing the
same ceremonies as the Japanese do themselves" (Cooper, *Southern Barbarians*,
p. 137).

Valignano went on to found two colleges for well-born Christian boys in the hope
these institutions would in time produce vocations to the religious life. Still extant
today are his written instructions spelling out the students' daily timetable and their

course of studies. (There was perhaps a limit to even Valignano's willingness to conform to Japanese life, for he stipulates that the boys should be allowed only one bath every week in summer, and every two weeks in winter.) The content of the classes was international for the boys also studied Latin, while the more talented applied themselves to western painting and music. From this modest beginning began the Southern Barbarian genre of art in which Japanese used western painting styles and techniques to copy religious (and, later, secular) pictures imported from Europe. That these early efforts never reached a high artistic standard need cause no surprise, for this training was allowed to continue for only a short time before persecution brought the experiment to an end. Still, paintings such as *Our Lady of the Rosary*, now in the possession of Kyoto University, exhibit considerable talent and skill (Cooper, *Southern Barbarians*, fig. 72).

The list of Valignano's imaginative innovations contains two more items of interest. He imported a European printing press of movable type, and in the course of 24 years the Jesuit Press produced a total of some 60 titles, including language textbooks, devotional works, and liturgical manuals. The celebrated Japanese–Portuguese dictionary, *Vocabulario da Lingoa de Iapam* (Nagasaki, 1603), includes 32,000 entries, many of them neatly classified as Buddhist, Shinto, literary, or women's words, or used in either the Kyoto region or Kyushu. The dictionary lists some colloquial words not found elsewhere in any other source, and is a standard work still used by scholars researching the language spoken in the early seventeenth century. While João Rodrigues's two Portuguese grammars of the Japanese language (1604 and 1620) admittedly leave much to be desired as textbooks for beginners, they contain a mass of information about not only the grammar and structure of the language as spoken at that time but also different aspects of contemporaneous life in Japan. The volume of the press's publications is even more impressive in view of the fact that the machinery had to be packed up several times and transported to different places owing to local persecutions (Moran, *Japanese and the Jesuits*, pp. 145–60).

Economic problems beset the mission from the beginning and obliged the Jesuits to take the controversial step of investing in the Portuguese silk trade between China and Japan. For clerics to engage in commerce was considered unseemly and was forbidden by church law, but because of their financial predicament Rome reluctantly granted the Jesuits in Japan permission for a limited participation. Nobody, least of all Valignano, was happy about this method of raising money, and it in fact brought down much criticism on the Jesuits' heads, but then nobody could suggest any alternative for financing such a remote mission lying outside the parameters of the Iberian empires (Moran, *Japanese and the Jesuits*, pp. 115–28).

To make the mission better known in Europe and hopefully attract greater economic aid, Valignano hit upon the novel plan of organizing an embassy to Rome. Two Christian teenage boys, accompanied by two companions and some Jesuits, represented three Kyushu daimyo and left Japan in 1582 for the long journey to Europe. The embassy's official purpose was to present to the pope letters of greeting and reverence from Japan, but in fact its twofold aim was to arouse European interest in the mission and then, on their return, for the boys to give eyewitness accounts of the glory of Renaissance Europe to their countrymen. In modern parlance the expedition was a PR exercise on a spectacularly ambitious scale. The boys were warmly greeted in Rome by Gregory XIII and later his successor Sixtus V, both of whom showered on them favors, perhaps hoping that the gains the church was making in Japan might offset its losses in Europe. The delegates' journey through Italy took on the form of a triumphal progress with local authorities vying to entertain them with lavish banquets, receptions, and festivals. Valignano's bold plan to publicize in Catholic Europe the work and progress of the Japanese church certainly succeeded beyond expectation, although the mission's financial problems still persisted.

One aspect of Valignano's policy, however, gave rise to resentment and controversy in Catholic circles, and even produced divisions within his own religious order. Receiving reports about the success of Jesuit work in Japan, other religious orders understandably wished to join the enterprise and thus increase the inadequate number of priests working in the country. This plan would seem to be laudable enough, but Valignano opposed it and in fact obtained a papal brief in 1585 reserving the Japanese mission exclusively to the Jesuits. Chief among his objections to the arrival of other orders was his fear that Spanish friars accustomed to conditions in Latin America or the Philippines would introduce outdated and unsuitable methods and might thus undo much of the success the Jesuits had achieved over the previous 30 or 40 years.

Relying on another papal brief, dated 1586, that appeared to favor their cause, four Spanish friars arrived from the Philippines in 1593; more of their colleagues joined them in due course, later to be followed by some Dominicans and Augustinians, although the total number of friars in Japan remained small. Relations between some, but not all, of the Jesuits and the friars became acrimonious, and this division presents a sad spectacle in the early history of the church in Japan. Possibly some of the controversy can also be attributed to the fact that the Jesuits, whether Portuguese or not, always departed Europe from Lisbon, stopped at the Portuguese settlement of Goa, then stayed at the Portuguese enclave of Macao, before finally reaching Nagasaki. But in 1580 King Philip II of Spain became also King Philip I of Portugal, thus initiating what the Portuguese bitterly called their 60 years of captivity. Obviously this was not a good time for Spanish friars to enter what the Portuguese considered their exclusive sphere of activity. Further, the friars belonged to venerable orders founded centuries earlier by canonized saints, and probably resented being barred from the rich harvest field of Japan by members of a religious order that had begun a mere 50 years earlier (Boxer, *Christian Century*, pp. 137–87).

Development

The above account about Valignano has necessarily diverted this narrative from the course of the church's history in Japan. In addition to Kyushu, missionary activity also developed in the capital region around Kyoto; here the work of evangelization was not related in any way with the Portuguese silk trade, and the Christian flock, so it seemed to Valignano, was in general more deeply grounded in the faith. The appointment of a bishop to Japan reflected the mission's growing importance, and Bishop Pedro Martins arrived in 1596. His stay in Japan was brief, but his successor, Luis de Cerqueira (1552–1614), labored indefatigably from 1598 until his death in Nagasaki, ordaining to the priesthood 15 Japanese candidates during his tenure of office. A strong supporter of Valignano's policy of acculturation, the bishop instituted a new liturgical feast to be observed on January 1 every year so that Christians could celebrate New Year's Day, the most important date in the Japanese calendar, in a religious fashion along with the rest of the populace.

As regards the political situation, the era of civil wars gradually drew to a close with the rise to power of three national unifiers in succession. Oda Nobunaga (1543–82) began as a petty daimyo, but ruthlessness and good fortune enabled him to win control of half the country by the time of his violent death. He was naturally curious about westerners, and Jesuit letters have left valuable reports about lengthy interviews with the powerful ruler. Part of the Buddhist establishment was a source of opposition to his authority, and Nobunaga undoubtedly showed favor to the Christian cause to score off his Buddhist adversaries.

Nobunaga's lieutenant, Toyotomi Hideyoshi (1536–98), continued the work of national unification. Initially favorable to the missionaries, his attitude changed when, during a visit to Kyushu in 1586, he realized Christianity's considerable influence in the western part of the country. His suspicions were further aroused when, in a misguided attempt to please him, the Jesuit superior, Gaspar Coelho (d. 1590), promised to obtain Portuguese support for the ruler's planned war against China. Not content with this blunder, he declared that he would also encourage Christian daimyo to help in his military campaign in Kyushu. The proposal, doubtless made in good faith, was obvious interference in domestic affairs, and Hideyoshi reacted accordingly by abruptly issuing an edict expelling missionaries from the country. In the event the decree was neither strictly enforced nor obeyed, and was probably intended as a warning to the foreigners not to meddle in the political arena.

Matters took a violent turn, however, when the Spanish ship *San Felipe* was wrecked off the Japanese coast in 1596 and its valuable cargo was seized by local officials. In the aftermath the elderly and increasingly irrational Hideyoshi ordered the execution of the Franciscan friars and Jesuits in Kyoto together with their Christian flock. The victims were escorted to Nagasaki, where on February 27, 1597, 26 Christians – friars, Jesuits, and laymen (including three young boys) – were crucified for their faith (Yuuki, *Twenty-Six Martyrs*, passim). It is not a little ironic that if Christian charity and unity were not sufficient to unite the Jesuits and friars, then a non-Christian ruler achieved that happy result through violence. On the eve of his martyrdom the Spanish Franciscan Pedro Bautista met with the Portuguese Jesuit João Rodrigues, and both men wept as they embraced and asked for mutual forgiveness.

Hideyoshi died in the following year and his successor, Tokugawa Ieyasu (1542–1616), assumed control of the country after winning the battle of Sekigahara in 1600 and receiving the office of shogun three years later. Initially, he and his son, Hidetada, showed no particular animosity toward Christians, although with the arrival of Dutch and English merchants at the beginning of the century the Iberian monopoly of European trade with Japan was broken, thus diminishing the need to favor Portuguese commerce and the related work of the Catholic missionaries.

Within a dozen years into the new century, political events produced a military showdown between the house of Tokugawa and the forces loyal to the late Hideyoshi. The shogun enjoyed no divine right to rule Japan, and he governed merely on account of his superior military and economic power. But his position was not totally secure, for a coalition of disaffected barons might bring about the downfall of the Tokugawa, and any catalyst, such as Christianity, uniting hostile daimyo in Kyushu, where the religion was at its strongest, was to be feared. The possibility of Christian daimyo joining forces on account of their religion was remote as they had never been united by their shared faith, indeed, some of them had fought among themselves. But the Tokugawa government was taking no chances. Knowing that it was only a matter of time before a military showdown would inevitably take place, Ieyasu decided to eliminate any influence that might prove harmful to his cause. In 1614 the authorities issued a decree expelling missionaries from Japan and outlawing Christianity, and this time the order was meant to be obeyed. In the following year the Tokugawa defeated their foes at Osaka and established a regime that would rule Japan for two and a half centuries, until the arrival of Commodore Matthew Perry and his American fleet in 1853 set in train events leading to the restoration of imperial power 15 years later.

Persecution

Despite the expulsion decree, many missionaries remained in the country and continued their work underground. Convinced that Christianity was a threat to Tokugawa rule, the shogunate increased its pressure to eliminate the religion, posting rewards for information leading to the arrest of priests and laity. The mission suffered one of the severest persecutions in church history. In the Great Martyrdom of Nagasaki in 1622, for example, 50 Christians, both European and Japanese, were beheaded or died at the stake in one day, while in Edo (present-day Tokyo) ten years later, 50 priests and laity were burned to death in a mass execution. The campaign was not confined to the cities, and Christians were hunted down and killed throughout the country. But to the authorities' exasperation, their efforts only seemed to increase the fervor of the Christians; at the Nagasaki mass martyrdom, for example, thousands of onlookers gathered to pray and sing hymns to encourage their condemned brethren to persevere to the end.

The government therefore changed its policy: no longer interested in producing martyrs, it now sought to bring about apostasy through the use of torture, the most effective of which was the *ana-tsurushi*, or suspension of a victim upside down for days until death or retraction ensued. Other forms of torment were devised to break the spirit of the apprehended Christians. The Protestant Dutchman Ryer Gyspertz witnessed the persecution in the Nagasaki region and describes the sufferings of the faithful; he ends his catalogue of atrocities with the words, "I cannot bring myself to write of them any more" (Cooper, *They Came to Japan*, p. 397). Many of the martyrdoms took place in remote areas or in crowded prisons, and have therefore gone unrecorded. The precise number of deaths is not available, but modern sources have traced between 2,000 and 4,000 specific instances; if unreported cases are included, this figure would be greatly increased. Efforts were made to smuggle priests into the country, but the newcomers were inevitably apprehended, and subsequent torture often resulted in apostasy. Whether this denial of faith was genuine or merely outward was of little concern to the authorities.

The finale came in 1638 when peasants and former samurai in the Shimabara region of Kyushu rose up against oppression and crushing taxes, and barricaded themselves in a local fortress. The region had formerly been a center of Christian activity, and what began as a social protest developed into a religious crusade with flags bearing Christian emblems boldly unfurled. It took four months before government troops, reportedly numbering 100,000 men, were able to overcome the peasants through starvation and take the besieged castle by storm. In the aftermath thousands of men, women, and children were put to the sword.

Disturbed by the difficulty experienced in subduing this uprising, the government ordered suspension of Portuguese trade, wrongly suspecting that the ships were smuggling missionaries and supplies to hidden Christians. In an attempt to restore its profitable trade with Japan, Macao sent an unarmed and unladen ship to Nagasaki in 1640 to plead for resumption of commerce. On orders from Edo, the ship's officials and crew were executed, with a dozen sailors spared to sail back to Macao with the somber news. The proclamation at the execution site threatened the same penalty would be inflicted on all future visitors, including "even the GOD of the Christians." From then on, Japan was closed to Europeans except for a handful of Dutch traders living in semi-confinement in Nagasaki. To prevent further contact with foreigners, Japanese were forbidden under pain of death to leave the country and travel abroad. Japan would remain closed for the following 200 years. Once more Marco Polo's Zipangu became a mysterious island kingdom shut off from the rest of the world.

Conclusion

As mentioned above, the history of the Christian church in Japan in the early period presents an interesting mixture of the old and the new, the tried and the innovative. Japan differed from other countries in which missionaries worked at that time. It was not part of the Iberian empires and there was not the remotest possibility that it could ever be overcome by European force of arms. Despite the political and military turmoil of the sixteenth century, it could boast of a sophisticated society, a rich cultural tradition, and a recorded history extending back for many centuries. Men such as Valignano (and later Ricci in China) realized that conventional missionary methods used elsewhere were no longer valid or appropriate in these two nations. Other missionaries, men of goodwill but unable or unwilling to shed their Euroethnocentric outlook and national prejudices, were content to follow the tried and traditional methods of evangelization.

In this chapter, reference has been made to Japanese history, politics, and commerce. Such information is required to set this account in context and to provide a better understanding of the initial success but eventual destruction of Christianity in that country. Other works (such as those of Jennes, Pacheco, and Fujita) offer detailed surveys that are more chronological in nature. The top-down policy and its inherent dangers have also been discussed in these pages. In other mission fields Iberian colonial authority bolstered missionary activity, but this was not possible in Japan. Instead of relying on colonial support, the missionaries there depended largely on the goodwill of influential rulers. Later in China Valignano's policies would reach their fulfillment, for there the carefully selected missionaries exerted influence among the literati class not as a result of colonial support, commerce, or political connections but solely thanks to their learning and scholarship.

Whatever the policy followed by the missionaries of that time, insular Japan, so remote from Europe and aloof from the mainstream of even Asian history, was not ready to receive and accept the Christian message in whichever form it might have been presented. In the volatile situation of the time, the authorities viewed the religion as a subversive system of thought that tended to complicate the already complex political scene. So Christianity had to be eliminated, not for strictly religious reasons (the Japanese have always been tolerant in religious matters), but for social and political purposes. As a result, the church was persecuted and wiped out, but not before a religious and cultural meeting, albeit impermanent, had been established between Japan and the West.

Envoi

When westerners were finally allowed to return to Japan in the middle of the nineteenth century, the world was astonished to learn that communities of hidden Christians still survived in remote communities in Kyushu. For more than two centuries these people had gathered in secret to recite their prayers, many of which at the time of their discovery existed in only garbled form. In rural areas where Christianity had been firmly planted and allowed to take deep root through four or five generations, the harsh Tokugawa campaign had been unable to completely eradicate the religion. Sadly these people were again oppressed during the closing years of Tokugawa rule. Ironically, even when the imperial Meiji period, the era of "enlightenment and culture," began in 1868, the persecution continued. Several thousand Christians were uprooted from Kyushu and shipped to other parts of the country, with hundreds dying of cold and starvation. It was only through western diplomatic pressure that the government finally withdrew its religious ban in 1873 and a new Christian era could begin in Japan.

BIBLIOGRAPHY

Boxer, C. R., *The Christian Century in Japan 1549–1650*. Berkeley: University of California Press, 1951, 1967.
Cartas que os padres e irmãos da Companhia de Iesus escreverão dos Reynos de Iapão e China ..., 2 vols. Evora, 1598; facsimile edition, Tenri, 1972.
Cooper, M., S.J., ed., *They Came to Japan: An Anthology of European Reports on Japan, 1543–1640*. Berkeley: University of California Press, 1965; Ann Arbor: Center for Japanese Studies, University of Michigan, 1995.
Cooper, M., S.J., ed., *The Southern Barbarians: The First Europeans in Japan*. Tokyo: Kodansha International, 1971.
Cooper, M., S.J., *Rodrigues the Interpreter: An Early Jesuit in Japan and China*. New York and Tokyo: Weatherhill, 1974.
Fróis, L., S.J., *Historia de Japam*, ed. J. Wicki, S.J., 5 vols. Lisbon: Biblioteca Nacional, 1976–84.
Fróis, L., S.J., *La Première Ambassade du Japon en Europe, 1582–1592*, ed. J. A. Abranches Pinto, Yoshitomo Okamoto, and Henri Bernard, S.J. Tokyo: Sophia University, Monumenta Nipponica Monograph 6, 1942.
Fujita, N. S., *Japan's Encounter with Christianity: The Catholic Mission in Pre-Modern Japan*. Mahwah, NJ: Paulist Press, 1991.
Jennes, J., C.I.C.M., *A History of the Catholic Church in Japan*. Tokyo: Oriens Institute, 1973.
Moran, J. F., *The Japanese and the Jesuits: Alessandro Valignano in Sixteenth-Century Japan*. London and New York: Routledge, 1993.

Pacheco, D., S.J., "The Europeans in Japan, 1543–1640," in M. Cooper, ed., *The Southern Barbarians: The First Europeans in Japan*. Tokyo: Kodansha International, 1971, pp. 35–96.

Perez, L., O.F.M., *Cartas y Relaciones del Japón*, 3 vols. Madrid, 1916–23.

Rodrigues, J., S.J., *This Island of JapOn: João Rodrigues' Account of 16th-Century Japan*, trans. Michael Cooper. Tokyo: Kodansha International, 1973.

Ross, A. C., *A Vision Betrayed: The Jesuits in Japan and China, 1542–1742*. Maryknoll, NY: Orbis Books, 1994.

Ruiz-de-Medina, J., S.J., ed., *Documentos del Japan, 1547–1557, 1558–1562*, 2 vols. Rome: Instituto Histórico de la Compañía de Jesús, 1990–5.

Schurhammer, G., S.J., *Francis Xavier: His Life and Times*. Vol. 4: *Japan and China, 1549–1552*, trans. M. Joseph Costelloe, S.J. Rome: Jesuit Historical Institute, 1982.

Schütte, J. F., S.J., *Introductio ad Historiam Societatis Jesu in Japonia 1549–1650*. Rome: Institutum Historicum Soc. Jesu, 1968.

Schütte, J. F., S.J., *Textus Catalogorum Japoniae*. Rome: Monumenta Historica Soc. Jesu, 1975.

Schütte, J. F., S.J., *Valignano's Mission Principles for Japan*, trans. John J. Coyne, S.J., 2 vols. St. Louis: Institute of Jesuit Sources, 1980–5.

Uyttenbroeck, T., O.F.M., *Early Franciscans in Japan*. Himeji, 1958.

Valignano, A., S.J., *II Cerimoniale per i Missionari del Giappone: Advertimentos e Avisos acerca dos Costumes e Catangues de Jappão*, ed. Giuseppe Fr. Schütte, S.J. Rome: Storia e Letteratura, 1946.

Valignano, A., S.J., *Sumario de las Cosas de Japon (1583), Adiciones del Sumario de Japon (1592)*, ed. José Luis Alvarez-Taladriz, 2 vols. Tokyo: Sophia University, Monumenta Nipponica Monograph 9, 1954.

Yuuki, D., S.J., *The Twenty-Six Martyrs of Japan*. Tokyo: Enderle, 1998.

FURTHER READING

The definitive history of the Japanese church in the sixteenth and seventeenth centuries has yet to be written, but Boxer, *Christian Century*, is by far the best account, although the author did not make use of the voluminous primary sources in the Jesuit archives in Rome. Earlier works rely on secondary sources and are often uncritical in their treatment of materials. As regards Jesuit letters from Japan during this period, *Cartas*, 2 vols. (Evora, 1598) is a rich source of information, and the 1972 facsimile edition has made this material more readily accessible. Ruiz-de-Medina's two volumes of Jesuit letters from Japan presents the texts with rigorous scholarship, but his recent death places in doubt the future of this valuable series. The publication of Fróis, *Historia*, 5 vols., provides an immense amount of primary material on church history. Schütte's *Introductio* and *Textus* offer encyclopedic detail about Jesuit work in Japan, and are based on primary materials. Schütte's *Valignano's Mission Principles* and Moran's *Japanese and the Jesuits* present valuable accounts of Valignano's contribution, while Ross, *Vision Betrayed*, compares Jesuit work in Japan and China. José Luis Alvarez-Taladriz's editing of primary documents provides an enormous amount of detailed material on missionary work in Japan. Cooper, *They Came to Japan*, is an anthology of European reports, both religious and secular, about Japan in this period, while Cooper, *Rodrigues the Interpreter*, deals with one particular Jesuit who played an important role in the development of the mission. For general surveys of the Japanese mission, Jennes, *History*, and Fujita, *Japan's Encounter*, provide standard accounts, based mainly on secondary sources. Perez, *Cartas*, and Uyttenbroeck, *Early Franciscans*, present the Franciscan viewpoint. The ten-page bibliography in Cooper, *Rodrigues the Interpreter*, provides further information about materials on Japan.

PART VI

Structures of
the Reformation World

TWENTY-FOUR

The New Parish

BRUCE GORDON

The most serious issue facing sixteenth-century reform movements in their transition from protest to institutionalization was the provision of pastoral care for the laity by a trained, educated clergy. Across Europe, reformers and magistrates, both Catholic and Protestant, faced a common and equally daunting dilemma: how to establish an ordered clerical estate on a firm financial basis which, on the one hand, could be politically and theologically controlled whilst, on the other, would not be rejected by the laity as alien, intrusive, and economically burdensome. The problem had many dimensions (historical, theological, legal, social, economic), and went to the core of the Reformation itself. The very nature of Christian ministry was up for grabs following Martin Luther's rejection of the sacrificial priesthood of the medieval church. Ministry was inextricably linked to the doctrine of justification, and by the middle of the sixteenth century Catholics and Protestants had adopted irreconcilable positions on the role of the Christian minister.

The Emergence of the Protestant Ministry

The Protestant teaching on ministry was a necessary consequence of the reformers' repudiation of the medieval Catholic priesthood and the doctrines of transubstantiation and penance. This theological revolt, however, was far in advance of any considered plan of what should replace the Catholic priesthood. A Protestant ministry emerged piecemeal out of the early debates of the Reformation during the 1520s. Luther's early theological positions were formative, and in particular we need to consider the implications of justification by grace alone and the priesthood of all believers. The former made untenable the sacrificial nature of the mass and thus the priest's role as intercessor between God and humanity. Luther's earliest statements on Christian ministry, which emerged during the chaotic period of the early 1520s, indicated his belief that the essence of the Christian ministry lay in the Word of God. This did not require preaching alone, but the proclamation of God's saving message through language and deed. The Word, he argued, must not be confused with the printed words on the page of the Bible; properly understood, it is the content of God's gift in Christ, and the minister, therefore, is the means by which the saving nature of this message is realized in the world through preaching, sacraments, and pastoral care.

Yet, if all Christians have received God's grace through the gift of faith and not by means of the church, why is a separate clergy necessary? And if ministers are required, what, we might further press, should be the relationship between ordinary Christians and the ministry? This point proved particularly knotty for the reformers, and scholars have been troubled by Luther's seemingly contradictory statements. To be sure, the so-called priestly functions of performing God's will in the world belong to the whole of the church and are the responsibility of every man and woman. Indeed, Luther, in places, indulged himself the sanguine hope of the possibility of a church without clergy. That, however, remained a table-talk fantasy, and the more dominant chord in his writings argued for an organized, properly constituted clerical estate with ordained ministers.

For Luther, men set apart for the ordained Christian ministry were distinguished by their calling to perform a public office connected to a specific congregation. This takes us to a fundamental point about the Protestant reform of the clergy in the early Reformation. As Luther, Zwingli, Bucer, and others believed that change should be dictated by theological principles alone, their doctrines of *sola fide* and *sola scriptura* required a ministry of proclamation but not, crucially, any change to the social and legal structures of the church. Thus they held that the parish system of the medieval church was an essential and necessary ecclesiastical and societal control ordained by God on account of human frailty and sustained by his ministering angels. Luther believed that without angelic support all human structures would be overthrown by the legions of devils who seek to bring chaos and despair. Parishes, with their material structures and financial and legal arrangements, were the proper forum for the prosecution of the Christian ministry. This still does not address the question of why there should be a ministry if all Christians are priests. For this we must turn to the issues of order and structure, and here we find that all the reformers grounded their argument for an ordained ministry in their distinction between the different, though equal, vocations of the Christian ministry.

The term "vocation" became central to the Protestant vocabulary of ministry. This meant the fulfillment of an individual's calling as a "priest" as realized in the divinely ordained institutions of the family and community. Despite the equality of all believers through faith (priesthood of all believers), Luther readily recognized that individuals could not perform all Christian activities required of them by their priesthood. Thus it was reasonable and necessary that Christians, in order to devote themselves to the fulfillment of their diverse vocations (artisan, mother, magistrate, minister, etc.), should delegate particular men to perform the public ministry of the church – that ministry involved the preaching of the Gospel and the administration of the sacraments of baptism and the Lord's Supper.

In its embryonic form, therefore, we can detect in the Protestant ministry strong echoes of both medieval conciliarism and the reform decrees which flowed across Europe after the Council of Basel. These older ideas were, however, refashioned in light of the startling theological formulations of the Luther affair. Zwingli began with a similar stance on ministry as delegated authority, but his route to this position was through the strong traditions of communalism which flourished in southern German and Swiss lands, where the idea that the minister should be chosen by the people had taken hold in the late Middle Ages. For both reformers this concept of pastoral authority from below proved to be a preliminary position that would be severely revised in light of events in the mid-1520s; for Luther it was the Peasants' War of 1525, and for Zwingli it was the rise of Anabaptism. These crises precipitated a fundamental shift toward a more authoritarian view of ministry in which the clergy took their place within the hierarchies of power.

The evolution of ministry from delegated authority to that of an office ordained by God is found in the writings of Philip Melanchthon, Heinrich Bullinger, Martin Bucer, and Jean Calvin. The change was also evident in Luther's own writings after 1525, in particular his preference for an ordered succession of ministers through ordination, which he understood as an expression of apostolic succession in the church. There was something of a studied ambiguity in this, for ordination was not a means of conferring grace, but rather a public confirmation of a minister's election. For Luther, proper (meaning "public") ordination ensured the continuity of the church's mission, and this then secured the maintenance of the hierarchy and order in the ongoing battle against the devil and chaos. Yet, at the same time, Luther was adamant that the office of minister was not attached to the person ordained; it left no indelible mark and could be withdrawn on account of either indolence or violation of the position. This tension over the nature of the office became a principal feature of the early modern Protestant clergy, and the reformers struggled with how to establish a ministry imbued with divine authority without slipping back toward the priesthood as a separate order in society.

The reformers responded to this challenge by explicitly linking the validity of the office with moral conduct in the public ministry. No longer were the people to see their minister as a sacred official who, despite any personal shortcomings or foibles, was endowed with sacramental powers. Rather, what an individual minister did or, crucially, said was an unequivocal indication of his fitness to hold his position as a representative of the church. He was a legitimate minister of the church only at the pleasure of the ruling authorities, and the measure of his ministry was his fidelity to the church ordinances drafted by Protestant reformers for their territorial and urban masters. These church ordinances across the empire detailed *in extenso* the "life and learning" of a minister. Life and learning formed the crucial diptych of the Protestant clerical office, derived from late medieval advocates of reform such as John Colet, Egidio de Viterbo, and, most importantly, from Erasmus.

The parish minister, then, was to embody the very principles he advocated from the pulpit, shared in pastoral visits, and taught from the catechisms. In many ways what was intended to distinguish him was not his office but his exemplary life as a Christian. Because the Protestants invested so heavily in the exemplary and pedagogical character of ministry, they had to construct a system by which ministers could be carefully monitored. The Protestant minister, consequently, was the object of scrutiny by church and secular officials as well as by the laity, three constituencies that did not necessarily hold a common view of what was desirable. This rendered the minister's position quite insecure and, as we shall see, both ruling officials and lay communities developed effective strategies for dealing with undesirable ministers. What this new system of exemplary clergy rooted in public discipline brought to the fore was the personality of the minister himself. Church leaders such as Heinrich Bullinger, Johannes Brenz, and Johannes Bugenhagen had to assess carefully the characters of the men they were about to send into parishes, to weigh up how that community would respond to a man of such a temperament. The minister's conduct in the community was now of heightened importance, for it determined the authority of his ministry.

Huldrych Zwingli concurred with Luther on many crucial points of the Christian ministry, but what emerged in Zürich had a distinct character, molded largely by Zwingli's emphasis on preaching and pastoral care. Zwingli was himself a talented preacher and in his early writings on the office of minister he continued to emphasize the proclamation of God's Word, declaring "know no priests, except those who proclaim the Word of God" (Stephens, *Theology of Huldrych Zwingli*, p. 274). His first extended treatment of the pastoral office is found in *The Shepherd* from October 1523, in which he outlined the essential components. It was the rise of Anabaptism in Zürich, rather than the Peasants' War, which brought Zwingli to a view of ministry in which he ultimately placed, like Luther and Melanchthon, greater emphasis on vocation and calling. His distinction between the internal and external calling enabled him to embed the Christian ministry in the state. The former is the work of the Spirit, and while it cannot be dependent on the latter, such confirmation of a person's fitness for the Christian ministry is required by the magistrates to ensure the ordered running of Christian society. Thus in the external calling of a minister the established temporal authorities played a crucial role. Zwingli increasingly spoke of the institutional nature of the Christian office. In Zwingli's view the magistrate held the sword of justice while the minister the sword of proclaiming God's Word. This led to conflict over what a minister might preach, given that he might have to criticize his political masters. Following Zwingli's death in 1531 his successor Heinrich Bullinger sought to resolve the relationship between the freedom to preach and the political realities of the magisterial church by making ministers servants of the state, controlled by institutions that were ultimately under the firm hand of secular rulers. This arrangement, devised in 1532, was a harbinger of the future for the Protestant clergy in the sixteenth century. The price of success for the Protestant churches would be obedience to temporal authorities and integration into the new instruments of state-building.

A key figure in the emergence of the Protestant ministry was Martin Bucer in Strasbourg, for whom the ministry of the church was instituted by Christ as the means of salvation; its central message is Christ himself. That ministry in the church, according to Bucer, has many branches and different people are to perform different tasks according to their abilities. Bucer made a crucial contribution to the Reformed Church through his division of ministry into ministers, elders, overseers, and deacons, each with a distinct function in the community. The first three are concerned with preaching the Gospel, teaching the faithful, administering the sacraments, and with the implementation of godly discipline. The deacons are committed to the care of the poor and sick. The function of all these offices was to teach the message of salvation and to apply it in the care of souls. The purpose of ministry, for Bucer, was to remain flexible because the pastoral needs of the people were so diverse.

Martin Bucer was the decisive influence on Jean Calvin, whose well-known four-fold division of the ministry was first expressed in the Genevan *Ecclesiastical Ordinances* of 1541: "First there are four orders of offices instituted by our Saviour for the government of his Church: namely the pastors, then the doctors, next the elders and fourthly the deacons. If we wish to see the Church well ordered and maintained we ought to observe this form of government" (Potter and Greengrass, *John Calvin*, p. 71). The pastors were to preach the Word of God and administer the sacraments, while the doctors were to "instruct the faithful in sound doctrine." The elders and deacons, following Bucer, had a more pastoral role; they were to admonish the faithful and care for the sick and needy. Humans are bound to the church on account of their fallen nature and the ministry exists to stir the faithful from their slumber, to feed them with the divine Word, and to promote the sanctification of the community through godly discipline. Far more than the Zwinglians, and again as a result of the influence of Bucer, Calvin stressed the importance of the institutional, visible church. Like all Protestants after Luther he taught that the church was the invisible body of the elect, but Calvin underscored the importance of the local, parochial church as an integral component of this body; it was a visible body of Christians gathered together to promote sanctification.

England offered an interesting variation from the empire, the Swiss Confederation, and France in that the episcopal system remained intact. Elizabethan churchmen had a highly developed sense of vocation which focused on preaching as the distinctive feature of the clerical office. As Bishop John Jewel wrote, in preaching "God lighteneth our darkness, he declareth his mind to us, he gathereth together his sacred sheep and publish unto the world the glad tidings of salvation" (Parker and Carlson, *"Practical Divinity,"* p. 60). Preaching was central to the emerging identity of the English Protestant clergy, yet the English reformers remained sensitive to the pastoral value of confession. Richard Greenham, a distinguished voice on the English pastoral office, wrote that Christians should "read the Bible," "frequent godly sermons," and "often confer with zealous preachers, for thy better instruction and sound confirmation" (ibid., p. 65).

With the ordinances of the German and Swiss churches of the 1530s the Protestant ministry came into existence. The first obvious consequence was the drastic reduction of the number of clerics in the parish as the lower clergy were removed, leaving each church with only one minister. In both Lutheran and Reformed lands the ministry assumed a roughly similar character. The head of the church, who was usually given a title such as superintendent or Antistes, was closely connected to the secular rulers. The authority of these men, such as Brenz, Bugenhagen, and Bullinger, was decisive. In the southern German and Swiss cities the heads of the church sat together with the Bürgermeister and leading members of the civic councils on the ruling commissions of the church. In the territorial principalities the leading Lutheran churchmen were often councilors to the prince.

There was a crucial second level of authority in the Protestant churches known as the superintendents or rural deans (in Swiss lands). These men were responsible for the preservation of order in a collection of parishes known as a chapter. The superintendent, who was generally a more senior minister, was required to watch over the activities of the parish ministers under his care and report problems to relevant authorities. Where problems arose it was the superintendent or dean who was expected to visit and admonish the minister. If such pastoral guidance failed to have the desired effect, the secular authorities would be brought in and the minister punished by fine or even imprisonment, should that prove necessary. The superintendent/deans were also required to hold consistory meetings at which the local clergy would gather to discuss events in the region and to be informed of decisions of the government. The parish minister would likely be the only ordained person in his community, although he might have an apprentice. Alongside the parish minister, however, there were other non-ordained officials, such as sacristans and churchwardens, involved in the running of the church. They would tend to the financial and material concerns of the parish, while the local bailiff would be responsible for the policing of the community. Although the effectiveness of the parish depended on harmonious relations between these officials, it often proved difficult to fill these positions on account of the hostility created in the community against those required to enforce the ordinances.

Across the churches of the Reformation we find broadly similar patterns of expectations for ministers. They were to hold services on Sundays, on several days through the week, on church holidays, and then during times of crisis, such as plague or war. In addition, Sunday afternoons were generally designated for the instruction of children. The celebration of the sacraments varied somewhat: the Swiss Reformed generally celebrated the Lord's Supper four times a year, a similar pattern was to be found among many German Lutheran churches, while in England communion was more frequent. Clerical vestments were abandoned. For urban reformers they were replaced by academic dress; whilst among the rural clergy a standard clerical dress seems not to have been widespread in the sixteenth century. To distinguish themselves from the Roman priesthood, the Protestant clergy adopted beards as the clerical fashion.

Church Discipline and Penance

The Reformation had begun with a dramatic rejection of the authority of the church when Luther publicly burned the bull of excommunication issued against him. Such defiance, soon to become part of the heroic myth of Luther as defender of liberty against institutional tyranny, greatly troubled the nascent Protestant churches as they struggled to stamp their authority on the laity and to work out their relationship to temporal authority. Central to this evolving identity was ecclesiastical discipline, the authority of the church to deal with public sinners. Having divested themselves of the sacramental authority of confession and penance, the new churches had to find alternative ways of dealing with communities in which, according to their theologies, the elect and the reprobate lived side by side.

Martin Luther addressed the issue of ecclesiastical discipline early in the 1520s. He argued that it was to be practiced in line with the Scriptural teaching of Matthew 18: 15–18, and therefore it was primarily about the conversion of the penitent sinner and the reconciliation with the community of one who had strayed. For Luther the church could enforce punishment on the sinner by refusing admission to the Lord's Supper, prohibiting the person from being a godparent, refusing marriage in the church, and finally, by forbidding Christian burial. What the church should not do, however, was to prevent any person from hearing the Word of God, the very instrument of reconciliation. The person excommunicated by the church should not be treated as a pariah, but rather as a lost brother. Luther was little interested in the means of discipline; his thoughts were occupied by Christian reconciliation, the means to which were visitations, personal conversations, and education (both public and in the home). Thus, ecclesiastical discipline was an integral part of pastoral care. Luther's views were largely shared by Melanchthon, who in his 1528 work *Unter-*

richt der Visitatoren placed church discipline firmly in the life of the local Christian community.

By the end of the 1530s, however, the situation in Germany had begun to change as the Lutheran churches put down roots. Discipline, which both Luther and Melanchthon had interpreted in terms of the spiritual work of the community, was being subsumed as part of the emergence of territorial states in the empire. A key person in this evolution was Justus Jonas, who in 1538 argued for the establishment of consistoria (morals courts) supported by secular authorities. In the German Lutheran churches ecclesiastical discipline, as the spiritual prerogative of the Christian community, gave way to a new constellation in which the churches worked with secular rulers to discipline the subjects of the state. Central to this construct was the superintendent, who, as head of the local chapters of churches, worked closely with the officials of the ruling prince to ensure that the ecclesiastical and civil ordinances were upheld in the communities. The superintendents took a leading role in the life and work of marriage courts, the consistoria, and visitations of parishes. By the second half of the sixteenth century, the Protestant rulers held regular visitations of their lands: villagers, both the laity and the local clergy, were publicly interrogated on their knowledge of the faith. These visitation committees consisted of superintendents, theologians, and representatives from the ruling council. The clergy were examined on their pastoral practices, the quality of preaching and worship, and their relations with parishioners. Where fault was found the first step was a fraternal admonition. When this failed more draconian measures were imposed. These could range from fines to suspension from office; quite common, however, was for a minister to be moved to another parish.

In the Swiss and German churches, in contrast to England, the minister was deployed as a servant of the state, and this proved an extremely uneasy relationship, fraught with complications on account of the centrality of the pulpit. It is fair to say that the magisterial churches of the sixteenth century only came to terms with the doctrine of *sola scriptura* by codifying Protestant beliefs through a wealth of confessional, catechistical, sermonic, and pastoral literature. The secular authorities had demanded their pound of flesh in return for supporting the new churches; Protestant ministers had to stick to the script or face the consequences. Assertions of Scriptural freedom, whether in preaching in Germany or the vestarian controversy of Bishop Hooper in England, would not be tolerated. The Protestant ministry, having shed its sacramental and hierarchical character, was something of a loose canon. Where, its critics asked, did authority reside within the new order? For many Protestants it was through the guidance of the Holy Spirit, but this proved very difficult to administer. The ultimate resolution was for the Protestant clergy to be bolted down by disciplinary institutions. Authority and structure in the Protestant ministry was to be imposed through the use of synods, visitations, and by pairing up ministers with civil officials.

Parish ministers were expected by church and state to lead the Christianizing of the community through preaching, visiting, teaching the catechism, and admonishing. In the ordinances of the German and Swiss churches, however, it was made clear that the power of the clergy was limited to admonition and supervision; ministers were not to excommunicate. Only the princes, or their officials, could mete out physical or monetary punishment. There was no firm division between ecclesiastical and secular offenses and the German Lutheran rulers punished men and women for transgressions against both civil and church ordinances. All activities in the parish were under the supervision of the secular rulers, although the minister was an important part of the disciplinary process.

Crucial to the Lutheran disciplinary process was confession. Although Luther had been in favor of retaining private confession in order that Christians might unburden themselves and relieve their consciences, he would not entertain any notion of sacramental absolution. Thus private confession became part of the German Lutheran churches, though utterly rejected by the Swiss Reformed. As Ron Rittgers has argued, this was reflected in the 1533 Nuremberg-Brandenburg church order. According to the order, each layperson was to submit to an examination of his/her knowledge of the faith before the minister would hear his/her confession and pronounce absolution, though this absolution was distinguished as a pastoral reassurance of God's forgiveness, and not the Catholic sacramental cleansing. Yet, despite this new model, it is clear that many laypeople did not wish to confess to ministers, preferring to participate in the general confessions held during worship. In an attempt to ameliorate lay fears about confessing to a minister, Lutheran churchmen like Johannes Brenz set limits on how deeply a clergyman should probe in helping an individual to relieve a troubled conscience. Thus, to a certain degree, Lutheran confession was dependent on the extent to which a layperson was willing to unburden him/herself. Confession was intended to relieve the conscience, not to incite anxiety.

In the Reformed tradition, discipline emerged as a central, if contested, aspect of the church's identity. In Zürich, Huldrych Zwingli had argued that the Christian magistrates should exercise the role of elders in the church and take responsibility for the punishment of sinners. The magistrates, as God's chosen rulers, should be advised by the ministers, who would interpret God's Word, but they should retain unto themselves full authority for wielding the sword. This view was opposed by Zwingli's friend and colleague Johannes Oecolampadius in Basel, who argued for a separate ecclesiastical court that would exercise authority over sinners. The civil authorities, he believed, should deal with crime, while the church dealt with those who offended against God's laws. Calvin developed the line taken by Oecolampadius in arguing that the church and magistrates had two separate polities, and that the church should retain the power of excommunication.

Discipline, for many early Calvinists (though not Calvin himself), was a mark of the true church. What did they mean by this term? That is not entirely easy to answer, but we can assert with Robert Kingdon that discipline meant both an ecclesiastical organization that had its roots in the apostolic church and a serious attempt to control all human behavior. In Geneva it took the form of the consistory, created in 1541, and was made up of lay elders, a syndic, and all the ministers of the city. This court was highly interventionist in the community and would summon large numbers of inhabitants – it has been estimated that up to a fifteenth of the population might appear before the consistory in a year. It examined all aspects of people's lives, but not simply to control them; for Calvin and his supporters discipline was a natural expression of the charge of Christ to the apostles in Matthew 18. Discipline was not about punishment alone, although there was an element of that, it was about conflict resolution, education in the faith, and helping people to live more Christian lives. It was intended to keep scandal out of the life of the community, and its invasive activities must be understood in terms of a world that had no concept of a private life. Additionally in Geneva the Company of Pastors, a gathering of all the ministers, were to discuss doctrine and to examine both themselves and all candidates for ordination.

Discipline became a hallmark of the Calvinist churches, but away from the established orders in Geneva and the Swiss cities it took different forms. In the Low Countries ecclesiastical discipline was central to the activities of the Dutch Calvinists during the 1570s and 1580s as national synods drew up plans for church organizations. But, unlike the Swiss churches, the Dutch Calvinist church was public but not official. That is, it was supported by the ruling authorities without being the official religion of the state, and the discipline of the church applied only to those who chose to join. Only a small number of people became members (perhaps 20 percent), thereby severely complicating the relationship between the church and civil magistrates. The disciplinary practices were formulated by the leaders of the Dutch exile churches Johann à Lasco and Marten Micron and owed much to Martin Bucer. The punishment and reconciliation of members of the church community were intimately connected with the Lord's Supper. The sacrament was celebrated six times a year and on each occasion the minister was to admonish publicly members whose sins had become known, and just before communion he would enumerate the offenses of the guilty. Each sinner had to make a public confession and express his/her remorse before being received back into the community and participating in the sacrament. The humiliation of public confession elicited a variety of responses from the congregations, but the willingness of many to undergo the ritual speaks to the importance of assuaging consciences.

In France every local Huguenot church possessed a consistory to which belonged the minister and half a dozen elders. The minister generally served as the moderator and the consistory was responsible for poor relief and discipline. When a problem arose in the community, at least two members of the consistory were sent to investigate. The suspected sinners were required to appear before the consistory and answer a series of questions. After a confession of wrongdoing was obtained the consistory expected the sinner to express remorse, though this did not result in an escape from punishment. Depending on the seriousness of the offense, the sinner could expect anything from a temporary suspension from the Lord's Supper to complete excommunication (Mentzer, "Notions of Sin," in Lualdi and Thayer, *Penitence*, p. 91). Frequently, however, a severe telling off from the minister was the most those caught playing card games or dancing might expect. Recent research has shown us the ritualistic nature of the discipline meted out by the French Huguenot consistories. The most common problems in these Huguenot communities, as across Europe, were feuding, strife, and violence. Ministers repeatedly had to broker peace agreements between members of the community who not infrequently had turned to violence. French Calvinist ministers often required penitents to engage in public acts of reconciliation in front of the community.

The Protestant Reformation replaced the sacrificial priesthood with a ministry based on preaching, education, and discipline. What made this possible was the support of the secular authorities, and without doubt the clergy became part of the system of social control. To leave it at this, however, is crudely reductionist. The three components of Protestant ministry were intended to bring about the moral and spiritual improvement of the people; confession, church discipline, and penance were intended to offer relief to afflicted consciences, and make reconciliation possible. It was realized that ministers could not make an assault on sin in all its forms, so the disciplinary systems of early modern Protestantism concentrated on what was known as "public sin." This was understood to be those things which did most harm to the life of the community. Private sins, it was well understood, would remain for God's judgment.

Clergy and the Laity

Religion in the sixteenth century was intensely local. Laypeople wanted services to be available within their community, and not at some distance. This poses one of the most perplexing conundrums for historians of early modern religion: why did the people want a clergyman, and full rites of the church, yet vehemently reject what they regarded as overbearing interference on the part of the church? To understand this, we must consider the complex relations which constituted the parish community. In the feudal system, when clergy were holders of parochial livings, they had various obligations to their patrons, which might be a cathedral chapter, a monastic house, or a local lord. Such benefices were regarded as property, and the obligations of the holder could include financial and economic matters, making the clergyman something of a local agent of the patron, responsible for administering property and collecting tithes. Resentment against the clergy's part in this oppressive regime was rife, particularly in southern German and Swiss lands, where it led to the communalism described by the German historian Peter Blickle. This growth of local control over the church reflected the desire of the people both to resist the feudal system and its tithes and to secure the rites of the church essential to salvation; it enabled the people to ensure that the priest was resident, sober, and diligent, and that the money generated by the church remained in the community. This idea was fueled by both the communal traditions of this region and the breakdown in political authority during the late Middle Ages with the collapse of the lower nobility and the rise of towns.

Much of the early success of the Protestant Reformation was through its alignment with anticlericalism. Across Europe, issues such as absenteeism, drunkenness, sexual promiscuity, and brawling caused outrage and, occasionally, a violent response on the part of the laity. One of the most powerful arguments deployed by the Protestant reformers focused on the figure of the fraudulent priest, the man who fleeced the members of the community and provided nothing in return. The fat, drunk, avaricious priest or friar was wickedly satirized in the pamphlet literature of the 1520s to much jeering on the part of men and women, because they recognized him in their community. Equally sinister and reviled was the mean-spirited cleric as agent of the landlord – often a religious house – who demanded payment in money or goods regardless of the severity of the times. Protestant propaganda made much of this, telling the people that these priests were not only driven by greed but that they were agents of the devil, deliberately working to impede their journey to salvation. This point was driven home by associating the rites of the medieval church with the false religions proscribed in the Bible and by the assertion of seemingly straightforward messages such as "faith alone" and "Scripture alone." The tables, however, were quickly turned and as soon as the new Protestant churches were established a new anticlericalism emerged, this time directed at the ministers who had replaced the priests.

In the wake of the disastrous Peasants' War of 1525 the Reformation ceased to be a popular movement; the mistrust engendered by Luther's support of the princes, the newly established Protestant churches' need for an ordered ministry, and the reemergence of the distinction made by most laity between the offensive character of their local cleric and their desire for a priest in the community created a new culture. The problem, or perhaps we should say challenge, was that if the Reformation was to take root it had to address the most fundamental issue of all, pastoral care. Here the laity proved to be anything but pliant, for men and women had clear ideas of what they wanted from a minister. He was to perform the sacraments, visit the sick, comfort the troubled and bereaved, and bury the dead. Certain aspects which troubled the Reformers greatly were of little consequence in the mostly rural parishes; the minister's level of education, for example, hardly seems to have brought a complaint, nor do we hear much about concubinage, so widespread in southern Germany and Swiss lands. The laity judged their minister on different terms, mostly on his ability to provide what they regarded as essential care. They took little notice of matters such as theological orientation and the minister's domestic life, unless they were a source of scandal, and they were prepared, unlovingly, to pay their dues in money and kind to support his work.

In most areas of the Protestant Reformation the shift to the new religion brought remarkably little change at the local level. In German and Swiss lands, priests became ministers overnight with the issuing of the new ordinances and they were expected to change their services accordingly. The problems were predictable: most local clergy had little sense of the new form of preaching, the teaching of the new faith, or of the services they were to hold. The 1528 visitation of Ernestine Saxony dramatically brought home to Luther and his supporters the depth of clerical and lay ignorance. The building of a new ministry required a tool which the reformers simply did not have in their bag: a new educational system. A new generation of clergy needed to be educated in the faith and prepared for a very different form of ministry. Philip Melanchthon in Germany and Huldrych Zwingli in Zürich turned their minds immediately to this task, but it would be a long time before the fruits would become evident. For the first few decades the Protestant churches had to make do with existing resources, and for the most part that was with former priests with only a rudimentary education. Canny decisions were made, beginning with the principle that it was better that each community have a minister, whatever his limitations, than for the local church to remain vacant. It was also decided that virtually all of the parish structures inherited from the late medieval church were to be kept intact; ideally the minister was to be supported by the churchwarden and a sacristan, while the local official, like a bailiff, would play an active role in the church as the representative of the ruling authorities.

For most of the sixteenth century following the Reformation we cannot speak of the clergy as a homogeneous body; social background and standards of education did not become fixed until the start of the seventeenth century. Although the social composition of the Reformation clergy still needs to be studied in detail, some trends can be observed: the new Protestant ministers mostly came from the towns and cities, many were displaced foreigners, and they frequently came from clerical families, that is, sons often followed their fathers. Also striking are the marriage patterns that emerged in both the German and English churches. Clerical families tended to marry one another, further reinforcing the trend toward dynasties within the churches. This endogenous tendency tells us something about the system of networks that emerged among the early modern clergy. The uneasy relations with the laity determined by their new brief accelerated the emergence of a new clerical estate in Protestant lands related not only by vocation but by blood. The result, primarily for the rural parishes, was a considerable social discrepancy between the clergy and their parishioners. The ministers were generally "outsiders." This raised a number of practical issues. Communities frequently complained, for example, that the minister foisted on them by the ruling authorities did not speak the local language and could not be understood. It was deep in the second half of the sixteenth century before the Protestant churches of Germany and the Swiss lands were able to recruit and train sufficient numbers of "home-grown" candidates, and this would become a foundation of the professional clerical class that would emerge by the end of the century. Until then, the appointment of ministers remained somewhat ad hoc as churches struggled to provide communities with an acceptable person.

Something similar is to be found in France, where the Huguenot formed only a small minority of the population. As Mark Greengrass has recently shown, the French church had 15 provinces and 50 colloquies spread through the kingdom. The French Protestant Church was disparate and often isolated, and the appointment of ministers to serve these communities was a complicated process. In contrast to the relatively well-appointed churches of the Protestant lands of the Swiss Confederation and the empire, the French churches struggled to support their clergy, if they could find any at all. Ministers had to be shared between communities and rivalries ensued as villages and towns were reluctant to relinquish a preacher when there was no certainty of a replacement. A recent examination of the correspondence of Huguenot ministers has shown that many suffered from loneliness and anxiety in the face of Catholic hostility; they would often undertake the arduous journeys to synods and colloquies in order to find comfort and support in gatherings of the faithful.

Local friction was intensified by a fundamental difference between the clergy and laity over what constituted acceptable conditions for the minister. Throughout the German and Swiss lands, parish buildings were in advanced decrepitude and the issue of the minister's income was extremely vexatious. Ministers argued that if they were to support a family, sufficient material recompense, such as a home, was required. The income generated by many rural parishes was insufficient to repair or build churches and houses, making these parishes extremely unattractive for prospective ministers. The Protestant churches faced problems on both sides, for the territorial and civic authorities, mindful of the political instability brought by the Reformation, were eager to employ many of the resources garnered in the dissolution of religious houses and other institutions for their own needs, such as fortifications. The reformers, having believed that resources of the old church were to be designated for the new, were bitterly disappointed and deeply resented having to go cap in hand for money to provide for the material fabric of urban and rural churches. As a result, many ministers in the sixteenth century had to resort to other means to stave off impecunity, and we find that ministers often had multiple roles in the community.

They took up trades or engaged in subsistence farming, thus bringing them into contact, and even competition, with other members of the community in ways that had little to do with the church. Such resourcefulness could create local tensions as farmers and tradesmen found themselves being preached to and admonished by a man with whom they might be doing business the next day.

This tension played itself out in other significant ways, reflecting the reality that whilst the Protestant churches had developed a new form of ministry they had, if anything, widened the gap between clergy and laity. All were agreed that the minister should reside in the community, but the reformers, and not the laity, had insisted on that minister having a family. The minister's family was held up, by writers such as Luther and Heinrich Bullinger, as an example to the community. But what sort of example could they provide? For the sixteenth-century reformers, the family was seen as the microcosm of the universe, with the minister presiding over the home in the same manner that God governed creation. The wife and children had their place in this pyramid and were to fulfill their appointed duties of looking after the household, providing for the children, and, in the case of the young ones, being educated in their Christian faith and a useful trade. The minister, as father, was to ensure the hierarchical stability of the family by a heady mixture of benevolence and severity, providing an example to his wife and children, as he was to his parishioners. In this vision, moral rectitude was essential, as was the ability to discern and admonish according to the needs of others.

The minister's family, therefore, was a sign that he was like other people and was to live like them, but the moral standard was such that this family simply could not be like the others. Disciplinary records of the sixteenth-century churches overflow with accounts of hostilities between clerical families and the communities in which they found themselves, reflecting the liminal nature of the relationship. The minister and his family were to be both part of and separate from the people they lived with, and this was no light burden. The minister was expected to preside over the essential ritual occasions of life (baptism, marriages, funerals) but not allow himself to become involved in the attendant festivities, with eating, drinking, and dancing, which were an integral part of the community's expression of joy or grief. To join in risked censure from the church or civil authorities, while to remain aloof only widened the distance from the parishioners. From what we read in the records, few ministers were able to balance these competing demands and most erred on the side of participation.

Likewise the minister's wife found herself in a difficult position, for the church regarded her as part of his ministry, yet no provision was made for her and her ambiguous situation in the community resulted in a variety of problems. Her role was a new one created by the Reformation, and for the sixteenth century we know very little about the plight of women who served in parishes. From marriage court records we can tell that infidelity was no less common among the clergy than the laity, and that the reputation of "clergy kids" is not a modern phenomenon. Neglect of one's own household seems to have been a not infrequent consequence of having to attend to a parish of other households. Ministers were frequently warned to control the behavior of their wives and children, but this was clearly more easily said than done, for the whole family was placed under enormous strain brought on by social and economic exigencies. Such negative pronouncements can, clearly, be read as an indication of the influence of the minister's wife in the community. Her daily contact with the parishioners was an integral part of the ministry, whether through conversations in the English town market or the spinning bees that became so important in Lutheran Germany.

It is difficult to generalize about the Protestant clergy of the sixteenth century. Despite theological tracts and church ordinances it was an amorphous body ranging from the well educated to the nearly illiterate. There have been several attempts to trace the growth of a professional clergy in the post-Reformation period, but before the seventeenth century this is highly problematical. It is only after 1600 that we find consistent patterns of a university-educated, well-paid clergy emerging from an urban middle class. These ministers had a distinct social and cultural status in early modern society. In the decades following the Reformation, however, we can find evidence for just about everything. The nascent Protestant churches struggled to impose a new model of Christian ministry during the ebb and flow of political tides. The theological, social, and economic implications of these changes were enormous; it was, however, with the clergy that we find most immediately the complexities of the relationship between new ideas and human behavior. The world of the parish minister – whether he was reading one of Luther's sermons from the pulpit to the sound of crying babies and barking dogs or admonishing a neighbor for failing to attend church – maps for us the profundity and uncertainty of religious change in the sixteenth century.

BIBLIOGRAPHY

Collinson, P., "Shepherds, Sheepdogs, and Hirelings: The Pastoral Ministry in Post-Reformation England," in W. J. Sheils and Diana Wood, eds., *The Ministry: Clerical and Lay*. Studies in Church History, 26. Oxford: Blackwell, 1989, pp. 185–220.

Dixon, C. S., *The Reformation and Rural Society: The Parishes of Brandenburg-Ansbach-Kulmbach, 1528–1603*. Cambridge: Cambridge University Press, 1996.

Dixon, C. S. and Schorn-Schütte, L., *The Protestant Clergy of Early Modern Europe*. Basingstoke: Palgrave, 2003.

Gordon, B., *Clerical Discipline and the Rural Reformation: The Synod in Zurich, 1532–1580*. Bern, 1992.

Green, I., "'Reformed Pastors' and Bons Curés: The Changing Role of the Parish Clergy in Early Modern Europe," in W. J. Sheils and Diana Wood, eds., *The Ministry: Clerical and Lay*. Studies in Church History, 26. Oxford: Blackwell, 1989, pp. 249–86.

Greengrass, M., "Informal Networks in Sixteenth-Century French Protestantism," in Raymond A. Mentzer and Andrew Spicer, eds., *Society and Culture in the Huguenot World 1559–1685*. Cambridge: Cambridge University Press, 2002, pp. 78–97.

Hunt, A., "The Lord's Supper in Early Modern England," *Past and Present*, 161 (1998), pp. 39–83.

Kooi, C., "Pharisees and Hypocrites: A Public Debate over Church Discipline in Leiden, 1586," *Archiv für Reformationsgeschichte*, 88 (1997), pp. 258–78.

MacCulloch, D. and Blatchly, J., "Pastoral Provision in the Parishes of Tudor Ipswich," *Sixteenth Century Journal*, 22 (1991), pp. 457–74.

Parker, K. L. and Carlson, E. J., *"Practical Divinity": The Life and Works of Revd Richard Greenham*. Aldershot: Scolar Press, 1998.

Schorn-Schütte, L., "The Christian Clergy in the Early Modern Holy Roman Empire: A Comparative Social Study," *Sixteenth Century Journal*, 29 (1998), pp. 717–31.

Schorn-Schütte, L., "Priest, Preacher, Pastor: Research on the Clerical Office in Early Modern Europe," *Central European History*, 33 (2000), pp. 1–39.

FURTHER READING

Dixon, C. S., *The Reformation in Germany*. Oxford: Blackwell, 2002.

Hsia, R. Po-chia, *Social Discipline in the Reformation: Central Europe, 1550–1750*. London: Routledge, 1989.

Karant-Nunn, S., *The Reformation of Ritual: An Interpretation of Early Modern Germany*. London and New York: Routledge, 1997.

Lualdi, K. J. and Thayer, A. T., eds., *Penitence in the Age of Reformations*. Aldershot: Scolar Press, 2000. In particular this chapter has made use of Raymond A. Mentzer, "Notions of Sin and Penitence within the French Reformed Community," pp. 84–100; Charles H. Parker, "The Rituals of Reconciliation: Admonition, Confession and Community in the Dutch Reformed Church," pp. 101–15; Ronald K. Rittgers, "Private Confession and Religious Authority in Reformation Nürnberg," pp. 49–70.

O'Day, R., *The English Clergy: The Emergence and Consolidation of a Profession, 1558–1642*. Leicester: Leicester University Press, 1979.

TWENTY-FIVE

Making Peace

OLIVIER CHRISTIN

On September 14, 1572, the Catholic and Protestant townspeople of St.-Affrique, in the south of the Massif Central, having been informed of the massacres committed some days earlier in Paris and other towns during St. Bartholomew, met in the town hotel to sign a mutual "accord" intended to preserve their peaceful coexistence and to avoid potential problems (*Archives nationales*, TT 268 [1] ff. 169sq.). Many participants solemnly proclaimed that "all the townspeople of both religions will be of but one body in which one will cause no offense against the other in order to protect and safeguard their living together"; they finally engaged jointly to protect the town against potential assailants and constituted a mixed government with a counsel of 12 members in which six Catholics and six Protestants took a seat. At a particularly dramatic moment in the history of the religious wars in the kingdom of France, the confessional parties could thus find local forms of an accord to preserve peace amongst themselves and to attempt to escape the spiral of violence. If this episode might *a priori* seem unusual, in fact it is not isolated from anything particular to the kingdom of France; it is related, on the contrary, in a specific European context, to religious peace treaties.

Religious Peace in Europe

The appearance and legal organization of the peaceful confessional coexistence between Catholics and Protestants illustrates a specific moment in the religious history of Europe. The countries of the south remained globally faithful to Rome while the Nordic countries turned to Protestantism. In the middle of the sixteenth century, numerous regions found themselves confronted with the end of Christian unity and with problems that created the rapid deepening of divergences amongst confessions: mounting violence, increasing powerlessness in the face of persecutions, and paralysis of institutions. Scarcely more than 20 years later (from 1555 to 1578), if one excludes the exceptional and exemplary case of Switzerland in 1531, several states or territories were to experience something which contemporaries in general called "peace," "pacification," or even "religious peace." This concerned the Holy

Roman Empire in 1555 with the Peace of Augsburg, France from 1563 with the Peace of Amboise, the principality of Transylvania during the 1560s and notably in 1568, the hereditary states of Habsburg in 1568 and at the beginning of the 1570s, Poland in 1573 with the famous religious clause of the Warsaw Confederation, the Netherlands in 1576 with the Pacification of Ghent and the Religious Peace of 1578. With the turn of the century and the turbulent course of the Counter-Reformation, relationships among the confessions in some areas paradoxically improved, in France with the Edict of Nantes (1598) and the Edict of Grace of Alès (1629), and in Bohemia with the Majesty of 1609.

Lasting or fleeting, respected or ridiculed, these religious peace treaties jointly outlined the legal and peaceful coexistence of several confessions within the same jurisdiction and under the theoretical authority of the same sovereign, prince, or magistrate. The more striking proof is undoubtedly found in the south of the Netherlands, where the decreasing prospect of reunification after the 1590s accompanied a growing lack of interest in the compromises of the 1570s: religious coexistence was losing the force of reality. Inspired and applied by the secular powers, often without or against the advice of the theologians and ministers of the rival churches, or at least part of them, the peace treaties thus not only constituted a decisive stage in the relationship between confessions in the second half of the sixteenth century and in the formation of the confessional map of Europe, but were also a test for certain states and secular authorities, who were obliged to redefine political and religious relationships and to base them on new theoretical justifications and practices, especially since other political entities led to the opposite, a policy of religious unification.

The religious peace from 1555 to 1578 aimed to settle or suspend the religious controversy by institutional balances, political concessions, territorial installations, and a great diversity of legal innovations. However, behind the "particularisms" which seem *a priori* to discourage any attempt at systematic comparison, the rules that were concluded almost simultaneously in order to bring an end to the religious wars show fundamental similarities. It is possible to provide a brief overview of these similarities, provided we keep in mind the distinctions between the technical and concrete provisions that were specific to each particular situation and each country, which cannot be taken into account here, and the general context in various countries. The similarities are so striking and so evident that they need to be stated. However, we also have to try to explain them by invoking the existence at the time of a common context for the majority of European countries in the middle of the sixteenth century, and the importance of a process of diffusion and imitation of pacification in several countries. It is surely the general context of central Europe that allows us to understand in part the rapid succession and the relative similarity of peace agreements in the middle of the sixteenth century. The confessional breakup of the first half of the sixteenth century and the rapid expansion of Calvinist reform (notably in France, the Netherlands, and Transylvania) in effect left sovereigns to confront their own powerlessness: not only had they failed to maintain or restore religious unity within their states, either by violence or by negotiation, but their attempts had only increased the distance and mistrust among adversaries everywhere, except in Transylvania, and demonstrated the failure of religious talks. Neither the edicts of persecution nor the military violence nor the efforts at doctrinal reconciliation had led to the expected results or filled the growing gaps between confessions. Peace came after disillusion, and most often in the hope of putting an end to civil war. In France, it was after the failure of the Poissy colloquy (1561) and the first religious war (1562–3) that the Peace of Amboise took shape; in the empire, it was in the wake of the fiasco of the Interim (1548) and the wars of Charles V that the successful compromise of Augsburg (1555) was framed; in the Netherlands, the efforts at religious pacification in 1576–8 were followed by nearly ten years of troubles and violence; in Transylvania, the accords concluded in 1552–7, 1564, and 1571 to avoid internal dissension only further weakened the country in the face of its powerful Habsburg and Ottoman neighbors.

As they were meant to appease the religious conflicts that endangered political society and were not to be succeeded by a definitive doctrinal accord or a unification of rival churches, the peace treaties introduced two general devices intended to settle the disputes and prevent the return of violence. On the one hand, they always, or nearly always, comprised a solemn promise of amnesty for the events of the past. Thus the first article of the Pacification of Ghent asserts that "all offenses, insults, wrongdoings, and damage, as a result of the unrest [. . .] will be forgiven, forgotten, and deemed not to have occurred" (*Representative Government*, pp. 433–47). Similarly, the Edict of Amboise commanded that "all insults and offenses [. . .] and all other past events and causes of the present turmoil shall remain obsolete, as dead, buried, and not having occurred" (Stegmann, *Édits*, pp. 35–6). On the other hand, they granted virtually all privileges to the nobility, who found themselves closely associated with the new institutional and religious balance that was established. In France, the lords who were the supreme dispensers of justice thus received the freedom of Protestant worship for themselves, their family, and their subjects; in the empire, the higher nobility and the imperial knights were the subject of an ad hoc article that made apparent the free choice of their confession; in Poland also, the nobility benefited from exceptional privileges that made individual religious freedom a characteristic of the nobility; in the hereditary Habsburg territories, lords and knights were the only ones able to enjoy the binding compromise granted by the sovereign, even if, locally, this restriction sometimes seemed to disappear rather quickly. In granting the nobles – or a certain portion of them at least – specific advantages in religious matters, the peace entailed the creation of passive coexistence and attempted to neutralize the factions and supporters who structured the confessional parties. As beneficiaries of the peace, the nobility were therefore to understand that they had nothing to gain by renewing hostilities.

With these religious peace treaties that aimed to put an end to violence and move away from the risk of civil and foreign wars related to religious quarrels, the political authorities thus embarked on an unfamiliar path toward institutional coexistence, in the name of the common good, the interests of the nation or those of the state. Charles IX consequently saw in the Peace of Amboise "the one thing in this world that we recognize to be the most useful for the good of our kingdom" (Christin, *Paix de religion*, p. 181). In a similar sense, the first article of the peace treaty of Augsburg underlines that this had been concluded "at last [. . .] to protect the German Nation, our beloved homeland, from definitive division and decline" (ibid., p. 37).

It can hardly be surprising if some of the most influential actors in the religious peace treaties or their most enthusiastic supporters saw established confessional coexistence as the occasion and perfect justification for an increase in the sovereign's powers, thus making him the guarantor of the civil peace and impartial arbiter among the parties and factions. We are familiar with the arguments of Michel de l'Hôpital or of Lazarus von Schwendi, who ended up assuming a role in the Holy Roman Empire not unlike that of a French chancellor. For Schwendi, by granting full religious freedom to all – prohibited in the peace treaty of Augsburg – the emperor was not weakening his political position; on the contrary, he "displays his peaceful and impartial wit [. . .] and, consequently, the government of your majesty, authority and obedience end up being reinforced" (Christin, *Paix de religion*, p. 193). Schwendi thus did not see any contradiction between the assertion of the modern state and the coexistence of several churches. Rather, the need for peace appeared favorable to him as an expression of new ambitions for imperial power. Reading the works of the French *politiques* yields other comparable examples. It is even more revealing to encounter this type of reasoning in the context of weak central power, as if the ideal of impartiality were still essential to it. At the diet of 1557 which sealed the legal recognition of Lutheranism in Transylvania, the regent Isabella Jagellon thus declared: "By our royal position and office, we are obligated to protect every church." In the middle of the sixteenth century, favoring the first systematic and successful efforts to leave the confessional confrontations behind, the ideal of the protective prince and impartial arbiter of confessions thus expressed itself on several occasions in Europe, within the framework of both a centralized monarchy and the federations of state (*Stände*).

The Law and the Contract

It seems essential, however, to distinguish between peace treaties granted or sanctioned by the sovereign, as in France or the empire, from peace contracts founded above all by the notion of reciprocity following the example of the Peace of Kappel or of the Religious Peace of 1578 in the Netherlands.

In the first case, by working directly to conclude the peace treaty and by propagating the peace treaty under his authority using the full force of the institutions available, the sovereign was careful to assume a central position in the organization of legal coexistence. In doing so, he at once became the ultimate guarantee and guarantor, architect and executor, and, above all, the principal beneficiary. Whatever his personal convictions, he was forced to protect religious rebels, at least those recognized in the letter of the peace. Thus between 1563 and 1567, with each new pacification edict, French Protestants, like German Lutherans after 1555, enjoyed the theoretical protection of the law, which gave them respite from persecution and the clauses of canon law concerning heretics; they even had judicial recourse to have their case heard and were usually eligible to apply for most offices. There is, of course, a big difference between the explicit intention and effective practice of peace, notably in France, but the contrast between attempts to grant religious dissidents the legal protection of the sovereign and what was observed in Poland and reinforced in the Netherlands does not remain any less striking. Peace thus found in the state the arbiter and guarantor of the common good, its justification and its internal structure: a solemn pact between old adversaries sanctioned and established by the state.

The Swiss cantons and the Low Countries succeeded in finding solutions that were very far from this model; in these two cases there was minimal reference to the central state, which was either absent or perceived as hostile. Peace was therefore constructed in the mode of an agreement between parties, or more precisely, of a contract by which the signatories made a mutual commitment. In the absence of sovereign authority and a perfectly legitimate method of validation – the Estates General of 1576 were united under unusual conditions and an unaccustomed constitution – and lacking the power to design an institution capable of judging infractions of the peace, it was only in the reciprocity of contracts that the form of confessional coexistence could take place. Even the text from the Peace of Kappel provides proof of this, as do the open debates concerning the Pacification of Ghent in 1576 and the Religious Peace of 1578. The controversial Protestant Duplessis-Mornay, for example, felt that the peace treaty of 1578 could only succeed on this condition: "to not prevent one another from freedom of thought and freedom of religion in these countries, since each one of us desires to live freely; and this since our country can only recover through this peace treaty, and the peace can only enter through this door" (Lecler, *Histoire de la tolérance*, p. 577). Only the mutual agreement of the contracts thus opened the door to peace: here we have a solution that is both audacious, since it dispensed with the need for the sovereign's approval, and precarious, since it is predicated upon each side's unreserved support for its principle, or at least upon the equilibrium of force and fear.

In practice, the contrast between these two forms of construction of agreement – one founded on the designation of an authority having sole arbitration in the name of all parties, the other on mutual agreement – is not as clear-cut as is suggested here. There were many transitional cases, imposed by institutional structures, political circumstances, and the relationship of religious forces, as in Poland, the Austrian Habsburg states (where the religious rights granted to the Lutherans in 1560–70 had a fragile official character, following the example of the Styrian dispositions which were never registered in the privileges of province), and Bohemia. It also appears obvious that some of those who brokered the peace of the state, with coexistence embedded in the law, were attempting to gain greater advantages in reference to the terms of pacts or contracts. In the second half of the sixteenth century, for example, many commentators of the Peace of Augsburg, concerned in general with its restrictions and even progressive abolition, questioned its contractual character and the possibility of unilateral revocation. Moreover, the burning question of the sincerity and validity of the peace settlements emerged especially surrounding the problem *De fide haereticis servanda*: was one bound by promises made to heretics or papists? Was not the prince entitled to free himself if the need arose, without fear of committing perjury? In contrast, to consolidate the terms of the 1531 pacification, the Swiss cantons eventually, at the beginning of the seventeenth century, designated a common court charged with adjudicating cases concerned with religious peace and thus achieved a manner of impartial arbitration. If between the two opposing styles in the creation of peace – the law, the contract – there existed many correspondences and many nuances, this distinction, however, remains essential if one wants to understand the opposing consequences of religious pacification for the political and religious evolution of different countries.

Because the peace treaty was ubiquitous, we have an opportunity to rethink the principal question of "two kingdoms," or, more precisely, of dual association. Could the prince agree to certain of his subjects adhering to another confession besides his own? Could he count on their political loyalty and their obedience? Did he not renounce an important part of his legitimacy and sovereignty in recognizing or tolerating religious dissidence? Some of the protagonists who played an essential part in the pacification settlements endeavored to supply coherent responses to these questions without resorting to the prince as the church's secular branch or resuming the logic of the religious wars: the views of Michel de l'Hôpital, who believed that "even the excommunicated do not stop being citizens," were shared by the author of a Protestant pamphlet in favor of the Religious Peace of 1578 in the Netherlands (Lecler, *Histoire de la tolérance*, p. 580). In this perspective, reinforcement of the state and religious rights were not contradictory: partisans and artists of the peace treaties unfailingly emphasized that the religious adversaries were co-citizens, subjects of the same prince and the same law, that they defended and followed together. In their eyes, the *Res Publica* transcended religious antagonisms.

The similarities between the different peace treaties – a general amnesty, prohibition of violence and abuse, particular rights for the nobility, partial agreement of political power – therefore inspire a comparative history, one that is attentive to the circulation of experiences and the programs and people that conveyed them. Even with a European perspective extended beyond France and Germany, there is no doubt that the second peace treaty of Kappel (1531) served as a model for all the countries confronted with confessional breakup and looking for a rapid exit, a political and secularized solution to the religious hostility: the Swiss precedent was in effect explicitly cited during the debates of the diet of Augsburg in 1555 and in the many works and pamphlets that accompanied the first French attempt at pacification, as well as in those written by adversaries or partisans. But in its turn, the path borrowed from the French monarchy was to serve as a reference in Europe and as a model, despite its repeated failures, which made the final criticisms of French pacification less fragile: if it had been as disappointing, unworkable, and condemned in advance as some historians have suggested, would it have been so praised by contemporaries and above all by certain informed observers? Lazarus von Schwendi, notably, who played an important role in the empire, did not hide his admiration for the work accomplished by L'Hôpital and the regent with the Peace of Amboise: from April 1563, in a letter to Duke Heinrich of Wolfenbüttel, he mentioned the peace treaty of Amboise, concluded a month earlier, and considered "that what is seen in France is that it is no longer possible to oppose change in religion only by sword and force," and "that we must tolerate the existence of a religion of another framework until God and time provide us with other means" (Mohrmann, "Bemerkungen zur Staatsauffassung Lazarus' von Schwendi," p. 520). Some years later, uneasy at the resumption of France's wars after 1567 and after St. Bartholomew, the signatories of the Religious Peace of 1578 in the Netherlands also referred explicitly to the French edicts.

In comparing the peace treaties of Europe, we free ourselves from the double illusion of particularism and finalism. We can demonstrate that attempts to bring about the peaceful institutional coexistence of several confessions were not the prerogative of one country or one political system alone but were born of a general context and a political reflection under a common party. We should recall that for contemporaries these attempts were not stillborn but were open, full of possibilities and promise, simultaneously allowing them to restore their true meaning and to question the reasons for their very different ways of functioning.

Freedom of Thought and *cuius regio*

The peace treaties of the sixteenth century and their inspirations were, in effect, driven by two distinct founding principles, whose opposition reflects rather well the political organization of the territories concerned and the state of prevailing power relationships: the axiom *cuius regio, eius religio* ("whose territory, his religion") and the idea of freedom of thought or freedom of choice of confession for all. Formulated tardily by Lutheran lawyers to define the principal line of the peace treaty of Augsburg, *cuius regio, eius religio* constituted in fact one of the major principles of organization for numerous other confessional coexistences that were institutionalized in Europe. Certainly, the beneficiaries of this concise axiom varied from one context to another, but the political logic of this type of compromise remained the same, that of freedom of religion, granted to single political authorities and to a part of the nobility: in Switzerland the peace treaty of Kappel left the cantons sovereign in religious matters without exceptions; in the empire, the peace treaty of Augsburg granted the *ius reformandi* to imperial estates only, which was not without ambiguity, for example concerning the imperial towns whose imperial status many contemporaries questioned; in Poland or in France it was the Szlachta nobles, who were the supreme dispensers of justice, who received the biggest benefit from this principle, by using it in the manner of a true *ius reformandi*. At first glance, the religious map of Europe consequently organized itself in the image of a leopard's skin, with a multitude of small sovereign entities in religious matters all strictly monoconfessional.

On closer examination, however, we see that this principle of *cuius regio* suffered from numerous exceptions. If in the empire and Switzerland these were rather marginal (ecclesiastical territories, biconfessional cities, imperial knighthood; common bailiwicks and mixed cantons), they were decisive for France, Poland, the Netherlands, and Transylvania, at which point it seems impossible to recognize them by applying the general principle. Some examples are sufficient to demonstrate this. In France as in Poland, the rights granted to a part of the nobility were primarily personal rights without territorial foundation: the lords who were supreme dispensers of justice benefited from the clauses that guaranteed them freedom of religion anywhere they found themselves (except in the entourage of the king), and not only in their everyday residence. Moreover, in the kingdom of France, it was the king in council who designated certain towns where the Protestant religion could be practiced, not the urban magistrates themselves or the local lords.

Here, therefore, it was the principle of freedom of thought that prevailed and structured the peace treaty, as was suggested in Article 6 of the Edict of Nantes: "Having allowed and allowing those of the aforementioned alleged reformed religion to live and remain in *all the villages and places* of our kingdom and country of our obedience without being questioned [persecuted], upset, mistreated, or com-

pelled to do anything for the sake of religion against their thought." The king turned
his back on a territorial solution, in reestablishing the Catholic religion everywhere
but in authorizing his Protestant subjects to reside where they saw fit. Their religion,
in contrast, was only authorized in certain places. The same choice was observed in
the Letter of Majesty of 1609 in Bohemia, which made the following assurance: "we
allow and grant the possibility in the 'Utraquist' States [. . .] to their subjects and
generally to all people without exception, who have professed or are professing the
Bohemia confession subject to the Emperor Maximilian, of glorious memory, our
well-loved father, of glorious memory, to the Diet of 1575, and subject again to ourselves, to practice their Christian religion under these two forms." In Transylvania
and in the Netherlands, the peace treaty turned its back still more on the theoretical bases of *cuius regio* in giving religious choice a definition that put it beyond the
reach of any secular power: faith was a divine gift to humanity, which no prince or
magistrate could obstruct. Like the Protestant apologist of the Religious Peace of
1578 already cited, "it is to each person in particular that this right pertains of not
having to change his religion except when he sees fit" (Lecler, *Histoire de la tolérance*,
p. 579).

The existence of several places of mixed confessions was the direct consequence
of these distortions of the principle of *cuius regio*. In numerous cities in France,
Germany, the Netherlands, Transylvania, Bohemia, and royal Prussia, in Swiss Glaris
and Appenzell, in Thurgau, members of the two (or more) confessions came together
daily. It was here that the concrete forms of coexistence were tested and the new
forms of relationship among confessions practiced: the division of time and space (for
example, the sharing of places of religious worship with different forms of *Simultaneum*), regulation of ceremonies (notably, the processions or burials that took up
public space), and the observance of forbidden times and forbidden foods.

The more religious peace distanced itself from the principle of *cuius regio* in order
to adopt the idea of freedom of conscience, the more it increased the number of such
cohabitations in the same place, as shown in the examples from France (the peace
treaty of Amboise permitted the Protestant service in a town by bailiwick and in all
those towns where it had already been present from March 7, 1563, a considerable
number), the Netherlands (the peace treaty of 1578 provided that the minority religion, Catholic or Calvinist, would be permitted wherever 100 families made a petition), and Transylvania. The paradox is worth emphasizing: it is the centralized
French monarchy and certain parts of the Netherlands that opened the widest door
to the concrete coexistence of Protestantism and Catholicism. This presented them
with a considerable challenge: to prevent daily contact between rival churches generating quarrels and disorder. Without the security of people and places of worship,
the freedoms granted by the peace treaty would indeed remain a dead letter. The
history of the religious peace of the sixteenth century cannot therefore be written
without taking into account the most basic everyday relationships among the
members of the rival confessions. Did they trade, did they discuss, did they intermarry? Did they live in the same streets and in the same neighborhoods? Did they
participate jointly in supervising the town and the management of its affairs? Did
they attend the same schools? Were they buried in the same cemeteries? These are
so many questions that cannot be ignored if we want to understand the effective
functioning of a peace treaty.

Challenges of the Peace

The first difficulties encountered by the actors in religious pacification arose when they had to put the peace into effect. Indeed, it was necessary not only to establish the exact text of the peace and make it known at least to those who would have the responsibility of applying it – police, lords, royal judges or urban magistrates, provincial governors or military leaders – but also to obtain as quickly as possible the resumption of order and the suspension of violence, reprisals, and provocation, and to bring back into the hands of legitimate authorities the instruments for exercising public control. In France and in the Netherlands, it is possible to observe the setting up of a genuine publishing network for disseminating the texts of the religious peace, backed by public readings and proclamations: the peace treaty of Amboise (1563) was published by local printers throughout a great number of French cities, including Orléans, Lyon, and Paris, and was also proclaimed as widely as possible to the subjects. Again and again, the king of France required his officers, ecclesiastical authorities, and local magistrates to make the text of the peace treaty known and to keep a copy in their possession "in order that each one of the townspeople can turn to it if need be" (*Archives Départementales Drôme*, B 996, ff. 44–6). Similarly, on November 8, 1576, the day on which the Pacification of Ghent was concluded, public readings were organized in Brussels and Ghent. The Brussels printer Michels van Hamont also received the right to print the text. This immediate publication of the peace treaties did not, however, prevent the appearance of different versions, which quickly became the source of interminable legal and judicial wrangling that constituted the most striking aspect of the juridification of religious conflicts in the second half of the sixteenth century, in France as in the empire, the Swiss cantons, and Poland. In France, for example, copies of the peace treaty of Amboise with the provisions concerning Paris deleted – where the Protestant religion was forbidden – were in wide circulation. In the Netherlands, dissimilar copies of the text of the pacification of 1576 also circulated, giving rise to some confusion.

The most difficult task, however, remained bringing about order and stopping the violence and threats that had preceded the signing of the peace treaty. The day after the peace treaty of Amboise of 1563, the king of France had to increase the number of edicts prohibiting adversaries from continuing private revenge and instructing all parties to lay down their weapons. It was these that were relayed by local authorities – governors, parliaments, or town councils – which, like Caen, banned "all the townspeople from carrying swords, daggers, or other prohibited weapons" (1567). The sovereign also planned a long tour of France that eventually lasted more than two years in order to bring tranquility to his kingdom and to strengthen his still fragile authority. These efforts were not excessive in relation to the immensity of the task: almost everywhere, armed groups continued to terrorize some of the townspeople, carrying out squalid acts of vengeance or refusing to apply provisions of the pacification edict. In Le Mans, for example, in the months that followed the return of peace, some of the leading protagonists of the first civil war were attacked, injured, or killed by strangers. The end of the most prominent violence, the disarmament of factions, and the installation of new judicial proceedings or the renewal of negotiation (imperial chamber court in the empire and mixed tribunals in France, which were composed of roughly equal numbers of Protestant and Catholic judges) only constituted the first stage of the true implementation of the peace treaty and the experience of daily coexistence. This first arrangement therefore had to be completed by a series of particular measures: condemnation of injuries and reciprocal threats, close monitoring of the circulation of books, and prohibition of controversial preaching.

During the debates of the diet of Augsburg in 1555, the idea of a specific article prohibiting controversial preaching was mentioned several times before being postponed indefinitely in the summer. The definitive test of the peace treaty remained, however, explicit in emphasizing that "each party must allow the other to maintain itself in calm and peace." The peace treaty of Amboise clearly forbade all subjects, whatever their condition, from "fighting, quarreling, and disputing together over religion, offending or provoking in actions or in words," a provision that we find again in most subsequent French appeasements, but also outside of the kingdom and notably in the Letter of Majesty of 1609.

To actually enforce interdictions was evidently not easy, even if the adversaries sometimes facilitated the work of the court and the local authorities by informing on provocateurs and offenders against the edicts, contributing to the considerable juridification of confessional confrontations. In Lyon in 1564, the townspeople insulted Franciscans in the streets; in Montélimar in the same year, some people overturned holy water in the town's church and insulted a Franciscan by yelling, "The fat bean eater! He ate them in his temple!" In the confessionally mixed town of Augsburg in 1561, a certain Caspar Herzog wrote abusive words against the Jesuits, Canisius, and the priests of the cathedral, especially the preacher. In the confessionally mixed district of Appenzell, at the end of 1579, Konrad Tanner, a recently converted Catholic, used the visit of the papal nuncio to leave abusive graffiti: on the representation of the Last Judgment in the parish church, he engraved the names of Zwingli, Luther, Gwalther, and Calvin above the condemned. Local authorities everywhere seemed to be working hard to prevent reciprocal provocation, verbal violence, and obscene gestures. But we must also note the revealing examples of almost unanimous condemnation of agitators who jeopardized the return to a peace that everyone knew to be fragile. In some cases, most townspeople of both confessions seemed effectively to refrain from serious offenses against pacification, as if they feared bearing the responsibility for failure or seeming to act against the sovereign's will. Thus one can see both Protestants and Catholics disassociating from their most aggressive coreligionists in an attempt to keep the peace.

Efforts for Peace

At the point where, for one reason (genuine adhesion to the peace treaty) or another (concern over obeying the sovereign, fear of retaliation, economic interest), supporters followed through with the peace treaty, we see the appearance of institutions and radically new political practices whose purpose was to organize and consolidate the local peaceful coexistence of confessions. This concerned mainly the councils of biconfessional or mixed-confessional towns, as in the empire (notably Augsburg, Biberach, Ravensburg, Dinkelsbühl), but also in France (Caen, Lyon, Orléans, Montélimar, and many others), in which Catholics and Protestants managed the business of the city together, although not without conflicts or difficulties. Also noteworthy was the less well-known existence of biconfessional committees of townspeople who were responsible for enforcing the essential clauses of the peace treaty and putting a stop to the belligerence of the most radically opposed. In Grenoble, Montélimar, Pamiers, and Valence, such groups of notables, consisting of equal numbers of Protestants and Catholics and sometimes armed, thus found themselves charged with supervising the progress of both religions, preventing attacks against the clergy, and calming opinions. In Montélimar, for example, it was decided that "there should be four of the most visible and prominent members of the town who will undertake to watch principally on Sundays and holidays during the services of both religions and the streets between the St. Croix church (where the Catholic religion is observed) and the 'Cordeliers' (where the Protestant religion is observed)" (*Archives communales Montélimar*, BB 46, f. 7). This principle recalls the spies (*stille Kundschaften*) of Augsburg who watched over the two religions and reported any incidents to the city council.

It is clear that the success of the peace treaty implied the implementation of an important set of rules and regulations that created the common instances of judicial negotiation toward the meticulous organization of biconfessional daily life. In this regard, the central powers and local authorities set themselves an immense task, which they approached in various ways and with unequal results, in attempting to invent new forms and new places of negotiation while simultaneously reviving old practices of friendly compromise. The groups of notables offering their services to the community recalled the "peacemakers" or "pacifiers" of villages from the Middle Ages and certain traditions in the creation of harmony within the cities.

The task of authorities who were appointed to implement the peace and who wished to bring it about (many only paid lip service to the idea of coexistence and failed to do their utmost) was made more difficult because the opportunities for confrontation in places of mixed confession were innumerable, and minor incidents could rapidly degenerate into large-scale riots. Anything, or almost anything, could spark off a conflict or dispute, since most disagreements among rival communities arose not from theological differences (the real presence, salvation by faith, predestination) but from tangible problems affecting the daily lives of townspeople of both confessions. The division of urban space – notably in relation to the recurring question of Catholic processions, which frequently aroused disputes and violence – the distribution of places of worship and cemeteries, the organization of the calendar and respect for feast days by Protestants, the excessive use of bells, the selection of schoolmasters, especially in small towns that could not increase the number of scholastic institutions and had to make do with one school, were almost everywhere liable to provoke antagonism and disorder. This does not even take into account the routine refusal of burials, disinterred corpses, cemeteries desecrated or situated as far as possible from town, Catholic processions jeered at or attacked, or Protestants instructed to decorate their houses, against their wishes, along processional routes.

Local coexistence, therefore, was carried through by the invention of compromises that were more or less equitable and sought to deal with the issues that threatened the way in which Protestants and Catholics thought of their belonging to the town. Besides the *Simultaneum*, two solutions were proposed: the division of places of worship, cemeteries, schools, bells, and an attempt at evenhandedness in the strict separation of the two bodies, on the one hand, and the creation of neutral spaces for common use, on the other. This last solution was practiced, for example, in measures adopted by some local French people around the issue of schools and bells. In 1652, the town council of Condorcet in the Drôme decided to keep the Protestant school-master because "in former times the children of Catholics were taught by the school-master of those belonging to this religion [Protestant] without anyone ever having been persuaded to change religions" (*Archives départementales de la Drôme*, E 4504 [BB1]). This decision was not exceptional: in 1697, the townspeople of Pont-de-Veyle, in Bresse, made a similar choice. This attempt at compromise was also observed in regard to the issue of bells. In towns with mixed confessions, commissioners who were responsible for implementing the provisions of the Edict of Nantes laid down strict rules in this matter in order to avoid provocation by the seizure of time by one of the parties. In the Dauphiné in particular, they reserved "the bell of the clock" for "the hours, gatherings in town, fires, and other matters concerning the public only" (Rabut, *Le Roi, l'Eglise et le Temple*, p. 174, in relation to Nyons). Protestants or Catholics could, however, acquire bells at their own expense to announce offices, prayers, or deaths, on condition that this was done in the hours when "there will be no competition between the two religious services" (ibid., pp. 70–1). While recognizing the legitimate rights of each confession, the commissioners thus tried to promote a confessionally neutral form of town administration.

Behind these compromises a specific type of argument can be identified: the inhabitants of a town shared common interests and together constituted a sort of common political body. Beyond their religious differences, they remained above all fellow citizens, sharing similar honors and being responsible for similar tasks. What is expressed here is a particular definition of citizenship that was shared by those known as "the *politiques*," since they placed the continuation of the state above the pursuit of religious unity, and especially in the writings of one of their chief inspirers, Jean Bodin. In a decisive chapter of *La Republique*, Bodin predicted that "several citizens [. . .] make a Republic for themselves [. . .] and still they are diverse in law, language, customs, *religions*, and nations. And if all citizens are governed by the same laws and customs, it is not only a Republic [but] also a City" (Rabut, *Le Roi, l'Eglise et le Temple*, pp. 94–5). Religious diversity did not prevent Catholics and Protestants from becoming fellow citizens if they recognized the full sovereignty of the prince in public affairs.

It is therefore not surprising that, in exceptional circumstances, certain French towns, like St.-Affrique at the beginning of the chapter, made extraordinary efforts to consolidate the unity of their townspeople despite religious dissent in order to avoid the resumption of civil war. In 1567, when the second religious war commenced, in 1572 after St.-Bartholomew, or during the period of wars in Rohan at the beginning of the seventeenth century, Protestant and Catholic townspeople concluded amongst themselves solemn pacts by which they promised each other assistance and mutual protection, friendship and fraternity. Signed by members of the general assembly, indeed by the gathering of men from the town, these pacts amply demonstrate the specific consequences of French peace treaties which made politics the point of conciliation and reconciliation of religious factions. It was only within the political sphere that religious divisions could be overcome or put in parentheses for the benefit of a new definition of the common good.

Peace-making amongst rival confessions in the sixteenth century cannot therefore be reduced to the search for hypothetical doctrinal accommodations: it always involved a genuine long-term task, both political and judicial. Little by little, not without difficulties and, above all, not without failures, the adversaries created specific intellectual and institutional tools – religious parity, the *Simultaneum*, the idea of non-confessional fellow citizens – which permitted, here and there, the development of genuine experiences of peaceful coexistence in which Protestants and Catholics could maintain economic, political, and symbolic exchanges with one another.

BIBLIOGRAPHY

Binder, L., *Grundlagen und Formen der Toleranz in Siebenbürgen bis zur Mitte des 17. Jahrhunderts*. Vienna and Cologne: Böhlau.

Blockmans, W. P. and Peteghem, P. van, "La pacification de Gand à la lumière d'un siècle de continuité constitutionnelle dans les Pays-Bas, 1477–1576," in R. Vierhaus, ed., *Herrschaftsverträge, Wahlkapitulationen, Fundamentalgesetze*. Göttingen: Vandehoeck & Ruprecht, 1977, pp. 220–34.

Christin, O., *Une revolution symbolique: L'iconoclasme huguenot et la reconstruction catholique*. Paris: Éditions de Minuit, 1991.

Die Chroniken der deutschen Städte vom 14. bis 16. Jahrhundert, ed. Historische Kommission bei der Bayerischen Akademie der Wissenschaften. *Die Chroniken der schwäbischen Städte*, Augsburg, vol. 8, Leipzig, 1928: "Das Diarium Paul Hektor Mairs, 1560–1563," pp. 123–4.

Clemns-Denys, C., "Les apaiseurs de Lille à la fin de l'Ancien Régime," *Revue du Nord*, 309 (1995).

Espinas, G., "Les guerres familiales dans la commune de Douai au XIII–XIVe siècles. Les trêves et les paix," *Nouvelle revue de droit français et étranger*, 1899.

Mentzer, R. A., "Bipartisan Justice and the Pacification of Late Sixteenth-Century Languedoc," in J. Friedman, ed., *Regnum, Religio et Ratio: Essays presented to Robert M. Kingdon*. Kirksville, Mo.: Sixteenth Century Essays and Studies, 1987, pp. 125–32.

Mohrmann, W. D., "Bemerkungen zur Staatsauffassung Lazarus' von Schwendi," in H. Maurer and H. Patze, eds., *Festschrift für Berent Schwineköper*. Sigmaringen, 1982.

Müller, M. G., "Protestant Confessionalisation in the Towns of Royal Prussia and the Practice of Religious Toleration in Poland-Lithuania," in O. P. Grell and R. Scribner, eds., *Tolerance and Intolerance in the European Reformation*. Cambridge: Cambridge University Press, 1996, pp. 262–81.

Nicklas, T., *Um Macht und Einheit des Reiches: Konzeption und Wirklichkeit der Politik bei Lazarus von Schwendi (1522–1583)*. Husum, 1995.

Peter, K., "Tolerance and Intolerance in Sixteenth-Century Hungary," in O. P. Grell and R. Scribner, eds., *Tolerance and Intolerance in the European Reformation*. Cambridge: Cambridge University Press, 1996.

Rabe, H., "Der Augsburger Religionsfriede und das Reichskammergericht 1555–1600," in H. Rabe et al., eds., *Festgabe für Ernst Walter Zeeden*. Münster, 1976.

Rabut, E., *Le Roi, l'Église et le Temple [Texte imprimé]: L'exécution de l'Édit de Nantes en Dauphiné*. Grenoble: La Pensée sauvage, 1987.

Representative Government in Western Europe in the Sixteenth Century: Commentary and Documents for the Study of Comparative Constitutional History. Oxford, 1968.

Ruthmann, B., *Die Religionsprozesse am Reichskammergericht*. Cologne, Weimar, Vienna, 1996.

Scheurmann, I., ed., *Frieden durch Recht: Das Reichskammergericht von 1495 bis 1806*. Mainz, 1994.

Stegmann, A., *Édits des Guerres de Religion*. Paris: J. Vrin, 1979.
Tazbir, J., *Geschichte der polnischen Toleranz*. Warsaw: Interpress, 1977.
Walder, E., ed., *Religionsvergleiche des 16. Jahrhunderts*. Bern, 1945.
Warmbrunn, P., "Simultaneen in der Pfalz," *Jahrbuch für westdeutsche Landesgeschichte*, 14 (1988), pp. 97–122.

FURTHER READING

Christin, O., *La Paix de religion: L'autonomisation de la raison politique au XVIe siècle*. Paris: Éditions du Seuil, 1997.
Cottret, B., *1598, l'édit de Nantes: Pour en finir avec les guerres de religion*. Paris: Perrin, 1997.
Grell, O. P. and Scribner, B., eds., *Tolerance and Intolerance in the European Reformation*. Cambridge: Cambridge University Press, 1996.
Lecler, J., *Histoire de la tolérance au siècle de la Réforme*. Paris: Montaigne-Desclées de Brouwer, 1955.
Ruthmann, B., *Die Religionsprozesse am Reichskammergericht*. Cologne, Weimar, Vienna, 1996.
Tazbir, J., *Geschichte der polnischen Toleranz*. Warsaw: Interpress, 1977.
Warmbrunn, P., *Zwei Konfessionen in einer Stadt: Das Zusammenleben von Katholiken und Protestanten in den paritätischen Reichsstädten Augsburg, Biberach, Ravensburg und Dinkelsbühl von 1548 bis 1648*. Wiesbaden, 1983.

Twenty-Six

Magic and Witchcraft

James A. Sharpe

Belief in magic and witchcraft was one of the distinctive elements in the intellectual life of Europe in the era of the Reformation. Representatives of all social classes, from the highly educated man of letters to the illiterate peasant, accepted that their world was subject to occult (that is, "secret" or "hidden") forces, and that individuals were able to harness these forces, sometimes for good, sometimes for evil. For many modern readers, these beliefs frequently serve as an indicator of the backwardness and ignorance of past societies, mere superstitions which were to be swept away by the onward march of progress, and in particular of rationality and science. But such an attitude is both ahistorical and intellectually limiting. Early modern Europeans were not stupid people: they thought in different ways from their modern equivalents, and with a different intellectual toolkit, while the writings of both intellectuals concerned with the magical arts and theologians concerned with the problem of witchcraft frequently show intellectual subtlety and immense learning. And, as mention of the writings of theologians on witchcraft suggests, magic and witchcraft presented the Christian Church with a number of intellectual and theological problems.

Defining magic and witchcraft is difficult. Broadly, magic can be regarded as the ability to control, summon, and direct such occult powers and forces as are believed to exist in natural creation, usually with the intention of altering or adjusting the course of nature to produce a desired effect. The man or (less usually in the Reformation era) woman doing this controlling, summoning, or directing does so through techniques or rituals which have been learned. In other words, one can acquire the ability to perform magic through study, and hence magic can be (and in fifteenth-, sixteenth-, and seventeenth-century Europe certainly was) regarded as a learned activity which can place severe intellectual demands on the magical practitioner. Witchcraft was a concept that was undergoing severe alterations in our period. Most human societies, as anthropologists remind us, believe in witchcraft or something very like it, and witches had been thought to exist in Europe from the early Middle Ages at least. The witch was felt to be somebody who had innate powers that could be mobilized for good or (much more worryingly) evil. Traditionally, it was felt that those powers could be inherited (most frequently by a female witch from her mother) or learned. But from the fifteenth century a new model of witchcraft emerged in which Christian theologians, taking a new interest in the issue, argued that witches were not isolated magical practitioners but rather members of a heretical and Satanic sect, and that their powers came from a pact they had made with the devil.

The dividing lines between magic and witchcraft in early modern Europe are hard to define, and one is left with the distinct impression that "magic" was the label attached to the activities of occult practitioners who were upper class, educated, and male, while "witchcraft" was the label attached to the activities of those occult practitioners who were poor, uneducated, and female. Certainly, as we have noted, that area of intellectual speculation which we categorize as "magic" attracted the attention of some very intelligent and educated men.

Magic

One of the key magical texts of the period was the *De Occulta Philosophia*, written in 1510 and published in 1531, the work of the great German physician and occultist Henry Cornelius Agrippa von Nettesheim (1486–1535). Magic, to Cornelius Agrippa, was

> a faculty of wonderful power, full of most high mysteries, containing the most profound contemplation of most secret things, together with the nature, power, quality, substance and virtues thereof, and the knowledge of whole nature, and it doth instruct concerning the differing and agreement of things amongst themselves, whence it produceth its wonderful effects, by uniting the virtues of things through the application of them one to the other, and to their inferior suitable subjects, joining and knitting them together thoroughly by the powers and virtues of superior bodies. This is the most perfect and chief science, that sacred and sublimer kind of philosophy, and lastly the most absolute perfection of all excellent philosophy. (Agrippa, *Philosophy of Natural Magic*, pp. 38–9)

Given his exalted view of magic, it is appropriate that this writer should insist that the would-be student of magic should be expert in natural philosophy (or, in modern terminology, science), mathematics, and astrology, for without this knowledge "he cannot possibly be able to understand the rationality of magic." Thus, for this most celebrated of occult writers, magic was something which operated on a high intellectual and moral level, and was a demanding and (in modern terminology) "scientific" activity.

Magic as an intellectual system and occult learning more generally had been given a tremendous impetus by developments in the second half of the fifteenth century. One of the major factors in this process was the spread of Greek translations of Plato's works, a development often associated with the fall of Constantinople to the Ottoman Empire in 1453 and the subsequent westward movement of Ancient Greek texts. Plato's works were not unknown in the Middle Ages, but now Platonic, or perhaps more accurately Neoplatonic, learning attracted considerable attention, and this learning was virtually designed to reinforce a belief in the occult. The differences between spiritual and physical matter became blurred, the earth was construed as a living entity, and the universe was represented as being filled with a hierarchy of spirits and was thought to be riddled with occult influences and sympathies. But as well as

Platonic texts, there became available a body of writing associated with the mythical Egyptian magician Hermes Trismegistus, a corpus of occult works which were thought, incorrectly, to be of very ancient origins, predating Moses. And, to cite a third major influence, there was the cabala, a body of traditional Jewish knowledge which entered the European intellectual mainstream via Spain. Cabala (also rendered "kabbalah" in modern English-language works) is derived from an Arabic word meaning "tradition," and was thought, among other things, to lead the contemplator to a deeper comprehension of the nature of God and of how divine power operates in what was construed as an ascending hierarchy of planes or worlds. The knowledge acquired in this process could be put to use by manipulating the names of power, which gave tremendous potency to the person who had learned how to master the appropriate techniques. Thus, of course, cabalistic writings assumed massive significance for those interested in magic.

The crystallization of this newly acquired magical and occult thinking is associated with the Florentine Renaissance and, in particular, with two major thinkers, Marsilio Ficino (1433–99) and Giovanni Pico della Mirandola (1463–94). Ficino became famous for his translation of Platonic texts into Latin, and was also responsible for rendering into that language a body of Greek texts, supposedly composed by Hermes Trismegistus, which became known as the *Hermetica*. Pico della Mirandola wrote widely on magical subjects, and, in particular, attempted to demonstrate that the cabala supported Christianity by showing how the coming and life of Jesus were prefigured in Jewish mystical literature (his efforts, sadly, provoked the condemnation of Pope Innocent VIII). Magic as a matter of intellectual concern rapidly became established throughout Europe, being spread northwards from Italy by the works of Cornelius Agrippa and Paracelsus (the pen name of the Swiss physician and alchemist Theophrast Bombastus von Hohenheim, 1493–1541). The various elements in this new occult thinking interacted with each other, with the existing canons of Aristotelian science and Galenic medicine, and, of course, with official Christianity, Catholic and Protestant alike. Many thinkers were able to combine facets of these different and sometimes seemingly antipathetic intellectual systems into a fascinating and, in their minds at least, effective synthesis, an interesting example here being the English thinker Robert Fludd (1574–1637).

But, of course, not all magical practitioners of the late medieval and early modern periods were educated or indeed scholarly individuals bent on constructing or unlocking the secrets of sophisticated intellectual systems. Far more common, if infinitely worse documented, were the practitioners and purveyors of popular magic. Most of what we know of their beliefs and activities comes either from court records describing their prosecution, or from the writings of learned critics of what were regarded as theologically erroneous popular superstitions. What is obvious is that magic was very much a live issue among the population at large, but that this magic was in many respects different from that of the Renaissance intellectual. Magic on this level does not seem to have operated as an intellectual system in the same way as it did for, let us say, Cornelius Agrippa. Nor did magic constitute an alternative intellectual system, still less religion, to Christianity. There were, without doubt, many pre-Christian elements in folk magic, but most popular magical practitioners, and most of those seeking help from them, would have regarded themselves as good Christians. So throughout Europe, and throughout Europe's American colonies (New England included), practitioners of popular magic, known under a variety of names (cunning man or woman was most common in England), offered the population at large a number of services: using charms and divinatory techniques, they could help find stolen goods, provide folk remedies for illness, tell fortunes, and help identify and develop counter-magic against those whom individuals thought to be bewitching them. The worlds of village cunning folk and of the educated magical practitioner were very distant, although the spread of literacy over the early modern period meant that at least a few popular magicians were reading books on natural magic, the occult, and astrology as they went about their business.

The activities of these local magical practitioners were almost universally condemned, either as manifestations of the credulity and superstition of the masses, or as manifestations of demonic magic. The reactions to educated magic were more mixed. Magic on an elite level was an activity, and a body of beliefs, which, as we have noted, created problems for the Christian Church, yet the church's position on the matter was in many ways ambivalent. Most contemporaries would have agreed that there were two types of magic: "demonic" magic, which everybody condemned, and "natural" magic, whose status in the eyes of the church was less clear-cut. Most Christian theologians who committed their thoughts on the subject to print apparently regarded magic as something of a gray area. They were aware that some of the more extreme claims made by occultists seemed to bring even God under the powers of the magician, which was clearly unacceptable, and at the very least the natural magic of the educated believer or speculator suggested a distinctive perspective on the nature of the relationship between God, humankind, and the universe. Yet mostly magicians claimed to be attempting to control occult powers inferior to the Almighty, while the fact that neither the magical thinking of the period nor Christian thinking about it were monolithic left the way open for the adoption of a variety of positions on the subject among Christian thinkers. There was a general nervousness about at least some aspects of magic, but few Christian thinkers, some extreme Protestants apart, were able to reject it entirely.

The Witch-Hunts

This ambivalence was absent, on an initial level at least, in the Christian Church's attitude to witchcraft. The belief in witchcraft was, let us remind ourselves, long established in Europe by the Reformation period. But now there came the innovation of the development of a new image of the witch which saw her (for most of those, maybe 80 percent over Europe as a whole, accused as witches were women) not as an isolated doer of evil but rather as the member of a newly arrived heretical sect who owed her power to do harm to having made a pact with the devil, this power being given to her in exchange for her soul. The exact reasons remain obscure, but it is currently accepted that the new image of the demonic witch originated and became established in a number of trials that occurred in Switzerland and the extreme north of Italy in the first half of the fifteenth century. At about the same time, a number of tracts were written, largely on the basis of these trials, describing the new witch stereotype: hence the science of demonology came into being.

The formative phase of witchcraft beliefs was encapsulated in 1486 with the publication of what is probably the most notorious of demonological texts, the *Malleus*

Maleficarum, once thought to have been co-authored by two Dominican inquisitors, Jacob Sprenger and Heinrich Kramer (or Institoris), but attributed by the most recent scholarship solely to the second of these men. Although the *Malleus* has been widely, and sometimes carelessly, cited by modern commentators, its influence was probably less than has occasionally been claimed: it stated a contested position rather than a new hegemony, it did not initiate a new wave of witch-hunts, and a number of later judges and writers were to treat it with extreme caution. It did, however, play an important role in three respects. Firstly, as we have suggested, it acted as a summation of the new notion of the demonic witch, although, interestingly, it had little to say on the sabbat. Secondly, it was important in reminding secular judges that they, as well as ecclesiastical inquisitors, could try persons suspected of witchcraft, and encouraged them to do so; and, thirdly, it emphasized the connections between witchcraft and the female sex (Institoris appears to have been both prurient and rabidly misogynistic). A large, disorganized, yet learned and powerful work, it still must be regarded as a landmark in the history of witch-hunting in Europe.

Curiously, on the strength of the current state of our knowledge, the publication of the *Malleus* did not encourage a wave of witch-hunting. Witches were prosecuted, and a number of tracts written, over the first half of the sixteenth century, but there was little to match either the levels of witch-trials, or the flurry of publications about witchcraft, which were to occur in the years after 1560. It is impossible not to see this development as operating within the context provided by the Reformation and the Counter-Reformation. Correct religious beliefs were now being more rigorously defined, these definitions were being more rigorously enforced, and there was a widespread acceptance that, either in the face of a purified Christianity or as a consequence of the knowledge that the world was near its end anyway, the devil and his minions were becoming more active. A number of European territories were to experience severe witch-hunts in the 1590s, while there was also a stream of demonological publications warning their readers of the danger of witchcraft and the urgent necessity of extirpating it. Among the most noteworthy of these were the *De la Démonomanie des Sorciers* of 1580, written by probably the most important intellectual of the day, Jean Bodin; the Jesuit Martin del Rio's *Disquisitionum Magicarum Libri Sex* of 1599, regarded as a latter-day *Malleus Maleficarum*; and Pierre De Lancre's *Le Tableau de l'Inconstance des mauvais Anges et Démons* of 1612, this last based on confessions extracted by its author while trying witches in the French Basque country, and containing unusually full and vivid descriptions of the sabbat.

It should be noted, however, that despite some recent popular histories and the tone of some previous scholarly work, the witch-hunts were limited in their extent, and varied greatly in their intensity between regions. The figure of 9 million executed witches, so freely bandied about a generation ago, has been substantially reduced, and it is now estimated that the period of the European witch-hunts, beginning in the early fifteenth century and ending in the late eighteenth, saw maybe 100,000 individuals accused of witchcraft, of which perhaps 40,000 were executed. Some areas experienced heavy witch-hunts, others saw virtually no witch executions, while, to address an issue which considerably exercised some nineteenth-century commentators, it is difficult to see any consistent difference between Catholicism, Protestantism, and the willingness to prosecute witches. Calvinist Scotland saw mass hunts in 1590–1, 1597, the late 1620s, 1649, and 1661–2, while the Calvinist Palatinate and the (in formal terms at least) Calvinist Dutch Republic saw almost no witch-trials. Conversely, those trying to link a propensity to hunt witches to Catholicism should note that neither the Spanish Inquisition nor its Italian counterpart were much concerned with hunting witches. Witch-trials were almost unknown in many areas, were usually spasmodic and episodic in areas where they were known, and yet (as was demonstrated in eastern England in 1645–7, in Sweden in 1668–76, and in Salem, Massachusetts, in 1692) could break out with appalling ferocity in areas where there was little reason for either contemporaries or later historians to expect them.

The mass trials which did occur continue to horrify modern observers, their sensibilities over such matters being sharpened by an awareness of the much greater horrors which occurred in twentieth-century Europe. There was, for example, that wave of mass trials and mass burnings which occurred in a number of southwest German territories, most of them Catholic and some of them prince-bishoprics, in the early seventeenth century. The small prince-provostship of Ellwangen experienced, on what might be a conservative estimate, some 400 burnings between 1611 and 1618, while around 1616 burnings began in the prince-bishoprics of Würzburg, Bamberg, and Eichstätt. In Würzburg the famous Reforming Bishop Julius Echter von Mespelbrunn presided over the burning of more than 300 witches between July 1616 and June 1617. In Bamberg another 300 supposed witches were burned between 1616 and 1618. These levels of persecutory zeal were, however, exceeded in the small bishopric of Eichstätt, where witches were burned every year between 1617 and 1630, estimates of the total executed over this period varying between 122 and 274. The region experienced a new wave of burnings in 1625–30: maybe 600 people in Bamberg, perhaps 900 in Würzburg, and with high, although undetermined, levels of executions slightly further north in Mainz. These southwest German trials were distinguished by indiscriminate torturing of suspects, and by prolonged interrogations under torture which induced individuals suspected of witchcraft to name large numbers of associates: thus a fishwife from a village near Eichstätt denounced 22 persons as witches, a peasant woman 261. Under such conditions, it is hardly surprising that members of social groups usually unaffected by accusations of witchcraft were tried and burned: among them were burgomasters and their wives, town councilors, other officials and their wives and dependants, young noblemen, and clergymen, including some of reasonably high rank.

Happily, witch-burnings on this scale were the exception rather than the rule, while in some areas (notably France) by about 1630 the propensity to persecute people as witches was declining. By the later seventeenth century many European states which had previously witnessed trials, among them France, England, Denmark, some German territories, and (perhaps less certainly) Scotland, were experiencing a very low intensity of witch-hunting. By this time, however, the witch-hunts were to be breaking out anew in eastern Europe. In Hungary witch-trials and witch-executions, albeit running at a level lower than that of southwest Germany in the late 1620s, peaked between 1710 and 1730. At about the same time, serious witch-hunting broke out in Poland. This Polish episode is currently being researched, and there is a strong possibility that the extent of the persecution has been exaggerated by previous historians. On the strength of current interpretations, however, there does seem to have been extensive witch-hunting in early eighteenth-century Poland, in this case linked to an aggressive campaign of Catholicization. Many other parts of Europe experienced scattered trials and the occasional execution until well into the eighteenth century: but by about 1750 the desire to burn witches, and the theological and intellectual bases which encouraged such a desire, were in near-total abeyance.

Explaining the Witch-Hunts

Thus we have a brief chronology of the European witch-hunts. Even before the last legal execution occurred (so far as is known in Switzerland, where the witch-hunts had begun, in 1782), people were trying to find an explanation for an episode in European history which, in the eyes of Europeans enmeshed in the new values of the Enlightenment, seemed irrational, striking evidence of the barbarity and bigotry of past ages. Ever since the mid-eighteenth century, explanations for the witch-hunts, some more convincing than others, have never failed to be forthcoming.

There can be little doubt that at the center of that phenomenon that we might still describe, for the sake of custom and convenience, as the European witch craze lay the context provided by developments in the late medieval and early modern Christian Church. The new stereotype of the devil-worshipping witch was essentially created by inquisitors in the fifteenth century, evidence of a continued concern for achieving religious purity. This concern was increased enormously in the sixteenth century with the coming of the Reformation and the Counter-Reformation, two movements which demanded a higher level of Christian understanding, a higher level of Christian knowledge and Christian conduct, and which were, as is the nature of campaigns for ideological purity, likely to encourage the imagining of and hunting for deviants. This is not to say that either the Reformation or Counter-Reformation encouraged witch-hunting in any simplistic manner: it is rather to argue that ideas about what witches did, why they existed, and why they had to be extirpated were, for most educated and many uneducated Europeans, linked at least to some extent with the greater intensity over matters religious that permeated European society, region by region, in the two centuries after Luther nailed his Theses to the door of Wittenburg cathedral.

Also of considerable importance was the running together of the concerns of the church authorities and those of secular rulers into what early modern English observers would have called the godly commonwealth and what modern historians describe as the confessional state. This connection was, for example, stressed by the great historian of the witch-hunts in Scotland, Christina Larner. For Larner, the early modern period was one which saw "the emergence of Christianity as a political ideology" (Larner, *Enemies of God*, p. 194), and she went on to note that:

> From the late fifteenth century, the evangelization of the populace coincided with the development of what can loosely be termed the nation state. Nation states could not depend on old ties to bind their people to them. Like all new regimes they demanded both ideological conformity and moral cleansing. Ideological conformity in the sixteenth century meant overt adherence to the form of Christianity preferred within the region concerned. (Larner, *Witchcraft and Religion*, p. 124)

The rise of witch-hunting was, for Larner, closely connected with the emergence of godly states of this type, their ideological bases so clearly imbued with that new, more demanding, view of Christianity which was both the cause and product of the Reformation and Counter-Reformation.

This line of argument raises the question of whether there actually was an organized, coherent "witchcraft" for the authorities to struggle against. This idea is one which has gained some currency from the early twentieth century, and is, of course, central to the beliefs of many modern pagans and Wiccans. Its origins, in relatively modern times, probably lay with the publication of Jules Michelet's *La Sorcière* of 1862, which argued that what was prosecuted as "witchcraft" was, in fact, the pre-Christian religion of the peasantry, and as such was an important ideological element in their continual conflict with landlords and the clergy. Michelet was a romantic radical who threw this book together in a few weeks with scant regard for historical evidence. Something like this idea was revived in 1921, with the publication of Margaret Murray's *The Witch-Cult in Western Europe*. This work, which, after a slow start, was to achieve a wide readership, argued a slightly different variation on the theme, but in effect maintained again that those persecuted as witches were actually adherents of a pre-Christian religion, and that the devils which were supposed to be present at witches' meetings were in fact the priests of that religion.

Murray's work was subjected to severe criticism from its publication, and is now completely discredited among serious historians; Michelet is largely forgotten, and there are now few serious scholars suggesting that there was, as so many demonologists claimed, an organized sect of witches. This should not obscure the fact that there was, as we have noted, a pervasive popular magic which represented not an organized counter-religion but a fusion of Christian, pre-Christian, and extra-Christian ideas. This popular magic was increasingly being identified as "superstition" by mainstream theological writers, while a close reading of some of the demonological tracts suggests elements of this folk magic were being identified by the authorities as having demonic overtones. A well-documented (if perhaps worryingly atypical) example of what might have been happening more widely is that of the *Benandante* in the Friuli, a region of Italy to the north of Venice. Here, something like a real fertility cult seems to have existed, although it should be noted that its members saw themselves as devout Christians and were adamant that they did good. Basically, the *Benandante* (the term, indeed, could be translated as "those who do good") believed that their souls left their bodies while they slept, and did battle with witches to ensure the fertility of the crops. At first the local agents of the Roman Inquisition, to whose records we owe our knowledge of this sect, had some trouble in knowing how to deal with people with these beliefs when they first came before them in the late sixteenth century. But the inquisitors, obviously having no other way to classify them, soon came to categorize them as witches: by the mid-seventeenth century, much of the local population had been educated into this interpretation of the *Benandante*, while even individual *Benandanti* under interrogation could be brought round to this point of view (Ginzburg, *Night Battles*). Fortunately, by the mid-seventeenth century, the Italian Inquisition had more or less rejected the notion of demonic witchcraft. We can imagine, however, what would have happened to the *Benandante* or people like them had they fallen foul of Heinrich Kramer a century and a half earlier. The new, better-defined, and more rigorous Christianity that was being spread across Europe not only marginalized popular magical beliefs as superstition, but also had the capacity to turn them into the symptoms of demonic witchcraft.

Another interpretation of popular beliefs, and one which in effect created a new perspective on the history of witchcraft, was offered by two British historians, Alan Macfarlane and Keith Thomas, in the early 1970s. Macfarlane, in an important regional study of witchcraft in the English county of Essex, argued that witchcraft accusations in that area needed to be understood not in terms of pressure to prosecute "from above," but rather in terms of tensions between members of the peasantry. His researches, based on an exhaustive study of surviving court records and informed by anthropological models, demonstrated a typical background to accusations. This involved an incident in which an elderly and poor woman would beg for alms, food, drink, the chance to work, or some other favor from a neighbor. If this was refused, the woman would often go away displeased, and sometimes muttering threats or curses. A little later misfortune would befall the household refusing to help the woman: animals might die, a child might fall sick with a mysterious illness, or something similar might happen to the head of household. This misfortune would then be attributed to harmful witchcraft, *maleficium*, of the elderly woman, especially if she had an existing reputation for being a witch. Macfarlane, noting that it was typically richer villagers who did the accusing and poorer ones who were the suspected witches, linked the pattern of accusations to the socioeconomic changes of the period. Demographic growth was creating a mass of poor people, and the spread of rural capitalism (Essex was an economically advanced region) was creating different attitudes to them. Macfarlane therefore related witchcraft accusations to changing attitudes to the poor, and to a transferral of the guilt that might be felt about not helping them in an era of ambivalent attitudes: it was not the refuser of charity who was breaking village norms, but rather the woman perpetrating witchcraft (Macfarlane, *Witchcraft in Tudor and Stuart England*).

Macfarlane's approach was very much reinforced by the description of witchcraft accusations given in Keith Thomas's *Religion and the Decline of Magic*, a work which was also of considerable importance in charting the wider belief system in which belief on a popular level in witchcraft and magic could flourish. Between them, these two historians offered a refreshingly novel approach to witchcraft accusations, which was soon recognized as having an importance that went far beyond English materials. What has become evident, however, is that Macfarlane and Thomas's "charity refused" model of witchcraft accusations, although found fairly widely, is by no means as universally pervasive as it apparently was in late sixteenth-century Essex. In many areas the initial accusations against a witch were typically brought before officialdom by neighbors who thought themselves to have suffered at her hands, but the tensions and disputes which underlay these accusations were almost infinite in their variety. In general, however, it seems that, certainly for the period ca. 1560 to 1650, worsening economic conditions for Europe's peasantry helped provide a context for witchcraft accusations. In a world where conditions at the base of society were becoming harder, and where resources (land, food, money, and chances of finding employment) were becoming scarcer, and hence more competitively struggled for, rivalries and disputes on a village level were bound to become more common, and frequently led to a witchcraft accusation when one party thought that they were being harmed or disadvantaged by the *maleficium* triggered by the greed, envy, or malice of a neighbor (Briggs, *Witches and Neighbours*).

It should also be noted that most frequently, in 90 percent of cases in Macfarlane's Essex and 80 percent on a European average, that neighbor would be female. One of the major themes of recent research has been the investigation of the connection between witchcraft accusations and late medieval and early modern attitudes to women. The initial approach, first popularized by non-specialist commentators writing within the context of the 1970s women's movement, was to see the connection between women and witchcraft purely in terms of male aggression against women: the misogyny of a patriarchal society led (in the view of some of these commentators) to men wishing to eradicate troublesome women, or perhaps women more generally, through the medium of the witch-burning. This campaign of male aggression was made to seem all the more terrible by the oft-quoted, but ludicrously exaggerated, claim that 9 million women had been burned as witches. Without doubt, Europe between the fifteenth and eighteenth centuries was a society where women were heavily disadvantaged, and where the moral, physical, and intellectual inferiority of women was taken for granted by male commentators and opinion formers. Yet it remains uncertain why this should lead to witchcraft accusations, while it remains to be proven that the misogyny of educated writers was widely shared among a largely illiterate peasantry. The importance of the connection between witchcraft and women had been highlighted, but explanations for it remained imperfect.

More recent research has still not altogether elucidated the issue, although we now have a better-informed confusion. Historians working on a variety of regional contexts have noted that a large number of witchcraft accusations were actually launched by women against other women. This finding could be explained by claiming that the accusing women were simply the lackeys of patriarchy, but if we take a more optimistic view of the potential for female historical agency, we are left with the impression that witchcraft on a village level was very much something that operated within the female sphere. Many of the disputes between women which led to accusations or suspicions of witchcraft involved either the invasion of domestic space or the disruption of domestic order by the supposed witch, or *maleficium* directed against a child, childcare being, in this period, a predominantly female activity (Purkiss, *Witch in History*). Evidently, the connection between women and witchcraft can no longer be seen in terms of straightforward oppression of women by men: the exact nature of the connection does, however, remain elusive. Some of the most adventurous research into witchcraft, in fact, currently involves attempts to reconstruct the psychological makeup of confessing witches and of the women accusing them (Roper, *Oedipus and the Devil*). At the very least one of the most frequent patterns of accusation, that of a woman of childbearing age accusing a post-menopausal woman of bewitching a child, suggests that, accustomed as we are to analyzing witchcraft in terms of social hierarchy and gender relations, we now have also to consider the problem in terms of age hierarchy.

The student of European witchcraft in and around the Reformation era has, therefore, no shortage of materials to work on and no shortage of interpretations to evaluate (and it should be noted that here we have only discussed the more mainstream interpretations: others, such as those which attribute the witch-hunts to ergot poisoning, hallucinogenic drugs, or the psychological shock of the impact of epidemic syphilis on Europe, have been passed over here). Historians, frequently led by the sources relating to the region, or sometimes particular case, they are studying, vary in their interpretations, but most of them would see the framework for understanding the European witch-hunts as embracing the heightened theological concerns of the period, the world of peasant tensions and rivalries, and the lived experience of women, and especially peasant women.

The Decline of Magic and Witchcraft

In 1550 most educated Europeans believed in, or were at least unwilling or unable to discount the possibility of, magic and witchcraft: by 1750 most educated Europeans had rejected magic and witchcraft, although, as the researches of nineteenth-century folklorists demonstrated, these remained live issues for Europe's peasant population. Explaining why this major intellectual transition took place presents us with a further set of rather difficult problems.

For the Enlightenment *philosophe*, and the nineteenth-century rationalist, this transition would have been easily explained: "science" had replaced magic as the way in which the world was understood, and the way was thus made open for intellectual, and subsequently technical, progress. Ultimately, there is, of course, much of value in this view: the universe as imagined by the great natural philosopher Sir Isaac Newton (1642–1727) obviously left less space for occult forces than the universe as imagined by the Neoplatonists. But simply to attribute the end of elite belief in witchcraft and magic to that bundle of intellectual changes which we term the scientific revolution in many ways obscures more than it reveals.

If we restrict ourselves to considering witchcraft, the main point to grasp is that there had always been skepticism on the subject. Famously, in 1563 Johann Weyer, court physician to the duke of Cleves, published his *De Praestiges Daemonum*, a work which challenged many existing assumptions about witches, while in 1584 Reginald Scot, an obscure English gentleman, published a thoroughgoingly skeptical tract, *The Discoverie of Witchcraft*. These two works, commonly interpreted as harbingers of progress, have attracted considerable attention among later scholars, although it should be noted that Scot, writing in English, had little impact in continental Europe. More importantly, perhaps, there existed within Christian thinking a perfectly sustainable theological position which allowed witchcraft as it was understood by the bulk of the population to be marginalized. A crucial issue was the degree of agency allowed to the devil. Demonological writers had to steer an uneasy course between asserting that the devil had immense power and avoiding a dualistic position which skirted the heretical proposition that the devil was as powerful as God. More skeptical writers were able to downgrade the devil's importance: indeed, one of the major skeptical works, Balthasar Bekker's *De Betoverde Wereld* of 1691, argued that the devil's agency on earth was very limited. Another, and connected, set of arguments revolved around the proposition that many of the misfortunes attributed to witches were in fact the outcome of divine providence. Thus to claim that the death of cattle, the sickness of a child, or the blasting of the crops was the outcome of *maleficium* displayed both an ignorance of God's purposes and a refusal to face up to one's relationship with the Almighty.

Perhaps curiously to the modern reader, something of this attitude was also present in many of those tracts of the period that completely accepted the notion of the demonic witch and that advocated witch-hunting. This was perhaps especially true of Protestant demonology. For many Protestant writers, witchcraft was part of a broader set of problems which centered on the need to evangelize the population at large, and to bring correct ideas about Christianity to them. As far as witchcraft was concerned, the main problem was to convince the population that it was the pact with the devil, not the doing of harm through *maleficium*, which was the central issue in witchcraft, and the reason why witches should be executed. This line of argument meant that even Protestant demonologists had to challenge large areas of popular beliefs about witches, so that it was possible to regard many commonly held beliefs about witches as vulgar superstition (Clark, *Thinking with Demons*, pp. 461–8). Thus Protestant demonologists were hostile to popular counter-measures against witchcraft, on the grounds that there was no Scriptural basis for them, were opposed to cunning folk, arguing that their ability to do good by magic came as surely from the devil as did the malefic witch's ability to hurt, and also generally rejected that central element of educated witch-belief, the sabbat, on the grounds that it too was not mentioned in Scripture.

There were, therefore, currents in the Christian thinking of the period which helped to minimalize and marginalize witchcraft: at the time of those mass southwest German trials we have mentioned, for example, the most potent voices against witch-hunting came not from proto-rationalists but from a number of Protestant universities in the area which, asked to give an opinion on witchcraft accusations, followed the line that the misfortunes attributed to witchcraft should more properly be ascribed to divine providence (Midelfort, *Witch Hunting in Southwestern Germany*). Another skeptical line, found among sixteenth-century writers such as Scot but becoming more widespread in the late seventeenth century, was to question the accuracy of the translation of those passages of the Bible that were concerned with witchcraft and related matters, and to question the comparability of the Scriptural and the early modern European witch. There was little new in the skeptical arguments that were being advanced around 1700, and certainly little that can be connected in any very direct way to the new scientific thinking of the period. What was new was a more widespread willingness to accept these arguments.

Part of this willingness may have been derived from an awareness that in many areas judges were becoming increasingly unwilling to convict in witchcraft trials. Judicial systems varied widely across Europe, with witches being tried in a range of institutions varying from central courts presided over by experienced and educated judges to local, even village, tribunals where the judges might be local amateurs who had minimal legal training and who were likely to be steeped in local prejudices against witches. As the seventeenth century progressed, it became evident that the more educated judges were finding it difficult to convict in cases of witchcraft. Perhaps the fullest evidence comes from the Parlement of Paris, an institution which heard appeals against capital sentences delivered in local courts in much of northern France. As early as the 1630s, the very senior lawyers of the Parlement were regularly quashing capital verdicts brought against witches in the inferior courts. Apparently the Parisian lawyers, while no doubt accepting the possibility of witchcraft, were very unhappy with the standards of proof and types of evidence upon which convictions were brought in local courts. It was easy to move from this position to one which became common in the later seventeenth century, in which senior judges, members of the educated elite, came to reject most of what they heard in witch-trials as mere vulgar superstition (Soman, *Sorcellerie et justice criminelle*).

This tendency was reinforced by changes in elite attitudes to Christianity. This is perhaps a contentious area, and it may be best to interpret these changes in terms of shifts of emphasis rather than absolute changes. Generally, however, the spread of what Europeans in the early eighteenth century would have described as a more rational approach to Christianity marginalized for the educated Christian that mental world of wonders and providences which had been so widely shared around 1600, but which by the time of the early Enlightenment was becoming regarded as more appropriate to the vulgar masses. At the same time (and here too we are speaking of a relative rather than an absolute change), the old notions of the "godly commonwealth" were becoming redundant in many European states. As Christina Larner put it, the witch-hunts ceased when "the establishment of the kingdom of God ceased to be a political objective and was replaced by the pursuit of liberty, the defence of property, the belief in progress, enlightenment, patriotism, and other secular alternatives" (Larner, *Witchcraft and Religion*, p. 90). Certainly, the final stages of witch-belief among the English elite in the early eighteenth century, and the end of that belief, have been linked to the final efforts, and failure, to promulgate the notion of the sacral state (Bostridge, *Witchcraft and its Transformations*).

There were, therefore, a number of tendencies running together which, by the early eighteenth century, were making elite Europeans less willing to believe in the concept of the demonic witch that had been created three centuries earlier. The belief in witchcraft as an abstract possibility may not have disappeared on this social level, but the acceptance of the reality of witchcraft in individual cases was proving more difficult to maintain. Obviously, new developments in religion and in scientific knowledge were of some importance here, but perhaps the crucial factor was a growing gap between the intellectual worlds of the elite and the population at large. There had always been a strand of thought in demonological writing which had been concerned to counter popular superstitions about witchcraft, and it was perhaps not so great a step to write off all belief in witchcraft, at least on the level of peasant fears of *maleficium*, as signs of popular ignorance and backwardness. A number of factors ran together to create the elite retreat from belief in witchcraft and magic over western and central Europe in the decades around 1700, but perhaps the most potent of them was straightforward snobbery. Among the lower orders, fear of the malefic witch, trust in the cunning man or woman, and a religious mentality imbued with the old Christianity of wonders and direct divine intervention in human affairs persisted throughout the nineteenth and into the twentieth century (Devlin, *Superstitious Mind*).

BIBLIOGRAPHY

Agrippa, H. C. von Nettesheim, *The Philosophy of Natural Magic*, ed. Leslie Sheppard. Secaucus, NJ: University Books, 1974.

Barry, J., Hester, M., and Roberts, G., eds., *Witchcraft in Early Modern Europe: Studies in Culture and Belief*. Cambridge: Cambridge University Press, 1996.

Behringer, W., *Witchcraft Persecutions in Bavaria: Popular Magic, Religious Zealotry and Reason of State in Early Modern Europe*. Cambridge: Cambridge University Press, 1997.

Bostridge, I., *Witchcraft and its Transformations c.1650–c.1750.* Oxford: Clarendon Press, 1997.

Briggs, R., *Witches and Neighbours: The Social and Cultural Context of European Witchcraft,* 2nd ed. Oxford: Blackwell, 2002.

Clark, S., *Thinking with Demons: The Idea of Witchcraft in Early Modern Europe.* Oxford: Clarendon Press, 1997.

Devlin, J., *The Superstitious Mind: French Peasants and the Supernatural in the Nineteenth Century.* New Haven, Conn.: Yale University Press, 1987.

Ginzburg, C., *The Night Battles: Witchcraft and Agrarian Cults in the Sixteenth and Seventeenth Centuries.* London: Routledge & Kegan Paul, 1983.

Larner, C., *Enemies of God: The Witch-Hunt in Scotland.* London: Chatto & Windus, 1981.

Larner, C., *Witchcraft and Religion: The Politics of Popular Belief.* Oxford: Blackwell, 1984.

Levack, B., *The Witch-Hunt in Western Europe,* 2nd ed. London: Longman, 1995.

Macfarlane, A. D. J., *Witchcraft in Tudor and Stuart England: A Regional and Comparative Study.* London: Routledge & Kegan Paul, 1970.

Maxwell-Stuart, P. G., *The Occult in Early Modern Europe: A Documentary History.* Houndmills: Macmillan, 1999.

Midelfort, H. C. E., *Witch Hunting in Southwestern Germany, 1562–1684: The Social and Intellectual Foundations.* Stanford, Calif.: Stanford University Press, 1972.

Murray, M., *The Witch-Cult in Western Europe.* Oxford: Clarendon Press, 1921.

Purkiss, D., *The Witch in History: Early Modern and Twentieth-Century Representations.* London: Routledge, 1996.

Roper, L., *Oedipus and the Devil: Witchcraft, Sexuality and Religion in Early Modern Europe.* London: Routledge, 1994.

Sharpe, J., *Instruments of Darkness: Witchcraft in England 1550–1750.* London: Hamish Hamilton, 1996.

Shumaker, W., *The Occult Sciences in the Renaissance.* Berkeley: University of California Press, 1972.

Soman, A., *Sorcellerie et justice criminelle (16e–18e siècles).* Croft Road, Hants., and Brookfield, Vt.: Variorum, 1992.

Thomas, K. V., *Religion and the Decline of Magic: Studies in Popular Beliefs in Sixteenth- and Seventeenth-Century England.* London: Weidenfeld & Nicolson, 1971.

Thorndike, L. A., *A History of Magic and Experimental Science,* 8 vols. New York: Columbia University Press, 1923–58.

Vickers, B., ed., *Occult and Scientific Mentalities in the Renaissance.* Cambridge: Cambridge University Press, 1984.

Wilson, S., *The Magical Universe: Everyday Ritual and Magic in Pre-modern Europe.* London and New York: Hambledon, 2000.

FURTHER READING

There has been an explosion over the past two decades in publications on the witch-hunts in Europe, much of this work being of a very high quality. S. Clark, *Thinking with Demons,* is a masterly exposition of the demonological theory which underpinned witch persecution. W. Behringer, *Witchcraft Persecutions in Bavaria,* is an excellent and detailed study of a regional experience, while James Sharpe, *The Bewitching of Anne Gunter: A Horrible and True Story of Football, Witchcraft, Murder and the King of England* (London: Profile, 1999) is one of a growing number of microcosmic case studies. The belief systems and tensions that underlay individual accusations are explored in Robin Briggs, *Witches and Neighbours,* 2nd ed., while the sheer diversity of European experiences of witchcraft and witch-hunting is demonstrated by B. Ankarloo and G. Henningsen, *European Witchcraft: Centres and Peripheries* (Oxford: Clarendon Press, 1990). A number of older studies are, however, still essential reading. Key works might include K. V. Thomas, *Religion and the Decline of Magic*; A. D. J. Macfarlane, *Witchcraft in Tudor and Stuart England* (in fact a study of witchcraft in the county of Essex); H. C. E. Midelfort, *Witch Hunting in Southwestern Germany*, and H. Trevor Roper, *The European Witch Craze of the Sixteenth and Seventeenth Centuries* (Harmondsworth: Penguin, 1969). On magic and related matters, P. G. Maxwell-Stuart, *The Occult in Early Modern Europe*, provides a lively and wide-ranging introduction with an excellent bibliography.

Twenty-Seven

Martyrs and Saints

Brad S. Gregory

Of all the renaissances in late medieval and early modern Europe, few were as dramatic or divisive as the rebirth of Christian martyrdom. Few phenomena reveal so clearly the continuities and discontinuities between late medieval and Reformation-era Christianity, or disclose so well the commitments of devout Christians in divergent traditions that were partly forged or sustained by martyrdom itself. Across western Europe, chiefly in the Low Countries, France, and England, some 5,000 men and women were judicially executed as either heretics or religious traitors between 1523 and the mid-seventeenth century, the large majority of them before 1600.[1] Sympathizers memorialized them as genuine martyrs for Christian truth, however defined, whereas detractors denounced them as false martyrs, justly executed for their obstinate persistence in dangerous beliefs and practices. In either case, the recognition of martyrs and the definition of sanctity were inseparable from true doctrine and its social cognate, communities of belief, whether this connection was expressly articulated by learned theologians or merely intuited by common folk. The relevant sources from the Reformation era make clear that each of its main martyrological traditions – Protestant, Anabaptist, and Roman Catholic – belongs to a larger story that stretches from the late Middle Ages into the seventeenth century, despite longstanding tendencies to study each tradition separately. By eschewing confessional history and its legacies, we can analyze martyrdom in the Reformation era as a cross-confessional whole and discern what was shared among and distinctive of these particular traditions. Such an approach also offers insights into the collective influence of martyrdom and religious disagreement on the subsequent course of western ideologies and institutions. Across confessional divides, martyrs literally embodied the doctrinal and devotional disagreements at the heart of early modern Christianity. Through the multiple facets of martyrdom and the related disputes over sanctity, the period's religious history is broadcast with the volume turned up.

But how closely should we listen? The backbone of the social history of the Reformation is the story of authorities' long-term endeavor to inculcate Protestant or Catholic beliefs and behaviors in the population at large. In various forms this issue, building on broader historiographical trends of the 1960s and 1970s, has guided much Reformation scholarship during the past generation, and in so doing has vastly increased our knowledge of the ways in which religious changes were received, resisted, or rejected. Five thousand executions for religious heterodoxy is a minuscule fraction of the millions of people whom the Reformations affected through more mundane social and political processes of confessionalization. Martyrs are not statistically representative of early modern Christians, and studying them obviously cannot substitute for the careful, local study of religious change across the population in early modern Europe. Nevertheless, there are good reasons not to marginalize the martyrs, whose influence transcended their numbers and whose convictions were shared with their contemporaries in important respects.

We could more readily ignore early modern martyrs were there not so many sources about them. Their profuse memorialization by contemporaries is a strong indication that martyrs were important in ways vastly disproportionate to their numbers. The plethora of sources extends far beyond the massive Protestant martyrological collections by Ludwig Rabus, John Foxe, Jean Crespin, Adriaen van Haemstede, and Heinrich Pantaleon, which first appeared in the 1550s and early 1560s. Despite their indisputable importance, these famous works have attracted scholarly attention to the relative neglect of the period's many other martyrological sources: pamphlets, poems, plays, woodcuts, engravings, paintings, and exhortatory treatises, in addition to the mention of martyrs and issues related to martyrdom in theological works, memoirs, correspondence, and chronicles. Already by the late 1520s, for example, dozens of different German pamphlets, many of them in multiple editions, were circulating in thousands of copies throughout the imperial cities of central Europe.[2] Both German- and Dutch-speaking Anabaptists, including the Swiss Brethren, the Hutterites, and the Mennonites, produced hundreds of different songs about their respective martyrs and about perseverance in the midst of persecution.[3] Eleven editions of the Dutch Mennonite martyrology, *The Sacrifice unto the Lord* [*Het Offer des Heeren*], had been published by the end of the sixteenth century, compared to five editions of John Foxe's far better-known *Acts and Monuments*. And between 1580 and 1619, during the high tide of Roman Catholic martyrological sensibility in England, a staggering 163 editions of dozens of works devoted wholly or in part to the martyrdom or persecution of English Catholics were published *in languages other than English*.[4] The vast majority of judicial executions were carefully orchestrated public spectacles, witnessed by hundreds or even thousands of onlookers, directly exposing the central events in the drama of martyrdom to more than simply a literate minority. After the executions themselves, oral reports streamed outward through traditional channels of communication. Although those judicially executed for their religious convictions were themselves a tiny percentage of the population, virtually everyone, in towns and rural areas alike, must have known about them in one way or another.

Just as we should not underestimate early modern awareness of the martyrs, we should beware of pigeonholing them too narrowly in a nook of radical exceptionalism. They were atypical in their manifest willingness to die for their beliefs, to be sure, but their beliefs were no different than those found throughout the period's sermons, catechisms, liturgies, and spiritual literature. Like those ordinary Christians of whatever tradition who knew at least the basics of their faith, the martyrs believed that the Bible was God's word, that Christ was humanity's savior, that the afterlife was their destiny, and that God was their judge. Further, the martyrs' fervent religiosity and uncompromising commitment were consistent with those of their devout Christian contemporaries. The martyrs' abundant prison writings reveal evidence of frequent prayer, unstinting trust in God, and intimate familiarity with Scripture, exhortations to which are ubiquitous in the Reformation era. Context, not content, distinguished the martyrs from other devout Christians: circumstances of persecution shaped the sensibilities of Elizabethan missionary priests or French Calvinists, for example, in ways that Italian clergy or Genevan Calvinists never had to confront. Indeed, martyrs simply *were* that subset of devout Christians who persevered through death in circumstances of persecution. Nor can the martyrs be marginalized through any neat social or gender categories, because in addition to transcending confessional divides, they included men and women, clergy and laity, young and old, the well-off, middling sorts, and the poor. If one is interested, then, in the *full* range of ways in which religion was received and lived across the breadth of the population, one cannot ignore devout Christians in general or martyrs in particular.

The comparative, cross-confessional study of Protestant, Anabaptist, and Roman Catholic martyrdom and sanctity makes clear striking similarities as well as obvious differences. All three traditions inherited late medieval values linked to martyrdom, and martyrs from all three traditions evinced similar attitudes and experiences in anticipation of their deaths. We will enhance our understanding of the divisiveness of martyrdom and the distinctiveness of each tradition if we first grasp what the three main traditions shared in common.

The Augustinian monks Hendrik Vos and Johann van den Esschen were proclaimed by evangelicals as the first martyrs for the restored Gospel immediately after they were burned in Brussels on July 1, 1523. Luther had word of their deaths three weeks later, and shortly thereafter published his *Letter to the Christians of the Low Countries*, one of four pamphlets about them printed by the end of the year.[5] The earliest executed Anabaptists, too, were instantly extolled as martyrs by their fellow believers in Switzerland. Whatever their rejections of the Roman Church and its saints, neither evangelicals nor Anabaptists moved incrementally toward a martyrological interpretation of the executions of their fellow believers, as though martyrdom were a forgotten mode of Christian sanctity that required gradual rediscovery. On the contrary, the interpretative framework of martyrdom was there from the very outset of the Reformation. Its vitality derived not only from the fact that the Bible, in which both evangelicals and Anabaptists grounded their versions of Christian truth, includes so many passages about persecution and suffering. In addition, the first generation of evangelicals and Anabaptists had not ceased to be late medieval Christians. As such, they inherited a host of values and practices that were directly relevant to martyrdom.

This is not necessarily apparent at first sight. The gradual Christianization of medieval Europe had meant the decline of active martyrdom. For well over two centuries, from 1254 to 1481, popes canonized no one who had died a violent death. With good reason André Vauchez has written that "at the end of the Middle Ages, the identification of sanctity with martyrdom is no more than a memory," while Richard Kieckhefer has noted that "the fantasy of dying for the faith was seldom more than a fantasy except for the missionaries."[6] In a society whose institutions were devoted to protecting the church against its enemies, the opportunities for martyr-

dom were indeed negligible. Yet whether Christianity is politically protected or persecuted, it remains a religion based on a martyr-savior, a fact unlikely to make certain
values linked to martyrdom simply vanish altogether. Martyrdom implies more than
the simple endurance of violent death as such: it also entails patience, commitment,
perseverance, suffering, and trust, each of which is much broader than its role in
martyrdom itself. Beginning more than a millennium before the Reformation, after
Constantine's conversion to Christianity, patristic writers had elaborated ways in
which the virtue of patience and the practice of asceticism permitted all Christians to
share obliquely in martyrdom despite the lack of overt persecution. By the decades
just prior to the Reformation, the lack of late medieval opportunities for actual
martyrdom was all but inversely proportional to the opportunities to participate in
its sublimation.

The virtue of patient suffering almost certainly would have been less important to
late medieval Christians had not Christ himself suffered a brutal martyrdom by crucifixion. His passion and death had made human salvation possible in the first place;
hence his specific martyrdom, together with his incarnation and resurrection, literally comprised the most important events in all of human history. Fittingly, then,
late medieval Christians honored their martyr-savior through multiple media and
many forms, including crucifixes, roadside shrines, woodcuts, processions, medals,
and plays.[7] Committed Christian men and women sought affective identification with
the stages of their Lord's ordeal, while *The Imitation of Christ*, a fifteenth-century
devotional treatise published over 120 times in seven languages between 1470 and
1520, captured in its title one of their guiding aspirations.[8] At the same time, Christ's
death taught lessons in the patient endurance of adversity regardless of the tribula-
tions that one faced: the extreme *imitatio Christi* of actual martyrdom was only the
limiting case of the exercise of patience open to all Christians. Life in late medieval
Europe, rife with bodily suffering, epidemic disease, agricultural uncertainty, and
sheer material hardship, provided virtually unlimited occasions to practice the virtue.
Patience and perseverance had eternal ramifications in the face of death itself, with
the afterlife looming, when fidelity to Christ and resistance to Satan mattered most.
However unlikely the possibility of martyrdom, one's eventual death was a certainty.
Consequently there emerged after the Council of Constance that most pragmatic of
all works, the *Ars moriendi*, which literally sought to teach Christians how well to
prepare for the inevitable. It became another fifteenth-century bestseller, the most
popular xylographic book of the fifteenth century. When evangelicals and Anabaptists faced persecution under changed religio-political circumstances in the 1520s,
they did so as part of a religious culture that for over a century had reverberated with
devotion to Christ's passion, prescriptions of patient suffering, and the art of dying
well.

That same religious culture was saturated with the veneration of the saints, those
extraordinary men and women whose exalted status in heaven made them powerful
intercessors for ordinary Christians in need on earth. Their relics, the bodily remains
of the saints embedded beneath Christendom's altars and scattered at pilgrimage sites
from Compostela and Canterbury to the Holy Land, were sites of divine power and
presence. Just as God had become incarnate in Christ, just as the sacraments were
material channels of his grace, so he displayed his providence preferentially in the
physical remains of his nearest and dearest followers. Supplications to his special

friends and the veneration of their relics led God to answer prayers and work miracles. Many of the most popular saints in late medieval Europe – including Peter, Paul, Sebastian, Lawrence, Andrew, Lucy, Barbara, Dorothy, and many more – were (or were believed to have been) ancient martyr-saints, pre-Constantinian imitators of the Lord from the heroic centuries of Christianity. In addition to their relics, real or not, vividly imagined depictions of the ancient martyrs' passions and deaths were everywhere in late medieval Europe, from hagiographical works to paintings, sculptures, woodcuts, and sermons. Christianization and the concomitant waning of active martyrdom had rendered the ancient martyr-saints largely irrelevant as models for imitation, but did not diminish their importance as intercessory patrons. In the sixteenth century, Protestants and Anabaptists would turn this view upside down. They would reject the martyr-saints' intercessory role as a Biblically unwarranted usurpation of Christ's mediatory uniqueness and spurn the veneration of their relics as idolatrous superstition, while reinvoking the direct relevance of their exemplary deaths. If the initial spread of the Gospel had provoked oppression and martyrdom, why should its rediscovery have been any different? Stripped of their status as intercessors, previous martyrs reemerged as paradigmatic predecessors in times of persecution.

Taken together, the ubiquity of martyr-saints, the prevalence of the *ars moriendi*, the emphasis on the virtue of patience, and the devotion to Christ's passion were elements of a powerful interpretative framework directly related to martyrdom. This continuity between the late Middle Ages and the Reformation era explains, at least in part, why right from the 1520s fellow evangelicals and Anabaptists saw the executions of their respective fellow believers as martyrdom. Indeed, these late medieval lenses not only persisted but were arguably strengthened during the course of the sixteenth century, across confessional divides. Anabaptist, Protestant, and Catholic martyrs, for example, together with their committed fellow believers, maintained that the highest *imitatio Christi* would be to follow the crucified martyr-savior in his passion. Consider the following passage, only one of many that might have been chosen:

> My dear brothers, since we are members of Jesus, it must be neither remarkable nor astonishing if we are participants in his cross and suffering. For if we want to reign with him, we must suffer together with him. Since he is our head, we are his members; the head cannot proceed by one path and the members by another, but rather the entire body and the members follow the head who guides and governs them. If therefore our head was crowned with thorns, we cannot be part of the body without feeling their sting and without grief piercing our heart. If our king and sovereign master has been hoisted and hung on wood completely naked, completely bloodied, completely burdened with reproaches, insults, and blasphemies, it cannot be that we wait in this world to sleep always at our leisure, to be exalted with honors and dignities, being dressed in purple, velour, and silk like the rich evildoer, having all our pleasures and sensual delights on this lowly earth.[9]

Who wrote this? Nothing in its content, tone, or word choice points to a particular tradition, or even to whether it is from the fifteenth or the sixteenth century, because it expresses attitudes shared across the divide between late medieval and early modern Christianity no less than across the confessions of the Reformation era. It might have been written by that master of the *devotio moderna*, Thomas à Kempis, in the 1420s, or by an anonymous evangelical pamphleteer a century later, the Dutch Anabaptist leader Menno Simons in the 1550s, or the Elizabethan Jesuit Robert Southwell in the 1580s. In fact, Calvin's colleague Pierre Viret wrote it in 1541. Yet nothing in it smacks distinctively of Reformed Protestantism.

A comparative approach to early modern martyrdom sheds light not only on the significance of the late medieval legacy for the Reformation era, but also on how Protestant, Catholic, and Anabaptist martyrs understood themselves and what they were doing. Their surviving prison writings, together with sympathetic and hostile depictions of their public deaths, permit the substantial reconstruction of the self-understanding that underpinned their willingness to die. Naturally, such reconstruction depends upon what survives; the lack of sources renders unrecoverable the particular experience of many individual martyrs. Nevertheless, hundreds of letters, songs, and confessions of faith provide access to bygone beliefs and behaviors and reveal remarkable similarities across confessional divides.

First and foremost, the martyrs believed that Christianity was true, because revealed by God. The implications of Christian truth led them radically to relativize temporal concerns, including even horrific death. Understood on their terms – the terms that render their actions thoroughly intelligible – perseverance in the truth was literally *more* than a matter of life and death: it was a matter of eternal salvation and damnation. Christian truth – that is, God's truth – embraced a world-view that embraced human origins, meaning, purpose, and destiny. The content of the world-view as well as the martyrs' willingness to die were grounded in faith and its relationship to Scripture. Catholics no less than Protestants and Anabaptists taught that the Bible was God's word, that it was true, that it was as relevant in the sixteenth century as it had been when first revealed, and that right faith was necessary for eternal salvation. Accordingly, all that the Bible had to say about suffering, persecution, and the threat of death for the truth applied directly to would-be martyrs.

Hence, the martyrs' prison writings are laced with Biblical passages relevant to their ordeals. Whether in Thomas More's Tower works written in 1534–5, or in the letters that Anabaptist leader Jakob Huter wrote to his beleaguered followers before his execution in 1536, or in the correspondence of Wallonian Calvinist François Varlut from 1562, it is abundantly clear that the martyrs connected specific Biblical verses to their concrete situations.[10] Who could have mistaken the applicability of Christ's words in Matthew 10: 28, "Do not fear those who kill the body but cannot kill the soul; rather fear him who can destroy both soul and body in hell," or the follow-up in verses 32–3, "Everyone who acknowledges me before others, I also will acknowledge before my Father in heaven, but whoever denies me before others, I also will deny before my Father in heaven"? Ecclesiastical and/or secular authorities were pressuring the martyrs to recant their faith, yet God's word commanded the opposite and promised them eternal reward: "Be faithful until death, and I will give you the crown of life" (Revelation 2: 10). Indeed, their savior had explicitly told them to *expect* persecution for maintaining the truth: "Remember the word that I said to you, 'Servants are not greater than their master.' If they have persecuted me, they will persecute you" (John 15: 20). God's word was both an authoritative exhortation and a definitive hermeneutic: it explained the meaning of persecution and told Christians how to respond. Joos Verkindert, a Dutch Mennonite executed in Antwerp in 1570, provides one among countless such examples of this practical application of Scripture, weaving together verses from several different New Testament books. As he told his wife, "[God] says, 'Whomever I love, I chastise,' and blessed is he who bears this chastisement, but the one who hates it is lost; and like as we meet much with the sufferings of Christ, so we also receive much consolation through Christ. For as Paul says, it is given to you not only to believe in Christ, but also to suffer for him, and to have the same struggle that you see in me and hear about from me."[11] In this context the Protestant and Anabaptist emphasis on Scripture did not break with the late Middle Ages, but rather intensified attitudes that previous Christians had applied to their everyday hardships.

This shared understanding of Biblical prescription also grounded an anti-Nicodemism common to Protestants, Catholics, and Anabaptists alike. Once again a cross-confessional approach pays dividends, revealing that most scholarly discussions of anti-Nicodemism – the condemnation of dissembling one's religious views in order to avoid punishment for nonconformity – have focused too narrowly on Reformed Protestantism, above all on writers such as Calvin and Viret. This is understandable, given Calvin's caustic reference to "Messieurs les Nicodemites" in the title of his 1544 treatise, and his decades-long concern with dissimulation among persecuted Protestants.[12] Yet exhortations to perseverance and condemnations of capitulation were part of the early evangelical movement in the 1520s and recur throughout the century among Anabaptists and Catholics. This becomes apparent if one compares, for example, the opening pages of Tyndale's *Obedience of a Christian Man* (1528) to Menno Simons's *Comforting Admonition* (1554–5) and to Thomas Hide's *Consolatory Epistle to the Afflicted Catholics* (1579). Anti-Nicodemism addressed issues inescapable for persecuted Christians regardless of creed, and so shows up not only in treatises, sermons, and songs but also in correspondence and reports of face-to-face encouragement. To be sure, the emphases in different traditions varied: Catholics, especially after the Council of Trent, waxed eloquent about the desire for and merit of martyrdom in ways that Reformed Protestants, who stressed the avoidance of idolatry, did not. Still, the similarity of anti-Nicodemism across confessional boundaries is unmistakable, as is its relationship to the martyrs who enacted its demands.

In all three traditions, anti-Nicodemism was built upon social relationships: it was fellow believers in communities of faith who urged Anabaptist, Protestant, and Catholic martyrs to stand fast unto death. Not individualist fanaticism but rather social embeddedness in their respective communities of belief helped to sustain the martyrs' willingness to die. In prison, they often received letters from family members, friends, and fellow believers urging them to persevere, and they reciprocated with epistles commenting on their experiences and disposition. "My dearest sister in Jesus Christ," the Calvinist minister Pierre Brully wrote to his wife in recounting his interrogation, "I have seen your letter that you sent me by way of Marguerite, which deeply touched my heart, inasmuch as you and all the brothers care about and are solicitous towards me."[13] Such passages are commonplace in the martyrs' correspondence. No less than their English and Dutch counterparts had done, persecuted Japanese Catholics consoled one another in the early seventeenth century, admonishing one another to remain steadfast, reading from the lives of martyr-saints, and praying together that they might merit the honor of martyrdom.[14]

Besides this contemporary solidarity with fellow believers, the martyrs and marty-rologists in all three traditions viewed themselves as standing in a historical commu-nity of God's chosen people. Renewed in their own days, this genealogy stretched back through the early Christian martyrs to Biblical martyrs such as Stephen, John the Baptist, and the Maccabees. Catholics mentioned the early Christian martyrs as paradigms more often than did Protestants and especially Anabaptists, for whom the Biblical martyrs were more exclusively important. Yet despite the variety of their accents, once again early modern Christians spoke the same language across confes-sional divides. In 1555, exiled bishop John Scory told persecuted Marian Protestants back in England to identify with specific Biblical martyrs for a wide range of types of execution: Jonah for drowning, Stephen for stoning, John the Baptist for behead-ing, and Shadrach, Meshach, and Abednego (from Daniel 3) for burning.[15] Before he was executed in Dordrecht on March 28, 1572, the imprisoned Mennonite Jan Wouters van Cuyck ruminated on his situation: "It is no wonder that this is hap-pening to me – look at John [the Baptist], no one more holy born of woman; he lived such a strict life and was imprisoned and killed. Indeed, Christ himself, Stephen, Peter, James worked so many miracles and did so many good works and were nevertheless killed."[16] The sixteenth-century martyrs were not blazing a new trail but seeking to conform as nearly as possible to an ancient one, epitomized by Christ's crucifixion and enacted by the early Christian martyrs.

When martyrdom is studied cross-confessionally, it becomes clear how much Protestant, Catholic, and Anabaptist martyrs shared in common. They all appropri-ated key elements of late medieval Christianity, maintained an uncompromising faith, relied explicitly on Scripture and its promises, were socially grounded in communi-ties of belief, and understood themselves to be enacting the latter-day chapters in a venerable history of God's persecuted people.

Yet the martyrs and their respective sympathizers were also deeply divided over doctrine, differences exacerbated by executions. They agreed that Christianity was true, but not about what it was. Following medieval practice, inquisitors asked spe-cific questions to determine whether heresy suspects were in error, just as Elizabethan officials sought precisely to determine the views of missionary priests and their sup-porters on papal and royal authority. Accordingly, martyrological writers linked doc-trines and deaths no less than had the authorities who condemned the martyrs, only with an opposite assessment of the doctrines for which they had been killed. Depend-ing on what one thought of the teachings – Anabaptist believers' baptism, say, or Protestant justification by faith alone, or Catholic papal primacy, to name three central doctrines – those killed for them were either justly executed criminals or genuine Christian martyrs. The sources prove that contemporaries paid close attention to who died for what: the mutual exclusivity of the three traditions and the longstanding dispute over true versus false martyrs follow doctrinal lines.

The study of martyrdom should thus help to correct recent scholarly tendencies to downplay the importance of doctrine, theology, and religious controversy in the Reformation era. There was nothing rarefied, abstract, inaccessible, or esoteric about bloody, public executions for religion. Martyrs rendered religious controversy unavoidably social and dramatic: from 1523 on, they were the living embodiment of what they believed and practiced as members of their respective religious communi-ties. In dying for disputed doctrines – the same doctrines taught in catechisms and

preached from pulpits – martyrs infused religious controversy with human concrete-
ness, making every would-be compromise a negotiation with murderous authorities.
Such compromise would have dishonored the martyrs' deaths with an implicit,
retrospective judgment that by dissembling they might have saved themselves.
Ultimately, doctrinal compromise would have denied that the doctrines for which
the martyrs had died were worth dying for. Instead of compromise, the widespread
celebration of martyrs amplified already existing dissonance over Christian truth and
pushed disputed doctrines beyond any realistic threshold for negotiation. Indeed, in
the 1520s martyrdom itself helped to distill from the mix of the "reform-minded"
more clearly separate camps of heroic witnesses and tyrannical persecutors. When
Hendrik Vos and Johann van den Esschen were given a final chance to recant
their Lutheran views in Brussels, minutes before the flames would make them the
Reformation's first two martyrs, they are reported to have said to their would-be
confessors, "we believe in God and in one Christian Church. *But we do not believe
your church* [*Aber euwer kirchen glauben wir nit*]."[17] The concretely divisive logic of
martyrdom was active from the outset of its sixteenth-century renaissance. As the
decades passed, martyrological memorialization would help to forge and strengthen
distinct Christian identities among Protestants, Anabaptists, and Catholics, reinforcing processes of confessionalization. The connotations of and prospects for martyrdom varied across these traditions, as did memorialization and its transformation over
time.

Beginning in the 1520s, Protestant interpreters reconfigured the legacy of late
medieval martyr-saints by redefining "martyrs" and "saints" in ways consistent with
their new theologies. They needed to honor their slain heroes for the rediscovered
Gospel, but not confound them with the bogus intercessors whose rejection the rediscovered Gospel demanded. Christ was the sole mediator between God and human
beings, to whom Christians could and should pray directly. Correctly understood,
"saints" simply referred to other, living Christians (even if many ordinary folk in
Protestant regions proved their attachment to the saints as heavenly intercessors). At
the same time, Greek etymology grounded a proper understanding of martyrs and
witnesses. Signs of impending apocalypse, they had witnessed to the Gospel without
distorting it or impinging on its truth. The imperative to preserve the martyrs' words
and deeds emerged slowly at first, but by the 1550s it was touted as a duty of the
faithful, so that the martyrs might inspire persecuted Protestants and document
the action of God's grace in his children. The Calvinist martyrologist Jean Crespin,
for example, instructed his readers to "collect . . . their words and writings, their
responses, the confession of their faith, their speeches and final exhortations."[18]
Depending upon where one lived, the prospect of martyrdom might be genuine, as
in Marian England or Charles V's Flanders, or all but inconceivable, as in Lutheran
Wittenberg or Calvinist Geneva. As always, prosecution for heterodoxy, in this case
by Catholic authorities, remained contingent on many local factors.

To study Protestant martyrdom beginning with the famous mid-century martyrologies is an approach destined to exaggerate their role in creating Protestant martyrological awareness. The collections by Foxe, Crespin, van Haemstede, and Rabus
synthesized and extended an *already existing* Protestant martyrological sensibility.
The major themes of the mid-century martyrologies – the connection between doctrines and deaths, the wicked world's inevitable persecution of God's truth, the par-

allel between ancient and latter-day martyrs, the final triumph of the just against an apocalyptic horizon – are already present in *Flugschriften*, songs, and correspondence from the 1520s and 1530s, across linguistic and national boundaries. This is not to diminish the martyrologies' importance or influence, but rather to locate their significance in their timing and scope rather than in any conceptual originality or role in creating a martyrological awareness as such. During a particularly difficult decade for Protestants – on the heels of the Schmalkaldic War in the empire, with the Marian restoration in England and the crackdown against Calvinists in France and the Low Countries – these collections made martyrs the anchor of a Protestant historical vision seen in Augustinian terms. The current persecution of God's children was not a here-and-there, sixteenth-century aberration but the culmination of a persistent, on-and-off pattern stretching from Biblical times to the present, with fifteenth-century precursors in the persecution of Lollards and Hussites. According to Tyndale, God's word could not exist without persecution, "no more than the sun can be without his light."[19] A generation later, Crespin wrote that "Among the marks of the true Church of God, this is among the principal ones, namely that it has at all times sustained the attacks of persecutions."[20] In between the 1520s and the 1550s, Reformed Protestantism pushed an uncompromising anti-Nicodemism to confront the more determined prosecution of heresy that began late in the reigns of Francis I and Charles V. The result was more executions, as the Gospel's full recovery elicited a final apocalyptic surge from the Romish Antichrist.

Protestant martyrologists and their continuators laid claim to restored Christian truth despite the embarrassing fact of intra-Protestant doctrinal disagreement that kept different groups apart. For example, the creation of the Protestant collections depended upon overlooking doctrinal differences that divided Lutherans from Reformed Protestants on the Lord's Supper. In the mid-1550s, the very years when martyrologists were overlooking doctrinal differences to fashion an inclusive, Protestant community of witnesses, the Lutheran theologian Joachim Westphal and Calvin hotly disputed over the sacrament.[21] Yet despite traces of their respective confessional commitments in their works, Rabus's collection was not a narrowly "Lutheran" martyrology, or Crespin's an expressly "Calvinist" martyrology. Later in the century, however, as more and more territorial princes shed their Lutheranism for Calvinism, Lutheran pastors were denouncing executed *Calvinists* as "the devil's martyrs," an epithet previously reserved for Anabaptists and Catholics. Because Protestantism in its national contexts followed radically different paths in the late sixteenth century and beyond, the place of the frequently reprinted martyrologies differed accordingly. Foxe's book became an important (if contentious) ideological pillar within England's established Protestant regime; Crespin's remained a bulwark for a vulnerable Huguenot minority; and van Haemstede's acquired a more rigorously Calvinist character after his death in response to martyrological competition from Dutch Mennonites and Catholics.

Anabaptists confronted different political realities and saw martyrdom in a different light. With the exception of the tenuous refuge sometimes afforded the Hutterites by Moravian nobles, and the toleration of the Mennonites in the northern Netherlands from the last quarter of the sixteenth century, Anabaptists endured persecution from Catholics and Protestants alike. The Kingdom of Münster in 1534–5 cemented authorities' association of heresy with sedition, as if confirmation were needed in the wake of the Peasants' War. Once the "Reformation of the Common Man" was crushed in 1525, Anabaptist leaders such as Conrad Grebel and Leonhard Schiemer concluded that if the world rejected truth, then truth must reject the world. Indeed, even before a single execution, Grebel had written that "Genuine, believing Christians are sheep in the midst of wolves, sheep for the slaughter."[22] The result was Anabaptist separatism, whether among the Swiss Brethren, the Hutterites, or the Dutch Mennonites. Anabaptists spurned infant baptism as an extra-Biblical invention and flawed cornerstone supporting a woeful "Christian society." Only men and women who understood what faith *was* and what discipleship entailed could become Christians. *Nachfolge Christi* implied an openness to oppression and violent death for the truth, the same truth for which Jesus had been crucified. Anabaptists thus effectively collapsed the late medieval distinction between extraordinary and ordinary Christians implied in the relationship between saints and those who sought their intercession. To become an Anabaptist implied both a commitment characteristic of traditional saints and a willingness to die as a martyr.

Martyrological songs played a much more important part among Anabaptist groups than they did among Protestants or Catholics. Numbering in the hundreds, their two principal types of songs are narrative hymns commemorating the words, deeds, and names of individual martyrs or groups of martyrs, and what might be called anti-Nicodemite songs, which urge steadfastness and proclaim the blessedness of those who suffer for Christ's sake. From the outset of their movements, the early Swiss and south German Anabaptists were no less sensitized to martyrological interpretation than were their evangelical counterparts. The rhyming lines of their songs set to familiar tunes aided memorization, helped Anabaptists overcome their relative lack of access to printers in the early decades of the sixteenth century, and served men and women who seem generally to have been less literate than their Protestant counterparts. Anabaptists sang their songs and occasionally printed them as broadsheets by the late 1520s. They were subsequently published in collections by the Swiss Brethren and Dutch Mennonites, as well as copied in Hutterite codices.

In the last third of the century, Dutch Mennonites printed dozens of pamphlets containing martyrs' prison writings. Their first collection of letters by and songs about the martyrs, *The Sacrifice unto the Lord* (1562–3), became the core of a Dutch Mennonite martyrological tradition that culminated in Thieleman Jans van Braght's huge *Martyr's Mirror* (1660), in many respects the Anabaptist analogue of Foxe or Crespin. Within the umbrella category of Anabaptism, just as within Protestantism, doctrine and martyrological recognition mingled unstably and was frequently the source of conflict. The internationalization of Anabaptist martyrology in the seventeenth century by the doctrinally liberal Dutch Waterlanders depended upon overlooking doctrinal differences upon which sixteenth-century Anabaptist groups had insisted. By 1685, as urban Mennonites ascended the golden-age ladder of Dutch prosperity, their martyrology had expanded into the second, illustrated edition of the *Martyr's Mirror*, essentially a luxurious coffee-table book. With supreme irony, van Braght himself, the last major Mennonite martyrologist, all but longed for the invigorating persecution that lay three or more generations in the past.[23] The faith for which heroic martyrs had once shed their blood was now being slowly eroded by a flood of material prosperity.

For Roman Catholics, both the meaning of and prospects for martyrdom were different yet again. In most of early modern Europe, Catholics were almost as unlikely to be martyred as they had been in the late Middle Ages. Only in Britain were Catholics judicially tried and executed as religious traitors (and understood by fellow Catholics as martyrs), beginning under Henry VIII in 1535. Even during the height of persecution in late Elizabethan England, however, martyrdom was a remote possibility provided that one avoided missionary priests. Mission fields abroad were quite another story: Japan and the Americas produced many more Catholic martyrs in the sixteenth and seventeenth centuries than did Europe. Far from the status quo expectation simply of being a Christian, martyrdom was an exalted calling that Christ bestowed only upon his most favored followers. Catholics esteemed it accordingly. After all, latter-day martyrs bypassed purgatory at a stroke and, like their ancient and medieval forebears, took their place in heaven as intercessory patrons for Catholics in need. Popes showed themselves as reluctant to canonize martyrs as their late medieval predecessors had been, yet both clergy and laity, high and low, did not wait for formal canonization before praying to the new saints. (None of the Catholics killed for their faith in the sixteenth and seventeenth centuries was canonized before 1700, and only the 19 Gorcum martyrs of 1572 and the 26 Nagasaki martyrs of 1597 were beatified.[24]) Clergy and laity also zealously sought the relics of the martyrs and other saints, which they pursued, preserved, divided up, parceled out, and honored, both in Europe and abroad. As in the late Middle Ages, the distinction between ordinary Christians and extraordinary intercessors remained fundamental. Yet because the new martyrs, unlike the ancient martyr-saints, were often well known as real people, they were also touted as paradigms of virtue in living, if not necessarily as models to imitate in dying. Where the prospect of persecution was nil, as in Spain or seventeenth-century France, there persisted the traditional notion of patience as a form of sublimated martyrdom.

Despite the continuity between late medieval and early modern Catholicism, at first the memorialization of Catholic martyrs was more sluggish than that of their Protestant and Anabaptist counterparts. Whereas obscure early evangelical martyrs such as Johannes Heuglin were publicized in multiple pamphlets, Henrician Catholic martyrs even as prominent as Thomas More and John Fisher inspired little memorialization, especially in England, in the years just after their deaths. The Henrician martyrs, however, belonged to a church blindsided by the Reformation and perplexed by the return of Catholic martyrdom in Europe after its lengthy medieval dormancy. By contrast, apocalyptic Protestants and Anabaptists each saw in their own persecution a sign that they had indeed recovered and dared to proclaim Christian truth. As the decades passed, Catholic leaders came to believe that God had renewed persecution of his church in Europe so that new martyrs might help beat back the worst spread of heresy since antiquity. Thrilled by the paleo-Christian recovery of the Roman catacombs in the 1570s, reassured by the clarifications of Trent, Catholic martyrological writers saw God using martyrs to convert pagans throughout the world, just as he had employed them in the Roman Empire. A Catholic martyrological mentality reached its highest pitch during the second half of Elizabeth's reign, among those associated with the Catholic mission and the priests trained at the English Colleges in Douai-Rheims and in Rome. The many publications about the persecution of English Catholics supplemented a vast production of Catholic martyrological art across the continent, not to mention scores of Jesuit plays that took ancient and modern martyrs as their subject matter. Publications devoted only to Franciscan or Carthusian martyrs, for example, reflected certain internal exclusivities in the celebration of Catholic martyrs. But the persistent Catholic emphases on the visible church and on unity of doctrine prevented the internal divisions characteristic of the Protestant and Anabaptist martyrological traditions. Martyrs were playing their part in the globalization of the universal church.

Catholic, Anabaptist, and Protestant martyrs in the Reformation era both shared common convictions and were divided by incompatible beliefs. Like their respective traditions, all laid claim to the one Christian truth, revealed by God, a truth neither subjective nor relative nor self-contradictory. Once this is understood, the logical relationship of martyrological *celebration* to anti-martyrological *denunciation* becomes clear. Since doctrines were tightly tied to deaths in martyrdom, to die for false doctrines necessarily made one a false martyr, no matter how heroically or horrifically one died. All attempts to find non-doctrinal criteria for telling true from false martyrs proved unsuccessful: whether constancy in death, how many people had suffered and what they had endured, alleged patterns in the fates of false martyrs and persecutors, social status and educational background, the purported presence of lack of charity, the fact of punishment for non-religious crimes, or the presence or absence of posthumous miracles. Consequently, the dictum that Augustine had wielded against the Donatists – "not the punishment, but the cause, makes a martyr" – was used by controversialists on all sides, employing doctrine (the "cause") to tell true from false martyrs. As surely as contradictory doctrines could not both be true, as surely as Catholics were not Lutherans and Calvinists were not Mennonites, martyrology necessarily excluded as it included. The doctrinal differences that separated Christians from each other to begin with doubled as the only means for telling true from false martyrs, solidifying the respective traditions in turn. Christians in all three traditions remembered and honored hundreds of fellow believers who indisputably had shed their blood for contested versions of Christian truth, directly linked to divergent communities of faith.

At the heart of Christian martyrdom in early modern Europe were committed Christians willing to die and to kill over rival versions of God's teachings. Ultimately this willingness derived from yet another shared conviction, the belief that so much more than mere life and death was at stake. The small numbers of both martyrs and the authorities responsible for their deaths should not mislead us about their influence, whether in the Reformation era or in the eventual making of the modern world. In the sixteenth century, it was zealous minorities much more than conformist majorities that shaped events and molded identities. Among such minorities were the martyrs and the fellow believers who celebrated their memory. It turned out that the apocalypse was not imminent, as Protestants and Anabaptists thought, nor was the Roman tyranny about to crumble. Neither were these heresies, as Catholic leaders believed in the light of medieval precedent, going to be contained or even controlled. Rather, to the chagrin of all sides, Christendom was socially and doctrinally sundered far beyond anything known in the late Middle Ages. Tertullian was mistaken: martyrdom proved to be not the seed of the church but the seed of the churches. In time, too, the Reformation era helped to create a world that its leading actors could not have foreseen and would have deplored. It would be a secular world of individualized, privatized, domesticated religion, for those who continued to bother with such things.

NOTES

1   The rough figure of 5,000 is compiled from data given in William Monter, "Heresy Executions in Reformation Europe," in Ole Peter Grell and Bob Scribner, eds., *Tolerance and Intolerance in the European Reformation*, pp. 48–65; Geoffrey F. Nuttall, "The English Martyrs 1535–1680: A Statistical Review," *Journal of Ecclesiastical History*, 22 (1971), pp. 191–97; and É. de Moreau, *Histoire de L'Église de Belgique*, vol. 5 (Brussels: L'Édition universelle, 1952), pp. 172–206.

2   See Hildegard Hebenstreit-Wilfert, "Märtyrerflugschriften der Reformationszeit," in Hans-Joachim Köhler, ed., *Flugschriften als Massenmedium der Reformationszeit* (Stuttgart: Klett-Cotta, 1981), pp. 397–446; Bernd Moeller, "Inquisition und Martyrium in Flugschriften der frühen Reformation in Deutschland," in Silvana Seidel Menchi, *Ketzerverfolgung im 16. und frühen 17. Jahrhundert*, pp. 21–48.

3   For the German songs, see Ursula Lieseberg, *Studien zum Märtyrerlied der Täufer im 16. Jahrhundert*.

4   This figure is derived from A. F. Allison and D. M. Rogers, *The Contemporary Printed Literature of the English Counter-Reformation between 1158 and 1640*, vols. 1–2 (Aldershot: Scolar Press, 1989, 1994).

5   Luther mentioned the martyrs in a letter written July 22 or 23, 1523; see *WA Briefwechsel*, vol. 3, no. 635, p. 115. For the pamphlet, see *Brief an die Christen im Niederland*, in *WA*, vol. 12, pp. 77–80. For the other three pamphlets about Vos and van den Esschen, see Hebenstreit-Wilfert, "Märtyrerflugschriften," pp. 432–6.

6   André Vauchez, *La Sainteté aux derniers siècles du moyen âge d'après les processus de canonisation et les documents hagiographiques*, 2nd ed. (Rome: École Française de Rome, 1988), pp. 482, 484 (quotation); Richard Kieckhefer, *Unquiet Souls: Fourteenth-Century Saints and their Religious Milieu* (Chicago: University of Chicago Press, 1984), p. 66.

7   On late medieval devotion to Christ's passion, see Johan Huizinga, *The Autumn of the Middle Ages*, trans. Rodney J. Payton and Ulrich Mammitzsch (Chicago: University of Chicago Press, 1996), pp. 220–1; Eamon Duffy, *The Stripping of the Altars: Traditional Religion in England c.1400–c.1580* (New Haven, Conn.: Yale University Press, 1992), pp. 234–56; Ellen M. Ross, *The Grief of God: Images of the Suffering Jesus in Late Medieval England* (New York: Oxford University Press, 1997).

8   Augustin de Backer, *Essai bibliographique sur le livre "De imitatione Christi"* (1864; reprint, Amsterdam: Desclee de Brouwer, 1966).

9   Pierre Viret, *Epistre consolatoire, envoyée aus fideles qui souffrent persecution pour le Nom de Jesus et Verité evangelique* (Geneva: Jean Girard, 1541), partially reprinted in *Correspondance des Réformateurs dans des pays de langue française*, ed. A. L. Herminjard, vol. 6 (Geneva: H. Georg, 1883), p. 430, translation mine.

10 Among More's Tower works, see his *Dialogue of Comfort Against Tribulation*, vol. 12 of *The Complete Works of St. Thomas More*, ed. Louis L. Martz and Frank Manley (New Haven, Conn.: Yale University Press, 1976); for Huter, see *Jakob Huter: Leben, Froemmigkeit, Briefe*, ed. Hans Fischer (Newton, Kans.: Mennonite Publication Office, 1956); and for Varlut's letters, see Jean Crespin, *Histoire des vrays Tesmoins de la verite de l'Evangile* . . . ([Geneva]: Jean Crespin, 1570), ff. 600v–610.

11 Joos Verkindert and Laurens Andries, *Sommige Brieven, Testamenten, ende Belijdingen geschreven door Joos Verkindert* . . . (n.p., 1572), f. 23.

12 Jean Calvin, *Excuse de Iehan Calvin a Messieurs les Nicodemites, sur la complaincte qu'ilz font de sa trop grand' rigeur* ([Geneva: Jean Girard], 1544), repr. in *Ioannis Calvini opera quae supersunt omnia*, vol. 6, ed. G. Baum, E. Cunitz, and E. Reuss (Brunswick, 1867), cols. 593–614.

13 Crespin, *Histoire*, f. 135.

14 See e.g. *Histoire de l'estat de la Chrestienté au Iapon, et du glorieux martyre de plusieurs Chrestiens en la grande persecution de l'an 1612, 1613, et 1614* . . . (Douai: Balthazar Beller, 1618).

15 John Scory, *An Epistle written by John Scory* . . . ([Emden: Gilles van der Erve], 1555), sigs. [A8]–B2.

16 Jan Wouters van Cuyck and Adriaenken Jans, *Sommighe belijdinghen schriftlijcke Sent-brieven, geschreven door Jan Wouterszoon van Cuyck* . . . (n.p., 1579), sig. G3r–v.

17 *Der actus und handlung der degradation und verprenung der Christlichen Ritter und merter Augustiner ordens geschechen zu Brussel* . . . , reprinted in *Bibliotheca Reformatoria Neerlandica*, vol. 8, ed. Frederik Pijper (The Hague: Martinus Nijhoff, 1911), pp. 16–17 (my emphasis).

18 [Crespin], *Recueil de plusieurs personnes, qui ont constamment enduré la mort, pour le nom du Seigneur* . . . ([Geneva]: Jean Crespin, 1555), sig. *4v.

19 William Tyndale, *The Obedience of a Christen man and how Christen rulers ought to governe* . . . ([Antwerp: Jacob Hoochstraten], 1528), f. 2.

20 Crespin, *Recueil*, sig. *2.

21 For an overview of the dispute, see François Wendel, *Calvin: Origins and Development of His Religious Thought*, trans. Philip Mairet (1963; reprint, Durham, NC: Labyrinth Press, 1987), pp. 102–5.

22 Conrad Grebel to Thomas Müntzer, September 5, 1524, in Leonhard von Muralt and Walter Schmid, eds., *Quellen zur Geschichte der Taüfer in der Schweiz*, vol. 1, *Zürich* (Zürich: S. Hirzel, 1952), p. 17.

23 Thieleman Jans van Braght, *Het Bloedigh Tooneel der Doops-gesinde, en Weereloose Christenen* . . . (Dordrecht: Jacob Braat, 1660), sigs. [(*)4v]–(**)1v.

24 Peter Burke, "How to Be a Counter-Reformation Saint," p. 51.

BIBLIOGRAPHY

Burke, P., "How to Be a Counter-Reformation Saint," in Kaspar Von Greyerz, ed., *Religion and Society in Early Modern Europe, 1500–1800*. London: German Historical Institute, 1984, pp. 45–55.

Dillon, A., *The Construction of Martyrdom in the English Catholic Community, 1535–1603*. Aldershot: Ashgate, 2002.

Dyck, C. J., "The Suffering Church in Anabaptism," *Mennonite Quarterly Review*, 59 (1985), pp. 5–23.

El Kenz, D., *Les Búchers du roi: La culture protestante des martyres 1523–1572*. Seyssel: Champs Vallon, 1997.

Gregory, B. S., *Salvation at Stake: Christian Martyrdom in Early Modern Europe*. Cambridge, Mass.: Harvard University Press, 1999.

Grell, O. P. and Scribner, B., eds., *Tolerance and Intolerance in the European Reformation*. Cambridge: Cambridge University Press, 1996.

Knott, J. R., *Discourses of Martyrdom in English Literature, 1563–1694*. Cambridge: Cambridge University Press, 1993.

Kolb, R., *For All the Saints: Changing Perceptions of Martyrdom and Sainthood in the Lutheran Reformation*. Macon, Ga.: Mercer University Press, 1987.

Kreider, A. F., "'The Servant is Not Greater than His Master': The Anabaptists and the Suffering Church," *Mennonite Quarterly Review*, 58 (1984), pp. 5–29.

Lieseberg, U., *Studien zum Märtyrerlied der Täufer im 16. Jahrhundert*. Frankfurt a.M.: Peter Lang, 1991.

Loades, D., ed., *John Foxe and the English Reformation*. Aldershot: Scolar Press, 1997.

Luther, M., *D. Martin Luthers Werke: Kritische Gesamtausgabe, Abteilung Werke*. Weimar: H. Böhlau, 1883–1993. [*WA*]

Mâle, É., *L'Art réligieux de la fin du XVIe siècle, du XVIIe siècle et du XVIIIe siècle: Étude sur l'iconographie après le concile de Trent*, 2nd ed. Paris: Armand Colin, 1951.

Nicholls, D., "The Theatre of Martyrdom in the French Reformation," *Past and Present*, 121 (1988), pp. 49–73.

Seidel Menchi, S., ed., *Ketzerverfolgung im 16. und frühen 17. Jahrhundert*. Wolffenbüttel: Harrassowitz, 1992.

White, H., *Tudor Books of Saints and Martyrs*. Madison: University of Wisconsin Press, 1963.

Wood, D., ed., *Martyrs and Martyrologies*. Studies in Church History, 30. Oxford: Blackwell, 1993.

FURTHER READING

Many of the themes in this essay are developed in detail in the first synthetic, comparative, cross-confessional analysis of Christian martyrdom in the Reformation era, Brad S. Gregory's *Salvation at Stake*. There exists a great deal of specialized scholarship devoted to specific early modern martyrs, martyrologists, and martyrological traditions. On Protestants, for brief introductory overviews of the martyrologies see A. G. Dickens et al., "Weapons of Propaganda: The Martyrologies," in *The Reformation in Historical Thought* (Cambridge, Mass.: Harvard University Press, 1985), pp. 39–57, and Jean-François Gilmont, "Books of Martyrs," in *The Oxford Encyclopedia of the Reformation*, vol. 1 (Oxford: Oxford University Press, 1996), pp. 195–200. On Anabaptists, two fine introductory articles include Cornelius J. Dyck, "The Suffering Church of Anabaptism," and Alan F. Kreider, "'The Servant is Not Greater than His Master.'" Also in print in English translation is Theileman Jans van Braght, *The Bloody Theater or Martyrs' Mirror of the Defenseless Christians*, translated by Joseph F. Sohm (1886; reprint, Scottdale, Pa: Herald Press, 1990). For a brief overview of post-Tridentine Catholic martyrs, see R. Po-chia Hsia, *The World of Catholic Renewal 1540–1770* (Cambridge: Cambridge University Press, 1998), pp. 80–91. The best introduction to the topic remains the chapter on martyrdom in Émile Mâle, *L'Art réligieux de la fin du XVIe siècle, du XVIIe siècle et du XVIIIe siècle*, pp. 109–49. Two other fine art-historical articles are David Freedberg, "The Representation of Martyrdoms during the Early Counter-Reformation in Antwerp," *Burlington Magazine*, 118 (1976), pp. 128–38, and Alexandra Herz, "Imitators of Christ: The Martyr-Cycles of late Sixteenth-Century Rome Seen in Context," *Storia dell'arte*, 62 (1988), pp. 53–70.

TWENTY-EIGHT

Jews in a Divided Christendom

MIRIAM BODIAN

When Martin Luther broke with the Roman Church and found a protector in the elector of Saxony, some Jews in the German states may have toyed with hopeful speculations, but for the most part they were confronted with fundamentally unchanged realities. At the time, they were a reviled minority living under severe economic and social restrictions. They were threatened by the prospect of blood libels, violence, and expulsion – sometimes all three, in quick succession. Their spokesman and representative before the authorities, the resourceful Josel of Rosheim, found himself occupied, both before and after Luther took the stage, with heading off expulsions, refuting calumnies, and trying to halt the revocation of privileges.

A climate of severe hostility to Jews had prevailed since the twelfth and thirteenth centuries, when popular Christian representations of the Jews, already negative, turned sinister. Jews were not only blind and obstinate in their error; they were also actively menacing. They sought to subvert Christian society and overthrow its authorities; they despoiled Christians with their usurious practices; they abducted children and killed them for their blood. More generally, they were an ally of the devil, a dangerous pollutant, a fiendish presence that had to be contained and suppressed, if not expelled. Reformation leaders came of age in a milieu permeated with such notions. It is striking, for example, that Luther appropriated an image from his environment – the obscene stone carving of the *Judensau*, "here at Wittenberg, in our parish church" – to defame the Talmud, suggesting its origins in the nether parts of a sow (*WA*, vol. 53, p. 600).[1] Such notions, in their extreme form, were largely independent of the formal teaching of the Catholic Church. It might even be said that they continued to satisfy popular psychic needs in a way the church was widely failing to do.

Hostile feelings were routinely translated into action by expulsion. The list of German towns and principalities from which Jews were expelled in the century before Luther's appearance makes for dreary reading. But the list is also deceptive. Typically, Jews would be expelled from a town by decree of the emperor at the behest of the burghers, and would scatter to villages where they would be granted protection by a local lord. They might eventually be allowed to return to the town – with new restrictions or taxes. (Not surprisingly, a significant number migrated to Poland-Lithuania or the Ottoman Empire, where conditions were better.) Collective survival entailed an endless round of negotiations with magistrates, bishops, princes, counts, margraves, and emperors, who, as recipients of Jews' taxes, had an interest in their continued presence.

In the early stages of his break with Rome, Martin Luther seemed to make a startling break with prevalent attitudes about Jews. In a treatise written in 1523, he held Jews up as models of probity and common sense: "If I had been a Jew and seen such oafs and numbskulls governing and teaching the Christian faith," he wrote, "I would have rather become a sow than a Christian" (*WA*, vol. 11, pp. 314–15). He urged reformers to use loving persuasion to bring about the Jews' conversion to the purified Christian faith.

Much has been written about Luther's volte-face in the 1540s, when he shifted from flattering rhetoric to unbridled attacks on "these venomous serpents and devil's children, who are the most vehement enemies of Christ our Lord and of us all" (*WA*, vol. 53, p. 530). The psychic factors behind Luther's shift are a matter of conjecture. But however anomalous Luther's early courting of the Jews might have been in the contemporary German context, it was not an innovation. If anything it is Luther's *later* attitude to the Jews, not his earlier, that reflects his break with the Roman Church.[2] Friendly persuasion had always been a strategy for achieving the Jews' conversion. Luther's 1543 "program" for dealing with the Jews, on the other hand, is quite another matter. It called for setting fire to the Jews' synagogues and homes, confiscating their prayer books and talmudic writings, prohibiting their rabbis from teaching, prohibiting their practice of usury, and confiscating their wealth; eventually, he believed, they should be driven from "our land" (*WA*, vol. 53, pp. 523–9). This program (which was never implemented) constituted a breach both of customary law, according to which the Jews paid for a charter that granted them basic protections, and Roman Church policy, which in principle protected the Jews' property and their right to unimpeded religious practice. Luther's dismissal of time-honored legal protections did not go unnoticed by the Jews. Wrote Josel of Rosheim, "Never has it been contended by any scholar that we Jews ought to be treated with violence and much tyranny; that none was bound to honor any obligation toward us or keep the peace of the land" just because the Jews refused to accept Christianity (Ben-Sasson, "Reformation," pp. 286–8).

Not every reformer was as immoderate as Luther. But Luther's "program" reflected a simple and important fact – namely, that hostile attitudes to the Jews were not inconsistent with Protestant theology. None of the major theological innovators of the age – not Erasmus or Reuchlin, Bucer or Müntzer, Calvin or Zwingli – produced a significantly new theological position *vis-à-vis* the Jews. They all reiterated the longstanding doctrine that Jews were willfully perverse in their refusal to accept the truth of the Gospels, despite the fact that this truth had been demonstrated to them through Christian teaching.

This is not to belittle the importance of differences in emotional attitudes among the reformers. The spectrum was a wide one – from Luther, on the one hand, with his poisonous invective, to Andreas Osiander, on the other, who sent a letter to the learned Jew Elias Levita apologizing for Luther's tirades (Oberman, *Roots of Anti-Semitism*, p. 47). But these differences had no lasting impact on the contours of Protestant thinking, any more than did similar variations in the Catholic world.

In any case, even for the moderate in spirit it was strategically unwise to be associated unnecessarily with Jews and Judaism. The accusation of "judaizing" was flung routinely at reformers of all stripes. The implication was that Protestant rejection of the authority of church dogma, in favor of the direct authority of Scripture, reflected a Jewish influence. (Luther, despite the fact that he himself was a target of such attacks, did not hesitate to hurl the charge at those even more radical adherents of *sola scriptura*, the Anabaptists.) The resilience of the charge was such that reformers could also fling it back at the "papist" enemy, as an allusion to the Roman Church's emphasis on outward ceremony and works righteousness. Relatively harmless as such mudslinging was, it did not make for a climate that encouraged magnanimity toward the Jews.

In terms of political realities, the immediate upheaval was far from favorable to the Jews. The bargaining and negotiating continued. But, in the charged atmosphere of the pamphlet wars, so did the expulsions. Noteworthy was the expulsion of the Jews in 1537 from Luther's Saxony. While the circumstances that led the elector to expel the Jews are somewhat obscure, there is no question that Luther refused Jewish appeals to intervene on their behalf.

In the face of new threats of expulsion at the local level, Josel of Rosheim appears to have adopted a cautious strategy, maintaining contacts with all parties but cultivating an alliance with the emperor, Charles V. For pragmatic reasons, the emperor did generally act to protect the Jews when local authorities sought to expel them. But an alliance with the stabilizing conservative forces of Catholic Church and empire was of limited value at a time when the territorial German states were becoming increasingly independent of imperial power. Under the circumstances, the power of the guilds and municipal councils was growing; these bodies were governed by the burghers, traditionally the most anti-Jewish group in the empire after the friars. It is they who were responsible for the continuing expulsions. But the German Jews, whatever the precise political realities, tended to hold the reformers responsible. One of the Jews expelled from Brunswick in 1547 reflected widespread attitudes when he lamented that the Jews had been driven out of that town "on the advice of this foul priest Martin Luther and the other scoundrels who derive from the stock of this archheretic" (Ben-Sasson, "Reformation," p. 289).

As fate would have it, in the one region in western Europe where Jewish exiles from Spain and the German states had found refuge – namely, in the papal states and northern Italy – the upheaval of the Reformation contributed to an abrupt change in policy toward greater repression of the Jews. In the previous century and a half, popes, princes, and urban governments in Italy had tended to adopt a pragmatic attitude to the Jews, yielding when expedient to popular anti-Jewish sentiment while ensuring that Jews be allowed to continue generating tax revenue. To be sure, this left the Jews in a precarious position, especially in light of the incendiary preaching of the Franciscans. (Significantly, the accusation of the ritual murder of Simon of Trent on Easter Sunday, 1475, was preceded by the anti-Jewish preaching of the celebrated Franciscan friar Bernardino da Feltre [Hsia, *Trent 1475*, p. 25].) Nevertheless, the conditions of Jewish settlement did not change radically until the 1550s. At that time, prompted by the various anxieties of the Reformation period,

Julius III and Paul IV decreed several severe measures aimed at bringing about conversions. These were not inherently novel. On the contrary, they reflected a European trend toward active interference by the authorities in the internal affairs of the Jews. But they did signal an end to an interlude of benign neglect under the Renaissance popes.

An early measure was the endorsement by Julius III, in 1554, of the burning of the Talmud the previous year by the Inquisition in Rome. While other cases of confiscation and destruction of rabbinic works followed, church opinion was by no means unanimous in supporting such action, and opposing views prevented the systematic destruction of the Talmud (Stow, "Burning of the Talmud"). Three measures from this period did, however, have far-reaching consequences for the Jews: the forced sale of all real estate to Christians, forced ghettoization, and the censorship of Hebrew books. To be sure, the need for Jewish loans and taxes meant that secular authorities often applied the new restrictions only partially. But virtually every Jewish community in Italy was ghettoized by the 1630s, resulting in restrictions of the most concrete sort. Among other things, Jews were confined within the ghetto walls after sunset, and were forced to pay rents for their cramped quarters, often exorbitant, to Christian landlords.

Viewed from 1570, it must have appeared that the Reformation had done little but erode the precarious foothold of the Jews in Christian Europe. But the Reformation, like other major historical upheavals, triggered diverse and unanticipated consequences. It also coincided with (and in some places served to spur) the interrelated processes of state-building, capitalist expansion, the diffusion of print culture, and the "decline of magic." Indirectly, these trends, and the impulses set off or reinforced by them – including the mental shifts that produced mercantilist/*politique* thinking, philosophical skepticism, and the notion of freedom of conscience – led to a gradual reversal almost everywhere of the deterioration of the conditions of Jewish life. (The notable exceptions were in Spain and Portugal and, by the late sixteenth century, Poland; of course the process was at best uneven elsewhere, too.)

Scholars are still debating the ways in which religious reform – both Protestant and Catholic – was enmeshed with other developments. Surveying the impact on the Jews of so complex a transformation thus raises an array of interpretative problems. I would not presume to attack the Gordian knot in a new way; but I will try to separate out some of the strands and suggest some points of convergence.

If we look at the most basic requirement of Jewish existence, namely the right of settlement, the late sixteenth century saw the beginnings of a trend toward reopening places of settlement to Jews in western and central Europe. Bohemia offers a dramatic early example. Earlier in the century, under the Habsburg emperors Charles V and Ferdinand I, Jews had been driven from the crown cities of Bohemia by pogroms and expulsion orders, leaving only a tiny rump population in Prague by the 1560s. But under Maximilian II and Rudolf II, charters were issued allowing Jews to resettle in Prague and in the countryside. Jews flocked there from Poland, and by 1600 the Jewish population of Prague had grown to at least several thousand.[3]

The Bohemian case manifests some of the characteristic elements of changing Jewry policies in most of the emerging absolutist states. The extraordinary fiscal pressures on rulers, at a time when the religious conflict had reached an impasse, meant that these rulers were routinely declining to force the issue of religious conformity.

This was strikingly evident in Bohemia, where a Catholic monarch had to gain consent to raise taxes from the predominantly Protestant estates. (As it happened, both Maximilian and Rudolf were also most un-Tridentine Catholics, and refused to adopt a repressive style for personal as well as political reasons.)

Jews who settled in Bohemia (many of them from Poland) became *the* traders in rural areas, where they served the nobility by marketing agricultural surpluses and providing luxuries in exchange. In Prague, they engaged in goldsmithing, printing, and moneylending. The capital accumulation from these activities enabled the emergence of the so-called "court Jews," creatures of the developing absolutist fiscal state who, with their international commercial ties (especially with Jewish grain merchants in Poland), financial skills, and readiness to accept risk, were able to supply services to monarchs that Christian merchants could not. They provided large-scale loans, provisioned armies, supplied metal to the mints, and promoted manufacture. One early such figure appeared in late sixteenth-century Prague in the person of Markus Meysl, who in recognition of his loans to the crown received unprecedented privileges and became a maecenas to the Jewish community – a routine corollary of court Jew status.

Not only in Bohemia but wherever centralization and commercial expansion became key aims of government, Jews tended to benefit. For rulers and bureaucrats, Jews became tools in the effort to break the monopoly of Christian guilds. In the 1660s, for example, the elector of Brandenburg-Prussia, hoping to develop maritime trade, attracted a Jewish merchant from Holland to settle in Memel, and local merchants were soon protesting that this Jew deviated from their own traditional, anti-competitive patterns of trade – precisely what the elector had in mind (Stern, *Preussische Staat*, vol. 1, pt. 1, pp. 57–61). The protests of the clergy were also increasingly ignored: in the Netherlands, the merchant ruling class routinely turned a deaf ear when the Reformed clergy complained of the "great freedom" of the Jews (Bodian, *Hebrews*, pp. 56–62). Louis XIV's minister Colbert put the matter succinctly when he wrote to his sovereign concerning protests about the Jews being made by merchants in Marseilles, who were invoking religious objections. "Since, at this moment, commerce is the only issue," he wrote, "there is no reason to pay any attention to [these] arguments" (Hertzberg, *French Enlightenment*, pp. 23–4).

An increasingly demystified, utilitarian view of the Jews (at least in ruling circles) facilitated their resettlement (or at least consideration of their resettlement) in virtually every European region from which they had been driven in the medieval period.[4] In evaluating this resettlement, however, it is impossible to ignore the specific role played by the Sephardi Jews, both exiles from Spain (and their descendants) and so-called *conversos*, descendants of forcibly baptized Jews in Spain and Portugal. In Italy, even at the height of the Catholic Reformation, princes and governments of the various Italian states competed to attract members of this merchant population, with its strong ties to the Ottoman Empire. (Many of them were actually Turkish subjects.) As early as 1538, the importance of these Jews in Balkan commerce induced the duke of Ferrara to grant them a favorable settlement charter. This set off a domino reaction. In 1541 the Venetian Senate offered "temporary" settlement rights to "Levantine Jews"; in 1551 the grand duke of Tuscany offered them favorable terms to settle in Pisa; and in 1553, the very year the Talmud was burned in Rome, the papacy followed suit to develop the port of Ancona. (It should be added, though, that as part of the crackdown of the 1550s, 24 Jews in Ancona – ex-*conversos* who had been baptized in the Iberian peninsula – were burned at the stake, leading to an exodus of recently settled Jews from that town.) In 1572 the duke of Savoy, ignoring pressure from Spain and the pope, offered privileges to Levantine Jews to settle in Nice and other Savoyard towns. In 1589, the Venetian Senate offered full rights of settlement to Levantine *and* "Ponentine" Jews, the latter being a euphemism for ex-*conversos* – "an act of defiant *raison d'État*," in the words of one scholar (Israel, *Age of Mercantilism*, p. 47). The grand duke of Tuscany aced all of the competition by offering a charter in 1593 with unprecedented privileges and protections, drawing Sephardi Jews of every background to settle in Livorno.

The historical accident by which decisions of the Spanish crown arising from religio-ethnic anxieties created an adaptive and mobile ex-*converso* Jewish merchant population outside the peninsula, precisely at the moment when Europe was poised for a commercial revolution, appears to have little to do with the Reformation. But in the case of the resettlement of Jews in France, the Netherlands, England, and the German states, there was a convergence of trends.[5] War-driven fiscal and commercial policies were certainly a factor. But no less important was a crystallizing *politique* outlook on religious issues – an outlook produced in part by weariness with the wars of religion that drove fiscal policy.

Conversos fleeing the Inquisition were certainly aware both of changing Jewry policies and shifting economic conditions. Now that Atlantic trade had overtaken Mediterranean, northern Europe became an increasingly attractive destination. At mid-century, Henry II of France issued *lettres patentes* to "the merchants and other Portuguese called New Christians" to settle and trade freely in his realm. His *politique* successors Henry III and Henry IV offered further protections. *Conversos* began settling in significant numbers in southwest France, where they pursued their former activity in the new Atlantic colonial trade, increasingly assured that royal authorities would protect them from local merchants jealous of their interests, as well as from clergy enraged by their lightly concealed "judaizing." The merchant colonies these settlers founded gave rise to the thriving Jewish communities of Bordeaux and Bayonne in the eighteenth century.

A similar story could be told, *mutatis mutandis*, about the settlement of Spanish and Portuguese Jews of *converso* origins in the Netherlands (from the late sixteenth century onward) and in England (from the mid-seventeenth century onward). In the latter case, mercantilist arguments were part of the negotiations. As a reason for readmitting Jews to England, the Dutch rabbi Menasseh ben Israel argued in his *Humble Addresses* to Oliver Cromwell that "there are none so profitable and beneficial to the place where they trade and live, as is the Nation of the Jews." By the following year, Jews in London were worshiping openly in a synagogue, with verbal assurances, apparently, that there would be no objection.

While it was the Sephardi population of ex-*conversos* that spearheaded the resettlement, Yiddish-speaking Ashkenazi Jews soon followed, fleeing persecutions in eastern Europe and taking advantage of new opportunities in German lands, as rulers there rebuilt economies shattered by the Thirty Years' War. Jews continued to suffer legal disabilities everywhere until the late eighteenth century – quite severe ones, in fact, in eastern Europe, the German states and Austria, some Italian states, and the papal states in France. But despite the relatively rapid growth of Jewish populations in central and western Europe, anti-Jewish violence, while occasionally erupting, had largely disappeared; the last major outbreak occurred in Frankfurt and Würms in 1614–15.

To generalize greatly about trends in this period, it could be said that the reappearance of Jews on landscapes from which they had been expelled or driven for generations was a consequence of the shift from a popular public sphere permeated by the *Weltanschauung* of the friars – one that was otherworldly, intensely fearful, and associated with the life of the towns – to one increasingly dominated by monarchs and bureaucrats: this-worldly, confident of humanity's power to change and control, and associated with capital cities. Within the new context of thinking, Jews lost much of their fantastic, "enchanted" image and assumed a more instrumental, utilitarian one.

There were somewhat different developments in thinking about the Jews that, while eventually impacting on political life, were initially associated with the world of letters and the privacy of the home. These developments have their roots in humanistic scholarship and Protestant Bible-reading. To elaborate on these, I would like to abandon the political scene momentarily and backtrack, picking up a different thread.

In the first half of the sixteenth century, a slowly shifting sensibility encouraged a number of Christian scholars to approach some fields of Jewish learning – the Hebrew language, rabbinic interpretation of the Old Testament, the Talmud, and kabbalah – with less anxiety and greater adventurousness of mind. (This is not to say that the phobic view did not persist: Erasmus, observing his contemporaries' enthusiasm for Hebrew studies, expressed concern that the revival of Hebrew letters might lead to a revival of Judaism, "the most pernicious plague and bitterest enemy that one can find to the teaching of Christ."[6]) Motivations ranged from an academic interest in Hebrew philology to an occult interest in kabbalistic numerology, making it difficult to generalize. But these efforts together did reflect a relatively widespread break with the cautious traditional approach of the church, one that endorsed the Vulgate as the authoritative text of the Old Testament and discouraged involvement with Hebrew and rabbinic literature except for the purposes of anti-Jewish polemics. The implications of the awakened interest in Hebrew learning for Christian perceptions of the Jews, though modest at first, were eventually far-reaching.

There was no way to gain an intimate acquaintance with the Hebrew text except through the medium of Jewish scholars. (Baptized Jews were an alternative but they often proved inadequately trained.) It is not surprising that Italy was the first focus of Christian Hebraist activity. Here the Jewish and Christian communities were less isolated from one another than they were in the German states, both culturally and psychologically. (This remained the case even after the ghettoization of Italian Jewry.) Johannes Reuchlin and Pico della Mirandola, two of the earliest Christian Hebraists, were instructed by Italian Jews – Reuchlin by the physician and exegete Obadiah Sforno and Pico by the thinker Yochanan Alemanno. Among humanist churchmen in Rome, Hebrew study became a natural adjunct to classical studies; several bishops turned to the papal physician Jacob Mantino for instruction, while the erudite Cardinal Egidio de Viterbo exchanged Greek lessons for Hebrew with the Jewish scholar Elias Levita.

Hebrew studies were soon pursued throughout Europe, even in places where Jews had not lived for generations. Given the Protestant affirmation of *sola scriptura* (and of the importance of lay Bible-reading), it is not surprising that Luther and many of the early reformers worked to promote Hebrew studies. Some of the reformers, like Müntzer, Zwingli, and Melanchthon, were themselves Hebraists. (A greater number *thought* themselves Hebraists.) An "infrastructure" for Hebrew studies was created rather rapidly: university chairs and trilingual colleges were established, and Hebrew grammars, dictionaries, and practice texts were printed for the Christian novice. Some of the finest of the grammatical works for Christian use were produced by the Christian printer Daniel Bomberg in Venice, in collaboration with Elias Levita.

Through their tutors and, for the very few whose proficiency was sufficient, through the texts themselves, Christian Hebraists became familiar with rabbinic exegesis, particularly through the commentaries of Rashi, Abraham ibn Ezra, and David Kimchi. This was to have a profound effect in the Protestant sphere in particular. The explicit rationale for turning to Jewish exegesis may have been purely technical. (As the Alsatian reformer Conrad Pellican put it, "In difficult passages recourse must be had to Hebrew truth" [Friedman, *Most Ancient Testimony*, p. 32].) But contact with the Jewish exegetical tradition eroded the boundary between the true, Christological, "spiritual" reading of the text and the erroneous, literal, "carnal" one. This was one of the routes by which Protestant scholars began to view the narrative passages of the Old Testament in historical, non-Christological terms.

It was not immediately obvious that Christian interest in Hebrew studies had benefits for the Jews beyond the fees some of them received for their services. Many of the Christian Hebraists manifested a remarkable affective split that allowed them to love the Hebrew language while loathing the Jews. This is nicely illustrated by the behavior of Otto Henry, the Calvinist elector of the Palatinate and an ardent Hebraist, who expelled the Jews from his territory in 1556, making sure, however, to appropriate valuable Hebrew books and manuscripts from the exiles before they left, so as to add them to the rich collection of Heidelberg's University which he had helped to build (Baron, *Social and Religious History*, p. 257). Johannes Reuchlin, for his part, looked on actions like Otto Henry's with some anxiety: the expulsion and emigration of Jews from Christian lands, he feared, would lead to the extinction of the Hebrew language there. Luther, however, saw Christian Hebraism as a solution. Not only would the Hebraists provide the needed expertise in Hebrew; they would purify what he regarded as a corrupted Jewish Biblical text. In his *On the Ineffable Name*, he praised a Hebraist in Leipzig for being "an exceptional enemy of the *jüdischen Judas pisse*," a man capable of "cleansing" the Hebrew Bible (*WA*, vol. 53, p. 647). Reuchlin, Luther, Zwingli, Müntzer, Melanchthon – all placed great value, in one way or another, on Hebrew texts; none had any particular sympathy for the Jews.

But in general, Christian Hebraism did serve to check extreme anti-rabbinic voices that had been active in the Catholic world from the thirteenth century onward. The outstanding illustration of this is the Reuchlin–Pfefferkorn affair. In 1509 Johannes Pfefferkorn, an apostate Jew who had been agitating (with Dominican support) against rabbinic learning, entered a Frankfurt synagogue with authorization from the emperor to confiscate Hebrew books found there. The Jews protested to local authorities who in turn appealed to the emperor, who ordered that Pfefferkorn's accusations about the rabbinic texts be judged by several theologians, including the prominent churchman and Hebraist Johannes Reuchlin. The resulting polarization of camps around Reuchlin, on the one hand, and Pfefferkorn, on the other, reflected the growing fissures in ecclesiastical ranks between the humanist-reformers and the conservatives. True, no one was defending the Jews; but for the first time in the history of Christian Europe their texts were vigorously defended by figures of authority. The controversy was eventually submitted to the Fifth Lateran Council, which in 1516 upheld Reuchlin's opinion – namely, that in matters of faith, Jews (and their texts) were not subject to Christian judgment.

The truly momentous change brought by the new focus on Scripture was not in the return of Christian scholars to Hebrew texts but in the wide dissemination of the Hebrew Bible itself, whether in Hebrew, Latin, or the vernacular. The Bible had always been the most widely read book in Christian Europe. But before the Reformation it had been read mainly by a tiny minority of educated, Latin-trained clerics. With the advent of vernacular translations in print, with increasing numbers of educated lay people, and with the strong encouragement of lay Bible-reading by reformers, a radically different relationship developed between lay Christians and the Scripture of the Jews.

It was one of the very few ways in which Reformation theology had a direct impact on the way Christians saw Jews. Vernacular Bibles became a common household object in Protestant Europe. Protestants and sectarians were reading the Bible freshly, unshackled by a theologically driven exegetical tradition. Familiarity entailed a certain demystification, even desacralization of the text. Fathers who were now responsible for the religious life of the household integrated the Bible into domestic life; its reading became a form of sacred entertainment and folksy instruction, and its narratives took on the flavor of popular epic, with heroes and villains, love stories and war sagas. Perhaps nothing testifies to this humanization of the Bible narrative so powerfully as Rembrandt's Biblical scenes. As Rembrandt saw it, a deliriously drunk Lot was indistinguishable from any dissolute figure in a contemporary tavern scene. There is the same everyday quality about Judah eagerly fondling a passive, compliant Tamar, or Sarah, eavesdropping from behind the door as Abraham presides over a meal.

A striking indication of increasing Protestant identification with figures from the Hebrew Bible was the trend to name boys after Old Testament figures – Abraham, Daniel, Elias, Benjamin. The fact that the Jews in one's midst bore such names – and, with the resettlement, such Jews were visible in more places – no longer marked them as outsiders or relics of a dead Law. Jewish law and custom also became more familiar. Bible-reading revealed the sources in Scripture for such prominent sights as *mezuzot* on the doorposts of Jewish homes and the booths built for the holiday of Sukkot. A market developed for engravings and books on the subject of Jewish ceremony. Thomas Godwyn's *Moses and Aron* (1625) in the English-speaking world and Buxtorf the Elder's *Synagoga judaica* (1603) in the German-speaking world presented Jewish ritual in a reasonably matter-of-fact way. The Venetian rabbi Leon de Modena produced such a volume for Christian consumption, published in Paris in 1637; the Dutch edition of 1683 was illustrated with detailed, graceful engravings of Jewish rites by Jan Luyken. As the Buxtorfs' careers testify, such popular works grew out of the tradition of Christian Hebraism. But they appeared at a time when budding comparative notions of religion, and curiosity about religious custom in general, had brought forth illustrated compilations about the religious practices of various exotic (and by now mostly conquered) peoples.

It is no wonder that with such a wealth of visual and verbal imagery in the atmosphere, it seeped into political discourse as well. As Michael Walzer has shown vividly in his *Exodus and Revolution*, the political rhetoric of the English Puritans was suffused with allusions to the Israelites in Egypt and the Wilderness. A less pervasive but parallel phenomenon can be found in the Netherlands as well, where defiant Dutch Calvinists depicted their liberation from Spanish tyranny as a second crossing of the Red Sea. In a less poetic vein, political thinkers weighed the virtues of Hebrew Biblical government and law in their ruminations about ideal government.[7] And while in general the Biblical archetypes remained just that, and did not interfere with reality, the imaginative hold of the Biblical narrative on the imagination was such that radical reformers like Thomas Müntzer in the sixteenth century or the Ranters and Fifth Monarchy men in the seventeenth identified with the ancient Israelites in the most immediate way.

The latter were among the millenarian voices in the Protestant world, sectarian voices that echoed the new Bible-reading with a focus not on history but on prophecy. The debate among the English millenarians about the role the Jews would play in the Second Coming threw a spotlight on contemporary Jews and prompted action during the Puritan regime aimed at obtaining their resettlement on English soil. The millenarian assumption that the Jews would convert just prior to the Second Coming was not, of course, compatible with the Jewish scenario. Nevertheless, some Jews were energized by the atmosphere of common expectation – not least among them the Amsterdam rabbi Menasseh ben Israel, who addressed Oliver Cromwell with arguments that the Jews should be readmitted to England for both mercantilist and millenarian reasons.

The cacophony of Protestant and sectarian voices by the seventeenth century makes generalization about attitudes to Jews risky. Yet certain trends seem to cut across confessional lines. Bible-reading Protestants tended to associate Jews somewhat less with the murderous Pharisees of the Gospels, and more with the flesh-and-blood heroes of the Pentateuch and historical books of the Old Testament, as discussed above. The more human, realistic view of the Jews that thus emerged was reinforced by another current in Protestant life, namely, the suppression of magical belief. As Keith Thomas has persuasively argued, the fierce Protestant propaganda campaign against the Roman Church, a campaign which targeted miracles, pilgrimages, and devotion to saints, had the effect of rendering magical practices ludicrous in the eyes of an ever-widening public. Where Jews were concerned, the demystification of the Eucharist, an object associated with Christ's physical suffering and as such liable to arouse desecration of the Host charges, was particularly significant. Popular fantasies persisted, to be sure, but a public that heaped scorn on "papist" fantasies was less likely to entertain demonic fantasies about the Jews.[8]

Perhaps the single most consequential change for Jews put in motion by the Reformation had little to do with Jews *per se*. It had to do partly with the eventual recognition in Christian society that a divided Christendom was going to remain that way. Less concretely, it had to do with changing ideas about how religious authority should be exercised. Christopher Hill was perhaps a bit categorical when he declared that the so-called priesthood of all believers "put down the priests from their judgment-seat; and ushered in a secular, Erastian society, in which sin was no longer defined and punished by public authority" (Hill, *Society and Puritanism*, p. 327). But eventually societies did emerge in which public authority refrained from punishing errors of conscience or otherwise applying coercion in matters of belief.

It was in the Netherlands in the seventeenth century that Jews first discerned in European public discourse the notion of a principle of universal religious toleration. That this happened where it did had to do both with the special characteristics of Dutch society and with the special characteristics of the Jews who settled there in the early seventeenth century – namely, ex-*conversos* from Spain and Portugal, a group that was keenly aware of currents in European society in a way that the more isolated (and self-isolating) Yiddish-speaking Ashkenazi Jews were not.

A grasp of the novelty of this toleration was expressed by one of the early rabbis of the Amsterdam community, who wrote in 1615 in evident wonder that the city authorities there "allow every man to believe in divine matters as he chooses, and each lives according to his faith, as long as he does not go about the markets and streets displaying his opposition to the faith of the residents of the city." What impressed him was not that the government permitted the practice of Judaism. (There was nothing new about this. The author was most likely Joseph Pardo, who grew up in Salonica and lived for a time in the Venetian ghetto, in both of which places the practice of Judaism was permitted.) It was the recognition that a (largely) Calvinist government tolerated *Christians* of various creeds. The Jews in Amsterdam were not tolerated by virtue of a special privilege, then, but by virtue of a universal right. The reality of life in Amsterdam may have been more complex than the passage suggests, but the rabbi was not wrong in understanding that the principle of universal toleration was already powerful in Dutch public opinion.

The toleration practiced in early seventeenth-century Amsterdam was not, however, without limits. Indeed, Hugo Grotius had argued that Jewish settlement be conditional on each Jew accepting the Hebrew Bible as revealed truth. While Grotius's recommendations had not in the end been adopted, the Jewish community clearly accepted the right of the government to suppress unacceptable beliefs, and took responsibility for disciplining its own heterodox members. Its ban on Spinoza in 1656, for example, was probably carried out in part to protect the community before the authorities. Ultimately, it would be the expression of opinions by individualists like Spinoza, or by radical sectarian groups who remained outside major church frameworks, that would undermine the practice of religious discipline. In fact, Jewish communal officials would soon find themselves in the same predicament as consistory officials, trying in vain to hold onto their disciplinary powers.

If the first Jewish encounter with state-sanctioned toleration involved Portuguese Jews in Amsterdam, the experience soon included Ashkenazi Jews, and embraced Jewish settlements in England, Dutch Brazil and the Dutch Caribbean, and British colonial America. By 1750, however, the number of Jews in Christian Europe living under these conditions was tiny. The vast majority of Jews, most of them living in eastern Europe, suffered disabilities inherited from the late medieval period; they were subject to heavy special taxes, settlement restrictions, and restrictions on their economic activity. The growing gulf in terms of legal status was one of the factors that contributed to ongoing migration of Jews from east to west, a migration that would peak only at the turn of the twentieth century.

How did early modern European Jews come to view the Protestant Reformation, after the initial upheaval? In general, in the medieval period, Jews tended to be "favorable" or "unfavorable" to one Christian ruler over another not because of the greater acceptability of his theology, but because of his treatment of them. In the Ashkenazi communities in central and eastern Europe, the theological differences between Catholic and Protestant were of no great interest. Characteristically, Josel of Rosheim reacted warmly to Luther as long as he expressed friendly views toward the Jews; once he turned hostile, Josel put his trust in Charles V, that "angel of the Lord."

It was only when Portuguese Jews settled in Amsterdam in the seventeenth century that we find Jews who were able to evaluate the differences not only between Protestants and Catholics, but between different Protestant groups as well. From the outset the "Portuguese" held strongly negative ideas about Catholicism that disposed them favorably to just about anything else. Moreover, their criticisms of the church often closely paralleled Protestant attacks – for example, in the matter of saint worship or the magical powers of the Eucharist. On the other hand, the Calvinists held to beliefs that the Portuguese Jews continued to repudiate no less vehemently than saint worship – above all, the messiahship of Jesus and the doctrine of the Trinity. While their views about Catholics and Protestants were unquestionably colored by their contrasting experience under the regimes of each, a few of them tried to understand the new theology (or theologies) in a critical way.

The most elaborate, nuanced, and learned Jewish evaluation of the Protestant world in the pre-Enlightenment period was a polemical treatise by the Amsterdam rabbi Saul Levi Mortera composed in 1659.[9] This massive treatise of more than 400 manuscript pages sought to stake out a Jewish position *vis-à-vis* a wide spectrum of Christian belief – Catholic, Calvinist, and Socinian. Mortera was predictably consistent in his hostility to Catholicism. His well-informed opinion of Calvinism (he had read Calvin's *Institutes* in Spanish translation) was more complex. He noted the admirable measures of the Calvinists: they had successfully defended their consciences, defeated the Spanish enemy, rejected "the great idolatry of the Host, the worship of the crucifix and other images," and spurned the ideal of celibacy. But in Mortera's view, their "return to the Bible" fell far short of what might be expected from a rereading of that text. "What astonishes me," he wrote, "is that the *Reformados* (who in everything try to govern themselves by Sacred Scripture, and to abandon the ordinances of the popes, particularly those contrary to [Scripture]), did not include in their reforms this matter of Sunday [i.e., the observance of the sabbath on Sunday]." While Mortera gave the Calvinists credit for removing statues from the church, here too, in his view, the job was incomplete. The Calvinists, he argued, may have rid themselves of "material, visible images" – crucifixes and statues of saints – but they remained deceived by what Mortera called "mental, invisible images" – that is, the conception of the plurality of God (i.e., the Trinity) and the corporeality of the Son.

It was only the "*novos reformados*," as he called the Socinian Antitrinitarians, who had truly eliminated idolatry, rejecting the doctrines of the Trinity and Incarnation.[10] But they still clung to certain errors, in particular the belief that the Gospels were divinely revealed, and that Jesus was the messiah. Interestingly, Mortera speculated about the possibility that the Socinians might eventually reject the divinity of the Gospels. Overall, Mortera discerned in the Reformation a considerable degree of dynamic change toward greater truth. Significantly, in his view it was rational thought (rather than miraculous events) that had the power to liberate gentiles from deluded thinking – and, by extension, from hostility to the Jews.

This is the view of a member of the rabbinic establishment, for whom the prose-lytizing Christian world, Calvinist as well as Catholic, posed dangers to the integrity of the Jewish community. No consideration of Jews in Reformation Europe, however, can neglect the powerful ways in which the rupture of boundaries within the Christian sphere brought about new points of contact between members of the Christian intelligentsia and nonconformist Jews – nonconformist Portuguese Jews in particular, with their command of European culture, their involvement in inter-national diplomacy, and their rabbinic education. Towering above them all is Baruch (Benedict) Spinoza, who was singular in belonging to no confessional group at all after his break with the Jewish community. Others, less gifted but equally schooled in conflict, were among the first to develop from a Jewish point of view such ideas accessible in European culture as a return to *sola scriptura* (Uriel da Costa), a re-pudiation of the revealed nature of Scripture (Juan de Prado), and democratic ideas of government (Daniel Levi de Barrios).[11]

The encounter of highly Europeanized Portuguese Jews with some of the most innovative trends in Christian Europe in seventeenth-century Amsterdam was highly exceptional, however, and had parallels only in Venice, southwest France, and London. The vast majority of Europe's Jews remained well outside the orbit of high-velocity ideological exchange with the Christian world. This is not to diminish what was happening elsewhere. By 1750, on the eve of the successive partitions of Poland, the largest Jewry in the world, that of Poland, was about to be transformed by the Hassidic movement. The annexed territories of Poland would remain the center of gravity of the Jewish world until World War II, both culturally and demographically. But the dynamic repercussions of the Reformation were felt most powerfully among Jews in the urban centers of western and central Europe, and it was in these centers that Christian–Jewish interaction would be most intense and fateful in the modern period.

NOTES

1 On the *Judensau*, see Isaiah Schacher, *The Judensau: A Medieval Anti-Jewish Motif and its History* (London, 1974).

2 Jeremy Cohen has argued that Luther's attitude "originated in late medieval Christen-dom, deriving from the generally increasing intensity and friction in Jewish–Christian rela-tions during the twelfth, thirteenth, and fourteenth centuries" ("Traditional Prejudice and Religious Reform: The Theological and Historical Foundations of Luther's Anti-Judaism," in Sander Gilman and Steven Katz, eds., *Anti-Semitism in Times of Crisis* [New York and London, 1991], p. 94). But while a radical popular anti-Jewish current did indeed develop within the late medieval church, the conservatism of papal government generally held it in check, sanctioning coercion for conversionist aims, but not violence or punitive actions lacking foundation in church law.

3 A Czech scholar has estimated a figure of 1,000 in 1546, and from 6,000 to 15,000 in 1600. See Jirina Žedinova, "The Jewish Town in Prague," in E. Fučíková, ed., *Rudolf II and Prague: The Imperial Court and Residential City as the Cultural and Spiritual Home of Central Europe* (Prague, 1997), p. 309 n.3.

4 Even in Spain, for a brief period in the seventeenth century, there were voices calling for Jewish resettlement, on grounds of *raison d'état*. See Israel, *Age of Mercantilism*, p. 112.

5   Medieval persecutions and expulsions had made England, France, and the Netherlands essentially *Judenrein* by the Reformation period. The Jews were expelled from England in 1290, from France over the course of the fourteenth century (however, France inherited a Jewish population in Alsace in the seventeenth century), and from the Netherlands by the end of the sixteenth century.

6   Letter of 1517 to Wolfgang Capito. See *The Correspondence of Erasmus* (Toronto, 1977), vol. 4, p. 261.

7   On the use of Biblical models in early modern political thinking, see S. B. Robinson, "The Biblical Hebrew State as an Example of the Ideal Government in the Writings of Political Thinkers of the Seventeenth and Eighteenth Centuries" (Hebrew), in Robinson, ed., *Hinukh ben hemshekhiut u-petihut* (Jerusalem, 1975), pp. 13–69. On the ambivalent attitudes to Mosaic law as judicial precedent among Protestant reformers, see P. D. L. Avis, "Moses and the Magistrate: A Study in the Rise of Protestant Legalism," *Journal of Ecclesiastical History*, 26 (1975), pp. 149–72.

8   The persistence of these fantasies in popular circles long after their "psychological and intellectual foundations began to disintegrate" has been argued persuasively for Germany by Hsia, *Myth of Ritual Murder*, pp. 136–230.

9   The manuscript work has been published by H. P. Salomon, *Tratado da verdade da lei de Moisés* (Coimbra, 1988). Mortera was not a Portuguese Jew of *converso* origin – he was apparently of mixed Italianate and Ashkenazi origins – but he had become a part of the ex-*converso* diaspora quite early in his life, and devoted himself to serving its needs until his death.

10 Ibid., p. 192.

11 On the latter's ideas, see Miriam Bodian, "Biblical Hebrews and the Rhetoric of Republicanism: Seventeenth-Century Portuguese Jews on the Jewish Community," *AJS Review*, 22 (1997), pp. 209–18.

BIBLIOGRAPHY

Baron, S., *A Social and Religious History of the Jews*, 18 vols. Philadelphia: Jewish Publication Society, vol. 13, 1969.

Ben-Sasson, H. H., "Jewish–Christian Disputation in the Setting of Humanism and Reformation in the German Empire," *Harvard Theological Review*, 59 (1966), pp. 369–90.

Bernardini, P. and Fiering, N., eds., *The Jews and the Expansion of Europe to the West, 1450–1800*. New York and Oxford: Berghahn Books, 2001.

Breuer, M. and Graetz, M., eds., *German–Jewish History in Modern Times*. Vol. 1: *Tradition and Enlightenment, 1600–1780*. New York: Columbia University Press, 1996.

Davis, R. and Ravid, B., eds., *The Jews of Early Modern Venice*. Baltimore: Johns Hopkins University Press, 2001.

Ettinger, S., "The Beginnings of Change in the Attitude of European Society Towards the Jews," *Scripta Hierosolymitana*, 7 (1961), pp. 193–219.

Friedman, J., *The Most Ancient Testimony: Sixteenth-Century Christian-Hebraica in the Age of Renaissance Nostalgia*. Athens, OH: Ohio University Press, 1983.

Hertzberg, A., *The French Enlightenment and the Jews*. New York: Columbia University Press, 1968.

Hill, C., *Society and Puritanism in Pre-Revolutionary England*. New York: Schocken Books, 1964.

Hsia, R. Po-chia, *The Myth of Ritual Murder: Jews and Magic in Reformation Germany*. New Haven, Conn.: Yale University Press, 1988.

Hsia, R. Po-chia, *Trent 1475: Stories of a Ritual Murder Trial*. New Haven, Conn.: Yale University Press, 1992.

Katz, D., *Philosemitism and the Readmission of the Jews to England, 1603–1655*. Oxford: Clarendon Press, 1982.

Katz, J., *Tradition and Crisis: Jewish Society at the End of the Middle Ages*, trans. Bernard Dov Cooperman. New York: Schocken Books, 1993.

Luther, M., *D. Martin Luthers Werke: Kritische Gesamtausgabe, Abteilung Werke*. Weimar: H. Böhlau, 1883–1993. [*WA*]

Menasseh ben Israel's Mission to Oliver Cromwell: Being a Reprint of the Pamphlets Published by Menasseh ben Israel to Promote the Re-Admission of the Jews to England, 1649–1656, ed. with an introduction by Lucien Wolf. London: Macmillan, 1901.

Oberman, H., *The Roots of Antisemitism in the Age of Renaissance and Reformation*, trans. James Porter. Philadelphia: Fortress Press, 1984.

Rosman, M., *The Lords' Jews: Magnate–Jewish Relations in the Polish-Lithuanian Commonwealth during the Eighteenth Century*. Cambridge, Mass.: Harvard University Press, 1990.

Ruderman, D., *Jewish Thought and Scientific Discovery in Early Modern Europe*. New Haven, Conn.: Yale University Press, 1995.

Stern, S., *Der preussische Staat und die Juden*, 4 vols. in 8. Tübingen: J. C. B. Mohr, 1962–75.

Stern, S., *Josel of Rosheim: Commander of Jewry in the Holy Roman Empire of the German Nation*, trans. Gertrude Hirschler. Philadelphia: Jewish Publication Society, 1965.

Stow, K., "The Burning of the Talmud in 1553, in Light of Sixteenth-Century Catholic Attitudes toward the Talmud," *Bibliothèque d'Humanisme et Renaissance*, 34 (1972), pp. 435–49.

Stow, K., *Catholic Thought and Papal Jewry Policy, 1555–1593*. New York: Jewish Theological Seminary of America, 1977.

Trachtenberg, J., *The Devil and the Jews: The Medieval Conception of the Jew and its Relation to Modern Antisemitism*, 2nd ed. Philadelphia: Jewish Publication Society of America, 1983.

FURTHER READING

Ben-Sasson, H. H., "The Reformation in Contemporary Jewish Eyes," *Proceedings of the Israel Academy of Sciences and Humanities*, 4 (1971), pp. 239–326.

Bodian, M., *Hebrews of the Portuguese Nation: Conversos and Community in Early Modern Amsterdam*. Bloomington: Indiana University Press, 1997.

Hsia, R. Po-chia and Lehmann, H., eds., *In and Out of the Ghetto: Jewish–Gentile Relations in Late Medieval and Early Modern Germany*. New York: Cambridge University Press, 1995.

Israel, J., *European Jewry in the Age of Mercantilism, 1550–1750*. Oxford: Clarendon Press, 1989.

Israel, J. and Katz, D., eds., *Sceptics, Millenarians, and Jews: Essays in Honour of Richard Popkin*. Leiden: Brill, 1990.

Manuel, F., *The Broken Staff: Judaism through Christian Eyes*. Cambridge, Mass.: Harvard University Press, 1992.

Twenty-Nine

Coexistence, Conflict, and the Practice of Toleration

Benjamin J. Kaplan

Of all the legacies scholars have attributed to the religious upheavals of the sixteenth century, from the triumph of individual liberty to the oppression of a new social discipline, at least one has never been disputed: the permanent division of western Christendom into rival churches. The Protestant and Catholic Reformations shattered the religious unity of Europe, initiating a period of bitter antagonism and conflict lasting some 200 years. This was not Europeans' first experience of religious difference. In the Middle Ages, some had known Jews, although a series of expulsions had made such contact increasingly rare. Muslims had maintained a large presence on the Iberian peninsula. Yet these "unbelievers" had always remained ethnically distinct peoples. In the sixteenth century, Christians suddenly found themselves divided by faith from their own kind – from family and friends, fellow citizens and parishioners. From Britain in the west to Hungary and Poland in the east, thousands of towns and villages found themselves split internally and still more had to reckon with "heretics" living just down the road or across the field. It was a profound shock, and it evoked extreme responses. France's "Most Christian King" Francis I declared in 1535 that he wanted heresy banished from his realm "in such manner that if one of the arms of my body was infected with this corruption, I would cut it off, and if my children were tainted with it, I would myself offer them in sacrifice" (Diefendorf, *Beneath the Cross*, p. 47). In episodes like the St. Bartholomew's Day massacres of 1572, Europeans acted out such convictions with breath-catching ferocity.

For Christians of opposing beliefs and practices, the obstacles to peaceful coexistence in early modern Europe were enormous. One was a form of religiosity historians call "confessional," which affirmed intolerance as a virtue and essential mark of genuine piety. Another was the role played by religion in defining the identity of communities. A heritage of the late Middle Ages, this role operated on the local level and, with increasing government centralization, also on the national. Contrary, though, to the images of inquisition and religious warfare that color our picture of the age, most Europeans were neither martyrs nor butchers. Large parts of early modern Europe were religiously mixed, and within them, as recent research attests, peaceful coexistence prevailed more widely than often supposed. Some of these areas, like France between 1598 and 1685, were officially multi-confessional; others, like the Dutch Republic, maintained a semblance of religious unity but were mixed *de facto*. In either case, coexistence never lacked for strains. Because the idea of religious tolerance suffered from a basic illegitimacy, the forms of it practiced in early modern Europe were always quite limited, bearing little resemblance to those characteristic of the West in our own day.

For more than a hundred years after Martin Luther's break with Rome, it was far from clear to most Europeans that western Christendom would remain permanently divided. After all, the Roman Catholic Church had suppressed heresies, resolved schisms, and absorbed reform movements many times in its past; why, declared its apologists, should this new challenge be any different? For their part, mainstream Protestants never sought to establish alternate churches but to restore Christianity everywhere to its pristine form. For generations they retained supreme confidence in the power of the Gospel – of God's Word unleashed on earth by its preaching – to effect such a reformation. Divine power, Catholics and Protestants agreed, would eventually suppress false worship and spread the true faith to the ends of the earth. The only questions were how and how soon. Preaching and teaching, accompanied by moral reform and the building of sound ecclesiastic institutions, were the first recourse of all parties. But what if these failed to persuade? Catholic authorities in Brussels burned the first martyrs of the Reformation in 1523; within a few years evangelicals too accepted the use of governments' coercive power for religious ends. The first religious wars, pitting the Protestant and Catholic cantons of Switzerland against one another, flared between 1529 and 1531. The next one, the Schmalkaldic War in the Holy Roman Empire, erupted in 1546. These conflicts were small compared to the wars that would consume France and the Netherlands from the 1560s and the empire beginning in 1618. For long decades, the militants who fought in these wars held out hopes of total victory over their religious foes.

Conciliators on all sides of the religious split found permanent schism equally inconceivable. For them, if peaceful measures did not suffice to bring dissenters into the true church, then compromise seemed necessary. Not that the church should compromise its essential principles and practices, they argued, but on other points of difference it should show flexibility. It should take care to distinguish accurately between what was "fundamental" to true Christianity and what was "adiaphoral," or indifferent. And it should engage in dialogue with its opponents to clarify points of agreement. By these means it could hope to reunite as members of a single church Christians currently divided into separate communions. In the sixteenth century, this goal was usually called Christian "peace" or "concord"; later it was often called "comprehension" or "ecclesiastical toleration." It was one of the earliest and most persistent forms taken by calls for tolerance in the early modern world (Rouse and Neill, *History of the Ecumenical Movement*). The English philosopher John Locke explained neatly the difference between it and toleration in the modern sense. Reporting on the parliamentary debates that led to the passage in 1689 of England's famous Toleration Act, he wrote,

> Toleration is now discussed under two forms "comprehension" and "indulgence." By the first, it is proposed to enlarge the bounds of the church, so that by the abolition of some ceremonies, many people may be made to conform. By the other is designed the

toleration of those who are either unwilling or unable to unite with the Church of England, even on the proposed conditions. (Cranston, "John Locke and the Case for Toleration," p. 87)

Of course, all Christian groups distinguished between *fundamenta* and *adiaphora*. Hopes of achieving concord were based on defining the former narrowly and the latter widely. Georg Calixtus, Lutheran professor of theology at the University of Helmstedt, equated the former with the teachings of early Christianity. William Chillingworth, one of a group of "Latitudinarian" thinkers in England in the 1630s–1640s, reduced Christianity to a lowest common denominator. The true church, he asserted, is nothing more than the "common profession of those articles of faith wherein all consent; a joint worship of God, after such a way as all esteem lawful; and a mutual performance of all those works of charity, which Christians owe one to another" (Jordan, *Development of Religious Toleration*, vol. 2, p. 393). A related approach was to minimize the importance of those matters over which the churches split. Erasmian humanists located the essence of Christianity not in any set of doctrines but in a morality that took Christ as preeminent model of Christian behavior. Spiritualists expressed indifference to the form church ceremonies took, seeking salvation instead in a wholly personal, internal union with the divine.

The broadest visions of a common Christianity inspired schemes to heal the breach between Protestants and Catholics. Such was the goal of the most ambitious conciliators: to restore the lost unity of medieval Christendom. Predictably, these schemes foundered time and again on specifics. Perhaps the closest conciliators ever came to forging agreement was at the Colloquy of Regensburg in 1541. There negotiators arrived at a compromise formula for the doctrine of justification but got nowhere on the issues of papal authority and the sacraments. The Council of Trent (1545–63) slammed the door shut on all such accommodations. Nevertheless, so powerful was the ideal of a "common corps of Christendom" that calls for the convening of a general church council to restore it continued to be issued through the following centuries.

Efforts to reconcile different Protestant groups appeared to have more realistic prospects, and they did book some limited successes, like the Consensus of Sandomierz (1570), which strengthened ties between Lutherans, Calvinists, and Bohemian Brethren in Poland. These efforts often attracted support for political reasons. It took the threat of annihilation by Catholic armies in the Thirty Years' War to bring the leader of Saxony's Lutheran Church to discuss unity in 1631 with Brandenburg's Reformed theologians (Nischan, "Reformed Irenicism and the Leipzig Colloquy of 1631"). The Calvinist electors of Brandenburg-Prussia had special domestic reasons to promote Protestant unity, since they ruled over a mostly Lutheran populace. One of their many initiatives, involving the philosopher Leibniz, proposed taking the Church of England as model. From the days of Queen Elizabeth, the Anglican Church had striven to include Protestants of different stripes, from Catholic-leaning to Puritan. These efforts failed to prevent the fragmentation of English Protestantism into separate churches – Presbyterian, Independent, Baptist, Quaker – but they did leave the Anglican still the most comprehensive Protestant denomination, including both "High" and "Low" churchmen, as they came to be called.

Tolerance in the modern sense, involving the coexistence of multiple churches, stood on far shakier ideological ground than did comprehension. Such tolerance went by various names: "indulgence," "civil" as opposed to "ecclesiastic toleration," or just plain "toleration." Until the eighteenth century, all these terms invariably carried negative connotations. French dictionaries offered "souffrir" and "endurer" as synonyms for the verb "tolérer," suggesting it was an inherently unpleasant experience, a subjection to some unpreventable evil (Benedict, "Un roi, une loi, deux foix", p. 67; Huseman, "Expression of the Idea of Toleration"). More often than not, it was proposed merely as a temporary expedient. Erasmus set the pattern when in 1526 he counseled an imperial official, "it would perhaps be better if cities where the [Protestant] evil has taken root were asked only to leave each party to its own place and each citizen to his own conscience, until the passage of time brings an opportunity for peace" (Tracy, "Erasmus, Coornhert and the Acceptance of Religious Disunity," p. 53). Later intellectuals like the Dutchman Dirck Coornhert cited the counsel of Gamaliel from Acts 5: 38–9: "for if this counsel or this work be of men, it will come to nought: But if it be of God, ye cannot overthrow it." They quoted also the parable of the wheat and the chaff from Matthew 13: 24–30. Both passages conveyed an eschatological optimism that the true faith would eventually emerge victorious, without human action. Even the Peace of Westphalia in 1648, often said to mark the final acceptance of Germany's religious divisions, contained a clause – little more than a pious wish, by then – making its terms provisional "until, through God's grace, agreement is reached over religion" (Müller, *Instrumenta pacis Westphalicae*, pp. 25, 113).

In fact, from Sebastian Castellio in the 1550s to Locke in the 1680s, proponents of toleration drew on a fairly fixed repertoire of arguments. One of the most fundamental dated to antiquity, that a person cannot be coerced into having faith. As France's chancellor Michel de l'Hôpital put it, "conscience, by its nature, cannot be forced, but must be instructed, nor can it be tamed or violated, but must be persuaded by true and cogent reasons; if faith is constrained, it is no longer faith" (L'Hôpital, *Oeuvres complètes*, vol. 1, p. 471). Efforts to coerce, it was claimed, only produced dissemblers and hypocrites, or atheists. The remedy was thus worse than the illness itself. The impossibility of coercing faith testified, in the view of many, to a crucial problem of jurisdiction: heresy was a spiritual evil which it fell to spiritual authorities, not secular ones, to punish with the spiritual "sword" God had given them. That sword consisted of Scripture and the church's powers of ecclesiastic discipline. It was futile for magistrates to direct their "civil sword" against heretics. Doing so violated the fundamental distinction between the "two kingdoms" God was said to have created, his own and that of "the world." On this point Castellio quoted Luther himself, who wrote in 1523,

> Civil government has laws which extend only to bodies and goods on earth. God, who alone has jurisdiction and authority over the soul will not suffer it to be subject to mundane laws. . . . Heresy is a spiritual thing which can be cut with no iron, burned with no fire, and drowned with no water. Only with the Word of God can it be cut, burned, and drowned. (Castellio, *Concerning Heretics*, pp. 141–2, 149)

Abstaining from coercion, then, by no means meant that one accepted others' right to believe what they wished. On the contrary, it could be justified simply as a more

effective, if less speedy, means of achieving their conversion. Rigorous Catholic casu-
ists approved tolerance only for this end – a spiritual good greater than the evil of
the means. Others approved tolerance to achieve important, primarily secular goals
as well, such as political stability. This again involved no acceptance of heresy, only a
balancing of good against evil. Justus Lipsius, one of the era's most influential political philosophers, declared religious uniformity highly desirable but added that if
a state could not suppress dissent without starting a civil war, it should leave it be.
Economic arguments too, never absent, gained greater acceptance over time. Pieter
de la Court was one of many who attributed the unrivaled prosperity of the Dutch
Republic in the seventeenth century to the toleration that prevailed there.

Given the high ground occupied by spiritual concerns, however, religious
arguments for toleration carried special weight. Some, following Castellio, claimed
that the Gospel itself taught tolerance. These proponents identified tolerance
with Christian love and with the virtues of gentleness, compassion, and humility practiced by Christ himself, whom they called on Christians to imitate. Many, again
following Castellio, expressed a sharp anticlericalism. Drawing on the rhetoric of
the early Reformation, they accused clergy of using persecution to tyrannize over the
laity. Some, like Coornhert and his fellow Dutchman Hubert Duifhuis, went so far
as to equate the clergy's doctrinal creeds with the "human additions" to Scripture
that the Reformation had supposedly cast off (Kaplan, *Calvinists and Libertines*,
chap. 2).

Tolerance, then, was fully compatible with the belief that one knew the correct
path to heaven. It did not, as some scholars have suggested, require skepticism concerning the ability of humans to distinguish true Christianity from false. Certainly,
though, the rival claims of the competing churches engendered, from the beginning,
much uncertainty and skepticism. Pierre du Chastel, bishop of Orléans, preached a
sermon on the death of Francis I that would have offended the deceased. "Since no
mortal man, whoever he may be, can through any human argument or reasoning
judge with certainty what is true," argued du Chastel, no one should be executed
for heresy (Smith, "Early French Advocates," p. 34). By the early seventeenth
century, skepticism had gained the coherence of a philosophical system, yet it never
led everyone to the same conclusion. Catholic apologists wielded it to prove the need
for a final arbiter in doctrinal disputes, such as the pope. Others, like Lipsius, concluded that, in the absence of certainty, one should obey one's ruler and conform to
the official religion of the state (Tuck, "Scepticism and Toleration").

Until the eighteenth century, the weight of educated, established opinion was
firmly on the side of intolerance, which was the insistent teaching of all the mainstream churches. They too drew on an intellectual tradition that went back to antiquity, in particular to Augustine (Nelson, "Theory of Persecution"; Goldie, "Theory
of Religious Intolerance in Restoration England"). While conceding that one could
not force a person to have faith, Augustine had held that limited forms of coercion
could serve as an effective pastoral tool: heretics could be forced at least to hear the
truth, ponder it, and reconsider their views. For such coercion Augustine had found
Scriptural warrant in the story of the banquet in Luke 14: 23, with its famous phrase
"compel them to enter." Persecution, he had argued, was for heretics' own good, as
their salvation was at stake; indeed, not to persecute was to leave them in the clutches
of the devil. Augustine's logic made persecution an act of Christian love, toleration

one of uncaring neglect. The paradox was echoed by Luther in words Castellio chose not to quote: "no persecution is total persecution" (*WA*, vol. 3, p. 424).

The Church Fathers had further legitimized intolerance by defining heresy not as a product of misunderstanding, ultimately, but as an act of will. In fact, the very term "heresy," from the Greek *hairesis*, meaning choice, implied such a definition. God had implanted in all human souls an ability to recognize the divine truth. Failing to accept that truth after being exposed to it was an act of perverse stubbornness – of rebellion against God, his agents on earth, and one's own conscience. Christian tradition thus called into doubt the very possibility of a sincerely held erroneous belief. It also suggested that Christian magistrates, following Old Testament models, had a duty to persecute: first, because God had entrusted them with the spiritual as well as material well-being of their subjects, and second, because they had a duty to uphold God's honor, which was harmed by blasphemy, idolatry, and false prophesying. For these offenses, with which heresy was equated, the punishment set in Deuteronomy and Leviticus was death.

These arguments formed part of a heritage common to all the churches that emerged from the sundering of western Christendom. That sundering, though, created a radically new context for their application, a crucial part of which was the rise of "confessionalism." The term refers to a type of religious culture promoted by Catholic, Lutheran, and Reformed churches equally, despite their obvious differences and conflicts. One of its characteristics was a sharply polarized, almost Manichean world-view that divided the cosmos into binary oppositions: good versus evil, God versus Satan, true versus false Christianity. These forces were seen as locked in an apocalyptic struggle with one another. In 1581 an anonymous Dutch Protestant wrote:

> either the Reformed religion is good or it is bad; there is no middle, since the affairs of heaven permit no averages . . . truth and falsehood are as much at odds as Belial and Christ, and hence there is as little in common between the Reformed teaching and Roman fantasies as there is between white and black. (Fredericq, *Het Nederlandsch proza*, pp. 107–8)

Such a mentality encouraged people of different faiths to regard one another as "servants of Satan." More than that, it encouraged them to define their own religious identities through such oppositions. No small part of being Protestant in England, for example, was to be virulently anti-Catholic. In this context, intolerance was raised to the status of an essential mark of true piety, while its absence could by itself bring down suspicion and punishment. "Whoever contends that punishing heretics and blasphemers is wrong," Calvin had written, "is himself guilty of blasphemy" (Calvin, "Defensio Orthodoxae Fidei," p. 476).

The same mentality tended to reduce complex conflicts to simple us-versus-them terms. Spokesmen for the Church of England frequently accused Quakers, Baptists, and, in the eighteenth century, Methodists of being "papists" in disguise. The accusation seems too patently false to have been believed, yet anyone who undermined the unity and strength of the Protestant front against Catholicism might, in a confessional culture, be suspected of serving Catholic interests. International politics might be viewed through the same prism, with countries divided into two camps based on their Protestant or Catholic affiliation. Such a view ignored messy realities,

Plate 1 William Hogarth, *Credulity, Superstition, and Fanaticism*, 1762. This satiric representation of a Methodist service shows the preacher's wig popping off, revealing beneath it the tonsured head of a Catholic priest.
Source: Ashmolean Museum, Oxford.

like the sharp rivalry that pitted Spain and France, both Catholic, against one another, or the Lutheran–Reformed split; but it also had the power to create new realities. It did so especially between the 1580s and 1620s, when all of Europe became polarized along religious lines, forming two great politico-military alliances at war with one another.

The conjuncture that gave religion such primacy then in international politics never repeated itself, but the confessional mentality that produced it did not simply disappear, even after the conclusion in 1648 of the Thirty Years' War. Popular sensitivity to international affairs remained so keen that distant events could spark riots. The Revocation of the Edict of Nantes in 1685, accompanied by Catholic advances elsewhere, sent shockwaves across Protestant Europe. So did the execution in 1724 of a group of Lutherans in the Polish town of Thorn, and the expulsion in 1732 of some 20,000 Lutherans from Salzburg. Jesuit conspirators and bloodthirsty inquisitors remained the bogeymen of fearful Protestants, as did Calvinist rebels and monarchomachs for Catholics. Indeed, recent research on Germany suggests that on the popular level confessionalism only grew stronger in the decades after 1648. By the eighteenth century, Catholics in Augsburg named their boys Franz Joseph while Protestants named theirs Friedrich Wilhelm (after Prussia's great elector); Catholics dressed their girls in "bolt" bonnets, Protestants theirs in "wing" bonnets (François, *Die unsichtbare Grenze*, pp. 168–80). In Metz and Speyer the two groups read different books and bought different paintings. In these and other facets of daily life, German Catholics and Protestants grew more distinct from one another, their antagonism climaxing between 1700 and 1720 in a wave of urban clashes.

The role traditionally played by religion in communal life made confessionalism doubly problematic. The Church Father Tertullian had written, "the religion of an individual neither harms nor profits anybody else" (Lecler, *Toleration and the Reformation*, vol. 1, p. 35). But in early modern Europe, religion was anything but a purely individual matter, and the sacred could not be separated from the profane. The intertwining was especially close in large villages and small towns, where parish and commune often had the same membership, territory, and leaders. The parish church, with its surrounding churchyard, served not only as place of worship but as site for assemblies, markets, and other events. On behalf of all, its bells pealed with joy on princely birthdays and intoned with grief when someone died; they summoned the community to services, but also to put out fires or flee invading armies. Parish schools provided elementary education, while parish funds provided alms to the poor. Communion services celebrated social harmony and sanctified it; public meetings opened with prayers; oaths invoked the divine to cement political allegiances. Saints' days and sabbaths set the rhythm of work and leisure, for Catholics and Protestants respectively. Whole communities participated together, standing as units before God, in Catholic processions and on Protestant days of repentance and thanksgiving. And as units, they feared, they would be punished for the sins of their members. God's wrath would descend on them if they tolerated heresy or vice in their midst. Persecution, then, was an act of communal self-defense. It was also an act of ritual purification, purging the community of a disease that threatened to infect the entire "body social" (Davis, "Rites of Violence").

The equation of civic and sacral community made religious divisions deeply problematic on the local level, but the same equation operated also on higher ones.

Europe's sovereign territories and countries never came close, in the early modern period, to eliminating the entrenched localism that prevailed. With the rise, though, of absolutist forms of government, they did make increasingly strong claims to their subjects' primary allegiance. Religion was a key component of emerging national identities. John Bull, the stereotypical Englishman, was as Protestant as the Spanish conquistador was Catholic. His real-life countrymen proudly proclaimed their freedom from tyranny, both papal and princely, which they linked. Their national church embodied, however imperfectly, an ideal of nation as "corpus Christianum." Scandinavian countries had similar national churches, as Protestant territories in the empire had territorial ones. And in Catholic lands, princely control of ecclesiastic patronage went far, though never all the way, toward creating similar national units. A shared religion united citizens with one another and subjects with their rulers. Indeed, from below as well as above, it was viewed as an essential prerequisite for loyalty and obedience. The principle *cuius regio, eius religio* – that a ruler could impose his religion on his subjects – had a compelling logic to most Europeans. For their part, rulers like the Habsburgs, who cultivated an exemplary devotion to the Eucharist and the Virgin Mary, made conscious use of religious rites and symbols to legitimize their power and unite their subjects (Hsia, *Social Discipline*, chap. 4). In such a context, it was not pure fantasy to equate heresy with treason.

All these factors made it painfully difficult for communities officially to acknowledge and redefine themselves as multi-confessional. With few exceptions, they did so only under duress. For national communities, the most common circumstance was stalemate in a religiously inspired civil war. The Second Peace of Kappel, which cemented in 1531 Switzerland's religious divisions, resulted from such a stalemate. So did the empire's Peace of Augsburg in 1555 and its Peace of Westphalia in 1648 (Walder, *Religionsvergleiche*; Müller, *Instrumenta pacis Westphalicae*). The Swiss Confederation barely constituted a unified polity in any event; peace meant that each of its cantons could pick its official religion and suppress rival faiths within its borders. The failure of emperors Charles V and Ferdinand II to impose Catholicism on the empire had the same result, leaving the princes and magistrates of the empire's 300-odd constituent units to choose the official religion of their territories. In both Switzerland and the empire, then, the weakness of central authorities contributed crucially to stalemate. The same was true in sixteenth-century Poland, though no religious war was fought there. By the Warsaw Confederation of 1573, Polish nobles gained a free hand to determine the religion of the peasants living on their estates – a *cuius dominium* principle similar to the *cuius regio* of the German princes (Tazbir, *State Without Stakes*, p. 99). Each of these treaties put multiple faiths on a footing of "parity" with one another, ratifying the multi-confessionalism of the polity as a whole. They left most parts of the latter, though, with a single official faith.

Exceptions did exist. A group of eight imperial free cities – Ulm, Donauwörth, Kaufbeuren, Leutkirch, Biberach, Ravensburg, Dinkelsbühl, and the great commercial center of Augsburg – formed the chief ones in the empire after 1555. In these towns both Protestants and Catholics enjoyed full citizenship, exercised their faiths publicly, and had members on the city council (Warmbrunn, *Zwei Konfessionen in einer Stadt*). Here parity operated on the local level but was far from neutral: Charles V used it to reintroduce a religion (the Catholic) that the local populace had largely rejected and to give its adherents power disproportionate to their numbers. France's

Louis XIV used parity to the same effect in the 1680s when he put Catholicism on an equal footing with Protestantism in Alsace, which he had just detached from the empire and incorporated into his kingdom.

The peace that France achieved in 1598, with the Edict of Nantes, was likewise a fruit of stalemate and royal weakness. By granting Huguenots, who dominated the south and west of the kingdom, 200 "places de sûreté," which they could garrison, the edict created a "state within a [Catholic] state." Yet given the condition of the kingdom after a string of eight brutal religious wars, the edict must be appreciated as an effective tool for reconstructing central government and strengthening royal authority. The edict allowed for public Protestant worship under three rubrics, "possession," "concession," and "exercices de fief" (English text in Mousnier, *Assassination of Henry IV*, pp. 316–63). Protestants could continue to worship where they had been doing so as of 1596 or 1597; they could build a "temple" in the suburbs of one or two towns in each administrative unit of the kingdom; and they could worship in the homes of Huguenot nobles. Under these stipulations, about 1,400 Calvinist congregations operated as of 1600. At the same time, the edict returned to the Catholic Church its property and reestablished Catholic worship across the kingdom, even in such Huguenot bastions as Nîmes and La Rochelle. Repression and closures reduced the number of Calvinist congregations by half, and with it the number of mixed communities, by the 1660s (Benedict, *Huguenot Population of France*; Quéniart, *Révocation de l'Édit de Nantes*).

Another circumstance producing official biconfessionalism was divided sovereignty. This took various forms, including "condominium," by which multiple rulers held jointly, as common property, all authority over an area. Thus the cantons of the Swiss Confederation jointly ruled their mandated territories (*Gemeine Herrschaften*). Among these were the Thurgau and Rheintal, whose populations were fairly evenly split between Catholic and Reformed faiths. Another condominium was the city of Maastricht, in the Netherlands. Since the early Middle Ages it had had two lords, the dukes of Brabant and the prince-bishops of Liège. When the Dutch army conquered the city in 1632, the Dutch States-General took over the powers of the former dukes. Together with Liège, it introduced a system of parity by which Catholics and Reformed Protestants each had use of two parish churches and received half the municipal revenues for charity, education, and worship. Magistrates swore to protect and maintain both religions (Ubachs, *Twee heren, twee confessies*).

Divided sovereignty was most common, however, within the empire, where it also took the form of "Ganerben," areas over which different rulers held different powers. In Franconia, for example, the prince-bishop of Würzburg held spiritual jurisdiction over dozens of villages that in other respects were subject to Lutheran princes. He and his officials would examine, on the basis of the Augsburg Confession, and install the villagers' Lutheran pastors, who were required to attend regional meetings of the Catholic clergy. The empire was full of such seeming anomalies. Another was Jülich-Cleves, partitioned in 1614 between Brandenburg and Catholic Pfalz-Neuburg. A series of treaties between these two territories guaranteed an extraordinary mix of publicly practiced faiths in their Rhineland possessions, particularly in Cleves and Mark, which belonged to Brandenburg. A few convents there were even cohabited by Catholic and Protestant "nuns." The situation in the bishopric of Osnabrück was equally remarkable. From 1650, it was ruled in alternating succession by a bishop whom the cathedral chapter elected and a Lutheran prince of the house of Braunschweig-Lüneburg. Of the bishopric's 59 parishes, 31 had Catholic pastors, 20 Lutheran, and eight both. In four of the mixed parishes Catholics and Lutherans had separate church buildings, while in the other four they shared use of a single church (Schindling and Ziegler, *Die Territorien des Reichs*, vol. 5, pp. 87–106; vol. 3, pp. 131–46).

Such shared use was called *Simultaneum*. Difficult to practice, it required rival religious groups to care jointly for the church building, agree on its decoration, coordinate times of services, and rub shoulders – sometimes literally – in coming and going. It required them to share their most sacred space with one another, allowing rituals that church leaders had declared perverse, even satanic, to be performed in it. It is therefore remarkable how widely the practice was adopted, with instances attested in Hungary, Royal Prussia, the Grisons, Silesia, Lusatia, Baden-Baden, Brandenburg, Berg, Draheim, the diocese of Strasbourg, and the Dutch Republic. By the early seventeenth century, most of the parish churches in the Swiss canton of Glarus and half of those in the Thurgau had become *Simultankirchen*. At the end of that century, *Simultaneum* was introduced by force to the Palatinate and Alsace, where it endured in almost 300 villages.

Usually *Simultaneum* involved a division of the church building: Catholics would attend mass in the choir, Protestants hear sermons in the nave, and in many *Simultankirchen* a partition was erected to separate the two spaces. Still, the arrangement left countless opportunities for squabbling and petty harassment. In the small town of Biberach, for example, with its single parish church, Catholics were scandalized in 1638 to find that someone had blown their nose into the vessel containing holy water. In retaliation, they locked the metal door to the choir, preventing Lutherans from passing through it to take communion. The next year, a Catholic sexton disturbed a Lutheran wedding by ringing the great alarm bell that hung in the church tower. While Catholics subsequently claimed the ringing was a simple mistake, Lutherans darkly construed it as an effort to provoke a religious riot. The episode quickly escalated into a political showdown, with both parties mobilizing the support of regional allies. It took an imperial commission to resolve the dispute (Stievermann, Press, and Diemer, *Geschichte der Stadt Biberach*; Pfeiffer, "Das Ringen um die Parität").

As the episode suggests, coexistence could be intimate without being friendly. One can generalize a step further: maintaining peace in biconfessional communities did not entail resolving tensions as much as managing and containing them. How was this achieved? First, by assuring both religious groups of their survival. Legal and military guarantees that eliminated the threat of annihilation reduced the aggressive behavior so often born of fear. Second, by granting both groups a high degree of autonomy, so that they could order their own religious affairs without interference. Third, by strict regulations that limited what the religious parties could fight over. The more precisely and rigidly assets like church buildings, government offices, and charitable funds were divided between the groups, the more they were excluded from the field of subsequent contest. And fourth, by establishing legal mechanisms for the peaceful resolution of disputes once they broke out.

All these principles of conflict management were incorporated in the Edict of Nantes and Peace of Westphalia, which built on the experience of past failures to create relatively stable frameworks for coexistence. The provisions of Westphalia dealing with the parity cities of the empire exemplify this successful adaptation. In four of the cities Westphalia replaced the looser form of parity instituted in 1555 with a stricter, numerical one. Henceforth, all municipal offices and resources were divided exactly half-and-half between Protestants and Catholics. Protestant magistrates caucused separately to decide Protestant religious matters, Catholic ones did the same (*itio in partes*). By the eighteenth century, what Étienne François calls a "mania" for division and distinction reached a point that struck many observers as absurd (François, *Die unsichtbare Grenze*, pp. 178–9, 225–6). Enlightenment *philosophes* ridiculed Augsburg's two pigsties, one for Catholic pigs, the other for Protestant. But the very rigidity of the system offered the ultimate in protection to the religious minority. Not that the system ended all disputes: on the contrary, it generated many but focused them on relative trivia.

Nantes and Westphalia imposed a protective rigidity also by freezing the status quo, or some version of it. Nantes set 1596–7 as the normative date for determining where Huguenots could operate churches by virtue of "possession." Westphalia set 1624 as *Normaljahre* for Catholics and Protestants: groups worshiping in a locale as of that date retained a permanent right to worship there, at least privately. The year 1648 served as *Normaljahre* for Reformed Protestants in Lutheran territories, and vice versa. Divided lordship tended to have a similarly stabilizing effect, for any change in religious arrangements required the agreement of all lords.

Of course, the Edict of Nantes did not preserve the status quo forever in France. From the beginning of his personal rule in 1661, Louis XIV waged a fierce campaign of conversion and repression against the Huguenots. Finally, in 1685, he declared that there simply were no more in the kingdom and revoked the edict. The principle of *cuius regio*, of "one king, one law, one faith," triumphed, and France rejoined the ranks of European lands with a single official church established by law. Some such lands, like Italy, Spain, and the Scandinavian kingdoms, were true bastions of one or another Christian orthodoxy. In others, though, the uniformity proclaimed by their rulers belied a more complex reality. Under circumstances ranging from comfortable and secure to furtive and dangerous, religious dissenters lived and worshiped in various parts of Europe that were officially mono-confessional.

They did so only under strictest secrecy and threat of severe punishment in post-Revocation France. Between 1685 and 1700, about 70 "new converts" were executed for apostasy and another 1,000 sentenced to life service on the galleys of the French navy. Some had been caught trying to flee abroad, the illegal recourse of more than 200,000. Others took refuge in the caves and woods of the Cévennes mountains, where a brutal religious war, that of the Camisards, was fought in the 1700s. For the next five decades the French government used troops sporadically to disrupt Huguenot assemblies in southern France. Local curés denied Huguenots all civil rights by withholding the sacraments of baptism and marriage. Despite such persecution, the "Eglise du Désert," as Huguenots called their church, survived. More than that, the situation provoked such religious fervor, often apocalyptic, that scholars have credited it with the spiritual renewal of French Calvinism (Joutard, "Revocation of the Edict of Nantes").

The Cévennes was not the only region whose rugged terrain offered a measure of protection to religious dissenters. In the high Alpine valleys of Austria, Salzburg, and Tirol, Lutherans lived for much of the seventeenth century beyond the reach of church and state. Memories of the Reformation, seasonal trips to Germany for work, and above all books nourished their confessional identity. Lacking organization, they worshiped at home as single families. If asked, they protested their loyalty to Catholicism, but mostly they avoided questions by staying away from church. The authorities began to penetrate this world of "secret Protestantism" only in the 1680s. Most Protestants remained untroubled until the 1730s, when the first mass expulsions took place (Mecenseffy, *Geschichte des Protestantismus in Österreich*).

One reason, then, for the survival of dissent was the weakness of early modern authorities. It was no coincidence that the great majority of English Catholics lived in the "dark corners" of the land, up north and west, above all in Lancashire. The diocesan and parochial structure of the Church of England had always been weak in those regions, making them prime missionary territory for Baptists and Quakers too. Scotland exhibited the same pattern, with pockets of Catholicism tenaciously hanging on for centuries in the highlands and islands (Bossy, *English Catholic Community*; Mullett, *Catholics in Britain and Ireland*).

Yet it was almost impossible for religious dissent to remain entirely secret. Except for the largest cities, early modern communities were too small, relations in them too intimate for people to mask their religious inclinations. More important, therefore, than the weakness of authorities was their willingness to turn a blind eye, to settle for the appearance rather than the reality of uniformity. And the same was true of neighbors and fellow citizens: more often than not, they knew each other's religious leanings. Peaceful coexistence depended, then, on a set of agreements, usually tacit, between dissenters, authorities, and rank-and-file members of the official church (Kaplan, "Fictions of Privacy"). Dissenters agreed not to challenge the monopoly of the official church over public religious life, thereby helping the community preserve a semblance of religious unity. In return, the other parties allowed dissenters to worship in a setting that was at least minimally acceptable. Without giving dissent their approval, they tolerated its presence. In this way, all three parties cooperated to avoid facing the full implications of their religious differences. They deferred to the dominant ideology of the confessional age that equated civic and sacral community, social and religious cohesion, even as they departed from its dictates.

In practice, these agreements took two forms. In the first, dissenters were permitted, either formally or "by connivance," to worship as they pleased, but only outside the physical boundaries of their town or village. They might attend church in a neighboring community, cross the border to an adjacent territory, or in a pinch organize services of their own in a suburb or field. In any case, by traveling outside their own community, they preserved the latter as an exclusive enclave of the official church at least with regard to worship. Thus enacted, their beliefs gave less "offense" to others, causing less "scandal," and were less likely to provoke either popular violence or official crackdown.

Known in German as *Auslauf*, such travel can be documented as early as the 1530s, when Catholics in such newly Protestant cities as Strasbourg and Ulm began to attend church in neighboring villages. By the end of the sixteenth century, it had grown common in the politically fragmented southwestern part of the empire. Catholics living in the Palatinate, for example, trekked regularly to the bishopric of Speyer, while Calvinists in the bishopric made the reverse trip. The Peace of Westphalia subsequently guaranteed dissenters throughout the empire the right to perform *Auslauf*, but the latter was never an exclusively German phenomenon. In the late sixteenth century, Viennese Protestants flocked to services on the rural estates of Protestant noblemen. In the seventeenth century, Parisian Huguenots obeyed the prohibition against Protestant worship in the capital by attending church in nearby Charenton. Dutch Catholics living near the border with the Spanish Netherlands crossed it regularly.

Worship outside the physical boundaries of the community could be arranged other ways as well. In the empire, entire satellite communities populated by religious dissenters grew in the vicinity of certain major urban centers. Near Hamburg, for example, rose Altona, populated by Catholics, Calvinists, Mennonites, and Jews who did business in the Lutheran city. Frankfurt, also Lutheran, had a similarly symbiotic relationship with Hanau, as did Catholic Cologne in the eighteenth century with Mülheim, in the county of Berg.

The second arrangement for accommodating dissenters was to allow them to worship in their home communities, but only in private. Like the first, this arrangement preserved in restricted form the monopoly of the official church and with it a semblance of religious unity. It did so, however, by creating a new distinction between public and private worship. Fluid and subject constantly to negotiation, the distinction hinged above all on appearances. Private worship took place in buildings that, viewed from any public thoroughfare, did not look like churches. They had no tower, bells, or external symbol that signaled their function. Often they were simply dissenters' homes, with a room adapted to serve as chapel. At the other end of the spectrum, they might be specially built structures, capacious and ornate internally but hidden from street view. Such places of worship could be found in many parts of western and central Europe. The Catholic gentry of England and Scotland had private chapels in their manor houses. So did the Lutheran nobility of Austria until the 1620s, and the Huguenot nobility of France until the Revocation. Irish Catholics had what their persecutors called "mass houses." It was the Dutch Republic, though, that developed furthest the public–private distinction and relied on it most heavily to accommodate religious dissent.

Uniquely, the Republic was neither officially multi-confessional nor did it have an established church. The Dutch Reformed was its official, "public" church, enjoying special privileges and shouldering special duties, but the law never required membership in it (Schilling, "Religion and Society"). From its emergence in the 1570s, the Republic had among the most religiously mixed populations in Europe, including Catholics, Mennonites, Lutherans, and a host of sects. While some foreigners enjoyed special religious privileges (as they did elsewhere in Europe), native dissenters worshiped overwhelmingly in what historians call *schuilkerken*, clandestine churches. A major city like Haarlem had 11 of them, Utrecht 15. Most commonly, they were houses whose facades were left intact but whose interiors were renovated to serve as churches. Although their true function was an open secret, they maintained the appearance of being ordinary houses. This pretense of domesticity stamped the worship conducted in these buildings all the more sharply as private.

In 1673, England's ambassador Sir William Temple remarked how strong "the force of Commerce, Alliances, and Acquaintance" was in the Republic. The ties formed by trade, family, and friendship went a long way, in his view, toward explaining why Dutch society was the most tolerant in Europe (Temple, *Observations*,

Plate 2 J. L. van Beek, etcher, after a drawing by C. van Waardt, *The Blossoming of the Roman Catholic Church in Amsterdam*. The etching shows the facades of all 20 Catholic churches (in the rectangles) and 12 Catholic charitable institutions (in the ovals) in Amsterdam as of 1795. Note that all but two of the churches are unrecognizable from the outside as churches. *Source*: Museum Amstelkring, Amsterdam.

p. 107). Temple's observation serves as a reminder that peaceful coexistence entailed more than allowing one's religious opponents to worship in their own manner. It meant getting along with them on the street, in the marketplace, over a tankard of ale in a tavern, and around the family hearth. Or did it? Did people of different faiths intermarry? Live in the same neighborhoods? Employ or buy goods from one another? Attend school together? Lie ill in the same hospitals? Clearly the answer varies with time and place, but few studies have yet examined the details of social life in Europe's religiously mixed communities. These few invariably present a complex picture. On the one hand, they suggest a long-term trend toward confessionally distinct subcultures and separate institutions; on the other, they testify to the enduring power of a common language, shared values, and close familiarity with one another to bind people of different faiths. A complaint by a Catholic magistrate of Biberach in 1750 exemplifies the ambiguity. According to him, the town's Catholic pastor, Ivo Brack, had lost all his "religious fervor": not only did he socialize too much with Lutherans, inviting them even into his parsonage, "but he also bought all the clothes he needed and other things at their shops, not without [giving] offense to Catholics" (Stievermann, Press, and Diemer, *Geschichte der Stadt Biberach*, p. 316). An adequate religious history of Biberach would have to capture both the pastor's socializing and the magistrate's complaint, both the economic boundary-crossing and the "offense" it caused. The same challenge, writ large, awaits all who would characterize social relations in religiously mixed communities.

Of course, by 1750 a significant shift in attitudes was taking place, at least among certain elites. Traditionally, historians have associated the shift with the Enlightenment. Reacting against Puritanism and the turmoil of civil war, English intellectuals began in the late seventeenth century to repudiate religious "enthusiasm" and "fanaticism." Calling for the application of reason to all spheres, they declared tolerance an essential trait of any "reasonable" form of Christianity. Around the same time, John Locke's political theory, based on the concept of a social contract, inspired a new definition of religious freedom as an inalienable, "natural" right inherent in the individual. Huguenot refugee Pierre Bayle championed the duty of every person to follow his or her conscience. And the Jewish philosopher Spinoza suggested that religious freedom was just one aspect of a broader freedom of thought and expression. The luminaries of the eighteenth century, from Gibbon to Voltaire and Lessing, embraced and propagated these ideas, making the cause of toleration their own.

Yet the tolerance of Enlightenment *philosophes* had decided limits, and that of Europe's rulers even sharper ones (Grell and Porter, *Toleration in Enlightenment Europe*). England's Toleration Act of 1689 had no continental counterparts. Licensing Protestant dissenters to build public places of worship, in effect it partially disestablished the Church of England. In France, by contrast, persecution began decisively to trail off only in the 1750s, and Huguenots had to wait until 1787 for the restoration of their civil rights. Elsewhere too, legal change came late. As for popular prejudices and the practice of coexistence among ordinary folk, it remains unclear whether Enlightenment theory had any contemporary impact on them.

Was Europe in the wake of the Reformations, then, a "persecuting society," as some have claimed (for the concept see Moore, *Formation of a Persecuting Society*), or was religious tolerance widespread? The answer depends largely on how one defines tolerance. Defined as respect for the right of all humans to religious freedom, it is a modern phenomenon born of the Enlightenment. Defined as a positive valuation of differentness, it had at least a handful of earlier supporters, like Coornhert, but no place in the mainstream of early modern culture. Defined as the practice of peaceful coexistence, though, it was more common than often recognized – common but limited, tense, a matter of conflict management not conflict resolution, and as often *de facto* as *de jure*. Such toleration might reveal its limits in the dynamic of social interactions, as in Biberach, or it might be rooted in the ambivalence of individual psyches, like that of Arnoldus Buchelius. This elder in the Dutch Reformed Church, not atypically, maintained friendships and family ties with Catholics even as he muttered imprecations against "papists" and their "idolatries" (Pollmann, *Religious Choice in the Dutch Republic*). Perhaps the truest answer to the question, then, is that it presents a false antithesis. In early modern Europe, tolerance and intolerance often went together.

BIBLIOGRAPHY

Benedict, P., *The Huguenot Population of France, 1600–1685: The Demographic Fate and Customs of a Religious Minority*. Philadelphia: American Philosophical Society, 1991.

Benedict, P., "Un roi, une loi, deux foix: Parameters for the History of Catholic-Reformed Co-existence in France, 1555–1685," in Ole Peter Grell and Bob Scribner, eds., *Tolerance and Intolerance in the European Reformation*. Cambridge: Cambridge University Press, 1996, pp. 65–93.

Berkvens-Stevelinck, C., Israel, J. I., and Posthumus Meyjes, G. H. M., eds., *The Emergence of Tolerance in the Dutch Republic*. Leiden/New York: Brill, 1997.

Bossy, J., *The English Catholic Community 1570–1850*. New York: Oxford University Press, 1976.

Calvin, J., "Defensio Orthodoxae Fidei de Sacra Trinitate, Contra Prodigiosos Errores Michaelis Serveti Hispani," in Guilielmus Baum, Eduardus Cunitz, and Eduardus Reuss, eds., *Ioannis Calvini Opera Quae Supersunt Omnia*, 59 vols. Brunsvigae: Apud C. A. Schwetschke et Filium, 1863–1900, vol. 8, pp. 453–644.

Cameron, K., Greengrass, M., Leslie, M., and Roberts, P., eds., *The Adventure of Religious Pluralism in Early Modern France: Papers from the Exeter Conference, April 1999*. Oxford: Peter Lang, 2000.

Castellio, S., *Concerning Heretics: Whether They are to be Persecuted and How they are to be Treated*, ed. Roland Bainton. New York: Octagon Books, 1965.

Christin, O., *La Paix de religion: L'autonomisation de la raison politique au XVIe siècle*. Paris: Éditions du Seuil, 1997.

Coffey, J., *Persecution and Toleration in Protestant England, 1558–1689*. London: Longman, 2000.

Cranston, M., "John Locke and the Case for Toleration," in John Horton and Susan Mendus, eds., *John Locke: A Letter Concerning Toleration in Focus*. London: Routledge, 1991, pp. 78–97.

Davis, N. Z., "The Rites of Violence," in N. Z. Davis, *Society and Culture in Early Modern France: Eight Essays*. Stanford, Calif.: Stanford University Press, 1975, pp. 152–87.

Diefendorf, B. B., *Beneath the Cross: Catholics and Huguenots in Sixteenth-Century Paris*. Oxford and New York: Oxford University Press, 1991.

François, É., *Die unsichtbare Grenze: Protestanten und Katholiken in Augsburg 1648–1806*. Sigmaringen: Jan Thorbecke, 1991.

Fredericq, P., ed., *Het Nederlandsch proza in de zestiendeeuwsche pamfletten uit den tijd der beroerten*. Brussels, 1907.

Goldie, M., "The Theory of Religious Intolerance in Restoration England," in Ole Peter Grell, Jonathan I. Israel, and Nicholas Tyacke, eds., *From Persecution to Tolerance*. Oxford: Clarendon Press, 1991, pp. 331–68.

Grandjean, M. and Roussel, B., eds., *Coexister dans l'intolérance: L'édit de Nantes (1598)*. Geneva: Labor et Fides, 1998.

Grell, O. P. and Porter, R., eds., *Toleration in Enlightenment Europe*. Cambridge: Cambridge University Press, 2000.

Grell, O. P. and Scribner, B., eds., *Tolerance and Intolerance in the European Reformation*. Cambridge: Cambridge University Press, 1996.

Haydon, C., *Anti-Catholicism in Eighteenth-Century England, c.1714–80: A Political and Social Study*. Manchester: Manchester University Press, 1993.

Heyd, D., ed., *Toleration: An Elusive Virtue*. Princeton, NJ: Princeton University Press, 1996.

Hsia, R. Po-chia, *Social Discipline in the Reformation: Central Europe, 1550–1750*. London: Routledge, 1989.

Hsia, R. Po-chia and Van Nierop, H. F. K., eds., *Calvinism and Religious Toleration in the Dutch Golden Age*. Cambridge: Cambridge University Press, 2002.

Huseman, W. H., "The Expression of the Idea of Toleration in French During the Sixteenth Century," *Sixteenth Century Journal*, 15 (1984), pp. 293–310.

Jordan, W. K., *The Development of Religious Toleration in England*, 4 vols. Cambridge, Mass.: Harvard University Press, 1932–40.

Joutard, P., "The Revocation of the Edict of Nantes: End or Renewal of French Calvinism?," in Menna Prestwich, ed., *International Calvinism 1541–1715*. Oxford: Clarendon Press, 1985, pp. 339–68.

Kamen, H., *The Rise of Toleration*. New York: McGraw-Hill, 1967.

Kaplan, B. J., *Calvinists and Libertines: Confession and Community in Utrecht, 1578–1620*. Oxford: Oxford University Press, 1995.

Kaplan, B. J., "Fictions of Privacy: House Chapels and the Spatial Accommodation of Religious Dissent in Early Modern Europe," *American Historical Review*, 107 (2002), pp. 1031–64.

Laursen, J. C. and Nederman, C. J., eds., *Beyond the Persecuting Society: Religious Toleration Before the Enlightenment*. Philadelphia: University of Pennsylvania Press, 1997.

Lecler, J., *Toleration and the Reformation*, 2 vols. London: Longman, 1960.

L'Hôpital, Michel de, *Oeuvres complètes*, ed. P. J. S. Duféy, 3 vols. Paris: A. Boulland, 1824–5.

Luther, M., *D. Martin Luthers Werke: Kritische Gesamtausgabe, Abteilung Werke*. Weimar: H. Böhlau, 1883–1993. [*WA*]

McClendon, M. C., *The Quiet Reformation: Magistrates and the Emergence of Protestantism in Tudor Norwich*. Stanford, Calif.: Stanford University Press, 1999.

Mecenseffy, G., *Geschichte des Protestantismus in Österreich*. Graz: H. Bohlau, 1956.

Mendus, S., *Toleration and the Limits of Liberalism*. Atlantic Highlands, NJ: Humanities Press, 1993.

Moore, R. I., *The Formation of a Persecuting Society: Power and Deviance in Western Europe, 950–1250*. Oxford: Blackwell, 1987.

Mousnier, R., *The Assassination of Henry IV: The Tyrannicide Problem and the Consolidation of the French Absolute Monarchy in the Early Seventeenth Century*. London, 1973.

Müller, K., ed., *Instrumenta pacis Westphalicae – Die Westfälischen Friedensverträge: vollst. lateinischer Text mit Übers. der wichtigsten Teile und Regesten*. Bern: Herbert Lang, 1975.

Mullett, M. A., *Catholics in Britain and Ireland, 1558–1829*. New York: St. Martin's Press, 1998.

Nelson, E. W., "The Theory of Persecution," in *Persecution and Liberty: Essays in Honor of George Lincoln Burr.* New York: Century, 1931, pp. 3–20.

Nirenberg, D., *Communities of Violence: Persecution of Minorities in the Middle Ages.* Princeton, NJ: Princeton University Press, 1995.

Nischan, B., "Reformed Irenicism and the Leipzig Colloquy of 1631," *Central European History,* 9 (1976), pp. 3–26.

Pfeiffer, G., "Das Ringen um die Parität in der Reichsstadt Biberach," *Blätter für Württembergische Kirchengeschichte,* 56 (1956), pp. 3–75.

Pollmann, J., *Religious Choice in the Dutch Republic: The Reformation of Arnoldus Buchelius (1565–1641).* Manchester: Manchester University Press, 1999.

Quéniart, J., *La Révocation de l'Édit de Nantes: Protestants et catholiques en France de 1598 à 1685.* Paris: Desclée de Brouwer, 1985.

Rouse, R. and Neill, S. C., eds., *A History of the Ecumenical Movement, 1517–1948.* Philadelphia: Westminster Press, 1954.

Schilling, H., "Religion and Society in the Northern Netherlands," in H. Schilling, *Religion, Political Culture and the Emergence of Early Modern Society: Essays in German and Dutch History.* Leiden: Brill, 1992, pp. 353–412.

Schindling, A. and Ziegler, W., eds., *Die Territorien des Reichs im Zeitalter der Reformation und Konfessionalisierung: Land und Konfession 1500–1650,* 7 vols. Münster: Aschendorff, 1989.

Smith, M. C., "Early French Advocates of Religious Freedom," *Sixteenth Century Journal,* 25 (1994), pp. 29–51.

Spaans, J., *Haarlem na de Reformatie: Stedelijke cultuur en kerkelijk leven, 1577–1620.* The Hague: Stichting Hollandse Historische Reeks, 1989.

Spufford, M., ed., *The World of the Rural Dissenters, 1520–1795.* Cambridge: Cambridge University Press, 1995.

Stievermann, D., Press, V., and Diemer, K., eds., *Geschichte der Stadt Biberach.* Stuttgart: Konrad Theiss, 1991.

Tazbir, J., *A State Without Stakes: Polish Religious Toleration in the Sixteenth and Seventeenth Centuries.* New York: Kościuszko Foundation, 1973.

Temple, Sir W., *Observations upon the United Provinces of the Netherlands,* ed. G. N. Clark. Oxford, 1972.

Tracy, J. D., "Erasmus, Coornhert and the Acceptance of Religious Disunity in the Body Politic: A Low Countries Tradition?," in Christiane Berkvens-Stevelinck, Jonathan I. Israel, and G. H. M Posthumus Meyjes, eds., *The Emergence of Tolerance in the Dutch Republic.* Leiden: Brill, 1997, pp. 49–62.

Tuck, R., "Scepticism and Toleration in the Seventeenth Century," in Susan Mendus, ed., *Justifying Toleration: Conceptual and Historical Perspectives.* Cambridge: Cambridge University Press, 1988, pp. 21–35.

Ubachs, P. J. H., *Twee heren, twee confessies: De verhouding van staat en kerk te Maastricht, 1632–1673.* Assen: Van Gorcum, 1975.

Walder, E., ed., *Religionsvergleiche des 16. Jahrhunderts.* Bern: Herbert Lang, 1974.

Walzer, M., *On Toleration.* New Haven, Conn.: Yale University Press, 1997.

Wanegffelen, T., *L'Édit de Nantes: Une histoire européenne de la tolérance du XVIe au XXe siècles.* Paris: Librairie générale française, 1998.

Warmbrunn, P., *Zwei Konfessionen in einer Stadt: Das Zusammenleben von Katholiken und Protestanten in den paritätischen Reichsstädten Augsburg, Biberach, Ravensburg und Dinkelsbühl von 1548 bis 1648.* Wiesbaden: Franz Steiner, 1983.

Whaley, J., *Religious Toleration and Social Change in Hamburg 1529–1819.* Cambridge: Cambridge University Press, 1985.

Whelan, R. and Baxter, C., eds., *Toleration and Religious Identity: The Edict of Nantes and its Implications in France, Britain and Ireland.* Dublin: Four Courts, 2003.

Zschunke, P., *Konfession und Alltag in Oppenheim: Beiträge zur Geschichte von Bevölkerung und Gesellschaft einer gemischtkonfessionelleen Kleinstadt in der frühen Neuzeit*. Wiesbaden: Franz Steiner, 1984.

FURTHER READING

The most recent overviews of the history of toleration are Wanegffelen, *L'Édit de Nantes*, and Coffey, *Persecution and Toleration in Protestant England*. Focusing on the ideas of intellectuals and on the laws and policies of rulers, these works are in the same traditional vein as the classic studies by Jordan, *The Development of Religious Toleration in England*; Lecler, *Toleration and the Reformation*; and Kamen, *The Rise of Toleration*. By contrast, recent specialized studies tend to draw more on the methods of social and cultural history. Many of these works take the form of local case studies, including Warmbrunn, *Zwei Konfessionen in einer Stadt*; Zschunke, *Konfession und Alltag in Oppenheim*; Whaley, *Religious Toleration and Social Change in Hamburg*; Spaans, *Haarlem Na De Reformatie*; Diefendorf, *Beneath the Cross* (Paris); François, *Die unsichtbare Grenze* (Augsburg); Kaplan, *Calvinists and Libertines* (Utrecht); and McClendon, *The Quiet Reformation* (Norwich). Other innovative works include Benedict, *The Huguenot Population of France*; Haydon, *Anti-Catholicism in Eighteenth-Century England*; Spufford, *The World of the Rural Dissenters*; and Christin, *La Paix de religion*. The past few years have seen a flood of essay collections: Grell and Scribner, *Tolerance and Intolerance in the European Reformation*; Grell and Porter, *Toleration in Enlightenment Europe*; Laursen and Nederman, *Beyond the Persecuting Society*; Berkvens-Stevelinck, Israel, and Posthumus Meyjes, *The Emergence of Tolerance in the Dutch Republic*; and Hsia and Van Nierop, *Calvinism and Religious Toleration in the Dutch Golden Age*. Several were occasioned by the quincentennial of the Edict of Nantes: Cameron, Greengrass, Leslie, and Roberts, *The Adventure of Religious Pluralism in Early Modern France*; Whelan and Baxter, *Toleration and Religious Identity*; and Grandjean and Roussel, *Coexister dans l'intolérance*. Certain older national studies, like Bossy, *The English Catholic Community*, and Tazbir, *A State Without Stakes* (Poland), remain useful, while for the empire a crucial guide is offered by Schindling and Ziegler, *Die Territorien des Reichs im Zeitalter der Reformation und Konfessionalisierung*. For theories of tolerance, see *inter alia* Walzer, *On Toleration*; Heyd, *Toleration: An Elusive Virtue*; and Mendus, *Toleration and the Limits of Liberalism*. Important insights into the relationship between coexistence and conflict, tolerance and intolerance, are offered by Nirenberg, *Communities of Violence*.

Bibliography

Abels, P. and Wouters, T., *Nieuw en ongezien: Kerk en samenleving in de classis Delft en Delfland 1572–1621*, 2 vols. Delft: Eburom, 1994.

Adorni-Braccesi, S., *"Una città infetta": La repubblica di Lucca nella crisi religiosa del Cinquecento*. Florence: Olschki, 1994.

Agrippa, H. C. von Nettesheim, *The Philosophy of Natural Magic*, ed. Leslie Sheppard. Secaucus, NJ: University Books, 1974.

Ahlgren, G. T. W., *Teresa of Avila and the Politics of Sanctity*. Ithaca, NY: Cornell University Press, 1996.

Aland, K., *Hilfsbuch zum Lutherstudium*, 4th ed. Bielefeld: Luther-Verlag, 1996.

Alberro, S., *Inquisición y sociedad en Mexico (1571–1700)*. Mexico: Fondo de Cultura Económica, 1988.

Albuquerque, L. de, *Martim Afonso de Sousa*. Lisbon: Biblioteca da Expansão Portuguesa, 1989.

Albuquerque, V. A. C. B. de, "Congregação do Oratório de S. Felippe Nery em Goa," *O Oriente Portuguez*, 2 (1905).

Alden, D., *The Making of an Enterprise: The Society of Jesus in Portugal, its Empire, and Beyond, 1540–1750*. Stanford, Calif.: Stanford University Press, 1996.

Almeida, A. F. de, "Da demanda do Preste João à missão jesuíta da Etiópia: A cristandade da Abissínia e os portugueses nos séculos XVI e XVII," *Lusitania Sacra*, 11, 2nd ser. (1999), pp. 247–94.

Almeida, F. de, *História da Igreja em Portugal*, 2nd ed. Porto and Lisbon, vol. 2, 1968.

Althaus, P., *The Theology of Martin Luther*, trans. Robert C. Schultz. Philadelphia: Fortress Press, 1966.

Althaus, P., *The Ethics of Martin Luther*, trans. Robert C. Schultz. Philadelphia: Fortress Press, 1972.

Alvarez-Taladriz, J. L., ed., *Sumario de las Cosas de Japon (1583), Adiciones del Sumario de Japon (1592)*, 2 vols. Tokyo: Sophia University, Monumenta Nipponica Monograph 9, 1954.

Alves, J. M. Dos Santos, *Portugal e a missionação no século XVI: O Oriente e o Brasil*. Lisbon: Imprensa Nacional-Casa da Moeda (Portuguese and English version), 1997.

Amaladass, A. and Young, R. F., *The Indian Christiad*. Gujarat, 1995.

Ambrosini, F., *Storie di patrizi e di eresia nella Venezia del '500*. Milan: Angeli, 1999.

Amiel, C., "Les archives de l'Inquisition portugaise: Regards et réflexions," *Arquivos do Centro cultural português*, 14 (1979).

Amiel, C. and Lima, A., eds., *L'Inquisition de Goa: La relation de Charles Dellon (1687)*. Paris: Chandeigne, 1997.

Andor, E. and Tóth, I. G., eds., *Frontiers of Faith: Religious Exchange and the Constitution of Religious Identities 1400–1750*. Budapest: Central European University/European Science Foundation, 2001.

Antonio, T. de, "Coleccionismo, devoción, y contrarreforma," in *Felipe II. Un monarca y su epoca: Un principe del Renacimiento*. Madrid: Sociedad Estatal para la Conmemoración de los centenarios de Felipe II y Carlos V, 1998, pp. 135–57.

Arand, C. P., *That I May Be His Own: An Overview of Luther's Catechisms*. St. Louis: Concordia, 2000.

Asch, R. G., *The Thirty Years' War: The Holy Roman Empire and Europe 1618–1648*. Basingstoke: Macmillan, 1997.

Asch, R. G., "Warfare in the Age of the Thirty Years' War 1598–1648," in Jeremy Black, ed., *European Warfare 1453–1815*. Basingstoke: Macmillan, 1999, pp. 45–68, 250–6.

Asche, M. and Schindling, A., eds., *Das Strafgericht Gottes: Kriegserfahrungen und Religion im Heiligen Römischen Reich Deutscher Nation im Zeitalter des Dreißigjährigen Krieges*. Münster: Aschendorff, 2001.

Aston, M., *Lollards and Reformers: Images and Literacy in Late Medieval Religion*. London: Hambledon Press, 1984.

Aston, M., *England's Iconoclasts*. Oxford: Oxford University Press, 1988.

Audisio, G., *Les Vaudois du Luberon: Une minorité en Provence, 1460–1560*. Aix-en-Provence: Association d'études vaudoises et historiques du Luberon, 1984.

Augustijn, C., "Anabaptisme in de Nederlanden," *Doopsgezinde Bijdragen*, 12–13 (1986–7), pp. 13–28.

Augustijn, C., "De opmars van de calvinistische beweging in de Nederlanden," *Theoretische Geschiedenis*, 20 (1993), pp. 424–38.

Aulén, G., *Christus Victor*, trans. A. G. Hebert. London: SPCK, 1945.

Bagchi, D., *Luther's Earliest Opponents: Catholic Controversialists, 1518–1525*. Minneapolis: Fortress Press, 1991.

Bahlcke, J. and Strohmeyer, A., eds., *Konfessionalisierung in Ostmitteleuropa: Wirkungen des religiösen Wandels im 16. und 17. Jahrhundert in Staat, Gesellschaft und Kultur*. Forschungen zur Geschichte und Kultur des östlichen Mitteleuropa, 7. Wiesbaden: Franz Steiner, 1999.

Baião, A., *A Inquisição de Goa, tentativa de história da sua origem, estabelecimento, evolução e extinção*, 2 vols. Lisbon and Coimbra: Academia das Ciências, 1930–45.

Bailey, G. A., *Art on the Jesuit Missions in Asia and Latin America, 1542–1773*. Toronto: University of Toronto Press, 2000.

Bainton, R. H., *Here I Stand*. New York: Abingdon, 1950.

Bangert, W. V., *A History of the Society of Jesus*. St. Louis: Institute of Jesuit Sources, 1972.

Baptista, J. C., "A formação do clero na diocese de Évora," *A Cidade de Évora*, 61–2 (1978–9), pp. 5–90.

Barnavi, E., *Le Parti de Dieu: Étude sociale et politique des chefs de la Ligue parisienne, 1585–1594*. Louvain: Nauwelaerts, 1980.

Baron, S., *A Social and Religious History of the Jews*, 18 vols. Philadelphia: Jewish Publication Society, vol. 13, 1969.

Barrett, D., Kurian, G., and Johnson, T., eds., *World Christian Encyclopedia: A Comparative Study of Churches and Religions in the Modern World*. Vol. 1: *The World by Countries: Religionists, Churches, Ministries*. Oxford: Oxford University Press, 2001.

Barrio Gonzalo, M., "El clero diocesano: Beneficios y beneficiados," in *Historia de la diocesis de Valladolid*. Valladolid: Arzobispado de Valladolid; Diputación Provincial de Valladolid, 1996, pp. 23–149.

Barrio Gonzalo, M., "El clero regular: Monasterios y conventos," in *Historia de la diocesis de Valladolid*. Valladolid: Arzobispado de Valladolid; Diputación Provincial de Valladolid, 1996, pp. 191–214.

Barrio Gonzalo, M., *Los obispos de Castilla y Léon durante el Antiguo Régimen (1556–1834): Estudio socioeconómico*. Zamora, Junta de Castilla y León: Consejeria de Educación y Cultura, 2000.

Barros, J. de, *Ropica Pnefma*. Lisbon: Germão Galharde, 1532.

Barry, J., Hester, M., and Roberts, G., eds., *Witchcraft in Early Modern Europe: Studies in Culture and Belief*. Cambridge: Cambridge University Press, 1996.

Bastide, R., *The African Religions of Brazil*. Baltimore: Johns Hopkins University Press, 1978.

Baumann, C., *Gewaltlosigkeit im Täufertum*. Leiden: Brill, 1968.

Bayer, O., *Promissio: Geschichte der reformatorischen Wende in Luthers Theologie*. Göttingen: Vandenhoeck & Ruprecht, 1971.

Bayly (née Kaufmann), S. B., "A Christian Caste in Hindu Society: Religious Leadership and Social Conflict among the Paravas of Southern Tamilnadu," *Modern Asian Studies*, 15/2 (1981).

Bayly, S., *Saints, Goddesses and Kings: Muslims and Christians in South Indian Society, 1700–1900*. Cambridge: Cambridge University Press, 1992 (Indian ed.).

Beaver, D. C., *Parish Communities and Religious Conflict in the Vale of Gloucester, 1590–1690*. Cambridge, Mass.: Harvard University Press, 1998.

Behringer, W., *Witchcraft Persecutions in Bavaria: Popular Magic, Religious Zealotry and Reason of State in Early Modern Europe*. Cambridge: Cambridge University Press, 1997.

Beinart, H., ed., *Records of the Trials of the Spanish Inquisition in Ciudad Real*, 4 vols. Jerusalem: Israel National Academy of Sciences and Humanities, 1974–85.

Bell, C., *Ritual Theory, Ritual Practice*. Oxford: Oxford University Press, 1992.

Bell, T., *Divus Bernhardus: Bernhard von Clairvaux in Martin Luthers Schriften*. Mainz: Zabern, 1993.

Benedict, P., "The Saint Bartholomew's Massacres in the Provinces," *Historical Journal*, 21/2 (1978), pp. 205–25.

Benedict, P., *Rouen during the Wars of Religion*. Cambridge: Cambridge University Press, 1981.

Benedict, P., *The Huguenot Population of France, 1600–1685: The Demographic Fate and Customs of a Religious Minority*. Philadelphia: American Philosophical Society, 1991.

Benedict, P., "Un roi, une loi, deux foix: Parameters for the History of Catholic-Reformed Co-existence in France, 1555–1685," in Ole Peter Grell and Bob Scribner, eds., *Tolerance and Intolerance in the European Reformation*. Cambridge: Cambridge University Press, 1996, pp. 65–93.

Benedict, P. et al., eds., *Reformation, Revolt and Civil War in France and the Netherlands, 1555–1585*. Amsterdam: Royal Netherlands Academy of Arts and Sciences, 1999.

Bennassar, B., *L'Inquisition espagnole, Xve–XIXe siècles*. Paris: Hachette, 1979.

Bennassar, B. and Bennassar, L., *Les Chrétiens d'Allah*. Paris: Perrin, 1989.

Ben-Sasson, H. H., "Jewish–Christian Disputation in the Setting of Humanism and Reformation in the German Empire," *Harvard Theological Review*, 59 (1966), pp. 369–90.

Ben-Sasson, H. H., "The Reformation in Contemporary Jewish Eyes," *Proceedings of the Israel Academy of Sciences and Humanities*, 4 (1971), pp. 239–326.

Bergier, J.-F. and Kingdon, R. M., eds., *The Register of the Company of Pastors of Geneva in the Time of Calvin*, trans. Philip E. Hughes. Grand Rapids, Mich.: Eerdmans, 1966.

Berkvens-Stevelinck, C., Israel, J. I., and Posthumus Meyjes, G. H. M., eds., *The Emergence of Tolerance in the Dutch Republic*. Leiden/New York: Brill, 1997.

Bernard, H., S.J., *Le Frère Bento de Goes chez les Musulmans de la Haute Asie (1603–1651)*. Tientsin, 1934.

Bernard, H., *Le P. Matthieu Ricci et la société chinoise de son temps (1552–1610)*, 2 vols. Tientsin: Hautes Études, 1937.

Bernardini, P. and Fiering, N., eds., *The Jews and the Expansion of Europe to the West, 1450–1800*. New York and Oxford: Berghahn Books, 2001.

Besse, L., S.J., *La Mission du Maduré: Historiques de ses Pangous*. Trichinopoly, 1914.

Bethencourt, F., *O imagináro da magia*. Lisbon: Centro de estudos de História e cultura portuguesa, 1987.

Bethencourt, F., *L'Inquisition à l'époque moderne: Espagne, Portugal, Italie XVe–XIXe siècles*. Paris: Fayard, 1995.

Betts, R. R., *Essays in Czech History*. London: Athlone Press, 1969.

Białostocki, J., *The Art of the Renaissance in Eastern Europe: Hungary, Bohemia, Poland*. Ithaca, NY: Cornell University Press, 1976.

Bijsterveld, A. J. A., *Laverend tussen kerk en wereld: De pastoors in Noord-Brabant 1400–1570*. Amsterdam: VU Uitgeverij, 1993.

Bilinkoff, J., *The Avila of St. Theresa*. Cornell, NY: Cornell University Press, 1989.

Bilinkoff, J., "Teresa of Jesus and Carmelite Reform," in R. L. DeMolen and J. C. Olin, eds., *Religious Orders of the Catholic Reformation: In Honor of John C. Olin on his Seventy-Fifth Birthday*. New York: Fordham University Press, 1994, pp. 165–86.

Biller, P., "The Preaching of the Waldensian Sisters," in *La Prédication sur un mode dissident: Laïcs, femmes, hérétiques*, in *Heresis*, 30 (1999), pp. 137–68.

Binder, L., *Grundlagen und Formen der Toleranz in Siebenbürgen bis zur Mitte des 17. Jahrhunderts*. Vienna and Cologne: Böhlau.

Bireley, R., *Religion and Politics in the Age of the Counterreformation: Emperor Ferdinand II, William Lamormaini, S.J., and the Formation of Imperial Policy*. Chapel Hill: University of North Carolina Press, 1981.

Bireley, R., "The Thirty Years' War as Germany's Religious War," in K. Repgen, ed., *Krieg und Politik 1618–1648*. Munich: R. Oldenbourg, 1988, pp. 85–106.

Bizer, E., *Fides ex auditu: Eine Untersuchung über die Entdeckung der Gerechtigkeit Gottes durch Martin Luther*. Neukirchen: Erziehungsverein, 1958.

Blaisdell, C. J., "Angela Merici and the Ursulines," in R. L. DeMolen and J. C. Olin, eds., *Religious Orders of the Catholic Reformation: In Honor of John C. Olin on his Seventy-Fifth Birthday*. New York: Fordham University Press, 1994, pp. 99–136.

Blanco, M. M. V., "Notas sobre o poder temporal da Companhia de Jesus na India," *Studia*, 49 (1989).

Blickle, P., *The Revolution of 1525: The German Peasants' War from a New Perspective*, trans. from 2nd ed. (1981) by Thomas A. Brady, Jr. and H. C. Erik Midelfort. Baltimore: Johns Hopkins University Press, 1982.

Blickle, P., *Die Reformation im Reich*, 2nd ed. Munich: Beck, 1988.

Blickle, P., *From the Communal Reformation to the Revolution of the Common Man*, trans. Beat Kümin. Leiden: Brill, 1998.

Bloch, E., *Thomas Münzer als Theologe der Revolution*. Frankfurt a.M.: Suhrkamp, 1962.

Block, D., *Mission Culture on the Upper Amazon: Native Tradition, Jesuit Enterprise, and Secular Policy in Moxos, 1660–1880*. Lincoln: University of Nebraska Press, 1994.

Blockmans, W. P. and Peteghem, P. van, "La pacification de Gand à la lumière d'un siècle de continuité constitutionnelle dans les Pays-Bas, 1477–1576," in R. Vierhaus, ed., *Herrschaftsverträge, Wahlkapitulationen, Fundamentalgesetze*. Göttingen: Vandehoeck & Ruprecht, 1977, pp. 220–34.

Bodian, M., *Hebrews of the Portuguese Nation: Conversos and Community in Early Modern Amsterdam*. Bloomington: Indiana University Press, 1997.

Bogucka, M., "Die Wirkungen der Reformation in Danzig," *Zeitschrift für Ostforschung*, 42 (1993), pp. 195–206.

Bontinck, F., *La Lutte autour de la liturgie chinoise aux XVIIe et XVIIIe siècles*. Louvain: Nauwelaerts, 1962.

Borges, C. J., *The Economics of the Goa Jesuits, 1542–1759: An Explanation of their Rise and Fall*. New Delhi: Oxford University Press, 1994.

Borges, C. J., "The Portuguese Jesuits in Asia: Their Economic and Political Networking within Asia and with Europe," in *A Companhia de Jesus e a Missionação no Oriente*. Lisbon: Brotéria & Fundação Oriente, 2000, pp. 203–24.

Borromeo, A., "Felipe II y el absolutismo confesional," in *Felipe II. Un monarca y su epoca: La monarquia Hispanica*. Madrid: Sociedad Estatal para la Conmemoración de los centenarios de Felipe II y Carlos V, 1998, pp. 185–95.

Bosbach, F., *Monarchia universalis: Ein politischer Leitbegriff der Frühen Neuzeit*. Göttingen: Vandenhoeck & Ruprecht, 1988.

Bossy, J., *The English Catholic Community 1570–1850*. New York: Oxford University Press, 1976.

Bossy, J., *Christianity in the West, 1400–1700*. Oxford: Oxford University Press, 1985.

Bostridge, I., *Witchcraft and its Transformations c.1650–c.1750*. Oxford: Clarendon Press, 1997.

Bouchon, G., *Premières expériences d'une société coloniale: Goa au XVIe siècle*. Paris, 1987.

Bouchon, G., *Albuquerque: Le lion des mers d'Asie*. Paris, 1992.

Bouza Alvarez, J. L., *Religiosidad contrarreformista y cultura simbolica del barroco*. Madrid: Consejo Superior de Investigaciones Científicas, 1990.

Boxer, C. R., *The Christian Century in Japan 1549–1650*. Berkeley: University of California Press, 1951, 1967.

Boxer, C. R., *The Great Ship from Amacon: Annals of Macao and the Old Japan Trade, 1555–1640*. Lisbon: CEHU, 1959.

Boxer, C. R., *Race Relations in the Portuguese Colonial Empire*. Oxford: Oxford University Press, 1963.

Boxer, C. R., *Fidalgos in the Far East, 1550–1770*. The Hague: Martinus Nijhoff, 1948 (rpt. 1968, Hong Kong).

Boxer, C. R., *The Portuguese Seaborne Empire, 1425–1825*. London and New York: Weidenfeld & Nicolson, 1969.

Boxer, C. R., *The Church Militant and Iberian Expansion, 1440–1770*. Baltimore: Johns Hopkins University Press, 1978.

Boxer, C. R., *Portuguese India in the Mid-Seventeenth Century*. New Delhi: Oxford University Press, 1980.

Boyd, R. H. S., *India and the Latin Captivity of the Church: The Cultural Context of the Gospel*. Cambridge: Cambridge University Press, 1974.

Brading, D., *The First America: The Spanish Monarchy, Creole Patriots, and the Liberal State, 1492–1867*. Cambridge: Cambridge University Press, 1991.

Brady, T. A., Jr., "Jacob Sturm of Strasbourg and the Lutherans at the Diet of Augsburg, 1530," *Church History*, 42 (June 1973), pp. 183–202.

Brady, T. A., "Luther and the State: The Reformer's Teaching in its Social Setting," in James D. Tracy, ed., *Luther and the Modern State in Germany*. Kirksville, Mo.: Sixteenth Century Journal, 1986, pp. 31–44.

Brambilla, E., *Alle origini del Sant'Uffizio, Penitenza, confessione e giustizia spirituale dal medioevo al XVI secolo*. Bologna: Il Mulino, 2000.

Brandão, M., *A Inquisição e os professores do Colégio das Artes*, 2 vols. Coimbra: Universidade de Coimbra, 1948–69.

Brazão, E., *Em demanda do Cataio: A viagem de Bento de Goes à China (1603–1607)*. Lisbon, 1954.

Brecht, M., *Martin Luther*, trans. James L. Schaaf, 3 vols. Philadelphia: Fortress Press, 1985–93.

Bredekamp, H., *Kunst als Medium sozialer Konflikte: Bilderkämpfe von der Spätantike bis zur Hussitenrevolution*. Frankfurt a.M.: Suhrkampf, 1975.

Brenon, A., "The Waldensian Books," in P. Biller and A. Hudson (eds.), *Heresy and Literacy, 1000–1530*. Cambridge: Cambridge University Press, 1994, pp. 137–59.

Breuer, M., and Graetz, M., eds., *German–Jewish History in Modern Times*. Vol. 1: *Tradition and Enlightenment, 1600–1780*. New York: Columbia University Press, 1996.

Bricker, V., *The Indian Christ, The Indian King: The Historical Substrate of Maya Myth and Ritual*. Austin: University of Texas Press, 1981.

Brigden, S., *London and the Reformation*. Oxford: Clarendon Press, 1989.

Briggs, R., *Witches and Neighbours: The Social and Cultural Context of European Witchcraft*, 2nd ed. Oxford: Blackwell, 2002.

Brock, P., *The Political and Social Doctrines of the Unity of the Czech Brethren in the Fifteenth and Early Sixteenth Centuries*. The Hague: Mouton, 1957.

Brockey, L. M., "Harvest of the Vine: The Jesuit Missionary Enterprise in China, 1575–1710," PhD dissertation, Brown University, 2002.

Brodrick, J., *Saint Peter Canisius*. London: Sheed & Ward, 1935.

Brou, A., "Notes sur les origines du clergé indigène au pays Tamoul," *Revue d'histoire des missions*, 7/2 (June 1930), pp. 188–210.

Brown, J. C., *Immodest Acts: The Life of a Lesbian Nun in Renaissance Italy*. New York: Oxford University Press, 1986.

Brown, L., *The Indian Christians of St. Thomas*. Cambridge: Cambridge University Press, 1982 (1st ed., 1956).

Brügisser, T., "Frömmigkeitspraktiken der einfachen Leute in Katholizismus und Reformiertentum: Beobachtungen des Luzerner Stadtschreibers Renward Cysat (1545–1614)," *Zeitschrift für historische Forschung*, 17 (1990), pp. 1–26.

Buescu, A. I., "O mito das origens da nacionalidade: O milagre de Ourique," in Francisco Bethencourt and Diogo Ramada Curto, eds., *A memória da Nação*. Lisbon: Livraria Sá da Costa, 1991, pp. 49–69.

Burckhardt, P., ed., *Das Tagebuch des Johannes Gast (Basler Chroniken*, vol. 8). Basel: Schwabe, 1945.

Burgaleta, C. M., *José de Acosta, S. J. (1540–1600): His Life and Thought*. Chicago: Loyola University Press, 1999.

Burke, P., "How to Be a Counter-Reformation Saint," in Kaspar Von Greyerz, ed., *Religion and Society in Early Modern Europe, 1500–1800*. London: German Historical Institute, 1984, pp. 45–55.

Burke, P., *The Italian Renaissance: Culture and Society in Italy*, 2nd ed. Princeton, NJ: Princeton University Press, 1986.

Burkhardt, J., "Der Dreißigjährige Krieg als frühmoderner Staatsbildungskrieg," in *Geschichte in Wissenschaft und Unterricht*, 45. Seelze: Erhard Friedrich, 1994, pp. 487–99.

Burkhardt, J., *Der Dreißigjährige Krieg*. Frankfurt a.M.: Suhrkamp, 1992; new ed., 1996; rev. ed., Darmstadt: Wissenschaftlichen Buchgesellschaft, 1997.

Burkhardt, J., "Die Friedlosigkeit in der Frühen Neuzeit: Grundlegung einer Theorie der Bellizität Europas," in *Zeitschrift für Historische Forschung*, 24. Berlin: Duncker & Humblot, 1997, pp. 509–74.

Burkhardt, J., "Die entgipfelte Pyramide: Kriegsgrund und Friedenskompromiß der europäischen Universalmächte," in Klaus Bußmann and Heinz Schilling, eds., *1648: Krieg und Frieden in Europa*, 3 vols. Vol. 2: *Politik, Religion, Recht und Gesellschaft*. Münster and Osnabrück: Verlagsgesellschaft 350 Jahre Westfälischer Friede, 1998, pp. 51–60.

Burkhardt, J., " 'Ist noch ein Ort, dahin der Krieg nicht kommen sey?' Katastrophenerfahrungen und Überlebensstrategien (misprinted: Kriegsstrategien) auf dem deutschen Kriegsschauplatz," in Horst Lademacher and Simon Groenveld, eds., *Krieg und Kultur: Die Rezeption von Krieg und Frieden in der Niederländischen Republik und im Deutschen Reich 1568–1648*. Münster: Waxmann, 1998, pp. 3–19.

Burkhardt, J., "Schlußkommentar und Ausblick," in B. von Krusenstjern and H. Medick, eds., *Zwischen Alltag und Katastrophe: Der Dreißigjährige Krieg aus der Nähe*. Göttingen: Vandenhoeck & Ruprecht, 1998, pp. 595–600.

Burkhardt, J., *Das Reformationsjahrhundert: Deutsche Geschichte zwischen Medienrevolution und Institutionenbildung 1517–1617*. Stuttgart: Kohlhammer, 2002.

Burkhart, L., *The Slippery Earth: Nahua-Christian Moral Dialogue in Sixteenth-Century Mexico*. Tucson: University of Arizona Press, 1989.

Burkhart, L., *Holy Wednesday: A Nahua Drama from Early Colonial Mexico*. Philadelphia: University of Pennsylvania Press, 1996.

Burleigh, M., *Germany Turns Eastwards: A Study of Ostforschung in the Third Reich*. Cambridge: Cambridge University Press, 1988.

Bůžek, V., Hrdlička, J., Král, P., and Vybíral, Z., eds., *Věk urozených: Šlechta v českých zemích na prahu novověku*. Prague, Litomyšl: Paseka, 2002.

Bylina, S., "Krisen – Reformen – Entwicklungen," in F. Seibt and W. Eberhard, eds., *Europa 1400. Die Krise des Spätmittelalters*. Stuttgart: Klett-Cotta, 1984, pp. 82–302.

Bylina, S., "The Church and Folk Culture in Late Medieval Poland," *Acta Poloniae Historica*, 68 (1993), pp. 27–42.

Cameron, E., *The Reformation of the Heretics: The Waldenses of the Alps 1480–1580*. Oxford: Clarendon Press, 1984.

Cameron, E., *The European Reformation*. Oxford: Clarendon Press, 1991.

Cameron, E., "Medieval Heretics as Protestant Martyrs," in *Martyrs and Martyrologies: Papers Read at the 1992 Summer Meeting and the 1993 Winter Meeting of the Ecclesiastical History Society*, ed. D. Wood, Studies in Church History, vol. 30. Oxford: Blackwell, 1993, pp. 185–207.

Cameron, E., *Waldenses: Rejections of Holy Church in Medieval Europe*. Oxford: Blackwell, 2000.

Cameron, K., Greengrass, M., Leslie, M., and Roberts, P., eds., *The Adventure of Religious Pluralism in Early Modern France: Papers from the Exeter Conference, April 1999*. Oxford: Peter Lang, 2000.

Camille, M., *Gothic Art: Glorious Visions*. New York: Harry N. Abrams, 1996.

Camps, A., O.F.M., *Jerome Xavier, S.J., and the Muslims of the Mogul Empire: Controversial Works and Missionary Activity*, Schöneck-Beckenried: Neue Zeitschrift für Missionwissenschaft (Nouvelle Revue de Science Missionaire), 1957.

Candau Chacon, M. L., *El clero rural de Sevilla en el siglo XVIII*. Seville: Caja Rural de Sevilla, 1994.

Canosa, R., *Storia dell'Inquisizione in Italia, della metà del Cinquecento alla fine del Settecento*, 5 vols. Rome: Sapere 2000, 1986–90.

Caponetto, S., *La Riforma protestante nell'Italia del Cinquecento*. Turin: Claudiana, 1992. Published in English as *The Protestant Reformation in Sixteenth-Century Italy*. Kirksville, Mo.: Truman State University Press, 1998.

Capp, B. S., *The Fifth Monarchy Men: A Study in Seventeenth-Century English Millenarianism*. London: Faber, 1972.

Caraman, P., *The Lost Empire: The Story of the Jesuits in Ethiopia*. London, 1985.

Carpintero Aguado, L., "Iglesia y corte castellana en el siglo XVI: Contribucion y tributos," *Hispania Sacra*, 41 (1989), pp. 547–67.

Carrasco, R., *Inquisición y repression sexual en Valencia*. Barcelona: Laertes, 1986.

Carroll, S., *Noble Power during the French Wars of Religion: The Guise Affinity and the Catholic Cause in Normandy*. Cambridge: Cambridge University Press, 1998.

Carvalho, J. R. de, "A jurisdição episcopal sobre leigos em matéria de pecados públicos: As visitas pastorais e o comportamento moral das populações portuguesas de Antigo Regime," *Revista Portuguesa de História*, 24 (1988), pp. 121–63.

Carvalho, J. R. de, *As visitas pastorais e a sociedade de Antigo Regime: Notas para o estudo de um mecanismo de normalização social*. Coimbra: Faculdade de Letras da Universidade de Coimbra, 1985.

Cassan, M., *Le Temps des Guerres de Religion: Le cas du Limousin (vers 1530-vers 1630)*. Paris: Publisud, 1996.

Castañeda Delgado, P., and Hernández Aparicio, P., *La Inquisición de Lima (1570–1635)*. Madrid: Deimos, 1989.

Castro, J. de, "Os portugueses em Trento," *Lumen*, 25 (1961), pp. 739–76.

Cervantes, F., *The Devil in the New World: The Impact of Diabolism in New Spain*. New Haven, Conn.: Yale University Press, 1994.

Chan, A., *Chinese Books and Documents in the Jesuit Archives in Rome: A Descriptive Catalogue*. Armonk, NY and London: M. E. Sharpe, 2002.

Chen Yuan, ed., *Kangxi yu Luoma shijie guanxi wenshu yingyin ben* (1932). Reprinted in *Zhongguo shixue congshu xubian*, 23. Taipei: Xuesheng shuju, 1973.

Christian, W. A., Jr., *Local Religion in Sixteenth-Century Spain*. Princeton, NJ: Princeton University Press, 1981.

Christin, O., *Une révolution symbolique: L'iconoclasme huguenot et la reconstruction catholique*. Paris: Éditions de Minuit, 1991.

Christin, O., *La Paix de religion: L'autonomisation de la raison politique au XVIe siècle*. Paris: Éditions du Seuil, 1997.

Clark, S., *Thinking with Demons: The Idea of Witchcraft in Early Modern Europe*. Oxford: Clarendon Press, 1997.

Clasen, C.-P., *Anabaptism: A Social History, 1525–1618. Switzerland, Austria, Moravia, South and Central Germany*. Ithaca, NY: Cornell University Press, 1972.

Clemns-Denys, C., "Les apaiseurs de Lille à la fin de l'Ancien Régime," *Revue du Nord*, 309 (1995).

Cline, S. L., *Colonial Culhuacan, 1580–1600: A Social History of an Aztec Town*. Albuquerque: University of New Mexico Press, 1986.

Coates, T. J., *Degredados e Órfãs: Colonização dirigida pela coroa no império português, 1550–1755*. Lisbon: CNCDP, 1998.

Coffey, J., *Persecution and Toleration in Protestant England, 1558–1689*. London: Longman, 2000.

Cohen, A. P., *The Symbolic Construction of Community*. London: Routledge, 1985.

Cohen, T. M., *The Fire of Tongues: António Vieira and the Missionary Church in Brazil and Portugal*. Stanford, Calif.: Stanford University Press, 1998.

Cohn, H. J., "Anticlericalism in the German Peasants' War," *Past and Present*, 83 (1979), pp. 3–31.

Cohn, N., *Europe's Inner Demons: An Enquiry Inspired by the Great Witch-Hunt*. London: Chatto, Heinemann, 1975; rev. ed., Chicago: University of Chicago Press, 2000.

Collinson, P., *The Religion of Protestants: The Church in English Society 1559–1625*. Oxford: Clarendon Press, 1982.

Collinson, P., *Godly People: Essays on English Protestantism and Puritanism*. London: Hambledon Press, 1983.

Collinson, P., *The Birthpangs of Protestant England*. Basingstoke: Macmillan, 1988.

Collinson, P., "Shepherds, Sheepdogs, and Hirelings: The Pastoral Ministry in Post-Reformation England," in W. J. Sheils and Diana Wood, eds., *The Ministry: Clerical and Lay*. Studies in Church History, 26. Oxford: Blackwell, 1989, pp. 185–220.

Collinson, P., "The English Reformation 1945–1995," in M. Bentley, ed., *Companion to Historiography*. London: Routledge, 1997.

Conrad, A., *Zwischen Kloster und Welt: Ursulinen und Jesuitinnen in der katholischen Reformbewegung des 16./17. Jahrhunderts*. Mainz: Philipp von Zabern, 1991.

Conrad, R. E., *Children of God's Fire: A Documentary History of Black Slavery in Brazil*. University Park: Pennsylvania State University Press, 1994.

Constant, J.-M., *Les Guise*. Paris: Hachette, 1994.

Constant, J.-M., *La Ligue*. Paris: Fayard, 1996.

Contreras, J., *El Santo Oficio de la Inquisición de Galicia (poder, sociedad y cultura)*. Madrid: Akal, 1982.

Contreras, J., *Pouvoir et Inquisition en Espagne au XVIe siècle*. Paris: Aubier, 1997 (French version of *Sotos contra Riquelmes*. Madrid, 1992).

Cooke, K., "The English Nuns and the Dissolution," in B. F. Harvey, J. Blair, and B. Golding, eds., *The Cloister and the World: Essays in Medieval History in Honour of Barbara Harvey*. Oxford and New York: Clarendon Press, 1996, pp. 287–301.

Cooper, M., S.J., ed., *They Came to Japan: An Anthology of European Reports on Japan, 1543–1640*. Berkeley: University of California Press, 1965; Ann Arbor: Center for Japanese Studies, University of Michigan, 1995.

Cooper, M., S.J., ed., *The Southern Barbarians: The First Europeans in Japan*. Tokyo: Kodansha International, 1971.

Cooper, M., S.J., *Rodrigues the Interpreter: An Early Jesuit in Japan and China*. New York and Tokyo: Weatherhill, 1974.

Cooper, T., *The Last Generation of English Catholic Clergy*. Woodbridge: Boydell Press, 1999.

Cordara, G. C., *On the Suppression of the Society of Jesus: A Contemporary Account*, trans. John P. Murphy. Chicago: Loyola University Press, 1999.

Correia-Afonso, J., S.J., *Jesuit Letters and Indian History*. Bombay: St. Xavier's College, 1955.

Correia-Afonso, J., S.J., "More about Akbar and the Jesuits," *Indica*, 14 (1977).

Correia-Afonso, J., S.J., *Indo-Portuguese History: Sources and Problems*. Bombay: Oxford University Press, 1981.

Costa, Fr. C. J., *Life and Achievements of Blessed Joseph Vaz*. Goa, 1996.

Costa, J. P. O. e, "Em torno da criação do Bispado do Japão," in A. T. de Matos and L. F. F. R. Thomaz, eds., *As relações entre a India Portuguesa, a Asia do Sueste e o Extremo Oriente*. Macao and Lisbon: CNCDP, 1993.

Costa, J. P. O. e, "Os Portugueses e a cristandade siro-malabar (1498–1530)," *Studia*, 52 (1994).

Costa, J. P. O. e, "A crise financeira da missão jesuítica do Japão no início do século XVIII," in *A Companhia de Jesus e a Missionação no Oriente*. Lisbon: Brotéria & Fundação Oriente, 2000, pp. 235–46.

Costa, M. O., "Spanish Women in the Reformation," in S. Marshall, ed., *Women in Reformation and Counter-Reformation Europe: Public and Private Worlds*. Bloomington: Indiana University Press, 1989, pp. 89–119.

Cottret, B., *1598, l'édit de Nantes: Pour en finir avec les guerres de religion*. Paris: Perrin, 1997.

Cottret, B., *Calvin: A Biography*. Grand Rapids, Mich.: Eerdmans, 2000.

Coutinho, F., *Le Régime paroissial des diocèses de rite latin de l'Inde des origines (XIVe siècle) à nos jours*. Louvain/Paris: Publications Universitaires de Louvain/Béatrice-Nauwelaerts, 1958.

Couto, D. do, *O Soldado Prático*, ed. M. Rodrigues Lapa. Lisbon: Livraria Sá da Costa Editora, 1937.

Cranston, M., "John Locke and the Case for Toleration," in John Horton and Susan Mendus, eds., *John Locke: A Letter Concerning Toleration in Focus*. London: Routledge, 1991, pp. 78–97.

Cranz, F. E., *An Essay on the Development of Luther's Thought on Justice, Law and Society*. Cambridge, Mass.: Harvard University Press, 1959.

Crew, P. M., *Calvinist Preaching and Iconoclasm in the Netherlands 1544–1569*. Cambridge: Cambridge University Press, 1978.

Criveller, G., *Preaching Christ in Late Ming China: The Jesuits' Presentation of Christ from Matteo Ricci to Giulio Aleni*. Taipei: Ricci Institute, 1997.

Crouzet, D., *Les Guerriers de Dieu: La violence au temps des troubles de religion (vers 1525–vers 1610)*, 2 vols. Seyssel: Champ Vallon, 1990.

Cruz, M. A. L., "Exiles and Renegades in Early Sixteenth-Century Portuguese India," *Indian Economic and Social History Review*, 23/3 (1986).

Cuevas, M., *Historia de la iglesia en México*, 5 vols. Mexico: Editorial Patria, 1946–7.

Cummins, J. S., *A Question of Rites: Friar Domingo Navarrete and the Jesuits in China*. Aldershot: Scolar Press, 1993.

Cunha, A. C. da, *A Inquisição no Estado da Índia: Origens (1539–1560)*. Arquivos Nacionais/Torre do Tombo, 1995.

Curto, D. R., "Cultura escrita e práticas de identidade," in F. Bethencourt and K. Chaudhuri, eds., *História da Expansão Portuguesa*. Navarre: Círculo de Leitores, 1998, vol. 2., pp. 458–531.

Cust, R. and Hughes, A., eds., *Conflict in Early Stuart England: Studies in Religion and Politics 1603–1642*. London: Longman, 1989.

Dalgado, S. R., *Glossário Luso-Asiático*, 2 vols. Coimbra, 1919–21.

Damme, D. van, *Armenzorg en de Staat*. Ghent: Author, 1990.

Das, K., *Mughal Painting during Jahangir's Time*. Calcutta: The Asiatic Society, 1978.

David, Z. V., "Bohusslav Bílejovský and the Religious *via media*: Czech Utraquism in the Sixteenth Century," in David R. Holeton, ed., *The Bohemian Reformation and Religious Practice*, vol. 1. Prague: Academy of Sciences of the Czech Republic Main Library, 1996, pp. 73–90.

David, Z. V., "The Strange Fate of Czech Utraquism: The Second Century, 1517–1621," *Journal of Ecclesiastical History*, 47/4 (1995), pp. 641–68.

David, Z. V., "A Brief Honeymoon in 1564–1566: The Utraquist Consistory and the Archbishop of Prague," *Bohemia*, 39 (1998), pp. 265–84.

David, Z. and Holeton, D. R., eds., *The Bohemian Reformation and Religious Practice*. Vol. 2: *Papers from the XVIII World Congress of the Czechoslovak Academy of Arts and Sciences, Brno, 1996*. Prague: Česká akademie věd, 1998.

Davies, A., *The Quakers in English Society, 1655–1725*. Oxford: Oxford University Press, 2000.

Davies, G., *The Restoration of Charles II, 1658–1660*. San Marino, Calif.: Huntington Library, 1955.

Davis, J. F., *Heresy and Reformation in the South-East of England, 1520–1559*, Royal Historical Society Studies in History, vol. 34. London: Royal Historical Society, 1983.

Davis, N. Z., "The Rites of Violence," in N. Z. Davis, *Society and Culture in Early Modern France: Eight Essays*. Stanford, Calif.: Stanford University Press, 1975, pp. 152–87.

Davis, N. Z., *Society and Culture in Early Modern France: Eight Essays*. Stanford, Calif.: Stanford University Press, 1975.

Davis, R., and Ravid, B., eds., *The Jews of Early Modern Venice*. Baltimore: Johns Hopkins University Press, 2001.

D'Costa, A., *Christianization of the Goa Island, 1510–1567*. Bombay: St. Xavier's College, 1965.

Deanesly, M., *The Lollard Bible and Other Medieval Biblical Versions*. Cambridge: Cambridge University Press, 1920.

Debergh, M., "Premiers jalons de l'évangélisation de l'Asie," in J.-M. Mayeur, Ch. and L. Pietri, A. Vauchez, and M. Venard, eds., *Histoire du Christianisme: Le temps des confessions (1530–1620)*. Paris: Desclée, 1992.

Decavele, J., *De dageraad van de Reformatie in Vlaanderen (1520–1565)*. Brussels: Koninklijke Academie voor Wetenschappen, Letteren en Schone Kunsten van België, 1975.

Dedieu, J.-P., "Les causes de foi de l'Inquisition de Tolède (1483–1820)," *Mélanges de la Casa de Velázquez*, 14 (1978), pp. 143–71.

Dedieu, J.-P., *L'Administration de la foi: L'Inquisition de Tolède, XVI–XVIIe siècles*. Madrid: Casa de Velázquez, 1989.

Dehergne, J., "Les Chrétientés de Chine de la période Ming, 1581–1650," *Monumenta Serica*, 16 (1957), pp. 1–136.

Dehergne, J., *Répertoire des Jésuites de Chine de 1552 à 1800*. Rome and Paris: Institutum Historicum Societatis Iesu/Letouzey & Ané, 1973.

Dejung, C., *Wahrheit und Häresie: Untersuchungen zur Geschichtsphilosophie bei Sebastian Franck*. Zürich: Samisdat, 1980.

Del Col, A., *Domenico Scandella Known as Menocchio: His Trials before the Inquisition (1583–1599)*, trans. J. and A. Tedeschi. Binghamton, NY: SUNY Press, 1996 (original ed. Pordonene, 1990).

Del Col, A. and Paolin, G., eds., *L'Inquisizione romano in Italia nell'età moderna*. Rome: Ufficio centrale per I beni archivistici, 1991.

Delumeau, J., *Catholicism Between Luther and Voltaire: A New View of the Counter-Reformation*, trans. Jeremy Moiser. London: Burns & Oates, 1977.

Deppermann, K., *Melchior Hoffman: Soziale Unruhen und apokalyptische Visionen im Zeitalter der Reformation*. Göttingen: Vandenhoeck & Ruprecht, 1979.

Descimon, R., *Qui étaient les Seize? Mythes et réalités de la Ligue parisienne (1585–1594)*. Paris: Fédération des Sociétés historiques et archéologiques de Paris et de l'Île-de-France, 1983.

Devlin, J., *The Superstitious Mind: French Peasants and the Supernatural in the Nineteenth Century*. New Haven, Conn.: Yale University Press, 1987.

Dharampal, G., *La Religion des Malabars, Tessier de Quéralay et la contribution des missionnaires européens à la naissance de l'indianisme*. Immensee: Nouvelle Revue de Science Missionnaire, 1982.

Dias, J. S. S., *O erasmismo e a Inquisição em Portugal: O processo de Fr. Valentim da Luz*. Coimbra: Faculdade de Letras Universidad de Coimbra, 1975.

Díaz del Castillo, B., *The Conquest of New Spain*, trans. J. M. Cohen. London: Penguin, 1963.

Dickens, A. G., ed., *Tudor Treatises*. Yorkshire Archaeological Society Record Series, vol. 123, 1959.

Dickens, A. G., *The English Reformation*. London: Batsford, 1964; 2nd ed., 1989.

Dickmann, F., *Der Westfälische Frieden*. Münster: Aschendorff, 1972.

Didier, H., "António de Andrade à l'origine de la tibétophilie européenne," *Aufsätze zur Portugiesischen Kulturgeschichte*, 20 (1988–92).

Diefendorf, B. B., *Beneath the Cross: Catholics and Huguenots in Sixteenth-Century Paris*. Oxford and New York: Oxford University Press, 1991.

Diefendorf, B. B., "Give Us Back Our Children: Patriarchal Authority and Parental Consent to Religious Vocations in Early Counter-Reformation France," *Journal of Modern History*, 68 (1996), pp. 265–307.

Dillon, A., *The Construction of Martyrdom in the English Catholic Community, 1535–1603*. Aldershot: Ashgate, 2002.

Dinan, S. E., "Confraternities as a Venue for Female Activism during the Catholic Reformation," in J. P. Donnelly and M. W. Maher, eds., *Confraternities and Catholic Reform in Italy, France, and Spain.* Kirksville, Mo.: Truman State University Press, 1999, pp. 191–214.

Dingel, I., *Concordia controversa: Die öffentlichen Diskussionen um das lutherische Konkordienwerk am Ende des 16. Jahrhunderts.* Gütersloh: Gütersloher Verlagshaus, 1996.

Dipple, G. L., *Antifraternalism and Reformation. Anticlericalism in the German Reformation: Johann Eberlin von Günzburg and the Campaign against the Friars.* Aldershot: Scolar Press, 1996.

Di Simplicio, O., *Inquisizione Stregoneria Medicina: Siena e il suo stato 1580–1721.* Siena: Il Leccio, 2000.

Dixon, C. S., *The Reformation and Rural Society: The Parishes of Brandenburg-Ansbach-Kulmbach, 1528–1603.* Cambridge: Cambridge University Press, 1996.

Dixon, C. S., *The Reformation in Germany.* Oxford: Blackwell, 2002.

Dmitrieva, M. and Lambrecht, K., eds., *Krakau, Prag und Wien: Funktionen von Metropolen im frühmodernen Staat.* Stuttgart: Franz Steiner, 2000.

Döllinger, J. Ignaz v., ed., *Dokumente vornehmlich zur Geschichte der Valdesier und Katharer (Beiträge zur Sektengeschichte des Mittelalters),* vol. 2. Munich: C. H. Beck, 1890.

Domínguez Ortiz, A., "Aspectos sociales de la vida eclesiastica en los siglos XVII y XVIII," in Ricardo García-Villoslada, ed., *Historia de la Iglesia en España.* Madrid: Biblioteca de Autores Cristianos, 1979, vol. 4, pp. 5–72.

Domínguez Ortiz, A., "Regalismo y relaciones Iglesia–Estado en el siglo XVII," in Ricardo García-Villoslada, ed., *Historia de la Iglesia en España.* Madrid: Biblioteca de Autores Cristianos, 1979, vol. 4, pp. 73–121.

Domínguez Ortiz, A., *El Antiguo Regimen: Los reys catolicos y los Austrias.* Madrid: Alianza editorial, 1988.

Dommann, F., "Der barocke Staat in der Schweiz," in O. Eberle, ed., *Barock in der Schweiz.* Einsiedeln: Benziger, 1930.

Donnelly, J. P., "The New Religious Orders, 1517–1648," in T. A. Brady, Jr., H. A. Oberman, and J. D. Tracy, eds., *Handbook of European History, 1400–1600: Late Middle Ages, Renaissance, and Reformation.* Grand Rapids, Mich.: Eerdmans, 1995, pp. 283–307.

Douglass, J. D., "Women and the Continental Reformation," in R. R. Ruether, ed., *Religion and Sexism.* New York: Simon & Schuster, 1974, pp. 292–318.

Douie, D. L., *The Nature and the Effect of the Heresy of the Fraticelli.* Manchester: Manchester University Press, 1932.

Duchhardt, H., ed., *Der Westfälische Friede: Diplomatie – politische Zäsur – kulturelles Umfeld – Rezeptionsgeschichte.* Munich: R. Oldenbourg, 1998.

Duchrow, U., *Christenheit und Weltverantwortung: Traditionsgeschichte und systematische Struktur der Zweirechelehre.* Stuttgart: Klett, 1970.

Duffy, E., *The Stripping of the Altars: Traditional Religion in England 1400–1580.* New Haven, Conn.: Yale University Press, 1992.

Duggan, L., "Fear and Confession on the Eve of the Reformation," *Archiv für Reformationsgeschichte,* 75 (1984).

Duke, A., *Reformation and Revolt in the Low Countries.* London/Ronceverte: Hambledon Press, 1990.

Dunne, G. H., *Generations of Giants: The Story of the Jesuits in China in the Last Decades of the Ming Dynasty.* South Bend, Ind.: University of Notre Dame Press, 1962.

Dupront, A., "Religion and Religious Anthropology," in J. Le Goff and P. Nora, eds., *Constructing the Past: Essays in Historical Methodology.* Cambridge: Cambridge University Press, 1985, pp. 123–50.

Dúran, D. de, *Book of the Gods and Rites and the Ancient Calendar,* trans. and ed. F. Horcasitas and D. Heyden. Norman: University of Oklahoma Press, 1971.

Dúran, D. de, *The History of the Indies of New Spain*, trans. D. Heyden. Norman: University of Oklahoma Press, 1994.

Durston, C. and Eales, J., eds., *The Culture of English Puritanism, 1560–1700*. Basingstoke: Macmillan, 1996.

Duteil, J.-P., *Le Mandat du Ciel: Le rôle des Jésuites en Chine*. Paris: Éditions Arguments, 1994.

Dyck, C. J., "The Suffering Church in Anabaptism," *Mennonite Quarterly Review*, 59 (1985), pp. 5–23.

Dykema, P. A. and Oberman, H. A. *Anticlericalism in Late Medieval and Early Modern Europe*. Leiden: Brill, 1993.

Ebeling, G., *Evangelische Evangelienauslegung, eine Unterschung zu Luthers Hermeneutik*. Munich: Lempp, 1942.

Ebeling, G., *Luther: An Introduction to his Thought*, trans. R. A. Wilson. Philadelphia: Fortress Press, 1970.

Eberhard, W., *Konfessionsbildung und Stände in Böhmen 1478–1530*. Veröffentlichungen des Collegium Carolinum, vol. 38. Munich: R. Oldenbourg, 1981.

Eberhard, W., *Monarchie und Widerstand: Zur ständischen Oppositionsbildung im Herrschaftssystem Ferdinands I. in Böhmen*. Veröffentlichungen des Collegium Carolinum, vol. 54. Munich: R. Oldenbourg, 1985.

Eberhard, W., "Entwicklungsphasen und Probleme der Gegenreformation und katholischen Erneuerung in Böhmen," *Römische Quartalschrift für christliche Altertumskunde und Kirchengeschichte*, 84 (1989), pp. 235–57.

Eberhard, W., "Die deutsche Reformation in Böhmen 1520–1620," In Hans Rothe, ed., *Deutsche in den Böhmischen Ländern*. Cologne: Böhlau, 1992.

Eberhard, W., "Konflikt und Integration: Die Dynamik in den Ergebnissen der Hussitenrevolution," *Studia Comeniana et Historica*, 22/48 (1992), pp. 31–55.

Edwards, M. U., Jr., *Luther and the False Brethren*. Stanford, Calif.: Stanford University Press, 1975.

Edwards, M. U., Jr., *Luther's Last Battles: Politics and Polemics, 1531–1546*. Ithaca, NY: Cornell University Press, 1983.

Edwards, M. U., Jr., *Printing, Propaganda, and Martin Luther*. Berkeley: University of California Press, 1994.

Egido, T., *Las claves de la Reforma y la Contrarreforma 1517–1648*. Barcelona: Editorial Planeta, 1991.

El Kenz, D., *Les Bûchers du roi: La culture protestante des martyres 1523–1572*. Seyssel: Champs Vallon, 1997.

Elliot, J. H., "Foreign Policy and Domestic Crisis: Spain 1598–1659," in K. Repgen, ed., *Krieg und Politik 1618–1648*. Munich: R. Oldenbourg, 1988, pp. 185–202.

Elton, G. R., *Policy and Police: The Enforcement of the Reformation in the Age of Thomas Cromwell*. Cambridge: Cambridge University Press, 1972.

Elton, G. R., *Reform and Reformation: England 1509–1558*. London: Edward Arnold, 1977.

Elton, G. R., *The Tudor Constitution*, 2nd ed. Cambridge: Cambridge University Press, 1982.

Englund, P., *Ofredsår: Om den svenska stormaktiden och en man i dess mitt*. Stockholm: Atlantis, 1993. German translation: *Die Verwüstung Deutschlands: Eine Geschichte des Dreißigjährigen Krieges*, trans. Wolfgang Butt. Stuttgart: Klett-Cotta, 1998.

Espinas, G., "Les guerres familiales dans la commune de Douai au XIII–XIVe siècles. Les trêves et les paix," *Nouvelle revue de droit français et étranger*, 1899.

Estié, P., *Het vluchtige bestaan van de eerste Nederlandse Lutherse gemeente, Antwerpen 1566–1567*. Amsterdam: Rodopi, 1986.

Etiemble, R., *Les Jésuites en Chine: La Querelle des Rites 1552–1773*. Paris: Julliard-Gallimard, 1966.

Etiemble, R., *L'Europe chinoise*, 2 vols. Paris: Gallimard, 1988, 1989.

Ettinger, S., "The Beginnings of Change in the Attitude of European Society Towards the Jews," *Scripta Hierosolymitana*, 7 (1961), pp. 193–219.

Evangelisti, S., "Wives, Widows, and the Brides of Christ: Marriage and the Convent in the Historiography of Early Modern Italy," *Historical Journal*, 43 (2000), pp. 233–47.

Evans, R. J. W., *Rudolf II and His World: A Study in Intellectual History, 1576–1612.* Oxford: Clarendon Press, 1973.

Evans, R. J. W., *The Wechsel Presses: Humanism and Calvinism in Central Europe 1572–1627.* Oxford: Oxford University Press, 1975.

Evans, R. J. W., *The Making of the Habsburg Monarchy, 1550–1700.* Oxford: Clarendon Press, 1979.

Evans, R. J. W., "Calvinism in East Central Europe: Hungary and Her Neighbours, 1500–1700," in Menna Prestwich, ed., *International Calvinism 1541–1715.* Oxford: Clarendon Press, 1986, pp. 167–96.

Evans, R. J. W. and Thomas, T. V., eds., *Crown, Church and Estates: Central European Politics in the Sixteenth and Seventeenth Centuries.* New York: St. Martin's Press, 1991.

Evennett, H. O., *The Spirit of the Counter-Reformation.* Notre Dame and London: University of Notre Dame Press, 1968.

Everitt, A., *The Community of Kent and the Great Rebellion, 1640–1660.* Leicester: Leicester University Press, 1966.

Fajardo Spinola, F., *Hechicería y brujería en Canarias en la Edad Moderna.* Las Palmas: Cabildo Insular de Gran Canaria, 1992.

Fang Hao, *Zhongguo tianzhujiao shi renwu zhuan*, 3 vols. Hong Kong/Taizhong: Gongjiao zhenli hui/Guangqi, 1973.

Farquhar, J. N., *Modern Religious Movements in India.* London: Munshiram Manoharlal, 1929.

Farriss, N. M., *Crown and Clergy in Colonial Mexico, 1759–1821.* London: Athlone Press, 1968.

Farriss, N. M., *Maya Society Under Colonial Rule: The Collective Enterprise of Survival.* Princeton, NJ: Princeton University Press, 1984.

Fast, H., ed., *Der linke Flügel der Reformation: Glaubenszeugnisse der Täufer, Spiritualisten, Schwärmer und Antitrinitarier.* Bremen: Carl Schünemann, 1962.

Fedorowicz, J. K., Bogucka, M., and Samsonowicz, H., eds., *A Republic of Nobles: Studies in Polish History to 1864.* Cambridge: Cambridge University Press, 1982.

Fernandes, M. de L. C., "Da reforma da Igreja à reforma dos cristãos," in Carlos Moreira Azevedo, ed., *História Religiosa de Portugal.* Lisbon: Círculo de Leitores, 2000, vol. 2, pp. 15–38.

Fernández Albaladejo, P., "Iglesia y configuración del poder en la monarquia católica (siglos XV–XVII): Algunas consideraciones," in *État et Église dans la génèse de l'État Moderne: Actes du colloque organisé par le Centre National de la Recherche Scientifique et la Casa de Velázquez.* Madrid: Casa de Velázquez, 1986, pp. 209–16.

Fernández Collado, A., "Felipe II y su mentalidad reformadora en el concilio provincial toledano de 1565," *Hispania Sacra*, 50/101 (1998), pp. 447–66.

Fernández Terricabras, I., *Felipe II y el clero secular: La aplicacion del Concilio de Trento.* Madrid: Sociedad Estatal para la Conmemoración de los Centenarios de Felipe II y Carlos V, 2000.

Ferroli, D., S.J., *The Jesuits in Malabar*, 2 vols. Bangalore: Bangalore Press, 1939–51.

Fincham, K., ed., *The Early Stuart Church, 1603–1642.* Basingstoke: Macmillan, 1993.

Firpo, M., *Tra alumbrados e "spirituali": Studi su Juan de Valdés e il valdesianesimo nella crisi religiosa del '500 italiano.* Florence: Olschki, 1990.

Firpo, M., *Inquisizione romana e Controriforma: Studi sul cardinal Giovanni Morone e il suo processo d'eresia.* Bologna: Il Mulino, 1992.

Firpo, M., *Riforma protestante ed eresie nell'Italia del Cinquecento*. Rome/Bari: Laterza, 1993.

Firpo, M., *Gli affreschi di Pontormo a San Lorenzo: Eresia, politica e cultura nella Firenze di Cosimo I.* Turin: Einaudi, 1997.

Firpo, M., *Dal sacco di Roma all'Inquisizione: Studi su Juan de Valdés e la Riforma italiana*. Alessandria: Edizioni dell'Orso, 1998.

Firpo, M. and Marcatto, D., eds., *Il processo inquisitoriale del Cardinal Giovanni Morone*, 6 vols. Rome: Istituto Storico Italiano per l'Età moderna e contemporanea, 1981–95.

Flogaus, R., *Theosis bei Palamas und Luther*. Göttingen: Vandenhoeck & Ruprecht, 1997.

Flores, J. M., "'Cael Velho', 'Calepatanão' and 'Punicale': The Portuguese and the Tambraparni Ports in the Sixteenth Century," *Bulletin de l'École française d'Extrême-Orient*, 1995.

Flores, J. M., *Os Portugueses e o Mar de Ceilão: Trato, Diplomacia e Guerra (1498–1543)*. Lisbon: Cosmos, 1998.

Flores, J. M., *"Um Curto História de Ceylan"*: *Five Hundred Years of Relations between Portugal and Sri Lanka*. Lisbon: Fundação Oriente, 2001.

Fonseca, F. T. da, "Origem social do clero conimbricense no século XVI (1581–1585)," *Actas do simpósio internacional comemorativo do IV Centenário da morte de Juão de Ruão*. Coimbra: Epartur, 1982, pp. 27–56.

Forde, G. O., *Justification by Faith: A Matter of Death and Life*. Philadelphia: Fortress Press, 1982.

Forde, G. O., *On Being a Theologian of the Cross: Reflections on Luther's Heidelberg Disputation, 1518*. Grand Rapids, Mich.: Eerdmans, 1997.

Foxe, J., *The Acts and Monuments of John Foxe*, ed. Josiah Pratt, 8 vols. London: The Religious Tract Society [1877].

Fragnita, G., *La Bibbia al rogo: La censura ecclesiastica e I volgarizzamenti della Scrittura (1471–1605)*. Bologna: Il Mulino, 1997.

Fróis, L., S.J., *La Première Ambassade du Japon en Europe, 1582–1592*, ed. J. A. Abranches Pinto, Yoshitomo Okamoto, and Henri Bernard, S. J. Tokyo: Sophia University, Monumenta Nipponica Monograph 6, 1942.

Fróis, L., S.J., *Historia de Japam*, ed. J. Wicki, S.J., 5 vols. Lisbon: Biblioteca Nacional, 1976–84.

François, É., *Die unsichtbare Grenze: Protestanten und Katholiken in Augsburg 1648–1806*. Sigmaringen: Thorbecke, 1991.

Frank, G., ed., *Der Theologe Melanchthon*. Sigmaringen: Thorbecke, 2000.

Fredericq, P., ed., *Het Nederlandsch proza in de zestiendeeuwsche pamfletten uit den tijd der beroerten*. Brussels, 1907.

Friedman, J., *The Most Ancient Testimony: Sixteenth-Century Christian-Hebraica in the Age of Renaissance Nostalgia*. Athens, OH: Ohio University Press, 1983.

Fuchs, W. P., ed., *Akten zur Geschichte des Bauernkriegs in Mitteldeutschland*, vol. 2. Jena/Aalen: Scientia, 1942/1964.

Fuchs-Mansfeld, R. G., *De Sefardim in Amsterdam tot 1795: Aspecten van een joodse minderheid in een Hollandse stad*. Hilversum: Verloren, 1989.

Fučíková, E., ed., *Rudolf II and Prague: The Imperial Court and Residential City as the Cultural and Spiritual Home of Central Europe*. Prague, London, Milan: Prague Castle Administration, Thames & Hudson, Skira, 1997.

Fudge, T. A., *The Magnificent Ride: The First Reformation in Hussite Bohemia*. Aldershot: Ashgate, 1998.

Fujita, N. S., *Japan's Encounter with Christianity: The Catholic Mission in Pre-Modern Japan*. Mahwah, NJ: Paulist Press, 1991.

Gagliano, J. A. and Ronan, C. E., eds., *Jesuit Encounters in the New World: Jesuit Chroniclers, Geographers, Educators, and Missionaries in the Americas, 1549–1767*. Rome: Institutum Historicum Societatis Iesu, 1997.

Gal, S., *Grenoble au temps de la Ligue: Étude politique, sociale et religieuse d'une cité en crise (vers 1562–vers 1598)*. Grenoble: Presses Universitaires de Grenoble, 2000.

Galpern, A. N., *The Religions of the People in Sixteenth-Century Champagne*. Cambridge: Cambridge University Press, 1976.

García Cárcel, R., *Orígines de la Inquisición española: El tribunal de Valencia (1478–1530)*. Barcelona: Península, 1976.

García Cárcel, R., *Herejía y sociedad: La Inquisición en Valencia 1530–1609*. Barcelona: Península, 1980.

García Carcél, R., "La iglesia triunfante," in *Arte y saber: La cultura en tiempos de Felipe III y Felipe IV*. Madrid: Ministerio de Educación y Cultura, 1999, pp. 77–87.

García-Gallo, A., "Las Bullas de Alejandro VI y el ordenamiento jurídico de la expansión portuguesa y castellana en Africa e Indias," in *Los orígines españoles de las instituciones americanas: Estudios de derecho indiano*. Madrid: R. Academia de Jurisprudencia y Legislación, Conmemoración del V Centenario del descubrimiento de América, 1987.

García Icazbalceta, J., *Bibliografía mexicana del siglo XVI: Catálogo razonado de libros impresos en México de 1539 a 1600*. Mexico: Fondo de Cultura Económica, 1954.

Garcilaso de la Vega el Inca, *Royal Commentaries of the Incas and General History of Peru*, 2 vols. trans. H. V. Livermore. Austin: University of Texas Press, 1966.

Gardiner, S. R., *History of the Great Civil War, 1642–1649*, 4 vols. Adlestrop: Windrush Press, 1987, 1991.

Garrisson, J., *Les Protestants au XVIe siècle*. Paris: Fayard, 1988.

Gaubil, A., *Correspondance de Pékin 1722–1759*, ed. Renée Simon. Geneva: Droz, 1970.

George, T., "The Spirituality of the Radical Reformation," in Jill Raitt, ed., *Christian Spirituality: High Middle Ages and Reformation*. New York: Crossroad, 1987.

Gernet, J., *China and the Christian Impact*. Cambridge: Cambridge University Press, 1985.

Ghesquière, T., *Mathieu de Castro, premier vicaire apostolique aux Indes*. Louvain: Apostolat monastique et missionnaire, 1937.

Gibson, C., *The Aztecs Under Spanish Rule: A History of the Indians of the Valley of Mexico, 1519–1810*. Stanford, Calif.: Stanford University Press, 1964.

Giles, M., ed., *Women in the Inquisition: Spain and the New World*. Baltimore: Johns Hopkins University Press, 1999.

Ginzburg, C., *The Cheese and the Worms*, trans. J. and A. Tedeschi. Baltimore: Johns Hopkins University Press, 1980 (original ed. Turin, 1975).

Ginzburg, C., *The Night Battles: Witchcraft and Agrarian Cults in the Sixteenth and Seventeenth Centuries*. London: Routledge & Kegan Paul, 1983.

Girard, P., *Os Religiosos Ocidentais na China na Época moderna*. Macao: Fundação Macáu, 1999.

Godinho, V. M., *Estrutura da antiga sociedade portuguesa*. Lisbon: Arcádia, 1977.

Godman, P., *The Saint as Censor: Robert Bellarmine Between Inquisition and Index*. Leiden: Brill, 2000.

Goertz, H.-J., *Innere und äussere Ordnung in der Theologie Thomas Müntzers*. Leiden: Brill, 1967.

Goertz, H.-J., ed., *Umstrittenes Täufertum 1525–1975: Neue Forschungen*, 2nd ed. Göttingen: Vandenhoeck & Ruprecht, 1977.

Goertz, H.-J., ed., *Radikale Reformatoren: 21 biographische Skizzen von Thomas Müntzer bis Paracelsus*. Munich: Beck, 1978.

Goertz, H.-J., *Pfaffenhass und gross Geschrei: Reformatorische Bewegungen in Deutschland 1517 bis 1529*. Munich: Beck, 1987.

Goertz, H.-J., *Die Täufer: Geschichte und Deutung*, 2nd ed. Munich: Beck, 1988.

Goertz, H.-J., *Thomas Müntzer: Mystiker, Apokalyptiker, Revolutionär*. Munich: Beck, 1989.

Goertz, H.-J., *Religiöse Bewegungen in der Frühen Neuzeit*. Munich: Beck, 1993.

Goertz, H.-J., *Thomas Müntzer: Apocalyptic, Mystic and Revolutionary*, trans. Jocelyn Jaquiery, ed. Peter Matheson. Edinburgh: T. & T. Clark, 1993.

Goertz, H.-J., *Antiklerikalismus und Reformation: Sozialgeschichtliche Untersuchungen*. Göttingen: Vandenhoeck & Ruprecht, 1995.

Goldie, M., "The Theory of Religious Intolerance in Restoration England," in Ole Peter Grell, Jonathan I. Israel, and Nicholas Tyacke, eds., *From Persecution to Tolerance*. Oxford: Clarendon Press, 1991, pp. 331–68.

Gonçalves, S., S.J., *Primeira Parte da Historia dos Religiosos da Companhia de Jesus e do que fizeram com a divina graça na conversão dos infieis a nossa sancta fee catholica nos reynos e provincias da India Oriental*, ed. José Wicki, S. J. Coimbra: Atlântida, Coimbra, 1957–62.

González, J. M., *Historia de las Misiones Dominicanas de China*. Vol. 1: *1632–1700*; vol. 2: *1700–1800*. Madrid: Juan Bravo, 1962, 1964.

González García, J. L., "La sombra de Dios: Imitatio Christi y contrición en la piedad privada de Felipe II," in *Felipe II. Un monarca y su epoca: Un príncipe del Renacimiento*. Madrid: Sociedad Estatal para la Conmemoración de los centenarios de Felipe II y Carlos V, 1998, pp. 185–201.

Goodbar, R. L., ed., *The Edict of Nantes: Five Essays and a New Translation*. Bloomington, Minn.: The National Huguenot Society, 1998.

Goosens, A., *Les Inquisitions modernes dans les Pays-Bas Méridionaux (1520–1633)*, 2 vols. Brussels: Éditions de l'Université de Bruxelles, 1998.

Gordon, B., *Clerical Discipline and the Rural Reformation: The Synod in Zurich, 1532–1580*. Bern, 1992.

Gordon, B., "Toleration in the Early Swiss Reformation: The Art and Politics of Niklaus Manuel of Berne," in O. P. Grell and B. Scribner, eds., *Tolerance and Intolerance in the European Reformation*. Cambridge: Cambridge University Press, 1996, pp. 128–44.

Gosner, K., *Soldiers of the Virgin: The Moral Economy of a Colonial Maya Rebellion*. Tucson: University of Arizona Press, 1992.

Gouveia, A. C., "A sacramentalização dos ritos de passagem," in Carlos Moreira Azevedo, ed., *História Religiosa de Portugal*. Lisbon: Círculo de Leitores, 2000, vol. 2, pp. 529–57.

Gracias, F. da Silva, *Health and Hygiene in Colonial Goa (1510–1961)*. New Delhi: Oxford University Press, 1994.

Gracias, F. da Silva, *Beyond the Self: Santa Casa da Misericórdia de Goa*. Panaji, Goa: Surya Publications, 2000.

Graciotti, S., *Italia e Boemia nella cornice del Rinascimento europeo*. Florence: L. S. Olschki, 1999.

Grandjean, M. and Roussel, B., eds., *Coexister dans l'intolérance: L'édit de Nantes (1598)*. Geneva: Labor et Fides, 1998.

Grane, L., *Martinus Noster: Luther in the German Reform Movement, 1518–1521*. Mainz: Zabern, 1994.

Graus, F., "Das Spätmittelalter als Krisenzeit: Eine Literaturbericht als Zwischenbilanz," *Mediaevalia Bohemica*, 1 (1969), Supplement.

Green, I., "'Reformed Pastors' and Bons Curés: The Changing Role of the Parish Clergy in Early Modern Europe," in W. J. Sheils and Diana Wood, eds., *The Ministry: Clerical and Lay*. Studies in Church History, 26. Oxford: Blackwell, 1989, pp. 249–86.

Green, I. M., *The Reestablishment of the Church of England*. Oxford: Oxford University Press, 1978.

Greengrass, M., "A Day in the Life of the Third Estate: Blois, 26th December 1576," in Adrianna E. Bakos, ed., *Politics, Ideology and the Law in Early Modern Europe*. Rochester, NY: University of Rochester Press, 1994, pp. 73–90.

Greengrass, M., *France in the Age of Henri IV*, 2nd ed. London and New York: Longman, 1995.

Greengrass, M., "Informal Networks in Sixteenth-Century French Protestantism," in Raymond A. Mentzer and Andrew Spicer, eds., *Society and Culture in the Huguenot World 1559–1685*. Cambridge: Cambridge University Press, 2002, pp. 78–97.

Greenleaf, R. E., *The Mexican Inquisition of the Sixteenth Century*. Albuquerque: University of New Mexico Press, 1969.

Greenleaf, R. E., ed., *The Roman Catholic Church in Colonial Latin America*. New York: Knopf, 1971.

Gregory, B. S., *Salvation at Stake: Christian Martyrdom in Early Modern Europe*. Cambridge, Mass.: Harvard University Press, 1999.

Grell, O. P. and Porter, R., eds., *Toleration in Enlightenment Europe*. Cambridge: Cambridge University Press, 2000.

Grell, O. P., and Scribner, B., eds., *Tolerance and Intolerance in the European Reformation*. Cambridge: Cambridge University Press, 1996.

Grendler, P., *The Roman Inquisition and the Venetian Press, 1540–1605*. Princeton, NJ: Princeton University Press, 1977.

Greyerz, K. von, *Religion und Kultur: Europa, 1500–1800*. Göttingen: Vandenhoeck & Ruprecht, 2000.

Gruzinski, S., *Man-Gods in the Mexican Highlands: Indian Power and Colonial Society, 1520–1800*. Stanford, Calif.: Stanford University Press, 1989.

Gruzinski, S., *The Conquest of Mexico: The Incorporation of Indian Societies into the Western World, 16th–18th Centuries*. Cambridge: Polity Press, 1993.

Gruzinski, S., "Les mondes mêlés de la monarchie catholique et autres 'connected histories,'" *Annales*, 56/1 (Jan.–Feb. 2001), pp. 85–117.

Guerreiro, F., S.J., *Relação Annual das Coisas que Fizeram os Padres da Companhia de Jesus nas suas Missões nos anos de 1600 a 1609*, 3 vols. Coimbra: Imprensa da Universidade, 1929–42.

Guggisberg, H. R., *Basel in the Sixteenth Century: Aspects of the City Republic before, during, and after the Reformation*. St. Louis, Mo.: Center for Reformation Research, 1982.

Guggisberg, H. R., "Tolerance and Intolerance in Sixteenth-Century Basle," in O. P. Grell and B. Scribner, eds., *Tolerance and Intolerance in the European Reformation*. Cambridge: Cambridge University Press, 1996, pp. 145–63.

Guy, J., "Henry VIII and the *Praemunire* Manoeuvres of 1530–1531," *English Historical Review*, 97 (1982), pp. 481–503.

Guy, J., *Tudor England*. Oxford: Oxford University Press, 1988.

Haan, H., "Prosperität und Dreißigjähriger Krieg," *Geschichte und Gesellschaft*, 7 (1991), pp. 91–118.

Hagen, K., *Luther's Approach to Scripture as Seen in his "Commentaries" on Galatians 1519–1538*. Tübingen: Mohr/Siebeck, 1993.

Haigh, C., "The Recent Historiography of the English Reformation," in C. Haigh, *The English Reformation Revised*. Cambridge: Cambridge University Press, 1987.

Haigh, C., *English Reformations: Religion, Politics, and Society under the Tudors*. Oxford: Oxford University Press, 1993.

Haliczer, S., *Inquisition and Society in the Kingdom of Valencia, 1478–1834*. Berkeley: University of California Press, 1990.

Haliczer, S., *Sex in the Confessional*. Berkeley: University of California Press, 1996.

Halliday, P., *Dismembering the Body Politic*. Cambridge: Cambridge University Press, 1998.

Hamm, B., Moeller, B., and Wendebourg, D., *Reformationstheorien: Ein kirchenhistoricher Disput über Einheit und Vielfalt der Reformation*. Göttingen: Vandenhoeck & Ruprecht, 1995.

Hanke, L., *All Mankind is One: A Study of the Disputation between Bartolomé de Las Casas and Juan Ginés de Sepúlveda in 1550 on the Intellectual and Religious Capacity of the American Indians*. De Kalb: Northern Illinois University Press, 1974.

Hanke, L., *The Spanish Struggle for Justice in the Conquest of America*. New York: American Historical Association, 1949.

Hanke, L., *Aristotle and the American Indians: A Study in Race Prejudice in the Modern World*. Chicago: Henry Regnery, 1959.

Han Qi, *Zhongguo kexue jishu de xichuan jiqi yingxiang*. Shijiazhuang: Hebei Remin chubanshe, 1999.

Hanzal, J., "Rekatolizace v Čechách: jeji historický smysl a význam," *Sborník historický*, 37 (1990), pp. 37–91.

Harasimowicz, J., *Treści i funkcje ideowe sztuki śląskiej reformacji, 1520–1650*. Wrocław, 1986.

Harasimowicz, J., "Die Glaubenskonflikte und die kirchliche Kunst der Konfessional-isierungszeit in Schlesien," *Berichte und Beiträge des Geisteswissenschaftliches Zentrums Osmitteleuropas* (1997), pp. 149–69.

Harding, R. R., "The Mobilization of Confraternities Against the Reformation in France," *Sixteenth Century Journal*, 11/2 (1980), pp. 85–107.

Harline, C., *The Burdens of Sister Margaret*. New York: Doubleday, 1994.

Harline, C., "Actives and Contemplatives: The Female Religious of the Low Countries Before and After Trent," *Catholic Historical Review*, 89 (1995), pp. 541–67.

Harline, C. and Put, E., *A Bishop's Tale*. New Haven, Conn.: Yale University Press, 2000.

Harnack, T., *Luthers Theologie*, 2 vols. Erlangen: Blaesing, 1862, 1886.

Harrington, J. F., *Reordering Marriage and Society in Reformation Germany*. Cambridge: Cambridge University Press, 1995.

Harris, R., *Lourdes: Body and Spirit in the Secular Age*. New York: Viking, 1999.

Harris, T., Seaward, P., and Goldie, M., eds., *The Politics of Religion in Restoration England*. Oxford: Blackwell, 1990.

Hausenblasová, J. and Šroněk, M., *Gloria & Miseria 1618–1648: Prague during the Thirty Years' War*. Prague, 1998.

Haydon, C., *Anti-Catholicism in Eighteenth-Century England, c.1714–80: A Political and Social Study*. Manchester: Manchester University Press, 1993.

Head, R. C., "Shared Lordship, Authority, and Administration: The Exercise of Dominion in the *Gemeine Herrschaften* of the Swiss Confederation, 1417–1600," *Central European History*, 30 (1997), pp. 489–512.

Head, R. C., "Catholics and Protestants in Graubünden: Confessional Discipline and Confessional Identities without an Early Modern State," *German History*, 17 (1999), pp. 321–45.

Hebdige, D., *Subculture: The Meaning of Style*. London: Methuen, 1979.

Hendrix, S., *Luther and the Papacy: Stages in a Reformation Conflict*. Philadelphia: Fortress Press, 1981.

Hendrix, S., "Luther's Impact on the Sixteenth Century," *Sixteenth Century Journal*, 16 (1985), pp. 3–14.

Hendrix, S., "American Luther Research in the Twentieth Century," *Lutheran Quarterly*, 15 (2001), pp. 1–23.

Hendrix, S., "Martin Luther und die Lutherischen Bekenntnisschriften in der englis-chsprachigen Forschung seit 1983," *Lutherjahrbuch*, 68 (2001), pp. 115–36.

Henningsen, G., "El 'banco de datos' del Santo Oficio: las relaciones de causas de la Inquisi-ción española (1550–1700)," *Boletín de la Real Academia de la Historia*, 174 (1977), pp. 547–70.

Henningsen, G., *The Witches' Advocate: Basque Witchcraft and the Spanish Inquisition*. Reno: University of Nevada Press, 1980.

Henningsen, G., "The Database of the Spanish Inquisition: The *relaciones de causas* Project Revisited," in H. Mohnhaupt and D. Simon, eds., *Vorträge zur Justizforschung: Geschichte und Theorie*, 2 vols. Frankfurt a.M., 1993, vol. 2, pp. 43–85.

Henningsen, G., and Tedeschi, J., eds., *The Inquisition in Early Modern Europe: Studies in Sources and Methods*. De Kalb: Northern Illinois University Press, 1986.

Herlihy, D., *Medieval Households*. Cambridge, Mass.: Harvard University Press, 1985.

Hernandes, A. S., S.J., "La obra Persa da un Jesuita Navarro, E. P. Jerónimo Javier," *Estudios Eclesiasticos*, 29 (1955).

Hertzberg, A., *The French Enlightenment and the Jews*. New York: Columbia University Press, 1968.

Heyd, D., ed., *Toleration: An Elusive Virtue*. Princeton, NJ: Princeton University Press, 1996.

Heymann, F. G., *John Zizka and the Hussite Revolution*. Princeton, NJ: Princeton University Press, 1955.

Heymann, F. G., *George of Bohemia, King of Heretics*. Princeton, NJ: Princeton University Press, 1965.

Hill, C., *Society and Puritanism in Pre-Revolutionary England*. New York: Schocken Books, 1964.

Hlaváček, P., "Beginnings of the Bohemian Reformation in the Northwest: The Waldensians and the Reformers in the Deanery of Kadaň at the Turn of the Fourteenth Century," in Z. V. David and D. R. Holeton, eds., *The Bohemian Reformation and Religious Practice*, vol. 4. Prague: Main Library of the Academy of Sciences of the Czech Republic, 2002, pp. 43–56.

Hojda, Z., "Zastavení nad novým soupisem italik od Jaroslavy Kašparové a nad literaturou k českoitalským vztahům vůbec," *Folio Historica Bohemica*, 15 (1991), pp. 481–95.

Hojda, Z., ed., *Kultura baroka v Čechách a na Moravě*. Prague: Historický ústav Českosloven-ské akademie věd, 1992.

Holeton, D. R., "The Bohemian Eucharistic Movement in its European Context," In David R. Holeton, ed., *The Bohemian Reformation and Religious Practice*, vol. 1. Prague: Academy of Sciences of the Czech Republic Main Library, 1996, pp. 23–48.

Holl, K., "Die Rechtfertigungslehre in Luthers Vorlesung über den Römerbrief," in *Gesammelte Aufsätze zur Kirchengeschichte*. Vol. 1: *Luther*. Tübingen: Mohr/Siebeck, 1921, pp. 111–54.

Holt, M. P., *The French Wars of Religion, 1562–1629*. Cambridge and New York: Cambridge University Press, 1995.

Hornedo, R. M., "Teatro e Iglesia en los siglos XVII y XVIII," in Ricardo García-Villoslada, ed., *Historia de la Iglesia en España*. Madrid: Biblioteca de Autores Cristianos, 1979, vol. 4, pp. 309–58.

Howell, R., Jr., *Newcastle upon Tyne and the Puritan Revolution: A Study of the Civil War*. Oxford: Oxford University Press, 1967.

Hroch, M., "Wirtschaftliche und gesellschaftliche Voraussetzungen des Dreißigjährigen Krieges: Einige Überlegungen zu einem offenen Problem," in K. Repgen, ed., *Krieg und Politik 1618–1648*. Munich: R. Oldenbourg, 1988, pp. 133–50.

Hsia, R. Po-chia, *Society and Religion in Münster, 1535–1618*. New Haven, Conn.: Yale University Press, 1984.

Hsia, R. Po-chia, ed., *The German People and the Reformation*. Ithaca, NY: Cornell University Press, 1988.

Hsia, R. Po-chia, *The Myth of Ritual Murder: Jews and Magic in Reformation Germany*. New Haven, Conn.: Yale University Press, 1988.

Hsia, R. Po-chia, *Social Discipline in the Reformation: Central Europe, 1550–1750*. London: Routledge, 1989.

Hsia, R. Po-chia, *Trent 1475: Stories of a Ritual Murder Trial*. New Haven, Conn.: Yale University Press, 1992.

Hsia, R. Po-chia, "Mission und Konfessionalisierung in Übersee: Die Chinamission und das Heilige Römische Reich," in Wolfgang Reinhard and Heinz Schilling, eds., *Katholische Konfessionalisierung*. Münster: Aschendorff, 1995, pp. 114–19.

Hsia, R. Po-chia and Lehmann, H., eds., *In and Out of the Ghetto: Jewish–Gentile Relations in Late Medieval and Early Modern Germany*. New York: Cambridge University Press, 1995.

Hsia, R. Po-chia and Van Nierop, H. F. K., eds., *Calvinism and Religious Toleration in the Dutch Golden Age*. Cambridge: Cambridge University Press, 2002.

Huang Yilong, "Ming Qing tianzhujiao zai Shanxi Jiangzhou de fazhan ji qi fantan," *Zhongyang yanjiuyuan jindaishi yanjiusuo jikan*, 26 (1996), pp. 3–39.

Hu-De Hart, E., *Missionaries, Miners, and Indians: Spanish Contact with the Yaqui Nation of Northwestern New Spain, 1533–1820*. Tucson: University of Arizona Press, 1981.

Hudson, A., ed., *Selections from English Wycliffite Writings*. Cambridge: Cambridge University Press, 1978.

Hudson, A., *The Premature Reformation: Wycliffite Texts and Lollard History*. Oxford: Clarendon Press, 1988.

Hudson, A. and Gradon, P., eds., *English Wycliffite Sermons*, 5 vols. Oxford: Clarendon Press, 1983–96.

Huertas Vallejos, L., *La religion en una sociedad rural andina, siglo XVII*. Ayacucho: Universidad Nacional de San Cristóbal de Huamanga, 1981.

Hughes, A., *Politics, Society, and Civil War in Warwickshire, 1620–1660*. Cambridge: Cambridge University Press, 1987.

Hughes, A., *The Causes of the English Civil War*, 2nd ed. Basingstoke: Macmillan, 1998.

Huizinga, J., *The Waning of the Middle Ages*. New York: Doubleday, repr. 1954.

Hunt, A., "The Lord's Supper in Early Modern England," *Past and Present*, 161 (1998), pp. 39–83.

Huseman, W. H., "The Expression of the Idea of Toleration in French During the Sixteenth Century," *Sixteenth Century Journal*, 15 (1984), pp. 293–310.

Hutchison, A. M., "Syon Abbey: Dissolution, No Decline," *Birgittiana*, 2 (1996), pp. 245–59.

Hutton, R., *The Restoration*. Oxford: Oxford University Press, 1985.

Hutton, R., *Charles II*. Oxford: Oxford University Press, 1989.

Ingram, M., *Church Courts, Sex, and Marriage in England, 1570–1640*. Cambridge: Cambridge University Press, 1987.

Israel, J., *European Jewry in the Age of Mercantilism, 1550–1750*. Oxford: Clarendon Press, 1989.

Israel, J., *The Dutch Republic, Its Rise, Greatness and Fall 1477–1806*. Oxford: Oxford University Press, 1995.

Israel, J. and Katz, D., eds., *Sceptics, Millenarians, and Jews: Essays in Honour of Richard Popkin*. Leiden: Brill, 1990.

Jankofsky, K., "National Characteristics in the Portrayal of English Saints in the South English Legendary," in R. Blumenfeld-Kosinski and T. Szells, eds., *Images of Sainthood in Medieval Europe*. Ithaca, NY: Cornell University Press, 1991, pp. 81–93.

Janz, D., *Luther on Thomas Aquinas*. Stuttgart: Franz Steiner, 1989.

Jennes, J., C.I.C.M., *A History of the Catholic Church in Japan*. Tokyo: Oriens Institute, 1973.

Jones, C., Newitt, M., and Roberts, S., eds., *Politics and People in Revolutionary England: Essays in Honour of Ivan Roots*. Oxford: Blackwell, 1986.

Jones, J. R., ed., *The Restored Monarchy, 1660–1688*. Totowa, NJ: Rowman & Littlefield, 1979.

Jones, N., *Faith by Statute: Parliament and the Settlement of Religion 1559*. London: Royal Historical Society, 1982.

Jordan, W. K., *The Development of Religious Toleration in England*, 4 vols. Cambridge, Mass.: Harvard University Press, 1932–40.

Jouanna, A., *La France du XVIe siècle (1483–1598)*. Paris: Presses Universitaires de France, 1996.

Jouanna, A., *Le Devoir de révolte: La noblesse française et la gestation de l'État moderne, 1559–1661.* Paris: Fayard, 1989.

Joutard, P., "The Revocation of the Edict of Nantes: End or Renewal of French Calvinism?," in Menna Prestwich, ed., *International Calvinism 1541–1715.* Oxford: Clarendon Press, 1985, pp. 339–68.

Junghans, H., ed., *Leben und Werk Martin Luthers von 1526 bis 1546,* 2 vols. Göttingen: Vandenhoeck & Ruprecht, 1983.

Junghans, H., *Der junge Luther und die Humanisten.* Göttingen: Vandenhoeck & Ruprecht, 1985.

Jussie, J. de, *Petite chronique,* ed. H. Feld. Mainz: Philipp von Zabern, 1996.

Kafka, F. and Skýbová, A., *Husitský epilog na koncilu tridenském a koncepce habsburské rekatolizace Čech: Počátky obnoveného pražského arcibiskupství.* Prague: Univerzita Karlova, 1969.

Kagan, R., *Lucrezia's Dreams.* Baltimore: Johns Hopkins University Press, 1990.

Kaiser, M., *Politik und Kriegführung: Maximilian von Bayern und die Katholische Liga im Dreißigjährigen Krieg.* Münster: Aschendorff, 1999.

Kaiser, M., "Die Söldner und die Bevölkerung: Überlegungen zu Konstituierung und Überwindung eines lebensweltlichen Antagonismus," in Stefan Kroll and Kersten Krüger, eds., *Militär und ländliche Gesellschaft in der frühen Neuzeit.* Münster: Lit, 2000, pp. 79–120.

Kalivoda, R., "Husitství a jeho vyústění v době předbělohorské a pobělohorské," *Studia Comeniana et Historica,* 25/13 (1993), pp. 3–44.

Kamat, P., *Farar Far (Crossfire): Local Resistance to Colonial Hegemony in Goa, 1510–1912.* Panaji, Goa: Institute Menezes Braganza, 1999.

Kamen, H., *The Rise of Toleration.* New York: McGraw-Hill, 1967.

Kamen, H., *Spain, 1469–1714: A Society of Conflict.* London: Longman, 1983.

Kamen, H., *The Phoenix and the Flame: Catalonia and the Counter-Reformation.* New Haven, Conn.: Yale University Press, 1993.

Kamen, H., *The Spanish Inquisition: A Historical Revision.* New Haven, Conn.: Yale University Press, 1997.

Kaminsky, H., "The Prague Insurrection of 30 July 1419," *Medievalia et Humanistica,* 17 (1966), pp. 106–26.

Kaminsky, H., *A History of the Hussite Revolution.* Berkeley: University of California Press, 1967.

Kaminsky, H., "The Problematics of 'Heresy' and 'The Reformation,'" in František Šmahel, ed., *Häresie und vorzeitige Reformation in Spätmittelalter.* Munich: R. Oldenbourg, 1998, pp. 1–22.

Kampmann, C., *Reichsrebellion und kaiserliche Acht: Politische Strafjustiz im Dreißigjährigen Krieg und den Verfahren gegen Wallenstein 1634.* Münster: Aschendorff, 1992.

Kaplan, B. J., *Calvinists and Libertines: Confession and Community in Utrecht, 1578–1620.* Oxford: Oxford University Press, 1995.

Kaplan, B. J., "Fictions of Privacy: House Chapels and the Spatial Accommodation of Religious Dissent in Early Modern Europe," *American Historical Review,* 107 (2002), pp. 1031–64.

Karant-Nunn, S., *Luther's Pastors: The Reformation in the Ernstine Countryside.* Philadelphia: American Philosophical Society, 1979.

Karant-Nunn, S., "Tolerance and Intolerance in Sixteenth-Century Hungary," in Ole Peter Grell and Bob Scribner, eds., *Tolerance and Intolerance in the European Reformation.* Cambridge: Cambridge University Press, 1996.

Karant-Nunn, S., *The Reformation of Ritual: An Interpretation of Early Modern Germany.* London and New York: Routledge, 1997.

Katz, D., *Philosemitism and the Readmission of the Jews to England, 1603–1655.* Oxford: Clarendon Press, 1982.

Katz, J., *Tradition and Crisis: Jewish Society at the End of the Middle Ages*, trans. Bernard Dov
   Cooperman. New York: Schocken Books, 1993.
Kaufmann, T. D., *Court, Cloister, and City: The Art and Culture of Central Europe 1450–1800*.
   Chicago: University of Chicago Press, 1995.
Kaye, J. W., *Christianity in India: An Historical Narrative*. London, 1859.
Kenyon, J. P., *Stuart England*, 2nd ed. Harmondsworth: Penguin, 1985.
King, G., "Couplet's Biography of Madame Candida Xu (1607–1680)", *Sino-Western
   Cultural Relations Journal*, 18 (1996), pp. 41–56.
King, R., *Orientalism and Religion: Postcolonial Theory, India and "The Mystic East."* New
   Delhi: Oxford University Press, 1999.
Kingdon, R. M., *Geneva and the Coming of the Wars of Religion in France, 1555–1563*. Geneva:
   Droz, 1956.
Kingdon, R. M., *Geneva and the Consolidation of the French Protestant Movement, 1564–1572*.
   Geneva: Droz, 1957.
Kingdon, R. M., "The Church in Calvin's Geneva," a section of four articles in *Church and
   Society in Reformation Europe*. London: Variorum Reprints, 1985.
Kingdon, R. M., "Popular Reactions to the Debate between Bolsec and Calvin," in Willem
   van 't Spijker, ed., *Calvin: Erbe und Auftrag, festschrift für Wilhelm Neuser*. Kampen: Kok,
   1991.
Kittelson, J. M., "Successes and Failures in the German Reformation: The Report from
   Strasbourg," *Archiv für Reformationsgeschichte*, 73 (1982), pp. 153–75.
Kittelson, J. M., *Martin Luther: The Story of the Man and his Career*. Minneapolis: Fortress
   Press, 1986.
Klassen, J. K., *The Nobility and the Making of the Hussite Revolution*. New York: Columbia
   University Press, 1978.
Klassen, J. K., *Warring Maidens, Captive Wives and Hussite Queens*. New York: Columbia
   University Press, 1999.
Klapisch-Zuber, C., "The Griselda Complex: Dowry and Marriage Gifts in the Quattrocento,"
   in *Women, Family, and Ritual in Renaissance Italy*. Chicago: University of Chicago Press,
   1985, pp. 213–46.
Kleinberg, A., *Prophets in their Own Country: Living Saints and the Making of Sainthood in
   the Later Middle Ages*. Chicago: University of Chicago Press, 1992.
Kłoczowski, J., *A History of Polish Christianity*. Cambridge: Cambridge University Press, 2000.
   Revised and extended English translation of *Dzieje Chrześcijaństwa Polskiego*, 2 vols. Paris:
   Éditions du Dialogue, 1987, 1991.
Kłoczowski, J., Kras, P., and Polak, W., eds., *Christianity in East Central Europe: Late Middle
   Ages/La Chrétienté en Europe du Centre-Est: Le Bas Moyen Age*. Proceedings of the Com-
   mission internationale d'histoire ecclésiastique comparée. Lublin: Instytut Evropy Środkowo
   Wschodniej, 1999.
Kłoczowski, J., Plisiecki, P., and Łaszkiewicz, H., eds., *Frontières et l'espace en Europe du
   Centre-Est. Exemples de quatre pays: Biélorussie, Lituanie, Pologne et Ukraine/The Borders and
   National Space in East-Central Europe. The Example of the Following Four Countries: Belarus,
   Lithuania, Poland and Ukraine*. Lublin: Instytut Europy Środkowo Wschodniej, 2002.
Knott, J. R., *Discourses of Martyrdom in English Literature, 1563–1694*. Cambridge:
   Cambridge University Press, 1993.
Knottnerus, O. S., "Menno als tijdverschijnsel," *Doopsgezinde Bijdragen*, n.s. 22 (1996),
   pp. 79–118.
Kobelt-Groch, M., *Aufsässige Töchter Gottes: Frauen im Bauernkrieg und in den Täuferbewe-
   gungen*. Frankfurt a.M.: Campus, 1993.
Köhler, W., *Zürcher Ehegericht und Genfer Konsistorium*, vol. 1 (*Quellen und Abhandlungen
   zur Schweizer Reformationsgeschichte*, vol. 7). Leipzig: Heinsius, 1932.

Köhler, W., *Zwingli und Luther: Ihr Streit über das Abendmahl nach seinen politischen und religiösen Beziehungen*, 2 vols. Leipzig: Heinsius, 1924, 1953.

Kohlmann, C., "'Von unsern Widersachern den Bapisten vil erlitten und ussgestanden': Kriegs- und Krisenerfahrungen von lutherischen Pfarrern und Gläubigen im Amt Hornberg des Herzogtums Württemberg während des Dreißigjährigen Krieges und nach dem Westfälischen Frieden," in M. Asche and A. Schindling, eds., *Das Strafgericht Gottes: Kriegserfahrungen und Religion im Heiligen Römischen Reich Deutscher Nation im Zeitalter des Dreißigjährigen Krieges*. Münster: Aschendorff, 2001, pp. 123–211.

Kohnle, A., *Reichstag und Reformation: Kaiserliche und ständische Religionspolitik von den Anfängen der Causa Lutheri bis zum Nürnberger Religionsfrieden*. Gütersloh: Gütersloher Verlagshaus, 2001.

Kolb, R., *For All the Saints: Changing Perceptions of Martyrdom and Sainthood in the Lutheran Reformation*. Macon, Ga.: Mercer University Press, 1987.

Kolb, R., *Martin Luther as Prophet, Teacher, and Hero: Images of the Reformer, 1520–1620*. Grand Rapids, Mich.: Baker, 1999.

Kolb, R. and Wengert, T. J., eds., *The Book of Concord*. Minneapolis: Fortress Press, 2000.

Konnert, M., *Civic Agendas and Religious Passion: Châlons-sur-Marne during the French Wars of Religion, 1560–1594*. Kirksville, Mo.: Sixteenth Century Essays and Studies, 1997.

Konrad, H. W., *A Jesuit Hacienda in Colonial Mexico: Santa Lucía, 1576–1767*. Stanford, Calif.: Stanford University Press, 1980.

Kooi, C., "Pharisees and Hypocrites: A Public Debate over Church Discipline in Leiden, 1586," *Archiv für Reformationsgeschichte*, 88 (1997), pp. 258–78.

Köpeczi, B., ed., *History of Transylvania*. Budapest: Akademiai, 1994.

Korade, M., Aleksic, M., and Matos, J., *Jesuits and Croatian Culture*. Zagreb: Croatian Writers' Association, 1992.

Kosa, L., *A Cultural History of Hungary*, vols. 1–2. Budapest: Osiris-Corvina, 2000.

Köstlin, J., *The Life of Martin Luther*, trans. John G. Morris, 2 vols. Philadelphia: Lutheran Publication Society, 1883.

Köstlin, J., *The Theology of Martin Luther*, trans. Charles E. Hay. Philadelphia: Lutheran Publication Society, 1897.

Kramář, V., *Zpustošení Chrámu svatého Víta v roce 1619*, ed. Michal Šroněk. Prague: Artefactum, 1998.

Kras, P., *Husyci w piętnastowicznej Polsce*. Lublin: Towarzystwo Naukowe KUL, 1998.

Krebs, M. and Rott, H. G., eds., *Quellen zur Geschichte der Täufer*, vols. 7–8, parts 1 and 2. Gütersloh: G. Mohn, 1959, 1960.

Kreider, A. F., "'The Servant is Not Greater than His Master': The Anabaptists and the Suffering Church," *Mennonite Quarterly Review*, 58 (1984), pp. 5–29.

Krmíčková, H., *K počátkám kalicha v Čechách: Studie a texty*. Brno, 1997.

Krusenstjern, B. von and Medick, H., eds., *Zwischen Alltag und Katastrophe: Der Dreißigjährige Krieg aus der Nähe*. Göttingen: Vandenhoeck & Ruprecht, 1998.

Kubler, G., *Mexican Architecture in the Sixteenth Century*, 2 vols. New Haven, Conn.: Yale University Press, 1948.

Lach, D. F., *Asia in the Making of Europe*, vol. 1, book 1. Chicago: Chicago University Press, 1994 (1965).

Lacouture, J., *Jesuits: A Multibiography*, trans. Jeremy Leggatt. Washington, DC: Counterpoint, 1995.

Lademacher, H., and Groenveld, S., eds., *Krieg und Kultur: Die Rezeption von Krieg und Frieden in der niederländischen Republik und im Deutschen Reich 1568–1648*. Munich: Waxmann, 1998.

Lake, P., *The Boxmaker's Revenge*. Stanford, Calif.: Stanford University Press, 2001.

Lambert, M., *Medieval Heresy: Popular Movements from the Gregorian Reform to the Reformation*, 2nd ed. Oxford: Blackwell, 1992.

Lambert, M., *The Cathars*. Oxford: Blackwell, 1998.

Lambert, T. A. and Watt, I. M., eds., *Registers of the Consistory of Geneva in the Time of Calvin*, vol. 1, trans. M. Wallace McDonald. Grand Rapids, Mich.: Eerdmans, 2000.

Lancashire, D., "Anti-Christian Polemics in 17th-Century China," *Church History*, 38 (1969), pp. 218–41.

Langer, E. and Jackson, R. H., eds., *The New Latin American Mission History*. Lincoln: University of Nebraska Press, 1995.

Langer, H., *1648, der Westfälische Frieden: Pax Europae und Neuordnung des Reiches*. Berlin: Brandenburgisches Verlagshaus, 1994.

Larner, C., *Enemies of God: The Witch-Hunt in Scotland*. London: Chatto & Windus, 1981.

Larner, C., *Witchcraft and Religion: The Politics of Popular Belief*. Oxford: Blackwell, 1984.

Las Casas, fray B. de, *Historia de las Indias*, 3 vols., ed. A. Millares Carlo. Mexico: Fondo de Cultura Económica, 1951.

Las Casas, fray B. de, *In Defense of the Indians*, trans. and ed. S. Poole. De Kalb: Northern Illinois University Press, 1974.

Las Casas, fray B. de, *A Short Account of the Destruction of the Indies*. London: Penguin, 1992.

Lášek, J. B., ed., *Jan Hus mezi Epochami, Národy a Konfesemi*. Sborník z mezinárodního sympozia, konaného 22.–26. září 1993 v Bayreuth, SRN. Prague: Česká křest'anská akademie, Husitská teologická fakulta Univerzity Karlovy, 1995.

Lau, F., "Der Bauernkrieg und das angebliche Ende der lutherischen Reformation als spontaner Volksbewegung," *Lutherjahrbuch*, 26 (1959), pp. 109–34.

Launay, A., *Histoire des Missions de l'Inde: Pondichéry, Maïssour, Coïmbatour*, 4 vols. Paris, 1898.

Laursen, J. C. and Nederman, C. J., eds., *Beyond the Persecuting Society: Religious Toleration Before the Enlightenment*. Philadelphia: University of Pennsylvania Press, 1997.

Lecler, J., *Histoire de la tolérance au siècle de la Réforme*. Paris: Montaigne-Desclées de Brouwer, 1955.

Lecler, J., *Toleration and the Reformation*, 2 vols. London: Longman, 1960.

Leite, B., *D. Gonçalo de Silveira*. Lisbon, 1946.

Leite, S., *História da Companhia de Jesus no Brasil*, 10 vols. Lisbon: Livraria Portugalia, 1938–50.

Leonard, A. E., " 'Nails in the Wall': Dominican Nuns in Reformation Strasbourg," PhD dissertation, University of California at Berkeley, 1999.

Leppin, V., "Luther-Literatur seit 1983," *Theologische Rundschau*, 65 (2000), pp. 350–7, 431–54.

Levack, B., *The Witch-Hunt in Western Europe*, 2nd ed. London: Longman, 1995.

Liebman, S., *The Jews in New Spain*. Coral Gables: University of Miami Press, 1970.

Lienhard, M., *Luther, Witness to Jesus Christ*, trans. Edwin H. Robertson. Minneapolis: Fortress Press, 1982.

Lierheimer, L., "Redefining Convent Space: Ideals of Female Community among Seventeenth-Century Ursuline Nuns," *Proceedings of the Western Society for French History*, 24 (1997), pp. 211–20.

Lieseberg, U., *Studien zum Märtyrerlied der Täufer im 16. Jahrhundert*. Frankfurt a.M.: Peter Lang, 1991.

Lin Jinshui, "Ai Rulüe yu Fujian shidafu jiaoyou biao," *Zhongwai guanxishi luncong*, 5 (1996), pp. 182–202.

Lin Jinshui, *Li Madou yu Zhongguo*. Beijing: Zhongguo she hui ke xue chubanshe, 1996.

Li Tiangang, *Zhongguo liyi zhi zheng: Lishi, wenxian he yiyi*. Shanghai: Guji chubanshe, 1998.

Loades, D., ed., *John Foxe and the English Reformation*. Aldershot: Scolar Press, 1997.

Lockhart, J., *The Nahuas After the Conquest: A Social and Cultural History of the Indians of Central Mexico, Sixteenth through Eighteenth Centuries*. Stanford, Calif.: Stanford University Press, 1992.

Lockhart, J. and Schwartz, S., *Early Latin America: A History of Colonial Spanish America and Brazil*. Cambridge: Cambridge University Press, 1983.

Loehr, J., ed., *Dona Melanchthoniana: Festgabe für Heinz Scheible*. Stuttgart-Bad Cannstatt: fromann-holzboog, 2001.

Loewenich, W. von, *Luther's Theology of the Cross*, trans. Herbert J. A. Bouman. Minneapolis: Augsburg, 1976.

Lohse, B., ed., *Der Durchbruch der reformatorischen Erkenntnis bei Luther*. Darmstadt: Wissenschaftliche Buchgesellschaft, 1958.

Lohse, B., *Martin Luther*, trans. Robert C. Schultz. Philadelphia: Fortress Press, 1986.

Lohse, B., ed., *Der Durchbruch der reformatorischen Erkenntnis bei Luther: Neuere Untersuchungen*. Wiesbaden: Franz Steiner, 1988.

Lohse, B., *Martin Luther's Theology: Its Historical and Systematic Development*, trans. Roy A. Harrisville. Minneapolis: Fortress Press, 1999.

Lopes, M. de Jesus dos Mártires, *Goa Setecentista: Tradição e Modernidade*. Lisbon: Universidade Católica Portuguesa, 1996.

Lopes, M. de Jesus dos Mártires, "A Inquisição de Goa na primeira metade do século XVIII: Uma visita pelo seu interior," *Mare Liberum*, 15 (1998).

Lopes, M. de Jesus dos Mártires, "Negócios e convivências dos jesuítas de Goa no século XVIII: Contributo para a sua história," in *A Companhia de Jesus e a Missionação no Oriente*. Lisbon: Brotéria & Fundação Oriente, 2000, pp. 235–58.

Lopez Martin, J., "Don Antonio Carrionero, obispo de Almeria, Padre conciliar en Trento," *Anthologica Annua*, 30–1 (1983–4), pp. 11–44.

Lortz, J., *Kardinal Stanislaus Hosius: Beiträge zur Erkenntnis der Persönlichkeit und des Werkes*. Münster, 1931.

Lortz, J., *Die Reformation in Deutschland*. Freiburg i.B.: Herder, 1940.

Loureiro, R. M., "O descrobrimento da civilização indiana nas caratas dos jesuítas (século XVI)," in *Encontro sobre Portugal e a Índia*. Lisbon: Fundação Oriente/Livros Horizonte, 2000, pp. 107–25.

Loureiro, R. M. and Gruzinski, S., eds., *Passar as fronteiras: II Colóquio International sobre Mediadores Culturais, séculos XV a XVIII*. Lagos: Centro de Estudos Gil Eanes, 1999.

Lualdi, K. J. and Thayer, A. T., eds., *Penitence in the Age of Reformations*. Aldershot: Scolar Press, 2000.

Lucas, T. M., *Landmarking: City, Church, and Jesuit Urban Strategy*, Chicago: Loyola University Press, 1997.

Luo Kuang, *Jiao Ting yu Zhongguo shi jie shi*. Taipei, 1962.

Luther, M., *D. Martin Luthers Werke: Kritische Gesamtausgabe, Abteilung Werke*. Weimar: H. Böhlau, 1883–1993.

Luther, M., *Luther's Works*. St. Louis: Concordia/Philadelphia: Fortress Press, 1958–86.

Luther, M., *Sermons of Martin Luther*, ed. John Nicolaus Lenker, 8 vols. (1903–9). Grand Rapids, Mich.: Baker, 1993.

Lutz, H., "Karl V.: Biographische Probleme," in Günter Vogler, ed., *Europäische Herrscher: Ihre Rolle bei der Gestaltung von Politik und Gesellschaft vom 16. bis zum 18. Jahrhundert*. Weimar: Böhlau, 1988, pp. 31–57.

MacCormack, S., *Religion in the Andes: Vision and Imagination in Early Colonial Peru*. Stanford, Calif.: Stanford University Press, 1991.

MacCulloch, D. *Thomas Cranmer: A Life*. New Haven, Conn.: Yale University Press, 1996.

MacCulloch, D., *Tudor Church Militant: Edward VI and the Protestant Reformation*. London: Allen Lane, 1999.

MacCulloch, D. and Blatchly, J., "Pastoral Provision in the Parishes of Tudor Ipswich," *Sixteenth Century Journal*, 22 (1991), pp. 457–74.

McAndrew, J., *The Open-Air Churches of Sixteenth-Century Mexico*. Cambridge, Mass.: Harvard University Press, 1965.

McClendon, M. C., *The Quiet Reformation: Magistrates and the Emergence of Protestantism in Tudor Norwich*. Stanford, Calif.: Stanford University Press, 1999.

McCoog, T. M., *The Society of Jesus in Ireland, Scotland, and England 1541–1588: "Our Way of Proceeding?"* Leiden: Brill, 1996.

Macek, J., *Jagellonský věk v českých zemích*. Prague: Academia, 1992–9.

Macfarlane, A. D. J., *Witchcraft in Tudor and Stuart England: A Regional and Comparative Study*. London: Routledge & Kegan Paul, 1970.

McGregor, J. F. and Reay, B., eds., *Radical Religion in the English Revolution*. Oxford: Oxford University Press, 1986.

Maclagan, E., *The Jesuits and the Great Mogul*. New York: Octagon Books/Farrar, Straus & Giroux, 1972 (1st ed., 1932).

McLaughlin, R. E., *Caspar Schwenckfeld, Reluctant Radical: His Life to 1540*. New Haven, Conn.: Yale University Press, 1986.

McNamara, J. A. K., *Sisters in Arms: Catholic Nuns through Two Millennia*. Cambridge, Mass.: Harvard University Press, 1996.

McSheffrey, S., *Gender and Heresy: Women and Men in Lollard Communities, 1420–1530*. Philadelphia: Pennsylvania University Press, 1995.

McSorley, H. J., *Luther: Right or Wrong? An Ecumenical-Theological Study of Luther's Major Work, The Bondage of the Will*. New York: Newman/Minneapolis: Augsburg, 1969.

Magalhães, J. R., "O rei," in José Mattoso, ed., *História de Portugal*. Lisbon: Círculo de Leitores, 1993, vol. 3, pp. 61–73.

Mâle, É., *L'Art religieux de la fin du XVIe siècle, du XVIIe siècle et du XVIIIe siècle: Étude sur l'iconographie après le concile de Trent*, 2nd ed. Paris: Armand Colin, 1951.

Maltby, J., *Prayer Book and People in Elizabethan and Early Stuart England*. Cambridge: Cambridge University Press, 1998.

Mannermaa, T., *Der im Glauben gegenwärtige Christus, Rechtfertigung und Vergottung. Zum ökumenischen Dialog*. Hanover: Lutherisches Verlagshaus, 1989.

Manning, B., *The English People and the English Revolution 1640–1649*, 2nd ed. London: Bookmarks, 1991.

Mannová, E., ed., *A Concise History of Slovakia*. Bratislava: Historical Institute, 2000.

Manuel, F., *The Broken Staff: Judaism through Christian Eyes*. Cambridge, Mass.: Harvard University Press, 1992.

Mariéjol, J.-H., *La Réforme, la Ligue, l'Édit de Nantes (1559–1598)*. Paris: Tallandier, 1983 (originally published 1904).

Marinus, M. J., "Het verdwijnen van het protestantisme in de Zuidelijke Nederlanden," *De Zeventiende Eeuw*, 13 (1997), pp. 261–72.

Marnef, G., "Het protestantisme te Brussel, ca. 1567–1585," *Tijdschrift voor Brusselse geschiedenis*, 1 (1984), pp. 57–81.

Marnef, G., *Het calvinistisch bewind te Mechelen*. Kortrijk-Heule: UGA, 1987.

Marques, J., *A arquidiocese de Braga no século XV*. Lisbon: Imprensa Nacional Casa da Moeda, 1988, pp. 1122–72.

Marques, J., "Os jesuítas, confessores da corte portuguesa na época barroca (1550–1700)," *Revista da Faculdade de Letras – História*, 12 (1995), pp. 231–70.

Marques, J., "Rituais e manifestações de culto," in Carlos Moreira Azevedo, ed., *História Religiosa de Portugal*. Lisbon: Círculo de Leitores, 2000, vol. 2, pp. 517–601.

Marshall, P., *The Catholic Priesthood and the English Reformation*. Oxford: Oxford University Press, 1994.

Marshall, P., ed., *The Impact of the English Reformation 1500–1640*. London: Edward Arnold, 1997.

Marshall, S., "Protestant, Catholic, and Jewish Women in the Early Modern Netherlands," in S. Marshall, ed., *Women in Reformation and Counter-Reformation Europe: Public and Private Worlds*. Bloomington: Indiana University Press, 1989, pp. 120–39.

Martin, A. L., *The Jesuit Mind: The Mentality of an Elite in Early Modern France*. Ithaca, NY: Cornell University Press, 1988.

Martin, H., *Les Ordres mendiants en Bretagne, vers 1230–vers 1530: Pauvreté volontaire et prédication à la fin du moyen âge*. Rennes: Institut armoricain de recherches historiques, 1975.

Martin, H., *Le Métier du prédicateur à la fin du moyen âge, 1350–1520*. Paris: Cerf, 1988.

Martin, J., *Venice's Hidden Enemies: Italian Heretics in a Renaissance City*. Berkeley/Los Angeles/London: University of California Press, 1993.

Martin, L., *The Intellectual Conquest of Peru: The Jesuit College of San Pablo, 1568–1767*. New York: Fordham University Press, 1968.

Martin Hernandez, F., *Los seminarios españoles: Historia y pedagogia*. Salamanca: Ediciones Sígueme, 1964.

Martin Rego, M., "La eucaristia en la archidiócesis hispalense a través de los libros de visitas pastorales. Siglo XVIII," *Isidorianum*, 3 (1993), pp. 203–30.

Martínez de Vega, M. E., "Santa Ana de Valencia de Alcantara: Un convento clariano bajo la jurisdiccion de la orden de Alcantara," in Enrique Martinez Ruiz and Vicente Suarez Grimon, eds., *Iglesia y Sociedad en el Antiguo Regimen*. Madrid: Associación Española de Historia Moderna, 1994, vol. 1, pp. 335–48.

Martins, J. F. F., *História de Misericórdia de Goa*, 3 vols. Nova Goa: Imprensa Nacional, 1910–14.

Matheson, P., ed., *The Collected Works of Thomas Müntzer*. Edinburgh: T. & T. Clark, 1988.

Maxwell-Stuart, P. G., *The Occult in Early Modern Europe: A Documentary History*. Houndmills: Macmillan, 1999.

Mecenseffy, G., *Geschichte des Protestantismus in Österreich*. Graz: H. Bohlau, 1956.

Meersman, A., *The Ancient Franciscan Provinces in India 1500–1835*. Bangalore: Christian Literature Society Press, 1971.

Megged, A., *Exporting the Catholic Reformation: Local Religion in Early-Colonial Mexico*. Leiden: Brill, 1996.

Melo, C. M. de, S. J., *The Recruitment and Formation of the Native Clergy in India*. Lisbon: Agência Geral do Ultramar, Divisão de Publicações et Biblioteca, 1955.

Mendus, S., *Toleration and the Limits of Liberalism*. Atlantic Highlands, NJ: Humanities Press, 1993.

Mentzer, R. A., "Bipartisan Justice and the Pacification of Late Sixteenth-Century Langue-doc," in J. Friedman, ed., *Regnum, Religio et Ratio: Essays presented to Robert M. Kingdon*. Kirksville, Mo.: Sixteenth Century Essays and Studies, 1987, pp. 125–32.

Mentzer, R. A., "The Persistence of Superstition and Idolatry among Rural French Calvinists," *Church History*, 65 (1996), pp. 220–33.

Metzler, J., O.M.I., *Sacrae Congregationis de Propaganda Fidei Memoria Rerum: 350 Years in the Service of the Missions*, vol. 1, part 1 (1522–1700). Rome/Freiburg/Vienna: Herder, 1972.

Michalski, S., *The Reformation and the Visual Arts: The Protestant Image Question in Western and Eastern Europe*. London and New York: Routledge, 1993. Revised English translation of *Protestanti a Sztuka*. Warsaw, 1989.

Midelfort, H. C. E., *Witch Hunting in Southwestern Germany, 1562–1684: The Social and Intellectual Foundations*. Stanford, Calif.: Stanford University Press, 1972.

Miguel García, I., "El arzobispo reformador," in *Don Hernando de Aragón: Arzobispo de Zaragoza y Virrey de Aragón*. Saragossa: Caja de Ahorros de la Immaculada de Aragón, 1998, pp. 75–131.

Mikulec, J., "Pobělohorská rekatolizace: téma stále problematické," *Český časopis historický*, 96 (1998), pp. 824–30.

Mikulec, J., *Barokní náboženská bratrsva v Čechách*. Prague: Knižnice dějin a současnosti, 2000.

Milhou, A., "Découvertes et christianisation lointaine," in J.-M. Mayeur, Ch. and L. Pietri, A. Vauchez, and M. Venard, eds., *Histoire du Christianisme: De la réforme à la Réformation (1450–1530)*. Paris, 1994.

Mills, K., *Idolatry and its Enemies: Colonial Andean Religion and Extirpation, 1640–1750*. Princeton, NJ: Princeton University Press, 1997.

Minamiki, G., *The Chinese Rites Controversy from its Beginning to Modern Times*. Chicago: Chicago University Press, 1985.

Mitter, P., *Much Maligned Monsters: A History of European Reactions to Indian Art*. Chicago: Chicago University Press, 1992 (1st ed., 1977).

Moeller, B., "Die Kirche in den evangelischen freien Städten Oberdeutschlands im Zeitalter der Reformation," *Zeitschrift für Geschichte des Oberrheins*, 112 (1964), pp. 147–62.

Moeller, B., "Piety in Germany around 1500," in Steven Ozment, ed., *The Reformation in Medieval Perspective*. Chicago: Triangle, 1971.

Moeller, B., "Religious Life in Germany on the Eve of the Reformation," in G. Strauss, ed., *Pre-Reformation Germany*. London: Macmillan, 1972, pp. 13–42.

Mohrmann, W. D., "Bemerkungen zur Staatsauffassung Lazarus' von Schwendi," in H. Maurer and H. Patze, eds., *Festschrift für Berent Schwineköper*. Sigmaringen, 1982.

Mol, J. A., "Friezen en het hiernamaals: Zieleheilsbeschikkingen ten gunste van kerken, klosoters en armen in testamenten in Friesland tot 1580," in J. A. Mol, ed., *Zorgen voor zekerheid: Studies over Friese testamenten in de vijftiende en zestiende eeuw*. Leeuwarden: Fryske Akademy, 1994.

Molnár, A., "Husovo místo v evropské reformaci," *Československý časopis historický*, 14 (1966), pp. 1–14.

Monaghan, J., *The Covenants of Earth and Rain: Exchange, Sacrifice, and Revelation in Mixtec Sociality*. Norman: University of Oklahoma Press, 1995.

Monson, C. A., "Disembodied Voices: Music in the Nunneries of Bologna in the Midst of the Counter-Reformation," in C. A. Monson, ed., *The Crannied Wall: Women, Religion, and the Arts in Early Modern Europe*. Ann Arbor: University of Michigan Press, 1992, pp. 191–210.

Monteiro, M., *Geestelijke maagden: Leven tussen klooster en wereld in Noord-Nederland gedurende de zeventiende eeuw*. Hilversum: Verloren, 1996.

Monter, W., *Calvin's Geneva*. New York: Wiley, 1967.

Monter, W., *Judging the French Reformation: Heresy Trials by Sixteenth-Century Parlements*. Cambridge, Mass.: Harvard University Press, 1999.

Monter, W., *Frontiers of Heresy: The Spanish Inquisition from the Basque Lands to Sicily*. Cambridge: Cambridge University Press, 2003.

Mooij, C. de, *Geloof kan Bergen verzetten: Reformatie en katholieke herleving te Bergen op Zoom 1577–1795*. Hilversum: Verloren, 1998.

Moore, R. I., *The Formation of a Persecuting Society: Power and Deviance in Western Europe, 950–1250*. Oxford: Blackwell, 1987.

Moran, J. F., *The Japanese and the Jesuits: Alessandro Valignano in Sixteenth-Century Japan*. London and New York: Routledge, 1993.

Moreno Gallego, V., "Dominicos y letras en la España ortosecular del XVII," in Enrique Martinez Ruiz and Vicente Suarez Grimon, eds., *Iglesia y Sociedad en el Antiguo Regimen*. Madrid: Associación Española de Historia Moderna, 1994, vol. 1, pp. 349–65.

Mörner, M., *The Political and Economic Activities of the Jesuits in the La Plata Region: The Hapsburg Era*. Stockholm: Victor Pettersons Bokindustri Aktiebolag, 1953.

Mörner, M. ed., *The Expulsion of the Jesuits from Latin America*. New York: Knopf, 1965.

Morrill, J., *The Nature of the English Revolution*. London: Longman, 1993.

Mosse, D., "The Politics of Religious Synthesis: Roman Catholicism and Hindu Village Society in Tamil Nadu, India," in C. Stewardt and R. Shaw, eds., *Syncretism/Antisyncretism: The Politics of Religious Synthesis*. London: Routledge, 1994.

Motolinia, fray T. de Benavente, *Historia de los indios de la Nueva España*. Madrid: Historia 16, 1985.

Mousnier, R., *The Assassination of Henry IV: The Tyrannicide Problem and the Consolidation of the French Absolute Monarchy in the Early Seventeenth Century*. London, 1973.

Muir, E., *Ritual in Early Modern Europe*. Cambridge: Cambridge University Press, 1997.

Mulakara, G., S.J., *History of the Diocese of Cochin*, vol. 1: *1298–1558*. Rome, 1986.

Müller, K., ed., *Instrumenta pacis Westphalicae – Die Westfälischen Friedensverträge: vollst. lateinischer Text mit Übers. der wichtigsten Teile und Regesten*. Bern: Herbert Lang, 1975.

Müller, L., ed., *Glaubenszeugnisse oberdeutscher Taufgesinnter*, vol. 1. Leipzig: M. Heinsius, 1938.

Müller, M. G., "Protestant Confessionalisation in the Towns of Royal Prussia and the Practice of Religious Toleration in Poland-Lithuania," in O. P. Grell and B. Scribner, eds., *Tolerance and Intolerance in the European Reformation*. Cambridge: Cambridge University Press, 1996, pp. 262–81.

Muller, R. A., *The Unaccommodated Calvin*. New York: Oxford University Press, 2000.

Mullett, M. A., *Catholics in Britain and Ireland, 1558–1829*. New York: St. Martin's Press, 1998.

Mundadan, M., C.M.I., *History of Christianity in India*. Vol. 1: *From the Beginning up to the Middle of the Sixteenth Century (up to 1542)*. Bangalore: Church History Association of India, 1989.

Mungello, D. E., *Curious Land: Jesuit Accommodation and the Origins of Sinology*. Stuttgart: Franz Steiner, 1985.

Mungello, D. E., ed., *The Chinese Rites Controversy: Its History and Meaning*. Nettetal: Steyler, 1994.

Mungello, D. E., *The Forgotton Christians of Hangzhou*. Honolulu: University of Hawaii Press, 1994.

Murdock, G., *Calvinism on the Frontier 1600–1660: International Calvinism and the Reformed Church in Hungary and Transylvania*. Oxford: Oxford University Press, 2000.

Muriel de la Torre, J., *Conventos de monjas en la Nueva España*. Mexico: Editorial Santiago, 1946.

Murphy, J. M., *Santería: An African Religion in America*. Boston: Beacon Press, 1988.

Murr, S., *L'Inde philosophique entre Bossuet et Voltaire – I, Moeurs et coutumes des Indiens (1777). Un inédit du Père G.-L. Coeurdoux, S. J., dans la version de N.-J. Desvaulx, & II, L'Indologie du Père Coeurdoux, S.J., Stratégies, apologétique et scientificité*. Paris: EFEO, 1987.

Murray, M., *The Witch Cult in Western Europe*. Oxford: Clarendon Press, 1921.

Nalle, S. T., *God in La Mancha: Religious Reform and the People of Cuenca, 1500–1650*. Baltimore: Johns Hopkins University Press, 1992.

Nalle, S. T., *Mad for God: Bartolomé Sánchez, the Secret Messiah of Cardenete*. Charlottesville: University of Virginia Press, 2001.

Naphy, W. G., *Calvin and the Consolidation of the Genevan Reformation*. Manchester: Manchester University Press, 1994.

Nayagam, X. S. T., "The First Books Printed in Tamil," *Tamil Culture*, 4 (1956).

Neil, S., *A History of Christianity in India*. Cambridge: Cambridge University Press, 1985.

Nelson, E. W., "The Theory of Persecution," in *Persecution and Liberty: Essays in Honor of George Lincoln Burr*. New York: Century, 1931, pp. 3–20.

Netanyahu, B., *Origins of the Inquisition in 15th-Century Spain*, 2nd ed. New York: Random House, 2000.

Newman, R. S., *Of Umbrellas, Goddesses and Dreams: Essays on Goan Culture and Society*. Mapusa: Other India Press, 2001.

Ngien, D., *The Suffering of God According to Martin Luther's "Theologia Crucis."* New York: Lang, 1995.

Nicholls, D., "The Theatre of Martyrdom in the French Reformation," *Past and Present*, 121 (1988), pp. 49–73.

Nicholson, W., ed., *The Remains of Edmund Grindal*. Cambridge: Parker Society, 1843.

Nicklas, T., *Um Macht und Einheit des Reiches: Konzeption und Wirklichkeit der Politik bei Lazarus von Schwendi (1522–1583)*. Husum, 1995.

Nirenberg, D., *Communities of Violence: Persecution of Minorities in the Middle Ages*. Princeton, NJ: Princeton University Press, 1995.

Nischan, B., "Reformed Irenicism and the Leipzig Colloquy of 1631," *Central European History*, 9 (1976), pp. 3–26.

Nolan, M. L. and Nolan, S., *Christian Pilgrimage in Modern Western Europe*. Chapel Hill: University of North Carolina Press, 1989.

Noll, R. R. and Sure, D. F., eds., *100 Roman Documents Concerning the Chinese Rites Controversy (1645–1941)*. San Francisco: Ricci Institute, 1992.

Norberg, K., "The Counter-Reformation and Women Religious and Lay," in J. O'Malley, ed., *Catholicism in Early Modern History: A Guide to Research*. St. Louis, Mo.: Center for Reformation Research, 1988, pp. 133–46.

Nunes, M. da Costa, *Documentação para a História da Congregação do Oratório da Santa Cruz dos Milagres do Clero Natural de Goa*. Lisbon: Instituto de Investigação Científica Tropical, 1966.

Nutini, H. G., *Todos Santos in Rural Tlaxcala: A Syncretic, Expressive, and Symbolic Analysis of the Cult of the Dead*. Princeton, NJ: Princeton University Press, 1988.

Oberman, H. A., *The Harvest of Medieval Theology: Gabriel Biel and Late Medieval Nominalism*. Cambridge, Mass.: Harvard University Press, 1963.

Oberman, H. A., *Forerunners of the Reformation: The Shape of Medieval Thought Illustrated by Key Documents*, 2nd ed. Philadelphia: Fortress Press, 1981.

Oberman, H. A., *Masters of the Reformation: The Emergence of a New Intellectual Climate in Europe*, trans. D. Martin. Cambridge: Cambridge University Press, 1981.

Oberman, H., *The Roots of Antisemitism in the Age of Renaissance and Reformation*, trans. James Porter. Philadelphia: Fortress Press, 1984.

Oberman, H. A., "The Impact of the Reformation: Problems and Perspectives," in E. I. Kouri and T. Scott, eds., *Politics and Society in Reformation Europe: Essays for Sir Geoffrey Elton on his Sixty-Fifth Birthday*. London: Macmillan, 1987, pp. 3–31.

Oberman, H. A., *Luther: Man Between God and the Devil*, trans. Eileen Walliser-Schwarzbart. New Haven, Conn.: Yale University Press, 1989.

O'Day, R., *The English Clergy: The Emergence and Consolidation of a Profession, 1558–1642*. Leicester: Leicester University Press, 1979.

Oddie, G. A., *Hindu and Christian in South-East India*. London: Curzon/Riverdale, 1991.

Odlozilik, O., *The Hussite King: Bohemia in European Affairs, 1440–1471*. New Brunswick, NJ: Rutgers University Press, 1965.

Ogg, D., *England in the Reign of Charles II*, 2nd ed. Oxford: Clarendon Press, 1956.

Olivier, D., *Luther's Faith*, trans. John Tonkin. St. Louis: Concordia, 1982.

Olson, J. E., *Calvin and Social Welfare: Deacons and the Bourse Française*. Selinsgrove: Susquehanna University Press, 1989.

O'Malley, J. W. et al., eds., *The Jesuits: Cultures, Sciences, and the Arts, 1540–1773*. Toronto: University of Toronto Press, 1999.

O'Malley, J. W., *The First Jesuits*. Cambridge, Mass.: Harvard University Press, 1993.

Oredsson, S., *Gustav Adolf, Sverige och Trettioåriga kriget: Historieskrivning och kult*. Lund: Lund University Press, 1992. German translation: *Geschichtsschreibung und Kult: Gustav Adolf, Schweden und der Dreißigjährige Krieg*, trans. Klaus R. Böhme. Berlin: Duncker & Humblot, 1994.

Oschmann, A., *Der Nürnberger Exekutionstag 1649–1650: Das Ende des Dreißigjährigen Krieges in Deutschland*. Münster: Aschendorff, 1991.

Ozment, S., *The Reformation in the Cities: The Appeal of Protestantism to Sixteenth-Century Germany and Switzerland*. New Haven, Conn.: Yale University Press, 1975.

Ozment, S., *When Fathers Ruled: Family Life in Reformation Europe*. Cambridge, Mass.: Harvard University Press, 1983.

Pacheco, D., S.J., "The Europeans in Japan, 1543–1640," in M. Cooper, ed., *The Southern Barbarians: The First Europeans in Japan*. Tokyo: Kodansha International, 1971, pp. 35–96.

Padipara, P. J., C.M.I., *The Hierarchy of the Syro-Malabar Church*. Alleppey, 1976.

Pagden, A., *The Fall of Natural Man: The American Indian and the Origins of Comparative Ethnology*. Cambridge: Cambridge University Press, 1982.

Pagden, A., *European Encounters with the New World: From Renaissance to Romanticism*. New Haven, Conn.: Yale University Press, 1993.

Pagano, S., ed., *I documenti del processo di Galileo Galilei*. Vatican City: Biblioteca Apostolica Vaticana, 1984.

Paiva, J. P., "A administração diocesana e a presença da Igreja: O caso da diocese de Coimbra nos séculos XVII e XVIII," *Lusitania Sacra*, 3 (1991), pp. 71–110.

Paiva, J. P., *Bruxaria e superstição num país sem caça às bruxas, 1600–1774*. Lisbon: Editorial Notícias, 1997.

Paiva, J. P., "A Igreja e o poder," in Carlos Moreira Azevedo, ed., *História Religiosa de Portugal*. Lisbon: Círculo de Leitores, 2000, vol. 2, pp. 135–85.

Paiva, J. P., "Os mentores," in Carlos Moreira Azevedo, ed., *História Religiosa de Portugal*. Lisbon: Círculo de Leitores, 2000, vol. 2, pp. 201–37.

Paiva, J. P., "The Portuguese Secular Clergy in the Sixteenth and Seventeenth Centuries," in Eszter Andor and István György Tóth, eds., *Frontiers of Faith*. Budapest: Central European University and European Science Foundation, 2001, pp. 157–66.

Paiva, J. P., "Public ceremonies ruled by the ecclesiastical-clerical sphere: A language of political assertion (16th–18th centuries)," in J. P. Paiva, ed., *Religious Ceremonials and Images: Power and Social Meaning (1400–1750)*. Coimbra: Centro de História da Sociedade e da Cultura; European Science Foundation; Palimage Editores, 2002, pp. 415–25.

Palmer, C. A., *Slaves of the White God: Blacks in Mexico, 1570–1650*. Cambridge, Mass.: Harvard University Press, 1976.

Palmitessa, J. R., *Material Culture and Daily Life in the New City of Prague in the Age of Rudolf II*. Krems: Medium Aevum Quotidianum, 1997.

Palomo del Barrio, F., *Fazer dos campos escolas excelentes: Los jesuitas de Évora, la misión de interior y el disciplinamiento social en la época confesional (1551–1630)*. Florence: Instituto Universitario Europeo, 2000.

Pánek, J., *Stavovská opozice a její zápas s Habsburky 1547–77. K politické krizi feudální třídy v předbělohorském období*. Prague: Československá akademie věd, 1982.

Pánek, J., *Poslední Rožemberkové: velmoci české renesance*. Prague: Panorama, 1989.

Pánek, J. and Polívka, M., eds., *Jan Hus ve Vatikánu*. Prague: Historický ústav, 2000.

Pannenberg, W., *Christliche Spiritualität: Theologische Aspekte*. Göttingen: Vandenhoeck & Ruprecht, 1986.

Papini, C., *Valdo di Lione e i "poveri nello spirito": Il primo secolo del movimento valdese (1170–1270)*. Turin: Claudiana, 2001.

Paradas Pena, M. S., "Pere García, obispo de Barcelona (1490–1505), y la reforma," in
    Enrique Martinez Ruiz and Vicente Suarez Grimon, eds., *Iglesia y Sociedad en el Antiguo
    Regimen*. Madrid: Associación Española de Historia Moderna, 1994, vol. 1, pp. 65–80.

Pardo Tomás, J., *Ciencia y censura: La Inquisición española y los libros científicos en los siglos
    XVI y XVII*. Madrid: CSIC, 1991.

Parker, G., *The Dutch Revolt*. Harmondsworth: Penguin, 1977.

Parker, G., *The Thirty Years' War*. London: Routledge & Kegan Paul, 1984.

Parker, K. L. and Carlson, E. J., *"Practical Divinity": The Life and Works of Revd Richard
    Greenham*. Aldershot: Scolar Press, 1998.

Patschovsky, A., "The Literacy of Waldensianism from Valdes to *c*.1400," in P. Biller and A.
    Hudson, eds., *Heresy and Literacy, 1000–1530*. Cambridge: Cambridge University Press,
    1994, pp. 112–36.

Pearson, M. N., *The Portuguese in India*. Cambridge: Cambridge University Press, 1987.

Pennec, H., "Des jésuites au royaume du Prêtre Jean (Éthiopie): Stratégie, rencontres et ten-
    tatives d'implantation (1495–1633)," unpublished PhD dissertation, Université de Paris I-
    Sorbonne.

Perera, S. G., S.J., *Life of the Venerable Father Joseph Vaz*. Colombo, 1953 (1st ed., 1943).

Perez, L., O.F.M., *Cartas y Relaciones del Japón*, 3 vols. Madrid, 1916–23.

Perez Muñoz, I., *Pecar, delinquir y castigar: El tribunal eclesiastico de Coria en los siglos XVI
    y XVII*. Salamanca: Institucion Cultural "El brocense", Diputation Provincial de Caceres,
    1992.

Pérez-Romero, A., " 'Get Thee to a Nunnery': Women's Empowerment in Golden Age Spain,"
    Bulletin of Hispanic Studies, 75 (1998), pp. 293–316.

Pérez Villanueva, J., ed., *La Inquisición Española: Nueva visión, nuevos horizontes*. Madrid:
    Siglo XXI, 1980.

Perrone, L., ed., *Lutero in Italia*. Casale Monferrato: Marietti, 1983.

Perry, M. E. and Cruz, A. J., eds., *Cultural Encounters: The Impact of the Inquisition in Spain
    and the New World*. Berkeley and Los Angeles: University of California Press, 1991.

Pesch, O. H., *Theologie der Rechtfertigung bei Martin Luther und Thomas von Aquin*. Mainz:
    Grünewald, 1967.

Pešek, J., "Knihovny pražských předbělohorských farářů," *Documenta Pragensia*, 9/2 (1991),
    pp. 417–38.

Pešek, J., *Měšťanská vzdělanost a kultura v předbělohorských Čechách 1547–1620 (Všední dny
    kulturního života)*. Prague: Univerzita Karlova, 1993.

Péter, K., "Hungary," in B. Scribner, R. Porter, and M. Teich, eds., *The Reformation in
    National Context*. Cambridge: Cambridge University Press, 1994.

Péter, K., "Tolerance and Intolerance in Sixteenth-Century Hungary," in O. P. Grell and B.
    Scribner, eds., *Tolerance and Intolerance in the European Reformation*. Cambridge:
    Cambridge University Press, 1996.

Peters, A., *Kommentar zu Luthers Katechismen*, ed. Gottfried Seebaß, 5 vols. Göttingen:
    Vandenhoeck & Ruprecht, 1990–4.

Peterson, D., "Out of the Margins: Religion and the Church in Renaissance Italy," *Renais-
    sance Quarterly*, 53 (2000), pp. 835–79.

Peterson, W. J., "Learning from Heaven: The Introduction of Christianity and Other Western
    Ideas into Late Ming China," in D. Twitchett and F. W. Mote, eds., *The Cambridge History
    of China: The Ming Dynasty 1368–1644*, pt. 2. Cambridge: Cambridge University Press,
    1998, pp. 789–839.

Pettegree, A., *Emden and the Dutch Revolt: Exile and the Development of Reformed Protes-
    tantism*. Oxford: Clarendon Press, 1992.

Peura, S., *Mehr als Mensch? Die Vergöttlichung als Thema der Theologie Martin Luthers von
    1513 bis 1519*. Mainz: Zabern, 1994.

Peyer, H. C., *Verfassungsgeschichte der alten Schweiz*. Zürich: Schulthess Polygraphischer Verlag, 1978.

Peyronel Rambaldi, S., *Dai Paesi Bassi all'Italia. "Il Sommario della sacra Scrittura": Un libro proibito nella società italiana del Cinquecento*. Florence: Olschki, 1997.

Pfanner, J., ed., *Die "Denkwürdigkeiten" der Abtissin Caritas Pirckheimer (aus den Jahren 1524–1528)*. Landshut: Solanus, 1962.

Pfeiffer, G., "Das Ringen um die Parität in der Reichsstadt Biberach," *Blätter für Württembergische Kirchengeschichte*, 56 (1956), pp. 3–75.

Phelan, J. L., *The Millennial Kingdom of the Franciscans in the New World: A Study of the Writings of Gerónimo de Mendieta*. Berkeley and Los Angeles: University of California Press, 1956.

Pinto Crespo, V., *Inquisición y control ideologico en la España del siglo XVI*. Madrid: Taurus, 1983.

Polišenský, J., ed., *War and Society in Europe 1618–1648*. Cambridge: Cambridge University Press, 1978.

Polišenský, J., *Komenský, muž labyrintů a naděje*. Prague: Academia, 1996.

Pollmann, J., *Religious Choice in the Dutch Republic: The Reformation of Arnoldus Buchelius (1565–1641)*. Manchester: Manchester University Press, 1999.

Poole, S., *Pedro Moya de Contreras: Catholic Reform and Royal Power in New Spain, 1571–1591*. Berkeley and Los Angeles: University of California Press, 1987.

Poole, S., "The Declining Image of the Indian among Churchmen in Sixteenth-Century New Spain," in S. E. Ramírez, ed., *Indian–Religious Relations in Colonial Spanish America*. Syracuse, NY: Maxwell School of Citizenship and Public Affairs, Syracuse University, 1989.

Poole, S., *Our Lady of Guadalupe: The Origin and Sources of a Mexican National Symbol, 1531–1797*. Tucson: University of Arizona Press, 1995.

Popp, D. and Suckale, R., eds., *Die Jagiellonen: Kunst und Kultur einer europäischen Dynasti an der Wende zur Neuzeit*. Nuremberg: Germanisches Nationalmuseum, 2002.

Poppi, A., *Cremonini e Galilei inquisiti a Padova nel 1604: Nuovi documenti d'archivio*. Padua: Antenore, 1992.

Porter, S., ed., *London and the Civil War*. London: Macmillan, 1996.

Poska, A. M., *Regulating the People: The Catholic Reformation in Seventeenth-Century Spain*. Leiden: Brill, 1998.

Post, R. R., *Kerkelijke verhoudingen in Nederland voor de Reformatie*. Utrecht/Amersfoort: Het Spectrum, 1965.

Powell, P. W., *Soldiers, Indians, and Silver: The Northward Advance of New Spain, 1550–1600*. Berkeley and Los Angeles: University of California Press, 1952.

Priolkar, A. K., *The Goa Inquisition*, 2nd ed. New Delhi: Voice of India, 1991.

Prodi, P., ed., *Disciplina dell'anima, disciplina del corpo e disciplina della società tra medioevo ed etá moderna*. Bologna: Il Mulino, 1994.

Prodi, P., "Il concilio di Trento di fronte alla politica e al diritto moderno," in Paolo Prodi and Wolfgang Reinhard, eds., *Il concilio di Trento e il moderno*. Bologna: Il Mulino, 1996, pp. 7–26.

Prosperi, A., *Tribunali della coscienza: Inquisitri, confessori, missionari*. Turin, 1996.

Prosperi, A., *L'eresia del Libro Grande: Storia di Giorgio Siculo e della sua setta*. Milan: Feltrinelli, 2000.

Pullan, B., *The Inquisition of Venice and the Jews of Europe*. Totowa, NJ: Barnes & Noble, 1987.

Purkiss, D., *The Witch in History: Early Modern and Twentieth-Century Representations*. London: Routledge, 1996.

Quéniart, J., *La Révocation de l'Édit de Nantes: Protestants et catholiques en France de 1598 à 1685*. Paris: Desclée de Brouwer, 1985.

Rabe, H., "Der Augsburger Religionsfriede und das Reichskammergericht 1555–1600," in H. Rabe et al., eds., *Festgabe für Ernst Walter Zeeden*. Münster, 1976.

Rabut, E., *Le Roi, l'Église et le Temple [Texte imprimé]: L'exécution de l'Édit de Nantes en Dauphiné*. Grenoble: La Pensée sauvage, 1987.

Rajamanickam, S., S.J., *The First Oriental Scholar*. Tirunelveli, 1972.

Rajamanickam, S., S.J., *His Star in the East*. Madras, 1995.

Ramírez, S. E., *The World Upside Down: Cross-Cultural Contact and Conflict in Sixteenth-Century Peru*. Stanford, Calif.: Stanford University Press, 1996.

Ramos, J. M., "The Invention of a Mission: The Brief Establishment of a Portuguese Catholic Minority in Renaissance Ethiopia," in E. J. Mucha, ed., *Dominant Culture as Foreign Culture: Dominant Group(s) in the Eyes of the Minorities*. New York: East European Monographs and Columbia University Press, 1999.

Ramos, J. M., "Machiavellian Empowerment and Disempowerment: The Violent Struggle for Power in XVIIth Century Ethiopia," in Angela Cheater, ed., *The Anthropology of Power: Empowerment and Disempowerment in Changing Structures*. London: Routledge, 1999, pp. 191–205.

Rapley, E., *The Dévotes: Women and Church in Seventeenth-Century France*. Montreal and Buffalo: McGill-Queen's University Press, 1990.

Reay, B., "The Quakers, 1659, and the Restoration of the Monarchy," *History*, 63 (1978), pp. 193–213.

Reay, B., "The Authorities and Early Restoration Quakerism," *Journal of Ecclesiastical History*, 34 (1983), pp. 69–84.

Reder Gadow, M., "Felipe II, Trento y la diocesis de Málaga," *Hispania Sacra*, 52/105 (2000), pp. 389–401.

Redondi, P., *Galileo Heretic*. Princeton, NJ: Princeton University Press, 1987 (Italian ed., 1983).

Reese, A. and Uffelmann, U., eds., *Pax sit Christiana: Die westfälischen Friedensverhandlungen als europäisches Ereignis*. Düsseldorf: Schwann-Bagel, 1988.

Rego, A. da Silva, *História das Missões do Padroado Português do Oriente: Índia (1500–1542)*. Lisbon: Agência Geral do Ultramar, 1949.

Rego, A. da Silva, "A primeira missão religiosa ao Grão Mogol," *Temas Sociomissionológicos e Históricos*, Lisbon, 1962.

Reguera, I., *La Inquisición española en el País Vasco (El tribunal de Calahorra, 1513–1570)*. San Sebastian: Txertoa, 1985.

Reinhard, W., *Ausgewählte Abhandlungen*. Berlin: Duncker & Humblot, 1997.

Reinhard, W., *Geschichte der Staatsgewalt: Eine vergleichende Verfassungsgeschichte Europas von den Anfängen bis zur Gegenwart*. Munich: R. Oldenbourg, 1999.

Rejchrtová, N., *Václav Budovec z Budova*. Prague: Melantrich, 1984.

Rempel, J. D., *The Lord's Supper in Anabaptism: A Study in the Christology of Balthasar Hubmaier, Pilgrim Marpeck, and Dirk Philips*. Scottdale, Pa.: Herald Press, 1993.

Repgen, K., *Die römische Kurie und der Westfälische Friede: Idee und Wirklichkeit des Papsttums im 16. und 17. Jahrhundert*, 2 vols. Tübingen: Niemeyer, 1962, 1965.

Repgen, K., ed., *Krieg und Politik 1618–1648*. Munich: R. Oldenbourg, 1988.

Repgen, K., *Dreißigjähriger Krieg und Westfälischer Friede: Studien und Quellen*. Paderborn: Schöningh, 1998.

Restall, M. B., *The Maya World: Yucatec Culture and Society, 1550–1850*. Stanford, Calif.: Stanford University Press, 1997.

Rey Castelao, O., "Los fundamentos económicos de la Iglesia en la España del periodo Moderno: Quiebras y conflictos de mantenimiento," in Enrique Martinez Ruiz and Vicente Suarez Grimon, eds., *Iglesia y Sociedad en el Antiguo Regimen*. Madrid: Associación Española de Historia Moderna, 1994, vol. 1, pp. 391–408.

Ricard, R., *The Spiritual Conquest of Mexico: An Essay on the Apostolate and the Evangelizing Methods of the Mendicant Orders in New Spain, 1523–72*, trans. Lesley Byrd Simpson. Berkeley and Los Angeles: University of California Press, 1966.

Richards, J. F., *The Mughal Empire*. Cambridge: Cambridge University Press, 1993.

Richardson, R. C., ed., *Town and Countryside in the English Revolution*. Manchester: Manchester University Press, 1992.

Rieth, R., *"Habsucht" bei Martin Luther: Ökonomisches und Theologisches Denken*. Weimar: Böhlau, 1996.

Ringmar, E., *Identity, Interest and Action: A Cultural Explanation of Sweden's Intervention in the Thirty Years' War*. Cambridge: Cambridge University Press, 1996.

Ritter, G., "Romantic and Revolutionary Elements in German Theology on the Eve of the Reformation," in S. E. Ozment, ed., *The Reformation in Medieval Perspective*. Chicago: Quadrangle Books, 1971, pp. 15–49.

Rivara, J. H. da Cunha, *Archivo Portueuz-Oriental*, 6 fasc. in 10 vols., 1st ed. Nova Goa: Imprensa Nacional, 1857–75; New Delhi/Madras, 1992.

Roberts, P., *A City in Conflict: Troyes during the French Wars of Religion*. Cambridge: Cambridge University Press, 1996.

Roche, P. A., *Fishermen of the Coromandel*. Manohar, New Delhi: Oxford University Press, 1984.

Rodrigues, J., S.J., *This Island of JapOn: João Rodrigues' Account of 16th-Century Japan*, trans. Michael Cooper. Tokyo: Kodansha International, 1973.

Rodrigues, M. A., *A cátedra de Sagrada Escritura na Universidade de Coimbra (1537–1640)*. Coimbra: Faculdade de Letras da Universidade de Coimbra, 1974.

Rodríguez, P., *El Catecismo romano ante Felipe II y la Inquisición española*. Madrid: Rialp, 1998.

Rogier, L. J., *Geschiedenis van het katholicisme in Noord-Nederland in de 16e en 17e eeuw*, 2 vols. Amsterdam: Urbi et Orbi, 1947.

Ronan, C. E. and Oh, B. B. C., eds., *East Meets West: The Jesuits in China, 1582–1773*. Chicago: Loyola University Press, 1982.

Rooze-Stouthamer, C., *Hervorming in Zeeland*. Goes: De Koperen Tuin, 1996.

Roper, L., *The Holy Household: Women and Morals in Reformation Augsburg*. Oxford: Clarendon Press, 1989.

Roper, L., *Oedipus and the Devil: Witchcraft, Sexuality and Religion in Early Modern Europe*. London: Routledge, 1994.

Rosman, M., *The Lords' Jews: Magnate–Jewish Relations in the Polish-Lithuanian Commonwealth during the Eighteenth Century*. Cambridge, Mass.: Harvard University Press, 1990.

Ross, A. C., *A Vision Betrayed: The Jesuits in Japan and China, 1542–1742*. Maryknoll, NY: Orbis Books, 1994.

Rosso, A. S., *Apostolic Legations to China: 18th Century*. South Pasadena: P. D. and I. Perkins, 1948.

Rothkrug, L., "Popular Religion and Holy Shrines: Their Influence on the Origins of the German Reformation and their Role in German Cultural Development," in J. Obelkevich, ed., *Religion and the People, 800–1700*. Chapel Hill: University of North Carolina Press, 1979, pp. 20–86.

Rothkrug, L., "Religious Practices and Collective Perceptions: Hidden Homologies in the Renaissance and Reformation," *Historical Reflections/Réflexions historiques*, 1980.

Rouleau, F. A., "Chinese Rites Controversy," in *New Catholic Encyclopedia*, Washington, DC: Catholic University of America Press, 1967, vol. 3, pp. 611–17.

Rouse, R. and Neill, S. C., eds., *A History of the Ecumenical Movement, 1517–1948*. Philadelphia: Westminster Press, 1954.

Rowlands, M. B., "Recusant Women, 1560–1640," in M. Prior, ed., *Women in English Society, 1500–1800*. London, 1985, pp. 149–80.

Royt, J., *Obraz a kult v Čechách 17. a 18 století*. Prague: Karolinum, 1999.

Rubiés, J.-P., *Travel and Ethnology in the Renaissance: South India through European Eyes, 1250–1625*. Cambridge: Cambridge University Press, 2000.

Rubiés, J.-P., "The Jesuit Discovery of Hinduism: Antonio Rubino's Account of the History and Religion of Vijayanagara (1608)," *Archiv für Religonsgeschichte*, 3 (2001), pp. 210–56.

Rubin, M., *Corpus Christi: The Eucharist in Late Medieval Culture*. Cambridge: Cambridge University Press, 1991.

Rublack, H.-C., ed., *Die lutherische Konfessionalisierung in Deutschland*. Gütersloh: Mohn, 1992.

Ruderman, D., *Jewish Thought and Scientific Discovery in Early Modern Europe*. New Haven, Conn.: Yale University Press, 1995.

Rudolph, H. U., *Der Dreißigjährige Krieg: Perspektiven und Strukturen*. Darmstadt: Wissenschaftliche Buchgesellschaft, 1977.

Ruiz de Adana, J. C., *El clero en el siglo XVII: Estudio de una visita secreta a la ciudad de Córdoba*. Cordoba: Imprenta San Pablo, 1976.

Ruiz de Alarcón, H., *Treatise on the Heathen Superstitions That Today Live Among the Indians Native to This New Spain, 1629*, trans. and ed. J. R. Andrews and R. Hassig. Norman: University of Oklahoma Press, 1984.

Ruiz-de-Medina, J., S.J., ed., *Documentos del Japan, 1547–1557, 1558–1562*, 2 vols. Rome: Instituto Histórico de la Compañía de Jesús, 1990–5.

Rule, P. A., *K'ung-tzu or Confucius? The Jesuit Interpretation of Confucianism*. Sydney: Allen & Unwin, 1986.

Russell-Wood, A. J. R., *Fidalgos and Philanthropists: The Santa Casa de Misericórdia of Bahia, 1550–1755*. Berkeley and Los Angeles: University of California Press, 1968.

Ruthmann, B., *Die Religionsprozesse am Reichskammergericht*. Cologne, Weimar, Vienna, 1996.

Sá, I. dos Gimarães, *Quando o rico se faz pobre: Misericórdias, caridade e poder no império português, 1500–1800*. Lisbon: CNCDP, 1997.

Saarinen, R., *Gottes Wirken auf Uns*. Wiesbaden: Franz Steiner, 1989.

Saarnivaara, U., *Luther Discovers the Gospel: New Light upon Luther's Way from Medieval Catholicism to Evangelical Faith*. St. Louis: Concordia, 1951.

Sahagún, fray B. de, *Historia general de las cosas de Nueva España*, 4 vols. Mexico: Editorial Porrua, 1996.

Sahagún, fray B. de, *The Florentine Codex: General History of the Things of New Spain*, trans. A. J. O. Anderson and C. E. Dibble, 13 parts. Salt Lake City and Santa Fe: University of Utah Press and School of American Research, 1950–82.

Salmon, J. H. M., *Society in Crisis: France in the Sixteenth Century*. New York: St. Martin's, 1975.

Salomon, F. and Urioste, G., eds. and trans., *Huarochirí Manuscript: A Testament of Ancient and Colonial Andean Religion*. Austin: University of Texas Press, 1991.

Sanchez González, A., "El clero rural en el arzobispado de Toledo en el Seiscientos," *Hispania Sacra*, 46/94 (1994), pp. 427–47.

Sandstrom, A., *Corn is Our Blood: Culture and Ethnic Identity in a Contemporary Aztec Indian Village*. Norman: University of Oklahoma Press, 1991.

Santos, C. M., *"Goa é a chave da toda a Índia": Perfil político da captal do Estado da Índia (1505–1570)*. Lisbon: CNCDP, 1999.

Saraiva, A. J., *Inquisição e critãos novos*. Porto: Inova, 1969.

Sasse, H., *This is my Body: Luther's Contention for the Real Presence*. Minneapolis: Augsburg, 1959.

Scaglione, A., *The Liberal Arts and the Jesuit College System*. Amsterdam and Philadelphia: Benjamins, 1986.

Scaramella, P., *"Con la Croce al core": Inquisizione ed eresia in Terra di Lavoro (1551–1564)*. Naples, 1995.

Scarisbrick, J. J., *The Reformation and the English People*. Oxford: Blackwell, 1984.

Schär, M., *Seelennöte der Untertanen: Selbstmord, Melancholie und Religion im Alten Zürich, 1500–1800*. Zürich: Chronos, 1985.

Scheible, H., ed., *Melanchthons Briefwechsel*. Stuttgart-Bad Cannstatt: fromann-holzboog, 1977–95.

Scheurmann, I., ed., *Frieden durch Recht: Das Reichskammergericht von 1495 bis 1806*. Mainz, 1994.

Schilling, H., "Religion and Society in the Northern Netherlands," in H. Schilling, *Religion, Political Culture and the Emergence of Early Modern Society: Essays in German and Dutch History*. Leiden: Brill, 1992, pp. 353–412.

Schilling, H., "Confessional Europe," in Thomas A. Brady, Jr., Heiko A. Oberman, and James D. Tracy, eds., *Handbook of European History 1400–1600: Late Middle Ages, Renaissance and Reformation*. Leiden: Brill, 1995, vol. 2, pp. 641–70.

Schilling, H., "Confessionalisation and the Rise of Religious and Cultural Frontiers in Early Modern Europe," in Eszter Andor and István György Tóth, eds., *Frontiers of Faith*. Budapest: Central European University and European Science Foundation, 2001, pp. 21–36.

Schindling, A., "Erfolgsgeschichte und Konfessionalisierung," in M. Asche and A. Schindling, eds., *Das Strafgericht Gottes: Kriegserfahrungen und Religion im Heiligen Römischen Reich Deutscher Nation im Zeitalter des Dreißigjährigen Krieges*. Münster: Aschendorff, 2001, pp. 11–51.

Schindling, A. and Ziegler, W., eds., *Die Territorien des Reichs im Zeitalter der Reformation und Konfessionalisierung: Land und Konfession 1500–1650*, 7 vols. Münster: Aschendorff, 1989.

Schmidt, G., *Der Dreißigjährige Krieg*, 2nd rev. ed. Munich: C. H. Beck, 1996.

Schmitt, J.-C., *The Holy Greyhound: Guinefort, Healer of Children Since the Thirteenth Century*, trans. M. Thom. Cambridge: Cambridge University Press, 1983.

Schmitt, J.-C., "Religion, Folklore, and Society in the Medieval West," in L. K. Little and B. Rosenwein, eds., *Debating the Middle Ages: Issues and Readings*. Malden, Mass., and Oxford: Blackwell, 1998, pp. 376–87.

Schnyder, C., "Durch Reformation zur frühneuzeitlichen Demokratie: Das Wallis zwischen 1524 und 1613," unpublished PhD dissertation, University of Bern, 2001.

Schormann, G., *Der Dreißigjährige Krieg*, 2nd ed. Göttingen: Vandenhoeck & Ruprecht, 1993.

Schorn-Schütte, L., "The Christian Clergy in the Early Modern Holy Roman Empire: A Comparative Social Study," *Sixteenth Century Journal*, 29 (1998), pp. 717–31.

Schorn-Schütte, L., "Priest, Preacher, Pastor: Research on the Clerical Office in Early Modern Europe," *Central European History*, 33 (2000), pp. 1–39.

Schraepler, H., *Die rechtliche Behandlung der Täufer in der deutschen Schweiz, Südwestdeutschland und Hessen, 1525–1618*. Tübingen: E. Fabian, 1957.

Schramm, G., *Der polnische Adel und die Reformation 1548–1607*. Wiesbaden: Franz Steiner, 1965.

Schroeder, S., *Chimalpahin and the Kingdoms of Chalco*. Tucson: University of Arizona Press, 1991.

Schurhammer, G., S.J., *The Malabar Church and Rome during the Early Portuguese Period and Before*. Trichinopoly, 1934.

Schurhammer, G., S.J., "Jugendprobleme des hl. Franz Xaver," *Studia Missionalia*, 2 (1946).

Schurhammer, G., S.J., "Cartas de Martim Afonso de Sousa," *Orientalia* [collected studies, vol. 2]. Rome/Lisbon: IHSI/Centro de Estudos Históricos Ultramarino, 1963, pp. 185–205.

Schurhammer, G., S.J., *Francis Xavier: His Life and Times*, trans. M. J. Costelloe, S.J., 4 vols. Rome: Jesuit Historical Institute, 1973–82.

Schurhammer, G., S.J., and Cottrell, G. W., S.J., "The First Printing in Indic Characters," *Orientalia*, Lisbon: Centro de Estudos Históricos Ultramarino, 1963.

Schutte, A. J., ed. and trans., *Autobiography of an Aspiring Saint*. Chicago: Chicago University Press, 1996.

Schütte, J. F., S.J., *Introductio ad Historiam Societatis Jesu in Japonia 1549–1650*. Rome: Institutum Historicum Soc. Jesu, 1968.

Schütte, J. F., S.J., *Textus Catalogorum Japoniae*. Rome: Monumenta Historica Soc. Jesu, 1975.

Schütte, J. F., S.J., *Valignano's Mission Principles for Japan*, trans. John J. Coyne, S.J., 2 vols. St. Louis: Institute of Jesuit Sources, 1980–5.

Schwaller, J. F., *The Church and Clergy in Sixteenth-Century Mexico*. Albuquerque: University of New Mexico Press, 1987.

Schwarz, R., *Luther*. Göttingen: Vandenhoeck & Ruprecht, 1986.

Schwarzwäller, K., *Shibboleth: Die Interpretation von Luthers Schrift De servo arbitrio seit Theodosius Harnack*. Munich: Kaiser, 1969.

Schwarzwäller, K., "Verantwortung des Glaubens, Freiheit und Liebe nach der Dekalogauslegung Martin Luthers," in Dennis D. Bielfeldt and Klaus Schwarzwäller, eds., *Freiheit als Liebe bei/Freedom as Love in Martin Luther*. Frankfurt/M.: Lang, 1995, pp. 133–58.

Schwarzwäller, K., *Kreuz und Auferstehung*. Göttingen: Vandenhoeck & Ruprecht, 2000.

Scott, T., *Freiburg and the Breisgau: Town–Country Relations in the Age of Reformation and Peasants' War*. Oxford: Clarendon Press, 1986.

Scott, T., *Thomas Müntzer: Theology and Revolution in the German Reformation*. Houndmills: Macmillan, 1989.

Scott, T., "The German Peasants' War and the 'Crisis of Feudalism': Reflections on a Neglected Theme," *Journal of Early Modern History*, 6 (2002), pp. 265–95.

Scott, T. and Scribner, R., eds., *The German Peasants' War: A History in Documents*. Atlantic Highlands, NJ: Humanities Press, 1991.

Scribner, R. W., *For the Sake of Simple Folk: Popular Propaganda for the German Reformation*. Cambridge: Cambridge University Press, 1981.

Scribner, R., "A Comparative Overview," in B. Scribner, R. Porter, and M. Teich, eds., *The Reformation in National Context*. Cambridge: Cambridge University Press, 1994, pp. 215–27.

Scribner, R. W. and Benecke, G., eds., *The German Peasant War of 1525: New Viewpoints*. London: George Allen & Unwin, 1979.

Seaver, P. S., *Wallington's World: A Puritan Artisan in Seventeenth-Century London*. Stanford, Calif.: Stanford University Press, 1985.

Seaward, P., *The Cavalier Parliament and the Reconstruction of the Old Regime*. Cambridge: Cambridge University Press, 1989.

Seed, P., *Ceremonies of Possession in Europe's Conquest of the New World, 1492–1640*. Cambridge: Cambridge University Press, 1995.

Seibt, F., *Hussitica: Zur Struktur einer Revolution*. Cologne and Graz: Böhlau, 1965.

Seibt, F., *Utopica: Modelle totaler Sozialplanung*. Düsseldorf: L. Schwann, 1972.

Seibt, F. and Eberhard, W., *Europa 1400. Die Krise des Spätmittelalters*. Stuttgart: Klett-Cotta, 1984.

Seibt, F. and Eberhard, W., *Europa 1500. Integrationsprozesse im Widerstreit: Staaten, Regionen, Personenverbände, Christenheit*. Stuttgart: Klett-Cotta, 1987.

Seidel Menchi, S., *Erasmo in Italia 1520–1580*. Turin: Bollati Boringhieri, 1987.

Seidel Menchi, S., ed., *Ketzerverfolgung im 16. und frühen 17. Jahrhundert.* Wolffenbüttel: Harrassowitz, 1992.

Shahar, S., *Women in a Medieval Heretical Sect: Agnes and Huguette the Waldensians,* trans. Y. Lotan. Woodbridge: Boydell Press, 2001.

Sharpe, J., *Instruments of Darkness: Witchcraft in England 1550–1750.* London: Hamish Hamilton, 1996.

Sharpe, K., *The Personal Rule of Charles I.* New Haven, Conn.: Yale University Press, 1992.

Shumaker, W., *The Occult Sciences in the Renaissance.* Berkeley: University of California Press, 1972.

Sider, R. J., *Andreas Bodenstein von Karlstadt: The Development of his Thought.* Leiden: Brill, 1974.

Siggins, I., *Martin Luther's Doctrine of Christ.* New Haven, Conn.: Yale University Press, 1970.

Silva, A. M. P., *O cardeal infante D. Henrique arcebispo de Évora: Um prelado no limiar da viragem tridentina.* Porto: Faculdade de Letras da Universidade do Porto, 1989.

Silva, C. R. de, "The Portuguese and Pearl Fishing off South India and Sri Lanka," *South Asia,* 1/1 (March 1978).

Sluhovsky, M., *Patroness of Paris: Rituals of Devotion in Early Modern France.* Leiden: Brill, 1998.

Šmahel, F., *Husitská revoluce,* 4 vols. Prague: Univerzita Karlova, 1993.

Šmahel, F., ed., *Häresie und vorzeitige Reformation in Spätmittelalter.* Munich: R. Oldenbourg, 1998.

Šmahel, F., ed., *Geist, Gesellschaft, Kirche im 13.–16. Jahrhundert.* Colloquia medievalia Pragensia, 1. Prague: Centrum medievistických studií, 1999.

Šmahel, F., *Idea národa v husitských Čechách.* Prague: Argo, 2000.

Smith, M. C., "Early French Advocates of Religious Freedom," *Sixteenth Century Journal,* 25 (1994), pp. 29–51.

Smith, N., *Literature and Revolution in England, 1640–1660.* New Haven, Conn.: Yale University Press, 1994.

Smith, V. A., *Akbar the Great Mogul.* Oxford: Oxford University Press, 1926.

Snyder, C. A. and Hecht, L. A. H., eds., *Profiles of Anabaptist Women: Sixteenth-Century Reforming Pioneers.* Waterloo, Ont.: Wilfrid Lauvier University Press, 1966.

Soman, A., *Sorcellerie et justice criminelle (16e–18e siècles).* Croft Road, Hants., and Brookfield, Vt.: Variorum, 1992.

Sousa, I. C. de, "Algumas hipóteses de investigação quantitativa acerca da Bibliografia Cronológica da Literatura de Espiritualidade em Portugal (1501–1700)," in *Congresso internacional Bartolomeu Dias e a sua época.* Porto: Tipografia Barbosa Xavier, 1989, vol. 5, pp. 115–38.

Sousa, L., Poole, S., and Lockhart, J., eds. and trans., *The Story of Guadalupe: Luis Laso de Vega's Huei tlamahuiçoltica of 1649.* Stanford and Los Angeles: Stanford University Press and UCLA Latin American Center, 1998.

Sousa, T. R. de, *The Medieval Goa: A Socio-Economic History.* New Delhi: Oxford University Press, 1979.

Soustiel, J. and David, M.-C., *Miniatures orientales de l'Inde,* 4. Paris: Galerie Soustiel, 1986.

Spaans, J., *Haarlem na de Reformatie: Stedelijke cultuur en kerkelijk leven, 1577–1620.* The Hague: Stichting Hollandse Historische Reeks, 1989.

Spaans, J., "Catholicism and Resistance to the Reformation in the Northern Netherlands," in Philip Benedict, Guido Marnef, Henk van Nierop, and Marc Venard, eds., *Reformation, Revolt and Civil War in France and the Netherlands 1555–1585.* Amsterdam: Koninklijke Nederlandse Academie van Wetenschappen, 1999, pp. 149–63.

Spaans, J., "Religious Policies in the Seventeenth-Century Dutch Republic," in Ronnie Po-chia Hsia and Henk van Nierop, eds., *Calvinism and Religious Toleration in the Dutch Golden Age.* Cambridge: Cambridge University Press, 2002, pp. 72–86.

Spalding, K., *Huarochirí: An Andean Society under Inca and Spanish Rule.* Stanford, Calif.: Stanford University Press, 1984.

Spence, J. D., *The Memory Palace of Matteo Ricci.* London and Boston: Faber, 1985.

Sperling, J., *Convents and the Body Politic in Late Renaissance Venice.* Chicago: University of Chicago Press, 1999.

Spicer, E. H., *Cycles of Conquest: The Impact of Spain, Mexico, and the United States on the Indians of the Southwest, 1533–1960.* Tucson: University of Arizona Press, 1962.

Spitz, L. W., *The Religious Renaissance of the German Humanists.* Cambridge, Mass.: Harvard University Press, 1963.

Spitz, L. W. *The Protestant Reformation 1517–1559.* New York: Harper & Row, 1985.

Spufford, M., "Literacy, Trade and Religion in the Commercial Centres of Europe," in Karel Davids and Jan Lucassen, eds., *A Miracle Mirrored: The Dutch Republic in International Perspective.* Cambridge: Cambridge University Press, 1995, pp. 229–83.

Spufford, M., ed., *The World of the Rural Dissenters, 1520–1795.* Cambridge: Cambridge University Press, 1995.

Spurr, J., *The Restoration Church of England, 1646–1689.* New Haven, Conn.: Yale University Press, 1991.

Stadler, P., "Eidgenossenschaft und Reformation," in H. Angermeier, ed., *Säkulare Aspekte der Reformationszeit (Schriften des Historischen Kollegs, Kolloquien,* vol. 5). Munich and Vienna: R. Oldenbourg, 1983, pp. 91–9.

Standaert, N., *Yang Tingyun, Confucian and Christian in Late Ming China: His Life and Thought.* Leiden: Brill, 1988.

Standaert, N., "New Trends in the Historiography of Christianity in China," *Catholic Historical Review*, 83/4 (1997), pp. 573–613.

Standaert, N., ed., *Handbook of Christianity in China.* Vol. 1: *635–1800.* Leiden: Brill, 2001.

Standaert, N. and Dudink, A., eds., *Chinese Christian Texts from the Roman Archives of the Society of Jesus,* 12 vols. Taipei: Ricci Institute, 2002.

Standaert, N., Dudink, A., Huang Yilong, and Zhu Pingyi, eds., *Chinese Christian Texts from the Zikawei Library,* 5 vols. Taipei: Fujen University, Faculty of Theology, 1996.

Starkey, D., *The Reign of Henry VIII: Personalities and Politics.* London: George Philip, 1985.

Stayer, J. M., *Anabaptists and the Sword,* 2nd ed. Lawrence, Ks.: Coronado Press, 1976.

Stayer, J. M., *The German Peasants' War and Anabaptist Community of Goods.* Montreal: McGill-Queen's University Press, 1991.

Stayer, J. M., *Martin Luther, German Saviour: German Evangelical Theological Factions and the Interpretation of Luther, 1917–1933.* Montreal and Kingston: McGill-Queens University Press, 2000.

Steen, C. R., *A Chronicle of Conflict: Tournai, 1559–1567.* Utrecht: Hes Publishers, 1985.

Stegmann, A., *Édits des Guerres de Religion.* Paris: J. Vrin, 1979.

Steinmetz, D. C., *Misericordia Dei: The Theology of Johannes von Staupitz in its Late Medieval Setting.* Leiden: Brill, 1968.

Stern, S., *Der preussische Staat und die Juden,* 4 vols. in 8. Tübingen: J. C. B. Mohr, 1962–75.

Stern, S., *Josel of Rosheim: Commander of Jewry in the Holy Roman Empire of the German Nation,* trans. Gertrude Hirschler. Philadelphia: Jewish Publication Society, 1965.

Stern, S. J., *Peru's Indian Peoples and the Challenge of the Spanish Conquest: Huamanga to 1640.* Madison: University of Wisconsin Press, 1982.

Stievermann, D., Press, V., and Diemer, K., eds., *Geschichte der Stadt Biberach.* Stuttgart: Konrad Theiss, 1991.

Stow, K., "The Burning of the Talmud in 1553, in Light of Sixteenth-Century Catholic Attitudes toward the Talmud," *Bibliothèque d'Humanisme et Renaissance*, 34 (1972), pp. 435–49.

Stow, K., *Catholic Thought and Papal Jewry Policy, 1555–1593*. New York: Jewish Theological Seminary of America, 1977.

Strasser, U., "Brides of Christ, Daughters of Men: Nuremberg Poor Clares in Defense of their Identity (1524–1529)," *Magistra*, 1 (1995), pp. 193–248.

Strasser, U., "Bones of Contention: Cloistered Nuns, Decorated Relics, and the Contest Over Women's Place in the Public Sphere of Counter-Reformation Munich," *Archiv für Reformationsgeschichte*, 90 (1999), pp. 255–88.

Strauss, G., *Luther's House of Learning: Indoctrination of the Young in the German Reformation*. Baltimore: Johns Hopkins University Press, 1978.

Subrahmanyam, S., *The Portuguese Empire in Asia, 1500–1700: A Political and Economic History*. London: Longman, 1993.

Subrahmanyam, S., *The Career and Legend of Vasco da Gama*. Cambridge: Cambridge University Press, 1997.

Subrahmanyam, S., "Connected Histories: Notes Towards a Reconfiguration of Early Modern Eurasia," *Modern Asian Studies*, 31/3 (1997), pp. 735–62.

Subrahmanyam, S., ed., *Sinners and Saints: The Successors of Vasco da Gama*. New Delhi: Oxford University Press, 1998.

Subrahmanyam, S., "Du Tage au Gange au XVIe siècle: Une conjoncture millénariste à l'échelle eurasiatique," *Annales, Histoire, Sciences Sociales*, 56 (Jan.–Feb. 2001), pp. 51–84.

Swanson, R. N., trans. and annot., *Catholic England: Faith, Religion and Observance Before the Reformation*. Manchester: Manchester University Press, 1993.

Swanson, R. N., *Religion and Devotion in Europe, c.1215–c.1515*. Cambridge: Cambridge University Press, 1995.

Tanner, N. P., ed., *Heresy Trials in the Diocese of Norwich, 1428–31*, Camden 4th series, vol. 20. London: Offices of the Royal Historical Society, 1977.

Tanner, N. P., ed., *Decrees of the Ecumenical Councils*. London and Washington, DC: Sheed & Ward and Georgetown University Press, 1990.

Tavares, P. V. B., "Em torno da história do Luteranismo ibérico do séc. XVI: Breves reflexões sobre alguns pressupostos, equívocos e encruzilhadas," *Humanística e Teologia*, 15 (1994), pp. 205–23.

Tavim, J. A. R. da Silva, "From Setúbal to the Sublime Porte: The Wandering of Jácome de Olivares, New Christian and Merchant of Cochin (1540–1571)," in S. Subrahmanyam, ed., *Sinners and Saints: The Successors of Vasco da Gama*. New Delhi: Oxford University Press, 1998.

Taylor, L., *Soldiers of Christ: Preaching in Late Medieval and Reformation France*. New York: Oxford University Press, 1992.

Taylor, L., "God of Judgment, God of Love: Preaching in France, 1460–1560," *Historical Reflections/Réflexions historiques*, 26 (2000), pp. 264–8.

Taylor, L., "Dangerous Vocations: The Social History of Preaching in France in the Late Medieval Period and Reformations," in L. Taylor, ed., *Preachers and People in the Reformations and Early Modern Period*. Leiden: Brill, 2001, pp. 91–124.

Taylor, W. B., *Magistrates of the Sacred: Priests and Parishioners in Eighteenth-Century Mexico*. Stanford, Calif.: Stanford University Press, 1996.

Taylor, W. B. and Pease, F., eds., *Violence, Resistance, and Survival in the Americas: Native Americans and the Legacy of Conquest*. Washington, DC: Smithsonian Institution Press, 1994.

Tazbir, J., *A State Without Stakes: Polish Religious Toleration in the Sixteenth and Seventeenth Centuries*. New York: Kościuszko Foundation, Twayne Publishers, 1973.

Tazbir, J., *Geschichte der polnischen Toleranz*. Warsaw: Interpress, 1977.

Tazbir, J., *Reformacja w Polsce*. Warsaw: Ksivążka i Wiedza, 1993.

Tedeschi, J. A., *The Pursuit of Heresy*. Binghamton, NY: SUNY Press, 1991.

Tedeschi, J. (in association with J. M. Lattis), *The Italian Reformation of the Sixteenth Century and the Diffusion of Renaissance Culture: A Bibliography of the Secondary Literature (ca. 1750–1996)*. Modena: Franco Cosimo Panini, 1999.

Tellechea Idígoras, J. I., *El arzobispo Carranza y su tiempo*. Madrid: Ediciones Guadarrama, 1968.

Tellechea Idígoras, J. I., *La reforma tridentina en San Sebastian: El libro de "Mandatos de visita" de la parroquia de San Vicente (1540–1670)*. San Sebastian, 1970.

Tellechea Idígoras, J. I., "Clemente VIII y el episcopado español en las postrimerías del reinado de Felipe II (1596–1597)," *Anthologica Annua*, 44 (1997), pp. 204–53.

Terraciano, K., *The Mixtecs of Colonial Oaxaca: Ñudzahui History, Sixteenth through Eighteenth Centuries*. Stanford, Calif.: Stanford University Press, 2001.

Thayer, A., "Penitence and Preaching on the Eve of the Reformation: A Comparative Overview from Frequently Printed Model Sermon Collections, 1450–1520." Harvard University PhD dissertation, 1996.

Thekkedath, J., S.D.B., *History of Christianity in India*. Vol. 2: *From the Middle of the Sixteenth Century to the End of the Seventeenth Century (1542–1700)*. Bangalore: Church History Association of India, 1982.

Thijs, A. K. L., *Van Geuzenstad tot katholiek bolwerk: Antwerpen en de Contrareformatie*. Antwerp: Brepols, 1990.

Thomas, K. V., *Religion and the Decline of Magic: Studies in Popular Beliefs in Sixteenth- and Seventeenth-Century England*. London: Weidenfeld & Nicolson, 1971.

Thomaz, L. F. F. R., "Le Portugal et l'Afrique au XVe siècle: Les débuts de l'expansion," *Arquivos do Centro Cultural Português*, 26 (1989).

Thomaz, L. F. F. R., "L'idée impériale manueline," in J. Aubin, ed., *La Découverte, le Portugal et l'Europe*. Paris: Fondation Calouste Gulbenkian/Centre Culturel Portugais, 1990.

Thomaz, L. F. F. R., "Factions, Interests and Messianism: The Politics of Portuguese Expansion in the East, 1500–1521," *Indian Economic and Social History Review*, 28/1 (1991).

Thomaz, L. F. F. R., *De Ceuta a Timor*. Lisbon: Difel, 1994.

Thomaz, L. F. F. R., "A crise de 1565–1575 na história do estado da Índia," *Mare Liberum*, 9 (1995).

Thomson, J. A. F., *The Later Lollards 1414–1520*. Oxford: Clarendon Press, 1965.

Thorndike, L. A., *A History of Magic and Experimental Science*, 8 vols. New York: Columbia University Press, 1923–58.

Tóth, I. G., ed., *Relationes missionariorum de Hungaria et Transilvania*. Rome/Budapest: Accademia d'Ungheria a Roma, 1994.

Tóth, I. G., ed., *Litterae missionariorum de Hungaria et Transilvania*. Rome/Budapest: Accademia d'Ungheria a Roma, 2002.

Tóth, I. G., ed., *Millennium History of Hungary*. Budapest: Osiris-Corvina, 2003.

Toussaert, J., *Le Sentiment religieux en Flandre à la fin du moyen âge*. Paris: Plon, 1963.

Trachtenberg, J., *The Devil and the Jews: The Medieval Conception of the Jew and its Relation to Modern Antisemitism*, 2nd ed. Philadelphia: Jewish Publication Society of America, 1983.

Tracy, J., "Believers, Non-Believers, and the Historian's Unspoken Assumptions," *Catholic Historical Review*, 86 (2000), pp. 403–19.

Tracy, J. D., "Erasmus, Coornhert and the Acceptance of Religious Disunity in the Body Politic: A Low Countries Tradition?," in Christiane Berkvens-Stevelinck, Jonathan I. Israel, and G. H. M Posthumus Meyjes, eds., *The Emergence of Tolerance in the Dutch Republic*. Leiden: Brill, 1997, pp. 49–62.

Trigg, J. D., *Baptism in the Theology of Martin Luther*. Leiden: Brill, 1994.

Tuck, R., "Scepticism and Toleration in the Seventeenth Century," in Susan Mendus, ed., *Justifying Toleration: Conceptual and Historical Perspectives*. Cambridge: Cambridge University Press, 1988, pp. 21–35.

Tyacke, N., *Anti-Calvinists: The Rise of English Arminianism, c.1590–1640*. Oxford: Clarendon Press, 1987.

Ubachs, P. J. H., *Twee heren, twee confessies: De verhouding van staat en kerk te Maastricht, 1632–1673*. Assen: Van Gorcum, 1975.

Uhalley, S. and Xiaoxin Wu, eds., *China and Christianity: Burdened Past, Hopeful Future*. Armonk, NY: M. E. Sharpe, 2001.

Underdown, D., *Revel, Riot, and Rebellion: Popular Politics and Culture in England 1603–1660*. Oxford: Oxford University Press, 1987.

Underdown, D., *Fire from Heaven: Life in an English Town in the Seventeenth Century*. London: Fontana, 1993.

Uyttenbroeck, T., O.F.M., *Early Franciscans in Japan*. Himeji, 1958.

Valignano, A., S.J., *Il Cerimoniale per i Missionari del Giappone: Advertimentos e Avisos acerca dos Costumes e Catangues de Jappão*, ed. Giuseppe Fr. Schütte, S.J. Rome: Storia e Letteratura, 1946.

Valignano, A., S.J., *Sumario de las Cosas de Japon (1583), Adiciones del Sumario de Japon (1592)*, ed. José Luis Alvarez-Taladriz, 2 vols. Tokyo: Sophia University, Monumenta Nipponica Monograph 9, 1954.

Válka, J., "Tolerance či koexistence? (K povaze soužití různých náboženských vyznání v českých zemích v 15. až 17. století)." *Studia Comeniana et Historica*, 18/35 (1988), supplement.

Válka, J., "Komenský a nadkonfesijní křest'anství," *Studia Comeniana et Historica*, 24/51 (1994), pp. 124–9.

Vargas Ugarte, R., *Historia de la iglesia en el Peru*. Lima: Impresa Santa María, 1953.

Vauchez, A., *The Laity in the Middle Ages: Religious Beliefs and Devotional Practices*, ed. D. E. Bornstein and trans. M. J. Schneider. Notre Dame and London: University of Notre Dame Press, 1993.

Vaz, Can. F. X., "Primeiros clerigos indios," *O Oriente Portuguez*, 6 (1909).

Vázquez, I., "Las controversias doctrinales postridentinas hasta finales del siglo XVII," in Ricardo García-Villoslada, ed., *Historia de la Iglesia en España*. Madrid: Biblioteca de Autores Cristianos, 1979, vol. 4, pp. 419–74.

Veiga Torres, J., "Uma longua Guerra social: os ritmos da repressão inquisitorial em Portugal," *Revista de História Económico e Social*, 1 (1978), pp. 55–68.

Verhoeven, G., *Devotie en negotie: Delft als bedevaartplaats in de late middeleeuwen*. Amsterdam: VU Uitgeverij, 1992.

Vickers, B., ed., *Occult and Scientific Mentalities in the Renaissance*. Cambridge: Cambridge University Press, 1984.

Vinay, V., *Le Confessioni di fede dei Valdesi riformati*. Turin: Claudiana, 1975.

Vincent, B., *Minorias y marginados en la España del siglo XVI*. Granada, 1987.

Vis, G. N. M., *Jan Arentsz., de mandenmaker van Alkmaar, voorman van de Hollandse Reformatie*. Hilversum: Verloren, 1992.

Visser, C. Ch. G., *De lutheranen in Nederland tussen katholicisme en calvinisme, 1566 tot heden*. Dieren: De Bataafsche Leeuw, 1983.

Visvanathan, S., *The Christians of Kerala*. Madras: Oxford University Press, 1993.

Vlnas, V., *Jan Nepomucký: Česká legenda*. Prague: Mladá fronta, 1993.

Vogler, G., *Europäische Herrscher: Ihre Rolle bei der Gestaltung von Politik und Gesellschaft vom 16. bis zum 18. Jahrhundert*. Weimar: Böhlau, 1988.

Vroede, M. de, *"Kwezels" en "zusters": De geestelijke dochters in de Zuidelijke Nederlanden*. Brussels: Koninklijke Academie voor Wetenschappen, Letteren en Schone Kunsten van België, 1994.

Wagner, C., "Los Luteranos ante la Inquisicion de Toledo en el siglo XVI," *Hispania Sacra*, 46/94 (1994), pp. 474–505.

Walder, E., ed., *Religionsvergleiche des 16. Jahrhunderts*. Bern: Herbert Lang, 1974.

Walder, E., "Reformation und moderner Staat," in *450 Jahre Berner Reformation* (*Archiv des Historischen Vereins des Kantons Bern*, vol. 64/65). Bern: Stämpfli, 1980, pp. 441–583.

Walker, C., "Prayer, Patronage, and Political Conspiracy: English Nuns and the Restoration," *Historical Journal*, 43 (2000), pp. 1–23.

Walter, J., *Understanding Popular Violence in the English Revolution: The Colchester Plunderers*. Cambridge: Cambridge University Press, 1999.

Walzer, M., *On Toleration*. New Haven, Conn.: Yale University Press, 1997.

Wandel, L. P., *Voracious Idols and Violent Hands*. Cambridge: Cambridge University Press, 1995.

Wanegffelen, T., *L'Édit de Nantes: Une histoire européenne de la tolérance du XVIe au XXe siècles*. Paris: Librairie générale française, 1998.

Wang Xiaochao, *Christianity and Imperial Culture: Chinese Christian Apologetics in the Seventeenth Century and their Latin Patristic Equivalent*. Leiden: Brill, 1998.

Warmbrunn, P., *Zwei Konfessionen in einer Stadt: Das Zusammenleben von Katholiken und Protestanten in den paritätischen Reichsstädten Augsburg, Biberach, Ravensburg und Dinkelsbühl von 1548 bis 1648*. Wiesbaden: Franz Steiner, 1983.

Warmbrunn, P., "Simultaneen in der Pfalz," *Jahrbuch für westdeutsche Landesgeschichte*, 14 (1988), pp. 97–122.

Warnicke, R., *Women of the English Renaissance and Reformation*. Westport, Conn.: Greenwood Press, 1983.

Wartburg-Ambühl, M.-L. von, *Alphabetisierung und Lektüre: Untersuchung am Beispiel einer ländlichen Region im 17. und 18. Jahrhundert* (*Europäische Hochschulschriften*, series l, vol. 459). Bern and Frankfurt a.M.: Peter Lang, 1981.

Watanabe, J., *Maya Saints and Souls in a Changing World*. Austin: University of Texas Press, 1992.

Watts, M., *The Dissenters*. Oxford: Clarendon Press, 1978.

Weber, A., *Teresa of Avila and the Rhetoric of Femininity*. Princeton, NJ: Princeton University Press, 1990.

Weber, D., *The Spanish Frontier in North America*. New Haven, Conn.: Yale University Press, 1992.

Weiss, R., "Grundzüge einer protestantischen Volkskultur," *Schweizerisches Archiv für Volkskunde*, 61 (1965), pp. 75–91.

Wendel, F., *Calvin: The Origins and Development of his Religious Thought*. New York: Harper & Row, 1963.

Wengert, T. J., *Law and Gospel: Philip Melanchthon's Debate with John Agricola of Eisleben over Poenitentia*. Grand Rapids, Mich.: Baker, 1997.

Wengert, T. J., *Human Freedom, Christian Righteousness: Philip Melanchthon's Exegetical Dispute with Erasmus of Rotterdam*. Oxford: Oxford University Press, 1998.

Wenz, G., *Theologie der Bekenntnisschriften der evangelisch-lutherischen Kirche*, 2 vols. Berlin: Aldine de Gruyter, 1996, 1998.

Whaley, J., *Religious Toleration and Social Change in Hamburg 1529–1819*. Cambridge: Cambridge University Press, 1985.

Whelan, R. and Baxter, C., eds., *Toleration and Religious Identity: The Edict of Nantes and its Implications in France, Britain and Ireland*. Dublin: Four Courts, 2003.

White, H., *Tudor Books of Saints and Martyrs*. Madison: University of Wisconsin Press, 1963.

Whitford, D., *Tyranny and Resistance: The Magdeburg Confession and the Lutheran Tradition*. St. Louis: Concordia, 2001.

Wicki, J., S.J., "Der einheimische Klerus in Indien," in J. Beckmann, ed., *Der einheimische Klerus in Geschichte und Gegenwart*. Schöneck-Beckenried: Neue Zeitschrift für Missionwissenschaft (Nouvelle Revue de Science Missionaire), 1950.

Wicki, J., S.J., "Pedro Luis, Brahmane und erster indischer Jesuit (ca. 1532–1596)," *Neue Zeitschrift für Missionswissenschaft*, 6 (1950).

Wicki, J., S.J., "Duas relações sobre a situação da Índia Portuguesa nos anos de 1568 e 1569," *Studia*, 8 (1961), pp. 123–221.

Wicki, J., S.J., *Missionskirche im Orient*. Immensee: Neue Zeitschrift für Missionwissenschaft (Nouvelle Revue de Science Missionaire), 1976.

Wicks, J., *Man Yearning for Grace: Luther's Early Spiritual Teaching*. Washington, DC: Corpus, 1968.

Wiesner, M. E., "Nuns, Wives, and Mothers: Women and the Reformation in Germany," in S. Marshall, ed., *Women in Reformation and Counter-Reformation Europe: Public and Private Worlds*. Bloomington: Indiana University Press, 1989, pp. 8–28.

Wiesner, M. E., "Ideology Meets the Empire: Reformed Convents and the Reformation," in A. C. Fix and S. C. Karant-Nunn, eds., *Germania Illustrata: Essays of Early Modern Germany Presented to Gerald Strauss*. Kirksville, Mo.: Sixteenth Century Journal, 1992, pp. 181–96.

Wilfred, F., S.J., "Christianity in Hindu Polytheistic Structural Mould: Converts in Southern Tamilnadu Respond to an Alien Religion During the 'Vasco da Gama Epoc,'" *Archives de sciences sociales des religions*, 103 (1998).

Willeke, B. H., *Imperial Government and Catholic Missions in China during the Years 1784–1785*. New York: Bonaventura, 1948.

Williams, G. H., *The Radical Reformation*, 3rd ed. Kirksville, Mo.: Sixteenth Century Essays and Studies, 15, 1992.

Wilson, S., *The Magical Universe: Everyday Ritual and Magic in Pre-modern Europe*. London and New York: Hambledon, 2000.

Wingren, G., *Luther on Vocation*, trans. Carl C. Rasmussen. Philadelphia: Muhlenberg, 1957.

Withington, P., "Views from the Bridge," *Past and Present*, 170 (2001), pp. 121–4.

Witte, C. M. de, "Les bulles pontificales et l'expansion portugaise au XVe siècle," *Revue d'histoire ecclésiastique*, 48 (1953); 49 (1954); 51 (1956); 53 (1958).

Wittkower, R. and Jaffe, I. B., eds., *Baroque Art: The Jesuit Contribution*. New York: Fordham University Press, 1972.

Wiznitzer, A., *Jews of Colonial Brazil*. New York: Columbia University Press, 1960.

Wolfe, M., *The Conversion of Henri IV: Politics, Power, and Religious Belief in Early Modern France*. Cambridge, Mass.: Harvard University Press, 1993.

Wolgast, E., *Die Wittenberger Theologie und die Politik der evangelischen Stände*. Gütersloh: Gütersloher Verlagshaus, 1977.

Woltjer, J. J., *Friesland in Hervormingstijd*. Leiden: Universitaire Pers, 1962.

Woltjer, J. J., *Tussen vrijheidsstrijd en burgeroorlog: Over de Nederlandse Opstand 1555–1580*. Amsterdam: Balans, 1994.

Wood, D., ed., *Martyrs and Martyrologies*. Studies in Church History, 30. Oxford: Blackwell, 1993.

Wood, J. B., *The King's Army: Warfare, Soldiers, and Society during the Wars of Religion in France, 1562–1576*. Cambridge: Cambridge University Press, 1996.

Wriedt, M., *Gnade und Erwählung: Eine Untersuchung zu Johann von Staupitz und Martin Luther*. Mainz: Zabern, 1991.

Wright, W. M., "The Visitation of Holy Mary: The First Years (1610–1618)," in R. L. DeMolen and J. C. Olin, eds., *Religious Orders of the Catholic Reformation: In Honor of John C. Olin on his Seventy-Fifth Birthday*. New York: Fordham University Press, 1994, pp. 217–50.

Xavier, Â. B., "Assistir diferenciadamente: Ordem social e mundo da caridade em Goa nos séculos XVI e XVII," *Vértice*, 2nd ser. (Mar.–Apr. 1997), pp. 11–20.

Xavier, Â. B., "Amores e desamores pelos pobres: Imagens, afectos e atitudes (sécs. XVI e XVII)," *Lusitania Sacra*, 11, 2nd ser. (1999).

Xavier, Â. B., "'Correo logo a fama do milagre': Narrativas missionárias, motivações e devoções num oriente imaginado," *Centro de Historia da Cultura, Terramar*, Lisbon, 1999, pp. 207–18.

Xavier, Â. B., "Between Conversion and Political Death: The Case of Carambolim in 16th-Century Goa," paper presented at the International Conference on Religion and Violence, New York University/Max-Planck Institut/Universiteit van Amsterdam, Amsterdam, May 25–7, 2000.

Xavier, Â. B., "The Martyrs of Cuncolim (Goa, 16th century): Portuguese Domination and the Resistance/Adaptation of Local Communities," paper presented at the Annual Conference of the Society for Spanish and Portuguese Historical Studies, New York, April 27–30, 2000.

Xavier, Â. B., "Uneasiness in the Village: Alliances, Conflicts and Conformity between Jesuits and Local Populations (Goa, 16th century)," paper presented at the workshop Jesuits as Intermediaries in the Early Modern World, October 11–13, 2001.

Yuuki, D., S.J., *The Twenty-Six Martyrs of Japan*. Tokyo: Enderle, 1998.

Zarri, G., "From Prophecy to Discipline, 1450 to 1650," in L. Scaraffia and G. Zarri, eds., *Women and Faith: Catholic Religious Life in Italy from Late Antiquity to the Present*. Cambridge, Mass.: Harvard University Press, 1999, pp. 85–112.

Zehnder, L., *Volkskundliches in der älteren schweizerischen Chronistik (Schriften der Schweizerischen Gesellschaft für Volkskunde*, vol. 60). Basel: Krebs, 1976.

Zhang Ze, *Qingdai jinjiao qi de Tianzhujiao*. Taipei: Guangqi chubanshe, 1992.

Zhu Pingyi, "Shenti, linghun yu tianzhu: Ming mo Qing chu xixue zhong de renti shengli zhishi," *Xinshixue*, 7 (1996), pp. 47–98.

Zijlstra, S., *Om de ware gemeente en de oude gronden: Geschiedenis van de dopersen in de Nederlanden 1531–1675*. Hilversum: Verloren, 2000.

Zschunke, P., *Konfession und Alltag in Oppenheim: Beiträge zur Geschichte von Bevölkerung und Gesellschaft einer gemischtkonfessionelleen Kleinstadt in der frühen Neuzeit*. Wiesbaden: Franz Steiner, 1984.

Zünd, A., *Gescheiterte Stadt- und Landreformationen des 16. und 17. Jahrhunderts in der Schweiz (Basler Beiträge zur Geschichtswissenschaft*, vol. 170). Basel: Helbing & Lichtenhahn, 1999.

Županov, I. G., "Aristocratic Analogies and Demotic Descriptions in the Seventeenth-Century Madurai Mission," *Representations*, 41 (1991).

Županov, I. G., "Prosélytisme et pluralisme religieux: Deux expériences missionnaires en Inde aux XVIe et XVIIe siècles," *Archives de sciences sociales des religions*, 87 (Jul.–Sept. 1994).

Županov, I. G., "Le repli du religieux: Les missionnaires jésuites du XVIIe siècle entre la théologie chrétienne et une éthique païenne," *Annales*, 6 (1996).

Županov, I. G., "The Prophetic and the Miraculous in Portuguese Asia: A Hagiographical View of Colonial Culture," in S. Subrahmanyam, ed., *Sinners and Saints: The Successors of Vasco da Gama*. New Delhi: Oxford University Press, 1998.

Županov, I. G., *Disputed Mission: Jesuit Experiments and Brahmanical Knowledge in Seventeenth-Century India*. New Delhi: Oxford University Press, 2000.

Županov, I. G., "Lust, Marriage and Free Will: Jesuit Critique of Paganism in South India (Seventeenth Century)," *Studies in History*, 12/2, n.s. (2000).

Zur Mühlen, K. H., *Nos extra nos: Luthers Theologie und zwischen Mystik und Scholastik*. Tübingen: Mohr/Siebeck, 1972.

Zürcher, E., "Bouddhisme et christianisme," in *Bouddhisme, christianisme et société chinoise (Conférences, essais et leçons du Collège de France)*, Paris: Julliard, 1990.

Zürcher, E., "Confucian and Christian Religiosity in Late Ming China," *Catholic Historical Review*, 83/4 (1997), pp. 614–53.

Index

Page references in *italic* are to illustrations